standard catalog of

CHEVROLET
1912-1998

2nd Edition

Edited by Ron Kowalke

Published by

700 E. State Street • Iola, WI 54990-0001
Telephone: 715/445-2214

Please call or write for our free catalog.
Our toll-free number to place an order or obtain a free catalog is 800-258-0929
or please use our regular business telephone 715-445-2214
for editorial comment and further information.

Library of Congress Catalog Number: 90-60576
ISBN: 0-87341-606-6

Printed in the United States of America

CATALOG STAFF

Editor:	Ron Kowalke
Cover Design Artist:	Tom Dupuis
Color Section Artist:	Kevin Sauter
Pagination Artist:	Stacy Bloch

CONTENTS

FOREWORD

Traditionally, the concept behind Krause Publications' Standard Catalogs is to compile massive amounts of information about motor vehicles and present it in a standard format which the hobbyist, collector or professional dealer can use to answer some commonly asked questions.

Those questions include: What year, make and model is the vehicle? What did it sell for new? How rare is it? What is special about it? Some answers are provided by photos and others by the fact-filled text.

Chester L. Krause, retired founder of Krause Publications, is responsible for the overall concept of creating the Standard Catalog series covering American automobiles. David V. Brownell undertook preliminary work on the concept while serving as editor of *Old Cars Weekly* in the 1970s. Then editor John A. Gunnell assumed the project in 1978. The first Standard Catalog, covering postwar models (1946-1975), was published in 1982, while Beverly Rae Kimes continued writing and researching the *Standard Catalog of American Cars 1805-1942*, which was published in 1985. In 1987, the *Standard Catalog of American Light-Duty Trucks* (1900-1986) was created by Gunnell, while the second edition of the 1946-1975 American car catalog was published. In 1988, the 1805-1942 American car catalog by Kimes appeared in its second edition. Also in 1988, James M. Flammang authored the *Standard Catalog of American Cars 1976-1986*, which went into its second edition in 1990. A third edition of the 1946-1975 catalog appeared in 1992. Ron Kowalke took over the editing of Standard Catalogs in 1995, and a third edition of the 1805-1942 volume by Kimes appeared in 1996 while a fourth edition of the 1946-1975 volume was printed in 1997. Currently the four-volume set of Standard Catalogs devoted to American cars and light-duty trucks enjoys good sales in the automotive/truck collector hobby, and provides a wealth of detailed information that car and truck collectors, hobbyists, restorers and investors will not find from any other publishing house.

The scope of these catalogs has been to cover the major manufacturers, which have survived into the Nineties: Chrysler, Ford and General Motors as well as companies they have absorbed and companies no longer with us today. Independent companies such as Checker, Hudson, Kaiser-Frazer, Nash, Packard, Studebaker and Willys are included in the earlier catalogs, as well as some 200 producers of low-volume nameplates from Airscoot to Yenko. In each case, the data compiled encompasses a physical description; list of known equipment and original specifications; technical data; historical footnotes and appraisal of the car's current 'ballpark value'.

In each catalog, all compilations were made by an experienced editorial team consisting of the automotive staff of Krause Publications and numerous contributors who are recognized experts on a certain marque or specific area of automotive history. A major benefit of combining teamwork with expertise has been the gathering of many significant facts about each model.

No claims are made about the catalogs being history textbooks or encyclopedias. Nor are they repair manuals or "bibles" for motor vehicles enthusiasts. They are, rather, intended as a contribution to the pursuit of greater knowledge about the many wonderful automobiles and trucks built in the United States since 1805. They are much larger in size, broader in scope and more deluxe in format than any previously published collectors' guides, buyers' digests or pricing guides.

The long-range goal of Krause Publications is to make all of these catalogs as nearly perfect as humanly possible. At the same time, we expect such catalogs will always raise new questions and bring forth new facts that were not previously unearthed in the countless hours of research by our team. All contributors are requested to maintain an ongoing file of new research, corrections and additional photos that can be used to refine and expand future editions.

With this second edition of *Standard Catalog of Chevrolet*, we continue our venture into researching a single automotive marque that has been responsible for millions of production vehicles since the early 1900s. And we thank the editors and contributors to the three volume *Standard Catalog of American Cars* for providing much of the material herein. For it is through their research and editing effort that we produce this *Standard Catalog of Chevrolet 1912-1998* with an assurance that the information that we've combined herein from those three catalogs is accurate and well-researched. Additionally, we have included some of the best Chevrolet-oriented articles from past issues of *Old Cars Weekly*, authored by experts in the field. Should you, as an individual Chevy enthusiast, member of a Chevy club, or historian, have access to expanded information that you wish to share, please do not hesitate to contact the editors, in care of Krause Publications, Standard Catalog of Chevrolet, 700 E. State St., Iola, WI 54990.

ABBREVIATIONS

A/C	Air conditioning	
A.L.A.M.	Assoc. of Licensed Automobile Mfgs.	
Adj.	Adjustable	
Aero.	Fastback	
AM, FM, AM/FM	Radio types	
Amp.	Amperes	
Approx.	Approximate	
Auto.	Automatic	
Auxil.	Auxiliary	
Avail.	Available	
Avg.	Average	
BxS	Bore x Stroke	
Base	Base (usually lowest-priced) model	
Bbl.	Barrel (carburetor)	
B.H.P.	Brake horsepower	
BSW	Black sidewall (tire)	
Brk/Brkwd/Brkwood	Brookwood	
Brdcl.	Broadcloth	
Bus.	Business (i.e. Business Coupe)	
C-A	Carryall	
C.C.	Close-coupled	
Cabr.	Cabriolet	
Carb.	Carburetor	
Capr.	Caprice	
Cass.	Cassette (tape player)	
Cav.	Cavalier	
CB	Citizens Band (radio)	
Celeb.	Celebrity	
CEO	Chief Executive Officer	
CFI	Cross Fire (fuel) Injection	
Chvt.	Chevette	
C.I.D.	Cubic inch displacement	
Cit.	Citation	
Clb	Club (Club Coupe)	
Clth.	Cloth-covered roof	
Col.	Colonnade (coupe body style)	
Col.	Column (shift)	
Conv/Conv.	Convertible	
Conv. Sed.	Convertible Sedan	
Corp Limo	Corporate Limousine	
Cpe	Coupe	
Cpe P.U.	Coupe Pickup	
C.R.	Compression ratio	
Crsr.	Cruiser	
Cu. In.	Cubic Inch (displacement)	
Cust.	Custom	
Cyl.	Cylinder	
DeL.	DeLuxe	
DFRS	Dual facing rear seats	
Dia.	Diameter	
Disp.	Displacement	
Dr.	Door	
Ea.	Each	
E.D.	Enclosed Drive	
E.F.I.	Electronic Fuel Injection	
E.W.B.	Extended Wheelbase	
Eight	Eight-cylinder engine	
8-tr.	Eight-track	
Encl.	Enclosed	
EPA	Environmental Protection Agency	
Equip.	Equipment	
Est. Wag.	Estate Wagon	
Exc.	Except	
Exec.	Executive	
F	Forward (3F - 3 forward speeds)	
F.W.D.	Four-wheel drive	
Fam.	Family	
Fml.	Formal	
"Four"	Four-cylinder engine	
4WD	Four-wheel drive	
4-dr.	Four-door	
4-spd.	Four-speed (transmission)	
4V	Four-barrel carburetor	
FP	Factory Price	
Frsm.	Foursome	
Frt.	Front	
FsBk	Fastback	
Ft.	Foot/feet	
FWD	Front wheel drive	
G.B.	Greenbrier	
GBR	Glass-belted radial (tire)	
Gal.	Gallon	
GM	General Motors (Corporation)	
GT	Gran Turismo	
G.R.	Gear Ratio	
H	Height	
H.B.	Hatchback	
H.D.	Heavy Duty	
HEI	High Energy Ignition	
H.O.	High-output	
H.P.	Horsepower	
HT/HT Hdtp.	Hardtop	
Hr.	Hour	
Hwg.	Highway	
I.	Inline	
I.D.	Identification	
Imp	Impala	
In.	Inches	
Incl.	Included or Including	
Int.	Interior	
King/Kingwd.	Kingswood	
Lan	Landau (coupe body style)	
Lb. or Lbs.	Pound-feet (torque)	
LH	Left hand	
Lift.	Liftback (body style)	
Limo	Limousine	
LPO	Limited production option	
Ltd.	Limited	
Lthr. Trm.	Leather Trim	
L.W.B.	Long Wheelbase	
Mag.	Wheel style	
Mast.	Master	
Max.	Maximum	
MFI	Multi-port Fuel Injection	
M.M.	Millimeters	
Monte	Monte Carlo	
MPG	Miles per gallon	
MPH	Miles per hour	
Mstr.	Master	
N/A	Not available (or not applicable)	
NC	No charge	
N.H.P.	Net horsepower	
No.	Number	
Notch or N.B.	Notchback	
OHC	Overhead cam (engine)	
OHV	Overhead valve (engine)	
O.L.	Overall length	
OPEC	Organization of Petroleum Exporting Countries	
Opt.	Optional	
OSRV	Outside rear view	
O.W. or O/W	Opera window	
OWL	Outline White Letter (tire)	
Oz.	Ounce	
P	Passenger	
Park/Parkwd	Parkwood	
PFI	Port fuel injection	
Phae.	Phaeton	
Pkg.	Package (e.g. option pkg)	
Prod.	Production	
Pwr.	Power	
R	Reverse	
RBL	Raised black letter (tire)	
Rbt.	Runabout	
Rds.	Roadster	
Reg.	Regular	
Remote	Remote control	
Req.	Requires	
RH	Right-hand drive	
Roch.	Rochester (carburetor)	
R.P.M.	Revolutions per minute	
RPO	Regular production option	
R.S. or R/S	Rumbleseat	
RV	Recreational vehicle	
RVL	Raised white letter (tire)	
S	Gm lowtrim model designation	
S.A.E.	Society of Automotive Engineers	
SBR	Steel-belted radials	
Sed.	Sedan	
SFI	Sequential fuel injection	
"Six"	Six-cylinder engine	
S.M.	Side Mount	
Spd.	Speed	
Spec.	Special	
Spt.	Sport	
Sq. In.	Square inch	
SR	Sunroof	
SS	Super Sport	
Sta. Wag.	Station wagon	
Std.	Standard	
Sub.	Suburban	
S.W.B.	Short Wheelbase	
Tach.	Tachometer	
Tax.	Taxable (horsepower)	
TBI	Throttle body (fuel) injection	
Temp.	Temperature	
THM	Turbo Hydramatic (transmission)	
3S	Three-seat	
Trans.	Transmission	
Trk.	Trunk	
2-Dr.	Two-door	
2 V	Two-barrel (carburetor)	
2WD	Two-wheel drive	
Univ.	Universal	
Utl.	Utility	
V.	Venturi (carburetor)	
V-6, V-8	Vee-type engine	
VIN	Vehicle Identification Number	
W	With	
W/O	Without	
Wag.	Wagon	
w (2w)	Window (two window)	
W.B.	Wheelbase	
Woodie	Wood-bodied car	
WLT	White-lettered tire	
WSW	White sidewall (tire)	
W.W.	Whitewalls	
W. Whl.	Wire wheel	

PHOTO CREDITS

Whenever possible, throughout the Catalog, we have strived to picture all cars with photographs that show them in their most original form. All photos gathered from reliable outside sources have an alphabetical code following the caption which indicates the photo source. An explanation of these codes is given below. Additional photos from Krause Publications file are marked accordingly. With special thanks to the editors of the previous *Standard Catalogs of American Cars* for their original research and obtaining many of these photos of Chevrolet over the years.

(AA)	Applegate & Applegate
(CH)	Chevrolet
(CP)	Crestline Publishing
(GM)	General Motors
(HAC)	Henry Austin Clark, Jr.
(HFM)	Henry Ford Museum
(IMSC)	Indianapolis Motor Speedway Corporation

(JAC)	John A. Conde
(JG)	John Gunnell
(NAHC)	National Automotive History Collection
(OCW)	Old Cars Weekly
(PH)	Phil Hall
(WLB)	William L. Bailey

APPEARANCE AND EQUIPMENT: Word descriptions identify cars by styling features, trim and (to a lesser extent) interior appointments. Most standard equipment lists begin with the lowest-priced model, then enumerate items added by upgrade models and option packages. Most lists reflect equipment available at model introductions.

I.D. DATA: Information is given about the Vehicle Identification Number (VIN) found on the dashboard. VIN codes show model or series, body style, engine size, model year and place built. Beginning in 1981, a standardized 17 symbol VIN is used. Earlier VINs are shorter. Locations of other coded information on the body and/or engine block may be supplied. Deciphering those codes is beyond the scope of this catalog.

SPECIFICATIONS CHART: The first column gives series or model numbers. The second gives body style numbers revealing body type and trim. Not all cars use two separate numbers. Some sources combine the two. Column three tells number of doors, body style and passenger capacity ('4-dr Sed-6P' means four-door sedan, six-passenger). Passenger capacity is normally the maximum. Cars with bucket seats hold fewer. Column four gives suggested retail price of the car when new, on or near its introduction date, not including freight or other charges. Column five gives the original shipping weight. The sixth column provides model year production totals or refers to notes below the chart. In cases where the same car came with different engines, a slash is used to separate factory prices and shipping weights for each version. Unless noted, the amount on the left of the slash is for the smallest, least expensive engine. The amount on the right is for the least costly engine with additional cylinders. 'N/A' means data not available.

ENGINE DATA: Engines are normally listed in size order with smallest displacement first. A 'base' engine is the basic one offered in each model at the lowest price. 'Optional' describes all alternate engines, including those that have a price listed in the specifications chart. (Cars that came with either a six or V-8, for instance, list the six as 'base' and V-8 'optional'). Introductory specifications are used, where possible.

CHASSIS DATA: Major dimensions (wheelbase, overall length, height, width and front/rear tread) are given for each model, along with standard tire size. Dimensions sometimes varied and could change during a model year.

TECHNICAL DATA: This section indicates transmissions standard on each model, usually including gear ratios; the standard final drive axle ratio (which may differ by engine or transmission); steering and brake system type; front and rear suspension description; body construction; and fuel tank capacity.

OPTIONAL EQUIPMENT LISTS: Most listings begin with drive-train options (engines, transmissions, steering/suspension and mechanical components) applying to all models. Convenience/appearance items are listed separately for each model, except where several related models are combined into a single listing. Option packages are listed first, followed by individual items in categories: comfort/convenience, lighting/mirrors, entertainment, exterior, interior, then wheels/tires. Contents of some option packages are listed prior to the price; others are described in the Appearance/Equipment text. Prices are suggested retail, usually effective early in the model year. ('N/A' indicates prices are unavailable.) Most items are Regular Production Options (RPO), rather than limited-production (LPO), special-order or dealer-installed equipment. Many options were available only on certain series or body types or in conjunction with other items. Space does not permit including every detail.

HISTORY: This block lists introduction dates, total sales and production amounts for the model year and calendar year. Production totals supplied by auto-makers do not always coincide with those from other sources. Some reflect shipments from the factories rather than actual production or define the model year a different way.

HISTORICAL FOOTNOTES: In addition to notes on the rise and fall of sales and production, this block includes significant statistics, performance milestones, major personnel changes, important dates and places and facts that add flavor to this segment of America's automotive heritage.

SERIES Z — V-8 — "The Corvette evolution continues," declared this year's catalog. Not much of that evolution was visible, however, after the prior year's massive restyle. Under the hood, the base engine got the dual-snorkel air intake introduced in 1978 for the optional L82 V-8. That added 10 horsepower. The L82 V-8 had a higher-lift cam, special heads with larger valves and higher compression, impact-extruded pistons, forged steel crankshaft, and finned aluminum rocker covers. The "Y" pipe exhaust system had new open-flow mufflers, while the automatic transmission got a higher numerical (3.55:1) rear axle ratio. All Corvettes now had the highback bucket seats introduced on the 1978 limited-edition Indy Pace Car. A high pivot point let the seat backrest fold flat on the passenger side, level with the luggage area floor. An AM/FM radio was now standard. Of ten body colors, only one (dark green metallic) was new this year. The others were Classic white, black and silver, plus Corvette dark or light blue, yellow, light beige, red, and dark brown. Interiors came in black, red, light beige, dark blue, dark brown, oyster, or dark green. Corvettes had black roof panel and window moldings. Bolt-on front and rear spoilers (also from the Pace Car) became available. Buyers who didn't want the full Gymkhana suspension could now order heavy-duty shocks alone. Standard equipment include the L48 V-8 with four-barrel carb, either automatic transmission or four-speed manual gearbox (close-ratio version available), power four-wheel disc brakes, and limited-slip differential. Other standards: tinted glass; front stabilizer bar; concealed wipers/washers; day/night inside mirror; wide outside mirror; anti-theft alarm system; four-spoke sport steering wheel; electric clock; trip odometer; heater/defroster; bumper guards; and luggage security shade. Tires were P225/70R15 steel-belted radial blackwalls on 15 x 8 in. wheels. Corvettes had four-wheel independent suspension. Bucket seats came with cloth/leather or all-leather trim. The aircraft-type console held a 7000 R.P.M. tachometer, voltmeter, oil pressure, temp and fuel gauges. Seat inserts could have either leather or cloth trim.

I.D. DATA: Coding of the 13-symbol Vehicle Identification Number (VIN) was similar to 1978. Engine codes changed to '8' base L48 and '4' optional L82. Model year code changed to '9' for 1979. Serial numbers began with 400001.

CORVETTE

Model Number	Body/Style Number	Body Type & Seating	Factory Price	Shipping Weight	Production Total
1Y	Z87	2-dr. Spt Cpe-2P	10220	3372	53,807

ENGINE DATA: BASE V-8: 90-degree, overhead valve V-8. Cast iron block and head. Displacement: 350 cu. in. (5.7 liters). Bore & stroke: 4.00 x 3.48 in. Compression ratio: 8.2:1. Brake horsepower: 195 at 4000 R.P.M. Torque: 285 lbs.-ft. at 3200 R.P.M. Five main bearings. Hydraulic valve lifters. Carburetor: 4Bbl. RPO Code: L48. VIN Code: 8. OPTIONAL V-8: Same as above, except C.R.: 8.9:1. B.H.P.: 225 at 5200 R.P.M. Torque: 270 lbs.-ft. at 3600 R.P.M. RPO Code: L82. VIN Code: 4.

CHASSIS DATA: Wheelbase: 98.0 in. Overall length: 185.2 in. Height: 48.0 in. Width: 69.0 in. Front Tread: 58.7 in. Rear Tread: 59.5 in. Wheel Size: 15 x 8 in. Standard Tires: P225/70R15 SBR. Optional Tires: P225/60R15.

TECHNICAL: Transmission: Four-speed manual transmission (floor shift) standard. Gear ratios: (1st) 2.85:1; (2nd) 2.02:1; (3rd) 1.35:1; (4th) 1.00:1; (Rev) 2.85:1. Close-ratio four-speed manual trans. optional: (1st) 2.43:1; (2nd) 1.61:1; (3rd) 1.23:1; (4th) 1.00:1; (Rev) 2.35:1. Three-speed automatic optional: (1st) 2.52:1; (2nd) 1.52:1; (3rd) 1.00:1; (Rev) 1.93:1. Standard final drive ratio: 3.36:1 w/4spd, 3.55:1 w/auto. Steering: Recirculating ball. Front Suspension: Control arms, coil springs and stabilizer bar.

Rear Suspension: Independent, with single transverse leaf spring and lateral struts. Brakes: Four-wheel disc (11.75 in. disc dia). Ignition: Electronic. Body construction: Fiberglass, on separate frame. Fuel tank: 24 gal.

CORVETTE OPTIONS: L82 350 cu. in., 4Bbl. V-8 engine ($565). Close-ratio four-speed manual transmission (NC). Turbo Hydra-matic (NC). Highway axle ratio ($19). Gymkhana suspension ($49). H.D. shock absorbers ($33). Heavy-duty battery ($21). Trailer towing equipment inc. H.D. radiator and Gymkhana suspension ($98). California emissions system (N/A). High-altitude emissions (N/A). Four season air cond. ($635). Rear defogger, electric ($102). Cruise-master speed control ($113). Tilt/telescopic leather-wrapped steering wheel ($190). Power windows ($141). Power windows and door locks ($272). Convenience group ($94). Sport mirrors, left remote ($45). AM/FM stereo radio ($90); with 8track or cassette player ($228-$234). AM/FM stereo radio w/CB and power antenna ($439). Dual rear speakers ($52). Power antenna ($52). Removable glass roof panels ($365). Aluminum wheels ($380). P225/70R15 SBR WL tires ($54). P225/60R15 Aramid-belted radial WL tires ($226).

HISTORY: Introduced: Sept. 25, 1978. Model year production: 53,807 (Chevrolet initially reported a total of 49,901 units.) Calendar year production: 48,568. Calendar year sales by U.S. dealers: 38,631. Model year sales by U.S. dealers: 39,816.

Historical Footnotes: For what it's worth, 7,949 Corvettes this year were painted in Classic White, while 6,960 carried silver paint. Only 4,385 Corvettes had the MM4 four-speed manual gearbox, while 4,062 ran with the close-ratio M21 version.

BODY STYLES

Body style designations describe the shape and character of an automobile. In earlier years automakers exhibited great imagination in coining words to name their products. This led to names that were not totally accurate. Many of those **'car words'** were taken from other fields: mythology, carriage building, architecture, railroading, and so on. Therefore, there was no 'correct' automotive meaning other than that brought about through actual use. Inconsistences have persisted into the recent period, though some of the imaginative terms of past eras have faded away. One manufacturer's 'sedan' might resemble another's 'coupe.' Some automakers have persisted in describing a model by a word different from common usage, such as Ford's label for Mustang as a 'sedan.' Following the demise of the true pillarless hardtop (two- and four-door) in the mid-1970s, various manufacturers continued to use the term 'hardtop' to describe their offerings, even though a 'B' pillar was part of the newer car's structure and the front door glass may not always have been frameless. Some took on the description 'pillared hardtop' or 'thin pillar hardtop' to define what observers might otherwise consider, essentially, a sedan. Descriptions in this catalog generally follow the manufacturers' choice of words, except when they conflict strongly with accepted usage.

One specific example of inconsistency is worth noting: the description of many hatchback models as 'three-door' and 'five-door,' even though that extra 'door' is not an entryway for people. While the 1976-1986 domestic era offered no real phaetons or roadsters in the earlier senses of the words, those designations continue to turn up now and then, too.

TWO-DOOR (CLUB) COUPE: The Club Coupe designation seems to come from club car, describing the lounge (or parlor car) in a railroad train. The early postwar club coupe combined a shorter-than-sedan body structure with the convenience of a full back seat, unlike the single-seat business coupe. That name has been used less frequently in the 1976-86 period, as most notchback two-door models (with trunk rather than hatch) have been referred to as just 'coupes.' Moreover, the distinction between two-door coupes and two-door sedans has grown fuzzy.

TWO-DOOR SEDAN: The term sedan originally described a conveyance seen only in movies today: a wheelless vehicle for one person, borne on poles by two men, one ahead and one behind. Automakers pirated the word and applied it to cars with a permanent top, seating four to seven (including driver) in a single compartment. The two-door sedan of recent times has sometimes been called a pillared coupe, or plain coupe, depending on the manufacturer's whim. On the other hand, some cars commonly referred to as coupes carry the sedan designation on factory documents.

TWO-DOOR (THREE-DOOR) HATCHBACK COUPE: Originally a small opening in the deck of a sailing ship, the term 'hatch' was later applied to airplane doors and to passenger cars with rear liftgates. Various models appeared in the early 1950s, but weather-tightness was a problem. The concept emerged again in the early 1970s, when fuel economy factors began to signal the trend toward compact cars. Technology had remedied the sealing difficulties. By the 1980s, most manufacturers produced one or more hatchback models, though the question of whether to call them 'two-door' or 'three-door' never was resolved. Their main common feature was the lack of a separate trunk. 'Liftback' coupes may have had a different rear-end shape, but the two terms often described essentially the same vehicle.

TWO-DOOR FASTBACK: By definition, a fastback is any automobile with a long, moderately curving, downward slope to the rear of the roof. This body style relates to an interest in streamlining and aerodynamics and has gone in and out of fashion at various times. Some (Mustangs for one) have grown quite popular. Others have tended to turn customers off. Certain fastbacks are, technically, two-door sedans or pillared coupes. Four-door fastbacks have also been produced. Many of these (such as Buick's late 1970s four-door Century sedan) lacked sales appeal. Fastbacks may or may not have a rear-opening hatch.

TWO-DOOR HARDTOP: The term hardtop, as used for postwar cars up to the mid-1970s, describes an automobile styled to resemble a convertible, but with a rigid metal (or fiberglass) top. In a production sense, this body style evolved after World War II, first called 'hardtop convertible.' Other generic names have included sports coupe, hardtop coupe or pillarless coupe. In the face of proposed rollover standards, nearly all automakers turned away from the pillarless design to a pillared version by 1976-77.

COLONNADE HARDTOP: In architecture, the term colonnade describes a series of columns, set at regular intervals, usually supporting an entablature, roof or series of arches. To meet Federal rollover standards in 1974 (standards that never emerged), General Motors introduced two- and four-door pillared body types with arch-like quarter windows and sandwich type roof construction. They looked like a cross between true hardtops and miniature limousines. Both styles proved popular (especially the coupe with louvered coach windows and canopy top) and the term colonnade was applied. As their 'true' hardtops disappeared, other manufacturers produced similar bodies with a variety of quarter-window shapes and sizes. These were known by such terms as hardtop coupe, pillared hardtop or opera-window coupe.

FORMAL HARDTOP: The hardtop roofline was a long-lasting fashion hit of the postwar car era. The word 'formal' can be applied to things that are stiffly conservative and follow the established rule. The limousine, being the popular choice of conservative buyers who belonged to the Establishment, was looked upon as a formal motorcar. So when designers combined the lines of these two body styles, the result was the Formal Hardtop. This style has been marketed with two or four doors, canopy and vinyl roofs (full or partial) and conventional or opera-type windows, under various trade names. The distinction between a formal hardtop and plain pillared-hardtop coupe (see above) hasn't always followed a strict rule.

CONVERTIBLE: To Depression-era buyers, a convertible was a car with a fixed-position windshield and folding top that, when raised, displayed the lines of a coupe. Buyers in the postwar period expected a convertible to have roll-up windows, too. Yet the definition of the word includes no such qualifications. It states only that such a car should have a lowerable or removable top. American convertibles became extinct by 1976, except for Cadillac's Eldorado, then in its final season. In 1982, though, Chrysler brought out a LeBaron ragtop; Dodge a 400; and several other companies followed it a year or two later.

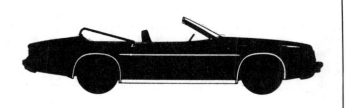

ROADSTER: This term derives from equestrian vocabulary where it was applied to a horse used for riding on the roads. Old dictionaries define the roadster as an open-type car designed for use on *ordinary* roads, with a single seat for two persons and, often, a rumbleseat as well. Hobbyists associate folding windshields and side curtains (rather than roll-up windows) with roadsters, although such qualifications stem from usage, not definition of term. Most recent roadsters are either sports cars, small alternative-type vehicles or replicas of early models.

RUNABOUT: By definition, a runabout is the equivalent of a roadster. The term was used by carriage makers and has been applied in the past to light, open cars on which a top is unavailable or totally an add-on option. None of this explains its use by Ford on certain Pinto models. Other than this inaccurate usage, recent runabouts are found mainly in the alternative vehicle field, including certain electric-powered models.

FOUR-DOOR SEDAN: If you took the wheels off a car, mounted it on poles and hired two weightlifters (one in front and one in back) to carry you around in it, you'd have a true sedan. Since this idea isn't very practical, it's better to use the term for an automobile with a permanent top (affixed by solid pillars) that seats four or more persons, including the driver, on two full-width seats.

FOUR-DOOR HARDTOP: This is a four-door car styled to resemble a convertible, but having a rigid top of metal or fiberglass. Buick introduced a totally pillarless design in 1955. A year later most automakers offered equivalent bodies. Four-door hardtops have also been labeled sports sedans and hardtop sedans. By 1976, potential rollover standards and waning popularity had taken their toll. Only a few makes still produced a four-door hardtop and those disappeared soon thereafter.

FOUR-DOOR PILLARED HARDTOP: Once the 'true' four-door hardtop began to fade away, manufacturers needed another name for their luxury four-doors. Many were styled to look almost like the former pillarless models, with thin or unobtrusive pillars between the doors. Some, in fact, were called 'thin-pillar hardtops.' The distinction between certain pillared hardtops and ordinary (presumably humdrum) sedans occasionally grew hazy.

FOUR-DOOR (FIVE-DOOR) HATCHBACK: Essentially unknown among domestic models in the mid-1970s, the four-door hatchback became a popular model as cars grew smaller and front-wheel-drive versions appeared. Styling was similar to the orignal two-door hatchback, except for — obviously — two more doors. Luggage was carried in the back of the car itself, loaded through the hatch opening, not in a separate trunk.

LIMOUSINE: This word's literal meaning is 'a cloak.' In France, Limousine means any passenger vehicle. An early dictionary defined limousine as an auto with a permanently enclosed compartment for 3-5, with a roof projecting over a front driver's seat. However, modern dictionaries drop the separate compartment idea and refer to limousines as large luxury autos, often chauffeur-driven. Some have a movable division window between the driver and passenger compartments, but that isn't a requirement.

TWO-DOOR STATION WAGON: Originally defined as a car with an enclosed wooden body of paneled design (with several rows of folding or removable seats behind the driver), the station wagon became a different and much more popular type of vehicle in the postwar years. A recent dictionary states that such models have a larger interior than sedans of the line and seats that can be readily lifted out, or folded down, to facilitate light trucking. In addition, there's usually a tailgate, but no separate luggage compartment. The two-door wagon often has sliding or flip-out rear side windows.

FOUR-DOOR STATION WAGON: Since functionality and adaptability are advantages of station wagons, four-door versions have traditionally been sales leaders. At least they were until cars began to grow smaller. This style usually has lowerable windows in all four doors and fixed rear side glass. The term 'suburban' was almost synonymous with station wagon at one time, but is now more commonly applied to light trucks with similar styling. Station wagons have had many trade names, such as Country Squire (Ford) and Sport Suburban (Plymouth). Quite a few have retained simulated wood paneling, keeping alive the wagon's origin as a wood-bodied vehicle.

LIFTBACK STATION WAGON: Small cars came in station wagon form too. The idea was the same as bigger versions, but the conventional tailgate was replaced by a single lift-up hatch. For obvious reasons, compact and subcompact wagons had only two seats instead of the three that had been available in many full-size models.

DIMENSIONS

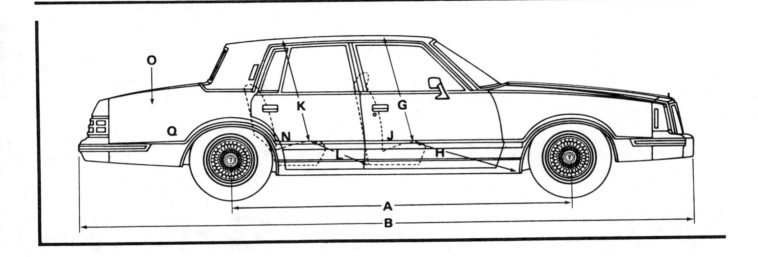

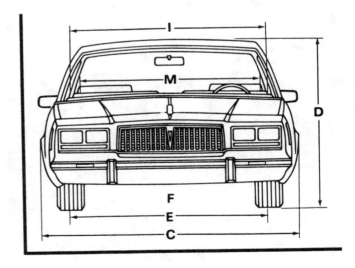

DIMENSIONS

Exterior:

A Wheelbase

B Overall length

C Width

D Overall height

E Tread, front

F Tread, rear

Interior—front:

G Headroom

H Legroom

I Shoulder room

J Hip room

Interior—rear:

K Headroom

L Legroom

M Shoulder room

N Hip room

O Trunk capacity (liters/cu. ft.)

P Cargo index volume (liters/cu. ft.)

Q Fuel tank capacity (liters/gallons)

CHEVROLET

1912-1942

CHEVROLET — Detroit and Flint, Michigan — (1912-1942 et. seq.) — The Chevrolet was a car built for a purpose. It was the vehicle by which William C. Durant intended to regain control of General Motors, the corporation he had founded in 1908 and that he lost to the bankers in 1910. A businessman/entrepreneur of the swashbuckling adventurer sort, Billy Durant was not always wise, but he was ever resourceful. Initially his Chevrolet — which he envisioned as a light car of "French type" to be sold at popular prices — didn't work out exactly as planned, but that was Louis' fault. To put his plan into operation, Durant had contacted Louis Chevrolet, one of the stalwarts on the successful racing team Durant had established while heading Buick. Durant was aware that Chevrolet had ambitions to build a car of his own, and since the Chevrolet name was already well known in motorsport, and since Chevrolet had been born in Europe and knew what "French type" meant, Durant was sure he was the man for the job. Chevrolet hired a Frenchman to help him, Etienne Planche, whom he had known from his days with the Walter in Brooklyn and who had designed the Roebling-Planche (antecedent to the Mercer) — and this Billy thought boded well, too. In May of 1911 a Detroit newspaper leaked the news of the forthcoming Chevrolet car from Durant. Meanwhile Durant began organizing a whole bunch of companies: the Chevrolet Motor Company in Detroit (initially Chevrolet Motor Car but the "Car" was soon dropped), the Little Motor Car Company in Flint (to build a less expensive car called the Little to bring some quick cash into the coffers), the Mason Motor Company in Flint (to build engines for these cars, with former Buick engineer Arthur Mason at its head), the Republic Motor Company (for which he bought an entire block in New York City to be used as an auxiliary assembly plant), among others. And meanwhile, too, Louis was taking his time coming up with the new Chevrolet. The Little arrived first, during the summer of 1912, as a $650 four. Some months later a $1,285 Little Six was added, this a last-minute decision because the car Louis Chevrolet was building was turning out to be not a light French type at all, but a big car that Durant knew he couldn't sell for less than $2,150. Still, when Louis Chevrolet finally had the car ready, Durant felt he had no other choice but to get it on the market right away, since a year-and-a-half had passed since that first press mention it was coming. And thus it was, late in 1912, that the Chevrolet Six Type C Clas-

Louis Chevrolet driving the first Chevrolet automobile built in 1911. (Photo courtesy of Detroit Public Library Automotive History Collection)

Louis Chevrolet (white duster) and W.C. Durant (to left of windshield) pose with the first Chevrolet, a six-cylinder-powered model with folding top and adjustable windshield. Durant's son, Cliff, and his wife occupy the front seat. Chevrolet produced 2,999 automobiles in 1912. (Photo courtesy of Chevrolet Public Relations)

sic arrived, with an overhead valve T-head engine of 299 cubic inches (the largest displacement of any Chevrolet engine until introduction of the 348-cubic-inch V-8 in 1958) and a wheelbase of 120 inches (as long as any Chevy ever). The car was well built — three point motor suspension, a three-speed selective transmission on a full-floating rear axle — but it was also ponderous, and sales were modest. Billy Durant definitely had a problem. With cheaper prices, the Little was selling, but it had been a shoestring operation and Durant was aware that the cars were not durable. His solution was to combine the good points of the Chevrolet and the Little into one new car to be sold as a Chevrolet. And to gather all the various companies he had organized under the Chevrolet banner, and to move the whole operation to Flint, where he had enjoyed boy-wonder status since his carriage-making days. This irritated Louis Chevrolet, who took off on his own to build the Frontenac; thereafter, Etienne Planche received an offer he couldn't refuse from Durant's old partner J. Dallas Dort and took off to build the Dort. Subsequently Durant finished the run of Chevrolet Classic Sixes for which parts remained, and introduced the Chevrolet Light Six or Model L for the 1914 model year (this the former Little Six, and the only L-head in Chevrolet history). More important in 1914 was the arrival of the H Series, powered by a 170.9-cubic inch four-cylinder engine designed by Arthur Mason that would remain in production until 1928. These were the first Chevrolets not to include a self-starter as standard equipment (it was available optionally), but they were also the first Chevrolets to be sold for under a thousand dollars. Baby Grand for the $875 touring and Royal Mail for the $750 roadster were the delightful names for these automobiles and there was a sporty Amesbury Special available at $985, too. All these cars carried a new emblem, the famous Chevrolet bowtie, which was Durant's idea and one that he'd carried around with him for a long time, having been inspired to it by either the wallpaper in a Paris hotel room (as he liked to say) or something he saw in the rotogravure section of a Hot Springs, Virginia, newspaper (which is the way his wife remembered it). Durant's plan to assemble Chevrolets in the heart of New York City, however, ran into an indisputable snag, the factory being located in one of the worst sections in town with the result that he had to buy protection from both Tammany Hall and street toughs. Thus when the former Maxwell-Briscoe plant became available in Tarrytown, he bought it up right away. A few months later, on December 16, 1914, he introduced the Chevrolet Four-Ninety, that figure being its price tag and just happening to be also the price tag at which Henry Ford was selling his Model T. The car designed by Alfred Sturt — another former Buick man — was essentially a Series H stripped to essentials and offered in any color so long as it was black. This copycat approach from Chevrolet brought an immediate rejoinder from Ford; he lowered the Model T's price to $440. Durant began selling Four-Ninetys by the tens of thousands anyway, though by 1917 their price tag was $550, this including a self-starter which of course the Model T did not have. Because of Henry Ford's headstart with mass production of the T, however, he could consistently lower his car's price tag with the result that the differential between the cars widened through the years — and the Model T swamped the Chevrolet in sales. But as this was happening, Billy Durant was otherwise occupied. Mysteriously, large chunks of General Motors stock were being bought up, and proxies procured, and on September 16, 1915 — the seventh anniversary of

Trade-in time? This well-used 1914 Chevrolet "Royal Mail" roadster with homemade front bumper was driven by the couple posing with it to the Downtown Chevrolet dealership filled with 1929 models powered by Chevy's new six-cylinder engine, according to the poster in the window. This photo was most likely taken at the beginning of the Great Depression in October of 1929.

Billy Durant's founding of General Motors — he had the corporation back again. "Chevrolet Buys General Motors" was the headline — and though that was a simplification of the Durant maneuvers, it pretty much told the story. Unfortunately, with GM again his, Billy Durant began to neglect Chevrolet. The $1,400 Model D — ohv 90 degree V-8 on a 120-inch wheelbase designed by Mason and Sturt, and an admirable car — was really a step backwards insofar as the Chevrolet marketing philosophy was concerned; introduced late in 1917, it was ushered out at the end of 1918. The Series F had replaced the H for 1917, and was a bigger car, and bigger yet with the FB for 1919. Bigger, too, were the Chevrolet's price tags. Bigger yet was the trouble Billy Durant was getting himself into at the helm of General Motors. Just as the first time around, Durant was on a buying spree, and many of his purchases (especially Samson tractor that he hoped to be a competitor to the Fordson) proved disastrous. When the postwar recession hit in 1920, Billy Durant lost everything: Chevrolet, General Motors, the whole works. Undaunted, he would come back, of course, with Durant Motors, but the question now was what would happen to Chevrolet. Heading GM

was Pierre du Pont who initially favored scuttling the car, but Alfred Sloan, Jr., the man du Pont brought in to make sense of the wreckage of Durant's empire, talked him out of it. Instead of eliminating Chevrolet, Sloan eliminated most of the Durant men in the organization and replaced them with his own people: K.W. Zimmerscheid as Chevrolet general manager and president, O.E. Hunt (formerly of Packard and Mercer) as chief engineer. And recognizing that tackling Henry Ford head-on was ludicrous ("suicidal," Sloan said), the decision was made to create a price class of its own for the Chevrolet, low but not the lowest, a step up in dollars but a step up also in refinement and creature comforts that those dollars bought and that the Model T didn't have. Billy Durant himself had moved the Chevrolet toward this concept, but hadn't followed through. Sloan would — and it worked beautifully, though not immediately. First there was the misstep of the copper-cooled Chevrolet. It was an interesting idea; its engine, at 135 cubic inches, was the smallest in Chevrolet history but it promised fewer parts, less weight, lower cost and higher performance than a water-cooled unit; air-cooling was certainly something the Model T didn't have, and the promotional potential for the car looked terrific. Unfortunately, the copper-cooled Chevrolet was terrible. Some 759 of the cars were built, 239 of which were scrapped before ever leaving the factory. Of the cars dispatched to dealers, in June 1923 the company asked for every one of them back, in the first massive recall in Chevrolet history. Fortunately, there had been another Chevrolet to sell that year called Superior, successor to the Four-Ninety, the Model FB being dropped because it encroached on Oldsmobile and Oakland territory that was a market area in which Sloan didn't want the Chevrolet anyway. Meanwhile, Zimmerscheid, who had suffered a nervous breakdown during the copper-cooled fiasco, elected to retire. On January 15, 1924, Danish-born William S. Knudsen, Henry Ford's former production manager, became Chevrolet's president and general manager. "I vant vun for vun," he said at a dealer meeting in Chicago. That would take a while, but unquestionably the Chevrolet was making inroads into Model T territory. In 1924 Ford outsold Chevrolet by more than eight to one, in 1925 four to one, in 1926 less than three to one. Among the reasons for this was the, literally, superior Superior beginning in 1925 when the "infamous rear end," as Sloan called it — or the "Chevrolet hum" as had been the nickname for the noise made by the car's bevel gear rear axle since the first Four-Ninety days — was at last eliminated. Chevy's new rear axle was a one-piece banjo type with the entire differential mounted in a carrier that included the torque tube. Also new for 1925 was variety of colors: Chevrolet was the first low-priced car to go Duco. And the car's standard transmission, sported since the beginning, was by now an even greater plus in the marketplace, since the jokes about the Model T's planetary were no longer as funny as they used to be. In 1927 Knudsen went all out: "The Most Beautiful Chevrolet in Chevrolet History" read the ads. The bodies of the new Capitol series had a double belt, full crown fenders, bullet-shaped headlamps, and the $715 sport cabriolet was America's first low-priced car with a rumbleseat. In 1927 Chevrolet built over 1.7 million cars. For the first time since 1906 a car other than a Ford was number one in the industry. But Ford had virtually given away the number one spot in 1927 by shutting down his factory for six months, and ensuing production delays with the new Model A Ford would give Chevrolet easy victory in 1928, too. Thereafter the top spot would have to be earned. Like the new Model A, the new National series Chevrolet for 1928 had four-wheel brakes. But the all-new Chevrolet for 1929 had something the Ford didn't have: two more cylinders. The Cast Iron Wonder had arrived, Chevy now had a six for the price of a four, and a sturdy overhead valve engine that would endure into the early Fifties. The new cars were called International, appropriately since their body styling had the Continental flair that Harley Earl of GM's Art and Colour Department was trying to introduce to all corporation cars. Nonetheless, Ford, having sorted out the Model A production problems, was now in full swing and delivering cars to the tens of thousands of people who had never driven anything else but a Ford and who had been des-perately waiting for a new one since the T assembly line shutdown. Ford won the sales race in 1929 and in 1930, when the Chevrolet was called the Universal. In 1931 Chevy had it back with the Independence series, and retained the top spot in 1932 when Ford went to a V-8, which Chevy countered with the Confederate series offering synchromesh, freewheeling, four-point rubber engine mounts, downdraft carburetion and further engine tweaks to get 60 hp out of the Cast Iron Wonder, only five less than Ford's V-8. With the Great Depression in full cry, Chevrolet ushered in a cheaper six called the Standard in 1933, which made a Master of the old six — and first place again in the industry. In 1933 the cast of characters in the Chevrolet management team changed, as the corporation moved top men around to trouble spots within the GM family. William Knudsen was appointed executive vice-president for General Motors, his place at Chevrolet taken by his understudy of many years, Marvin Coyle. Harry Klingler, the super sales manager of Chevrolet since 1929, moved over to help troubled Pontiac, his place taken by the aptly named William Holler, who was a super salesman, too. Only chief engineer Jim Crawford (who had replaced O.E. Hunt in 1929) remained at Chevy, and he begged Knudsen to do what he could to get Knee Action for Chevrolet for 1934, initial thought having been that it should be reserved for the top-of-the-line GM cars. Knudsen won the argument, a good thing, too, since Plymouth also went independent front suspension in 1934. Ford stuck to transverse springs — and Chevy won the sales race again. Chevy lost in 1935, partly because of a labor strike, partly because the new Ford V-8 had pizzazz and was advertising 90 hp, as opposed to the 80 of Chevy's Blue Flame six (it had been called the Blue Streak in 1934 and there was no explicable reason for the name change to Blue Flame, though probably both designations were coined by Chevrolet public relations in hopes that people would start using them instead of Stovebolt Six, which Chevrolet's venerable engine was nicknamed). Henry Ford helped Chevrolet regain the top spot in 1936 by offering nothing new, which made Chevy's introduction of hydraulic brakes (Ford wouldn't have them until 1939) something to shout about. But the 1937 Chevrolet gave William Holler even more crowing opportunity, because the car was all-new, with a more compact and powerful (85 hp) version of the Cast Iron Wonder, a stiffer box-girder frame and hypoid rear axle. The 15 millionth Chevrolet was built in 1939; in 1940 a General Motors dealer from Argentina, Juan Manuel Fangio, began his remarkable racing career behind the wheel of a Chevrolet Master 85 that he drove to victory in the 5,900-mile Buenos Aires-Lima-Buenos Aires race at an average of 53.6 mph. From 1937 Chevrolet had remained solidly in first place in the industry, a position it would not relinquish for the remainder of the years before America's entrance into World War II brought a halt to automobile production. Postwar, Chevrolet's status as number one — indeed as the best-selling car in the world — would become a virtual tradition.

LITTLE

1912 Little, roadster, WLB

LITTLE — Flint, Michigan — (1912-1913) — The Little was one of two cars William C. Durant decided to build following his first ouster from General Motors. It was the first announced, on October 30th, 1911 — and the first to arrive, during late summer of 1912. The Little Motor Car Company was named for a huge bear of a man, William H. Little, Durant's former general manager at Buick. The car was more appropriately named than the man: it was little and cute as a button. A 20 hp $690 four on a 90-inch wheelbase, it was "simple to the point of innocence," according to Alex Hardy, the Durant man in charge of Little production. The car was produced at the Flint Wagon Works, which had previously seen manufacture of the Whiting. Meantime Bill Little himself was in Detroit, assigned as liaison to hurry Louis Chevrolet along in the design of the other car Billy Durant was planning to build. The new Chevrolet had been announced November 8th, 1911, a week after the Little, but Louis was taking his time finishing it. When finally during the summer of 1912 the prototype Chevrolet was completed, Durant was displeased. The car was too big, too heavy, too expensive; he knew he couldn't sell it for less than $2150. But at least it was a car to sell, so he ordered the

1913 Little Six, touring, HAC

Chevrolet into production. Meantime, aware of the costly direction the Chevrolet was taking, Durant had also decided to build a Little Six to sell for $1285, which was closer to his desired price range for the Chevrolet. Both cars arrived in the marketplace at the same time, which was unfortunate since each was a Durant car and tended to be confused or compared in the automotive press. This was to the benefit of neither, since the Chevrolet was sturdily built and expensive, and the Little was hastily built and inexpensive, Durant aware that it would be "driven to its death in less than 25,000 miles." A road test of that duration that Durant had ordered for the Little had proved it. Naturally, since the public was unaware of this, the Little's sales figures were far better than the Chevrolet's. Durant thus found himself with two cars, one that could be driven forever and wasn't selling, one that couldn't and was selling. His solution was to take the individual virtues of each car and combine them into one. Chevrolet was to be the one car. Among other factors, as Alex Hardy pointed out, the Little's name would ultimately have proved a negative, few people buying a small, inexpensive car wishing to be so pointedly reminded of it. And so the Little was discontinued without regrets in May of 1913 after approximately 3500 were built. All efforts now were focused on the Chevrolet. It appeared to be a wise decision.

MONROE

1915 Monroe, model M-2, roadster, WLB

1917 Monroe, model M-3, roadster, WLB

MONROE — Flint, Michigan — (1914-1916) / Pontiac, Michigan — (1916-1918) / Indianapolis, Indiana — (1918-1923) — Initially, the Monroe was a collaboration. R.F. Monroe headed the Monroe Body Company in Pontiac, William C. Durant was the man behind the Chevrolet in Flint. Although the Monroe Motor Company, which was organized in Flint in August of 1914, was separate and distinct from Chevrolet, there were a good many ties that bound. Monroe's president was R.F. Monroe; its vice-president was Durant. All of the stockholders of the Monroe company were also stockholders of Chevrolet, manufacture of the Monroe was begun in a plant formerly used by Chevrolet in Flint, and distribution of the Monroe was through the Chevrolet sales organization. The Monroe-Durant collaboration was short-lived, however. In April of 1916 Durant resigned his Monroe vice-presidency, and Monroe moved his company into the former Welch plant in Pontiac. Capital stock in the reorganized Monroe Motor Car Company was increased to $1 million, and R.F. Monroe announced that henceforth he would sell his cars himself. This he did for the two years following, and then went bankrupt. In the fall of 1918, the Monroe assets were purchased by the William Small Company of Indianapolis, the former distributor for Monroes in that city. The plant at Pontiac was leased to General Motors for production of its Samson tractors, and Monroe now moved to Indianapolis. Monroe had begun as a small light car fitted with a proprietary engine and offered in open body styles only. Now it sported an engine of its own make, a sedan was added — and Louis Chevrolet was recruited by William Small as a consulting engineer to "work out designing problems for the Monroe car." There was a nice irony in this, Chevrolet long since having disassociated himself from William C. Durant. The extent of Chevrolet's influence on the Monroe production car was limited, but he did move into the Small premises in Indianapolis where, with the help of Corne-

1918 Monroe, model MM-6, sedan, HAC

lius Van Ranst, he put together seven race cars, four of them to be campaigned under the Monroe name, three as Frontenacs. His brother Gaston Chevrolet drove a Monroe to victory in the 1920 Indianapolis 500, the first win by an American car at the Brickyard since 1912. Unfortunately, three months later, in August of 1920 William Small went into receivership. Refinancing schemes were tried thereafter, but ultimately in January of 1922 the Monroe assets were acquired at the receiver's sale for $175,000 in cash by the Fletcher American National Bank in Indianapolis. By March of 1923, Monroe had a new owner: Strattan Motors Corporation which had just been organized by Frank E. Strattan, who was also reported to have his eye on purchase of the Premier plant in town. Strattan announced that he would continue the Monroe and introduce a new lower-priced car to be called the Strattan. By June, however, he had sold his interest in the Monroe in order to concentrate all energies on the new lowpriced Strattan, which didn't survive the year. Meanwhile, Monroe had been bought from Strattan by Frederick Barrows of Premier. Initially, he organized this venture as Monroe Motors, Inc., but rather quickly the Monroe was simply absorbed into the Premier company. The last Monroes were sold as the Premier Model B.

1921 Monroe, model S, touring, JAC

1912

CHEVROLET — CLASSIC SIX — SERIES C — SIX:
The first Chevrolet bore a resemblance to the Republic Four, but was primarily an all-new automobile. Only one model — the Classic Six touring car — was available. It was built on a 120-inch wheelbase chassis. Features included ignition by dual system and dry cells, an English Air starter, drop-forged "I" front axle, full-floating rear axle, and cone clutch. The springs were semi-elliptic up front and three-quarter platform in the rear. The steering gear was of the worm and gear type. The body, frame, and wheels were finished in Chevrolet Blue-Black. The fenders, splash aprons, and hood were black. A light gray stripe decorated the body and wheels. A German silver radiator bore the Chevrolet name in script. Standard equipment included a top, top boot, windshield, speedometer, electric speedometer light, self starter, demountable rims, extra tire holders, electric lights, gas gauge, two-gallon auxiliary oil tank, 20-gallon gas tank and runningboard mounted tool kit.

1912 Chevrolet, Classic Six, touring, OCW

I.D. DATA: Serial numbers were not used.

Model No.	Body Type & Seating	Price	Weight	Prod. Total
C	4-dr. Tr.-5P	2250	NA	2999

ENGINE: T-head. Twin cam. Six (Cast in three banks of two). Cast iron block. B & S: 3-9/16 x 5 in. Disp.: 299 cu. in. Brake H.P.: 40. Net H.P.: 30 N.A.C.C. Main bearings: three. Valve lifters: solid.

CHASSIS: W.B.: 120 in. Front/Rear Tread: 56/56 in. Tires: 35 x 4.5.

TECHNICAL: Rear axle mounted selective sliding transmission. Speeds: 3F/1R. Floor-mounted gearshift controls. Cone type clutch. Full-floating rear axle. Internal expanding rear brakes. Wood spoke artillery wheels.

OPTIONS: Front bumper, Moto-meter. Spare tire(s). 60 in. Southern tread. Outside rear view mirror. Running-board luggage gate. Whitewall tires.

HISTORICAL: Introduced November 1911. Calendar year production: 2,999. Innovations: First car to bear Chevrolet nameplate. Chevrolet Motor Company was incorporated November 3, 1911.

1913

CHEVROLET — CLASSIC SIX — SERIES C — SIX:
The 1913 Classic Six was virtually unchanged from the original, except for the design of the windshield. The method of mounting the windshield was now to bolt it to a swept back cowl, instead of directly to the dashboard. Also, the braces ran from the dash to the center hinges of the windshield frame. There is no record of exactly when the change took place — it may have been phased into production in late 1912. Thus, the later design cannot be used to date a car, but all 1913 models have swept back cowls. Colors and equipment were as in 1912.

1913 Chevrolet, Classic Six, touring, OCW

I.D. DATA: Serial numbers were not used. Engine numbers identified the cars. Numbers are not available.

Model No.	Body Type & Seating	Price	Weight	Prod. Total
C	4-dr. Tr.-5P	2500	NA	5987

ENGINE: T-head. Twin cam. Six (Cast in three banks of two). Cast iron block. B & S: 3-9/16 x 5 in. Disp.: 299 cu. in. Brake H.P.: 40. Net H.P.: 30 N.A.C.C. Main bearings: three. Valve lifters: solid. Carb.: Stromberg (exhaust heated type).

CHASSIS: W.B.: 120 in.

TECHNICAL: Rear axle mounted selective sliding transmission. Speeds: 3F/1R. Floor-mounted gearshift controls. Cone type clutch. Full-floating rear axle. Internal expanding rear wheel brakes.

OPTIONS: Front bumper. Moto-meter. Spare tire(s). 60 in. Southern tread. Outside rear view mirror. Running-board luggage gate. Whitewall tires.

HISTORICAL: Introduced late 1912. Calendar year production: 5,987. Innovations: New windshield mounting and bracing system. W.C. Durant merged the Little Motor Car Company with Chevrolet in 1913. He gave the Chevrolet name to the Little car and moved the Detroit plant to his Flint Wagon Works. A second assembly plant was leased in New York City. The Chevrolet "bow-tie" trademark was used for the first time this year, on all Light Six models.

1914

CHEVROLET — SERIES H — FOUR: The all-new 1914 H Series came in two body styles called the "Royal Mail" roadster and "Baby Grand" touring. (These names would be used on Chevrolet F, FA, and FB models built through 1922.) Early versions had a flat wooden dash. This was replaced in mid-year with a streamlined, all-metal dash and cowl. The folding windshield was braced to the cowl. The touring had a two-man top and came in Chevrolet gray or plum color finish with black chassis and gray wheels. The roadster was finished only in Chevrolet gray with black chassis and gray wheels. The Royal Mail had a flat rear deck. "Standard" equipment included top, curtains, windshield, speedometer, horn, spare tire, and complete tool kit. Early Royal Mails had 30 x 3-1/2 clincher type tires.

1914 Chevrolet, roadster, OCW

CHEVROLET — LIGHT SIX — SERIES L — SIX: Available only as a touring car, the new Light Six came in Chevrolet blue or gun metal gray. The chassis and wheels were blue. Standard equipment included mohair top, top boot, side curtains, ventilating windshield, foot rail, robe rail, speedometer, electric horn, demountable rims, spare tire carrier on rear (with extra rim), two double bulb electric headlamps, electric taillamp, Auto-Lite starter, LBA battery, and complete tool kit.

CHEVROLET — CLASSIC SIX — SERIES C — SIX: This large touring car was in its last season. The Chevrolet name appeared in script on the front. The radiator shell and Chevrolet nameplate were silver. The finish color was a dark (almost black) color called Chevrolet blue. It was used on the body, frame, and wheels. The fenders and splash aprons and hood were black. Light gray striping was seen on the body and wheels. Standard equipment included a top, boot, windshield, speedometer, electric lights, self-starter, demountable rims, extra tire holders, electric lights, and gas gauge. A two-gallon auxiliary oil tank was under the seat. Side curtains were stored in a compartment under the rear seat. Tools were stored in a box located under the runningboard, which was integral with it. There was a console-like storage fixture between the front seats.

I.D. DATA: [Series H] Serial numbers were not used. Engine numbers identified the cars. Starting: 1. Ending: 6243. [Series L] Serial numbers were not used. Engine numbers identified the cars. Starting: 1. Ending: 6243. [Series C] Serial numbers were not used. Engine numbers identified the cars. Engine numbers are not available.

Model No.	Body Type & Seating	Price	Weight	Prod. Total
H-2	2-dr. Rds.-2P	750	1975	Note 3
H-4	4-dr. Tr.-5P	875	2500	Note 3

NOTE 1: Above price is for cars with Prest-o-Lite lights and magneto. With an Auto-Lite system the roadster was $875 and the touring was $1,000.

L	4-dr. Tr.-5P	1475	3050	Note 3

NOTE 2: With Prest-o-Lite lighting and magneto the price was $125 higher.

C	4-dr. Tr.-5P	2500	3750	Note 3

NOTE 3: Total production was 5,005 Chevrolets of all models.

ENGINE: [Model H] Engine: Ohv. Inline (cast enbloc). Four-cylinder. Cast iron block. B & S: 3-11/16 x 4 in. Disp.: 171 cu. in. Brake H.P.: 24. Net H.P.: 21.75 N.A.C.C. Main bearings: three. Valve lifters: solid. Carb.: Zenith two-jet. [Model L] Engine: L-head. Inline (cast in blocks of three). Six. Cast iron block. B & S: 3-5/16 x 5-1/4 in. Disp.: 271 cu. in. Brake H.P.: 35. Net H.P.: 26 N.A.C.C. Main bearings: three. Valve lifters: solid. Carb.: Zenith two-jet. [Model C] Engine: T-head. Twin cam. Inline. Six (cast in three banks of two). Cast iron block. B & S: 3-9/16 x 5 in. Disp.: 299 cu. in. Brake H.P.: 40. Net H.P.: 30 N.A.C.C. Main bearings: three. Valve lifters: solid. Carb.: Stromberg (exhaust heated type).

CHASSIS: [Series H] W.B.: 104 in. Front/Rear Tread: 56/56 in. Tires: 32 x 3.5. [Series L] W.B.: 112 in. Front/Rear Tread: 56/56 in. Tires: 34 x 4. [Series C] W.B.: 120 in. Front/Rear Tread: 56/56 in. Tires: 35 x 4.5. A special 60 in. tread for use on roads in the South was available.

TECHNICAL: Selective sliding (mounted on rear axle on Light/Classic sixes). Speeds: 3F/1R. Floor-mounted gearshift controls. Cone type clutch. Rear axle: [Model

C] full-floating. [Model L] three-quarter floating. [Model H] semi-floating. [Classic Six] Internal expanding rear wheel brakes. [Others] External contracting rear wheel brakes. Wood spoke artillery wheels. Drivetrain options: Free-wheeling. Vacuum clutch. Hill-holder. Automatic transmission. Overdrive.

OPTIONS: Front bumper. Moto-meter. Auto-Lite electrical system. Spare tire(s). 60-in. Southern tread. Outside rear view mirror. Runningboard luggage gate. Houk wire wheels on "H" series.

1914 Chevrolet, touring, OCW

HISTORICAL: Introduced late 1913. Calendar year production: (All) 5,005. Innovations: (H) First Chevrolet ohv four-cylinder engine. (L) only L-head Chevrolet ever built. Large 112-inch wheelbase. (C) Gray & Davis electric starter. Simms ignition. Longest wheelbase in Chevrolet history (also used on 1917-19 V-8). Louis Chevrolet leaves company over dispute with W.C. Durant. In June 1914 the Maxwell Motor Company's Tarrytown, New York, plant was purchased by Chevrolet. A new sales office was set up in Oakland, California.

1915

CHEVROLET — SERIES H — FOUR: The 1915 Chevrolet fours had the same general appearance as 1914 editions, but the wheelbase grew to 106 in. Another change was the use of concealed door hinges. Larger tires with demountable rims were a new feature. The windshield cowl braces were removed. A starter became standard equipment. The diameter of the steering wheel went up to 17 inches. A new "Amesbury Special" roadster was introduced. It had the racy lines of an imported car and an exposed wooden dashboard. A lockable rear deck was featured. The one-piece windshield was fitted behind the seat. Standard on all models were the top, top hood, windshield, speedometer, and demountable rims.

CHEVROLET — SERIES L — SIX: The Light Six, Model L was the only Chevrolet ever to use an L-head engine. It came only as a touring car available in Chevrolet blue or gun metal gray. The chassis and wheels were blue. Standard equipment included mohair top, cover, side curtains, ventilating windshield, foot rail, robe rail, speedometer, electric horn, demountable rims, spare tire carrier on rear, extra rim, two double-bulb electric headlamps, electric taillamp, Auto-Lite starter, LBA battery, and complete tool equipment.

I.D. DATA: [Series H] Serial numbers were not used. Engine numbers located on flywheel and on the left front engine mount. Starting: 6244. Ending: 13000. [Series L] Serial numbers ran from 501 to 1000.

Model No.	Body Type & Seating	Price	Weight	Prod. Total
H-2	2-dr. Rds.-2P	750	2000	Note 1
H-4	4-dr. Tr.-5P	850	2500	Note 1
H-3	2-dr. Spl. Rds.-2P	985	2100	Note 1

NOTE 1: Total production for calendar 1915 was 13,605 Chevrolets including 313 cars built in Canada.

NOTE 2: Model H-2 also called "Royal Mail"; Model H-4 also called "Baby Grand"; Model H-3 also called "Amesbury Special."

L	4-dr. Tr.-5P	1475	3050	1000

1915 Chevrolet, roadster, HAC

ENGINE: [Series H] Ohv. Inline. Four. Cast iron block. B & S: 3-11/16 x 4 in. Disp.: 171 cu. in. Brake H.P.: 24. Net H.P.: 21.75 N.A.C.C.: Main bearings: three. Valve lifters: solid. Carb.: Zenith two-jet. [Series L] L-head. Inline (three banks of two each). Six. Cast iron block. B & S: 3-5/16 x 5-1/4 in. Disp.: 271 cu. in. Brake H.P.: 30. Net H.P.: 26.3. Main bearings: three. Valve lifters: solid. Carb.: Zenith double-jet.

CHASSIS: [Series H] W.B.: 106 in. Front/Rear Tread: 56/56 in. Tires: 32 x 3.5. [Series L] W.B.: 112 in. Front/Rear Tread: 56/56 in. Tires: 34 x 4.

TECHNICAL: Selective sliding gear transmission. Speeds: 3F/1R. Floor-mounted gearshift controls. Cone type clutch. Rear axles: (H) semi-floating; (L) three-quarter floating. Contracting and expanding rear wheel brakes. Wood artillery spoke wheels. Transaxle on Series L six.

OPTIONS: Front bumper. Spare tire. Outside rear view mirror. Houk quick-detachable wire wheels ($125). Auto Lite electric system, on H ($60); on L ($125). Moto-meter. "Fat Man" steering wheel. Southern gauge (60 in. track).

HISTORICAL: Introduced 1915 (490 introduced in January 1915 and placed on sale June 1, 1915). Innovations: (H) Larger wheelbase. Starter option mounted on flywheel at rear of engine. New "Amesbury Special" roadster. Electric lights became standard equipment. Calendar year production: 13,605. Model year production: (H) 13,600; (L) 1,000; (Total) 14,600.

Chevrolet sales offices opened in Kansas City, Missouri, and Atlanta, Georgia. New factories established in St. Louis, Missouri, and Oshawa, Canada. Chevrolet also licensed Gardner Buggy Co. to assemble cars in St. Louis. Within 17 days of putting the new 490 on the market, Chevrolet Motor Co. had accepted 46,611 orders for the car, valued at $23,329,390.

1916

CHEVROLET — SERIES 490 — FOUR: Named after the price of the two basic models, the Chevrolet 490 series was new for 1916. Neither the touring nor the roadster had a left front door. A vertical windshield was one styling trait. Front fenders followed a straight line from behind the center of the front wheels to the front of the running-boards and no splash guards were used. Standard equipment included a top, top hood and the windshield. The rear curtain in the top hood had a single celluloid window. With an electric lighting and starting system the price was $550. Cars so equipped had a Connecticut automatic ignition system instead of a magneto.

1916 Chevrolet, Series 490, touring, HAC

CHEVROLET — SERIES H — FOUR: The Model H Chevrolet was about the same as in 1915. Both the flat deck "Royal Mail" and the "Baby Grand" touring were carried over. The Model H-2-1/2 Special Roadster replaced the "Amesbury Special." It had a conventional rear deck and Brewster green finish. The other cars were finished in French gray with green patent leather upholstery. Standard equipment included a top, top hood, windshield, speedometer, ammeter and demountable rims on all models.

I.D. DATA: Serial numbers were not used on 1916 models in the 490 series. Series H serial numbers were not used. Engine numbers located on the flywheel. Engine numbers for 1916 were 13001 to 29390.

Model No.	Body Type & seating	Price	Weight	Prod. Total
490	1-dr. Rds.-2P	490	1820	Note 1
490	3-dr. Tr.-5P	490	1910	Note 1
H-2	2-dr. Rds.-2P	720	2000	Note 1
H-4	4-dr. Rds.-5P	720	2500	Note 1
H-2-1/2	2-dr. Spl. Rds.-2P	750	2100	Note 1

NOTE 1: Total production was 70,701 Chevrolets including 7,721 cars made in Canada.

NOTE 2: Model H-2 also called "Royal Mail"; Model H-4 also called "Baby Grand"; Model H-2-1/2 also called "Royal Mail" Turtledeck Roadster.

ENGINE: Ohv. Inline. Four. Cast iron block. B & S: 3-11/16 x 4 in. Disp.: 171 cu. in. Brake H.P.: 24. Net H.P.: 21.74 N.A.C.C. Main bearings: three. Valve lifters: solid. Carb.: Zenith one-inch double-jet.

CHASSIS: [Series 490] W.B.: 102 in. Front/Rear Tread: 56/56 in. Tires: (front) 30 x 3; (rear) 30 x 3.5. [Series H] W.B.: 106 in. Front/Rear Tread: 56/56 in. Tires: 32 x 3.5.

TECHNICAL: Selective sliding transmission. Speeds: 3F/1R. Floor-mounted gearshift controls. Cone type clutch. Rear axles: (490) three-quarter floating; (H) semi-floating. External contracting rear wheel brakes. Wood spoke artillery wheels.

OPTIONS: Front bumper. Spare tire. Outside rear view mirror. Moto-meter. Southern gauge (60-in. track). (H) A Simms high tension magneto was standard equipment. For $125 extra buyers could order the Auto-Lite starting, generating, and lighting system with battery. Cars so equipped had a Connecticut coil and distributor in place of magneto. (490) Similar electrical equipment was $60 extra. "Fat Man" steering wheel.

HISTORICAL: Introduced during late 1915. Calendar year production: 62,898. Model year production: (490) 18,000 approximate; (H) 52,000 approximate. Innovations: (490) New Series 490 designed as low cost auto to compete with Model T Ford. (H) Open Hotchkiss drive used on cars built at Tarrytown. Radius rods for improved rear axle alignment.

Chevrolet was now operating plants in Ft. Worth, Texas, and Bay Cities, Michigan. The Warner Gear factory in Toledo, Ohio, was purchased as a Chevrolet manufacturing plant. Chevrolet also opened the auto industry's first West Coast plant in Oakland, California. First closed car bodies built by Chevrolet this year. Production hits 70,701 unit mark.

1917

CHEVROLET — SERIES 490 — FOUR: For 1917 the 490 was changed little in appearance. A left front door was added. Electric lamps became standard equipment. A new model called the All-Season touring car had a permanent hardtop replacing the folding top. Flexible sliding windows disappeared into the roof and removable side sections were used. The top even had a dome lamp. The interior was trimmed in cloth upholstery. All models were finished in black. A self-starter was now standard equipment. New touring car body improvements included foot and robe rails, a tilted windshield, a one-man top with curtains of the improved type, protection flaps on the door tops, door storage pockets, a kickpad at the rear of the front seat, and demountable rims.

1917 Chevrolet, touring, HAC

CHEVROLET — SERIES F — FOUR: A new Series F replaced the Series H for the 1917 season. It had a longer wheelbase. Two models were offered. The "Royal Mail" was the roadster and the "Baby Grand" was the touring car. On both models the front fenders followed a straight line from just behind the center of the front wheels to the runningboard. A vertical, nonfolding windshield was standard equipment. An Auto-Lite generator, starter, and lighting system with Remy ignition was standard.

I.D. DATA: [Series 490] Serial number system same as on Model F except 490s were also built in St. Louis (code 3), Oakland (code 6) and Ft. Worth (code 7) plants. Serial numbers not used prior to July 1. Starting: 1-8972. Ending: 1-37468. Also: 2-22507 to 2-36488; 3-8512 to 3-15000; 6-5977 to 6-10089; 7-3001 to 7-5842 and 9-151 to 9-1935. Engine numbers located on flywheel. Engine numbers not available. [Series F] Serial number located on dashboard nameplate. Factory codes: 1 is Flint, 2 is Tarrytown, and 9 is Oshawa (Canada). Starting: 1-1222. Ending: 1-3430. Also: 2-2894 to 2-4113 and 9-466 to 9-532. Engine numbers located on flywheel. Engine numbers not available.

Model No.	Body Type & Seating	Price	Weight	Prod. Total
490	2-dr. Rds.-2P	535	1820	Note 1
490	4-dr. Tr.-5P	550	1890	Note 1
490	4-dr. All-Season Touring-5P	625	NA	Note 1
F-2	2-dr. Rds.-2P	800	2640	Note 1
F-5	4-dr. Tr.-5P	800	2745	Note 1

NOTE 1: Total production was 125,882 Chevrolets including 14,005 cars built in Canada.

NOTE 2: Price of both models increased to $875 during the year.

ENGINE: [Series 490] Ohv. Inline. Four. Cast iron block. B & S: 3-11/16 x 4 in. Disp.: 171 cu. in. Brake H.P.: 24. Net H.P.; 21.75 N.A.C.C. Main bearings: three. Valve lifters: solid. Carb.: Zenith double-jet. [Series F] Ohv. Inline. Four. Cast iron block. B & S: 3-1/16 x 4 in. Disp.: 171 cu. in. Brake H.P.: 24. Net H.P.: 21.75 N.A.C.C. Main bearings: three. Valve lifters: solid. Carb.: Zenith double-jet.

CHASSIS: [Series 490] W.B.: 108 in. Front/Rear Tread: 56/56 in. Tires: 32 x 3-1/2. [Series F] W.B.: 102 in. Front/Rear Tread: 56/56 in. Tires: (front) 30 x 3. (rear) 30 x 3.5.

TECHNICAL: Selective sliding transmission. Speeds: 3F/1R. Floor-mounted gearshift controls. Cone type clutch. Three-quarter floating rear axle. Overall ratio: 3.5:1. External contracting rear wheel brakes. Artillery spoke wood wheels.

OPTIONS: Self-starter and electric lights ($60). Motometer. Outside rear view mirror. Spare tire. Demountable rims (on roadster). Southern gauge (60-in. track). "Fat Man" steering wheel. Front bumper.

HISTORICAL: Introduced 1917. Innovations: (490) Plunger type oil pump. Open valve train. Cone type clutch. Ball bearing front wheels. Quarter elliptic springs. Duplex type front spring deleted. New all-season car. (F) Larger wheelbase. Calendar year production: 110,839. Model year production: (490) 57,692; (F) 3,493; (Total) 61,185. Company president: William C. Durant.

Early in 1917 the Monroe Motor Co. was sold to William Small of Flint, Michigan. Thereafter, this brand was no longer sold by Chevrolet dealers. Also on the business front, the Mason Motor Co. of Flint merged with Chevrolet to build engines. Chevrolet was not yet part of General Motors. Chevrolet introduced its V-8 Model D in 1917. Specifications for this model are given in the 1918 chapter.

1918

CHEVROLET — SERIES 490 — FOUR: New models this year were all-season coupes and sedans with removable center posts. Open cars had a windshield with a 15-degree backward slant. Wheel felloes were square and demountable rims were standardized. Closed cars featured a rear mounted gas tank. Standard equipment included a top, top hood, windshield, speedometer, ammeter, tire pump, electric horn, and demountable rims. The bodies were built by Ionia Body Co. and finished by Chevrolet.

CHEVROLET — SERIES FA — FOUR: The FA series replaced the F. It was much the same as far as appearance. Open cars had a windshield with a 15-degree slant. The sedan had removable roof center posts. Standard equipment included top, top hood, windshield, speedometer, ammeter, tire pump, electric horn, and demountable rims.

1918 Chevrolet, center-door sedan, OCW

CHEVROLET — SERIES D — V-8: The Chevrolet V-8 Series D came in two models. The D-4 was a four-passenger roadster, the D-5 a five-passenger touring. Both were finished in Chevrolet green and had French-pleated leather upholstery. A 20-gallon gas tank was mounted at the rear of the frame. The touring was a four-door model. The roadster was actually more of a two-door "dual-cowl" touring car. Rear slanting hood louvers were used. The body was described as "a delight to the eye" and "a series of curves that blend harmoniously." All visible woodwork was of genuine mahogany and metal parts were nickel. The body foundation was of pressed steel. Standard equipment included a one-man waterproof top with side curtains and Bair brackets; windshield; 16 candle power headlights; speedometer; demountable rims with extra rim; tire carrier; license holder; and tools. Experts believe that production started late in 1917, and that the car was discontinued late in 1918. This was most likely the only full year for the model. To conserve space we are listing specifications in this book under 1918 only, although the Master Price Lists from Chevrolet include the model in 1917, 1918, and 1919. Production breakdown for those three years are indicated below.

I.D. DATA: [Series 490] Serial number located on dash nameplate. Factory codes were: 1 is Flint; 2 is Tarrytown; 3 is St. Louis; 6 is Oakland; 7 is Ft. Worth; and 9 is Oshawa (Canada). Starting: 1-37469. Ending: 1-59674. Also: 2-36489 to 2-59958; 3-15001 to 3-24000; 6-10090 to 6-20097; 7-5843 to 7-15110 and 9-1936 to 9-1935. Engine numbers located on flywheel. Engine numbers not available. [Series FA] Serial number sys-

tem same as on 490. Starting: 1-3431. Ending: 1-10241. Also: 2-4114 to 2-7432 and 9-772 to 9-2047. Engine numbers located on flywheel. Engine numbers not available. [Series D] Serial number system same as on 490 and FB. Starting: (1917) 1-8; (1918) 1-242. Ending: (1917) 1-241; (1918) 1-1557. Also: (1917) 2-2894 to 2-4112; (1918) 2-4113 to 2-7437 and (1917) 9-466 to 9-532; (1918) 9-533 to 9-727.

Model No.	Body Type & Seating	Price	Weight	Prod. Total
490	4-dr. Tr.-5P	685	1890	Note 1
490	2-dr. Rds.-2P	660	1820	Note 1
490	2-dr. A/W Cpe.-3P	1060	2040	Note 1
490	3-dr. A/W Sed.-4P	1060	2160	Note 1
FA-2	2-dr. Rds.-2P	935	2640	Note 1
FA-5	3-dr. Tr.-5P	935	2680	Note 1
FA-4	2-dr. A/W Sed.-4P	1475	2950	Note 1
D-4	2-dr. Rds.-4P	1550	3150	Note 1
D-5	4-dr. Tr.-5P	1550	3200	Note 1

NOTE 1: Total production of the Chevrolet 490 was 95,660 cars including 13,840 made in Canada. Total production of the Series D (V-8) was 511 in 1917; 2,199 in 1918; and 71 in 1919.

NOTE 2: Prices in 1917 were $1,385 for both models.

1918 Chevrolet, Series 490, touring, JAC

ENGINE: [Series 490] Ohv. Inline. Four. Cast iron block. B & S: 3-11/16 x 4 in. Disp.: 171 cu. in. Brake H.P.: 26 @ 1800 R.P.M. Net H.P.: 21.75 N.A.C.C. Main bearings: three. Valve lifters: solid. Carb.: IV. [Series FA] Ohv. Inline. Four. Cast iron block. B & S: 3-11/16 x 5-1/4 in. Disp.: 224 cu in. Brake H.P.: 37 @ 2000 R.P.M. Net H.P.: 21.75 N.A.C.C. Main bearings: three. Valve lifters: solid. Carb.: one-barrel. [Series D] 90# V-Block. Ohv. Eight. Cast iron block. B & S: 3-3/8 x 4 in. Disp.: 288 cu. in. Net H.P.: 36 N.A.C.C. Main bearings: three. Valve lifters: solid. Carb.: Zenith double-jet.

CHASSIS: [Series 490] W.B.: 102 in. Front/Rear Tread: 56/56 in. Tires: 30 x 3.5. [Series FA] W.B.: 108 in. Front/Rear Tread: 56/56 in. Tires: 33 x 4. [Series D] W.B.: 120 in. Tires: 34 x 4 (non-skid on rear).

TECHNICAL: Selective sliding transmission. Speeds: 3F/1R. Floor-mounted gearshift controls. Cone type clutch. Three-quarter rear axle. Overall ratio: (490) 3.63:1; (FB) 4.62:1; (D) 4.25:1. External contracting rear wheel brakes. Wood spoke wheels.

OPTIONS: Spare tire. Moto-meter. Outside rear view mirror (fender mount). "Fat Man" steering wheel. 60-in. Southern tread.

HISTORICAL: Introduced late 1917. Calendar year production: 80,434. Model year production: (490) 86,200; (FA) 11,403; (D) 4,833. Innovations: (490) New water pump. New gear oil pump. Spur and gear steering with one-piece main shaft. New oil pressure gauge. (FA) larger displacement engine. New water pumps. (D) All new V-8 (introduced in late 1917 as 1917 model).

Chevrolet joined GM in 1918. St. Louis assembly plant opens. Truck production started, Chevrolet headquarters still at 57th St. and Broadway in New York City. Royal Mail and Baby Grand names dropped. Same styles continue as roadster and touring in FA series.

1919

CHEVROLET — SERIES 490 — FOUR: Only a few minor changes were made in 1919 models. On open cars a Bair top saddle replaced the old-fashioned, bolt-on type. The spare tire carrier was now of three-quarter circle design with a lever. Fixed center posts and a full frame door were now used on the 490 coupe. Prices included top, top hood, windshield, speedometer, ammeter, tire pump, electric horn, and demountable rims.

CHEVROLET — SERIES FB — FOUR: The first 1,514 Chevrolet sedans built used the body and all chassis sheet metal from the FA. Later sedans and all other body types were completely new for 1919. New front fenders featured a stylish reverse curve. A new 110-inch wheelbase was used. The later sedans were four-door models. The new FB coupe had fixed center posts and a full frame door. Prices included top, top hood, windshield, speedometer, ammeter, tire pump, electric horn, and demountable rims.

I.D. DATA: [Series 490] Serial number located on dash nameplate. Factory codes: 1 is Flint; 2 is Tarrytown; 3 is St. Louis; 6 is Oakland; 7 is Ft. Worth; and 9 is Oshawa (Canada). Starting: 1-59675. Ending: 1-92474. Also: 259959 to 2-90421; 3-24001 to 3-47100; 6-20098 to 6-36684; 7-15111 to 7-25429; and 9-14187 to 9-28153. Engine numbers located on flywheel. Engine numbers not available. [Series FB] Serial number system was same as on 490. Starting: 1-100. Ending: 1-9384. Also: 2-100 to 2-4738; 6-1001 to 6-1289; and 9-104 to 9-1335. Engine numbers located on flywheel. Engine numbers unknown.

Model No.	Body Type & Seating	Price	Weight	Prod. Total
490	2-dr. Rds.-2P	715	1820	Note 1
490	4-dr. Tr.-5P	735	1890	Note 1
490	4-dr. Sed.-4P	1185	2160	Note 1
490	2-dr. Cpe.-3P	1100	2040	Note 1
FB-20	2-dr. Rds.-2P	1110	2640	Note 1
FB-30	4-dr. Tr.-5P	1235	2880	Note 1
FB-50	2-dr. Cpe.-3P	1635	2820	Note 1
FB-40	4-dr. Sed.-4P	1685	2950	Note 1
FB-40	2-dr. Sed.-4P*	1685	2950	Note 1

NOTE 1: Total production of Chevrolets was 149,904 including 17,431 cars made in Canada.

NOTE 2: * This was the FB sedan using the old FA body with a center opening door on passenger side.

· 1919 Chevrolet, touring, HAC

ENGINE: [Series 490] Ohv. Inline. Four. Cast iron block. B & S: 3-11/16 x 4 in. Disp.: 171 cu. in. Brake H.P.: 26 @ 1800 R.P.M. Net H.P.: 21.75 N.A.C.C. Main bearings: three. Valve lifters: solid. Carb.: one-barrel. [Series FB] Ohv. Inline. Four. Cast iron block. B & S: 3-11/16 x 5-1/4 in. Disp.: 224 cu. in. Brake H.P.: 37 @ 2000 R.P.M. Net H.P.: 21.75. Main bearings: three. Carb.: one barrel.

CHASSIS: [Series 490] W.B.: 102 in. Front/Rear Tread: 56/56 in. Tires: 30 x 3.5. [Series FB] W.B.: 110 in. Front/Rear Tread: 56/56 in. Tires: 33 x 4.

TECHNICAL: Selective sliding transmission. Speeds: 3F/1R. Floor-mounted gearshift controls. Cone type clutch. Three-quarter floating rear axle. Overall ratio: (490) 3.63:1; (FB) 4.62:1. External contracting two-wheel brakes. Artillery spoke wheels.

OPTIONS: Out side rear view mirror (fender mounted). Spare tire. Moto-meter. "Fat Man" steering wheel. 60-in. Southern gauge.

HISTORICAL: Introduced late 1918. Calendar year production: 123,371. Model year production: [Series 490] 127,231; [Series FB] 14,516. Innovations: (490) Speedometer drive taken from universal joint. Four-button switch changed to lever type. Fixed center post coupe. (FB) completely new line introduced this year.

This was Chevrolet's first full year as part of General Motors Corp. Some sources show the Series D V-8 as a 1919 model, but there are no 1919 serial numbers for V-8s. Some 1918 models may have been sold as 1919s.

1920

CHEVROLET — SERIES 490 — FOUR: Although automotive styling wasn't around in 1920, Chevrolet did make a change in the 490's appearance. It was done by replacing the old straight fenders with a reverse curve type. They also mounted the headlights on steel brackets and eliminated the tie-bar. New for open models was a top with two round windows in the rear.

CHEVROLET — SERIES FB — FOUR: Reverse curve front fenders were also used on the FB Series Chevrolets for 1920. Otherwise there was little change from the first FB models of 1919.

1920 Chevrolet, coupe, HAC

I.D. DATA: [Series 490] Serial number located on nameplate on dash. Prefix indicates plant. 1 is Flint; 2 is Tarrytown; 3 is St. Louis; 6 is Oakland; 7 is Ft. Worth; and 9 is Oshawa (Canada). Starting: 1-92475. Ending: 1A-20160. Also: 2-90422 to 2A-23673; 3-47101 to 3A-70100; 6-36685 to 6A-51094; 7-25430 to 7A-34121; 9-28154 to 9-A40225. Engine numbers located on flywheel. Engine numbers not available. [Series FB] Serial number system same as on Series 490. Starting: 1-9385. Ending: 1-20516. Also: 2-4739 to 2-10634; 3-54 to 3-1600; 6-1290 to 6-4990; and 9-1336 to 9-4604. Engine numbers located on flywheel. Engine numbers not available.

Series 490

Model No.	Body Type & Seating	Price	Weight	Prod. Total
490	2-dr. Rds.-2P	795	1820	Note 2
490	4-dr. Tr.-5P	810	1895	Note 2
490	4-dr. Sed.-5P	1285	2160	Note 2
490	2-dr. Cpe.-3P	1210	2040	Note 2

NOTE 1: Prices dropped about $100 during 1920 model year.

Series FB

FB	2-dr. Rds.-2P	1270	2160	Note 2
FB	4-dr. Tr.-5P	1355	2800	Note 2
FB	4-dr. Sed.-5P	1885	2950	Note 2
FB	2-dr. Cpe.-3P	1855	2820	Note 2

Note 2: Total production was 150,226 Chevrolets including 18,847 cars made in Canada.

Note 3: Prices dropped $60-$100 during 1921.

ENGINE: [Series 490] Ohv. Inline. Four. Cast iron block. B & S: 3-11/16 x 4 in. Disp.: 171 cu. in. Brake H.P.: 26 @ 1800 R.P.M. Net H.P.: 21.75 N.A.C.C. Main bearings: three. Valve lifters: solid. Carb.: one-barrel. [Series FB] Ohv. Inline. Four. Cast iron block. B & S: 3-11/16 x 5-1/4 in. Disp.: 224 cu. in. Brake H.P.: 37 @ 2000 R.P.M. Net H.P.: 21.75. Main bearings: three. Valve lifters: solid. Carb.: one-barrel.

CHASSIS: [Series 490] W.B.: 102. Tires: 30 x 3-1/2. [Series FB] W.B.: 110. Tires: 33 x 4.

TECHNICAL: Selective sliding transmission. Speeds: 3F/1R. Floor-mounted gearshift controls. Cone type clutch. (490) two-piece rear axle. (FB) 3/4 floating rear axle. Overall ratio: (490) 3.63:1; (FB) 4.62:1. External contracting rear brakes. Wood spoke wheels.

OPTIONS: Front bumper. Rear bumper. Spare tire. Spare tire cover. Step plates. "Fat Man" steering wheel. Moto-meter. Cowl lights. Wind wings. Outside rear view mirror. Special paint.

HISTORICAL: Introduced January 1920. Model year production: (490) 129,106; (FB) 17,137; total: 146,243 approximate. Calendar year production: 121,908. Innovations: Gravity fuel feed on 490. Vacuum fuel feed on FB.

W.C. Durant leaves General Motors for second time. Karl W. Zimmerscheid becomes president of Chevrolet.

1921

CHEVROLET — SERIES 490 — FOUR: The 1921 Chevrolet 490 was virtually unchanged in appearance from last year. The passenger side door on the sedan was moved to a position in the center of the car. Larger size 31 x 4 tires were used on closed models only.

CHEVROLET — SERIES FB — FOUR: There were no basic changes in Series FB Chevrolets from 1920. The same four body styles remained in production.

I.D. DATA: [Series 490] Serial number located on nameplate on dash. Prefix indicates plant. 1A is Flint; 2A is Tarrytown; 3 is St. Louis; 6 is Oakland; and 9 is Oshawa (Canada). Starting: 1A-20161. Ending: 1A-59938. Also: 2A-23674 to 2A-55239; 3-70101 to 3A-53241; 6-51095 to 6A-54958; 9-40226 to 9A-47848. Engine numbers on flywheel. Engine numbers not available. [Series FB] The serial number system was the same as on the 490 series. Starting: 1-20517. Ending: 1-24853. Also: 2-10635 to 2-15651; 3-1601 to 3-2316; 6-4991 to 6-6121; 9-4605 to 9-6436. Engine numbers located on flywheel. Engine numbers not available.

Series 490

Model No.	Body Type & Seating	Price	Weight	Prod. Total
490	Chassis	NA	NA	Note 2
490	2-dr. Rds.-2P	795	1820	Note 2
490	4-dr. Tr.-5P	820	1890	Note 2
490	2-dr. Cpe.-3P	1325	2040	Note 2
490	3-dr. Sed.-5P	1375	2160	Note 2

NOTE 1: During the year prices dropped to the 1922 factory prices.

Series FB

FB	2 dr. Rds.-2P	1320	2640	Note 2
FB	4-dr. Touring-5P	1345	2780	Note 2
FB	2-dr. Cpe.-3P	2075	2820	Note 2
FB	4-dr. Sed.-5P	2075	2950	Note 2

NOTE 2: Total production was 76,370 Chevrolets including 8,187 cars made in Canada.

NOTE 3: Prices dropped about $500 in late 1921 due to recession.

1921 Chevrolet, Series 490, sedan, HAC

ENGINE: [Series 490] Ohv. Inline. Four. Cast iron block. B & S: 3-11/16 x 4 in. Disp.: 171 cu. in. Brake H.P.: 26 @ 1800 R.P.M. N.A.C.C. H.P.: 21.75. Main bearings: three. Valve lifters: solid. Carb.: one-barrel. [Series FB] Ohv. Inline. Four. Cast iron block. B & S: 3-11/16 x 5-1/4 in. Disp.: 224 cu. in. Brake H.P.: 37 @ 2000 R.P.M. N.A.C.C. H.P.: 21.75. Main bearings: three. Valve lifters: solid. Carb.: one-barrel.

CHASSIS: [Series 490] W.B.: 102 in. Tires: 30 x 3-1/2 (open); 31 x 4 (closed). [Series FB] W.B.: 110 in. Tires: 33 x 4.

TECHNICAL: Selective sliding transmission. Speeds: 3F/1R. Floor mounted gearshift controls. Cone clutch. Shaft drive (torque tube). Rear axle: (FB) 3/4-floating; (490) two-piece. Overall ratio: (FB) 4.62:1; (490) 3.63:1. External contracting rear brakes. 12-spoke wood artillery wheels.

OPTIONS: Spare tire. Spare tire cover. Step plates. "Fat Man" steering wheel. Motometer. Cowl lights. Wind wings. Outside rear view mirror. Special paint.

HISTORICAL: Introduced January 1921. Innovations: New center door sedan. Larger tires on 490 closed models. Calendar year production: 61,717. Model year production: (490) 117,827 approximate; (FB) 13,028 approximate.

A management survey recommended the discontinuance of Chevrolet production.

1922

CHEVROLET — SERIES 490 — FOUR: The appearance of 490 models stayed about the same. Steel wheel felloes were new. The sedan became a four-door model. Gypsy style rear curtains were now seen on open cars. Also, the windshield was lower and a hand-operated emergency brake was used for the first time. A utility coupe was added to the line in March 1922.

1922 Chevrolet, sedan, OCW

CHEVROLET — SERIES FB — FOUR: This was the final season for the FB Chevrolet. There were no basic styling changes. New features included steel felloe wheels, a 10-gallon gas tank, a shorter steering column, and a 4-1/2 in. lower seat cushion. New 32 x 4 size tires were introduced during the year. An ad in the *Saturday Evening Post* of March 4, 1922, introduced the "Superior" designation.

I.D. DATA: [Series 490] Serial number located on nameplate on dash. Prefixes indicated plant: 1 is Flint; 2 is Tarrytown; 3 is St. Louis; 6 is Oakland; and 9 is Oshawa (Canada). Starting: IA-59939. Ending: 1A-92881. Also: 2A-55240 to 2A-88765. 3A-33242 to 3A-66294. 6A-54959 to 6A-72319. 9A-47849 to 9A-70543. Engine numbers on flywheel. Engine numbers not available. [Series FB] Serial number system same as on 490 Series. Starting: 1-24854. Ending: 1A-39542. Also: 2-15652 to 2A-30267; 3-2317 to 3A-30599; 6-6122 to 6A-30704; 9-6436 to 9A-7593. Engine numbers located on flywheel. Engine numbers not available.

Model No.	Body Type & Seating	Price	Weight	Prod. Total
490	Chassis	NA	1435	Note 1
490	2-dr. Rds.-2P	510	1725	Note 1
490	4-dr. Tr.-5P	525	1770	Note 1
490	2-dr. Utl. Cpe.-2P	850	1945	Note 1
490	2-dr. Cpe.-4P	680	2015	Note 1
490	4-dr. Sed.-5P	875	2150	Note 1

FB	2-dr. Rds.-2P	865	2310		Note 1
FB	4-dr. Tr.-5P	885	2595		Note 1
FB	2-dr. Cpe.-4P	1325	2735		Note 1
FB	4-dr. Sed.-4P	1395	2890		Note 1

NOTE 1: Total production was 243,479 Chevrolets including 19,895 cars made in Canada.

ENGINE: [Series 490] Ohv. Inline. Four. Cast iron block. B & S: 3-11/16 x 4 in. Disp.: 171 cu. in. Brake H.P.: 26 @ 1800 R.P.M. Main bearings: three. Valve lifters: solid. Carb.: one-barrel. [Series FB] Ohv. Inline. Four. Cast iron block. B & S: 3-11/16 x 5-1/4 in. Disp.: 224 cu. in. Brake H.P.: 37 @ 2000 R.P.M. N.A.C.C. Horsepower 21.75. Main bearings: three. Valve lifters: solid. Carb.: one-barrel.

1922 Chevrolet, touring, JAC

CHASSIS: [Series 490] W.B.: 102 in. Tires: 30 x 3-1/2 or 31 x 4. [Series FB] W.B.: 110 in. Tires: 32 x 4.

TECHNICAL: Selective sliding transmission. Speeds: 3F/1R. Floor-mounted gearshift controls. Cone clutch. Shaft drive (torque tube). Rear axle: (FB) 3/4-floating; (490) two-piece. Overall ratio: (FB) 4.62:1; (490) 3.63:1. External contracting rear brakes. Steel felloe wheels.

OPTIONS: Spare tire. Spare tire cover. Step plates. "Fat Man" steering wheel. Motometer. Cowl lights. Wind wings. Outside rear view mirror. Special paint.

HISTORICAL: Introduced January 1922. Innovations: (Series FB) New poured con rods. New crank with two-inch longer throws. Improved cylinder head with three exhaust ports. Reverse Elliot front axle. (Series 490) Valve adjustment on rocker arms. Larger diameter king pins. Single pedal brakes. Spiral cut ring and pinion. Calendar year production: 208,848. Model year production: (490) 109,473 approximate; (FB) 29,459 approximate. W.S. Knudsen became the new president of Chevrolet.

1923

CHEVROLET — COPPER COOLED — SERIES C — FOUR: The Copper Cooled Chevrolet looked like a conventional 1923 Series B Superior model, except that the radiator was replaced by louvers and the "bow-tie" emblem had a copper colored background. The word "Copper" appeared above the Chevrolet logo and the word "Cooled" was below it. There was a functional nickel-plated hood ornament.

1923 Chevrolet, Copper Cooled, coupe, HAC

The unusual air-cooled engine in these Chevrolets was designed by Charles F. Kettering. The model evolved from two years of experimentation with the air-cooled concept, but the car was still unperfected when released for sale at the New York Automobile Show in January 1923. Production was suspended five months later and a complete recall was issued.

Only 759 of the cars were built, of which 239 were scrapped before leaving the factory. Of the 500 cars shipped, 150 were used by Chevrolet representatives and about 300 were sent to dealerships. About 100 were sold before the recall. Two are known to survive today. One is part of the Harrah's Automobile Collection. The other is in the Henry Ford Museum. In addition, several engines still survive. Well-known Chevrolet collector "Pinky" Randall says, "I have one of them. They were used as stationary engines in Chevrolet factories."

CHEVROLET — SUPERIOR — MODEL B — FOUR: The 1923 Chevrolet Superior had much smoother lines for open models. The hood line was raised and the cowl section was narrowed. Drum type headlights were featured. The radiator was higher and had a flatter curvature at its top. Late in the year, deluxe versions of the touring, coupe, and sedan were introduced. They featured disc wheels, bumpers, nickel-plated radiator shells, deluxe radiator caps, motometers, runningboard kick plates and locking steering wheels. The deluxe touring had outside door handles and deluxe upholstery.

I.D. DATA: [Series C] Serial numbers were located on a plate on the left side of the front seat frame. They took the form 1-C-1001 and up. Ending number is not recorded. The Copper Cooled car in Michigan is 1-C-1109; the car in Nevada is 1-C-1268. The location of engine numbers is not recorded. [Series B] Serial number located on nameplate on the left side of front seat frame. Prefixes indicated the plant: 1 is Flint; 2 is New York; 3 is St.

Louis; 6 is Oakland. Up to the later part of 1923 a 9 is Oshawa; later 9 is Norwood; 12 is Buffalo; and 21 is Janesville. Starting: 1-B20391. Ending: 1-B98854. Also: 2-B19269 to 2-B111787; 3-624459 to 3-B132178; 6-B8087 to 6-B51547; 9-B1928 to 9-B9077; 12-B1190 to 12-B7340; and 21-B1000 to 21-B38352. Engine numbers located on flywheel. Engine numbers not available.

Model No.	Body Type & Seating	Price	Weight	Prod. Total
M	2-dr. Rds.-2P	710	NA	Note 3
M	4-dr. Tr.-5P	695	NA	Note 3
M	4-dr. Sed.-5P	1060	NA	Note 3
M	2-dr. Coach-5P	1050	NA	Note 3
M	2-dr. Utility Cpe.-2P	880	1700*	Note 3
M	4-dr. Del. Tr.-5P	725	NA	Note 3

1923 Chevrolet, Superior, touring, OCW

NOTE 1: * Based on *Special Interest Autos* "Drive Report" Sept.-Oct. 1975. Indicated that Copper Cooled was 215 lbs. lighter than a conventional Chevrolet.

NOTE 2: Total production: 500; total sales: 100.

B	Chassis	NA	1390	Note 3
B	2-dr. Rds.-2P	510	1715	Note 3
B	4-dr. Tr.-5P	495	1795	Note 3
B	2-dr. Utility Cpe.-2P	680	1915	Note 3
B	2-dr. S'net-4P	850	2055	Note 3
B	4-dr. Sed.-5P	860	2095	Note 3

1923 Chevrolet, Superior, roadster, JAC

NOTE 3: Total production was 480,737 Chevrolets including 25,751 cars made in Canada.

NOTE 4: Prices for deluxe models slightly lower than prices for 1924 deluxe models.

ENGINE: [Copper Cooled] Ohv. Inline. Four. Cast iron block with corded copper fins. B & S: 3.5 x 3.5 in. Disp.: 135 cu. in. C.R.: 4.0:1. Brake H.P.: 22 @ 1750 R.P.M. Main bearings: three. Valve lifters: solid. Carb.: Carter one-barrel (updraft). Torque: 50 lb.-ft. @ 1300 R.P.M. [Superior] Ohv. Inline. Four. Cast iron block. B & S: 3-11/16 x 4 in. Disp.: 171 cu. in. Brake H.P.: 26 @ 2000 R.P.M. N.A.C.C. H.P.: 21.75. Main bearings: three. Valve lifters: solid. Carb.: Carter one-barrel.

1923 Chevrolet, Superior, four-door sedan, OCW

CHASSIS: [Both Series] W.B.: 103 in. O.L.: 142 in. O.H.: 74.25 in. Front/Rear Tread: 58/58 in. Tires: 30 x 3.5.

TECHNICAL: Selective sliding transmission. Speeds: 3F/1R. Floor-mounted gearshift controls. Cone clutch. Shaft drive. Semi-floating rear axle. Overall ratio: [Model M] 4.44:1; [Model B] 3.77:1. External contracting rear wheel brakes. Wood spoke wheels 24.75 x 3.0.

OPTIONS: Front bumper. Rear bumper. Disc wheels. Plated radiator. Wind wings. Spare tire. Tire cover. Moto-meter. Kick plates. Deluxe upholstery. Deluxe radiator cap. Locking steering wheel. Outside rear view mirror. Sun visor (open cars). Special paint. Cowl lamps.

HISTORICAL: Superior B introduced October 1922. Innovations: Increased wheelbase. Copper Cooled Series. New serial number system used letter or number to identify model year. Calendar year registrations: 291,761. Calendar year production: 415,814. Model year production: 323,182 (approx.).

New plants opened in Norwood, Ohio; Buffalo, New York; and Janesville, Wisconsin. Some Model B engines had Holley carburetors.

1924

CHEVROLET — SUPERIOR — SERIES F — FOUR: The Superior Series F was virtually unchanged in appearance from 1923 models. New body styles included a two-door coach and four-passenger coupe. The sedanette was dropped. Standard equipment on open cars included tools; jack; speedometer; ammeter; oil pressure gauge;

dash light; choke pull; electric horn; ignition theft lock; demountable rims with extra rim; spare tire carrier; legal headlights; headlight dimmer; license bracket; and double adjustable windshield. Closed models also had a windshield cleaner; plate glass windows; window regulator; sun visor; and door locks. Deluxe equipment available for some mid-year models included disc wheels; bumpers; nickel radiator shells; runningboard kick plates; and (on the touring) outside door handles.

1924 Chevrolet, Superior, touring, OCW

I.D. DATA: Serial numbers were located on the right or left side of dash under cowl and seat frame. Starting: IB72774. Ending: 1F38881. Also: 2B92892 to 2F51140; 3B98371 to 3F56585; 6B41756 to 6F29296; 9B1166 to 9F27125; 12B1064 to 12F35270; and 21B22374 to 21F33581. Note: Cars built late in the run were sold as 1925 models. They had the following serial numbers: 1F38882 to 1K-1; 2F51141 to 2K-1; 3F56586 to 3K-1; 6F297 to 6K-1; 9K27126 to 9K-1; 12F35271 to 12K-1; and 21F33582 to 21 K-1.1924

Chevrolet, Superior, coach, OCW

Model No.	Body Type & Seating	Price	Weight	Prod. Total
F	2-dr. Rds.-2P	490	1690	Note 1
F	4-dr. Tr.-5P	495	1875	Note 1
F	4-dr. Sed.-5P	795	2070	Note 1
F	2-dr. Cpe.-2P	640	1880	Note 1
F	2-dr. Cpe.-4P	725	2005	Note 1
F	2-dr. Coach-5P	695	2030	Note 1
Deluxe Equipped				
F	4-dr. Del. Tr.-5P	640	1955	Note 1
F	4-dr. Del. Sed.-5P	940	2240	Note 1
F	2-dr. Del. Cpe.-4P	775	2050	Note 1

NOTE 1: Total production was 307,775 Chevrolets including 20,587 cars made in Canada.

ENGINE: Ohv. Enbloc. Four. Cast iron block. B & S: 3-11/16 x 4 in. Disp.: 171 cu. in. Brake H.P.: 26 @ 2000 R.P.M. N.A.C.C. H.P.: 21.7. Main bearings: three. Valve lifters: solid. Carb.: one-barrel.

CHASSIS: W.B.: 103 in. Tires: 30 x 3-1/2 non-skid.

TECHNICAL: Selective sliding transmission. Speeds: 3F/1R. Floor-mounted gearshift controls. Semi-floating rear axle. 3.82:1. External contracting rear brakes. Steel felloes, wood spoke wheels.

OPTIONS: Step plates. Outside rear view mirrors. Tire cover. Moto-meter. Special paint. Spare tire. Disc wheels. Deluxe equipment.

HISTORICAL: Introduced August 1, 1923. Innovations: New coach and four-passenger coupe. New Deluxe models. Improved front axle. Improved brakes. Calendar year registrations: 289,962. Calendar year production: 262,100. Model year production: 264,868 (August 1, 1923, to August 1, 1924).

Curved front axles and cable-operated brakes characterized early models in this series. Straight front axles and brake rods were used on later Series F Superior Chevrolets. New plant in Norwood, Ohio, opened this year. Cars built before August 1, 1923, were Series B Superior Chevrolets.

1925

CHEVROLET — SUPERIOR — SERIES K — FOUR: The 1925 Chevrolet had a new radiator design. The upper part of the nickel-plated shell curved down at the center. Fisher Body vertical ventilating (v.v.) windshields were used on closed cars. A cadet-style visor was another new feature. Wood spoke wheels were standard on open cars; sedans and coupes in late production had steel disc wheels. New Klaxon horns and a new steering wheel with walnut-like rim were other features of Superior K Chevrolets built after August 1, 1925.

I.D. DATA: Serial numbers were located on the right or left side of dash under cowl and seat frame. Starting: 1K1000. Ending: 1K33571. Also: 2K1000 to 2K45727; 3K1000 to 3K48220; 6K1000 to 6K27866; 9K1000 to 9K27519; 12K1000 to 12K36081; and 21K1000 to 21K32544.

Note: Cars built late in the run were sold as 1926 models. They had the following serial numbers: 1K33752 to 1V-1; 2K45728 to 2V-1; 3K48221 to 3V-1; 6K27867 to 6V-1; 9K27520 to 9V-1; 12K36082 to 12V-1; and 21K32545 to 21V-1.

Model No.	Body Type & Seating	Price	Weight	Prod. Total
K	2-dr. Rds.-2P	525	1690	Note 1
K	4-dr. Tr.-5P	525	1855	Note 1
K	2-dr. Cpe.-2P	715	1880	Note 1
K	4-dr. Sed.-5P	825	2070	Note 1
K	2-dr. Coach-5P	735	2030	Note 1

NOTE 1: Total production was 519,229 Chevrolets including 30,968 cars made in Canada.

1925 Chevrolet, Superior, Series K, coupe, JAC

ENGINE: Ohv. Inline. Four. Cast iron block. B & S: 3-11/16 x 4 in. Disp.: 171 cu. in. Brake H.P.: 26 @ 2000 R.P.M. N.A.C.C. H.P.: 21.7. Main bearings: three. Valve lifters: solid. Carb.: one-barrel Model RXO.

CHASSIS: W.B.: 103 in. Tires: 30 x 3-1/2 (open cars); 29 x 4.40 (closed cars).

TECHNICAL: Selective sliding transmission. Speeds: 3F/1R. Floor-mounted gearshift controls. Clutch: single plate dry disc. Semi-floating rear axle. Overall ratio: 3.82:1. External contracting rear wheel brakes. Spoke wheels (open); Disc wheels (closed).

1925 Chevrolet, Superior, Series K, coach, OCW

OPTIONS: Front bumper. Rear bumper. Step plates. Outside rear view mirrors. Tire cover. Moto-meter. Special paint. Spare tire. Heater. Clock. Wood spoke wheels (closed cars). Steel disc wheels (open cars).

HISTORICAL: Introduced January 1925. Innovations: Redesigned engine with new block, rods, and crank. New disc clutch. Semi-elliptic springs. Calendar year registrations: 341,281. Calendar year production: 444,671. Model year production: 306,479 (January 1925-August 1925).

Cars built after August 1, 1925, had the new Klaxon horns and walnut steering wheel. They also had spark/throttle controls on the dash above the steering wheel and a headlight brace bar. They were sold as 1926 models. Bloomfield, New Jersey, factory purchased. First year of production over 500,000 units (including early 1926 models).

1926

CHEVROLET — SUPERIOR — SERIES V — FOUR: The Super Series V was introduced in mid-1926 and was marketed into the first part of the 1927 sales year. It was similar to the previous Series K except that a tie-bar connected the drum-shaped headlights.

I.D. DATA: Serial number located on right or left side of dash under cowl and seat frame. Starting: 1V1000. Ending: 1V48499. Also: 2V100 to 2V49550; 3V1000 to 3V83277; 6V1000 to 6V27138; 9V100 to 9V52906; 12V1000 to 12V38701; and 21V1000 to 21V54755.

Model No.	Body Type & Seating	Price	Weight	Prod. Total
V	2-dr. Rds.-2P	510	1790	Note 1
V	4-dr. Tr.-5P	510	1950	Note 1
V	2-dr. Cpe.-2P	645	2035	Note 1
V	4-dr. Sed.-5P	735	2225	Note 1
V	2-dr. Coach-5P	645	2150	Note 1
V	4-dr. Lan. Sed.-5P	765	2220	NA

NOTE 1: Total production was 732,147 Chevrolets including 39,967 cars made in Canada.

1926 Chevrolet, Superior, Series V, four-door sedan, OCW

ENGINE: Ohv. Inline. Four cylinder. Cast iron block. B & S: 3-11/16 x 4 in. Disp.: 171 cu. in. Brake H.P.: 26 @ 2000 R.P.M. Net H.P.: 21.7 N.A.C.C. Main bearings: three. Valve lifters: solid. Carb.: one-barrel.

CHASSIS: W.B. 103 in. Tires: 29 x 4.40.

TECHNICAL: Selective sliding transmission. Speeds: 3F/1R. Floor-mounted gearshift controls. Clutch: single plate dry disc. Semi-floating rear axle. Overall ratio: 3.82:1. External contracting rear wheel brakes. Wood spoke wheels.

OPTIONS: Step plates. Outside rear view mirror. Tire covers. Whitewall tires. Moto-meter. Special paint. Spare tire. Wood spoke wheels. Commercial pickup equipment.

HISTORICAL: Introduced mid-1926. Calendar year registrations: 486,366. Calendar year production: 588,962. Model year production: 547,724. Innovations: Belt driven generator. Cam operated oil pump. Improved brakes. New landau sedan.

Spark/throttle control moved above steering wheel on late models. Combination stop/taillamp (instead of round taillight) on late models. New Detroit axle factory. Eight million dollars appropriated to make Chevrolet more competitive with Ford.

1927

1927 Chevrolet, Capitol, landau sedan, AA

CHEVROLET — CAPITOL — SERIES AA — FOUR:
The 1927 Chevrolets had a new radiator shell on which the top portion no longer bowed downwards. There was a downward pointing "peak" in the center of the upper shell. New bullet shaped headlight buckets were finished in black enamel with bright metal trim rings. Fuller crown fenders were seen. Rectangular brake and clutch pedals were used. There was a new parking brake release and a coincidental ignition/steering wheel lock. A new body style was the sports cabriolet. An Imperial landau sedan was introduced in May 1927. Equipment on open cars included tools; jack; speedometer; ammeter; oil pressure gauge, dash light; choke pull, electric horn, extra rim; spare tire carrier; bullet type cowl lamps; headlight dimmer; license brackets; double-adjustable windshield; foot accelerator; air cleaner; oil filter; pedal enclosure; rear-vision mirror; gas gauge; and automatic stop light. Closed cars also had V.V. windshields; wipers; plate glass windows; window regulators; sun visor; door locks; dome lights; rear window roller shade; door pockets; and remote control door handles.

I.D. DATA: Serial number located on right or left side of dash under cowl and seat frame. Starting: AA1 & up. Engine numbers located on base ahead of oil filter.

Model No.	Body Type & Seating	Price	Weight	Prod. Total
AA	2-dr. Rds.-2P	525	1960	41,313
AA	4-dr. Tr.-5P	525	1895	53,187
AA	2-dr. Cpe.-2P	625	2090	124,101
AA	2-dr. Spt. Cabr.-2/4P	715	2135	41,137
AA	2-dr. Coach-5P	695	2190	239,566
AA	4-dr. Sed.-5P	695	2275	99,400
AA	4-dr. Imp. Lan.-5P	NA	NA	37,426
AA	4-dr. Lan. Sed.-5P	745	2270	42,410

1927 Chevrolet, Capitol, coach (with Alfred Sloan), JAC

NOTE 1: The sports cabriolet was a closed car, not a convertible.

ENGINE: Ohv. Inline. Four. Cast iron block. B & S: 3-11/16 x 4 in. Disp.: 171 cu. in. Brake H.P.: 26 @ 2000 R.P.M. Net H.P.: 21.7. Main bearings: Three. Valve lifters: solid. Carb.: one-barrel; Model: Carter.

1927 Chevrolet, Capitol, coach (C.F. Barth, Chevy factory manager, behind the wheel, W.S. Knudsen, president and general manager, leaning on door. Other two men unidentified), AA

CHASSIS: W.B.: 103 in. Tires: 29 x 4.40 (balloon).

TECHNICAL: Selective sliding transmission. Speeds: 3F/1R. Floor-mounted gearshift controls. Single plate dry disc. Semi-floating rear axle. Overall ratio: 3.82:1. External contracting rear-wheel brakes. Steel disc wheels.

OPTIONS: Window awnings. Step plates. Whitewall tires. Wood spoke wheels. Moto-meter. Special paint. Outside rear view mirror. Spare tire. Tire cover.

HISTORICAL: Introduced January 1927. Total production: 1,001,820 Chevrolets including 61,740 cars made in Canada. Innovations: First Chevrolet rumbleseat on Capitol AA sports cabriolet. First year for natural wood spoke wheel option. New Remy distributor and Carter carburetor. Air and oil filters standard for first time.

In 1927, Chevrolet outsold Ford for the first time. Saginaw gray iron foundry was opened. First million car sales year for Chevrolet. General manager: William S. Knudsen.

1928

CHEVROLET — NATIONAL — MODEL AB — FOUR:
The 1928 Chevrolets were larger cars. New, full crown fenders were used. There were larger, bullet-type headlamps and a higher cowl line. Standard equipment included: Fisher V.V. windshield, vacuum wiper, inside rear view mirror, stop light, parking lights, door pockets, and gas gauge. Smoking set and robe rails on sedans.

1928 Chevrolet, National, Imperial landau, HAC

I.D. DATA: Serial numbers on front seat heel board at left or right side. Starting: AB1000 and up. A numerical prefix indicated assembly plant as follows: "1" — Flint, Michigan; "2" — Tarrytown, New Jersey; "3" — St. Louis; "5" Kansas City, Missouri; "6" — Oakland, California; "8" — Atlanta, Georgia; "9" — Norwood, Ohio; "12" — Buffalo, New York; and "21" — Janesville, Wisconsin. Engine number on base ahead of oil filter. Codes not available.

Model No.	Body Type & Seating	Price	Weight	Prod. Total
AB	2-dr. Rds.-2P	495	2030	NA
AB	4-dr. Tr.-5P	495	2090	26,973
AB	2-dr. Cpe.-2P	595	2235	150,356
AB	2-dr. Cabr.-2/4P	665	2270	NA
AB	2-dr. Cpe. Spt. Conv.-2P	695	2265	38,268
AB	2-dr. Coach-5P	585	2360	346,976
AB	4-dr. Sed.-5P	675	2435	127,819
AB	4-dr. Imp. Lan.-5P	715	2405	54,998

ENGINE: Ohv. Inline. Four. Cast iron block. B & S: 3-11/16 x 4 in. Disp.: 171 cu. in. Brake H.P.: 35 @ 2200 R.P.M. N.A.C.C. H.P.: 21.7. Valve lifters: solid. Carb. Carter one-barrel.

CHASSIS: W.B.: 107 in. Length: 156 in. (less bumpers). Tread: 56 in. Tires: 30 x 4.50 in.

1928 Chevrolet, National, coach, OCW

TECHNICAL: Manual transmission. Straight cut gears. Speeds: 3F/1R. Floor shift controls. Overall ratio: 3.82:1. Mechanical brakes on four wheels. Disc wheels.

OPTIONS: Front bumper. Rear bumper. Heater. Wood spoke wheels. Outside rear view mirror. Leatherette spare tire cover. Spare tire (rim standard). Fluid canisters. Runningboard step plates. Wind wings (open cars).

HISTORICAL: Introduced January 1928. Indirect lighted instrument panel. Four-wheel brakes. Thermostat. Alemite chassis lubrication. Total production: 1,193,212 Chevrolets including 69,217 cars made in Canada. Hibbard & Darrin constructed at least one custom-bodied National series AB sedan. General manager: W.S. Knudsen.

1929

CHEVROLET — INTERNATIONAL — MODEL AC — SIX:
The 1929 Chevrolets had a more rectangular radiator with the company "bow-tie" logo in an upright oval at the top of the chrome-plated radiator shell. Fewer vertical louvers were seen towards the rear of the hood side panels. Wider, single belt moldings decorated the body. New, one-piece full crown fenders and new bullet-type lamps were used. A rumbleseat sport roadster was a mid-year addition to the line.

I.D. DATA: Serial number on right body sill under floor mat, except roadster and phaeton (right side of seat frame on these models). Starting: AC1000 and up. Numerical prefixes used for each factory; same as 1928. Each factory built only one body style. Engine numbers on right side of block behind fuel pump. Codes not available.

Model No.	Body Type & Seating	Price	Weight	Prod. Total
1AC	2-dr. Rds.-2P	525	2175	27,988
2AC	4-dr. Phae.-5P	525	2240	8,632
3AC	2-dr. Cpe.-2P	595	2425	Note 1
5AC	2-dr. Spt. Cpe.-2/4P	645	2470	Note 1
6AC	2-dr. Cabr.-2/4P	695	2440	45,956
8AC	2-dr. Coach-5P	595	2500	367,360
9AC	4-dr. Sed.-5P	675	2585	196,084
21AC	4-dr. Imp. Sed.-5P	695	2555	41,983
12AC	4-dr. Lan. Conv.-5P	725	2560	300
5AC	2-dr. Spt. Rds.-2/4P	545	2230	1,210

1929 Chevrolet, International, coach, OCW

NOTE 1: Combined production total for coupe and sport coupe was 157,230 cars.

NOTE 2: Model number prefix shown above indicates assembly point. Refer to factory codes in 1928 Chevrolet serial number data.

ENGINE: Ohv. Inline. Six. Cast iron block. B & S: 3-5/16 x 3-3/4 in. Disp.: 194 cu. in. Brake H.P.: 46 @ 2600 R.P.M. N.A.C.C. H.P.: 26.3. Main bearings: three. Valve lifters: solid. Carb.: Carter one-barrel.

1929 Chevrolet, International, four-door sedan, HFM

CHASSIS: W.B.: 107 in. Length: 156 in. (less bumpers). Tread: 56 in. Tires: 20 x 4.50.

TECHNICAL: Manual transmisson. Straight cut gears. Speeds: 3F/1R. Floor shift controls. Banjo rear axle. Single plate dry disc clutch. Overall ratio: 3.82:1. Four wheel mechanical brakes. Rod activated. Internal front/external rear. Disc wheels.

OPTIONS: Front bumper. Rear bumper. Single sidemount. Dual sidemount. Sidemount cover(s). Rear spare cover. Trunk rack. Steamer type trunk. Heater. Outside rear view mirror. Cigar lighter. Runningboard step plates. Wire spoke wheels. Wind wings (open cars). Accessory hood mascot.

1929 Chevrolet, International, roadster, OCW

1929 Chevrolet, International, landau convertible, OCW

HISTORICAL: Introduced December 1928. Banjo type rear axle. Electro lock. Rubber covered 17-in. steering wheel. New six-cylinder engine. Total production: 1,328,605 Chevrolets including 73,918 cars made in Canada. Advertised as "A Six for the Price of a Four." Fuel consumption: approx. 19 mpg. General manager: W.S. Knudsen.

1930

CHEVROLET — UNIVERSAL — SERIES AD — SIX: The major change in 1930 Chevrolets was the addition of a slanting, non-glare windshield. The gas gauge was moved to the dashboard. Other instruments had a new, circular shape with dark colored faces. Smaller tires were used. The special sedan replaced the Imperial sedan. Its standard equipment included six wire wheels with fender wells, front and rear bumpers, robe rail, dome light, and silk assist cords.

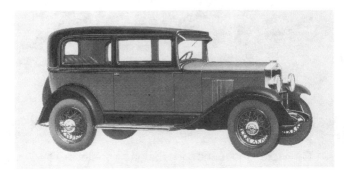

1930 Chevrolet, Universal, coach, OCW

I.D. DATA: Serial numbers in same locations as 1929. AD1000 and up. Numerical prefixes used for each factory; same as 1929. Each factory built one body style. Engine numbers same location; codes not available.

Model No.	Body Type & Seating	Price	Weight	Prod. Total
1AD	2-dr. Rds.-2P	495	2195	5,684
2AD	2-dr. Spt. Rds.-2/4P	515	2250	27,651
3AD	4-dr. Phae.-5P	495	2265	1,713
5AD	2-dr. Cpe.-2P	565	2415	100,373
6AD	2-dr. Spt. Cpe-2/4P	615	2525	45,311
8AD	2-dr. Coach-5P	565	2515	255,027
9AD	4-dr. Club Sed.-5P	625	2575	24,888
12AD	4-dr. Sed.-5P	675	2615	135,193
21AD	4-dr. Spec. Sed.-5P	685	2665	35,929
5AD	2-dr. R/S Cpe.-2/4P	—	—	9,211

NOTE 1: Model number prefix shown above indicates assembly point. Refer to factory codes in 1928 Chevrolet serial number data.

1930 Chevrolet, Universal, coupe, JAC

ENGINE: Ohv. Inline. Six. Cast iron block. B & S: 3-5/16 x 3-3/4 in. Disp.: 194 cu. in. C.R.: 5.02:1. Brake H.P.: 50 @ 2600 R.P.M. N.A.C.C. H.P.: 26.3. Main bearings: three. Valve lifters: solid. Carb.: Carter one-barrel.

CHASSIS: W.B.: 107 in. Tires: 19 x 4.75.

TECHNICAL: Manual transmission. Speeds: 3F/1R. Floor shift controls. Single plate clutch. Semi-floating rear axle. Overall ratio: 4.1:1. Four wheel internal (mechanical) brakes. Disc wheels.

1930 Chevrolet, Universal, sport roadster, JAC

OPTIONS: Front bumper. Rear bumper. Single sidemount. Dual sidemount. Sidemount cover(s). Trunk rack. Steamer trunk. Wood spoke wheels. Heater. Wire spoke wheels (standard on sports models). Cigar lighter. Rear spare cover. Outside rear view mirror.

HISTORICAL: Introduced January 1930. New type manifold. Three-spoke steering wheel. Hydraulic shock absorbers added. Total production: 864,243 Chevrolets, including 39,773 cars made in Canada. The seven-millionth Chevrolet since 1912 was built on May 28, 1930, at Flint, Michigan. General manager: W.S. Knudsen.

1931

1931 Chevrolet, Independence, roadster, OCW

CHEVROLET — INDEPENDENCE — SERIES AE — SIX: The 1931 Chevrolet had a higher, larger radiator. The headlights were mounted on a bowed tie-bar. The hood sides featured multiple vertical louvers within a raised panel. There were new type panel and body moldings. Wire spoke wheels became standard equipment.

I.D. DATA: Serial numbers in same location as 1930. Starting: AE1000 and up. Numerical prefixes used for each factory; same as 1929. Each factory built one body style. Engine numbers same location. Starting: 2100285. Ending: 2951552.

1931 Chevrolet, Independence, coupe, OCW

Model No.	Body Type & Seating	Price	Weight	Prod. Total
1AE	2-dr. Rds.-2P	475	2295	2939
2AE	2-dr. Spt. Rds.-2/4P	495	2340	24,050
3AE	4-dr. Phae.-5P	510	2370	852
5AE	2-dr. Cpe.-2P	535	2490	57,741
6AE	2-dr. Spt. Cpe.-2/4P	575	2565	66,029
8AE	2-dr. 5-W Cpe.-2P	545	2490	28,379
21AE	2-dr. Cpe.-5P	595	2610	20,297
21AE	2-dr. Conv. Cabr.-2/4P	615	2520	23,077
9AE	2-dr. Coach-5P	545	2610	228,316
12AE	4-dr. Sed.-5P	635	2685	52,465
21AE	4-dr. Spec. Sed.-5P	650	2725	109,775
21AE	2-dr. Lan. Phae.-5P	650	2610	5634

NOTE 1: Model number prefixes shown above indicate assembly point. Refer to factory codes in 1928 Chevrolet serial number data.

ENGINE: Ohv. Inline. Six. Cast iron block. B & S: 3-5/16 x 3-3/4 in. Disp.: 194 cu. in. C.R.: 5.02:1. Brake H.P.: 50 @ 2600 R.P.M. N.A.C.C. H.P.: 26.3. Main bearings: three. Valve lifters: solid. Carb.: Carter one-barrel.

CHASSIS: W.B.: 109 in. Tires: 19 x 4.75.

TECHNICAL: Manual transmission. Speeds: 3F/1R. Floor shift controls. Disc clutch. Semi-floating rear axle.

Overall ratio: 4.1:1. Internal mechanical brakes on four wheels. Wire wheels standard.

1931 Chevrolet, Independence, landau phaeton, OCW

OPTIONS: Front bumper. Rear bumper. Single sidemount. Dual sidemount. Sidemount cover(s). Rear spare cover. Pedestal mirrors. Dual taillamps. Heater. Dual chrome sidemount trim rings. Cigar lighter. Luggage rack. Touring trunk. Spotlight. Wind wings. Quail radiator mascot. Guide lamps.

1931 Chevrolet, Independence, sedan, JAC

HISTORICAL: Introduced November 1930. Lovejoy shock absorbers. Semi-elliptic springs. Engine vibration dampener added. Heavier frame. More rigid crankshaft. Improved flywheel. New ribbed block and crankcase castings. Calendar year registrations: 583,429. Calendar year production: 627,104. Model year production: 623,901. General managers: W.S. Knudsen and M.E. Coyle. Chevrolet produced its eight-millionth car on August 25, 1931.

1932

CHEVROLET — CONFEDERATE — SERIES BA — SIX: Styling changes for 1932 Chevrolets included a longer hood and new deep crown front fenders. Door type louvers were used in the hood. They were chrome plated on Deluxe models. A built-in radiator grille was part of the new design. New 18-inch wire wheels were adopted. Standard equipment included a built-in sun visor, tilting windshield, and adjustable seat. New technical features included a downdraft carburetor, counterbalanced crankshaft, and added frame crossmember.

1932 Chevrolet, Confederate, sport roadster, OCW

I.D. DATA: Serial numbers on closed cars were on the right body sill under floor mat. Serial numbers on open cars were on the right side of the seat frame. Starting: BA1000 and up. Numerical prefixes used for each factory; same as 1931. Each factory built one body style. Engine number1932 Chevrolet, Confederate, sport roadster, OCW

1932 Chevrolet, Confederate, landau phaeton, OCW

Model No.	Body Type & Seating	Price	Weight	Prod. Total
1BA	4-dr. Phae.-5P	495	2495	419
1BA	2-dr. Rds.-2P	445	2410	1118
2BA	2-dr. Spt. Rds.-2/4P	485	2480	8552
5BA	2-dr. Cpe.-2P	490	2580	8874
6BA	2-dr. Spt. Cpe.-2/4P	535	2645	2226
8BA	2-dr. 5W Cpe.-2P	490	2580	34,796
21BA	2-dr. Cpe.-5P	575	2700	7566
21BA	2-dr. Del. 5W Cpe.-2P	510	2580	26,623
21BA	2-dr. Conv.-2/4P	595	2590	Note 2
9BA	2-dr. Coach-5P	495	2665	132,109
12BA	2-dr. Del. Coach-5P	515	2665	9346
12BA	4-dr. Sed.-5P	590	2750	27,718
21BA	4-dr. Spec. Sed.-5P	615	2800	52,446
21BA	2-dr. Lan. Phae.-5P	625	2700	1602

NOTE 1: Model number prefix shown above indicated assembly point. Refer to factory codes in 1928 Chevrolet serial number data.

NOTE 2: No production total available.

ENGINE: Ohv. Inline. Six. Cast iron block. B & S: 3-5/16 x 3-3/4 in. Disp.: 194 cu. in. C.R.: 5.2:1. Brake H.P.: 60 @ 3000 R.P.M. N.A.C.C. H.P.: 26.3. Main bearings: three. Valve lifters: solid. Carb.: Carter one-barrel Model 150S.

CHASSIS: W.B.: 109 in. Tires: 18 x 5.24.

TECHNICAL: Manual synchromesh transmission. Speeds: 3F/1R. Floor shift controls. Single plate clutch. Semi-floating rear axle. Overall ratio: 4.1:1. Four wheel internal (mechanical) brakes. Wire wheels standard. Drivetrain options: Free-Wheeling.

1932 Chevrolet, Confederate, coupe, JAC

OPTIONS: Front bumper. Rear bumper. Single sidemount. Dual sidemount. Trunk rack. Standard tire cover ($1.00). Deluxe tire cover (2.50). Heater. Outside mirror. Pedestal mirrors. Dual wipers. Cowl lights. Dual horns. Metal tire covers (6.00). Fender well tire lock (5.00). Rear tire lock (2.50). DeLuxe equipment included chrome hood louvers; two ashtrays; assist cords; armrests; curtains for rear and rear quarter windows; and vanity case.

1932 Chevrolet, Confederate, special sedan, JAC

HISTORICAL: Introduced December 5, 1931. Innovations: Synchromesh transmission. Selective freewheeling. Counter-balanced crankshaft. Added frame member. Calendar registrations: 332,860. Calendar year production: 306,716. Model year production: 323,100. General manager: M.E. Coyle.

The 1932 Chevrolet sports roadster could travel from 0-35 mph in 6.7 seconds. Some station wagon bodies were constructed on Chevrolet chassis by Mifflinburg Body Co. of Mifflinburg, Pennsylvania.

1933

CHEVROLET — MASTER EAGLE — SERIES CA — SIX: A slightly larger, more streamlined car was Chevrolet's Master Eagle series for 1933. New styling features included a vee-shaped radiator, rear slanting hood door louvers, skirted fenders, and a beaver tail back panel. This was called "Airstream" design. It also brought in a fixed position windshield and Fisher Body No-Draft ventilation system. Door lock buttons were on the window sills. Chrome headlight buckets were used. An eagle radiator mascot was available to identify cars in this series.

1933 Chevrolet, Master Eagle, sedan, OCW

CHEVROLET — STANDARD MERCURY — SERIES-CC — SIX: Chevrolet introduced an all-new series in the middle of the year. These cars had slanting vee-type radiators and skirted fenders. The headlight buckets were painted black and had chrome-plated rims. Conventional hood louvers were featured. Overall dimensions were scaled down from those of the Master Eagle Series. Otherwise the two lines looked similar.

I.D. DATA: [Series CA] Serial number locations were as on 1932 models. Starting: CA1000 & up. Engine numbers in same location; codes not available. [Series CC] Serial number locations were the same as on Master Eagle models. Starting: CC1000 & up. Engine numbers in same location as on Master Eagle Motors; codes not available.

Model No.	Body Type & Seating	Price	Weight	Prod. Total
CA	2-dr. Spt. Rds.-2/4P	485	2555	2876
CA	4-dr. Phae.-5P	515	2600	543
CA	2-dr. Cpe.-2P	495	2665	60,402
CA	2-dr. Spt. Cpe.-2/4P	535	2730	26,691
CA	2-dr. Conv.-2/4P	565	2820	4276
CA	2-dr. Coach-5P	515	2770	162,629
CA	4-dr. Sed.-5P	565	2830	162,361
CA	4-dr. Twn. Sed.-5P	545	2795	30,657
CC	2-dr. Cpe.-2P	445	2425	8909
CC	2-dr. Spt. Cpe.-2/4P	475	2485	1903
CC	2-dr. Sed.-5P	455	2515	25,033

ENGINE: [Series CA] Ohv. Inline. Six. Cast iron block. B & S: 3-5/16 x 4 in. Disp.: 194 cu. in. C.R.: 5.2:1. Brake H.P.: 65 @ 2800 R.P.M. N.A.C.C. H.P.: 26.3 Main bearings: three. Valve lifters: solid. Carb.: Carter one-barrel Model W1. [Series CC] Ohv. Inline. Six. Cast iron block.

B & S: 3-5/16 x 3-1/2 in. Disp.: 181 cu. in. C.R.: 5.2:1. Brake H.P.: 60 @ 3000 R.P.M. N.A.C.C. H.P.: 26.3. Main bearings: three. Valve lifters: solid. Carb.: Carter one-barrel Model W1.

1933 Chevrolet, Master Eagle, phaeton, JAC

CHASSIS: [Master Eagle Series] W.B.: 110 in. Tires: 18 x 5.25. [Mercury Series] W.B.: 107 in. Tires: 17 x 5.25.

1933 Chevrolet, Master Eagle, sport coupe, OCW

TECHNICAL: Manual transmission (synchromesh on Master Eagle). Speeds: 3F/1R. Floor shift controls. Single plate clutch. Semi-floating rear axle. Overall ratio: (Master Eagle) 4.11:1; (Standard) 4.4:1. Four wheel internal mechanical brakes. Wire wheels standard. Selective standard on Master Eagle; not available on Standard Mercury.

1933 Chevrolet, Master Eagle, four-door sedan, OCW

NOTE: Synchromesh transmission with Master Eagles. Selective constant mesh transmission on Mercury standard models.

OPTIONS: Oval wipers. Fog lights. Trunk rack. Twin horns. Step plates. Outside mirrors. Sidemount pedestal mirrors.

NOTE: Deluxe equipment for Chevrolets included dual horns, dual taillights, vanity set and other special interior furnishings.

HISTORICAL: (Master Eagle) December 1932; (Mercury) March 1933. Innovations: An airplane type dashboard was employed on Master Eagle models. Both Chevrolet engines featured an octane selector. Safety plate glass used in Mercury series windshield. Model year production: (Eagle Series) 450,530; (Mercury Series) 35,848; (Total) 486,378. General manager: M.E. Coyle.

1933 Chevrolet, Master Eagle, town sedan, JAC

Chevrolet dealers sponsored the first Soap Box Derby in Dayton, Ohio, this year. It was created by M.E. Scott, who later joined the company's public relations department.

1934

CHEVROLET — MASTER — SERIES DA — SIX: Cars in Chevrolet's top priced series grew slightly larger in 1934, but the basic features of "Airstream" styling were unchanged. A new vee-type radiator and grille appeared. The hood was even longer and wider, too. Deeper crown fenders were seen. There were three horizontal hood louvers that decreased in length from top to bottom. A new, winged hood ornament graced the radiator shell. Prices increased significantly this year.

CHEVROLET — STANDARD — SERIES DC — SIX: The Standard models for 1934 were much the same as last year. A new longer hood with horizontal streamlined louvers was used. The No-Draft ventilation system was also improved. A fancier, winged hood ornament made the cheaper Chevrolets look more like the expensive ones. The standard models had painted headlight buckets and less bright metal trim. The vertical grille bars were spaced wider apart than on the Master Series models.

I.D. DATA: [Series DA] Serial number locations were the same as on 1933 models. Starting: DA-1001 & up. Engine numbers were in the same location. Master series engine numbers were M-3964078 to M-4708994.

[Series DC] Serial number locations were the same as on Master Series models. Starting: DC-1001 & up. Engine numbers were in same location as on Master Series motors. Starting: M-40549. Ending: M-166168.

1934 Chevrolet, roadster, OCW

Model No.	Body Type & Seating	Price	Weight	Prod. Total
DA	2-dr. Rds.-2/4P	540	2830	1974
DA	2-dr. Bus. Cpe.-2P	560	2895	53,018
DA	2-dr. Spt. Cpe.-2/4P	600	2995	18,365
DA	2-dr. Cabr.-2/4P	695	2990	3276
DA	2-dr. Coach-5P	580	2995	163,948
DA	4-dr. Sed.-5P	640	3080	124,754
DA	2-dr. Twn. Sed.-5P	615	3020	49,431
DA	4-dr. Spt. Sed.-5P	675	3155	37,646

NOTE 1: The sport sedan was a touring sedan style with integral rear trunk.

DC	2-dr. Spt. Rds.-2/4P	465	2380	1038
DC	4-dr. Phae.-5P	520	2400	234
DC	2-dr. Cpe.-2P	485	2470	16,765
DC	2-dr. Coach-5P	495	2565	69,082
DC	4-dr. Sed.-5P	540	2655	11,840

NOTE 2: The four-door Sedan was added to the Standard Series as a mid-year model in October 1934.

1934 Chevrolet, coach, JAC

ENGINE: [Series DA] Ohv. Inline. Six. Cast iron block. B & S: 3-5/16 x 4 in. Disp.: 206.8 cu. in. C.R.: 5.45:1. Brake H.P.: 80 @ 3300 R.P.M. N.A.C.C. H.P.: 26.3. Main bearings: three. Valve lifters: solid. Carb.: Carter one-barrel Model W1. [Series DC] Ohv. Inline. Six. Cast iron block. B & S: 3-5/16 x 3-1/2 in. Disp.: 181 cu. in. C.R.: 5.2:1. Brake H.P.: 60 @ 3000 R.P.M. N.A.C.C. H.P.: 26.3. Main bearings: three. Valve lifters: solid. Carb.: Carter one-barrel Model W1.

CHASSIS: [Master Series] W.B.: 112 in. Tires: 5.50 x 17. Note: The Master Chevrolet featured "Knee Action" front suspension with coil springs. [Standard Series] W.B.: 107 in. Tires: 5.25 x 17.

TECHNICAL: Manual transmission. Speeds: 3F/1R. Floor shift controls. Single-plate clutch. Semi-floating rear axle. Overall ratio: 4.11:1. Four wheel mechanical brakes. Wire wheels. Selective free-wheeling optional on Master.

OPTIONS: Front bumper. Rear bumper. Dual taillights. Dual sidemount ($30.00). Sidemount cover(s). Fender skirts (8.00). Bumper Guards. Radio. Heater. Clock. Cigar lighter. Radio antenna. Seat covers. Rear view mirror. Spotlight.

1934 Chevrolet, four-door sedan, JAC

HISTORICAL: Introduced: (Master) January 1934; (Standard) January 1934. Innovations: Knee Action coil spring front suspension on Master Chevrolet. External horns not available. New X-Y frame on Master. New type valve and rocker arm arrange for Master "Blue Flame" six. Calendar year registrations: 534,906. Calendar year production: 620,726. Model year production: (Master) 457,167; (Standard) 99,499; (Total) 556,666. General manager: M.E. Coyle.

The phaeton, offered only in the Standard Series, is rare today. Fender skirts were a new Chevrolet accessory in 1934. In an unusual promotion to prove the power of the improved Chevrolet engine, a 1934 Chevy six was used to tow a train called the Burlington Zephyr into a Chicago railroad station.

1935

CHEVROLET — STANDARD — SERIES EC — SIX: Standard series 1935 Chevrolets had styling that was similar to 1934 models. Two changes were painted headlight shells and the repositioning of gauges in the center of the dashboard. Semi-elliptic front springs were carried over on these models. An 11-gallon fuel tank was used on Standard Chevrolets.

CHEVROLET — MASTER DELUXE — SERIES ED/EA — SIX: The Master DeLuxe series 1935 Chevrolets had completely new styling. They featured Fisher Body Division's latest innovation — all-steel "Turret Top" body construction. It allowed smoother, rounder, more streamlined designs. Cars in the EA series featured "Knee-Action" front suspension with coil springs. (Dubonnet suspension.) An option was semi-elliptic front springs and a straight front axle. Cars so equipped were designated ED series models and cost $20.00 less. A split-type front windshield was part of the all-new body styling. The doors opened from the front in "suicide door" style. There were no open cars in the Master DeLuxe series. A 14-gallon fuel tank was used on Master DeLuxe models.

1935 Chevrolet, Standard, coach, OCW

I.D. DATA: [Series EC] Serial numbers were on the body sill under the floor mat at right front door, near front seat; also on seat frame on right side. Starting: EC-1001. Ending: EC-39050. Engine numbers were on right side of block near fuel pump. Starting: M4709885. Ending: M5500178. [Series ED/EA] Serial numbers were in the same location as on Standard models. Starting: ED-1001/EA-1001. Ending: ED-3043/EA-54937. Engine numbers were in the same location as on Standard models. Starting: 4708995. Ending: 5500178.

Model No.	Body Type & Seating	Price	Weight	Prod. Total
EC	2-dr. Spt. Rds.-2/4P	465	2410	1176
EC	4-dr. Phae.-5P	485	2465	217
EC	2-dr. Cpe.-2P	475	2520	32,193
EC	2-dr. Coach-5P	485	2625	126,138
EC	4-dr. Sed.-5P	550	2675	42,049

Series ED (Without Knee-Action)

ED	2-dr. Cpe.-2P	560	2910	40,201
ED	2-dr. Spt. Cpe.-2/4P	600	2940	11,901
ED	2-dr. Coach-5P	580	3010	102,996
ED	4-dr. Sed.-5P	640	3055	57,771
ED	2-dr. Twn. Sed.-5P	615	3050	66,231
ED	4-dr. Spt. Sed.-5P	675	3120	67,339

NOTE 1: Cars with "Knee Action" were designated EA models. They cost $20 more and weighed 30 pounds more. Production of ED and EA models was lumped together as a single total.

ENGINE: [Series EC] Ohv. Inline. Cast iron block. B & S: 3-5/16 x 4 in. Disp.: 206.8 cu. in. C.R.: 5.45:1. Brake H.P.: 74 @ 3200 R.P.M. N.A.C.C. H.P.: 26.3. Main bearings: three. Valve lifters: solid. Carb.: Carter one-barrel Model 284S. [Series ED/EA] Ohv. Inline. Six. Cast iron block. B & S: 3-5/16 x 4 in. Disp.: 206.8 cu. in. C.R.: 5.45:1. Brake H.P.: 80

@ 3300 R.P.M. N.A.C.C. H.P.: 26.3. Main bearings: three. Valve lifters: solid. Carb.: Carter one-barrel Model 284S.

CHASSIS: [Standard Series] W.B.: 107 in. Tires: 17 x 5.25. [Master DeLuxe ED Series] W.B.: 113 in. Tires: 17 x 5.50 without Knee-Action. [Master DeLuxe EA Series] W.B.: 113 in. Tires: 17 x 5.50 with Knee Action.

1935 Chevrolet, Standard, coupe, OCW

TECHNICAL: Manual transmission. Speeds: 3F/1R. Floor shift controls. Single-plate clutch. Semi-floating rear axle. Overall ratio: 4.11:1. Four wheel mechanical brakes. Wire wheels. Selective free-wheeling (optional on Master DeLuxe).

OPTIONS: Bumper guards. Radio. Heater. Clock. Cigar lighter. Radio antenna. Seat covers. Spotlight. Cowl lamps. Fender skirts. License plate frame. Wire wheels. Rear view mirror. Dual sidemounts (rare).

1935 Chevrolet, Master DeLuxe, sport sedan, JAC

HISTORICAL: Introduced December 15, 1934. Introduced Fisher Body with "Turret Top." The 1935 "Blue Flame" six-cylinder engine had an improved head design, better lubrication, and redesigned combustion chambers. Calendar year registrations: 656,698. Calendar year production: 793,437. Model year production: (Standard) 207,976; (Master DeLuxe) 346,481; (total) 554,457. General manager: M.E. Coyle.

The 10 millionth Chevrolet ever produced was built on November 13, 1934. The car — a 1935 model — was donated to the City of Flint (Mich.) for police safety patrol duties. The Standard sports roadster and phaeton were discontinued in the early part of the 1935 production run. A new assembly plant (Code 14) opened in Baltimore. New manufacturing plants were added in Saginaw, Michigan, and Muncie, Indiana.

1936

CHEVROLET — STANDARD — SERIES FC — SIX: The Standard series Chevrolets adopted the all-steel Fisher Body with "Turret Top" styling. They had more rounded front fenders and radiator grilles and shells. A split front windshield (as used on 1935 Master DeLuxes) was new. The number of horizontal hood louvers was reduced to two, with the top ones being longer. Rear fenders were skirted and more streamlined. Steel disc wheels were used this year. A 14-gallon fuel tank was now used on all Chevrolets.

1936 Chevrolet, Standard, town sedan, OCW

MASTER DELUXE — SERIES FD/FA — SIX: A thicker, rounder radiator shell characterized cars in the Master DeLuxe lines. The grille was also larger and more rounded at the top; more pointed at the bottom. A lower hood ornament had its wings pointing back horizontally. The doors were now hinged toward the rear; no more "suicide" style front doors. The FD designation was for cars without coil spring front suspension; the FA designation was for cars with this feature. There were still no open cars in the Master DeLuxe series. In mid-year, steel spoke wheels were adopted for all models.

Model No.	Body Type & Seating	Price	Weight	Prod. Total
FC	2-dr. Cpe.-2P	495	2645	59,356
FC	2-dr. Cabr.-2/4P	595	2745	3629
FC	2-dr. Coach-5P	510	2750	76,646
FC	4-dr. Sed.-5P	575	2775	1142
FC	2-dr. Twn. Sed.-5P	535	2775	220,884
FC	4-dr. Spt. Sed.-5P	600	2805	46,760
Series FD (without knee action)				
FD	2-dr. Cpe.-2P	560	2895	49,319
FD	2-dr. Spt. Cpe.-2/4P	590	2940	10,985
FD	2-dr. Coach-5P	580	2985	40,814
FD	4-dr. Sed.-5P	640	3060	14,536
FD	2-dr. Twn. Sed.-5P	605	3030	244,134
FD	4-dr. Spt. Sed.-5P	665	3080	140,073

NOTE 1: Cars with Knee-Action were designated FA models. They cost $20.00 more and weighed 30 pounds more. Production of FD and FA models was lumped together as a single total.

1936 Chevrolet, convertible coupe, OCW

ENGINE: Ohv. Inline. Six. Cast iron block. B & S: 3-5/16 x 4 in. Disp.: 206.8 cu. in. C.R.: 6.0:1. Brake H.P.: 79 @ 3200 R.P.M. N.A.C.C. H.P.: 26.3. Main bearings: three. Valve lifters: solid. Carb.: Carter one-barrel Model 319S.

1936 Chevrolet, Master DeLuxe, sedan, HAC

NOTE 2: The same engine was used in both series in 1936.

CHASSIS: [Standard Series] W.B.: 109 in. Tires: 17 x 5.25. [Master DeLuxe FD Series] W.B.: 113 in. Tires: 17 x 5.50 without Knee-Action. [Master DeLuxe FA Series] W.B.: 113 in. Tires: 17 x 5.50 with Knee-Action.

1936 Chevrolet, Master Deluxe, coupe, OCW

TECHNICAL: Manual transmission. Speeds: 3F/1R. Floor shift controls. Single-plate clutch. Semi-floating rear axle. Overall ratio: 4.11:1. Four-wheel hydraulic brakes. Steel spoke wheels (slotted).

OPTIONS: Fender skirts. Bumper guards. Radio. Heater. Clock. Cigar lighter. Radio antenna. Seat covers. External sun shade. Spotlight. Cowl lamps. Fog lamps. License plate frame. Wire wheels. Rear view mirror. Dual sidemounts (rare).

HISTORICAL: Introduced November 2, 1935. Innovations: Hydraulic brakes introduced for Chevrolets. Cabriolet reintroduced in Standard series. Box-girder frame on Standard models. Early Standards had composite wood/steel doors. Later cars were all-steel. Calendar year registrations: 930,250. Calendar year production: 975,238. Model year production: (Standard) 431,016; (DeLuxe) 499,996; (total) 975,238. General manager: M.E. Coyle.

Chevrolet reclaimed the number one position in U.S. automobile sales this season. A new transcontinental speed record was set by Bob McKenzie driving a 1936 Standard Chevrolet.

1937

CHEVROLET — MASTER — SERIES GB — SIX: Chevrolets had completely new "Diamond Crown" styling with safety glass in all windows and straight side fenders. A streamline groove ran from the fenders onto the doors, where it blended into the sheet metal. The grille was swept in on each side. Headlamp buckets on all models were painted body color. Master models had less trim, single taillamps, single wipers, and no front fender parking lamps. Inside there was no front seat armrest or dashboard head indicator gauge. The sides of the hood were decorated with a tapering, spear-shaped panel incorporating cooling louvers. Semi-elliptic springs and a straight axle suspension were at the front of these cars. The standard cabriolet featured Master DeLuxe style bumper guards. Safety-Plate glass was used in all Chevrolets. Trunks on most models were now larger, with enclosed spare tires.

MASTER DELUXE — SERIES GA — SIX: The Master DeLuxe models had the same size and styling features as Masters. Knee-Action front suspension was standard. Other standard equipment included dashboard heat indicator; front passenger armrest; dual taillamps; double wipers; twin sun visors, fancy bumpers with guards.

I.D. DATA: Starting: GB-1001. Ending: GB-60674. Engine numbers were on the right side of block near fuel pump. Starting: 1. Ending: 1187821. Series GA serial numbers were in the same location as on Master models. Starting: GA-1001. Ending: GA-82134. Engine numbers were the same as on Master models.

Model No.	Body Type & Seating	Price	Weight	Prod. Total
GB	2-dr. Cpe.-2P	619	2770	54,683
GB	2-dr. Cabr.-2/4P	725	2790	1724
GB	2-dr. Coach-5P	637	2800	15,349

Model No.	Body Type & Seating	Price	Weight	Prod. Total
GB	2-dr. Twn. Sed.-5P	655	2830	178,645
GB	4-dr. Sed.-5P	698	2845	2755
GB	4-dr. Spt. Tr. Sed.-5P	716	2885	43,240
GA	2-dr. Cpe.-2P	685	2840	56,166
GA	2-dr. Spt. Cpe.-2/4P	724	2870	8935
GA	2-dr. Coach-5P	703	2910	7260
GA	2-dr. Twn. Sed.-5P	721	2935	300,332
GA	4-dr. Sed.-5P	770	2935	2221
GA	4-dr. Spt. Sed.-5P	788	2960	144,110

1937 Chevrolet, Master, town sedan, OCW

ENGINE: [Series GA] OHV. Inline. Six. Cast iron block. B & S: 3-1/2 x 3-3/4 in. Disp.: 216.5 cu. in. C.R.: 6.25:1. Brake H.P.: 85 @ 3200 R.P.M. N.A.C.C. H.P.: 29.4. Main bearings: four. Valve lifters: solid. Carb.: Carter one-barrel Model W1.

CHASSIS: [Master Series] W.B.: 112-1/4 in. Tires: 16 x 6.00. [Master DeLuxe Series] W.B.: 112-1/4 in. Tires: 16 x 6.00.

1937 Chevrolet, Master Deluxe, four-door sedan, PH

TECHNICAL: Manual transmission. Speeds: 3F/1R. Floor shift controls. Single-plate clutch. Semi-floating rear axle. Overall ratio: (Master) 3.73:1; (Master DeLuxe) 4.22:1. Four wheel hydraulic brakes. Steel spoke wheels.

OPTIONS: Fender skirts. Bumper guards. Radio. Heater. Clock. Cigar lighter. Radio antenna. Seat covers. External sun shade. Spotlight. Fog lamps. License frames. Whitewall tires. Front fender marker lamps. Rear tire cover. Slide in express box. Wheel trim rings.

NOTE 1: Sidemounts were no longer a standard accessory.

HISTORICAL: Introduced November 1936. Innovations: Completely new all-steel Unisteel Body by Fisher with updated styling. Completely re-engineered six-cylinder engine with larger bore; shorter stroke. Four main bearings. Box-girder type frame now used on all models. Available in the Master and Master DeLuxe, according to a *Town & Country* ad of April 1937, were the Suburban station wagons by Cantrell. Calendar year registrations: 768,040. Calendar year production: 868,250. Model year production: (Master) 306,024; (Master DeLuxe) 519,196; (total) 825,220. General manager: M.E. Coyle. Chevrolet was again America's best selling automobile.

1938

CHEVROLET — MASTER — SERIES HB — SIX: Chevrolet advertised that its 1938 models had new modern body styling. In reality, the body shell, fenders, and runningboards were the same as in 1937. A new grille was composed of horizontally arranged chromium bars, alternating one wide and four narrow. It was in two pieces, right and left. A center molding divided them. New bumper had a full width indentation, about one-half inch wide, that was painted black. Headlights and taillamps were of a carryover design. The hood had ventilators highlighted by three chrome horizontal moldings. The bullet-shaped headlights were mounted closely to the radiator grille. Inside, the seats were two inches wider. Improved worm and roller sector steering was used. The front suspension was of semi-elliptic springs and a straight axle on all Master series models, plus the Master DeLuxe cabriolet. Master Chevrolets had single taillamps as standard equipment.

1938 Chevrolet, Master DeLuxe, four-door sedan, AA

CHEVROLET — MASTER DELUXE — SERIES HA — SIX: The Master DeLuxe featured styling changes identical to Master models. The main difference was that bumper guards were standard equipment on the Master DeLuxe. These guards were now braced to the frame. The Master DeLuxe designation appeared on the center chrome molding running across the oblong shaped hood ventilators. Dual taillamps were standard equipment.

I.D. DATA: [Series HB] Serial numbers were on a plate under hood on right side of cowl. Starting: HB-1001. Ending: HB-30097. Engine numbers were on the right side of block near fuel pump. National 1938 and later series on milled pad on crankcase to rear of distributor on right side of engine. Engines with a "B" prefix were built at Buffalo, New York. Starting: 1187822. Ending: 11915446; also B-1 to B-10502. [Series HA] Serial numbers were in the same location as on Master models. Starting: HA-1001. Ending: HA-46134. Engine numbers were the same as on Master models.

Model No.	Body Type & Seating	Price	Weight	Prod. Total
HB	2-dr. Cpe.-2P	648	2770	39,793
HB	2-dr. Cabr.-4P	755	2790	2787
HB	2-dr. Coach-5P	668	2795	3326
HB	2-dr. Twn. Sed.-5P	689	2825	95,050
HB	4-dr. Sed.-5P	730	2840	522
HB	4-dr. Spt. Sed.-5P	750	2845	20,952
HA	2-dr. Cpe.-2P	714	2840	36,106
HA	2-dr. Spt. Cpe.-4P	750	2855	2790
HA	2-dr. Coach-5P	730	2900	1038
HA	2-dr. Twn. Sed.-5P	750	2915	186,233
HA	4-dr. Sed.-5P	796	2915	236
HA	4-dr. Spt. Sed.-5P	817	2940	76,323

NOTE 1: The slant-back four-door sedan is an unusually rare Chevrolet. Other sedans were trunk-back models.

1938 Chevrolet, Master DeLuxe, sport coupe, HAC

ENGINE: Ohv. Inline. Six. Cast iron block. B & S: 3-1/2 x 3-3/4 in. Disp.: 216.5 cu. in. C.R.: 6.25:1. Brake H.P.: 85 @ 3200 R.P.M. N.A.C.C. H.P.: 29.4. Main bearings: four. Valve lifters: solid. Carb.: Carter one-barrel Model W1.

CHASSIS: [Master Series] W.B.: 112-1/4 in. Tires: 16 x 6.00. [Master DeLuxe Series] W.B.: 112-1/4 in. Tires: 16 x 6.00.

TECHNICAL: Manual transmission. Speeds: 3F/1R. Floor shift. Single-plate clutch. Semi-floating rear axle. Overall ratio: (Master) 3.73:1; (Master DeLuxe) 4.22:1. Four wheel hydraulic brakes. Steel spoke wheels.

OPTIONS: White sidewall tires. Fender marker lamps. Rear tire cover. Dual sidemount (rare). Sidemount cover (rare). Fender skirts ($8.00). Bumper Guards (standard on Master DeLuxe). Radio. Heater. Clock. Cigar lighter. Radio antenna. Seat covers. External sun shade. Spotlight. Fog lamps. Wheel trim rings. License plate holder.

NOTE 2: At least one U.S. built 1938 Chevrolet had factory equipment dual sidemounts. This car is owned by a Dutch collector who lives in Holland.

1938 Chevrolet, Master Deluxe, town sedan, PH

HISTORICAL: Introduced October 23, 1937. Innovations: Heavier valve springs. Cutoff exhaust valve guides. Longer water pump shaft. New ball bearing water pump (mid-year). Improved generator and starter systems. New diaphragm spring type clutch. New Departure throw-out bearing. Lighter flywheel. Longer rear axle housing and shaft. Calendar year registrations: 464,337. Calendar year production: 490,447. Model year production: (Master) 167,926; (Master DeLuxe) 302,840; (total) 470,766. General manager: M.E. Coyle.

1939

CHEVROLET — MASTER 85 — SERIES JB — SIX: The 1939 Chevrolets had longer hoods. Their redesigned hoods, fenders, wheels and runningboards made for a lower, longer appearance. The body shell was basically the same as 1938, but looked more modern. The grille extended back along the fender line at the top and narrowed to around four inches at the bottom. It had a well rounded look with horizontal grille mouldings and a horizontal bar effect on the splash aprons. The radiator was more upright. Headlights were mounted atop the front fenders. The door panel creases were eliminated and all four fenders were raised at the rear. Mounted at the center of the decklid, except on sedans and coaches, was the license plate lamp. Combination taillamps were of smaller size and incorporated stop lamps. The front bumpers had a more rounded face bar and were otherwise unchanged. Four-spoke steel wheels replaced the old eight-spoke type. Inside, the hand brake lever was moved to the cowl. A vacuum gearshift mounted on the steering column was a $10.00 option.

CHEVROLET — MASTER DELUXE — SERIES JA — SIX: The Master DeLuxe was a fancy version of the Master. It had bumper guards as standard equipment. Twin taillights were regular equipment. An all-new body style was the four-passenger coupe with folding opera seats replacing the rumbleseat. The Knee-Action coil spring front suspension was utilized.

I.D. DATA: [Series JB] Serial numbers were on a plate underhood on right side of cowl. Starting: JB-1001. Ending: JB-33221. Engine numbers were on the right side of engine on milled pad on crankcase near rear of distributor. Starting: 1915447. Ending: 2697267; also B-10503 to B-105461. [Series JA] Serial numbers were in the same location as on Master 85 models. Starting: JA-1001. Ending: JA-58510. Engine numbers were the same as on Master models.

Model No.	Body Type & Seating	Price	Weight	Prod. Total
JB	2-dr. Cpe.-2P	628	2780	41,770
JB	2-dr. Coach-5P	648	2795	1404
JB	.2-dr. Twn. Sed.-5P	669	2820	124,059
JB	4-dr. Sed.-5P	689	2805	336
JB	4-dr. Spt. Sed.-5P	710	2845	22,623
JB	4-dr. Sta. Wag.-8P	848	3010	430

NOTE 1: The four-door slantback sedan continued to sell poorly. The new station wagon came in two variations. Production total given above includes 229 station wagons with folding end gates and 201 with rear door.

JA	2-dr. Bus. Cpe.-2P	684	2845	33,809
JA	2-dr. Spt. Cpe.-4P	715	2845	20,908
JA	2-dr. Coach-5P	699	2865	180
JA	2-dr. Twn. Sed.-5P	720	2875	220,181
JA	4-dr. Sed.-5P	745	2875	68
JA	4-dr. Spt. Sed.-5P	766	2910	110,521
JA	4-dr. Sta. Wag.-8P	883	3060	989

1939 Chevrolet, Master DeLuxe, four-door sedan, AA

NOTE 2: Rare models included the Master DeLuxe coach and four-door slantback sedan.

ENGINE: Ohv. Inline. Six. Cast iron block. B & S: 3-1/2 x 3-3/4 in. Disp.: 216.5 cu. in. C.R.: 6.25:1. Brake H.P.: 85 @ 3200 R.P.M. N.A.C.C. H.P.: 29.4. Main bearings: four. Valve lifters: solid. Carb.: Carter one-barrel Model W1-4205.

CHASSIS: [Master Series] W.B.: 112-1/4 in. Tires: 16 x 6.00. [Master DeLuxe Series] W.B.: 112-1/4 in. Tires: 16 x 6.00.

TECHNICAL: Manual transmission. Speeds: 3F/1R. Floor shift controls. Single-plate clutch. Semi-floating rear axle. Overall ratio: (Master) 3.23:1; (Master DeLuxe) 4.22:1. Four wheel hydralic brakes. Four spoke steel wheels. Vacuum clutch ($10.00).

NOTE 3: Column gearshift used with vacuum clutch option.

OPTIONS: White sidewall tires. Rearview mirror. Single sidemount (standard on station wagon). License plate frame. Sidemount cover (on station wagon). Fender skirts ($8.90). Bumper guards. Radio. Heater. Clock. Cigar lighter. Radio antenna. Seat covers. External sun shade. Spotlight. Fog lamps. Wheel trim rings. Slip-in coupe pickup box. Fender marker lamps.

1939 Chevrolet, Master DeLuxe, coach, HAC

HISTORICAL: Introduced October 1938. Innovations: Double-acting (airplane type) shock absorbers on Master 85. Rubber bushed front suspension on Master. Diaphragm clutch spring riveted to clutch cover. New open spring front suspension on Master DeLuxe. Double-acting rear shock absorbers. New folding trunk guard braced to frame. Town and Country deluxe horn package. Calendar year registrations: 598,341. Calendar year production: 648,471. Model year production: (Master) 200,058; (Master DeLuxe) 387,119; (total) 587,177. General manager: M.E. Coyle.

The new station wagon bodies were built by Mid-States Body Corp. The Master DeLuxe was said to be the fastest accelerating American passenger car of 1939: 10 to 60 mph in high gear. A new manufacturing plant in Tonawanda, New York, was opened this year. The 15-millionth Chevrolet was built in 1939. No convertible cabriolets were built this year.

1940

CHEVROLET — MASTER 85 — SERIES KB — SIX: A longer wheelbase and completely new body and sheet metal were changes for 1940. The New "Royal Clipper" styling started with an "alligator" type front opening hood. The side panels were removable to get at the engine. The grille had a narrow vertical center bar, topped in name by a horizontal bar. It was of one-piece design. The headlights were on top of the fenders and featured sealed beam bulbs. Parking lights were mounted on top of the front fenders. The trunk had more flowing lines with flush taillamps. The license plate lamp was again in the center of the trunk lid. The bumpers featured two black-finished indentations running the length of the face bar. The Master 85 models did not have stainless steel belt hood or runningboard moldings. They had plainer upholstery and slightly less standard equipment. Front suspension was still of the leaf-spring, I-beam axle design.

CHEVROLET — MASTER DELUXE — SERIES KH — SIX:
Master DeLuxe was now Chevrolet's mid-priced line. These cars had the same styling as Master 85s, with more trim. Master DeLuxe identification appeared at the rear of the hood side ventilators. Stainless steel body and hood moldings were omitted. Knee-Action front suspension was standard equipment.

CHEVROLET — SPECIAL DELUXE — SERIES KA — SIX:
The Special DeLuxe, Chevrolet's new top-priced line, was a fancier edition of the Master DeLuxe. Stainless steel moldings trimmed the hood and body belt line. Standard equipment included a 30 hour clock, front door armrests, right-hand windshield wiper, twin air horns, and a deluxe steering wheel with horn ring. A convertible with a full width rear seat and power-operated top was new. The opera seat coupe was replaced with a five-passenger coupe having a full rear seat. A choice of different colors of upholstery and convertible tops was offered for the first time by Chevrolet.

1940 Chevrolet, Special DeLuxe, convertible coupe, OCW

I.D. DATA: [Series KB] Serial numbers were on a plate on right side of floor pan in front of front seat. Starting: KB-1001. Ending: KB-20946. Engine numbers were on the right side of engine on milled pad on crankcase near rear of distributor. Starting: 2697268. Ending: 3665902; also B-105462 to B-221935. "B" prefix on engine number indicates Buffalo, New York, factory. [Series KH] Serial numbers were in the same location as on Master 85 models. Starting: KH-1001. Ending: KH-37644. Engine numbers were the same as on Master 85 models. [Series KA] Serial numbers were in the same location as on other models. Starting: KA-1001. Ending: KA-72089. Engine numbers were the same as on other models.

Model No.	Body Type & Seating	Price	Weight	Prod. Total
KB	2-dr. Bus. Cpe.-2P	659	2865	25,734
KB	2-dr. Twn. Sed.-5P	699	2915	66,431
KB	4-dr. Spt. Sed.-5P	740	2930	11,468
KB	4-dr. Sta. Wag.-8P	903	3106	411

NOTE 1: Station wagon was low production model.

Model No.	Body Type & Seating	Price	Weight	Prod. Total
KH	2-dr. Bus. Cpe.-2P	684	2920	28,090
KH	2-dr. Spt. Cpe.-2/4P	715	2925	17,234
KH	2-dr. Twn. Sed.-5P	725	2965	143,125
KH	4-dr. Spt. Sed.-5P	766	2990	40,924
KA	2-dr. Bus. Cpe.-2P	720	2930	25,537
KA	2-dr. Spt. Cpe.-4P	750	2945	46,628
KA	2-dr. Conv.-4P	898	3160	11,820
KA	2-dr. Twn. Sed.-5P	761	2980	205,910
KA	4-dr. Spt. Sed.-5P	802	3010	138,811
KA	4-dr. Sta. Wag.-8P	934	3158	2493

1940 Chevrolet, Special DeLuxe, sport sedan, PH

NOTE 2: A total of 367 station wagons had double rear doors.

ENGINE: Ohv. Inline. Six. Cast iron block. B & S: 3-1/2 x 3-3/4 in. Disp.: 216.5 cu. in. C.R.: 6.25:1. Brake H.P.: 85 @ 3400 R.P.M. N.A.C.C. H.P.: 29.4. Main bearings: four. Valve lifters: solid. Carb.: Carter one-barrel Model W1-420S.

CHASSIS: [Master 85 Series] W.B.: 113 in. Tires: 16 x 6.00. [Master DeLuxe Series] W.B.: 113 in. Tires: 16 x 6.00. [Special DeLuxe Series] W.B.: 113 in. Tires: 16 x 6.00.

1940 Chevrolet, Special DeLuxe, coupe, JAC

TECHNICAL: Manual synchromesh transmission. Speeds: 3F/1R. Column gearshift (vacuum type) controls. Single-plate clutch. Semi-floating rear axle. Overall ratio: (Master) 3.73:1; (others) 4.11:1. Four wheel hydraulic brakes. Steel spoke wheels.

OPTIONS: Whitewall tires. Wheel trim rings. Rear view mirror. Master grille guard. Full wheel discs. Fender skirts. Bumper guards. Radio. Heater. Clock. Cigar lighter. Radio antenna. Seat covers. External sun shade. Spotlight. Fog lamps. Accessory (plastic) hood ornament.

HISTORICAL: Introduced September 1939. Innovations: First use of plastic parts. First stainless steel trim. New shape oil pan. Redesigned valve lifters. Higher charging rate. Helical gear transmission. Cross trunion type u-joint. Redesigned front cross member. Calendar year registrations: 853,529. Calendar year production: 895,734. Model year production: (Master) 116,618; (Master DeLuxe) 232,510; (Special DeLuxe) 430,945; (total) 775,073. General manager: M.E. Coyle.

1940 Chevrolet, Master DeLuxe, four-door sedan, OCW

A Model 85 business coupe driven by Juan Manuel Fangio won the 6,000 mile Gran Primo Internacional Del Norte race in Argentina. Fangio averaged 55 mph. He came in over an hour ahead of the second-place car. Three Chevys were among the top ten finishers in this contest. Chevrolet also signed its first contract for U.S. Government weapons production in April 1940.

1941

CHEVROLET — MASTER DELUXE — SERIES AG — SIX: Longer, lower, wider bodies were mounted on a Chevrolet chassis with a three inch longer wheelbase. The grille resembled last year's, but was new. It had six chrome-plated die-cast moldings. The hood was a front opening type with side panels eliminated. The headlights were now blended into the fenders. Chrome moldings decorated the front fender tops. There were parking lamps below each headlight. The new body featured concealed safety steps instead of runningboards. The slope of the windshield, rear window, and upper bodysides was increased. Concealed hinges were used on the doors and hood. The Master DeLuxe had body belt moldings and model identification plates at the rear of the hood sides. Standard upholstery and trimmings were plain. There were no armrests on the front doors.

CHEVROLET — SPECIAL DELUXE — SERIES AH — SIX: The Special DeLuxe had the same new body and basic styling as the Master DeLuxe. The series name appeared in chrome block letters on the rear sides of the hood. Additional standard equipment included a deluxe steering wheel with horn ring, stainless steel hood moldings, stainless steel window reveal moldings, a chrome-plated license plate lamp, and armrests on the front doors. Richer upholstery material

was used. In the spring, the Fleetline sedan was introduced. It was a close-coupled four-door model without ventipanes.

I.D. DATA: [Series AG] Serial numbers were on a plate on right side of floor pan in front of front seat. Starting: AG-1001. Ending: AG-62708. Engine numbers were on the right side of engine on milled pad on crankcase near rear of distributor. Starting: AA-1001. Ending: AA-1163729. Engines built in Tonawanda factory were numbered AC-1001 to AC-195459. [Series AH] Serial numbers were in the same location as on Master DeLuxe. Starting: AH-1001. Ending: AH-102375. Engine number were the same as Master DeLuxe.

1941 Chevrolet, Master Deluxe, sport sedan, PH

Model No.	Body Type & Seating	Price	Weight	Prod. Total
AG	2-dr. Bus. Cpe.-2P	712	3020	48,763
AG	2-dr. Cpe.-5P	743	3025	79,124
AG	2-dr. Twn. Sed.-5P	754	3050	219,438
AG	4-dr. Spt. Sed.-5P	795	3090	59,538
AH	2-dr. Bus. Cpe.-2P	769	3040	17,602
AH	2-dr. Cpe.-5P	800	3050	155,889
AH	2-dr. Cabr.-5P	949	3285	15,296
AH	2-dr. Twn. Sed.-5P	810	3095	228,458
AH	4-dr. Spt. Sed.-5P	851	3125	148,661
AH	4-dr. Sta. Wag.-8P	995	3410	2045

1941 Chevrolet, Special DeLuxe, convertible coupe, OCW

FLEETLINE SERIES

AH	4-dr. Sed.-5P	877	3130	34,162

ENGINE: Ohv. Inline. Six. Cast iron block. B & S: 3-1/2 x 3-3/4 in. Disp.: 216.5 cu. in. C.R.: 6.5:1. Brake H.P.: 90 @ 3300 R.P.M. N.A.C.C. H.P.: 29.4. Main bearings: four. Valve lifters: solid. Carb.: Carter one-barrel Model W1-483S.

CHASSIS: [Master DeLuxe] W.B.: 116. in. Tires: 16 x 6.00. [Special DeLuxe Series] W.B.: 116 in. Tires: 16 x 6.00.

TECHNICAL: Manual synchromesh transmission. Speeds: 3F/1R. Column gearshift controls. Single-plate clutch. Semi-floating rear axle. Overall ratio: 4.11:1. Four wheel hydraulic brakes. Steel spoke wheels.

1941 Chevrolet, Special Deluxe, town sedan, PH

OPTIONS: Whitewall tires. Stainless steel fender trim. Short wave radio. Exhaust deflector. Fender skirts. Bumper guards. Radio. Heater. Clock. Cigar lighter. Radio antenna. Seat covers. External sun shade. Spotlight. Fog lamps. Wheel trim rings. Full wheel discs. License plate frame. Accessory hood ornament. Bumper wing guards. Rear view mirror.

1941 Chevrolet, Special DeLuxe, station wagon, JAC

HISTORICAL: Introduced September 1940. Innovations: Increased compression ratio. Flat top pistons. Smaller combustion chamber. New 10mm spark plugs. New design rocker arms. Redesigned water pump. Improved ignition points. Knee-Action front coil spring suspension standard on all Chevrolets. Calendar year registrations: 880,346. Calendar year production: 930,293. Model year production: (Master DeLuxe) 419,044; (Special DeLuxe) 602,327; (total) 1,021,371. General manager: M.E. Coyle.

Last full production year prior to World War II. Chevrolet conducted a promotional contest in which Spencer Tracy was picked as America's top movie star. He was given a new Chevrolet station wagon.

1942

CHEVROLET — MASTER DELUXE — SERIES BG — SIX: A heavier "American Eagle" grille with lower and wider

horizontal bars characterized the 1942 Chevrolet. A front bumper gravel shield was added. Parking lights were in the grille side moldings. A new hood extended back to the edge of the door. The cowl panel was eliminated. Headlights were flush-mounted in the front fenders. Bolt-on caps extended the fenders onto the doors. At the rear the fenders and taillights were unchanged, but the license lamp and gravel shields were of new designs. There was no nameplate on the sides of the Master DeLuxe hood. Seats, steering wheel and interior trim were plain. On January 1, 1942, all bright metal trim — with the exception of bumpers and guards — was eliminated as part of the war effort. These "black out" models had trim parts painted in body color.

1942 Chevrolet, Special DeLuxe Fleetline, Aerosedan, AA

CHEVROLET — SPECIAL DELUXE — SERIES BH — SIX: Better upholstery, more trim and a longer list of standard equipment were seen on Special DeLuxe Chevrolets. Extras included a deluxe steering wheel with horn ring, chrome hood nameplates, and front door armrests. The cabriolet now had rear quarter windows. A new model was a fastback two-door Fleetline Aerosedan. Like the Fleetline sport master sedan it had three stainless steel trim strips on the sides of the fenders and fender caps. After January 1, Special DeLuxes were also sold with painted, rather than plated, trim.

I.D. DATA: [Series BG] Serial numbers were on a plate on right side of floor pan in front of front seat. Starting: BG-1001. Ending: BG-13310. Engine numbers were on the right side of engine on milled pad on crankcase near rear of distributor. Starting: 2AA-1001 & up; BA-1001 & up; 2AC-1001 & up. [Series BH] Serial numbers were in the same locations as on Master DeLuxe. Starting: BH-1001. Ending: BH-27530. Engine numbers were the same as on Master DeLuxe.

Model No.	Body Type & Seating	Price	Weight	Prod. Total
Master DeLuxe Series				
BG	2-dr. Cpe.-2P	760	3055	8089
BG	2-dr. Cpe.-5P	790	3060	17,442
BG	2-dr. Twn. Sed.-6P	800	3090	41,872
BG	4-dr. Spt. Sed.-6P	840	3110	14,093
Fleetmaster Series				
BH	2-dr. Cpe.-2P	815	3070	1716
BH	2-dr. Cpe.-5P	845	3085	22,187
BH	2-dr. Cabr.-5P	1080	3385	1182

46

BH	2-dr. Twn. Sed.-6P	855	3120	39,421	
BH	4-dr. Spt. Sed.-6P	895	3145	31,441	
BH	4-dr. Sta. Wag.-8P	1095	3425	1057	

Fleetline Series

BH	2-dr. Aerosedan-6P	880	3105	61,855	
BH	4-dr. Spt. Master-6P	920	3165	14,530	

NOTE 1: The new Aerosedan was a fastback model.

1942 Chevrolet, Master Deluxe, coupe, OCW

ENGINE: Ohv. Inline. Six. Cast iron block. B & S: 3-1/2 x 3-3/4 in. Disp.: 216.5 cu. in. C.R.: 6.5:1. Brake H.P.: 90 @ 3300 R.P.M. N.A.C.C. H.P.: 29.4. Main bearings: four. Valve lifters: solid. Carb.: Carter one-barrel Model 483S.

CHASSIS: [Master DeLuxe Series] W.B.: 116 in. Tires: 16 x 6.00. [Special DeLuxe Series] W.B.: 116 in. Tires: 16 x 6.00.

TECHNICAL: Manual synchromesh transmission. Speeds: 3F/1R. Column gearshift controls. Single-plate clutch. Semi-floating rear axle. Overall ratio: 4.11:1. Four wheel hydraulic brakes. Steel spoke wheels.

OPTIONS: Whitewall tires. Short wave radio. Signal-seeking radio. Exhaust deflector. Fender skirts. Bumper guards. Radio. Heater. Clock. Cigar lighter. Radio antenna. Seat covers. External sun shade. Spotlight. Fog lamps. Wheel trim rings. License plate lamp. Bumper wing guards. Rear view mirror.

1942 Chevrolet, Special DeLuxe, Fleetmaster cabriolet, HAC

HISTORICAL: Introduced September 1941. Innovations: Signal-seeking radio with station tuner introduced as an option. Aerosedan introduced. Calendar year production: 45,472. Model year production: (Master DeLuxe) 84,806; (Special DeLuxe) 173,989; (total) 258,795. General manager: M.E. Coyle.

All automobile production halted February 1, 1942. Last prewar Chevrolet built January 30. All factories except Saginaw Service Manufacturing plant converted for war production.

1941 Chevrolet, Special Deluxe, sport sedan, PH

CHEVROLET

1946-1975

1971 Chevrolet, Monte Carlo two-door hardtop, V-8 (PH)

Although Chevrolet entered the postwar era with a warmed-over version of its 1942 model, the marque quickly assumed its traditional role as America's best selling car. The 1946-1948 Chevys were conservative in styling and engineering, but earned a reputation as value leaders in the low-price field. The "Stovebolt Six," dating back to 1937, was not a performance engine, but provided dependable service.

By Tony Hossain

Chevrolet's brand new 1949 models were, once again, conservatively styled and ruggedly built. Although arch-rival Ford also fielded a new 1949 model, with more modern slab-sided body lines, Chevrolet remained far ahead in the sales race.

The big news for 1950 was the addition of a sporty Bel Air two-door hardtop and a new option, the fully automatic Powerglide transmission. Sales went over the 1.5 million mark for the first time in history.

Chevrolet strengthened its hold on the low-price field in the early 1950s, but these were not exciting years for

enthusiasts ... with one notable exception. In 1953, Chevy introduced the fiberglass Corvette sports car. The first Corvette used a Chevy sedan chassis, engine and Powerglide transmission, but the car would soon become a creditable sports car.

Nineteen fifty-five was Chevrolet's renaissance. It was year one for the hot Chevy and marked the division's first assault on the growing youth market. With a sharp new style and a hot new 265-cid V-8 under the hood, as optional power, Chevrolet was no longer grandma's car. Model year production soared to over 1.7 million, a record figure for any automaker.

Chevrolet built upon a good thing in 1956, with an extensive face lift and some potent new power options for the 265-cid 'Turbo-Fire' V-8. But, if there ever was a 'Classic Chevy', it was the 1957 model. In the 1950s, people regarded it as a 'baby Cadillac' and the Bel Air Sport Coupe, convertible and two-door Nomad station wagon quickly developed a cult following that still lasts to this day. In a 1974 advertisement, Chevy referred to the 17-year-old car as "the most popular used car in history." It still is. Performance enthusiasts will remember 1957 as the year Chevy bored out the small-block

V-8 to 283 cid and made available that most prestigious of options, Ramjet Fuel-Injection. Chevy claimed one horsepower per cubic inch of displacement.

The 1958 Chevrolet was totally redesigned, inside and out. The new Impala Sport Coupe and convertible joined the Bel Air series as Chevy's top-of-the-line offering. The Impala was immediately popular and, in ensuing years, would become known as 'the pre-eminent American car.'

Chevrolet called its 1959 models "all new all over again." Although they shared the cruciform frame design, which debuted in 1958, the 1959 body styling was all new and highly controversial. Especially disconcerting, to many longtime Chevrolet buyers, were the extreme horizontal tailfins and dramatically larger size. The Impala became a separate line, rather than a Bel Air sub-series. While young people scoured used car markets for sharp 1955-1957 models in powerpacked form, Chevrolet, responding to criticism of past performance merchandising, toned down the styling of its 1960 models.

The big news for 1960 was the introduction of the compact Corvair. Initially available in four-door sedan form only, the Corvair was a revolution in American automotive design with its rear-mounted aluminum six, fully independent suspension and clean styling. At first, sales were disappointing, but the mid-1960 addition of two-door models and the luxurious Monza Club Coupe sent sales upward. The Corvair quickly developed a following among automotive enthusiasts.

The Chevrolet product line continued to proliferate in the early 1960s, with the addition of the traditionally engineered, compact Chevy II in model year 1962. Then came the popular Chevelle, two years later. Chevrolets from the early 1960s that collectors find particularly appealing today include the 1962-1964 Impala SS (Super Sport), the Corvair Monza Spyder and all Corvettes.

Nineteen sixty-five would be known as the year of records for the Chevrolet Motor Division. Large Chevrolets were restyled with pleasing, flowing lines. Also new, from the ground up, was the Corvair. With continental-like styling and an all-new suspension system, the new Corvair received rave reviews from the motoring press. The 1965 Corvette received a four-wheel disc brake system and a robust 396-cid V-8 became Chevy's latest stormer.

It replaced the big Chevy's top-option '409;' an engine that had become a legend from 1961 to early 1963.

The late 1960s were years of declining market share for Chevrolet products. Ralph Nader's attack on the Corvair, in 1965, hurt auto sales in general, but had a particularly severe impact on Chevrolet. The Corvair was quietly withdrawn from the market in 1969.

The Camaro, Chevy's belated answer to the enormously successful Ford Mustang, was introduced in model year 1967. First-generation Camaros (1967-1969) are popular among collectors today. Particularly desirable are the Z28 or SS performance packages and all convertible models.

Chevrolet regained lost market share in the early 1970s, with new products and aggressive marketing. New for 1970 was the Monte Carlo and a redesigned Camaro, hailed as a contemporary classic. The smart new, sporty design lasted, with few changes, through the 1981 model year. Chevrolet's combined car and truck sales, in 1971, totaled over three million units.

Chevy had entered the 1970s as the world's largest producer of motor vehicles. Notable new entries in 1971 included a redone full-size Chevrolet and the subcompact Vega. Although it was a strong contender in its market segment, the Vega suffered numerous quality and engineering problems and was withdrawn at the end of the 1977 model year. Highly desirable today, however, are the limited edition, high-performance 1975-1976 Cosworth Vegas.

Chevrolets from the 1970s attracting collector interest today include the 1970-1972 Monte Carlos, Chevelle SSs, Camaros of all years and the 1975 Caprice convertible. That car was Chevrolet's last production ragtop for the 1970s.

1946 Chevrolet, Fleetline two-door Aerosedan, 6-cyl

1948 Chevrolet, Custom Country Club Coupe, 6-cyl

1948 Chevrolet, Fleetmaster station wagon, 6-cyl

1949 Chevrolet, Fleetline four-door sedan, 6-cyl

1954 Chevrolet, Bel Air four-door sedan, 6-cyl

1954 Chevrolet, Bel Air station wagon, 6-cyl

1964 Chevrolet, Impala two-door hardtop (Sport Coupe), V-8 (PH)

1958 Chevrolet, Impala two-door hardtop (Sport Coupe), V-8 (PH)

1946

STYLEMASTER — SIX — SERIES DJ — The 1946 Chevrolet Stylemaster models were updated 1942 Master Deluxes. The grille was modified, the parking lamps were relocated and chrome plated trim features returned to replace plastic parts used in prewar cars. Plain fenders, notchback styling and Stylemaster block lettering on hoodside moldings were identifiers. On the interior, three-spoke steering wheels, painted window sills and a minimum of bright metal trim moldings were used. Pile fabric upholstery, standard rubber floor mats and single left-hand sun visors were seen.

1946 Chevrolet, Stylemaster four-door sedan, 6-cyl

STYLEMASTER I.D. NUMBERS: Serial numbers were stamped on a plate on the right front door hinge pillar. Engine numbers were stamped on the right side of block near fuel pump The numerical prefix in serial number indicated assembly plant as follows: (1) Flint, Mich.; (2) Tarrytown, N.Y.; (3) St. Louis, Mo.; (5) Kansas City, Mo.; (6) Oakland, Calif.; (8) Atlanta, Ga.; (9) Norwood, Ohio; (14) Baltimore, Md.; (21) Janesville, Wis. The letters on the number plate indicated year and model, for example: DJ was for 1946 Stylemasters. A Fisher Body/Style Number was located on the vehicle data plate, on engine side of firewall. It began with a two-digit prefix designating model year, followed by a dash and four numbers indicating body type and sometimes having a letter suffix designating trim level or equipment installations. Serial numbers for Michigan-built 1946 Stylemasters were DJ-1001 to 56896; engine numbers were DAA1001 to 546865. Chevrolet model numbers appear in second column in charts below.

STYLEMASTER SIX SERIES DJ

Model No.	Body/Style No.	Body Type & Seating	Factory Price	Shipping Weight	Prod. Total
46-DJ	1504	2-dr Bus Cpe-2P	1022	3080	14,267
46-DJ	1524	2-dr Spt Cpe-5P	1059	3105	19,243
46-DJ	1502	2-dr Twn Sed-6P	1072	3145	61,104
46-DJ	1503	4-dr Spt Sed-6P	1123	3150	75,349

FLEETMASTER — SIX — SERIES DK — The Fleetmaster series replaced the prewar Special Deluxe group. The moldings on the sides of the hood carried this name. Richer upholstery trims were available and included two sun visors; front seat armrests and woodgrained window sills. No business coupe was offered, but a convertible and station wagon were. A Deluxe, two-spoke steering wheel with a stylized "bird" horn button insert was seen.

1946 Chevrolet, Fleetline two-door Aerosedan, 6-cyl

FLEETMASTER I.D. NUMBERS: Serial, engine and body style coding was based on the Stylemaster system, but different series codes and additional body nomenclature were used. Fleetmasters built in Michigan were numbered DK-1001 to 58678. The first two symbols in the main Style Number were '21' for Fleetmaster DK Series. Engine numbering range was the same as Stylemaster.

1946 Chevrolet, Fleetline Sportmaster four-door sedan, 6-cyl

FLEETMASTER SIX SERIES DK

Model No.	Body/Style No.	Body Type & Seating	Factory Price	Shipping Weight	Prod. Total
46-DK	2124	2-dr Spt Cpe-5P	1130	3120	27,036
46-DK	2134	2-dr Conv-5P	1381	3420	4,508
46-DK	2102	2-dr Twn Sed-6P	1143	3165	56,538
46-DK	2103	4-dr Spt Sed-6P	1194	3200	73,746
46-DK	2109	4-dr Sta Wag-8P	1604	3435	804

FLEETLINE — SIX — SUB-SERIES DK — As was the case in prewar times, a Fleetmaster sub-series was available as the two model Fleetline group. Both of these cars had the fastback GM 'Sport Dynamic' body shell and a Super Deluxe level of trim. Fleetline lettering adorned the hoodside molding. Triple speedline moldings were stacked on the flanks of all fenders. A distinctive bright metal windshield surround was seen. Interior appointments were generally of the Fleetmaster level, with special non-pile 'Fleet weave' fabrics used only in these two models. There was no way to overlook their extra-fancy appearance.

FLEETLINE I.D. NUMBERS: As a Fleetmaster sub-series, Fleetlines shared the same numbering system, except for style codes.

FLEETLINE SUB-SERIES DK

Model No.	Body/Style No.	Body Type & Seating	Factory Price	Shipping Weight	Prod. Total
46-DK	2113	4-dr Spt Mas Sed-6P	1222	3215	7,501
46-DK	2144	2-dr Aero Sed-6P	1165	3140	57,932

ENGINE: Six-cylinder. Overhead valve. Cast iron block. Displacement: 216.5 cid. Bore and stroke: 3-1/2 x 3-3/4 inches. Compression ratio: 6.5:1. Brake horsepower: 90 at 3300 rpm. Four main bearings. Solid valve lifters. Carburetors: Carter one-barrel as follows: (standard transmission with Climate Control) YF-765S or YF-765SA: (manual choke with standard transmission) YF-787S or YF-787SA or YF-787SB; (all standard transmission) WI-574S or YF-787S or YF-787SB or YF-789S or YF-789SB.

CHEVROLET CHASSIS FEATURES: Three-speed manual transmission was exclusively available. Wheelbase: (all) 207-1/2 inches. Front tread: (all) 57.6 inches. Rear tread: (all) 60 inches. Rear axle ratio: 4.11:1. Tires: 16 x 6.00.

CONVENIENCE OPTIONS: Radio. Heater. Whitewall tire disks. Spotlight. Radio antenna. Fog lamps. Cowl windshield washer. Center bumper guards. Deluxe steering wheel. Deluxe push-button radio. Heater and defroster. Wheel trim rings. Deluxe in-dash heater and defroster.

HISTORICAL FOOTNOTES: The first postwar Chevy was built Oct. 3, 1945. The business coupe had front seat only. The Fleetmaster station wagon was a true 'woodie' wagon.

1947

STYLEMASTER — SIX — SERIES 1500 EJ — There was minimal change for 1947 at Chevrolet. The radiator grille had a softer, more horizontal appearance with the blades contoured into three distinct sections and Chevrolet lettering on the uppermost bar. A more horizontal hood emblem with bow-tie insignia was used. The horizontal moldings, which ran from hood to rear, were eliminated from all models, but a short, spear-shaped molding at the rear sides of the hood carried the series name in block letters. A three-spoke steering wheel with no horn ring was seen. Pile fabric upholstery was used. The floor mats lacked carpet inserts and a single left-hand sun visor appeared.

STYLEMASTER I.D. NUMBERS: Serial numbers were stamped on a plate on the right front door hinge pillar. Engine numbers were stamped on the right side of block near fuel pump. The numerical prefix in serial number indicated

assembly plant as follows: (1) Flint, Mich.; (2) Tarrytown, N.Y.; (3) St. Louis, Mo., (5) Kansas City, Mo.; (6) Oakland, Calif.; (8) Atlanta, Ga.; (9) Norwood, Ohio; (14) Baltimore, Md.; (21) Janesville, Wis. The letters on the number plate indicated year and model, for example: EJ was for 1947 Stylemaster. A Fisher Body/Style Number was located on the vehicle data plate, on engine side of firewall. It began with a two-digit prefix designating model year, followed by a dash and four numbers indicating body type and sometimes having a letter suffix designating trim level or equipment installations. Serial numbers for Michigan-built 1947 Stylemasters were EJ-1001 to 56896; engine numbers were EA-1001 to 683120. Chevrolet model numbers appear in column two in charts below.

1947 Chevrolet, Stylemaster four-door sedan, 6-cyl

SYTLEMASTER SIX SERIES 1500 EJ

Model No.	Body/Style No.	Body Type & Seating	Factory Price	Shipping Weight	Prod. Total
47-EJ	1504	2-dr Bus Cpe-2P	1160	3050	27,403
47-EJ	1524	2-dr Spt Cpe-5P	1202	3060	34,513
47-EJ	1502	2-dr Twn Sed-6P	1219	3075	88,534
47-EJ	1503	4-dr Spt Sed-6P	1276	3130	42,571

1947 Chevrolet, Fleetline two-door Aerosedan, 6-cyl

FLEETMASTER — SIX — SERIES 2100 EK — Quick identification of Fleetmaster models came from the lettering on hoodside spears, the appearance of bright metal window reveal moldings and use of trim below taillamps. A Deluxe two-spoke steering wheel was standard. Two-tone, Bedford cloth upholstery was optional, with leatherette scuff covering used in all trim combinations on doors, front seats and rear seats. Carpet inserts highlighted Fleetmaster front floor mats. Two sun visors were used. An illuminated radio grille and package compartment with lock was featured. Fleetline fastbacks lacked speedline fender trim, but again came with special "Fleetweave' upholstery and all Fleetmaster appointments.

FLEETMASTER I.D. NUMBERS: The numbers followed the same general system with new alphabetical codes. Serial numbers EK-1001 to 72404. Engine numbers fit into the same sequence listed for Stylemaster above.

FLEETMASTER SIX SERIES 2100 EK

Model No.	Body/Style No.	Body Type & Seating	Factory Price	Shipping Weight	Prod. Total
47-EK	2103	4-dr Spt Sed-6P	1345	3185	91,440
47-EK	2102	2-dr Twn Sed-6P	1286	3125	80,128
47-EK	2124	2-dr Spt Cpe-5P	1281	3090	59,661
47-EK	2134	2-dr Conv-5P	1628	3390	28,443
47-EK	2109	4-dr Sta Wag-8P	1893	3465	4,912

FLEETLINE 2100 EK SUB-SERIES

Model No.	Body/Style No.	Body Type & Seating	Factory Price	Shipping Weight	Prod. Total
47-EK	2113	4-dr Spt Mas Sed-6P	1371	3150	54,531
47-EK	2144	2-dr Aero Sed-6P	1313	3125	159,407

1947 Chevrolet, Fleetmaster station wagon, 6-cyl

ENGINE: Six-cylinder. Overhead valve. Cast iron block. Displacement: 216.5 cid. Bore and stroke: 3-1/2 x 3-3/4 inches. Compression ratio: 6.5:1. Brake horsepower: 90 at 3300 rpm. Four main bearings. Solid valve lifters. Carburetors: Carter one-barrel as follows: (standard transmission with Climate Control) YF-765S or YF-765SA: (manual choke with standard transmission) YF-787S or YF-787SA or YF-787SB; (all standard transmission) WI-574S or YF-787S or YF-787SB or YF-789S or YF-789SB.

CHEVROLET CHASSIS FEATURES: Three-speed manual transmission. Wheelbase: (all) 116 inches. Overall length: (passenger cars) 197-3/4 inches; (station wagons) 207-1/2 inches. Front tread: (all) 57.6 inches. Rear tread: (all) 60 inches. Rear axle ratio: 4.11:1. Tires: 16 x 6.00.

CONVENIENCE OPTIONS: Heater. Whitewall tire disks. Spotlight. Radio antenna. Fog lamps. Cowl windshield washer. Center bumper guards. Deluxe steering wheel. Deluxe push-button radio. Heater and defroster. Wheel trim rings. Deluxe in-dash heater and defroster.

HISTORICAL FOOTNOTES: Model year sales of 684,145 units made Chevrolet America's number one producer of autos. Dealer introductions were held Feb. 8, 1947. The business coupe had a front seat only. The Fleetmaster station wagon was a true 'woodie' wagon.

1948

STYLEMASTER — SIX — SERIES 1500 FJ — A T-shaped vertical center bar was added to the 1947 grille to make a 1948 Chevy. A new hood ornament and slightly revised nose emblem appeared. Black rubber windshield surrounds; plain side fenders; rubber mud guards; and Stylemaster lettering on the rear hoodside spears characterized the exterior of the low-priced Chevrolet. Inside was found a three-spoke steering wheel (without horn ring); painted dashboard; unlighted glovebox; plain trim; pile fabric upholstery; plain rubber floor mats; painted window sills and all-cloth seats without leather topped armrests.

STYLEMASTER I.D. NUMBERS: Serial numbers were stamped on a plate on the right front door hinge pillar. Engine numbers were stamped on the right side of block near fuel pump. The numerical prefix in serial number indicated assembly plant as follows: (1) Flint, Mich.; (2) Tarrytown, N.Y.; (3) St. Louis, Mo., (5) Kansas City, Mo.; (6) Oakland, Calif.; (8) Atlanta, Ga.; (9) Norwood, Ohio; (14) Baltimore, Md.; (21) Janesville, Wis. The letters on the number plate indicated year and model, for example: FJ was for 1948 Stylemaster. A Fisher Body/Style Number was located on the vehicle data plate, on engine side of firewall. It began with a two-digit prefix designating model year, followed by a dash and four numbers indicating body type and sometimes having a letter suffix designating trim level or equipment installations. Serial numbers for Michigan-built 1948 Stylemasters were FJ-1001 to 30590, engine numbers were FA-1001 to 825234. Chevrolet model numbers appear in column two in charts below.

1948 Chevrolet, Stylemaster two-door sport coupe, 6-cyl

STYLEMASTER SIX SERIES 1500 FJ

Model No.	Body/Style No.	Body Type & Seating	Factory Price	Shipping Weight	Prod. Total
48-FJ	1503	4-dr Spt Sed-6P	1371	3115	48,456
48-FJ	1502	2-dr Twn Sed-6P	1313	3095	70,228
48-FJ	1524	2-dr Spt Cpe-6P	1323	3020	34,513
48-FJ	1504	2-dr Bus Cpe-3P	1244	3045	18,396

1948 Chevrolet, Fleetline two-door Aerosedan, 6-cyl (AA)

FLEETMASTER — SIX — SERIES 2100 FK — Short, stylized spears on the rear corners of hoods read 'Fleetmaster.' So did the inclusion of features such as chrome windshield surrounds; two-spoke Deluxe steering wheel (with horn ring); woodgrained dashboard and window sills; illuminated glove locker; leatherette rear seat scuff covers; front floor mat carpet inserts and leather-topped front seat armrests. An equipment change was that the clock and cigarette lighter were now considered standard on Fleetmasters and Fleetlines only. A dome lamp with automatic switch at driver's door was also a regular extra feature on these lines. On the Fleetmaster, buyers could select two-tone Bedford cloth upholstery options or stick with the standard pile fabric choice. Triple, stacked speedline moldings once again graced front and rear fenders of Fleetline fastbacks. These cars had other Super Deluxe features as well such as five vertical slashes of chrome beneath the taillights and Fleetline signature script on the center of the deck lid. There was also a three-quarter length belt molding.

1948 Chevrolet, Fleetmaster four-door Sport Sedan, 6-cyl (PH)

FLEETMASTER I.D. NUMBERS: The numbers followed the same general system with new alphabetical codes. Serial numbers FK-1001 to 81603. Engine numbers fit into the same sequence listed for Stylemaster above.

1948 Chevrolet, Fleetline two-door Aerosedan, 6-cyl

FLEETMASTER SIX SERIES 2100 FK

Model No.	Body/Style No.	Body Type & Seating	Factory Price	Shipping Weight	Prod. Total
48-FK	2103	4-dr Spt Sed-6P	1439	3150	93,142
48-FK	2102	2-dr Twn Sed-6P	1381	3110	66,208
48-FK	2124	2-dr Spt Cpe-6P	1402	3050	58,786
48-FK	2134	2-dr Conv-5P	1750	3340	20,471
48-FK	2109	4-dr Sta Wag-8P	2013	3430	10,171

FLEETLINE 2100 FK SUB-SERIES

Model No.	Body/Style No.	Body Type & Seating	Factory Price	Shipping Weight	Prod. Total
48-FK	2113	4-dr Spt Mas-6P	1492	3150	83,760
48-FK	2144	2-dr Aero Sed-6P	1434	3100	211,861

ENGINE: Six-cylinder. Overhead valve. Cast iron block. Displacement: 216.5 cid. Bore and stroke: 3-1/2 x 3-3/4 inches. Compression ratio: 6.5:1. Brake horsepower: 90 at 3300 rpm. Four main bearings. Solid valve lifters. Carburetors: Carter one-barrel as follows: (standard transmission with Climate Control) YF-765S or YF-765SA; (manual choke with standard transmission) YF-787S or YF-787SA or YF-787SB; (all standard transmission) WI-574S or YF-787S or YF-787SB or YF-789S or YF-789SB.

CHEVROLET CHASSIS FEATURES: Three-speed manual transmission. Wheelbase: (all) 116 inches. Overall length: (passenger cars) 197-3/4 inches; (station wagons) 207-1/2 inches. Front tread: (all) 57.6 inches. Rear tread: (all) 60 inches. Rear axle ratio: 4.11:1. Tires: 16 x 6.00.

CONVENIENCE OPTIONS: Standard radio. Deluxe push-button radio. Standard below dash heater and defroster. Deluxe in-dash heater and defroster. White sidewall tires. Spotlight cowl windshield washer. Low-pressure tires on wide rim 15-inch wheels. Bedford cord Fleetmaster upholstery. Front and rear bumper wing guards. Chrome plated gravel shields. Radio antenna. Clock in Stylemaster. Cigarette lighter in Stylemaster. Engine oil filter, external canister type. Oil bath air cleaner. Country Club trim package (see Historical Footnotes for details). Wheel trim rings. Directional signals. External windshield sun shade (visor).

HISTORICAL FOOTNOTES: Model introductions were held February 1948. Calendar sales of 775,982 units were recorded for the year. Precision interchangeable main engine bearings were adopted this season, in place of poured babbitt bearings. The business coupe had a front seat only. The Fleetmaster station wagon was a true 'woodie' wagon. A unique accessory sold by Chevrolet dealers this year was the woodgrained 'Country Club' trim package, produced by Engineered Enterprises of Detroit, Mich., but sold only through factory authorized dealers for $149.50. It could be ordered for the Fleetline Aero Sedan and the Fleetmaster Town Sedan or convertible coupe, but few cars were so-equipped.

1949

SPECIAL SERIES — SIX — 1500 GJ — Series designations were now determined by trim level, not body style. Each line had Styleline (notchback) and Fleetline (fastback) sub-series. All new, postwar designs were seen with integral front fenders and lower styling lines for fenders, roofs and hoods. The grille had a bowed upper bar with Chevrolet lettering; a horizontal center bar with round parking lamps (where bars intersected); and seven, short vertical bars dividing the lower opening. Standard equipment for Specials included dual tail and stop lights; dual license lights; dual windshield wipers; stainless steel body belt molding; body sill molding; rear fender crown moldings; front door push-button handles (with integral key locks); black rubber rear fender shields; gas filler door in left rear fender; hood ornament and emblem; rear deck lid emblem; chrome headlamp rims; five extra-low pressure 6.70 x 15 tires on five-inch rims; front and rear bumpers and guards; and license guard on front bumper. Seats were upholstered with tan, striped-pattern, pile fabric with rubberized backs. Black rubber floor mats were used in the front compartment, carpets in rear of sedans and sport coupes. Three-spoke steering wheels with horn buttons appeared.

SPECIAL I.D. NUMBERS: Serial numbers were stamped on a plate on the right front door hinge pillar. Engine numbers were stamped on the right side of block near fuel pump. The numerical prefix in serial number indicated assembly plant as follows: (1) Flint, Mich.; (2) Tarrytown, N.Y.; (3) St. Louis, Mo., (5) Kansas City, Mo.; (6) Oakland, Calif.; (8) Atlanta, Ga.; (9) Norwood, Ohio; (14) Baltimore, Md.; (21) Janesville, Wis. The letters on the number plate indicated year and model, for example: 'GJ' for Special series; 'GK' for Deluxe. Number plate locations changed to left-hand door pillar. Engine number also stamped on crankcase to rear of distributor. Serial numbers GJ-1001 to 47213. Engine numbers GA-1001 to 1031807. Fisher Body/Style Numbers now appear on second column of charts; Chevrolet model numbers in first column; series code in head above.

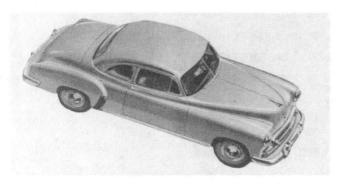

1949 Chevrolet, Styleline Special two-door business coupe, 6-cyl

SPECIAL SERIES 1500 GJ

STYLELINE SUB-SERIES

Model No.	Body/Style No.	Body Type & Seating	Factory Price	Shipping Weight	Prod. Total
1503	49-1269	4-dr Sed-6P	1460	3090	46,334
1502	49-1211	2-dr Sed-6P	1413	3070	69,398
1524	49-1227	2-dr Spt Cpe-6P	1418	3030	40,239
1504	49-1227B	2-dr Bus Cpe-3P	1339	3015	20,337

FLEETLINE SUB-SERIES

Model No.	Body/Style No.	Body Type & Seating	Factory Price	Shipping Weight	Prod. Total
1553	49-1208	4-dr Sed-6P	1460	3095	58,514
1552	49-1207	2-dr Sed-6P	1413	3060	36,317

DELUXE SERIES — SIX — SERIES 2100 GK —
In addition to body equipment found, on Special Series models, Deluxes had series nameplate (Deluxe) on front fenders; stainless steel moldings on front fenders and doors; windshield reveal moldings; stainless steel rear fender shields (gravel guards); window reveal moldings (except station wagon and convertible); short lower belt molding sections; rear wheel cover panels (fender skirts); left-hand outside rearview mirror on convertible and chrome-plated side window frames, also on convertible. Seats were upholstered with tan, striped pattern, flat cloth in sedans and coupe; genuine leather and tan Bedford cord in convertibles; tan leather fabric in station wagon. Also included were Deluxe two-spoke steering wheel, two sun visors, simulated carpet floor mat inserts, two-tone tan and brown dashboard finish and many other Deluxe appointments.

DELUXE I.D. NUMBERS: The numbers followed the same general system with new alphabetical code. Serial numbers GK-1001 to 128201. Engine numbers fit into the same sequence listed for Special Series above.

DELUXE SERIES 2100 GK

STYLELINE SUB-SERIES

Model No.	Body/Style No.	Body Type & Seating	Factory Price	Shipping Weight	Prod. Total
2103	49-1069	4-dr Sed-6P	1539	3125	191,357
2102	49-1011	2-dr Sed-6P	1492	3100	147,347
2124	49-1027	2-dr Spt Cpe-6P	1508	3065	78,785
2134	49-1067	2-dr Conv-5P	1857	3355	32,392
2109	49-1061	4-dr Wood Wag-8P	2267	3485	3,342
2119	49-1062	4-dr Steel Wag-8P	2267	3435	2,664

FLEETLINE SUB-SERIES

Model No.	Body/Style No.	Body Type & Seating	Factory Price	Shipping Weight	Prod. Total
2153	49-1008	4-dr Sed-5P	1539	3135	130,323
2152	49-1007	2-dr Sed-5P	1492	3100	180,251

NOTE 1: Body/Style Number 1061, the wood station wagon, was replaced by Style Number 1062, the steel station wagon, in the middle of the model run, with both styles available concurrently early in the year

1949 Chevrolet, Styleline Deluxe two-door convertible, 6-cyl (AA)

ENGINE: Six-cylinder. Overhead valve. Cast iron block. Displacement: 216.5 cid. Bore and stroke: 3-1/2 x 3-3/4 inches. Compression ratio: 6.5:1. Brake horsepower: 90 at 3300 rpm. Four main bearings. Solid valve lifters. Carburetor: Carter one-barrel W1-684.

CHEVROLET CHASSIS FEATURES: Box girder frame. In convertible a 'VK' structure of I-beam members takes place of engine rear support cross member. Knee-action front suspension with direct, double-acting shock absorbers. Ride stabilizer. Rubber insulated semi-elliptic rear springs with metal covers. Direct double-acting hydraulic rear shock absorbers. Four-wheel hydraulic brakes with 11-inch drums. Wheelbase: (all) 115 inches. Overall length: (passenger cars) 197 inches; (station wagon) 198 inches. Front tread: (all) 57 inches. Rear tread: (all) 58-3/4 inches. Rear axle: Semi-floating with hypoid drive and 4.11:1 gear ratio. Torque tube drive with tubular propeller shaft; both fully enclosed. Tires: 6.70 x 15 blackwall on widebase rims.

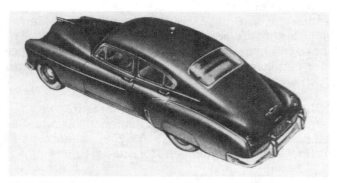

1949 Chevrolet, Fleetline Deluxe four-door sedan, 6-cyl

CONVENIENCE OPTIONS: Standard manual radio. Deluxe push-button radio. Radio antenna. Under dash heater and defroster. In-dash Deluxe heater and defroster. White sidewall tires. Wheel trim rings. Spotlight. Fog lamps. Directional signals. Back-up light. External windshield sun shade (visor). Tan striped pattern, free-breathing pile fabric. Deluxe series upholstery trim. San-Toy seat covers. Outer bumper tips. Master grille guard. Locking gas filler cap. Other standard factory and/or dealer installed accessories.

HISTORICAL FOOTNOTES: Dealer introduction in January 1949. Interior trims varied per body style and are fully explained in 1949 Chevrolet sales catalogs. Model year production was 1,037,600 cars. Calendar year sales total was 1,109,958 cars. Chevrolet was America's number one automaker again. Steel station wagon (not wood) has front bodyside molding. Business Coupe has black rubber mat on rear compartment floor; single sun visor for driver. Lowerable quarter windows in two-door sedans. Lowerable forward sections and fixed ventipanes in four-door sedan rear door windows. Fixed quarter windows in coupes. Sliding rear quarter windows in sport coupe. Genuine carpet inserts for convertible front floor mat. Convertible features dome light in roof bow. Station wagon has sliding quarter windows; woodgrained leatherette headliner; tan rubber floor mats; tan linoleum cargo area deck and no rear seat armrests, coat hooks or assist straps.

1950

SPECIAL SERIES — SIX — 1500 HJ — Few styling changes appeared. New grille deletes vertical division bars, except for new triple ribbed-type directly under

front parking lamps. Nose and deck lid ornaments restyled; new hood ornament. Deck lid handle slightly revised for easier locking and lifting. Styleline Specials have bustle back; no chrome body strip. Fleetline Specials have sweeping fastback lines; no chrome body strip. Curved windshield with chrome center strip on both. Equipment features similar to list for 1949. Upholstery is gray-striped modern weave flat cloth with dark gray broadcloth; plain light gray fabric back, side and sidewall panels. Light gray control knobs replace ivory-type used in 1949. Floor mat, lamp and steering wheel features follow trends of earlier years. Exact equipment varies per model and is fully outlined in 1950 factory sales literature.

SPECIAL I.D. NUMBERS: Serial numbers were stamped on a plate on the right front door hinge pillar. Engine numbers were stamped on the right side of block near fuel pump. The numerical prefix in serial number indicated assembly plant as follows: (1) Flint, Mich.; (2) Tarrytown, N.Y.; (3) St. Louis, Mo.; (5) Kansas City, Mo.; (6) Oakland, Calif.; (8) Atlanta, Ga.; (9) Norwood, Ohio; (14) Baltimore, Md.; (21) Janesville, Wis. The letters on the number plate indicated year and model, for example: HJ was for 1950 Special. A Fisher Body/Style Number was located on the vehicle data plate, on engine side of firewall. It began with a two-digit prefix designating model year, followed by a dash and four numbers (shown in second column of charts below) indicating body type and sometimes having a letter suffix designating trim level or equipment installations. Serial numbers for Michigan-built 1950 Specials were HJ-1001 to 49801; engine numbers were HA-1001 to 1320152.

SPECIAL SERIES 1500 HJ

STYLELINE SUB-SERIES

Model No.	Body/Style No.	Body Type & Seating	Factory Price	Shipping Weight	Prod. Total
1503	50-1269	4-dr Sed-6P	1450	3120	55,644
1502	50-1211	2-dr Sed-6P	1403	3085	89,897
1524	50-1227	2-dr Spt Cpe-6P	1408	3050	28,328
1504	50-1227B	2-dr Bus Cpe-3P	1329	3025	20,984

FLEETLINE SUB-SERIES

| 1553 | 50-1208 | 4-dr Sed-6P | 1450 | 3115 | 23,277 |
| 1552 | 50-1207 | 2-dr Sed-6P | 1403 | 3080 | 43,682 |

1950 Chevrolet, Styleline Deluxe four-door sedan, 6-cyl

NOTE 1: Fisher Body/Style Numbers: First two symbols are prefix indicating model year: 50=1950. First two symbols in main number identify series (12=Special). Second two symbols in main number identify body type (69=four-door sedan; 11=two-door sedan, etc.). This number is located on vehicle data plate under hood and is the best way to positively identify Chevrolet body styles.

1950 Chevrolet, Styleline Deluxe two-door Sport Coupe, 6-cyl

DELUXE SERIES — SIX — 2100 HK — Styleline Deluxe models have bustle back; fender skirts; chrome body strip; word Deluxe on fender; and same extra equipment features outlined for 1949 Deluxe series. Bel Air 'hardtop convertible,' with three-piece wraparound curved backlight, is a new style. Fleetline Deluxe models have sweeping fastback body with same higher trim level features inside and out. Bel Air interior features are same as in convertible coupe, except two rear compartment lamps are used at roof quarter panels; neutral gray headliner with chrome roof bows appears; and transmission lever knob is black plastic. Other Deluxe models trimmed with gray striped broadcloth material having 'off shoulder' dark gray broadcloth contrast panels and dark gray front seatback cushions, seat risers, upper sidewalls and center pillars. Light gray headliner and lower sidewalls used. Features vary per body style and are fully detailed in 1950 Chevrolet sales catalogs.

1950 Chevrolet, Styleline Deluxe two-door convertible, 6-cyl

DELUXE I.D. NUMBERS: The numbers followed the same general system with new 'HK' alphabetical code. Serial numbers HK-1001 to 187118. Engine numbers fit into same sequence listed for Special Series above.

DELUXE SERIES 2100 HK

STYLELINE SUB-SERIES

Model No.	Body/Style No.	Body Type & Seating	Factory Price	Shipping Weight	Prod. Total
2103	50-1069	4-dr Sed-6P	1529	3150	316,412
2102	50-1011	2-dr Sed-6P	1482	3100	248,567
2124	50-1027	2-dr Spt Cpe-6P	1498	3090	81,536
2154	50-1037	2-dr Bel Air-6P	1741	3225	76,662
2134	50-1067	2-dr Conv-5P	1847	3380	32,810
2119	50-1062	4-dr Sta Wag-8P	1994	3460	166,995

FLEETLINE SUB-SERIES

2153	50-1008	4-dr Sed-6P	1529	3145	124,287
2152	50-1007	2-dr Sed-6P	1482	3115	189,509

NOTE: Style Number 50-1037 is a two-door pillarless hardtop coupe.

1950 Chevrolet, Fleetline Deluxe two-door sedan, 6-cyl

ENGINE: Six-cylinder. Overhead valve. Cast iron block. Displacement: 216.5 cid. Bore and stroke: 3-1/2 x 3-3/4 inches. Compression ratio: 6.5:1. Brake horsepower: 90 at 3300 rpm. Four main bearings. Solid valve lifters. Carburetor: Rochester one-barrel 7002050.

CHEVROLET CHASSIS FEATURES: Box girder frame. In convertible a 'VK' structure of I-beam members takes the place of engine rear support cross member. Knee-action front suspension with direct, double-acting shock absorbers. Ride stabilizer. Rubber insulated semi-elliptic rear springs with metal covers. Direct double-acting hydraulic rear shock absorbers. Four-wheel hydraulic brakes with 11-inch drums. Wheelbase: (all) 115 inches. Overall length: (passenger cars) 197.5 inches; (station wagon) 198.25 inches. Front tread: (all) 57 inches. Rear tread: (all) 58-3/4 inches. Rear axle: Semi-floating with hypoid drive and 4.11:1 gear ratio. Torque tube drive with tubular propeller shaft; both fully enclosed. Tires: 6.70 x 15 blackwall on widebase rims.

POWERTRAIN OPTIONS: Powerglide two-speed automatic transmission was introduced as a $159 option for Deluxe series only. Cars so equipped were provided with a modified Chevrolet truck engine with 3-9/6 x 3-15/16 inch bore and stroke and 235 cubic inches of piston displacement. Hydraulic valve lifters and larger intake valves were used. Horsepower was rated the familiar 90 at 3300 rpm. A slightly lower 3.55:1 rear axle gear ratio was used on Powerglide-equipped models. Also, 7.10 x 15 tires ($14.75 extra) were optional for convertibles equipped with Powerglide.

1950 Chevrolet, Styleline Deluxe Bel Air two-door hardtop, 6-cyl

CONVENIENCE OPTIONS: Standard manual radio. Deluxe push-button radio. Radio antenna. Under dash heater and defroster. In-dash Deluxe heater and defroster. White sidewall tires. Wheel trim rings. Spotlight. Fog lamps. Directional signals. Back-up light. External windshield sun shade (visor). Tan striped pattern, free-breathing pile fabric Deluxe Series upholstery trim. San-Toy seat covers. Outer bumper tips. Master grille guard. Locking gas filler cap. Other standard factory and/or dealer installed accessories.

HISTORICAL FOOTNOTES: Dealer introduction was Jan. 7, 1950. Model year production was 1,371,535 units. Calendar year sales totaled 1,520,577. Chevrolet is America's number one automaker again. Bel Air hardtop introduced. Powerglide automatic transmission introduced. Hydraulic valve lifters adopted for Powerglide six-cylinder engine. Body style features were the same as detailed under 1949 Historical Footnote. New Rochester carburetor was B or BC type ('C' indicating automatic choke). Some cars also had Stromberg BXVD-2 or BXXD-35 carburetors.

1951

SPECIAL SERIES — SIX — 1500JJ — A subtle, but attractive face lift characterized the 1951 Chevrolet. By moving the parking lamps into the lower grille opening under the headlamps a wider look was achieved. Styleline Specials had bustle backs and no chrome body strip. Fleetline Specials had fastbacks and no chrome body strip. Black Rubber mud guards were seen on both Special lines. Two-tone gray interiors with light gray striped pattern cloth upholstery were used. Equipment features followed the 1949-1950 assortment. Variations are fully detailed in factory sales catalogs. New, smaller taillamps with a nearly square red plastic lens were used. A small round reflector was positioned at the bottom of the same housing. Bendix 'Jumbo Drum' brakes replaced the old Huck units. A simplified trunk ornament bearing the Chevrolet bow-tie emblem was used. Specials still came only with the base engine and conventional transmission.

SPECIAL I.D. NUMBERS: Serial numbers were stamped on a plate on the right front door hinge pillar. Engine numbers were stamped on the right side of block near fuel pump. The numerical prefix in serial number indicated assembly plant as follows: (1) Flint, Mich.; (2) Tarrytown, N.Y.; (3) St. Louis, Mo., (5) Kansas City, Mo.; (6) Oakland, Calif.; (8) Atlanta, Ga.; (9) Norwood, Ohio; (14) Baltimore, Md.; (21) Janesville, Wis. The letters on the number plate indicated year and model, for example: JJ was for 1951 Special. A Fisher Body/Style Number was located on the vehicle data plate, on engine side of firewall. It began with a two-digit prefix designating model year, followed by a dash and four numbers (shown in second column of charts below) in-dicating body type and sometimes having a letter suffix designating trim level or equipment installations. Serial numbers for Michigan-built 1951 Specials were JJ-1001 to 32061; engine numbers were JA-1001 to 1261301.

1951 Chevrolet, Styleline Deluxe two-door sedan, 6-cyl

SPECIAL SERIES 1500 JJ

STYLELINE SUB-SERIES

Model No.	Body/Style No.	Body Type & Seating	Factory Price	Shipping Weight	Prod. Total
1503	1269	4-dr Sed-6P	1594	3110	63,718
1502	1211	2-dr Sed-6P	1540	3070	75,566
1524	1227	2-dr Spt Cpe-6P	1545	3060	18,981
1504	1227B	2-dr Bus Cpe-3P	1460	3040	17,020

FLEETLINE SUB-SERIES

Model No.	Body/Style No.	Body Type & Seating	Factory Price	Shipping Weight	Prod. Total
1553	1208	4-dr Sed-6P	1594	3130	3,364
1552	1207	2-dr Sed-6P	1540	3090	6,441

DELUXE SERIES — SIX — 2100 JK — Deluxe models also used the newly designed grille that had the lower two horizontal bars extended to form a circular frame for oblong parking lamps with five vertical sectioned bars beside the parking lamps. Chevrolet was written, in script, on the chrome grille frame molding. Deluxes had a stainless steel molding starting above the front wheel openings and extending onto doors with a Deluxe nameplate on front fenders. Chrome rear fender gravel shields and painted fender skirts were standard equipment. Interiors were two-tone gray with gray striped broadcloth upholstery. Four different, special two-tone combinations were offered for Bel Air interiors. Bel Air upholstery was in two-tone gray striped pilecord fabric with genuine deep buff leather bolsters. Station wagons were trimmed with tan imitation pigskin. Cars with Powerglide had a special script, denoting this feature, on deck lids.

DELUXE I.D. NUMBERS: The numbers followed the same general system with new 'JK' alphabetical code. Serial numbers JK-1001 to 174408. Engine numbers fit into same sequence listed for Special Series above.

DELUXE SERIES 1500 JK

STYLELINE SUB-SERIES

Model No.	Body/Style No.	Body Type & Seating	Factory Price	Shipping Weight	Prod. Total
2103	1069	4-dr Sed-6P	1680	3150	380,270
2102	1011	2-dr Sed-6P	1629	3110	262,933
2124	1027	2-dr Spt Cpe-6P	1647	3090	64,976
2154	1037	2-dr Bel Air-6P	1914	3215	103,356
2134	1067	2-dr Conv-5P	2030	3360	20,172
2119	1062	4-dr Sta Wag-8P	2191	3450	23,586

FLEETLINE SUB-SERIES

2153	1008	4-dr Sed-6P	1680	3155	57,693
2152	1007	2-dr Sed-6P	1629	3125	131,910

NOTE: Style Number 1037 is a two-door pillaress hardtop coupe.

1951 Chevrolet, Styleline Deluxe four-door sedan, 6-cyl

ENGINES

(INLINE SIX): Overhead valve. Cast iron block. Displacement: 216.5 cid. Bore and stroke: 3-1/2 x 3-3/4 inches. Compression ratio: 6.6:1. Brake horsepower: 92 at 3400 rpm. Four main bearings. Solid valve lifters. Carburetor: Single-barrel Rochester, Carter and Stromberg models used in mixed production.

(POWERGLIDE SIX): Inline six. Overhead valve. Cast iron block. Displacement: 235.5 cid. Bore and stroke: 3-9/16 x 3-15/16 inches. Four main bearings. Hydraulic valve lifters. Compression ratio: 6.7:1. Brake horsepower: 105 at 3600 rpm. Carburetor: Rochester one-barrel BC.

CHEVROLET CHASSIS FEATURES: Box girder frame. In convertible a 'VK' structure of I-beam members takes the place of engine rear support cross member. Knee-action front suspension with direct double-acting shock absorbers. Ride stabilizer. Rubber insulated semi-elliptic rear springs with metal covers. Direct double-acting hydraulic rear shock absorbers. Four-wheel hydraulic brakes with 11-inch drums. Wheelbase: (all) 115 inches. Overall length: (passenger cars) 197.75 inches; (station wagon) 198-7/8. Front tread: (all) 57 inches. Rear tread: (all) 58-3/4 inches. Rear axle: Semi-floating with hypoid drive and 4.11:1 gear ratio. Torque tube drive with tubular propeller shaft; both fully enclosed. Tires: 6.70 x 15 blackwall on widebase rims; 7.10 x 15 on convertible.

CONVENIENCE OPTIONS: Directional signals. Dash panel ashtray (standard in Deluxe). Manual radio. Deluxe push-button radio. Under dash heater and defroster. Deluxe in-dash heater and defroster. Full wheel discs. Wheel trim rings. Whitewall tires. Thirty-nine hour stem wind clock (standard in Deluxe). Fender skirts (standard on Deluxe). No-Mar Fuel door guard. Door handle shields. Front and rear bumper wing tips. Master grille guard. Spotlight. Fog lamps. External sun shade (visor). Locking gas filler door. Front fender stainless steel gravel shields. Impala-style hood ornament. Tissue dispenser. San-Toy seat covers. Left-hand outside rearview mirror (standard in convertible). Right-hand outside rearview mirror. Radio antenna. License plate frame. Back-up lamp. Vacuumatic ashtray. Rubber heel protector. Underhood lamp. Luggage compartment lamp. Other standard factory and dealer-installed accessories. Powerglide, Deluxe only ($169).

HISTORICAL FOOTNOTES: Dealer introductions were held Dec. 9, 1950. Model year production totaled 1,250,803 units. Calendar year sales were 1,118,096 cars. Chevrolet remained America's number one automaker. Attractive new dashboard and steering wheel with 'bow tie' spoke and horn ring design (Deluxe type).

1952

SPECIAL SERIES — SIX — 1500 KJ — A new grille for 1952 had five vertical bars that soon became known as Chevrolet "teeth." They were mounted to the horizontal center divider bar and equally spaced out from the center. The parking lamps were again in the lower grille opening and again oblong-shaped, but now "floated" in their housings. The word Chevrolet trimmed a wider new nose emblem, which still had a "bow-tie" logo. The Special Series no longer included fastback Fleetline models. Specials had notchback styling, no chrome body molding, rubber gravel deflectors and open rear wheelhousings. Nine exterior colors and four two-tone combinations were provided for all sedans, sport coupes and business coupes, including Styleline Specials. Two-tone gray interiors were featured, with seat upholstery of checkered pattern cloth.

SPECIAL I.D. NUMBERS: Serial numbers were stamped on a plate on the right front door hinge pillar. Engine numbers were stamped on the right side of block near fuel pump. The numerical prefix in serial number indicated assembly plant as follows: (1) Flint, Mich.; (2) Tarrytown, N.Y.; (3) St Louis, Mo., (5) Kansas City, Mo.; (6) Oakland, Calif.; (8) Atlanta, Ga.; (9) Norwood, Ohio; (14) Baltimore, Md.; (21) Janesville, Wis. The letters on the number plate indicated year and model, for example: KJ was for 1951 Special. A Fisher Body/Style Number was located on the vehicle data plate, on engine side of firewall. It began with a two-digit prefix designating model year, followed by a dash and four numbers (shown in second column of charts below) indicating body type and sometimes having a letter suffix designating trim level or equipment installations. Serial numbers for Michigan-built 1951 Specials were KJ-1001 to 19286; engine numbers were KA-1001 to 860773.

STYLELINE SPECIAL SERIES 1500 KJ

Model No.	Body/Style No.	Body Type & Seating	Factory Price	Shipping Weight	Prod. Total
1503	1269	4-dr Sed-6P	1659	3115	35,460
1502	1211	2-dr Sed-6P	1603	3085	54,781
1524	1227	2-dr Spt Cpe-6P	1609	3050	8,906
1504	1227B	2-dr Bus Cpe-6P	1519	3045	10,359

1952 Chevrolet, Styleline Deluxe two-door sedan, 6-cyl

DELUXE SERIES — SIX — 2100 KK — The new 1952 styling was particularly attractive when packaged in Deluxe trim. Easily noticed distinctions included body rub moldings on front fenders and doors; bright metal rear fender gravel guards (with long extension moldings sweeping up over the fender-skirted wheelhousings) and Deluxe script logos directly above the gravel guards on the rear fender pontoons. Bright metal windshield and window reveals were featured as well. A two-spoke steering wheel, with full blowing ring, replaced the three-spoke Special-type with horn button. Deluxes also had ivory plastic control knobs with bright metal inserts; dome lamps with automatic door switches; two inside sun visors and richer interior trims with foam rubber cushions. Upholstery combinations were reversed, with dark gray chevron pattern cloth and lighter toned upper contrast panels. As usual, convertibles, Bel Airs and station wagons had their own exclusive trim. There were also four exterior paint colors for Bel Airs and 11 two-tone combinations, while convertibles came in 10 colors (with five different top tones) and wagons offered four types of finish in combination with woodgrained trim panels. In the model lineup, the two-door Fleetline sedan was the sole fastback car in the Chevrolet line. It came only with Deluxe trim, as did the Powerglide transmission option. Cars with Powerglide again had lettering to the effect attached on the rear deck lid.

DELUXE I.D. NUMBERS: The numbers followed the same general system with new 'KK' alphabetical code. Serial numbers KK-1001 to 115255. Engine numbers fit into same sequence given for Special series above.

DELUXE SERIES 2100 KK

STYLELINE SUB-SERIES

Model No.	Body/Style No.	Body Type & Seating	Factory Price	Shipping Weight	Prod. Total
2103	1069	4-dr Sed-6P	1749	3145	319,736
2102	1011	2-dr Sed-6P	1696	3110	215,417
2124	1027	2-dr Spt Cpe-6P	1715	3100	36,954
2154	1037	2-dr Bel Air-6P	1992	3215	74,634
2134	1067	2-dr Conv-5P	2113	3380	11,975
2119	1062	4-dr Sta Wag-8P	2281	3475	12,756

FLEETLINE SUB-SERIES

2152	1007	2-dr Sed-6P	1696	3110	37,164

NOTE: Style number 1037 is a two-door pillarless hardtop coupe.

ENGINES

(INLINE SIX): Overhead valve. Cast iron block. Displacement: 216.5 cid. Bore and stroke: 3-1/2 x 3-3/4 inches. Compression ratio: 6.6:1. Brake horsepower: 92 at 3400 rpm. Four main bearings. Solid valve lifters. Carburetor: Rochester one-barrel B or BC (automatic choke on BC), or Stromberg BXOV-2 Model 380286, or Stromberg BXOV-25 Model 380270.

(POWERGLIDE SIX): Inline six. Overhead valve. Cast iron block. Displacement: 235.5 cid. Bore and stroke: 3-9/16 x 3-15/16 inches. Four main bearings. Hydraulic valve lifters. Compression ratio: 6.7:1. Brake horsepower: 105 at 3600 rpm. Carburetor: Rochester one-barrel BC (Note: 3.55:1 gear ratio rear axle used with Powerglide transmission both years).

1952 Chevrolet, Styleline Deluxe Bel Air two-door hardtop, 6-cyl

CHEVROLET CHASSIS FEATURES: Box girder frame. In convertible a 'VK' structure of I-beam members takes place of engine rear support cross member. Knee-action front suspension with direct double-acting shock absorbers. Ride stabilizer. Rubber insulated semi-elliptic rear springs with metal covers. Direct double-acting hydraulic rear shock absorbers. Four-wheel hydraulic brakes with 11-inch drums. Wheelbase: (all) 115 inches. Overall length: (passenger cars) 197.75 inches; (station wagon) 198-7/8 inches. Front tread: (all) 57 inches. Rear tread: (all) 58-3/4 inches. Rear axle: Semi-floating with hypoid drive and 4.11:1 gear ratio. Torque tube drive with tubular propeller shaft; both fully enclosed. Tires: 6.70 x 15 blackwall on widebase rims; 7.10 x 15 on convertible.

CONVENIENCE OPTIONS: Directional signals. Dash panel ashtray (standard in Deluxe). Manual radio. Deluxe push-button radio. Under dash heater and defroster. Deluxe in-dash heater and defroster. Full wheel discs. Wheel trim rings. Whitewall tires. Thirty-nine hour stem wind clock (standard in Deluxe). Fender skirts (standard on Deluxe). No-Mar Fuel door guard. Door handle shields. Front and rear bumper wing tips. Master grille guard. Spotlight. Fog lamps. External sun shade (visor). Locking gas filler door. Front fender stainless steel gravel shields. Impala-style hood ornament. Tissue dispenser. San-Toy seat covers. Left-hand outside rearview mirror (standard in convertible). Right-hand outside rearview mirror. Radio antenna. License plate frame. Back-up lamp. Vacuumatic ashtray. Rubber heel protector. Underhood lamp. Luggage compartment lamp. Other standard factory and dealer-installed accessories. Powerglide, Deluxe only ($178). E-Z-Eye glass. Ashtray (dash-type) now standard in both series. Availability of whitewalls limited due to Korean War material restrictions.

HISTORICAL FOOTNOTES: Dealer introductions began Jan. 19, 1952. Model year sales reached 827,317 despite Korean War manufacturing limitations. Calendar year sales totaled 877,947 despite war. Whitewall tires were uncommon. Inferior chrome plating process was used this year. Chevrolet again ranked as number one American automaker. In October 1952, the one-millionth Powerglide-equipped Chevrolet was assembled; the option was just 34 months old. The 28-millionth U.S. or Canadian Chevrolet car or truck was built in December 1952.

1953

SPECIAL 150 SERIES — SIX — 1500 A — The subseries designations Styleline and Fleetline were dropped since there was no fastback Chevrolet for 1953. Cars with Special level features and trim were called One-Fifty or 150 models, this designation coming from the first three digits of the numerical series code. The sport coupe became the 'club coupe' and a 'Handyman' station wagon was a new Special model. New styling details included one-piece curved windshields; new chrome hood ornament and nose nameplate; new grille with three vertical fins on the center horizontal bar and extensions encircling the parking lamps; and new vertical dual stop and taillamps. Easy identifiers included rubber windshield molding; plain bodysides without moldings; rubber gravel guards; no rocker panel molding; unskirted rear wheel housings; and no series nameplate. On the inside of Special 150s there was a standard steering wheel; single sun visor; and plain upholstery. The One-Fifty station wagon had safety sheet side door windows in place of Safety Plate glass and was rated a six-passenger car.

1953 Chevrolet, Two-Ten four-door sedan, 6-cyl

CHEVROLET I.D. NUMBERS: Serial numbers were stamped on a plate on the right front door hinge pillar.

Engine numbers were stamped on the right side of block near fuel pump. Style Number was located on the vehicle data plate, on engine side of firewall. It began with a two-digit prefix designating model year, followed by a dash and four numbers (shown in second column of charts below) indicating body type and sometimes having a letter suffix designating trim level or equipment installations. Alphabetical code 'A' for Special series. Serial numbers A53( )-001001 to A53-228961. Engine numbers LA-1001 to 1183450. The blank space ( ) in serial number was filled with a letter indicating assembly plant as follows: A-Atlanta; B-Baltimore; F-Flint; J-Janesville, Wis.; K-Kansas City; L-Los Angeles; N-Norwood, Ohio; O-Oakland; S-St. Louis; T-Tarrytown, N.Y. It should be noted that engine numbers consisted of four to seven numbers with a prefix or suffix. The prefix or suffix indicated year, engine size, factory, type of valve lifter and other peculiarities. It is impossible to tabulate all these codes in a small amount of space. Restorers can consult Chevrolet shop manuals or master parts catalogs for this type of information.

1953 Chevrolet, One-Fifty station wagon, 6-cyl

SPECIAL 150 SERIES

Model No.	Body/Style No.	Body Type & Seating	Factory Price	Shipping Weight	Prod. Total
1503	1269	4-dr Sed-6P	1670	3215	54,207
1502	1211	2-dr Sed-6P	1613	3180	79,416
1524	1227	2-dr Clb Cpe-6P	1620	3140	6,993
1504	1227B	2-dr Bus Cpe-3P	1524	3140	13,555
1509	1262F	4-dr Sta Wag-6P	2010	3420	22,408

1953 Chevrolet, Two-Ten station wagon, 6-cyl

NOTE 1: Style Number 1227B has single seat (front), fixed rear quarter windows and rear storage space with raised floor. Style Number 1262F has two seats (folding second seat) and plexiglass 'Safety Seal' side windows.

SPECIAL 150 SERIES ENGINE: Inline six. Overhead valve. Cast iron block. Displacement: 235.5 cid. Bore and stroke: 3-9/16 x 3-15/16. Compression ratio: 7.1:1. Brake horsepower: 108 at 3600 rpm. Four main bearings. Solid valve lifters. Carburetor: Rochester one-barrel B-type Model 7007181 or Carter one-barrel Model 2101S.

DELUXE 210 SERIES — SIX — 2100 B — Cars with Deluxe level features and trim were now called Two-Ten or 210 models, the new designation taken from the first three digits of numerical series code. The Sport Coupe became the 'Club Coupe.' The pillarless hardtop was not a Bel Air. The six-passenger station wagon with folding second seat was called the 'Handyman' (as was the same version with Special trim). The eight-passenger station wagon was called the 'Townsman.' The Townsman had three seats, the second and third units being stationary, but completely removable. The 210 convertible was deleted in midyear and the 210 Townsman station wagon was also dropped for 1954, along with the 210 sport coupe. External identification of Two-Tens was afforded by horizontal lower belt moldings running from front to rear; chrome windshield and window moldings; rocker panel moldings; and bright metal rear gravel guards with short spears at the top. A two-spoke steering wheel with horn ring was used. Standard equipment also included cigarette lighter; dash panel ashtray; dual sun visors and 39-hour stem wind clock. Heaters and radios were optional and, when not fitted, blocker plates were used to cover the cutouts on the dashboard for heater and radio controls. Interior door handles used on 210 models had bright metal inserts in the black plastic knobs. Other interior appointments included foam rubber seat cushion pads in front seats and in rear seats of sedans and coupes; front armrests in all models; rear armrests in sedans and coupes; rear compartment ashtray in four-door sedans; one ashtray in each armrest of two-door sedans and coupes; and bright metal moldings on rear quarter panels of sedans and coupes.

DELUXE 210 I.D. NUMBERS: The numbers followed the same general system with new 'B' alphabetical code. Serial numbers B53( )001001 to 228961 with blank ( ) showing assembly plant code. Engine numbers fit into same sequence given above for Special 150 series.

DELUXE 210 SERIES

Model No.	Body/Style No.	Body Type & Seating	Factory Price	Shipping Weight	Prod. Total
2103	1069W	4-dr Sed-6P	1761	3250	332,497
2102	1011W	2-dr Sed-6P	1707	3215	247,455
2124	1027	2-dr Clb Cpe-6P	1726	3190	23,961
2154	1037	2-dr Spt Cpe-6P	1967	3295	14,045
2134	1067	2-dr Conv-5P	2093	3435	5,617
2109	1062F	4-dr Sta Wag-6P	2123	3450	18,258
2119	1062	4-dr Sta Wag-8P	2273	3495	7,988

NOTE 1: Two-Ten body/style numbers are similar to Bel Air body/style numbers except for suffixes. Style Number 1011W, 1037 and 1067 have lowering rear quarter windows. The Style Number 1062F 210 Townsman station wagon varies from the '150' Townsman in that Safety Plate glass door windows are used.

1953 Chevrolet, Bel Air four-door sedan, 6-cyl (AA)

BEL AIR — SIX — SERIES 2400 C — The Bel Air designation was applied to a four car lineup this season. It now identified a level of trim, instead of a particular body style. The numerical code 2400C applied to all Bel Air models, but was rarely used in place of the descriptive series name. To identify this new luxury series, Chevrolet added a double molding on the rear fender pontoon. It enclosed a panel that was decorated with a short, wide-ribbed beauty molding, Bel Air script and Chevrolet crest on the leading edge above a chrome gravel shield. All Two-Ten trim features and equipment were incorporated, plus rear fender skirts; double windshield pillar moldings; extra wide window reveals on sedans; and saddle moldings on sport coupes and convertibles. Exposed bright metal roof bows and dashboard mounted rearview mirrors were standard in Bel Air sport coupes.

BEL AIR I.D. NUMBERS: The numbers followed the same general system with new 'C' alphabetical code. Serial numbers C53( )-001001 to 228961 with ( ) showing assembly plant code. Note that serial numbers, as well as engine number, fit into same sequence given above for Deluxe 210 series.

BEL AIR SERIES

Model No.	Body/Style No.	Body Type & Seating	Factory Price	Shipping Weight	Prod. Total
2403	1069WD	4-dr Sed-6P	1874	3275	246,284
2402	1011WD	2-dr Sed-6P	1620	3230	144,401
2454	1037D	2-dr Spt Cpe-6P	2051	3310	99,047
2434	1067D	2-dr Conv-5P	2175	3470	24,047

ENGINES

(INLINE SIX): Overhead valve. Cast iron block. Displacement: 235.5 cid. Bore and stroke: 3-9/16 x 3-15/16. Compression ratio: 7.1:1. Brake horsepower: 108 at 3600 rpm. Four main bearings. Solid valve lifters. Carburetor: Rochester one-barrel B-type Model 7007161 or Carter one-barrel Model 2101S.

(POWERGLIDE INLINE SIX): Overhead valve. Cast iron block. Displacement: 235.5 cid. Bore and stroke: 3-9/16 x 3-15/16 inches. Compression ratio: 7.5:1. Brake horsepower: 115 at 3600 rpm. Four main bearings. Hydraulic valve lifters. Carburetor: Rochester BC type one-barrel Model 7007200 or Carter one-barrel Model 2101S. (A transmission oil cooler and 3.55:1 axle ratio were used with Powerglide.)

CHEVROLET CHASSIS FEATURES: Wheelbase: (all series) 115 inches. Overall length: (all passenger cars)

195-1/2 inches; (all station wagons) 197-7/6 inches. Front tread: (all) 56.69 inches. Rear tread: (all) 58.75 inches. Tires: (convertible with Powerglide) 7.10 x 15 four-ply; (Townsman station wagon) 6.70 x 15 six-ply; (all others) 6.70 x 15 four-ply. Standard rear axle ratio: 3.7:1.

CONVENIENCE OPTIONS: Power steering ($178). Custom radio push-button. Custom Deluxe radio. Recirculating heater and defroster (under dash type). Air Flow heater and defroster (dashboard type). E-Z-Eye tinted glass. Autronic Eye automatic headlamp dimmer. White sidewall tires. Directional signals. Back-up lights. Bumper guards (second pair, front or rear). Front fender gravel shields. Door handle shields. Windshield sun shade (visor). Full wheel discs. Accessory "Bird-type" hood ornament. Fender skirts on 150 models. License plate frame. Front and rear bumper tip guards. Stem-wind clock on 150 models. Radio antenna. Locking gas filler door. Venti-pane wind deflectors. Left-hand outside rearview mirror. Fog lights. Traffic light viewer. Tissue dispenser. Vacuumatic ashtray. Non-glare rearview mirror. No-Mar fuel door trim. Underhood light. San-Toy seat covers. Powerglide ($178). Other standard factory and dealer-installed accessories.

HISTORICAL FOOTNOTES: Dealer introductions occurred January 1953. Model year sales totaled 1,356,413. Calendar year sales reached 1,477,287. A completely new body was offered with wraparound and backlight on all models except club coupe, convertible and station wagon. Chevrolet introduced the Corvette. Powerglide models now had full-pressure lubrication. Powerglide available in Two-Ten and Bel Air only. Seventeen models were the most ever offered by Chevrolet. First year for Chevrolet power steering. Chevrolet remained America's number one automaker.

1954

SPECIAL 150 SERIES — SIX — 1500 A — Styling improvements for 1954 Chevrolets, although minor, gave the impression of a wider, more modern car. New was a full-width horizontal center grille bar housing wraparound horizontal parking lamp housings at each outer end. Five vertical teeth were equally spaced from the center of the main bar out. The front bumper was redesigned with its ends bulged out to wrap around the body corners. New bumper guards, headlight rims, front ornament and hood mascot were seen. The taillight housings were hooded to create a fin-like look in profile view. They housed a vertical red and white cigar-shaped lens, the white portion provided in case optional back-up lamp wiring was added. Powerglide was now available in One-Fifty models, cars so equipped having Powerglide badges, in place of the normal Chevrolet scripts, on the deck lid. Inside, the 150 Specials had black window crank knobs and plainer interior appoint-

ments described as being "smartly fashioned of durable materials." Rubber windshield moldings; black rubber gravel guards; hubcaps and plain body sides were a few ways to spot cars in this line. The club coupe was gone and the business coupe was renamed the 'utility sedan,' which had no back seat. It had a raised rear compartment load floor.

1954 Chevrolet, One-Fifty two-door utility sedan, 6-cyl

CHEVROLET I.D. NUMBERS: Serial numbers were stamped on a plate on the right front door hinge pillar. Engine numbers were stamped on the right side of block near fuel pump. Style Number was located on the vehicle data plate, on engine side of firewall. It began with a two-digit prefix designating model year, followed by a dash and four numbers (shown in second column of charts below) indicating body type and sometimes having a letter suffix designating trim level or equipment installations. Alphabetical code 'A' for Special Series. Serial numbers A54( )-001001 to A54-174684. Engine numbers 01001Z54 to 1024930. The blank space ( ) in serial number was filled with a letter indicating assembly plant as follows: A-Atlanta; B-Baltimore; F-Flint; J-Janesville, Wis.; K-Kansas City; L-Los Angeles; N-Norwood, Ohio; O-Oakland; S-St. Louis; T-Tarrytown, N.Y. It should be noted that engine numbers consisted of four to seven numbers with a prefix or suffix. The prefix or suffix indicated year, engine size, factory, type of valve lifter and other peculiarities. It is impossible to tabulate all these codes in a small amount of space. Restorers can consult Chevrolet shop manuals or master parts catalogs for this type of information.

SPECIAL 150 SERIES

Model No.	Body/Style No.	Body Type & Seating	Factory Price	Shipping Weight	Prod. Total
1503	1269W	4-dr Sed-6P	1680	3210	32,430
1502	1211W	2-dr Sed-6P	1623	3165	64,855
1509	1262F	4-dr Sta Wag-6P	2020	3455	21,404
1512	1211WB	2-dr Utl Sed-3P	1539	3145	10,770

DELUXE 210 SERIES — SIX — 2100 B — Two-Ten identification features were similar to 1953 and included chrome bodyside moldings; chrome windshield molding; chrome window moldings; rocker panel moldings; bright metal gravel guards; genuine carpets in rear compartment; and durable cloth seats with vinyl contrasting panels in four different color schemes. The Two-Ten club coupe was sometimes called the 'Del Ray' and came with all-vinyl, waffle pattern upholstery and matching two-tone door panels. The Two-Ten 'Handyman' station wagon was upholstered with long-wearing vinyl materials of contrasting colors and tex-

tures including horizontally ribbed door panel inserts. The Two-Ten convertible and 'Townsman' station wagon were dropped.

1954 Chevrolet, Two-Ten Del Ray two-door sedan, 6-cyl

DELUXE 210 I.D. NUMBERS: The numbers followed the same general system. Serial numbers 8-54( )-001001 to 174684. Engine numbers fit into the same sequence given above for Special 150 series.

DELUXE 210 SERIES

Model No.	Body/Style No.	Body Type & Seating	Factory Price	Shipping Weight	Prod. Total
2103	1069W	4-dr Sed-6P	1771	3230	235,146
2102	1011W	2-dr Sed-6P	1717	3185	194,498
2124	1011WA	2-dr Del Ray Cpe-6P	1782	3185	66,403
2109	1062F	4-dr Sta Wag-6P	2133	3470	27,175

NOTE: Style Number 1062F was the Handyman station wagon with two seats. The rear most often was a folding type.

1954 Chevrolet, Two-Ten four-door sedan, 6-cyl

BEL AIR — SIX — SERIES 2400 C — The new Bel Air had the traditional assortment of extra equipment and features such as full genuine carpeting; newly designed full wheel discs; horizontally ebbed vinyl door panels and an electric clock. The sport coupe had special 'fashion fiesta' two-tone upholstery; rear pillar courtesy lights; chrome-plated inside roof garnish moldings; and rear window frame and bright metal exposed roof bows. The convertible interior seemed even richer, with two-tone all-vinyl trims and snap-on boot cover. The rearview mirror was no longer mounted atop the dashboard. Identifying all Bel Airs externally were full-length sweepspear moldings with double moldings on rear fenders enclosing the name Bel Air and a Chevrolet crest; bright metal double windshield pillar moldings and window molding; body belt molding; rocker panel moldings; bright metal gravel guards; and rear wheel fender skirts.

1954 Chevrolet, Bel Air two-door convertible, 6-cyl

BEL AIR I.D. NUMBERS: The numbers followed the same general system. Serial numbers C54( )-001001 to 174684. Engine numbers fit into the same sequence given above for Special 150 series.

BEL AIR SERIES

Model No.	Body/Style No.	Body Type & Seating	Factory Price	Shipping Weight	Prod. Total
2403	1069WD	4-dr Sed-6P	1684	3255	248,750
2402	1011WD	2-dr Sed-6P	1830	3220	143,573
2454	1037D	2-dr Spt Cpe-6P	2061	3300	66,378
2434	1067D	2-dr Conv-5P	2165	3445	19,383
2419	1062D	4-dr Sta Wag-8P	2263	3540	8,156

NOTE: Style Number 1062D was the Bel Air Townsman station wagon with Di-Noc simulated woodgrain exterior trim and color-keyed interior. It had three stationary seats, the rear two being entirely removable for extra cargo capacity.

ENGINES

(SYNCHROMESH) Inline Six: Overhead valve. Cast iron block. Displacement: 235.5 cid. Bore and stroke: 3-9/16 x 3-15/16. Compression ratio: 7.5:1. Brake horsepower: 115 at 3700 rpm. Four main bearings. Solid valve lifters. Carburetor: Rochester one-barrel 'B' type Model 7007181 or Carter one-barrel 2102S.

(POWERGLIDE) Inline Six: Overhead valve. Cast iron block. Displacement: 235.5 cid. Bore and stroke: 3-9/16 x 3-15/16. Compression ratio: 7.5:1. Brake horsepower: 125 at 4000 rpm. Four main bearings. Hydraulic valve lifters. Include transmission oil cooler; new high-lift camshaft; full-pressure lubrication; new aluminum pistons. (Standard with Powerglide and available in all car lines.)

CHEVROLET CHASSIS FEATURES: Wheelbase: (all series) 115 inches. Overall length: (all passenger cars) 196-7/16 inches; (all station wagons) 198-15/16 inches. Front tread: (all) 56.69 inches. Rear tread: (all) 58.75 inches. Tires: (convertible with Powerglide) 7.10 x 15 four-ply; (Townsman station wagon) 6.70 x 15 six-ply; (all others) 6.70 x 15 four-ply. Standard rear axle ratio: 3.7:1.

CONVENIENCE OPTIONS: Custom radio push-button. Custom Deluxe radio. Recirculating heater and defroster (under dash type). Air Flow heater and defroster (dashboard type). E-Z-Eye tinted glass. Autronic Eye automatic headlamp dimmer. Directional signals. Back-up lights. Bumper guards (second pair, front or rear). Front fender gravel shields. Door handle shields. Windshield sunshade (visor). Full wheel discs. Accessory "Bird-type" hood ornament. Fender skirts on 150 models. License plate frame. Front and rear bumper tip guards. Stem-wind clock on 150 models. Radio antenna. Locking gas filler door. Venti-pane wind deflectors. Left-hand outside rearview mirror. Fog lights. Traffic light viewer. Tissue dispenser. Vacuumatic ashtray. Non-glare rearview mirror. No-Mar fuel door trim. Underhood light. San-Toy seat covers. Powerglide ($178). Power brakes ($38). Power operated front window lifts ($86). Power operated seat ($86). Power steering ($135). White sidewall tires ($27 exchange).

1954 Chevrolet, Bel Air Townsman station wagon, 6-cyl

HISTORICAL FOOTNOTES: New models were introduced in December 1953. Model year sales totaled 1,151,486. Calendar year sales reached 1,414,352. Ford actually out-produced Chevrolet on a model year basis this season, but Chevrolet 'dumped' cars on dealers to increase factory shipments and capture first place on a calendar year basis. Thus, Ford was America's largest automaker, but Chevrolet was the number one selling American car again. Last season for woodgrained station wagon trim through 1966 model year, when Caprice station wagon reintroduced this feature. First year automatic transmission was available in all Chevrolets. Last year for exclusive use of six-cylinder powerplants in Chevrolet.

1955

ONE-FIFTY — SERIES 1500 A — The One-Fifty series was Chevrolet's lowest-priced line. Standard equipment included rubber floor mats front and rear; full-width, all-steel seat frames with 'S' springs; all-vinyl upholstery for station wagon and one-piece wraparound windshield. Exterior bright metal decoration was limited to a Chevrolet script on front fender and standard chrome-plated bumpers; grille; door handles; hood ornament; lamp rims; and wheel hub center caps.

ONE-FIFTY I.D. NUMBERS: Serial number stamped on plate on right (front) door hinge pillar. Engine numbers stamped on crankcase to rear of distributor on right side of engine. The beginning serial numbers for the 1955 One-Fifty series were A55-001001 (six-cylinder) and VA55-001001 (V-8). Six-cylinder engine numbers began 01001-55Z and up. V-8 engine numbers began 01001-55G and up.

1955 Chevrolet, Two-Ten four-door sedan, V-8 (AA)

ONE-FIFTY SERIES

Model No.	Body/Style No.	Body Type & Seating	Factory Price	Shipping Weight	Prod. Total
1503	55-1219	4-dr Sed-6P	1726/1827	3165/3135	29,898
1502	55-1211	2-dr Sed-6P	1685/1784	3110/3080	66,416
1512	55-1211B	2-dr Sed-3P	1593/1692	3065/3055	11,196
1529	55-1263F	2-dr Sta Wag-6P	2030/2129	3290/3260	17,936

NOTE 1: The V-8 was considered a separate series, not an option.

NOTE 2: Data for six above slash/V-8 below slash.

1955 Chevrolet, Bel Air two-door hardtop, V-8

TWO-TEN — SERIES 2100 B — The Two-Ten series was Chevrolet's middle-priced line. Standard equipment included all One-Fifty equipment listed above, plus stainless steel windshield and backlight reveals; chrome front seat and sidewall moldings; glove compartment light; ash receptacles; cigarette lighter; armrests; and assist straps. Additional exterior bright metal decoration included upper beltline and rear fender side and sash moldings.

TWO-TEN I.D. NUMBERS: The beginning serial numbers for the 1955 Two-Ten series were B55-001001 (six-cylinder) and VB55-001001 (V-8). The engine number sequence was the same for all series.

TWO-TEN SERIES

Model No.	Body/Style No.	Body Type & Seating	Factory Price	Shipping Weight	Prod. Total
2103	55-1019	4-dr Sed-6P	1819/1918	3180/3150	317,724
2102	55-1011	2-dr Sed-6P	1775/1674	3145/3125	249,105
2124	55-1011A	2-dr Clb Cpe-6P	1635/1934	3145/3115	115,584
2154	55-1037F	2-dr Spt Cpe-6P	1959/2058	3172/3144	11,675
2129	55-1063F	2-dr Sta Wag-6P	2079/2176	3330/3300	29,916
2109	55-1062F	4-dr Sta Wag-6P	2127/2226	3370/3340	62,303

NOTE 1: The V-8 was considered a separate series, not an option.

NOTE 2: Data for six above slash/V-8 below slash.

1955 Chevrolet, Bel Air two-door convertible, V-8

BEL AIR — SERIES 2400 C — The Bel Air was Chevrolet's top series. Standard equipment included most features found on the lower priced lines, plus carpets on closed body styles; chrome ribbed headliner on the Sport Coupe; richer upholstery fabrics; horizontal chrome strip on sides of front fender and doors; narrow white painted insert on rear fender horizontal side molding; gold Bel Air script and Chevrolet crest behind slanting vertical sash molding; ribbed vertical trim plate on sides above rear bumper ends; wide chrome window and door post reveals; and full wheel discs. A midyear introduction was the Nomad, a two-door station wagon featuring hardtop-style doors, slanted B-pillars, wraparound rear quarter windows, open rear wheel wells and Bel Air-level interior trim.

1955 Chevrolet, Bel Air Nomad two-door station wagon, V-8 (M)

BEL AIR I.D. NUMBERS: The beginning serial numbers for the 1955 Bel Air series were C55-001001 (six-cylinder) and VC55-001001 (V-8). The engine number sequence was the same for all series.

BEL AIR SERIES

Model No.	Body/Style No.	Body Type & Seating	Factory Price	Shipping Weight	Prod. Total
2403	55-1019D	4-dr Sed-6P	1932/2031	3200/3170	345,372
2402	55-1011D	2-dr Sed-6P	1668/1987	3155/3125	168,313
2454	55-1037D	2-dr HT-6P	2067/2166	3195/3165	185,562
2434	55-1067D	2-dr Conv-5P	2206/2305	3315/3285	41,292
2429	55-1064DF	2-dr Nomad Wag-6P	2472/2571	3300/3270	6,103
2409	55-1062DF	4-dr Sta Wag-6P	2262/2361	3385/3355	24,313

NOTE 1: The V-8 was considered a separate series, not an option.

NOTE 2: Data for six above slash/V-8 below slash.

ENGINES

SIX-CYLINDER: Overhead valve. Cast iron block. Displacement: 235.5 cid. Bore and stroke: 3-9/16 x 3-15/16 inches. Compression ratio: 7.5:1. Brake horsepower: 123 at 3800 rpm (standard shift); 136 at 4200 rpm (Powerglide). Four main bearings. Solid valve lifters (standard shift); Hydraulic valve lifters (Powerglide). Carburetor: Rochester one-barrel Model 7007181.

1955 Chevrolet, Bel Air Beauville station wagon, 6-cyl

V-8: Overhead valve. Cast iron block. Displacement: 265 cid. Bore and stroke: 3-3/4 x 3 inches. Compression ratio: 8.0:1. Brake horsepower: 162 at 4400 rpm (all V-8s). Five main bearings. Powerglide engine has hydraulic valve lifters. Carburetor: Rochester two-barrel Model 7008006.

1955 Chevrolet, Bel Air four-door sedan, 6-cyl

POWERTRAIN OPTIONS: A three-speed manual gearbox with column-mounted gearshift was standard on all models. Overdrive was available on the manual transmission at $108 extra. Powerglide two-speed automatic transmission was available at $178 extra. The V-8 engine was available with an optional 'power-pack' that included single four-barrel carburetor and dual exhaust. Optional horsepower rating with 'power-pack' was 180 at 4600 rpm.

CHASSIS FEATURES: Wheelbase: 115 inches. Overall length: (passenger cars) 195.6 inches; (station wagons) 197.1 inches. Front tread: 58 inches. Rear tread: 58.8 inches. Tires: 6.70 x 15 tubeless.

CONVENIENCE OPTIONS: Power steering ($92). Power brakes ($38). Directional signals. Electric windshield wipers. Power windows. Power seat. Heater and defroster. Air conditioning. White sidewall tires. Fender antenna. Locking gas cap. Continental tire kit. Outside sun visor. Self de-icing wiper blades. Wiring junction block. Electric clock. Compass. Seat covers. Accelerator pedal cover. Wire wheel covers. Tissue dispenser. Exhaust extension. Filter and element. License plate frame. Glare-shields. Grille guard. Fender guard. Door edge guard. Gasoline filler guard. Tool kit. Back-up lamps. Courtesy lamps. Cigarette lighter. Floor mats. Outside rearview mirrors. Inside non-glare rearview mirrors. Vanity visor. Manual radio. Push-button radio. Signal-seeking radio. Automatic top riser armrests. Wheel trim rings. Safety light with mirror. Sport lamp. Electric shaver. Parking brake signal. Door handle shields. Front fender shields. Rear speaker. Vent shades. Inside sun visor. Traffic light viewer. Foot-operated windshield washer. Vacuum operated windshield washer.

HISTORICAL FOOTNOTES: Body style 55-1211B was a utility sedan. Body style 55-1263F was a Handyman station wagon. Body style 55-1062F was a Handyman station wagon. Body style 55-1063F was a Townsman station wagon. Body style 55-1011A was the Del Ray. Body style 55-1037F was a midyear model. Body style 55-1062DF was the Beauville station wagon. Body Style 55-1064DF was the Nomad, a two-door station wagon with special hardtop styling, introduced as a midyear model.

1956

ONE-FIFTY — SERIES 1500 A — A minor restyling for 1956 Chevrolets included a full-width grille; large, rectangular front parking lamps; new front and rear bumpers and guards (except station wagons); inward angled dome-shaped taillamp lenses set into chrome ribbed decorative housings (with back-up lamp lens provided); new side trims that varied per series; and squarer headlamp hoods. One-Fifty models had Chevrolet rear fender nameplates; chrome moldings around the windshield and rear window; and a horizontal bodyside molding. This chrome strip ran from just behind the headlamp hood crease line to a point below the rear side window, where it was intersected by a slanting sash molding embossed in windsplit style. Standard equipment included a two-spoke steering wheel with horn ring; lockable glovebox; dome light and cloth and vinyl upholstery (all-vinyl on station wagons). Features such as the upholstery fabrics or provision of a dashboard ashtray varied per body style, but all had black rubber floor mats and small hubcaps as standard features. Just one interior sun visor, on the driver's side, was provided as base One-Fifty equipment.

CHEVROLET I.D. NUMBERS: Serial number stamped on plate on right (front) door hinge pillar. Engine numbers stamped on crankcase to rear of distributor on right side of engine. Serial numbers were A56-001001 to 220555 (six-cylinder) and VA56-001001 to 220555 (V-8). Six-cyl-

inder engine numbers 01001-56Z to 525227 were used. V-8 engine numbers 01001-56G to 676997 were used.

ONE-FIFTY SERIES

Model No.	Body/Style No.	Body Type & Seating	Factory Price	Shipping Weight	Prod. Total
1503	1219	4-dr Sed-6P	1869/1968	3206/3186	29,898
1502	1211	2-dr Sed-6P	1826/3164	3164/3144	66,416
1512	1211B	2-dr Utl Sed-3P	1734/1833	3127/3107	11,196
1529	1263F	2-dr Sta Wag-6P	2171/2270	3309/3289	17,936

NOTE 1: The V-8 was considered a separate series, not an option.

NOTE 2: Data for six above slash/V-8 below slash.

1956 Chevrolet, One-Fifty four-door sedan, V-8 (AA)

TWO-TEN — SERIES 2100 B — The Two-Ten series was Chevrolet's middle-priced line. These cars also carried Chevrolet rear fender nameplates and had chrome moldings around the windshield and backlight, plus on the side window sills. The side trim was distinctive in that the single horizontal molding swept downward, towards the rear bumper end, from the point where the sash molding intersected it below the rear side window. Exterior and interior details varied per body style, but all models had two sunshades (visors), ashtrays and cigarette lighters and richer interior trims. The Del Ray coupe featured deep-pile carpets and all-vinyl upholstery, while others had vinyl coated rubber floor mats and vinyl and cloth trims. A two-spoke steering wheel with horn ring was used. Small hubcaps were standard equipment. Specific interior colors were standard, but custom colored upholstery was optional. A brand new style was a pillarless four-door hardtop, which was called a Sport Sedan.

1956 Chevrolet, Two-Ten two-door hardtop (Sport Coupe), V-8 (AA)

TWO-TEN I.D. NUMBERS: The Chevrolet numbering system and number locations were used and numbers assigned were the same as on One-Fifty models, except the serial number prefix was a 'B'.

TWO-TEN SERIES

Model No.	Body/Style No.	Body Type & Seating	Factory Price	Shipping Weight	Prod. Total
2103	1019	4-dr Sed-6P	1955/2054	3212/3192	283,125
2113	1039	4-dr HT-6P	2117/2216	3262/3242	20,021
2102	1011	2-dr Sed-6P	1912/2011	3177/3157	205,545
2124	1011A	2-dr Cpe-6P	1971/2070	3182/3162	56,382
2154	1037	2-dr HT-6P	2063/2162	3204/3184	18,616
2129	1063F	2-dr Sta Wag-6P	2215/2314	3344/3324	22,038
2109	1062F	4-dr Sta Wag-6P	2263/2362	3381/3361	113,656
2119	1062FC	4-dr Sta Wag-9P	2348/2447	3500/3480	17,988

NOTE 1: The V-8 was considered a separate series, not an option.

NOTE 2: Data for six above slash/V-8 below slash.

BEL AIR — SERIES 2400 C — The luxurious Bel Air was richly appointed inside and out. Bel Air nameplates and emblems appeared on rear fenders. The slanting sash molding blended into a horizontal chrome belt that ran forward to the headlamp crease and doubled back, running horizontally to below rear side windows and then, sweeping down towards the rear bumper ends. Chrome wheel covers were standard equipment. There was an extra chrome treatment around and between all window groups. Three-spoke steering wheels and deep-pile carpets graced all models except the Beauville nine-passenger station wagon, which had vinyl coated rubber floor mats as standard equipment. Exclusive Bel Air models included a convertible and the Milestone two-door Nomad station wagon, the latter having a unique two-door hardtop roof treatment. All Bel Airs had electric clocks and lighted, lockable glove compartments. All 1956 Chevrolets with V-8 power had large V-shaped emblems below the crest ornaments on the hood and deck.

CHEVROLET I.D. NUMBERS: Serial number stamped on plate on right (front) door hinge pillar. Engine numbers stamped on crankcase to rear of distributor on right side of engine. The Chevrolet system was also used on Bel Air with the same range of numbers seen for other lines, but with a 'C' prefix for serial numbers.

1956 Chevrolet, Bel Air Nomad two-door station wagon, V-8

BEL AIR SERIES

Model No.	Body/Style No.	Body Type & Seating	Factory Price	Shipping Weight	Prod. Total
2403	1019D	4-dr Sed-6P	2068/2167	3231/3211	269,798
2413	1039D	4-dr HT-6P	2230/2329	3280/3260	103,602
2402	1011D	2-dr Sed-6P	2025/2124	3197/3177	104,849
2454	1037D	2-dr HT-6P	2176/2275	3232/3212	128,382
2434	1067D	2-dr Conv-5P	2344/2443	3340/3320	41,268
2429	1064DF	2-dr Nomad-6P	2608/2707	3362/3342	7,886
2419	1062DF	4-dr Sta Wag-9P	2482/2581	3516/3496	13,268

NOTE 1: The V-8 was considered a separate series, not an option.

NOTE 2: Data for six above slash/V-8 below slash.

ENGINES

SIX-CYLINDER: Overhead valve. Cast iron block. Displacement: 235.5 cid. Bore and stroke: 3-9/16 x 3-15/16 inches. Compression ratio: 8.0:1. Brake horsepower: 140 at 4200 rpm. Four main bearings. Hydraulic valve lifters. Carburetor: (Powerglide) Rochester one-barrel Model 7007200 or Carter one-barrel Model 2101S; (standard shift) Rochester one-barrel Model 7007181.

1956 Chevrolet, Bel Air four-door sedan, V-8

V-8: Overhead valve. Cast iron block. Displacement: 265 cid. Bore and stroke: 3-3/4 x 3 inches. Compression ratio: 8.0:1. Brake horsepower: (standard transmission or 'Touch-down' overdrive) 162 at 4400 rpm; (Powerglide) 170 at 4400 rpm. Five main bearings. Hydraulic valve lifters. Carburetor: (Powerglide) Carter two-barrel Model 2286S; Rochester two-barrel Model 7009910; (standard shift) Rochester two-barrel Model 7009909.

1956 Chevrolet, Bel Air two-door convertible, V-8

POWERTRAIN OPTIONS: Three-speed manual transmission with column-mounted control was standard. Overdrive was available on the manual transmission at $108 extra. Powerglide two-speed automatic transmission was available at $189 extra. A four-barrel Super Turbo-Fire V-8 with 205 horsepower and 9.25:1 compression ratio was optional with all transmissions. Also a 225 horsepower dual four-barrel carburetor. Study of the specifications charts will reveal that Chevrolet V-8s were lighter than sixes. The resulting power-to-weight ratio is one reason 1956 Chevrolet V-8s became known as the 'Hot Ones'.

CHASSIS FEATURES: Wheelbase: 115 inches. Overall length: (station wagons) 200.8 inches; (all other models) 197.5 inches. Front tread: 58 inches. Rear tread: 58.9 inches. Tires: (station wagons) 6.70 x 15 six-ply on nine-passenger models; (all other models) 6.70 x 15 four-ply; (optional) 7.10 x 15 four-ply.

1956 Chevrolet, Bel Air four-door hardtop (Sport Sedan), V-8

CONVENIENCE OPTIONS: Power steering ($92). Power brakes ($38). Accelerator cover. Oil bath air cleaner. Air conditioner (V-8 only). Armrests for One-Fifty. Autronic Eye. Back-up lights. Chrome sill moldings. Park brake signal lamp. Power seat (except One-Fifty). Lighted cigarette lighter. Electric clock (except Bel Air). Eleven inch diameter heavy-duty clutch. Optional colors (paint or convertible top). Compass. Courtesy lights. Custom Color interior. Door edge guards. Door handle shields. Exhaust extension. Fender guards. Fender top moldings. Floor mats. Locking gas cap. Heavy-duty generators. Deluxe heater and defroster. Recirculating heater and defroster. Tinted glass. Glovebox lamp as option. Six-cylinder governor. Vibrator horn. License frames. Power convertible top. Vanity mirror. Oil filter. Chrome grille guard. Insect screen. Radio antennas. Radios (manual, push-button or signal-seeking). Rear speaker. Rain deflectors. Rearview mirrors (three-types). Seat covers. Ventilated seat pad. Electric shaver. Spotlights. Heavy-duty springs. Right-hand sun visor for One-Fifty. Whitewall and oversize tires. Tissue dispenser. Tool kit. Traffic light viewer. Trunk light. Underhood light. Continental wheel carrier. Wheel covers. Wire wheel covers. Power windows (except One-Fifty). Plastic windshield glare shield. Outside sun visor. Windshield washers (automatic or foot operated). De-icing wiper blades. Dual electric wipers. Wiring junction block.

1956 Chevrolet, Bel Air Beauville station wagon, V-8

HISTORICAL FOOTNOTES: Dealer introductions were held in November 1955. Model year production equalled 1,574,740 units. Calendar year sales hit 1,621,004. Chevrolet was America's number one automaker. The Two-Ten Club Coupe was called the Del Ray coupe. The One-Fifty utility coupe was the equivalent of the traditional business coupe and had a single front bench seat with raised storage compartment platform behind. All four-door hardtops were called Sport Sedan; two-door hardtops were called Sport Coupe. Nine-passenger station wagons were called Beauville. Four-door conventional station wagons were called Townsman. Two-door conventional station wagons were called Handyman. The two-door Nomad station wagon had a slanting pillar roofline, cross ribbed roof and slanting tailgate with seven chrome 'slat' moldings. An innovation on all 1956 Chevrolets was that the left-hand taillamp functioned as the fuel filler door. The Nomad station wagon is recognized as a Milestone Car.

1957

1957 Chevrolet, One-Fifty two-door sedan, V-8 (AA)

ONE-FIFTY — SERIES 1500 — One of the most popular models in the modern collector car hobby, the 1957 Chevrolet was highlighted by a new oval shaped front bumper grille complete with bomb-type bumper guards. Round front parking lamps were seen at each end of a horizontal center bar that seemed to float against the delicately cross-hatched grille insert. A Chevrolet medallion was set into a center cavity within this horizontal bar. Windsplit bulges ran along both sides of the flat hood panel, decorated in front by bombsight ornaments. The headlamps were set into small grilles housed in square-looking fender openings. New side moldings appeared, but varied for each series, looking a little richer as they moved up the scale. The rear fenders were shaped into broad, flat tailfins. Although based on the previous body structure, the new Chevrolet image seemed more modern and sportier. The One-Fifty models were the plainest. They had exclusive use of the 1955-'56 style sash molding (below rear side windows), which intersected an approximately half-length, single horizontal molding. This strip of chrome ran from the front door region to the trailing edge of the tailfins. Chevrolet script was affixed to the upper side of the front fenders. The fins had only partial outline moldings near their rear tips, which dropped to the taillight housing. The grille insert was done in anodized aluminum finish. Interior trims were the most basic, although the Handyman station wagon had a two-tone look inside. Round horn buttons were used with standard steering wheels.

1957 Chevrolet, One-Fifty four-door sedan, V-8 (AA)

CHEVROLET I.D. NUMBERS: Serial number stamped on plate on right (front) door hinge pillar. Engine numbers stamped on crankcase to rear of distributor on right side of engine. Serial numbers used on One-Fifty models were A57-100001 to 314393 for sixes; VA57-100001 to 314393 for V-8s. Engine numbers are difficult to catalog and factory shop manuals or master parts catalogs should be consulted.

1957 Chevrolet, One-Fifty Handyman two-door station wagon, 6-cyl

ONE-FIFTY SERIES

Model No.	Body/Style No.	Body Type & Seating	Factory Price	Shipping Weight	Prod. Total
1503	1219	4-dr Sed-6P	2048/2148	3241/3232	52,266
1502	1211	2-dr Sed-6P	1996/2096	3216/3207	70,774
1512	1211B	2-dr Utl Sed-3P	1885/1985	3168/3159	8,300
1529	1263F	2-dr Sta Wag-6P	2307/2407	3411/3402	14,740

NOTE 1 : The V-8 was considered a separate series, not an option.

NOTE 2: V-8s are priced uniformly $100 above six-cylinder models.

NOTE 3: Data for six above slash/V-8 below slash.

TWO-TEN — SERIES 2100 — Distinguishing this line from the lowest series was the distinct side trim treatment; richer interiors; and not really much else. The body rub moldings began just behind the headlight area and gently sloped to the rear bumper ends, although the sweep was most pronounced towards the rear half of the body. However, there was a second, upper molding, that branched off just below (and behind) the body belt dip. This top molding just about paralleled the general contour of the fins and ran rearward, to hit the back edge of the fender. Inside the two moldings, near the taillamp, a Chevrolet script was placed. In many cases, this 'inside' area was painted a contrasting color, as part of many optional two-tone finish schemes. Other trim features were the same as used on One-Fifty models. For instance, rear fendertop moldings on the rear third of the fins only and silver aluminized grilles. Three

two-tone interior schemes, with cloth and vinyl combinations, were available at standard prices. Despite its kinship to the lowest priced line, this year's Two-Ten looked more Bel Air-like, especially when done up in optional two-tone exterior finish. As in 1956, all Chevrolets with V-8 power had large, V-shaped hood and deck lid ornaments, which were bright metal finished on the lower series.

1957 Chevrolet, Bel Air two-door sedan, V-8

TWO-TEN I.D. NUMBERS: The only VIN numbering variation for the mid-range models was a 'B' prefix (instead of 'A') for the serial numbers with VB indicating V-8 attachment. The range of numbers was the same as used on One-Fifty models, which indicates mixed production runs.

TWO-TEN SERIES

Model No.	Body/Style No.	Body Type & Seating	Factory Price	Shipping Weight	Prod. Total
2103	1019	4-dr Sed-6P	2174/2274	3275/3266	260,401
2113	1039	4-dr HT Spt Sed-6P	2270/2370	3325/3316	16,178
2102	1011	2-dr Sed-6P	2122/2222	3230/3221	162,090
2124	1011A	2-dr Del Ray Cpe-6P	2162/2262	3225/3216	25,664
2154	1037	2-dr HT Spt Cpe-6P	2204/2304	3265/3256	22,631
2109	1062F	4-dr Sta Wag-6P	2456/2556	3466/3457	27,803
2119	1062FC	4-dr Sta Wag-9P	2563/2663	3566/3557	21,083
2129	1063F	2-dr Sta Wag-6P	2402/2502	3411/3402	17,528

NOTE 1: The V-8 was considered a separate series, not an option.

NOTE 2: V-8s are priced uniformly $100 above six-cylinder models.

NOTE 3: Data for six above slash/V-8 below slash.

BEL AIR — SERIES 2400 C — Extra richness characterized the Bel Air line in all regards. Side trim was arranged as on Two-Tens, except the area between the molding 'branches' was filled with a silver anodized aluminum beauty panel. Three gold chevrons marked the forward side of each front fender. Also done in gold were such things as the grille insert, V-8 ornaments (when used) and Bel Air beauty panel script. Rocker sills, roof and window outlines and the entire edge of the fins were all trimmed with bright metal moldings. There were also traditional Chevrolet/Bel Air crests on the rear fenders, near the golden script. Distinctive two-tone interiors were another highlight. The Nomad station wagon had carryover features with new 1957 styling.

BEL AIR I.D. NUMBERS: The Chevrolet numbering system was also used on Bel Air with the same range of numbers seen for other lines, but with 'C' or 'VC' serial number prefixes.

1957 Chevrolet, Two-Ten four-door sedan, V-8

BEL AIR SERIES

Model No.	Body/Style No.	Body Type & Seating	Factory Price	Shipping Weight	Prod. Total
2403	1019D	4-dr Sed-6P	2290/2390	3281/3272	254,331
2413	1039D	4-dr HT Spt Sed-6P	2364/2464	3336/3304	137,672
2402	1011D	2-dr Sed-6P	2238/2338	3237/3228	62,751
2454	1037D	2-dr HT Spt Cpe-6P	2299/2399	3283/3274	166,426
2434	1067D	2-dr Conv-5P	2511/2611	3414/3405	47,562
2409	1062DFC	4-dr Sta Wag-6P	2580/2680	3465/3456	27,375
2429	1064DF	2-dr Nomad-6P	2757/2857	3470/3461	6,103

NOTE 1: The V-8 was considered a separate series, not an option.

NOTE 2: V-8s are priced uniformly $100 above six-cylinder models.

NOTE 3: Data for six above slash/V-8 below slash.

1957 Chevrolet, Two-Ten nine-passenger station wagon, V-8

ENGINES

SIX-CYLINDER: Overhead valve. Cast iron block. Displacement: 235.5 cid. Bore and stroke: 3-9/16 x 3-15/16 inches. Compression ratio: 8.0:1. Brake horsepower: 140 at 4200 rpm. Four main bearings. Hydraulic valve lifters. Carburetor: (Powerglide) Rochester one-barrel Model 7007200 or Carter one-barrel Model 2101S; (standard shift) Rochester one-barrel Model 7007181. (The 'Blue Flame' six came with synchromesh, overdrive or Powerglide attachment.)

V-8: Overhead valve. Cast iron block. Displacement: 265 cid. Bore and stroke: 3-3/4 x 3 inches. Compression ratio: 8.0:1. Brake horsepower: (standard transmission or 'Touch-down' overdrive) 162 at 4400 rpm; (Powerglide) 170 at 4400 rpm. Five main bearings. Hydraulic valve lifters. Carburetor: (Powerglide) Carter two-barrel Model 2286S; Rochester two-barrel Model 7009910; (standard shift) Rochester two-barrel Model

7009909. (Note: This 'Turbo-Fire 265' was available as the base V-8 powerplant for 1957 Chevrolets with synchromesh or overdrive transmissions.) Other engines are listed under Powertrain Options below.

1957 Chevrolet, Bel Air two-door hardtop (Sport Coupe), V-8

POWERTRAIN OPTIONS: According to the 1957 Chevrolet Passenger Car Shop Manual, six extra-cost power options were available in conventional (non-Corvette) models along with six gearbox selections. This provided a total of 17 optional engine/transmission combinations as follows:

CID	Comp. Ratio	Carb Barrels	Exhaust	HP @ rpm	Trans Combo	Valve Lifters
283	8.5	2V	1	185 @ 4600	3-4	H
SUPER TURBO-FIRE V-8						
283	9.5	4V	2	220 @ 4800	1-2-3-4	H
CORVETTE V-8						
283	9.5	2 x 4V	2	245 @ 5000	1-2-4-5-6	H
283	9.5	F.I.	2	250 @ 5000	1-4-5-6	H
283	9.5	2 x 4V	2	270 @ 6000	5	S
283	10.5	F.I.	2	283 @ 6200	5	S

1957 Chevrolet, Bel Air Nomad two-door station wagon, V-8

1957 Chevrolet, Bel Air six-passenger station wagon, V-8

NOTES: F.I. — Fuel-injection. Transmission choices: (1) Three-speed manual; (2) Overdrive; (3) Regular Powerglide; (4) Turboglide; (5) Close-ratio three-speed and (6) Corvette-type Powerglide. H=hydraulic lifters.

S=solid (mechanical) lifters. Corvette V-8s were not available in sedan deliveries. Lightweight valves were used only with SR high-performance camshaft and solid lifters. Some collectors maintain that a limited number of 1957 Chevrolet passenger cars came with four-speed manual transmission attachments, perhaps dealer-installed. This cannot be verified with normal factory literature. Cars with fuel injection engines wore special badges denoting this fact.

1957 Chevrolet, Two-Ten Handyman two-door station wagon, V-8 (AA)

CHASSIS FEATURES: Wheelbase: 115 inches. Overall length: 200 inches. Front tread: 58 inches. Rear tread: 58.8 inches. Tires: 7.50 x 14 four-ply tubeless blackwall.

1957 Chevrolet, Bel Air four-door hardtop (Sport Sedan), V-8 (M)

CONVENIENCE OPTIONS: Power brakes ($38). Power steering ($70). Overdrive ($108). Powerglide ($188).Turboglide ($231). Accelerator cover. Oil bath air cleaner. Air conditioner (V-8 only). Armrests for One-Fifty. Autronic Eye. Back-up lights. Chrome sill moldings. Park brake signal lamp. Power seat (except One-Fifty). Lighted cigarette lighter. Electric clock (except Bel Air). Eleven inch diameter heavy-duty clutch. Optional colors (paint or convertible top). Compass. Courtesy lights. Custom Color interior. Door edge guards. Door handle shields. Exhaust extension. Fender guards. Fender top moldings. Floor mats. Locking gas cap. Heavy-duty generators. Deluxe heater and defroster. Recirculating heater and defroster. Tinted glass. Glovebox lamp as option. Six-cylinder governor. Vibrator horn. License frames. Power convertible top. Vanity mirror. Oil filter. Chrome grille guard. Insect screen. Radio antennas. Radios (manual, push-button or signal-seeking). Rear speaker. Rain deflectors. Rearview mirrors (three-types). Seat covers. Ventilated seat pad. Electric shaver. Spotlights. Heavy-duty springs. Right-hand sun visor for One-Fifty. Whitewall

and oversize tires. Tissue dispenser. Tool kit. Traffic light viewer. Trunk light. Underhood light. Continental wheel carrier. Wheel covers. Wire wheel covers. Power windows (except One-Fifty). Plastic windshield glare shield. Outside sun visor. Windshield washers (automatic or foot operated). De-icing wiper blades. Dual electric wipers. Wiring junction block. The fuel-injection V-8 was priced $484 over the base price of a six. Safety seat belts and shoulder harnesses were new options this season.

HISTORICAL FOOTNOTES: Dealer introductions for 1957 Chevrolets were held October 1956. Model year production peaked at 1,515,177 cars. Calendar year sales were counted at 1,522,536 units. Chevrolet outsold Ford by only 136 cars on a calendar year basis, but Ford actually built more 1957 specifications models than Chevrolet. It was a neck-and-neck battle between the two firms this season. Turboglide transmission was a running production change, so some early cars may have had 265-cid V-8s with Powerglide attachment. Chevrolet advertised that its solid lifter fuel-injection V-8 was the first American production car engine to provide one horsepower per cubic inch of displacement (283 cid/283 hp). This year the Chevrolet gas filler was incorporated into the chrome molding at the rear edge of the left-hand tailfin. Body style nomenclature (Sport Sedan; Sport Coupe; Del Ray; Beauville; Townsman; Handyman and Nomad) was similar, in application, to the previous year.

1958

DEL RAY — 1100 SERIES (6-CYL) — 1200 SERIES (V-8) — By adopting an all-new Safety Girder chassis for 1958, Chevrolet brought to market a completely re-engineered and restyled line. Body revisions included lower, wider, longer sheet metal; a new front end with dual headlamps and a dream car look; gull-wing rear fender and deck sculpturing and revamped side trim treatments. New names identified two series, while models available within each line were altered, too. The sedan delivery was cataloged as a conventional model but strangely not with the station wagons, which were now a series unto themselves. Del Ray nameplates marked the rear fender coves (indentations) of four styles in the low-priced line that had single belt moldings and lacked bright metal side window trim. Del Ray interior appointments were, needless to say, the most basic types with standard steering wheels, rubber floor mats and fewer bright highlights.

CHEVROLET I.D. NUMBERS: Serial numbers were stamped on a plate affixed to the left front door hinge pillar. The first symbol, a letter, identified series as follows: A - Del Ray six; B - Del Ray V-8; C - Biscayne six; D - Biscayne V-8; E - Bel Air six; F - Bel Air V-8. The second and third symbols were '58' for the 1958 model year. The fourth symbol indicated assembly plant, as follows: A - Baltimore; F - Flint; J - Janesville; K - Kansas City; L - Los Angeles; N - Norwood; O - Oakland: S - St Louis and T - Tarrytown. The last six symbols were numbers indicating production sequence. Numbers for each series at each factory began at 100001 and up. For example, Number A58(F)100101: 100th Del Ray six manufactured in Flint, Mich. Sedan deliveries used Body/Style Number and letter prefix (G - six; H - V-8). For example, 1171G48(F)-100001 for Del Ray six. Sedan delivery built at Flint. Engine numbers are not given in general reference sources.

DEL RAY SERIES

Model No.	Model No. (V-8)	Body Type & Seating	Factory Price	Shipping Weight	Prod. Total
(PASSENGER CARS)					
1149	1249	4-dr Sed-6P	2155/2262	3439/3442	Note 1
1141	1241	2-dr Sed-6P	2101/2208	3396/3399	Note 1
1121	1221 B	2-dr Utl Sed-3P	2013/2120	3351/3356	Note 1
1171	1271	2-dr Sed DeL-1P	2123/2230	3529/3531	Note 1
(STATION WAGONS)					
1193	1293	4-dr Sta Wag-6P	2467/2574	3740/3743	Note 1
1191	1291	2-dr Sta Wag-6P	2413/2520	3693/3696	Note 1

NOTE 1: Most Chevrolet production totals, after 1957, are available only in a form that indicates all series. There are no breakouts per series, model or engine type. For 1958, the totals were: four-door sedan - 491,441; two-door sedan - 256,182; four-door station wagon - 170,473; Sport Coupe - 142,592; Sport Sedan - 83,330; convertible - 55,989 and two-door station wagon - 16,590.

NOTE 2: Chevrolet station wagons were officially listed as a separate series, but will be grouped under passenger cars with the same level of trim in this catalog. Station wagons with Del Ray trim were called Yeoman models.

1958 Chevrolet, Del Ray two-door sedan, 6-cyl (AA)

NOTE 3: The model numbering system changed in 1958. Model numbers and Body/Style Numbers are now identical. The first column in chart above shows model/body numbers for sixes. The second column in chart shows model/body numbers for V-8s. This system will be applied for post 1958 models.

BISCAYNE — SERIES 1500 (6-CYL) — 1600 SERIES (V-8) — Only two body styles came under the Biscayne name, although two Brookwood station wagons wore the same level trim. Since sixes and V-8s were considered separate series, the result is eight Biscaynes to catalog. The passenger styles wore Biscayne nameplates at the leading edge of the rear fender cove, but station wagons had Brookwood script in the same location. All 1958 Chevrolets with V-8 power had additional, large, V-shaped ornaments on the hood and deck (or tailgate). Biscayne side trim moldings outlined the upper and lower edges of the cove but did not connect. Ahead of the cove, a bi-level belt molding, with slight forward taper, was seen. It was connected to the single, lower cove outline trim at the rear. Like the Del Ray models, Biscaynes came standard with small hubcaps, no sill moldings, no chevrons and no fender ornaments, but they did feature slightly up-market interior trims.

1958 Chevrolet, Biscayne two-door sedan, V-8

BISCAYNE SERIES

Model No.	Model No. (V-8)	Body Type & Seating	Factory Price	Shipping Weight	Prod. Total
(PASSENGER CARS)					
1549	1649	4-dr Sed-6P	2290/2397	3447/3450	Note 1
1541	1641	2-dr Sed-6P	2236/2343	3404/3407	Note 1
(STATION WAGONS)					
1593	1693	4-dr Sta Wag-6P	2571/2678	3748/3751	Note 1
1594	1694	4-dr Sta Wag-9P	2678/2785	3837/3839	Note 1

NOTE 1: Most Chevrolet production totals, after 1957, are available only in a form that indicates all series. There are no breakouts per series, model or engine type. For 1958, the totals were: four-door sedan - 491,441; two-door sedan - 256,182; four-door station wagon - 170,473; Sport Coupe - 142,592; Sport Sedan - 83,330; convertible - 55,989 and two-door station wagon - 16,590.

NOTE 2: Station wagons with Biscayne trim are Brookwoods and were actually part of the separate Chevrolet station wagon series.

NOTE 3: The V-8 was considered a separate series, not an option. Data for six above slash/V-8 below slash.

1958 Chevrolet, Bel Air four-door hardtop (Sport Sedan), V-8 (AA)

BEL AIR — 1700 SERIES (6-CYL) — 1800 SERIES (V-8) — This series was enriched over others and was also endowed with two even more luxurious Impala models. The base Bel Air had series name script and Chevrolet crests at the rear of the coves. The upper edge of the indentation was outlined with a single level molding that slashed down and back, below the body belt dip, to intersect an elaborated horizontal molding arrangement. This could best be described as spear-shaped moldings, with indented concave contrast band towards the rear and a horizontally grooved, missile-shaped 'spear tip' at the front. Also seen were four chevrons on the sides of the front fenders; four short vertical strips on the lower rear fender bulge; front fendertop ornaments; chrome outlined side windows; grooved rear roof pillar beauty plates; and full wheel discs. Interior appointments were rich and fancy. The Impala Sport Coupe and convertible were even more impressive. Trim features included Impala script; insignia and crossed-flag emblems at the front of the cove; broad, ribbed body sill panels; large dummy chrome plated chrome air scoops ahead of rear wheelwells; competition style two-spoke deep hub steering wheels (with Impala medallions); Impala dashboard script; standard rear radio speaker grille (with Impala script and medallion between rear seatback dip); and triple taillamp arrangements (replacing two taillights on other cars; one on all station wagons). The Impala Sport Coupe had a chrome-edged, rear-facing dummy air scoop and curved contour crease molded into the back of the roof.

1958 Chevrolet, Bel Air Impala two-door hardtop (Sport Coupe), V-8

BEL AIR SERIES

Model No.	Model No. (V-8)	Body Type & Seating	Factory Price	Shipping Weight	Prod. Total
(PASSENGER CARS)					
1749	1849	4-dr Sed-6P	2440/2547	3467/3470	Note 1
1739	1839	4-dr HT Spt Sed-6P	2511/2618	3511/3514	Note 1
1741	1841	2-dr Sed-6P	2386/2493	3424/3427	Note 1
1731	1831	2-dr HT Spt Cpe-6P	2447/2554	3455/3458	Note 1
(IMPALA)					
1747	1847	2-dr HT Spt Cpe-5P	2586/2693	3458/3459	Note 1
1767	1867	2-dr HT Spt Conv-5P	2724/2841	3522/3523	Note 1
(STATION WAGONS)					
1793	1893SD	4-dr Nomad-6P	2728/2835	3738/3771	Note 1

NOTE 1: Most Chevrolet production totals, after 1957, are available only in a form that indicates all series. There are no breakouts per series, model or engine type. For 1958, the totals were: four-door sedan - 491,441; two-door sedan - 256,182; four-door station wagon - 170,473; Sport Coupe - 142,592; Sport Sedan - 83,330; convertible - 55,989 and two-door station wagon - 16,590.

NOTE 2: Impalas were considered part of the Bel Air line and were not listed as a sub-series. The Nomad station wagon was now a four-door style with conventional styling, but high-level trim. The Nomad was actually a part of the separate station wagon series, but had Impala trim with Nomad rear fender nameplates.

NOTE 3: The V-8 was considered a separate series, not an option. Data for six above slash/V-8 below slash.

ENGINES

SIX-CYLINDER: Overhead valve. Cast iron block. Displacement: 235.5 cid. Bore and stroke: 3.56 x 3.94 inches. Compression ratio: 8.25:1. Brake horsepower: 145 at 4200 rpm. Four main bearings. Hydraulic valve lifters. Carburetor: Rochester two-barrel Model 7012127.

V-8: Overhead valve. Cast iron block. Displacement: 283 cid. Bore and stroke: 3.875 x 3 inches. Compression ratio: 8.5:1. Brake horsepower: 185 at 4600 rpm. Five main bearings. Hydraulic valve lifters. Carburetor: Rochester two-barrel Model 7012133.

POWERTRAIN OPTIONS: Optional engine and transmission combinations were as follows:

CID	Comp. Ratio	Carb Barrels	Exhaust	HP @ rpm	Trans Combo	Valve Lifter
SUPER TURBO-FIRE V-8						
283	9.5	4V	1	230 @ 4800	1-2-3-5	H
TURBO-THRUST V-8						
348	9.5	4V	2	250 @ 4400	1-4-5-6	H
SUPER TURBO-THRUST V-8						
348	9.5	3 x 2V	2	280 @ 4800	1-4-5	H
348 (M)	11.0	3 x 2V	2	315 @ 5600	1-5	S
RAM-JET FUEL INJECTION V-8						
283	9.5	F.I.	1	250 @ 5000	1-4-5-6	H

NOTES: (M) - Maximum performance V-8. F.I. - fuel injection. Transmission choices: (1) - Three-speed manual; (2) - Overdrive; (3) - Two-Speed Powerglide; (4) Turbo-glide; (5) - Close-ratio three-speed; (6) - Corvette-type Powerglide; H=Hydraulic lifters; S=Solid lifters. (M) includes special performance-type camshaft and high-speed valve trains. Some of the transmission attachment data that has been interpolated as nominal factory literature is not specific about types of three-speed manual or automatic transmissions used.

1958 Chevrolet, Bel Air Impala two-door convertible, V-8 (AA)

CHASSIS FEATURES: Wheelbase: 117.5 inches. Overall length: 209.1 inches. Overall width: 77.7 inches. Overall height: (Impala Convertible) 56.5 inches; (Impala Sport Coupe) 56.4 inches; (other models) 57.4 inches. Tires: (convertibles and station wagons) 8.00 x 14; (other models) 7.50 x 14. Full coil spring suspension; high-level ventilation; anti-dive braking and built-in leveling and foot-operated parking brakes were used this year.

CONVENIENCE OPTIONS: Four-barrel carburetor for 283 cid/230 hp V-8 ($27). Turbo-Thrust 250-hp V-8 ($59). Super Turbo-Thrust 280-hp V-8 ($70). Base fuel-injection 250-hp V-8 ($484). Powerglide transmission ($188). Turbo-glide transmission ($231). Overdrive ($108). Power steering ($70). Power brakes ($38). Power window control ($102). Front power seat ($43). Oil filter ($9). Oil bath air cleaner ($5). Dual exhaust as option ($16). Deluxe heater ($77). Recirculating heater ($49). Whitewall tires, size 7.50 x 14, four-ply ($32). E-Z-I tinted glass ($38). Electric wipers ($7). Safety panel padding ($16). Manual radio ($61); push-button radio ($84). Air conditioning ($468). Air suspension ($124). Two-tone paint ($32). Posi-traction rear axle with 3.36:1 or 3.55:1 ratio ($48). Other standard dealer installed accessories.

HISTORICAL FOOTNOTES: Dealer introductions of 1958 Chevrolets took place October 1957. Model year total was 1,217,047 cars. Calendar year total was 1,255,935 cars. Gas filler now under door in trunk latch lid panel. On Impalas the center taillamps housed a back-up lamp. A great deal of bright metal trim on 1958 Chevrolets was made of aluminum.

1959

BISCAYNE — SERIES 1100 (6-CYL) — 1200 SERIES (V-8) — Chevrolet for 1959 featured new "Slimline Design" styling with wider, roomier bodies; a new radiator grille;

"Spread Wing" rear treatment; cat's eye taillights; increased glass area and flat-top roof styling on Sport Sedans. Standard equipment on Biscaynes included rear foam cushions; electric wipers; and oil bath air cleaner for V-8s.

CHEVROLET I.D. NUMBERS: Serial numbers were stamped on a plate affixed to the left front door hinge pillar. The first symbol, a letter, identified series as follows: A - Del Ray six; B - Del Ray V-8; C - Biscayne six; D - Biscayne V-8; E - Bel Air six; F - Bel Air V-8. The second and third symbols were '59' for 1959 model year. The fourth symbol indicated assembly plant, as follows: A - Baltimore; F - Flint; J - Janesville; K - Kansas City; L - Los Angeles; N - Norwood; O - Oakland: S - St Louis; T - Tarrytown; and W - Willow Run, Mich. The last six symbols were numbers indicating production sequence. Numbers for each series at each factory began at 100001 and up. For example, Number A59(F)100101: 100th Biscayne six manufactured in Flint, Mich. Engine numbers are not given in general reference sources.

BISCAYNE SERIES

Model No.	Model No. (V-8)	Body Type & Seating	Factory Price	Shipping Weight	Prod. Total
(PASSENGER CARS)					
1119	1219	4-dr Sed-6P	2301/2419	3605/3600	Note 1
1111	1211	2-dr Sed-6P	2247/2365	3535/3530	Note 1
1121	1221	2-dr Utl Sed-3P	2160/2278	3480/3490	Note 1
(STATION WAGONS)					
1135	1235	4-dr Brkwd-6P	2638/2756	3965/3955	Note 1
1115	1215	2-dr Brkwd-6P	2571/2689	3870/3860	Note 1

NOTE 1: Chevrolet production totals are now available by body style only. For 1959, the totals were: four-door sedan - 525,461; two-door sedan - 281,924; four-door station wagon - 188,623; Sport Sedan - 182,520; Sport Coupe - 164,901; convertible - 72,765 and two-door station wagon - 20,760. No breakouts by series, model or body style are available.

NOTE 2: First column shows six-cylinder Model Number; second column shows V-8 Model Number.

NOTE 3: Data above slash for six/V-8 below slash.

BEL AIR — SERIES 1500 (6-CYL) — SERIES 1600 (V-8) — Bel Airs had model script nameplates and crests on front fenders. While Biscayne side moldings ran from the headlights to center front doors, Bel Air moldings ran full length and had painted inserts. Another enrichment was front fendertop ornaments. Kingswood and Parkwood station wagons had Bel Air trim, but their own model script on front fenders. Standard equipment was the same as Biscayne, plus Deluxe features, front foam seat cushions, Deluxe steering wheel and power tailgate on Kingswood.

BEL AIR SERIES

Model No.	Model No. (V-8)	Body Type & Seating	Factory Price	Shipping Weight	Prod. Total
(PASSENGER CARS)					
1519	1619	4-dr Sed-6P	2440/2558	3600/3615	Note 1
1539	1639	4-dr HT Spt Sed-6P	2556/2674	3660/3630	Note 1
1511	1611	2-dr Sed-6P	2386/2504	3515/3510	Note 1

(STATION WAGONS)

1535	1635	4-dr Pkwd-6P	2749/2867	3965/3970	Note 1
1545	1645	4-dr Kgwd-9P	2852/2970	4020/4015	Note 1

1959 Chevrolet, Bel Air four-door sedan, 6-cyl (AA)

NOTE 1: Chevrolet production totals are now available by body style only. For 1959, the totals were: four-door sedan - 525,461; two-door sedan - 281,924; four-door station wagon - 188,623; Sport Sedan - 182,520; Sport Coupe - 164,901; convertible - 72,765 and two-door station wagon - 20,760. No breakouts by series, model or body style are available.

NOTE 2: First column shows six-cylinder Model Number; second column shows V-8 Model Number.

NOTE 3: Data above slash for six/below slash for V-8.

IMPALA — SERIES 1700 (6-CYL) — SERIES 1700 (V-8) — For the "upper crust" Chevrolet, identification features included Impala nameplates and crossed racing flags emblems. Both identifiers were mounted inside the painted insert area of the full length side trim moldings, below the rear side windows. The front fendertop ornaments also had rear extension strips. Bright metal trim marked the deck lid center crease and taillamp lenses. Closed models had simulated Impala-style roof scoops. Nomads had Impala trim with different I.D. script. Standard equipment was the same as on Bel Airs, plus electric clock, dual sliding sun visors and aluminum trim.

IMPALA SERIES

Model No.	Model No. (V-8)	Body Type & Seating	Factory Price	Shipping Weight	Prod. Total
(PASSENGER CARS)					
1719	1819	4-dr Sed-6P	2592/2710	3625/3620	Note 1
1739	1839	4-dr HT Spt Sed-6P	2664/2782	3665/3670	Note 1
1737	1837	2-dr HT Spt Cpe-6P	2599/2717	3570/3580	Note 1
1767	1867	2-dr Conv-5P	2849/2967	3660/3650	Note 1
(STATION WAGONS)					
1735	1835	4-dr Nomad-6P	2891/3009	3980/3975	Note 1

NOTE 1: Chevrolet production totals are now available by body style only. For 1959, the totals were: four-door sedan - 525,461; two-door sedan - 281,924; four-door station wagon - 188,623; Sport Sedan - 182,520; Sport Coupe - 164,901; convertible - 72,765 and two-door station wagon - 20,760. No breakouts by series, model or body style are available.

NOTE 2: First column shows six-cylinder Model Number; second column shows V-8 Model Number.

NOTE 3: Data above slash for six/below slash for V-8.

1959 Chevrolet, Impala two-door convertible, V-8 (AA)

ENGINES

SIX-CYLINDER: Overhead valve. Cast iron block. Displacement: 235.5 cid. Bore and stroke: 3-9/16 x 3-15/16 inches. Compression ratio: 8.25:1. Brake horsepower: 135 at 4000 rpm. Four main bearings. Hydraulic valve lifters. Carburetor: Rochester two-barrel Model 7013003.

V-8: Overhead valve. Cast iron block. Displacement: 283 cid. Bore and stroke: 3.875 x 3 inches. Compression ratio: 8.5:1. Brake horsepower: 185 at 4600 rpm. Five main bearings. Hydraulic valve lifters. Carburetor: Rochester two-barrel Model 7013007.

1959 Chevrolet, Impala two-door hardtop (Sport Coupe), 6-cyl

POWERPLANT OPTIONS: Optional engine and transmission combinations were:

CID	Comp. Ratio	Carb Barrels	Exhaust	HP @ rpm	Trans Combo	Valve Lifters
SUPER TURBO-FIRE V-8						
283	9.5	4V	1	230 @ 4800	1-2-3-4-5-6	H
RAM-JET FUEL INJECTION V-8						
283	9.5	F.I.	1	250 @ 5000	1-3-4-5-6-7	H
283	10.5	F.I.	1	290 @ 6200	1-5-7	H
TURBO-THRUST V-8						
348	9.5	4V	2	250 @ 4400	1-3-4-5-6-7	H
SUPER TURBO-THRUST V-8						
348	9.5	3x2V	2	280 @ 4800	1-3-4-5-6-7	H

SPECIAL TURBO-THRUST V-8

348	11.0	4V	2	300 @ 5600	1-3-5-6-7	S

SPECIAL SUPER TURBO-THRUST V-8

348	11.0	3x2V	2	315 @ 5600	1-5-7	S

NOTES: F.I. - Fuel-injection. Transmission choices: (1) Three-speed manual; (2) Overdrive; (3) Two-Speed Powerglide; (4) Turboglide; (5) Close-ratio three-speed; (6) Corvette-type Powerglide; (7) Four-speed.

1959 Chevrolet, Impala four-door hardtop, (Sport Sedan), V-8

1959 Chevrolet, Bel Air four-door hardtop (Sport Sedan), V-8

CHASSIS FEATURES: Wheelbase: 119 inches. Overall length: 210.9 inches. Overall width: 79.9 inches. Overall height: (hardtops) 54 inches; (sedans) 56 inches; (station wagons) 56.3 inches. Tires: (convertible and station wagons) 8.00 x 14; (all other models) 7.50 x 14.

CONVENIENCE OPTIONS: Powerglide transmission ($199). Turboglide transmission ($242). Overdrive ($108). Super Turbo-fire V-8 ($147). Turbo-thrust V-8 ($199). Super Turbo-thrust V-8 ($269). Power steering ($75). Power brakes ($43). Power windows ($102). Power seat ($102). Oil filter ($9). Oil bath air cleaner ($5). Dual exhaust ($19). Deluxe heater ($80). Recirculating heater ($52). Whitewall 7.50 x 14 tires ($32). Whitewall 8.00 x 14 tires, for convertibles and station wagons ($35); other models ($51). E-Z-I tinted glass ($43). Windshield washer ($12). Padded dash ($18). Manual radio ($65). Push-button radio ($87). Air conditioner, including heater ($468). Air suspension ($135). Positraction with 3.36:1, 3.55:1 or 4.11:1 gears ($48). Two-tone paint, on Biscayne ($22); on Brookwood, Bel Air, Impala ($27); on Parkwood, Kingswood, Nomad ($32). Power tailgate window ($32). Deluxe steering wheel ($4). Close-ratio four-speed transmission ($188). Wheel discs ($16). Two-speed wipers and washers ($16). Shaded rear window ($22). Front air foam cushion ($8). Deluxe Group including sun visor; front arm-

rest; fender ornaments and cigarette lighter ($16). Heavy-duty 35-amp generator ($8).

HISTORICAL FOOTNOTES: Dealer introductions were held October 1958. The Del Ray name was dropped. Calendar year sales were 1,528,592 units. Model year production totaled 1,481,071 cars. Ford and Chevy ran neck-and-neck, but Chevrolet turned out more cars built to 1959 specifications. Magic-Mirror deep-luster acrylic lacquer was introduced, along with improved Safety-Master brakes.

1960

BISCAYNE — SERIES 1100/1300 (6-CYL) — SERIES 1200/1400 (V-8) — This year a new oval grille enclosed dual headlamps. Missile inspired side trim was seen. The seagull-like "Spread Wing" fins were more angular. Small circular taillamps were set into a beauty panel at the rear. Identification came from Biscayne front fender script; a painted rear beauty panel; and single molding quarter panel trim. Brookwoods, actually part of a separate station wagon series, were trimmed like Biscaynes, except for front fender script. Cataloged as standard equipment were dual sun visors, electric wipers, cigarette lighter and front armrests, all formerly considered Deluxe equipment. An economy sub-series for corporate fleet use was provided in two Fleetmasters, which were marketed without these Deluxe-type items.

1960 Chevrolet, Bel Air two-door hardtop (Sport Coupe), 6-cyl

CHEVROLET I.D. NUMBERS: Serial numbers were stamped on a plate affixed to the left front door hinge pillar. The first symbol identified the model year: 0=1960. The second and third symbols identified the series (see first two digits of Model Number columns in charts below). The fourth and fifth symbols identified body style (see last two digits of Model Number columns in charts below). The sixth symbol indicated assembly plant, as follows: A=Atlanta, Ga.; B=Baltimore, Md.; F=Flint, Mich.; J=Janesville, Wis.; K=Kansas City, Mo.; L=Los Angeles, Calif.; N=Norwood, Ohio; O=Oakland, Calif.; S=St. Louis, Mo.; T=Tarrytown, N.Y.; W=Willow Run, Mich.; G=Framingham, Mass. The last six symbols were the sequential production number, with numbers for each series at each factory starting at 100001 and up. Fisher Body plate attached to left-hand cowl starts with two-digit model year prefix (60-) and Fisher Body/Style Number (Model Number) and also shows factory code, production sequence, trim and body color data. Engine numbers: (six) right side of block behind distributor; (V-8) right front of engine block.

BISCAYNE SERIES

Model No.	Model No. (V-8)	Body Type & Seating	Factory Price	Shipping Weight	Prod. Total
(BASE PASSENGER CARS)					
1169	1269	4-dr Sed-6P	2316/2423	3500/3505	Note 1
1111	1211	2-dr Sed-6P	2262/2369	3415/3425	Note 1
1121	1221	2-dr Utl Sed-6P	2175/2282	3390/3395	Note 1
(FLEETMASTER 1300 SUB-SERIES)					
1369	1469	4-dr Sed-6P	2284/2391	3495/3500	Note 1
1311	1411	2-dr Sed-6P	2230/2337	3410/3415	Note 1
(STATION WAGON)					
1145	1245	4-dr Brkwd-9P	2756/2863	3900/3895	Note 1
1135	1235	4-dr Brkwd-6P	2653/2760	3850/3845	Note 1

NOTE 1: Chevrolet production totals are again available by body style only. For 1960, the totals were: four-door sedan - 497,048; two-door sedan - 228,322; Sport Coupe - 204,467; four-door station wagon - 198,066; Sport Sedan - 169,016; convertible - 79,903 and two-door station wagon - 14,663. No breakouts by series, model or engine are available.

NOTE 2: Data for six above slash/for V-8 below slash.

BEL AIR — SERIES 1500 (6-CYL) — SERIES 1600 (V-8) — A shield medallion split the words Bel Air on front fenders. A single rear quarter extension molding flew rearward from the missile ornament. The rear beauty panel was horizontally grooved and outlined with bright metal trim. All Biscayne features were standard, plus front foam cushions; Deluxe steering wheel and power tailgate on Kingswood station wagon.

BEL AIR SERIES

Model No.	Model No. (V-8)	Body Type & Seating	Factory Price	Shipping Weight	Prod. Total
(PASSENGER CARS)					
1519	1619	4-dr Sed-6P	2438/2545	3565/3580	Note 1
1539	1639	4-dr HT Spt Sed-6P	2554/2661	3605/3620	Note 1
1511	1611	2-dr Sed-6P	2384/2491	3490/3505	Note 1
1537	1637	2-dr HT Spt Cpe-5P	2489/2596	3515/3530	Note 1
(STATION WAGON)					
1545	1645	4-dr Kgswd-9P	2850/2957	3990/4000	Note 1
1535	1635	4-dr Pkwd-6P	2747/2854	3945/3950	Note 1

1960 Chevrolet, Bel Air Kingswood station wagon, 6-cyl

NOTE 1: Chevrolet production totals are again available by body style only. For 1960, the totals were: four-door sedan - 497,048; two-door sedan - 228,322; Sport Coupe - 204,467; four-door station wagon - 198,066;

Sport Sedan - 169,016; convertible - 79,903 and two-door station wagon - 14,663. No breakouts by series, model or engine are available.

NOTE 2: Data for six above slash/for V-8 below slash.

IMPALA — SERIES 1700 (6-CYL) — SERIES 1800 (V-8) — The Impala was dressy from stem to stern. A short molding strip extended back from the headlights. Twin pairs of bar moldings were above and below this strip on the fender tips. The quarter panel missile ornaments had two moldings streaking rearward, the area between them filled with a white insert and Impala script with crossed racing flags insignia. Triple taillights and a vertically ribbed aluminum rear beauty panel were seen. All, except convertibles, had simulated vents on the lower rear window molding. Standard equipment was as on Bel Airs, plus parking brake, glove compartment and back-up lights; anodized aluminum trim; electric clock; and, on V-8s, oil filters and oil bath air cleaners.

IMPALA SERIES

Model No.	Model No. (V-8)	Body Type & Seating	Factory Price	Shipping Weight	Prod. Total
(PASSENGER CARS)					
1719	1819	4-dr Sed-6P	2590/2697	3575/3580	Note 1
1739	1839	4-dr HT Spt Sed-6P	2662/2769	3635/3625	Note 1
1737	1837	2-dr HT Spt Cpe-5P	2597/2704	3540/3530	Note 1
1767	1867	2-dr Conv-5P	2847/2954	3635/3625	Note 1
(STATION WAGON)					
1735	1835	4-dr Nomad-6P	2889/2996	3960/3955	Note 1

NOTE 1: Chevrolet production totals are again available by body style only. For 1960, the totals were: four-door sedan - 497,048; two-door sedan - 228,322; Sport Coupe - 204,467; four-door station wagon - 198,066; Sport Sedan - 169,016; convertible - 79,903 and two-door station wagon - 14,663. No breakouts by series, model or engine are available.

NOTE 2: Data for six above slash/for V-8 below slash.

1960 Chevrolet, Impala two-door hardtop (Sport Coupe), V-8 (AA)

ENGINES: There were no changes in specifications from 1959, except in Biscayne V-8 attachments, where a detuned 170 horsepower rating was cataloged for the 283-cid V-8. In other Chevrolets, the base engines were:

SIX-CYLINDER: Overhead valve. Cast iron block. Displacement: 235.5 cid. Bore and stroke: 3-9/16 x 3-15/16 inches. Compression ratio: 8.25:1. Brake horsepower: 135 at 4000 rpm. Four main bearings. Hydraulic valve lifters. Carburetor: Rochester two-barrel Model 7013003.

V-8: Overhead valve. Cast iron block. Displacement: 283 cid. Bore and stroke: 3.875 x 3.00 inches. Compression ratio: 8.5:1. Brake horsepower: 185 at 4600 rpm. Five main bearings. Hydraulic valve lifters. Carburetor: Rochester two-barrel Model 7013007.

1960 Chevrolet, Impala two-door convertible, V-8

POWERPLANT OPTIONS: Optional engine and transmission combinations were:

CID	Comp. Ratio	Carb Barrels	Exhaust	HP @ rpm	Trans Combo	Valve Lifters
283	8.5	4V	1	230 @ 4800	1-3-4-5-6	H
348	9.5	4V	1	250 @ 4400	1-3-4-5-6-7	H
348	9.5	3x2V	2	280 @ 4800	1-3-4-5-6-7	H
348	11.25	4V	2	320 @ 5600	1-5-6-7	H
348	11.25	3x2V	2	335 @ 5800	1-5-6-7	H

NOTES: F.I. - Fuel injection. Transmission choices: (1) Three-speed manual; (2) Overdrive; (3) Two-Speed Powerglide; (4) Turboglide; (5) Close-ratio three-speed; (6) Corvette-type Powerglide; (7) Four-speed.

CHASSIS FEATURES: Wheelbase: 119 inches. Overall length: 210.8 inches. Overall width: 79.9 inches. Overall height: (hardtops) 54 inches; (sedans) 56 inches; (station wagons) 56.3 inches. Tires: (convertible and station wagons) 8.00 x 14; (all other models) 7.50 x 14.

CONVENIENCE OPTIONS: Oil bath air cleaner ($5). Air conditioner, including heater; requires automatic drive ($468). Positraction ($43). Heavy-duty battery ($8). Biscayne economy carburetor ($8). Heavy-duty clutch for six-cylinder ($5). Foam front cushion ($8). PCV valve ($12). Dual exhaust ($19). Temperature Control fan ($16). Generators, 35-amp ($8); 40-amp ($27). Tinted glass, windshield ($22); all windows ($38); shaded backlight for Sport Coupe ($14). Deluxe heater ($74). Recirculating heater ($46). Padded dash ($18). Nonglare inside mirror ($4). Six-cylinder oil filter ($9). Two-tone paint ($16). Power brakes ($43). Power seat, except 1100/1200/1300/1400, Six-Way ($97); Four-Way ($65). Power steering ($75). Power tailgate window ($32). Power windows, except 1100/1200/1300/1400 ($102). Manual radio ($56). Push-button radio ($72). Heavy-duty rear coil springs ($3). Deluxe steering wheel ($4). Whitewalls, priced by size and model ($16-$36). Overdrive ($188). Powerglide, on six ($188); on V-8 ($199). Turboglide V-8 only ($210). Four-speed close-ratio, V-8 only ($188). Wheel discs ($15). Windshield washer ($11). Electric wipers with washer ($16). Super Turbo-fire V-8 ($136). Turbo-thrust V-8 ($188). Special Turbo-thrust V-8 ($268). Special Turbo-glide thrust 320 horsepower V-8 ($311). Super Turbo-thrust V-8 ($258). Special Super Turbo-thrust V-8 ($333). Seatbelt ($16). Electric clock ($21). Wheel covers ($24). Edge guards, two-door ($4); four-door ($7). Lamps, ashtray ($3); back-up ($13); courtesy ($7); glovebox ($3); luggage ($4) and underhood ($4). Mats front ($7), rear ($7). Outside rearview mirror, body-mounted ($6). Vanity mirror ($2). Body sill molding ($15). Brake signal ($5). Rear speaker ($15).

HISTORICAL FOOTNOTES: Model introduction occurred in October 1959. Calendar year production reached 1,863,598. Model year production totaled 1,391,485. Corvair was introduced. Totals include Corvettes and Corvairs, which are listed separately in this catalog.

1961

BISCAYNE — SERIES 1100/1300 (6-CYL) — SERIES 1200/1400 (V-8) — The 1961 Chevrolets followed the General Motors' pattern in adopting a brand new, downsized body, but varied from the corporate trend in that strictly carryover engineering was used. Grille and front areas were rather flat and square, while the rearend sported a flat V-type fin. At the front, a full-width air slot stretched above the grille, below the beveled front lip of the hood. The bevel line swept around the front body corners and ran, in a straight line, down and back towards the rear quarter panel. There, it angled upwards again, to connect with the flat V-type fin. Biscaynes had twin circular taillamps, small hubcaps and model nameplates on upper rear fender tips, while lacking side body moldings along the bevel line. Rocker panel steps were used on 1100/1200 level cars, but not on the Series 1300/1400 Fleetmaster economy models. Standard equipment consisted of dual sun visors, electric windshield wipers, cigarette lighter, front armrests and five 7.50 x 14 black tubeless tires.

CHEVROLET I.D. NUMBERS: Serial numbers were stamped on a plate affixed to the left front door hinge pillar. The first symbol identified model year: 1=1961. The second and third symbols identified the series (see first two digits of Model Number columns in charts below). The fourth and fifth symbols identified body style (see last two digits of Model Number columns in charts below). The sixth symbol, a letter, indicated assembly plant, as follows: A=Atlanta, Ga.; B=Baltimore, Md.; F=Flint, Mich.; J=Janesville, Wis.; K=Kansas City, Mo.; L=Los Angeles, Calif.; N=Norwood, Ohio; O=Oakland, Calif.; S=St. Louis, Mo.; T=Tarrytown, N.Y.; W=Willow Run, Mich.; G=Framingham, Mass. The last six symbols are the sequential production number, with numbers for each series at each factory starting at 100001 and up. Fisher Body plate attached to left-hand cowl starts with two-digit model year prefix (61-) and Fisher Body/Style Number (Model Number) and also shows factory code, production sequence, trim and body color data. Engine numbers: (six) right side of block behind distributor; (V-8) right front of engine block.

BISCAYNE SERIES

Model No.	Model No. (V-8)	Body Type & Seating	Factory Price	Shipping Weight	Prod. Total
(FLEETMASTER LINE)					
1369	1469	4-dr Sed-6P	2284/2391	3495/3500	Note 1
1311	1411	2-dr Sed-6P	2230/2337	3410/3415	Note 1
(DELUXE LINE)					
1169	1269	4-dr Sed-6P	2316/2423	3500/3505	Note 1
1111	1211	2-dr Sed-6P	2262/2369	3415/3425	Note 1
1121	1221	2-dr Utl Sed-3P	2175/2282	3390/3395	Note 1
(STATION WAGONS)					
1145	1245	4-dr Brkwd-9P	2756/2863	3900/3895	Note 1
1135	1235	4-dr Brkwd-6P	2643/2760	3850/3845	Note 1

NOTE 1: Chevrolet production was recorded, by body style only, as follows: four-door sedan - 452,251; Sport Coupe - 177,969; Sport Sedan - 174,141; four-door station wagon - 168,935; two-door sedan - 153,988 and convertible - 64,624. No further breakouts by model, series or engine were provided by Chevrolet except in the case of Super Sport models, of which 142 were reported as built.

NOTE 2: Industry statistics provide some additional information. First, on a model year basis, approximately 137,300 station wagons were two-seat types and approximately 31,649 others had three-seat configuration. Second, Chevrolet production by series, again on a model year basis, included the following: (Fleetmaster) 3,000 units; (Biscayne) 201,006 units; (Bel Air) 330,000 units; (Impala) 491,000 units and (station wagons) 169,000 units. These figures are slightly rounded-off, as is the figure of 513,000 six-cylinder Chevrolets built this season.

NOTE 3: Data above slash for six/below slash for V-8.

NOTE 4: Station wagons were grouped by the manufacturer as a separate series, but are being grouped under passenger cars with similar trim level in this catalog.

1961 Chevrolet, Bel Air four-door sedan, 6-cyl

BEL AIR — SERIES 1500 (6-CYL) — SERIES 1600 (V-8) —

A chrome trim bar, extending from the front parking lights rearward to the trunk, distinguished Bel Airs from Biscaynes. Bel Air nameplates appeared at the upper rear fender; twin taillamps were seen; small hubcaps were standard equipment; and no rocker sill strips were used. As in other lines, regular sedans, Sport Sedans, Sport Coupes and station wagons all had individual rooflines with the flat-top look on regular sedans, a formal look on Sport Sedans, a rounded semi-

fastback on Sport Coupes and boxy, conventional station wagon styling. Station wagons had Bel Air trim but Parkwood rear fender script. Standard equipment matched that of Biscayne, plus foam seat cushions and Deluxe steering wheel.

BEL AIR SERIES

Model No.	Model No. (V-8)	Body Type & Seating	Factory Price	Shipping Weight	Prod. Total
(PASSENGER CARS)					
1569	1669	4-dr Sed-6P	2438/2545	3515/3520	Note 1
1539	1639	4-dr HT Spt Sed-6P	2554/2661	3550/3555	Note 1
1511	1611	2-dr Sed-6P	2384/2491	3430/3435	Note 1
1537	1637	2-dr HT Spt Cpe-5P	2489/2596	3475/3480	Note 1
(STATION WAGONS)					
1545	1645	4-dr Pkwd-9P	2850/2957	3910/3910	Note 1
1535	1635	4-dr Pkwd-6P	2747/2854	3865/3860	Note 1

1961 Chevrolet, Impala two-door convertible, V-8

NOTE 1: Chevrolet production was recorded, by body style only, as follows: four-door sedan - 452,251; Sport Coupe - 177,969; Sport Sedan - 174,141; four-door station wagon - 168,935; two-door sedan - 153,988 and convertible - 64,624.

NOTE 2: On a model year basis, approximately 137,300 station wagons were two-seat types and approximately 31,649 others had three-seat configuration. Chevrolet production by series: (Fleetmaster) 3,000 units; (Biscayne) 201,006 units; (Bel Air) 330,000 units; (Impala) 491,000 units and (station wagons) 169,000 units. These figures are rounded-off, as is a figure of 513,000 six-cylinder Chevrolets.

NOTE 3: Data above slash for six/below slash for V-8.

NOTE 4: Station wagons were grouped by the manufacturer as a separate series, but are being grouped under passenger cars with similar trim level in this catalog.

IMPALA — SERIES 1700 (6-CYL) — SERIES 1800 (V-8) —

Impalas were easily identified by their triple taillight treatment. They also had crossed racing flags insignia at the center of the rear deck and at the rear fenders with model identification script in the latter location as well. Deluxe wheel discs and wide side moldings, with contrasting insert panels, were other visual distinctions of the top Chevrolet line. Nomad station wagons had Impala level trim, but Nomad rear fender signatures. Standard equipment lists began with Bel Air features and added parking brake glovebox and back-up lights; anodized aluminum trim; electric clock and 8.00 x 14 tires on convertibles. All 1961 Chevrolet V-8s had oil filters and oil bath-type air cleaners, all station wagons had 8.00 x 14 tires and nine-passenger models had power tailgates.

IMPALA SERIES

Model No.	Model No. (V-8)	Body Type & Seating	Factory Price	Shipping Weight	Prod. Total
(PASSENGER CARS)					
1769	1869	4-dr Sed-6P	2590/2697	3530/3525	Note 1
1739	1839	4-dr HT Spt Sed-6P	2662/2769	3575/2570	Note 1
1711	1811	2-dr Sed-6P	2536/2643	3445/3440	Note 1
1737	1837	2-dr HT Spt Cpe-5P	2597/2704	3485/3480	Note 1
1767	1867	2-dr Conv-5P	2847/2954	3605/3600	Note 1
(STATION WAGONS)					
1745	1845	4-dr Nomad-9P	2922/3099	3935/3930	Note 1
1735	1835	4-dr Nomad-6P	2889/2996	3885/3885	Note 1

NOTE 1: Chevrolet production was recorded, by body style only, as follows: four-door sedan - 452,251; Sport Coupe - 177,969; Sport Sedan - 174,141, four-door station wagon - 168,935; two-door sedan - 153,988 and convertible - 64 624. No further breakouts by model, series or engine were provided by Chevrolet except in the case of Super Sport models, of which 142 were reported as built.

NOTE 2: On a model year basis, approximately 137,300 station wagons were two-seat types and approximately 31,649 others had three-seat configuration. Chevrolet production by series: (Fleetmaster) 3,000 units; (Biscayne) 201,006 units; (Bel Air) 330,000 units; (Impala) 491,000 units and (station wagons) 169,000 units. These figures are rounded-off, as is a figure of 513,000 six-cylinder Chevrolets.

NOTE 3: Data above slash for six/below slash for V-8.

NOTE 4: Station wagons were grouped by the manufacturer as a separate series, but are being grouped under passenger cars with similar trim level in this catalog.

1961 Chevrolet, Impala four-door hardtop (Sport Sedan), V-8

NOTE 5: The 1961 Super Sport package was a dealer installed kit available on any Impala model. It consisted of 'SS' emblems on rear fenders and deck lid; instrument panel pad; special wheel covers with spinners; power brakes and steering; heavy-duty springs and shocks; sintered metallic brake linings; 7000 rpm tachometer and 8.00 x 14 narrow band white sidewall tires. A choice of five performance power teams was available. Price for the equipment package was in the $54 range, according to sources.

1961 Chevrolet, Impala two-door hardtop (Sport Coupe), V-8

ENGINES

SIX-CYLINDER: Overhead valve. Cast iron block. Displacement: 235 cid. Bore and stroke: 3.56 x 3.94 inches. Compression ratio: 8.25:1. Brake horsepower: 135 at 4000 rpm. Four main bearings. Hydraulic valve lifters. Carburetor: Rochester one-barrel Model 7013003.

1961 Chevrolet, Impala Nomad station wagon, 6-cyl

V-8: Overhead valve. Cast iron block. Displacement: 283 cid. Bore and stroke: 3.875 x 3.00 inches. Compression ratio: 8.5:1. Brake horsepower: 170 at 4200 rpm. Five main bearings. Hydraulic valve lifters. Carburetor: Rochester two-barrel Model 7019007.

POWERTRAIN OPTIONS: Six optional engine choices were provided for 1961 Chevrolets as follows:

SUPER TURBO-FIRE V-8

CID	Comp. Ratio	Carb Barrels	Exhaust	HP @ rpm	Trans Combo	Valve Lifters
283	9.5	4V	1	230 @ 4800	N/A	H

TURBO-THRUST V-8

348	9.5	4V	2	250 @ 4400	N/A	H

SPECIAL TURBO THRUST V-8

348	9.5	4V	2	305 @ 5200	N/A	S
348	11.25	4V	2	340 @ 5800	N/A	S

SUPER TURBO-THRUST V-8

348	11.25	3x2V	2	280 @ 4800	N/A	H

SPECIAL SUPER TURBO-THRUST V-8

348	11.25	3x2V	2	350 @ 6000	N/A	S

TURBO-FIRE 409 V-8

409	11.0	1x4V	2	360 @ 5800	N/A	S

CHASSIS FEATURES: Wheelbase: 119 inches. Overall length: 209.3 inches. Front tread: 60.3 inches. Rear tread: 59.3 inches. Width: 78.4 inches. Height: 55.5 inches.

CONVENIENCE OPTIONS: Oil bath air cleaner ($5). Deluxe air conditioner, with V-8 only, includes heater ($457). Cool pack air conditioner ($317). Positraction rear axle ($43). Heavy-duty battery ($8). Group A body equipment package including outside rearview mirror, front and rear bumper guards, grille guard and inside non-glare mirror, for all models except Impala and Nomad ($48). Group B body equipment package with electric clock, door guards and back-up lights for all models except Impala and Nomad; two-door ($23); four-door ($26). Economy carburetor ($8). Heavy-duty clutch for six-cylinder models ($5). Crankcase ventilation system, required on California cars ($5). Air Foam front seat cushions for Biscayne and Brookwood models ($8). Positive engine ventilation for six-cylinder models ($12). Dual exhaust combined with 230 horsepower V-8 ($25). Temperature controlled radiator fan for V-8 models ($16). Optional generators, three types ($8-$97). Tinted glass, all windows ($38), windshield only ($22); shaded rear windows on two-door Sport Coupe ($14). Deluxe heater ($74); recirculating heater ($47). Padded instrument panel ($18). Oil filter with six-cylinder models ($9). Two-tone paint ($16). Power brakes ($43). Six-Way power seat, except Biscayne and Brookwood ($97); Four-Way power seat, except Biscayne and Brookwood ($65). Power steering ($75). Power tailgate window ($32). Power windows, except Biscayne and Brookwood ($102). Heavy-duty radiator ($11). Radios, manual ($54), push-button ($62). Heavy-duty rear coil springs ($3). Deluxe steering wheel ($4). Overdrive transmission ($108). Powerglide transmission with six-cylinder ($188). Powerglide transmission with V-8 ($199). Turbo-glide transmission with V-8 ($210). Four-speed, close-ratio manual transmission with V-8 ($188). Wheel covers ($15). Windshield washers ($11). Two-speed electric windshield wipers and washers ($16). Super Turbo-fire V-8 ($136). Turbo-thrust V-8 ($201). Special Turbo-thrust V-8 ($317). Special Turbo-thrust 340 horsepower V-8 ($344). Super Turbo-thrust V-8 ($271). Special Super Turbo-thrust V-8 ($365).

HISTORICAL FOOTNOTES: Chevrolets were introduced to the public Oct. 8, 1960. The division's model year production peaked at 1,204,917 cars, including Corvettes, but excluding 297,881 Corvairs. (See separate catalog listing for Corvettes and Corvairs). A total of 142 Impalas were manufactured with Super Sport equipment and the 409-cid V-8, which went into production in January 1961. Prod. of models built to 1961 specifications ceased on Aug. 2, 1961. Calendar year production of 1,604,805 units in all lines made Chevrolet America's number one automaker again. Semon E. 'Bunkie' Knudsen was general manager of the division this season. The 1961 Impala SS hardtop with the 409 cid/360 hp V-8 was reported capable of 0-to-60 mph times of 7.8 seconds and 15.8 second quarter-mile runs. The 1961 Bel Air Sport Coupe with the 409 cid/409 hp engine was reported to do the quarter-mile in 12.83 seconds. Don Nicholson wasTop Stock Eliminator at the 1961 National Hot Rod Association Winter Nationals in a 409/409 Super Stock Chevy.

1962

CHEVY II — ALL SERIES — Designed to combat the popularity of the Falcon, Ford Motor Co.'s conventional compact car, the Chevy II line made its debut in 1962. This no-nonsense economy model featured simple, squarish styling with unitized body and front stub-frame construction. Major front end components, including fenders, were of bolt-on design for easy replacement. There were 11 basic models arranged in four different series, according to powerplant applications. At the bottom were the 100 series (four-cylinder/six-cylinder) having, as standard equipment, five 6.00 x 13 tires; heater and defroster; front foam cushions; cigarette lighter; electric windshield wipers; oil filter; and power tailgate on three-seat station wagons. These cars lacked moldings around the side windows, rear deck panel and bodysides and had spartan interiors. A 200 series (interim-priced model between the 100 and 300 series) was announced, but discontinued shortly after introduction. The 300 series four and six had all moldings mentioned above, plus slightly enriched interiors. The Nova 400 series came only with six-cylinder power. Identification features included Nova rear fender nameplates; side body, window and deck trim; rocker sill strips; front fender tip windsplit moldings and full wheel discs. Nova equipment included all found on the lower series, plus 6.50 x 13 tires (also used on base station wagons); rear foam seat cushions; floor carpets; and special interior upholstery and trim. The engines used in all Chevy IIs were completely new.

CHEVY II I.D. NUMBERS: Vehicle numbers were on the left front body hinge pillar. Engine numbers, for both engines, were on the right side of the block to the rear of distributor. The first symbol was a '2' indicating the 1962 model year. This was followed by four symbols shown in charts below as Model Numbers. The first pair of symbols in these Model Numbers indicate the series (01=Chevy II 100 four-cylinder; 02=Chevy II 100 six-cylinder; 03=Chevy II 300 four-cylinder and 04=Chevy II 300 and Nova six-cylinder) and the second pair of symbols in the Model Number indicate body style. The next letter (sixth symbol of VIN) shows the assembly plant code with Chevy II production limited to factories coded W=Willow Run, Mich., and N=Norwood, Ohio. The last six numbers were the sequential production code starting with 100001 at each plant. A Fisher Body Style plate is under the hood on left and gives Style Number, Body Number, Trim Code and Paint Code.

1962 Chevrolet, Chevy II 300 station wagon, 6-cyl

CHEVY II SERIES (ALL)

SERIES 100 (4-CYL)/SERIES 100 (6-CYL)

Model No.	Model No. (6-CYL)	Body Type & Seating	Factory Price	Shipping Weight	Prod. Total
0169	0269	4-dr Sed-6P	2041/2101	2445/2535	Note 1
0111	0211	2-dr Sed-6P	2003/2063	2410/2500	Note 1
0135	0235	2-dr Sta Wag-6P	2339/2399	2665/2755	Note 1

SERIES 300 (4-CYL)/SERIES 300 (6-CYL)

0369	0469	4-dr Sed-6P	2122/2182	2460/2550	Note 1
0311	0411	2-dr Sed-6P	2084/2144	2425/2515	Note 1
0345	0445	2-dr Sta Wag-9P	2517/2577	2765/2855	Note 1

SERIES NOVA 400 (6-CYL)

N/A	0449	4-dr Sed-6P	2236	2575	Note 1
N/A	0441	2-dr Sed-6P	2198	2540	Note 1
N/A	0437	2-dr Spt Cpe-5P	2264	2550	Note 1
N/A	0467	2-dr Conv-5P	2475	2745	Note 1
N/A	0435	4-dr Sta Wag-6P	2497	2775	Note 1

1962 Chevrolet, Chevy II Nova 400 two-door convertible, 6-cyl

NOTE 1: Production totals were recorded by body style only, with no breakouts by series, model or engine. Totals for 1962 were as follows: four-door sedan - 139,004; four-door station wagons - 59,886; two-door Sport Coupe - 59,586; two-door sedan - 44,390 and two-door convertible - 23,741.

NOTE 2: First column shows four-cylinder codes and second column shows six-cylinder codes.

NOTE 3: Data above slash for fours/below slash for sixes. Nova 400 is six-cylinder only, no slashes used.

NOTE 4: There was a factory-offered kit for dealer installation of either a 283-cid or 327-cid V-8 engine, with outputs up to 360 hp.

BISCAYNE — SERIES 1100 (6-CYL) — SERIES 1200 (V-8) — The plainest full-size Chevrolet benefited from the bodyside sculpturing of the 1962 design. Standard features included heater and defroster; dual sun visors; crank-operated ventipanes; directional signals; parallel action windshield wipers; front door armrests; ashtray; coat hooks; and color-keyed vinyl-coated rubber floor coverings. Interiors were trimmed in cloth and leather grain vinyl with all-vinyl sidewalls. Exterior bright metal decoration included an anodized aluminum grille with pairs of flanking headlamps. Biscaynes had a slender, full-length lower body sill molding and four taillights at the rear. The series script appeared on the rear fenders. Small hubcaps were standard.

CHEVROLET I.D. NUMBERS: Serial numbers were stamped on a plate affixed to the left front door hinge pillar. The first symbol identified the model year: 2=1962. The second and third symbols identified the series (see first two digits of Model Number columns in charts below). The fourth and fifth symbols identified body style (see last two digits of Model Number columns in charts below). The sixth symbol, a letter, indicated assembly plant, as follows: A=Atlanta, Ga.; B=Baltimore, Md.; F=Flint, Mich.; G=Framingham, Mass.; J=Janesville, Wis.; K=Kansas City, Mo.; L=Los Angeles, Calif.; N=Norwood, Ohio; O=Oakland, Calif.; S=St. Louis, Mo.; T=Tarrytown, N.Y.; W=Willow Run, Mich. The last six symbols are the sequential production number, with numbers for each series at each factory starting at 100001 and up. Fisher Body plate attached to left-hand cowl starts with two-digit model year prefix (62-) and Fisher Body/Style Number (Model Number) and also shows factory code, production sequence, trim and body color data. Engine numbers: (six) right side of block behind distributor; (V-8) right front of engine block.

1962 Chevrolet, Chevy II 300 four-door sedan, 6-cyl (PH)

BISCAYNE SERIES

Model No.	Model No. (V-8)	Body Type & Seating	Factory Price	Shipping Weight	Prod. Total
(PASSENGER CARS)					
1169	1269	4-dr Sed-6P	2378/2485	3480/3475	Note 1
1111	1211	2-dr Sed-6P	2324/2431	3405/3400	Note 1
(STATION WAGONS)					
1135	1235	4-dr Bis Sta Wag-6P	2725/2832	3845/3840	Note 1

NOTE 1: Production totals were recorded by body style only, with no breakouts by series, model or engine. Totals for 1962 'Regular Chevrolets' were as follows: four-door sedan - 533,349; two-door hardtop Sport Coupe - 323,427; four-door station wagon - 187,566; four-door hardtop Sport Sedan - 176,077; two-door sedan - 127,870 and two-door convertible - 75,719.

NOTE 2: In rounded-off figures, production of Biscaynes, excluding station wagons, was 166,000 units. Production of all Chevrolet station wagons was 187,600.

NOTE 3: Production of all full-size Chevy V-8s was 921,900 units. Production of all full-size Chevy sixes was 502,100 units.

NOTE 4: Data above slash for six/below slash for V-8.

NOTE 5: Model Numbers and Body/Style Numbers are the same. The first column in chart shows six-cylinder codes and the second column in chart shows V-8 codes.

BEL AIR — SERIES 1500 (6-CYL) — SERIES 1600 (V-8) — This was Chevrolet's popular mid-priced line. Standard equipment included all Biscayne features, plus extra quality interior appointments; foam front and rear seats; color-keyed carpeting; foam backed luggage compartment mat; and a specific steering wheel hub. Interiors were higher grade cloth and vinyl combinations. A full-length upper bodyside molding was used, with Bel Air script appearing on the rear fenders, just below it. A stainless bright gutter cap molding was another Bel Air feature. Four taillights, arranged two on each side, were seen. A bright rear cove molding added a touch of distinction.

1962 Chevrolet, Bel Air four-door sedan, V-8 (PH)

BEL AIR SERIES

Model No.	Model No. (V-8)	Body Type & Seating	Factory Price	Shipping Weight	Prod. Total
(PASSENGER CARS)					
1569	1669	4-dr Sed-6P	2510/2617	3480/3475	Note 1
1511	1611	2-dr Sed-6P	2456/2563	3410/3405	Note 1
1537	1637	2-dr HT Spt Cpe-6P	2561/2668	3445/3440	Note 1
(STATION WAGONS)					
1545	1645	4-dr Sta Wag-9P	2922/3029	3895/3890	Note 1
1535	1635	4-dr Sta Wag-6P	2819/2926	3845/3840	Note 1

NOTE 1: Production totals were recorded by body style only, with no breakouts by series, model or engine. Totals for 1962 'Regular Chevrolets' were as follows: four-door sedan - 533,349; two-door hardtop Sport Coupe - 323,427; four-door station wagon - 187,566; four-door hardtop Sport Sedan - 176,077; two-door sedan - 127,870 and two-door convertible - 75,719.

NOTE 2: In rounded-off figures, production of Bel Airs, excluding station wagons, was 365,500 units. Production of all Chevrolet station wagons was 187,600.

NOTE 3: Production of all full-size Chevy V-8s was 921,900 units. Production of all full-size Chevy sixes was 502,100 units.

NOTE 4: Data above slash for six/below slash for V-8.

NOTE 5: Model Numbers and Body/Style Numbers are the same. The first column in chart shows six-cylinder codes and the second column in chart shows V-8 codes.

1962 Chevrolet, Bel Air two-door hardtop (Sport Coupe), V-8

1962 Chevrolet, Impala four-door sedan, V-8

IMPALA — SERIES 1700 (6-CYL) — SERIES 1800 (V-8) — Chevrolet's top models were in the Impala line. Standard equipment included most features found on lower priced lines, plus bright aluminum front seat end panels; bright metal backed rearview mirror; extra-long front and rear armrests (with fingertip door release handles); built-in door safety panel reflectors; rear seat radio grille (built into Sport Coupe and convertible); and Sport-type steering wheel with Impala center emblem. The instrument panel included an electric clock; parking brake warning light; glove compartment light; and bright metal valance panels. Interiors were plusher cloth and leather grain vinyl combinations, with embossed vinyl headlining. Exterior bodyside trim consisted of a full-length upper molding with color-keyed insert; a wide, ribbed body sill molding; stainless steel window reveals (except convertible); and Impala script badge on the rear fenders. Front fender ornaments were standard while at the rear, a brushed aluminum cove panel with six taillamps was found. Back-up lights were built-in. A simulated rear window vent was seen, below the glass, on all styles except the convertible.

IMPALA SERIES

Model No.	Model No. (V-8)	Body Type & Seating	Factory Price	Shipping Weight	Prod. Total
(PASSENGER CARS)					
1769	1869	4-dr Sed-6P	2662/2769	3510/3505	Note 1

1739	1839	4-dr HT Spt Sed-6P	2734/2841	3540/3535	Note 1
1747	1847	2-dr HT Spt Cpe-5P	2669/2776	3455/3450	Note 1
1767	1867	2-dr Conv-5P	2919/3026	3565/3560	Note 1

(STATION WAGON)

1745	1845	4-dr Sta Wag-9P	3064/3171	3935/3930	Note 1
1735	1835	4-dr Sta Wag-6P	2961/3068	3870/3865	Note 1

NOTE 1: Production totals were recorded by body style only, with no breakouts by series, model or engine. Totals for 1962 'Regular Chevrolets' were as follows: four-door sedan - 533,349; two-door hardtop Sport Coupe - 323,427; four-door station wagon - 187,566; four-door hardtop Sport Sedan - 176,077; two-door sedan - 127,870 and two-door convertible - 75,719.

1962 Chevrolet, Impala two-door hardtop (Sport Coupe), V-8

NOTE 2: In rounded-off figures, production of Impalas, excluding station wagons, was 704,900 units. Of these, 99,311 had the Super Sport option. Production of all Chevrolet station wagons was 187,600.

NOTE 3: Production of all full-size Chevy V-8s was 921,900 units. Production of all full-size Chevy sixes was 502,100 units.

NOTE 4: Production of 409-cid V-8s was 15,019.

NOTE 5: Data above slash for six/below slash for V-8.

NOTE 6: Model Numbers and Body/Style Numbers are the same. The first column in chart shows six-cylinder codes and the second column in chart shows V-8 codes.

1962 Chevrolet, Impala two-door convertible, V-8

SUPER SPORT EQUIPMENT: The Option Code 240 Super Sport package added or substituted the following items on regular Impala equipment: Swirl-pattern bodyside moldings; 'SS' rear fender emblems; 'SS' deck lip badge; specific Super Sport full wheel discs with simulated knock-off spinners; locking center console and passenger assist bar. Super Sport equipment was available on the Impala Sport Coupe and convertible at $53.80 extra, plus $102.25 for bucket seats.

1962 Chevrolet, Impala four-door hardtop (Sport Sedan), V-8

CHEVY II ENGINES

FOUR-CYLINDER: Overhead valve. Cast iron block. Displacement: 153.3 cid. Bore and stroke: 3.875 x 3.25 inches. Compression ratio: 8.5:1. Brake horsepower: 90 at 4000 rpm. Five main bearings. Hydraulic valve lifters. Carburetor: Rochester one-barrel Model 7020103.

SIX-CYLINDER: Overhead valve. Cast iron block. Displacement: 194.4 cid. Bore and stroke: 3.562 x 3.25 inches. Compression ratio: 8.5:1. Brake horsepower: 120 at 4400 rpm. Seven main bearings. Hydraulic valve lifters. Carburetor: Rochester one-barrel Model 7020105.

CHEVROLET ENGINES

SIX-CYLINDER: Overhead valve. Cast iron block. Displacement: 235 cid. Bore and stroke: 3.56 x 3.94 inches. Compression ratio: 8.25:1. Brake horsepower: 135 at 4000 rpm. Four main bearings. Hydraulic valve lifters. Carburetor: Rochester one-barrel Model 7013003.

V-8: Overhead valve. Cast iron block. Displacement: 283 cid. Bore and stroke: 3.875 x 3.00 inches. Compression ratio: 8.5:1. Brake horsepower: 170 at 4200 rpm. Five main bearings. Hydraulic valve lifters. Carburetor: Rochester two-barrel Model 7020007. Base engines for Impalas were the same as for Biscaynes. See 1962 Biscayne engine data.

CHEVROLET POWERTRAIN OPTIONS: Optional engine choices provided for 1962 were:

CID	Comp. Ratio	Carb Barrels	Exhaust	HP @ rpm	Trans Combo	Valve Lifters
327	10.5	4V	2	250 @ 4400	M/PG	H
327	10.5	4V	2	300 @ 5000	M/PG	H
409	11.1	4V	2	380 @ 6000	M	S
409	11.1	4V	2	409 @ 5800	M	S

NOTE: V=Venturi; 1=single exhaust; 2=dual exhaust; M=manual transmission; PG=Powerglide automatic transmission; H=hydraulic valve lifters; S=solid valve lifters.

CHASSIS FEATURES: Wheelbase: (Chevy II) 110 inches; (Chevrolet) 119 inches. Overall length: (Chevy

II station wagon) 197.4 inches; (all other Chevy IIs) 183 inches; (Chevrolet, all models) 209.6 inches. Front tread: (Chevy II) 56.8 inches; (Chevrolet) 60.3 inches. Rear tread: (Chevy II) 56.3 inches; (Chevrolet) 59.3 inches. Tires: (Chevy II, all station wagons and Sport models) 6.50 x 13; (all other Chevy II) 6.00 x 13; (Biscayne) 7.00 x 14, (Chevrolet station wagons) 8.00 x 14; (all other Chevrolets) 7.50 x 14.

CHEVY II OPTIONS: Air conditioning ($317). Rear armrest for 100 series models only ($10). Front seat driver's safety belt ($11). Two front seat safety belts ($20). Group A body equipment, station wagons ($29); passenger cars ($34). Heavy-duty brakes ($38). Comfort and Convenience group ($39). Tinted glass, all windows ($27); windshield only ($13). Padded dash ($16). Two-tone paint, except convertible ($11). Power brakes ($43). Power steering ($75). Power tailgate window on six-passenger station wagon ($27). Manual radio and antenna ($48). Push-button radio and antenna ($57). Station wagon divided second seat ($38). Nova 400 front bucket seats, except station wagon ($70). Heavy-duty rear shock absorbers ($1). Heavy-duty springs, front ($1); rear ($3). Whitewall tires ($30). Full wheel covers ($13) and wire wheel covers ($38). Rear axles with 3.36:1 or 3.55:1 gear ratio ($2). Positraction rear axle ($40). Heavy-duty battery ($8). Heavy-duty clutch ($5). Crankcase ventilation ($4). Generator, 35-amp ($8). Delcotron generator, 42-amp ($27). Heavy-duty radiator ($3). Powerglide transmission ($167).

CHEVROLET OPTIONS: Deluxe air conditioning with automatic transmission, includes heater ($364). Cool Pack air conditioner ($317). Group A body equipment including outside rearview mirror, rear bumper guards, grille guard and inside non-glare mirror, for station wagons ($29); other models ($34). Heavy-duty metallic-faced brakes ($38). Impala Comfort and Convenience Group ($30); same for Bel Air ($41); same for Biscayne ($44). Air foam front seat cushions for Biscayne ($8). Tinted glass, all windows ($38); windshield only ($22). Shaded Sport Coupe backlight ($14). Padded dash ($16). Lockable station wagon rear compartment ($11). Two-tone paint ($16). Power brakes ($43). Six-Way power seat ($97). Power steering ($75). Power tailgate window ($32). Power windows except Biscayne ($102). Manual radio ($48). Push-button radio ($57). Station wagon divided second seat ($38). Impala Sport Coupe and convertible bucket seats ($102). Heavy-duty front and rear shock absorbers, except station wagons ($1). Heavy-duty front coil springs ($1). Heavy-duty rear coil springs ($3). Deluxe steering wheel for Biscayne ($4). Tachometer for V-8s ($49). Vinyl trim for Biscayne sedan ($5). Wheel discs ($18). Electric two-speed wipers with washers ($17). Various whitewall and oversize tire options ($31-$36). The Option Code 240 Super Sport (SS) package was available on the Impala Sport Coupe and convertible at $53.80 extra, plus $102.25 for bucket seats. Turbo-Fire 327 cid/250 hp V-8 with four-barrel carburetor and dual exhaust ($191). Turbo-Fire 327 cid/300 hp V-8 with four-barrel carburetor and dual exhaust ($245). Turbo-Fire 409 cid/380 hp V-8 with four-barrel carburetor, dual exhaust, high-lift camshaft and solid valve lifters ($428). Turbo-Fire 409 cid/409 hp V-8 with dual four-barrel carburetors, lightweight valve train, dual exhaust and solid valve lifters ($484). Economy carburetor ($8). Heavy-duty six-cylinder clutch ($30). Positive crankcase ventilation system ($5). Positive six-cylinder engine ventilation ($12). Heavy-duty battery ($8). Oil bath air cleaner ($5). Temperature controlled 170 horsepower V-8 radiator fan ($16). Generator, 35-amp ($8). Delcotron 45-amp generator ($27). Delcotron 52-amp generator, with Deluxe air conditioner ($8); without air ($34).

NOTE: Generator options not available with 409-cid V-8s. Heavy-duty radiator ($11). Positraction rear axle ($43). Overdrive transmission ($108). Six-cylinder Powerglide attachment ($188). V-8 Powerglide attachment, not available with 409-cid engine ($199). Close-ratio four-speed transmission with Turbo-Fire V-8 ($188).

HISTORICAL FOOTNOTES: Chevrolets and Chevy IIs built to 1962 specifications appeared in dealer showrooms Sept. 29, 1961. Model year production hit 1,424,000 units excluding Corvairs, Corvettes and Chevy IIs. The new Chevy II series saw production of 326,600 additional units for the model year, which included 47,000 cars in the 100 series (35,500 sixes); 103,200 cars in the 300 series (92,800 sixes); 116,500 Nova 400s (all sixes) and 59,900 station wagons (57,800 sixes) in rounded-off totals. Calendar year output peaked at 2,161,398 units, making Chevrolet America's number one automaker by a substantial margin. The first Chevrolets with a lightweight Z11 drag racing package were constructed late in the year. They had an aluminum hood, aluminum inner fenders and aluminum front fenders. The Bel Air "bubbletop" two-door sedan was the basis of most Chevrolet race cars and weighed in at about 3,360 pounds with Z11 equipment. Many sources indicate "about 100" Z11s were built (57 is given as the specific number made in 1963). Hayden Profit's Z11 took AA/S Stock Eliminator honors at the U.S. Nationals in Indianapolis with a run of 12.83 seconds/113.92 mph in the quarter-mile. Top Stock Eliminator in S/S was Dave Stickler's Z11 with a 12.97 second/113.35 mph run. Don Nicholson's B/FX Z11 ran a 12.93 second quarter-mile at 113.63 mph. Ronnie Sox campaigned two Z11s on the East Coast. Chevrolets took 14 NASCAR victories on the short tracks. The 1962 Impala SS two-door hardtop with the 409 cid/409 hp engine was reported to do the quarter-mile in 14.9 seconds. A 1962 Bel Air "bubbletop" with the same engine covered the distance in 12.2 seconds!

1963

CHEVY II/NOVA — ALL SERIES — Detail refinements and new freshness for its basically simple lines were the major exterior changes for this year's Chevy II. On the inside, new upholstery and trim set off the cars. The three series, 100, 300 and Nova 400 were continued with a total of 10 regular models, plus a new Super Sport (SS) option exclusive to Nova 400 Sport models. A new grille consisted of five, slightly thicker horizontal bars. The main divider bar of the previous year was gone. Chevrolet lettering on the front of the hood replaced the thin, wide medallion of 1962. Base level 100 series models were plain, without bodyside trim. Series 300 models had moldings along the bodysides, window reveals and edges of the rear cove panel. Novas had similar trim, plus wheel discs and rocker sill moldings, with identification script on the rear fenders. Cars with the Super Sport option had special finned wheel covers, wider bodyside moldings, aluminized rear panels and 'SS' badges on the rear fenders and right-hand side of the deck lid. Standard equipment included five 6.00 x 13 black tubeless tires on most cars (6.50 x 13 on station wagon and Nova 400 SS models); heater; defroster; front foam cushions; cigarette lighter; electric windshield wipers; oil filter and power tailgate windows on three-seat station wagons. In addition, Nova 400s had rear foam seats; floor carpets; special upholstery; Deluxe trim; and back-up lights.

1963 Chevrolet, Chevy II Nova 400 two-door hardtop (Sport Coupe), 6-cyl

CHEVY II/NOVA I.D. NUMBERS: Vehicle numbers were on the left front body hinge pillar. Engine numbers, for both engines, were on the right side of the block to the rear of the distributor. The first VIN symbol was a '3' indicating the model year 1963. This was followed by four symbols shown in charts below as Model Numbers. The first pair of symbols in these Model Numbers indicate the series (01=Chevy II 100 four-cylinder; 02=Chevy II 100 six-cylinder; 03=Chevy II 300 four-cylinder and 04=Chevy II 300 and Nova six-cylinder) and the second pair of symbols in the Model Number indicate body style. The next letter (sixth symbol of VIN) shows the assembly plant code with Chevy II production limited to factories coded W=Willow Run, Mich., and N=Norwood, Ohio. The last six numbers were the sequential production code starting with 100001 at each plant. A Fisher Body Style plate is under the hood on left and gives Style Number, Body Number, Trim Code and Paint Code.

CHEVY II/NOVA SERIES (ALL)

Model No.	Model No. (6-CYL)	Body Type & Seating	Factory Price	Shipping Weight	Prod. Total
SERIES 100 (4-CYL)/SERIES 100 (6-CYL)					
0169	0269	4-dr Sed-6P	2040/2099	2455/2545	Note 1
0111	0211	2-dr Sed-6P	2003/2062	2430/2520	Note 1
0135	0235	4-dr Sta Wag-6P	2338/2397	2725/2810	Note 1

SERIES 300 (4-CYL)/SERIES 300 (6-CYL)					
0369	0469	4-dr Sed-6P	2121/2180	2470/2560	Note 1
0311	0411	2-dr Sed-6P	2084/2143	2440/2530	Note 1
0345	0445	4-dr Sta Wag-9P	2516/2575	2810/2900	Note 1
SERIES NOVA 400 (6-CYL)					
N/A	0449	4-dr Sed-6P	2235	2590	Note 1
N/A	0437	2-dr HT Spt Cpe-5P	2262	2590	Note 1
N/A	0467	2-dr Conv-5P	2472	2760	Note 1
N/A	0435	4-dr Sta Wag-6P	2494	2835	Note 1

1963 Chevrolet, Chevy II Nova SS two-door hardtop (Sport Coupe), 6-cyl

NOTE 1: Chevy II production totals were recorded by body style only, with no breakouts by series, model or engine. Totals for 1963 were as follows: four-door sedan - 146,097; two-door hardtop Sport Coupe - 87,415; four-door station wagon - 72,274; two-door sedan - 42,017 and two-door convertible - 24,823.

NOTE 2: Nova SS production - 42,432 Sport Coupes and convertibles (combined).

NOTE 3: Model year production of 1963 Chevy IIs was approximately 375,600 cars. This included 50,400 in the 100 series (48,200 six-cylinder); 78,800 in the 300 series (77,700 six-cylinder); 171,100 in the Nova 400 series and 75,300 station wagons (74,800 six-cylinder). Of these station wagons, 67,347 had two-seats and 7,927 had three-seats. Also, 470 station wagons with four-cylinder engines were made.

NOTE 4: First column above shows four-cylinder Model Number; second column above shows six-cylinder Model Number.

NOTE 5: Data above slash for four-cylinder/below slash for six-cylinder. The Nova 400 line came only with six-cylinder power, so no slashes are used.

BISCAYNE — SERIES 1100 (6-CYL) — SERIES 1200 (V-8) — Chevrolet's new 1963 styling was seen as a move to make the company's products look more like luxury cars. Grilles, bumpers, hoods, sculptured side panels and rear deck contours were all new yet the overall alteration level was minor. Seen in profile, both front and rear fenders had a V-shape. The basic Biscayne was a little brighter this year with its slender full-length upper body molding. Standard features included heater and defroster; dual sun visors; crank-operated ventipanes; directional signals; parallel action electric windshield wipers; front door armrests; vinyl embossed headliners; ashtray; and color coordinated vinyl-coated rubber front covering. Interiors were trimmed in cloth and leather grained vinyls (all-vinyl on station wagons) with full vinyl door panels. The front seat was foam-cushioned. Exterior brightwork included the full-length body trim strip; anodized bright grille, hood and deck emblems and bright trim rings for the twin unit taillights. A series script and Chevrolet badge were seen on rear fenders and small hubcaps were standard.

1963 Chevrolet, Biscayne four-door sedan, 6-cyl

CHEVROLET I.D. NUMBERS: Serial numbers were stamped on a plate affixed to the left front door hinge pillar. The first VIN symbol identified the model year: 3=1963. The second and third symbols identified the series (see first two digits of Model Number columns in charts below). The fourth and fifth symbols identified bodystyle (see last two digits of Model Number columns in charts below). The sixth symbol, a letter, indicated assembly plant, as follows: A=Atlanta, Ga.; B=Baltimore, Md.; F=Flint, Mich.; G=Framingham, Mass.; J=Janesville, Wis.; K=Kansas City, Mo.; L=Los Angeles, Calif.; N=Norwood, Ohio; O=Oakland, Calif.; R=Arlington, Texas; S=St. Louis, Mo.; T=Tarrytown, N.Y.; W=Willow Run, Mich. The last six symbols are the sequential production number, with numbers for each series at each factory starting at 100001 and up. Fisher Body plate attached to left-hand cowl starts with two-digit model year prefix (63-) and Fisher Body/Style Number (Model Number) and also shows factory code, production sequence, trim and body color data. Engine numbers: (six) right side of block behind distributor; (V-8) right front of engine block.

BISCAYNE SERIES

Model No.	Model No. (V-8)	Body Type & Seating	Factory Price	Shipping Weight	Prod. Total
(PASSENGER CARS)					
1169	1269	4-dr Sed-6P	2376/2483	3280/3415	Note 1
1111	1211	2-dr Sed-6P	2322/2429	3205/3340	Note 1
(STATION WAGON)					
1135	1235	4-dr Sta Wag-6P	2723/2830	3685/3810	Note 1

NOTE 1: Production totals for 1963 'Regular Chevrolets' were as follows: four-door sedan - 561,511; two-door hardtop Sport Coupe - 399,224; four-door station wagon - 198,542; four-door hardtop Sport Sedan - 194,158; two-door sedan - 135,636 and two-door convertible - 82,659.

NOTE 2: Model year production (rounded-off) of Biscaynes, excluding station wagons, was approximately 186,500 cars (37,000 V-8s; 149,500 sixes). Production of all station wagons was 198,500 (146,200 V-8s; 52,300 sixes).

NOTE 3: Data above slash for sixes/below slash for V-8s.

NOTE 4: First column in chart above shows six-cylinder Model Numbers and the second column in chart shows V-8 Model Numbers.

BEL AIR SERIES — SERIES 1500 (6-CYL) — SERIES 1600 (V-8) — Chevrolet's medium-priced line was refined for 1963. Standard equipment included most Biscayne features, plus extra-quality interior trim; front and rear foam seat cushions; Deluxe steering wheel; glove compartment light; carpets; automatic dome light and dual rear ashtrays. A foam backed luggage compartment mat was another Bel Air additive. A bright metal lower body ridge molding, with accent stripe, was used. Bel Air signature script and Chevrolet badges appeared on the rear fenders. Stainless steel drip gutter moldings were found above the side windows. A bright finished rear cove with embossed Chevrolet lettering was seen at the rear, as well as twin unit taillights.

BEL AIR SERIES

Model No.	Model No. (V-8)	Body Type & Seating	Factory Price	Shipping Weight	Prod. Total
(PASSENGER CARS)					
1569	1669	4-dr Sed-6P	2508/2615	3280/3415	Note 1
1511	1611	2-dr Sed-6P	2454/2561	3215/3345	Note 1
(STATION WAGONS)					
1545	1645	4-dr Sta Wag-9P	2921/3028	3720/3850	Note 1
1535	1635	4-dr Sta Wag-6P	2818/2925	3685/3810	Note 1

NOTE 1: Production totals for 1963 'Regular Chevrolets' were as follows: four-door sedan - 561,511; two-door hardtop Sport Coupe - 399,224; four-door station wagon - 198,542; four-door hardtop Sport Sedan - 194,158; two-door sedan - 135,636 and two-door convertible - 82,659.

NOTE 2: Model year production (rounded-off) of 1963 Bel Airs, excluding station wagons, was approximately 354,100 cars (177,200 V-8s; 176,900 sixes). Production of all station wagons was 198,500 (146,200 V-8s; 52,300 sixes).

NOTE 3: Data above slash for sixes/below slash for V-8s.

NOTE 4: First column in chart above shows six-cylinder Model Numbers and the second column in chart shows V-8 Model Numbers.

IMPALA — SERIES 1700 (6-CYL) — SERIES 1800 (V-8) — Chevrolet's plushest line had most standard equipment found on lower lines, plus bright aluminum front seat end panels; patterned cloth and leather grained vinyl upholstery (in color-coordinated materials); extra thick foam seat cushions; tufted grain and cobble pattern vinyl door and side panels; paddle-type armrests with lift-up door releases; bright metal rear-view mirror backing; added insulation and foam backed trunk mats. A specific Sport-style steering wheel with half-circle and thumb control horn ring was used. Other extras included electric clock; parking brake warning lamp; glovebox lamp; bright metal, textured instrument cluster accents; and dashboard face panels of similar texture. The steering wheel had duo-tone finish on cars with fawn, aqua, green and blue interiors. Exterior bodyside trim included front fender accent bars; stainless steel belt moldings with stainless steel drip caps (except convertible); a full-length lower body molding with colored insert; and Impala lettering on the rear quarter section. An Impala emblem also appeared high on rear fenders. The rear cove was filled with satin aluminum finish and trimmed by bright metal outline moldings. Triple unit taillight groups were used and incorporated built-in back-up lamps.

1963 Chevrolet, Impala SS two-door convertible, V-8

IMPALA SERIES

Model No.	Model No. (V-8)	Body Type & Seating	Factory Price	Shipping Weight	Prod. Total
(PASSENGER CARS)					
1769	1869	4-dr Sed-6P	2662/2768	3310/3435	Note 1
1739	1839	4-dr HT Spt Sed-6P	2732/2839	3350/3475	Note 1
1747	1847	2-dr HT Spt Cpe-5P	2667/2774	3265/3390	Note 1
1767	1867	2-dr Conv-5P	2917/3024	3400/3870	Note 1
(STATION WAGONS)					
1745	1845	4-dr Sta Wag-9P	2063/3170	3745/3870	Note 1
1735	1835	4-dr Sta Wag-6P	2960/3067	3705/3835	Note 1

NOTE 1: Production totals for 1963 'Regular Chevrolets' were as follows: four-door sedan - 561,511; two-door hardtop Sport Coupe - 399,224; four-door station wagon - 198,547; four-door hardtop Sport Sedan - 194,158; two-door sedan - 135,636 and two-door convertible - 82,659.

NOTE 2: The 1963 Super Sport equipment package (RPO Z03) was expanded this season. It now included swirl pattern side molding inserts; matching cove inserts; red-filled 'SS' overlays for rear fender Impala emblems; specific full wheel covers; all-vinyl front bucket seat interiors and, also, a center console with locking storage compartment (when optional Powerglide or four-speed manual transmissions were ordered). In addition, the Super Sport's dashboard was trimmed with bright, swirl pattern inserts and 'SS' steering wheel center hubs were used.

NOTE 3: Model year production (rounded-off) of 1963 Impalas, excluding station wagons, was approximately 832,600 cars (735,900 V-8s; 96,700 sixes). Production of all station wagons was 198,500 (146,200 V-8s; 52,300 sixes).

1963 Chevrolet, Impala four-door hardtop (Sport Sedan), V-8

NOTE 4: A total of 16,920 cars had the 409-cid V-8 installed during the 1963 model run. Most of these units were Super Sports.

NOTE 5: Chevrolet Motor Division released a figure of 153,271 cars built in 1963 with the Super Sport equipment package, but no breakout of SS cars per body style.

NOTE 6: Data above slash for sixes/below slash for V-8s.

NOTE 7: First column in chart above shows six-cylinder Model Numbers and the second column in chart shows V-8 Model Numbers.

CHEVY II ENGINES

FOUR-CYLINDER: Overhead valve. Cast iron block. Displacement: 153.3 cid. Bore and stroke: 3.875 x 3.25 inches. Compression ratio: 8.5:1. Brake horsepower: 90 at 4000 rpm. Five main bearings. Hydraulic valve lifters. Carburetor: Rochester one-barrel Model 7020103.

SIX-CYLINDER: Overhead valve. Cast iron block. Displacement: 194.4 cid. Bore and stroke: 3.562 x 3.25 inches. Compression ratio: 8.5:1. Brake horsepower: 120 at 4400 rpm. Seven main bearings. Hydraulic valve lifters. Carburetor: Rochester one-barrel Model 7023103.

CHEVROLET ENGINES

SIX-CYLINDER: Overhead valve. Cast iron block. Displacement: 230 cid. Bore and stroke: 3.875 x 3.25 inches. Compression ratio: 9.25:1. Brake horsepower: 140 at 4400 rpm. Seven main bearings. Hydraulic valve lifters. Carburetor: Rochester one-barrel Model 7023003.

V-8: Overhead valve. Cast iron block. Displacement: 283 cid. Bore and stroke: 3.875 x 3.00 inches. Compression ratio: 9.25:1. Brake horsepower: 195 at 4800 rpm. Five main bearings. Hydraulic valve lifters. Carburetor: Rochester two-barrel Model 7023007.

CHEVROLET POWERTRAIN OPTIONS: Optional engine choices provided for 1963 were:

CID	Comp. Ratio	Carb Barrels	Exhaust	HP @ rpm	Trans Combo	Valve Lifters
327	10.5	4V	2	250 @ 4400	M/PG	H
327	10.5	4V	2	300 @ 5000	M/PG	H
327	10.5	4V	2	340 @ 6000	M/PG	S
409	11.1	4V	2	400 @ 5800	M	S
409	11.1	2x4V	2	425 @ 6000	M	S
427	13.5	2x4V	2	430 @ 6000	M	S

NOTE: V=venturi; 1=single exhaust; 2=dual exhaust; 2x4V= dual four-barrel carburetor; M=manual transmission; PG=Powerglide automatic transmission; H=hydraulic valve lifters; S=solid valve lifters.

1963 Chevrolet, Impala two-door hardtop (Sport Coupe), V-8

CHEVROLET CHASSIS FEATURES: Wheelbase: (Chevy II) 110 inches; (Chevrolet) 119 inches. Overall length: (Chevy II station wagon) 187.4 inches; (other Chevy IIs) 183 inches; (all Chevrolets) 210.4 inches. Front tread: (Chevy II) 56.8 inches; (Chevrolet) 60.3 inches. Rear tread: (Chevy II) 56.3 inches; (Chevrolet) 59.3 inches. Tires: (Chevy II station wagon) 6.50 x 13; (Chevy II) 6.00 x 13; (Chevrolet station wagon) 8.00 x 14; (Chevrolet convertible) 7.50 x 14; (Chevrolet) 7.00 x 14.

CHEVY II OPTIONS: Air conditioning ($317). Rear armrests ($10). Pair of front seat belts ($19). Heavy-duty brakes ($38). Comfort and Convenience Group, on Nova ($28); on others ($39). Tinted glass, all windows ($27); windshield only ($13); Grille guard ($15). Rear bumper guard ($10). Padded dash ($16). Station wagon roof luggage rack ($43). Two-tone paint, except convertible ($11). Power brakes ($3). Power steering ($75). Power tailgate window ($27). Power convertible top ($54). Push-button radio with antenna and rear speaker ($70). Manual radio and antenna ($48). Push-button radio and antenna ($57). Station wagon divided second seat ($38). Super Sport equipment for Nova Sport Coupe and convertible ($161). Full wheel covers ($13). Wire design wheel covers ($13). Various whitewall and oversize tire options ($9-$42). Positraction rear axle ($38). Heavy-duty clutch ($5). Delcotron 42-amp generator ($11). Heavy-duty radiator ($3). Powerglide transmission ($167).

CHEVROLET OPTIONS: Deluxe air conditioning, including heater ($364). Cool Pack air conditioning ($317). Driver seat belt ($10). Pair of front seat belts ($19). Heavy-duty brakes with metallic facings ($38). Comfort and Convenience Group, for Impala ($31); for Bel Air ($41); for Biscayne ($44). Biscayne front air foam seat cushion ($8). Tinted glass, all windows ($38); windshield only ($22). Grille guard ($19). Passenger car rear bumper guard ($10). Padded dash ($18). Station wagon luggage locker ($11). Station wagon luggage carrier ($43). Two-tone paint ($16). Power brakes ($43). Six-Way power seat ($97). Power steering, except Biscayne ($75). Power tailgate window ($32). Power windows except Biscayne ($102). Manual radio ($48). Push-button radio ($57). Push-button radio with antenna and rear speaker ($70). Vinyl roof for Impala Sport Coupe ($75). Station wagon divided second seat ($38). Deluxe steering wheel ($4). Super Sport equipment package ($161). Tachometer with V-8s ($48). Wheel discs ($18). Wire wheel discs on Super Sports ($25); on others ($43). Two-speed electric washers and wipers ($17). Turbo-Fire 327 cid/250 hp V-8 with four-barrel carburetor and dual exhaust ($191). Turbo-Fire 327 cid/300 hp V-8 with four-barrel carburetor and dual exhaust ($245). Turbo-Fire 327 cid/340 hp V-8 with four-barrel carburetor and dual exhaust ($349). Turbo-Fire 409 cid/400 hp V-8 with four-barrel carburetor, dual exhaust, high-lift camshaft and solid valve lifters ($428). Turbo-Fire 409 cid/425 hp V-8 with dual four-barrel carburetors, dual exhaust, high-lift camshaft and solid valve lifters ($484). (Note: 427-cid V-8 came with Z11 package). Overdrive transmission with six-cylinder or 283-cid V-8 engines ($108). Six-cylinder Powerglide ($188). Powerglide with 283 cid/327 cid V-8s ($199). Close-ratio four-speed manual transmission with 250 horsepower V-8 ($188). Four-speed transmission with 340/400/425 horsepower V-8s ($237). Positraction rear axle ($43). Delcotron 42-amp generator, standard with air conditioning, optional on others at ($11). Heavy-duty radiator ($11). Heavy-duty battery, standard with 340 horsepower V-8, optional on others at ($8). Six-cylinder temperature controlled cooling fan ($16). Delcotron 52-amp generator ($32). Delcotron 62-amp generator ($65-$75).

HISTORICAL FOOTNOTES: For 1963, the widest range of Chevrolets ever offered in history was available in dealer showrooms on Sept. 28, 1962. The division sold three out of every 10 cars retailed in the United States this season. Model year sales of Chevrolets and Chevy IIs peaked at 1,947,300 units. Calendar year production reached 2,303,343 cars, including Corvettes and Corvairs, which are covered separately in this catalog. Semon E. Knudsen remained general manager of Chevrolet Motor Division. In July 1963, prototypes for a new, intermediate-size line, to be called Chevelle, were introduced at the long-lead press preview. The cast iron crankshaft, used in the all-new seven main bearing six-cylinder engine, was a first for Chevrolet. This was a peak year for factory drag racing options, such as improved-for-'63 lightweight Z11 drag package (RPO Z11). This was available for the Model 1847 Impala Sport Coupe. The $1,245 option now had an aluminum front bumper and stripped interior, in addition to the aluminum front fenders, inner fenders and hood. A new 427 cid/430 hp version of the Chevy big-block used a .100 stroke increase to achieve the extra 18 cubic inches of displacement. It had a bore and stroke of 4.312 x 3.65 inches. This engine also included a new dual four-barrel intake manifold that isolated the intake runners from the engine valves, which were covered by a separate valve cover. The cylinder heads were slightly different on the intake manifold mating the surface, in order to match this new manifold setup. There was also a special cowl induction air cleaner; heavy-duty clutch; four-speed gearbox; Positraction rear axle; semi-metallic brakes and tachometer. On Dec. 1, 1962, Chevrolet issued 25 cars with the Z11 package. On Jan. 1, 1963, the company issued 25 more and seven more were sold soon after that date for a total of 57. The aluminum front end saved 112 pounds. Other weight-saving measures, such as the lack of center bumper backing and bracing helped, too. By cutting another 121 pounds, the car weight dropped to about 3,340 pounds. Also in 1963, five Mark 11 NASCAR 427 "mystery engines" were built and raced at Daytona, winning the two 100-mile preliminary races and setting the track stock car speed record. While these engines were rare, they were the prototype of the 1965 396-cid engine that was brought up to 427 cid in 1966 and 454 cid in 1970. These first five engines were closely related to the 409 and the Z11-optioned 427. They even shared crankshaft and piston rods with the Z11, but differed completely in having the combustion chamber in the cylinder head. That means the cylinder block deck surfaces were angled to parallel the piston dome, and also incorporated the stagger-valve or "porcupine" valve layout. The bore and stroke was the same as the Z11, 4.312 x 3.65 inches. The GM decision to adhere strictly to the Auto Manufacturers Association's anti-racing ban put a tragic end to these great engines, but not before the cat was, at least briefly, out of the bag.

1964

CHEVY II/NOVA — ALL SERIES — The 1964 Chevy II had a redesigned grille. Nine vertical bars were equally spaced along the five full-width horizontal blades. This gave a quadrant effect. Side trim treatments were more like the 1962 look, than the 1963 style. The base level 100 series models had no belt moldings. The 300 series was discontinued. Novas had constant-width belt moldings and Nova signature script at the upper trailing edge of front fenders. The top series consisted of only one model, the Nova Super Sport Sport Coupe, with 'SS' trim and equipment. Body style and engine availability was shuffled as indicated by the chart below. New technical features included an optional 283-cid V-8 and self-adjusting 9.6-inch drum brakes.

CHEVY II/NOVA I.D. NUMBERS: Vehicle numbers were on the left front body hinge pillar. Engine numbers for both engines were on the right side of the block to the rear of the distributor. The first VIN symbol was a '4' indicating the 1964 model year. This was followed by four symbols shown in charts below as Model Numbers. The first pair of symbols in these Model Numbers indicate the series (01 =Chevy II 100 four-cylinder; 02=Chevy II 100 six-cylinder; 04=Nova six-cylinder) and the second pair of symbols in the Model Number indicate body style. The next letter (sixth symbol of VIN) shows the assembly plant code with Chevy II production limited to factories coded W=Willow Run, Mich., and N=Norwood, Ohio. The last six numbers were the sequential production code starting with 100001 at each plant. A Fisher Body Style plate is under the hood on left and gives Style Number, Body Number, Trim Code and Paint Code.

CHEVY II ALL SERIES

Model No.	Model No. (6-CYL)	Body Type & Seating	Factory Price	Shipping Weight	Prod. Total
SERIES 100 (4-CYL)/SERIES 100 (6-CYL)					
0169	0269	4-dr Sed-6P	2048/2108	2495/2580	Note 1
0111	0211	2-dr Sed-6P	2011/2070	2455/2540	Note 1
N/A	0235	4-dr Sta Wag-6P	N/A/2406	N/A/ 2840	Note 1
NOVA 400 SERIES (6-CYL)					
N/A	0469	4-dr Sed-6P	N/A/2243	N/A/2595	Note 1
N/A	0411	2-dr Sed-6P	N/A/2206	N/A/2560	Note 1
N/A	0437	2-dr Spt Cpe-5P	N/A/2271	N/A/2660	Note 1
N/A	0435	4-dr Sta Wag-6P	N/A/2503	N/A/2860	Note 1
NOVA SUPER SPORT SERIES					
N/A	0447	2-dr Spt Cpe-4P	N/A/2433	N/A/2675	Note 1

1964 Chevrolet, Chevy II Nova four-door sedan, 6-cyl

NOTE 1: Production was recorded only by body styles, as follows; four-door sedan - 84,846; two-door sedan - 40,348; four-door station wagon - 35,670 and two-door Sport Coupe - 30,827.

NOTE 2: Industry production figures vary by source. One indicates 165,487 sixes; 1,121 fours and 25,083 V-8s. Another indicates 800 fours in the 100 series, 52,300 cars in the 100 series, 102,900 cars in the Nova Series (including Super Sports) and 35,700 station wagons. Apparently, the new V-8 option caused some confusion in record keeping.

NOTE 3: Data above slash for four/below slash for six. A V-8 was optional.

NOTE 4: Top section of charts shows four-cylinder Model Number in first column; six-cylinder Model Number in second column. The Series 100 station wagon and all Novas were available with the base six or optional V-8, but not with the four-cylinder engine.

CHEVELLE/MALIBU — ALL SERIES — Anticipating a general improvement in the market for cars priced and sized below regular models, Chevrolet introduced its all-new Chevelle, a car that fit between the compact Chevy II and full-size models, and was soon being called a "senior compact." Assembly was quartered at plants in Baltimore and Kansas City and a brand new factory in Fremont, Calif. The car was styled with square looking lines in the Chevy II model, but curved side window glass and an emphasis on width provided a distinctive look. Eleven models were available in two basic lines called Chevelle 300 and Chevelle Malibu, with a convertible as an exclusive upper level offering. Base editions lacked bodyside moldings. Malibu models had a full-length strip of bright metal along the lower beltline, with an insert at the rear and Malibu rear fender script. A Super Sport option was released and cars so-equipped had no lower belt trim. Instead, there was a molding running along the full-length of the upper body ridge and continuing along the rear fender edge, plus SS rear fender and rear panel badges and specifically styled wheel covers. Bucket front seats were popular features in the Chevelle Malibu Super Sport.

1964 Chevrolet, Chevelle 300 two-door station wagon, 6-cyl

CHEVELLE/MALIBU I.D. NUMBERS: Vehicle numbers were on the left front body hinge pillar. Engine numbers, for both engines, were on the right side of the block to the rear of the distributor. The first VIN symbol was a '4' indicating the 1964 model year. This was followed by four symbols shown in charts below as Model Numbers. The first pair of symbols in these Model Numbers indicate the series (53=Chevelle six-cylinder; 54=Chevelle V-8; 55=Malibu six-cylinder; 56=Malibu V-8; 57=Malibu SS six-cylinder; 58=Malibu SS V-8) and the second pair of symbols in the Model Number indicate body style. The next letter (sixth symbol of VIN) shows the assembly plant code with Chevelle production limited to factories coded B (Baltimore, Md.); K (Kansas City, Mo.) and Z (Fremont, Calif.). The last six numbers were the sequential production code starting with 100001 at each plant. A Fisher Body Style plate is under the hood on left and gives Style Number, Body Number, Trim Code and Paint Code.

CHEVELLE/MALIBU ALL SERIES

Model No.	Model No. (V-8)	Body Type & Seating	Factory Price	Shipping Weight	Prod. Total
SERIES 300 (6-CYL)/SERIES 300 (V-8)					
5369	5469	4-dr Sed-6P	2268/2376	2850/2980	Note 1
5311	5411	2-dr Sed-6P	2231/2339	2825/2955	Note 1
5335	5435	4-dr Sta Wag-6P	2566/2674	3130/3250	Note 1
5315	5415	2-dr Sta Wag-6P	2528/2636	3050/3170	Note 1
MALIBU SERIES (6-CYL)/MALIBU SERIES (V-8)					
5569	5669	4-dr Sed-6P	2349/2457	2870/2995	Note 1
5537	5637	2-dr Spt Cpe-5P	2376/2484	2850/2975	Note 1
5567	5667	2-dr Conv-5P	2587/2695	2995/3120	Note 1
5545	5645	4-dr Sta Wag-8P	2744/2852	3240/3365	Note 1
5535	5635	2-dr Sta Wag-6P	2647/2755	3140/3265	Note 1

1964 Chevrolet, Chevelle Malibu 'SS' two-door hardtop (Sport Coupe), V-8

NOTE 1: Production was recorded by body style, as follows: two-door Sport Coupe - 134,670; four-door sedan - 113,816; four-door station wagon - 41,374; two-door convertible - 23,158; two-door sedan - 22,568 and two-door station wagon - 2,710.

NOTE 2: Industry statistical breakouts show 142,034 Chevelle sixes and 196,252 Chevelle V-8s were built.

NOTE 3: Additional statistics record series production, in rounded-off figures, as follows (Chevelle 300) 53,000 sixes and 15,300 V-8s; (Malibu) 62,100 sixes and 86,900 V-8s; (Malibu SS) 67,100 V-8s and (station wagons) 17,100 sixes and 26,900 V-8s.

NOTE 4: Data above slash for six/below slash for V-8.

NOTE 5: First column on chart shows Model Numbers for sixes and the second column on chart shows Model Numbers for V-8s.

BISCAYNE — SERIES 1100 (6-CYL) — SERIES 1200 (V-8) — This was Chevrolet's most inexpensive line. Standard features included heater and defroster; dual sun visors; color-keyed floor carpeting; foam-cushioned seats; cigarette lighter; glove compartment lock; dual-spoke steering wheel with horn ring; front and rear armrests; ashtray; crank-operated ventipanes and two coat hooks. Interiors were trimmed in patterned cloth and leather grain vinyl combinations, with all-vinyl door panels and embossed vinyl headliners. Spatter pattern paint was used in the luggage compartment. Exterior bright metal decoration included a full-length lower body molding; rear cove upper molding; twin-style taillights; hood and deck emblems and nameplates; Biscayne rear fender signatures with Chevrolet emblems; small wheel center hubcaps; and bright windshield, rear window and ventipane frames.

CHEVROLET I.D. NUMBERS: Serial numbers were stamped on a plate affixed to the left front door hinge pillar. The first VIN symbol identified the model year:

4=1964. The second and third symbols identified the series (see first two digits of Model Number columns in charts below). The fourth and fifth symbols identified body style (see last two digits of Model Number columns in charts below). The sixth symbol, a letter, indicated assembly plant, as follows: A=Atlanta, Ga.; H=Baltimore, Md.; F=Flint, Mich.; G=Framingham, Mass.; H=Fremont, Calif.; J=Janesville, Wis.; K=Kansas City, Mo.; L=Los Angeles, Calif.; N=Norwood, Ohio; O=Oakland, Calif.; R=Arlington, Texas; S=St. Louis, Mo.; T=Tarrytown, N.Y.; U=Southgate, Calif.; W=Willow Run, Mich.; Y=Wilmington, Del. The last six symbols are the sequential production number, with numbers for each series at each factory starting at 100001 and up. Fisher Body plate attached to left-hand cowl starts with two-digit model year prefix (64-) and Fisher Body/Style Number (Model Number) and also shows factory code production sequence trim and body color data. Engine numbers: (six) right side of block behind distributor; (V-8) right front of engine block.

BISCAYNE SERIES

Model No.	Model No. (V-8)	Body Type & Seating	Factory Price	Shipping Weight	Prod. Total
1169	1269	4-dr Sed-6P	2417/2524	3300/3430	Note 1
1111	1211	2-dr Sed-6P	2363/2471	3230/3365	Note 1
1135	1235	4-dr Sta Wag-6P	2763/2671	3700/3820	Note 1

NOTE 1: Production (for all full-size Chevrolets) was recorded by body style only as follows: four-door sedan - 536,329; two-door Sport Coupe - 442,292; four-door Sport Sedan - 200,172; four-door station wagon - 192,627; two-door sedan - 120,951 and two-door convertible - 81,897.

NOTE 2: Breakouts show 383,647 Chevrolet sixes and 1,190,621 Chevrolet V-8s were built.

NOTE 3: Rounded-off series production figures were: (Biscayne six) 132,500; (Biscayne V-8) 41,400; (station wagon six) 39,700 and (station wagon V-8) 153,100. The station wagon totals are for Chevrolet wagons of all trim levels and not just Biscaynes.

NOTE 4: Data above slash for six/below slash for V-8.

NOTE 5: First column in chart above shows six-cylinder Model Number; second column shows V-8 Model Number.

BEL AIR — SERIES 1500 (6-CYL) — SERIES 1600 (V-8) —

Chevrolet's middle-priced line had less exterior distinction, but a plusher interior for 1964. Standard equipment included all the Biscayne features listed above, plus bright door trim accents; plastic cowl side panels with molded-in ventilation grilles; a bright instrument panel molding; glove compartment light; dome light door switches; Deluxe quality interior handles; and a patterned rubber luggage compartment mat. Interior trim was of a brighter color-keyed patterned cloth and leather grained vinyl combination on the seats, with all-vinyl door panels and embossed headliner. A narrow, full-length upper body bright molding and a slender body sill molding were used. Bel Air script and Chevrolet badges appeared on the rear fenders. Dual rear cove moldings were used, with twin-unit taillights. Bright roof drip cap moldings were a Bel Air feature.

1964 Chevrolet, Impala six-passenger station wagon, V-8

BEL AIR SERIES

Model No.	Model No. (V-8)	Body Type & Seating	Factory Price	Shipping Weight	Prod. Total
1569	1669	4-dr Sed-6P	2519/2626	3305/3440	Note 1
1511	1611	2-dr Sed-6P	2465/2573	3235/3370	Note 1
1535	1635	4-dr Sta Wag-6P	2626/2935	3705/3825	Note 1
1545	1645	4-dr Sta Wag-9P	2931/3039	3645/3665	Note 1

NOTE 1: Production (for all full-size Chevrolets) was recorded by body style only, as follows: four-door sedan - 536,329; two-door Sport Coupe - 442,292; four-door Sport Sedan - 200,172; four-door station wagon - 192,627; two-door sedan - 120,951 and two-door convertible - 81,897.

NOTE 2: Breakouts show 383,647 Chevrolet sixes and 1,190,821 Chevrolet V-8s were built.

NOTE 3: In rounded-off figures Bel Air production, by series, was as follows: (Bel Air six) 137,800 and (Bel Air V-8) 180,300. Bel Air station wagons are included in combined total previously noted.

NOTE 4: Data above slash for six/below slash for V-8.

NOTE 5: First column in chart above shows six-cylinder Model Number; second column shows V-8 Model Number.

IMPALA — SERIES 1700 (6-CYL) — SERIES 1800 (V-8) —

The separation of Impala Super Sport models into their own series made the regular Impala the second most expensive Chevrolet line for 1964. Standard equipment included most features found on lower-priced lines, plus extra-thick foam cushion seats; bright aluminum front seat end panels; bright instrument panel insert with nameplate molding; electric clock; parking brake warning light; Impala center emblem on steering wheel; chrome-backed rearview mirror; specific paddle-type front and rear armrests (with fingertip door release lever); dual dome lights; bright windshield, rear window and upper side window interior garnish moldings; and an automatic luggage compartment light. Interiors were of cloth and leather grain vinyl in a more intricate design, with bright-accented all-vinyl door panels and vinyl embossed headliner (convertible and station wagons had all-vinyl trim). Exterior trim included color-accented bodyside moldings; hood and deck windsplit moldings; rear cove outline moldings; satin-finish anodized cove insert; triple unit taillights (with back-up light built in); Impala lettering and emblem on rear fenders; roof rail and drip cap moldings; bright door windows glass edges (hardtop styles); and bright belt moldings.

1964 Chevrolet, Impala two-door hardtop (Sport Coupe), V-8

IMPALA SERIES

Model No.	Model No. (V-8)	Body Type & Seating	Factory Price	Shipping Weight	Prod. Total
1769	1869	4-dr Sed-6P	2671/2779	3340/3460	Note 1
1739	1839	4-dr HT Spt Sed-6P	2742/2850	3370/3490	Note 1
1747	1847	2-dr HT Spt Cpe-6P	2678/2786	3295/3415	Note 1
1767	1867	2-dr Conv-6P	2927/3035	3400/3525	Note 1
1735	1835	4-dr Sta Wag-6P	2970/3077	3725/3850	Note 1
1745	1845	4-dr Sta Wag-9P	3073/3181	3770/3895	Note 1

NOTE 1: Production (for all full-size Chevrolets) was recorded by body style only, as follows: four-door sedan - 536,329; two-door Sport Coupe - 442,292; four-door Sport Sedan - 200,172; four-door station wagon - 192,827; two-door sedan - 120,951 and two-door convertible - 81,897.

NOTE 2: Breakouts show 383,647 Chevrolet sixes and 1,190,821 Chevrolet V-8s were built.

NOTE 3: Production in rounded-off figures was as follows: (Impala six) 73,600 and (Impala V-8) 616,000. Impala station wagons are included in combined total for all wagons.

NOTE 4: Data above slash for six/below slash for V-8.

NOTE 5: First column in chart above shows six-cylinder Model Number; second column shows V-8 Model Number.

1964 Chevrolet, Malibu SS two-door convertible, V-8

IMPALA SUPER SPORT — SERIES 1300 (6-CYL) — SERIES 1400 (V-8) — Chevrolet's plushest and most sporting model was available only in two-door styles. Standard equipment approximated that of the Impala, with added interior features including leather grained vinyl upholstery with individual front bucket seats and locking compartment in a center console. Swirl-pattern instrument panel inserts and moldings were used. A built-in rear seat radio speaker grille was featured. Dual dome and floor courtesy lamps, with automatic door switches or manual instrument panel controls were used. Door safety reflectors were found on the all-vinyl door panels. Special SS emblems appeared on the console and door panels. Exterior distinction came from the use of a wider upper body molding, filled with a swirl-pattern silver anodized insert. Impala lettering and the SS badge appeared on the rear fenders, with another badge appearing on the deck lid. The rear cove outline moldings were filled with silver anodized inserts. Full wheel covers of specific Super Sport design were used.

IMPALA SUPER SPORT SERIES

Model No.	Model No. (V-8)	Body Type & Seating	Factory Price	Shipping Weight	Prod. Total
1347	1447	2-dr HT Spt Cpe-5P	2839/2947	3325/3450	Note 1
1367	1467	2-dr Conv-5P	3068/3196	3435/3555	Note 1

1964 Chevrolet, Impala SS two-door hardtop (Sport Coupe), V-8

NOTE 1: Chevrolet Motor Division recorded the production of 185,325 Impala Super Sport models in 1964. There is no breakout, by body style, available. It is most likely that six to 10 percent of these units were convertibles and the rest two-door hardtop Sport Coupes.

NOTE 2: A total of 8,684 Chevrolets were equipped with 409-cid engines during the 1964 model run, the majority being Impala Super Sports.

CHEVY II ENGINES

FOUR-CYLINDER: Overhead valve. Cast iron block. Displacement: 153 cid. Bore and stroke: 3.875 x 2.35 inches. Compression ratio: 8.5:1. Brake horsepower: 90 at 4000 rpm. Five main bearings. Hydraulic valve lifters. Carburetor: Carter one-barrel Model 3379.

SIX-CYLINDER: Overhead valve. Cast iron block. Displacement: 194.4 cid. Bore and stroke: 3.562 x 3.25 inches. Compression ratio: 8.5:1. Brake horsepower: 120 at 4400 rpm. Seven main bearings. Hydraulic valve lifters. Carburetor: Rochester one-barrel Model 7023105.

CHEVELLE ENGINES

SIX-CYLINDER: Overhead valve. Cast iron block. Displacement: 194.4 cid. Bore and stroke: 3.562 x 3.25 inches. Compression ratio: 8.5:1. Brake horsepower: 120 at 4400 rpm. Seven main bearings. Hydraulic valve lifters. Carburetor: Rochester one-barrel Model 7023105.

V-8: Overhead valve. Cast iron block. Displacement: 283 cid. Bore and stroke: 3.875 x 3.00 inches. Compression ratio: 9.25:1. Brake horsepower: 195 at 4800 rpm. Four main bearings. Hydraulic valve lifters. Carburetor: Rochester one-barrel Model 7024101.

CHEVROLET ENGINES

SIX-CYLINDER: Overhead valve. Cast iron block. Displacement: 230 cid. Bore and stroke: 3.875 x 3.25 inches. Compression ratio: 9.25:1. Brake horsepower: 140 at 4400 rpm. Seven main bearings. Hydraulic valve lifters. Carburetor: Rochester one-barrel Model 7023003.

V-8: Overhead valve. Cast iron block. Displacement: 283 cid. Bore and stroke: 3.875 x 3.00 inches. Compression ratio: 9.25:1. Brake horsepower: 195 at 4800 rpm. Five main bearings. Hydraulic valve lifters. Carburetor: Rochester two-barrel Model 7023007.

CHEVY II/NOVA POWERTRAIN OPTIONS: Optional engines for 1964 were:

CID	Comp. Ratio	Carb Barrels	Exhaust	HP @ rpm	Trans Combo	Valve Lifters
(SIX)						
230	6.5	1V	1	155 @ 4400	M/A	H
(V-8)						
283	9.25	2V	1	195 @ 4800	M/A	H

NOTE: V=venturi; 1=single exhaust; M=manual transmission; A=automatic transmission; H=hydraulic valve lifters.

CHEVELLE/MALIBU POWERTRAIN OPTIONS: Optional engines for 1964 were:

CID	Comp. Ratio	Carb Barrels	Exhaust	HP @ rpm	Trans Combo	Valve Lifters
(SIX)						
230	8.5	1V	1	155 @ 4400	M/A	H
(V-8)						
283	9.25	4V	2	220 @ 4800	M/A	H
327	10.5	4V	1	250 @ 4400	M/A	H
327	10.5	4V	2	300 @ 5000	M/A	H

NOTE: V=venturi; 1=single exhaust; 2=dual exhaust; M=manual transmission; A=automatic transmission; H=hydraulic valve lifters.

CHEVROLET POWERTRAIN OPTIONS: Optional V-8 engines for 1964 were:

CID	Comp. Ratio	Carb Barrels	Exhaust	HP @ rpm	Trans Combo	Valve Lifters
327	10.5	4V	2	250 @ 4400	M/A	H
327	10.5	4V	2	300 @ 5000	M/A	H
327	10.5	4V	2	340 @ 6000	M/A	S
409	11.0	4V	2	400 @ 5800	M	S
409	11.0	2x4V	2	425 @ 6000	M	S

NOTE: V=venturi; 1=single exhaust; 2=dual exhaust; 2 x 4V=dual four-barrel carburetor; M=manual transmission; A=automatic transmission; H=hydraulic valve lifters; S=solid valve lifters.

1964 Chevrolet, Impala six-passenger station wagon, V-8

CHASSIS FEATURES: Wheelbase: (Chevy II) 110 inches; (Chevelle) 115 inches; (Chevrolet) 119 inches. Overall length: (Chevy II station wagon) 167.6 inches; (Chevy II) 182.9 inches; (Chevelle station wagon) 198.8 inches; (Chevelle) 193.9 inches; (Chevrolet station wagon) 210.8 inches; (Chevrolet) 209.9 inches. Width: (Chevy II) 69.9 inches; (Chevelle) 74.6 inches; (Chevrolet) 79.6 inches. Tires: (Chevy II station wagons and Novas) 6.50 x 13; (Chevy II) 6.00 x 13; (Chevelle station wagons) 7.00 x 14; (Chevelles) 6.50 x 14; (Chevrolet station wagons) 8.00 x 14; (Chevrolet convertibles) 7.00 x 14; (other Chevrolets) 7.00 x 14.

CHEVY II/NOVA OPTIONS: Air conditioning ($317). Rear armrests ($10). Pair of front seat belts ($19). Heavy-duty brakes ($38). Comfort and Convenience Group, on Nova ($28); on others ($39). Tinted glass, all windows ($27); windshield only ($13). Grille guard ($15). Rear bumper guard ($10). Padded dash ($16). Station wagon roof luggage rack ($43). Two-tone paint, except convertible ($11). Power brakes ($3). Power steering ($75). Power tailgate window ($27). Power convertible top ($54). Push-button radio with antenna and rear speaker ($70). Manual radio and antenna ($46). Push-button radio and antenna ($57). Station wagon divided second seat ($38). Super Sport equipment for Nova Sport Coupe and convertible ($161). Full wheel covers ($13). Wire design wheel covers ($13). Various whitewall and oversize tire options ($9-$42). Positraction rear axle ($33). Heavy-duty clutch ($5). Delcotron 42-amp generator ($11). Heavy-duty radiator ($3). Powerglide transmission ($167).

CHEVELLE/MALIBU OPTIONS: Air conditioning ($317). Rear armrests ($10). Pair of front seat belts ($19). Heavy-duty brakes ($38). Comfort and Convenience Group, on Nova ($26); on others ($39). Tinted glass, all windows ($27); windshield only ($13). Grille guard ($15). Rear bumper guard ($10). Padded dash ($16). Station wagon roof luggage rack ($43). Two-tone paint, except convertible ($11). Power brakes ($3). Power steering ($75). Power tailgate window ($27). Power convertible top ($54). Push-button radio with antenna and rear speaker ($70). Manual radio and antenna ($48). Push-button radio and antenna ($57). Station wagon divided second seat ($38). Super Sport equipment for Nova Sport Coupe and convertible ($161). Full wheel covers ($13). Wire design wheel covers ($13). Various whitewall and oversize tire options ($9-$42). Positraction rear axle ($38). Heavy-duty clutch ($5). Delcotron 42-amp generator ($11). Heavy-duty radiator ($3). Powerglide transmission ($167). The 230 cid/155 hp six-cylinder engine with one-barrel carburetor was $43 extra. The 283-cid/220 hp V-8 with four-barrel carburetor and 9.25:1 compression returned as a $54 extra. The 327 cid/250 hp V-8 with four-barrel carburetor and 10.5:1 compression was $95 extra. The 327 cid/300 hp V-8 with four-barrel carburetor and 10.5:1 compression was a $138 option.

CHEVROLET OPTIONS: Deluxe air conditioning, including heater ($364). Cool Pack air conditioning ($317). Driver's seat belt ($10). Pair of front seat belts ($19). Heavy-duty brakes with metallic facings ($36). Comfort and Convenience Group, for Impala ($31); for Bel Air ($41); for Biscayne ($44). Biscayne front air foam seat cushion ($6). Tinted glass, all windows ($36); windshield only ($22). Grille guard ($19). Passenger car rear bumper guard ($10). Padded dash ($18). Station wagon luggage locker ($11). Station wagon luggage carrier ($43). Two-tone paint ($16). Power brakes ($43). Six-Way power seat ($97). Power steering, except Biscayne ($75). Power tailgate window ($32). Power windows, except Biscayne ($102). Manual radio ($46). Push-button radio ($57). Push-button radio with antenna and rear speaker ($70). Vinyl roof for Impala Sport Coupe ($75). Station wagon divided second seat ($38). Deluxe steering wheel ($4). Super Sport equipment package ($161). Tachometer with V-8s ($48). Wheel discs ($18). Wire wheel discs on Super Sport ($25); on others ($43). Two-speed electric washers and wipers ($17). Tilt Steering. Turbo-Fire 327 cid/250 hp V-8 with four-barrel carburetor and dual exhaust ($191). Turbo-Fire 327 cid/300 hp V-8 with four-barrel carburetor and dual exhaust ($245). Turbo-Fire 327 cid/340 hp V-8 with four-barrel carburetor and dual exhaust ($349). Turbo-Fire 409 cid/400 hp V-8 with four-barrel carburetor, dual exhaust, high-lift camshaft and solid valve lifters ($428). Turbo-Fire 409 cid/425 hp V-8 with dual four-barrel carburetors, dual exhaust, high-lift camshaft and solid valve lifters ($484). Overdrive transmission with six-cylinder or 283-cid V-8 engines ($108). Six-cylinder Powerglide ($188). Powerglide with 283 cid/327 cid V-8s ($199). Close-ratio four-speed manual transmission with 250 horsepower V-8 ($188). Four-speed transmission with 340/400/425 horsepower V-8s ($237). Positraction rear axle ($43). Delcotron 42-amp generator standard with air conditioning, optional on others at ($11). Heavy-duty radiator ($11). Heavy-duty battery, standard with 340 horsepower V-8, optional on others at ($3). Six-cylinder temperature controlled cooling fan ($16). Delcotron 52-amp generator ($32). Delcotron 62-amp generator ($65-$75).

HISTORICAL FOOTNOTES: Dealer introductions of new Chevrolet cars occurred on Sept. 28, 1964. Model year sales for the Chevrolet Motor Division totaled 2,125,200 cars. Semon E. Knudsen remained as general manager of Chevrolet Division.

1965

BISCAYNE — (6-CYL/V-8) — SERIES 153/154 — Chevrolets had larger bodies for 1965. A new stamped grille had a lower extension below the bumper, which was slightly veed. Curved window glass and taillamps mounted high at the rear characterized the new styling. Rear fender lines had a prominent kick up and a blunter and more rounded shape. Biscaynes had thin body sill moldings, thin rear fender ridge moldings, bright windshield moldings and dual style rear lamps with the Biscayne script on the rear quarters. Standard equipment for all Biscaynes included heater and defroster; foam-cushioned front seat; oil filter; electric wipers; front seat belts and five blackwall tires. Convertibles and all 327-cid V-8 cars had 7.75 x 14 tires, station wagons and 409-cid V-8 cars had a 8.25 x 14 tires. Interiors were vinyl and pattern cloth (all-vinyl on station wagons).

CHEVROLET I.D. NUMBERS: The Vehicle Identification Number was located on plate attached to left front door hinge pillar. The number had 13 symbols. The first symbol is a 1 for Chevrolet; the second and third symbols indicate series and the fourth and fifth symbols indicate body type. (Together, these first five symbols comprised the model number and appear in the Body/Style Number column of charts below). The sixth symbol indicated model year: 5=1965. The seventh symbol indicated assembly plant: A=Atlanta, Ga.; B=Baltimore, Md.; C=Southgate, Calif.; F=Flint, Mich.; G=Framingham, Mass.; J=Janesville, Wis.; K=Kansas City, Mo.; L=Los Angeles, Calif.; N=Norwood, Ohio; R=Arlington, Texas; S= St. Louis, Mo.; T=Tarrytown, N.Y.; W=Willow Run, Mich.; Y=Wilmington, Del.; Z=Fremont, Calif.; 1=Oshawa, Ontario (Canada); 2=St. Therese, Quebec (Canada) and P=Pontiac, Mich. The last six symbols were the sequential number. A Fisher Body Number tag on the cowl gives the style number, body number, trim and paint codes. Engine codes appear on the right side of six-cylinder blocks behind the distributor and right front of V-8 engine blocks: CHEVY II (153 cid/90 hp four) OA, OC, OG, OH, OJ; (194 cid/120 hp six) OK, ON, OQ, OR; (230 cid/140 hp six) PA, PC, PV, PX, PI; (283 cid/195 hp V-8) PD, PF, PL, PM, PN, PP; (283 cid/220 hp V-8) PB, PE, PG, PK, PO, PQ; (327 cid/250 hp V-8) ZA, ZE, ZK, ZM; (327 cid/300 hp V-8) ZB, ZF, ZL, ZN; CHEVELLE (194 cid/120 hp six) AA, AC, AG, AH, AK, AL, AN, AR;

(230 cid/140 hp six) BK, BN, BY, BZ, CA, CB, CC, CD; (283 cid/195 hp V-8) DA, DB, DE; (283 cid/220 hp V-8) DG, DH; (327 cid/250 hp V-8) EA, EE; (327 cid/300 hp V-8) ED, EF; (327 cid/350 hp V-8) EC, ED; (396 cid/375 hp V-8) IX. CHEVROLET (230 cid/140 hp six) FA, FE, FF, FK, FL, FM, FP, FR; (250 cid/150 hp six) FY, FZ; (283 cid/195 hp V-8) GA, GO, GF; (283 cid/220 hp V-8) GK, GL; (327 cid/250 hp V-8) HA, HC; (327 cid/300 hp V-8) HB, HD; (396 cid/325 hp V-8) IA, IB, IC, IE, IF, IG, II, IV, IW; (409 cid/340 hp V-8) JB, JC, JE, JF; (409 cid/400 hp V-8) JA, JD.

BISCAYNE SERIES

Model No.	Body/Style No.	Body Type & Seating	Factory Price	Shipping Weight	Prod. Total
153/4	15369	4-dr Sed-6P	2417/2524	3365/3515	Note 1
153/4	15311	2-dr Sed-6P	2363/2470	3305/3455	Note 1
153/4	15335	4-drSta Wag-6P	2417/2671	3765/3900	Note 2

NOTE 1: Some 107,700 six-cylinder and 37,600 V-8 Biscaynes were built. Total production, in figures rounded-off to the nearest 100 units, was 145,300 excluding station wagons.

NOTE 2: Some 29,400 six-cylinder and 155,000 V-8 Chevrolet station wagons were built during the 1965 model year. Total station wagon output, in figures rounded-off to the nearest 100 units, was 164,400 cars. This includes Biscayne, Bel Air and Impala station wagons.

NOTE 3: V-8s have the number '6' as the third digit of their series, model and serial number.

NOTE 4: Prices and weights above slash for six/below slash for V-8.

BEL AIR — (6-CYL/V-8) — SERIES 155/156 — External decor on the Bel Air included a narrow full-length bodyside molding; roof drip rail moldings; rear accent band; and Bel Air script (with Chevrolet emblems on rear quarters). All features found on Biscaynes were included, plus a glove compartment light and power tailgate window on nine-passenger station wagons. Interiors were plusher, with vinyl and pattern cloth trims.

BEL AIR SERIES

Model No.	Body/Style No.	Body Type & Seating	Factory Price	Shipping Weight	Prod. Total
155/6	15569	4-dr Sed-6P	2519/2626	3380/3530	Note 1
155/6	15511	2-dr Sed-6P	2465/2573	3310/3460	Note 1
155/6	15535	4-drSta Wag-6P	2970/2936	3810/3950	Note 2
155/6	15545	4-dr Sta Wag-6P	3073/3039	3765/3905	Note 2

NOTE 1: Some 107,600 six-cylinder and 163,600 V-8 Bel Airs were built. Total production, in figures rounded-off to the nearest 100 units, was 271,400, excluding station wagons (all full-sized Chevrolet station wagons being contained in a separate series).

NOTE 2: Some 29,400 six-cylinder and 155,000 V-8 Chevrolet station wagons were built during the 1965 model year. Total station wagon output, in figures rounded-off to the nearest 100 units, was 184,400 cars. This includes Biscayne, Bel Air and Impala station wagons.

NOTE 3: V-8s have the number '6' as the third digit of their series, model and serial number.

1965 Chevrolet, Impala two-door hardtop (Sport Coupe), V-8 (PH)

NOTE 4: Prices and weights above slash for six/below slash for V-8.

IMPALA — (6-CYL/V-8) — SERIES 163/164 — Impala features included wide lower, bright bodyside moldings (with rear fender extensions); bright wheelhouse moldings; bright rear cover panel trim; triple-unit taillamps and full wheel covers. Interiors were more detailed and plusher. Instrument panels had bright center panel moldings and woodgrained lower panel facings. Bright garnish moldings were seen. Extra features included on Impala were electric clock; parking brake light; trunk and back-up lights. Luxurious vinyl/pattern cloth trim combinations were used in pillared sedan models. Both convertibles and station wagons featured all-vinyl trims. Black, all-vinyl upholstery was available in Sport Coupes and pillarless Sport Sedans. The four-door (hardtop) Sport Sedans had dual roof side rail lamps.

1965 Chevrolet, Impala four-door hardtop (Sport Sedan), V-8 (PH)

IMPALA SERIES

Model No.	Body/Style No.	Body Type & Seating	Factory Price	Shipping Weight	Prod. Total
163/4	16369	4-dr Sed-6P	2672/2779	3460/3595	Note 1
163/4	16337	2-dr HT-6P	2676/2785	3385/3630	Note 1
163/4	16339	4-dr HT-6P	2742/2850	3490/3525	Note 1
163/4	16367	2-dr Conv-6P	2943/3051	3470/3605	Note 2
163/4	16335	4-dr Sta Wag-6P	2970/3076	3625/3960	Note 2
163/4	16345	4-dr Sta Wag-9P	3073/3181	3865/4005	Note 2

NOTE 1: Some 56,600 six-cylinder and 746,800 V-8 Impalas were built. Total production, in figures rounded off to the nearest 100 units, was 803,400 excluding station wagons (all full-sized Chevrolet station wagons were contained in a separate series).

NOTE 2: A total of 72,760 full-sized Chevrolet convertibles were built, including both Impalas and Impala Super Sports. About 45,800 of these were Impalas and about 27,000 were Impala Super Sports.

NOTE 3: V-8s have the number '4' as the third digit of their series, model and serial number.

NOTE 4: Prices and weights above slash for six/below slash for V-8.

1965 Chevrolet, Impala two-door convertible, V-8

CAPRICE CUSTOM SEDAN OPTION PACKAGE: RPO Z18 was the Caprice Custom Sedan option for Model 16439 (Impala four-door hardtop) and included a heavier stiffer frame, suspension changes, black-accented front grille and rear trim panel with Caprice nameplate, slender body sill moldings, Fleur-de-lis roof quarter emblems, color-keyed bodyside stripes, specific full wheel covers and Caprice hood and dash emblems.

IMPALA SUPER SPORT — (6-CYL/V-8) — SERIES 165/166 — The prestige Chevrolet was noted by its bright wheelhouse moldings (without bright lower body moldings); Super Sport front fender script; black-filled rear cove band with Impala SS badge at right; and a similar badge on the radiator grille, at the left. Specific Super Sport full wheel covers were used. The SS interior featured full carpeting; all-vinyl trim with front bucket seats and bright seatback outline moldings; combination vinyl and carpet door trim (with bright accents); foam cushions; courtesy lights; SS identification on the door panels; and a console with a built-in, Rally-type clock. A vacuum gauge was standard as well.

IMPALA SUPER SPORT

Model No.	Body/Style No.	Body Type & Seating	Factory Price	Shipping Weight	Prod. Total
165/6	16537	2-dr HT-6P	2839/2947	3435/3570	Note 1
165/6	16567	2-dr Conv-6P	3104/3212	3505/3645	Note 2

NOTE 1: 3,600 six-cylinder and 239,500 V-8 Impala Super Sports were built. Total production was exactly 243,114 units.

NOTE 2: Approximately 27,000 Impala Super Sport convertibles were built.

NOTE 3: V-8 models have the numeral '6' as the third digit of their series, style and serial number.

CHEVELLE 300 — (6-CYL/V-8) — SERIES 131/132 — Chevelles were mildly restyled for their second year. The nose was veed slightly outward and a new grille was used. At the rear were new taillamps. 300 models had lower body sill moldings; Chevelle 300 rear fender nameplates and emblems; bright ventipanes; wind-

shield and rear window reveal moldings; single unit taillamps with bright bezels; rear bumper back-up light opening covers; and small hubcaps. Interiors were pattern cloth and vinyl trim (all vinyl on station wagons) in a standard grade, with vinyl floor covering. Standard equipment included heater and defroster; front foam cushions; electric windshield wipers; front seat belts; and five 6.95 x 14 blackwall tires (station wagons had 7.35 x 14 blackwall tires).

CHEVELLE 300

Model No.	Body/Style No.	Body Type & Seating	Factory Price	Shipping Weight	Prod. Total
131/2	13169	4-dr Sed-6P	2193/2251	2910/3035	Note 1
131/2	13111	2-dr Sed-6P	2156/2215	2870/3010	Note 1
131/2	13115	2-dr Sta Wag-6P	2453/2505	3185/3275	Note 2

NOTE 1: Some 26,500 Chevelle 300 sixes and 5,100 V-8s were built. Total production, in figures rounded-off to the nearest 100 units, was 31,600 cars, excluding station wagons (all Chevelle station wagons being contained in a separate series).

NOTE 2: Some 13,800 six-cylinder and 23,800 V-8 Chevelle station wagons were built during the 1965 model year. Total Chevelle station wagon output, in figures rounded-off to the nearest 100 units, was 37,600 cars. This includes all station wagons in the Chevelle 300, Chevelle 300 Deluxe and Chevelle Malibu Series.

NOTE 3: V-8s have the number '2' as the third digit of their series, model and serial number.

NOTE 4: Prices and weights above slash for six/below slash for V-8.

CHEVELLE 300 DELUXE — (6-CYL/V-8) — SERIES 133/134 — Chevelle 300 Deluxe models had higher bright bodyside trim strips; Chevelle 300 rear fender emblems; roof drip cap moldings; and rear cove outline moldings (except station wagons). Interiors were a plusher vinyl and cloth with all-vinyl door trim and a unique dual-spoke steering wheel with horn ring. Standard equipment, in addition to that found on the Chevelle 300, included padded armrests.

CHEVELLE 300 DELUXE

Model No.	Body/Style No.	Body Type & Seating	Factory Price	Shipping Weight	Prod. Total
133/4	13369	4-dr Sed-6P	2220/2236	2910/3050	Note 1
133/4	13311	2-dr Sed-6P	2163/2266	2870/3010	Note 1
133/4	13335	4-dr Sta Wag-6P	2511/2616	3165/3320	Note 2

1965 Chevrolet, Chevelle Malibu two-door hardtop, V-8

NOTE 1: Some 32,000 six-cylinder and 9,600 V-8 Chevelle 300 Deluxes were built. Total production, in figures rounded-off to the nearest 100, was 41,600 cars, excluding station wagons (all Chevelle station wagons being contained in a separate series).

NOTE 2: Some 13,800 six-cylinder and 23,800 V-8 Chevelle station wagons were built during the 1965 model year. Total Chevelle station wagon output, in figures rounded-off to the nearest 100 units, was 37,600 cars. This includes all station wagons in the Chevelle 300, Chevelle 300 Deluxe and Chevelle Malibu series.

NOTE 3: V-8s have the number '4' as the third digit of their series, model and serial number.

NOTE 4: Prices and weights above slash for six/below slash for V-8.

CHEVELLE MALIBU — (6-CYL/V-8) — SERIES 135/136 —

Cars in the Malibu series had the following features added to, or replacing, 300 Deluxe equipment: color-accented bodyside moldings; bright wheelhouse moldings; Malibu rear fender script (with Chevelle emblems); hood windsplit moldings; ribbed upper and lower cove trim panels; ribbed tailgate lower trim panel on station wagon; back-up lights in rear bumper; luxurious pattern cloth and vinyl interior trims; color-keyed deep twist floor carpeting; foam cushioned rear seat; specific dual-spoke steering wheel (with horn ring); electric clock; bright glove compartment facing molding (with series nameplate); and glovebox light.

1965 Chevrolet, Chevelle Malibu SS two-door hardtop (Sport Coupe), V-8 (PH)

CHEVELLE MALIBU

Model No.	Body/Style No.	Body Type & Seating	Factory Price	Shipping Weight	Prod. Total
135/6	13569	4-dr Sed-6P	2299/2405	2945/3080	Note 1
135/6	13537	2-dr HT-6P	2326/2431	2930/3065	Note 1
135/6	13567	2-dr Conv-6P	2532/2637	3025/3160	Note 2
135/6	13535	4-dr Sta Wag-6P	2590/2695	3225/3355	Note 3

NOTE 1: Some 56,400 six-cylinder and 95,800 V-8 Malibus were built. Total production, in figures rounded-off to the nearest 100 units, was 152,200 cars, excluding station wagons (all Chevelle station wagons being contained in a separate series).

NOTE 2: Exactly 19,765 Chevelle convertibles were built during the 1965 model year. However, this total includes both Malibu and Malibu Super Sport convertibles.

NOTE 3: V-8s have the number '6' as the third digit of their series, model and serial number.

NOTE 4: Prices and weights above slash for six/below slash for V-8.

CHEVELLE SUPER SPORT — (6-CYL/V-8) — SERIES 137/138 —

A clean, sporty appearance was obtained by the use of wide bright body sill moldings; rear lower fender moldings; Malibu SS rear fender script; deck lid SS emblems; black-accented grille and rear cove (except silver rear cove with black exterior); specific Super Sport full wheel covers; front bucket seats with bright trim ends; center console with four-speed manual or automatic transmissions; and all-vinyl luxury interiors. Special instrument panel features included temperature, ammeter and oil pressure gauges.

CHEVELLE SS

Model No.	Body/Style No.	Body Type & Seating	Factory Price	Shipping Weight	Prod. Total
137/8	13737	2-dr HT-6P	2484/2590	2980/3115	Note 1
137/8	13767	2-dr Conv-6P	2690/2796	3075/3210	Note 2

NOTE 1: Some 58,600 six-cylinder and 72,500 V-8 Malibus were built. Total production, in figures rounded-off to the nearest 100, was 81,100 units.

NOTE 2: Exactly 19,765 Chevelle convertibles were built during the 1965 model year. However, this total included both Malibu and Malibu Super Sport convertibles.

NOTE 3: V-8s have the number '8' as the third digit of their series, model and serial number.

NOTE 4: Prices and weights above slash for six/below slash for V-8.

1965 Chevrolet, Chevelle Malibu SS two-door convertible, V-8

CHEVELLE SS-396

RPO Z16 was the midyear SS-396 package, which included a 396 cid/375 hp V-8 with dual exhaust and chrome accents; four-speed transmission; special shocks and suspension; 160 mph speedometer; and AM/FM stereo multiplex radio. Specific exterior trim included Malibu SS emblems mounted on front fenders, special rear cove panel and '396 Turbo-Jet' front fender emblems. An SS-396 emblem was mounted in the dash. Fifteen inch wide simulated mag style wheel covers were included. The cost for this option package was $1,501 and a total of just 201 cars were so-equipped.

CHEVELLE SS-396 SERIES

Model No.	Body/Style Number	Body Type & Seating	Factory Price	Shipping Weight	Prod. Total
138	13837	2-dr HT-5P	4091	N/A	Note 1
138	13867	2-dr Conv-5P	4297	N/A	Note 1

NOTE 1: Some 58,600 six-cylinder and 72,500 V-8 Malibus were built. Total production, in figures rounded-off to the nearest 100, was 81,100 units.

NOTE 2: Exactly 19,765 Chevelle convertibles were built during the 1965 model year. However, this total included both Malibu and Malibu Super Sport convertibles.

NOTE 3: V-8s have the number '8' as the third digit of their series, model and serial number.

CHEVY II — 100-4/100-6 — (4-CYL/6-CYL) — SERIES 111/113 — Chevy IIs for 1965 were mildly restyled with a new grille, new rear cove treatment and revised bright trim. Sedans benefited from a new roofline. Chevy II 100 models featured rear fender script emblems; bright ventipane frames; windshield and rear window reveal moldings (side and upper tailgate reveal moldings on station wagons); anodized aluminum grille with special emblems; single unit headlights with anodized aluminum bezels; grille opening moldings with Chevrolet hood nameplate; front fender engine identification emblems (with optional six and V-8); front bumper mounted parking and directional signal lights; small, bright hubcaps; cove divider molding (with nameplate and emblem); single-unit taillights with matching back-up light opening cover plates optional; back-up lights; cloth and vinyl trim interior; all-vinyl interior on station wagons; black rubber floor covering; and dual-spoke steering wheel with horn button. Standard equipment included heater and defroster; front seat belts; foam cushioned front seats; dual sun visors; 6.00 x 13 blackwall tubeless tires on four-cylinder models; and 6.50 x 13 blackwall tires on six-cylinder models. Station wagons had size 7.00 x 13 blackwall tires.

CHEVY II 100 SERIES

Model No.	Body/Style No.	Body Type & Seating	Factory Price	Shipping Weight	Prod. Total
111	11169	4-dr Sed-6P	2005	2520	Note 1
111	11111	2-dr Sed-6P	1966	2505	Note 1
113	11369	4-dr Sed-6P	2070	2620	Note 1
113	11311	2-dr Sed-6P	2033	2605	Note 1
113	11335	4-dr Sta Wag-6P	2362	2875	Note 2

NOTE 1: Total production, in figures rounded-off to the nearest 100 units, was 40,500 cars (excluding station wagons).

NOTE 2: A total of 21,500 Chevy II station wagons were built during the 1965 model year. This included station wagons in Chevy II '100' and Chevy II Nova series.

NOTE 3: Six-cylinder models have the numeral '3' as the third digit of the series, style and serial numbers.

CHEVY II NOVA — (6-CYL) — SERIES 115 — Nova features used in place of, or in addition to, Chevy II 100 series equipment included: full-length, color-accented bodyside moldings; rear quarter crown moldings; Nova nameplates and emblems on rear fenders; roof drip cap moldings; hood windsplit moldings; ribbed cove divider panel with nameplate and emblem; single-unit taillights with matching back-up lights; luxury pattern cloth and vinyl trim (all-vinyl on station wagons); bright accents on sidewall trim panels; armrests with built in ashtrays; series nameplate on glove compartment door; full-width instrument panel trim molding; specific dual-spoke steering wheel with horn ring; and color-keyed deep-twist carpet floor covering.

1965 Chevrolet, Chevy II Nova six-passenger station wagon, 6-cyl (PH)

CHEVY II NOVA SERIES

Model No.	Body/Style No.	Body Type & Seating	Factory Price	Shipping Weight	Prod. Total
115	11569	4-dr Sed-6P	2195	2645	Note 1
115	11537	2-dr HT-6P	2222	2645	Note 1
115	11535	4-dr Sta Wag-6P	2456	2680	Note 2

NOTE 1: Total production, in figures rounded-off to the nearest 100 units, was 51,700 cars (excluding station wagons).

NOTE 2: A total of 21,500 Chevy II station wagons were built during the 1965 model year. This includes station wagons in Chevy II '100' and Chevy II Nova series.

NOTE 3: V-8 models have the numeral '6' as the third digit of the series, style and serial numbers.

1965 Chevrolet, Chevy II Nova SS two-door hardtop, V-8 (PH)

CHEVY II NOVA SUPER SPORT — (6-CYL) — SERIES 117 — In addition to, or replacing Nova equipment on Nova SS models were: color-accented bodyside and rear quarter moldings; front and rear wheel opening moldings; belt moldings; Nova SS rear fender nameplates and SS emblems; Nova SS deck lid nameplate and emblem; rear cove outline molding; silver-painted rear cove area; special Super Sport wheel covers with 14-inch wheels and tires; luxurious all-vinyl trim and headliner; front bucket seats; floor-mounted shift and special trim plate (with optional four-speed and Powerglide transmissions); oil pressure, temperature and ammeter gauges (in place of warning lights); bright front seat outer end panels; SS glove compartment door nameplates and electric clock.

CHEVY II NOVA SUPER SPORT

Model No.	Body/Style No.	Body Type & Seating	Factory Price	Shipping Weight	Prod. Total
117	11737	2-dr HT-5P	2381	2690	4,300

CHEVROLET ENGINES

SIX-CYLINDER: Inline. Overhead valve. Cast iron block. Displacement: 230 cid. Bore and stroke: 3.87 x 3.25 inches. Compression ratio: 8.5:1. Brake hp: 140 at 4200 rpm. Seven main bearings. Hydraulic valve lifters. Carburetor: Rochester one-barrel Model 7025003.

V-8: Overhead valve. Cast iron block. Displacement: 283 cid. Bore and stroke: 3.75 x 3.00 inches. Compression ratio: 9.25:1. Brake hp: 195 at 4800 rpm. Five main bearings. Carburetor: Rochester two-barrel Model 7024101.

CHEVELLE ENGINES

SIX-CYLINDER: Inline. Overhead valve. Cast iron block. Displacement: 194 cid. Bore and stroke: 3.563 x 3.25 inches. Compression ratio: 8.5:1. Brake hp: 120 at 4400 rpm. Seven main bearings. Hydraulic valve lifters. Carburetor: Rochester one-barrel Model 7023105.

V-8: Overhead valve. Cast iron block. Displacement: 283 cid. Bore and stroke: 3.875 x 3.00 inches. Compression ratio: 9.25:1. Brake hp: 195 at 4800 rpm. Hydraulic valve lifters. Carburetor: Rochester two-barrel Model 7024101.

CHEVY II 100 SERIES ENGINES

FOUR-CYLINDER: Inline. Overhead valve. Cast alloy iron block. Displacement: 153 cid. Bore and stroke: 3.875 x 3.25 inches. Compression ratio: 8.5:1. Brake hp: 90 at 4000 rpm. Five main bearings. Hydraulic valve lifters. Carburetor: Carter one-barrel Model 3379.

SIX-CYLINDER: Inline. Cast alloy block. Displacement: 194 cid. Bore and stroke: 3.563 x 3.25 inches. Compression ratio: 8.5:1. Brake hp: 177 at 2400 rpm. Seven main bearings. Hydraulic valve lifters. Carburetor: Rochester one-barrel Model 7023105.

CHASSIS FEATURES: Wheelbase: (full-size Chevrolets) 119 inches; (Chevelle) 115 inches; (Chevy II) 110 inches. Overall length: (full-size Chevrolet passenger cars) 213.1 inches; (full-size Chevrolet station wagons) 213.3 inches; (Chevelle passenger cars) 196.6 inches; (Chevelle station wagons) 201.4 inches; (Chevy II passenger cars) 162.9 inches; (Chevy II station wagons) 187.6 inches. Front tread: (full-size Chevrolets) 61.2 inches; (Chevelle) 58.0 inches; (Chevy II) 56.6 inches. Rear tread: (full-size Chevrolets) 61.6 inches; (Chevelle) 58.0 inches; (Chevy II) 56.3 inches. Tires: (full-size six-cylinder passenger cars) 7.35 x 14; (full-size V-8 passenger cars) 7.35 x 14; (convertibles) 7.75 x 14; (full-size station wagons) 8.25 x 14 (Chevelle passenger cars) 6.95 x 14; (Chevelle station wagons) 7.35 x 14; (Chevy II 100-4) 6.00 x 13; (Chevy II, Nova passenger cars) 6.50 x 13; (Chevy II Nova SS) 6.95 x 14; (Chevy II and Nova station wagons) 7.00 x 13.

CHEVROLET OPTIONS: Power brakes ($43). Power steering ($96). Four-season air conditioning not available with 400 hp 409 ($363). Size 7.75 or larger tires required. Deluxe front seat belts with retractors ($8). Rear window defroster ($22). Tinted glass on all windows ($38); windshield only ($22). Rear bumper guards, not available on wagons ($10). Front bumper guards ($16). Heater/defroster delete ($72 credit). Tri-volume horn ($14). Padded instrument panel ($18.30). Rear luggage compartment lock on six-passenger wagons ($11). Roof luggage rack on wagons ($43). Six-Way power seat, not available on Biscayne, Super Sport or with four-speed transmission ($97). Power windows not available on Biscayne ($102.25). Manual radio ($50). Push-button radio ($59). AM/FM push-button radio ($137). AM/FM radio with stereo ($244). Rear seat speaker ($13). Vinyl roof cover on Impala, SS Sport Coupe, Impala Sport Sedan ($75). Foam front seat cushion on Biscayne ($8). Divided second seat on wagons ($38). Sport-styled steering wheel ($32). Comfort-lift steering wheel ($43). Vinyl interior on Biscayne sedan ($5). Wire design wheel covers, not available on Impala SS ($75). Wire wheel design wheel covers on Impala SS ($57). Electric two-speed windshield wipers with washer ($17). Three-speed manual transmission was standard in all models. Overdrive transmission ($107.60). Automatic transmission. Powerglide on six-cylinder models ($188.30); on V-8 models ($199.10). Turbo-Hydramatic with 327 and 396 V-8s. Four-speed manual floor shift transmission with 240 hp ($188.30); with 300, 340 and 400 hp engine ($236.75). Six-cylinder 250 cid/150 hp L22 engine. V-8 283 cid/220 hp L77 engine. V-8 327 cid/250 hp L30 engine ($95). V-8 327 cid/300 hp L74 engine ($138). V-8 396 cid/325 hp L35 engine. V-8 396 cid/425 hp L76 engine. V-8 409 cid/340 hp L33 engine ($242.10). V-8 409 cid/400 hp L31 engine ($320.65). V-8 409 cid/425 hp L31-L80. V-8 396 cid/425 hp L78. Positive traction rear axle ($43). Heavy-duty air cleaner ($5.40). Heavy-duty clutch ($11). Available rear axle gear ratios: 3.35:1; 3.55:1.

CHEVELLE OPTIONS: Power brakes ($43). Power steering ($86). Four season air conditioning ($364). Rear antenna, not available on station wagons (no charge). Front bumper guards ($10); rear bumper guards, not available on wagons ($10). Rear windshield defroster ($22). Tinted glass on all windows ($31); windshield only ($20). Heater and defroster deletion ($72 credit, not available with air). Tri-volume horn ($14). Instrument panel safety pad ($18). Luggage rack on station wagons ($43). Two-tone paint ($16). Four-way power seat not available on four-speed, SS or 300 series ($64). Power tailgate window on wagons ($27). Power top on convertible ($54). Power windows not available on 300 series ($102). Manual radio ($50). Push-button radio ($58). Push-button radio with rear seat speaker, not available on convertibles ($72). AM/FM radio ($137). Black vinyl roof cover on Sport Coupes ($75). Deluxe seat belts with retractors ($8). Divided second seat on wagons ($38). Sport-styled steering wheel ($32). Comfort-lift steering wheel with four-speed or Powerglide ($43). Tachometer on V-8s ($48). Full wheel covers, excluding Super Sport ($22). Simulated wire wheels, excluding Super Sport ($75). Simulated wire wheel covers, excluding Super Sport ($57). Three-speed manual transmission was standard. Overdrive transmission ($108). Powerglide automatic transmission on six-cylinder ($188); on V-8 ($199). Four-speed manual floor shift ($188). Six-cylinder 230 cid/140 hp L26 engine. V-8 283 cid/220 hp RPO L77 engine. V-8 327 cid/250 hp L30 engine. V-8 327 cid/300 hp L74 engine. V-8 327 cid/350 hp L79 engine. Positive traction rear axle ($38). Heavy-duty clutch, on six-cylinder only ($5). Available rear axle gear ratios: 3.08:1; 3.31:1; 4.70:1; 2.73:1.

CHEVY II/NOVA OPTIONS: Power brakes ($43). Power steering, not available on four-cylinder ($86). Air conditioning, not available on four-cylinder ($317). Rear antenna, not available on station wagon (no charge). Rear armrest, 100 series only ($10, standard on Novas). Front Custom Deluxe retractable seat belts ($8). Tinted glass on all windows ($27); on windshield only ($13). Grille guard ($15). Rear bumper guard, not available on station wagons ($10). Tri-Volume horn, not available on AC ($14). Padded instrument panel ($16). Roof luggage rack on station wagons ($43). Two-tone paint ($11). Power tailgate window on station wagons ($27). Push-button radio with front speaker ($59). Manual radio ($50). Push-button radio with front and rear speakers ($72). Push-button AM/FM radio ($137). Divided second seat on station wagons ($37). Tachometer ($48). Super Sport wire wheel covers ($57). Wire wheel covers on Nova and 100 series ($75). Wheel covers, not available on Nova and Super Sport ($13). Wheel covers for 13-inch wheels ($70). Three-speed manual transmission was standard. Automatic transmission, on V-8s ($178); on six- and four-cylinder ($167). Four-speed manual floor shift transmission on V-8 only ($188). Six-cylinder 230 cid/140 hp RPO L26 engine. V-8 283 cid/220 hp L77 engine. V-8 327 cid/250 hp L30 engine. V-8 327 cid/300 hp L74 engine. Positive traction rear axle ($38). Heavy-duty clutch, not available on V-8, AC ($5). Available rear axle gear ratios: 3.08:1; 3.55:1; 3.36:1; 3.07:1.

HISTORICAL FOOTNOTES: Model year production peaked at 2,382,509 units. Calendar year sales of 2,587,487 cars were recorded. E.M. Estes was the chief executive officer of the company this year. Chevy built 155,000 V-8 models including all Chevrolet, Chevelle and Chevy II models and station wagons. It built 29,400 six-cylinders. Total production was 184,400 units.

Chevy built 59,650 of its 396-cid V-8s and 2,828 of its 409-cid V-8s for 1965. This year was also the end of an era. The great W-block introduced in 1956 as a 348 cid, later the 409 of 1961, was phased out, and the Mark IV production version of the 1963 Mark II NASCAR engine in its 396-cid version superseded the 409.

1966

BISCYANE — (6-CYL/V-8) — SERIES 153/154 — Chevrolet was in the second season of a totally new body change, so a mild face lift sufficed. Front fenders were given blunt forward-thrusting shapes, while the four-unit headlamp system was placed in new anodized bezels flanking a revised anodized aluminum grille. At the rear, a break with the now traditional round taillamp units were made; the 1966 full-size cars had horizontal rectangles, with back-up lights built in on Biscayne and Bel Air models. Other Biscayne features included series rear fender script, bright ventipane frames, windshield and rear window reveal moldings, (tailgate and side reveal moldings on station wagons), and grille opening moldings. Interiors were upholstered in vinyl and cloth, with Deluxe door release handles featured, and a foam-cushioned front seat only. A silver-painted shatter-resistant rearview mirror was suspended above the instrument panel, which had a glove compartment lock, bright instrument cluster housing and padding. A dual-spoke steering wheel with horn ring was standard as was carpeting on the floor, dual sun visors and embossed vinyl headlining. A heater and defroster unit, front and rear ashtrays, front and rear seat belts and five tubeless blackwall tires were included in the base equipment.

CHEVROLET I.D. NUMBERS: The Vehicle Identification Number was located on plate attached to left front door hinge pillar. The number had 13 symbols. The first symbol is a 1 for Chevrolet; the second and third symbols indicate series and the fourth and fifth symbols indicate body type. (Together, these first five symbols comprised the model number and appear in the Body/Style Number column of charts below.) The sixth symbol indicated model year: 6=1966. The seventh symbol indicated assembly plant: A=Atlanta, Ga.; B=Baltimore, Md.; C=Southgate, Calif.; F=Flint, Mich.; G=Framingham, Mass.; J=Janesville, Wis.; K=Kansas City, Mo.; L=Los Angeles, Calif.; N=Norwood, Ohio; R=Arlington, Texas; S=St. Louis, Mo.; T=Tarrytown, N.Y.; U=Lordstown, Ohio; W=Willow Run, Mich.; Y=Wilmington, Del.; Z=Fremont, Calif.; 1=Oshawa, Ontario (Canada); 2=St. Therese, Quebec (Canada) and P=Pontiac, Mich. The last six symbols were the sequential number. A Fisher Body Number tag on the cowl gives the style number, body number, trim and paint codes. Engine codes appear on the right side of six-cylinder blocks behind the distributor and right front of

V-8 engine blocks: CHEVY II (153 cid/90 hp four) OA, OC, OG, OH, OJ; (194 cid/120 hp six) OK, OQ, OR, OS, OT, ZV, ZW, ZX, ZY; (230 cid/140 hp six) PC, PV, PX, PI; (263 cid/195 hp V-8) PO, PF, PL, PM, PE, PG, PQ, PS, PN, PP, PV, PO; (283 cid/220 hp V-8) QA, QB, QC, QF, PK, PP, QD, QE; (327 cid/275 hp V-8) ZA, ZB, ZC, ZD, ZF, ZK, ZM; (327 cid/350 hp V-8) ZG, ZH, ZI, ZJ; CHEVELLE (194 cid/120 hp six) AA, AC, AG, AH, AK, AL, AN, AR, AS, AT, AU, AV, AW, AX, AY; (230 cid/140 hp six) CA, CB, CC, CD, BL, BM, BN, BO; (283 cid/195 hp V-8) DA, DB, DE, DF, DK, DI, DJ (283 cid/220 hp V-8) DG, DO, DL, DM; (327 cid/250 hp V-8) EA, EB, EC, EE; (396 cid/325 hp V-8) ED, EH, EK, EM; (396 cid/360 hp V-8) EF, EJ, EL, EN; (396 cid/375 hp V-8) KG. CHEVROLET (250 cid/155 hp six) FA, FE, FF, FK, FL, FM, FP, FR, FV, FW, FX, FY, FZ, GP, GO, GR; (283 cid/195 hp V-8) GA, GO, GF, GK, GS, GT; (283 cid/220 hp V-8) GL, GW, GX, GZ; (327 cid/275 hp V-8) HA, HB, HO, HF; (327 cid/230 hp V-8) ID; (396 cid/325 hp V-8) IA, IB, IC, IG, IV, IN; (427 cid/390 hp V-8) IH, II, IJ; (427 cid/425 hp V-8) ID, IO.

BISCAYNE SERIES

Model No.	Body/Style No.	Body Type & Seating	Factory Price	Shipping Weight	Prod. Total
153/4	15369	4-dr Sed-6P	2431/2537	3375/3510	Note 1
153/4	15311	2-dr Sed-6P	2379/2484	3310/3445	Note 1
153/4	15335	4-dr Sta Wag-6P	2772/2677	3770/3895	Note 1

NOTE 1: 83,200 six-cylinder Biscaynes and 39,200 V-8 Biscaynes were built, excluding station wagons.

NOTE 2: V-8 models have the numeral '4' as the third digit of their model, series, style and serial numbers.

NOTE 3: Prices and weights above slash for six/below slash for V-8.

BEL AIR — (6-CYL/V-8) — SERIES 155/156 — One step up Chevrolet's price and prestige ladder was the Bel Air, readily distinguished from the Biscayne by its full-length bodyside molding along the dent-prone bodyside flare. In addition, Bel Air script and Chevrolet emblems were used on the rear fenders, while roof drip gutter moldings and a deck lip molding were also added. Interiors were a bit plusher, in cloth and vinyl (except the station wagon, which was all-vinyl) and features added to or replacing Biscayne equipment included: a glovebox lamp, automatic front door courtesy/dome lamp switches, third seat courtesy lamp and third seat foam padding on station wagons.

BEL AIR SERIES

Model No.	Body/Style No.	Body Type & Seating	Factory Price	Shipping Weight	Prod. Total
155/6	15569	4-dr Sed-6P	2531/2636	3390/3525	Note 1
155/6	15511	2-dr Sed-6P	2479/2584	3315/3445	Note 1
155/6	15545	4-dr Sta Wag-9P	2948/3053	3815/3990	Note 1
155/6	15535	4-dr Sta Wag-6P	2835/2940	3770/3895	Note 1

NOTE 1: 236,600 Bel Airs were built, excluding station wagons, of which 164,500 had V-8 engines and 72,100 had six-cylinder engines.

NOTE 2: V-8 models had the numeral '6' as the third digit of their series, style and serial numbers.

NOTE 3: Prices and weights above slash for six/below slash for V-8.

1966 Chevrolet, Impala station wagon, V-8

IMPALA — (6-CYL/V-8) — SERIES 163/164 — This was a more Deluxe Chevrolet with a color-accented full-length bodyside molding on the body flare peak, body sill bright moldings, front and rear wheel opening moldings, bright side window accents, Impala front fender nameplates and emblems, belt moldings, deck lid molding with color accent, triple-unit wraparound rear taillamps (dual unit on station wagon), back-up lamps in the rear bumper, hood windsplit molding and station wagon lower reveal molding. Interiors were plusher cloth and vinyl (all-vinyl on station wagon and convertible), with the following features added to, or replacing, Bel Air equipment: brushed aluminum lower instrument panel insert with bright bezel, fingertip door releases, foam cushioned rear seat, bright aluminum seat end panels, chrome-plated rearview mirror housings, bright windshield header (on convertible), rear seat speaker grille (convertible and two-door hardtop), and dual roof rear quarter panel interior lights on two-door hardtops (which also had dual instrument panel courtesy lamps along with the convertible).

IMPALA SERIES

Model No.	Body/Style No.	Body Type & Seating	Factory Price	Shipping Weight	Prod. Total
163/4	16369	4-dr Sed-6P	2678/2783	3425/3565	Note 1
163/4	16339	4-dr HT-6P	2747/2852	3525/3650	Note 1
163/4	16337	2-dr HT-6P	2684/2789	3430/3535	Note 1
163/4	16367	2-dr Conv-6P	2935/3041	3485/3610	Note 1
163/4	16345	4-dr Sta Wag-9P	3083/3189	3860/3985	Note 1
163/4	16335	4-dr Sta Wag-6P	2971/3076	3805/3930	Note 1

NOTE 1: Impala production totaled 654,900, of which 33,100 were six-cylinders and 621,800 were V-8s.

NOTE 2: V-8 models have the numeral '4' as the third digit of their series, model and serial numbers.

NOTE 3: Prices and weights above slash for six/below slash for V-8.

1966 Chevrolet, Impala SS two-door convertible, V-8

IMPALA SUPER SPORT — (6-CYL/V-8) — SERIES 167/168 — The sporting Impala lost some of its exterior distinction this year, with only the addition of Super Sport front fender nameplates, grille Impala SS indention bar, deck badge and specific tri-bar Super Sport wheel covers giving distinction. Interiors again featured all-vinyl trim, with front bucket seats, console and SS identification on the instrument panel. Standard features added to those found on base-line Chevrolets were the same as on the Impala models.

1966 Chevrolet, Caprice Custom station wagon, V-8

1966 Chevrolet, Caprice two-door Custom Coupe, V-8

IMPALA SUPER SPORT SERIES

Model No.	Body/Style No.	Body Type & Seating	Factory Price	Shipping Weight	Prod. Total
167/8	16737	2-dr HT-6P	2842/2947	3460/3485	Note 1
167/8	16767	2-dr Conv-6P	3093/3199	3505/3630	Note 1

NOTE 1: Impala Super Sport production totaled 119,300 of which 900 were six-cylinder and 116,400 were V-8s.

NOTE 2: V-8 models have the numeral '8' as the third digit of their series, style and serial numbers.

NOTE 3: Prices and weights above slash for six/below slash for V-8.

CAPRICE — (V-8) — SERIES 166 — A popular Sport Sedan option in 1965, the Caprice was expanded to series status for 1966. It included a new Custom Coupe with special formal roofline and two station wagon models with woodgrained bodyside trim. Interiors were plush cloth in the four-door hardtop Sport Sedan (bench front seat standard, Strato-back front seat optional), all-vinyl or cloth in the two-door hardtop Custom Coupe, and all-vinyl in the station wagons. A wood-look lower instrument panel insert was used, with wood-accented combination vinyl and carpet door panels (except on wagons) added. Exterior distinction came from color-keyed bodyside striping, wide ribbed body sill moldings, Caprice front fender and deck signatures, wraparound rear taillamps with bright horizontal ribs, specific Caprice wheel covers, roof rear quarter emblems, twin simulated exhaust ports below Custom Coupe backlight and a Caprice tailgate nameplate on the Custom Wagons.

CAPRICE SERIES

Model No.	Body/Style Number	Body Type & Seating	Factory Price	Shipping Weight	Prod. Total
166	16639	4-dr HT-6P	3063	3675	Note 1
166	16647	2-dr Cpe-6P	3000	3585	Note 1
166	16645	4-dr Sta Wag-9P	3347	4020	Note 1
166	16635	4-dr Sta Wag-6P	3234	3970	Note 1

NOTE 1: 181,000 Caprices were built, excluding station wagons.

CHEVELLE 300 — (6-CYL/V-8) — SERIES 131/132 — A new body graced 1966 Chevelles, with forward thrusting front fenders, new body contour lines, wider-appearing anodized aluminum grille and new rear body cove treatment. Chevelle 300 models were relatively lacking in ornamentation with series rear fender emblems, bright ventipane frames, windshield and rear window moldings, outside rearview mirror, four headlamps with anodized aluminum bezels, grille outline moldings, rear cove Chevelle nameplate, front bumper mounted park/turn lights, small hubcaps, single-unit rear lights (with bright bezels) and built-in back-up lights. Interiors were pattern cloth and vinyl trimmed, black rubber floor covering, plus all GM safety features and five blackwall tires, heater and defroster.

CHEVELLE 300 SERIES

Model No.	Body/Style No.	Body Type & Seating	Factory Price	Shipping Weight	Prod. Total
131/2	13169	4-dr Sed-6P	2202/2306	2935/3080	Note 1
131/2	13111	2-dr Sed-6P	2165/2271	2695/3040	Note 1

NOTE 1: A total of 28,600 Chevelle '300s' were built of which 23,300 were six-cylinders and 5,300 were V-8s.

NOTE 2: V-8 models had the numeral '2' as the third digit of their serial and style numbers.

NOTE 3: Prices and weights above slash for six/below slash for V-8.

CHEVELLE 300 DELUXE — (6-CYL/V-8) — SERIES 133/134 — This was a slightly upgraded Chevelle 300 with full-length bodyside moldings, Chevelle 300 Deluxe rear fender nameplates and painted rear quarter reveal moldings, bright tailgate molding and emblem on station wagon. A dual-spoke steering wheel with a horn ring was specific to this model, as was the color-keyed upper instrument panel with bright lower panel trim strip. Doors had bright accents on the trim panels and the rear armrests had built-in ashtrays. Interiors were cloth and vinyl upholstered.

CHEVELLE 300 DELUXE SERIES

Model No.	Body/Style No.	Body Type & Seating	Factory Price	Shipping Weight	Prod. Total
133/4	13369	4-dr Sed-6P	2276/2362	2945/3095	Note 1
133/4	13311	2-dr Sed-6P	2239/2345	2910/3060	Note 1
133/4	13335	4-dr Sta Wag-6P	2575/2661	3210/3350	Note 1

NOTE 1: A total of 37,500 Chevelle '300 Deluxes' were built (excluding station wagons), of which 27,100 were six-cylinders and 10,500 were V-8s.

NOTE 2: V-8 models had the numeral '4' as the third digit of their style and serial numbers.

NOTE 3: Prices and weights above slash for six/below slash for V-8.

CHEVELLE MALIBU — (6-CYL/V-8) —
This nicely trimmed series added to or replaced equipment on the Chevelle 300 Deluxe as follows: slender body sill and wheelhouse moldings were added, along with Malibu rear fender nameplates and a hood windsplit molding. A rear cove outline molding surrounded the single-unit rear lights with built-in back-up lamps (vertical light units were used on the station wagons). A rear cove emblem was used with Chevrolet script above on the deck lid. Station wagons in this series had a full-width ribbed molding and emblem and tailgate Chevelle nameplate. Interiors were plusher cloth and vinyl (all-vinyl on convertible and station wagon). A distinctive dual-spoke steering wheel was used. Black crackle-finish was used on the instrument panel upper section. A glove compartment light, bright-backed rearview mirror, bright roof rails and floor carpeting were additional Malibu features.

CHEVELLE MALIBU

Model No.	Body/Style No.	Body Type & Seating	Factory Price	Shipping Weight	Prod. Total
135/6	13569	4-dr Sed-6P	2352/2458	2960/3110	Note 1
135/6	13539	4-dr HT-6P	2458/2564	3035/3180	Note 1
135/6	13517	2-dr HT-6P	2378/2484	2935/3075	Note 1
135/6	13567	2-dr Conv-6P	2586/2693	3030/3175	Note 1
135/6	13535	4-dr Sta Wag-6P	2651/2756	2651/3375	Note 1

NOTE 1: A total of 241,500 Chevelle Malibus were built (excluding station wagons), of which 52,300 were six-cylinders and 189,300 were V-8s.

NOTE 2: V-8 models had the numeral '6' as the third digit of their style and serial numbers.

NOTE 3: Prices and weights above slash for six/below slash for V-8.

1966 Chevrolet, Chevelle SS-396 two-door hardtop, V-8

CHEVELLE SS-396 — (V-8) — SERIES 138 —
Chevelle's performance package for this year included twin simulated air intakes, ribbed color-accented body sill and rear fender lower moldings, SS-396 grille and rear cover emblems and Super Sport script on the rear fenders. Specific wheel covers were included, as were five nylon red-stripe tires. Interiors were all-vinyl, with bench front seat standard and included all Malibu features (except for color-keyed vinyl-coated cargo floor mat and textured vinyl cargo area sidewalls).

CHEVELLE SS-396 SERIES

Model No.	Body/Style No.	Body Type & Seating	Factory Price	Shipping Weight	Prod. Total
136	13617	2-dr HT-6P	2276	3375	Note 1
136	13667	2-dr Conv-6P	2964	3470	Note 1

NOTE 1: Chevelle Super Sport production was 72,272 units in both body styles.

NOTE 2: All 1966 Chevelle Super Sports were SS-396s.

CHEVY II — 100-4/100-6 — (4-CYL/6-CYL) — SERIES 111/113 —
A new body was used for 1966 featuring single unit headlamps in new bright bezels, a refined anodized aluminum front grille, and turn directional signal lights in the front bumper. At the rear were new vertical-type taillights, of the single unit type, with built-in back-up lamps. Chevy II '100' models had Chevy II rear fender emblems, bright ventipane frames, windshield and rear window reveal moldings, bright outside rearview mirror, grille opening moldings, small bright hubcaps, deck lid Chevy II emblem tailgate on wagons and cloth and vinyl interiors (all-vinyl on station wagons). Standard features included a dual-spoke steering wheel with horn button, padded instrument panel, glove compartment lock, vinyl door and sidewall trim panels, Deluxe-type door handles and regulators, foam-cushioned front seat, dual sun visors, two coat hooks and other convenience items.

CHEVY II SERIES

Model No.	Body/Style No.	Body Type & Seating	Factory Price	Shipping Weight	Prod. Total
111/3	11169	4-dr Sed-6P	2065/2127	2535/2635	Note 1
111/3	11111	2-dr Sed-6P	2026/2090	2520/2630	Note 1
113	11335	4-dr Sta Wag-6P	2430	2855	Note 1

NOTE 1: Six-cylinder and optional V-8 units had the numeral '3' as the third digit of their style and serial numbers.

NOTE 2: A total of 47,000 Chevy II '100s' were produced, of which 44,500 were six-cylinders and 4,900 were optional V-8s.

NOTE 3: Prices and weights above slash for four-cylinder/below slash for six-cylinder.

1966 Chevrolet, Chevy II Nova SS two-door hardtop, V-8

CHEVY II NOVA — (6-CYL) — SERIES 115 —
A plusher model, with exterior distinction derived from a color accent full-length bodyside molding, body sill moldings, Nova rear fender script and model badge, hood emblem, roof drip gutter bright moldings, door and rear quarter upper side moldings (on two-door hardtop Sport Coupe), bright roof rear quarter belt molding (on sedan) and full-width color accented deck trim with Chevy II nameplate. Interiors were cloth and vinyl (all vinyl on Sport Coupe and station wagon), with the following features added to equipment found on the Chevy II '100': distinctive dual-spoke steering wheel with horn ring,

glove compartment, door trim panel and nameplate, bright accents on door and sidewall trim, rear armrests with built-in ashtrays, foam cushioned rear seat, color-keyed floor carpeting and automatic front door dome light switches.

CHEVY II NOVA SERIES

Model No.	Body/Style No.	Body Type & Seating	Factory Price	Shipping Weight	Prod. Total
115	11569	4-dr Sed-6P	2245	2640	Note 1
115	11537	2-dr HT-6P	2271	2675	Note 1
115	11535	4-dr Sta Wag-6P	2518	2885	Note 1

NOTE 1: A total of 73,900 Chevy II Novas were built, excluding station wagons. Of these, 54,300 were six-cylinders and 19,600 were V-8s.

NOTE 2: V-8s were a Nova option, and are listed under options.

NOVA SS — (6-CYL) — SERIES 117 — The sporty Nova SS was identified on the exterior by color-accented wide body sill moldings, front and rear wheel opening moldings with extensions on both lower fenders, door and rear quarter upper bodyside moldings, an SS grille emblem, Nova SS rear fender script, a full-width ribbed rear deck panel with Chevy II nameplate and SS badge and special 14-inch Super Sport wheel covers. Interiors included all-vinyl front bucket seats (console with four-speed or automatic) and most features found on Nova models. An SS emblem was found on the glovebox door.

NOVA SS SERIES

Model No.	Body/Style No.	Body Type & Seating	Factory Price	Shipping Weight	Prod. Total
117	11737	2-dr HT-6P	2430	2740	10,100

NOTE 1: V-8s were a Nova SS option and are included in Powertrain Options.

CHEVROLET ENGINES

(SIX-CYLINDER) Inline. Overhead valve. Cast iron block. Displacement: 250 cid. Bore and stroke: 3.87 x 3.53 inches. Compression ratio: 8.5:1. Brake hp:155 at 4200 rpm. Hydraulic valve lifters. Carburetor: Down-draft single barrel.

(V-8) Overhead valve. Cast iron block. Displacement: 283 cid. Bore and stroke: 3.875 x 3.00 inches. Compression ratio: 9.25:1. Brake hp: 195 at 4800 rpm. Five main bearings. Carburetor: Downdraft two-barrel.

CHEVELLE ENGINES

(SIX-CYLINDER) Inline. Overhead valve. Cast iron block. Displacement: 194 cid. Bore and stroke: 3.563 x 3.25 inches. Compression ratio: 6.5:1. Brake hp: 120 at 4400 rpm. Seven main bearings. Hydraulic valve lifters. Carburetor: Rochester one-barrel Model 7023105.

(V-8) Overhead valve. Cast iron block. Displacement: 283 cid. Bore and stroke: 3.875 x 3.00 inches. Compression ratio: 9.25:1. Brake hp: 195 at 4800 rpm. Hydraulic valve lifters. Carburetor: Rochester two-barrel Model 7024101.

SS-396 ENGINE: V-8. Overhead valve. Cast iron block. Displacement: 396 cid. Bore and stroke: 4.094 x 3.76 inches. Compression ratio: 10.25:1. Brake hp: 325 at 4800 rpm. Five main bearings. Hydraulic valve lifters. Carburetor: Downdraft four-barrel.

CHEVY II ENGINES

FOUR-CYLINDER: Inline. Overhead valve. Cast alloy iron block. Displacement: 153 cid. Bore and stroke: 3.875 x 3.25 inches. Compression ratio: 8.5:1. Brake hp: 90 at 4000 rpm. Five main bearings. Hydraulic valve lifters. Carburetor: Carter one-barrel Model 3379.

SIX-CYLINDER: Inline. Cast alloy block. Displacement: 194 cid. Bore and stroke: 3.563 x 3.25 inches. Compression ratio: 8.5:1. Brake hp: 177 at 2400 rpm. Seven main bearings. Hydraulic valve lifters. Carburetor: Rochester one-barrel Model 7023105.

CHASSIS FEATURES: Wheelbase: (full-size Chevrolets) 119.0 inches; (Chevelle) 115.0 inches; (Chevy II) 110.0 inches. Overall length: (full-size Chevrolet) 213.2 inches; (full-size wagons) 212.4 inches; (Chevelle) 197.0 inches; (wagons) 197.6 inches; (Chevy II) 183.0 inches; (wagons) 187.4 inches. Front tread: (full-size Chevrolet) 62.5 inches; (full-size wagons) 63.5 inches; (Chevelle) 58.0 inches; (Chevy II) 56.8 inches; (wagons) 56.3 inches. Rear tread: (full-size Chevrolet) 62.4 inches; (full-size wagons) 63.4 inches; (Chevelle) 58.0 inches; (Chevy II) 56.3 inches; (wagons) 55.6 inches. Tires: (full-size Chevrolet) 7.35 x 14, 7.75 x 14, 8.25 x 14, 8.55 x 14 (depending on model, engine and options); (Chevelle) 6.95 x 14 or 7.35 x 14, (SS-396) 7.75 x 14; (Chevy II) six-cylinder 6.50 x 13; or V-8 6.95 x 14.

CHEVROLET OPTIONS: Power brakes ($42). Power steering ($95). Four-Season comfort air conditioning. Power rear antenna ($26). Rear window defroster. Emergency road kit. Tinted Soft-Ray glass on all windows ($37); windshield only ($21). Front bumper guards ($16); rear bumper guards ($16). Strato-ease front seat headrests ($53). Deletion heater and defroster ($71 credit). Tri-volume horn ($14). Special instrumentation ($79). Spare wheel lock. AM/FM push-button radio with front antenna ($134). AM/FM push-button radio with front antenna and rear speaker ($147). AM/FM push-button stereo radio with front antenna ($239). AM push-button radio with front antenna ($57). AM push-button radio with front antenna and rear speaker ($71). Vinyl roof cover in black or beige ($79). Front and rear Custom Deluxe color matched seat belts with front retractors. Four-Way power driver's seat ($70). Comfort-Tilt steering wheel ($42). Sport-styled steering wheel ($32). Tilt-telescopic steering wheel. Tachometer. Traffic hazard warning system. Set of five 14-inch wheels with 6JK rims ($21). Mag style wheel covers ($53). Simulated wire wheel covers ($56). Power windows ($100). A three-speed manual transmission, with column shift was standard on six-cylinder and 283-cid and 327-cid V-8 models. A heavy-duty three-speed, with floor shift was optional (required) with 396-cid and 427-cid V-8s ($79). Overdrive was optional for standard engines

($115). A four-speed manual transmission was optional for V-8 engines ($184). Close ratio version (2.20:1 low) was available for 396-427 V-8s. Powerglide two-speed automatic transmission was available with column shift (floor lever on bucket-seat equipped Series 163, 166, 167 cars) for six-cylinder ($184); for 283, 327 and 325 hp 396 V-8s ($195). Turbo Hydra-Matic was optional on 396 V-8 and 427 cid/390 hp V-8 ($226). Optional engines included: 263 cid/220 hp Turbo-Fire V-8 (RPO L77). 327 cid/275 hp Turbo-Fire V-8 (RPO-L30) ($93). 396 cid/325 hp Turbo-Jet V-8 (RPO L35) ($158). 427 cid/390 hp Turbo-Jet V-8 (RPO L36) ($316). 427 cid/425 hp Turbo-Jet V-8 (RPO L72).

CHEVELLE/CHEVY II OPTIONS: Power brakes ($42). Power steering ($84). Four-Season air conditioning on Chevelle; All-Weather on Chevy II ($310). Center console for strato-bucket seats. Rear window defroster. Tinted Soft-Ray glass on all windows ($31); on windshield only ($21). Front bumper guards ($10); rear bumper guards ($10). Strato-Rest headrest ($53). Tri-volume horn. AM/FM push-button radio, not available in Chevy II. AM/FM push-button radio with rear speaker, not available in Nova. AM push-button radio ($57). AM push-button radio with rear seat speaker ($71). Vinyl roof cover ($74). Custom Deluxe color matched seat belts ($8). Four-way power front seat not available in Chevy II. Strato-bucket front seats, not available in Chevy II. Comfort-Tilt steering wheel, not available in Chevy II. Sport-styled steering wheel ($32). Tachometer not available in Chevy II. Power-operated convertible top. Wheel covers ($21). Mag styled wheel covers ($74). Simulated wire wheel covers ($73). Power windows, Chevelle only. (CHEVELLE): A three-speed manual transmission, with column mounted shift, was standard on all Chevelle models. Overdrive was optional with standard engines ($116). A four-speed manual transmission, close ratio or wide range with floor shift was available for all V-8s ($184; $105 on SS-396). Powerglide two-speed automatic transmission was offered for six-cylinder and all cataloged V-8 engines except the 396 cid/360 hp V-8 ($164; $195 on SS-396). Optional engines included: 230 cid/140 hp six-cylinder RPO L26 ($37). 283 cid/220 hp V-8 RPO L77. 327 cid/275 hp V-8 RPO L30 ($93). 327 cid/350 hp V-8 RPO L79 ($198). 396 cid/360 hp V-8 RPO L34 ($105). 396 cid/375 hp V-8 RPO L78 for SS-396 only. (CHEVY II): A three-speed manual transmission was standard in all models. A four-speed manual transmission was optional for cars equipped with V-8s ($184). Powerglide two-speed automatic transmission was optional for all engines ($164-$174). Optional engines included: 230 cid/140 hp six-cylinder RPO L26 ($37). 283 cid/220 hp V-8 RPO L77. 327 cid/275 hp V-8 RPO L30 ($93). 327 cid/350 hp V-8 RPO L79 (only 200 built).

HISTORICAL FOOTNOTES: Model year production peaked at 2,215,979 units. Calendar year sales of 2,202,758 cars were recorded. E.M. Estes was the chief executive officer of the company this year. Of the total production of 1966 Chevrolets, 1,499,676 were full-size cars; 18,100 were six-cylinder station wagons; 167,400 were full-size V-8

Chevrolet station wagons; 8,900 were six-cylinder Chevelles; 23,000 were V-8 Chevelles; 16,500 were six-cylinder Chevy II/Novas; and 4,900 were Chevy II/Nova V-8s. Chevrolet called its two-door hardtops Sport Coupes in all lines. Style 16647 was the Caprice Custom Coupe.

1967

BISCAYNE — (6-CYL/V-8) — SERIES 153/154 — Chevrolet featured a new body for 1967. The Biscayne was the base line. It had an anodized aluminum grille with a bright bumper carrying the parking/turn signal lamps. Grille opening moldings were used, as were bright windshield and rear window reveal moldings. Biscayne script appeared on the rear fenders, while Chevrolet script was found on the deck lid and hood. Small bright metal hubcaps were standard and a chrome outside rearview mirror was included. Ventipane frames were plated. Dual unit taillamps were found at the rear with built-in back-up lights. Station wagons had tailgate reveal moldings and script on the tailgate. Interiors were cloth and vinyl or all-vinyl on station wagons. Standard features included a brake system warning light; cigarette lighter; illuminated heater control panel; padded instrument panel; glove compartment lock; front door armrests; rear armrests with built-in ashtrays; foam-cushioned front seat (with seatback latches on two-door models) and color-keyed floor carpeting.

BISCAYNE SERIES

Series No.	Body/Style No.	Body Type & Seating	Factory Price	Shipping Weight	Prod. Total
153/154	69	4-dr Sed-6P	2464/2589	3410/3525	Note 1
153/154	11	2-dr Sed-6P	2442/2547	3335/3465	Note 1
153/154	35	4-dr Sta Wag-6P	2817/2923	3765/3885	Note 2

NOTE 1: Some 92,800 Biscayne passenger cars were built in the 1967 model year. In figures rounded-off to the nearest 100 units, this includes 54,200 sixes and 36,600 V-8s. This does not include station wagons.

NOTE 2: Some 155,100 full-size station wagons were built in the 1967 model year. In figures rounded-off to the nearest 100 units, this included 14,400 sixes and 140,700 V-8s. Since production of all station wagons was grouped together, this includes Biscayne, Bel Air, Impala and Caprice output.

NOTE 3: Data above slash for six/below slash for V-8.

BEL AIR — (6-CYL/V-8) — SERIES 155/156 — The middle-priced Chevrolet line had a narrow full-length bodyside molding; roof drip cap moldings; triple unit taillamps with center back-up lights; lower deck lid or tailgate moldings; and Bel Air script on the rear fenders to give it distinction. Interiors were somewhat refined and standard equipment, added to that found on the Biscaynes, included a glove compartment light; illuminated ignition switch and the following station wagon features: foam-cushioned third seat; color-keyed textured vinyl cargo area; sidewalls (except two-seat wagon); and a third seat courtesy light.

BEL AIR SERIES

Series No.	Body/Style No.	Body Type & Seating	Factory Price	Shipping Weight	Prod. Total
155/156	69	4-dr Sed-6P	2484/2689	3395/3535	Note 1
155/156	11	2-dr Sed 6P	2542/2647	3340/3470	Note 1
155/156	45	4-dr Sta Wag-9P	2993/3098	3825/3940	Note 2

NOTE 1: Some 179,700 Bel Air passenger cars were built in the 1967 model year. In figures rounded-off to the neatest 100 units, this total included 41,500 sixes and 138,200 V-8s.

NOTE 2: Some 155,100 full-size station wagons were built in the 1967 model year. In figures rounded-off to the nearest 100 units, this included 14,400 sixes and 140,700 V-8s. Since production of all station wagons was grouped together, this includes Biscayne, Bel Air, Impala and Caprice output.

NOTE 3: Data above slash for six/below slash for V-8.

1967 Chevrolet, Impala SS two-door convertible, V-8

IMPALA (6-CYL/V-8) — SERIES 163/164 — Exterior
items giving the Impala its status included bright lower bodyside moldings; roof drip cap and reveal moldings on hardtops; bright side window accents on station wagons and sedans; deck lid center panel accents in silver (with Chevrolet center emblem flanking rear cove); black accented taillamp surrounds and lower tailgate reveal molding (on the station wagon). Full wheel covers were included. Interiors were cloth and vinyl or all-vinyl, depending on the model. These features were added to (or replaced) the equipment found on lower-priced lines: a brushed metal bright-outlined lower instrument panel facing; electric clock; fingertip door releases; foam-cushioned rear seat; bright seat end panels; bright garnish moldings on hardtop styles; bright foot pedal trim outlines (with power brakes); roof side rail lights; courtesy instrument panel (on two-door hardtop and convertible); and a power-operated convertible top.

IMPALA SERIES

Series No.	Body/Style No.	Body Type & Seating	Factory Price	Shipping Weight	Prod. Total
163/164	69	4-dr Sed-6P	2723/2828	3455/3575	Note 1
163/164	39	4-dr HT-6P	2793/2899	3540/3660	Note 1
163/164	37	2-dr HT-6P	2740/2845	3475/3590	Note 1
163/164	67	2-dr Conv-6P	2991/3097	3515/3625	Note 2
163/164	45	4-dr Sta Wag-9P	3129/3234	3860/3980	Note 3
163/164	35	4-dr Sta Wag-6P	3016/3122	3805/3920	Note 3

NOTE 1: Some 575,600 Impala passenger cars were built in the 1967 model year. In figures rounded-off to the nearest 100 units, this includes 18,800 sixes and 556,800 V-8s. It covers convertibles, but not station wagons.

NOTE 2: Exactly 29,937 full-size Chevrolet convertibles were built in the 1967 model year. This total is included in Note 1. It covers both Impala and Impala SS convertibles with sixes and V-8s.

NOTE 3: Some 155,100 full-size station wagons were built in the 1967 model year. In figures rounded-off to the nearest 100 units, this included 14,400 sixes and 140,700 V-8s. Since production of all station wagons was grouped together, this includes Biscayne, Bel Air, Impala and Caprice output.

1967 Chevrolet, Impala two-door hardtop, V-8

IMPALA SUPER SPORT — (6-CYL/V-8) — SERIES
167/168 — The sporting Impala once again featured an all-vinyl interior, with front Strato bucket seats and a division console housing the shift lever as standard equipment (Strato bench seating was a no charge substitution). Exterior identification was made by the use of black accents on the grille (with bright horizontal bars remaining); front and rear wheelhouse moldings; black-accented body sill and lower rear fender bright moldings; a black-accent deck lid latch panel; SS deck lid and grille badges and specific Impala SS full wheel covers.

IMPALA SUPER SPORT SERIES

Series No.	Body/Style No.	Body Type & Seating	Factory Price	Shipping Weight	Prod. Total
167/168	37	2-dr HT-6P	2898/3003	3500/3615	66,510
167/168	67	2-dr Conv-6P	3149/3254	3535/3650	9,545

NOTE 1: In figures rounded-off to the nearest 100 units, total model year production of Impala Super Sports included some 400 sixes and 75,600 V-8s.

NOTE 2: A total of exactly 2,124 Impala Super Sports were equipped with the SS-427 option.

NOTE 3: Data above slash for six/below slash for V-8.

CAPRICE — (V-8) — SERIES 116 — This posh Chevrolet included these exterior features on the Custom Sedan and Custom Coupe: front fender lights; front and rear wheelhouse moldings; bright lower bodyside moldings with rear quarter extensions; color-keyed bodyside stripes; belt reveal molding on Custom Coupe; black-accented deck lid panel with bright highlight trim; triple-

unit taillights with back-up lights in the rear bumper; Caprice deck lid signatures; roof side panel nameplates; and specific Caprice full wheel covers. Interiors were plush, being trimmed in cloth; cloth and vinyl or all-vinyl, depending on model. Caprice Custom station wagons had wood panels, with bright outline moldings on the bodysides and tailgate plus Caprice tailgate nameplates. Interior features, in addition to (or replacing) those found on lower-priced models, included walnut-look lower instrument panel facing (with bright outline); pattern cloth and vinyl door panels; wood-look door panel trim in sedan and coupe (wagons were all-vinyl); and front seat fold-down center armrest (on sedans).

CAPRICE SERIES

Series No.	Body/Style No.	Body Type & Seating	Factory Price	Shipping Weight	Prod. Total
166	39	4-dr HT-6P	3130	3710	Note 1
166	47	2-dr HT-6P	3078	3605	Note 1
166	45	4-dr Sta Wag-9P	3413	3990	Note 2
166	35	4-dr Sta Wag-6P	3301	3935	Note 2

NOTE 1: In figures rounded-off to the nearest 100 units, a total of some 124,500 Caprice passenger cars were built in the 1967 model year. All were V-8 powered. This does not include Caprice station wagons.

NOTE 2: Some 155,100 full-size station wagons were built in the 1967 model year. In figures rounded-off to the nearest 100 units, this included 14,400 sixes and 140,700 V-8s. Since production of all station wagons was grouped together, this includes Biscayne, Bel Air, Impala and Caprice output.

CHEVELLE 300 — (6-CYL/V-8) — SERIES 131/132
— Minor sheet metal changes, primarily in the front and rear fender edges, were made for Chevelle in 1967. A new anodized aluminum grille was used and all Chevelles had grille opening moldings with a Chevrolet badge; front bumper-mounted parking and directional signals; windshield bright reveal moldings; bright ventipane frames; rear window reveal moldings; and back-up lights in the rear bumper. Chevelle 300 models had rear fender series identification; single-unit taillights with bright bezels; a chromed outside rearview mirror; and Chevelle lettering in the deck cove. Interiors were trimmed in cloth and vinyl and included these features: parking brake and brake system warning light; cigarette lighter; glove compartment lock; lever-type door handles; front door armrests; foam-cushioned front seat; padded sun visors; black rubber floor covering; day/night rearview mirror; four-way hazard flasher system and center dome light.

CHEVELLE 300 SERIES

Series No.	Body/Style No.	Body Type & Seating	Factory Price	Shipping Weight	Prod. Total
131/132	69	4-dr Sed-6P	2250/2356	2955/3090	Note 1
131/132	11	2-dr Sed-6P	2221/2326	2935/3360	Note 1

NOTE 1: Some 24,700 Chevelle 300 models were built for the 1967 model year.

NOTE 2: In figures rounded-off to the nearest 100 units, production included 19,900 sixes and 4,800 V-8s.

NOTE 3: Data above slash for six/below slash for V-8.

CHEVELLE 300 DELUXE — (6-CYL/V-8) — SERIES 133/134 — A slightly embellished Chevelle series featured (in addition to or replacing Chevelle 300 equipment) bright exterior body sill moldings; rear cove lower trim moldings on the sedan; Chevelle 300 Deluxe rear fender nameplates; and a rear cove or tailgate center emblem. Interiors were cloth and vinyl (all-vinyl in station wagon) and the instrument panel had a silver-finished upper accent. Rear armrests had built-in ashtrays, while the floor was covered with color-keyed vinyl-coated rubber. Automatic interior light switches were found on the door jambs. Bodies had "Flush & Dry" rocker panels and inner fenders.

1967 Chevrolet, Chevelle Malibu four-door hardtop (Sport Sedan), V-8

CHEVELLE 300 DELUXE SERIES

Series No.	Body/Style No.	Body Type & Seating	Factory Price	Shipping Weight	Prod. Total
133/134	69	4-dr Sed-6P	2324/2930	2980/3110	Note 1
133/134	11	2-dr Sed-6P	2295/2400	2955/3090	Note 1
133/134	35	4-dr Sta Wag-6P	2619/2725	3230/3360	Note 2

NOTE 1: Some 26,300 Chevelle 300 Deluxe models were built during the 1967 model year.

NOTE 2: In figures rounded-off to the nearest 100 units, production included 19,300 sixes and 7,000 V-8s (station wagons not included).

NOTE 3: Some 27,300 Chevelle station wagons were built during the 1967 model year.

NOTE 4: In figures rounded-off to the nearest 100 units, station wagon production included 5,900 sixes and 21,400 V-8s including both Chevelle 300 Deluxe, Chevelle Malibu and Concours wagons.

NOTE 5: Data above slash for six/below slash for V-8.

MALIBU — (6-CYL/V-8) — SERIES 135/136 — A nicely appointed Chevelle, the Malibu found exterior distinction by the use of bright lower bodyside and rear quarter moldings; roof drip cap moldings; bright rear quarter window reveal moldings (on station wagons); Malibu rear fender nameplates; black-accented rear cove outline panel; single-unit taillights with black-accented bezels and bright horizontal strips; rear cove or tailgate Chevelle badge (to the right), and a tailgate molding on the station wagon. Full wheel covers were included. Interiors were plusher and included a specific steering wheel; a walnut-finish upper panel on the instrument panel; illuminated heater control panel; electric clock; bright accents on the vinyl

sidewall and door panel trim; bright bases on front armrests; a foam-cushioned rear seat; color-keyed floor carpeting; and courtesy lights in the convertible.

MALIBU SERIES

Series No.	Body/Style No.	Body Type & Seating	Factory Price	Shipping Weight	Prod. Total
135/136	69	4-dr Sed-6P	2400/2506	3000/3130	Note 1
135/136	17	2-dr HT-6P	2434/2540	2960/3115	Note 1
135/136	67	2-dr Conv-6P	2637/2743	3050/3165	Note 2
135/136	35	4-dr Sta Wag-6P	2695/2801	3260/3390	Note 3
135/136	39	4-dr HT-6P	2506/2611	3065/3200	Note 1

NOTE 1: Some 227,800 Malibu passenger cars were built during the 1967 model year.

NOTE 2: In figures rounded-off to the nearest 100 units, this total included 40,600 sixes and 187,200 V-8s (does not include station wagons).

NOTE 3: Some 27,300 Chevelle station wagons were built during the 1967 model year.

NOTE 4: In figures rounded-off to the nearest 100 units, station wagon production included 5,900 sixes and 21,400 V-8s including Chevelle 300 Deluxe, Chevelle Malibu and Concours wagons.

NOTE 5: Exactly 12,772 convertibles were built in the 1967 model year, including Chevelle Malibu and Malibu SS models. This figure is included in the rounded-off totals given above There is no SS breakout available.

NOTE 6: Data above slash for six/below slash for V-8.

1967 Chevrolet, Chevelle Concours Estate station wagon, V-8

CONCOURS — (6-CYL/V-8) — SERIES 137/138 — This
was a luxury station wagon of the Chevelle line featuring special black-accented grille; synthetic woodgrain exterior side and tailgate paneling (with bright outline trim); front and rear wheelhouse moldings; ribbed, gray accented body sill moldings; tailgate emblem badge for Concours identification and rear fender Concours script. Interiors were trimmed in textured vinyl. The passenger floor was carpeted and the cargo load floor had a vinyl coating.

CONCOURS SERIES

Series No.	Body/Style No.	Body Type & Seating	Factory Price	Shipping Weight	Prod. Total
137	35	4-dr Sta Wag-6P	2827/2933	3270/3405	Note 1

NOTE 1: Some 27,300 Chevelle station wagons were built during the 1967 model year.

NOTE 2: In figures rounded-off to the nearest 100 units, station wagon production included 5,900 sixes and 21,400 V-8s including Chevelle 300 Deluxe, Chevelle Malibu and Concours wagons.

NOTE 3: Data above slash for six/below slash for V-8.

CHEVELLE SS-396 — (V-8) — SERIES 138 — The
Chevelle SS-396 had a youthful flair and was identifiable by these exterior additions or changes from other Chevelles: special black-accented grille with SS-396 badge; front and rear wheelhouse bright outlines; ribbed, gray-accented body sill moldings; color-keyed bodyside accent stripes; simulated air intakes on a domed hood; Super Sport rear fender emblems; black-painted rear cove panel (with SS-396 center medallion); five Red Stripe special tires; and specific full wheel covers. Interiors were all-vinyl, with a black-accent upper panel on the instrument board. Bucket seats were an option.

CHEVELLE SS-396 SERIES

Series No.	Body/Style No.	Body Type & Seating	Factory Price	Shipping Weight	Prod. Total
138	17	2-dr HT-6P	2825	3415	Note 1
138	67	2-dr Conv-6P	3033	3495	Notes 1/2

NOTE 1: Exactly 63,006 Chevelle SS-396 models were built during the 1967 model year. This includes both hardtops and convertibles. All were V-8 powered. No further body style breakouts are available.

NOTE 2: No more than 29,937 Chevelle SS-396 convertibles were built.

CHEVY II 100 — (4-CYL/6-CYL) — SERIES 111/113 —
Minor trim changes occurred for the second year of the styling cycle. A new anodized aluminum grille had a distinct horizontal center bar motif, with a Chevy II nameplate to the driver's side. Chevy II '100' standard items included grille opening moldings; front bumper mounted parking and directional signal lamps; windshield bright reveal molding; small, bright hubcaps; bright ventipane frames; chromed outside rearview mirror; vertical, single-unit taillights (with built-in back-up lights); rearview reveal molding; and deck lid or tailgate Chevy II emblems. Chevy II rear fender emblems gave side identification. Interiors were trimmed in cloth and vinyl or all-vinyl, depending on model. Standard interior features included bright instrument cluster bezel; brake system warning light; glove compartment lock; front door armrests; foam-cushioned front seat; folding front seatback latches (on two-door sedan); black rubber floor covering; four-way hazard flasher; and center dome light.

CHEVY II 100 SERIES

Series No.	Body/Style No.	Body Type & Seating	Factory Price	Shipping Weight	Prod. Total
111/113	69	4-dr Sed-6P	2120/2182	2560/2650	Note 1
111/113	11	2-dr Sed-6P	2090/2152	2555/2640	Note 1
111/113	35	4-dr Sta Wag-6P	2478	2865	Note 2

NOTE 1: Some 35,900 Chevy II 100 passenger cars were built for the 1967 model year.

NOTE 2: In figures rounded-off to the nearest 100 units, production included 480 fours, 33,720 sixes and 1,700 V-8s (does not include station wagons).

NOTE 3: Some 12,900 Chevy II station wagons were built during model year 1967. In figures rounded-off to the nearest 100 units, this included 10,000 sixes and 2,900 V-8s. This includes Chevy II 100 and Nova wagons.

NOTE 4: Data above slash for four/below slash for six (V-8s optional).

CHEVY II NOVA — (6-CYL) — SERIES 115 — A more Deluxe Chevy II, the Nova had these features in addition to (or replacing) those found on the Chevy II 100: black-accented bodyside moldings; body sill moldings; roof drip cap bright moldings; door and rear quarter moldings on two-door hardtops; bright roof rear quarter belt molding on sedan; full-width deck lid or tailgate trim panel (with Chevy II badge and emblem); and bright metal extensions under station wagon rear lights. Interiors were cloth and vinyl (all-vinyl in station wagon). Standard features, in addition to those on lower-priced models, included an illuminated heater control panel; cigarette lighter; glove compartment door trim panel; glove compartment light; instrument panel nameplate; more distinctive door panels and sidewall trim (with bright accents); bright bases on front padded armrests; rear armrest bright bases and built-in ashtrays; foam cushioned rear seat; color-keyed floor carpeting; and automatic front door dome light switches.

1967 Chevrolet, Chevy II Nova SS two-door hardtop, V-8 (AA)

CHEVY II NOVA SERIES

Series No.	Body/Style No.	Body Type & Seating	Factory Price	Shipping Weight	Prod. Total
115	69	4-dr Sed-6P	2296	2660	Note 1
115	37	2-dr HT Cpe-6P	2330	2660	Note 1
115	35	4-dr Sta Wag-6P	2566	2690	Note 2

NOTE 1: Some 47,600 Nova passenger cars were built in the 1967 model year.

NOTE 2: In figures rounded-off to the nearest 100 units, this production included 34,400 sixes and 13,200 V-8s (does not include station wagons).

NOTE 3: Some 12,900 Chevy II station wagons were built during model year 1967. In figures rounded-off to the nearest 100 units, this included 10,000 sixes and 2,900 V-8s. This includes Chevy II 100 and Nova wagons.

NOVA SUPER SPORT — (6-CYL) — SERIES 117 — Revised for 1967, the taut, small Nova continued to make an excellent high-performance car when equipped with this model-option. The 1967 Nova Super Sport had these exterior distinctions: special black-accented grille (with Nova SS emblem low on the driver's side); lower body moldings (above black-painted sill area); bodyside accent stripes; front and rear bright wheelhouse moldings (with extensions along lower fender edges); specific Super Sport full wheel covers. Super Sport rear fender scripts and full-width color accent deck lid trim panel (with center emblem and Nova SS signature). Interiors were all-vinyl, with front Strato bucket seats and bright seat end panels standard. A floor shift trim plate was included on cars with four-speed or automatic transmission. A three-spoke steering wheel was used. Other standard features were the same as Nova.

1967 Chevrolet, Camaro two-door hardtop, 6-cyl

CHEVY II NOVA SUPER SPORT SERIES

Series No.	Body/Style No.	Body Type & Seating	Factory Price	Shipping Weight	Prod. Total
117	11737	2-dr HT Cpe-5P	2467	2690	10,100

NOTE 1: Total Nova SS production for the 1967 model year was 10,100 units.

NOTE 2: In figures rounded-off to the nearest 100 units, production included 1,900 sixes and 8,200 V-8s.

CAMARO — (6-CYL/V-8) — SERIES 123/124 — Chevrolet entered the pony car race with its sporty Camaro for 1967. A 'building block' system of option packages allowed for the creation of many varied and distinctive vehicles. The base model featured: slender body sill moldings; black plastic grille; single-unit headlights; grille-mounted parking lights; small bright metal hubcaps; taillights with bright bezels and built-in back-up lights; windshield pillar and rear belt moldings; and manual-operation top (on convertible). Standard interior features included color-keyed all-vinyl trim with Strato-bucket front seats; scuff-resistant cowlside panels with ventilator grilles; color-keyed carpeting; front armrests with bright bases; cigarette lighter; built-in instrument panel ashtray; automatic front door switches for dome or courtesy lights; locking glove compartment; friction-type ventipanes; and, in convertibles, built-in armrests and dual courtesy lights.

1967 Chevrolet, Camaro two-door convertible (prototype lacking fender script), 6-cyl (PH)

CAMARO SERIES

Series No.	Body/Style No.	Body Type & Seating	Factory Price	Shipping Weight	Prod. Total
123/124	37	2-dr HT Cpe-5P	2466/2572	2770/2920	195,765
123/124	67	2-dr Conv-5P	2704/2609	3025/3180	25,141

NOTE 1: Production included 602 Camaro Z-28 coupes; 64,642 Rally Sports (10,675 RS convertibles); 34,411 Super Sport coupes and convertibles (many with Rally Sport option also).

NOTE 2: Approximately 100-200 Indianapolis 500 Pace Car models and 200-300 Z-10 Pace Car replica hardtops were produced.

1967 Chevrolet, Camaro SS two-door hardtop, V-8

CHEVROLET ENGINES

(SIX-CYLINDER) Inline. Overhead valve. Cast-iron block. Displacement: 250 cid. Bore and stroke: 3.67 x 3.53 inches. Compression ratio: 8.5:1. Brake hp: 155 at 4200 rpm. Hydraulic valve lifters. Carburetor: Rochester one-barrel Model 7026027. (Base equipment for Biscayne/Bel Air/Impala/Impala SS.)

(V-8) Overhead valve. Cast iron block. Displacement: 283 cid. Bore and stroke: 3.875 x 3.00 inches. Compression ratio: 9.25:1. Brake hp: 195 at 4800 rpm. Five main bearings. Carburetor: Rochester two-barrel Model 7027101. (Base V-8 equipment for Biscayne/Bel Air/Impala/Impala SS and standard in Caprice).

CHEVELLE ENGINES

(SIX-CYLINDER) Inline. Overhead valve. Cast iron block. Displacement: 230 cid. Bore and stroke: 3.875 x 3.25 inches. Compression ratio: 8.5:1. Brake hp: 140 at 4400 rpm. Seven main bearings. Hydraulic valve lifters. Carburetor: Rochester one-barrel Model 7027003. (Base engine for all Chevelle models, except SS-396.)

(V-8) Overhead valve. Cast iron block. Displacement: 263 cid. Bore and stroke: 3.675 x 3.00 inches. Compression ratio: 9.25:1. Brake hp: 195 at 4800 rpm. Hydraulic valve lifters. Carburetor: Rochester two-barrel Model 7027101. (Base V-8 equipment for all Chevelle models, except SS-396.)

(SS-396 V-8) Overhead valve. Cast iron block. Displacement: 396 cid. Bore and stroke: 4.094 x 3.76 inches. Compression ratio: 10.25:1. Brake hp: 325 at 4600 rpm. Five main bearings. Hydraulic valve lifters. Carburetor: Rochester Quadra-Jet four-barrel Model 7027201. (Standard in SS-396 and not available in Chevelles otherwise.)

CHEVY II/NOVA ENGINES

(FOUR-CYLINDER) Inline. Overhead valve. Cast alloy iron block. Displacement: 153 cid. Bore and stroke: 3.875 x 3.25 inches. Compression ratio: 8.5:1. Brake hp: 90 at 4000 rpm. Five main bearings. Hydraulic valve lifters. Carburetor: Carter one-barrel Model 3905971. (Base engine for Chevy II 100 series.)

(SIX-CYLINDER) Inline. Cast alloy block. Displacement: 187.6 cid. Bore and stroke: 3.50 x 3.25 inches. Compression ratio: 6.5:1. Brake hp: 120 at 4000 rpm. Seven main bearings. Hydraulic valve lifters. Carburetor: Rochester one-barrel Model 7025105. (Base six for Chevy II 100 series and standard in Nova/Nova SS.)

(V-8) Overhead valve. Cast iron block. Displacement: 326.7 cid. Bore and stroke: 4.00 x 3.25 inches. Compression ratio: 10.0:1. Brake hp: 275 at 4800 rpm. Five main bearings. Hydraulic valve lifters. Carburetor: Rochester four-barrel. (There was not a Chevy II V-8 series, but this was the base V-8 option.)

CAMARO ENGINES

(SIX-CYLINDER) Inline. Overhead valve. Cast iron block. Displacement: 230 cid. Bore and stroke: 3.88 x 3.25 inches. Compression ratio: 8.5:1. Brake hp: 140 at 4400 rpm. Seven main bearings. Hydraulic valve lifters. Carburetor: Downdraft one-barrel. (Base six for all Camaros.)

(V-8) Overhead valve. Cast iron block. Displacement: 327 cid. Bore and stroke: 4.00 x 3.25 inches. Compression ratio: 8.8:1. Brake hp: 210 at 4600 rpm. Five main bearings. Carburetor: Downdraft two-barrel. (Base V-8 for Camaros.)

CHASSIS FEATURES: Wheelbase: (full-size Chevrolets) 119.0 inches; (Chevelle) 115.0 inches; (Chevy II) 110.0 inches; (Camaro) 108.1 inches. Overall length: (full-size Chevrolets) 213.2 inches; (full-size Chevrolet wagons) 212.4 inches; (Chevelle) 197.0 inches; (Chevy II) 163.0 inches; (Camaro) 164.6 inches. Front tread: (full-size Chevrolets) 62.5 inches; (full-size Chevrolet wagons) 63.5 inches; (Chevelle) 58.0 inches; (Chevy II) 56.8 inches; (Chevy II wagons) 56.3 inches; (Camaro) 59.0 inches. Rear tread: (full-size Chevrolets) 62.4 inches; (full-size Chevrolet wagons) 63.4 inches;

(Chevy II) 56.3 inches; (Chevy II wagons) 55.6 inches; (Camaro) 58.9 inches. Tires: (full-size Chevrolets) 8.25 x 14; (with disc brakes) 8.15 x 15; (Impala SS-427) 6.70 x 15; (Chevrolet station wagons) 8.55 x 14; (Chevelles) 7.35 x 14; (Chevelle 384 Sport Sedan/convertible/with 327 V-8s/and wagons) 7.75 x 14; (SS-396) F70-14; (Chevy II) 6.95 x 14; (Camaro) 7.35 x 14; (Camaro SS-350) D70-14; and (Camaro Z-28) 7.75 x 15.

1967 Chevrolet, Camaro Rally Sport two-door hardtop, V-8

FULL-SIZE CHEVROLET OPTIONS: Power brakes ($42). Power steering ($95). Four Season air conditioning ($356). Comfort-On air conditioning ($435). Rear window air deflector on wagons ($19). Rear manual antenna, not available on wagons or with AM/FM radio ($9.50). Custom Deluxe front and rear seat belts ($6). Front shoulder belts ($23). Load area carpets on Caprice and Impala wagons ($53). Electric clock on Biscayne and Bel Air ($16). Rear window defroster ($21). Tinted glass on all windows ($37); windshield only ($21). Door edge guards on two-doors ($3); on four-doors ($6). Rear bumper guards ($16). Front bumper guards ($16). Head rest with Strato-Back or bucket seats ($53). Head rests with standard bench front seats ($42). Heater and defroster deletion ($71 credit). Tri-Volume horn ($14). Special instrumentation, V-8 only ($79). Automatic superlift level control, not available on six-cylinder ($79). Roof luggage rack on wagons ($42). Color-keyed floor mats ($11). Left-hand outside remote control mirror ($10). Two-tone paint ($16). Rear power antenna ($28). Six-Way power seat not available on Biscayne or with bucket seats ($95). Four-Way power seat on Impala, Super Sport with bucket seats ($70). Power tailgate window, standard on three-seat wagons ($32). Power windows, not available on Biscayne ($100). Push-button radio with front antenna ($57). Push-button AM/FM radio with front antenna ($134). Push-button AM/FM radio with front antenna and rear speaker ($147). AM/FM stereo radio with front antenna ($239). Rear seat speaker ($13). Vinyl roof cover on black or beige hardtops ($79). Divided second seat on wagons ($37). Strato-back vinyl seat in Caprice Custom Sedan ($116). Strato-back vinyl seat in Impala SS (no charge). Strato-back cloth seat, Caprice Custom Sedan and Coupe ($105). Strato-back seats including console floor-mounted shift ($158). Rear fender skirts ($26).

Speed and cruise control ($50). Speed warning indicator ($11). Comfort-lift steering wheel with Powerglide Hydramatic or four-speed transmission required ($42). Sport-styled steering wheel ($32). Stereo tape system with four speakers ($129). Wheel covers, not available on Impala SS or Caprice ($21). Mag style wheel covers on all Chevrolets except Impala SS and Caprice ($74). Mag style wheel covers, Impala SS and Caprice ($53). Simulated wire wheel covers on Impala SS and Caprice ($56). Simulated wire wheel covers all except Impala SS and Caprice ($74). A three-speed manual transmission with floor shift was standard with six-cylinder and 283 cid/327 cid V-8s. A three-speed manual transmission with floor shift was optional for 396 cid/427 cid V-8s (RPO M13). Overdrive was optional for the base six-cylinder and base 283 cid V-8 ($16). A four-speed manual transmission with floor shift coded RPO M20 was optional for all V-8 engines ($184). Powerglide two-speed automatic transmission was optional for all engines, except the 427 cid V-8 ($184 with six-cylinder; $195 with V-8). Turbo-Hydramatic ($226). Three-speed automatic transmissions were available with 327/396/427 cid V-8s. Optional engines included: [RPO L30] 327 cid/275 hp V-8 ($92.70). [RPO L35] 396 cid/325 hp V-8 ($158). [RPO L36] 427 cid/385 hp V-8 (included with SS-427 package for $316 total). Posi-Traction rear axle.

CHEVELLE/CHEVY II OPTIONS: Power brakes ($42). Power steering ($84). Four-Season air conditioning. Chevelle ($356). All-Weather air conditioning, Chevy II ($311). Rear antenna ($10). Custom Deluxe front and rear seat belts ($6). Driver and passenger front shoulder belts, standard type ($23); Custom Deluxe type ($26). Front bumper guards, Chevelle ($13); Chevy II ($10). Rear bumper guards, Chevelle ($13, but not available on wagons); Chevy II ($10). Electric clock, Chevelle 300 and 300 Deluxe ($16); Chevy II and Nova ($16). Rear window defroster, sedan and Sport Coupe ($21). Door edge guards, two-doors ($3); four-doors ($6). Tinted glass, all windows ($31); windshield only ($21). Driver and passenger Strato-Ease headrests, in Chevelle with bucket seats and Nova SS ($53), in Chevelle/Nova 100 with standard bench front seat ($42). Heater and defroster deletion ($70 credit). Tri-Volume horn, all Chevelle except 300 ($14). Special instrumentation on Chevelle V-8 Sport Coupes and convertibles ($79). Luggage rack, wagons ($42). Front and rear color-keyed floor mats ($11). Left-hand outside remote control mirror ($10). Two-tone paint ($16). Power tailgate window, wagons ($32). Push-button radio with front antenna and rear speaker ($71). Push-button radio with front antenna ($57). Push-button AM/FM radio with front antenna, Chevelle only ($134). Rear speaker ($13). Vinyl roof cover, Chevelle ($74). Strato bucket seats, Chevelle Sport Coupe and convertible ($111). Speed and cruise control, Chevelle V-8 models ($60). Speed warning indicator ($10). Sport-styled steering wheel ($32). Stereo tape system with four speakers, Chevelle ($129). Tachometer in Chevelle V-8 models ($47). Wheel covers, not available with disc brakes ($21). Mag styled wheel covers for Chevy II/Nova SS/Chevelle SS-

396, not available with disc brakes ($53). Same for Nova Chevy II 100/Chevelle models ($74). Simulated wire wheel covers on Chevy II/Nova SS/SS-396, without disc brakes ($56); same on Nova Chevy II 100/Chevelle models ($74). A three-speed manual transmission, with column shift, was standard on all Chevy II/Novas. A four-speed manual transmission was available with optional Chevy II/Nova V-8s ($184). Powerglide two-speed automatic transmission was available with all Chevy II/Nova engines ($164 or $174 with V-8). Optional Chevy II/Nova engines included [RPO L22] 250 cid/155 hp six-cylinder ($37). [RPO L30] 327 cid/275 hp V-8 ($93). Chevy II/Nova Posi-Traction rear axle ($42). A three-speed manual transmission with column shift, was standard on Chevelles with six-cylinder engines and 283-cid or 327-cid V-8s. A three-speed, heavy-duty manual transmission, with floor shift, was standard with Chevelle SS-396s (optional other models for $79). An overdrive transmission was available for Chevelles with base sixes and 283-cid V-8s ($116). A four-speed manual transmission, with floor shift, was optional for all Chevelle V-8 engines (wide- or close-ratio SS-396 for $105; others for $184). Powerglide two-speed automatic transmission was available with all Chevelle engines, except SS-396 ($116 with six; $195 with V-8). Turbo-HydraMatic three-speed automatic transmission was available with 396-cid V-8s ($147). Optional engines included: [RPO L22] 250 cid/155 hp six-cylinder ($26). [RPO L30] 327 cid/275 hp V-8 ($198). [RPO L79] 327 cid/325 hp V-8 ($93). [RPO L34] 396 cid/350 hp V-8 ($105; SS-396 only). Chevelle Posi-Traction rear axle ($42.15).

CAMARO OPTIONS: All-weather air conditioning ($356). Manual rear antenna, not available with AM/FM radio ($10). Custom Deluxe seat belts ($6). Standard front shoulder belts ($23). Custom Deluxe front shoulder belts ($26). Electric clock, not available with stereo ($16). Floor console with shifter ($47). Rear window defroster, coupe ($21). Tinted glass on all windows ($31); windshield only ($21). Rear bumper guards ($10). Front bumper guards ($13). Door edge guards ($3). Strato-Ease headrests ($53). Heater and defroster deletion ($32 credit). Tri-Volume horn, coupe only ($14). Ashtray light, coupe only ($1.60). Courtesy lights ($4). Glove compartment light, when not included ($2.65). Front and rear floor mats ($42). Power steering ($84). Power windows ($100). Manual push-button radio ($57). Manual push-button radio with rear seat speaker ($71). AM/FM radio ($133). Vinyl roof cover, black or beige for Sport Coupe only ($74). Folding rear seat ($32). Strato-back front seat, not available on convertible with console ($26). Speed and cruise control with V-8 on Powerglide only ($50). Speed warning indicator ($11). Comfort-tilt steering wheel ($42). Sport-style steering wheel ($32). Stereo tape system with four speakers ($128). Simulated wire wheel covers, not available with disc brakes ($74). Simulated mag wheel covers, not available with disc brakes ($74). Special instrumentation group included ammeter, temperature, oil and fuel gauges; electric clock mounted on console; fuel indicator light and tachometer in instrument panel

($79). A three-speed manual transmission was standard on all models, except Z-28. A three-speed heavy-duty manual transmission with floor shift was available for 350 cid/396 cid V-8 engines. A four-speed manual transmission was optional for all engines ($184 with SS-350). Powerglide two-speed automatic transmission was available for six-cylinder ($184) and 327 cid/350 cid V-8s ($195). Turbo-Hydramatic was optional with 396 cid/325 hp V-8. Optional engines included: [RPO Z26] 302 cid/290 hp V-8 (see Z28 package price). [RPO L30] 327 cid/275 hp V-8 ($93). [RPO L48] 350 cid/295 hp V-8 (see L48 package below). [RPO L35] 396 cid/325 hp V-8. [RPO L78] 396 cid/375 hp V-8. Posi-Traction rear axle ($42).

CAMARO OPTION PACKAGES

(Z10) Indy Pace Car coupe package. Installed for a special promotional run of 200-300 cars made during the period of just a couple of weeks.

(Z21) Style trim group RPO Z21 adds front and rear wheelhouse moldings, drip gutter moldings on coupe, and bodyside accent stripes ($29).

(Z23) Special interior group RPO Z23 replaces standard equipment with these items: bright pedal pad frames, windshield pillar moldings in bright metal and roof rail moldings in coupe.

(Z87) Custom interior RPO Z87 replaces standard equipment with these special items: roof rear quarter dome lights on Sport Coupe, recessed door handles, color-keyed accent bands on front and rear seats, special front armrests, glove compartment light, three-spoke oval steering wheel with ornaments, carpeted scuff panels on doors, molded luggage compartment mat ($95).

(Z22) Camaro Rally Sport RPO Z22 includes style trim group and parking lights below bumper, special grille with electrically controlled panels concealing headlamps, 'RS' grille, fender and gas cap emblems, wide lower body moldings, hood drip bright moldings on coupe, bodyside accent strips, black-painted specific taillight bezels and back-up lights below rear bumper ($105).

(L48) Camaro SS-350 option RPO L48 features these additions: 295 hp Turbo-Fire 350 V-8; 'SS' grille, fender and gas cap emblems (even when 'RS' group is included); special hood and simulated intake grids; front hood stripes and five special D70-14 red stripe tires ($105).

(L34) The high-performance SS-396 package coded RPO L34 included equipment similar to the SS-350 package, plus the bigger engine.

(Indy Pace Car) Actual Official Pace Cars for the 1967 Indianapolis 500-Mile Race were equipped with TR 732-Z bright blue custom interior; matching top boot; Rallye wheels; D70-14 nylon cord red stripe tires; and a blue nose stripe. Under the hood was an L35 386 Turbo-Jet V-8 hooked to an M-40 Turbo-Hydramatic

114

and 3.07:1 positraction rear axle. Chevrolet's May 1967 *Pace Car Activity Book* listed 43 Camaro Pace Car convertible replicas built as "Festival" cars, plus 10 replicas for use by Indianapolis Motor Speedway officials and about 25 "Brass Hat" Camaro Pace Car convertibles for VIPs. Including the three actual Pace Cars, a total of at least 61 Camaro Pace Car convertible replicas were made for speedway activities. A total of 66 cars are known to exist and 19 of those have the 396-cid V-8. Information about the Camaro Pace Car Registry can be obtained from the International Camaro Owners Club, 2001 Pittston Ave., Scranton, PA 18503 or by calling (717)585-4082.

HISTORICAL FOOTNOTES: All Chevrolets appeared in dealer showrooms Sept. 29, 1966. Model year production peaked at 1,900,049 units. Calendar year sales of 1,978,550 cars were recorded. E.M. Estes was the chief executive officer of the company this year. In addition to Camaro convertible Pace Cars, Chevrolet supplied eight to 18 Impala station wagons, 10 three-quarter ton trucks and five half-ton pickups for official use during the Indianapolis 500.

1968

BISCAYNE — (6-CYL/V-8) — SERIES 153/154 — Chevrolets grew longer in 1966, with the addition of some bumper, grille, hood and fender modifications. The change that stood out the most was in the taillamp design, which now featured recessed lenses housed in rear bumper apertures. The hood was restyled to cover recessed windshield wipers. The front end featured a 'floating' type bumper design, in which a grille with slightly finer gridwork showed through below the bumper bar. Headlights were now mounted in rectangular bezels. The size of the parking lamps, notched into the front corners of the body, was reduced from 1967 and the lens was now smooth and light colored. Biscayne was the base series with standard equipment including all GM safety features; front seat shoulder belts; door-actuated light switches; heater and defroster; cigarette lighter; locking glovebox; carpeting; armrests; center dome light; Flush & Dry rocker panels; and either the base six or V-8. Passenger cars wore 8.25 x 14 blackwall tires, while station wagons had size 8.55 x 14.

CHEVROLET I.D. NUMBERS: The Vehicle Identification Number was on plate on left front door pillar. The first three symbols indicate make and series and appear as Series Number in first column of charts below. For example, the first car listed has numbers 153 (1=Chevrolet Division; 53=Biscayne six) for six-cylinder series and 154 (1=Chevrolet Division; 54=Biscayne V-8) for eight-cylinder series. Fourth and fifth symbols indicate body type and appear as Body/Style Number in second column of charts below. Sixth symbol indicates model

year: 8=1968. Seventh symbol identifies assembly plant: A=Atlanta, Ga.; B=Baltimore, Md.; C=Southgate, Calif.; D=Doraville, Ga.; F=Flint, Mich.; G=Framingham, Mass.; J=Janesville, Wis.; K=Kansas City, Mo.; U=Lordstown, Ohio; L=Los Angeles, Calif.; N=Norwood, Ohio; R=Arlington, Texas; S=St. Louis, Mo.; T=Tarrytown, N.Y.; W=Willow Run, Mich.; Y=Wilmington, Del.; Z=Fremont, Calif., 2=St. Therese, Canada. Next six symbols are sequential production number. Body Number tag riveted to cowl indicates some of the same information, plus trim and paint codes. Engine numbers are stamped on front right side of V-8 blocks and right side of six-cylinder block behind distributor. Consult factory or aftermarket sources for numerous Chevrolet engine codes.

BISCAYNE SERIES

Series No.	Body/Style No.	Body Type & Seating	Factory Price	Shipping Weight	Prod. Total
153/154	69	4-dr Sed-6P	2484/2589	3395/3525	Note 1
153/154	11	2-dr Sed-6P	2442/2547	3335/3465	Note 1
153/154	35	4-dr Sta Wag-6P	2817/2923	3765/3885	Note 3

NOTE 1: In rounded-off total 82,100 Biscayne 1968 passenger cars were built.

NOTE 2: Rounded-off total includes 44,500 sixes and 3,600 V-8s, not including station wagons.

NOTE 3: Rounded-off total of 175,600 full-size station wagons built in all lines.

NOTE 4: Station wagon total includes 7,700 sixes/167,900 V-8s, but no series breakout.

NOTE 5: Data above slash for six/below slash for V-8.

BEL AIR — (6-CYL/V-8) — SERIES 155/156 — The Bel Air series was Chevrolet's moderate-priced, full-size line for 1968. Bel Air had all standard equipment found in Biscaynes, plus mid-bodyside moldings; bright metal rear window, roof drip and windshield moldings; front and rear side marker lamps; glovebox and ignition switch lights; and upgraded interior trims. Station wagons featured all-vinyl interior; seat belts for all passengers; and automatic ignition key alarms. The three-seat station wagon also had a power tailgate window.

BEL AIR SERIES

Series No.	Body/Style No.	Body Type & Seating	Factory Price	Shipping Weight	Prod. Total
155/156	69	4-dr Sed-6P	2723/2626	3466/3562	Note 1
155/156	11	2-dr Sed-6P	2661/2786	3404/3518	Note 1
155/156	45	4-dr Sta Wag-9P	3183/3238	3878/3981	Note 3
155/156	35	4-dr Sta Wag-6P	3020/3125	3823/3926	Note 3

NOTE 1: In rounded-off total 152,200 Bel Air 1968 passenger cars were built.

NOTE 2: Rounded-off total includes 28,900 sixes and 123,400 V-8s, not including station wagons.

NOTE 3: Rounded-off total of 175,600 full-size station wagons in all lines.

NOTE 4: Station wagon total includes 7,700 sixes/167,900 V-8s, but no series breakout.

1968 Chevrolet, Impala SS two-door convertible, V-8

IMPALA — (6-CYL/V-8) — SERIES 163/164 — The Impala series was Chevrolet's top-selling full-size line. It had the same general styling features as the other big cars, except that a new formal-top roofline treatment was available. This gave buyers a choice between a fastback or "coach" style top. Standard equipment began with everything included for the Bel Air. However, bright roof drip moldings were not used on Impala two-door sedans or four-door sedans and station wagons. Additional features for the volume series included Deluxe steering wheel; door and window frame moldings; ignition switch and luggage lights; and front and rear foam seat cushions. The Impala Sport Coupe also had thin, bright metal rocker panel accent moldings below its doors and bright metal wheel lip trim. The convertible featured courtesy lights, all-vinyl upholstery and carpeting on lower door panels. The three-seat Impala station wagon had a built-in rear bumper step. Super Sport equipment returned to its original status as an optional equipment package.

IMPALA SERIES

Series No.	Body/Style No.	Body Type & Seating	Factory Price	Shipping Weight	Prod. Total
163/164	69	4-dr Sed-6P	2846/2951	3513/3623	Note 1
163/164	39	4-dr HT Sed-6P	2917/3022	3601/3711	Note 1
163/164	87	2-dr HT Cpe-6P	2663/2968	3517/3623	Note 1
164	47	2-dr FT Cpe-6P	3021	3628	Note 1
164	67	2-dr Conv-6P	3197	3677	Note 5
164	45	4-dr Sta Wag-9P	3358	4042	Note 3
164	35	4-dr Sta Wag-6P	3245	3984	Note 3

NOTE 1: In rounded-off total, 710,900 Impala 1968 passenger cars were built.

NOTE 2: Rounded-off total includes 11,500 sixes and 699,500 V-8s, not including station wagons.

NOTE 3: Rounded-off total of 175,600 full-size station wagons built in all lines.

NOTE 4: Station wagon total includes 7,700 sixes/167,900 V-8s, but no series breakout.

NOTE 5: Impala convertible production was 24,730 for model year.

NOTE 6: Data above slash for six/below slash for V-8.

CAPRICE — (V-8) — SERIES 166 — The Caprice represented the top of the full-size Chevrolet line. Its equipment assortment began with all Impala features, plus full wheel covers; courtesy and ashtray lamps; Caprice signature script; fender lights; distinctive side moldings; electric clock; and front center armrest seat. The Caprice coupe also included the Astro Ventilation System. Caprice station wagons had instrument panel courtesy lamps and, in three-seat styles, courtesy lights in the auxiliary passenger area.

1968 Chevrolet, Caprice two-door hardtop, V-8 (GM)

CAPRICE SERIES

Series No.	Body/Style No.	Body Type & Seating	Factory Price	Shipping Weight	Prod. Total
166	39	4-dr HT Sed-6P	3271	3754	Note 1
166	47	2-dr FT Cpe-6P	3219	3646	Note 1
166	45	4-dr Sta Wag-9P	3570	4062	Note 2
166	35	4-dr Sta Wag-6P	3458	4003	Note 2

NOTE 1: In rounded-off total 115,500 Caprice 1968 passenger cars were built.

NOTE 2: Rounded-off total of 175,600 full-size station wagons built in all lines.

1968 Chevrolet, Caprice six-passenger Estate Wagon, V-8 (PH)

NOTE 3: Station wagon total includes 7,700 sixes/167,900 V-8s, but no series breakout.

NOTE 4: Data above slash for six/below slash for V-8.

CHEVELLE 300 — (6-CYL/V-8) — SERIES 131/132 — The Chevelle was completely and attractively restyled for model year 1968, with one additional body style added to the line in the form of a new station wagon. Characteristics of the latest appearance included long hood/short deck characteristics with the front fenders swept back and cut under the feature line. Two wheelbases were provided, the shorter for two-doors and the longer for four-doors. The standard V-8 now displaced 307 cubic inches. Lowest in price was the base 300 line on which, other than the windshield surround and ventipane frames, practically no chrome moldings were used. A new front bumper was straighter-lined, with the only openings being large squares flanking the license plate, plus smaller, outboard rectangles incorporating amber parking light lenses. The horizontal, dual headlamps were mounted in individual, bright metal bezels of square shape and the full-width grille featured a fine gridwork of cross-hatched moldings with black-finished air slot directly above. Chevelle script appeared on the front fenders behind the wheel openings (at mid-body height) and above the left headlight. Standard equipment included all GM safety features; front armrests; heater and defroster; base six or V-8 and 7.35 x 14 two-ply (four-ply rated) tires. Base station wagons, however, used 7.75 x 14 blackwalls. Standard interiors were all textured vinyl in blue, gold or black.

CHEVELLE 300 SERIES

Series No.	Body/Style No.	Body Type & Seating	Factory Price	Shipping Weight	Prod. Total
131/132	27	2-dr Cpe-6P	2341/2447	3988/3124	Note 1
131/132	35	4-dr Nomad Wag-6P	2625/2731	3350/2731	Note 3

NOTE 1: In rounded-off total 12,600 Chevelle 300 1968 passenger cars were built.

NOTE 2: Rounded-off total includes 9,700 sixes and 2,900 V-8s, not including station wagons.

NOTE 3: Rounded-off total of 45,500 Chevelle station wagons built in all lines.

NOTE 4: Station wagon total includes 10,700 sixes/34,800 V-8s, but no series breakouts.

NOTE 5: Data above slash for six/below slash for V-8.

CHEVELLE 300 DELUXE — (6-CYL/V-8) — SERIES 133/134 —
The easiest way to distinguish the Chevelle 300 Deluxe was to look for the ribbed, bright metal rocker panels below the door. These were promoted as the 'Flush & Dry' type. Other equipment, above the most basic assortment, included a left-hand outside rearview mirror; front shoulder belts; Chevrolet badge on grille center and rear deck latch panel; door switch dome lamp; lane change turn signals; keyless door locking; suspended accelerator pedal; back-up lights and self-adjusting brakes. Four-doors had chrome window sill moldings, while two-doors had chrome trim along the upper window frame. As on all Chevelles when the base V-8 was added, a black, rectangular engine call-out badge was positioned ahead of the front fender side marker lens and framed in the same band of bright metal. The all-vinyl textured seating surfaces used in Chevelle 300 Deluxes came only in black, although blue, black or gold fabric/vinyl combinations were also provided.

CHEVELLE 300 DELUXE SERIES

Series No.	Body/Style No.	Body Type & Seating	Factory Price	Shipping Weight	Prod. Total
133/134	69	4-dr Sed-6P	2445/2550	3071/3207	Note 1
133/134	37	2-dr HT Cpe-6P	2479/2584	3036/3171	Note 1
133/134	27	2-dr Cpe-6P	2415/2521	3005/3141	Note 1
133/134	35	4-dr Nomad Wag-6P	2736/2641	3409/3554	Note 3

NOTE 1: In rounded-off total 43,200 Deluxe 300 1968 passenger cars were built.

NOTE 2: Rounded-off total includes 24,500 sixes and 17,700 V-8s, not including station wagons.

NOTE 3: Rounded-off total of 45,500 Chevelle station wagons built in all lines.

NOTE 4: Station wagon total includes 10,700 sixes/34,800 V-8s, but no series breakouts.

NOTE 5: Data above slash for six/below slash for V-8.

1968 Chevrolet, Chevelle Malibu four-door sedan, V-8

CHEVELLE MALIBU — (6-CYL/V-8) — SERIES 135/136 —
The new Malibu was trimmed to play its role as the top non-super-high-performance car in the Chevelle lineup. Like the 300 Deluxe, a Chevrolet insignia was carried in the center of its grille. The Malibu, however, did not have the 300 Deluxe's matching insignia on the rear deck latch panel. Instead, the panel was banded in chrome, with a Chevelle signature near the right rear taillamp. The taillamps themselves were different, as Malibu back-up lights were repositioned into the back bumper. Other added highlights included Malibu script on the front fender sides; chrome trim along the front feature line (also extending along the lower side feature line); twin pin stripes along the upper side feature line; and additional window frame accents. Standard equipment began at the Deluxe level and added hideaway two-speed wipers; Deluxe steering wheel; illuminated heater controls; ignition alarm system; crank-operated ventipanes; side marker lights; high level ventilation and wheel covers. Interior trim choices varied with body style and there was also a special Concours four-door hardtop. It came with all-vinyl seating; lockable glovebox with light; extra thick foam-cushioned seats; color-keyed wall-to-wall carpeting; black-accented wheel openings; black-trimmed lower body accents; ribbed bright metal rear deck lid latch panel plate; Concours signature script; chrome wheel lip moldings; special oval steering wheel with horn tabs; and woodgrained dash panel inlays. It was called the Concours Sport Sedan and had a lot of extra appeal. Malibu interior trims included the regular fab-

ric/vinyl patterns in gold, black, blue and gray-green; or all-vinyl in teal, gold, black, blue, red and parchment black or the Concours Sport Sedan's special Custom fabric choice in gold, blue, black or gray-green.

MALIBU SERIES

Series No.	Body/Style No.	Body Type & Seating	Factory Price	Shipping Weight	Prod. Total
135/136	69	4-dr Sed-6P	2524/2629	3090/3223	Note 1
135/136	39	4-dr HT Sed-6P	2929/2735	3165/3298	Note 1
135/136	37	2-dr HT Cpe-6P	2558/2663	3037/3170	Note 1
135/136	67	2-dr Conv-6P	2757/2663	3115/3245	Note 5
135/136	35	4-dr Sta Wag-6P	2846/2951	3421/3554	Note 3

NOTE 1: In rounded-off total 266,400 Malibu 1968 passenger cars were built.

NOTE 2: Rounded-off total includes 33,100 sixes and 233,200 V-8s, not including station wagons.

NOTE 3: Rounded-off total of 45,500 Chevelle station wagons built in all lines.

NOTE 4: Station wagon total includes 10,700 sixes/34,800 V-8s, but no series breakouts.

NOTE 5: Combined Malibu and SS-396 convertible production was 10,600.

NOTE 6: Data above slash for six/below slash for V-8.

CHEVELLE CONCOURS — (6-CYL/V-8) — SERIES 137/138
— In addition to the Concours Sport Sedan in the regular model line there was a separate Concours Estate station wagon sub-series. It included only one luxury wagon model, which was specially-trimmed. It came standard with all GM safety features, plus all-vinyl upholstery; lighted glovebox light; extra thick foam-cushioned seats; simulated walnut exterior side and rear paneling; hideaway two-speed wipers; chrome wheel lip moldings; and special oval steering wheel with the horn tabs.

CONCOURS ESTATE SUB-SERIES

Series No.	Body/Style No.	Body Type & Seating	Factory Price	Shipping Weight	Prod. Total
137/138	35	4-dr Cus Sta Wag-6P	2976/3063	3543/3561	Note 1

NOTE 1: Concours Estate production included with that of all Chevelle station wagons.

CHEVELLE SS-396 — (V-8) — SERIES 138 — Quick-
size convenience; floor-mounted shift; vinyl upholstery; carpeting; and brand-new looks characterized the high-performance Chevelle SS-396 series. Other standard extras on the two models in the line included fender mounted side marker lamps; lower bodyside moldings with front and rear extensions; black-accented finish below the feature line, front to rear; specific SS-396 identification at grille and latch panel centers; black-out grille treatment; black-finished deck panel plate; F70-14 four-ply rated special Red Stripe (or White Stripe) tires; concealed windshield wipers; 396 cid/325 hp V-8; full wheel covers with SS center medallions; and "Turbo-Jet 396" engine call-out badges ahead of side marker lenses.

1968 Chevrolet, Chevelle SS396 two-door hardtop, V-8 (PH)

CHEVELLE SS-396 SERIES

Series No.	Body/Style No.	Body Type & Seating	Factory Price	Shipping Weight	Prod. Total
138	37	2-dr HT Cpe-6P	2899	3475	Note 1
138	67	2-dr Conv-6P	3102	3551	Notes 1/3

NOTE 1: Rounded-off calendar production total was 57,600 Chevelle SS-396s.

NOTE 2: Model year production was 62,785 Chevelle SS-396s.

NOTE 3: No body style breakouts available.

NOTE 4: Chevy built 131,700 Turbo-Jet 396 V-8s in model year 1968 (all lines).

CHEVY II NOVA — (FOUR/6-CYL) — SERIES 111/113
— Chevrolet's senior compact underwent a basic styling change in 1968. The new body was longer and wider and featured a Chevelle-inspired semi-fastback roofline with wide, flaring sail panels. Another change was a reduction in base model offerings, with only two-door coupes and four-door sedans remaining. The four-cylinder engine remained available, but only slightly more than 1,000 were sold. The 230-cid engine was the base six and the 307-cid was the base V-8. Even the Turbo-Jet 396 high-performance V-8 was optional. So was a Super Sport equipment package. The Chevy II would stay with this basic body through 1974 and a just slightly modified one thereafter. However, the 1968 model can be identified by the positioning of the Chevy II name at the center of the upper grille surround. Other features included single headlamps set into square bezels; a full-width multiple bar grille; and the Chevelle-like rear end look. Standard equipment included all GM safety features; heater and defroster; front armrests; foot-operated emergency brake; ignition alarm system; concealed fuel filler; front and rear side marker lights and 7.35 x 14 (four-ply rated) two-ply blackwall tires.

CHEVY II SERIES

Series No.	Body/Style No.	Body Type & Seating	Factory Price	Shipping Weight	Prod. Total
FOUR					
111	69	4-dr Sed-6P	2229	2790	Note 1
111	27	2-dr Cpe-6P	2199	2760	Note 1
SIX					
113	69	4-dr Sed-6P	2291	2890	Note 2
113	27	2-dr Cpe-6P	2261	2860	Note 2
V-8					
114	69	4-dr Sed-6P	2396	N/A	Note 2
114	27	2-dr Cpe-6P	2367	N/A	Note 2

1968 Chevrolet, Chevy II Nova two-door coupe, V-8

NOTE 1: 1,270 four-cylinder 1968 Chevy IIs were built.

NOTE 2: Rounded-off totals include 146,300 sixes and 53,400 V-8s.

1968 Chevrolet, Camaro two-door hardtop, 6-cyl (PH)

CAMARO — (6-CYL/V-8) — The Camaro was virtually unchanged as it entered its second model year, although close inspection would show the addition of the new front and rear side marker lights and ventless door glass. Standard equipment included all GM safety features; integrated front headlamps and parking lights; Strato-bucket front seats; all-vinyl interior; carpeting; Astro Ventilation System; front shoulder belts; outside rearview mirror; the new side marker lights; heater and defroster; five 7.35 x 14 (two-ply) four-ply rated blackwall tires and courtesy lights in the convertible.

CAMARO SERIES

Series No.	Body/Style No.	Body Type & Seating	Factory Price	Shipping Weight	Prod. Total
123/124	37	2-dr HT Spt Cpe-4P	2638/2727	3040/3050	214,711
123/124	67	2-dr Conv-4P	2852/2941	3160/3295	20,440

NOTE 1: Production included 50,937 sixes and 184,178 V-8s.

NOTE 2: 40,977 Camaros had the RS equipment package.

NOTE 3: 27,634 Camaros had the SS equipment package.

NOTE 4: 7,199 Camaros had the Z/28 option.

NOTE 5: 12,997 Camaros were built for export.

NOTE 6: 54,948 three-speeds/47,572/ four-speeds/ 132,631 automatics built.

NOTE 7: 35,666 with air; 115,260 cars with power steering; 3,304 with power windows built.

NOTE 8: Data above slash for six/below slash for V-8.

1968 Chevrolet, Camaro SS-350 two-door hardtop, V-8 (AA)

CHEVROLET ENGINES

(CHEVY II) Inline four. Overhead valve. Cast iron block. Displacement: 153 cid. Bore and stroke: 3.875 x 3.25 inches. Compression ratio: 8.5:1. Brake hp: 90 at 4000 rpm. Five main bearings. Hydraulic valve lifters. Carburetor: Rochester one-barrel Model 7028009.

(CHEVELLE 300/CHEVY II NOVA/CAMARO) Inline six. Overhead valve. Cast iron block. Displacement: 230 cid. Bore and stroke: 3.875 x 3.25 inches. Compression ratio: 8.5:1. Brake hp: 140 at 4400 rpm. Seven main bearings. Hydraulic valve lifters. Carburetor: Rochester one-barrel Model 7028017.

(BISCAYNE/BELAIR/IMPALA) Inline six. Overhead valve. Cast iron block. Displacement: 250 cid. Bore and stroke: 3.875 x 3.53 inches. Compression ratio: 8.5:1. Brake hp: 155 at 4200 rpm. Seven main bearings. Hydraulic valve lifters. Carburetor: Carter one-barrel Model 3891593.

(BISCAYNE/BELAIR/IMPALA/CHEVELLE/CHEVY II/ CAPRICE) V-8. Overhead valve. Cast iron block. Displacement: 307 cid. Bore and stroke: 3.875 x 3.25 inches. Compression ratio: 10.0:1. Brake hp: 200 at 4600 rpm. Five main bearings. Carburetor: Rochester two-barrel Model 7026101.

(CAMARO) V-8. Overhead valve. Cast iron block. Displacement: 326.7 cid. Bore and stroke: 4.00 x 3.25 inches. Compression ratio: 8.75:1. Brake hp: 210 at 4000 rpm. Five main bearings. Hydraulic valve lifters. Carburetor: Rochester two-barrel Model 7028101.

(CAPRICE) V-8. Overhead valve. Cast iron block. Displacement: 307 cid. Bore and stroke: 3.875 x 3.25 inches. Compression ratio: 10.0:1. Brake hp: 200 at 4600 rpm. Five main bearings. Carburetor: Rochester two-barrel Model 7026101.

(CHEVELLE SS-396) V-8. Overhead valve. Cast iron block. Displacement: 396 cid. Bore and stroke: 4.09 x 3.76 inches. Compression ratio: 10.25:1. Brake hp: 325 at 4800 rpm. Five main bearings. Hydraulic valve lifters. Carburetor: Rochester Quadra-Jet four-barrel.

CHASSIS FEATURES: Wheelbase: (Chevrolet) 119 inches; (Chevelle two-door) 112 inches; (Chevelle four-door) 116 inches; (Nova) 111 inches; (Camaro) 106 inches. Overall length: (Chevrolet wagon) 214 inches; (Chevrolet) 215 inches; (Chevelle wagon) 208 inches;

(Chevelle four-door) 202 inches; (Chevelle two-door) 198 inches; (Nova) 190 inches; (Camaro) 185 inches. Front tread: (Chevrolet) 62.5 inches; (Chevelle) 59 inches; (Nova) 59 inches; (Camaro) 59 inches. Rear tread: (Chevrolet) 62.4 inches; (Chevelle) 59 inches; (Nova) 58.9 inches; (Camaro) 58 inches. Various tire options.

CHEVROLET OPTIONS: Dual stage air cleaner, with six ($5.30). Four Season air conditioning, except with 425 hp V-8 ($368.65). Comfort-On automatic temperature control air conditioning, except with 425 hp V-8 ($447.65). Posi-traction rear axle ($42.15). Station wagon load area carpeting ($52.70). Heavy-duty chassis equipment on Biscayne ($36 90). Electric clock, standard in Caprice ($15.80). Heavy-duty clutch ($10.55). Rear window defroster ($21.10). Turbo-Fire 327 cid/250 hp V-8 ($63.20). Turbo-Fire 327 cid/275 hp V-8 ($92.70). Turbo-Jet 396 cid/325 hp V-8 ($158). Turbo-Jet 427 cid/385 hp V-8, included with SS-427 option ($263.30). Turbo-Jet 427 cid/425 hp V-8 ($447.65). Dual exhaust with 250, 275 or 325 hp V-8 ($27.40). Tinted glass, windshield ($25.30); all windows ($39.50). Caprice retractable headlights ($79). Headrests with Strato bucket seats ($52.70); with bench seats ($42.15). Special instrumentation including ammeter, oil pressure, temperature gauges and tachometer, in Caprice ($79), in other models, including clock ($94 80). Remote control left and outside rearview mirror ($9.50). Station wagon rooftop luggage rack, fixed type ($44.25); adjustable type ($63.20). Power rear antenna ($28.45). Power drum brakes ($42.15). Power disc brakes, includes 15-inch hubcaps, wheels and tires ($121.15). Power door lock system, two-door ($44.80); four-door ($66.50). Six-Way power seat, except Biscaynes, cars with bucket seats or cars with four-speed manual transmission ($94.60). Four-Way power left-hand bucket seat ($69.55). Power steering ($94.60). Power tailgate window ($31.60). Power windows, except Biscayne and Styles 15511/15611 ($100.10). Heavy-duty radiator ($13.70). Push-button AM radio with antenna ($61.10). Push-button AM/FM radio with front antenna ($133.80). AM/FM radio and stereo ($239.15). Rear manual antenna ($9 50). Rear speaker ($13.20). Stereotape system with four speakers ($133.80). White or black vinyl roof for all hardtops ($89.55). Cloth Strato-Back seats ($105.35). Strato-Back seats, bucket style ($158). Superlift shock absorbers, standard type ($42.15); automatic level control type ($89.55). Cruise Master speed control ($92.70). Rear fender skirts, except station wagons and disc brakes ($26.35). Speed warning indicator ($10.55). Deluxe steering wheel ($4.25). Comfort-Tilt steering wheel ($42.15). Sport steering wheel ($31.60). Front and rear special purpose suspension ($21.10). Overdrive transmission ($115.90). Powerglide transmission, with six ($184.35); with V-8s, except '427' ($194.85). Close-Range four-speed manual transmission with '427' V-8 ($184.35). Heavy-duty Close-Range four-speed manual transmission with '427' V-8 only ($310.70). Wide-Range four-speed manual transmission, in all V-8 models ($184.35). Turbo-Hydramatic transmission ($226.45-$237). All-vinyl interior trim ($5.30-$10.55).

Wheel covers, standard 14 inch ($21.10), mag-style 14 inch — Caprice or Super Sport ($52.70); others ($73.75); simulated wire type — Caprice or Super Sport ($55.85); others ($73.75). Mag spoke 14-inch wheel covers. Caprice or Super Sport ($52.70); others ($73.75). Rallye wheels, on Caprice or SS-427 without disc brakes; ($21.10); others ($31.60); with discs ($10.55). Appearance Guard Group ($26.35-$49.55). Auxiliary Lighting Group ($2.65-$39). Convenience Operating Group ($9.50-$46.40). Decor Group ($21.10-$72.60). RPO Z03 Impala Super Sport Option, includes special all-vinyl interior; Strato-Bucket seats; center console; SS wheel covers and console shift with automatic or four-speed manual transmissions, on Impala Custom Coupe, Sport Coupe or convertible ($179.05). RPO Z24 Impala SS-427 Option, includes all the above plus special hood; Red Stripe tires; ornamentation; special suspension features and 15-inch wheels, with RPO L36 Turbo-Jet 385 hp V-8 ($358.10); with RPO L72 Turbo-Jet 425 hp V-8 ($542.45). Notes: V-8 engine option prices are in addition to cost of base V-8. Where a range of prices is indicated, retail varied according to model, trim level, body style or inclusion of other features. It was usually slightly less expensive to add some options to the top line models. Numerous tire options were provided for all 1968 Chevrolets.

CHEVELLE OPTIONS: Four-Season air conditioning ($360.20). Station wagon air deflector ($19). Posi-traction rear axle ($42.15). Economy or performance axle ($2.15). Heavy-duty battery ($7.40). Station wagon rooftop carrier ($44.25). Electric clock ($15 80). Heavy-duty clutch, with six ($5.30); with V-8 ($10.55). Center console, including electric clock and with bucket seats, gearshift lever is mounted in console/available with three-speed only in SS-396 ($50 60). Rear windshield defroster ($21.10). RPO L22 250 cid/155 hp six ($26.35). RPO L73 327 cid/250 hp V-8 ($63.20). RPO L30 327 cid/275 hp V-8 ($92.70). RPO L79 327 cid/325 hp V-8 ($198.05). RPO L34 396 cid/350 hp V-8 in SS-396 only ($105.35). RPO L76 396 cid/375 hp V-8 in SS-396 only ($237). Dual exhaust ($27.40). Temperature-controlled fan ($15.00). Tinted glass, all windows ($34.80); windshield only ($26.35). Special instrumentation, Malibu V-8s and SS-396 only ($94.80). Light monitoring system ($26.35). Remote control left-hand outside rearview mirror ($9.50). Two-tone paint ($21.10). Power disc front brakes ($100.10). Power front drum brakes ($42.15). Power steering ($94.80). Power convertible top ($52.70). Power windows, in Concours/Malibu/SS-396 only ($100.10). AM/FM radio with front antenna ($61.10). AM/FM radio with front antenna ($133.80). AM/FM radio with stereo and front antenna ($239.15). Rear seat speaker ($13.20). White or black vinyl top on hardtops ($84.30). Strato bucket seats in Malibu/SS-396 ($110.60). Superlift shock absorbers ($42.15). Speed and Cruise Control, automatic transmission required ($52.70). Speed warning indicator ($10.55). Comfort-Tilt steering wheel ($42.15). Sport-style steering wheel ($31.60). SS-396 accent striping ($29.50). Four-speed manual transmissions: special close-ratio type for SS-396 with 375 hp V-8

($237); close-ratio for all models with 325, 360 or 375 hp V-8s ($184.35); Wide-Range-type ($184.35). Turbo-Hydramatic in SS-396 with 325 or 350 hp V-8s ($237). Three-speed manual transmission with floor shift ($79). Powerglide transmission, with six ($184.35); with small V-8s ($194.85). Overdrive ($115.90). Vinyl interior trim, Malibu or 300s ($10.55). Wheel covers, regular type ($6.35); mag style ($21.10); simulated wire/mag-spoke Rallye styles, all ($73.75). Rallye wheels with special hubcaps and trim rings ($31 60). Hidden windshield wipers ($19).

CHEVY II OPTIONS: All-Season air conditioning, except four-cylinders ($347.60). Rear posi-traction axle ($42.15). Console with floor mounted shift, except four-cylinders (bucket seats required), not available on 295 or 325 hp engine with standard transmission ($50.60). Electric clock ($15.80). Heavy-duty clutch ($5.30). 250 cid/155 hp six-cylinder ($26.35). 327 cid/275 hp V-8 ($92.70). 327 cid/325 hp V-8 ($198.05). Dual exhaust, V-8 models with standard or 275 hp engine only ($27.40). Tinted glass, all windows ($30.55); windshield only ($21.10). Special instrumentation, V-8 coupes with console ($94.80). Left-hand outside remote-control mirror ($9.50). Power brakes, all with drum-type brakes except four-cylinder ($42.15). Power brakes, all with disc-type brakes except four-cylinder ($100.10). Power steering, except four-cylinder ($84.30). Vinyl roof cover in white or black, all except four-cylinder ($73.75). Sport-styled steering wheel ($31.60). Stereo tape system ($133.80). Powerglide, four- and six-cylinder models ($163.70). Powerglide, with 200, 275, 295 and 325 hp engines ($174.25). Four-speed wide range, with 200, 275, 295 and 325 hp engines ($184.35). Four-speed close range, with 325 hp engines ($79.00). Simulated wire wheel covers ($73.75). Mag-style wheel covers ($73.75). Mag spoke wheel covers ($31.60). Custom Exterior Group ($68.50). Exterior Decor Package ($31.60). Nova SS Option includes: 350 cid/295 hp Turbo-Fire engine, special steering wheel, hood ornaments, black-accented grilleand rear deck plate, hood insulation, nameplate, deck emblems, SS grille, red stripe tires on six-inch rims. Special Interior Group ($15.60).

CAMARO OPTIONS: Four-Season air conditioning ($360.20). Posi-traction rear axle ($42.15). Electric clock ($15.80). Rear window defroster ($21.10). 155 hp Turbo-Thrift six-cylinder ($26.25). 275 hp Turbo-Fire V-8 ($92.70). Dual exhaust, with deep tone mufflers with 210 or 275 hp engines ($27.40). Dual exhaust, with 210 or 275 hp engines ($27.40). Tinted glass on all windows, with air conditioning ($26.35); windshield only ($30.55). Special instrumentation, not available on 375 hp or 302 cid engines, includes ammeter, temperature, oil pressure and fuel gauges mounted on console, electric clock and tachometer mounted in instrument panel, in V-8 models with console ($94.80). Light monitoring system ($26.35). Power drum brakes ($42.15). Power disc brakes ($100.10). Power steering ($64.30). Power top in white, black or blue on convertible ($52.70). Power windows ($100.10). Heavy-duty radiator, standard with air; not available with 302-cid or 396-cid engines

($13.70). Push-button AM radio ($61.10). Push-button AM/FM radio ($133.80). Push-button AM/FM stereo radio ($239.15). Manual rear antenna, not available with AM/FM or auxiliary panel and valance ($9.50). Stereo tape system ($133.80). White or black vinyl roof cover, Sport Coupe ($73.75). Rear folding seat ($42.15). Strato-back front seat, Sport Coupe, not available with console ($32 65). Speed and Cruise Control, V-8 only, Powerglide required ($52.70). Speed warning indicator ($10.55). Special rear springs included. Rear bumper guards ($20.05). Special steering with quick response ($15.80). Comfort-Tilt steering wheel, automatic or floor-mounted transmission required ($42.15). Sport-style steering wheel ($31.60). Accent striping ($13.70). Powerglide, six-cylinder ($184.35). Powerglide, with all 210, 275 and 295 hp V-8s ($194 85). Three-speed special with 295, 325, 350 and 375 hp engines ($79.00). Four-speed wide range, except with 375 hp engines ($184.35). Four-speed close-ratio, with 350, 375 hp and 302 cid engines ($184.35). Four-speed heavy-duty close-ratio, with 375 hp engine ($310.70). Turbo-HydraMatic, with 325 and 350 hp engines ($237.00). Rallye wheels ($31.60). Bright metal wheel covers ($21.10). Simulated wire wheel covers ($73.75). Mag-style wheel covers ($73.75). Mag spoke wheel covers ($73.75). Appearance Guard Group ($40.10). Camaro SS Option includes: special hood, special red stripe tires, SS emblems, hood insulation, black accented grille, front accent band, engine accents, special suspension, V-8 engine (dual exhaust, no charge) with 295 hp L48 V-8 ($210.65); with 325 hp L35 V-8 ($263.30); with 350 hp L34 V-8 ($368.65); with 375 hp L78 V-8 ($500.30). Rally Sport Group ($105.35).

HISTORICAL FOOTNOTES: Style Number 47, the Formal-Top (FT) coupe was called the Custom Coupe. The Impala Super Sport option, RPO Z03 was available for styles 87, 47 and 67 at $179.05 extra. The Impala SS-427 package, RPO Z24 with 427 cid/385 hp L36 Turbo-Jet V-8 was available for the same models at $358.10 extra. The Impala SS-427 package, RPO Z24 with 427 cid/425 hp L72 Turbo-Jet V-8 was available for the same models at $542.45 extra. A total of 38,210 Impalas had one of these options installed. 105,858 Chevy IIs made for domestic sale had dual exhaust.

1969

BISCAYNE — (6-CYL/V-8) — SERIES 153/154 — Full-size Chevrolets were completely redesigned. While wheelbase was unchanged, cars grew an inch in length; station wagons three inches. A new, integrated bumper/grille imparted a narrower look, although the width of 80 inches was the same as the previous year. The area around the front and rear wheelhousings was flared out, giving a more highly sculptured appearance. The lower body feature line kicked-up, between the flares, giving a 'pinched' bodyside effect. A straight, upper feature line ran between the wraparound ends of the front and back bumpers. The grille surround was a heavy chrome molding completely encircling head-lamps and grille. The grille insert was a grid-patterned type, with bright, prominent cross-hatched moldings forming large, square openings that were filled with mul-tiple, smaller blades. Parking lamps were set into the front gravel pan, which had a wide slot at the center allowing a portion of the grille to show through. Vertical, rectangular side markers were positioned at the ex-treme forward edge of front fenders. Taillights were of a round-cornered rectangular shape and set into the rear bumper. Twin lamps were seen on Biscaynes (triple lamps on upper series cars). Identification trim consist-ed of a Chevrolet insignia at the center of the grille, Chevrolet script on the left hood and right deck lid edges and a model script behind the front wheelwell at mid-fender height. New transmissions, some new engines, ventless side window glass and an anti-theft steering column were promoted advances. New options includ-ed a headlight washing device and automatic liquid 'tire chain' dispensing system. Basic equipment on the Bis-cayne included all GM safety features; head restraints (as a mandatory option); door-actuated light switches; heater and defroster; cigarette lighter; locking glove-box; carpeting; armrests; center dome light; 8.25 x 14 two-ply (four-ply rated) black sidewall tires and either the 155 hp six or 235 hp V-8 as base powerplants. Stan-dard equipment in Biscayne and all other full-size Chev-rolet station wagons included all GM safety features; heater and defroster; front head restraints (mandatory option); all-vinyl trim; dual-speed electric wipers and washers; carpeting; Hide-Away windshield wipers; Astro Ventilation; dual-action tailgate and ashtray light.

CHEVROLET I.D. NUMBERS: Serial numbers on all Chevrolet products were now found on the top left-hand surface of the instrument panel. They were visible through the windshield. The Vehicle Identification Num-ber had 13 symbols. The first three symbols indicate make and series and appear as Series Number in first column of charts below. For example, the first car listed has number 153 (1=Chevrolet; 53=Biscayne six) for six-cylinder series and 154 (1=Chevrolet; 54=Biscayne V-8) for eight-cylinder series. Fourth and fifth symbols in-dicate body type and appear as Body/Style Number in second column of charts below. Sixth symbol indicates model year: 9=1969. Seventh symbol identifies assem-bly plant: A=Atlanta, Ga.; B=Baltimore, Md.; C=South-gate, Calif.; D=Doraville, Ga.; F=Flint, Mich.; G=Framingham, Mass.; J=Janesville, Wis.; K=Kansas City, Mo.; L=Los Angeles, Calif.; N=Norwood, Ohio; R=Arlington, Texas; S=St. Louis, Mo.; T=Tarrytown, N.Y.; U=Lordstown, Ohio; W=Willow Run, Mich.; Y=Wilmington, Del.; Z=Fremont, Calif.; 2=Canada. Next six symbols are sequential production number. Body tag riveted to cowl indicates some of the same information, plus paint and trim codes. Engine numbers are stamped on right side of V-8 blocks and right side of six-cylinder blocks behind distributor. Consult factory or aftermarket sources for numerous Chevrolet engine codes.

BISCAYNE SERIES

Series No.	Body/Style No.	Body Type & Seating	Factory Price	Shipping Weight	Prod. Total
153/154	69	4-dr Sed-6P	2687/2793	3590/3725	Note 1
153/154	11	2-dr Sed-6P	2645/2751	3630/3670	Note 1
153/154	36	4-dr Sta Wag-6P	3064/3169	4045/4170	Note 1

NOTE 1: In rounded-off total 68,700 Biscayne cars and station wagons were built.

NOTE 2: Rounded-off total includes 27,400 sixes and 41,300 V-8s.

NOTE 3: Data above slash for six/below slash or no slash is V-8 data.

BEL AIR — (6-CYL/V-8) — SERIES 155/156 — The Bel Air represented the next step up from Biscayne. Cars in this line featured a thin, horizontal molding along the full-length of the upper body feature line; Bel Air front fender side script and twin taillamps. Interiors were slightly upgraded. Standard equipment included all items found on Biscaynes, plus side moldings; bright metal rear window, roof drip and windshield moldings; front and rear side marker lamps and glovebox light. Base powerplants were the same as in Biscaynes, but the Bel Air-level Townsman station wagon came only with the V-8 this season. Townsman (Bel Air) and Kings-man (Impala) station wagons also had courtesy lights; bodyside moldings and, on Kingswood only, Deluxe steering wheel and extra thick front foam seat cushions.

BEL AIR SERIES

Series No.	Body/Style No.	Body Type & Seating	Factory Price	Shipping Weight	Prod. Total
155/156	69	4-dr Sed-6P	2787/2893	3590/3725	Note 1
155/156	11	2-dr Sed-6P	2745/2851	3540/3670	Note 1
156	46	4-dr TwnMn Wag-9P	3345	4230	Note 1
156	36	4-dr TwnMn Wag-6P	3232	4175	Note 1

NOTE 1: In rounded-off total 155,700 Bel Air cars and station wagons were built.

NOTE 2: Rounded-off total includes 16,000 sixes and 137,700 V-8s.

NOTE 3: Data above slash for six/below slash or no slash is V-8 data.

IMPALA — (6-CYL/V-8) — SERIES 163/164 — The Impala, being a bit fancier than Biscayne/Bel Air mod-els, came with the triple taillight arrangement. There were also wide, bright metal underscores along the lower portion of the body, between the wheel openings. Bodyside script bore the Impala name. The two-door sedan was not offered, but four other styles joined the four-door sedan in this line. Sportier models such as the convertible and Custom Coupe with formal (blind rear quarter) roof came with V-8 power only. Other mod-els, including two- and four-door hardtops offered buy-ers the choice of a six or V-8. Impala-level Kingswood station wagons also came solely with V-8 engines. Standard equipment included everything used for Bel Airs except that bright roof drip moldings were deleted from all the full-pillared models. In addition, all Impalas added a Deluxe steering wheel; door and window frame moldings; glovebox and luggage compartment lighting and extra-thick front foam seat cushions. The Sport Coupe also had bright metal moldings below the doors combined with wheel lip moldings. The convertible had all of this plus all-vinyl upholstery and carpeted lower door panels. Kingsman station wagons also had courtesy lights and bodyside moldings.

1969 Chevrolet, Impala four-door hardtop (Sport Sedan), 6-cyl (PH)

IMPALA SERIES

Series No.	Body/Style No.	Body Type & Seating	Factory Price	Shipping Weight	Prod. Total
163/164	69	4-dr Sed-6P	2911/3016	3640/3760	Note 1
163/164	39	4-dr HT Spt Sed-6P	2981/3086	3735/3855	Note 1
163/164	37	2-dr HT Spt Cpe-6P	2927/3033	3650/3775	Note 1
164	47	2-dr FT Cus Cpe-6P	3085	3800	Note 1
164	67	2-dr Conv-6P	3261	3835	Notes 1/2
164	46	4-dr KgWd Wag-9P	3465	4285	Note 1
164	36	4-dr KgWd Wag-6P	3352	4225	Note 1

1969 Chevrolet, Impala two-door Custom Coupe, V-8

NOTE 1: In rounded-off total 777,000 Impalas and Kingswood station wagons were built.

NOTE 2: Rounded-off total includes 8,700 sixes and 768,300 V-8s.

NOTE 3: 14,415 Chevrolet Impala convertibles built in 1969 model year.

NOTE 4: 2,425 full-size 1969 Chevrolets had the Super Sport option.

NOTE 5: Data above slash for six/below slash or no slash is V-8 data.

1969 Chevrolet, Caprice two-door Custom Coupe, V-8 (PH)

CAPRICE — (V-8) — SERIES 166 — The Caprice was the top-rung offering in the Chevrolet full-size lineup. Standard features included the complete assortment of Impala equipment plus full wheel covers; Caprice signature script; front fender marker lamps; distinctive side molding treatment; electric clock and front seat with center armrest. The Caprice Sport Coupe also provided the Astro Ventilation System at its base price. The Caprice-level station wagon was the luxurious Kingswood Estate, which came with all items used on Impala-level Kingswood models, plus full wheel covers; electric clock; glovebox light; window moldings; two-spoke steering wheel; sculptured wheel openings; Look-of-Wood side paneling; recessed step-in boarding-type rear bumper; wheel lip moldings and Kingswood Estate identification script on the rear fender sides. Passenger styles had rear fender skirts, but the Kingswood Estate wagons did not. Retractable headlights were optional on all Caprices. Variable-ratio power steering was a new extra-cost feature offered for Impala/Caprice models only.

CAPRICE SERIES

Series No.	Body/Style No.	Body Type & Seating	Factory Price	Shipping Weight	Prod. Total
166	39	4-dr HT Spt Sed-6P	3346	3895	Note 1
166	47	2-dr FT Cus Cpe-6P	3294	3815	Note 1
166	46	4-dr KgWd Est Wag-9P	3678	4300	Note 1
166	36	4-dr KgWd Est Wag-6P	3565	4245	Note 1

Note 1: Rounded-off total of 166,900 Caprices and Kingswood Estates built.

CHEVELLE 300 DELUXE — (6-CYL/V-8) — SERIES 133/134 — For 1969, this Chevrolet intermediate had new frontal styling. The forward edge of the hood and fenders was more beveled than in 1968. The square-shaped housings containing the circular headlight lenses were changed from the former bright-finished appearance, with the new dull-finish look emphasizing negative space effects. This treatment was carried to the grille insert, which also had a dull-finish treatment that gave prominence to a bright, horizontal molding stretching, full width, between the headlights. A Chevrolet insignia was placed at the center of this bar. A new front bumper with wider, horizontal slots on either side of the license plate area was seen. The parking lamps were set into the slots. At the rear, there were larger taillight lenses mounted in the body corners. The front side marker lamps, although still rectangular, grew smaller and were repositioned closer to the upper feature line. Different wheelbases once again appeared: 112 inches on two-door styles and 116 inches on four-doors. Standard equipment on Chevelle 300 Deluxe models included all GM safety features; head restraints (as a mandatory option); heater and defroster; front armrests; dual headlights; 7.35 x 14 four-ply rated blackwall tires; and either a 140 hp six or 200 hp V-8 as base powerplant. The low-level Chevelles were characterized by thin rocker panel moldings; bright metal windshield and rear window framing; bright metal roof drip moldings and series identification badges on the front fenders behind the wheel opening. With all factors totaled, the Chevelle was a handsome machine, even in its most basic forms.

Chevelle station wagons proliferated in 1969. Although non-Deluxe passenger cars were dropped, the comparable Nomad station wagon was carried over as an economy model, which is listed with the 300 Deluxe line below. Extra station wagon features included all-vinyl interior trim; dual-speed electric wipers; and windshield washers. Nomad series coding is the same as that of 1968 Chevelle 300s. Some Chevelle station wagons had a new "Dual-Action" tailgate (indicated on chart with symbols /D). The Greenbrier was the true Chevelle 300 Deluxe trim station wagon.

CHEVELLE 300 DELUXE SERIES

Series No.	Body/Style No.	Body Type & Seating	Factory Price	Shipping Weight	Prod. Total
133/134	69	4-dr Sed-6P	2488/2577	3100/3230	Note 1
133/134	37	2-dr HT Spt Cpe-6P	2521/2611	3075/3205	Note 1
133/134	27	2-dr Cpe-6P	2458/2548	3035/3165	Note 1
131/132	35	4-dr Nomad-6P	2668/2758	3390/3515	Note 3
131/132	36	4-dr Nomad/D-6P	2710/2800	N/A/N/A	Note 3
133/134	35	4-dr Grn Br Wag-6P	2779/2669	3445/2565	Note 3
133/134	36	4-dr Grn Br Wag-9P	2821/2911	N/A/N/A	Note 3
134	46	4-dr Grn Br/D Sta Wag	3024	3740	Note 3

1969 Chevrolet, Chevelle SS-396 two-door hardtop, V-8

NOTE 1: In rounded-off total 42,000 Chevelle 300 passenger cars were built in 1969.

NOTE 2: Rounded-off total includes 21,000 sixes and 21,000 V-8s, not including station wagons.

NOTE 3: Rounded-off total of 45,900 Chevelle station wagons built in all lines.

NOTE 4: Station wagon total includes 7,400 sixes/38,500 V-8s, but no series breakouts.

NOTE 5: Data above slash for six/below slash or no slash is V-8 data.

CHEVELLE MALIBU — (6-CYL/V-8) — SERIES 135/136 — The Malibu was the mid-priced, mid-sized series and included all equipment found on the base line, plus Hide-Away two-speed wipers; Deluxe steering wheel; glovebox light; window moldings and carpets. Specific identification features varied by body type and optional equipment packages that a buyer ordered. It was possible to order Chevelles and Malibus in over 300 different variations. Some that collectors look for are the Malibu four-door hardtop (Sport Sedan) with the RPO Z16 Concours package or the Malibu two-door hardtop (Sport Coupe) with Argent Silver lower bodyside treatment, both of which added greatly to a sporty appearance. Several pages of new or revised options packages were released by Chevrolet in May 1969. A convertible was also available in Malibu trim and had all of the above standard equipment, plus courtesy lights. The SS-396 (Z25) was still offered as an option package.

MALIBU SERIES

Series No.	Body/Style No.	Body Type & Seating	Factory Price	Shipping Weight	Prod. Total
135/136	69	4-dr Sed-6P	2567/2657	3130/3265	Note 1
135/136	39	4-dr HT Sed-6P	2672/2762	3205/3340	Note 1
135/136	37	2-dr HT Spt Cpe-6P	2601/2690	3095/3230	Note 1
135/136	67	2-dr Conv-6P	2800/2889	3175/3300	Note 5
136	46	4-dr Estate Wag-9P	3266	3730	Note 3
136	36	4-dr Estate Wag-6P	3153	3680	Note 3

NOTE 1: In rounded-off total 367,100 Malibu passenger cars were built in 1969.

NOTE 2: Rounded-off total includes 25,000 sixes and 343,600 V-8s, not including station wagons.

NOTE 3: Rounded-off total of 45,900 Chevelle station wagons built in all lines.

NOTE 4: Station wagon total includes 7,400 sixes/38,500 V-8s, but no series breakouts.

NOTE 5: 8,927 cars in rounded-off total were Malibu or SS-396 convertibles.

NOTE 6: 86,307 cars in rounded-off total had SS-396 option.

NOTE 7: Data above slash for six/below slash or no slash is V-8 data.

NOVA — (FOUR/6-CYL/V-8) — The Chevy II name was dropped from the 'senior' compact offerings, which were now simply called Novas. Due to this change, a Chevrolet emblem was placed on the center of the upper grille bar. Vertical louvers were optional on the side of the cowl, behind the front wheel opening. A Nova script was seen on the right-hand corner of the deck lid. The front side marker lights were enlarged and moved slightly closer to the body corner. A vast selection of options, including Super Sport equipment, could be ordered. Standard equipment included the corporate safety assortment; head restraints (mandatory option); heater and defroster; front armrests; concealed fuel filler; and 7.35 x 14 four-ply rated black sidewall tires. Base engines were the 90 hp four; 140 hp six or 200 hp V-8 from the Chevrolet power team lineup.

1969 Chevrolet, Nova two-door coupe, V-8 (AA)

NOVA SERIES

Series No.	Body/Style No.	Body Type & Seating	Factory Price	Shipping Weight	Prod. Total
FOUR					
111	69	4-dr Sed-6P	2267	2610	Note 1
111	27	2-dr Cpe-6P	2237	2785	Note 1

SIX

113	69	4-dr Sed-6P	2345	2920	Note 2
113	27	2-dr Cpe-6P	2315	2895	Note 2

V-8

114	69	4-dr Sed-6P	2434	N/A	Note 3
114	27	2-dr Cpe-6P	2405	N/A	Note 3

NOTE 1: 6,103 four-cylinder Novas were built; no body style breakouts.

NOTE 2: Rounded-off total of 157,400 six-cylinder Novas built in model year.

NOTE 3: Rounded-off total of 88,400 Nova V-8s built in model year.

NOTE 4: 17,654 Novas included above were equipped with the Super Sport option.

1969 Chevrolet, Camaro Z/28 two-door hardtop, V-8 (AA)

CAMARO — (6-CYL/V-8) — SERIES 123/124 — A new body gave the 1969 Camaro a longer and lower appearance. Sport coupe and convertible styles were offered, with option package selections having a great effect on final appearance features. The formerly smooth-sided body was now more highly sculptured with a side feature line tracing the forward edge of the front wheelhousing and running straight from the top of the opening to the rear of the car. A second line traced the front of the rear wheel opening and blended into the main one. Simulated vertical air slots were positioned ahead of the rear wheel. The Rally Sport option offered a special black grille with concealed headlights, the retractable headlamp doors being decorated by a triple-slot design motif. A functional 'Super Scoop' hood was available with Z/28 or Super Sport (SS) packages. Standard equipment began at the safety-oriented level and included the mandatory headrest option plus heater and defroster; integrated front headlight and parking light unit; Strato-Bucket front seats; all-vinyl interior; carpeting; Astro Ventilation System; front shoulder safety belts; left-hand outside rearview mirror; side marker lights; E78-14 two-ply (four-ply rated) black sidewall tires; 140 hp six or 210 hp V-8 and, in convertibles, interior courtesy lights. In terms of power, the rare ZL-1 Camaros became one of the year's hottest and most collectible cars. Optioned with a 427-cid V-8 featuring aluminum block construction and three two-barrel carburetors, these 425 hp screamers were built in limited numbers for factory experimental racing purposes. Production of only 69 units has been reported. Nearly as desirable to car collectors, although not quite as rare, is the Indianapolis

Pace Car replica Camaro. According to several articles, about 100 original editions were built and provided as official cars for dignitaries and press personalities attending the 500-mile race. The actual Pace Car was an RS/SS-396 convertible and most of the replicas were SS-350 ragtops. A Pace Car replica package was issued to the general public on Feb. 4, 1969. This led to the sale of 3,675 cars with the Z11 Indy Sport Convertible option. Also made for a few weeks was the Z10 Indy Sport Coupe option. About 200-300 cars in a special promotional run had this package.

CAMARO SERIES

Series No.	Body/Style No.	Body Type & Seating	Factory Price	Shipping Weight	Prod. Total
123/124	37	2-dr HT Spt Cpe-4P	2638/2727	3040/3050	214,280
123/124	67	2-dr Conv-4P	2852/2941	3160/3295	16,519

ADDITIONAL NOTES: The figures above are for domestic market units only. Production included 65,008 sixes; 178,087 V-8s; 37,773 Rally Sports; 33,980 Super Sports (some cars had both Rally Sport and Super Sport packages); 19,014 cars with the Z/28 option; 72,395 cars with three-speed manual transmission; 50,128 cars with four-speed manual transmission; 120,572 cars with automatic transmission; 37,878 cars with air conditioning; 120,060 cars with power steering and 2,913 cars with power windows. A total of 12,316 Camaros were built for export.

ENGINES

(NOVA) Inline four. Overhead valve. Cast iron block. Displacement: 153.3 cid. Bore and stroke: 3.675 x 3.25 inches. Compression ratio: 8.5:1. Brake hp: 90 at 4000 rpm. Four main bearings. Hydraulic valve lifters. Carburetor: Rochester one-barrel Model 7028017.

(BISCAYNE/BEL AIR/IMPALA SIX) Inline six. Overhead valve. Cast iron block. Displacement: 250 cid. Bore and stroke: 3.88 x 3.53 inches. Compression ratio: 8.5:1. Brake hp: 155 at 4200 rpm. Seven main bearings. Hydraulic valve lifters. Carburetor: Rochester one-barrel Model 7029017.

(BISCAYNE/BEL AIR/IMPALA/CAPRICE V-8) Overhead valve. Cast iron block. Displacement: 326.7 (327) cid. Bore and stroke: 4.00 x 3.25 inches. Compression ratio: 9.0:1. Brake hp: 235 at 4800 rpm. Five main bearings. Hydraulic valve lifters. Carburetor: Rochester two-barrel Model 7029127.

(CHEVELLE/MALIBU/NOVA/CAMARO SIX) Inline six. Overhead valve. Cast iron block. Displacement: 230 cid. Bore and stroke: 3.875 x 3.25 inches. Compression ratio: 8.5:1. Brake hp: 140 at 4400 rpm. Seven main bearings. Hydraulic valve lifters. Carburetor: Rochester one-barrel Model 7029017.

(CHEVELLE/MALIBU/NOVA V-8) Overhead valve. Cast iron block. Displacement: 306.6 (307) cid. Bore and stroke: 3.875 x 3.25 inches. Compression ratio: 9.0:1. Brake hp: 200 at 4600 rpm. Five main bearings. Hydraulic valve lifters. Carburetor: Rochester two-barrel.

(CAMARO BASE V-8) Overhead valve. Cast iron block. Displacement: 326.7 (327) cid. Bore and stroke: 4.00 x 3.25 inches. Compression ratio: 9.0:1. Brake hp: 210 at 4600 rpm. Five main bearings. Hydraulic valve lifters. Carburetor: Rochester two-barrel.

(TURBOJET SS-396) V-8. Overhead valve. Cast iron block. (Aluminum cylinder heads optional after mid-year). Displacement: 396 cid. Bore and stroke: 4.09 x 3.76 inches. Compression ratio: 10.25:1. Brake hp: 325 at 4600 rpm. Hydraulic valve lifters. Five main bearings. Carburetor: Rochester four-barrel Quadra-Jet.

1969 Chevrolet, Camaro RS two-door convertible, V-8

CHASSIS FEATURES: Wheelbase: (Chevrolet) 119 inches; (Chevelle two-door) 112 inches; (Chevelle four-door) 116 inches; (Nova) 111 inches; (Camaro) 108 inches. Overall length: (Chevrolet wagon) 217 inches; (Chevrolet) 216 inches; (Chevelle two-door) 197 inches; (Chevelle wagon) 206 inches; (Chevelle four-door) 201 inches; (Nova) 190 inches; (Camaro) 166 inches. Front tread: (Chevrolet) 62.5 inches; (Chevelle/Nova/Camaro) 59 inches. Rear tread: (Chevrolet) 62.4 inches; (Chevelle) 59 inches; (Nova) 58.9 inches; (Camaro) 58 inches. Base tires: (Chevrolet) 8.25 x 14 cars; 8.55 x 14 wagons; (Chevelle/Nova) 7.35 x 14 cars; 7.75 x 14 wagons; (Camaro) E78-14-B.

OPTIONS: [Early 1969] Four-Season air conditioning ($363.40-$384.45). Comfort-On air conditioning ($463.45). Station wagon rear deflector ($19). Custom Deluxe shoulder belts ($12.15-$16.90). Power drum brakes, except Nova four ($42.15). Power front disc brakes, except Nova four ($64.25). Special Camaro front bumper ($42.15). Load floor carpeting in Kingswood and Kingswood Estate ($52.70). Adjustable roof rack ($52.70). Electric clock ($15.80). Heavy-duty clutch ($47.50-$52.00). Console with courtesy light ($53.75). ElectroClear rear defroster ($32.65). Power door locks: Chevelle two-door ($44.80); four-door ($68.50). Retractable headlights, Caprice/Estate ($79). Headlight washer ($15.80). Special instrumentation; in Chevelle/Camaro ($94.80). Light monitoring system ($26.35). Two-tone paint, all except Camaro ($23.20); on Camaro, includes roof molding ($31.60). AM push-button radio ($61.10). AM/FM push-button radio ($133.60). AM/FM radio and stereo ($239.10). Rear manual antenna ($9.50-$10.55). Vinyl roof ($79.00-$88.55). Camaro folding rear seat ($42.15). Six-Way power seat ($100.10). Strato Bucket seat, in Caprice, includes front center armrest and Custom knit black cloth trim ($115.90). Strato Bucket in Malibu

coupe/convertible ($121.15); in Caprice, including console with shift if automatic or four-speed, plus center console ($168.55). Automatic level control, Chevrolets ($89.66). Rear fender skirts, Chevrolets with 14-inch wheels ($31.60). Speed and Cruise Control, V-8 and automatic required ($57.95). Power steering ($89.55-$105.35). Special steering with Quick-Response feature in Camaro, power steering required with air conditioner or 396-cid V-8 ($15.80). Comfort-Tilt steering column ($45.30). Sport-styled steering wheel, except Nova ($34.80). Chevelle SS-396 fender accent striping ($26.35). Camaro front accent or Sport striping ($25.30). Liquid tire chain ($23.20). Power convertible top on Chevelle/Camaro ($52.70). Power trunk opener on Chevrolet ($14.75). Power tailgate window, standard in three-seat wagon; in two-seat styles ($34.80). Hide-Away wipers as option ($19). Full wheel covers ($21.10). Mag-spoke wheel covers, Caprice and Kingswood Estate ($52.70); all others ($73.75). Simulated wire wheels, Caprice and Kingswood Estate ($55.85). Special wheel covers and Caprice and Kingswood Estate ($57.95); on other full-size Chevrolets ($79.00). [May 1, 1969, changes]: Adjustable wagon roof rack ($52.70). ElectroClear rear defroster ($47.40). Special ducted hood for Camaro SS with performance package ($79). Front and rear spoiler, Camaro without performance package ($32.65). Special rear springs, on Camaro, includes rear bumper guards ($20.05). [Early 1969]: Turbo-Thrift 250-cid six, in Chevelle/Camarov Nova ($26.35). Turbo-Fire 350-cid V-8 in Chevrolet/Camaro ($52.70); in Chevelle/Nova ($68.50). RPO L66 396 cid/265 hp Turbo-Jet V-8, in Chevrolets ($68.50) RPO L48 350 cid/300 hp V-8, in Chevrolet ($52.70); in Chevelle ($68.50). RPO L35 396 cid/325 hp Turbo-Jet V-8 in Camaro SS only ($63.20). RPO LS1 427 cid/335 hp V-8, in Chevrolets only ($163.25). RPO L34 396 cid/350 hp Turbo-Jet V-8, in Chevelle SS-396 ($121.15); in Camaro SS/Nova SS ($184.35). RPO L78 396 cid/375 hp Turbo-Jet V-8 in Chevelle SS-396 ($252.60); in Camaro SS/Nova SS ($316.00). RPO L78-89 375 hp Turbo-Jet V-8 with special aluminum cylinder heads, in Chevelle SS-396 ($647.75); in Camaro SS ($710.95). RPO L36 427 cid/390 hp Turbo-Jet V-8, in Chevrolet ($237.00). RPO L72 427 cid/425 hp Turbo-Jet V-8, in Chevrolet ($447.65); in Chevrolet with SS option ($183.35). Dual exhaust ($30.55). Wide-Range four-speed manual transmission, in Camaro ($195.40); in others ($184.80). Close-ratio four-speed manual transmission, in Camaro ($195.40); in others ($184.80). Heavy-duty four-speed manual transmission, in Nova ($312.55); in Camaro ($322.10); in Chevelle ($264.00); in Chevrolet ($313.00). Powerglide automatic transmission, with Nova V-8 ($158.40); with Nova four/six ($147.85); with other V-8s ($174.25); with other sixes ($163.70). Special three-speed manual transmission, standard with SS-427/SS-396 and Camaro SS/Nova SS; in others ($79.00). TorqueDrive, in Camaro/Nova six only ($68.65). Turbo-HydraMatic (M40 type), in Nova six ($174.25); in other six ($190.10); in all, except Nova, with 255/300 hp V-8 ($200.65); in Nova with 255/300 hp V-8 ($190.10); in all with 375/425 hp V-8 ($290.40); in all with other V-8s ($221.80). Floor-mounted shift lever, as optional equipment ($10.55). Posi-traction axle ($42.15). [May 1,1969, changes]: RPO L65 350 cid/250 hp Turbo-Fire V-8, in Chevelle/Nova/Camaro ($21.10); RPO LMI 350 cid/255 hp Turbo-Fire V-8, in Chevrolet and Camaro ($52.70); in Chevelle/Nova ($68.50). RPO NC8 dual chambered exhaust system, in Chevelle SS-396/Z28/Camaro SS with 325/350/375 hp V-8s ($15.80).

OPTION PACKAGES

RPO Z27: Camaro SS-350 option includes: special hood; Sport striping; hood insulation; F70-14 white-letter tires; 14 x 7-inch wheels; power disc brakes; special three-speed manual transmission; bright fender louvers; engine accents; emblems; and 350 cid/300 hp V-8 ($295.95); after May 1, 1969 ($311.75).

RPO Z16: Chevelle Concours sedan (hardtop) includes: luxury cloth seat and sidewall trim; steering wheel emblem; panel trim plate; black-accented lower bodyside and wheel opening moldings; deck lid nameplate and special insulation ($131.65).

RPO ZJ2: Nova Custom exterior package includes: simulated front fender louvers with bright accents; bodysill and rear fender moldings; black bodysill and lower rear fender trim panels; and accent striping. Coupe also had bright side window moldings and lower body accent band. Sedan also had bodyside molding with black vinyl insert, on coupe ($97.95); on sedan ($79).

RPO Z67: (Camaro)/ZJI (Nova with bench)/A51 (Nova with buckets) Custom interior trim. Included on Camaro: molded vinyl door panel with built-in armrest; assist grip; carpeted lower door panel; woodgrain panel accents; woodgrain steering wheel; bright pedal trim; glovebox light; insulation and baggage mat. Included, on Nova, luxury seats and sidewalls; bright accents; rear armrest ashtrays; carpets; Deluxe mirror; interior or light switches; baggage mat and insulation. Price for bucket seat Nova ($231.75); price for other ($110.60).

RPO Z24: Impala SS-427 option, on Custom Coupe, Sport Coupe or convertible includes: power disc brakes; special three-speed transmission; ornamentation; chassis and suspension features; 15-inch wheels; Red Stripe tires and 427 cid/390 hp V-8 ($422.35).

RPO Z26: Nova SS option package, on coupe only, includes simulated air intakes on hood; simulated front fender louvers; black accents; black accent grille and rear panel; SS emblems; Red Stripe F70-14 tires; 14 x 7-inch wheels; special suspension and three-speed gearbox; power disc brakes; bright engine accents; hood insulation; and 350 cid/300 hp V-8 ($280.20).

RPO Z22: Camaro Rally Sport (RS) option package includes special grille with concealed headlights; headlight washers; fender striping (except with SS); bright accents on simulated rear fender louvers; front and rear wheel lip moldings; black bodysills; RS emblems; nameplates; accented tail and parking lights; back-up lights below bumper; steering wheel accents and coupe roof drip moldings ($131.85).

RPO Z35: Camaro SS-396 option includes special hood, ornamentation and suspension; Sport wheels; white letter tires (Wide-Oval); power disc brakes; special three-speed transmission; black accented grille and 396 cid/325 hp V-8 ($347.60).

RPO Z28: Camaro Special Performance Package includes dual exhaust with deep-toned muffler; special front and rear suspension; heavy-duty radiator and temperature controlled fan; quick-ratio steering; 15 x 7-inch Rally wheels; E70-15 white letter tires; 3.73:1 ratio axle; Rally stripes on hood and rear deck and special 302-cid V-8 (estimated hp rating 350). Four-speed manual transmission and power disc brake options were additional mandatory options (at regular price in addition to Z/28 retail). Posi-traction rear axle was also recommended. Cost ($458.15); after May 1, 1969 ($506.60). A total of 503 were equipped with disc brakes.

RPO Z11/RPO Z10: Camaro Indy Pace Car packages. Contact International Camaro Owners Association, 2001 Pittston Ave., Scranton, PA 18503 for full details.

HISTORICAL FOOTNOTES: The 1969 Chevrolet line-up was introduced Sept. 26, 1968. John Z. DeLorean was general manager of Chevrolet Division. Model year output figures included exactly 1,109,013 full-size Chevrolets; 439,611 Chevelles; 269,988 Novas and 243,085 Camaros. Market penetration, including Corvettes and Corvairs, was an even 25 percent. The 1969 Camaro captured top honors in SCCA Trans-Am Championship racing for cars in the over 2.5-liter class. Mark Donohue and Roger Penske were the top Chevrolet drivers.

1970

NOTE: 1970 and later Chevrolet models cataloged by platform groupings.

FULL-SIZE CHEVROLET — (SIX/V-8) — ALL SERIES — The 'big' Chevrolets were the same in size as the previous models. There were changes front and rear. The front fenderline, hood and grille were redone, eliminating the encircling, integrated bumper/grille look. Round dual headlamps were set horizontally in square bezels flanking a finer-textured grille, although a cross-hatched insert design was retained. The gravel pan was re-shaped to round the front body corners and incorporate slightly larger parking lamps as well as triple-slit side markers. At the rear, the taillights took a new vertical-slot shape and were recessed into the bumper. A base '350' V-8, optional regular-fuel '400' V-8 and transmission-controlled vacuum spark advance were technical refinements. Standard equipment for Biscaynes included all safety features; windshield antenna; Astro Ventilation; Hide-Away wipers; Delco-Eye battery; side-guard door beams; heater/defroster; cigarette lighter; locking glovebox; carpets; ashtray light; center dome lamp; F78-15 blackwalls; and either the '250' six or '350' V-8. The Bel Air was equipped likewise, plus having side and roof drip moldings and a glovebox light. The Impala had all the above, plus foam seat cushions; fabric and vinyl trim (all-vinyl in convertible); Deluxe steering wheel; trunk light; door/window frame moldings; vinyl-insert bodyside moldings; and luggage lamps. The Impala Sport Coupe also had bright metal moldings below the doors and on its wheel lips. The Custom Coupe had power front disc brakes and the convertible had courtesy lights and carpeted lower door panels. Tires were size F78-15 on sixes; G78-15 on V-8s. The Caprice was equipped with all of the above, plus power front disc brakes; distinctive side moldings; color-keyed wheel covers; electric clock; G78-15/B bias-belted blackwalls; 250 hp base engine; and in sedans a center armrest seat. Station wagons had items such as vinyl trim; Dual-Action tailgates and glovebox light plus all Biscayne passenger car equipment. The Kingswood station wagon compared to the Impala trim level, with courtesy lights; bodyside moldings; and foam cushions included. The Kingswood Estate was the Caprice-level counterpart with a Deluxe steering wheel; clock and window moldings; and exterior woodgrain paneling. Base engine for all wagons was the '350' V-8 and H78-15/D tires were used. Power disc brakes were standard with Kingswood Estates.

1970 Chevrolet, Caprice two-door hardtop, V-8

CHEVROLET I.D. NUMBERS: Serial numbers on all Chevrolet products were now found on the top left-hand surface of the instrument panel. They were visible through the windshield. The Vehicle Identification Number had 13 symbols. The first three symbols indicate make and series and appear as Series Number in first column of charts below. For example, the first car listed has number 153 (1=Chevrolet; 53=Biscayne six) for six-cylinder series and 154 (1=Chevrolet; 54=Biscayne V-8) for eight-cylinder series. Fourth and fifth symbols indicate body type and appear as Body/Style Number in second column of charts below. Sixth symbol indicates model year: 0=1970. Seventh symbol identifies assembly plant: A=Atlanta, Ga.; B=Baltimore, Md.; C=Southgate, Calif.; F=Flint, Mich.; G=Framingham, Mass.; I=Oshawa, Canada; J=Janesville, Wis.; K=Kansas City, Mo.; L=Los Angeles, Ca-

lif.; N=Norwood, Ohio; R=Arlington, Texas; S=St. Louis, Mo.; T=Tarrytown, N.Y.; U=Lordstown, Ohio; W=Willow Run, Mich.; Y=Wilmington, Del.; Z=Fremont, Calif. Next six symbols are sequential production number. Body tag riveted to cowl indicates some of the same information, plus paint and trim codes. Engine numbers are stamped on right side of V-8 blocks and right side of six-cylinder blocks behind distributor. Consult factory or aftermarket sources for numerous Chevrolet engine codes.

1970 Chevrolet, Impala two-door convertible, V-8

FULL-SIZE CHEVROLET

Series No.	Body/Style No.	Body Type & Seating	Factory Price	Shipping Weight	Prod. Total
BISCAYNE SERIES (INCLUDES BROOKWOOD WAGON)					
153/154	69	4-dr Sed-6P	2787/2998	3600/3759	Note 1
154	36	4-dr Sta Wag-6P	3294	4204	Note 2

1970 Chevrolet, Caprice four-door hardtop, V-8 (PH)

BEL AIR SERIES (INCLUDES TOWNSMAN WAGONS)

Series No.	Body/Style No.	Body Type & Seating	Factory Price	Shipping Weight	Prod. Total
155/156	69	4-dr Sed-6P	2887/2998	3604/3763	Note 3
156	46	4-dr Sta Wag-9P	3469	4263	Note 2
156	36	4-dr Sta Wag-6P	3357	4208	Note 2

IMPALA SERIES (INCLUDES KINGSWOOD WAGONS)

163/164	69	4-dr Sed-6P	3021/3132	3655/3602	Note 4
163/164	37	2-dr HT Spt Cpe-6P	3038/3149	3641/3788	Note 4
164	39	4-dr HT Spt Sed-5P	3203	3871	Note 4
164	47	2-dr Cus Cpe-6P	3266	3801	Note 4
164	67	2-dr Conv-6P	3377	3643	Notes 4/5
164	46	4-dr Sta Wag-9P	3589	4321	Note 2
164	36	4-dr Sta Wag-6P	3477	4269	Note 2

CAPRICE SERIES (INCLUDES KINGSWOOD ESTATE WAGONS)

166	39	4-dr HT Sed-6P	3527	3905	Note 7
166	47	2-dr HT Sed-6P	3474	3621	Note 7
166	46	4-dr Sta Wag-9P	3866	4361	Note 2
166	36	4-dr Sta Wag-6P	3753	4295	Note 2

FIGURES BELOW ARE ROUNDED-OFF (except Note 5):

NOTE 1: 35,400 Biscayne cars were built (12,300 sixes/343,600 V-8s).

NOTE 2: 162,800 full-size Chevrolet station wagons were built (all V-8s).

NOTE 3: 75,800 Bel Air cars were built (9,000 sixes/66,800 V-8s).

1970 Chevrolet, Impala two-door Custom Coupe, V-8 (PH)

NOTE 4: 612,800 Impala cars were built (6,500 sixes/606,300 V-8s).

NOTE 5: Exactly 9,562 Impala convertibles are included in Note 4.

NOTE 6: 86,307 cars in rounded-off total had SS-396 option.

NOTE 7: 92,000 Caprice V-8s built.

NOTE 8: Data above slash for six/below slash or no slash is V-8 data.

MONTE CARLO — (V-8) — SERIES 138 — The original Monte Carlo was said to combine action and elegance in a sporty, personal luxury package. Based on the same platform as the re-designed 1969 Pontiac Grand Prix, the Monte Carlo was bigger than the Chevelle and had a price tag in the Impala range. A long hood/short deck image and smart interior and exterior appoint-

ments were incorporated. Styling features included large, single headlamps mounted in square-shaped bright housings; a rectangular front opening with a grid-textured grille of thin bright horizontal moldings (with a center badge); and a profile emphasizing the popular 'venturi' shape, enhanced by a crisply sculptured upper feature line. Although mainly luxurious in overall character, the Monte Carlo turned out to be quite a fine high-performance machine. The potent, SS-454 version was capable of 0-to-60 mph in under eight seconds. This package was found to be extremely suitable to short track stock car racing. This was due to a combination of good power-to-weight distribution along with aerodynamic factors. The only available body style was a coupe. Standard equipment included all features found on Malibu, plus power front disc brakes; electric clock; assist straps; elm-burl dash panel inlays; G78-15-B bias-belted black sidewall tires; and a 350-cid V-8. Although commonly seen on most Monte Carlos, fender skirts were optional.

1970 Chevrolet, Monte Carlo two-door hardtop, V-8

MONTE CARLO SERIES

Series No.	Body/Style No.	Body Type & Seating	Factory Price	Shipping Weight	Prod. Total
136	57	2-dr HT Cpe-5P	3123	3460	145,975

NOTE 1: The production total includes 3,823 cars built with SS-454 equipment, including 454 cid/360 hp V-8 and 10 cars ordered with the LS-6 454-cid V-8 rated at 450 hp.

MID-SIZE CHEVELLE — (SIX/V-8) — ALL SERIES — The more highly sculptured 1970 Chevelle featured a bold-looking frontal treatment with split grille and dual, blending headlights. A new slotless front bumper incorporated rectangular parking ramps directly below the headlamps. The swept-back front fender look was gone, replaced by a blunter image. An upper feature line ran from above the headlight level to the top of the back bumper, with a prominent dip at mid-waist height. Rear side markers with a slotted and segmented look were seen. The Chevelle 300

Deluxe name was dropped. The Chevelle was the base model and the Malibu was one step up. A wide range of station wagons included the Nomad (comparable to the old standard 300 line); the Deluxe Greenbriers; Malibu-level Concours and the top-of-the-line Concours Estate Wagon (essentially with Monte Carlo-level appointments). Chevelle level standard equipment included the safety assortment: heater/defroster; locking glovebox; cigarette lighter; rubber floor mats; and either a 250 cid/155 hp six or 307 cid/200 hp V-8. The blackwall tires were size E78-14-B on both sixes and V-8s. Malibus had all of the above features, plus hidden antenna; Astro Ventilation; sideguard door beam construction; Delco-Eye battery; Hide-Away wipers; and a glovebox light. The convertible also came with interior courtesy lights. Malibu six engines and tires were the same. On Malibu V-8s, larger F78-14-B rubber was used. All station wagons came with GM safety features; Dual-Action tailgates; in-the-windshield hidden antenna; Hide-Away wipers; side beam doors; heater/defroster; all-vinyl trim; and cigarette lighter. Concours also had courtesy lights. Concours Estates added carpeting; door edge moldings; and simulated woodgrain exterior paneling. Engines were the same used on passenger cars and V-8s had power front disc brakes. All station wagons had G78-14-B blackwalls.

1970 Chevrolet, Chevelle SS-396 two-door hardtop, V-8

INTERMEDIATE-SIZE SERIES

Series No.	Body/Style No.	Body Type & Seating	Factory Price	Shipping Weight	Prod. Total
NOMAD STATION WAGONS					
131/132	36	4-dr Sta Wag-6P	2835/2925	3615/3718	Note 1
CHEVELLE (GREENBRIER STATION WAGONS)					
133/134	69	4-dr Sed-6P	2537/2627	3196/3312	Note 2
133/134	37	2-dr Cpe-6P	2572/2662	3142/3260	Note 2
133/134	36	4-dr Sta Wag-6P	2946/3100	3644/3748	Note 1
134	46	4-dr Sta Wag-9P	3213	3794	Note 1
CHEVELLE MALIBU SERIES (CONCOURS STATION WAGON)					
135/136	69	4-dr Sed-6P	2665/2775	3221/3330	Note 3
135/136	39	4-dr HT Sed-6P	2790/2881	3302/3409	Note 3
135/136	37	2-dr Spt Cpe-6P	2719/2809	3197/3307	Note 3
135/136	67	2-dr Conv-6P	2919/3009	3243/3352	Note 4
135/136	36	4-dr Sta Wag-6P	3056/3210	3687/3794	Note 1
136	46	4-dr Sta Wag-9P	3323	3836	Note 1

CONCOURS ESTATE STATION WAGON

138	46	4-dr Sta Wag-9P	3455	3880	Note 1
138	36	4-dr Sta Wag-6P	3342	3621	Note 1

1970 Chevrolet, Chevelle two-door hardtop, 6-cyl (PH)

FIGURES BELOW ARE ROUNDED-OFF (except Note 4):

NOTE 1: 40,600 Chevelle station wagons (5,600 sixes/35,000 V-8s) built in all series.

NOTE 2: 23,900 base Chevelles built (10,700 sixes/13,200 V-8s).

NOTE 3: 375,800 Malibus built (21,100 sixes/354,700 V-8s).

NOTE 4: Exactly 7,511 Malibu/Malibu SS convertibles included in Note 3 total.

NOTE 5: Data above slash for six/below slash or no slash is V-8 data.

1970 Chevrolet, Chevelle Malibu four-door hardtop (Sport Sedan), V-8

1970 Chevrolet, Nova two-door coupe, V-8

NOVA — (FOUR/SIX/V-8) — SERIES 111/113/114 —
The 1970 Nova had a grille insert with squarer openings than the previous model. The Chevrolet badge at the center of the upper grille molding was slightly fatter and not quite as wide as before. Options included simulated bright vertical cowlside louvers; in-the-windshield radio antennas; and new variable-ratio power steering. The sporty Nova SS package included a hefty 350 cid/300

hp V-8. Regular equipment included GM safety hardware; front armrests; heater/defroster; Delco-Eye battery and E78-14 black sidewall tires. Base engines were the 90 hp four-cylinder; 230 cid/140 hp six and the 307-cid V-8.

NOVA SERIES

Series No.	Body/Style No.	Body Type & Seating	Factory Price	Shipping Weight	Prod. Total
FOUR					
111	69	4-dr Sed-6P	2205	2843	Note 1
111	27	2-dr Cpe-6P	2176	2820	Note 1
SIX					
113	69	4-dr Sed-6P	2264	2942	Note 2
113	27	2-dr Cpe-6P	2254	2919	Note 2
V-8					
114	69	4-dr Sed-6P	2533	N/A	Note 3
114	27	2-dr Cpe-6P	2503	N/A	Note 3

NOTE 1: Exactly 2,247 Nova fours were built for the 1970 model year.

NOTE2: Exactly 173,632 Nova sixes were built for the 1970 model year.

NOTE 3: Exactly 139,243 Nova V-8s were built for the 1970 model year.

1970 Chevrolet, Camaro two-door hardtop, V-8

CAMARO SERIES — (SIX/V-8) — Due to slow sales of 1969 Camaros, no new design was introduced for this series at 1970 model introduction time in the fall of 1969. Chevrolet dealers continued to sell leftover units until supplies ran out. This may have led to some cars with 1969 specifications being sold and titled as 1970s. The true 1970 models (often called 1970-1/2 Camaros) did not go on sale until Feb. 26, 1970. They had completely new styling with high intensity headlamps; a semi-fastback roofline; snout-styled grille (with egg-crate insert); and a much smoother-looking rear end. The only body style available was the Sport Coupe. Standard equipment included all GM safety features; Strato-Bucket front seats; all-vinyl interior; carpeting; Astro Ventilation; left-hand outside rearview mirror; side marker lights; and E78-14-B bias-belted blackwall tires. The 155 hp six was base engine while the 307-cid V-8 was standard in the V-8 line. Desirable options were the SS, RS and Z/28 special-performance packages. The latter carried a retail price of $572.95 and featured the 350 cid/360 hp V-8.

CAMARO SERIES

Series No.	Body/Style No.	Body Type & Seating	Factory Price	Shipping Weight	Prod. Total
123/124	87	2-dr HT Spt Cpe-4P	2749/2839	3058/3172	117,604

NOTE 1: Figures above are for domestic market units only.

NOTE 2: Figures include 12,566 sixes/112,323 V-8s.

NOTE 3: Figures include 27,135 RS/12,476 SS (some cars had both packages).

NOTE 4: Figures include 8,733 Z/28s.

NOTE 5: Transmissions: 11,859 three-speed; 18,676 four-speed; 91,352 automatic.

NOTE 6: 36,565 with air conditioning; 92,640 with power steering.

NOTE 7: 7,295 Camaros were exported.

NOTE 8: Data above slash for six/below slash or no slash is V-8 data.

ENGINES

(NOVA) Inline four. Overhead valve. Cast iron block. Displacement: 153.3 cid. Bore and stroke: 3.875 x 3.25 inches. Compression ratio: 8.5:1. Brake hp: 90 at 4000 rpm. Four main bearings. Hydraulic valve lifters. Carburetor: Rochester one-barrel Model 7028017.

(CHEVROLET/CHEVELLE/NOVA/CAMARO SIX) Inline six. Overhead valve. Cast iron block. Displacement: 250 cid. Bore and stroke: 3.875 x 3.53 inches. Compression ratio: 8.5:1. Brake hp: 155 at 4200 rpm. Seven main bearings. Hydraulic valve lifters. Carburetor: Rochester one-barrel.

(CHEVROLET/MONTE CARLO V-8) Overhead valve. Cast iron block. Displacement: 350 cid. Bore and stroke: 4.00 x 3.48 inches. Compression ratio: 9.0:1. Brake hp: 250 at 4500 rpm. Five main bearings. Hydraulic valve lifters. Carburetor: Rochester two-barrel.

(CHEVELLE/NOVA/CAMARO V-8) Overhead valve. Cast iron block. Displacement: 307 cid. Bore and stroke: 3.875 x 3.53 inches. Compression ratio: 9.0:1. Brake hp: 200 at 4600 rpm. Five main bearings. Hydraulic valve lifters. Carburetor: Rochester two-barrel.

CHASSIS FEATURES: Wheelbase: (Chevrolet) 119 inches; (Chevelle two-door) 112 inches; (Chevelle four-door) 116 inches; (Monte Carlo) 116 inches; (Nova) 111 inches; (Camaro) 106 inches. Overall length: (Chevrolet wagon) 217 inches; (Chevrolet) 216 inches; (Chevelle wagon) 207 inches; (Chevelle two-door) 198 inches; (Chevelle four-door) 202 inches; (Monte Carlo) 206 inches; (Nova) 190 inches; (Camaro) 188 inches. Width: (Chevrolet) 80 inches; (Chevelle) 76 inches; (Monte Carlo) 76 inches; (Nova) 73 inches; (Camaro) 75 inches. Tires: Refer to text.

OPTIONS: Comfort-On air conditioning ($463.45). Four Season air conditioning ($363.40-$384.15). Deflector, station wagon ($19). Power drum brakes ($41.15-$43.05). Power front disc brakes ($64.25-$65.65). Carpeted load floor ($52.70). Monte Carlo console ($53.75). Console in Malibu/Nova with bucket seats ($53.75). Electro-Clear rear defroster ($41.70). Standard rear defroster ($20.85-$29.20). Power door locks, two-door ($35.45); four-door ($54.12). Tinted glass ($24.83-$30.00). Headlight delay system ($18.36). Special instrumentation, includes tachometer, ammeter and temperature gauges. Malibu coupe/convertible ($84.30); Monte Carlo ($68.50); Camaro and Nova V-8 with console ($94.80). Vigilante light monitoring system, except Nova ($26.35). AM push-button radio ($61.10). AM/FM push-button radio ($133.80). AM/FM radio with FM stereo ($239.10). Stereotape, with AM radio ($194.85); with AM/FM radio and FM stereo ($372.85). Black, blue, dark gold, green or white vinyl tops; on Monte Carlo ($126.40); on Chevrolet ($105.35); on Nova six/V-8 ($84.30); on Camaro Sport Coupe, including roof rail molding ($84.30); on Chevelle ($94.80). Six-Way power front seat ($100.10). Power Strato-Bucket seat ($121.15). Rear fender skirts; on Monte Carlo and Chevrolet, except station wagons ($31.60). Power steering ($89.55-$105.35). Comfort-Tilt steering wheel ($46). Wheel covers ($21). Monte Carlo color-keyed wheel covers ($15.80). Special wheel covers ($57.95-$80.70). Six 15 x 7JK wheels on Monte Carlo ($10.55). Rally-styled wheels, on Caprice and Kingswood Estate ($21); others ($36). Nova sport-styled wheels ($79). Fingertip windshield wiper control ($19). Rear deck lid spoiler, on 1970-1/2 Camaro, standard with Z/28 package ($32.65). Air conditioning, 1970-1/2 Camaro ($380.25). Console, including compartment, ashtray and automatic shift lever, in 1970-1/2 Camaro ($59). Vinyl roof on 1970-1/2 Camaro ($89.55). RPO L65 350 cid/250 hp V-8, in 1970-1/2 Camaro ($31.60); in base Chevelle ($21.10) in Malibu and Nova ($16.70). RPO L34 396 cid/350 hp V-8 in 1970-1/2 Camaro with RPO Z27 ($152.75). RPO L78 396 cid/375 hp V-8 in 1970-1/2 Camaro with RPO Z27, posi-traction required ($365.50). RPO L46 300 hp Turbo-Fire V 8, in 1970-1/2 Chevelles and Malibus ($68.50). RPO LS3 400 cid/330 hp Turbo-Jet V-8, in 1970-1/2 Chevelles ($162.20); in Malibu and Chevelle station wagons ($128.32); in Monte Carlo ($111.67). RPO LS6 454 cid/450 hp Turbo-Jet V-8, in 1970-1/2 Chevelle with SS-454 option package ($263.30). RPO LF6 400 cid/265 hp Turbo-Fire V-8 ($50.00). RPO LS4 454 cid/345 hp Turbo-Jet V8, except Novas and Chevelles ($133.35). RPO L22 250 cid/155 hp Turbo-Thrift six, in Camaro and Nova ($20.85). Wide-range type four-speed manual transmission in 1970-1/2 Camaro ($205.96); in 1970-1/2 Chevelle ($184.80); in Malibu/Nova/Monte Carlo ($184.80). Special close-ratio four-speed manual transmission in 1970-1/2 Chevelle ($221.80); in 1970-1/2 Camaro ($232.35). Regular close-ratio four-speed manual transmission in Malibu/Nova ($184.80); in 1970-1/2 Camaro ($205.95); in 1970-1/2 Chevelle ($184.80). Turbo-Hydramatic transmission, in 1970-1/2 Chevelle with 330/350/360 hp V-8s ($221.80); in same model with 450 hp V-8 ($290.40); in Nova six ($174.25); in other sixes ($190.10); in 200/250/300 hp V-8s, except Nova ($200.65); in Nova with 250/300 hp V-8s ($190.10); in all with 265/330/345/350/390 hp V-8s ($221.80); in all with 325/425 hp V-8s (N/A). Torque-Drive transmission, in Nova four/six ($68.65). Powerglide transmission in sixes, except Nova ($163.70); in V-8s, except Nova ($174.25); in Nova six ($147.85); in Nova V-8 ($158.40). RPO ZL2 Chevelle cowl-induction hood, SS-396/SS-454 option required ($147.45). Posi-traction axle ($42.15). Heavy-duty battery ($15.80). Dual exhaust ($24.17). 63-amp generator without air conditioning ($21.00); with air conditioning ($4). Engine block heater ($10.55). Heavy-duty radiator ($15-$32, per size of car).

OPTION PACKAGES:

Nova Custom Exterior Package, includes simulated front fender louvers; bright accents; rear panel trim plate; body sill and rear fender moldings; black bodysill and lower rear fender accent striping on coupe; bright side window and lower body moldings; black lower accent band and black vinyl insert-type side molding; on coupes ($97.95); on sedans ($79.00).

Nova Custom Interior Package, includes luxury seat and sidewall trim with bright accents; rear armrest ashtrays; carpeting; bright rearview mirror support, dome light bezel and pedal trim; right front hood light switch; glovebox light; trunk mat; and insulation.

RPO Z23 1970-1/2 Camaro interior accent group, includes additional instrument cluster lighting; woodgrain dash accents and steering wheel ($21.10) or included with Z/28 package at no charge.

1970-1/2 Chevrolet, Camaro Rally Sport two-door hardtop, V-8

RPO Z27 1970-1/2 Super Sport (SS) package, includes 350 cid/300 hp V-8; bright engine accents; power brakes; special ornamentation; hood insulation; F70-14 white-letter tires; 14 x 7-inch wheels; black-painted grille; Hide-Away wipers with black arms; and SS emblems ($289.65).

RPO Z22 1970-1/2 Camaro RS (Rally Sport) package, includes black-painted grille with rubber-tipped vertical center bar and resilient body-color grille frame; independent left and right front bumpers; license plate bracket mounted below right front bumper; parking lights with bright accents molded on grille panel; Hide-Away wipers; bright window, hood panel and bodysill moldings; body-colored door handle inserts; RS emblems; nameplate; bright accented taillamps and back-up lamps; F78-14 or E70-14 tires required ($188.35).

RPO Z28 1970-1/2 Camaro Special Performance Package, includes special 350 cid/360 hp V-8 with bright engine accents; heavy-duty radiator, dual exhaust; black painted grille; Z/28 emblems; special performance suspension; heavy-duty front and rear springs; 15 x 7-inch wheels; special center caps and trim rings; hood insulation; F60-15-B white-lettered tires; rear deck spoiler; and special paint stripes on hood and deck ($572.95).

RPO Z15 1970-1/2 Chevelle SS-454 Package, includes bright engine accents; dual exhaust with bright tips; black-painted grille; wheel opening moldings; power front disc brakes; special rear suspension and rear bumper with black insert; special 'power bulge' hood; SS emblems; 454 cid/360 hp Turbo-Jet V-8; heavy-duty battery; F70-14 white-letter tires; 14 x 7-inch wheels (sport-type); deletion of bodysill molding; and deletion of beltline molding, on Malibu V-8 Sport Coupe or convertible, with M40 Turbo-Hydramatic or four-speed manual transmissions only ($503.45).

RPO Z20 Monte Carlo SS Package, includes 454 cid/360 hp V-8; Superlift with Automatic Level Control; dual exhaust; G70-15/B white-letter tires; 15 x 7-inch wheels; 454 emblems on bodysill moldings; and requires Turbo-Hydramatic ($420.25).

RPO Z26 Nova SS Package, includes 350 cid/300 hp V-8; dual exhaust; power front disc brakes; simulated air intake on hood; simulated front fender louvers; bright accents; black-finished grille and rear panel; 14 x 7-inch wheels; E70-14 white-stripe tires; hood insulation and SS emblems. Four-speed manual or Turbo-Hydramatic transmission required ($290.70).

RPO L34 Nova SS-396 package, includes same as above with 350 hp Turbo-Jet V-8 ($184.35 extra).

RPO L38 Nova SS-396 package, includes same as above with 375 hp Turbo-Jet V-8 ($316.00).

RPO Z25 Chevelle SS-396 package, includes 396 cid/350 hp Turbo-Jet V-8; power front disc brakes; dual exhaust with bright tips; black-painted grille; wheel opening moldings; special rear bumper with black inserts; 'power dome' hood; special suspension; 14 x 7-inch sport-style wheels; G70-14 white-lettered tires; and SS emblems. Four-speed or Turbo-Hydramatic required ($445.55).

RPO Z25 with L78 Chevelle SS-396 with 375 hp V-8 and cast iron heads. Includes same as above, except engine ($210.65).

RPO Z25 with L78/L89 Chevelle SS-396, includes same as above with 375 hp V-8 and aluminum heads ($394.95).

HISTORICAL FOOTNOTES: The 1970-1/2 Camaro was not introduced until Feb. 26, 1970. The other new Chevrolet products hit the showrooms on Sept. 18, 1969. John Z. DeLorean was general manager of the Chevrolet Motor Division this year. Calendar year production of models included in this section was as follows: (Chevrolet) 550,596; (Monte Carlo) 130,659; (Nova) 247,344; (Chevelle) 354,839; and Camaro (143,675). Model year output included 143,664 Camaros; 354,855 Chevelles; 130,657 Monte Carlos; 550,571 Chevrolets; and 254,242 Novas. A total of 53,599 Malibu SS models left the factory, including 3,733 with the 454-cid V-8. Also carrying SS equipment were 3,823 Monte Carlos and 19,558 Novas.

1971

FULL-SIZE CHEVROLET — (SIX/V-8) — ALL SERIES — All-new styling and increased size were characteristics of the big Chevrolets for 1971. All models grew, but the station wagon showed the largest gain in inches and was now on a longer wheelbase than passenger cars. The grille had an eggcrate look and was higher, but narrower. Parking lamps were re-situated on the front body corners, where the large, ribbed, vertical lenses were set into fender extension caps. The dual horizontal headlamps were housed in square bezels. The hood panel bulged at the center and carried Chevrolet block lettering on its front edge. Bodyside contours were more rounded and straighter. The rear fenders kicked-up at the upper rear quarter region, then slanted back towards the tail. New taillight treatments were seen. Power disc brakes became standard on all full-size models, as well as on Monte Carlos and Camaros. Standard equipment for Bel Airs included hidden (in-the-windshield) antenna; Astro-Ventilation; concealed wipers; sideguard beam doors; heater and defroster; cigarette lighter; locking glovebox; center dome light; armrests; 145 hp six or 245 hp V-8; inside hood release; and left-hand outside rearview mirror. Bel Airs had all these features, plus glovebox light and cloth with vinyl trim interior. Impalas had the same equipment as Bel Airs, plus luggage compartment light; vinyl-trimmed pattern cloth upholstery; woodgrain accented dash; Deluxe steering wheel; foam front seat cushions; and, on convertibles, courtesy lights; lower door carpeting; and all-vinyl seats. Tires were F78-15 on Bel Air/Biscayne, G78-15 on Impala. The Caprice added ashtray and courtesy lights; electric clock; rear fender skirts; distinctive cloth and vinyl trim; color-keyed wheel covers; and 225 hp V-8. It also used G78-15 tires The Caprice sedan was equipped with a fold-down center armrest in the front seat. Features of full-size station wagons were a concealed storage bin; cushioned-center steering wheel; Flush & Dry rocker panels; all-vinyl interior; power disc/drum brakes; Hide-Away wipers; Glide-Away tailgate with power window; Air-Flow rear contour; recessed dual headlights; flush-style curved side glass; Flow-through power ventilation; open rocker panels; inside hood release; forward-facing rear seat on nine-passenger station wagon; 350 cid/245 hp V-8; and L78-15 tires mounted on 15 x 6-inch wheels. Brookwoods added a map light. Townsman/Kingswood models added mirror map and glovebox lights and the Kingswood Estate also had ashtray, courtesy glovebox and mirror map lights; door edge guards; electric clock; and woodgrained side and rear panels.

CHEVROLET I.D. NUMBERS: Serial numbers on all Chevrolet products were now found on the top left-hand surface of the instrument panel. They were visible through the windshield. The Vehicle Identification Number had 13 symbols. The first three symbols indicate make and series and appear as Series Number in first column of charts below. For example, the first car listed has number 153 (1=Chevrolet; 53=Biscayne six) for six-cylinder series and 154 (1=Chevrolet; 54=Biscayne V-8) for eight-cylinder series. Fourth and fifth symbols indicate body type and appear as Body/Style Number in second column of charts below. Sixth symbol indicates model year: 1=1971. Seventh symbol identifies assembly plant: A=Atlanta, Ga.; B=Baltimore, Md.; C=Southgate, Calif.; F=Flint, Mich.; G=Framingham, Mass.; I=Oshawa, Canada; J=Janesville, Wis.; K=Kansas City, Mo.; L=Los Angeles, Calif.; N=Norwood, Ohio; R=Arlington, Texas; S=St. Louis, Mo.; T=Tarrytown, N.Y.; U=Lordstown, Ohio; W=Willow Run, Mich.; Y=Wilmington, Del.; Z=Fremont, Calif. Next six symbols are sequential production number. Body tag riveted to cowl indicates some of the same information, plus paint and trim codes. Engine numbers are stamped on right side of V-8 blocks and right side of six-cylinder blocks behind distributor. Consult factory or aftermarket sources for numerous Chevrolet engine codes.

FULL-SIZE CHEVROLET SERIES

Series No.	Body/Style No.	Body Type & Seating	Factory Price	Shipping Weight	Prod. Total
BISCAYNE (BROOKWOOD STATION WAGON)					
153/154	69	4-dr Sed-6P	3096/3448	3732/3888	Note 1
154	35	4-dr Sta Wag-6P	3929	4542	Note 2
BEL AIR (TOWNSMAN STATION WAGONS)					
155/156	69	4-dr Sed-6P	3232/3585	3732/3888	Note 3
156	45	4-dr Sta Wag-9P	4135	4598	Note 2
156	35	4-dr Sta Wag-6P	4020	4544	Note 2
IMPALA (KINGSWOOD STATION WAGONS)					
163/164	69	4-dr Sed-6P	3391/3742	3760/3914	Note 4
163/164	57	2-dr HT Cpe-6P	3408/3759	3742/3896	Note 4
164	39	4-dr HT Sed-6P	3813	3978	Note 4
164	47	2-dr Cus Cpe-6P	3826	3912	Note 4
164	67	2-dr Conv-6P	4021	3960	Notes 4/5
164	45	4-dr Sta Wag-9P	4227	4648	Note 2
164	35	4-dr Sta Wag-6P	4112	4568	Note 2
CAPRICE (KINGSWOOD ESTATE WAGONS)					
166	39	4-dr HT Sed-6P	4134	4040	Note 3
166	47	2-dr Cus Cpe-6P	4081	3964	Note 6
166	45	4-dr Sta Wag-9P	4498	4738	Note 2
166	35	4-dr Sta Wag-6P	4384	4678	Note 2

1971 Chevrolet, Caprice Kingswood Estate station wagon, V-8

FIGURES BELOW ARE ROUNDED-OFF (except Note 5):

NOTE 1: 37,600 Biscayne cars were built (2,900 sixes/34,700 V-8s).

NOTE 2: 91,300 full-size Chevrolet station wagons were built (all V-8s).

NOTE 3: 20,000 Bel Air cars were built (5,000 sixes/15,000 V-8s).

NOTE 4: 427,700 Impala cars were built (2,300 sixes/425,400 V-8s).

NOTE 5: Exactly 4,576 Impala convertibles are included in Note 4.

NOTE 6: 91,300 Caprice V-8s were built.

NOTE 7: Data above slash for six/below slash or no slash is V-8 data.

1971 Chevrolet, Caprice two-door Custom Coupe, V-8 (PH)

MONTE CARLO — (V-8) — SERIES 138 — A new grille with a finer insert mesh appeared on 1971 Monte Carlos. A front bumper with rectangular parking lamps was used in this model's second year. Another change was a raised hood ornament. The original wheelbase was carried over, but overall length grew an inch. The headlight bezels were squarer. This was the last year for the

Monte Carlo SS-454, of which only 1,919 examples were built in 1971. Standard Monte Carlo features included all safety equipment; power front disc brakes; power ventilation system; electric clock; sideguard door beam structure; assist straps; vinyl burled elm finish instrument panel; concealed wipers; 350 cid/245 hp V-8; glovebox light; and left-hand outside rearview mirror. Size G78-15 tires were used.

MONTE CARLO SERIES

Series No.	Body/Style No.	Body Type & Seating	Factory Price	Shipping Weight	Prod. Total
138	57	2-dr HT Cpe-5P	3416	3488	112,599

1971 Chevrolet, Monte Carlo two-door hardtop, V-8

NOTE 1: The production total includes 1,919 cars with SS-454 equipment, including the 454 cid/365 hp V-8. An unspecified, but extremely limited number of cars were ordered with the LS-6 454-cid V-8 rated at 425 hp.

INTERMEDIATE-SIZE CHEVELLE — (SIX/V-8) — ALL SERIES — The Chevelle models received changes to the front and rear for 1971. A new twin level grille was divided by a bright, horizontal bar with a Chevrolet 'bow tie' insignia at the middle. The grille inserts were of multiple, horizontal blades segmented by wide-spaced vertical dividers. Single headlamps in square bezels were used. Parking lamps were moved from the previous bumper location into the front fenders. There were two parking lamp lenses, set into individual rectangular housings that wrapped around the body corners. The upper lens was amber and the lower lens was white. At the rear, circular taillights were deeply recessed into the bumper. Standard equipment for base editions consisted of Astro-Ventilation; cigarette lighter; sideguard door beam structure; concealed wipers; and either the 250 cid/145 hp six or 307 cid/200 hp V-8. The Malibu convertible also had interior courtesy lamps, while all Malibus featured a glovebox light and left outside rearview mirror. Size E78-14 tires were used. Equipment included on Nomad, Concours and Greenbriers was comprised of Dual-Action tailgate; concealed storage compartment; cushioned-center steering wheel; Flush & Dry rocker panels; all-vinyl interior; bias-belted G78-14 tires; carpeting; vinyl-coated textured metal cargo floor; and Guard-Beam side door construction. The Nomad came as a six or V-8, while the other station wagons came V-8 only. Concours and Concours Estates also had Hide-Away wipers; power front disc/rear drum brakes; and a glovebox light. The Estate also included door edge guards and woodgrained exterior paneling, with rear-facing third seats and power tailgate window in nine-passenger models.

1971 Chevrolet, Chevelle Malibu two-door hardtop, V-8

INTERMEDIATE-SIZE CHEVELLE SERIES

Series No.	Body/Style No.	Body Type & Seating	Factory Price	Shipping Weight	Prod. Total
NOMAD STATION WAGONS					
131/132	36	4-dr Sta Wag-6P	2997/3097	3632/3746	Note 1
CHEVELLE (GREENBRIER STATION WAGONS)					
133/134	69	4-dr Sed-6P	2677/2773	3210/3336	Note 2
133/134	37	2-dr HT Cpe-6P	2712/2807	3166/3296	Note 2
134	46	4-dr Sta Wag-9P	3340	3882	Note 1
134	36	4-dr Sta Wag-6P	3226	3820	Note 1
CHEVELLE MALIBU (CONCOURS STATION WAGONS)					
135/136	69	4-dr Sed-6P	2851/2947	3250/3380	Note 3
135/136	37	2-dr HT Cpe-6P	2885/2980	3212/3342	Note 3
136	39	4-dr HT Sed-6P	3052	3450	Note 3
136	67	2-dr Conv-6P	3260	3390	Notes 3/4
136	46	4-dr Sta Wag-9P	3450	3908	Note 1
136	36	4-dr Sta Wag-6P	3337	3664	Note 1
CONCOURS ESTATE STATION WAGONS					
138	46	4-dr Sta Wag-9P	3626	3944	Note 1
138	36	4-dr Sta Wag-6P	3514	3692	Note 1

1971-1/2 Chevrolet, (Chevelle) "Heavy Chevy" two-door hardtop, V-8 (PH)

GENERAL NOTE: All model year production figures given below are expressed to the nearest 100 units. No body style breakouts are available, except for convertibles.

NOTE 1: Some 43,200 Chevelle intermediate-size station wagons were built during the 1971 model year. This includes 2,800 sixes (all Nomads) and 39,500 V-8s.

This includes all Nomad, Greenbrier, Concours and Concours Estate wagons, with no additional breakout by series available.

NOTE 2: Some 35,600 base Chevelles were built during the 1971 model year. This included 11,500 sixes and 24,100 V-8s.

1971-1/2 Chevrolet, "Rally Nova" two-door coupe, V-8 (PH)

NOTE 3: Some 249,300 Chevelle Malibus were built during the 1971 model year. This included 9,100 sixes and 240,200 V-8s.

NOTE 4: Exactly 5,089 Chevelle Malibu convertibles were built during the 1971 model year. This breakout is included in the rounded-off total in Note 3 above. All convertibles were V-8s. There is no additional breakout available as to the number of Super Sport convertibles built.

ADDITIONAL NOTE: In rounded-off figures, a total of some 80,000 Chevelles were sold with Super Sport equipment packages. Exactly 19,992 of these cars were Chevelle SS-454s.

1971 Chevrolet, Nova two-door coupe, V-8

NOVA SERIES — (SIX/V-8) — SERIES 113/114 — The disappearance of the Nova four was one change for the 'senior' compact models. There was also a slight amount of revision to the grille. It seemed to highlight the vertical elements more than the year before. A vertical molding was also seen in the front fender corner trim panels. Amber plastic parking lamp lenses were new. Simulated fenderside louvers were on the optional equipment list, but many new packages were added.

The body was essentially the same design introduced in 1968. Standard features included front armrests; foot-operated brake; ignition key alarm system; anti-theft steering wheel column lock; heater and defroster; and either the 250-cid six or 307-cid V-8. The Nova wore E78-14 tires in standard trim.

NOVA SIX/V-8 SERIES

Series No.	Body/Style No.	Body Type & Seating	Factory Price	Shipping Weight	Prod. Total
111/113	69	4-dr Sed-6P	2205/2284	2843/2942	Note 1
111/113	27	2-dr Cpe-6P	2176/2254	2820/2919	Note 1

NOTE 1: 194,878 Novas were built (94,928 sixes/99,950 V-8s).

NOTE 2: 7,015 Novas included in the total above had Super Sport option.

1971 Chevrolet, Vega 2300 two-door notchback sedan, 4-cyl

VEGA 2300 — (FOUR) — SERIES 2300 — The Vega was a completely new sub-compact car from Chevrolet. Three two-door models: notchback sedan, hatchback coupe and Kammback station wagon were offered. Single headlights, round parking lamps and a slightly 'veed' rectangular grille with eggcrate insert characterized the front of the car. A full-width wraparound bumper ran across the grille. The rear panel had a slightly concave treatment, with twin rectangular taillamps at each side. Three sets of louvers were punched in the deck of the notchback and on the rear quarter of station wagons. The hatchback had its louvers at the rear roof pillar. Power came from an aluminum four with overhead camshaft. A dome-shaped bulge was on the hood of all three styles. A nameplate was placed ahead of the forward hood seam, above the upper left-hand corner of the grille. It read 'Chevrolet Vega 2300.' Standard features included side marker lights and reflectors; functional vent louvers; Flush & Dry rocker panels; left outside rearview mirror; front bucket seats; rear bucket-style bench seats; Flow-Through ventilation; three-speed manual transmission with floor shift control; windshield washers; dual speed wipers; ashtray; all-vinyl upholstery; exhaust emission control system; storage well in driver's door; and 80 hp four. The coupe also had hatchback rear deck construction; fold-down back seat; front area carpeting; passenger sliding seat adjustment; cargo area rubber mats; and concealed-under-floor storage area. Sedans and station wagons had front manual disc brakes. The wagon included carpeting. All featured a three-point safety belt system. Size 6.00 x 13 tires were used as standard equipment.

VEGA 2300 SERIES

Series No.	Body/Style No.	Body Type & Seating	Factory Price	Shipping Weight	Prod. Total
141	11	2-dr Sed-4P	2090	2146	58,800
141	77	2-dr Cpe-4P	2196	2190	166,300
141	15	2-dr Sta Wag-4P	2328	2230	42,800

NOTE 1: 274,699 Vegas were built during the 1971 model year.

NOTE 2: Chart shows rounded-off totals for each passenger body style.

NOTE 3: Some 7,800 Vega panel wagons were also included in the model year total.

1971 Chevrolet, Vega 2300 two-door Kammback station wagon, 4-cyl

CAMARO — (SIX/V-8) — SERIES 123/124 — There was hardly any change in the 1971 Camaro. As on other Chevrolets, the grille insert seemed to have a more vertical character, although the design elements remained basically unchanged. Trim details varied according to the options ordered for each car. New options were brown or blue vinyl top coverings. Power disc brakes were standard. So was side marker lights; reflectors; defroster; washers and dual speed wipers; inside day/nite mirror; outside rearview mirror; all-vinyl interior; bucket seats; rear bucket-style seat cushions; front disc brakes; steel side guard rails; three-speed manual transmission with floor shift; cigarette lighter; carpeting; Astro-Ventilation; and either the 250-cid six or 307-cid V-8. Size E78-14 tires were standard equipment. The Camaro SS package included dual exhaust; power brakes; left-hand remote-control sport mirror; special ornamentation and hood insulation; F70-14 white-lettered tires; 14 x 7-inch wheels; black-finished grille, Hide-Away wipers; and the 350 cid/270 hp V-8 with bright engine accents. Rally sport equipment included special black-finished grille with rubber-tipped vertical center bar and resilient body-color grille frame; independent front left- and right-hand bumpers; license plate bracket below right bumper; parking lights with bright accents mounted on grille panel; Hide-Away wip-

ers; bright roof drip, window and hood panel moldings; body-color insert on door handles; RS emblem on steering wheel; RS front fender nameplates; and bright accented taillights and back-up lamps (RS emblems were deleted when SS or Z/28 packages were ordered). The Z/28 package also included special 350 cid/330 hp V-8 with bright engine trim; remote-control left-hand outside rearview mirror; special instrumentation; power brakes; 3.73:1 ratio posi-traction rear axle; heavy-duty cooling; dual exhaust; black-accented grille; Z/28 front fender emblems; rear bumper guards; sport suspension; rear deck spoiler with Z/28 decal; special paint stripes on hood and rear deck (choice of black or white stripes except with vinyl top or roof with black or white paint finish); heavy-duty front and rear springs; 15 x 7-inch wheels with chrome lugnuts; special center hubcaps with trim rings; and F60-15/B bias-belted white-letter tires.

1971 Chevrolet, Camaro SS-396 two-door hardtop, V-8

CAMARO SERIES

Series No.	Body/Style No.	Body Type & Seating	Factory Price	Shipping Weight	Prod. Total
123/124	87	2-dr HT Cpe-4P	2921/3016	3094/3218	107,496

NOTE 1: Production included 18,404 Rally Sports.

NOTE 2: Production included 8,377 Super Sports.

NOTE 3: Production included 4,862 Z/28s.

NOTE 4: 103,452 cars had V-8s/11,191 had sixes.

NOTE 5: Transmissions: 13,042 with three-speed; 10,614 with four-speed; 90,987 with automatic.

NOTE 6: Options: 42,537 cars with air conditioning; 93,163 cars with power steering.

NOTE 7: 7,147 Camaros were built in the U.S. for export market sales.

ENGINES

(ALL SIX-CYLINDER) Inline six: Cast iron block. Displacement: 250 cid. Bore and stroke: 3.875 x 3.53 inches. Compression ratio: 8.5:1. Brake hp: 145 at 4200 rpm. Seven main bearings. Hydraulic valve lifters. Carburetor: Rochester one-barrel.

(V-8 BISCAYNE/BEL AIR/IMPALA/MONTE CARLO) Overhead valve. Cast iron block. Displacement: 350 cid. Bore and stroke: 4.00 x 3.48 inches. Compression ratio: 8.5:1. Brake hp: 245 at 4800 rpm. Five main bearings. Hydraulic valve lifters. Carburetor: Rochester two-barrel.

(V-8 CAPRICE AND STATION WAGONS) Overhead valve. Cast iron block. Displacement: 400 cid. Bore and stroke: 4.125 x 3.75 inches. Compression ratio: 8.5:1. Brake hp: 255 at 4400 rpm. Five main bearings. Hydraulic valve lifters. Carburetor: Rochester two-barrel.

(CHEVELLE/MALIBU/NOVA/CAMARO) V-8. Overhead valve. Cast iron block. Displacement: 307 cid. Bore and stroke: 3.875 x 3.25 inches. Compression ratio: 8.5:1. Brake hp: 200 at 4600 rpm. Five main bearings. Hydraulic valve lifters. Carburetor: Rochester two-barrel.

(VEGA) Inline OHC-four. Aluminum block. Displacement: 140 cid. Bore and stroke: 3.501 x 3.625 inches. Compression ratio: 8.0:1. Brake hp: 90 at 4800 rpm. Hydraulic valve lifters. Carburetor: one-barrel.

CHASSIS FEATURES: Wheelbase: (Chevrolet wagon) 125 inches; (Chevrolet) 121.5 inches; (Monte Carlo/Chevelle four-door) 116 inches; (Chevelle two-door) 112 inches; (Nova) 111 inches; (Camaro) 108 inches; (Vega) 97 inches. Overall length: (Chevrolet wagon) 224 inches; (Chevrolet) 217 inches; (Monte Carlo/Chevelle wagon) 207 inches; (Chevelle two-door) 198 inches; (Chevelle four-door) 202 inches; (Nova) 190 inches; (Camaro) 188 inches; (Vega) 170 inches. Width: (Chevrolet) 80 inches; (Monte Carlo/Chevelle) 76 inches; (Nova) 73 inches; (Camaro) 75 inches; (Vega) 66 inches. Tires: Refer to text.

OPTIONS: Vega power steering ($95). Vega air conditioning ($360). Nova vinyl top ($84). Nova power steering ($103). Nova air conditioning ($392). Chevelle vinyl top ($95). Monte Carlo/Camaro/Chevelle air conditioning ($408). Camaro vinyl top ($90). Monte Carlo vinyl top ($126). Chevrolet AM/FM stereo ($239). Chevrolet power windows ($127). Vega GT coupe package ($349). Nova SS package ($328). Chevelle SS package ($357). Malibu SS package ($357). Camaro SS package ($314). Monte Carlo SS-454 package ($485). Camaro RS package ($179). Three-speed manual transmission was standard. Automatic transmission. Special three-speed manual floor shift transmission. Four-speed manual floor shift transmission. Wide-ratio four-speed manual transmission with floor shift. Close-ratio four-speed manual transmission with floor shift. Vega four 140 cid/110 hp two-barrel engine. Chevrolet V-8 400 cid/255 hp two-barrel engine. Chevrolet V-8 402 cid/300 hp four-barrel engine. Chevrolet V-8 454 cid/365 hp four-barrel engine. Monte Carlo/Corvette 402 cid/300 hp four-barrel engine. Monte Carlo/Chevelle V-8 454 cid/365 hp four-barrel engine. Chevelle V-8 350 cid/245 hp two-barrel engine. Chevelle V-8 350 cid/270 hp four-barrel engine. Nova V-8 350 cid/245 hp two-barrel engine. Camaro V-8 350 cid/245 hp two-barrel engine. Camaro

V-8 350 cid/270 hp four-barrel engine. Camaro V-8 350 cid/330 hp four-barrel engine. Camaro V-8 402 cid/300 hp four-barrel engine.

HISTORICAL FOOTNOTES: The full-size Chevrolets were introduced on Sept. 29, 1970, and the Vega appeared in dealer showrooms Sept. 10. Calendar year production of 2,275,694 cars was recorded. John Z. DeLorean was the chief executive officer of the company this year. In the high-performance car field, Chevrolet built some 60,000 Chevelle Super Sports; 7,015 Nova Super Sports; 1,919 Monte Carlo SS-454 models and 6,377 Camaro Super Sports. Only 19,292 Chevelle SS models had the 454-cid V-8 installed. Monte Carlos continued to compete and win on the NASCAR short tracks, even with horsepower reduced to 425 due to lower 9.0:1 compression ratio. This compared to 460 hp in the late 1970 LS6-equipped Chevelles. Most other Chevrolets were limited to an 8.5:1 maximum compression ratio to ensure adaptability of the new engines to low-lead or no-lead fuel. However, the Camaro Z/28 was an exception. It came with a 9.0:1 compression, 350 cid/330 hp V-8.

1972

FULL-SIZE CHEVROLET — (SIX/V-8) — ALL SERIES — Chevrolet's standard models continued to get bigger, with a slight increase in passenger car wheelbase as well. The front lip of the hood dipped deeper creating a slimmer grille above the full-width bumper. However, more of the grille showed through underneath. Parking lamps, while still in the fender extension caps, were smaller. The grille had a finer texture and a Chevrolet insignia was seen at the center of the hood. A lower body feature line was used on the bodysides and the upper rear fender edge was somewhat raised. Tires were size G78-15/B on Impala/Caprice, F78-15/B on Biscayne/Bel Air; and H78-15 on station wagons. Power brakes; power steering; and automatic transmission became standard in all full-size lines. For this season only, engine horsepower ratings were expressed in both the traditional way and in the new SAE Net (nhp) format.

1972 Chevrolet, Caprice two-door hardtop, V-8

CHEVROLET I.D. NUMBERS: Serial numbers on all Chevrolet products were now found on the top left-hand surface of the instrument panel. They were visible through the windshield. The Vehicle Identification Number had 13 symbols. The first symbol indicated make: 1=Chevrolet, and the second symbol indicated car-line: B=Nomad; C=Chevelle/Greenbrier; D=Malibu/Concours; H=Monte Carlo/Concours Estate; K=Biscayne/Brookwood; L=Bel Air/Townsman; M=Impala/Kingswood; N=Caprice/Kingswood Estate; Q=Camaro; V=Vega; X=Nova. (These appear in Series Number column of charts below). The third and fourth digits indicated body type and appear in Body/Style Number column of charts below. Fifth symbol indicates engine: B=140-cid four; D=250-cid six; F=307-cid V-8; H=350-cid V-8 2V; J=350-cid V-8 (L48); L=Camaro Z28 four-barrel 350-cid V-8 (high-output); R=400-cid V-8; S=402-cid (LS3) V-8 single exhaust; U=402-cid (LS3) V-8 dual exhaust; V=454-cid V-8 4V (LS5) single exhaust; W=454-cid V-8 4V (LS5) dual exhaust. Sixth symbol indicates model year: 2=1972. Seventh symbol indicates assembly plant: A=Lakewood, Ga.; B=Baltimore Md.; C=Southgate, Calif.; D=Doraville, Ga.; F=Flint, Mich.; J=Janesville, Wis.; K=Leeds, Mo.; L=Van Nuys, Calif.; N=Norwood, Ohio; R=Arlington, Texas; S=St. Louis, Mo.; T=Tarrytown, N.Y.; U=Lordstown, Ohio; V=Pontiac, Mich.; W=Willow Run, Mich.; Y=Wilmington, Del.; Z=Fremont, Calif.; 1=Oshawa, Canada; 2=St. Therese, Quebec, Canada. Next six symbols are sequential production number. Body tag riveted to cowl indicates some of the same information, plus paint and trim codes. Engine numbers are stamped on right side of V-8 blocks and right side of six-cylinder blocks behind distributor. Consult factory or aftermarket sources for numerous Chevrolet engine serial numbers.

1972 Chevrolet, Caprice four-door sedan, V-8 (PH)

FULL-SIZE CHEVROLET SERIES K-L-M-N

Series No.	Body/Style No.	Body Type & Seating	Factory Price	Shipping Weight	Prod. Total
BISCAYNE (BROOKWOOD STATION WAGON)					
1K	69	4-dr Sed-6P	3074/3406	3857/4045	Note 1
1K	35	4-dr Sta Wag-6P	3882	4686	Note 2
BEL AIR (TOWNSMAN STATION WAGONS)					
1L	69	4-dr Sed-6P	3204/3536	3854/4042	Note 3
1L	45	4-dr Sta Wag-9P	4078	4769	Note 2
1L	35	4-dr Sta Wag-6P	3969	4687	Note 2
IMPALA (KINGSWOOD STATION WAGONS)					
1M	69	4-dr Sed-6P	3369/3704	3928/4113	Note 4
1M	57	2-dr HT Cpe-6P	3385/3720	3864/4049	Note 4
1M	39	4-dr HT Sed-6P	3771	4150	Note 4
1M	47	2-dr Cus Cpe-6P	3767	4053	Note 4
1M	67	2-dr Conv-6P	3979	4125	Notes 4/5
1M	45	4-dr Sta Wag-9P	4165	4617	Note 2
1M	35	4-dr Sta Wag-6P	4056	4734	Note 2

CAPRICE (KINGSWOOD ESTATE STATION WAGONS)

1N	69	4-dr Sed-6P	4009	N/A	Note 6
1N	47	2-dr Cus Cpe-6P	4026	4102	Note 6
1N	45	4-dr Sta Wag-9P	4423	4883	Note 2
1N	35	4-dr Sta Wag-6P	4314	4796	Note 2

1972 Chevrolet, Impala two-door convertible, V-8

FIGURES BELOW ARE ROUNDED-OFF (except Note 5):

NOTE 1: 20,500 Biscayne cars were built (1,500 sixes/19,000 V-8s).

NOTE 2: 171,700 full-size Chevrolet station wagons were built (all V-8s).

NOTE 3: 41,900 Bel Air cars were built (900 sixes/41,000 V-8s).

NOTE 4: 597,500 Impala cars were built (1,500 sixes/596,000 V-8s).

NOTE 5: Exactly 6,456 Impala V-8 convertibles are included in Note 4.

NOTE 6: 178,500 Caprice V-8s were built.

NOTE 7: Data above slash for six/below slash or no slash is V-8 data.

1972 Chevrolet, Caprice four-door hardtop, V-8

1972 Chevrolet, Impala two-door Custom Coupe, V-8

MONTE CARLO — (V-8) — SERIES 1H

MONTE CARLO — (V-8) — SERIES 1H — The new Monte Carlo grille covered the entire area between the square-bezeled headlamps. It had horizontal blades divided by prominent vertical blades. Parking lamps were moved from the bumper and were vertically positioned at the outboard grille segments. It was the last season for the original Monte Carlo body style. Standard equipment tires were size G78-15/B blackwalls.

1972 Chevrolet, Caprice Kingswood Estate station wagon, V-8

MONTE CARLO SERIES

Series No.	Body/Style No.	Body Type & Seating	Factory Price	Shipping Weight	Prod. Total
1H	57	2-dr HT Cpe-6P	3362	3506	180,819

INTERMEDIATE-SIZE CHEVELLE — (SIX/V-8) — ALL SERIES

INTERMEDIATE-SIZE CHEVELLE — (SIX/V-8) — ALL SERIES — Changes to the Chevelle were of a minor nature. The grille had a new texture and was divided horizontally by two even-spaced moldings giving a three-tier look. Parking lamps were still found in the fender cap, but now had a larger, one-piece plastic lens of square shape. It wrapped around the body corner, serving double duty as a side marker lamp. A new molding treatment with some trim levels included a stainless steel spear at mid-body height running only between the front and rear wheel openings. Tires for base models were size E78-14/B blackwalls. Station wagons had G78-14/B tires. Chevelle V-8s built for California sale were equipped with the 350-cid engine in 165 or 175 hp form. Federal cars had either the 250-cid six or the 307-cid two-barrel V-8.

INTERMEDIATE-SIZE CHEVELLE SERIES B-C-D-H

Series No.	Body/Style No.	Body Type & Seating	Factory Price	Shipping Weight	Prod. Total
NOMAD STATION WAGON					
1B	36	4-dr Sta Wag-6P	2926/3016	3605/3732	Note 1
CHEVELLE (GREENBRIER STATION WAGONS)					
1C	69	4-dr Sed-6P	2636/2726	3204/3332	Note 2
1C	37	2-dr HT Cpe-6P	2669/2759	3172/3300	Note 2
1C	46	4-dr Sta Wag-9P	3247	3870	Note 1
1C	36	4-dr Sta Wag-6P	3140	3814	Note 1

1972 Chevrolet, Chevelle Malibu two-door hardtop, V-8

MALIBU (CONCOURS STATION WAGONS)

Series No.	Body/Style No.	Body Type & Seating	Factory Price	Shipping Weight	Prod. Total
1D	69	4-dr Sed-6P	2801/2891	3240/3371	Note 3
1D	39	4-dr HT Sed-6P	2991	3438	Note 3
1D	37	2-dr HT Cpe-6P	2833/2923	3194/3327	Note 3
1D	67	2-dr Conv-6P	3187	3379	Notes 3/4
1D	46	4-dr Sta Wag-9P	3351	3909	Note 1
1D	36	4-dr Sta Wag-6P	3244	3857	Note 1

CONCOURS ESTATE STATION WAGONS

Series No.	Body/Style No.	Body Type & Seating	Factory Price	Shipping Weight	Prod. Total
1H	46	4-dr Sta Wag-9P	3588	3943	Note 1
1H	36	4-dr Sta Wag-6P	3431	3887	Note 1

FIGURES BELOW ARE ROUNDED-OFF (except Note 4):

NOTE 1: 54,400 Chevelle station wagons were built in all series (3,000 sixes/51,400 V-8s).

NOTE 2: 49,400 base Chevelles were built (13,800 sixes/35,600 V-8s).

NOTE 3: 290,100 Malibus were built (8,400 sixes/281,700 V-8s).

1972 Chevrolet, Nova two-door coupe (with optional Super Sport package and Skyroof), V-8 (PH)

NOTE 4: 4,853 Malibu/Malibu SS convertibles included in above total.

NOTE 5: 24,946 SS models counted in Note 3 total (including 3,000 SS-454s).

NOTE 6: Data above slash for six/below slash or no slash is V-8 data.

1972 Chevrolet, Nova two-door sedan, V-8

NOVA — (SIX/V-8) — SERIES X — The Nova was carried over from 1971 without any obvious change, except for an indented license plate housing on the front bumper. If closely examined, a slight change in the bevel of the hood could be seen. There were numerous decor packages available to create anything from a hot

rod to personal/luxury car look. However, true high-performance hardware was no longer provided. Base engines in all states were the 250-cid six or 307-cid V-8. A 350 cid/245 hp V-8 was optional. Regular tires were E78-14/B blackwalls.

NOVA SERIES

Series No.	Body/Style No.	Body Type & Seating	Factory Price	Shipping Weight	Prod. Total
1X	69	4-dr Sed-6P	2405/2501	2976/3108	Note 1
1X	27	2-dr Cpe-6P	2376/2471	2952/3084	Note 1

NOTE 1: 349,733 Novas built in model year (139,769 sixes and 209,964 V-8s).

NOTE 2: Above total includes 12,309 cars sold with Nova SS equipment package.

VEGA 2300 — (FOUR) — SERIES 1V — The grille on the Vega was finished in a manner that made its vertical elements slightly less prominent. A model identification emblem was positioned on the side of the cowl. A change to A78-13 tires was made for standard equipment. Otherwise, there was little difference from 1971.

VEGA 2300 SERIES

Series No.	Body/Style No.	Body Type & Seating	Factory Price	Shipping Weight	Prod. Total
1V	11	2-dr Sed-4P	2060	2158	55,800
1V	77	2-dr Cpe-4P	2160	2294	262,700
1V	15	2-dr Sta Wag-4P	2285	2333	72,000

1972 Chevrolet, Vega two-door hatchback coupe, 4-cyl

NOTE 1: Model year production was 394,592 units.

NOTE 2: Model year production includes 4,114 panel express trucks.

NOTE 3: Chart shows body style production rounded-off to nearest 100 units.

CAMARO — (SIX/V-8) — SERIES Q — The Camaro, for 1972, had a slightly different grille mesh and new high-back bucket seats. The fate of the car was said to be in danger, since a strike at the Camaro assembly plant (Lordstown, Ohio) turned into a disaster. The walk-out stranded thousands of bodies on the assembly line and, by the time it was over, these cars were unfit for sale under new federal safety standards. General Motors was forced to scrap the bodies and almost decided to do the same with the Camaro/Firebird program. Chevrolet engineer Alex Mair fought successfully for survival of the Camaro, which went on to higher sales. Camaros wore E78-14 tires in standard trim and base engine selections were the same as in Chevelles, with different V-8s used for federal and California cars.

CAMARO SERIES

Series No.	Body/Style No.	Body Type & Seating	Factory Price	Shipping Weight	Prod. Total
1Q	87	2-dr HT Cpe-4P	2730/2820	3121/3248	68,656

NOTE 1: Production total includes 11,364 RS; 6,562 SS; 2,575 Camaro Z/28s.

NOTE 2: 63,832 cars had V-8s; 4,824 cars had sixes.

NOTE 3: Transmission: 6,053 had three-speed; 5,835 had four-speed; 56,768 had Turbo-HydraMatic.

NOTE 4: Options: 31,737 had air conditioning, 59,857 had power steering.

NOTE 5: 3,698 cars were built in the U.S. for export sales.

1972 Chevrolet, Camaro two-door hardtop (with optional Super Sport package), V-8

ENGINES

(CHEVROLET/CHEVELLE/NOVA) Inline six. Overhead valve. Cast iron block. Displacement: 250 cid. Bore and stroke: 3.875 x 3.53 inches. SAE Net hp: 110 at 3800 rpm. Seven main bearings. Hydraulic valve lifters. Carburetor: one-barrel.

(V-8 BISCAYNE/BEL AIR/IMPALA/MONTE CARLO/CHEVELLE CALIFORNIA) Overhead valve. Cast iron block. Displacement: 350 cid. Bore and stroke: 4.00 x 3.48 inches. SAE Net hp: 165 at 4000 rpm. Five main bearings. Hydraulic valve lifters.

1972 Chevrolet, Camaro two-door hardtop, V-8

(V-8 CAPRICE/ALL STATION WAGONS) Overhead valve. Cast iron block. Displacement: 400 cid. Bore and stroke: 4.126 x 3.75 inches. SAE Net hp: 170 at 3400 rpm. Five main bearings. Hydraulic valve lifters. Carburetor: two-barrel.

CAMARO FEDERAL V-8: See 1972 Nova series V-8 engine data.

CAMARO CALIFORNIA V-8: See 1972 Chevrolet series V-8 engine data.

(V-8 NOVA/CHEVELLE FEDERAL/CAMARO) Overhead valve. Cast iron block. Displacement: 307 cid. Bore and stroke: 3.875 x 3.25 inches. Brake hp: 130 at 4400 rpm. Five main bearings. Hydraulic valve lifters. Carburetor: two-barrel.

(VEGA) Inline four. Overhead valve. Cast aluminum block. Displacement: 140 cid. Bore and stroke: 3.50 x 3.625 inches. Brake hp: 80 at 4400 rpm. Carburetor: one-barrel.

CHASSIS FEATURES: Wheelbase: (Chevrolet passenger) 122 inches; (all other models) same as 1971. Overall length: (Chevrolet wagon) 226 inches; (Chevrolet) 220 inches; (all other models) same as 1971. Tires: (all models) Refer to text.

OPTIONS: Vega power steering ($92). Vega air conditioning ($349). Nova vinyl top ($82). Nova power steering ($100). Nova air conditioning ($381). Nova Super Sport Package ($320). Chevelle vinyl top ($92). Monte Carlo/Chevelle air conditioning ($397). Chevelle SS Package ($350). Chevrolet/Monte Carlo/Chevelle AM/FM stereo ($233). Chevrolet/Monte Carlo/Chevelle

AM/FM stereo with tape ($363). Camaro vinyl top ($87). Camaro air conditioning ($397). Camaro SS package ($306). Camaro RS Package ($116). Monte Carlo vinyl top ($123). Monte Carlo Custom trim ($350). Chevrolet vinyl top ($106). Chevrolet air conditioning ($405). Chevrolet power windows ($113). Vega GT Package ($339). Camaro Z/28 Special Performance option ($598). Three-speed manual transmission was standard on all sixes and non-full-size lines. Automatic transmission was standard on full-size V-8s. Overdrive transmission. Automatic transmission. Three-speed manual floor shift transmission. Four-speed manual floor shift transmission. Wide-ratio four-speed manual transmission with floor shift. Close-ratio four-speed manual transmission with floor shift. Vega four-cylinder 140 cid/90 hp two-barrel engine. Chevrolet V-8 350 cid/255 hp four-barrel engine ($168). Chevrolet V-8 400 cid/170 hp four-barrel engine. Chevrolet V-8 402 cid/210 hp four-barrel engine. Chevrolet V-8 454 cid/270 hp four-barrel engine. Monte Carlo V-8 350 cid/175 hp two-barrel dual-exhaust. Monte Carlo V-8 402 cid/240 hp four-barrel engine ($142). Monte Carlo V-8 454 cid/270 hp four-barrel engine ($261). Chevelle V-8 350 cid/165 hp two-barrel engine. Chevelle V-8 350 cid/175 hp two-barrel dual exhaust. Chevelle V-8 402 cid/240 hp four-barrel engine ($166). Chevelle V-8 454 cid/270 hp four-barrel engine ($272). Nova V-8 350 cid/165 hp two-barrel engine. Camaro V-8 350 cid/165 hp two-barrel engine. Camaro V-8 350 cid/200 hp four-barrel engine. Camaro V-8 350 cid/255 hp high-output engine. Camaro V-8 402 cid/240 hp four-barrel engine.

HISTORICAL FOOTNOTES: The full-size Chevrolets were introduced on Sept. 23, 1971, and the other models appeared in dealer showrooms at the same time. Calendar year production of 2,252,892 cars was recorded. Sales of models covered here made by U.S. franchised dealers in calendar 1973, peaked at 2,300,812 cars. This figure excludes Corvettes and Sports Vans, which Chevrolet Motor Division normally accounted with auto production. F. James McDonald was the chief executive officer of the company this year.

1973

FULL-SIZE CHEVROLET — (SIX/V-8) — ALL SERIES
— New styling, front and rear, characterized 1973 Chevrolet model offerings made up of Bel Airs, Impalas, Caprice Classics and three station wagon lines. A wider, bolder grille design was featured. On Caprice Classics, the grille had an open grid texture and a Caprice medallion was placed at the center of the hood lip. Grilles on other series had additional vertical bars and a Chevrolet 'bow tie' badge at the grille center instead of the hood medallion. On all cars, the upper grille border was at a level even with the top of the headlamp surrounds. The front lamp treatment used dual, round lenses

housed in side-by-side square bezels. Parking lamps were moved from the fender extension caps into the bumper, which was a new hydraulically-cushioned, energy-absorbing type. The rear bumper panel slanted forward and housed rectangular lamps. Following the pattern established in 1958, the higher-priced models had triple taillamps, while Biscaynes and Bel Airs had a dual lens design. All station wagons had single-unit taillights in the fenders and Dual-Action tailgate construction. At the front of all models, the license plate housing was moved to the center of the bumper, instead of to one side. The only full-size convertible remaining was in the Caprice Classic lineup. Power steering and power front disc brakes were standard equipment. All V-8 models included automatic transmission at base price. A new, 22-gallon fuel tank provided a longer cruising range. The first cars of the year were assembled August 7, 1972. With the discontinuance of the Biscayne, the Bel Air became the low-priced Chevrolet and the only model available with the 250-cid six. A 350 cid/145 hp V-8 was base powerplant in the Bel Air station wagon and all Impalas. The 400-cid V-8, now rated at 150 SAE Net hp, was standard in all Caprice Classics and Caprice Estate wagons. The station wagons no longer used distinctive nameplates, such as Brookwood or Kingswood. Standard size tires were G78-15/B on Bel Air; H78-15/B on Bel Air station wagons and L78-15/B on Impala coupes/Caprice/Estate and Impala station wagons.

1973 Chevrolet, Caprice two-door Custom Coupe, V-8

CHEVROLET I.D. NUMBERS: The Vehicle Identification Number was located on the top left side of dash, visible through windshield. First symbol 1=Chevrolet. Second symbol indicates car-line: C=Chevelle Deluxe; D=Malibu; E=Laguna; G=Malibu Estate; H=Monte Carlo/Laguna Estate; K=Bel Air; L=Impala; N=Caprice; Q=Camaro; S=Type LT; V=Vega; X=Nova; Y=Nova Custom. Third and fourth symbols indicate body type and appear in Body/Style Number column of charts below. Fifth symbol indicates engine: A=140-cid four one-barrel; B=140-cid four two-barrel; D=250-cid six; F=307-cid V-8 2V; H=350-cid V-8 2V; K=350-cid V-8 4V; T=350-cid V-8 (Z/28); R=400-cid V-8 2V; X=454-cid V-8 (L54) single exhaust; Y=454-cid V-8 dual exhaust. Sixth symbol 3=1973. Seventh symbol indicates assembly plant: A=Lakewood; B=Baltimore; C=Southgate; D=Doraville; F=Flint; J=Janesville; K=Leeds; L=Van Nuys; N=Norwood; R=Arlington; S=St. Louis; T=Tarrytown; U=Lordstown; V=Pontiac; W=Willow Run; Y=Wilmington; Z=Fremont; 1=Oshawa; 2=St. Therese. Next six symbols are sequential production number. Body tag on right or left of firewall gives some of same information, plus plant production sequence, trim code, paint code and date code. Engine numbers stamped on right side of V-8 block and left side of four-cylinder and six-cylinder blocks behind distributor. Consult factory or aftermarket reference sources for numerous Chevrolet engine serial numbers.

1973 Chevrolet, Caprice Classic two-door convertible, V-8

FULL-SIZE CHEVROLET SERIES

Series No.	Body/Style Number	Body Type & Seating	Factory Price	Shipping Weight	Prod. Total
BEL AIR SERIES					
1K	69	4-dr Sed-6P	3247/3595	3895/4087	Note 1
1K	45	4-dr Sta Wag-9P	4136	4770	Note 1
1K	35	4-dr Sta Wag-6P	4022	4717	Note 1
IMPALA SERIES					
1L	69	4-dr Sed-6P	3752	4138	Note 1
1L	39	4-dr HT Sed-6P	3822	4162	Note 1
1L	57	2-dr Spt Cpe-6P	3769	4096	Note 1
1L	47	2-dr Cus Cpe-6P	3836	4110	Note 1
1L	45	4-dr Sta Wag-9P	4233	4607	Note 1
1L	35	4-dr Sta Wag-6P	4119	4742	Note 1

1973 Chevrolet, Caprice Estate station wagon, V-8 (PH)

CAPRICE CLASSIC SERIES

1N	69	4-dr Sed-6P	4064	4176	Note 1
1N	39	4-dr HT Sed-6P	4134	4208	Note 1
1N	47	2-dr Cus Cpe-6P	4082	4143	Note 1
1N	67	2-dr Conv-6P	4345	4191	Notes 1/2
1N	45	4-dr Sta Wag-9P	4496	4858	Note 1
1N	35	4-dr Sta Wag-6P	3282	4779	Note 1

NOTE 1: Model year of all full-size Chevrolets totaled 941,104 units.

NOTE 2: 7,339 Caprice Classic convertibles included in above total.

NOTE 3: Bel Air sedan only available with a six; see data above slash.

1973 Chevrolet, Monte Carlo two-door hardtop, V-8

MONTE CARLO — (V-8) — SERIES 1H — The 1973 Monte Carlo saw extensive styling changes. It was four inches longer and had a heavily sculptured look with new rear quarter sheet metal. The upper grille border was lowered and the front lip of the hood extended down to meet it. Parking lamps were placed vertically in the front fender ends. The grille insert had a neat, cross-hatched texture. There was a badge at its center, plus a script on the left side of the hood. A wide, U-shaped guard was built into the new front bumper, which was reengineered to conform with federal standards. Headlights were round units set into circular housings, which blended in the rounded upper fender contour. The outer fender surface swooped in a radical curve, to the middle of the door. The rear fenderline had a prominent kickup, with extra crisp sculpturing seen here as well. A V-shaped rear window was used and opera window treatments were optional. At the back, the fenders tapered to a crisply shaped tail, which was highlighted by a U-shaped panel. It curved upwards around the trapezoid-shaped taillamps, which were accented with multiple horizontal moldings. Back-up lights were incorporated into the bumper again. The Monte Carlo was now offered in three basic levels of trim with countless option packages available. There was the base Monte Carlo, the 'S' series and the Landau. The latter model featured wide lower body accents and bright wheel lip moldings. Standard equipment included power front disc brakes, power steering and automatic transmission. The base engine was the same 350-cid V-8 used in Impalas. Regular tires were G78-15 blackwalls.

1973 Chevrolet, Monte Carlo two-door hardtop (with optional skyroof), V-8

MONTE CARLO SERIES

Series No.	Body/Style No.	Body Type & Seating	Factory Price	Shipping Weight	Prod. Total
MONTE CARLO					
1H	57	2-dr HT Cpe-5P	3415	3713	Note 1
MONTE CARLO 'S'					
1H	57	2-dr HT Cpe-5P	3562	3720	Note 1
MONTE CARLO LANDAU					
1H	57	2-dr HT Cpe-5P	3806	3722	Note 1

NOTE 1: Exactly 233,689 Monte Carlos were built in the 1973 model year.

CHEVELLE INTERMEDIATES — (SIX/V-8) — ALL SERIES — Totally new 'Colonnade hardtop' styling was seen on 1973 Chevelles. Primarily a safety advance engineered to meet new federal rollover standards, this innovative design consisted of a body with inner and outer shells; side guard door beam construction; and improved fuel tank isolation. Extremely heavy roof pillars and a side window treatment similar to that used in building limousines created a car that looked like a hardtop, but really was not. The Colonnade hardtop look was great on coupes and sedans, but seemed somewhat awkward for station wagons. General styling highlights included cross-hatched grilles with a flat look that continued below the single headlights. They had extremely narrow extensions. Bodysides were quite plain with Malibus wearing rocker panel moldings. All models carried their nameplates at the left of the grille and on the fenders in back of the front wheel opening. New energy-absorbing front bumpers incorporated rectangular parking lights at the outer ends. Taillamps were circular units, recessed into a back panel that was 'veed' horizontally along its centerline. The top-of-the-line entry was the Laguna, with a special die-cast grille accented with double horizontal moldings and circular rally lights. It had a racy European flavor. The Chevelle convertible was discontinued. Each of three series — Chevelle Deluxe, Malibu and Laguna — offered the Colonnade coupe, sedan and station wagons. Base powerplants in the Deluxe and Malibu lines were the 250-cid six or the 307-cid V-8. Laguna offerings started with the 350-cid V-8 under the hood. The big-block 454-cid V-8 was down to 245 nhp. Tire sizes varied by model: E78-14 on most passengercars; G78-14 on most wagons and Lagunas; and H78-14 on the Laguna Estate.

CHEVELLE SERIES

Series No.	Body/Style No.	Body Type & Seating	Factory Price	Shipping Weight	Prod. Total
DELUXE SERIES					
1C	29	4-dr Col Sed-6P	2719/2635	3435/3585	Note 1
1C	37	2-dr Col Cpe-6P	2743/2860	3423/3580	Note 1
1C	35	4-dr Sta Wag-6P	3331	4054	Note 1
1C	35	4-dr Sta Wag-6P	3106/3198	3849/4006	Note 1

1973 Chevrolet, Chevelle Laguna two-door Colonnade Coupe, V-8

Series No.	Body/Style No.	Body Type & Seating	Factory Price	Shipping Weight	Prod. Total
MALIBU SERIES					
1D	29	4-dr Col Sed-6P	2871/2987	3477/3627	Note 1
1D	37	2-dr Col Cpe-6P	2894/3010	3430/3580	Note 1
1D	35	4-dr Sta Wag-8P	3423	4075	Note 1
1D	35	4-dr Sta Wag-6P	3290	4027	Note 1

1973 Chevrolet, Chevelle Malibu four-door Colonnade Sedan, V-8

Series No.	Body/Style No.	Body Type & Seating	Factory Price	Shipping Weight	Prod. Total
MALIBU ESTATE					
1G	35	4-dr Sta Wag-8P	3608	4080	Note 1
1G	35	4-dr Sta Wag-6P	3475	4032	Note 1
LAGUNA SERIES					
1E	29	4-dr Col Sed-6P	3179	3627	Note 1
1E	37	2-dr Col Cpe-6P	3203	3678	Note 1
1E	35	4-dr Sta Wag-8P	3616	4158	Note 1
1E	35	4-dr Sta Wag-6P	3483	4110	Note 1
LAGUNA ESTATE					
1H	35	4-dr Sta Wag-8P	3795	4189	Note 1
1H	35	4-dr Sta Wag-6P	3662	4141	Note 1

1973 Chevrolet, Nova Custom four-door sedan, 6-cyl (PH)

NOTE 1: 328,533 Chevelles were built in the 1973 model year.

NOTE 2: 28,647 Chevelle SS-396 option packages were installed on above cars.

NOTE 3: 2,500 Chevelle SS-454 option packages were installed on above cars.

NOVA — (SIX/V-8) — ALL SERIES — The Nova was 'customized' this season, but could still be purchased in standard trim, too. The new Nova Custom series was simply a bit richer inside and out. General appearance changes were 'hatched' out of a program that emphasized refinements, instead of major revamps. One change, in fact, was a hatchback coupe with an easily lifted, counter-balanced panel that flipped-up to give rear compartment access. Side guard door beam construction; flow-through ventilation; improved sound deadening and a 21-gallon fuel tank were standard equipment revisions. A new grille design featured a more open cross-hatch texture and built-in parking lights. Dual, rectangular taillight treatments were seen on each side at the rear. A heftier, safer bumper protected both ends of the car, with the rear unit having a new center dip and both using black vinyl impact strips. The Nova nameplate was above the left side of the grille. Attractive half-vinyl tops made the options list. Base engines were the 250-cid six or 307-cid V-8. Standard tires were E78-14 blackwalls.

1973 Chevrolet, Nova two-door hatchback coupe, V-8

NOVA SERIES

Series No.	Body/Style No.	Body Type & Seating	Factory Price	Shipping Weight	Prod. Total
NOVA					
1X	69	4-dr Sed-6P	2407/2497	3065/3194	Note 1
1X	27	2-dr Cpe-6P	2377/2467	3033/3162	Note 1
1X	17	2-dr Hatch-6P	2528/2616	3145/3274	Note 1
NOVA CUSTOM					
1Y	69	4-dr Sed-6P	2580/2671	3105/3234	Note 1
1Y	27	2-dr Cpe-6P	2551/2641	3073/3203	Note 1
1Y	17	2-dr Hatch-6P	2701/2791	3152/3261	Note 1

NOTE 1: 369,511 Novas were built in the 1973 model year.

NOTE 2: 35,542 Nova Super Sports were built for the 1973 model year.

VEGA — FOUR — The 1973 Vega had a new front bumper with stronger mountings. It provided better protection for the carryover sheet metal. The name-plate was changed to read 'Vega by Chevrolet' with the 2300 engine size call-out being dropped. Unaccustomed to using cubic centimeter measurements for engine displacement, American buyers had trouble relating to the meaning of the original nomenclature. New Chevrolet-built three- and four-speed transmissions, with improved shift linkages and a better emissions control system were featured in the third generation Vega. Using the new SAE system, the base, one-barrel four was rated at just 72 hp; the optional two-barrel engine at 85. The standard tire size was, again, A78-13. Vega's new grille had a handsome, eggcrate texture.

1973 Chevrolet, Vega two-door notchback sedan, 4-cyl

VEGA SERIES

Series No.	Body/Style No.	Body Type & Seating	Factory Price	Shipping Weight	Prod. Total
1V	11	2-dr Notch-4P	2087	2219	Note 1
1V	77	2-dr Hatch-4P	2192	2313	Note 1
1V	15	2-dr Sta Wag-4P	2323	2327	Note 1

NOTE 1: 395,792 Vegas were built; no breakout as to body style available.

1973 Chevrolet, Vega GT two-door Kammback station wagon, 4-cyl

1973 Chevrolet, Vega two-door hatchback coupe, 4-cyl

CAMARO — (SIX/V-8) — SERIES 1Q — The 1973 Camaro had few changes from the previous style. The texture of the grille insert was modified by using slightly heavier, deeper moldings and reducing the number of vertical moldings from 12 to seven. Those trim packages featuring a full-width front bumper bar had new, black rubber faced guards. They protruded both above and below the bumper, housing the license plate at the bottom center. Fifteen new colors were available. A new soft-rim steering wheel with four spokes was used and the rear seats received a bit more foam padding. A new decor treatment was the 'luxury touring' Camaro LT package, which included rocker panel accents; dual outside rearview mirrors; Hide-Away wipers; full instrumentation (with tachometer); 14 x 7-inch Rally wheel rims and extra sound-deadening insulation. A new option was a set of Turbine I wheels, for all models except those with the Z/28 package. Air conditioning was, however, available for the first time with Z/28 'special performance' equipment. Base Camaro engines were the 250-cid six or 307-cid V-8 and E78-14 tires were used. Standard in Z/28s was a hydraulic lifter 350-cid V-8 with a new low-restriction air cleaner and rated at 245 nhp.

CAMARO SERIES

Series No.	Body/Style No.	Body Type & Seating	Factory Price	Shipping Weight	Prod. Total
BASE LEVEL					
1Q	87	2-dr Spt Cpe-4P	2781/2872	3119/3238	Note 1
LT LEVEL					
1S	87	2-dr Spt Cpe-4P	3268	3349	Note 1

NOTE 1: 89,988 Camaros were built in the United States.

NOTE 2: Total includes 32,327 LT; 16,133 RS; 11,574 Camaro Z/28s.

NOTE 3: Total includes 93,138 V-8s; 3,616 sixes.

NOTE 4: Transmissions: 5,964 had three-speed; 11,388 had four-speed; 79,404 had Turbo-HydraMatic.

NOTE 5: Options: 49,504 with air conditioning; 96,752 power steering; 217 with power windows.

NOTE 6: 6,766 cars made in the United States for export markets.

ENGINES

(BEL AIR/CHEVELLE/NOVA/CAMARO SIX) Inline six. Cast iron block. Displacement: 250 cid. Bore and stroke: 3.875 x 3.53 inches. Compression ratio: 8.25:1. SAE Net hp: 100 at 3600 rpm. Seven main bearings. Hydraulic valve lifters. Carburetor: one-barrel.

1973 Chevrolet, Camaro LT two-door hardtop, V-8

(V-8 BEL AIR/IMPALA/MONTE CARLO/LAGUNA) Overhead valve. Cast iron block. Displacement: 350 cid. Bore and stroke: 4.00 x 3.48 inches. Compression ratio: 8.5:1. SAE Net hp: 145 at 4000 rpm. Five main bearings. Hydraulic valve lifters. Carburetor: two-barrel.

(V-8 CAPRICE) Overhead valve. Cast iron block. Displacement: 400 cid. Bore and stroke: 4.126 x 3.75 inches. Compression ratio: 6.5:1. SAE Net hp: 150 at 3200 rpm. Five main bearings. Hydraulic valve lifters. Carburetor: two-barrel.

(V-8 CHEVELLE DELUXE/MALIBU/NOVA/CAMARO) Overhead valve. Cast iron block. Displacement: 307 cid. Bore and stroke: 3.87 x 3.25 inches. Compression ratio: 8.5:1. SAE Net hp: 115 at 3600 rpm. Five main bearings. Hydraulic valve lifters. Carburetor: two-barrel.

(VEGA) Inline four. Overhead camshaft. Aluminum block. Displacement: 140 cid. Bore and stroke: 3.501 x 3.625 inches. Compression ratio: 8.0:1. Brake hp: 72 at 4400 rpm. Hydraulic valve lifters. Carburetor: one-barrel.

CHASSIS FEATURES: Wheelbase: (Chevrolet wagon) 125 inches; (Chevrolet) 121.5 inches; (Monte Carlo/Chevelle four-door) 116 inches; (Chevelle two-door) 112 inches; (Nova) 111 inches; (Vega) 97 inches; (Camaro) 108 inches. Overall length: (Chevelle wagon) 229 inches; (Chevrolet) 223 inches; (Monte Carlo) 211 inches; (Chevelle four-door) 207 inches; (Chevelle two-door) 203 inches; (Chevelle wagon) 214 inches; (Nova) 195 inches; (Vega) 173 inches; (Camaro) 189 inches. Width: (Chevrolet) 80 inches; (Monte Carlo) 78 inches; (Chevelles) 77 inches; (Novas) 73 inches; (Vega) 66 inches; (Camaro) 75 inches. Tires: Refer to text.

POPULAR OPTIONS: Vega power steering ($92). Vega air conditioning ($349). Vega Estate Wagon package ($212). Vega hatchback GT package ($340). Vega station wagon GT package ($314). Vega Custom interior ($115). Nova vinyl top ($82). Nova air conditioning ($381). Nova Super Sport package ($123). Nova skyroof ($179). Chevelle/Camaro/Nova power brakes ($46). Nova power brakes with front discs ($68). Chevelle vinyl top ($92). Chevelle/Monte Carlo/Camaro AM/FM stereo ($233). Chevrolet/Monte Carlo/Chevelle AM/FM stereo with tape ($363). Chevelle Malibu SS package ($243). Monte Carlo vinyl top ($123). Chevelle/Monte Carlo skyroof ($325). Camaro vinyl top ($87). Monte Carlo/Camaro air conditioning ($397). Camaro LT Special Performance package ($502). Camaro Z/28 Special Performance package ($598). Chevrolet vinyl top ($106). Chevrolet power seats ($103). Chevrolet power windows ($124). Chevrolet air conditioning ($462). Nova power steering ($100). Three-speed manual transmission was standard in Vega/Nova/Chevrolet/Chevelle/Monte Carlo and Camaro with fours or sixes. Automatic transmission was standard in Chevrolet V-8s and Camaro LTs and was also a no-cost option in the Z/28. Automatic transmission was optional, except in above models. Four-speed manual floor shift transmission was optional in Vega/Nova/Monte Carlo/Chevelle/Camaro. Vega four-cylinder 140 cid/85 hp two-barrel engine ($41*). Chevrolet V-8 350 cid/175 hp four-barrel engine. Chevrolet V-8 400 cid/150 hp two-barrel engine. Chevrolet V-8 454 cid/215 hp four-barrel engine ($231). Chevrolet V-8 454 cid/245 hp four-barrel dual exhaust engine. Monte Carlo V-8 350 cid/175 hp four-barrel engine. Monte Carlo V-8 454 cid/245 hp four-barrel dual exhaust engine ($209). Chevelle V-8 350 cid/145 hp two-barrel engine. Chevelle V-8 350 cid/175 hp four-barrel engine. Chevelle V-8 454 cid/245 hp four-barrel engine ($235). Camaro V-8 350 cid/145 hp two-barrel engine. Camaro V-8 350 cid/175 hp four-barrel engine. Camaro V-8 350 cid/245 hp Z/28 engine (**). Nova V-8 350 cid/145 hp two-barrel engine. Nova V-8 350 cid/175 hp four-barrel engine. Positive traction rear axle. NOTES: *The Vega GT package included the two-barrel four. **The Camaro Z/28 package included the 350 cid/245 hp V-8.

HISTORICAL FOOTNOTES: The 1973 Chevrolets were introduced on Sept. 21, 1972. Model year production peaked at 2,365,381 units. Calendar year sales of 2,434,890 cars were recorded. F.J. MacDonald was the chief executive officer of the company this year. Early (1971 and 1972) Vegas came with steel head gaskets, which were easily 'done-in' by water and heat. The result was that dealers had to replace many engines under the original 12,000-mile engine warranty. The early engines earned such a bad reputation that the warranty was later extended to 50,000 miles to help prevent a too large drop in sales due to the problem.

1974

FULL-SIZE CHEVROLET — (V-8) — ALL SERIES — Caprice Classics had a different appearance than Bel Airs and Impalas this year, and all models were changed at the front and rear. A new grille on the low-/medium-priced cars was completely above the bumper and the number of vertical bars was cut more than 50 percent. Their new front bumper had no parking light or grille reveal openings, but rubber-faced protective guards were standard. The license plate attachment was moved from the center to the left. On these Bel Airs and Impalas, the parking lamps were placed in the fender extension caps, outboard of the dual, square headlamp housings. A 'bow tie' insignia was at the center of the grille, with a Chevrolet inscription on the left side of the upper grille frame molding. A model identification script was seen behind the front wheel housings. Standard equipment for Bel Airs included all regulation safety features; body sill moldings; power steering; power brakes (with front disc and rear finned drums); inside day/nite mirror; foam seats; power ventilation system; glovebox light; cigarette lighter; recessed wipers; inside hood release; left-hand outside rearview mirror; windshield antenna; pattern cloth and vinyl interior; and Turbo-Hydramatic transmission on V-8s. Most sources indicate that all big Chevrolets were V-8 powered, but the Bel Air sedan was available with a six and three-speed manual gearbox, at least at the beginning of the year. There is no record of any such cars being built and sold. The Impalas had all of the above plus bright bodyside moldings (with a black vinyl insert on the Custom Coupe); triple taillights with silver accents; front and rear wheel lip moldings (on Custom Coupe) and a luggage compartment mat. The base V-8 was the two-barrel 350-cid engine and regular tires were G78-15 blackwalls. All front end sheet metal on the Caprice was distinctive and had a more swept back look with different fenders; hood; grille; header bar and lamps. The grille was more elaborate with 11 prominent bright moldings forming a dozen segments. Each segment was filled with multiple horizontal and vertical members. A signature script was placed in the left-hand side of the grille and a Caprice crest was seen at the center of the wider upper border bar. The Caprice parking lights were moved to a position between the headlights and the grille. The Custom Coupe had a form of Colonnade styling, in which oversized opera windows were used at the upper rear roof quarters. Bodysides were decorated with a low, full-length molding, which was extra-wide and carried color-keyed vinyl protective strips. A Caprice crest was placed on the coupe's central roof pillar. The Caprice had the same equipment as Impalas plus ashtray and courtesy lights; electric clock; rear fender skirts; distinctive cloth and vinyl interior; color-keyed wheel covers; GT8-15/B tires and a 400-cid V-8. The sedan used a fold-down center armrest seat. Station wagons were equipped like their passenger car counterparts, plus hidden storage compartment; Glide-Away tailgate; all-vinyl upholstery; power taillight window; L78-15/B tires and forward-facing rear seat on nine-passenger styles. The Caprice Estate also had a vertical bar grille; electric clock; ashtray and courtesy lights and 400-cid two-barrel V-8 engine. Woodgrained siding was optional.

1974 Chevrolet, Impala two-door hardtop, V-8

CHEVROLET I.D. NUMBERS: The Vehicle Identification Number was located on the top left side of dash, visible through the windshield. The first symbol 1 = Chevrolet. The second symbol indicates car-line: C = Chevelle and Malibu; D = Malibu Classic; E = Laguna; G = Malibu Estate; H = Monte Carlo; K = Bel Air; N = Caprice Classic/Caprice Estate; L = Impala; Q = Camaro; S = Type LT; V = Vega; X = Nova Custom. Third and fourth symbols indicate body type and appear in Body/Style Number column of charts below. Fifth symbol indicates engine: A = 140-cid four one-barrel; B = 140-cid four two-barrel; D = 250-cid six; F = 307-cid V-8 2V; H = 350-cid V-8 2V; K = 350-cid V-8 4V; T = 350-cid V-8 (Z/28); R = 400-cid V-8 2V; X = 454-cid V-8 (L54) single exhaust; Y = 454-cid V-8 dual exhaust. Sixth symbol 4 = 1974. Seventh symbol indicates assembly plant: A = Lakewood; B = Baltimore; C = Southgate; D = Doraville; F = Flint; J = Janesville; K = Leeds; L = Van Nuys; N = Norwood; R = Arlington; S = St. Louis; T = Tarrytown; U = Lordstown; V = Pontiac; W = Willow Run; Y = Wilmington; Z = Fremont; 1 = Oshawa; 2 = St. Therese. Next six symbols are sequestial production number. Body tag on right or left of firewall gives some of same information, plus plant production sequence, trim code, paint coat and date code. Engine numbers stamped on right side of V-8 block and left side of four-cylinder and six-cylinder blocks behind distributor. Consult factory or aftermarket reference sources for numerous Chevrolet engine serial numbers.

1974 Chevrolet, Caprice Classic two-door Custom Coupe, V-8

FULL-SIZE CHEVROLET SERIES

Series No.	Body/Style No.	Body Type & Seating	Factory Price	Shipping Weight	Prod. Total
BEL AIR SERIES					
1K	69	4-dr Sed-6P	3960	4148	Note 1
1K	45	4-dr Sta Wag-9P	4578	4884	Note 2
1K	35	4-dr Sta Wag-6P	4464	4629	Note 2

1974 Chevrolet, Caprice Estate station wagon, V-8

IMPALA SERIES					
1L	69	4-dr Sed-6P	4135	4205	Note 3
1L	39	4-dr HT Sed-6P	4215	4256	Note 3
1L	57	2-dr Spt Cpe-6P	4162	4167	Note 3
1L	47	2-dr Cus Cpe-6P	4229	4169	Note 3
1L	45	4-dr Sta Wag-9P	4675	4936	Note 2
1L	35	4-dr Sta Wag-6P	4561	4891	Note 2
CAPRICE CLASSIC					
1N	69	4-dr Sed-6P	4465	4294	Note 4

1N	39	4-dr HT Sed-6P	4534	4344	Note 4
1N	47	2-dr Cus Cpe-6P	4463	4245	Note 4
1N	67	2-dr Conv-6P	4745	4308	Notes 4/5
1N	45	4-dr Sta Wag-9P	4914	5004	Note 2
1N	35	4-dr Sta Wag-6P	4800	4960	Note 2

1974 Chevrolet, Caprice Classic two-door convertible, V-8

GENERAL NOTE : Domestic model year production of full-size Chevrolets totaled exactly 630,861 units. This total is again distorted by the fact that production of some models for U.S. sales was quartered in Canada. The exact number of full-size Chevrolets sold by dealers holding U.S. franchises was 565,376 cars. This means that some 65,485 Bel Airs, Impalas and Caprice Classics built in U.S. factories were shipped to Canada under the new trade agreements. A similar situation existed in other Chevrolet model lines. This should be kept in mind when using the series output figures given below.

NOTE 1: Exactly 34,095 Bel Air passenger cars were built for the 1974 model year. All were V-8s.

NOTE 2: Exactly 35,331 full-size station wagons were built for the 1974 model year. All were V-8s. This includes all station wagons with no further breakout by series available.

NOTE 3: Exactly 405,286 Impala passenger cars were built for the 1974 model year. All were V-8s.

1974 Chevrolet, Impala two-door hardtop (with 'Spirit of America' option), V-8

NOTE 4: Exactly 155,860 Caprice passenger cars were built for the 1974 model year. All were V-8s.

NOTE 5: Exactly 4,670 Caprice Classic convertibles were built for the 1974 model year. All were V-8s.

ADDITIONAL NOTE: Though listed as available early in the year, standard reference sources do not indicate the price or weight of a Bel Air six and Chevrolet production records indicate that no such cars were built.

MONTE CARLO — (V-8) — SERIES 1H — The 1974 Monte Carlo received minor appearance changes, the

most obvious a new eggcrate grille. Bodyside moldings used with some decor packages were of a new design that extended completely forward to hit the rear edge of the front wheelhousing. The front lip of the hood was decorated with a center medallion, instead of the former left side script. Landau or Monte Carlo 'S' packages replaced the mid-bodyside molding (described above) with wide, bright rocker panel accents having both front and rear extensions. At the rear, a new bumper was used. It incorporated two full-width vinyl impact strips and protruded out further, giving the cars three extra inches of length. Rubber faced rear bumper guards were also new. The back-up lights were moved, from the bumper to a license-plate-flanking position on the deck latch panel. The design of the trunk lock was simplified and the multiple, short accent moldings were removed from the taillights. Crests and chrome signatures called out the various levels of trim. Standard equipment included PowerBeam single-unit headlights; formal coupe roofline; rear quarter 'coach' style windows; Hide-Away wipers; rear stabilizer; power front disc brakes; power steering ignition key alarm; flow-thru power ventilation; electric clock; wood-bur dash and steering wheel accents; Delco-Eye battery; carpets; door map pockets; knit cloth and vinyl trim; cigarette lighter; inside hood release; GR70-15 radial tires and 350-cid V-8. The Landau also had a landau vinyl top; color-keyed rear window and belt moldings; fender accent stripes; body-color Sport mirrors (left remote-control); wheel covers; visor/vanity mirror; 15 x 7-inch Turbine II wheels; radial tuned suspension; passenger assist grips and door map pockets.

1974 Chevrolet, Monte Carlo two-door hardtop, V-8

1974 Chevrolet, Chevelle Malibu Classic Estate station wagon, V-8

MONTE CARLO SERIES

Series No.	Body/Style No.	Body Type & Seating	Factory Price	Shipping Weight	Prod. Total
MONTE CARLO SERIES					
1H	57	2-dr HT Cpe-5P	3885	3926	Note 1
MONTE CARLO LANDAU					
1H	57	2-dr HT Cpe-5P	4129	3950	Note 1

NOTE 1: Exactly 312,217 Monte Carlos were built for the 1974 model year. All were V-8s. No additional break-outs per trim level are available. Monte Carlo sales byU.S. dealers peaked at 284,667 cars. This indicates that over 25,000 U.S. built cars were shipped to Canada.

INTERMEDIATE-SIZE CHEVELLES — (SIX/V-8) — ALL SERIES —

The Nomad and Chevelle Deluxe series models were dropped in 1974 and the intermediate-size Chevrolet products now came in Malibu, Malibu Classic, Malibu Classic Estate and Laguna decor levels. Basic styling changes were modest. They included a bumper without the flattened license plate attachment panel in the center; twin-slot side marker lamps and a radiator-style grille that looked like a Mercedes-Benz unit stretched sideways. Decor option packages, however, had a big effect on final appearances. Chevelles came in a variety of 'flavors' ranging from the 'unmarked police car' look to the race-ready image of the Laguna Type S-3 coupe. One way to spot a 1974 model for sure, was to eyeball the round-corner trapezoid shape of the large rear lamps. Early models had round taillights; later versions became more rectangular so the 1974 types are distinctive. A new, stand-up hood ornament decorated the Malibu Classic, which also had wide, lower body accent panels. Optional innovations included the canopy top or louvered rear 'coach' window treatments. Standard equipment on the base Malibu included regulation safety equipment; flow-through power ventilation system; double panel steel acoustical roof; inside hood release; manual front disc brakes; side marker lamps and reflectors; defroster; dual speed wipers with washers; inside day/nite mirror; left outside rearview mirror; full foam rubber seats; color-keyed vinyl roof covering; cigarette lighter; Hide-Away wipers; windshield radio antenna; Delcotron generator; E78-14/B tires and either the 250-cid six or 350-cid two-barrel V-8. Malibu V-8s wore G78-14/B tires. The Malibu Classic came with all of the above, plus carpeting; glovebox light; mixed pattern cloth and vinyl interior; bodyside, roof drip and wheel opening moldings and Deluxe center armrest in front seat. The Laguna Colonnade Coupe came only in V-8 form. It featured, in addition to the above, patterned cloth and vinyl (or all-vinyl) interior; woodgrain vinyl accents on dash (with elm-burl center vinyl inlay); full wheel covers; bright accented dual-unit taillights; wheel lips and scalp-moldings; GR70-15/B steel-belted radial tires and the two-barrel 350-cid V-8. The high-performance image Laguna Type S-3 coupe added a custom eggcrate grille isolated within a body-color front end panel; bright grille crossbar with square rally lights at each end; nerf-bar bumper treatment; louvered 'coach' window styling; swivel bucket seats; variable-ratio power steering; heavy-duty Pliacell shock absorbers; radial-tuned suspension; specific Type S-3 nameplates at grille center and behind front wheels; engine call-out decals above side markers; lower body perimeter striping and black-accent treatment; body-color twin Sport mirrors (left remote-controlled); red or white stripe radial tires; body color reveal moldings; full-instrumentation (with round-faced gauges); four-spoke steering wheel and 15 x 7-inch Turbine II wheels. Top power option was the detuned — SAE rated — 235-hp, 454-cid V-8.

1974 Chevrolet, Chevelle Malibu Classic two-door Colonnade Coupe, V-8

CHEVELLE INTERMEDIATE SERIES

Series No.	Body/Style No.	Body Type & Seating	Factory Price	Shipping Weight	Prod. Total
MALIBU					
1C	29	4-dr Col Sed-6P	3049/3340	3638/3788	Note 1
1C	37	2-dr Col Cpe-6P	3054/3345	3573/3723	Note 1
1C	35	4-dr Sta Wag-8P	3834	4223	Note 2
1C	35	4-dr Sta Wag-6P	3701	4191	Note 2
MALIBU CLASSIC					
1D	29	4-dr Col Sed-6P	3304/3595	3695/3845	Note 3
1D	37	2-dr Col Cpe-6P	3307/3596	3609/3759	Note 3
1D	37	2-dr Lan Cpe-6P	3518/3800	N/A/N/A	Note 3
1D	35	4-dr Sta Wag-9P	4251	4315	Note 2
1D	35	4-dr Sta Wag-6P	4118	4283	Note 2
MALIBU CLASSIC ESTATE					
1G	35	4-dr Sta Wag-9P	4424	4338	Note 2
1G	35	4-dr Sta Wag-6P	4291	4306	Note 2
LAGUNA					
1E	37	2-dr Col Cpe-6P	3723	3951	Note 4
LAGUNA TYPE S-3					
1E	37	2-dr Col Cpe-5P	4504	N/A	Note 4

NOTE 1: Exactly 91,612 Malibu passenger cars were built for the 1974 model year, including 27,188 sixes and 64,424 V-8s.

NOTE 2: Exactly 44,108 Chevelle intermediate-size station wagons were built for the 1974 model year. All were V-8s. This includes all Malibu, Malibu Classic and Malibu Classic Estate station wagons, with no breakouts per trim level available.

1974 Chevrolet, Chevelle Laguna S-3 two-door Colonnade Coupe, V-8

NOTE 3: Exactly 204,870 Malibu Classic passenger cars were built for the 1974 model year, including 8,940 sixes and 195,930 V-8s.

NOTE 4: Exactly 21,902 Lagunas were built for the 1974 model year. All were V-8s. No breakout per trim level is available.

1974 Chevrolet, Nova two-door coupe (with 'Spirit of America' option), V-8

NOVA — (SIX/V-8) — ALL SERIES — Never a car to change for the sake of change, the 1974 Nova was basically unaltered. A 'bow tie' badge was added at the center of the grille and the nameplate on the left-hand side of the hood lip read 'Nova by Chevrolet'. Rubber-faced front bumper guards were standard now, and 11 new colors were available. Coupes or hatchbacks with the Super Sport option received the black-out grille treatment with prominent horizontal moldings badging the rectangular parking lamps top and bottom. Two-tone finish was available for body style 17. The designers also added new hubcaps, with a bright anodized look. Two-speed Powerglide automatic transmission was no longer offered. Standard equipment included color-keyed nubber floor coverings; flow-through ventilation system; full-foam front seats; foam rear seats; dual-speed electric wipers; left outside rearview mirror; cargo-guard luggage compartment (except hatchback) and 250-cid six. The hatchback added the swing-up rear deck and fold-down rear seat. The Nova Custom also had bright parking lights and liftgate accents; body sill and scalp moldings; Deluxe bumpers with black vinyl impact strips; carpets; inside day/nite mirror; glovebox light; right front door light switch; cigarette lighter and trunk mat. Standard tires were size E78-14/B blackwalls and the two-barrel 350 was base V-8.

1974 Chevrolet, Nova Custom four-door sedan, V-8

NOVA SERIES

Series No.	Body/Style No.	Body Type & Seating	Factory Price	Shipping Weight	Prod. Total
NOVA					
1X	69	4-dr Sed-6P	2841/2949	3192/3330	Note 1
1X	27	2-dr Cpe-6P	2811/2919	3150/3288	Note 1
1X	17	2-dr Hatch-6P	2935/3043	3260/3398	Note 1
NOVA CUSTOM					
1Y	69	4-dr Sed-6P	3014/3123	3233/3371	Note 1
1Y	27	2-dr Cpe-6P	2985/3093	3206/3344	Note 1
1Y	17	2-dr Hatch-6P	3108/3217	3299/3437	Note 1

NOTE 1: Exactly 390,537 Novas were built during the 1974 model year: 171,430 sixes and 219,107 V-8s. No breakouts per body style or trim level are available.

NOTE 2: Included in the total given above were exactly 21,419 cars equipped with the Nova SS option package. No additional breakout per coupes and hatchback styles is available.

1974 Chevrolet, Vega two-door Estate Wagon, 4-cyl

VEGA — (FOUR) — SERIES 1V — New for the Vega subcompact was a shovel-nosed look with a quad-level air-slot style grille divided into two halves with a vertical body colored center divider strip. The headlamps were recessed into slanting, square-shaped housings finished in bright metal style. A much thicker full-width wraparound bumper incorporated black rubber guards and vinyl black impact strips. Single-unit square taillamps (or vertical fender-mount lamps on wagons) were seen at the rear where a more protrusive bumper, with vinyl impact strips, was used. A three-inch length increase resulted. Standard equipment included all regulation safety devices; side marker lights and reflectors; left outside rearview mirror; back-up lights; bright hubcaps; foam-filled front bucket/rear bucket style seats; storage well in driver's door; glovebox; power vent system; folding seat-back latches; steel side guard beams; ashtray; inside windshield moldings; carpets; heater and defroster; windshield washer and electric wipers; inside hood release; manual front disc brakes; three-speed manual transmission with floor shift; OHC-Four engine and AT78-13 black sidewall tires. The hatchback added a fold-down rear seat and storage compartment. The station wagon (Kammback) also had a swing-up tailgate and folding rear seat. The Estate wagon featured Deluxe interior and exterior trim; full carpeting and concealed storage compartment.

1974 Chevrolet, Vega two-door hatchback coupe (with 'Spirit of America' option), 4-cyl

VEGA SERIES

Series No.	Body/Style No.	Body Type & Seating	Factory Price	Shipping Weight	Prod. Total
1V	11	2-dr Cpe-4P	2087	2219	63,591
1V	77	2-dr Hatch-4P	2192	2313	271,682
1V	15	2-dr Sta Wag-4P	2323	2327	113,326
1HV	05	2-dr Panel-2P	2404	2402	4,289

1974 Chevrolet, Vega two-door hatchback coupe, 4-cyl

NOTE 1: The production totals given in the chart above are the exact model year output figures per body style. The panel delivery is included to indicate Model Number, price and weight characteristics of this particular body style. The panel truck was marketed strictly as a commercial vehicle, although this model is popular with many involved in the modified vehicle segment of the old car hobby.

CAMARO — (SIX/V-8) — ALL SERIES — The Camaro got a major restyling for the 1974 model year. It followed the Vega's shovel-nose theme and included a soft ure-thane-cushioned front panel. The forward angled grille featured an eggcrate motif, with grille texture reveal below the new widened front bumper. At the rear, a new appearance was also achieved. The four round taillamps from previous models gave way to large lenses that slid around the body corners to serve double-duty as side marker lights. The area between the lamps was flattened. The Z/28 option included a bolder graphics treatment with decals calling out the model nomenclature within stripes that dominated the hood and deck lids. Parking lamps were now circular and housed inside slanting, scooped-out square recesses between the grille and front fenders. Standard equipment included safety features; side markers and reflectors; rear markers; rocker moldings; Astro vents; day/nite inside mirror; double-panel roof; pull-type door handles; color-keyed carpets; front bumper guards; bucket seats; all-vinyl interior; dual wipers and washers; left outside rearview mirror; rear bucket cushions; manual front disc brakes; three-speed with floor shift; E78-14 tires and 250-cid six or 350-cid two-barrel V-8. The Camaro LT coupe added electric clock; special instrumentation; outside rearview Sport mirrors (left remote-controlled); Rally wheels and Hide-Away wipers; plus the base V-8 as standard equipment.

CAMARO SERIES

Series No.	Body/Style No.	Body Type & Seating	Factory Price	Shipping Weight	Prod. Total
CAMARO LEVEL					
1Q	87	2-dr HT Cpe-4P	3162/3366	3309/3450	Note 1

CAMARO LT LEVEL

1S	87	2-dr HT Cpe-4P	3713	3566	Note 1

NOTE 1: Exactly 146,595 Camaros were built for the U.S. market in the 1974 model year. Exactly 4,412 Camaros were built for export, bringing total output to 151,006 units. This included 13,802 Camaros with the Z/28 package; 128,810 V-8s; 22,198 sixes; 11,174 with three-speeds; 11,175 with four-speeds; 128,659 with automatic; 79,279 with air conditioning and 151,006 with power steering. No breakout is available as to the number of cars equipped in LT level trim.

ENGINES

(V-8 BEL AIR/IMPALA/MONTE CARLO) Overhead valve. Cast iron block. Displacement: 350 cid. Bore and stroke: 4.00 x 3.48 inches. Compression ratio: 8.5:1. SAE Net hp: 145 at 2400 rpm. Five main bearings. Hydraulic valve lifters. Carburetor: two-barrel.

1974 Chevrolet, Camaro LT two-door hardtop, V-8

(V-8 CAPRICE): Overhead valve. Cast iron block. Displacement: 400 cid. Bore and stroke: 4.126 x 3.75 inches. Compression ratio: 6.5:1. SAE Net hp: 150 at 2400 rpm. Five main bearings. Hydraulic valve lifters. Carburetor: two-barrel.

CHEVELLE ENGINES

SIX: See 1973 Chevelle series six-cylinder engine data.

V-8: See 1974 Chevrolet series engine data.

NOVA ENGINES

SIX: See 1973 Chevelle series six-cylinder engine data.

V-8: See 1974 Chevelle series V-8 engine data.

VEGA ENGINE: See 1973 Vega series engine data. Specifications were basically unchanged, though a 75 hp rating was advertised in 1974.

CAMARO ENGINES

SIX: See 1973 Chevrolet series six-cylinder engine data.

V-8: See 1974 Chevrolet series V-8 engine data.

CHASSIS FEATURES: Wheelbase: (Chevrolet wagon) 125 inches; (Chevrolet) 121.5 inches; (Monte Carlo/Chevelle four-door) 116 inches; (Nova/Nova Custom) 111 inches; (Vega) 91 inches; (Camaro) 106 inches. Overall length: (Chevrolet wagon) 229 inches; (Chevrolet) 223 inches; (Monte Carlo) 214 inches; (Chevelle wagon) 216 inches; (Chevelle four-door) 211 inches; (Chevelle two-door) 207 inches; (Nova) 197 inches; (Nova Custom) 196 inches; (Vega) 176 inches; (Camaro) 196 inches. Width: Same as 1973 for all styles. Tires: Refer to text.

OPTIONS: Power brakes. Power steering. Monte Carlo/Camaro/Chevelle/Chevrolet AM/FM stereo ($233). Monte Carlo/Chevelle/Chevrolet AM/FM stereo with tape ($363). Chevrolet power seats ($106). Chevrolet wagon luggage rack ($77). Impala 'Spirit of America' sport coupe package ($399). Vega vinyl top ($75). Vega power steering ($95). Vega air conditioning ($362). Vega GT package ($359). Nova air conditioning ($396). Nova SS package ($140). Chevelle vinyl top ($92). Monte Carlo/Chevelle skyroof ($325). Camaro vinyl top ($87). Camaro air conditioning ($412). Three-speed manual transmission was standard in Chevelle/Nova/Camaro six Automatic transmission was standard in Bel Air/Impala/Caprice. Automatic transmission optional in others. Three-speed manual floor shift transmission, standard in Vega. Four-speed manual floor shift transmission was optional in Nova/Camaro/Vega. Vega four-cylinder 140 cid/85 hp two-barrel engine. Chevrolet V-8 350 cid/160 hp four-barrel engine. Chevrolet V-8 400 cid/150 hp two-barrel engine. Chevrolet V-8 400 cid/180 hp four-barrel engine. Chevrolet V-8 454 cid/235 hp four-barrel engine ($248). Monte Carlo V-8 350 cid/160 hp four-barrel engine. Monte Carlo V-8 400 cid/150 hp two-barrel engine. Monte Carlo V-8 400 cid/180 hp four-barrel engine. Monte Carlo 454 cid/235 hp four-barrel engine ($241). Chevelle V-8 400 cid/150 hp two-barrel engine. Chevelle V-8 400 cid/180 hp four-barrel engine. Chevelle V-8 454 cid/235 hp four-barrel engine ($293). Nova V-8 350 cid/160 hp four-barrel engine. Nova V-8 350 cid/185 hp four-barrel dual-exhaust engine. Camaro V-8 350 cid/160 hp four-barrel engine. Camaro V-8 350 cid/185 hp four-barrel dual-exhaust engine. Camaro V-8 350 cid/245 hp Z/28 engine (standard on Z/28). Posi-traction rear axle.

HISTORICAL FOOTNOTES: The 1974 Chevrolets were introduced Sept. 22, 1973. Model year production peaked at 2,396,284 units. Calendar year sales of 2,156,480 cars were recorded. Robert L. Lund was the chief executive officer of the company this year. Sales of Chevrolet's full-line of cars, Sport vans, and Vega panel express models dropped 12.3 percent from 1973 levels. Note: The model year production and calendar year sales figures given above cover only models included in this section, excluding Corvette and Sport van production and sales. Vega panel express models are, however, included in both totals.

1975

FULL-SIZE CHEVROLET — (SIX/V-8) — ALL SERIES — Model year 1975 is best known as the season of the catalytic converter and the 'last' Chevrolet convertible. Additional innovations included introduction of the standard High-Energy ignition system and new Colonnade-style rooflines for four-door sedans and hardtop sedans. The Bel Air and Impala received a revised frontal treatment that was similar to that of the 1974 Caprice Classic. This brought changes including the placement of parking lamps between grille and headlamps; a bright signature script on the left-hand face of the grille and repositioning of the Chevrolet 'bow tie' near the center of the hood lip. Bel Airs had no side spears and stuck with a two-unit taillight design. Impalas were highlighted with three-quarter length bodyside moldings that ran from behind the front upper wheel lip to the rear of the car. Bright-accented, triple taillamps were used. The Caprice Classic had a distinctive vertical barred grille that was even with the upper headlamp borders and partially revealed through an opening below the front bumper. A bright signature script was placed on the left of the grille; a Caprice Crest was seen at the upper center and parking lamps were moved into the bumper, directly under the headlamps. Tires were HR78-15/B blackwalls on passenger cars and LR78-15/C size on station wagons. The standard V-8 in all models was the 350 cid/145 hp engine. Other equipment features were comparable to those listed in 1974.

1975 Chevrolet, Caprice four-door hardtop sedan, V-8

CHEVROLET I.D. NUMBERS: The Vehicle Identification Number was located on the top left side of dash, visible through the windshield. First symbol 1=Chevrolet. Second symbol indicates car-line: C=Malibu; D=Malibu Classic; E=Laguna; G=Malibu Estate; H=Monte Carlo/Laguna Estate; K=Bel Air; M=Monza; N=Caprice Classic/Caprice Estate; L=Impala; Q=Camaro; R=Monza 2+2; S=Type LT; V=Vega; X=Nova; Y=Nova Custom. Third and fourth symbols indicate body type and appear in Body/Style Number column of charts below. Fifth symbol indicates engine: A=140-cid four one-barrel; B=140-cid four two-barrel; D=250-cid six; F=307-cid V-8 2V; G=262-cid 2V V-8; H=350-cid V-8 2V; K=350-cid V-8 4V; T=350-cid V-8 (Z/28); R=400-cid V-8 2V; X=454-cid V-8 (L54) single exhaust; Y=454-cid V-8 dual exhaust. Sixth symbol 5=1975. Seventh symbol indicates assembly plant: A=Lakewood; B=Baltimore; C=Southgate; D=Doraville; F=Flint; J=Janesville; K=Leeds; L=Van Nuys; N=Norwood; R=Arlington; S=St. Louis; T=Tarrytown; U=Lordstown; V=Pontiac; W=Willow Run; Y=Wilmington; Z=Fremont; 1=Oshawa; 2=St. Therese. Next six symbols are sequential production number. Body tag on right or left of firewall gives some of same information, plus plant production sequence, trim code, paint code and date code. Engine numbers stamped on right side of V-8 block and left side of four-cylinder and six-cylinder blocks behind distributor. Consult factory or aftermarket reference sources for numerous Chevrolet engine serial numbers.

FULL-SIZE CHEVROLET

Series No.	Body/Style No.	Body Type & Seating	Factory Price	Shipping Weight	Prod. Total
BEL AIR					
1K	69	4-dr Sed-6P	4345	4179	Note 1
1K	45	4-dr Sta Wag-9P	4998	4913	Note 2
1K	35	4-dr Sta Wag-6P	4878	4856	Note 2
IMPALA					
1L	69	4-dr Sed-6P	4548	4218	Note 3
1L	39	4-dr HT Sed-6P	4631	4265	Note 3
1L	57	2-dr Spt Cpe-6P	4575	4207	Note 3
1L	47	2-dr Cus Cpe-6P	4626	4190	Note 3
1L	47	2-dr Lan Cpe-6P	4901	N/A	Note 3
1L	45	4-dr Sta Wag-9P	5121	4959	Note 2
1L	35	4-dr Sta Wag-6P	5001	4910	Note 2
CAPRICE					
1N	69	4-dr Sed-6P	4819	4311	Note 4
1N	39	4-dr HT Sed-6P	4891	4360	Note 4
1N	47	2-dr Cus Cpe-6P	4837	4275	Note 4
1N	47	2-dr Lan Cpe-6P	5075	N/A	Note 4
1N	67	2-dr Conv-6P	5113	4342	Notes 4/5
1N	45	4-dr Sta Wag-9P	5351	5036	Note 2
1N	35	4-dr Sta Wag-6P	5231	4978	Note 2

1975 Chevrolet, Impala four-door sedan, V-8

NOTE 1: 13,168 Bel Air four-door sedans were built in 1975 model run.

NOTE 2: 58,529 full-size wagons were built in 1975 model year (all series).

NOTE 3: 176,376 Impala cars were built in 1975 model year; no body type breakouts available.

NOTE 4: 103,944 Caprice Classics built in 1975; one body type breakout below.

NOTE 5: 8,349 Caprice Classic convertibles were built in the 1975 model year.

1975 Chevrolet, Monte Carlo two-door hardtop, V-8

MONTE CARLO — (V-8) — SERIES H — Chevrolet's personal/luxury car was refined for model year 1975. A new grille treatment featured two rows of 14 chrome-framed squares, arranged horizontally above the bumper with an additional row revealed through a long oval slot below. Each of the 42 square segments was highlighted with three, short vertical moldings. A shield-shaped medallion was placed at the center of the upper grille opening, with a Monte Carlo signature on the left-hand hood lip. Parking lamps were housed at the front fender corners, with a strip of body-colored sheet metal dividing the lens vertically. A new taillight treatment featured a stack of four horizontal slats that wrapped around the rear body edges. The Monte Carlo signature was removed from the right-hand trunk corner and dropped to the rear deck lid latch panel, directly below. Wheel cover design details were changed. Luxurious interiors featured new trim and fabrics and a choice of options such as 50/50 reclining passenger seats or swivel bucket seats. Standard engine was the 350-cid V-8 in two-barrel form. Power front disc brakes were included.

MONTE CARLO

Series No.	Body/Style No.	Body Type & Seating	Factory Price	Shipping Weight	Prod. Total
MONTE CARLO 'S'					
1H	57	2-dr HT Cpe-5P	4249	3927	Note 1
MONTE CARLO LANDAU					
1H	57	2-dr HT Cpe-5P	4519	3950	Note 1

NOTE 1: 258,909 Monte Carlos were built in the 1975 model year; no series breakout available.

CHEVELLE — (SIX/V-8) — ALL SERIES — Appearance features of Chevelles were changed in small details from 1974. The grille was still of the "Mercedes-type" with a chromed radiator shell, but was modified with prominent division bars forming 10 vertical segments. Each segment had a screen-like texture within. On Malibu Classics, the screening was black-finished, making the bright metal elements standout with a look of increased elegance. The Classic models also featured stand-up hood ornaments. Taillamp designs were again based on a horizontal, rectangular-shaped lens. The lamps, however, were somewhat longer and narrower with nearly square back-up lights added at the inboard side. On Malibu Classics, the rectangular panel housing the taillights and center license plate indentation received a satin silver finish and held a model identifying signature script on the right side. It was midyear before the Laguna Type S-3 coupe was reintroduced, again featuring a unique styling treatment. Prime among its special touches was a sloping urethane plastic front end with a grille opening that was divided both horizontally and vertically. This formed four large rectangular slots with screen-textured inserts. Also included were Rally wheels, louvered opera windows and radial tuned suspension. The S-3 came in a choice of six colors with specific body striping and half-vinyl roofs on its optional equipment list. Technical innovations for Chevelles were a more efficient six, High-Energy ignition and catalytic converter. Base V-8 was the 350-cid two-barrel and tire sizes were FR78-15/B on passenger cars; HR78-15/B on wagons and special GR70-15/B wide profile type on Laguna Type S-3.

1975 Chevrolet, Chevelle Malibu Classic two-door hardtop (with optional Skyroof), V-8 (PH)

CHEVELLE SERIES

Series No.	Body/Style No.	Body Type & Seating	Factory Price	Shipping Weight	Prod. Total
MALIBU					
1C	29	4-dr Col Sed-6P	3402/3652	3713/3833	Note 1
1C	37	2-dr Col Cpe-6P	3407/3657	3642/3762	Note 1
1C	35	4-dr Sta Wag-6P	4463	N/A	Note 2
1C	35	4-dr Sta Wag-6P	4318	4207	Note 2
MALIBU CLASSIC					
1D	29	4-dr Col Sed-6P	3695/3945	3713/3898	Note 3
1D	37	2-dr Col Cpe-6P	3698/3948	3681/3801	Note 3
1D	37	2-dr Lan Cpe-6P	3930/4180	N/A/N/A	Note 3
1D	35	4-dr Sta Wag-9P	4701	N/A	Note 2
1D	35	4-dr Sta Wag-8P	4556	4275	Note 2
MALIBU CLASSIC ESTATE					
1G	35	4-dr Sta Wag-9P	4893	N/A	Note 2
1G	35	4-dr Sta Wag-6P	4748	4301	Note 2
LAGUNA TYPE S-3					
1E	37	2-dr Col Cpe-5P	4113	3908	Note 4

1975-1/2 Chevrolet, Chevelle Laguna S-3 two-door hardtop, V-8 (PH)

NOTE 1: 63,530 Malibus were built in model year 1975 (21,804 sixes/41,726 V-8s).

NOTE 2: 45,582 Chevelle station wagons (all types) were built in 1975 model year. All V-8s.

NOTE 3: 131,455 Malibu Classics were built in model year 1975 (3,844 sixes/127,611 V-8s).

NOTE 4: 6,714 Chevelle Laguna coupes were built in 1975 model year. All were V-8s.

NOTE 5: Data above slash for six/below slash or no slash is V-8 data.

1975 Chevrolet, Nova LN two-door coupe, V-8

NOVA — (SIX/V-8) — ALL SERIES — The 'senior compact' Novas underwent the most change in the Chevrolet lineup with their first big revisions in eight years. Patterned after the German Mercedes-Benz, the body was squarer and more luxurious looking. Rooflines received the major share of attention with thinner pillars on all models and a slimmer roof increasing the total area of glass. The windshield was 15 percent larger. A functional louver treatment for venting stale air from the interior was featured on two-door Novas. Swing-out rear quarter windows were optional on coupes, while the hatchback had lift gate improvements. The new Nova grille was a simple, but elegant rectangle with two full-width bright accent moldings and a bright vertical center trim bar. Rectangular parking lamps stood up in the outboard ends of the grille and circular headlights were placed into large, square, bright-finished housings. Rectangular taillamps were seen. Available lines included the base models, Nova Customs with thin rocker moldings and luxurious LNs (with fancy fender medallions and lower perimeter moldings that accented the front and rear quarters and wheel lips, plus the area between the wheel openings and above the rocker panel trim). The Nova LN also featured thick window reveal moldings and vertically grooved trim plates on the center body pillar. Technical innovations included either the improved six-cylinder engine or an all-new 262-cid (4.3-liter) V-8, except on cars certified for California sale. Three-speed manual transmission was standard (automatic with 350-cid V-8 in California cars); Turbo-Hydramatic was optional and a 'Muncie' four-speed could be ordered for attachment with only the most powerful optional engine. The High-Energy electronic ignition system was standard equipment. Regular tire equipment was size E78-14 bias-belted blackwalls. The new Nova six had an EPA fuel economy rating of 16 city/23 highway miles per gallon.

NOVA SERIES

Series No.	Body/Style No.	Body Type & Seating	Factory Price	Shipping Weight	Prod. Total
NOVA 'S'					
1X	27	2-dr Cpe-5P	3099/3174	N/A/N/A	Note 1
NOVA					
1X	69	4-dr Sed-5P	3209/3284	3306/3408	Note 1
1X	27	2-dr Cpe-5P	3205/3280	3276/3378	Note 1
1X	17	2-dr Hatch-5P	3347/3422	3391/3493	Note 1
NOVA CUSTOM					
1Y	69	4-dr Sed-5P	3415/3490	3367/3469	Note 1
1Y	27	2-dr Cpe-5P	3402/3477	3335/3437	Note 1
1Y	17	2-dr Hatch-5P	3541/3616	3421/3523	Note 1
NOVA LN					
1Y	69	4-dr Sed-5P	3795/3870	N/A/N/A	Note 1
1Y	27	2-dr Cpe-5P	3782/3857	N/A/N/A	Note 1

NOTE 1: Exactly 272,982 Novas were built in the 1975 model year, including 138,879 sixes and 134,103 V-8s. No breakouts per body style or trim level available. Exactly 9,087 Novas were sold with the Super Sport option.

NOTE 2: Adjusted on a new cumulative model year basis, the above total increased slightly to 273,014 units for the 1975 model year. In cases where shipping weights are not available, the car listed was not a distinct model, but a decor package (or decor package deletion, in the case of the stripped-down Nova 'S').

1975 Chevrolet, Vega GT two-door hatchback coupe, 4-cyl

VEGA — (FOUR) — SERIES V — While unchanged, in a basic sense when it appeared in the fall of 1974, the Vega built to 1975 specifications included a number of refinements ranging from a new catalytic converter and spark and carburetion improvements to redesigned front suspension equipment. Power brakes and a tilt steering wheel were optional for the first time. In the middle of the year, a special, limited-edition Cosworth Vega appeared on the scene (2,081 built). Its double overhead camshaft, 16 valve four-cylinder engine was designed by England's famed Cosworth Engineering, Ltd. (a renowned race car building firm) and underwent final development in the Chevrolet Engineering laboratories. A true, high-performance machine, the Cosworth Vega also featured a Bendix electronic fuel injection system; special pulse air injection hardware; Vega heavy-duty front suspension; Chevrolet torque-arm rear suspension; stainless steel exhaust headers; breakerless, High-Energy ignition; onboard Motorola computer;

black vinyl interior with adjustable driver's seatback; black carpeting; padded Sport steering wheel; 8000 rpm tachometer; electric clock; temperature gauges; volt meter; passenger grab bar; gold-colored cast aluminum wheels; black exterior finish with specific gold pin striping; dual Sport mirrors; black-finished wiper arms; blacked-out headlamp bezels and instrument panel; and 'Twin Cam' nameplate finished in gold and engraved with owner's name and car's serial number. The Vega engine in the Cosworth was extensively modified so as to qualify as a virtually hand-crafted powerplant. The engines were, in fact, built by hand assembly methods at Chevrolet's Tonawanda, New York, plant. They were then shipped to Lordstown, Ohio, where the installation took place in bodies constructed off-line apart from the regular production models. Special components included shot-peened rods; forged and magnafluxed crankshaft; the computer-controlled induction setup; 18-valve aluminum Cosworth cylinder head; deep-dish high-compression pistons; low-lift design performance camshaft (for smooth idle); solid valve lifters and oversized oval-shaped exhaust ports connected to scavenging-type steel tube headers and low-restriction pipes and mufflers. Engine displacement was actually reduced to 122 cubic inches (2 liter) and specifications included 3.16 x 3.50 bore and stroke, 8.5:1 compression ratio and 120 hp at 5200 rpm. However, experimental racing versions prepared by Cosworth Engineering's Keith Duckworth featured 11.5:1 compression and 270 hp at 8750 rpm. The production version (which was originally scheduled for 1974-1/2 introduction, but failed to achieve government certification due to a burned exhaust valve in the test prototype) came with a close-ratio four-speed manual transmission and rode on six-inch wide spoked wheels. The regular, single cam Vega, on the other hand, featured 78 hp in one-barrel carburetor/base engine form and had standard three-speed manual attachment and A78-13/B blackwall tires on conventional rims.

1975 Chevrolet, Vega GT two-door Kammback station wagon, 4-cyl

VEGA SERIES

Series No.	Body/Style No.	Body Type & Seating	Factory Price	Shipping Weight	Prod. Total
VEGA					
1V	11	2-dr Cpe-4P	2788	2415	35,133
1V	77	2-dr Hatch-4P	2899	2478	112,912
1V	15	2-dr Sta Wag-4P	3018	2531	58,133
VEGA ESTATE					
1V	15	2-dr Sta Wag-4P	3255	N/A	Note 1
VEGA 'LX'					
1V	11	2-dr Cpe-4P	3119	N/A	Note 2

COSWORTH VEGA

1V	77	2-dr Hatch-4P	5916	N/A	2,061

VEGA PANEL EXPRESS

1H	05	2-dr Panel-2P	2822	2401	1,525

1975 Chevrolet, Cosworth Vega two-door hatchback coupe, 4-cyl

NOTE 1: Included in two-door station wagon total. No breakout is available for number of wagons equipped with 'Estate' trim package.

NOTE 2: Included in two-door (notchback) coupe total. No breakout is available for number of coupes equipped with 'LX' decor package.

1975 Chevrolet, Monza 2 + 2 two-door hatchback coupe, 4-cyl.

MONZA — (FOUR) — ALL SERIES — A popular Chevrolet nameplate of the past appeared again in the fall of 1974, on an all-new subcompact with a sporty, European-like body. Originally planned to be called the Chaparral, this fastback 2 + 2 coupe was built off the Vega platform, but bore an uncanny resemblance to the Ferrari GTC-4. It was some four inches longer and 180 pounds heavier than its Vega counterpart, which left enough room for a small-block V-8 under the hood. Base engine, however, was the aluminum 2.3-liter four and the same V-8s used for Novas were optional. Standard features included front bucket seats in leather-look vinyl; armrests; door map pockets; added Sport steering wheel; woodgrain dash inserts; three-speed manual floor shift transmission; manual front disc/rear drum brakes. Firestone BR78-13 steel-belted radial tires on six-inch wide rims; tight-sealing rear hatch panel; carpeting and fold down rear seatback. In April 1975, to answer the threat of the new Mustang II Ghia coupe, the midyear Monza 'S' notchback was introduced as an addition to the line.

This Style was 1.5 inches shorter and 135 pounds lighter than the 2 + 2 and had increased headroom, a new instrument panel and single, round headlights in place of the fastback's dual, rectangular type. It was classified as the 'Towne Coupe'.

MONZA SERIES

Series No.	Body/Style No.	Body Type & Seating	Factory Price	Shipping Weight	Prod. Total
MONZA 'S'					
1M	27	2-dr Twn Cpe-4P	3570	2675	Note 1
1M	07	2-dr Hatch-4P	3648	N/A	Note 1
MONZA (2 + 2)					
1R	07	2-dr Hatch-4P	3953	2753	Note 1

1975-1/2 Chevrolet, Monza two-door Town Coupe, 6-cyl

NOTE: Exactly 66,615 Monzas were built during the 1975 model year, including 41,658 fours and 24,957 V-8s. No breakouts by body style or trim level available.

CAMARO — (SIX/V-8) — ALL SERIES — The Camaro featured a new, wraparound backlight for 1975. It provided a 10 percent increase in rear visibility. The Z/28 'Special Performance Package' was (temporarily) dropped, but the Rally Sport option was reissued to fill the gap. Standard equipment echoed that of the previous season, plus High-Energy ignition and the catalytic converter. The RS added Rally wheels; radial tuned suspension; specific ornamentation and graphics including black paint accents for the grille; hood; front fendertops; headlamp bezels; window reveal area; forward sail panels and roof header. Engine selections were down to just three EPA-era choices: improved 140 cid/105 hp six; RPO L65 350 cid/145 hp two-barrel V-8 (not available in cars for California sale) and the RPO LM1 350 cid/155 hp four-barrel V-8 (in California and high-altitude counties only).

CAMARO SERIES

Series No.	Body/Style No.	Body Type & Seating	Factory Price	Shipping Weight	Prod. Total
CAMARO					
1Q	87	2-dr HT Cpe-4P	3540/3685	3421/3532	141,629
CAMARO TYPE LT					
1S	87	2-dr HT Cpe-4P	4057	3616	Note 1

NOTE 1: Production of the Camaro LT is included in the total figure given for base Camaro in chart above. This represents domestic production for the U.S. market. An additional 4,160 cars were built for export. Of the full total, 29,359 were sixes and 116,430 were V-8s.

NOTE 2: The total above also included 8,688 cars with four-speeds; 10,568 with three-speeds; 126,533 with automatics; 77,290 with air conditioning; 7,000 with Rally Sport equipment; 145,755 with power steering and 10,596 with power windows.

BEL AIR/IMPALA/CAPRICE ENGINE: See 1974 Bel Air/Impala series engine data.

MONTE CARLO ENGINE: See 1974 Bel Air/Impala series engine data.

CHEVELLE ENGINES

SIX: See 1975 Nova series six-cylinder engine data.

V-8: See 1974 Bel Air/Impala V-8 engine data.

NOVA ENGINES

SIX: Inline. L-head six. Cast iron block. Displacement: 250 cid. Bore and stroke: 3.875 x 3.53 inches. Compression ratio: 8.2:1. SAE Net hp: 105 at 1800 rpm. Seven main bearings. Hydraulic valve lifters. Carburetor: one-barrel.

'FEDERAL' V-8: Overhead valve. Cast iron block. Displacement: 262 cid. Bore and stroke: 3.671 x 3.10 inches. Compression ratio: 8.5:1. SAE Net hp: 110 at 3600 rpm. Five main bearings. Hydraulic valve lifters. Carburetor: Rochester two-barrel.

1975 Chevrolet, Camaro Type LT two-door hardtop, V-8

'CALIFORNIA' V-8: Overhead valve. Cast iron block. Displacement: 350 cid. Bore and stroke: 4.00 x 3.48

inches. Compression ratio: 8.5:1. SAE Net hp: 155 at 3800 rpm. Five main bearings. Hydraulic valve lifters. Carburetor: four-barrel.

VEGA ENGINE: See 1974 Vega series engine data. Brake hp for the 1975 one-barrel four was 78 at 4200 rpm, but other specifications were unchanged. The two-barrel four (87 hp at 4400 rpm) was standard in cars built for California sale and was also included in Vega Estate and Vega LX packages. Refer to text for Cosworth Vega specifications.

MONZA ENGINES

FOUR: See 1974 and 1975 Vega series engine data.

V-8: See 1975 Nova series engine data.

CHASSIS FEATURES: Wheelbase: (Chevrolet/Monte Carlo/Camaro/Nova/Vega/Chevelle) same as 1974; (Monza) 97 inches. Overall length: (Chevrolet/Monte Carlo/Camaro/Nova/Vega/Chevelle wagons) same as 1974; (Chevelle two-doors) 206 inches; (Chevelle four-doors) 210 inches; (Monza 2 + 2) 160 inches; (Monza Town Coupe) 179 inches. Width: (Monza) 66 inches; (all other models) same as 1974. Tires: Refer to text.

OPTIONS: Vega vinyl top ($79). Vega power steering ($111). Monza/Vega air conditioning ($398). Vega wagon luggage rack ($50). Monza/Vega AM/FM stereo ($213). Vega hatchback GT packages ($425). Monza 5.7-liter engine ($296). Camaro/Nova vinyl top ($87). Nova air conditioning ($435). Nova tape deck ($199). Nova AM/FM stereo ($223). Chevelle wagons 454 V-8 engines ($285). Chevelle 454 V-8 engine ($340). Chevelle vinyl top ($96). Chevrolet/Monte Carlo/Camaro/Chevelle AM/FM stereo ($233). Chevrolet/Monte Carlo/Camaro/Chevelle AM/FM stereo with tape ($363). Monte Carlo/Chevelle skyroof ($350). Chevelle wagon luggage rack ($65). Chevrolet/Monte Carlo/Chevelle power seats ($113). Camaro/Chevelle Rally wheels ($46). Monte Carlo/Camaro power windows ($91). Monte Carlo vinyl top ($123). Monte Carlo 454 V-8 engine ($285). Chevrolet Group 454 V-8 engine ($315). Chevrolet wagon luggage rack ($77). Chevrolet Group wagons 454 V-8 engine ($172).

HISTORICAL FOOTNOTES: The full-size 1975 Chevrolets were introduced in September 1974 and the Cosworth Vega, Laguna Type S-3 and Monza Towne Coupe appeared in dealer showrooms during April 1975. Model year production peaked at 1,600,878 units. Calendar year production of 1,639,490 cars were recorded. R.L. Lund was the chief executive officer of the company this year. The Monza 2 + 2 coupe was selected as 1975 "Car of the Year" by *Motor Trend* magazine.

1964 Chevrolet, Corvair Monza Spyder two-door convertible, 6-cyl

The Chevrolet Corvair, introduced in the fall of 1959 as a 1960 model, is perhaps the most significant automobile of the postwar era. The controversy surrounding the handling qualities of the 1960-1963 Corvairs inspired Ralph Nader to write a best-selling book on "the designed-in dangers of the American automobile." Titled *Unsafe At Any Speed*, that book ushered in a new era of zealous governmental regulation that continues to this day.

By Tony Hossain

The Corvair was a wholly unconventional automobile. It measured a tight 180 inches in overall length and it sat on a compact 108-inch wheelbase. An aluminum, air-cooled, horizontally-opposed six-cylinder engine was rear-mounted, as in the popular German Volkswagen. The fully independent suspension system used coil springs all around and swing axles in the rear. An oddly shaped trunk was up front, where the engine was on all other American cars. The Corvair's primary competition, the Ford Falcon and the Plymouth Valiant,

were also introduced in the 1960 model year. But they were, basically, scaled down versions of bigger cars.

Auto enthusiasts loved the new Corvair. *Motor Trend* magazine proclaimed it 'Car of the Year.' The buff books liked the quick handling qualities, the gutsy sounding rear engine and the European flavor of Chevy's new small car.

Unfortunately, the public was unsure. The conventionally engineered Ford Falcon outsold the Corvair by a wide margin in 1960.

It was the Monza Club Coupe, introduced in April 1960, that saved the day for the Corvair. By 1961, the Monza, with its luxurious appointments and sporty bucket seats, was outselling every other Corvair model. The Corvair had found its niche, not as a small family compact, but as an economical sporty car. Monza owners found out that four-speed transmissions and agile handling made driving a lot more fun.

In mid-1962, the Corvair station wagon, never popular, was phased out. The Monza convertible took its place on the assembly line. Also making its debut in 1962 was the Monza Spyder option, with its handling suspension and turbocharged engine.

An all-new Corvair arrived in 1965. The lines were smooth and would characterize GM styling for years to come. Once again, the Corvair was one of America's style leaders. A new rear suspension, Corvette-inspired, corrected some of the oversteering tendencies of the original design, and in turbocharged form horsepower ratings went as high as 180. But it was too late. On April 17, 1964, Ford introduced the car that quickly took over the 'Monza market' that Chevy had discovered four years earlier. That car was the Mustang.

With the bad publicity stemming from Ralph Nader's book and the public's preference for the relatively unsophisticated but brutally powerful V-8 Mustang, Corvair sales plummeted in 1966. Chevy introduced the Camaro in 1967, but the Corvair limped along as an afterthought in the division's model line for two more years. The last Corvair built, a gold Monza coupe, left the Willow Run, Mich., assembly line on May 14, 1969.

1960 CORVAIR

1960 Chevrolet, Corvair Series 500 four-door sedan, 6-cyl

CORVAIR STANDARD — (SIX) — SERIES 500 — The first Corvair was publicly introduced on Oct. 2, 1959. Its lightweight air-cooled rear engine, unique suspension system and rear-mounted transaxle drive setup were a radical departure from other American cars of the day. All of the compact Corvairs were just over four feet high and 15 feet in overall length. All were designed to seat six people. Unitized construction of frame and body was a technical advance for Corvair. The Series 500 models were the standard line. Equipment features included electric windshield wipers; left-hand sun visor; turn signals and five tubeless black sidewall tires. Other items found in all 1960 Corvairs were friction-type ventipane latches; single key locking system; push-button outside door handles; dual horizontal headlamps; front ashtray; and center dome light with instrument panel switch. The sole model available at introduction time was the four-door sedan, but a standard 500 series two-door coupe was a running addition to the line in January 1960.

CORVAIR I.D. NUMBERS: The numbering system and code locations were the same as for Chevrolet models. Corvair serial numbers were located on the left center body pillar. Twelve numbers appeared. The first symbol designated the model year: '0' = 1960. The second and third symbols designated the series ('05' = 500; '07' = 700; '09' = 900 Monza). The fourth and fifth symbols designated the type of body (see last two digits in second column of charts below). The sixth symbol designated the assembly plant. The following group of symbols was the sequential unit production number. The Corvair production sequence began at 100001 and went up from there at each factory where Corvair production was quartered. Body/Style Numbers were comprised of the two-digit series and body type codes and appeared, on the vehicle, with a two-digit model year prefix (for example: 60-0569, for a 1960 Corvair 500 four-door sedan). In this catalog, the main Body/Style Number appears in the second column of charts: this prefix is not shown, but will always correspond to the year. The engine number for Corvairs is stamped on top of the block, ahead of the generator/oil filter adapter. It consists of six or seven symbols, the first identifying the point of manufacture; the next two indicating month of manufacture and the final one or two symbols identifying the horsepower and the type of transmission attachment.

STANDARD SERIES 500

Model No.	Body/Style No.	Body Type & Seating	Factory Price	Shipping Weight	Prod. Total
500	0569	4-dr Sed-6P	2038	2305	47,683
500	0527	2-dr Clb Cpe-6P	1984	2270	14,628

1960 Chevrolet, Corvair Series 700 four-door sedan, 6-cyl (AA)

CORVAIR DELUXE — (SIX) — SERIES 700 — Corvairs in the Series 700 line were Deluxe models. Standard equipment included everything found on Corvair 500s, plus right-hand sun visor; chrome exterior moldings; front armrest; cigarette lighter and upgraded upholstery design. There were also dual horns; automatic front door dome light switches; luggage compartment mat; colored-keyed floor mats and a choice of three different interior trims. Like the standard models, the Corvair Deluxe 700 came only as a four-door sedan at first, but a two-door coupe was added to the line in January 1960. As opposed to the four-door sedan's flat-top, overhanging roof styling, the two-door edition had a smooth, flowing roofline with large, curved glass backlight.

CORVAIR DELUXE SERIES 700

Model No.	Body/Style No.	Body Type & Seating	Factory Price	Shipping Weight	Prod. Total
700	0769	4-dr Sed-6P	2103	2315	139,208
700	0727	2-dr Clb Cpe-6P	2049	2290	36,562

1960 Chevrolet, Corvair, Series 700 two-door Club Coupe, 6-cyl

CORVAIR MONZA — (SIX) — SERIES 900 — The sporty Corvair Monza two-door Club Coupe made its debut at the Chicago Auto Show, in February 1960, as a show car. It was a dressed up Deluxe 700 coupe with bucket seats and a sun roof. Public response prompted the release of a production model, bearing the same name, in May of the year. Standard equipment included bucket seats with chrome trim; stainless steel rocker sill moldings; special wheel covers; bright metal seat and armrest moldings; leather-like vinyl upholstery; chrome simulated rear deck air vents; folding rear seat; rear ashtrays; dual sun visors and glovebox light plus all other Series 700 features.

MONZA SERIES 900

Model No.	Body/Style No.	Body Type & Seating	Factory Price	Shipping Weight	Prod. Total
900	0927	2-dr Clb Cpe-5P	2238	2280	11,926

ENGINE: (all) Horizontally opposed six. Overhead valve. Aluminum block. Displacement: 140 (139.6) cid. Bore and stroke: 3.375 x 2.60 inches. Compression ratio: 8.0:1. Brake hp: 80 at 4400 rpm. Four main bearings. Hydraulic valve lifters. Carburetor: Two Rochester one-barrel Model 7015311.

CHASSIS FEATURES: Wheelbase: (all models) 108 inches. Overall length: (all models) 180 inches. Front tread: (all models) 54 inches. Rear tread (all models) 54 inches. Tires: (all models) 6.50 x 13.

OPTIONS: Rear axle with 3.89:1 ratio gearing ($2). Heater ($74). Padded dash ($18). Manual radio ($54). Rear folding seat, standard in Monza ($32). Wheel trim rings ($11). Five white sidewall tires 6.50 x 13 four-ply ($21). Two-tone paint in selected schemes was offered as regular production option only. Undergear paint was always black. Wheel paint was determined by color and tire equipment. Comfort and Convenience Group: including left outside rearview mirror; push-button windshield washers; back-up lights and glovebox light ($32). Deluxe Body Equipment Group: including cigarette lighter; right-hand sun visor; front armrests; for standard models only ($11). Three-speed manual transmission was standard, Automatic transmission ($146). Six-cylinder 140 cid/95 hp dual one-barrel engine ($27). Heavy-duty battery ($3). Available rear axle gear ratios: (standard) 3.55:1; (optional) 3.89:1.

HISTORICAL FOOTNOTES: The first Corvairs were introduced Oct. 2, 1959, and the Monza appeared in dealer showrooms during May. Model year production peaked at 250,007 units. Calendar year sales of 250,000 cars were recorded. Ed Cole was the chief executive officer of Chevrolet this year. Automatic transmission (Powerglide) was installed in 83.5 percent of all 1960 Corvairs; 39.8 percent had radios; 90.2 percent had heaters; 55 percent had whitewall tires; 42.6 percent had windshield washers; 42.6 percent had back-up lamps and only 0.6 percent had E-Z-Eye tinted windshields. Series production amounted to 62,300 Standards; 175,800 Deluxes and 11,900 Monzas.

1961 CORVAIR

CORVAIR — (SIX) — SERIES 500 — The Corvair line was expanded for 1961. New models included a station wagon, van-type Sports Wagon and three half-ton trucks. On all models, the spare tire was relocated over the rear engine compartment. Corvairs were advertised and promoted as the lowest-priced Chevrolets. New styling features included a convex nose panel. Corvair lettering replaced Chevrolet lettering on the rear deck and there was a wider Chevrolet insignia housing on the front panel. Series nameplates on 500 models were repositioned to a point high on the sides of the front fenders, but below the belt molding, in the cowl region of the body. Standard equipment for the base series was comprised of directional signals; left-hand sun visor; dual electric windshield wipers; folding rear seat (in Lakewood station wagon) and five 6.50 x 13 black sidewall tubeless tires available except on Lakewood models, which used 7.00 x 13 blackwall tubeless. Gray, green or blue interior trims, of slightly improved quality, were provided. With the rear seat folded, the new Lakewood station wagon provided 58 cubic feet of load space. The 500 series Lakewood lasted only this one model year.

1961 Chevrolet, Corvair Series 700 two-door Club Coupe, 6-cyl

CORVAIR I.D. NUMBERS: The numbering system and code locations were the same as for previous models with the first symbol changed to a '1' to indicate the 1961 model year. New Body/Style Numbers identified the Lakewood station wagons.

CORVAIR SERIES 500

Model No.	Body/Style No.	Body Type & Seating	Factory Price	Shipping Weight	Prod. Total
500	0569	4-dr Sed-6P	1974	2355	18,752
500	0527	2-dr Clb Cpe-5P	1920	2320	18,857
500	0535	4-dr StaWag-6P	2266	2530	5,591

1961 Chevrolet, Corvair Series 700 Lakewood station wagon, 6-cyl

CORVAIR — (SIX) — SERIES 700 — Corvair's middle-priced models wore '700' nameplates on the cowl sides of the fenders. They had all equipment included on the base level cars, plus chrome exterior moldings; interiors with richer trims; dual horns; coat hooks and automatic light switches that were rigged to operate when the front door was opened.

CORVAIR DELUXE SERIES 700

Model No.	Body/Style No.	Body Type & Seating	Factory Price	Shipping Weight	Prod. Total
700	0769	4-dr Sed-6P	2039	2380	51,948
700	0727	2-dr Clb Cpe-5P	1985	2350	24,786
700	0735	4-dr Sta Wag-6P	2330	2555	20,451

CORVAIR MONZA — (SIX) — SERIES 900 — Behind the front wheelwell of Monza models, a special ornament bearing the 900 series designation could be seen. Wheel covers were the same as used on 1961 Corvair 500 and 700 models. Standard were all features of 700 series Corvairs, plus front bucket seats and carpeting. All-vinyl interior trim was standard on two-door Monzas only, while the four-door used a vinyl/cloth combination; front armrests; cigarette lighter; right-hand sun visor; back-up lights; Deluxe steering wheel; glovebox light; rear armrests (sedan) and folding rear seat. The Monza sedan was not available at fall introduction time, but became a running addition to the line soon-thereafter. Prices for both Monzas were identical. Interestingly, Chevrolet reduced the rated passenger capacity of all 1961 Club Coupes by one person. Thus, the coupes in the 500 and 700 Deluxe series were rated as five-passenger models, while the Monza coupe — with bucket seats — was classified a four-place car.

CORVAIR MONZA SERIES 900

Model No.	Body/Style No.	Body Type & Seating	Factory Price	Shipping Weight	Prod. Total
900	0969	4-dr Sed-6P	2201	2420	33,745
900	0927	2-dr Clb Cpe-4P	2201	2395	109,945

ENGINE: Horizontally opposed six. Overhead valve. Aluminum block. Displacement: 145 (144.8) cid. Bore and stroke: 3.438 x 2.609 inches. Compression ratio: 8.0:1. Brake hp: 80 at 4400 rpm. Four main bearings. Hydraulic valve lifters. Carburetor: Two Rochester one-barrel Model 7019101.

CHASSIS FEATURES: Wheelbase: (all models) 108 inches. Overall length: (all models) 180 inches. Front tread: (all models) 54 inches. Rear tread: (all models) 54 inches. Tires: (Lakewood) 7.00 x 13; (all other models) 6.50 x 13.

OPTIONS: Wheel covers, standard on Monza ($11). Rear door armrests for 500/700 four-door sedan ($10). Comfort and Convenience Group, 500/700 four-door sedan ($39). Comfort and Convenience Group, Monza ($28). Deluxe body equipment, 500/700 models ($11). Tinted glass, all windows ($27); windshield only ($13). Direct-air heater ($74). Gasoline-operated heater ($92). Padded dash, all models ($18). Spare wheel lock ($5). Two-tone paint finish ($11). Manual radio ($54). Push-button radio ($62). Folding rear seat 500/700 coupes and sedans ($27). Heavy-duty shock absorbers ($8). Windshield washer ($11). Two-speed windshield wipers ($16). Three-speed manual transmission was standard. Powerglide automatic transmission ($157). Four-speed manual floor shift transmission ($850). Six-cylinder 145 cid/98 hp dual one-barrel engine ($27). Heavy-duty battery ($5). Special crankcase vent ($4). Generator, 35-amp ($38). Available rear axle gear ratios: (standard) 3.27:1; (optional) 3.55:1, but standard in wagons; with air conditioning, or with automatic and 98 hp engine. 3 89:1 optional.

1961 Chevrolet, Corvair Series 700 four-door sedan, 6-cyl

HISTORICAL FOOTNOTES: The 1961 Corvairs were introduced Oct. 8, 1960, and the Monza sedan appeared in dealer showrooms at mid-season. Model year production peaked at 297,881 units. Calendar year sales of 316,028 cars were recorded. Semon E. 'Bunkie' Knudsen was the chief executive officer of the company this year. On a model year basis, 60.1 percent of 1961 Corvairs had automatic transmission installed; 49.2 percent had radios; 95.4 percent had heaters; 42.5 percent had bucket seats; 69.6 percent had whitewall tires; 48 percent had windshield washers; 24.4 percent had tinted glass; 50.9 percent had back-up lights and one percent had a new, midyear option, air conditioning. An interesting comparison can be made between the entire 1961 model year and the first few months of 1962 model production to show how fast the popularity of bucket seats was growing. A total of 132,000 models built to 1961 specifications had this option, but by December of 1961, there had been 70,470 Corvairs (1962 models) already built with bucket seats.

1962 CORVAIR

CORVAIR — (SIX) — SERIES 500 — There were no significant changes in the 1962 Corvair. After a year of strong sales, Chevrolet decided to leave well enough alone. Revision was seen in the front, side and rear trim; redesigned hubcaps and plusher interiors. A V-shaped ornament was placed at the center of the front panel. It was flanked by thin, horizontally divided, simulated air vents on either side. Model nameplates were still on the sides of the front fenders. Interiors on the 500 series models were comparable to the previous Deluxe trims. They came in vinyl and cloth combinations (with a checkered pattern) in colors of aqua, red or fawn (tan). Standard equipment included directional signals; leff-hand sun visor; electric windshield wipers; heater and defroster; rubber floor mats; front foam seat cushions and five 8.50 x 13 black sidewall tubeless tires. The Corvair 500 Lakewood station wagon was no longer on the market and the four-door sedan was gone also.

1962 Chevrolet, Corvair Monza Spyder two-door convertible, 6-cyl (M)

CORVAIR I.D. NUMBERS: The numbering system and code locations were the same as for previous models, with the first symbol changed to a '2' to indicate the 1962 model year. A new convertible used Body/Style Number '0967' (the '09' designating Monza series and the '67' designating the new body type).

1962 Chevrolet, Corvair Series 500 two-door Club Coupe, 6-cyl

CORVAIR SERIES 500

Model No.	Body/Style No.	Body Type & Seating	Factory Price	Shipping Weight	Prod. Total
500	0527	2-dr Clb Cpe-5P	1992	2350	16,245

CORVAIR — (SIX) — SERIES 700 — The Corvair 700 Deluxe series models had all equipment found on the basic line, plus extra chrome exterior moldings; dual horns; upgraded upholstery and, on station wagons, a folding rear seat and 7.00 x 13 black sidewall tires. The Lakewood was dropped in the middle of the model run, since it was in direct competition with the new Chevy II station wagon. The latter car was cheaper to build and easier to sell, due to its greater conventionality. Model nameplates on 700s were located ahead of the front wheelhousing. Another trim change was that the upper belt molding no longer ran entirely around the cars.

CORVAIR SERIES 700

Model No.	Body/Style No.	Body Type & Seating	Factory Price	Shipping Weight	Prod. Total
700	0769	4-dr Sed-6P	2111	2410	35,368
700	0727	2-dr Clb Cpe-5P	2057	2390	18,474
700	0735	4-dr Sta Wag-6P	2407	2590	3,716

1962 Chevrolet, Corvair Series 900 Monza two-door Club Coupe, 6-cyl

CORVAIR MONZA — (SIX) — SERIES 900 — The Monza was becoming the true star of the Corvair lineup, as Chevrolet's rear-engined wonder caught on with the sports car crowd. These cars included all items found on lower lines, plus all-vinyl interior trims standard in the coupe and convertible, while four-door Monzas and Monza wagons used cloth-vinyl upholstery as standard; carpets; rear armrests; cigarette lighter; right-hand sun visor; back-up lights; Deluxe steering wheel (with horn ring); glovebox light; wheel covers; folding rear seat and, in coupes and convertibles, bucket-type front seats. Model nameplates on Monzas were of a special design, located behind the front wheelwell. Bright ribbed metal rocker panel moldings were used along the lower body sills. New models included an extra-sporty mid-year Monza convertible, plus a short-lived Monza station wagon that was introduced in the fall and killed by the spring.

CORVAIR MONZA SERIES 900

Model No.	Body/Style No.	Body Type & Seating	Factory Price	Shipping Weight	Prod. Total
900	0969	4-dr Sed-6P	2273	2455	48,059
900	0927	2-dr Clb Cpe-4P	2273	2440	151,738
900	0967	2-dr Conv-4P	2483	2625	16,569
900	0935	4-dr Sta Wag-6P	2569	2590	2,362

CORVAIR MONZA SPYDER — (SIX) — SERIES 900 —
About the same time that the new convertible appeared, a car called the Monza Spyder began receiving attention in the press. One such car was tested in *Popular Science* magazine, April 1962, and *Motor Trend* magazine got its hands on another. Technically, Spyder equipment was an options package for the Monza convertible and coupe. At least that's the way it was cataloged in 1963, but most people thought of it as a new model. In either case, the package included a special 150-hp turbocharged version of the Corvair engine, plus identification badges on the rear deck and a round "turbocharged" emblem with opposing arrows and "bow tie" on the rear deck. It was not available on cars with air conditioning or two-speed Powerglide automatic transmission.

CORVAIR MONZA SPYDER

Model No.	Body/Style No.	Body Type & Seating	Factory Price	Shipping Weight	Prod. Total
900	0927	2-dr Clb Cpe-4P	2569	2490	(6,894)
900	0967	2-dr Conv-4P	2779	2675	(2,574)

NOTE 1: Figure in parentheses indicate the number of each body style equipped with the turbocharged six. These figures are included in the Monza series 900 body style production totals of coupes and convertibles.

1962 Chevrolet, Corvair Series 900 Monza two-door convertible, 6-cyl

ENGINES

(BASE SIX) Horizontally opposed six. Overhead valve. Aluminum block. Displacement: 145 cid. Bore and stroke: 3.43 x 2.60 inches. Compression ratio: 8.0:1. Brake hp: 80 at 4400 rpm. Four main bearings. Hydraulic valve lifters. Carburetor: Two Rochester one-barrel Model 702101.

(MONZA POWERGLIDE SIX) An 84 hp (at 4400 rpm) engine was used with Powerglide-equipped Monzas only. It came with a compression ratio of 9.0:1.

(MONZA SPYDER TURBO SIX) Horizontally opposed six. Overhead valve. Aluminum block. Displacement: 145 cid. Bore and stroke: 3.43 x 2.60 inches. Compression ratio: 8.0:1. Brake hp: 150 at 4400 rpm. Four main bearings. Hydraulic valve lifters. Induction: Carter YH one-barrel sidedraft carburetor Model 3817245 with turbocharger.

CHASSIS FEATURES: Wheelbase: (all models) 108 inches. Overall length: (all models) 180 inches. Front tread: (all models) 54.5 inches. Rear tread: (all models) 54.5 inches. Tires: (station wagons) 7.00 x 13; (passenger) 6.50 x 13.

OPTIONS: Air conditioning ($350). Pair of front seat belts, all ($20). Comfort and Convenience Equipment in 500/700 ($39). Comfort and Convenience Equipment in 900 ($28). Tinted glass, all windows ($27); windshield only ($13). Padded instrument panel ($16). Two-tone paint, all models ($11). Manual radio ($48). Push-button radio ($57). Folding rear seat, for 500 series and Styles 0727/0769 ($27). Front bucket seats for Monza sedan standard in 0927/0967 ($54). Heavy-duty suspension, all ($22). Whitewall tires, exchange ($29). Full wheel covers, standard on Monzas ($11). Wire wheel design hubcaps 500/700 ($38). Monzas ($27). Two-speed windshield wipers and washers ($16). Three-speed manual transmission was standard. Automatic transmission ($157). Four-speed manual floor shift transmission ($65). Six-cylinder 145 cid/102 hp, 9.0:1 compression engine ($27). Six-cylinder 145 cid/84 hp Powerglide engine. Generator, 35-amp ($5). Available rear axle gear ratios: (standard) 3.27:1, and the 3.55:1 axle ratio was standard in wagons; with air conditioning; with Spyder equipment and with the 102-hp engine and Powerglide.

HISTORICAL FOOTNOTES: The 1962 Corvairs were introduced Sept. 29, 1961, and the convertible and Spyder appeared in dealer showrooms around May 1962. Model year production peaked at 306,023 units. Calendar year sales of 292,531 cars were recorded. S.E. Knudsen was the chief executive officer of the company this year. Series production, expressed in round figures for the model year, included 16,300 Corvair 500s; 53,800 Corvair 700s; 216,400 Monza 900s and 19,500 station wagons. Of all Corvair passenger cars and station wagons built to 1962 model specifications, 48 percent had automatic transmissions; 38 percent had four-speed gearboxes; 55.1 percent had radios; 64.6 percent had bucket seats; 86.7 percent had white sidewall tires; 55 percent had windshield washers; 2.5 percent had air conditioning and 5.9 percent had limited-slip differentials.

1963 CORVAIR

CORVAIR — (SIX) — SERIES 500 — The pattern of minimum annual change continued for 1963 in the Corvair lineup. The trim on the front panel was changed once again. A strip of chrome was centered between the quad headlamps, running horizontally across the car. Its center section was finished in black paint. Amber colored front parking lamps were a new touch. So was a Corvair nameplate placed in the upper left-hand corner of the hood latch panel. On the side, model identification badges were placed above and ahead of the front wheel opening. Standard equipment included directional signals; electric windshield wipers; heater and defroster; front foam seat cushions; five 6.50 x 13 black sidewall tires and small hubcaps. There was little difference in the interior from 1962. The model lineup was unchanged. Standard power came from the rear-mounted, air-cooled six carried over from the previous season. It gave 80 hp with synchromesh transmission. Prices for the Corvair 500 coupe were unchanged from 1962.

CORVAIR I.D. NUMBERS: The numbering system and code locations were the same as for previous models with the first symbol changed to a '3' to indicate the 1963 model year.

CORVAIR 500 SERIES

Model No.	Body/Style No.	Body Type & Seating	Factory Price	Shipping Weight	Prod. Total
500	0527	2-dr Clb Cpe-5P	1992	2300	16,680

1963 Chevrolet, Corvair Monza four-door sedan, 6-cyl (AA)

CORVAIR (DELUXE) — (SIX) — SERIES 700 — The
Club Coupe and the four-door sedan remained available in the Corvair 700 series. Prices for both models decreased one dollar. Weights were down, too, indicating the deletion of some formerly standard hardware. One way to spot a 700 was to look for an upper belt molding that followed the body feature line from the middle of the front door forward, around the front end and down to the middle of the opposite door. A Corvair 700 nameplate was seen ahead of the front wheel opening, and a rocker panel molding was used. Standard features began with everything found on lower priced models, plus the chrome exterior moldings; fancier interior upholstery; color-keyed vinyl rubber floor mats; dual horns and automatic dome lamp switches. This was the last run for the Corvair 700 Club Coupe.

CORVAIR 700 SERIES

Model No.	Body/Style No.	Body Type & Seating	Factory Price	Shipping Weight	Prod. Total
700	0769	4-dr Sed-6P	2110	2385	20,684
700	0727	2-dr Clb Cpe-5P	2058	2355	12,378

CORVAIR MONZA — (SIX) — SERIES 900 — The Cor-
vair Monza had all standard equipment found on other models and more. For example, all-vinyl interiors with a new tufted pattern were used on four-door models and convertibles only. Equipment included a cigarette lighter; back-up lights; Deluxe steering wheel; glovebox light; full wheel covers; rocker panel moldings; and distinct model identification badges on the lower front fender in back of the wheel openings. Bucket seats were standard in all models including the four-door sedan. Spyder equipment was optional on the coupe and convertible at an attractive price. Sintered metallic brakes were no longer included. What did come on Spyders was a round "turbocharged" emblem on the rear deck; tachometer; 120 mph speedometer; full instrumentation; special

brushed metal dash insert panel and turbocharged flat six. This engine included heavy-duty engine bearings; hardened crank; chromed upper piston rings; special valves; and heavy-duty clutch. Spyders had Carter YH single-barrel sidedraft carburetors.

1963 Chevrolet, Corvair Series 900 Monza two-door convertible, 6-cyl

1963 Chevrolet, Corvair Series 900 Monza two-door Club Coupe, 6-cyl

CORVAIR 900 SERIES

Model No.	Body/Style No.	Body Type & Seating	Factory Price	Shipping Weight	Prod. Total
MONZA					
900	0969	4-dr Sed-6P	2326	2450	31,120
900	0927	2-dr Clb Cpe-4P	2272	2415	117,917
900	0967	2-dr Conv-4P	2481	2525	36,693
MONZA WITH SPYDER OPTION					
900	0927	2-dr Clb Cpe-4P	2589	2440	11,827
900	0967	2-dr Conv-4P	2798	2550	7,472

ENGINES

(CORVAIR 500/700/900 SERIES ENGINE): Horizontally opposed six. Overhead valve. Aluminum block. Displacement: 145 cid. Bore and stroke: 3.438 x 2.609 inches. Compression ratio: 8.0:1. Brake hp: 80 at 4400 rpm. Four main bearings. Hydraulic valve lifters. Carburetor: Two Rochester one-barrel Model 7017360.

(MONZA SPYDER TURBO SIX): Horizontally opposed six. Overhead valve. Aluminum block. Displacement: 145

cid. Bore and stroke: 3.438 x 2.609 inches. Compression ratio: 8.0:1. Brake hp: 150 at 4400 rpm. Four main bearings. Hydraulic valve lifters. Induction: Carter YH one-barrel sidedraft carburetor Model 3817245 with turbocharger.

CHASSIS FEATURES: Wheelbase: (all models) 108 inches. Overall length: (all models) 180 inches. Front tread: (all models) 54.5 inches. Rear tread: (all models) 54.5 inches. Tires: (all models) 6.50 x 13.

OPTIONS: Air conditioning ($350). Rear armrest, Style 0769 only ($10). Pair of front seat belts ($19). Comfort and Convenience equipment, Monza ($28); others ($39). Tinted glass, all windows ($27); windshield only ($13). Padded instrument panel ($16). Spare wheel lock ($5). Two-tone paint ($11). Manual radio ($48). Push-button radio ($57). Push-button radio and front and rear speaker, except convertible ($70). Folding rear seat, Styles 0727/0769 and all 500s ($27). Four-ply white sidewall tires ($29). Power convertible top ($54). Full wheel covers, standard on Monzas ($11). Wire design wheel covers, 500/700 ($38); Monza ($27). Kelsey-Hayes wire wheels with knock-off hubs, all models ($404). Three-speed manual transmission was standard. Powerglide automatic transmission ($157). Four-speed manual floor shift transmission ($92). Six-cylinder 164 cid/110 hp, 9.25:1 compression engine ($30). Six-cylinder 164 cid/150 hp turbocharged engine (*). Positive traction rear axle ($38). Heavy-duty air cleaner ($17). Heavy-duty clutch (*). Available rear axle gear ratios: 3.27:1; 3.55:1. Generator, 35-ampere ($38).

NOTE : Options marked (*) are included in Spyder equipment package at $317.45.

HISTORICAL FOOTNOTES: The 1963 Corvairs were introduced Sept. 28, 1962. Model year production peaked at 254,571 units. Calendar year production of 261,525 cars was recorded. S.E. Knudsen was the chief executive officer of the company this year. Optional equipment installation rates for Corvairs built to 1963 model specifications were as follows: automatic transmission (44.3 percent); four-speed manual gearbox (44.3 percent); radio (55.9 percent); heater (99.4 percent); bucket seats (80.5 percent); seat belts (17.6 percent); whitewall tires (77.4 percent); windshield washers (58.6 percent); tinted windshield (39.4 percent); all tinted glass (8.6 percent); air conditioning (2.5 percent); limited-slip differential (7.7 percent) and full wheel covers (92.0 percent). Introduced in 1963 was the Fitch Sprint, a modified Corvair Monza (costing $565 more than the Prod. version) upgraded by sports car racing champion John Fitch. The Sprint, sanctioned by Chevrolet, featured four carburetors; tuned dual exhaust; modified suspension; racing steering wheel; vinyl top; tachometer and racing stripes. Fitch continued to produce Sprints through 1968.

NOTE : Percentages are based on a slightly higher model year output figure (266,564) that includes Greenbrier trucks. See Krause Publications *Standard Catalog Of American Light-Duty Trucks* for information about Chevrolet and Corvair trucks.

1964 CORVAIR

CORVAIR — (SIX) — SERIES 500 — Seven models in four series comprised Corvair offerings for 1964. Improved brakes and redesigned suspensions were highlights of the year. The base powerplant now gave 95 hp with manual transmission attachments. A thicker crossbar stretched between the headlights. Below it was a triangular Chevrolet badge. Corvair block letters trimmed the edge of the hood and deck. The circular taillamp bezels were redone. Standard equipment on the 500 series Club Coupe was comprised of directional signals; electric wipers, heater and defroster; front foam seat cushions; rubber floor mats; locking glovebox; dual sun visors; cigarette lighter; front armrests; small hubcaps and five tubeless black sidewall tires. Model nameplates remained in their previous location ahead of front wheel cutouts. Interiors came in red, aqua and fawn (tan). They were slightly plainer in design this year. Many refinements made the 1964 Corvair truly the best of the early editions. It was a great machine for the money, which was less than $10 over the previous year's cost for most models.

Corvair 500 Club Coupe in Lagoon Aqua.

1964 Chevrolet, Corvair Series 500 two-door Club Coupe, 6-cyl

CORVAIR I.D. NUMBERS: The numbering system and code locations were the same as for previous models with the first symbol changed to a '4' to indicate the 1964 model year.

Corvair 700 4-Door Sedan in Meadow Green with optional wheel covers*.

1964 Chevrolet, Corvair Series 700 four-door sedan, 6-cyl

CORVAIR 500 SERIES

Model No.	Body/Style No.	Body Type & Seating	Factory Price	Shipping Weight	Prod. Total
500	0527	2-dr Clb Cpe-5P	2000	2365	22,968

CORVAIR (DELUXE) — (SIX) — SERIES 700 — Only the four-door sedan was available in the Corvair 700 series this season. It came with all features found on the base-level models, plus front fender model nameplates; chrome exterior moldings; upgraded interior and dual horns. A blue cloth and vinyl interior trim combination was offered and buyers could also select from these materials in the same colors available for Corvair 500s. The Series 700 Club Coupe was dropped due to lagging sales. There were three reasons for the dip in deliveries. First, the new Chevy II had more appeal to conservative buyers in the compact car market. Second, the Corvair hadn't changed much in five years and had lost much of its novelty. Its styling was growing too stale for the mass market, although not for the enthusiast buyer. Third, an unearned reputation for unsafe handling traits was beginning to gain publicity. The result of these three factors combined was that Corvair sales tapered off and also became concentrated in the sportier Monza series. However, the introduction of the Ford Mustang, in mid-1964, began hurting even the enthusiast market sales. Meanwhile, Chevrolet kept reducing the availability of low trim level Corvairs.

1964 Chevrolet, Corvair Series 900 Monza four-door sedan, 6-cyl

CORVAIR 700 SERIES

Model No.	Body/Style No.	Body Type & Seating	Factory Price	Shipping Weight	Prod. Total
700	0769	4-dr Sed-6P	2119	2415	16,295

1964 Chevrolet, Corvair Series 900 Monza two-door Club Coupe, 6-cyl

CORVAIR MONZA — (SIX) — SERIES 900 — Corvair Monzas could be most easily identified by their wider rocker panel moldings; inverted cross-shaped insignias mounted behind the front wheelhousing; stylish full wheel covers; and trim moldings along the lips of both front and rear wheel cutouts. A new interior feature was map pockets on the front door panels. Standard equipment included everything found on Series 700 models, plus all-vinyl upholstery on four-door and convertible body styles; rear armrests; back-up lights; Deluxe steering wheel with chrome horn ring; glovebox light; and simulated vents below rear window. The Monza Spyder officially became part of a separate series this year. All Monzas also featured bucket seats.

CORVAIR MONZA 900 SERIES

Model No.	Body/Style No.	Body Type & Seating	Factory Price	Shipping Weight	Prod. Total
900	0969	4-dr Sed-6P	2335	2470	21,926
900	0927	2-dr Clb Cpe-4P	2281	2445	88,440
900	0967	2-dr Conv-4P	2492	2555	31,045

1964 Chevrolet, Corvair Monza Spyder two-door convertible, 6-cyl (AA)

CORVAIR MONZA SPYDER — (SIX) — SERIES 600 — The Monza Spyder looked a great deal like the Series 900 Monza on the outside. There was a Spyder signature below the Monza badges on the lower front fender and a round "turbocharged" emblem on the rear deck. Also the full wheel covers had special Spyder center inserts. The interior featured full instrumentation and a brushed metal dash insert. While displacement was up 19 cubic inches over the 1963 engine, the 150 hp rating was the same (though the 1964 version developed it at 4000 rpm compared to the 1963 engine's 4400 rpm). Like all 1964 Corvair powerplants, this one had redesigned hardware and gaskets to better seal against oil leakage around the rocker arm covers as this had been a common problem in the past. Also new were finned rear brakes and the addition of a transverse leaf spring to the rear suspension. With all these changes, the 1964 Corvairs were significantly improved automobiles and the Spyder was the best of the lot. Sales, however, dropped by nearly 50 percent.

CORVAIR MONZA SPYDER SERIES 600

Model No.	Body/Style No.	Body Type & Seating	Factory Price	Shipping Weight	Prod. Total
600	0627	2-dr Cpe-4P	2599	2470	6,480
600	0667	2-dr Conv-4P	2811	2580	4,761

ENGINES

(CORVAIR): Horizontally opposed six. Overhead valve. Aluminum block. Displacement: 164 (163.6) cid. Bore and stroke: 3.438 x 2.938 inches. Compression ratio: 8.25:1. Brake hp: 95 at 3600 rpm. Four main bearings. Hydraulic valve lifters. Carburetor: Two Rochester one-barrel Model 7024023.

(MONZA SPYDER SERIES): Horizontally opposed six. Overhead valve. Aluminum block. Displacement: 164 cubic inches. Bore and stroke: 3.438 x 2.938 inches. Compression ratio: 8.25:1. Brake horsepower: 150 at 4000 rpm. Four main bearings. Hydraulic valve lifters. Carburetor: Carter YH one-barrel sidedraft carburetor Model 3817245 with turbocharger.

CHASSIS FEATURES: Wheelbase: (all models) 108 inches. Overall length: (all models) 180 inches. Front tread: (all models) 54.5 inches. Rear tread: (all models) 54.5 inches. Tires: (all models) 6.50 x 14.

OPTIONS: Air conditioning ($350). Rear armrest, Style 0769 only ($10). Pair of front seat belts ($19). Comfort and Convenience equipment, Monza ($28); others ($39). Tinted glass, all windows ($27); windshield only ($13). Padded instrument panel ($16). Spare wheel lock ($5). Two-tone paint ($11). Manual radio ($48). Push-button radio ($57). Push-button radio and front and rear speaker, except convertible ($70). Folding rear seat, Styles 0727, 0769 and all 500s ($27). Four-ply white sidewall tires ($29). Power convertible top ($54). Full wheel covers, standard on Monzas ($11). Wire design wheel covers, 500/700 ($38); Monza ($27). Kelsey-Hayes wire wheels with knock-off hubs, all models ($404). Three-speed manual transmission was standard. Powerglide automatic transmission ($157). Four-speed manual floor shift transmission ($92). Six-cylinder 164 cid/110 hp, 9.25:1 compression engine ($30). Six-cylinder 164 cid/150 hp turbocharged engine (*). Positive traction rear axle ($38). Heavy-duty air cleaner ($17). Heavy-duty clutch (*). Available rear axle gear ratios: 3.27:1; 3.55:1. Generator, 35-ampere ($38).

Options marked (*) are available only as standard equipment on the Monza Spyder.

HISTORICAL FOOTNOTES: The 1964 Corvairs were introduced Sept. 26, 1963. Model year production peaked at 199,387 units. Calendar year production of 195,770 cars was recorded. S.E. Knudsen was the chief executive officer of the company this year. Optional equipment installation rates for Corvairs built to 1964 specifications (including Greenbriers) were as follows: automatic transmission (47 percent); four-speed manual transmission (39.5 percent); radio (92.8 percent); heater (100 percent); bucket seats (79.5 percent); whitewall tires (75 percent); windshield washers (64.8 percent); tinted windshield only (40.5 percent); all tinted glass (7.3 percent); back-up lights (87.6 percent); air conditioning (3.1 percent); limited slip differential (6.8 percent); and wheel covers (82.4 percent).

1965 CORVAIR

CORVAIR 500 — (SIX) — SERIES 101 — The Corvair had a completely new body for 1965 and it was beautiful. *Car and Driver* magazine said, "It unabashedly borrows from the best of the already established foreign and domestic coachwork without losing any of its identity as a Corvair." The new styling was a direct adaptation of the Italian school of industrial design and highlighted smooth-flowing rounded lines; a 'venturi' shaped profile and a pillarless hardtop look on all closed body styles. The Corvair was also two inches wider than before, somewhat lower, and about three inches longer end-to-end. Curved side glass was another innovation. The base Corvair 500 series included Sport Coupe and Sport Sedan. Trim consisted of a horizontal front panel molding, red in color, set directly below the feature line, with a Chevrolet badge at its center; Corvair script above the left-hand headlight housing; rectangular parking lamps set into a smooth bumper underpan; roof gutter rails painted roof colors; nameplates above and behind front wheel opening; Corvair script on right side of engine lid; and small center hubcaps. Standard equipment included directional signals; electric wipers; heater and defroster; all-vinyl interior; twin sun visors; front seat belts; front armrests; locking glovebox; cigarette lighter; coat hooks and interior light.

CORVAIR I.D. NUMBERS: The numbering system and code locations were changed as follows: The Vehicle Identification Number was located on the top face of the left-hand frame side rail, behind the battery bolts. The engine number was on top of the block, behind the oil pressure sending unit. The VIN had 13 symbols. The first symbol '1' designated Chevrolet product. The second and third symbols designated car-line, as follows: '01' = Corvair 500; '05' = Corvair Monza and '07' = Corvair Corsa. The fourth and fifth symbols designated body style as follows: '39' = four-door hardtop (Sport Sedan); '37' = two-door hardtop (Sport Coupe); '67' = convertible. The sixth symbol designated the model year ('5' = 1965). The seventh symbol designated the Chevrolet assembly plant. The following group of symbols was the sequential unit production number, with series in mixed production at a specific plant. Body/Style Numbers (also called model number) were used and correspond to those in second column of the specifications charts below. These numbers were located on the vehicle data plate, on which they were preceeded by a two-digit prefix indicating model year ('65' for 1965). The 1965 Corvair engine number contained a two letter code indicating equipment features as follows: 'RA' = manual transmission; 'RB' = base engine; 'RD' = high-performance; 'RE' = manual transmission/air conditioning; 'RF' = high-performance w/air conditioning; 'RG' = Powerglide; 'RH' = high-performance w/Powerglide; 'RJ' = Powerglide w/air conditioning; 'RK' = high-performance w/Powerglide. RA manual transmission, 95 hp; RB Corsa manual transmission, 140 hp; RD optional manual transmission, 110 hp; RE manual transmission, 95 hp and air conditioning; RF optional manual transmission, 110 hp and air conditioning; RG automatic, 95 hp; RH optional automatic, 110 hp; RJ automatic, 95 hp and air conditioning; RK optional automatic, 110 hp and air conditioning; RL optional (Corsa only) manual, 180 hp; RM optional (except Corsa) manual, 140 hp; RN optional (except Corsa) automatic, 140 hp.

CORVAIR 500

Model No.	Body/Style No.	Body Type & Seating	Factory Price	Shipping Weight	Prod. Total
101	10139	4-dr HT Spt Sed-6P	2096	2405	17,560
101	10137	2-dr HT Spt Cpe-4P	2022	2385	36,747

1965 Chevrolet, Corvair Corsa two-door convertible, 6-cyl (AA)

CORVAIR MONZA — (SIX) — SERIES 105 — Monzas now represented the mid-price Corvair models, as the Corvair 700 line was dropped. Standard equipment included all items found on the lower priced cars plus full wheel covers; rocker sill moldings; front bucket seats; carpeting; courtesy and glovebox lights; front armrests; rear armrests were not standard (nor available) on two-door coupe styles; back-up lights; and folding rear seats on Sport Coupe and Sport Sedan. As in the past, a Monza badge, consisting of a vertical bar passing through a V-shaped horizontal ornament, was seen on the lower front fenders behind the wheel opening. Whereas the Corvair 500 had only red, aqua or fawn interior color choices, the Monza had no aqua, but blue, black, saddle, slate, and white available with aqua or black accents, depending on exterior color. The rear panel, to which the engine lid latched, was outlined with a chrome molding. A convertible was also provided in this series and came standard with a manual top and top boot. A handsome new feature of all Corvairs was a slanted-back instrument panel with deep tunnels containing the gauges. On Series 500 and Monza models they housed a speedometer, gas gauge, warning lights and, if ordered, an optional electric clock.

CORVAIR MONZA

Model No.	Body/Style No.	Body Type & Seating	Factory Price	Shipping Weight	Prod. Total
105	10539	4-dr HT Spt Sed-6P	2370	2465	37,157
105	10537	2-dr HT Spt Cpe-4P	2297	2440	88,954
105	10567	2-dr Conv-4P	2440	2675	26,466

CORVAIR CORSA — (SIX) — SERIES 107 — The Corvair Corsa models were the top line models in 1965. They earned Corsa lettering on the front fender cowlsides, below the main feature line (just under the new, square gas filler door). In addition, a Corsa badge was placed just ahead of the rear wheel opening. It had an oval-shaped ornament with a 'C' in the middle, flanked by vertical bars running up and down. Standard equipment included all items featured with Monzas, plus electric clock; tachometer; oil pressure gauge; temperature gauge; Satin Silver special ornamentation; and special interior trim. There was also a difference in base motivation, the Corsa coming standard with a high-compression 164-cid flat six that put out 140 hp and inducted

fuel and air through four single-barrel Rochester carburetors. An important advance on all 1965 Corvairs was a new, Corvette-like, fully independent rear suspension with upper axle half-shafts; lower equal-length trailing torque arms; rubber-bushed rods; and coil springs at each corner. It was complemented by an improved front suspension. Handling with this system was much better than in the past.

1965 Chevrolet, Corvair Corsa two-door hardtop Sport Coupe, 6-cyl

CORVAIR CORSA

Model No.	Body/Style No.	Body Type & Seating	Factory Price	Shipping Weight	Prod. Total
107	10731	2-dr HT Spt Cpe-4P	2465	2475	20,291
107	10767	2-dr Conv-4P	2608	2710	8,353

ENGINES

(500/MONZA SIX) Horizontally opposed six. Overhead valve. Aluminum block. Displacement: 164 cid. Bore and stroke: 3.438 x 2.938 inches. Compression ratio: 8.25:1. Brake hp: 95 at 3600 rpm. Four main bearings. Hydraulic valve lifters. Carburetor: Two Rochester one-barrel Model 7025023.

(CORSA SIX) Horizontally opposed six. Overhead valve. Aluminum block. Displacement: 164 cid. Bore and stroke: 3.438 x 2.938 inches. Compression ratio: 9.25:1. Brake hp: 140 at 5200 rpm. Four main bearings. Hydraulic valve lifters. Carburetor: Four Rochester one-barrel Model 7025023 with progressive linkage.

CHASSIS FEATURES: Wheelbase: (all models) 108 inches. Overall length: (all models) 183.3 inches. Front tread: (all models) 55 inches. Rear tread: (all models) 56.6 inches. Tires: (all models) 6.50 x 13.

OPTIONS: All-weather air conditioning, Series 500 or Monza, not with 140-hp six ($350). Rear antenna, in place of front-mounted antenna (no charge). Rear armrest, Style 10139 ($10). Tinted glass, all windows ($27); windshield only ($13). Front or rear bumper guards ($10). Padded instrument panels ($16). Spare wheel lock, all ($5). Two-tone paint, available on Style 10139 only ($11). Manual radio with front antenna ($50). Push-button radio with front antenna ($59). AM/FM push-button radio with front antenna ($137). Seat belts with retractor ($8). Folding rear seat, as option ($27). Sport-style steering wheel ($32). Telescopic steering shaft, includes Sport-style wheel ($75). White sidewall tires size 6.50 x 13, four-ply ($29). Power top for all convertibles ($54). Wheel covers, on 500 series models ($11). Wire design wheel covers, on 500 series ($70); on Monza/Corsa ($59). Delete options for credit, heater/defroster ($72 credit); seat belts ($11 credit). 500 Series Convenience Group, includes: left outside rearview mirror; non-glare inside mirror; two-speed wiper/washer; back-up and glovebox lights ($39). Monza/Corsa Comfort and Convenience Group, includes: all the above, less back-up and glovebox lights, which are standard. Comfort and Convenience Group 'B' includes all the above with left outside rearview remote-control mirror, 500 series ($48); others ($38). Three-speed manual transmission was standard. Powerglide automatic transmission, in 500 and Monza series ($157). Four-speed manual floor shift transmission ($92). Monza and 500 six-cylinder 164 cid/110 hp Turbo-Air engine ($27). Monza and 500 six-cylinder 164 cid/140 hp Turbo-Air engine ($81). Corsa series six-cylinder 164 cid/180 hp turbocharged engine ($161). Positive traction rear axle ($38). Heavy-duty air cleaner, 500 or Monza without air conditioning or 140-hp six ($32). Available rear axle gear ratios: 3.27:1 and 3.55:1. Heavy-duty 70-ampere battery ($8). Delcotron 47-ampere generator, standard with air conditioning; ($16) on others.

HISTORICAL FOOTNOTES: The 1965 Corvairs were introduced Sept. 24, 1964. Model year production peaked at 235,500 units. Calendar year sales of 204,007 cars were recorded. S.E. Knudsen was the chief executive officer of the company this year. Of all Corvairs built during the 1965 model year, 53.1 percent had automatic transmission; 33.6 percent had four-speed gearboxes; 62.9 percent had radios; 99.2 percent had heaters; 16.9 percent had bucket seats; 92.6 percent had seat belts; 73.9 had white sidewall tires; 69.2 percent had windshield washers; 40.2 percent had tinted windshields only; 9.6 percent had all windows tinted; 86.8 percent had back-up lights; 4.0 percent had air conditioning; 3.7 percent had telescopic steering shafts; 6.1 percent had limited-slip differential and 80.7 percent had wheel covers. The turbocharged Corsair could move from 0 to 60 mph in under 11 seconds and cover the quarter-mile in around 18 seconds hitting 79 mph in the process. Top speed was over 113 mph.

1966 CORVAIR

CORVAIR 500 — (SIX) — SERIES 101 — Styling refinements including a new one-piece rear grille and taillights were featured in the Corvair for 1966. Slimmer moldings were used to accent the wheel openings front and rear. The front panel trim bar was widened and had a blue painted center section. The V-shaped Chevrolet ornament in the center was not quite as large end-to-end, but a little fatter. The Corvair signature was moved (from above the headlights) back onto the front panel, where it was positioned, on the left-hand side, at a rakish angle. The 500 models featured an expanded list of standard equipment, such as padded dash; padded sun visors; back-up lights; two-speed wipers; windshield washers; left outside rear-

view mirror; cigarette lighter; coat hooks; locking glovebox; interior lamps; and rear seat belts. A more luxurious all-vinyl interior was seen. Technical advances included a fully-synchromesh three-speed transmission (with both manual gearboxes being highly refined); larger 7.00 x 13 standard tires; and the spoiler below the bumper, which improved both handling and gas mileage.

1966 Chevrolet, Corvair 500 Series four-door hardtop Sport Sedan, 6-cyl

CORVAIR I.D. NUMBERS: The numbering system and code locations were the same as for previous models with the sixth symbol changed to a '6' to indicate the 1966 model year. Several new engine number codes appeared as follows: 'RQ' = special high-performance with exhaust emissions system; 'RR' = air conditioned; 'RT' = base engine with exhaust emissions system; 'RV' = Powerglide with exhaust emissions system; 'RW' = high-performance with exhaust emissions system and 'RY' = special high-performance with Powerglide and air conditioning. Codes 'RV' and 'RX', as used in 1965, were changed or deleted, while all other 1965 codes were applicable again. RQ optional 140 hp, manual transmission, Air*; RR Corsa 140 hp, manual transmission, air conditioning; RS standard 95 hp, manual transmission, Air*; RV standard 95 hp, automatic transmission, Air*; RU optional 110 hp, manual transmission, Air*; RY optional 140 hp, automatic transmission, air conditioning; RW optional 110 hp, automatic transmission, Air*; RT Corsa 140 hp, Air*.

Air* — air injection reactor (Emissions Control)

CORVAIR 500

Model No.	Body/Style No.	Body Type & Seating	Factory Price	Shipping Weight	Prod. Total
101	10139	4-dr HT Spt Sed-6P	2157	2445	8,779
101	10137	2-dr HT Spt Cpe-5P	2083	2400	24,045

CORVAIR MONZA — (SIX) — SERIES 105 — The Monza was easy to spot. On the lower front fender, behind the wheel opening, was a badge that looked like a stylized airplane with delta wings flying straight down. The center of the badge was black-finished and carried the word Monza across its 'wings'. There were chrome outline moldings around the rear deck panel; thin rocker panel moldings; bright metal roof gutter trim and wheel covers with the delta-winged logo in the center. Standard extras included front bucket seats; carpeting; luggage compartment mat; automatic dome and glovebox lights; fold-down rear seat on closed styles; front and rear ashtrays and rear foam seat cushions. Pleated upholstery with metal buttons was seen.

1966 Chevrolet, Corvair Monza two-door Sport Coupe, 6-cyl (PH)

CORVAIR MONZA

Model No.	Body/Style No.	Body Type & Seating	Factory Price	Shipping Weight	Prod. Total
105	10539	4-dr HT Spt Sed-5P	2424	2495	12,497
105	10537	2-dr HT Spt Cpe-4P	2350	2445	37,605
105	10567	2-dr Conv-4P	2493	2675	10,345

1966 Chevrolet, Corvair Corsa two-door convertible, 6-cyl

CORVAIR CORSA — (SIX) — SERIES 107 — In its last season, the sporty high-performance Corsa still clung to a few visual distinctions to set it apart from more lowly models. Most evident was Corsa front fender lettering above and behind the wheel opening and below the body feature line. There were special Corsa ornaments ahead of the rear wheel openings; a Satin Silver finished engine lid latch panel; and an emblem that read "140" or "Turbocharged", depending upon the engine ordered, at the center of the engine lid. The wheel covers had special turbine-style center inserts with the Corsa "C-inside-an-oval" badge at the middle. This badge was also seen on the special steering wheel hub insert. Standard equipment included everything found with Monzas, plus full instrumentation; tachometer; oil pressure gauge and temperature gauge. For 1966, three special colors: Marina blue, Lemonwood yellow and Chateau slate came only on Monzas and Corsas.

CORVAIR CORSA

Model No.	Body/Style No.	Body Type & Seating	Factory Price	Shipping Weight	Prod. Total
107	10737	2-dr HT Spt Cpe-4P	2519	2485	7,330
107	10767	2-dr Conv-4P	2662	2720	3,142

ENGINES

(500/MONZA SIX) Horizontally opposed six. Overhead valve. Aluminum block. Displacement: 164 cid. Bore and stroke: 3.438 x 2.938 inches. Compression ratio: 8.25:1. Brake hp: 95 at 3600 rpm. Four main bearings. Hydraulic valve lifters. Carburetor: Two Rochester one-barrel Model 7026023.

(CORSA SIX) Horizontally opposed six. Overhead valve. Aluminum block. Displacement: 164 cid. Bore and stroke: 3.438 x 2.938 inches. Compression ratio: 9.25:1. Brake hp: 140 at 5200 rpm. Four main bearings. Hydraulic valve lifters. Carburetor: Four Rochester one-barrel Model 7026023 with progressive linkage.

CHASSIS FEATURES: Wheelbase: (all models) 108 inches. Overall length: (all models) 184 inches. Front tread: (all models) 55 inches. Rear tread: (All models) 56.6 inches. Tires: (all models) 7.00 x 14.

OPTIONS: All-weather air conditioning, Series 500 or Monza, not with 140-hp six ($350). Rear antenna, in place of front mounted antenna (no charge). Rear armrest, Style 10139 ($10). Tinted glass, all windows ($27); windshield only ($13). Front or rear bumper guards ($10). Padded instrument panels ($16). Spare wheel lock, all ($5). Two-tone paint available on Model 10139 only ($11). Manual radio with front antenna ($50). Push-button radio with front antenna ($59). AM/FM push-button radio with front antenna ($137). Seat belts with retractor ($8). Folding rear seat, as option ($27). Sport-style steering wheel ($32). Telescopic steering shaft, includes Sport-style wheel ($75). White sidewall tires, size 6.50 x 13, four-ply ($29). Power top for all convertibles ($54). Wheel covers, on 500 series models ($11). Wire design wheels covers, on 500 series ($70); on Monza/Corsa ($59). Delete options for credit, heater/defroster ($72 credit); seat belts ($11 credit). 500 Series Convenience Group, includes left outside rearview mirror; non-glare inside mirror; two-speed wiper/washer; back-up and glovebox lights ($39). Monza/Corsa Comfort and Convenience Group, includes all the above, less back-up and glovebox lights, which are standard. Comfort and Convenience Group 'B' includes all the above with left outside rearview remote-control mirror, 500 series ($48); others ($38). Three-speed manual transmission was standard. Powerglide automatic transmission, in 500 and Monza series ($157). Four-speed manual floor shift transmission ($92). Monza and 500 six-cylinder 164 cid/110 hp Turbo-Air engine ($27). Monza and 500 six-cylinder 164 cid/140 hp Turbo-Air engine ($81). Corsa series six-cylinder 164 cid/180 hp turbocharged engine ($161). Positive traction rear axle ($38). Heavy-duty air cleaner, 500 or Monza without air conditioning or 140-hp six ($32). Available rear axle gear ratios: 3.27:1 and 3.55:1. Heavy-duty 70-ampere battery ($8). Delcotron 47-ampere generator, standard with air conditioning; ($16) on others.

HISTORICAL FOOTNOTES: The 1966 Corvairs were introduced Oct. 7, 1965. Model year production peaked at 103,743 units. Calendar year production of 73,360 cars was recorded. E.M. Estes was the chief executive officer of the company this year. For the 1966 Corvair model year, optional equipment percentage installation rates were as follows (percentages in parenthesis): automatic transmission (57.2); four-speed manual transmission (26.7); radio (61.4); heater (99); telescopic steering shaft (2.2); bucket seats (68.4); whitewall tires (68); tinted windshield only (39.5); all glass tinted (8.4); air conditioning (4.6); limited-slip axle (6.8); wheel covers (73.6); power antenna (0.4) and non-glare rearview mirror (4.9). At the end of the year, Chevrolet announced plans for a major expansion of its Willow Run, Mich., assembly plant.

1967 CORVAIR

1967 Chevrolet, Corvair 500 Series two-door hardtop Sport Coupe, 6-cyl

CORVAIR 500 — (SIX) — SERIES 101 — The high-priced Corvair Corsa series was dropped for 1967, leaving only five models in hardtops and convertibles. New Strato bucket seats and oval-shaped steering wheels were seen. A wider bezel was used on the taillamps from early 1966 on. Dash padding was heavier; the window handle knobs were color-keyed plastic covered and the Powerglide transmission was no longer operated via a T-handle. Now a more conventional knob was used. Otherwise, appearance aspects were about identical to 1966. An eight-track solid state stereo tape player was a new option, and 7.00 x 13 tires were used. Standard in Corvair 500 models were all federally mandated safety equipment (called "GM Safety Features"); closed positive crankcase ventilation; all-vinyl interior; cigarette lighter; interior light; foam-cushioned front seat; front door armrest; three-speed manual full-synchromesh transmission and 95 hp 'Turbo-Air 164' six-cylinder engine.

CORVAIR I.D. NUMBERS: The numbering system and code locations were the same as for previous models with the sixth symbol changed to a '7' to indicate the 1967 model year. No new 'R' engine codes were used, although several were dropped. There was, however, a completely different group of codes, beginning with letter 'Q'. All of these included exhaust emission controls for California sale. They were as follows: 'QM' = manual transmission and air conditioning; 'QO' = Powerglide w/air conditioning; 'QP' = high-performance w/Powerglide and 'QS' = high-performance w/manual transmission and air conditioning. QM 95 hp manual, air conditioning and Air*; QO 95 hp automatic, air conditioning and Air*; QP 110 hp automatic, air conditioning and Air*; QS 110 hp manual, air conditioning and Air*.

*Air — air injection reactor (Emissions Control)

CORVAIR 500

Model No.	Body/Style No.	Body Type & Seating	Factory Price	Shipping Weight	Prod. Total
101	10139	4-dr HT Spt Sed-6P	2194	2470	2,959
101	10137	2-dr HT Spt Cpe-5P	2128	2435	9,257

1967 Chevrolet, Corvair Monza four-door Sport Sedan, 6-cyl (AA)

CORVAIR MONZA — (SIX) — SERIES 105 — Appearance distinctions of the 1967 Monza were the same as seen the year before. They included full wheel covers with Monza 'delta-wing' insignia; rocker panel moldings; 'delta-wing' fenderside badges behind front wheel openings; bright metal roof gutter rail moldings; wheel opening moldings and rear panel outline trim. The Monza came with all equipment included on Corvair 500 models plus dual headlamps; front lockable trunk; bucket seats; carpeting; luggage compartment mat; automatic dome and glovebox lights; fold-down rear seat (except convertibles); speedometer, odometer, fuel gauge, generator and temperature warning lights; front and rear ashtrays and rear foam seat cushions. The turbocharged engine was no longer available. The 140-hp option was deleted and, then, reinstated. New for this year was General Motors' first engine/drivetrain five-year warranty.

CORVAIR MONZA

Model No.	Body/Style No.	Body Type & Seating	Factory Price	Shipping Weight	Prod. Total
105	10539	4-dr HT Spt Sed-5P	2464	2515	3,157
105	10537	2-dr HT Spt Cpe-4P	2398	2465	9,771
105	10567	2-dr Conv-4P	2540	2695	2,109

CORVAIR ENGINE: Horizontally opposed six. Overhead valve. Aluminum block. Displacement: 164 cid. Bore and stroke: 3.438 x 2.938 inches. Compression ratio: 8.25:1. Brake hp: 95 at 3600 rpm. Four main bearings. Hydraulic valve lifters. Carburetor: Two Rochester one-barrel Model 7026023.

CHASSIS FEATURES: Wheelbase: (all models) 108 inches. Overall length: (all models) 183 inches. Front tread: (all models) 55 inches. Rear tread: (all models) 56.6 inches. Tires: (all models) 7.00 x 13.

OPTIONS: All-weather air conditioning ($342). Rear manual antenna, substitution (no charge). Center rear seat belt ($6). Front and rear Custom Deluxe seat belts ($6). Center rear seat belt, Custom Deluxe type ($8). Custom Deluxe front shoulder belts, with Custom Deluxe Group ($26). Standard front shoulder belt ($23). Electric clock, all models ($16). Door edge guards, four-door ($6); two-door ($3). Tinted glass, all windows ($31);

windshield only ($21). Front or rear bumper guards ($10). Two-tone paint, available on Model 10139 only ($16). Push-button radio; with front antenna ($57); and rear speaker ($71). AM/FM push-button radio, with front antenna and rear speaker ($133). Eight-Track stereo-tape system, includes quad speakers ($129). White, black or blue power convertible top ($53). Deluxe steering wheel, 500 ($7); Monza ($4); telescoping type ($42). Speed warning indicator ($11). Special purpose (heavy-duty) front and rear suspension ($11). Mag-style wheel covers, 500 ($73); Monza ($63). Simulated wire wheel covers, 500 ($69); Monza ($58). Whitewall tires ($28). Folding rear seat, 500 series ($26). Appearance Guard Group ($39-$42). Auxiliary Lighting Group ($714). Three-speed manual transmission was standard. Four-speed manual floor shift transmission, with 95 hp only ($90). Monza and 500 six-cylinder 184 cid/110 hp Turbo-Air engine ($26). Monza six-cylinder 164 cid/140 hp Turbo-Air engine ($79). Positive traction rear axle ($42). Heavy-duty air cleaner ($6). Available rear axle gear ratios: 3.27:1 and 3.55:1. Air injection reactor, mandatory California cars ($45). Heavy-duty 70-ampere battery ($7). Heavy-duty 47-ampere Delcotron ($16).

HISTORICAL FOOTNOTES: The 1967 Corvairs were introduced Sept. 29, 1966. Model year production peaked at 27,253 units. Calendar year production of 18,703 cars was recorded. E.M. Estes was the chief executive officer of the company this year. For the 1967 model year, optional equipment installation rates (percentages in parenthesis) were as follows: automatic (67.9); four-speed (14.8); AM radio (63.6); air conditioning (5.1); telescoping steering column (1.1); bucket seats (55.2); white sidewall tires (60.8); tinted windshield only (34.7); all tinted glass (7.5); limited-slip axle (4.8); wheel covers (64.2); AM/FM radio (1.3); and electric clock (6.9).

1968 CORVAIR

CORVAIR 500 — (SIX) — SERIES 101 — Model availability for the Corvair dropped from five to three for the 1968 model year. The Monza Sport Sedan and the 500 Sport Sedan were discontinued. This eliminated all four-door styles from the lineup. Side marker lamps on the front and rear fenders are the easy way to spot a 1968 model from past editions. A look inside will reveal a dash with even more stuffing and padded windshield pillar posts. What else was new? A larger floor shift lever knob; restyled, padded armrests; new vinyl upholstery fabrics and, on Jan. 1, 1968, shoulder safety belts became mandatory. The Corvair 500 coupe came with all GM Safety Features; cigarette lighter; heater and defroster (no longer deletable); 7.00 x 13 two-ply, four-ply rated blackwall tires and the 95 hp 'Turbo-Air' six. The four-carb 'TurboAir 140' engine was still optional. Hubcaps were standard.

CORVAIR I.D. NUMBERS: The numbering system and code locations were the same as for previous models with

the sixth symbol indicating 1968 model year. Engine/equipment combinations were down to eight choices, coded as follows: 'RS' = manual transmission; 'RM' = high-performance; 'RF' = high-performance with air conditioning; 'RW' = high-performance with Powerglide; 'RJ' = Powerglide with air conditioning; 'RK' = high-performance with Powerglide and air conditioning; 'RE' = air conditioning and 'RV' = Powerglide. NOTE: Not explained is why engine codes with air conditioning are listed, although this particular factory option was dropped! RS 95 hp, manual transmission; RU 110 hp, manual transmission; RV 95 hp, automatic transmission; RW 110 hp, automatic transmission; RY 140 hp, manual transmission; RZ 140 hp, automatic transmission.

1968 Chevrolet, Corvair 500 Series two-door Sport Coupe, 6-cyl

CORVAIR 500

Model No.	Body/Style No.	Body Type & Seating	Factory Price	Shipping Weight	Prod. Total
101	10137	2-dr HT Spt Cpe-5P	2243	2470	7,206

1968 Chevrolet, Corvair Monza two-door Sport Coupe, 6 cyl (AA)

CORVAIR MONZA — (SIX) — SERIES 105 — The Monza had all features found on the Corvair 500, plus glovebox light; dual headlamps; front bucket seats; carpeting; courtesy lights (in convertible) and folding rear seat (in coupe). Appearance extras were full wheel covers; chrome roof gutter strips; rocker panel moldings; rear panel outline trim strips and Monza inverted 'delta-wing' badges behind the front wheel opening, plus wheel lip moldings and high-grade interior trimmings in blue, black or gold. The folding rear seat had an improved latching mechanism instead of the old, hard to operate, friction type.

CORVAIR MONZA

Model No.	Body/Style No.	Body Type & Seating	Factory Price	Shipping Weight	Prod. Total
105	10537	2-dr HT Spt Cpe-4P	2507	2500	6,807
105	10567	2-dr Conv-4P	2626	2725	1,386

CORVAIR ENGINE: Horizontally opposed six. Overhead valve. Aluminum block. Displacement: 164 cid. Bore and stroke: 3.438 x 2.938 inches. Compression ratio: 8.25:1. Brake hp: 95 at 3600 rpm. Four main bearings. Hydraulic valve lifters. Carburetor: Two Rochester one-barrel Model 7028005.

CHASSIS FEATURES: Wheelbase: (all models) 108 inches. Overall length: (all models) 183 inches. Front tread: (all models) 55 inches. Rear tread: (all models) 56.6 inches. Tires: (all models) 7.00 x 13.

OPTIONS: Rear manual antenna, except with AM/FM ($10). Front and rear Custom Deluxe shoulder belts, with bucket seats ($8). Front and rear Custom Deluxe shoulder belts, with full-width seats ($10). Pair of front shoulder belts, standard type ($23); front and rear ($46). Custom Deluxe shoulder belts, front pair ($26); front and rear ($53). Electric clock ($16). Rear window defroster, except convertible ($21). Door edge guards, all ($4). Tinted glass, all windows ($31); windshield only ($21). Head restraints, pair, in 500 ($42); in Monza ($52). Spare wheel lock ($5). Twin front and rear floor mats, all ($11). Left outside rearview remote-control mirror, all ($10). Radios, push-button with front antenna ($61); same AM/FM ($134). Rear speaker, except with stereo ($13). Folding rear seat, 500 series, standard in Monza coupe ($32). Speed warning indicator ($11). Adjustable steering column ($42). Deluxe steering wheel, 500 coupe ($7); Monzas ($4); Sport-style steering wheel, all models ($32). Stereo tape system, includes quadraphonic ($134). Special purpose front and rear suspension ($11). Whitewall tires, 7.00 x 13 4-ply ($28). Power convertible top ($53). Wheel covers, standard in 500 ($21); mag-style, in 500 ($74); mag-style in Monza ($63); wire-style in 500 ($69); wire-style in Monza ($56). Appearance Guard Group ($34). Three-speed manual transmission was standard. Automatic transmission, all ($153). Four-speed manual floor shift transmission, all ($90). Turbo-Air six-cylinder 164 cid/110 hp, 9.25:1 compression engine ($26). Turbo-Air six-cylinder 164 cid/140 hp four-carb engine ($79). Heavy-duty 70-ampere battery ($7). Positive traction rear axle ($42). Heavy-duty air cleaner ($6). Available rear axle gear ratios: availability depends on power teams.

HISTORICAL FOOTNOTES: The 1968 Corvairs were introduced Sept. 21, 1967. Model year production peaked at 15,400 units. Calendar year production of 11,490 cars was recorded. John Z. DeLorean was the chief executive officer of the company this year. For the 1968 model year, optional equipment installation rates (percentages in parenthesis) were as follows: automatic (70); AM radio (66); telescoping steering wheel (1.5); bucket seats (53); whitewalls (58); tinted windshield only (23); all glass tinted (10); limited-slip axle (7); wheel covers (63); AM/FM radio (4) and stereo tape system (0.5).

1969 CORVAIR

CORVAIR 500 — (SIX) — SERIES 101 — Aside from color choices, the 1969 interiors were identical to 1968. Two coupes and one convertible were offered in the last season of Corvair production. Appearance changes were minor. They included a bigger rearview mirror and amber front side marker lens. The Corvair 500 came with front headrests as a mandatory option; cigarette lighter; heater and defroster; 7.00 x 13 four-ply rated blackwall tires and unchanged 95 hp Turbo-Air engine. Vinyl interiors now came in black, blue and medium green.

CORVAIR I.D. NUMBERS: The numbering system and code locations were the same as for previous models with the sixth symbol changed to a '9' to indicate 1969 model year. Engine identification codes were the same as in 1968.

CORVAIR 500

Model No.	Body/Style No.	Body Type & Seating	Factory Price	Shipping Weight	Prod. Total
101	10137	2-dr HT Cpe-5P	2258	2515	2,762

1969 Chevrolet, Corvair Monza two-door Sport Coupe, 6-cyl

CORVAIR MONZA — (SIX) — SERIES 105 — The Monza came with all equipment found on the base-line coupes, plus glovebox light; dual headlamps; front bucket seats; courtesy lights (in convertible) and folding rear seat (in coupe). Appearance distinctions were identical to those of the 1968 Monza. An Olympic gold Monza, serial number 105379W706000 was the last Covair built.

CORVAIR MONZA

Model No.	Body/Style No.	Body Type & Seating	Factory Price	Shipping Weight	Prod. Total
105	10537	2-dr HT Cpe-4P	2522	2545	2,717
105	10567	2-dr Conv-4P	2641	2770	521

HISTORICAL FOOTNOTES: The 1969 Corvairs were introduced Sept. 26, 1968. Model year production peaked at 6,000 units. Calendar year sales of 3,103 cars were recorded. John Z. DeLorean was the chief executive officer of the company this year. For the 1969 model year, optional equipment installation rates (percentages in parenthesis) were as follows: Powerglide (2); four-speed gearbox (14); AM radio (80); AM/FM radio (3); bucket seats (54); whitewall tires (55); tinted windshield (0.1); all tinted glass (26); posi-traction (8); standard wheel covers (54); optional wheel covers (13); electric clock (11); telescoping steering wheel (2.5). In mid-May 1969, Chevrolet offered Corvair buyers a $150 discount coupon to use in purchasing any new Chevrolet from then until 1973. The idea was to compensate for any lost resale value experienced due to the discontinuance of the Corvair. Today, these cars hold a small premium in the collector market for being last-year models.

CORVETTE

1953-1975

1964 Chevrolet, Corvette Sting Ray two-door coupe and convertible, V-8 (PH)

The 1953 Corvette was based on the 1952 EX-122 show car. It was one of the few Motorama dream cars to actually go into production with the styling virtually unchanged.

The Corvette was created as an economical sports car for young adults. It was also something that could be used as a performance-image builder while Chevrolet waited for its V-8. The car's fiberglass body was not only novel, but practical. It lowered the cost of production in limited numbers and expedited the Corvette's debut. Steel-bodied models were originally planned for later model years.

By Charles Webb

Sports car enthusiast and TV celebrity Dave Garroway heaped a lot of praise on the pretty new Corvette in the Chevrolet sales promotion film "Halls of Wonder." Yet, many of the sports car fans it was meant for snubbed it. They harbored a prejudice that nothing good could come out of Detroit and certainly not from Chevrolet. Remember, at the time, a "Chevy" was the car mothers drove to the grocery store to pick up peanut butter and jelly for their childrens' lunch. The marque did not have a hot-car image yet. The fact that Corvettes used standard 'family car' mechanical components and came with a Powerglide automatic transmission were other points of criticism.

Most of the people who knocked the 'Vette never drove one. As *Road & Track* said of the 1954 version, "The outstanding characteristic of the Corvette is probably its deceptive performance."

The car looked the same in 1955, but the 265-cid V-8 made it much hotter. Unfortunately, like a beautiful debutante with a black belt in karate, its appearance belied its power. Sales were so bad Chevrolet management was on the verge of killing the Corvette. However, when Ford came out with its two-passenger Thunderbird, the company was forced, for competitive reasons, to continue production.

Sales shot up dramatically in 1956. One of the main reasons was the Corvette now had looks to match its performance. A manual transmission, roll-up side windows and lockable doors also added to its appeal. And several prestigious racing victories contributed to its performance image.

With the introduction of fuel-injection in 1957, advertising proclaimed, "For the first time in automotive history — one horsepower for every cubic inch." Chrysler 300 fans knew better, but it did make good copy and sales once again increased.

The clean, classic styling of 1956 and 1957 was jazzed-up in 1958. Although the basic design was attractive, the chrome-laden 1958 is generally considered the gaudiest Corvette. But, apparently, that's what the public wanted and sales climbed significantly over the previous year's model.

Some of the excess glitter was removed in 1959. In 1961, the Corvette received a new 'duck tail' rear end treatment. Two years later, in a major restyling, the 1963s were an immediate hit. Demand was so great many customers had to wait two months or more to take delivery of their new Sting Ray coupe or ragtop. By now, Corvette's reputation as a powerful sports car was firmly established on the track and street.

A four-passenger Corvette was considered for 1963. It might have been quite successful. Thunderbird sales soared when it went that route in 1958. However, the T-bird never really claimed to be a true sports car; it was a 'sporty' personal car. Putting a back seat in the Corvette might have hurt its image.

The basic aerodynamic styling introduced in 1968 would remain until 1983. After the early 1970s, Corvettes became significantly tamer. Still, when you mention performance, the American car that comes first to most peoples' minds is Corvette.

1958 Chevrolet, Corvette two-door convertible, V-8

1959 Chevrolet, Corvette two-door convertible with hardtop, V-8

1954 Chevrolet, Corvette two-door roadster, 6-cyl

1954 Chevrolet, Corvette two-door roadster, 6-cyl

1960 Chevrolet, Corvette two-door convertible, V-8

1956 Chevrolet, Corvette two-door convertible, V-8

1961 Chevrolet, Corvette two-door convertible, V-8

1963 Chevrolet, Corvette Sting Ray two-door convertible, V-8

1966 Chevrolet, Corvette Sting Ray two-door convertible with hardtop, V-8

1969 Chevrolet, Corvette Stingray two-door T-top coupe, V-8

1963 Chevrolet, Corvette Sting Ray two-door convertible, V-8

Rodin's "The Thinker" seems to be pondering which of these 24 1956 Corvettes would he like to own.

1953 CORVETTE

CORVETTE — (6-CYL) — SERIES E2934 — The new 1953 Corvette had a fiberglass body, chrome-framed grille with 13 heavy vertical chrome bars, rounded front fenders with recessed headlights, no side windows or outside door handles, a wraparound windshield and protruding, fender-integrated taillights. The interior featured a floor-mounted shifter, Powerglide automatic and a full array of gauges including a tachometer. Each 1953 Corvette was virtually hand-built and a lot of minor changes were made during the production run.

CORVETTE I.D. NUMBERS: The Corvette used the standard Chevrolet coding system. It consisted of a total of 10 symbols, except for V-8s, which in some years utilized 11 symbols. The first symbol was an 'E' for 1953-1957 models and a 'J' for 1958-1959 models. The second and third symbols designated model year, for example '53' = 1953. The fourth symbol designated the manufacturing plant, as follows: F=Flint, Mich., and S=St. Louis, Mo. The following group of numbers (usually six digits) was the sequential unit production number. Corvettes, for 1953, were numbered E53F001001 to E53F001300. The serial number was located on the left front door hinge pillar post. Engine numbers were found on the right-hand side of the crankcase, behind the distributor. The engine numbers for 1953 models used the prefix 'LAY'. Since Corvette bodies were virtually handmade, they did not carry standard Fisher Body/Style Numbers, as did other GM cars. The Corvette model number consisted of four symbols, '2934', which also served as the body/style number for the early production years.

1953 Chevrolet, Corvette two-door roadster, 6-cyl (AA)

CORVETTE

Model No.	Body/Style No.	Body Type & Seating	Factory Price	Shipping Weight	Prod. Total
2934	2934	2-dr Rds-2P	3498	2705	300

ENGINE: Inline six. Overhead valve. Cast iron block. Displacement: 235.5 cid. Bore and stroke: 3.56 x 3.93 inches.

Compression ratio: 8.0:1. Brake hp: 150 at 4200 rpm. Carburetor: Three Carter Type YH one-barrel Model 2066S (early models); Model 2055S (late models).

CHASSIS FEATURES: Wheelbase: 102 inches. Overall length: 167 inches. Front tread: 57 inches. Rear tread: 59 inches. Tires: 6.70 x 15.

OPTIONS: Signal-seeking AM radio ($145.15). Heater ($91.40). White sidewall tires.

HISTORICAL FOOTNOTES: The first Corvette was built on June 30, 1953, at the Flint, Mich., assembly plant. Model year production peaked at 200 units. Calendar year sales of 300 cars was recorded. T.H. Keating was the chief executive officer of Chevrolet this year. By early 1954, Chevrolet announced that 315 Corvettes had been built and that production of the model had been shifted to the assembly plant in St. Louis. Programming, at that point, called for production of 1,000 Corvettes per month by June 1954. The company predicted that 10,000 per year could be built and sold.

1954 CORVETTE

CORVETTE SERIES — (6-CYL) — SERIES E2934 — For all practical purposes, the 1953 and 1954 Corvettes were the same. Minor changes were made to the window storage bag, air cleaners, starter and location of the fuel and brake lines. Unlike the previous year's model, 1954s were available in Pennant blue, Sportsman red and black in addition to Polo white. The softtop was now offered only in beige.

1954 Chevrolet, Corvette two-door roadster, 6-cyl (AA)

CORVETTE I.D. NUMBERS: The numbering system and code locations were the same as for previous models. Serial numbers were E54S001001 to E54S004640. Engine numbers, for 1954, had the suffix 'YG'.

CORVETTE

Model No.	Body/Style No.	Body Type & Seating	Factory Price	Shipping Weight	Prod. Total
2934	2934	2-dr Rds-2P	3523	2705	3,640

ENGINE: Inline Six. Overhead valve. Cast iron block. Displacement: 235.5 cid. Bore and stroke: 3.56 x 3.93 inches. Compression ratio: 8.0:1. Brake hp: 150 at 4200 rpm. Four main bearings. Solid valve lifters. Carburetor: Three Carter one-barrel Type YH Model 2066SA.

NOTE: Later in the model year, a new camshaft upped horsepower to 155.

CHASSIS FEATURES: Wheelbase: 102 inches. Overall length: 167 inches. Front tread: 57 inches. Rear tread: 59 inches. Tires: 6.70 x 15. Signal-seeking AM radio ($145.15). Heater ($91.40). Windshield washer ($11.85). Parking brake alarm ($5.65). Powerglide transmission standard. Various rear axle ratios.

HISTORICAL FOOTNOTES: Approximately 80 percent of 1954 Corvettes were painted white. About 16 percent had a blue exterior. A 1954 Corvette could go from 0-to-60 mph in 11 seconds. From 0-to-100 mph in 41 seconds.

1955 CORVETTE

1955 Chevrolet, Corvette two-door roadster, V-8

CORVETTE SERIES — (6-CYL) — SERIES E2934 — Corvette styling remained the same as last year's model. The big news was the availability of a V-8 engine. An enlarged gold 'V' within the word CheVrolet, on the front fenders, was a quick way to tell V-8-powered (12-volt electrical system) cars from those with a six-cylinder engine (and six-volt electrical system).

CORVETTE I.D. NUMBERS: The numbering system and code locations were the same as for previous models with the number symbols changed as follows: VE55S001001 to VE55S001700.

NOTE: Cars equipped with a six-cylinder engine did not have a 'V' in their Vehicle Identification Number. Engine number suffixes used were 'YG' (six-cylinder); 'FG' (V-8 and automatic) and 'GR' (V-8 with manual transmission).

CORVETTE

Model No.	Body/Style No.	Body Type & Seating	Factory Price	Shipping Weight	Prod. Total
2934	2934	2-dr Rds-2P	2934	2705	700

ENGINES

SIX: Inline. Overhead valve. Cast iron block. Displacement: 235.5 cid. Bore and stroke: 3.56 x 3.93 inches. Compression ratio: 8.0:1. Brake hp: 155 at 4200 rpm. Four main bearings. Solid valve lifters. Carburetor: Three Carter one-barrel Model 3706989.

V-8: Overhead valve. Cast iron block. Displacement: 265 cid. Bore and stroke: 8.0:1. Brake hp: 195 at 5000 rpm. Five main bearings. Solid valve lifters. Carburetor: Rochester four-barrel Model 7008005.

CHASSIS FEATURES: Wheelbase: 102 inches. Overall length: 167 inches. Front tread: 57 inches. Rear tread: 59 inches. Tires: 6.70 x 15.

OPTIONS: Parking brake alarm ($5.65). Signal-seeking AM radio ($145.15). Windshield washer ($11.85). Heater ($91.40). Automatic transmission with floor shift was standard. Six-cylinder 235.5 cid/155 hp 'Tri-Carb' engine standard. V-8 265 cid/195 hp four-barrel engine ($135).

HISTORICAL FOOTNOTES: The overwhelming majority of 1955 Corvettes were V-8 powered, but at least a half-dozen six-cylinder models were reportedly produced. A V-8-powered 1955 Corvette could go from 0-to-60 mph in 8.7 seconds; from 0-to-100 mph in 24.7 seconds. Harvest gold exterior finish was introduced along with Gypsy red and Corvette copper. Tops now came in white, dark green, or beige. Red, yellow, light beige and dark beige Elascofab interiors were available.

1956 CORVETTE

CORVETTE SERIES — (V-8) — SERIES E2934 — A lot of people would have been perfectly content if Chevrolet had frozen Corvette styling with the 1956 model. Although the same basic grille was kept, there were new front fenders with chrome-rimmed headlights; external door handles; chrome-outlined concave side body coves and sloping, taillight-integrated rear fenders. The dash layout remained the same as in the past. Upholstery colors were limited to beige or red, but six nitro-cellulose lacquer body colors were available. They were Onyx black, Polo white, Venetian red, Cascade green, Aztec copper and Arctic blue.

CORVETTE I.D. NUMBERS: Numbers were the same as for previous models with the number symbols changed as follows: E56S001001 to E56S004467. Beginning engine numbers were 0001001 and up at each assembly plant with 'F' = Flint, Mich., and 'T' = Tonawanda, N.Y. Suffixes were as follows: 'GV' for 265-cid V-8 with synchromesh; 'GU' for 265-cid V-8 with two four-barrel carburetors and high-lift camshaft; 'GR' for regular 265-cid dual four-barrel V-8; 'FK' for 265-cid V-8 with Powerglide and 'FG' for latter V-8 combinations with dual four-barrel carburetors.

CORVETTE

Model No.	Body/Style No.	Body Type & Seating	Factory Price	Shipping Weight	Prod. Total
2934	2934	2-dr Conv-2P	3120	2870	3,467

ENGINE: V-8. Overhead valve. Cast iron block. Displacement: 265 cid. Bore and stroke: 3.75 x 3.00 inches. Compression ratio: 9.25:1. Brake hp: 210 at 5200 rpm. Five main bearings. Solid valve lifters. Carburetor: Carter Type WCFB four-barrel Model 2419S.

CHASSIS FEATURES: Wheelbase: 102 inches. Overall length: 168 inches. Front tread: 57 inches. Rear tread: 59 inches. Tires: 6.70 x 15.

1956 Chevrolet, Corvette two-door convertible with and without hardtop, V-8 (AA)

OPTIONS: Power top ($100). Power windows ($60). Windshield washer ($11). Detachable hardtop ($200). Signal-seeking AM radio ($185). Heater ($115). A close-ratio three-speed manual floor shift transmission was standard. Automatic transmission ($175). V-8 265 cid/225 hp dual four-barrel carburetors, high-lift cam engine ($175). V-8 265 cid/240 hp dual four-barrel carb engine ($160). Available rear axle gear ratios: 3.27:1.

HISTORICAL FOOTNOTES: A 225-hp 1956 Corvette could go from 0-to-60 mph in 7.3 seconds; from 0-to-100 mph in 20.7 seconds.

1957 CORVETTE

CORVETTE SERIES — (V-8) — SERIES E2934 — The 1957 Corvette looked the same as the previous year's model. The big news was the availability of a 283 cid/283 hp fuel-injected V-8. Among the standard features were: dual exhaust; all-vinyl bucket seats; three-spoke competition-style steering wheel; carpeting; outside rearview mirror; electric clock and tachometer. It was available in seven colors: Onyx black; Polo white; Aztec copper; Arctic blue; Cascade green; Venetian red or silver. White, silver, and beige were optional color choices for the cove.

CORVETTE I.D. NUMBERS: The numbering system and code locations were the same as for previous models with the numbers changed as follows: E57S100001 to E57S106339. Engine number suffixes were: 'EF' four-barrel/synchromesh; 'EG' dual four-barrel/high-lift cam/synchromesh; 'EH' dual four-barrel/synchromesh; 'EL' fuel-injection/high-lift cam; 'EN' fuel-injection/high-lift cam; 'FG' Powerglide/dual four-barrel; 'FH' Powerglide and 'FK' Powerglide/fuel-injection.

1957 Chevrolet, Corvette two-door convertible, V-8 (AA)

CORVETTE

Model No.	Body/Style No.	Body Type & Seating	Factory Price	Shipping Weight	Prod. Total
2934	2934	2-dr Conv-2P	3465	2730	6,339

ENGINE: V-8. Overhead valve. Cast iron block. Displacement: 283 cid. Bore and stroke: 3.87 x 3.00 inches. Compression ratio: 9.50:1. Brake hp: 220 at 4800 rpm. Five main bearings. Valve lifters: (see note). Carburetor: Carter four-barrel Model 3744925.

NOTE: A solid lifter camshaft was used with 'EL' and 'EG' engines; hydraulic lifters with others.

CHASSIS FEATURES: Wheelbase: 102 inches. Overall length: 168 inches. Front tread: 57 inches. Rear tread: 59 inches. Tires: 6.70 x 15.

OPTIONS: Special 15 x 5.5-inch wheels ($14). Signal-seeking AM radio ($185). Detachable hardtop ($215). Power top ($130). Courtesy lights ($8). Heater ($118). Windshield washer ($12). Parking brake alarm ($5). Whitewall tires ($32). Dual carburetors ($151). Two-tone paint ($19). Motorola radio ($125). Electric windows ($55). Hydraulic power top ($99). Three-speed manual floor shift transmission was standard. Automatic transmission ($175). Four-speed manual floor shift transmission ($188). V-8 283 cid/245 hp dual four-barrel carb engine ($140). V-8 283 cid/270 hp dual four-barrel carb engine ($170*). V-8 283 cid/250 hp fuel-injection engine ($450). V-8 283 cid/283 hp fuel-injection engine ($450*). "RPO 579E" V-8 283 cid/283 hp fuel-injection engine ($675**). Positive traction rear axle ($45). Heavy-duty racing suspension ($725). Available rear axle gear ratios: 3.70:1, 4.11:1, 4 56:1.

(*) With competition camshaft. (**) With cold-air induction system.

HISTORICAL FOOTNOTES: Only 1,040 of the 1957 Corvettes were fuel-injected. A 283 hp fuel-injection 1957 Corvette could go from 0-to-60 mph in 5.7 seconds. From 0-to-100 mph in 16.8 seconds. It had a top speed of 132 mph.

1958 CORVETTE

CORVETTE SERIES — (V-8) — SERIES J800 — Corvette styling was jazzed up for 1958. There were now four chrome rimmed headlights with fender length chrome strips running between each pair of lights. As if that weren't enough glitter, fake louvers were placed on the hood. The grille was similar to the previous year's, but had four fewer vertical bars. Three horizontal chrome strips were added to the new cove. A couple of vertical chrome bars decorated the trunk. They detracted from an otherwise graceful rear end treatment. The wraparound front and rear bumpers were larger. The interior changed dramatically. The gauges were clustered together, rather than spread across the dash as before. A center console and passenger assist (sissy) bar were added. Upholstery was available in red, charcoal or blue-green. There were six acrylic lacquer exterior colors offered: charcoal, white, yellow, red, blue and turquoise. The cove could be painted silver or white.

1958 Chevrolet, Corvette two-door convertible with and without hardtop, V-8 (PH)

CORVETTE I.D. NUMBERS: The numbering system and code locations were the same as for previous models with the numbers changed as follows: J58S100001 to J58S109168. Engine codes were: 'CQ' = manual transmission; 'CR' = manual and fuel injection; 'CS' = manual transmission/high-lift cam and fuel injection; 'CT' = manual and dual four-barrels; 'CU' = manual/high-lift cam and dual four-barrels; 'DG' = Powerglide transmission; 'DH' = Powerglide and fuel injection and 'DJ' = Powerglide and dual four-barrel. Note: Both three- and four-speed manual transmissions used the same engine code suffixes.

CORVETTE

Model No.	Body/Style No.	Body Type & Seating	Factory Price	Shipping Weight	Prod. Total
J800	867	2-dr Conv-2P	3631	2781	9,168

ENGINE: V-8. Overhead valve. Cast iron block. Displacement: 283 cid. Bore and stroke: 3.87 x 3.00 inches. Compression ratio: 9.50:1. Brake hp: 230 at 4800 rpm. Five main bearings. Hydraulic valve lifters. Carburetor: Carter Type WCFB four-barrel.

CHASSIS FEATURES: Wheelbase: 102 inches. Overall length: 177.2 inches. Front tread: 57 inches. Rear tread: 59 inches. Tires: 5.70 x 15.

OPTIONS: Heater ($97). Power top ($140). Additional cove color ($16.15). Detachable hardtop ($2.15). Signal-seeking AM radio ($144). Power windows ($59.20). Special 15 x 5.5-inch wheels (no charge). Windshield washer ($16). Whitewall tires ($31.55). Courtesy lights ($6.50). Parking brake alarm ($5.40). Three-speed manual floor shift transmission was standard. Automatic transmission ($188). Four-speed manual floor shift transmission ($215). V-8 283 cid/245 hp dual four-barrel carb engine ($150). V-8 283 cid/270 hp dual four-barrel carb engine ($182.95). V-8 283 cid/250 hp fuel-injection engine ($484). V-8 283 cid/290 hp fuel-injection engine ($484). Positive traction rear axle ($48.45). Heavy-duty brakes and suspension ($780.10). Available rear axle gear ratios: 3.70:1; 4.11:1; 4.56:1.

HISTORICAL FOOTNOTES: Almost 11 percent of 1958 Corvettes were powered by the 283 cid/290 hp fuel-injected V-8. A 1958 Corvette with the standard 230 hp V-8 could go from 0-to-60 mph in 9.2 seconds. One with the 290 hp fuel-injected engine took only 6.9 seconds and got slightly better gas mileage.

1959 CORVETTE

CORVETTE SERIES — (V-8) — SERIES J800 — The 1959 Corvette was basically a cleaned-up 1958. The fake hood louvers and vertical chrome strips on the trunk were removed. Interior changes included redesigned bucket seats and door panels, a fiberglass package tray under the sissy bar and concave gauge lenses. A tachometer, outside rearview mirror, dual exhaust and electric clock were among the standard features. Seven exterior color choices were offered: black, white, cream, silver, red, blue and Crown Sapphire. The cove could be painted either silver or white. Blue, red, turquoise and (for the first time) black interiors were available.

CORVETTE I.D. NUMBERS: The numbering system and code locations were the same as for previous models with the numbers changed as follows: J59S100001 to J59S109670. Engine number suffixes were similar to those of 1958.

CORVETTE

Model No.	Body/Style No.	Body Type & Seating	Factory Price	Shipping Weight	Prod. Total
J800	867	2-dr Conv-2P	3875	2900	9,670

ENGINE: V-8. Overhead valve. Cast iron block. Displacement: 283 cid. Bore and stroke: 9.50:1. Brake hp: 230 at 4800 rpm. Five main bearings. Hydraulic valve lifters. Carburetor: Carter Type WCFB four-barrel Model 2816.

1959 Chevrolet, Corvette two-door convertible, V-8 (AA)

CHASSIS FEATURES: Wheelbase: 102 inches. Overall length: 177.2 inches. Front tread: 57 inches. Rear tread: 59 inches. Tires: 6.70 x 15.

OPTIONS: Power top ($139.90). Windshield washer ($16.15). Signal-seeking transistor radio ($149.80). Deluxe heater ($102.25). Two-tone paint ($16.15). Electric windows ($59.20). Courtesy light ($6.50). Parking brake alarm ($5.40). Sunshades ($10.80). Special 15 x 5.5-inch wheels (no charge). Detachable hardtop ($236.75). Three-speed manual floor shift transmission was standard. Automatic transmission ($199). Four-speed manual floor shift transmission ($188). V-8 283 cid/245 hp dual four-barrel carb engine ($150.65). V-8 283 cid/270 hp dual four-barrel carb engine ($182.95). V-8 283 cid/250 hp fuel-injection engine ($484). V-8 283 cid/290 hp fuel-injection engine ($484). Metal brakes ($26.90). Positive traction rear axle ($48.45). Heavy-duty brakes and suspension ($425.05).

HISTORICAL FOOTNOTES: A 290 hp fuel-injected 1959 Corvette could go from 0-to-60 mph in 6.6 seconds; from 0-to-100 mph in 15.5 seconds. It had a top speed of 128 mph.

1960 CORVETTE

CORVETTE SERIES — (V-8) — SERIES 0800 — The 1960 Corvette looked much the same as the previous year's model. A new rear suspension sway-bar improved the car's handling. Aluminum heads and radiator were introduced, but later withdrawn. Standard equipment included: tachometer, sun visors, dual exhaust, carpeting, outside rearview mirror and electric clock. Buyers could choose from eight exterior finishes: black, white, turquoise, blue, silver, green, red and maroon. The cove was available in silver or white. Three colors of convertible tops: black, white and blue, were offered.

CORVETTE I.D. NUMBERS: The numbering system and code locations were the same as for previous models with the numbers changed as follows: 00867S100001 to 00867S110261. The first symbol designated year. The second, third, fourth and fifth symbols designated Model Number ('0800') and Body/Style Number: '67' = convertible; '63' = coupe. The sixth symbol designated manufacturing plant, 'S' St. Louis. The last six digits were the sequential production numbers.

1960 Chevrolet, Corvette two-door convertible, V-8 (AA)

CORVETTE

Model No.	Body/Style No.	Body Type & Seating	Factory Price	Shipping Weight	Prod. Total
0800	67	2-dr Conv-2P	3872	2840	10,261

ENGINE: V-8. Overhead valve. Cast iron block. Displacement: 283 cid. Bore and stroke: 3.87 x 3.00 inches. Compression ratio: 9.25:1. Brake hp: 230 at 4800 rpm. Five main bearings. Hydraulic valve lifters. Carburetor: Carter Type WCFB four-barrel Model 3779178.

CHASSIS FEATURES: Wheelbase: 102 inches. Overall length: 177.2 inches. Front tread: 57 inches. Rear tread: 59 inches. Tires: 6.70 x 15.

OPTIONS: Power top ($139.90). Windshield washer ($16.15). Signal-seeking transistor radio ($137.75). Deluxe heater ($102.25). Detachable hardtop ($236.75). Two-tone paint ($16.15). Electric windows ($59.20). Whitewall tires ($31.55). Courtesy lights ($6.60). Parking brake alarm ($5.40). Sunshades ($10.80). Permanent anti-freeze ($5.00). Special 15 x 5.5-inch wheels (no charge). Three-speed manual floor shift transmission was standard. Automatic transmission ($199.10). Four-speed manual floor shift transmission ($188). V-8 283 cid/245 hp dual four-barrel carb engine ($150.65). V-8 283 cid/270 hp dual four-barrel carb engine ($182.95). V-8 283 cid/275 hp fuel-injection engine ($484). V-8 283 cid/315 hp fuel-injection engine ($484). Metallic brakes ($26.90). Positive traction rear axle ($43.05). Heavy-duty brakes and suspension ($333.60). Available rear axle gear ratios: 3.70:1, 4.11:1, 4.56:1.

HISTORICAL FOOTNOTES: The majority of 1960 Corvettes, 50.1 percent, were sold with a detachable hardtop. Most, 51.9 percent, also had a four-speed manual transmission.

1961 CORVETTE

CORVETTE SERIES — (V-8) — SERIES 0800 — A refined, thin, vertical and horizontal bar grille and 'duck tail' rear end treatment with four cylindrical taillights quickly set the new 1961 Corvette apart from its predecessor. The exhaust now exited under the car, rather than through bumper ports. Standard equipment included: tachometer; seat belts; sun visors; dual exhaust; carpeting; electric clock; and an outside rearview mirror. Seven exterior colors were available: black, white, red, maroon, beige, blue and silver.

1961 Chevrolet, Corvette two-door convertible, V-8 (AA)

CORVETTE I.D. NUMBERS: The numbering system and code locations were the same as for previous models with the numbers changed as follows: 10867S100001 to 10867S110939.

CORVETTE

Model No.	Body/Style No.	Body Type & Seating	Factory Price	Shipping Weight	Prod. Total
0800	67	2-dr Conv-2P	3934	2905	10,939

ENGINE: V-8. Overhead valve. Cast iron block. Displacement: 283 cid. Bore and stroke: 3.87 x 3.00 inches. Compression ratio: 9.5:1. Brake hp: 230 at 4800 rpm. Five main bearings. Hydraulic valve lifters. Carburetor: Carter Type WCFB four-barrel Model 3779178.

CHASSIS FEATURES: Wheelbase: 102 inches. Overall length: 177.2 inches. Front tread: 57 inches. Rear tread: 59 inches. Tires: 6.70 x 15.

OPTIONS: Power top ($161.40). Windshield washer ($16.15). Signal-seeking transistor radio ($137.75). Deluxe heater ($102.25). Detachable hardtop ($236.75). Two-tone paint ($16.15). Electric windows ($59.20). Whitewall tires ($31.55). Blackwall nylon tires ($5.40). Crankcase ventilating system ($5.40). Oversize 24 gallon fuel tank ($161.40). Permanent anti-freeze ($5.00). Special 15 x 5.5-inch wheels (no charge). Three-speed manual floor shift transmission was standard. Automatic transmission ($199). Four-speed manual floor shift transmission ($188). V-8 283 cid/245 hp dual four-barrel carb engine ($150.65). V-8 283 cid/270 hp dual four-barrel carb engine ($182.95). V-8 283 cid/275 hp fuel-injection engine ($484). V-8 283 cid/315 hp fuel-injection engine ($484). Metallic brakes ($37.70). Positive traction rear axle ($43.05). Heavy-duty brakes and suspension ($333.60).

HISTORICAL FOOTNOTES: Most 1961 Corvettes, 51.98 percent, came with a detachable hardtop and 64.1 percent had a four-speed manual transmission. This was the last year wide whitewall tires were available.

1962 CORVETTE

CORVETTE SERIES — (V-8) — SERIES 0800 — The most noticeable changes for 1962 were the removal of the side cove chrome, a blacked-out grille and ribbed chrome rocker panel molding. For the first time since 1955, Corvettes were offered in solid colors only. Standard features included: electric clock; dual exhaust; tachometer; heater and defroster; seat belts; outside rearview mirror and windshield washer. The wheels were available in black, beige, red, silver or maroon. The last time buyers had a choice of wheel colors was in 1957. In following years, wheels would be offered in only a single color.

CORVETTE I.D. NUMBERS: The numbering system and code locations were the same as for previous models with the numbers changed as follows: 20867S100001 to 20867S114531.

CORVETTE

Model No.	Body/Style No.	Body Type & Seating	Factory Price	Shipping Weight	Prod. Total
0800	67	2-dr Conv-2P	4038	2905	14,531

ENGINE: V-8. Overhead valve. Cast iron block. Displacement: 327 cid. Bore and stroke: 4.00 x 3.25 inches. Compression ratio: 10.5:1. Brake hp: 250 at 4400 rpm. Five main bearings. Hydraulic valve lifters. Carburetor: Carter Type WCFB four-barrel Model 3788246.

1962 Chevrolet, Corvette two-door convertible, V-8 (AA))

CHASSIS FEATURES: Wheelbase: 102 inches. Overall length: 177.2 inches. Front tread: 57 inches. Rear tread: 59 inches. Tires: 6.70 x 15.

OPTIONS: Power top ($161.40). Detachable hardtop ($236.75). Signal-seeking transistor radio ($137.75). 24 gallon fuel tank ($118.40). Electric windows ($59.20). Whitewall tires ($31.55). Blackwall nylon tires ($15.70). Crankcase ventilation system ($5.40). Heavy-duty brakes with metallic facings ($37.70). Permanent anti-freeze ($5.00). Special 15 x 5.5-inch wheels (no charge). Three-speed manual floor shift transmission was standard. Automatic transmission ($199). Four-speed manual floor shift transmission ($188). V-8 327 cid/300 hp dual four-barrel carb engine ($53.80). V-8 327 cid/340 hp dual four-barrel carb engine ($107.60). V-8 327 cid/360 hp fuel-injection engine ($484). Direct flow exhaust system (no charge). Metallic brakes ($37.70). Positive traction rear axle ($43.05). Heavy-duty brakes and suspension ($333.60).

HISTORICAL FOOTNOTES: A 360 hp fuel-injected 1962 Corvette could go from 0-to-60 mph in 5.9 seconds; from 0-to-100 mph in 14 seconds.

1963 CORVETTE

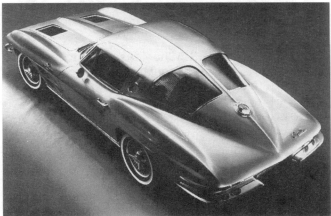

1963 Chevrolet, Corvette Sting Ray two-door coupe, V-8 (AA)

STING RAY SERIES — (V-8) — SERIES 0800 — The Corvette received major restyling in 1963, including a rear window divider. Although the rear deck treatment resembled that of the previous year's model, the rest of the car appeared totally new. The headlights were hidden in an electrically operated panel. This was more than a styling gimmick, as it added to the car's basic aerodynamic design. The recessed fake hood louvers were another matter. Front fender louvers, vents on the roof side panels (of the fastback sport coupe) and ribbed rocker panel molding were styling features used on the sides of the new Corvette. The interior had circular gauges with black faces. There was storage space under the seats of early models. Among the standard equipment was windshield washer; carpeting; outside rearview mirror; dual exhaust; tachometer; electric clock; heater and defroster; cigarette lighter; and safety belts. Seven exterior colors were offered: black, white, silver, silver-blue, Daytona blue, red and tan. For the first time since 1957, a beige softtop was available.

CORVETTE I.D. NUMBERS: The numbering system and code locations were the same as for previous models with the numbers changed as follows: 30867S100001 to 30867S121513, or 30837S100001 to 30837S121513.

STING RAY SERIES

Model No.	Body/Style No.	Body Type & Seating	Factory Price	Shipping Weight	Prod. Total
0800	37	2-dr FsBk Cpe-2P	4257	2859	10,594
0800	67	2-dr Conv-2P	4037	2881	10,919

185

1963 Chevrolet, Corvette Sting Ray two-door convertible, V-8

ENGINE: V-8. Overhead valve. Cast iron block. Displacement: 327 cid. Bore and stroke: 4.00 x 3.25 inches. Compression ratio: 10.5:1. Brake hp: 250 at 4400 rpm. Five main bearings. Hydraulic valve lifters. Carburetor: Carter Type WCFB four-barrel Model 3501S.

CHASSIS FEATURES: Wheelbase: 98 inches. Overall length: 175.2 inches. Front tread: 56.8 inches. Rear tread. 57.6 inches. Tires: 6.70 x 15.

CONVENIENCE OPTIONS: Power brakes ($43.05). Power steering ($73.35). Air conditioning ($421.80). Detachable hardtop ($236.75). Signal-seeking transistor radio ($137.75). Electric windows ($59.20). Whitewall tires ($31.55). Blackwall nylon tires ($15.70). Heavy-duty brakes with metallic facings ($37.70). Sebring Silver paint ($80.70). Woodgrain plastic steering wheel ($16.15). Aluminum knock-off wheels ($322.80). AM-FM radio ($174). Tinted windshield ($10.80). Tinted glass ($16.15). Leather seat trim ($80.70). Three-speed manual floor shift transmission was standard. Automatic transmission ($199.10). Four-speed manual floor shift transmission ($188). 'L75' V-8 327 cid/300 hp four-barrel carb engine ($53.80). 'L76' V-8 327 cid/340 hp four-barrel carb engine ($107 60). 'L84' V-8 327 cid/360 hp fuel-injection engine ($430.40). Sintered metallic brakes ($37.70). Off-road exhaust system ($37.70). RPO Z06 Special performance package (coupe): metallic power brakes; heavy-duty shocks; stabilizers; knock-off-type aluminum wheels; positraction rear axle; four-speed manual gearbox; 360 hp fuel injection V-8 ($1,818). Positive traction rear axle ($43.05). Available rear axle gear ratio: 4.11:1, 4.56:1, 3.08:1, 3.36:1, 3.55:1, 3.70:1.

HISTORICAL FOOTNOTES: A rare option in 1963 Corvettes is air conditioning. Only 1.3 percent were so-equipped. However, 83.5 percent came with four-speed manual transmission. An L84-powered Corvette could go from 0-to-60 mph in 5.9 seconds and from 0-to-100 mph in 16.5 seconds. The historic Corvette Grand Sport was constructed in 1963. A total of five were built before the program was canceled. The Grand Sport weighed 1,908 pounds, had a 377-cid version of the small-block V-8 equipped with aluminum cylinder block and aluminum hemi-head cylinder heads with twin ignition and port fuel-injection.

1964 CORVETTE

STING RAY SERIES — (V-8) — SERIES 0800 — Styling was cleaned up a bit for 1964. The previous year's distinctive rear window divider was replaced by a solid piece of glass. The fake hood vents were eliminated and the roof vents were restyled. A three-speed fan was available in the coupe to aid in ventilation. Seven exterior colors were offered: black, white, tan, Daytona blue, silver-blue, silver and red.

CORVETTE I.D. NUMBERS: The numbering system and code locations were the same as for previous models with the numbers changed as follows: 40867S100001 to 40867S122229, or 40837S100001 to 40837S122229.

1964 Chevrolet, Corvette Sting Ray two-door coupe, V-8 (AA)

STING RAY SERIES

Model No.	Body/Style No.	Body Type & Seating	Factory Price	Shipping Weight	Prod. Total
0800	37	2-dr FsBk Cpe-2P	4252	2945	8,304
0800	67	2-dr Conv-2P	4037	2960	13,925

ENGINE: V-8. Overhead valve. Cast iron block. Displacement: 327 cid. Bore and stroke: 4.00 x 3.25 inches. Compression ratio: 10.5:1. Brake hp: 250 at 4400 rpm. Carburetor: Carter Type WCFB four-barrel Model 3846247.

CHASSIS FEATURES: Wheelbase: 98 inches. Overall length: 175.2 inches. Front tread: 56.8 inches. Rear tread: 57.6 inches. Tires: 6.70 x 15.

OPTIONS: Power brakes ($43.05). Power steering ($73.35). Air conditioning ($421.80). Leather seat trim ($80.70). Soft-ray tinted windows ($16.15). Soft-ray tinted windshield ($10.80). Electric windows ($59.20). Detachable hardtop ($236.75). Sintered metallic power brakes ($53.80). Special 36 gallon fuel tank, coupe only ($202.30). Special cast aluminum knock-off wheels ($322.80). Blackwall nylon tires ($15.70). Whitewall rayon tires ($31.85). Back-up lights ($10.80). AM/FM radio ($176.50). Three-speed manual floor shift transmission was standard. Automatic transmission ($199.10). Four-speed manual floor shift transmission ($188). 'L75' V-8 327 cid/300 hp four-barrel carb engine ($53.80). 'L76' V-8 327 cid/365 hp four-barrel carb engine ($107.60). 'L84' V-8 327 cid/375 hp fuel-injection engine ($538). Positive traction rear axle ($43.50). Off-road exhaust system ($37.70). Special front and rear suspension ($37.70). Transistor ignition system ($73.75). Special sintered metallic brake package ($629.50). Available rear axle gear ratios: 4.11:1; 4.56:1; 3.08:1; 3.36:1; 3.55:1; 3.70:1.

1964 Chevrolet, Corvette Sting Ray two-door convertible, V-8

HISTORICAL FOOTNOTES: Only 3.2 percent of 1964 Corvettes were sold with the standard three-speed manual transmission. Most, 85.7 percent, were equipped with a four-speed manual transmission. An L84-powered 1964 Corvette could go from 0-to-60 mph in 6.3 seconds and from 0-to-100 mph in 14.7 seconds. It had a top speed of 138 mph.

1965 CORVETTE

STING RAY SERIES — (V-8) — SERIES 194 — Three functional, vertical front fender louvers; a blacked-out, horizontal bar grille and different rocker panel moldings were the main styling changes for 1965 Corvettes. Standard equipment included: tachometer; safety belts; heater and defroster; windshield washer; outside rearview mirror; dual exhaust; electric clock; carpeting; manually operated top (convertible); and sun visors. Eight exterior colors were available: black, white, yellow, red, blue, green, silver and maroon.

1965 Chevrolet, Corvette Sting Ray two-door coupe, V-8 (M)

CORVETTE I.D. NUMBERS: The numbering system and code locations were the same as for previous models with the numbers changed as follows: 194675S100001 to 194675S123562, or 194375-S100001 to 194375S123562. The first symbol designated make ('1' = Chevrolet). The second, third, fourth and fifth symbols designated Corvette series and Body/Style Number: '37' = coupe, '67' = convertible. The sixth symbol designated year. The last six digits were the sequential production number and started at 100001.

1965 Chevrolet, Corvette Sting Ray two-door convertible with and without removable hardtop, V-8

STING RAY SERIES

Model No.	Body/Style No.	Body Type & Seating	Factory Price	Shipping Weight	Prod. Total
194	37	2-dr FsBk Cpe-2P	2947	3570	8,187
194	67	2-dr Conv-2P	3212	3645	15,377

ENGINE: V-8. Overhead valve. Cast iron block. Displacement: 327 cid. Bore and stroke: 4.00 x 3.25 inches. Compression ratio: 10.5:1. Brake hp: 250 at 4400 rpm. Five main bearings. Hydraulic valve lifters. Carburetor: Carter Type WCFB four-barrel Model 3846247.

CHASSIS FEATURES: Wheelbase: 98 inches. Overall length: 175.2 inches. Front tread: 56.8 inches. Rear tread: 57.6 inches. Tires: 7.75 x 15.

OPTIONS: Power brakes ($43.05). Power steering ($96.85). Air conditioning ($421.80). Backup lights and inside rearview mirror ($16.15). Heater and defroster ($100.00). Tinted glass ($16.15). Tinted windshield ($10.80). Special 36-gallon fuel tank, coupe only ($202.30). Power windows ($59.20). AM/FM radio with power antenna ($203.00). Teakwood steering wheel ($48.15). Detachable hardtop ($236.75). Whitewall tires ($31.30). Goldwall tires ($51.00). Saddle trim leather seats ($80.70). Special 15-inch knock-off-type wheels ($322.80). Telescopic steering column ($43.05). Three-speed manual transmission was standard. Automatic transmission ($199.10). Four-speed manual floor shift transmission ($188). Close-ratio four-speed manual transmission with floor shift ($237). 'L75' V-8 327 cid/300 hp dual four-barrel carb engine ($53.80). 'L79' V-8 327 cid/350 hp dual four-barrel carb engine ($107.60). "L76" V-8 327 cid/365 hp four-barrel carb engine ($129.15). 'L84' V-8 327 cid/375 hp fuel-injection engine ($538). Special front and rear suspension ($37.70). Off-road exhaust system ($37.70), side-mount exhaust system ($134.50). Transistor ignition system ($75.35). Positive traction rear axle ($43.05). Available rear axle gear ratios: 4.11:1, 4.56:1, 3.08:1, 3.36:1, 3.55:1, 3.70:1.

HISTORICAL FOOTNOTES: Most 1965 Corvettes (89.6 percent) were sold with a four-speed manual transmission; 8.6 percent had Powerglide automatic transmission; 69.5 percent tinted glass; 10.3 percent air conditioning and 13.7 percent power steering. An L78-powered 1965 Corvette could go from 0-to-60 mph in 5.7 seconds; from 0-to-100 mph in 13.4 seconds.

1966 CORVETTE

STING RAY SERIES — (V-8) — SERIES 194 — An egg-crate grille; ribbed rocker panel molding; chrome-plated exhaust bezels; spoke-style wheel covers; vinyl covered headliner; and the elimination of roof vents helped set the 1966 Corvette apart from the previous year's model. Those equipped with the new 427-cid V-8 came with a power-bulge hood. The 10 lacquer exterior finishes offered included: black, white, Nassau blue, Laguna blue, Trophy blue, red, green, maroon, yellow and silver.

CORVETTE I.D. NUMBERS: The numbering system and code locations were the same as for previous models with the numbers changed as follows: 194676S100001 to 194676S127720, or 194376S100001 to 194376S127720.

STING RAY SERIES

Model No.	Body/Style No.	Body Type & Seating	Factory Price	Shipping Weight	Prod. Total
194	37	2-dr FsBk Cpe-2P	4295	2985	9,958
194	67	2-dr Conv-2P	4084	3005	17,762

1966 Chevrolet, Corvette Sting Ray two-door coupe, V-8 (AA)

ENGINE: V-8. Overhead valve. Cast iron block. Displacement: 327 cid. Bore and stroke: 4.00 x 3.25 inches. Compression ratio: 10.5:1. Brake hp: 300 at 5000 rpm. Five main bearings. Hydraulic valve lifters. Carburetor: Holley four-barrel Model 3884505.

CHASSIS FEATURES: Wheelbase: 98 inches. Overall length: 175.2 inches. Front tread: 56.8 inches. Rear tread: 57.6 inches. Tires: 7.75 x 15.

OPTIONS: Power brakes ($43.05). Power steering ($94.80). Air conditioning ($412.90). Leather seats ($79.00). Tinted windows ($15.80). Tinted windshield ($10.55). Electric windows ($59.20). Headrests ($42.15). Shoulder harness ($26.35). Detachable hardtop ($231.75). Special 36-gallon fuel tank ($198.05). Teakwood steering wheel ($48.45). Telescopic steering column ($42.15). Special cast aluminum knock-off wheels ($326.00). Whitewall tires ($31.30). Goldwall tires ($46.55). AM/FM radio ($199.10). Traffic-hazard lamp switch ($11.60). Three-speed manual transmission was standard. Automatic transmission ($194.85). Four-speed manual floor shift transmission ($184). Close-ratio four-speed manual transmission with floor shift ($184). Heavy-duty close-ratio four-speed manual transmission with floor shift ($237). 'L79' V-8 327 cid/350 hp four-barrel carb engine ($105). 'L39' V-8 427 cid/390 hp four-barrel carb engine ($181.20). 'L72' V-8

427 cid/425 hp four-barrel carb engine ($312). Positive traction rear axle ($42.15). Heavy-duty brakes ($342.30). Special front and rear suspension ($36.90). Transistor ignition system ($73.75). Off-road exhaust system ($36.90). Side-mount exhaust system ($131.65). Available rear axle gear ratios: 3.08:1; 3.36:1; 3.55:1; 3.70:1; 4.11:1; 4.56:1.

HISTORICAL FOOTNOTES: Only two percent of all 1966 Corvettes had a three-speed manual transmission; 89.3 percent came with a four-speed manual gearbox; 13.2 percent had a tilting steering wheel and 20.2 percent had power steering.

1967 CORVETTE

1967 Chevrolet, Corvette Sting Ray two-door coupe, V-8 (AA)

STING RAY SERIES — (V-8) — SERIES 194 — Some consider the 1967 the best looking of the early Sting Rays. Its styling, although basically the same, was cleaner. Unlike the others, it had five functional front fender louvers. Minor changes were made to the interior. The most noticeable was the relocation of the parking brake from under the dash to the center console. Standard equipment included: rally wheels; odometer; clock; carpeting; wheel trim rings; tachometer; and all-vinyl foam-cushioned bucket seats in black, white, Teal blue, saddle, bright blue or green.

CORVETTE I.D. NUMBERS: The numbering system and code locations were the same as for previous models with the numbers changed as follows: 194677S100001 to 194677S122940, or 194377S100001 to 194377S122940.

STING RAY SERIES

Model No.	Body/Style No.	Body Type & Seating	Factory Price	Shipping Weight	Prod. Total
194	37	2-dr FsBk Cpe-2P	4353	3000	8,504
194	67	2-dr Conv-2P	4141	3020	14,436

ENGINE: V-8. Overhead valve. Cast iron block. Displacement: 327 cid. Bore and stroke: 4.00 x 3.25 inches. Compression ratio: 10.0:1. Brake hp: 300 at 5000 rpm. Five main bearings. Hydraulic valve lifters. Carburetor: Holley four-barrel Model R3810A or R3814A.

CHASSIS FEATURES: Wheelbase: 98 inches. Overall length: 175.2 inches. Front tread: 56.8 inches. Rear tread: 57.6 inches. Tires: 7.75 x 15.

OPTIONS:Power brakes ($42.15). Power steering ($94.80). Air conditioning ($412.90). Front shoulder belts ($26.35). Special 36-gallon fuel tank ($198.05). Tinted windows ($15.80). Tinted windshield ($10.55). Strato-ease driver and passenger headrests ($42.15). Heater and defroster ($97.85). Power windows ($57.95). AM/FM radio with rear antenna ($172.75). Black vinyl roof cover ($52.70). Leather seats ($79.00). Speed warning indicator ($10.55). Telescope steering shaft ($42.15). Four-ply whitewall tires, size 7.75 x 15 ($31.35). Four-ply red stripe nylon tires, size 7.75 x 15 ($46.55). Detachable hardtop ($231.75). Headrests ($42.15). Cast aluminum bolt-on wheels ($263.30). Three-speed manual transmission was standard. Automatic transmission ($194.35). Heavy-duty close-ratio four-speed manual floor shift transmission ($237). Wide-ratio four-speed manual transmission with floor shift ($184). Close-ratio four-speed manual transmission with floor shift ($184). 'L79' V-8 327 cid/350 hp four-barrel carb engine ($105). 'L36' V-8 427 cid/390 hp four-barrel carb engine ($200.15). 'L68' V-8 427 cid/400 hp Tri-Power engine ($305). 'L71' 427 cid/435 hp Tri-Power engine ($437). Aluminum cylinder heads for 'L71' V-8 ($368). 'L88' V-8 427 cid/430 hp, actual output around 530 hp; aluminum heads included, $947.90 (L-88 features: single Holley four-barrel; no radio; heater; no fan shroud. About 20 built). Special front and rear suspension ($36.90). Heavy-duty brakes ($342.30). Off-road exhaust system ($36.90). Transistor ignition system ($74.75). Side-mount exhaust system ($131.65). Available rear axle gear ratios: 3.08:1, 3.36:1, 3.55:1, 3.70:1, 4.11:1.

HISTORICAL FOOTNOTES: Eighty-eight percent of 1967 Corvettes came with four-speed manual transmission; 10.1 percent had Powerglide automatic transmission; 20.8 percent had power brakes; 16.5 percent had air-conditioning; 10.5 percent had a tilting steering wheel and 25.1 percent came with power steering. A 327 cid/300 hp V-8-powered Corvette of this vintage would go from 0-to-60 mph in 7.8 seconds; from 0-to-100 mph in 23.1 seconds.

1968 CORVETTE

CORVETTE SERIES — (V-8) — SERIES 194 — The Corvette's first major restyling since 1963 occurred in this year. As the sales brochure read, "Corvette '68... all different all over." The fastback was replaced by a tunneled-roof coupe. It featured a removable back window and a two-piece detachable roof section or T-top. The convertible's optional hardtop had a glass rear window. The front end was more aerodynamic than those on previous Corvettes. As before, the headlights were hidden. Now they were vacuum-operated, rather than electrical. The wipers also disappeared when not in use. Except for the rocker panels, the sides were devoid of chrome. Conventional door handles were eliminated and in their place were push-buttons. The blunt rear deck contained four round taillights with the word Corvette printed in chrome in the space between them. The wraparound, wing-like rear bumper and license plate holder treatment resembled that used on the 1967 models. Buyers had their choice of 10 exterior colors.

CORVETTE I.D. NUMBERS: The numbering system and code locations were the same as for previous models with the numbers changed as follows: 194678S100001 to 194678S128566, or 194378S100001 to 194378S128566.

CORVETTE SERIES

Model No.	Body/Style No.	Body Type & Seating	Factory Price	Shipping Weight	Prod. Total
194	37	2-dr Spt Cpe-2P	4663	3055	9,936
194	67	2-dr Conv-2P	4347	3070	18,630

ENGINE: V-8. Overhead valve. Cast iron block. Displacement: 327 cid. Bore and stroke: 4.00 x 3.25 inches. Compression ratio: 10.0:1. Brake hp: 300 at 5000 rpm. Five main bearings. Hydraulic valve lifters. Carburetor: Rochester Type 4MV four-barrel Model 7028207.

CHASSIS FEATURES: Wheelbase: 98 inches. Overall length: 182.5 inches. Front tread: 58.7 inches. Rear tread: 59.4 inches. Tires: F70-15.

1968 Chevrolet, Corvette two-door convertible, with optional 427-cid V-8

OPTIONS: Power brakes ($42.15). Power steering ($94.80). Air conditioning ($412.90). Custom Deluxe front shoulder belts ($26.35). Rear window defroster ($31.60). Tinted windows ($15.80). Tinted windshield ($10.55). Driver and passenger head restraints ($42.15). Heavy-duty power brakes ($384.45). Power windows ($57.95). AM/FM radio with fixed height antenna ($172.75). AM/FM stereo radio ($278.10). Black vinyl roof ($52.70). Leather seats ($79.00). Speed warning indicator ($10.55). Adjustable steering shaft ($42.15). Detachable hardtop ($231.75). Four wheel covers ($57.95). Special red stripe F70-15 tires ($31.30). Special white stripe F70-15 tires ($31.30). Alarm system ($26.35). Three-speed manual transmission was standard. Automatic transmission ($226). Heavy-duty close-ratio four-speed manual floor shift transmission ($263). Wide-ratio four-speed manual transmission with floor shift ($164). Close ratio four-speed manual transmission with floor shift ($184). 'L79' V-8 327 cid/350 hp four-barrel engine ($105). 'L36' V-8 427 cid/390 hp four-barrel engine ($200.15). 'L68' V-8 427 cid/400 hp Tri-Power engine ($305). 'L71' V-8 427 cid/435 hp Tri-Power engine ($437.10). 'L71/89' V-8 427 cid/435 hp Tri-Power engine ($805.75). 'L88' V-8 427 cid/430 hp, actual output around 530 hp. (L88 features; aluminum heads included. Option price $947.90. Single Holley four-barrel. Production of 80 cars. Heater was standard as was a high-rise, fresh air, bubble hood.) Special front and rear suspension ($36.90). Heavy-duty brakes ($384.45). Off-road exhaust system ($36.90). Transistor ignition system ($73.75). Positive traction rear axle ($46.35). Available rear axle gear ratios: 2.73:1, 3.08:1, 3.36:1, 3.55:1, 4.11:1.

HISTORICAL FOOTNOTES: Just over 80 percent of 1968 Corvettes were equipped with four-speed manual transmission; 81 percent had tinted glass; 36.3 percent had power steering; 19.8 percent had air-conditioning and 33.7 percent had power brakes. The L79-powered Corvette of this year could go from 0-to-60 mph in 7.7 seconds and from 0-to-100 mph in 20.7 seconds.

1969 CORVETTE

STINGRAY SERIES — (V-8) — SERIES 194 — After a year's absence, the Stingray name (now spelled as one word) re-appeared on the front fenders. The back-up lights were integrated into the center taillights. The ignition was now on the steering column and the door depression button used in 1968 was eliminated. (A key lock was put in its place.) Front and rear disc brakes, headlight washers, center console, wheel trim rings, carpeting, and all-vinyl upholstery were standard.

CORVETTE I.D. NUMBERS: The numbering system and code locations were the same as for previous models with the numbers changed as follows: 194679S100001 to 194679S138762, or 194379S100001 to 194379S138762.

STINGRAY SERIES

Model No.	Body/Style No.	Body Type & Seating	Factory Price	Shipping Weight	Prod. Total
194	37	2-dr Spt Cpe-2P	4763	3091	22,129
194	67	2-dr Conv Cpe-2P	4420	3096	16,633

ENGINE: V-8. Overhead valve. Cast iron block. Displacement: 350 cid. Bore and stroke: 4.00 x 3.48 inches. Compression ratio: 10.25:1. Brake hp: 300 at 4800 rpm. Five main bearings. Hydraulic valve lifters. Carburetor: Rochester four-barrel Model 7029203.

CHASSIS FEATURES: Wheelbase: 98 inches. Overall length: 182.5 inches. Front tread: 58.7 inches. Rear tread: 59.4 inches. Tires: F70-15.

OPTIONS: Power brakes ($42.15). Power steering ($105.35). Air conditioning ($428.70). Auto alarm system ($26.35). Custom Deluxe front shoulder belts ($42.15). Rear window defroster ($32.65). Tinted windows ($16.90). Front fender louver trim ($21.10). Heavy-duty power brakes ($384.45). Power windows ($63.20). AM/FM radio with fixed height antenna ($172.75). AM/FM push-button stereo radio ($278.10). Black vinyl roof cover ($57.95). Leather seat trim ($79.00). Speed warning indicator ($11.60). Telescopic tilt steering wheel ($84.30). Special red stripe tires ($31.30). Special white stripe tires ($31.30). Detachable hardtop ($252.80). Four wheel covers ($57.95). Three-speed manual transmission was standard. Automatic transmission ($221.80). Heavy-duty close-ratio four-speed manual floor shift transmission ($290). Wide-ratio four-speed manual transmission with floor shift ($184). Close-ratio four-speed manual transmission with floor shift ($184). 'L46' V-8 350 cid/350 hp four-barrel carb engine ($131.65). 'L36' V-8 427 cid/390 hp four-barrel carb engine ($221.20). 'L68' V-8 427 cid/400 hp Tri-Power engine ($326). 'L71' V-8 427 cid/435 hp Tri-Power engine ($437.10). 'L88' engine option 427 cid/430 hp with actual output around 530 hp. Aluminum heads included. Option price $1,032.15. Single Holley four-barrel. Production of 116 cars. 'L88' 1967, '68, '69

Corvette-engined models were targeted at road racers. The drivetrain was quite different from other 427-equipped Corvettes, with many heavy-duty parts and performance assembly techniques. There were no standard visual changes in the body (aside from the '68, '69 hood). A decal on the parking brake console warned of engine damage unless run on 103 octane gasoline. ZL1 427 cid ($3,000). Only two were built. Special front and rear suspension ($36.90). Transistor ignition system ($81.10). Side-mount exhaust system ($147.45). Positive traction rear axle ($46.35). Available rear axle gear ratios: 2.73:1, 3.08:1, 3.36:1, 3.55:1, 3.70:1, 4.11:1, 4.56:1.

1969 Chevrolet, Corvette Stingray two-door coupe, V-8 (AA)

HISTORICAL FOOTNOTES: The majority of 1969 Corvettes, 59.2 percent, came with power steering; 78.4 percent had four-speed manual attachments and one-in-four had power windows. A 350 cid/300 hp V-8 was available this season. Cars with this powerplant and automatic transmission were capable of 0-to-60 mph speeds in the 8.4 second bracket and could move from 0-to-100 mph in approximately 21.7 seconds.

1970 CORVETTE

1970 Chevrolet, Corvette Stingray two-door convertible, V-8

STINGRAY SERIES — (V-8) — SERIES 194 — Refinements were made to the basic styling used since

1968. A new 'ice cube tray' design grille and side fender louvers; rectangular, amber front signal lights; fender flares and square exhaust exits were exterior changes. The bucket seats and safety belt retractor containers were also improved. Standard equipment included: front and rear disc brakes, headlight washers, wheel trim rings, carpeting, center console and all-vinyl upholstery (in either black, blue, green, saddle or red).

CORVETTE I.D. NUMBERS: The numbering system and code locations were the same as for previous models with the numbers changed as follows: 194670S100001 to 194670S117316, or 194370S100001 to 194370S117316.

STINGRAY SERIES

Model No.	Body/Style No.	Body Type & Seating	Factory Price	Shipping Weight	Prod. Total
194	37	2-dr Spt Cpe-2P	5469	3153	10,668
194	67	2-dr Conv-2P	5129	3167	6,648

1970 Chevrolet, Corvette Stingray two-door coupe, V-8

ENGINE: V-8. Overhead valve. Cast iron block. Displacement: 350 cid. Bore and stroke: 4.00 x 3.48 inches. Compression ratio: 10.25:1. Brake hp: 300 at 4800 rpm. Five main bearings. Hydraulic valve lifters. Carburetor: Rochester Type Quadra-Jet four-barrel Model 4MV.

CHASSIS FEATURES: Wheelbase: 98 inches. Overall length: 182.5 inches. Front tread: 58.7 inches. Rear tread: 59.4 inches. Tires: F70-15.

OPTIONS: Power brakes ($33.55). Power steering ($83.35). Air conditioning ($339.16). Audio alarm system ($20.85). Custom Deluxe front shoulder belts ($33.35). Rear window defroster ($25.83). Tinted windows ($13.38). Front fender louver trim ($16.70). Heavy-duty power brakes ($304.15). Power windows ($50.00). AM/FM radio with fixed height antenna ($136.67). AM/FM push-button stereo radio ($220.02). Black vinyl roof cover ($45.85). Genuine leather seat trim ($62.50). Speed warning indicator ($918). Telescopic tilt steering wheel ($66.70). Detachable hardtop ($200). Wheel covers ($45.85). Automatic transmission (no charge). A wide range four-speed manual floor shift transmission was standard. Close-ratio four-speed manual transmission with floor shift (no charge). Heavy-duty close-ratio four-speed manual transmission with floor shift ($95). 'L56' V-8 350 cid/350 hp four-barrel carb engine ($158). 'LT1' V-8 350 cid/370 hp four-barrel carb engine ($447.60). 'LS5' V-8 454 cid/390 hp four-barrel carb engine ($289.65). 'LS7' V-8 454 cid/460 hp Tri-Power engine ($3,000). Side-mounted exhaust system ($116.65). Full transistor ignition system ($64.16). Special front and rear suspension ($29.20). Positive

traction rear axle standard, but optional ratios cost $12. Heavy-duty clutch ($62.50). Available rear axle gear ratios: 2.73:1; 3.08:1; 3.36:1; 3.55:1; 4.11:1; 4.56:1.

HISTORICAL FOOTNOTES: Most 1970 Corvettes, 70.5 percent, came with four-speed manual transmission; 33.5 percent had tilting steering wheels; 27.9 percent power windows; 38.5 percent air-conditioning and 68.8 percent power steering. An LS6-powered 1970 Corvette would do 0-to-60 mph in seven seconds and go from 0-to-100 mph in 14 seconds.

1971 CORVETTE

1971 Chevrolet, Corvette Stingray two-door convertible with LT-1 package, V-8

STINGRAY SERIES — (V-8) — SERIES 194 — If you liked the 1970 Corvette, you'd like the 1971 version. They were virtually the same car. A new resin process (that supposedly improved the body) and a different interior were the major changes. Under the hood, the compression ratios were dropped a bit to enable Corvette engines to run on lower octane fuel. Standard equipment included: all-vinyl upholstery; dual exhaust; outside rearview mirror; carpeting; center console; wheel trim rings; electric clock; tachometer; heavy-duty battery; front and rear disc brakes with warning light; and tinted glass.

CORVETTE I.D. NUMBERS: The numbering system and code locations were the same as for previous models with the numbers changed as follows: 194671S100001 to 194671S21801, or 194371S100001 to 194371S121801.

STINGRAY SERIES

Model No.	Body/Style No.	Body Type & Seating	Factory Price	Shipping Weight	Prod. Total
194	37	2-dr Spt Cpe-2P	5536	3153	14,680
194	67	2-dr Conv-2P	5299	3167	7,121

ENGINE: V-8. Overhead valve. Cast iron block. Displacement: 350 cid. Bore and stroke: 4.00 x 3.48 inches. Compression ratio: 8.5:1. Brake hp: 270 at 4800 rpm. Five main bearings. Hydraulic valve lifters. Carburetor: Rochester Type Quadra-Jet four-barrel Model 4MV.

CHASSIS FEATURES: Wheelbase: 98 inches. Overall length: 182.5 inches. Front tread: 58.7 inches. Rear tread: 59.4 inches. Tires: F70-15.

1971 Chevrolet, Corvette Stingray two-door coupe, V-8

OPTIONS: Power brakes ($47.40). Power steering ($115.90). Air conditioning ($464.50). Audio alarm system ($31.60). Heavy-duty battery ($15.60). Custom Deluxe shoulder belts ($42.15). Rear window defroster ($42.15). AM/FM push-button radio ($178). AM/FM stereo radio ($283.35). Black vinyl roof cover ($63.20). Telescopic tilt steering wheel ($84.30). White stripe tires ($30.35). White letter tires ($43.65). Custom trim ($158). Custom wheel covers ($63.20). Power windows ($85.35). Automatic transmission (no cost with standard engine, $100 with others). Wide-range four-speed manual floor shift transmission was standard. Close-ratio four-speed manual transmission with floor shift (no charge). Heavy-duty close-ratio four-speed manual transmission with floor shift ($100). 'LT1' V-8 350 cid/350 hp four-barrel carb engine ($483). 'LS5' V-8 454 cid/385 hp four-barrel carb engine ($295). 'LS8' V-8 454 cid/425 hp four-barrel carb engine ($1,221). A 'ZR1' option package included heavy-duty brakes, close-ratio four-speed manual transmission, special front stabililizer bar, special springs and shock absorbers, fully-transistorized ignition system and the 'LT1' engine at a price of $1,010. A 'ZR2' option package included all ZR1 features listed, except that the 'LS6' powerplant was substituted, at a price of $1,747. Available rear axle gear ratios: 2.73:1; 3.08:1; 3.36:1; 3.55:1; 4.11:1; 4.56:1.

HISTORICAL FOOTNOTES: Slightly over one-third of 1971 Corvettes had a tilting steering wheel; 53.9 percent had a four-speed manual transmission; 82.1 percent had power steering; 52.7 percent had air conditioning and 28.4 percent had power windows.

1972 CORVETTE

STINGRAY SERIES — (V-8) — SERIES Z — The 1972 Corvette was basically the same as the 1971. Among the standard equipment was a positraction rear axle; outside rearview mirror; tinted glass; flo-thru ventilation system; front and rear disc brakes, electric clock; carpeting; wheel trim rings; all-vinyl upholstery; and anti-theft alarm system. Ten exterior colors were available. The convertible top could be ordered in white or black.

CORVETTE I.D. NUMBERS: The numbering system and code locations were changed as follows: 1Z67K2S500001 to 1Z67K2S527004 or 1Z37K2S500001 to 1Z37-K2S527004. The first symbol designated make ('1' = Chevrolet). The second symbol designated series ('Z' = Corvette). The third and fourth symbol designated Body/Style Number ('37' = coupe; '67' = convertible). The fifth symbol designated engine ('K' = standard 350 V-8 in 1972; 'J' = standard 350 V-8 in 1973-1976; 'L' = LT-1; 'T' = L-82; 'Y' = 454 V-8). The seventh symbol designated manufacturing-assembly plant ('S' = St. Louis). The last six digits were the sequential production number.

1972 Chevrolet, Corvette Stingray two-door coupe, V-8

STINGRAY SERIES

Model No.	Body/Style No.	Body Type & Seating	Factory Price	Shipping Weight	Prod. Total
Z	37	2-dr Spt Cpe-2P	5472	3215	20,496
Z	67	2-dr Conv-2P	5246	3215	6,508

1972 Chevrolet, Corvette Stingray two-door convertible, V-8

ENGINE: V-8. Overhead valve. Cast iron block. Displacement: 350 cid. Bore and stroke: 4.00 x 3.48 inches. Compression ratio: 8.5:1. Brake hp: 200 at 4400 rpm. Five main bearings. Hydraulic valve lifters. Carburetor: Rochester Type Quadra-Jet four-barrel Model 4MV.

CHASSIS FEATURES: Wheelbase: 98 inches. Overall length: 182.5 inches. Front tread: 58.7 inches. Rear tread: 59.4 inches. Tires: F70-15.

OPTIONS: Power brakes ($47.40). Power steering ($115.90). Air conditioning ($464.50). Custom interior ($158). Electric power windows ($85.35). Custom shoulder belts ($26.35). Detachable hardtop ($273.85). Vinyl roof covering for detachable hardtop ($158). Telescopic tilt steering column ($84.30). Rear window defroster ($42). White stripe nylon tires ($30.35). White lettered nylon tires ($42.65). Heavy-duty battery ($15.80). Stereo AM/FM radio ($283). AM/FM radio ($178). Automatic transmission (no charge with standard engine, $97 with others). Wide range four-speed manual floor shift transmission was standard. Close-ratio four-speed manual transmission with floor shift (no charge). 'LT1' V-8 350 cid/255 hp engine ($483.45). 'ZR1' V-8 350 cid/255 hp engine ($1,010.05). 'LS5' 454 cid/270 hp engine ($294.90). Note: Only 30 ZR1-equipped cars were built.

HISTORICAL FOOTNOTES: Over one-third of 1972 Corvettes came with power windows; 46.1 percent had a four-speed manual transmission; 88.1 percent had power steering; 63.8 percent had air conditioning; 48.1 percent had a tilting steering wheel and one percent were powered by the 'LT1' engine.

1973 CORVETTE

1973 Chevrolet, Corvette Stingray two-door coupe, V-8

STINGRAY SERIES — (V-8) — SERIES Z — There were predictions in the automotive press that Chevrolet would introduce a mid-engine Corvette this year. However, nothing as radical as that came to be. Major changes for 1973 were a new domed hood, body-color urethane plastic front bumper and a fixed rear window (which added a little extra trunk space). Radial tires became standard and an effort was made to reduce noise. It was generally effective but a *Road & Track* report found the 1973 to be louder than a 1971 in certain circumstances. Buyers who wanted a leather interior could select from black, medium saddle and dark saddle.

CORVETTE I.D. NUMBERS: The numbering system and code locations were the same as for previous models with

the numbers changed as follows: 1Z67J3S400001 to 1Z67J3S434464, or 1Z37J3S400001 to 1Z37J3S434464.

STINGRAY SERIES

Model No.	Body/Style No.	Body Type & Seating	Factory Price	Shipping Weight	Prod. Total
Z	37	2-dr Spt Cpe-2P	5921	3407	25,520
Z	67	2-dr Conv-2P	5685	3407	4,943

ENGINE: V-8. Overhead valve. Cast iron block. Displacement: 350 cid. Bore and stroke: 4.00 x 3.48 inches. Compression ratio: 8.5:1. Brake hp: 190 at 4400 rpm. Five main bearings. Hydraulic valve lifters. Carburetor: Rochester Type Quadra-Jet four-barrel Model 4MV.

CHASSIS FEATURES: Wheelbase: 98 inches. Overall length: 182.5 inches. Front tread: 58.7 inches. Rear tread: 59.4 inches. Tires: F70-15.

OPTIONS: Power brakes ($46). Power steering ($113). Air conditioning ($452). Custom interior ($154). Power windows ($83). Custom shoulder belts ($41). Detachable hardtop ($267). Vinyl roof covering for detachable hardtop ($62). Rear window defroster ($42). Telescopic tilt steering column ($82). Custom wheel covers ($62). White stripe radial tires ($32). White letter radial tires ($45). Heavy-duty battery ($15). Stereo AM/FM radio ($276). AM/FM radio ($173). Cast aluminum wheels ($175). Automatic transmission (no charge). Four-speed manual floor shift transmission was standard. Close-ratio four-speed manual transmission with floor shift (no charge). 'L82' V-8 350 cid/250 hp engine ($299). 'LS4' V-8 454 cid/275 hp engine ($250). Off-road suspension and brake package ($369).

HISTORICAL FOOTNOTES: The majority of 1973 Corvettes, 70.8 percent, were sold with air conditioning; 41.2 percent had a four-speed manual transmission; 91.5 percent had power steering; 79.3 percent had power brakes and 46 percent had power windows. A 1973 L82-powered Corvette could go from 0-to-60 mph in 7.2 seconds and from 0-to-100 mph in 17.9 seconds.

1974 CORVETTE

STINGRAY SERIES — (V-8) — SERIES Z — A restyled sloping rear end and the elimination of the conventional rear bumper with a body-color urethane bumper substitute were two noticeable changes for 1974 Corvettes. The power steering, seat belts and radiator were improved. The alarm system activator was relocated. Buyers once again had their choice of 10 exterior finishes: medium blue, gray, bright yellow, dark green, medium red, orange, white, dark brown, silver and Mille Miglia red.

CORVETTE I.D. NUMBERS: The numbering system and code locations were the same as for previous models with the numbers changed as follows: 1Z67J4S400001 to 1Z67J4S437502, or 1Z37J4S400001 to 1Z37J4S437502.

STINGRAY SERIES

Model No.	Body/Style No.	Body Type & Seating	Factory Price	Shipping Weight	Prod. Total
Z	37	2-dr Spt Cpe-2P	6372	3532	32,029
Z	67	2-dr Conv-2P	6156	3532	5,472

ENGINE: V-8. Overhead valve. Cast iron block. Displacement: 350 cid. Bore and stroke: 4.00 x 3.48 inches. Compression ratio: 9.0:1. Brake hp: 250 at 5200 rpm. Five main bearings. Hydraulic valve lifters. Carburetor: Rochester Type Quadra-Jet four-barrel Model 4MV.

CHASSIS FEATURES: Wheelbase: 98 inches. Overall length: 185.5 inches. Tires: GR70-15.

1974 Chevrolet, Corvette Stingray two-door coupe, V-8

OPTIONS: Power brakes ($49). Power steering ($117). Air conditioning ($467). Custom interior ($154). Power windows ($83). Custom shoulder belts ($41). Detachable hardtop ($267). Vinyl covered detachable hardtop ($329). Rear window defogger ($41). Telescopic tilt steering column ($82). White stripe radial tires ($32). White letter radial tires ($45). Dual horns ($4). AM/FM stereo radio ($276). AM/FM radio ($173). Heavy-duty battery ($15). Map light ($5). Cast aluminum wheel trim ($175). Automatic transmission (no charge with standard engine, $97 with others). Four-speed manual floor shift transmission was standard. Close-ratio four-speed manual transmission with floor shift (no charge). 'L82' V-8 350 cid/250 hp engine ($299). 'LS4' V-8 454 cid/270 hp engine ($250). Off-road suspension and brake package ($400). Gymkhana suspension ($7).

HISTORICAL FOOTNOTES: Most 1974 Corvettes, 95.6 percent, had power steering; 88.3 percent had power brakes; 63.1 percent had power windows; 72.9 percent had tilting steering wheel; 77.7 percent had air conditioning and 33.7 percent had a four-speed manual transmission.

1975 CORVETTE

STINGRAY SERIES — (V-8) — SERIES Z — Most of the changes on the Corvette for 1975 were hidden. The bumpers were improved (but looked the same). Under the hood were a catalytic converter and a new High-Energy ignition. On the inside, the speedometer included kilometers-per-hour for the first time. This was the last year for the Corvette convertible.

CORVETTE I.D. NUMBERS: The numbering system and code locations were the same as for previous models with the numbers changed as follows: 1Z67J5S400001 to 1Z67J5S438465, or 1Z37J5S400001 to 1Z37J5S438465.

STINGRAY SERIES

Model No.	Body/Style No.	Body Type & Seating	Factory Price	Shipping Weight	Prod. Total
Z	37	2-dr Spt Cpe-2P	7117	3532	33,836
Z	67	2-dr Conv-2P	6857	3532	4,829

ENGINE: V-8. Overhead valve. Cast iron block. Displacement: 350 cid. Bore and stroke: 4.00 x 3.48 inches. Compression ratio: 8.5:1. Brake hp: 165 at 3800 rpm. Five main bearings. Hydraulic valve lifters. Carburetor: Rochester Type Quadra-Jet four-barrel Model 4MV.

1975 Chevrolet, Corvette Stingray two-door coupe, V-8

CHASSIS FEATURES: Wheelbase: 98 inches. Overall length: 185.5 inches. Tires: GR70-15.

OPTIONS: Power brakes ($50). Power steering ($129). Air conditioning ($490). Custom interior ($154). Power windows ($93). Custom shoulder belts ($41). Detachable hardtop ($267). Vinyl covered detachable hardtop ($350). Rear window defroster ($46). Telescopic tilt steering column ($82). White stripe tires ($35). White letter tires ($48). Dual horns ($4). AM/ FM stereo radio ($284). AM/FM radio ($178). Heavy-duty battery ($15). Map light ($5). Automatic transmission (no charge). Four-speed manual floor shift transmission was standard. Close-ratio four-speed manual transmission with floor shift (no charge). 'L82' V-8 350 cid/205 hp engine ($336). Off-road suspension and brake package ($403). Gymkhana suspension ($7).

HISTORICAL FOOTNOTES: The 454-cid Corvette engine was dropped this year, as was the convertible style. *Car and Driver* tested a 1975 model and covered the quarter-mile in 16.1 seconds. The magazine timed the car at 0-to-60 mph in 7.7 seconds and found it to have a top speed of 129 mph. Robert D. Lund became Chevrolet general manager. Zora Arkus Duntov retired as the division's chief engineer. He was replaced by David R. McLellan.

The old and the new: A 1912 Chevrolet on display in a Wisconsin dealership next to a new 1954 Corvette. (PH)

1970 Chevrolet, Corvette Stingray two-door T-top coupe, V-8

1972 Chevrolet, Corvette Stingray two-door T-top coupe, V-8

CHEVROLET

1976-1998

1978 Chevrolet, Camaro two-door coupe (PH)

When Monte Carlo and the restyled Camaro appeared in 1970, few were surprised by their popularity. Similarly high expectations greeted the subcompact Vega when it emerged a year later, only to fizzle through half a dozen seasons, victim of unresolved technical difficulties (including its aluminum four-cylinder engine). Monza, an alternate subcompact, came to life for 1975. But Chevrolet's modest new Chevette for 1976 may have been most significant of all, heralding a trend toward small cars to rival the imports, which would eventually take over the industry. Based on GM's German-built Opel Kadett, Chevette even came in a two-passenger Scooter version, priced as low as $2,899.

In 1973, Chevrolet had turned away from the pillarless two-door hardtop, switching to the "Colonnade" design. This would be the final year for the true pillarless four-door hardtop in Impala/Caprice form. After a poor 1975, Chevrolet sales rose amply this year, but Oldsmobile's Cutlass was GM's best seller.

Full-size Chevrolets of 1976 were still mighty big, carrying V-8 engines up to 400 and 454 cubic inch displacement. Mid-sizes and Camaro, on the other hand, switched from a 350 to 305 cubic inch standard V-8. Nova compacts could have either a 305 or 350 V-8 instead of the basic inline six. Among the most noteworthy models was the Cosworth Vega with Twin Cam (16-valve) engine, in its final year. *Motor Trend* had named Monza "Car of the Year" for 1975. Monzas with the Spyder package draw the most interest today. So does the Nova Super Sport (SS) coupe and hatchback. Also of interest to enthusiasts: The last Chevelle Laguna S-3, sporting a "soft" aero front end and louvered coach windows. Camaro came in base or Luxury Touring (LT) trim, but the Z28 had faded away (temporarily).

Full-size Chevrolets weren't quite full after their 1977 downsizing, as the 350 became Impala/Caprice's biggest V-8. Caprice earned the *Motor Trend* honors this year, as overall Chevrolet sales rose moderately—and full-size models considerably. A Borg-Warner four-speed gearbox went into some Camaros, which didn't change at first. Later in the year, though, the Z28 was back, carrying a four-barrel 350 V-8. Though not so potent as its forerunners, it attracted considerable attention. For its final season, Vega's Cosworth was gone, but twin GT packages were available. Chevette's Scooter added a back seat. Monza's Spyder came in two separate packages; one for appearance, another for performance.

Downsizing hit the mid-size Malibu and Monte Carlo for 1978. Base engines were new too: A 200 cubic inch V-6 for Malibu and 231 cubic inch V-6 (from Buick) for the Monte Carlo. Chevrolet sales reached their third highest point ever for the model year, led by a whopping rise in Chevette interest. Monza continued in its previous form, and added the former Vega's hatchback and station wagon. Both Spyder and GT packages were available, as was a new 196 cubic inch Buick-built V-6. Monza's base four-cylinder engine came from Pontiac, but the 305 cubic inch V-8 was Chevrolet's. Chevette supplemented the original two-door with a four-door hatchback, and lengthened its standard equipment list. Camaro's Z28 added slanted fender louvers, rear spoiler and hood air scoop.

Except for a new small-block 267 cubic inch V-8 available under Monte Carlo hoods, not much changed for 1979. A new Berlinetta replaced Camaro's Type LT, while Z28 featured new flared front wheel openings and air dam.

Full-size models switched from the old familiar inline six-cylinder engine to a new standard 229 cubic inch V-6 for 1980, and enjoyed an aero restyle. That news was minor, though, compared to the introduction of the Citation X-car. Widely praised at first, Chevrolet's first front-drive model soon suffered a variety of recalls and charges of seriously flawed brakes—charges that were never fully resolved, even years later. For the moment, though, Citation found plenty of buyers, including nearly 25,000 for its sporty X-11 package. Monza Spyders were available again, but V-8 engines were not. Camaro's Z28 took on further bodily changes, this time rear fender flares and a rear-facing hood scoop. California Z28 fans couldn't have the 350 cubic inch V-8. Both 267 and 305 cubic inch V-8s were available in other Camaros, though, along with the new base V-6. Monte Carlos could now get Buick's turbocharged 231 cubic inch V-6, which delivered 55 more horsepower than the standard 229 cubic inch engine. Turbo-powered Chevrolets never quite took hold, as they did in other makes. Oldsmobile diesels were available in full-size station wagons. Overall, Chevrolet sales declined by some 20 percent in this rough year for the industry.

Citation's X-11 package included a high-output V-6 engine for 1981, but the recalls were already having an impact on sales. Monte Carlo got a wedge-shape aero restyle, but little else was new. A diesel engine, supplied by Isuzu, became available in Chevettes, with five-speed gearbox. Sales slipped again—even worse for full-size models, which seemed in danger of extinction. Within the next couple of years, however, they would enjoy a rebirth of popularity.

Front-wheel drive took on two additional forms for 1982: Subcompact Cavalier and family-size Celebrity, both of which quickly became popular. A downsized Camaro looked even sleeker than its predecessor, if also a lot more expensive. It was named "Car of the Year" by Motor Trend. Powerplants ranged from the base Pontiac "Iron Duke" four (now fuel-injected), to 173 cubic inch V-6 and 305 cubic inch V-8. More than 6,300 Indianapolis 500 Commemorative Editions of the Z28 were built. Z28 Camaros could also get a Cross-Fire fuel-injected engine, churning out 165 horsepower.

Most noteworthy event of the 1983 model year was the arrival of a Cavalier convertible. A new high-output, 190-horsepower, 305 cubic inch V-8 became available under Camaro hoods. Monte Carlo added an SS model, which gained a strong following, also with a high-output 305 V-8. Only four-door full-size models were offered this year, but Caprice's coupe would return for 1984. Five-speed gearboxes were available on Chevette, Cavalier and Camaro. Malibu, a long-standing nameplate, was in its final season. NHTSA's order to recall Citations for the alleged brake problems helped sales to plunge. Chevrolet sales went up somewhat, but largely as a result of increases in larger models.

A more powerful Monte Carlo SS lured youthful customers for 1984, with its wind-tunnel nose and lack of brightwork. Cross-Fire injection had lasted only two years as a Z28 option, but a four-barrel V-8 took its place. Camaro Berlinettas turned to a Corvette-inspired cockpit with digital instruments. A Eurosport option was added to Celebrity's possibilities; a Type 10 hatchback model to Cavalier's. So was a Celebrity station wagon. No more Chevette Scooters were built—hardly a major loss. Cavalier was America's best selling car, with Celebrity a strong second.

Excitement marked the 1985 model year, with the arrival of the IROC-Z Camaro. This Z28 option was styled like racing models, with foglamps, low air dam, and full-circle "ground effects" skirting. Three 305 cubic inch V-8s were available, including one with tuned-port fuel injection. A performance-oriented Z24 Cavalier was announced, but didn't arrive until later. Chevrolet's market share dropped by a percentage point (to 19 percent). Two new Chevrolet imports hit the market: The three-cylinder Sprint (from Suzuki) and four-cylinder Spectrum (from Isuzu).

Citation finally bit the dust after 1985, but something quite different emerged: The joint-venture Nova, produced in partnership with Toyota. One more nameplate disappeared: Impala. Cavalier had its Z24, with port-injected 173 cubic inch V-6 engine; and an RS series replaced the former Type 10. Monte Carlo added a luxurious and stylish LS model. On the sales front, Celebrity took over Cavalier's spot as Number One. Early in 1987, the Chevette dropped away. Even pioneers can't last forever, especially when front-drive had become the standard for small cars—and more than a few big ones.

Chevrolet observed 75 years of automaking in 1987. By this time, filling every niche in the market was more than a goal; it had become a necessity for a company that had dropped more than five percent in market share since 1980. With American buyers flocking to Japanese cars, Chevy's patriotic "baseball, hot dogs and apple pie" appeal was waning. After 1,200 workers lost their jobs in a $311 million shutdown and modernization of the 40-year-old Wilmington, Delaware, plant in February 1986, it became clear that the company's future was dependent upon success of the new Nova—coming out of its New United Motor Manufacturing joint-venture with Toyota, in Fremont, California—and its Corsica/Beretta "world class" models.

The importance of these new product plans was even greater by mid-year, by which time Chevrolet deliveries were running 133,500 units below the previous season and Ford was threatening to take over the Number One sales slot. Unfortunately, the introduction of Corsica and Beretta (as 1988 models) was delayed until March 1987, to allow a test of 17,000 cars by rental car companies and shipping of 45,000 to dealer showrooms nationwide. Hailed as "the slowest new car launch in history," this sluggish promotion induced Chevy General Manager Bob Burger to lower sales goals by some 50,000 units.

During 1987 model announcements, Chevrolet promised "cars with the latest technology and most advanced engineering available at affordable prices." The model lineup started with the Sprint, which was actually an import built by Suzuki and therefore outside the scope of this catalog. Next came the entry-level Chevette, in its 11th year and now lacking a diesel. It was followed by the smaller, but pricier Spectrum, a badge-engineered Isuzu built stateside. It had a re-calibrated suspension and optional turbocharged 1.5-liter four-cylinder engine capable of 0-to-60 mph in less than nine seconds. America's best selling car, the Cavalier, was back again in five models, including a convertible. A new Getrag five-speed manual transmission was available with the optional V-6.

Chevy's 1987 family fleet included the two Nova four-doors, three Celebritys and the full-sized Caprice. All Celebritys with the Eurosport package or optional V-6 could be had with a Getrag-like five-speed. Caprice buyers had a choice of a 4.3-liter V-6 or 5.0-liter V-8 and many picked the fancier Brougham trim level to emphasize old-fashioned splendor.

Additionally, the lineup included future collectibles such as the Camaro (especially IROC Camaros with the hot 190 hp Corvette V-8) and the Monte Carlo, which could still be had in limited-production Aero Coupe SS format boasting 80 hp.

With the 1988 Corsica/Beretta selling at over 30,000 units per month by June 1987, Chevrolet entered model year 1988 with Bob Burger predicting sales of 1.7 million cars. This projection equated to nearly 17 percent of the year's anticipated 10.3 million industry output and eventually matched the company's domestic and imported car production of 1,709,742 units in the model year. Retail sales of U.S.-built Chevys, in the calendar year, stood at 1,363,187.

Gone for 1988 was the Chevette, which left a niche for the Spectrum to fill completely. Another new "special interest" 1988 model was the Twin Cam Nova, featuring a potent 110 hp, 16-valve engine, stiff suspension, aluminum wheels and four-wheel disc brakes. It came with a 120-mph speedometer and found favor with about 10 percent of Nova buyers. New for the Cavalier was an Aero package with spoilers, flares and a 130 hp Z24 V-6. The convertible remained available for enthusiasts, too. In fact, it was upgraded to Z24 status and a $15,000-plus price tag.

Subtle refinements graced the 1988 Celebritys, along with a re-tuned Eurosport suspension and better anti-corrosion protection. The Monte Carlo returned, almost unchanged from the year previous, but now offering a third engine option: The High Output 5.0-liter V-8 rated at 200 hp at 4800 rpm.

Big news for Camaro enthusiasts was the release of a convertible, available in both sport coupe and IROC-Z trim levels. LT and Z28 models were discontinued. Four engines were offered: 130 hp, 165 hp, 190 hp and 220 hp. As *Motor Trend* read, "You can still play kick-the-Porsche with one of the best performing American anachronisms on the street."

An interesting new development for Chevrolet, in 1989, was the Suzuki-built Geo Metro, in two-door hatchback and four-door sedan versions, which replaced the Sprint. This model, as well as the renamed Geo Spectrum, is considered an import and is not covered in this catalog under its Geo affiliation (which would change to Chevrolet in 1998, where the coverage begins). Maintaining its sporty image was the 1989 Cavalier, with base, RS, Z24 and VL (Value Leader) trim levels. Only the coupe and convertible came with the 130 hp Z24 option and the VL—an entry-level variation—was available for just the coupe.

The Corsica and Beretta line—now housing the best-selling Chevys since 1980—reflected ongoing change for 1989. A hatchback Corsica sedan had been added, as well as the four-door LTZ with a sport suspension and stickshift and V-6. Performance-minded buyers could order the GTU package with Aero body modifications and 16-inch wheels and tires. Celebritys had a revamped cylinder head for the base 2.5-liter balance-shaft four-cylinder engine fitted with the three-speed automatic. When the V-6 was added, buyers could select a four-speed automatic or five-speed manual gearbox. Larger families, desiring more room, could opt for

a Caprice or Caprice Classic station wagon with 5.0-liter V-8. the wagon's engine used a four-barrel carburetor and generated 140 hp. Thirty additional horsepower were produced by a 5.0-liter EFI V-8. Camaros came in two trim levels, RS and IROC-Z, and two body styles, coupe and convertible, now with a Pass-Key anti-theft system. The RS looked a bit more like the discontinued Z-28, while top output for the IROC was increased to 225 hp at 4200 rpm.

A high-performance 180-hp Quad 4-powered Beretta GTZ coupe replaced the former GTU offering in 1990. Added to the Chevy lineup this year was the Lumina—a replacement for the Monte Carlo that was discontinued after 1988. The front-drive Lumina was available in coupe and sedan versions in base and Eurosport trim levels. All Cavaliers offered in 1990 had solid tops as ragtops were dropped from the series. Both the Cavalier's engines grew more powerful, with the former 2.0-liter four-cylinder replaced by the 2.2-liter four and the former 2.8-liter V-6 replaced by a 3.1-liter V-6. The Celebrity sedan was dropped leaving only the station wagon in that series, available in two-seat or three-seat versions in base or Eurosport trim. Both the Camaro and Caprice had short runs in 1990 as all-new 1991 models were expected.

When the 1991 Camaro arrived in early 1990, the Z28 returned as a replacement for the discontinued IROC-Z. Also dropped was the Celebrity series and the LTZ sedan from the Corsica lineup. Added were an RS convertible to the Cavalier stable and Z34 performance coupe in the Lumina series. The Z34 featured a 3.4-liter DOHC V-6 rated at 200 hp. The all-new-design Caprice and Caprice Classic also debuted this year with a more rounded appearance and including the LTZ sedan powered by a 5.7-liter V-8 capable of 0-to-60 mph in under 10 seconds.

The Z24 ragtop returned to the Cavalier series in 1992 after a two-year absence. It was powered by the 3.1-liter V-6. All Camaros could be ordered with the Heritage Edition exterior package commemorating the 25th Anniversary of the Camaro. The Z28 coupe could be ordered with the 5.7-liter V-8. Anti-lock brakes were now standard on most Chevrolet models including Cavalier, Corsica, Beretta and Lumina Euro and Z34. A Lumina Euro 3.4 sedan also debuted in 1992, offering a domestic choice in the upscale luxury/performance car category dominated by Japanese brands.

The fourth-generation Camaro debuted in 1993—only as a coupe in base and Z28 versions—and was dubbed the "closest thing to a 'Vette" by Chevrolet. Other lines were refined, with the Lumina's base powerplant now the 2.5-liter four-cylinder engine, which replaced the former 2.2-liter four. Also, all Caprice models were now lumped into the Caprice Classic series.

After a year of little change in '93, 1994 saw wholesale change within the ranks of Chevrolet models. The former Impala SS concept car, based on the Caprice Classic LTZ, was aligned with the Caprice Classic series as a production sedan. A ragtop rejoined the Camaro series, offered in both base and Z28 versions. The former Beretta GT and GTZ performance coupes were dropped in favor of a single, equally potent coupe called the Z26. The Cavalier VL station wagon and Lumina's base coupe were also dropped. Caprice Classic models received a new standard engine in the 4.3-liter V-8, which supplanted the 5.0-liter V-8 used previously.

(Continued on page 381)

1976

1976 Chevrolet, Chevette two-door hatchback coupe

1976 Chevrolet, Chevette Rally 1.6 two-door hatchback coupe (CH)

Chevrolet's lineup was largely a carryover from 1975, with one big (actually small) exception: the new subcompact Chevette. Throughout the line, improved gas mileage was the year's primary theme. Chevrolet also reduced its total number of models. A new 305 cu. in. engine replaced the former 350 as base V-8 under Chevelle, Monte Carlo and Camaro hoods. Vega and Monza also got new engines this year. Most models could have optional low axle ratios. Rectangular headlamps, first offered on full-size 1975 models, were now stacked vertically on Malibu Classic and Monte Carlo. All Chevrolets had a new roll-over fuel spillage control system. Brake materials were improved. Monza offered a sporty new Spyder option package. Rust resistance got considerable attention this year. Chevettes were protected by 17 anti-corrosion methods including wax base spray; epoxy paint; front inner fender plastic liners; zinc coated cowl side panels, hood, roof side rails and rear quarter panels; zinc-rich primer; galvanized metal front side rails, front valance and rocker panels; and oil base coating on rear springs. Promoted for Vega was a zinc-rich pre-prime coating on door surfaces; Plastisol-sealed door edges; aluminum wax spray applied to inner door areas after painting; plus four-layer fender protection, zinc-coated steel for lower radiator support and front fenders, and galvanized steel rocker panels.

CHEVETTE -- SERIES 1T -- FOUR -- "A new kind of American car" was promised by Chevette's catalog, "international in design and heritage." Target market was buyers of Datsun B-210, Toyota Corolla, and VW Rabbit. In addition to the basic four-passenger two-door hatchback, Chevrolet offered Sport, Woody and Rallye options, as well as a bare-bones two-passenger (no back seat) Scooter with a base price of just $2899. Chevette's design was based on GM's German-built Opel Kadett. Powered by a base 85 cu. in. (1.4-liter) four-cylinder overhead-cam engine, Chevette carried a fully synchronized four-speed manual transmission, rack-and-pinion steering, and front disc brakes. Chevrolet's new subcompact measured almost 17 inches shorter than Vega (formerly the smallest Chevrolet), and weighed over 600 pounds less (just under one ton). As for economy, EPA estimates with the base 1.4-liter engine and four-speed manual gearbox came to 28 MPG city and 40 MPG highway. And the optional 97.6 cu. in. (1.6-liter) OHC four was thriftier yet, reaching a 48 MPG highway estimate. Styling features included an aero-designed front spoiler and flush-type door handles. Chevette's simple grille consisted of four wide openings (two on each side) in an angled body-color panel. Front fenders held small marker lenses; rear quarters, similar red lenses. Round headlamps were recessed; park/signal lamps mounted below the bumper area. Front fenders held 'Chevette' script near rear edges. At the rear were "international" horizontal tri-color taillamps (red, amber and white). The full-width (48 in.) rear hatch had pneumatic supports. This was Chevrolet's first metric-measurement car, supplied with a simple self-servicing booklet. A built-in diagnostic connector (first one on a domestic car) helped do-it-yourselfers or mechanics analyze electrical system problems. The optional Four-Season air conditioner had its own diagnostic connector. Unibody construction plus a combined hood and grille gave easy underhood accessibility. Front fenders bolted on. High-strength bumpers were mounted on shock absorbers, which connected to solid underbody rails. The front suspension had a stabilizer bar, low-friction ball joints and high-caster geometry, mounted on a heavy-gauge crossmember. At the rear were variable-rate coil springs and torque tube axle. Chevette was the first Chevrolet to get a fingertip "Smart Switch" on the steering column to control headlamp dimmer, turn signals, lane-change and "flash-to-pass" signals, and wiper/washer. Up front were full-form, shell-type bucket seats; in back, a full-width seat with folding backrest. Body color choices were: antique white, silver, light or dark blue metallic, lime green, bright yellow, cream, burnt orange, medium orange, firethorn metallic, light red, black, buckskin, or dark green metallic. (Light blue metallic, lime green, burnt orange and light red were Chevette exclusives.) Soft vinyl upholstery came in black, dark blue, light buckskin or dark firethorn. Cloth-and-vinyl upholstery came in light buckskin or dark firethorn. The optional Custom interior was rattan-pattern vinyl in black, light buckskin, dark blue, dark firethorn or white; or Rutledge cloth-and-vinyl in the same colors (except white). Standard equipment included the 1.4-liter engine; four-speed manual gearbox with floor lever; blackwall tires on 13 x 5 in. disc wheels; heater/defroster; fuel gauge; courtesy light in windshield header; easy-access instrument panel; spare tire below cargo floor; mini do-it-yourself service manual; color-keyed wall-to-wall carpeting; fold-down rear seat; glove compartment with door latch; bright bumpers and trim moldings; and acoustical insulation. The Sport Coupe added bold sport stripes and black accents. The Rally Coupe package came with a 1.6-liter engine, special suspension with rear stabilizer bar, special instruments including tachometer and temperature gauge, sport shifter and steering wheel, passenger assist grip, Rally wheel covers, and black rocker panels. Woody Coupes had woodgrain vinyl body trim, custom interior with woodgrain vinyl accents on the instrument cluster, sport steering wheel, day/night mirror, bright window moldings, wheel trim rings, and deluxe grille with bright accents. The low-budget Scooter had only two bucket seats and less standard equipment, including an open glove compartment. It came only in light blue, antique white, cream, or light red. Chevette options included the larger 1.6-liter engine, AM/FM radio, twin sport mirrors, Four-Season air conditioning, sport steering wheel, deluxe bumpers with impact strips, bumper guards, rooftop luggage rack, rear defogger, custom exterior trim package, and swing-out rear quarter windows. Also optional: a sport shifter (with console), the $306 Woody package, and Rally equipment. Turbo Hydra-matic cost an extra $244.

1976 Chevrolet, Vega GT two-door hatchback coupe (CH)

VEGA -- SERIES 1H -- FOUR -- Chevrolet's first subcompact coupe, introduced in 1971, never quite managed to overcome its early so-so reputation. Vegas came in sport and hatchback coupe form, as well as a two-door station wagon and Estate wagon. The LX model was dropped this year. The base aluminum-block four added new hydraulic valve lifters, eliminating the need for tappet adjustment. Crankcase ventilation was improved to ease engine breathing. New valve stem seals improved overhead oil control. Instead of a catalytic converter, the base four used an air pump and manifold injection for emissions control. Torque arm rear suspension was new this year (introduced on the '75 Monza). Brakes used larger (9-1/2 x 2 in.) rear drums and new organo-metallic front disc pad material. Power brakes were optional. So was a new lightweight, aluminum-case four-speed manual gearbox, as well as a five-speed on the Cosworth twin-cam model (and others with the optional two-barrel engine). The four-speed came with a new 2.53:1 axle ratio, plus long 3.75:1 low-gear ratio. A new box-section design front cross-member added structural rigidity. Vega's new grille consisted of three wide louvered openings that reached almost to the recessed round headlamps, giving the car an ultra-wide appearance. Parking lamps sat behind the grille. At the back, new multi-color lights were divided into three top-to-bottom sections, with tiny square backup lenses in lower sections. (Wagons had narrower vertical taillamps.) Vega's unitized body had bolt-on front fenders. Body colors this year were antique white, silver, black, buckskin, cream, bright yellow, medium orange, and seven metallics: light or dark blue, firethorn, mahogany, lime green, medium saddle, and dark green. Both 140 cu. in. four-cylinder engines were called Dura-built: with one-barrel (70 horsepower) or two-barrel (84 horsepower) carburetion. Vegas rode 13 x 5 in. steel wheels, except 13 x 6 in. on the GT. Cosworths had 13 x 6 in. cast aluminum wheels. Standard equipment included the 140 cu. in. four with 1Bbl. carburetor, three-speed manual transmission (floor shift), electric fuel pump, heater/defroster, front bucket seats, and A78 x 13 blackwall tires. All models could have five-speed manual or Turbo Hydra-matic for the same $244 extra cost. All could get a new heavy-duty sealed Freedom battery. Vega's GT package included the two-barrel version of the 140 engine, F41 sport suspension, special instruments, woodgrain accents on instrument cluster, dual sport mirrors (left remote-controlled), black headlamp bezels, bright grille header moldings, 13 x 6 in. wheels with trim rings, and A70 x 13/B white-letter tires. Offered for both hatchback coupes and wagons, the GT package also included a sport steering wheel, belt and wheel opening moldings, adjustable driver's seatback, and black sill and lower bodyside moldings. Sport coupes could have a new Cabriolet appearance option. This would be the final season for the Cosworth Twin Cam Vega. Cosworths carried an aluminum 122 cu. in. engine developed by Chevrolet and Cosworth Engineering of England. It had twin overhead camshafts, 16 valves, electronic fuel injection and mechanical valve lifters, and developed 110 horsepower at 5600 R.P.M. Four-speed manual shift was standard. To boost performance, the axle ratio switched from the former 3.73:1 to a new 4.10:1. Cosworths came in nine colors with gold pin striping. Included were special gold-color aluminum wheels; 'Cosworth Twin Cam' decals on rear and both sides; gold-colored wheel opening stripes; and end panel striping. Custom interiors came in black or white, with Cosworth insert in the sport steering wheel. Also standard: an 8000 R.P.M. tachometer and adjustable driver's seatback.

1976 Chevrolet, Monza two-door Town Coupe (PH)

1976 Chevrolet, Monza 2 + 2 two-door hatchback coupe (PH)

MONZA -- SERIES 1H -- FOUR/V-8 -- Monza's 2 + 2 hatchback had been named *Motor Trend* "Car of the Year" after introduction in 1975. Part way through that model year, the Town Coupe debuted, with much different notchback styling. Both returned for 1976, along with a formal Cabriolet version of the Town Coupe. The base Towne Coupe had large rear quarter windows, hard bumpers, plus a sound-deadening and acoustical package. The $256 Cabriolet option included opera-type rear quarter windows and a vinyl top that covered the rear half of the roof, plus bright moldings, sport equipment, and woodgrain steering wheel shroud. Hatchbacks had a low body-color grille: just two rows of four wide holes, with that pattern repeated below the bumper. On the solid panel above the grille was a round emblem, plus 'Chevrolet' lettering off toward the driver's side. Parking lamps with rounded outer lower edges sat below the bumper. An engine identification plaque was at the front of front fenders, above the marker lens; 'Monza 2 + 2' lettering farther back, at the cowl. Quad rectangular headlamps were inset into a soft, resilient urethane front-end skin. The hood sloped down between the headlamps, but contained a bulge farther back. The 2 + 2 had bright-trimmed wraparound taillamps that tapered to a point on the bodyside, with square backup lenses toward the center. Town Coupes had an entirely different front-end and side look, including bright chrome bumpers and single headlamp bezels. A classic grid grille (six holes wide) held hidden parking/signal lights. Rear bumper cover and rocker panels were body-colored. Monza body colors were cream, bright yellow, medium orange, black, buckskin, silver and antique white, plus metallic light or dark blue, firethorn, mahogany, lime green, saddle brown, and dark green. Refinements for the aluminum-block 140 cu. in. (2.3-liter) four included new hydraulic lifters for quieter running, new valve stem seals to improve oil control, and improved crankcase ventilation. That engine again had a 60,000-mile, five-year guarantee. Monza also offered options of a two-barrel version of the 140 four, a 262 cu. in. (4.3-liter) V-8, or even a 305 (5.0-liter) V-8. That big V-8 was smaller in size, yet considerably stronger in horsepower, than the 350 offered in 1975. No V-8s were available on the base Towne Coupe. The two-barrel four was included in Sport and Cabriolet packages. Transmission choices included a new four-speed manual gearbox with aluminum case for the four-cylinder engine, plus an economy five-speed that had been introduced during the 1975 model year. A new underbody lowered the floor hump between bucket seats by more than two inches. An all-new brake system included larger rear drums with increased torque capacity, a new vented front rotor, new front disc pad material, and front-to-rear proportioning. A muffler replaced the catalytic converter on the Town Coupe's base four. Models that retained converters lost their exhaust system resonators this year. All models had a new floor shift and parking brake console. The new lighter weight four-speed gearbox, used with four-cylinder engines, had a 3.75:1 low gear. Monza standard equipment included the 2.3-liter four with one-barrel carburetor, three-speed manual transmission, heater/defroster, bucket seats, cigarette lighter, front disc brakes, A78 x 13/B tires, and cut-pile carpeting. Hatchback 2 + 2 models included Euro-style finned wheel covers with GT center hub and bright nuts. Towne Coupes had bright metallic wheel covers. The 4.3-liter V-8 engine cost an extra $224. Four- and five-speed manual gearboxes were optional, as was Turbo Hydra-matic. So were aluminum wheels, as well as a widened choice of entertainment options including AM/FM stereo radio and tape player. Inside, the 2 + 2 had a new deluxe "stitched" instrument panel pad, with woodgrain vinyl ornamentation color-keyed to the car interior. A two-spoke steering wheel had woodgrain vinyl insert. The 2 + 2 had knit cloth and vinyl upholstery in black, buckskin or firethorn; or all-vinyl in black, buckskin, firethorn or white. Town Coupes had sport cloth upholstery in black or buckskin. Cabriolet equipment for the Town Coupe included the padded vinyl roof in firethorn, mahogany, white, silver metallic, buckskin, or blue. Monza's Spyder package, available on the 2 + 2 or Town Coupe with sport equipment, had the two-barrel four; floor console; F41 suspension with large front and rear stabilizer bars and special shocks; wheel opening moldings; day/night mirror; sport steering wheel; distinctive Spyder identification; special instrumentation and stitched instrument panel pad with woodgrain vinyl accents; and BR70 or BR78 radial tires. Spyders required a five-speed manual gearbox or Turbo Hydra-matic. A total of 2,339 were produced. Town Coupes with Sport equipment had a black pillar appliqué with argent edges, ahead of large rear quarter windows. The package included body-colored finned wheel covers with argent painted edges; front stabilizer bar; plus body-contoured high-back front bucket seats. Knit cloth/vinyl upholstery came in black, buckskin or firethorn; all-vinyl in black, buckskin, firethorn or white.

1976 Chevrolet, Nova Concours two-door coupe (CH)

NOVA -- SERIES 1X -- SIX/V-8 -- Nova Concours joined the lineup this year as top-of-the-line member of the compact family. Both 111 in. wheelbase models showed a new front-end look. Novas displayed a new six-row crosshatch grille (6 x 12 pattern) split in half by a heavier horizontal bar, with single round headlamps. Regular Novas had vertical amber parking lamp lenses at grille ends. Twin side-by-side rectangular taillamps were split by two horizontal dividers. Concours models added chrome trim around the headlamps and hood

areas, as well as a special NC insignia and upright three-dimensional hood ornament. Concours' similar but bold grille had 24 square holes in two rows, each square containing 3 x 3 crosshatching, also with vertical parking lamps between grille and headlamps. Concours had a wide bright panel above the grille; regular Novas did not. Identifying features also included a fender nameplate, wheel cover insignia, and NC shield on the rear panel. Concours models also carried bumper guards and impact strips, bright moldings, plus dark-accented full-length bodyside louvers and rocker panel moldings. Inside, the Concours had rosewood-grain vinyl accents on the dash, steering wheel and upper door panels, along with identification on the right side of the instrument panel. A new 305 cu. in. engine became the basic V-8, replacing the former 262. Base engine continued to be the inline 250 cu. in. six. A four-barrel 350 V-8 was also optional again. Power brakes moved from the option list to standard equipment for V-8 Novas this year, and were available on six-cylinder models. Brake systems had new front disc pads and rear lining material, and larger-diameter rear cylinders. Air conditioners had a new seven-mode setting and maximum cooling position. Otherwise, changes were modest this year: altered fuel and exhaust system mountings, new interior colors and trim materials, and new instrument panel knobs. Nova's body colors were: medium orange, buckskin, cream, antique white, bright yellow, black and silver; plus metallic light or dark blue, firethorn, mahogany, lime green, saddle, and dark green. Regular Nova interiors came in three cloth and vinyl colors: black, buckskin or firethorn. All-vinyl colors were buckskin, blue or firethorn. Hatchbacks came only with all-vinyl interiors. Concours had three knit cloth and vinyl interiors: black, buckskin or firethorn. Or all-vinyl in buckskin or firethorn. White interiors were available in coupe and hatchback only. Optional: new high-pile deluxe carpeting. Standard equipment included the 250 cu. in. six-cylinder engine (one-barrel carb), three-speed manual shift, heater/defroster, front disc brakes, and cut-pile carpeting. Nova V-8s had power brakes. Four-speed wide-range manual shift cost $242, while a floor shift lever cost $29 extra. Both cabriolet and vinyl roofs were optional. So were heavy-duty and sport suspensions. The 350 cu. in. V-8 was available for $85 more than the standard 305 V-8. Nova Concours carried similar equipment but added bright moldings, front/rear bumper guards, full wheel covers, cigarette lighter, and FR78 x 14 steel-belted radial tires. Nova's Super Sport (SS) coupe and hatchback had a new black-finished diamond-mesh pattern grille with 'Nova SS' emblem, plus other black-accented trim. Styling features included black headlamp bezels and side window frame moldings; distinctive lower body side striping; Nova SS decals on fenders and rear end panel; dual black sport mirrors (left remote controlled); horizontal parking lamps with clear lenses; heavy-duty suspension; and four-spoke sport steering wheel. The $187 SS coupe package also included roof drip moldings, rally wheels with trim rings, and heavy-duty F40 front/rear suspension. All told, 7,416 SS Novas came off the line.

1976 Chevrolet, Nova SS two-door coupe (CP)

CAMARO -- SERIES 1F -- SIX/V-8 -- Chevrolet's sport coupe, in base or Type LT (Luxury Touring) form, looked similar to the 1975 version. The crosshatch grille was made up of thin bars peaked forward at the center, surrounded by a bright molding with rounded upper corners. Round, deeply recessed parking lamps sat between the grille and the recessed round headlamps. Front fenders held small side marker lenses. Taillamps with bright moldings wrapped around the side, tapering to a point. Small vertical backup lights were in the taillamp housings. Rectangular emblems sat on hood and deck. Type LT had a 'TYPE LT' nameplate on the right side of the bright rear end panel, but could also be spotted by its brushed aluminum appliqué across the full width of the rear end panel. LT seat trim now used vertical stitching for both cloth and vinyl upholstery (three knit cloth/vinyl choices or three all-vinyl). Standard sport coupes came with two cloth/vinyl interiors or four in all-vinyl. Styling features included a long hood and short deck, with swept-back roofline. Sport Coupes had new narrow bright rocker panel moldings, 14 x 6 in. wheels, contoured Strato-bucket front seats, cut-pile carpeting, padded vinyl-covered four-spoke steering wheel with crest, and a left outside mirror. Type LT added Hide-A-Way wipers and sport mirrors (left one remote-controlled), and 14 x 7 in. Rally wheels. Inside LT were a tachometer, clock, voltmeter and temp gauge, plus color-keyed steering wheel, glove compartment light, and simulated leather instrument panel trim. LT interiors also had special bucket seats with deep-contour backs and built-in padded armrests. A new small-block V-8 engine was available this year: a 305 cu. in. (5.0-liter) version that replaced the 350 as standard eight-cylinder engine. It came with either the standard or high-performance axle ratio. As before, the 250 cu. in. inline six was the base (Sport Coupe) powerplant, while a 350 (5.7-liter) V-8 with four-barrel carburetor was available for both models. Transmission choices were the same as in 1975, except that the four-speed manual gearbox came with a 2.85:1 low-gear ratio (formerly 2.54:1). Power brakes (front disc) were now standard with V-8s. Brake improvements included new front disc pad material and new rear linings, plus larger-diameter rear wheel cylinders. Base Sport Coupes had the standard inline six; LT the new 305 V-8. Standard equipment included a heater/defroster, variable-ratio power steering, finned rear brake drums, contoured Strato bucket seats, four-spoke steering wheel, and FR78 x 14 steel-belted radial tires. Three-speed manual transmission (floor shift) was standard. Turbo Hydra-matic was optional on all models, wide-range four-speed manual available with the optional 350 cu. in. engine (which cost $85 more than the 305). Both transmissions were priced at $260. Cruise-Master speed control was optional for the first time. Also available: Rally or styled wheels, sport suspension, power windows and door locks, Four-Season air conditioning, rear defogger, tinted glass, white-letter tires, front and rear spoilers, Positraction, two-position driver's seatback, and center console with storage area. This year's vinyl Sport Roof covered only the front, leaving a painted band exposed at the back. Of the 14 Camaro body colors this year, ten were new. Choices were: light or dark blue metallic, firethorn metallic, mahogany metallic, lime green or dark green metallic, buckskin, cream, bright yellow, medium orange or saddle metallic, black, silver, and antique white. Sport Coupes came with black or dark firethorn cloth/vinyl upholstery, or all-vinyl in black, white, dark firethorn or light buckskin. Type LT offered three Dover knit cloth/vinyl choices (black, dark blue and dark firethorn) or all-vinyl in black, white or light buckskin. A Rally Sport package, available on both models, included low-gloss black finish on forward roof, hood, grille, header panel, headlamp bezels, upper fenders, rockers and rear panel, as well as Rally wheels. Tri-color striping separated the black-accented areas from the basic body color. The package also included bright headlamp trim, 'Rally Sport' decals on decklid and front fender, and argent paint. Rally Camaros came in white, silver, light blue metallic, firethorn metallic, or bright yellow body colors.

1976 Chevrolet, Camaro Type LT two-door coupe (CP)

1976 Chevrolet, Camaro Rally Sport two-door coupe (CP)

1976 Chevrolet, Chevelle Malibu Classic Landau two-door coupe (CP)

CHEVELLE -- SERIES 1A -- SIX/V-8 -- Two Chevelle series were offered for 1976, Malibu and Malibu Classic, plus (for the last time) the sportier Laguna S-3. The Malibu Classic lineup included a Colonnade coupe and sedan, plus Landau coupe, two- and three-seat wagons, and two- or three-seat Estate wagons. Base Malibus came in coupe, sedan or wagon form (also two- or three-seat). Malibu Classic's restyled front end displayed new stacked rectangular headlamps, plus a lightweight diamond-pattern grille with script in lower corner, "classic" hood ornament, and new bumpers. Standard Malibus added a new horizontally-ribbed grille, but kept their single round headlamps with bright bezels. Both displayed a restyled rear end with tapered rear panel, with new horizontal rectangular taillamps and bumper in integrated design. Parking lamps were inset in the lower bumper. Landau coupes had new color-keyed paint stripes at front and rear, coach window styling, and distinctive vinyl roof. Malibu Classics had wide bright rocker panel moldings and window moldings, while base Malibus were plain. Biggest change in the powerplant parade was a new small-block 305 cu. in. (5.0-liter) standard V-8, which was supposed to emit fewer hydrocarbons as well as deliver better economy than the prior 350 V-8. Though the stroke of the 305 was the same as the 350, it was the only Chevrolet engine to have a 3.74 inch bore. Base engine was again the 250 cu. in. inline six, hooked to either three-speed manual or optional Turbo Hydra-matic. (V-8 Chevelles came only with automatic.) A 350 V-8 with two-barrel remained optional, as did a four-barrel 400 cu. in. V-8. Only in California was the four-barrel 350 offered. The big 454 was dropped as a Chevelle option this year. All Chevelles except the basic six-cylinder Malibu coupe and sedan now had standard power brakes. The brake system used new lining materials, plus larger rear drums in coupes and sedans. Standard equipment included the six-cylinder engine, three-speed manual (column) shift, front disc brakes, heater/defroster, cut-pile carpeting, lighter, hide-away wipers, and FR78 x 15/B steel-belted radial tires. Chevelle V-8s had a standard 305 engine and Turbo Hydra-matic, GR78 tires, as well as power brakes and steering. Wagons carried the 350 V-8. The Malibu Classic Landau added a vinyl roof, body-color sport mirrors (left one remote-controlled), deluxe bumpers, dual horns, and full wheel covers. 70-series radial tires and

sport suspension were available at extra cost. All models could have the 400 cu. in. V-8 powerplant for $148 or less. Of the 14 body colors this year, nine were new. Available were metallic light or dark blue, firethorn, mahogany, lime green, medium saddle, and dark green; plus cream, medium red, buckskin, cream gold, antique white, silver, and black. Interiors came in new knit vinyls as well as patterned cloths and expanded vinyls. Light buckskin, dark mahogany and lime white were new interior trim colors. Base Malibu interiors were sport cloth and vinyl, in black and buckskin. All-vinyl upholstery came in black, buckskin or blue, plus mahogany and white (with accents of black, lime or mahogany) for coupes only. Malibu Classic's interior was standard knit cloth and vinyl in black, blue or mahogany. (Coupes could have buckskin.) Or buyers could get all-vinyl in buckskin and blue, plus black, mahogany and white (with accents of black, blue, mahogany or lime) for coupe only. For its final season, the sporty Laguna S-3 added the new Chevelle rear end but otherwise looked largely the same as in 1975. Laguna had an angled, aerodynamically styled "soft" urethane front end, louvered coach windows, sport mirrors (driver's remote), rally wheels, color-keyed bumper impact strips, plus S-3 identification on grille, front fenders and rear panel. Optional on Laguna: sport roof and sport striping. Inside was a round-dial instrument panel and woodgrain vinyl accents. The radial-tuned suspension had large-diameter stabilizer bars and revalved shock absorbers. Not available on Laguna bodies were light blue metallic, cream, medium saddle metallic, dark green metallic, medium red, buckskin, and cream gold. Laguna interiors were sport cloth and vinyl in black and buckskin; or all-vinyl in black, buckskin, blue and mahogany; plus white with accents of black, lime or mahogany.

1976 Chevrolet, Monte Carlo Landau two-door coupe (CP)

MONTE CARLO -- SERIES 1A -- V-8 -- Chevrolet's personal-luxury coupe, in the lineup since 1970, came in regular 'S' or Landau coupe form. New front-end styling focused on new vertically-stacked rectangular headlamps, plus an integrated-look bumper. This year's grille was made up of three wide segments, one above the other, each with internal crosshatching. Both parking and backup lamps were repositioned. Rounded horizontal parking lamps sat below the bumper. New tapered vertical taillamps had emblems in the center and small rectangular backup lenses below. A characteristic bodyside bulge tapered from front fenders into doors, continuing again on the rear quarters. Base engine was the 305 cu. in. (5.0-liter) V-8 with two-barrel carburetor; optional, either a 350 two-barrel or 400 four-barrel. Only in California was the 350 with four-barrel carb available. The 454 cu. in. V-8 available in 1975 was dropped this year. Standard powertrain included Turbo Hydra-matic with a 2.73:1 axle ratio. Montes also had standard power steering and brakes, electric clock, hideaway wipers, cut-pile carpeting, full wheel covers, and 15 x 7 in. wheels with GR70 x 15/B steel-belted radial tires. The Landau model added a landau vinyl roof and body-color sport mirrors (left remote), visor vanity mirror, plus Turbine II wheels, pinstripe accents, dual horns, and landau body identification. The 350 cu. in. V-8 engines cost an extra $30 (two-barrel) or $85 (four-barrel); the 400 V-8, an extra $148. New to the option list: an electric rear window defogger. Of the 14 Monte body colors, nine were new. They included cream, buckskin, cream gold, medium red, white, black and silver; plus metallic mahogany, firethorn, medium saddle, lime green, light blue, dark blue, or dark green. Two-tones were available. Standard interiors had a full-foam bench seat; deep cut pile carpeting; color-keyed instrument panel and steering wheel; and tailored knit cloth or vinyl upholstery in choice of three shades. Optional swivel bucket seats could have rich velour fabric. Custom interiors came in velour, knit cloth or vinyl fabric; or three all-vinyl colors.

1976 Chevrolet, Impala S four-door sedan (CP)

1976 Chevrolet, Caprice Classic four-door Sport Sedan (CP)

IMPALA/CAPRICE -- SERIES 1B -- V-8 -- Full-size Chevrolets got new front styling and engine/brake refinements. For 1976 there were 13 models in two series (down from 17 in three series the year before). Bel Air sedans and wagons were dropped, as was the Caprice convertible. Impala's sport coupe was dropped; a new Impala sedan added. Impala's lineup now included a Custom coupe, Custom Landau coupe, sport sedan, four-door sedan, 'S' sedan, and station wagons (two or three seat). On the higher-priced Caprice Classic side, the choices were a coupe, sport sedan, four-door sedan, and Landau coupe; plus Caprice Estate station wagons (two or three seat). This would be the final year for the "true" pillarless four-door hardtop body. Impala refined its "swept back" front end look with round quad headlamps (as on the '75 Caprice). The grille had four full-width segments that appeared unconnected to each other. At the rear were triple-unit wraparound taillamps. The new Caprice front-end look featured new quad rectangular headlamps, plus a new grille with bold chrome horizontal and vertical bars and smaller inner bars. Both grilles repeated themselves in twin segments down in the front bumper. Both lines had hideaway windshield wipers. Caprice had wide bodyside moldings with color-keyed textured vinyl inserts (which could match the vinyl roof, if desired). Four V-8 choices were available: 350 cu. in. (5.7-liter) with two- or four-barrel carburetor; 400 cu. in. (6.6-liter) 4Bbl.; and big 454 (7.4-liter) with 4Bbl. Three-speed Turbo Hydra-matic was standard with each engine. Wagons kept the 400 V-8 as standard powerplant. Like all Chevrolet engines, the 454 V-8 got revised ignition tuning and carburetor metering, plus refinements to improve economy and performance at low- and mid-range speeds. Some models with the 454 got different brake lining materials and heavier brake drums, plus a new brake pedal ratio. Standard Caprice equipment included the 350 V-8 with two-barrel, power steering and brakes, carpeting, heater/defroster, deluxe bumpers, and accent stripes. Caprice also had rear fender skirts, a quiet sound group, electric clock, and GR78 x 15/B steel-belted radial tires. Wagons came with glide-away tailgate and LR78 x 15/C tires. Landau coupes added twin sport mirrors (left remote-controlled). The big 454 V-8 was optional on all models, priced from $223 to $375. Inside, Caprice Classic sported new bright steering wheel trim; plus new simulated rosewood accents on instrument cluster, steering wheel, and above the glove compartment. Impala's standard equipment was similar to Caprice, but the low-budget 'S' version had bias-ply tires rather than radials, and less acoustical material. Impala 'S' also had no bodyside chrome strip or door window trim. Impala had a soft-rimmed steering wheel with cushioned center; but the same dash as Caprice, with simulated rosewood. Landau versions of both coupes had an elk-grain padded vinyl roof cover in choice of colors to complement the body. Also included: landau identification on quarter-window glass, body-colored wheel covers with landau markings, twin body-color sport mirrors, deluxe bumpers with impact strips, accent stripes and bright moldings. Sport sedans had a bright metal vinyl top molding. Of the 14 Caprice/Impala body colors, nine were new this year. The list included cream, antique white, silver, black, medium red, buckskin and cream gold; plus metallic light or dark blue, lime or dark green, medium saddle, firethorn, and mahogany. Impala upholstery was new standard knit cloth and vinyl in black, dark blue, or dark firethorn; or buckskin sport cloth. Caprice's knit cloth and vinyl came in black, dark blue, or dark mahogany. All-vinyl white trim was now available in the Caprice Classic coupe. Wagons added a cargo light as auxiliary lighting, while an illuminated visor vanity mirror was available on all models. Options included aluminum door edge guards.

I.D. DATA: Like other GM passenger cars, Chevrolets used a 13-symbol Vehicle Identification Number (VIN) displayed on the upper left surface of the instrument panel, visible through the windshield. The first digit ('1') indicates Chevrolet Division. Next is a letter identifying the series (car line): 'B' = Chevette; 'J' = Chevette Scooter; 'V' = Vega; 'M' = Monza; 'R' = Monza 2 + 2; 'X' = Nova; 'Q' = Camaro; 'S' = Camaro Type LT; 'Y' = Nova Concours; 'C' = Chevelle Malibu; 'D' = Malibu Classic; 'E' = Laguna S-3; 'H' = Monte Carlo; 'L' = Impala; 'N' = Caprice Classic. Symbols 3-4 indicate body type: '08' = Chevette 2-dr. hatchback coupe; '11' = Vega 2-dr. notchback pillar coupe; '77' = Vega 2-dr. hatchback coupe; '07' = Monza hatchback pillar coupe; '17' = Nova 2-dr. hatchback coupe; '27' = 2-dr. notchback coupe; '87' = Camaro 2-dr. hardtop sport coupe; '37' = Chevelle 2-dr. notchback hardtop coupe; '47' = Caprice/Impala 2-dr. notchback hardtop coupe; '57' = Monte Carlo 2-dr. hardtop coupe; '69' = 4-dr. (4-window) pillar sedan; '39' = 4-dr. (4-window) hardtop sedan; '29' = Chevelle 4-dr. sedan; '35' = 4-dr. 2-seat station wagon; '45' = 4-dr. 3-seat station wagon; '15' = Vega 2-dr. station wagon. Symbol five is the engine code: '1' = L4-85 1Bbl.; 'E' = L4-97.6 1Bbl.; 'O' = L4-122 EFI; 'A' = L4-140 1Bbl.; 'B' = L4-140 2Bbl.; 'D' = L6-250 1Bbl.; 'G' = V8-262 2Bbl.; 'Q' = V8-305 2Bbl.; 'V' = V8-350 2Bbl.; 'L' = V8-350 4Bbl.; 'U' = V8-400 4Bbl.; 'S' = V8-454 4Bbl. Next is a code for model year ('6' = 1976). Symbol seven denotes assembly plant: 'B' = Baltimore, MD; 'C' = South Gate, CA; 'D' = Doraville, GA; 'J' = Janesville, WI; 'K' = Leeds, MO; 'U' = Lordstown, OH; 'L' = Van Nuys, CA; 'N' = Norwood, OH; 'R' = Arlington, TX; 'S' = St. Louis, MO; 'T' = Tarrytown, NY; 'W' = Willow Run, MI; 'Y' = Wilmington, DE; 'Z' = Fremont, CA; '1' = Oshawa, Ontario; '2' = St. Therese, Quebec; '4' = Scarborough, Canada. The last six digits are the sequential serial number. A Body Number Plate on the upper horizontal surface of the shroud (except X-bodies, on the vertical surface) identifies model year, car division, series, style, body assembly plant, body number, trim combination, modular seat code, paint code, and date build code. A three-symbol (sometimes two) code combined with a serial number identifies each engine. Inline sixes have that number on a pad at front right of block, at rear of distributor. On V-8s, it's on a pad at front right side of block. Chevette engine numbers are on a pad at right of block, below No. 1 spark plug. Vega numbers are on a pad at right side of block below No. 3 plug at head parting line.

CHEVETTE (FOUR)

Model No.	Body/Style No.	Body Type & Seating	Factory Price	Shipping Weight	Prod. Total
1T	B08	2-dr. Hatch-4P	3098	1924	178,007

CHEVETTE SCOOTER (FOUR)

1T	J08	2-dr. Hatch-4P	2899	1870	9,810

Chevette Production Note: 7,523 Chevettes were built for the Canadian market, called Acadians.

VEGA (FOUR)

1H	V11	2-dr. Spt Cpe-4P	2984	2443	27,619
1H	V77	2-dr. Hatch-4P	3099	2534	77,409
1H	V15	2-dr. Sta Wag-4P	3227	2578	46,114
1H	V15	2-dr. Est Wag-4P	3450	N/A	7,935

1976 Chevrolet, Cosworth Vega two-door hatchback coupe (CP)

COSWORTH VEGA (FOUR)

1H	V77	2-dr. Hatch-4P	6066	N/A	1,446

MONZA (FOUR/V-8)

1H	M27	2-dr. Twn Cpe-4P	3359	2625	46,735
1H	R07	2-dr. Hatch 2+2-4P	3727	2668	34,170

Monza Engine Note: Prices shown are for four-cylinder. Only 7,277 Towne Coupes and 10,085 hatchbacks had a V-8 engine, which cost an additional $224. Production totals include four-cylinder Monzas built in Canada.

NOVA (SIX/V-8)

1X	X27	2-dr. Cpe-6P	3248/3413	3188/3272	131,859
1X	X17	2-dr. Hatch-6P	3417/3579	3391/3475	18,719
1X	X69	4-dr. Sedan-6P	3283/3448	3221/3305	123,767

NOVA CONCOURS (SIX/V-8)

1X	Y27	2-dr. Cpe-6P	3795/3960	3324/3408	22,298
1X	Y17	2-dr. Hatch-6P	3972/4134	3401/3485	7,574
1X	Y69	4-dr. Sedan-6P	3830/3995	3367/3451	30,511

CAMARO (SIX/V-8)

1F	Q87	2-dr. Spt Cpe-4P	3762/3927	3421/3511	130,538
1F	S87	2-dr. LT Cpe-4P	----/4320	----/3576	52,421

CHEVELLE MALIBU (SIX/V-8)

1A	C37	2-dr. Col Cpe-6P	3636/4166	3650/3755	30,592
1A	C29	4-dr. Col Sed-6P	3671/4201	3729/3834	38,469
1A	C35	4-dr. Sta Wag-6P	----/4543	----/4238	13,581
1A	C35	4-dr. 3S Wag-9P	----/4686	----/ N/A	2,984

CHEVELLE MALIBU CLASSIC (SIX/V-8)

1A	D37	2-dr. Col Cpe-6P	3926/4455	3688/3793	82,634
1A	D37	2-dr. Lan Cpe-6P	4124/4640	N/A	30,167
1A	D29	4-dr. Col Sed-6P	4196/4490	3827/3932	77,560
1A	D35	4-dr. Sta Wag-6P	----/4776	----/4300	24,635
1A	D35	4-dr. 3S Wag-9P	----/4919	----/ N/A	11,617
1A	G35	4-dr. Est Wag-6P	----/4971	----/4326	5,518
1A	G35	4-dr. 3S Est Wag-6P	----/5114	----/ N/A	6,386

Malibu Classic Engine Note: Only 672 Landau coupes, 5,791 regular coupes and 4,253 sedans had a six-cylinder engine.

LAGUNA S-3 (V-8)

1A	E37	2-dr. Col Cpe-5P	4622	3978	9,100

Laguna Production Note: Total includes 864 built in Canada.

MONTE CARLO (V-8)

1A	H57	2-dr. 'S' Cpe-6P	4673	3907	191,370
1A	H57	2-dr. Lan Cpe-6P	4966	N/A	161,902

FULL-SIZE CHEVROLETS

IMPALA (V-8)

1B	L47	2-dr. Cust Cpe-6P	4763	4175	43,219
1B	L47	2-dr. Lan Cpe-6P	5058	N/A	10,841
1B	L69	4-dr. Sedan-6P	4706	4222	86,057
1B	L69	4-dr. 'S' Sed-6P	4507	N/A	18,265
1B	L39	4-dr. Spt Sed-6P	4798	4245	39,849
1B	L35	4-dr. Sta Wag-6P	5166	4912	19,657
1B	L45	4-dr. 3S Wag-9P	5283	4972	21,329

CAPRICE CLASSIC (V-8)

1B	N47	2-dr. Coupe-6P	5043	4244	28,161
1B	N47	2-dr. Lan Cpe-6P	5284	N/A	21,926
1B	N69	4-dr. Sedan-6P	5013	4285	47,411
1B	N39	4-dr. Spt Sed-6P	5078	4314	55,308
1B	N35	4-dr. Est Wag-6P	5429	4948	10,029
1B	N45	4-dr. 3S Est-6P	5546	5007	21,804

FACTORY PRICE AND WEIGHT NOTE: Where two prices and weights are shown, the figure to the left of the slash is for six-cylinder model, to right of slash for V-8 (except Monza, four-cylinder and V-8).

PRODUCTION NOTE: Chevelle and full-size totals include models built in Canada.

ENGINE DATA: BASE FOUR (Chevette): Inline. Overhead cam. Four-cylinder. Cast iron block and head. Displacement: 85.0 cu. in. (1.4 liters). Bore & stroke: 3.23 x 2.61 in. Compression ratio: 8.5:1. Brake horsepower: 52 at 5200 R.P.M. Torque: 70 lb.-ft. at 3600 R.P.M. Five main bearings. Hydraulic valve lifters. Carburetor: 1Bbl. Rochester 1ME. VIN Code: 1. **OPTIONAL FOUR** (Chevette): Inline. Overhead cam. Four-cylinder. Cast iron block and head. Displacement: 97.6 cu. in. (1.6 liters). Bore & stroke: 3.23 x 2.98 in. Compression ratio: 8.5:1. Brake horsepower: 60 at 4800 R.P.M. Torque: 82 lb.-ft. at 3400 R.P.M. Five main bearings. Hydraulic valve lifters. Carburetor: 1Bbl. Roch. 1ME. VIN Code: E. **BASE FOUR** (Cosworth Vega): Inline vee-slanted. Dual overhead cam. Four-cylinder 16-valve (four valves per cylinder). Cast aluminum alloy block and head. Displacement: 122 cu. in. (2.0 liters). Bore & stroke: 3.50 x 3.16 in. Compression ratio: 8.0:1. Brake horsepower: 110 at 5600 R.P.M. Torque: 107 lb.-ft. at 4800 R.P.M. Five main bearings. Solid valve lifters. Electronic fuel injection. VIN Code: O. **BASE FOUR** (Vega, Monza): Inline. Overhead cam. Four-cylinder. Aluminum block, cast iron head. Displacement: 140 cu. in. (2.3 liters). Bore & stroke: 3.50 x 3.63 in. Compression ratio: 8.0:1. Brake horsepower: 70 at 4400 R.P.M. Torque: 107 lb.-ft. at 2400 R.P.M. Five main bearings. Hydraulic valve lifters. Carburetor: 1Bbl. Rochester

1MV. VIN Code: A. **OPTIONAL FOUR** (Vega, Monza): Same as 140 cu. in. four above, except: Brake H.P.: 84 at 4400 R.P.M. Torque: 113 lb.-ft. at 3200 R.P.M. Carb: 2Bbl. Holley 5210C. **BASE SIX** (Nova, Chevelle, Camaro): Inline. OHV. Six-cylinder. Cast iron block and head. Displacement: 250 cu. in. (4.1 liters). Bore & stroke: 3.88 x 3.53 in. Compression ratio: 8.25:1. Brake horsepower: 105 at 3800 R.P.M. Torque: 185 lb.-ft. at 1200 R.P.M. Seven main bearings. Hydraulic valve lifters. Carburetor: 1Bbl. Roch. 1MV. VIN Code: D. **OPTIONAL V-8** (Monza): 90-degree, overhead valve V-8. Cast iron block and head. Displacement: 262 cu. in. (4.3 liters). Bore & stroke: 3.67 x 3.10 in. Compression ratio: 8.5:1. Brake horsepower: 110 at 3600 R.P.M. Torque: 195 lb.-ft. at 2000 R.P.M. Five main bearings. Hydraulic valve lifters. Carburetor: 2Bbl. Roch. 2GC. VIN Code: G. **BASE V-8** (Monte Carlo); **OPTIONAL V-8** (Monza, Nova, Camaro, Chevelle): 90-degree, overhead valve V-8. Cast iron block and head. Displacement: 305 cu. in. (5.0 liters). Bore & stroke: 3.74 x 3.48 in. Compression ratio: 8.5:1. Brake horsepower: 140 at 3800 R.P.M. Torque: 245 lb.-ft. at 2000 R.P.M. Five main bearings. Hydraulic valve lifters. Carburetor: 2Bbl. Roch. 2GC. VIN Code: Q. **BASE V-8** (Chevelle wagon, Caprice, Impala); **OPTIONAL V-8** (Chevelle, Monte Carlo): 90-degree, overhead valve V-8. Cast iron block and head. Displacement: 350 cu. in. (5.7 liters). Bore & stroke: 4.00 x 3.48 in. Compression ratio: 8.5:1. Brake horsepower: 145 at 3800 R.P.M. Torque: 250 lb.-ft. at 2200 R.P.M. Five main bearings. Hydraulic valve lifters. Carburetor: 2Bbl. Roch. 2GC. VIN Code: V. **OPTIONAL V-8** (Nova, Camaro, Chevelle, Monte Carlo, Caprice, Impala): Same as 350 cu. in. V-8 above, except four-barrel carburetor. Brake H.P.: 165 at 3800 R.P.M. Torque: 260 lb.-ft. at 2400 R.P.M. Carb: 4Bbl. Roch. M4MC. VIN Code: L. **BASE V-8** (Caprice/Impala wagon); **OPTIONAL V-8** (Chevelle, Monte Carlo, Caprice, Impala): 90-degree, overhead valve V-8. Cast iron block and head. Displacement: 400 cu. in. (6.6 liters). Bore & stroke: 4.13 x 3.75 in. Compression ratio: 8.5:1. Brake horsepower: 175 at 3600 R.P.M. Torque: 305 lb.-ft. at 2000 R.P.M. Five main bearings. Hydraulic valve lifters. Carburetor: 4Bbl. Roch. M4MC. VIN Code: U. **OPTIONAL V-8** (Caprice, Impala): 90-degree, overhead valve V-8. Cast iron block and head. Displacement: 454 cu. in. (7.4 liters). Bore & stroke: 4.25 x 4.00 in. Compression ratio: 8.25:1. Brake horsepower: 225 at 3800 R.P.M. Torque: 360 lb.-ft. at 2400 R.P.M. Five main bearings. Hydraulic valve lifters. Roch. M4ME. VIN Code: S.

CHASSIS DATA: Wheelbase: (Chevette) 94.3 in.; (Vega/Monza) 97.0 in.; (Camaro) 108.0 in.; (Nova) 111.0 in.; (Chevelle cpe) 112.0 in.; (Chevelle sed/wag, Monte Carlo) 116.0 in.; (Imp/Capr) 121.5 in.; (Imp/Capr wag) 125.0 in. Overall length: (Chvt) 158.7 in.; (Vega) 175.4 in.; (Monza twn cpe) 177.8 in.; (Monza hatch) 179.3 in.; (Camaro) 195.4 in.; (Nova) 196.7 in.; (Nova Concours) 197.7 in.; (Camaro) 195.4 in.; (Chevelle cpe) 205.3 in.; (Laguna) 207.3 in.; (Chevelle sed) 209.3 in.; (Chevelle wag) 215.2 in.; (Monte) 212.7 in.; (Imp/Capr) 222.9 in.; (Imp/Capr wag) 228.6 in. Height: (Chvt) 52.3 in.; (Vega spt cpe/wag) 51.8 in.; (Vega hatch) 50.0 in.; (Monza twn cpe) 49.8 in.; (Monza hatch) 50.2 in.; (Nova) 54.3 in.; (Camaro) 49.2 in.; (Chevelle/Laguna cpe) 53.1 in.; (Chevelle sed) 53.8 in.; (Chevelle wag) 55.7 in.; (Monte) 52.7 in.; (Imp/Capr cpe) 53.7 in.; (Imp/Capr sed) 54.4 in.; (Imp/Capr spt sed) 53.9 in.; (Imp/Capr 2S wag) 58.1 in.; (Imp/Capr 3S wag) 57.4 in. Width: (Chvt) 61.8 in.; (Vega/Monza) 65.4 in.; (Nova) 72.2 in.; (Camaro) 74.4 in.; (Chevelle) 76.6 in.; (Chevelle wag) 76.8 in.; (Monte) 77.6 in.; (Imp/Capr) 79.5 in. Front Tread: (Chvt) 51.2 in.; (Vega/Monza) 54.8 in.; (Nova/Camaro) 61.3 in.; (Camaro LT) 61.6 in.; (Chevelle) 61.5 in.; (Monte) 61.9 in.; (Imp/Capr) 64.1 in. Rear Tread: (Chvt) 51.2 in.; (Vega/Monza) 53.6 in.; (Nova) 59.0 in.; (Camaro) 60.0 in.; (Camaro LT) 60.3 in.; (Chevelle/Monte) 60.7 in.; (Imp/Capr) 64.0 in. Standard Tires: (Chvt) 155/80-13-B; (Vega/Monza) A78 x 13/B; (Nova) E78 x 14/B; (Nova Concours, Camaro) FR78 x 14/B; (Chevelle six) FR78 x 15/B; (Chevelle V-8) GR78 x 15/B; (Chevelle wag) HR78 x 15/B; (Monte) GR70 x 15/B; (Imp/Capr) G78 x 15/B; (Imp/Capr wag) LR78 x 15/C.

TECHNICAL: Transmission: Three-speed floor shift standard on Vega/Monza four and Camaro; column shift on Chevelle/Nova; floor shift available on Nova. Gear ratios: (1st) 3.11:1; (2nd) 1.84:1; (3rd) 1.00:1; (Rev) 3.22:1; except Nova V-8-350 (1st) 2.85:1; (2nd) 1.84:1; (3rd) 1.00:1; (Rev) 2.95:1. Four-speed floor shift standard on Chevette, optional on Vega/Monza four: (1st) 3.75:1; (2nd) 2.16:1; (3rd) 1.38:1; (4th) 1.00:1; (Rev) 3.82:1. Four-speed floor shift optional on Monza V-8, Cosworth: (1st) 3.11:1; (2nd) 2.20:1; (3rd) 1.47:1; (4th) 1.00:1; (Rev) 3.11:1. Four-speed floor shift optional on Nova/Camaro V8-350: (1st) 2.85:1; (2nd) 2.02:1; (3rd) 1.35:1; (4th) 1.00:1; (Rev) 2.85:1. Five-speed floor shift on Vega/Monza: (1st) 3.10:1; (2nd) 1.89:1; (3rd) 1.27:1; (4th) 1.00:1; (5th) 0.80:1; (Rev) 3.06:1. Three-speed Turbo Hydra-matic standard on Chevelle V-8 and Monte/Caprice/Impala, optional on others. Gear ratios: (1st) 2.52:1; (2nd) 1.52:1; (3rd) 1.00:1; (Rev) 1.94:1 except Caprice/Impala w/V8-454: (1st) 2.48:1; (2nd) 1.48:1; (3rd) 1.00:1; (Rev) 2.08:1. Chevette and Nova (exc. V8-350) THM gear ratios: (1st) 2.74:1; (2nd) 1.57:1; (3rd) 1.00:1; (Rev) 2.07:1. Standard final drive ratio: (Chevette) 3.70:1 exc. 4.11:1 w/1.6 engine; (Vega) 2.92:1 exc. 2.53:1 w/4-spd, 2.93:1 w/5-spd, 2.92:1 or 3.42:1 w/auto.; (Cosworth Vega) 4.10:1; (Monza) 2.92:1 exc. 2.56:1 or 2.93:1 w/5-spd or auto., 3.42:1 w/2Bbl. four, 2.56:1 w/V-8; (Nova) 2.73:1 exc. 3.08:1 w/V8-350, 2.73:1 or 3.08:1 w/auto.; (Camaro) 2.73:1 exc. 2.73:1 or 3.08:1 w/auto., 2.85:1 w/4-spd; (Chevelle) 2.73:1 exc. 2.73:1 or 3.08:1 w/auto.; (Monte) 2.73:1; (Caprice/Imp) 2.73:1 or 3.08:1. Steering: (Chevette) rack and pinion; (others) recirculating ball. Front Suspension: unequal-length control arms, coil springs, stabilizer bar. Rear Suspension: (Chevette) rigid axle, torque tube, longitudinal trailing radius arms, coil springs, transverse linkage bar; (Vega) rigid axle, lower trailing radius arms, upper oblique torque arms, coil springs, transverse linkage bar; (Monza) similar to Vega, with stabilizer bar; (Nova/Camaro) semi-elliptic leaf springs, stabilizer bar on Camaro; (others) rigid axle, lower trailing radius arms, upper oblique torque arms and coil springs, plus stabilizer bar on Laguna, Monte and Caprice Classic. Brakes: Front disc, rear drum. Ignition: High energy electronic. Body construction: (Chvt/Vega/Monza) unitized; (Nova/Camaro) integral, with separate partial front box frame; (Chevelle/Monte/Impala/Caprice) perimeter box frame with cross-members. Fuel tank: (Chvt) 13 gal.; (Vega) 16 gal.; (Monza) 18.5 gal.; (Nova/Camaro) 21 gal.; (Chevelle/Monte) 22 gal.; (Imp/Capr) 26 gal.; (Imp/Capr wag) 22 gal.

DRIVETRAIN OPTIONS: Engines: 1.6-liter four: Chevette ($51). 140 cu. in., 2Bbl. four: Vega/Monza ($56). 262 cu. in., 2Bbl. V-8: Monza ($224). 350 cu. in., 2Bbl. V-8: Chevelle/Monte ($30). 350 cu. in., 4Bbl. V-8: Nova/Camaro/Chevelle/Monte ($85); Chevelle wag ($55); Imp/Caprice cpe/sed ($56). 400 cu. in., 4Bbl. V-8: Chevelle/Monte ($148); Chevelle wag ($118); Imp/Capr cpe/sed ($120). 454 cu. in., 4Bbl. V-8: Imp ($375); Caprice ($350); Imp/Capr wag ($223). Transmission/Differential: Four-speed manual shift: Vega/Monza ($60). Four-speed wide-range manual shift: Nova ($242); Camaro ($260). Five-speed manual shift: Vega/Monza ($244). Turbo Hydra-matic transmission: Chevette/Vega/Monza ($244); Nova/Camaro, Chevelle six ($260). Sport shifter w/console: Chevette ($40). Floor shift lever: Nova ($29). Positraction axle: Vega/Monza ($48); Nova/Camaro/Chevelle/Monte ($51); Imp/Capr ($55). High-altitude or highway axle ratio: Chvt/Vega/Monza ($12); Chevelle/Monte/Imp/Capr ($13). High-altitude axle ratio: Nova/Camaro ($13). Power Accessories: Power brakes: Chvt/Vega/Monza ($55); Nova/Camaro/Chevelle six ($58). Power steering (variable ratio): Vega/Monza ($120); Nova/Chevelle ($136). Suspension: F40 H.D. suspension: Nova ($6-$29); Chevelle/Monte/Imp/Capr ($18). F41 sport suspension: Vega ($141); Monza ($26); Nova/Camaro ($25-$32); Imp ($32); Caprice ($7). FE8 radial-tuned suspension: Chevelle ($27); Imp/Capr cpe/sed ($25). Superlift rear shock absorbers: Imp/Caprice ($44). Rear stabilizer bar: Chevette ($26). Other: Heavy-duty radiator ($25-$34). H.D. alternator (61-amp): Chevelle/Monte/Imp/Capr ($27). H.D. battery ($15-$16). California emission certification ($50).

CHEVETTE/VEGA/MONZA CONVENIENCE/APPEARANCE OPTIONS: Option Packages: Woodie package: Chevette ($306). Rally equipment: Chevette ($230-$251). GT pkg.: Vega hatch ($457); Vega wagon ($340-$429). Cabriolet equipment (vinyl roof, opera windows, bright moldings, woodgrain steering wheel shroud, sport equipment): Monza ($256). Sport equipment: Monza ($118). Spyder equipment: Monza Twn Cpe ($421-$430); Monza hatch ($333-$342). Quiet sound group: Chvt ($29-$39); Vega ($32-$43). Comfort/Convenience: Air conditioning ($424). Rear defogger ($66). Tinted glass ($44). Sport steering wheel ($15). Comfortilt steering wheel: Vega/Monza ($48). Special instrumentation: Chvt ($56); Vega ($72); Monza ($56-$72). Econominder gauge: Monza ($10-$26). Electric clock: Chvt/Monza ($16). Cigarette lighter: Chvt ($5). Glove compartment lock: Chvt ($3). Lighting and

Mirrors: Aux. lighting: Vega ($15-$29); Monza ($15). Twin sport mirrors, left remote: Vega/Monza ($25). Driver's remote sport mirror: Chvt ($19). Twin remote sport mirrors: Chvt ($43). Day/night mirror ($7). Entertainment: Push-button AM radio ($70). Push-button AM/FM radio ($129). AM/FM stereo radio: Vega/Monza ($212). Stereo tape player w/AM radio: Monza ($196). Rear speaker ($20). Windshield antenna: Vega/Monza ($15); incl. w/radios. Exterior Trim: Vinyl roof: Chvt ($90). Swing-out windows: Chvt ($45); Vega cpe ($29-$35). Custom exterior: Chvt ($82); Vega ($59-$88). Decor group: Vega ($6-$34). Sport decor: Chvt ($77). Sport stripes: Vega ($76). Bodyside moldings ($36). Wheel opening moldings: Vega/Monza ($19). Side window reveal moldings: Chvt ($59). Door edge guards ($7). Roof carrier: Chvt/Vega ($53). Rear air deflector: Vega ($23). Deluxe bumpers, front/rear: Chvt ($27); Vega ($44). Deluxe bumpers w/guards: Monza ($60). Deluxe front bumper guards: Vega ($17). Deluxe bumper guards, front/rear: Chvt ($34-$61); Monza ($34). Interior Trim/Upholstery: Custom interior trim: Chevette ($152-$164). Console: Chvt ($16); Monza ($73). Bucket seats: Vega ($126-$158); Monza ($124-$140). Adjustable driver's seatback: Vega/Monza ($17). Load floor carpet: Chvt ($40). Color-keyed floor mats ($14). Front mats: Chvt ($8). Deluxe seatbelts ($15). Trunk mat: Monza ($10). Wheels and Tires: Aluminum wheels: Monza ($173-$204). Rally II wheels: Vega ($97). Wheel covers: Vega ($28). Sport wheel covers: Chvt ($36-$66). Wheel trim rings: Chvt ($30); Vega ($3-$30). 155/80-13/B WSW: Chvt ($32). 155/80-13/B SBR: Chvt ($99). 155/80-13/B SBR WSW: Chvt ($131). 155/80-13/B SBR WLT: Chvt ($145). A78 x 13/B WSW: Vega ($32); Monza ($26-$32). A78 x 13/B belted WSW: Vega ($53); Monza ($43-$53). BR78 x 13/B SBR: Vega ($34-$122); Monza ($98-$122). BR78 x 13/B SBR WSW: Vega ($66-$154); Monza ($123-$154). BR78 x 13/B SBR WLT: Vega ($80-$168); Monza ($135-$168). BR78 x 13/C SBR: Monza ($114-$146). BR78 x 13/C SBR WSW: Monza ($25-$178). BR78 x 13/C SBR WLT: Monza ($36-$192). BR70 x 13/B SBR WLT: Monza ($36-$46). Stowaway spare: Monza ($23).

NOVA/CAMARO/CHEVELLE/MONTE CARLO CONVENIENCE/APPEARANCE OPTIONS: Option Packages: SS equipment: Nova ($187). Rally Sport equipment: base Camaro ($260); Camaro LT ($173). Interior decor/quiet sound group: base Camaro ($53). Comfort/Convenience: Air conditioning ($452-$479). Rear defogger (forced-air): Nova/Camaro/Monte ($43); Chevelle ($43-$47). Rear defogger (electric): Monte ($77). Cruise-Master speed control: Nova/Chevelle/Monte ($73). Tinted glass: Nova/Camaro ($46); Chevelle ($49); Monte ($53). Sport steering wheel: base Nova, Chevelle ($16). Comfortilt steering wheel ($52). Six-way power seat: Chevelle/Monte ($124). Power windows ($99-$140). Power door locks: Nova/Chevelle ($62-$89); Camaro/Monte ($62). Power trunk release: Monte ($17). Power tailgate release: Chevelle 2S wag ($20). Electric clock: Nova/Camaro ($18); Chevelle ($19). Special instrumentation (incl. tach and console):

Nova ($160); Concours ($89). Special instrumentation (incl. tach and clock): base Camaro ($92). Econominder gauge pkg.: Chevelle/Monte ($45). Econominder light: Nova ($16). Intermittent wipers: Nova/Monte ($28). Hide-a-way wipers: base Camaro ($22). Lighting, Horns and Mirrors: Aux. lighting ($21-$41). Dual horns: Nova/Camaro/Chevelle ($6). Remote-control driver's mirror: Nova/Chevelle/Monte ($14). Twin sport mirrors, left remote ($27). Twin remote sport mirrors (body-color): Nova/Chevelle/Monte ($20-$46). Day/night mirror: Nova ($7). Visor vanity mirror: Chevelle/Monte ($4). Lighted visor mirror: Chevelle ($26); Monte ($23-$26). Entertainment: Push-button AM radio ($75). AM/FM radio: Nova/Camaro/Chevelle ($137); Monte ($146). AM/FM stereo radio ($226). Stereo 8-track tape player w/AM radio: Nova/Camaro/Chevelle ($209); Monte ($225). Stereo tape player with AM/FM stereo radio ($324). Rear speaker ($21). Windshield antenna ($16); incl. w/radios. Exterior Trim: Electric sky roof: Monte ($370). Vinyl roof: Nova/Camaro ($96); Chevelle ($109); Monte ($129). Cabriolet roof: Nova ($150). Spoilers, front/rear: Camaro ($81). Exterior decor pkg.: Nova ($73); Chevelle ($19-$51). Custom appearance group: Nova Concours ($65-$75). Exterior style trim: Camaro ($58). Fashion-tone paint: Monte ($104-$233). Two-tone paint: Nova/Chevelle ($40). Swing-out rear side windows: Nova ($48). Bodyside moldings: Nova/Camaro/Chevelle ($38); Nova Concours, Monte ($49). Door edge guards ($7-$11). Wheel opening moldings: Nova ($19). Roof drip moldings: base Nova, Camaro ($16). Bodyside pin striping: Nova ($26). Sport stripes: Chevelle cpe/sed ($81). Rear window air deflector: Chevelle wag ($23). Roof carrier: Chevelle wag ($68). Deluxe bumpers: Chevelle/Monte ($29). Deluxe bumpers w/guards, front/rear: Nova ($63). Bumper guards, front/rear: Camaro/Chevelle/Monte ($36); Chevelle wag ($18). Interior Trim/Upholstery: Interior decor pkg.: base Nova ($25). Console: base Nova, Camaro/Chevelle/Monte ($71). Bench seat w/custom interior: base Nova ($180). Bucket seats: Nova ($255); Nova Concours ($204). Knit or sport cloth seats: Camaro, Chevelle wag ($20). Vinyl bucket seats: Chevelle ($20). Bucket seats w/knit cloth or vinyl: Chevelle ($102-$140); Monte ($140). Custom cloth bucket seats: Monte ($265). 50/50 reclining passenger seat: Monte ($273). Adj. driver's seatback: Camaro ($19). Litter container: Chevelle/Monte ($6). Deluxe carpet: Nova/Camaro ($32). Removable load-floor carpeting: Chevelle wag ($42). Color-keyed mats ($15). Deluxe seatbelts ($14-$20). Wheels and Tires: Custom styled wheels: Nova ($116); Nova Concours ($86); Camaro ($79-$116). Rally wheels: base Nova/Camaro ($60); Nova Concours ($38); Chevelle ($35-$60); Monte ($46). Wire wheel covers: Chevelle ($59-$89); Monte ($79); Monte Landau ($23 credit). Full wheel covers: base Nova, Camaro ($30). Deluxe wheel covers: Monte ($19). Wheel trim rings: base Nova ($33). E78 x 14/B BSW: Camaro ($84-$106 credit). E78 x 14/B WSW: base Nova ($26-$33); Camaro ($58-$73 credit). FR78 x 14/B SBR: base Nova ($84-$106). FR78 x 14/B SBR WSW: Nova ($112-$141); Nova Concours, Camaro ($28-$35); Chevelle six ($30-$37). FR78 x 14/B SBR WLT: Nova ($123-$155); Nova Concours, Camaro ($39-$49). GR78 x 15/B SBR WSW: Chevelle/Laguna V-8 ($30-$37). HR78 x 15/B SBR BSW: Chevelle/Laguna V-8 ($38). HR78 x 15/B SBR WSW: Chevelle/Laguna V-8 ($78); Chevelle wag ($40). GR70 x 15/B SBR BSW: Chevelle V-8 ($43-$54); Laguna ($14-$17). GR70 x 15/B SBR WSW: Chevelle V-8 ($73-$91); Laguna ($43-$54); Monte ($30-$37). GR70 x 15/B SBR WLT: Chevelle V-8 ($84-$105); Laguna ($55-$68). Stowaway spare: base Nova, Camaro ($15); Concours/Chevelle/Monte (NC).

NOTE: Chevelle/Laguna GR70 tires included sport suspension.

1976 Chevrolet, Impala two-door Custom Coupe (CP)

IMPALA/CAPRICE CONVENIENCE/APPEARANCE OPTIONS: Comfort/Convenience: Four season air cond. ($485). Comfortron auto-temp air cond. ($567). Rear defogger, forced-air ($44-$48). Cruise-Master speed control ($74). Tinted glass ($63). Comfortilt steering wheel ($53). Power door locks ($63-$90). Six-way power seat ($126). Power windows ($105-$159). Power trunk release ($17). Power tailgate: wag ($52). Electric clock: Imp ($19). Econominder gauge pkg. ($34). Intermittent wipers ($28). Quiet sound group ($33-$45). Lighting, Horns and Mirrors: Aux. lighting ($20-$37). Dome reading light ($14). Dual horns: Imp ($6). Driver's remote mirror ($14). Dual remote mirrors ($42). Dual remote body-color sport mirrors ($19-$47). Visor vanity mirror ($4). Lighted visor mirror ($26). Entertainment: Push-button AM radio ($76). AM/FM radio ($148). AM/FM stereo radio ($229). Stereo 8-track tape player w/AM radio ($228); with AM/FM stereo radio ($328). Rear speaker ($21). Windshield antenna ($16); incl. w/radios. Exterior Trim: Vinyl roof ($125-$150). Rear fender skirts ($33); std. on Caprice. Two-tone paint ($41) incl. bright outline moldings. Roof carrier: wag ($82). Bodyside moldings: wag ($39). Deluxe bodyside moldings: Imp ($25-$50). Door edge guards ($7-$11). Wheel opening moldings: Imp ($19); std. on cpe. Deluxe bumpers ($40). Bumper guards ($43). Interior Trim/Upholstery: 50/50 reclining passenger seat ($142). Deluxe load-floor carpet: wag ($61). Removable load-floor carpet: wag ($43). Color-keyed mats ($15). Litter container ($6). Color-keyed deluxe seatbelts ($17-$20). Deluxe trunk trim ($35-$43). Wheels and Tires: Full wheel covers ($31). Wire wheel covers ($69-$100). G78 x 15/B WSW: cpe/sed ($37). HR78 x 15/B SBR BSW: Imp S ($132); others (NC). HR78 x

15/B SBR WSW: Imp S ($172); other cpe/sed ($41). LR78 x 15/C SBR BSW (NC); std. on wag. LR78 x 15/C SBR WSW ($47).

HISTORY: Introduced: Oct. 2, 1975. Model year production (U.S.): 1,920,200 (incl. Corvettes but not incl. 7,523 Acadians). Of total vehicles built for U.S. market, 411,883 were four-cylinder, 278,775 six, and 1,341,112 had a V-8. Calendar year production: 2,012,024 (incl. 47,425 Corvettes, 5,311 Acadians and 27,677 Sportvans). Calendar year sales by U.S. dealers: 2,104,142 for a 24.4 percent market share, down from almost 26 percent in 1975. (That total included 30,337 Sportvans and 41,673 Corvettes.) Model year sales by U.S. dealers: 2,077,119 (including 27,416 Sportvans and 41,027 Corvettes), up from 1,714,593 in 1975.

Historical Footnotes: Chevrolet hoped to sell 275,000 Chevettes in its initial season, taking 185,000 sales away from imports, to help the company into a strong year after poor sales in 1975. Only 1,686,062 Chevrolets had been built in calendar year 1975, the lowest total since 1970. Model year production was lower yet for 1975: just 1,614,491, far below the 2.4 million Chevrolets produced in model year 1973. As it turned out, neither Chevette nor Vega sold well in 1976. This year did indeed see a resurgence in sales, but GM's best seller was now the Olds Cutlass, not a Chevrolet. In fact, Chevrolet sales amounted to only 42.6 percent of the GM total--one of the lowest figures posted in recent years. Model year sales were up, however, by 21.1 percent over the 1975 total. Why? Because big cars continued to sell rather well. The new 305 cu. in. V-8 was particularly well received by the public. R.L. Lund was Chevrolet's general manager. Appearing at the Detroit Auto Show was an experimental (but fully operational) Monza Super Spyder, crafted from a 1975 Monza 2 + 2. Powered by the Cosworth Twin Cam four- and five-speed gearbox, it featured a hand-built fiberglass nose and tail panels, magnesium wheels, and fluorescent tube lighting up front. This was one more GM show car that never made it into production.

1977

Full-size Chevrolets were downsized for 1977, leading the first wave of shrinkage that would hit the entire domestic lineup in the next few years. The old reliable inline six and the 305 cu. in. V-8 each added five horsepower. At mid-year the renowned Camaro Z28 returned, adorned with graphics and carrying a four-barrel 350 V-8 under the hood. The one-barrel 140 cu. in. four and 262 cu. in. V-8 were dropped. Intermittent wipers became optional on subcompact to compact models. A new "Pulse Air" system replaced air injection on Chevette, Vega and Monza fours.

1977 Chevrolet, Chevette two-door hatchback coupe (CH)

CHEVETTE -- SERIES 1T -- FOUR -- As in its opening season, Chevette came in two models: standard four-passenger hatchback coupe, and Scooter. But this year, the Scooter added a standard back seat for the same four-passenger capacity (though the back seat could be deleted). The Woody option was dropped, but the Rally Sport was offered again. A new "Sandpiper" appearance package, available with white or yellow-gold body paint (a color not offered on other models) wasn't hard to spot with foot-long 'Sandpiper' decals on quarter panels. A custom interior included yellow-gold "Reef" vinyl seat trim with cloth insert, plus yellow-gold carpeting, instrument panel and door panels. Also in the package: a sport steering wheel, day/night mirror, and carpeted cargo area. Two engines were available again this year: the base 85 cu. in. (1.4-liter) four and bigger 97 cu. in. (1.6-liter). Both could have either standard four-speed manual gearbox or optional three-speed automatic. (In California and high-altitude regions, only the 1.6 was available.) The 1.4 gained five horsepower this year as a result of a larger carburetor flow capacity and revised hot air intake system. Positive carburetor outside air control also improved cold-weather driveability. The 1.4 had similar changes but a smaller power boost. New front disc brake pad and rear brake lining materials were meant to increase lining life. A smaller rear wheel cylinder was said to improve front-to-rear braking balance. Joining Chevette's option list: an intermittent "pulse" windshield wiper that operated either from the "smart switch" on the column or a separate dash control. Interiors had a new pattern of vinyl cloth, while custom interiors used perforated vinyl. Of the 14 Chevette body colors, nine were new: light lime, red, bright orange, light buckskin, and five metallics (silver, dark blue, brown, orange, and dark aqua). Carryover colors were white, black, firethorn metallic, light blue, and bright yellow.

1977 Chevrolet, Vega two-door notchback coupe

VEGA -- SERIES 1H -- FOUR -- For its seventh and final try at luring buyers, Vega again came in three body styles: notchback or hatchback coupe, plus station wagon and Estate wagon. The Cosworth Vega was gone. So were the GT Estate Wagon options and Cabriolet equipment package. This year's GT package came in two levels: one subtle, the other bold. The subtler one had a blacked-out trim theme with black paint around window openings, windshield and doors, plus black sport mirrors and wheels. For a more noticeable look, the alternate package featured bold horizontal stripes that broke along the bodyside to display huge 'Vega GT' lettering. It was hard to miss, since the lower-bodyside decal ran the full distance between wheel openings. Standard engine was the 140 cu. in. (2.3-liter) Dura-Built four with two-barrel carburetor, plus four-speed manual gearbox. A five-speed manual and three-speed automatic transmission were available. The one-barrel carb engine and three-speed manual shift, formerly standard, were dropped this year. A new, simpler Pulse-Air manifold injection system was standard on the base engine, replacing the Air Injection Reactor system. Vega was the only domestic production car with an all-aluminum engine block. Vega's standard interior added a color-keyed steering column, steering wheel, instrument cluster face, and parking brake cover. Of the 14 body colors this year, eight were new: dark blue, brown, orange, silver or dark aqua metallic; light buckskin; light lime; and bright orange. Carryover colors were white, black, firethorn metallic, light blue, red, and bright yellow. Vega's GT package included woodgrained dash accents, sport mirrors (left remote), black headlamp bezels, bright grille header molding, F41 sport suspension, Rally II wheels with trim rings and special center caps, black sill and lower bodyside moldings, gauge set (including tachometer and clock), and white-letter tires. The price was $401 for hatchbacks (including belt moldings) and $373 for wagons.

1977 Chevrolet, Vega GT two-door hatchback coupe (CP)

1977 Chevrolet, Monza Spyder two-door hatchback coupe (CH)

1977 Chevrolet, Monza 2 + 2 two-door hatchback coupe

1977 Chevrolet, Monza 2 + 2 two-door Town Coupe

MONZA -- SERIES 1H -- FOUR -- Once again, Monza fielded a notchback Towne Coupe and a 2 + 2 hatchback, with no significant styling changes this year. Towne Coupes had a new rear look with functional tricolor taillamps. A Sport Front End Appearance option package, introduced late in the prior model year, gave Towne Coupes the same soft-fascia front end and rectangular headlamps as the 2 + 2, along with a rear bumper impact strip. Other carryover options: large rear quarter windows, or opera windows. The Cabriolet Equipment package was dropped, but a Cabriolet vinyl roof and opera windows remained available. Two intertwined all-new options were offered, however: the Monza Spyder appearance and performance packages. The appearance package included bold striping, front air dam and rear spoiler; plus satin black accents around window openings, headlamp openings and bezels, parking lamps, taillamps and grille louvers, as well as rocker panel, quarter, rear panel and fender areas. A large 'Spyder' script identification decal appeared on both doors. Dual side stripes came in black or gold, with Spyder lettering outlined in red, white or gold. The $199 package (for 2 + 2 only) also included black sport mirrors, black Rally II wheels and bright trim rings. Spyder's equipment package sold separately at $274. That one included an F41 suspension, console, sport steering wheel, sport mirrors, large Spyder emblem, hood header panel, modified front stabilizer and rear shocks, and BR70 x 13 radial tires. Other Monza options included aluminum wheels, Sport equipment and front-end appearance packages, front/rear spoilers, and an instrument set (including tachometer). Added to the option list: a digital clock over the glove box, angled toward the driver. Fourteen body colors were available, plus three new luxury cloth interior trims and four colors of vinyl trim. Both hatchback and Towne Coupe carried a standard 140 cu. in. (2.3-liter) Dura-Built four-cylinder engine, with four-speed manual transmission. A 305 cu.

in. (5.0-liter) V-8 was also available, as were a five-speed manual gearbox and three-speed automatic. The 262 cu. in. V-8 was gone. The standard 2 + 2 came with finned wheel covers. In mid-model year, the Monza Mirage made its debut in dealer showrooms. The Mirage got its name from a special package of sport driving and trim equipment designed for it, and was a street version of racetrack winners bearing the Monza nameplate. The special supplier package included front air dam and rear spoiler, front and rear fender flares, special striping and the Monza Mirage identification. Other suggested optional equipment included the 5.0-liter V-8 engine, sport suspension, mirrors and steering wheel, special instrumentation and white lettered radial tires.

1977 Chevrolet, Nova Concours four-door sedan (CH)

1977 Chevrolet, Nova Rally two-door coupe (PH)

NOVA -- SERIES 1X -- SIX/V-8 -- The basic Nova carried over its 1976 styling, offered again as a two-door coupe, two-door hatchback, or four-door sedan. Nova's grille had square holes in a 2 x 12 arrangement, with vertical parking lamps at outer ends. The upscale Concours had a new fine-mesh grille made up of many thin vertical bars, separated into four rows, intended to offer a massive look. Lower-profile parking lamps sat slightly inboard of grille ends. A new chromed center filler panel was meant to give an illusion of depth, in company with the restyled hood molding, grille and bumper. Outer ends of the bumper filler panel were body-colored. Bright headlamp bezels were restyled, as were fender end caps. Concours also sported a stand-up hood ornament, new wide wheel opening moldings, and distinctive 'C' script insignias at front, side and rear, plus new triple rectangular taillamps. Inside, the Concours featured woodgrain appliqués on door panels, instrument panel and steering wheel. Powerplant possibilities included 305 and 350 cu. in. V-8s as well as the standard inline six (250 cu. in.). Three- and four-speed manual gearboxes were available, along with three-speed automatic. Of the 14 Nova body colors, nine were new (all metallic): medium green, dark aqua, light blue, buckskin, light buckskin, orange, silver, brown, or dark blue. Antique white, black, red, bright yellow and firethorn metallic were repeated from 1976. A new Nova Rally option for coupe and hatchback was announced for mid-year availability, to replace the Super Sport. It consisted of a new chrome-plated, diamond-pattern grille with inset horizontal parking lamps and five-color 'Nova Rally' nameplate in the center. The name was repeated on fenders and decklid (above right taillamp). Rally models also had black headlamp bezels with bright edges plus white, black or gold tri-band striping along lower bodysides and rear end panel. Rally wheels were color-keyed to the stripes (but argent-finished when ordered with black striping).

1977 Chevrolet, Camaro Type LT two-door coupe

CAMARO -- SERIES 1F -- SIX/V-8 -- Camaro changed little for 1977. The lineup included the standard Sport Coupe and luxury Type LT. A Rally Sport option came in three new contrasting accent colors for the satin black trim: medium gray, dark blue metallic, and buckskin metallic. Satin black treatment was found on Rally hood, front end, grille, headlamp bezels, forward roof section, rear end panel, and rocker panels. Otherwise, body color selection was the same as Nova: nine new colors and five carryovers. Inside was new cloth in the base interior. Type LT had new knit cloth and puffed-texture vinyl materials. The familiar inline 250 cu. in. (4.1-liter) six became the standard powerplant for Type LT this year. Optional were two V-8s: a 305 cu. in. (5.0-liter) and 350 (5.7-liter). Transmissions included the standard three-speed manual, four-speed manual, or three-speed automatic. Standard axle ratio for the V-8 with automatic changed from 2.73:1 to 2.56:1, to help boost gas mileage. The four-speed transmission shift pattern

was revised this year. Reverse was now engaged by a rearward (toward the driver) lifting motion, rather than forward as before. A new refillable carbon-dioxide canister replaced the disposable freon-filled unit used to inflate the stowaway spare tire. Intermittent wipers joined the option list, and all Camaro wipers were hidden. Away from the lineup for two years, the high-performance Z28 returned as a 1977-1/2 model, debuting at the Chicago Auto Show. Special wide-profile radial tires were mounted on 15 x 7 in. mag-type wheels. Under the hood was a special 350 cu. in. V-8; atop it, an identifying decal. The chassis held front and rear stabilizer bars, special spring rates and quicker steering. This new Z28 had body-color bumpers, spoilers, mirrors and wheels, plus a blackout grille, rear-end panel, rocker panels, moldings, headlamp bezels and taillamp bezels. Rounding out the Z28's appearance were rocker/wheelhouse stripes and emblems, and 'Z28' badge on the driver's side of the grille. Transmission was a Borg-Warner four-speed, and the "open" exhaust used dual resonators.

1977 Chevrolet, Chevelle Malibu Classic Landau two-door coupe (CH)

1977-1/2 Chevrolet, Camaro Z28 two-door coupe (PH)

CHEVELLE MALIBU -- SERIES 1A -- SIX/V-8 -- Chevelle dropped down to two series for 1977: Malibu and Malibu Classic. Two-door coupe, four-door sedan and station wagon bodies (two or three seat) were offered in both. The Laguna coupe and Malibu Classic Estate wagon were gone. Both series had new grilles and six-section taillamps this year. Malibu Classic's grille showed a vertical theme with many narrow bars. Malibu's was a mesh pattern of many wide rectangles. As before, Classics had stacked rectangular head-lamps, regular Malibus single round ones. Script was in the grille's lower corner (driver's side). Small horizontal rectangular parking lamps were again inset in the bumper. The Malibu coupe's rear side windows got "coach" style glass this year. Classic taillamps had fancier brightwork that reached toward the license plate, and rockers wore wide bright moldings. Station wagons had a standard 305 cu. in. (5.0-liter) V-8, and the Malibu Classic wagon held a 350 (5.7-liter) V-8, now with four-barrel carb. The 400 V-8 was gone. Base engine for other bodies was the inline 250 six. Three-speed manual transmission was standard on six-cylinder models except the Malibu Classic sedan, which had Turbo Hydra-matic. Wagons also had automatic plus power brakes and steering. Also standard: heater/defroster, carpeting, lighter, and FR78 x 15/B fiberglass-belted radial tires (HR78 x 15/B steel-belted radials on wagons). The Classic Landau added a vinyl roof, dual horns, sport mirrors (left remote-controlled), deluxe front/rear bumpers, and full wheel covers. Coupes rode a 112-inch wheelbase, sedans and wagons 116-inch. Chevelle's design went all the way back to 1964. Of ten body colors, four were new this year. And of seven vinyl top colors, three were new. Six new trim colors were available for Malibu Classic, five for Malibu.

1977 Chevrolet, Monte Carlo Landau two-door coupe (CH)

MONTE CARLO -- SERIES 1A -- V-8 -- Personal-luxury Montes entered another year with a restyled, bold grille texture: still three separate rows, but eight holes across each one. Stacked rectangular headlamps continued, but horizontal rectangular parking lamps below the headlamps had a more square look. New wider tail-lamps had horizontal divider bars. End caps were also new. A new hood ornament on "flip-flop" pedestal carried the Monte Carlo crest surrounded by a bright ring. Fourteen body colors (nine new) were offered, plus seven interior trim fabrics (two new) and seven vinyl tops (two new). Monte's chassis had new front springs for a softer ride, plus improved corrosion protection. A radiator pressure relief cap improved cooling. Wheelbase was still 116 inches, length 212.7 inches. Again, the 305 cu. in. (5.0-liter) V-8 was the base engine. The 400 cu. in. V-8 was no longer available, but the 350 cu. in. (5.7-liter) V-8 with four-barrel was optional. Turbo

Hydra-matic was standard with both engines. Standard equipment also included power steering and brakes, electric clock, hide-away wipers, deluxe wheel covers, heater/defroster, carpeting, lighter, inside hood release, wheel opening moldings, and GR70 x 15 steel-belted radial tires. The Landau coupe added a vinyl roof, dual body-color sport mirrors (left one remote-controlled), pin striping, and Turbine II wheels.

1977 Chevrolet, Impala two-door Custom Coupe (CH)

1977-1/2 Chevrolet, Caprice Landau two-door coupe (PH)

1977 Chevrolet, Caprice Classic four-door sedan (PH)

IMPALA/CAPRICE CLASSIC -- SERIES 1B -- SIX/V-8 -- Downsized full-size Chevrolet sedans were 5.5 inches shorter in wheelbase, 10.6 inches shorter overall and 4 inches narrower--but 2.5 inches taller. Both Impala and Caprice kept their "big car" look and ample interior dimensions, but lost some 700 pounds. Impala's silhouette was more angular than before, with flatter side panels and a blunt front and rear look. Now they came with a base six-cylinder engine (the familiar inline 250 cu. in.) and smaller (305 cu. in.) base V-8 for better mileage. Wagons had the 305 as standard. All models could also get a 350 cu. in. (5.7-liter) V-8 with four-barrel carburetor. A new diagnostic connector under the hood allowed up to 35 engine tests. Coupe/sedan fuel tanks shrunk from 26 to 21 gallons. The big 400 and 454 engines were gone, but full-size models could have an optional sport or heavy-duty suspension. Impala's 'S' model was dropped. So were sport sedans. All models now had pillars; the true hardtop had become a relic of the past. The rear-facing third seat for wagons was offered as a regular production option. The Landau coupe option emerged during the year. Of ten full-size body colors, four were new. Three new two-tone combinations were offered, along with seven vinyl top colors (three new). New interior trim came in six colors. Impalas had an 8 x 3 hole "eggcrate" grille pattern with center bowtie emblem, plus quad rectangular headlamps over quad park/signal lamps. Caprice's grille had a finer mesh pattern. Caprice also had wraparound marker lamps and small parking lamps inset down in the bumper. Back ends were similar, with taillamps in three side-by-side sections (outer one slightly angled). Caprice's version put backup lamps alongside the license plate. Caprice also displayed a stand-up hood ornament. Impala's new Custom coupe model had a distinctive back window treatment. Caprice wagons got a new two-way tailgate that opened either downward or to the side. Standard Impala/Caprice equipment included Turbo Hydra-matic transmission, power steering and brakes, heater/defroster, carpeting, cigarette lighter, hide-away windshield wipers, and FR78 x 15/B fiberglass-belted radial tires. Wagons had HR78 x 15/B steel-belted tires and a power tailgate. Caprice Estate added an electric clock, dual horns, and quiet sound group.

I.D. DATA: Chevrolets again had a 13-symbol Vehicle Identification Number (VIN) on the upper left surface of the instrument panel, visible through the windshield. Coding was similar to 1976. Body type codes '45' (three-seat station wagon) and '39' (full-size sport sedan) were dropped. Model year code changed to '7' for 1977. Engine codes 'N' (L4-110), 'O' (L4-122 EFI), 'G' (V8-262), 'A' (L4-140 1Bbl.) and 'S' (V8-454) were dropped. The code for V8-305 changed from 'Q' to 'U'.

1977-1/2 Chevrolet, Monza Mirage two-door coupe (PH)

CHEVETTE (FOUR)

Model No.	Body/Style No.	Body Type & Seating	Factory Price	Shipping Weight	Prod. Total
1T	B08	2-dr. Hatch-4P	3225	1958	120,278

CHEVETTE SCOOTER (FOUR)

1T	J08	2-dr. Hatch-4P	2999	1898	13,191

VEGA (FOUR)

1H	V11	2-dr. Coupe-4P	3249	2459	12,365
1H	V77	2-dr. Hatch-4P	3359	2522	37,395
1H	V15	2-dr. Sta Wag-4P	3522	2571	25,181
1H	V15	2-dr. Est Wag-4P	3745	N/A	3,461

MONZA (FOUR/V-8)

1H	M27	2-dr. Twn Cpe-4P	3560/3765	2580/ N/A	34,133
1H	R07	2-dr. Hatch 2+2-4P	3840/4045	2671/ N/A	39,215

NOVA (SIX/V-8)

1X	X27	2-dr. Cpe-6P	3482/3602	3139/3257	132,833
1X	X17	2-dr. Hatch-6P	3646/3766	3214/3335	18,048
1X	X69	4-dr. Sedan-6P	3532/3652	3174/3292	141,028

NOVA CONCOURS (SIX/V-8)

1X	Y27	2-dr. Cpe-6P	3991/4111	3285/3391	28,602
1X	Y17	2-dr. Hatch-6P	4154/4274	3378/3486	5,481
1X	Y69	4-dr. Sedan-6P	4066/4186	3329/3437	39,272

CAMARO (SIX/V-8)

1F	Q87	2-dr. Spt Cpe-4P	4113/4223	3369/3476	131,717
1F	S87	2-dr. LT Cpe-4P	4478/4598	3422/3529	72,787
1F	Q87	2-dr. Z28 Cpe-4P	----- /5170	-----/ N/A	14,349

CHEVELLE MALIBU (SIX/V-8)

1A	C37	2-dr. Cpe-6P	3885/4005	3551/3650	28,793
1A	C29	4-dr. Sed-6P	3935/4055	3628/3727	39,064
1A	C35	4-dr. Sta Wag-6P	----- /4734	----- /4139	18,023
1A	C35	4-dr. 3S Wag-9P	----- /4877	----- / N/A	4,014

CHEVELLE MALIBU CLASSIC (SIX/V-8)

1A	D37	2-dr. Cpe-6P	4125/4245	3599/3698	73,739
1A	D37	2-dr. Lan Cpe-6P	4353/4473	N/A	37,215
1A	D29	4-dr. Sed-6P	4475/4595	3725/3824	76,776
1A	D35	4-dr. Sta Wag-6P	----- /5065	----- /4233	31,539
1A	D35	4-dr. 3S Wag-9P	----- /5208	----- / N/A	19,053

MONTE CARLO (V-8)

1A	H57	2-dr. 'S' Cpe-6P	4968	3852	224,327
1A	H57	2-dr. Lan Cpe-6P	5298	N/A	186,711

FULL-SIZE CHEVROLETS

IMPALA (SIX/V-8)

1B	L47	2-dr. Cust Cpe-6P	4876/4996	3533/3628	55,347
1B	L47	2-dr. Lan Cpe-6P	N/A	N/A	2,745
1B	L69	4-dr. Sedan-6P	4901/5021	3564/3659	196,824
1B	L35	4-dr. Sta Wag-6P	---- /5289	---- /4042	37,108
1B	L35	4-dr. 3S Wag-9P	---- /5406	---- / N/A	28,255

CAPRICE CLASSIC (SIX/V-8)

1B	N47	2-dr. Coupe-6P	5187/5307	3571/3666	62,366
1B	N47	2-dr. Lan Cpe-6P	N/A	N/A	9,607
1B	N69	4-dr. Sedan-6P	5237/5357	3606/3701	212,840
1B	N35	4-dr. Est Wag-6P	---- /5617	---- /4088	22,930
1B	N35	4-dr. 3S Est-6P	---- /5734	---- / N/A	33,639

FACTORY PRICE AND WEIGHT NOTE: Where two prices and weights are shown, the figure to the left of the slash is for six-cylinder model, to right of slash for V-8 (except Monza, four-cylinder and V-8).

ENGINE DATA: BASE FOUR (Chevette): Inline. Overhead cam. Four-cylinder. Cast iron block and head. Displacement: 85.0 cu. in. (1.4 liters). Bore & stroke: 3.23 x 2.61 in. Compression ratio: 8.5:1. Brake horsepower: 57 at 5200 R.P.M. Torque: 71 lb.-ft. at 3600 R.P.M. Five main bearings. Hydraulic valve lifters. Carburetor: 1Bbl. Rochester 1ME. VIN Code: 1. OPTIONAL FOUR (Chevette): Inline. Overhead cam. Four-cylinder. Cast iron block and head. Displacement: 97.6 cu. in. (1.6 liters). Bore & stroke: 3.23 x 2.98 in. Compression ratio: 8.5:1. Brake horsepower: 63 at 4800 R.P.M. Torque: 82 lb.-ft. at 3200 R.P.M. Five main bearings. Hydraulic valve lifters. Carburetor: 1Bbl. Roch. 1ME. VIN Code: E. BASE FOUR (Vega, Monza): Inline. Overhead cam. Four-cylinder. Aluminum block and cast iron head. Displacement: 140 cu. in. (2.3 liters). Bore & stroke: 3.50 x 3.63 in. Compression ratio: 8.0:1. Brake horsepower: 84 at 4400 R.P.M. Torque: 117 lb.-ft. at 2400 R.P.M. Five main bearings. Hydraulic valve lifters. Carburetor: 2Bbl. Holley 5210C. VIN Code: B. BASE SIX (Nova, Chevelle, Camaro, Impala, Caprice): Inline. OHV. Six-cylinder. Cast iron block and head. Displacement: 250 cu. in. (4.1 liters). Bore & stroke: 3.88 x 3.53 in. Compression ratio: 8.3:1. Brake horsepower: 110 at 3800 R.P.M. Torque: 195 lb.-ft. at 1600 R.P.M. Seven main bearings. Hydraulic valve lifters. Carburetor: 1Bbl. Roch. 1ME. VIN Code: D. BASE V-8 (Monte Carlo, Malibu wagon, Impala/Caprice wagon); OPTIONAL V-8 (Monza, Nova, Chevelle, Camaro, Impala, Caprice): 90-degree, overhead valve V-8. Cast iron block and head. Displacement: 305 cu. in. (5.0 liters). Bore & stroke: 3.74 x 3.48 in. Compression ratio: 8.5:1. Brake horsepower: 145 at 3800 R.P.M. Torque: 245 lb.-ft. at 2400 R.P.M. Five main bearings. Hydraulic valve lifters. Carburetor: 2Bbl. Roch. 2GC. VIN Code: U. BASE V-8 (Malibu Classic wagon); OPTIONAL V-8 (Nova, Camaro, Chevelle, Monte Carlo, Impala, Caprice): 90-degree, overhead valve V-8. Cast iron block and head. Displacement: 350 cu. in. (5.7 liters). Bore & stroke: 4.00 x 3.48 in. Compression ratio: 8.5:1. Brake horsepower: 170 at 3800 R.P.M. Torque: 270 lb.-ft. at 2400 R.P.M. Five main bearings. Hydraulic valve lifters. Carburetor: 4Bbl. Roch. M4MC. VIN Code: L.

CHASSIS DATA: Wheelbase: (Chevette) 94.3 in.; (Vega/Monza) 97.0 in.; (Camaro) 108.0 in.; (Nova) 111.0 in.; (Chevelle cpe) 112.0 in.; (Chevelle sed/wag, Monte, Imp/Capr) 116.0 in. Overall length: (Chevette) 158.7 in.; (Vega) 175.4 in.; (Monza twn cpe) 177.8 in.; (Monza hatch) 179.3 in.; (Nova) 196.7 in.; (Nova Concours) 197.7 in.; (Camaro) 195.4 in.; (Chevelle cpe) 205.7 in.; (Chevelle sed) 209.7 in.; (Chevelle wag) 215.4 in.; (Monte) 213.3 in.; (Imp/Capr) 212.1 in.; (Imp/Capr wag) 214.7 in. Height: (Chevette) 52.3 in.; (Vega spt cpe/wag) 51.8 in.; (Vega hatch) 50.0 in.; (Monza twn cpe) 49.8 in.; (Monza hatch) 50.2 in.; (Nova) 53.6 in.; (Camaro) 49.2 in.; (Chevelle cpe) 53.4 in.; (Chevelle sed) 54.1 in.; (Chevelle wag) 55.8 in.; (Monte) 52.8 in.; (Imp/Capr cpe) 55.3 in.; (Imp/Capr sed) 56.0 in.; (Imp/Capr wag) 58.0 in. Width: (Chevette) 61.8 in.; (Vega/Monza) 65.4 in.; (Nova) 72.2 in.; (Camaro) 74.4 in.; (Chevelle) 76.9 in.; (Chevelle wag) 76.8 in.; (Monte) 77.6 in.; (Imp/Capr) 75.5 in.; (Imp/Capr wag) 79.1 in. Front Tread: (Chevette) 51.2 in.; (Vega/Monza) 54.8 in.; (Nova/Camaro) 61.3 in.; (Camaro LT) 61.6 in.; (Chevelle) 61.5 in.; (Monte) 61.9 in.; (Imp/Capr) 61.8 in.; (Imp/Capr wag) 62.2 in. Rear Tread: (Chevette) 51.2 in.; (Vega/Monza) 53.6 in.; (Nova) 59.0 in.; (Camaro) 60.0 in.; (Camaro LT) 60.3 in.; (Chevelle/Monte) 60.7 in.; (Imp/Capr) 60.8 in.; (Imp/Capr wag) 64.1 in. Standard Tires: (Chevette) 155/80 x 13/B; (Vega/Monza) A78 x 13/B; (Nova) E78 x 14/B; (Nova Concours, Camaro) FR78 x 14/B SBR; (Chevelle/Imp/Capr) FR78 x 15/B GBR; (Chevelle/Imp/Capr wag) HR78 x 15/B SBR; (Monte) GR70 x 15.

TECHNICAL: Transmission: Three-speed manual transmission (column shift) standard on Chevelle; floor shift on Camaro. Gear ratios: (1st) 3.11:1; (2nd) 1.84:1; (3rd) 1.00:1; (Rev) 3.22:1. Four-speed floor shift standard on Chevette: (1st) 3.75:1; (2nd) 2.16:1; (3rd) 1.38:1; (4th) 1.00:1; (Rev) 3.82:1. Four-speed floor shift standard on Vega, Monza four: (1st) 3.11:1; (2nd) 2.20:1; (3rd) 1.47:1; (4th) 1.00:1; (Rev) 3.11:1. Four-speed floor shift standard on Monza V-8, optional on Nova/Camaro V8-350: (1st) 2.85:1; (2nd) 2.02:1; (3rd) 1.35:1; (4th) 1.00:1; (Rev) 2.85:1. Five-speed floor shift available on Vega, Monza four: (1st) 3.40:1; (2nd) 2.08:1; (3rd) 1.39:1; (4th) 1.00:1; (5th) 0.80:1; (Rev) 3.36:1. Three-speed Turbo Hydra-matic standard on some Malibus, Monte Carlo and Caprice/Impala, optional on others. Automatic gear ratios: (1st) 2.52:1; (2nd) 1.52:1; (3rd) 1.00:1; (Rev) 1.94:1 except standard Caprice/Impala, Monza V-8, Chevette and Nova (V8-305) ratios: (1st) 2.74:1; (2nd) 1.57:1; (3rd) 1.00:1; (Rev) 2.07:1. Standard final drive ratio: (Chevette) 3.70:1 exc. w/1.4-liter engine and automatic, 4.11:1; (Vega) 2.92:1; (Monza four) 3.42:1; (Monza V-8) 2.73:1; (Nova) 2.73:1; (Camaro) 2.73:1 exc. 2.56:1 w/V-8 and automatic; (Z28) 3.73:1; (Chevelle six) 2.73:1; (Chevelle V-8) 2.56:1; (Monte) 2.56:1; (Imp/Capr six) 2.73:1; (Imp/Capr V-8) 2.56:1. Steering: (Chevette) rack and pinion; (others) recirculating ball. Suspension/Body: Same as 1976. Brakes: Front disc, rear drum. Ignition: Electronic. Fuel tank: (Chevette) 13 gal.; (Vega) 16 gal.; (Monza) 18.5 gal.; (Nova/Camaro) 21 gal.; (Chevelle/Monte) 22 gal.; (Imp/Capr) 21 gal.; (Imp/Capr wag) 22 gal.

DRIVETRAIN OPTIONS: Engines: 1.6-liter four: Chevette ($55). 305 cu. in., 2Bbl. V-8: Monza ($205); Nova/Camaro, Chevelle/Imp/Caprice cpe/sed ($120). 350 cu. in., 4Bbl. V-8: Nova/Camaro/Chevelle ($210); Chevelle/Imp/Capr wag, Monte ($90); Imp/Capr cpe/sed ($210). Transmission/Differential: Four-speed manual shift: Nova/Camaro ($252). Five-speed manual shift: Vega/Monza ($248). Turbo Hydra-matic transmission: Chevette/Vega/Monza ($248); Nova/Camaro, Chevelle cpe/sed ($282). Sport shifter w/console: Chevette ($43). Floor shift lever: Nova ($31). Positraction axle: Vega/Monza ($50); Nova/Camaro/Chevelle/Monte ($54); Imp/Capr ($58). Highway axle ratio: Monza ($13). Performance axle ratio ($13-$14). Power Accessories: Power brakes: Chvt/Vega/Monza ($58); Nova, Camaro, Chevelle cpe/sed ($61). Power steering: Vega/Monza ($129); Nova, Chevelle cpe/sed ($146). Suspension: F40 H.D. suspension: Nova ($8-$31); Chevelle/Monte/Imp/Capr ($19). F41 sport susp.: Vega ($149); Monza ($28); Nova, Camaro, Chevelle/Imp/Capr cpe/sed ($36). Superlift rear shock absorbers: Imp/Capr ($47). Rear stabilizer bar: Chevette ($28). Other: Heavy-duty radiator ($27-$37). H.D. alternator (61-amp): Chevelle/Monte/Imp/Capr ($29). H.D. battery ($16-$17). California emission system ($70). High altitude emission system ($22).

CHEVETTE/VEGA/MONZA CONVENIENCE/APPEARANCE OPTIONS: Option Packages: Sandpiper pkg.: Chevette (N/A). Rally sport equipment: Chevette

($295-$321). GT pkg.: Vega hatch ($401); Vega wagon ($373). Sport equipment: Monza ($134). Sport front-end appearance pkg.: Monza ($118). Spyder equipment pkg.: Monza ($274). Spyder appearance pkg.: Monza ($199). Quiet sound group: Chvt ($31-$42); Vega ($34-$46). Comfort/Convenience: Air conditioning ($442). Rear defogger ($71). Tinted glass ($48). Sport steering wheel ($16). Comfortilt steering wheel: Vega/Monza ($50). Special instrumentation: Chvt ($60); Vega ($77); Monza ($60-$77). Econominder gauge: Monza ($28). Electric clock: Chvt/Monza ($17). Digital clock: Monza ($43). Cigarette lighter: Chvt ($5). Glove compartment lock: Chvt ($3). Intermittent wipers: Chvt/Vega ($28). Lighting, Horns and Mirrors: Aux. lighting: Chvt ($33-$38); Vega ($16-$31); Monza ($16-$20). Sport mirrors, left remote: Vega/Monza ($28). Twin remote sport mirrors: Chevette ($46). Driver's remote sport mirror: Chvt ($20). Day/night mirror ($8). Entertainment: AM radio ($67). AM/FM radio ($129). AM/FM stereo radio: Vega/Monza ($212). Stereo tape player w/AM radio: Vega/Monza ($196). Stereo tape player with AM/FM stereo radio: Vega/Monza ($304). Rear speaker ($22). Windshield antenna: Vega/Monza ($16); incl. w/radios. Exterior Trim: Sky roof: Vega/Monza ($210). Vinyl roof: Monza ($145) incl. opera windows. Spoilers, front/rear: Monza ($87). Swing-out windows: Chvt ($48); Vega cpe ($33-$39). Custom exterior: Chvt ($86); Vega ($62-$92). Decor group: Vega ($6-$36). Sport stripes: Vega ($80). Bodyside moldings ($38). Wheel opening moldings: Vega/Monza ($20). Side window reveal moldings: Chvt ($63). Door edge guards ($8). Roof carrier: Chvt/Vega ($56). Rear air deflector: Vega ($24). Deluxe bumpers, front/rear: Chvt ($29). Deluxe bumpers w/guards: Monza ($65). Deluxe front bumper guards: Vega ($18). Deluxe bumper guards, front/rear: Chvt ($36-$65); Monza ($36). Bumper rub strips, front/rear: Vega ($47). Interior Trim/Upholstery: Custom interior trim: Chevette ($151-$199); Vega ($139-$188). Console: Chvt ($17); Vega/Monza ($77). Bucket seats (plaid cloth): Chvt ($9-$18); Vega ($18). Knit cloth bucket seats: Monza ($18). Custom knit cloth bucket seats: Monza ($135-$151). Leather bucket seats: Monza ($213). Adjustable driver's seatback: Vega/Monza ($17). Folding rear seat: Monza ($87). Rear seat delete: Chvt ($56 credit). Load floor carpet: Chvt ($43). Color-keyed floor mats ($15). Front mats: Chvt ($9). Deluxe seatbelts ($17). Wheels and Tires: Aluminum wheels: Monza ($186-$209). Rally II wheels: Vega ($74-$104). Wheel covers: Vega ($30). Deluxe wheel covers: Monza ($33). Sport wheel covers: Chevette ($71). Wheel trim rings: Chvt ($32); Vega ($2-$32). 155/80-13/B WSW: Chvt ($38). 155/80-13/B SBR: Chvt ($99). 155/80-13/B SBR WSW: Chvt ($137). 155/80-13/B SBR WLT: Chvt ($151). A78 x 13/B WSW: Vega ($38); Monza ($30-$38). BR78 x 13/B SBR: Vega ($35-$151); Monza ($94-$151). BR78 x 13/B SBR WSW: Vega ($73-$188); Monza ($124-$188). BR70 x 13/C SBR BSW: Monza (NC to $190). BR70 x 13/C SBR WSW: Monza ($30-$227). BR70 x 13/C SBR WLT: Vega ($126-$241); Monza ($42-$241). Conventional spare: Monza (NC).

NOVA/CAMARO/CHEVELLE/MONTE CARLO CONVENIENCE/APPEARANCE OPTIONS: Option Packages: Rally Sport equipment: base Camaro ($281); Camaro

LT ($186). Estate equipment: Chevelle wag ($185). Interior decor/quiet sound group: base Camaro ($57). Comfort/Convenience: Air conditioning ($478-$507). Rear defogger, forced-air ($48). Rear defogger (electric): Monte ($82). Cruise-master speed control ($80). Tinted glass: Nova/Camaro ($50); Chevelle ($54); Monte ($58). Comfortilt steering wheel ($57). Six-way power seat: Chevelle/Monte ($137). Power windows ($108-$151). Power door locks: Nova/Chevelle ($68-$96); Camaro/Monte ($68). Power trunk release: Chevelle/Monte ($18). Power tailgate release: Chevelle 2S wag ($22). Electric clock: Nova, base Camaro ($19); Chevelle ($20). Special instrumentation (incl. tach and clock): Nova/Camaro ($99). Econominder gauge pkg.: Nova/Chevelle/Monte ($47). Intermittent wipers ($30). Lighting, Horns and Mirrors: Aux. lighting ($22-$44). Dual horns: Nova, base Camaro, Chevelle ($6). Remote-control driver's mirror: Nova/Chevelle/Monte ($15). Twin sport mirrors (left remote): Nova, base Camaro, Chevelle/Monte ($30). Twin remote sport mirrors: Chevelle/Monte ($21-$51). Day/night mirror: base Nova ($8). Visor vanity mirror: Chevelle/Monte ($4). Lighted visor mirror: Chevelle ($28); Monte ($24-$28). Entertainment: AM radio ($72). AM/FM radio: Nova/Camaro/Chevelle ($137); Monte ($146). AM/FM stereo radio ($226). Stereo tape player w/AM radio: Nova/Camaro/Chevelle ($209); Monte ($225). Stereo tape player with AM/FM stereo radio ($324). Rear speaker ($23). Windshield antenna ($17); incl. w/radios. Exterior Trim: Electric sky roof: Monte ($394). Vinyl roof: Nova/Camaro ($96); Chevelle ($111); Monte ($131). Cabriolet roof: Nova ($162). Spoilers, front/rear: Camaro ($87). Exterior decor pkg.: base Nova ($78); Chevelle ($20-$54). Custom appearance group: Nova Concours ($70-$81). Exterior style trim pkg.: Camaro ($61). Fashion-tone paint: Monte ($112). Two-tone paint: Nova, Chevelle cpe/sed ($43). Swing-out rear side windows: Nova ($52). Swing-out rear window: Chevelle 2S wag ($52). Bodyside moldings: Nova/Camaro/Chevelle ($40). Deluxe bodyside moldings: Nova Concours, Monte ($51). Door edge guards ($8-$12). Wheel opening moldings: base Nova ($20). Roof drip moldings: base Nova, Camaro ($17). Bodyside pin striping: Nova ($28). Rear window air deflector: Chevelle wag ($26). Roof carrier: Chevelle wag ($71). Bumper rub strips: Chevelle/Monte ($32). Bumper rub strips and guards, front/rear: base Nova ($68). Bumper guards, front/rear: Camaro/Chevelle/Monte ($39); Chevelle wag ($20). Interior Trim/Upholstery: Interior decor pkg.: Nova ($27). Console: base Nova, Camaro/Chevelle/Monte ($75). Knit or plaid cloth bench seat: Nova ($20). Custom cloth interior: base Nova ($211). Custom vinyl interior: base Nova ($191). Vinyl bench seat: Monte ($20). Bench or notchback bench seat (sport cloth or vinyl): Chevelle ($20). Vinyl bucket seats: base Nova ($272); Chevelle ($109-$129); Monte ($169). Bucket seats (knit cloth): Nova Concours ($143-218). Sport cloth bucket seats: Camaro ($20). Monte custom 50/50 seating (reclining passenger): cloth ($293); vinyl ($313). Adj. driver's seatback: Camaro ($20). Litter container: Chevelle/Monte ($6). Load-floor carpeting: Chevelle wag ($45). Color-keyed mats ($16). Deluxe seatbelts ($16-$22). Deluxe trunk trim: Monte ($38). Wheels and Tires: Custom wheels: Camaro ($85-$125). Rally wheels: base Nova/Camaro ($65); Nova Concours ($42); Chevelle ($38-$65); Monte ($50). Wire wheel covers: base Nova ($108); Nova Concours ($75). Full wheel covers: base Nova, Camaro/Chevelle ($33). Deluxe wheel covers: Monte ($20). Sport wheel covers: Chevelle ($48-$81); Monte ($66). E78 x 14/B BSW: Camaro ($87-$107 credit). E78 x 14/B WSW: base Nova ($31-$39); Camaro ($56-$63 credit). FR78 x 14/B SBR: base Nova ($86-$107). FR78 x 14/B SBR WSW: base Nova ($119-$148); Nova Concours, Camaro ($33-$41). FR78 x 14/B SBR WLT: base Nova ($129-$161); Nova Concours, Camaro ($44-$55). FR78 x 15/B GBR WSW: Chevelle ($33-$41). FR78 x 15/B SBR BSW: Chevelle ($35-$45). FR78 x 15/B SBR WSW: Chevelle ($68-$86). GR78 x 15/B SBR BSW: Chevelle ($56-$71). GR78 x 15/B SBR WSW: Chevelle ($90-$114). HR78 x 15/B SBR BSW: Chevelle ($110). HR78 x 15/B SBR WSW: Chevelle ($157); Chevelle wag ($47). GR70 x 15/B SBR BSW: Chevelle ($74-$93). GR70 x 15/B SBR WSW: Chevelle ($108-$136); Monte ($34-$43). GR70 x 15/B SBR WLT: Chevelle ($119-$150). Stowaway spare: Nova w/o radials ($15); Camaro/Chevelle/Monte (NC).

1977 Chevrolet, Caprice Classic Estate Wagon (CH)

IMPALA/CAPRICE CONVENIENCE/APPEARANCE OPTIONS: Option Packages: Estate equipment: wag ($210). Value appearance group: bodyside and wheel opening moldings, full wheel covers ($69). Comfort/Convenience: Four season air cond. ($527). Comfortron auto-temp air cond. ($607). Rear defogger, forced-air: cpe/sed ($48). Rear defogger, electric ($83). Cruise-Master speed control ($84). Tinted glass ($69). Comfortilt steering wheel ($58). Power door locks ($70-$98). Six-way power driver's seat ($139). Power windows ($114-$171). Power trunk release ($18). Power tailgate lock: wag ($37). Electric clock: Imp ($20). Digital clock: Imp ($42); Caprice ($23). Econominder gauge pkg. ($47). Intermittent wipers ($30). Quiet sound group: Imp ($41). Lighting, Horns and Mirrors: Aux. lighting ($23-$38). Dome reading light ($15). Dual horns: Imp ($6). Driver's remote mirror ($15). Dual remote mirrors ($45). Dual sport mirrors, left remote ($30). Dual remote body-color sport mirrors ($51). Visor vanity mirror ($4). Lighted visor mirror ($28). Entertainment: AM radio ($73). AM/FM radio ($148). AM/FM stereo radio ($229). Stereo tape player w/AM radio ($228); with AM/FM stereo radio ($328). Rear speaker ($23). Power antenna ($57); w/radio ($40). Windshield antenna ($17); incl. w/radios. Exterior Trim: Vinyl roof ($135). Two-tone paint ($44). Custom two-tone ($99). Pin striping ($31). Roof carrier: wag ($104). Bodyside moldings ($41). Door edge guards ($8-$12). Wheel opening moldings ($20). Roof drip moldings: Imp ($17). Bumper rub strips, front/rear ($45). Bumper guards ($46). Interior Trim/Upholstery: Vinyl bench seat: cpe/sed ($20). Knit or sport cloth bench seat: wag ($20). Knit cloth 50/50 seat: cpe/sed ($153). Knit or sport cloth 50/50 seat: wag ($173). Vinyl 50/50 seat ($153-$173). Special custom cloth 50/50 seat: cpe/sed ($285). Deluxe load-floor carpet: wag ($66). Deluxe cargo area carpet: wag ($95). Color-keyed mats ($16). Litter container ($6). Deluxe seatbelts ($19-$22). Deluxe trunk trim ($38). Wheel Covers: Full wheel covers ($34). Sport wheel covers: Imp ($82); Capr ($48). Coupe/Sedan Tires: FR78 x 15/B GBR WSW ($41). FR78 x 15/B SBR BSW ($45). FR78 x 15/B SBR WSW ($86). GR78 x 15/B SBR BSW ($71). GR78 x 15/B SBR WSW ($114). GR70 x 15/B SBR WSW ($136). Wagon Tires: HR78 x 15/B SBR WSW ($47).

HISTORY: Introduced: Sept. 30, 1976. Model year production (U.S.): 2,079,798 (incl. Corvettes but not incl. 3,299 Acadians). Of the total North American production for U.S. market, 263,829 had four-cylinder engines, 283,874 sixes, and 1,872,643 V-8s. Calendar year production: 2,135,942 (including 36,605 Sportvans, 46,345 Corvettes and 4,678 Acadians). Calendar year sales by U.S. dealers: 2,280,439 (incl. 36,609 Sportvans and 42,571 Corvettes) for a 25.1 percent market share. Full-size Chevrolets sold the best. Model year sales by U.S. dealers: 2,239,538 (incl. 39,640 Sportvans and 40,764 Corvettes).

Historical Footnotes: Caprice Classic, in its new down-sized form, was voted *Motor Trend* "Car-of-the-Year" for 1977. That magazine considered Caprice "the most car you can get for your dollar" and applauded its "understated elegance." Model year sales rose by 8 percent over 1976, due largely to popular acceptance of the smaller full-sized models. Full-size sales rose by a healthy 38 percent, giving Chevrolet back the title of best selling passenger car in the industry (formerly held by Olds Cutlass). Calendar year production gained 4.5 percent. Only the discontinued Vega and soon-to-be-shrunk Malibu posted a loss for the calendar year. For the first time, Chevrolet began to supply other GM divisions with its 350 cu. in. V-8. Unfortunately, the installation of that V-8 in Oldsmobiles led eventually to class-action lawsuits and ultimate rebates to customers who felt they'd been cheated by not receiving a "real" Olds powerplant. In the four-cylinder engine marketplace, Pontiac's new cast iron "Iron Duke" powerplant was expected to tempt some customers away from Chevrolet with its all-aluminum 140 cu. in. four. But Chevrolet would soon obtain the Pontiac powerplant for its Monza. Chevette was the first serious attempt by a domestic automaker to compete against the smallest imports. That market began to fall, but Chevette remained a strong competitor. "It'll drive you happy" was Chevette's theme, and the rear-drive subcompact would hang around for another decade before being overrun by front-drive models. Monza's Spyder was thought by some observers to show revived Detroit interest in "muscle cars," though a Monza hardly seemed in the same league with some of the truly muscular beasts of the past.

1978

After downsizing of full-size models for 1977, the mid-size A-body Malibu and Monte Carlo got the same treatment this year. Each was a foot shorter and 500-800 pounds lighter than equivalent 1977 models. Vega was dropped, but that line's hatchback and wagon continued under the Monza name. Chevrolet offered two new V-6 engines: a 200 cu. in. that was now standard on the downsized Malibu, and a 231 (supplied by Buick) for the Monte Carlo. Monza's new small V-8 (196 cu. in.) also originated at Buick. A new four, dubbed the "Iron Duke," came from Pontiac.

1978 Chevrolet, Chevette four-door hatchback sedan (CH)

CHEVETTE – SERIES 1T – FOUR – After two seasons as a two-door, Chevette added a six-window four-door hatchback sedan on a three-inch longer wheelbase. Rear legroom stretched five inches over the two-door's. Rear door glass in the sedan retracted only partly; side quarter glass was fixed. This year's grille used new molding treatments around each air inlet louver, plus single horizontal and double vertical bars through each opening. The result: a dozen large, boxy holes arranged in 3 x 2 pattern on each half of the angled panel. Grille moldings were argent on the Scooter coupe, bright chrome on other models. Small amber rectangular parking lamps were below the bumper rub strip; similar amber side marker lenses on front fenders. 'Chevette' script was on the front fender, just ahead of the door. Standard engine was now the 98 cu. in. (1.6-liter) over-head-cam four, rated 63 horsepower, replacing the smaller 1.4-liter of 1977. A high-output version (not available in California) had a bigger carburetor, revised manifolds, reduced exhaust back pressure, and higher-speed camshaft. Even though Chevette's price rose only modestly, 18 items that had been optional now became standard. Standard equipment (except on Scooter) now included a front spoiler, AM radio, center console with coin pocket, whitewall tires, wheel trim rings, bumper rub strips, bodyside and sill moldings, sport steering wheel, and cigarette lighter. The coupe

had a swing-out rear window. Also standard: fully synchronized four-speed manual transmission, glove box lock, color-keyed dash, and carpeting. New options included tri-tone sport stripes (five color choices), and seven-position Comfortilt steering wheel. Most automatic transmissions were produced at Strasbourg, identical to those used on European Chevettes. Body acoustics were revised for quieter road operation. Zincro-metal inner fender skirts and galvanized fender reinforcements joined the list of special corrosion-protection treatments. All-vinyl interiors came in black, blue, carmine, green or camel. Cloth/vinyl upholstery came in black, carmine or camel. Scooters were upholstered with all-vinyl or Sport cloth/vinyl, in black or camel. Optional Custom interiors were "Rattan" all-vinyl or "Darby" woven cloth/vinyl. Of the 14 body colors, ten were new this year.

1978 Chevrolet, Monza S two-door hatchback coupe (CH)

1978 Chevrolet, Monza two-door Estate Wagon

MONZA -- SERIES 1H -- FOUR/V-6/V-8 -- With the departure of Vega, the subcompact Monza line grew to seven two-door models in two groups. Monza took over two carryover Vega body styles: the hatchback and wagon. That gave the standard lineup an 'S' hatchback, 2 + 2 hatchback, coupe, and two station wagons. Monza's Sport series, repeating the soft fascia of 1977, came in two body types: sport coupe and 2 + 2 hatchback. Standard models had single round headlamps with restyled housings, black-accented bright grille and moldings with single crossbars and center bowtie emblem, new header panel, and bright steel bumpers. A new body-colored filler strip at the rear closed the gap between bumper and body. Rear end of the wagon and hatchback coupe looked the same as their Vega predecessors, except for the steel bumper. Monza Sport displayed quad rectangular headlamps and the Euro-look soft fascia, restyled with new front cover and headlamp bezels. Bumper guards and strips (front and rear) switched to body color this year. Upper air intake slots were gone this year, replaced by a single wide opening over the bumper, with round emblem above. Separate 'Monza' block letters stood at the center of the thin, full-width grille opening. Engine choices were the new base 151 cu. in. (2.5-liter) four; new optional 196 cu. in. (3.2-liter) V-6; and optional 305 cu. in. (5.0-liter) V-8. All three had two-barrel carburetors. Both new engines came from other GM divisions. California Monzas carried a 231 cu. in. V-6 rather than the 196, and the four came only with automatic shift. Fours and the 196 cu. in. V-6 weren't available in high-altitude areas. The V-8 was available only in notchback or 2 + 2 models. The new base engine replaced the former aluminum 140 cu. in. four, which had its share of troubles. The 151 had a cast iron head, block and manifolds, with two-barrel two-stage carburetor. The new 196 V-6 also used cast iron construction. The California V-6 was similar but with larger bore. Transmissions were the standard four-speed manual or optional five-speed (available for four or V-6 engine). Turbo Hydra-matic was available for all engines. The acoustical package was upgraded this year, with full hood insulation. Front disc brakes had ventilated rotors. New GT coupe equipment packages featured 'GT' striping and BR70 x 13/C tires. Spyder performance equipment for the Sport 2 + 2 hatchback included special-handling suspension and BR70 x 13/C tires. V-8 versions had dual exhaust outlets. A 'Spyder' nameplate went on front fender; emblems on hood header and rear keylock cover. A companion Spyder appearance package could again be ordered separately. A new Estate package was offered for station wagons.

1978 Chevrolet, Nova Custom four-door sedan (CH)

NOVA -- SERIES 1X -- SIX/V-8 -- A new Nova Custom series combined the 1977 Concours body trim with the custom interior option. Otherwise, appearance was unchanged except for new colors, trims, emblems, and steering wheel. A two-door coupe and four-door sedan came in both levels, plus a two-door hatchback coupe in basic Nova dress only. The list of optional body moldings was expanded. A new front seatbelt retractor system provided greater rear seat comfort and more convenient operation. The "Nova Rally" coupe appearance option package for the Custom coupe was similar to the 1977 version, but the grille nameplate was

deleted. Custom models were identified by a modified block-letter 'Nova Custom' emblem on front fender. Styling features included a massive-look grille made of thin vertical bars, inset low-profile vertical parking lamps, chromed headlamp bezels, bright wide hood edge moldings, and tri-section taillamps. The former Concours' stand-up hood ornament did not continue. Small horizontal side marker lenses were again near the front of front fenders. New colors this year were silver, light camel, bright blue metallic, camel or dark camel metallic, saffron metallic, and carmine metallic. Carried over: black, white, light blue or green metallic, dark blue-green metallic, bright yellow, and light red. Standard engine was the inline 250 cu. in. (4.1-liter) six with three-speed manual transmission. Optional: 305 cu. in. (5.0-liter) and 350 (5.7-liter) V-8s. Four-speed manual transmission was required with the 305 V-8, while automatic was mandatory with the 350 V-8. California Novas came only with automatic. Novas could even be ordered with a police package, offering handling that some compared to a Camaro Z28. Nova's Rally Equipment package included striping at lower bodyside, rear end panel and over wheel openings; a chromed diamond-pattern grille; black headlamp bezels; Rally nameplates; and 14 x 6 in. (or 14 x 7 in.) Rally wheels.

1978 Chevrolet, Camaro two-door coupe (PH)

CAMARO -- SERIES 1F -- SIX/V-8 -- Though unchanged in basic design, Camaros managed a fresh look with a new body-colored soft nose section and rear bumper. The new design used the same cellular urethane as Corvette, to replace the former aluminum face bar and spring bumper system. Camaro's grille was similar to 1977, but with fewer horizontal bars and larger holes (ten rows across), and a deeper repeated lower section below the narrow bumper. At the rear were wedge-shaped wraparound taillamps with inboard amber directional signal lamps and clear backup lamps. Rally Sport became a model this year rather than an option, with new paint striping. Both standard and Type LT

Rally Sport coupe models had a bold contrasting paint scheme. The forward roof section, hood surface and front header (to below the grille opening) were black metallic. Tri-color striping separated those black surfaces from the basic body color. 'Rally Sport' decals were on front fenders and decklid. Standard engine was the 250 cu. in. inline six, now rated 110 horsepower, with three-speed manual transmission. Optional: 305 and 350 V-8s, now with base four-speed manual gearbox. California Camaros only came with automatic, while high-altitude buyers could get only the 350 V-8 and automatic. The six had improved exhaust system isolation this year. An aluminum intake manifold helped cut the 305 V-8's weight by 35 pounds. Chassis had improved front frame reinforcements. And the brake-pressure differential switch was now made of nylon. All axle ratios were lowered in an attempt to boost gas mileage. Body colors this year were white, silver, black, light or bright blue, orange-yellow, bright yellow, dark blue-green, camel, dark camel, saffron, light red, and carmine. New Rally wheels came in all body colors. Camaros had new standard cloth seat trim, a new door trim design, and could have new optional aluminum wheels. Also joining the option list: a T-bar twin hatch roof with tinted glass lift-out roof panels, operated by a single latch on each panel. A total of 9,875 T-roofs were installed this year. The high-performance Z28 added a new pointed hood panel air scoop with black throat, functional slanted front-fender air louvers, body-color rear spoiler, modified body striping, and simulated string-wrapped steering wheel. Powerplant was the 350 (5.7-liter) V-8 with four-barrel and dual exhaust outlets, putting out 170 or 185 horsepower. Z28s had a 3.42:1 or 3.73:1 axle ratio, special handling suspension, and GR70 x 15/B white-letter tires. Suspension revisions this year increased front-end rigidity and limited transverse movement of the rear axle. A 'Z28' decal was below the air louvers.

1978 Chevrolet, Malibu Classic Landau two-door coupe (CH)

1978 Chevrolet, Malibu Classic four-door sedan

MALIBU -- SERIES 1A -- V-6/V-8 -- New-size Malibus rode a 108 inch wheelbase and averaged 193 inches, overall. That was 12-1/2 to 22 inches shorter than 1977 equivalents. This year's editions were narrower, too, but as tall as before. Slimmer doors and reduced body-side curvature helped keep interior space ample. Broad glass area improved visibility. Rear armrests in sedans and wagons were now recessed into back door trim panels, so door glass was fixed rather than movable. Somehow, the newly shrunken Malibus managed to offer more interior and luggage space. Shell-type seats helped add head/leg room. Coupes lost 550 pounds, wagons closer to half a ton. Models included a two-door coupe, four-door sedan, and four-door (two-seat) station wagon, in both Malibu and Malibu Classic series. A Malibu Classic Landau coupe was available, as was an Estate option for the Malibu Classic wagon. The old Chevelle name faded away this year. Both Malibus had a new wide, chrome-plated plastic grille in horizontally-oriented lattice style, with 'Chevrolet' block lettering in the upper molding. Vertical rectangular parking lamps sat between the grille and single chrome-bezel rectangular headlamps. Bright steel bumpers had horizontal sculpture lines. Tapered, angled amber side marker lamps stood at front fender tips. 'Malibu' or 'Malibu Classic' identification was at the rear of quarter panels. Both models had bright roof drip moldings and wheel covers. Six-window sedans had large pivoting quarter vent windows. At the rear were large tri-section taillamps, level with the license plate, with outboard lenses wrapping around to form side markers. (Wagon taillamps sat in the back bumper.) A 'Chevrolet' block-letter nameplate was on the lower right of the decklid. Malibu Classic added extra rear moldings and bright taillamp trim, plus wheel opening moldings (also on Malibu wagon). Standard powerplant was a new Chevrolet 200 cu. in. (3.3-liter) V-6, derived from the popular small-block V-8. The new engine had a cast iron block and cylinder heads, new "Dualjet" carburetor, and lightweight aluminum intake manifold. New dynamic balancing was supposed to ensure smooth running. California models, though, required a 231 V-6. Standard transmission was the three-speed manual, except in California where the otherwise optional Turbo Hydra-matic was mandatory. An optional 305 cu. in. (5.0-liter) V-8 could have either four-speed manual or automatic. Wagons in high-altitude areas had to have the four-barrel 350 cu. in. V-8. A new vertical-style instrument panel, mounted well forward, helped to enhance the spacious feeling. A separate module held radio/heater controls and instruments. Plug-in components and a swing-down glove compartment made behind-dash servicing easier. The dimmer switch moved to the turn-signal lever. A new ventilation system delivered outside air under all driving conditions, whether power assisted or ram vented. Sedans and wagons had standard swing-out rear vent windows. Drivers had a delta-spoke soft vinyl steering wheel. Wagons had a much wider cargo opening than before, plus a split tailgate instead of the previous swing-up version. As in full-size wagons, storage compartments were in the rear quarter trim panels, just inside the tailgate. The new Malibus used a full perimeter frame to keep their "big car" ride. The chassis featured coil springs all around, a single-piece propeller shaft, lower rear axle ratios, relay-type steering, and front disc (rear drum) brakes. The new fuel tank held 17.5 gallons. Malibus rode on radial-ply tires on 14 inch wheels. All had a modular mini-enersorber bumper system. A new temporary spare tire saved 15 pounds and allowed greater trunk space. Fourteen tuned rubber body mounts helped keep road noise down. In addition to 14 solid colors, five custom two-tone combinations were optional: dark blue and light blue metallic; gold and light camel; carmine and dark carmine metallic; green and light green metallic; and silver with medium gray accent. Standard equipment included heater/defroster, carpeting, bright windshield and back window reveal moldings, bright belt side moldings, front stabilizer bar, Freedom battery, and P185/75R14 fiberglass-belted radial tires (wagons had P195/75R14). Malibu Classic added dual horns. Malibu Classic Landau had a vinyl roof, bodyside striping, rally wheels, and sport wheel covers. Power brakes and steering, V-8 engines and Turbo Hydra-matic were optional.

1978 Chevrolet, Monte Carlo two-door coupe (CH)

MONTE CARLO -- SERIES 1A -- V-6/V-8 -- The third-generation Monte, according to Chevrolet, was "reengineered to meet the need for modern levels of vehicle efficiency" to provide "a new dimension in affordable luxury." Weight was cut by over 800 pounds. Overall length shrunk by 12.9 inches, wheelbase by nearly 8 inches (down to 108.1), while height rose slightly. Even so, interior dimensions managed to grow instead of shrink. The downsized version displayed a more formal roofline with sweeping fender and body lines (but lacking the former body bulges), much larger quarter windows, and frameless door glass. Single bright-bezeled rectangular headlamps sat between large parking lamps (which wrapped around to amber marker lamps) and the bright, fine-mesh grid-pattern grille. At the rear were distinctive five-segment taillamps. Lower body contours retained the look of former Montes. Large, soft bumper impact areas held bright impact strips. Up front was a standup header emblem and 'Monte Carlo' script nameplate. Nameplates were also on front fenders; nameplate with bowtie emblem on decklid; Monte crest on the sail panel. Basic mechanical (and bodily) changes were similar to Malibu. The new standard 231 cu. in. (3.8-liter) V-6 engine with two-barrel carburetor was claimed to deliver 24 percent better

gas mileage than the former base V-8. Sole V-8 option this year was the 305 cu. in. (5.0-liter). Base transmission was three-speed manual, with four-speed manual and automatic available. The V-8 came with automatic, but could have four-speed manual. Automatics were required in California. For improved handling, Monte got a special frame, front and rear stabilizer bars, and P205/70R14 steel-belted radial tires. The new body used aluminum inner and outer decklid panels to save weight. Rear brake drums were finned aluminum. Improved corrosion protection included zincro-metal, aluminum, galvanized metal, zinc priming, anti-corrosion dip, plus special sealers and coatings. Front and rear bumper reinforcement bars were aluminum. The new integrated-look outer covering was injection-molded and pliable, finished in body color. Monte's standard interior used a bench seat with split back, in vinyl or woven cloth. Optional: a 55/45 split bench seat (velour or vinyl), or vinyl buckets with individual adjustments. Standard equipment included the 231 V-6, three-speed manual transmission, manual front disc brakes, electric clock, day/night mirror, dual horns, bright wheel opening and roof drip moldings, bumper impact strips, front and rear stabilizer bars, heater/defroster, and carpeting. Body colors this year were white, silver, black, light blue, light camel, or nine metallics: light or dark blue, light or medium green, camel, dark camel, saffron, carmine, or dark carmine. A new Landau model had a vinyl half-roof with unique white-metalized rear quarter window treatment, sport mirrors, special wheel covers, wide sill moldings, lower body appliqué, upper body pin striping, and 'Landau' nameplates with decorative crest. As before, Landaus came with standard automatic transmission, power brakes and steering. Added to the option list: a twin hatch sunroof with removable tinted glass panels. Still available was the power-operated steel sunroof.

1978 Chevrolet, Impala two-door coupe (PH)

1978 Chevrolet, Caprice Classic four-door sedan (CH)

IMPALA/CAPRICE CLASSIC -- SERIES 1B -- SIX/V-8 -- Apart from revised front and rear styling treatments, the full-size Chevrolets were carryovers from their 1977 downsizing. Impalas carried a new horizontal-bar grille, with bowtie above rather than on the grille itself. Caprice's version had a lattice crosshatch pattern (with fewer divider bars than before). Taillamps and moldings were also restyled. Both Caprice and Impala were again available in two-door coupe, four-door sedan and four-door station wagon (two- or three-seat) body styles. Powertrains were the same as 1977, except for reduced axle ratios to achieve greater economy. Standard engine was again the 250 cu. in. (4.1-liter) inline six, with both 305 and 350 V-8s available. The six now had an integral distributor cap and coil, while the 305 V-8 lost 35 pounds as a result of a new aluminum intake manifold. A larger power brake booster reduced pedal effort. Of the 14 standard body colors, ten were new this year. In addition to styling differences, Caprice added a few items of standard equipment absent on Impalas. They included a dual-note horn, full wheel covers, wheel opening moldings, clock, interior lighting, and fold-down center armrest on sedans. The Caprice Classic Landau coupe, introduced during the 1977 model year, was continued this year. That appearance package included an elk-grain forward vinyl top with bright rear-edge molding, sport mirrors, wire wheel covers with Landau hub identification, accent striping, and belt moldings painted to match the vinyl top. Roof panels held a Landau nameplate. New options this year: new wheel trim covers for Impala, an electrically-powered sliding steel sunroof for coupes and sedans, and 40-channel CB built into AM/FM radio.

I.D. DATA: As before, Chevrolet used a 13-symbol Vehicle Identification Number (VIN) displayed on the upper left surface of the instrument panel, visible through the windshield. The first digit ('1') indicates Chevrolet division. Next is a letter identifying the series (car line): 'B' = Chevette; 'J' = Chevette Scooter; 'M' = Monza; 'R' = Monza Sport; 'X' = Nova; 'Y' = Nova Custom; 'Q' = Camaro; 'S' = Camaro Type LT; 'Y' = Nova Concours; 'T' = Malibu; 'W' = Malibu Classic; 'Z' = Monte Carlo; 'L' = Impala; 'N' = Caprice Classic. Symbols 3-4 indicate body type: '08' = 2-dr. (4-pass.) hatchback coupe; '07' = 2-dr. (2 + 2) hatchback coupe; '77' = 2-dr. hatchback coupe; '17' = Nova 2-dr. (6-pass.) hatchback coupe; '27' = 2-dr. coupe or notchback coupe; '87' = 2-

dr. (4-pass.) sport coupe; '37' = 2-dr. (6-pass.) sport coupe; '47' = 2-dr. (6-pass.) coupe; '19' = 4-dr. (6-pass.) sedan; '68' = 4-dr. (4-pass.) hatchback sedan; '69' = 4-dr. (6-pass.) sedan; '15' = 2-dr. (4-pass.) station wagon; '35' = 4-dr. station wagon. Symbol five is the engine code: 'E' = L4-97.6 1Bbl.; 'J' = L4-97.6 H.O.; 'V' = L4-151 2Bbl.; 'C' = V6-196 2Bbl.; 'M' = V6-200 2Bbl.; 'A' = V6-231 2Bbl.; 'D' = L6-250 1Bbl.; 'U' = V8-305 2Bbl.; 'L' = V8-350 4Bbl. Next is a code for model year ('8' = 1978). Symbol seven denotes assembly plant: 'B' = Baltimore, MD; 'C' = South Gate, CA; 'D' = Doraville, GA; 'J' = Janesville, WI; 'K' = Leeds, MO; 'U' = Lordstown, OH; 'L' = Van Nuys, CA; 'N' = Norwood, OH; 'R' = Arlington, TX; 'S' = St. Louis, MO; 'T' = Tarrytown, NY; 'W' = Willow Run, MI; 'Y' = Wilmington, DE; 'Z' = Fremont, CA; '1' = Oshawa, Ontario. The last six digits are the sequential serial number. A Body Number Plate on the upper horizontal surface of the shroud (except X-bodies, on the vertical surface) identifies model year, car division, series, style, body assembly plant, body number, trim combination, modular seat code, paint code, and date build code. A two- or three-symbol code (combined with a serial number) identifies each engine. Chevette engine numbers are on a pad at right of block, below No. 1 spark plug. Pontiac (151) fours have a number pad at the right side of the block, by distributor shaft hole. On sixes, the pad is at the right side of the block, to rear of distributor. On V-8s, that pad is just forward of the right cylinder head.

CHEVETTE (FOUR)

Model No.	Body/Style No.	Body Type & Seating	Factory Price	Shipping Weight	Prod. Total
1T	B08	2-dr. Hatch Cpe-4P	3354	1965	118,375
1T	B68	4-dr. Hatch Sed-4P	3764	2035	167,769

CHEVETTE SCOOTER (FOUR)

1T	J08	2-dr. Hatch Cpe-4P	2999	1932	12,829

Chevette Production Note: 11,316 Chevettes were built for sale in Canada as Acadians.

MONZA (FOUR/V-6/V-8)

1H	M07	2-dr. Hatch 2+2-4P	3609	2732	36,227
1H	M77	2-dr. 'S' Hatch-4P	3527	2643	2,326
1H	M27	2-dr. Cpe-4P	3462	2688	37,878
1H	M15	2-dr. Sta Wag-4P	3698	2723	24,255
1H	M15/YC6	2-dr. Est Wag-4P	3932	N/A	2,478

1978 Chevrolet, Monza Sport two-door coupe (CH)

HOT ONES FROM CHEVROLET

V8 1955

The launch of Chevrolet's "Hot Ones" occurred in 1955 with a totally new automobile design and a new small-block V-8. Chevy touted this revolutionary powerplant as "...the most modern V-8 on the road." This was the beginning of a long line of muscle-machines from Chevrolet that continues today, almost a half-century later.

Chevrolet's *red-hot* hill-flatteners !
162 H.P. V8 - 180 H.P. V8

See that fine fat mountain yonder?

You can iron it out, flat as a flounder . . . and easy as whistling!

Just point one of Chevrolet's special hill-flatteners at it (either the 162-h.p. "Turbo-Fire V8," or the 180-h.p. "Super Turbo-Fire"*) . . . and pull the trigger!

Barr-r-r-r-o-o-O-O-OOM!

Mister, you got you a flat mountain!

. . . At least it *feels* flat. Because these silk-and-dynamite V8's gobble up the toughest grades you can ladle out. And holler for more. They love to climb, because that's just about the only time the throttle ever comes near the floorboard.

And that's a pity. For here are engines that sing as sweetly as a dynamo . . . built to pour out a torrent of pure, vibrationless power. Big-bore V8's with the shortest stroke in the industry, designed to gulp huge breaths of fresh air and transmute it into blazing acceleration.

So most of the time they loaf. Even at the speed limit they just dream along, light and easy as a zephyr, purring out an effortless fraction of their strength.

You don't have to be an engineer to know that these are the sweetest-running V8's you ever piloted. Just drop in at your Chevrolet dealer's, point the nose at the nearest hill, and feather the throttle open. *These* V8's can do their own talking . . . and nobody argues with them!

SEE YOUR CHEVROLET DEALER
*Optional at extra cost.

motoramic *Stealing the thunder from the high-priced cars with the most modern V8 on the road!*

One of the most desirable collector cars today is the 1957 Chevrolet Bel Air Sport Coupe powered by a fuel-injected 283-cid V-8 capable of producing 283 hp at 6200 rpm. The license plates of this black beauty reflect the one horsepower per cubic inch capability of the car's powerplant, which was a Corvette engine with a 10.5:1 compression ratio.

CORVETTE

America's sports car, the Chevrolet Corvette, had a distinctive interior including this version from its 1959 model. Promoted as a jewel-box cockpit, the interior was keyed to the car's exterior finish. It featured foam-rubber padded vinyl bucket seats that were individually adjustable. Instruments featured concave lenses to reduce distortion and glare, including a speedometer, tachometer and ammeter gauge as well as fuel, oil pressure and coolant temperature gauges. The competition-type steering wheel and seat belts were indicators that the Corvette had a higher purpose than just cruising the boulevard.

As of 1964, the Super Sport was no longer just a trim package available on Chevrolet Impala models but, instead, a series of its own. As shown on this convertible model, the Impala Super Sport featured special SS badges on the rear quarter panels, silver anodized side molding and tri-bar wheel covers. While the standard powerplant of the Impala SS continued to be a six-cylinder engine, the majority of these cars were ordered with optional V-8s. These option choices included the potent 409-cid big-block V-8 with 11.0:1 compression and rated at 425 hp at 6000 rpm when equipped with dual four-barrel carburetors.

With the phasing out of Chevrolet's 409 engine beginning in 1965, the 396- and 327-cid V-8s became the engines of choice for the Super Sport set, including the buyers of Impala SS convertibles. This particular Impala SS had the 327-cid V-8. The Impala SS received major restyling over the previous year's model, but still retained the distinctive tri-bar wheel covers. Super Sport script now adorned the front fenders and an Impala SS badge was found on the grille.

The 1966 Chevrolet Corvette Sting Rays—including this road warrior—that were powered by the optional 427-cid/425-hp V-8 were also fitted with a "power bulge" hood. This particular 'Vette featured the optional cast aluminum wheels with knock-off hubs and side-mount exhaust system. The vents in the fender were functional and necessary due to the excessive heat produced by the big-block engine, which reportedly produced way more than the 425 hp claimed by Chevrolet.

"A little like driving a storm," stated the ad copy for this 1967 Chevrolet Chevelle SS396 sport coupe. This particular Chevelle featured an optional vinyl roof. The Chevelle SS396 was identified by its black-accented grille with a SS396 badge, Super Sport rear quarter panel script and simulated air intakes on its domed hood. Special wheel covers and Red Stripe tires were also part of the package. The 396-cid Turbo-Jet V-8 was rated at 325 hp at 4600 rpm and featured a 10.25:1 compression ratio.

SS 396 Sport Coupe with all of Chevrolet's new safety feature

Cubes, red lines, ft.-lbs., torque, tach. An SS 396 will even change the way you talk.

If you could bottle and sell what a new car like an SS 396 does for a guy, you could retire now. Rich.

You look out over a louver-styled hood. You ride on red stripe tires. You control 396 cubic inches of Turbo-Jet V8 (which is a little like driving a storm).

You can add a 4-speed and Strato-bucket seats with center console, disc brakes up front and Positraction in back. It's quick to turn, quick to shift, quick to do what you tell it to.

It's one of those cars you think about driving when you're not and hardly think about anything else when you are.

You'd like to give it a go? Now you're talking.

THE QUICK-SIZE
'67 CHEVELLE
MANEUVERS LIKE MAGIC

CHEVROLET

GM
MARK OF EXCELLENCE

The Chevrolet Corvette's first major restyling since 1963 took place in 1968 as evidenced by this T-top coupe. For this year only, the Sting Ray name was not used and would be spelled as one word, Stingray, upon its return in 1969. This particular Corvette was powered by the optional 427-cid V-8, according to the badge visible on the hood. The spoked wheel covers shown and Red Stripe tires were also optional equipment. The Corvette coupe featured a power-operated rear window that could be lowered for enhanced ventilation.

Chevrolet's Chevelle was also restyled for 1968, including a "rakish" front end design. This Chevelle SS396 convertible featured optional SS396 striping that swept across the car's front and down and across its lower bodysides. The Turbo-Jet 396-cid V-8 was rated at 325 hp and engine call-out badges were located ahead of the side marker lenses. Standard Chevelle SS396 features included: black-out grille treatment, Red Stripe tires and wheel covers with SS center medallions.

Chevrolet offered the "purrfect" pair of automobiles in 1957 with its Corvette and Bel Air Sport Coupe. Promoting its new-for-1957 Super Turbo-Fire small-block 283-cid V-8, the ad copy read: "It's sassy, sure— but as tame to your touch as a purring pussycat."

Promoting its 1963 line of cars as the "Go Show" in dealers' showrooms, two headliners in that year's Chevrolet showcase were the Corvette Sting Ray (top) and Corvair Monza Spyder. The Sting Ray featured the controversial split-window design that obscured rearward vision. One of the Monza Spyder's new features was its taillight ring that, as Chevy stated in ad copy, allowed for "...all the people you pass will know you're driving a '63."

You had to read the fine print of this ad copy to get the "scoop" on the 1969 Chevrolet Camaro SS, shown with Rally Sport equipment and Super Scoop hood (offered only on SS and Z28 versions of that year's Camaro). The Rally Sport package, which could be combined with any SS package, included: black-out grille treatment and concealed headlights, fender striping, RS emblems and bright metal trim on simulated louvers located ahead of the rear wheels. The Camaro SS350 was powered by the 350-cid/300-hp V-8. The vinyl roof shown was optional equipment whether the Camaro was ordered with the RS or SS package or both.

GM

Camaro SS Sport Coupe with Rally Sport equipment and Super Scoop hood.

Equipped with the "air-gulping" Cowl Induction Hood, this 1970 Chevrolet Chevelle SS396 offered 350 hp with standard powerplant and was available with engine options including the LS6 rated at 454 cid and 450 hp. The Cowl Induction Hood featured a small "trap door" at the base of the hood dome that opened when the car was under acceleration. This allowed high-pressure air from around the windshield to surge into the carburetor. The Chevelle SS396 featured a pin-lock hood, black-out grille treatment, special striping and mag-style wheels.

Based on the Chevelle Sport Coupe, this 1972 "Heavy Chevy" was more of a graphics package than a true performance machine. It came standard with the rather tame 307-cid V-8, but one of three optional engines was the Turbo-Jet 400, which increased the car's "snort factor" considerably. Called a "low-buck SS" by some, the "Heavy Chevy" featured black-out grille treatment, domed hood with lock pins, special side striping and pressed steel rally-type wheels with bright center caps.

Derived from the Chevrolet Caprice—and sporting a version of the Corvette LT1 V-8 engine—the Impala SS made its debut in 1993 as a concept car on the auto show circuit. The Impala SS was based on the Caprice LTZ, utilizing the drivetrain and suspension from the car's police equipment package. The LT1 engine produced 300 hp and was mated to a four-speed automatic transmission. The Impala SS was finished in monochromatic paint and featured 17-inch aluminum wheels and low-profile radial tires.

The 1996 return of Chevrolet's Grand Sport Corvette evoked memories of the five lightweight Corvette Grand Sport race cars constructed in 1962-'63 under the direction of the late Zora Arkus-Duntov. These five racing machines—three coupes and two roadsters—were driven by racing legends including Roger Penske, A.J. Foyt and Jim Hall. The 1996 Grand Sport mimicked its predecessors with its Admiral blue metallic paint, white stripe and red "hash marks" on its left front fender. Chromed Corvette emblems on the hood and fuel door and 17-inch spoked aluminum wheels further distinguished the 1996 Grand Sport, which was powered by a 330-hp LT4 small-block V-8 mated to a six-speed manual transmission.

A mid-year debut in 1993, details of the fourth generation Chevrolet Camaro Z28 are visible in this cutaway rendering of the T-top coupe, including power rack-and-pinion steering and four-wheel disc brakes. The Z28's exterior was a completely new design, and power was supplied by the 5.7-liter LT1 V-8—also found in the Corvette—rated at 275 hp at 5000 rpm.

To commemorate the Camaro's 30th anniversary in 1997, Chevrolet, in conjunction with SLP Engineering, developed a limited-edition Z28 SS loaded with special features. Only 1,000 of the orange-stripes-on-white Camaro Z28 SS models were produced. Only the show car depicted was finished in reverse fashion, white stripes on orange. This show Camaro Z28 SS featured: chrome-plated alloy wheels, Level II suspension, high-performance exhaust, Torsen limited-slip differential, Hurst short-throw shifter and enhanced decklid airfoil. It was powered by the 350-hp 5.7-liter LT4 V-8 mated to a six-speed manual transmission.

The 1998 Chevrolet Camaro Z28, offered in both coupe and convertible versions, was powered by the 5.7-liter LS1 V-8 mated to a four-speed automatic transmission. This engine featured an aluminum block, composite intake manifold and air intake system. the Z28's updated exterior appearance featured a new front fascia, composite headlamps and optional foglamps. The Z28 also featured traction control and four-wheel disc brakes as part of the package.

MONZA SPORT (FOUR/V-6/V-8)

| 1H | R27 | 2-dr. Spt Cpe-4P | 3930 | 2730 | 6,823 |
| 1H | R07 | 2-dr. Hatch 2+2-4P | 4077 | 2777 | 28,845 |

Monza Engine Note: Prices shown are for four-cylinder engine. The 196 cu. in. V-6 cost $130 extra; a 231 V-6, $170. Monza could also have a 305 V-8 for $320 over the four-cylinder price. A total of 41,995 Monzas had a 196 V-6 installed, and 16,254 a 231 V-6. Only 9,478 had a V-8 engine.

NOVA (SIX/V-8)

1X	X27	2-dr. Cpe-6P	3702/3887	3132/3277	101,858
1X	X17	2-dr. Hatch-6P	3866/4051	3258/3403	12,665
1X	X69	4-dr. Sedan-6P	3777/3962	3173/3318	123,158

NOVA CUSTOM (SIX/V-8)

| 1X | Y27 | 2-dr. Cpe-6P | 3960/4145 | 3261/3396 | 23,953 |
| 1X | Y69 | 4-dr. Sedan-6P | 4035/4220 | 3298/3443 | 26,475 |

CAMARO (SIX/V-8)

| 1F | Q87 | 2-dr. Spt Cpe-4P | 4414/4599 | 3300/3425 | 134,491 |
| 1F | Q87/Z85 | 2-dr. Rally Cpe-4P | 4784/4969 | N/A | 11,902 |

CAMARO TYPE LT (SIX/V-8)

| 1F | S87 | 2-dr. Spt Cpe-4P | 4814/4999 | 3352/3477 | 65,635 |
| 1F | S87/Z85 | 2-dr. Rally Cpe-4P | 5065/5250 | N/A | 5,696 |

CAMARO Z28 (V-8)

| 1F | Q87 | 2-dr. Spt Cpe-4P | ---- /5604 | ---- / N/A | 54,907 |

MALIBU (V-6/V-8)

1A	T27	2-dr. Spt Cpe-6P	4204/4394	3001/3138	27,089
1A	T19	4-dr. Sed-6P	4279/4469	3006/3143	44,426
1A	T35	4-dr. Sta Wag-6P	4516/4706	3169/3350	30,850

MALIBU CLASSIC (V-6/V-8)

1A	W27	2-dr. Spt Cpe-6P	4461/4651	3031/3167	60,992
1A	W27/Z03	2-dr. Lan Cpe-6P	4684/4874	N/A	29,160
1A	W19	4-dr. Sed-6P	4561/4651	3039/3175	102,967
1A	W35	4-dr. Sta Wag-6P	4714/4904	3196/3377	63,152

Malibu Engine Note: Only 8,930 Malibus had the 231 V-6 engine, and only 802 had the 350 V-8 (code (LM1).

MONTE CARLO (V-6/V-8)

| 1A | Z37 | 2-dr. Spt Cpe-6P | 4785/4935 | 3040/3175 | 216,730 |
| 1A | Z37/Z03 | 2-dr. Lan Cpe-6P | 5678/5838 | N/A | 141,461 |

IMPALA (SIX/V-8)

1B	L47	2-dr. Spt Cpe-6P	5208/5393	3511/3619	33,990
1B	L47/Z03	2-dr. Lan Cpe-6P	5598/5783	N/A	4,652
1B	L69	4-dr. Sedan-6P	5283/5468	3530/3638	183,161
1B	L35	4-dr. Sta Wag-6P	---- /5777	---- /4037	40,423
1B	L35/AQ4	4-dr. 3S Wag-8P	---- /5904	---- /4071	28,518

CAPRICE CLASSIC (SIX/V-8)

1B	N47	2-dr. Spt Cpe-6P	5526/5711	3548/3656	37,301
1B	N47/Z03	2-dr. Lan Cpe-6P	5830/6015	N/A	22,771
1B	N69	4-dr. Sedan-6P	5626/5811	3578/3686	203,837
1B	N35	4-dr. Sta Wag-6P	---- /6012	---- /4079	24,792
1B	N35/AQ4	4-dr. 3S Wag-8P	---- /6151	---- /4109	32,952

FACTORY PRICE AND WEIGHT NOTE: Where two prices and weights are shown, the figure to the left of the slash is for six-cylinder model, to right of slash for V-8.

BODY/STYLE NO. NOTE: Some models are actually option packages. Figure after the slash (e.g., Z03) is the number of the option package that comes with the model listed.

ENGINE DATA: BASE FOUR (Chevette): Inline. Overhead cam. Four-cylinder. Cast iron block and head. Displacement: 97.6 cu. in. (1.6 liters). Bore & stroke: 3.23 x 2.98 in. Compression ratio: 8.6:1. Brake horsepower: 63 at 4800 R.P.M. Torque: 82 lb.-ft. at 3200 R.P.M. Five main bearings. Hydraulic valve lifters. Carburetor: 1Bbl. Rochester 1ME. VIN Code: E. **OPTIONAL FOUR (Chevette):** Same as above except: Brake H.P.: 68 at 5000 R.P.M. Torque: 84 lb.-ft. at 3200 R.P.M. VIN Code: J. **BASE FOUR (Monza):** Inline. Overhead valve. Four-cylinder. Cast iron block. Displacement: 151 cu. in. (2.5 liters). Bore & stroke: 4.00 x 3.00 in. Compression ratio: 8.3:1. Brake horsepower: 85 at 4400 R.P.M. Torque: 123 lb.-ft. at 2800 R.P.M. Five main bearings. Hydraulic valve lifters. Carburetor: 2Bbl. Holley 5210C. VIN Code: V. **OPTIONAL V-6 (Monza):** 90-degree, overhead-valve V-6. Cast iron block and head. Displacement: 196 cu. in. (3.2 liters). Bore & stroke: 3.50 x 3.40 in. Compression ratio: 8.0:1. Brake horsepower: 90 at 3600 R.P.M. Torque: 165 lb.-ft. at 2000 R.P.M. Four main bearings. Hydraulic valve lifters. Carburetor: 2Bbl. Rochester 2GE. VIN Code: C. **BASE V-6 (Malibu):** 90-degree, overhead-valve V-6. Cast iron block and head. Displacement: 200 cu. in. (3.3 liters). Bore & stroke: 3.50 x 3.48 in. Compression ratio: 8.2:1. Brake horsepower: 95 at 3800 R.P.M. Torque: 160 lb.-ft. at 2000 R.P.M. Four main bearings. Hydraulic valve lifters. Carburetor: 2Bbl. Rochester 2GC. VIN Code: M. **BASE V-6 (Monte Carlo); OPTIONAL (Monza, Malibu):** 90-degree, overhead-valve V-6. Cast iron block and head. Displacement: 231 cu. in. (3.8 liters). Bore & stroke: 3.80 x 3.40 in. Compression ratio: 8.0:1. Brake horsepower: 105 at 3400 R.P.M. Torque: 185 lb.-ft. at 2000 R.P.M. Four main bearings. Hydraulic valve lifters. Carburetor: 2Bbl. Rochester 2GE. VIN Code: A. **BASE SIX (Nova, Camaro, Impala, Caprice):** Inline. OHV. Six-cylinder. Cast iron block and head. Displacement: 250 cu. in. (4.1 liters). Bore & stroke: 3.88 x 3.53 in. Compression ratio: 8.1:1. Brake horsepower: 110 at 3800 R.P.M. Torque: 190 lb.-ft. at 1600 R.P.M. Seven main bearings. Hydraulic valve lifters. Carburetor: 1Bbl. Rochester 1ME. VIN Code: D. **BASE V-8 (Impala/Caprice wagon); OPTIONAL (Monza, Nova, Camaro, Malibu, Monte Carlo, Impala, Caprice):** 90-degree, overhead valve V-8. Cast iron block and head. Displacement: 305 cu. in. (5.0 liters). Bore & stroke: 3.74 x 3.48 in. Compression ratio: 8.4:1. Brake horsepower: 145 at 3800 R.P.M. Torque: 245 lb.-ft. at 2400 R.P.M. Five main bearings. Hydraulic valve lifters. Carburetor: 2Bbl. Rochester 2GC. VIN Code: U. **BASE V-8 (Camaro Z28); OPTIONAL (Nova, Camaro, Malibu wagon, Impala, Caprice):** 90-degree, overhead valve V-8. Cast iron block and head. Displacement: 350 cu. in. (5.7 liters). Bore & stroke: 4.00 x 3.48 in. Compression ratio: 8.2:1. Brake horsepower: 170 at 3800 R.P.M. Torque: 270 lb.-ft. at 2400 R.P.M. Five main bearings. Hydraulic valve lifters. Carburetor: 4Bbl. Rochester M4MC. VIN Code: L. **OPTIONAL V-8 (Camaro Z28):** Same as 350 V-8 above except: Brake H.P.: 185 at 4000 R.P.M. Torque: 280 lb.-ft. at 2400 R.P.M.

CHASSIS DATA: Wheelbase: (Chevette 2-dr.) 94.3 in.; (Chvt 4-dr.) 97.3 in.; (Monza) 97.0 in.; (Camaro) 108.0 in.; (Nova) 111.0 in.; (Malibu/Monte) 108.1 in.; (Caprice/Imp) 116.0 in. Overall length: (Chevette 2-dr.) 159.7 in.; (Chvt 4-dr.) 162.6 in.; (Monza) 178.0-179.3 in.; (Nova) 196.7 in.; (Camaro) 197.6 in.; (Malibu) 192.7 in.; (Malibu wag) 193.4 in.; (Monte) 200.4 in.; (Capr/Imp) 212.1 in.; (Capr/Imp wag) 214.7 in. Height: (Chevette 2-dr.) 52.3 in.; (Chvt 4-dr.) 53.3 in.; (Monza cpe) 49.8 in.; (Monza hatch) 50.2 in.; (Monza wag) 51.8 in.; (Nova 2-dr.) 52.7 in.; (Nova 4-dr.) 53.6 in.; (Camaro) 49.2 in.; (Malibu cpe) 53.3 in.; (Malibu sed) 54.2 in.; (Malibu wag) 54.5 in.; (Monte) 53.9 in.; (Capr/Imp cpe) 55.3 in.; (Capr/Imp sed) 56.0 in.; (Capr/Imp wag) 58.0 in. Width: (Chevette) 61.8 in.; (Monza) 65.4 in.; (Nova) 72.2 in.; (Camaro) 74.5 in.; (Malibu/Monte) 71.5 in.; (Malibu wag) 71.2 in.; (Capr/Imp) 76.0 in.; (Capr/Imp wag) 79.1 in. Front Tread: (Chevette) 51.2 in.; (Monza) 54.8 in.; (Nova/Camaro) 61.3 in.; (Camaro LT) 61.6 in.; (Malibu/Monte) 58.5 in.; (Capr/Imp) 61.8 in.; (Capr/Imp wag) 62.2 in. Rear Tread: (Chevette) 51.2 in.; (Monza) 53.6 in.; (Nova) 59.0 in.; (Camaro) 60.0 in.; (Camaro LT) 60.3 in.; (Malibu/Monte) 57.8 in.; (Capr/Imp) 60.8 in.; (Capr/Imp wag) 64.1 in. Standard Tires: (Chevette) P155/80 x 13; (Monza) A78 x 13; (Monza wag) B78 x 13; (Nova) E78 x 14; (Camaro) FR78 x 14/B SBR; (Malibu) P185/75R14 GBR; (Malibu wag) P195/75R14 GBR; (Imp/Capr) FR78 x 15 GBR; (Imp/Capr wag) HR78 x 15 SBR; (Monte) P205/70R14 SBR.

1978 Chevrolet, Camaro Z28 two-door coupe (CP)

TECHNICAL: Transmission: Three-speed manual transmission (floor shift) standard on Camaro, Nova and Monte Carlo six. Gear ratios: (1st) 3.50:1; (2nd) 1.81:1; (3rd) 1.00:1; (Rev) 3.62:1. Four-speed floor shift standard on Chevette: (1st) 3.75:1; (2nd) 2.16:1; (3rd) 1.38:1; (4th) 1.00:1; (Rev) 3.82:1. Four-speed floor shift optional on Monza four and Monte V-6: (1st) 3.50:1; (2nd) 2.48:1; (3rd) 1.66:1; (4th) 1.00:1; (Rev) 3.50:1. Four-speed floor shift standard on Nova (V8-350) and Camaro V-8, optional on Chevette, Monza, Monte: (1st) 2.85:1; (2nd) 2.02:1; (3rd) 1.35:1; (4th) 1.00:1; (Rev) 2.85:1. Camaro Z28 four-speed floor shift: (1st) 2.64:1; (2nd) 1.75:1; (3rd) 1.34:1; (4th) 1.00:1; (Rev) 2.55:1. Five-speed floor shift available on Monza V-6: (1st) 3.40:1; (2nd) 2.08:1; (3rd) 1.39:1; (4th) 1.00:1; (5th) 0.80:1; (Rev) 3.36:1. Three-speed Turbo Hydra-matic standard on Caprice/Impala, optional on others. Gear ratios: (1st) 2.52:1; (2nd) 1.52:1; (3rd) 1.00:1; (Rev) 1.94:1 except standard Caprice/Impala V-8, Monza V-6, Malibu six and Monte (V8-305) ratios: (1st) 2.74:1; (2nd) 1.57:1; (3rd) 1.00:1; (Rev) 2.07:1. Chevette/Mon-

za four automatic trans.: (1st) 2.40:1; (2nd) 1.48:1; (3rd) 1.00:1; (Rev) 1.92:1. Standard final drive ratio: (Chevette) 3.70:1; (Monza four) 2.73:1 exc. 3.23:1 w/5-spd; (Monza V-6) 2.56:1 exc. 2.73:1 w/5-spd or auto.; (Monza V-8) 3.08:1 w/4-spd, 2.29:1 w/auto.; (Nova) 2.73:1 exc. 3.08:1 w/V-8 or 2.41:1 w/V8-305 and auto.; (Camaro six) 2.73:1; (Camaro V-8) 3.08:1; (Camaro Z28) 3.42:1 or 3.73:1; (Malibu) 2.73:1 exc. 2.29:1 w/V-8; (Malibu wag) 2.41:1; (Monte V-6) 2.93:1 w/3-spd, 2.56:1 w/auto.; (Monte V-8) 2.73:1 w/4-spd, 2.29:1 w/auto.; (Capr/Imp six) 2.73:1; (Capr/Imp V-8) 2.41:1; (Capr/Imp wag) 2.56:1. Steering/Suspension/Body: Same as 1976-77. Brakes: Front disc, rear drum. Fuel tank: (Chevette) 12.5 gal.; (Monza cpe) 18.5 gal.; (Monza hatch/wag) 15 gal.; (Nova/Camaro) 21 gal.; (Malibu/Monte) 17.5 gal.; (Malibu wag) 18 gal.; (Capr/Imp) 21 gal.; (Capr/Imp wag) 22 gal.

DRIVETRAIN OPTIONS: Engines: 1.6-liter H.O. four: Chevette ($55). 196 cu. in. V-6: Monza ($130). 231 cu. in. V-6: Monza ($170); Malibu ($40). 305 cu. in., 2Bbl. V-8: Monza ($320); Nova/Camaro ($185); Malibu ($190); Monte ($150); Imp/Caprice cpe/sed ($185). 350 cu. in., 4Bbl. V-8: Nova/Camaro ($300); Malibu wag ($305); Imp/Capr cpe/sed ($300); Imp/Capr wag ($115). Transmission/Differential: Four-speed manual shift: Nova/Camaro/Malibu/Monte ($125). Close-ratio four-speed manual shift: Camaro (NC). Five-speed manual shift: Monza ($175). Turbo Hydra-matic: Chevette/Monza ($270); Nova/Camaro/Malibu/Monte ($307); Camaro Z28 ($45). Sport shifter: Chvt ($28). Positraction axle: Monza ($55); Nova/Camaro ($59); Malibu/Monte ($60); Imp/Capr ($63). Performance axle ratio ($14-$17). Power Accessories: Power brakes: Chvt/Monza ($66); Nova/Camaro/Monte, Malibu cpe/sed ($69). Power steering: Monza ($134); Nova/Malibu/Monte ($152). Suspension: F40 H.D. suspension: Nova ($9-$33); Malibu cpe/sed, Monte/Imp/Capr ($20). F41 sport suspension: Monza ($30); Nova ($41); Camaro, Malibu/Imp/Capr cpe/sed ($38). Superlift rear shock absorbers: Imp/Capr ($50). Rear stabilizer bar: Chvt ($30). Other: Heavy-duty radiator ($29-$31) exc. Imp/Capr ($40). H.D. alternator (61-amp): Malibu/Monte/Imp/Capr ($31). H.D. battery ($17-$18). California emission system ($75) exc. Monza four ($100). High altitude emission system ($33).

CHEVETTE/MONZA CONVENIENCE/APPEARANCE OPTIONS: Option Packages: Spyder equipment pkg.: Monza ($252). Spyder appearance pkg.: Monza ($216). Quiet sound group: Chvt ($33-$45); Monza ($24-$34). Comfort/Convenience: Air conditioning ($470). Rear defogger, electric ($79). Tinted glass ($54). Sport steering wheel: Monza ($17). Comfortilt steering wheel: Monza ($62). Special instrumentation: Chvt ($64); Monza ($64-$82). Electric clock ($18). Digital clock: Monza ($45). Cigarette lighter: Scooter ($5). Intermittent wipers ($30). Lighting, Horns and Mirrors: Aux. lighting: Chvt ($34-$35); Monza ($17-$33). Twin sport mirrors, left remote: Monza ($31). Driver's remote sport mirror: Chvt ($22). Twin remote sport mirrors: Chvt ($49). Day/night mirror ($9). Entertainment: AM radio ($71); std. on base Chevette. AM/FM radio: Chvt

($68); Scooter/Monza ($139). AM/FM stereo radio: Monza ($215). Stereo tape player w/AM radio: Monza ($216). Stereo tape player with AM/FM stereo radio: Monza ($308). Rear speaker ($23). Windshield antenna: Monza ($24); incl. w/radios. Exterior Trim: Sky roof ($215). Cabriolet vinyl roof: Monza ($153) incl. opera windows. Spoilers, front/rear: Monza ($93). Swing-out windows: Chvt ($51) but std. on base; Monza ($42). Custom exterior (wheel opening, side window and rocker panel moldings): Chvt ($99). Tri-tone sport stripes: Chvt ($67); w/o bodyside moldings ($27). Bodyside moldings ($40); std. on base Chevette. Wheel opening moldings: Monza ($21). Side window reveal moldings: Chvt ($67). Door edge guards ($11-$18). Roof carrier: Chvt ($60). Rear air deflector: Monza ($26). Deluxe bumpers, front/rear: Scooter ($33). Bumper guards, front/rear: Chvt ($38-$71); Monza ($38). Interior Trim/Upholstery: Console: Monza ($77). Bucket seats (sport cloth): Chvt ($10-$19); Monza ($19). Custom Chevette bucket seats: cloth ($170); vinyl ($151). Custom vinyl bucket seats: Monza (NC to $192). Custom sport cloth bucket seats: Monza ($19-$211). Adjustable driver's seatback: Monza ($19). Folding rear seat: Monza ($93) but std. on 2 + 2. Rear seat delete: Chvt ($56 credit). Load floor carpet: Chvt ($46). Color-keyed floor mats ($18). Deluxe seatbelts ($19). Wheels and Tires: Aluminum wheels: Monza ($178-$258). Rally II wheels: Monza ($43-$80). Styled gold wheels: Monza ($101-$181). Deluxe wheel covers: Monza ($37). Sport wheel covers: Chvt ($42). Wheel trim rings: Scooter ($34). 155/80-13/B WSW: Scooter ($43). 155/80-13/B SBR: Chvt ($62); Scooter ($105). 155/80-13/B SBR WSW: Chvt ($105); Scooter ($148). 155/80-13/B SBR WLT: Chvt ($120); Scooter ($163). B78 x 13 WSW: Monza (NC to $19). BR78 x 13 SBR BSW: Monza ($65-$117). BR78 x 13 SBR WSW: Monza ($125-$160). BR70 x 13 SBR BSW: Monza (NC to $157). BR70 x 13 SBR WSW: Monza ($132-$200). BR70 x 13 SBR WLT: Monza ($47-$215). Conventional spare: Monza (NC).

NOVA/CAMARO/MALIBU/MONTE CARLO CONVENIENCE/APPEARANCE OPTIONS:

Option Packages: Rally equipment: Nova cpe ($199). Estate equipment: Malibu wag ($235). Interior decor/quiet sound group: Camaro ($61); std. on LT. Quiet sound group: Malibu ($46). Security pkg.: Malibu wag ($35). Comfort/Convenience: Air conditioning: Nova/Camaro ($508-$539); Malibu/Monte ($544). Rear defogger, forced-air ($51). Rear defogger (electric): Malibu/Monte ($92). Cruise-master speed control ($90). Tinted glass: Nova/Camaro ($56); Malibu/Monte ($62). Comfortilt steering wheel ($69). Six-way power seat: Malibu/Monte ($151). Power windows: Nova ($118-$164); Camaro/Monte ($124); Malibu ($124-$172). Power door locks: Nova/Malibu ($74-$112); Camaro/Monte ($80). Power trunk release: Malibu/Monte ($21). Electric clock: Nova, base Camaro ($20); Malibu ($21). Special instrumentation: Nova, base Camaro ($106); Malibu ($118); Monte ($97). Econominder gauge pkg.: Nova ($50). Gauge pkg.: Malibu ($53); Monte ($32). Intermittent wipers ($32). Lighting, Horns and Mirrors: Aux. lighting ($28-$52). Dome reading light: Malibu/Monte ($16). Dual horns: Nova, base Camaro, Z28, base Malibu ($7). Remote-control driver's mirror: Nova/Malibu/Monte ($16). Twin sport mirrors (left remote): Nova, base Camaro, Malibu/Monte ($33). Twin remote sport mirrors: Malibu/Monte ($57); Monte Lan ($24). Day/night mirror: Nova ($9). Visor vanity mirror: Malibu/Monte ($4). Lighted visor mirror: Malibu ($37); Monte ($33-$37). Entertainment: AM radio ($77-$79). AM/FM radio: Nova/Camaro/Malibu ($149); Monte ($154). AM/FM stereo radio ($229). Stereo tape player w/AM radio: Nova/Camaro ($229); Malibu/Monte ($233). Stereo tape player with AM/FM stereo radio ($328). Rear speaker ($24). Dual front speakers: Malibu/Monte ($20). Windshield antenna ($25); incl. w/radios. Power antenna: Malibu/Monte ($45). Exterior Trim: Removable glass roof panels: Camaro/Monte ($625). Power sky roof: Malibu cpe/sed, Monte ($499). Vinyl roof: Nova ($97); Camaro ($102); Malibu ($116); Monte ($131). Cabriolet roof: Nova ($179). Rear spoiler: Camaro/LT ($55). Style trim pkg.: Camaro ($70). Two-tone paint: Nova ($46); Malibu ($62-$110). Swing-out rear side windows: Nova ($56). Bodyside moldings: Nova/Camaro ($42). Deluxe bodyside moldings: Nova/Malibu/Monte ($53). Door edge guards ($11-$18). Bright rocker moldings and extensions: Nova ($37). Bright sill moldings: Monte ($44). Wheel opening moldings: Nova/Malibu ($21). Wide wheel opening moldings: Nova ($39). Side window sill moldings: Monte ($31). Side window reveal moldings: Nova/Malibu ($41). Roof drip moldings: Nova ($18); Camaro ($23). Bodyside pin striping: Nova ($30); Malibu ($48); Monte ($33). Rear window air deflector: Malibu wag ($28). Roof carrier: Malibu wag ($85). Bumper rub strips: Malibu/Monte ($36). Bumper rub strips and guards, front/rear: Nova ($73). Bumper guards, front/rear: Malibu ($40). Interior Trim/Upholstery: Interior decor pkg.: base Nova ($29). Console ($80). Vinyl bench seat: Malibu cpe/sed, Monte ($24). Sport cloth bench seat: Nova ($21). Custom vinyl bench seat: Nova (NC). Custom vinyl bucket seats: Nova ($110). Vinyl bucket seats: Malibu cpe/sed, Monte ($110). Custom vinyl bucket seats: Camaro Z28 ($294). Sport cloth bucket seats: Camaro ($21). Custom cloth or sport cloth bucket seats: Camaro LT ($21); Z28 ($315). Knit cloth 50/50 seating: Malibu cpe/sed ($164). Vinyl 50/50 seating: Malibu cpe/sed ($188); Malibu wag ($164). Monte custom 55/45 seating: cloth ($340); vinyl ($364). Adj. driver's seatback: Camaro ($21). Litter container: Malibu/Monte ($6). Color-keyed mats ($20). Deluxe seatbelts ($19-$21). Deluxe trunk trim: Malibu/Monte ($41). Wheels and Tires: Aluminum wheels: Camaro ($180-$265). Custom styled wheels: Camaro ($91-$133). Rally wheels: Nova ($69); Camaro ($85) but std. on LT; Malibu ($41-$78); Malibu Lan (NC); Monte ($41). Color-keyed Rally wheels: Nova ($82). Full wheel covers: Nova, Camaro, Malibu cpe/sed ($37). Sport wheel covers (silver or gold): Malibu ($49-$86). Wire wheel covers: Nova ($120); Malibu ($60-$146); Monte ($109); Monte Landau ($60). E78 x 14/B BSW: Camaro ($90-$113 credit). E78 x 14/B WSW: Nova

($36-$44); Camaro ($55-$69 credit). FR78 x 14/B SBR: Nova ($91-$113). FR78 x 14/B SBR WSW: Nova ($128-$159); Camaro ($37-$46). FR78 x 14/B SBR WLT: Nova ($140-$174); Camaro ($49-$61). P185/75R14 GBR WSW: Malibu cpe/sed ($37). P195/75R14 SBR WSW: Malibu cpe/sed ($96); Malibu wag ($78). P205/75R14 SBR WSW: Malibu cpe/sed ($148). P195/75R14 GBR WSW: Malibu wag ($39). P205/75R14 SBR WLT: Malibu cpe/sed ($160). P205/70R14 SBR WSW: Monte ($42). Stowaway spare: Nova ($17); Camaro (NC).

IMPALA/CAPRICE CONVENIENCE/APPEARANCE OPTIONS: Option Packages: Estate equipment: wag ($235). Value appearance group: bodyside and wheel opening moldings, full wheel covers ($73). Comfort/Convenience: Four season air cond. ($569). Comfortron auto-temp air cond. ($655). Rear defogger, forced-air: wag ($51). Rear defogger, electric ($94). Cruise-Master speed control ($95). Tinted glass ($76). Comfortilt steering wheel ($70). Power door locks ($82-$114). Six-way power driver's seat ($151). Power windows ($130-$190). Power trunk release ($21). Power tailgate lock: wag ($40). Electric clock: Imp ($21). Digital clock: Imp ($49); Caprice ($28). Econominder gauge pkg. ($50). Intermittent wipers ($32). Quiet sound group: Imp ($51-$55). Lighting, Horns and Mirrors: Aux. lighting ($32-$46). Dual horns: Imp ($7). Driver's remote mirror ($16). Dual remote mirrors ($48). Dual sport mirrors, left remote ($33). Dual remote body-color sport mirrors ($57) exc. Lan ($24). Visor vanity mirror ($4). Lighted visor mirror ($37). Entertainment: AM radio ($80). AM/FM radio ($160). AM/FM stereo radio ($232). Stereo tape player with AM/FM radio ($250); with AM/FM stereo radio ($332). AM/FM/CB radio and power antenna ($498). Rear speakers ($24). Dual front speakers ($20). Power antenna ($45). Windshield antenna ($25); incl. w/radios. Exterior Trim: Power sky roof: cpe/sed ($595). Vinyl roof: cpe/sed ($142). Two-tone paint ($47). Custom two-tone ($115). Pin striping ($33). Roof carrier ($110). Color-keyed bodyside moldings ($43). Door edge guards ($11-$18). Wheel opening moldings: Imp ($21). Bumper rub strips, front/rear ($50). Bumper guards ($46). Interior Trim/Upholstery: Vinyl bench seat: cpe/sed ($24). Knit cloth 50/50 seat: cpe/sed ($224). Sport cloth 50/50 seat: wag ($248). Vinyl 50/50 seat ($224-$248). Special custom cloth 50/50 seat: cpe/sed ($365). Deluxe load-floor carpet: wag ($71). Deluxe cargo area carpet: wag ($102). Color-keyed mats ($20). Litter container ($6). Color-keyed seatbelts ($21-$24). Deluxe trunk trim ($44). Wheel Covers: Full wheel covers ($38). Sport wheel covers: Imp ($88); Caprice ($50). Coupe/Sedan Tires: FR78 x 15/B GBR WSW ($46). FR78 x 15/B SBR BSW ($48). FR78 x 15/B SBR WSW ($94). GR78 x 15/B SBR WSW ($124). GR70 x 15/B SBR WSW ($147). Wagon Tires: HR78 x 15/B SBR WSW ($52).

HISTORY: Introduced: Oct. 6, 1977. Model year production (U.S.): 2,197,861 (incl. Corvettes but not incl. 11,316 Acadians). The North American total of 2,474,547 units for the U.S. market included 381,394 four-cylinder engines, 521,162 sixes and 1,571,991 V-8s. Chevrolet reported a total of 2,252,111 passenger cars shipped. Calendar year production: 2,347,327 (including 30,150 Sportvans, 48,522 Corvettes and 13,585 Acadians). Calendar year sales by U.S. dealers: 2,349,781 (incl. 43,582 Sportvans and 42,247 Corvettes) for a 25.3 percent market share. Model year sales by U.S. dealers: 2,342,035 (incl. 43,594 Sportvans and 43,106 Corvettes).

Historical Footnotes: Model year sales rose by 4.6 percent (from 2,239,538 to 2,342,035), making 1977 the third highest year in Chevrolet history. After two sluggish years, Chevette seemed to finally catch on, showing a whopping 71 percent sales gain. The freshly downsized Malibu and Monte Carlo took a while to get moving in sales. But the full-size (downsized in '77) Caprice and Impala continued to move well, taking 22.5 percent of the company's sales. In recent years, other GM divisions had been using more shared components and body style offerings. Chevrolet continued to retain more individuality, at least for the time being. The new 200 cu. in. V-6 was built at Chevrolet's Tonawanda, New York, plant. However, the 231 cu. in. V-6 came from Buick, as did the 196 V-6. And 151 cu. in. four-cylinder engines were supplied by Pontiac. Late in the model year, a handful of Chevettes came off the line with a passive restraint system--the first examples on a domestic automobile.

1979

This was primarily a carryover year, with some engine changes, horsepower boosts (and losses) and appearance restyles, but nothing drastic. The 305 cu. in. V-8 managed to lose 15 horsepower, down to 130. Biggest news would actually be the mid-year introduction of the new Citation X-car as an early 1980 model--the first front-drive Chevrolet--which replaced the Nova.

1979 Chevrolet, Chevette two-door hatchback coupe (CP)

CHEVETTE -- SERIES 1T -- FOUR -- Chevrolet's sub-compact got a new front-end look including a "real" separate brightwork crosshatch grille insert with bright/black bowtie emblem in the center, rather than the previous slots in a body-colored panel. Also new: a shorter hood and single recessed rectangular headlamps with bright bezels. Parking lamps remained down below the bumper rub strips. Bumpers, rub strips and valance panel were the same as in 1978. A driver's side lower duct increased air flow to the interior. The low-budget Scooter carried no bodyside trim. Standard tires were now glass-belted radials. A new two-stage carburetor, tuned intake manifold, valve port refinements, heavier pistons and improved EGR valve added to the driveability and gas mileage of the standard 97.6 cu. in. (1.6-liter) four. A trapped vacuum spark system gave it better cold-start qualities. Axle ratio was again 3.70:1 with either the standard or high-output engine, coupled to standard four-speed manual or optional three-speed automatic transmission. The formerly optional 4.11:1 ratio was dropped. A new F41 Sport Suspension option replaced the previous rear stabilizer bar option. It included a larger front stabilizer bar and bushings, plus a new and bigger eyeless-type rear stabilizer with new bushings and linkage. Steel-belted radial tires were required with the package. Other new options included an AM/FM stereo radio with three speakers, and a pair of sport mirrors (left one remote-controlled and the right one convex). The twin-remote sport mirror option was dropped. Chevettes kept their full coil suspension with torque tube drive. All Chevettes had a front stabilizer bar, Delco Freedom battery, heater/defroster, front bucket seats, and courtesy dome light. All but the Scooter also had an AM radio, fold-down back seat, color-keyed instrument panel, sport steering wheel, mini console, bumper impact strips, and cigarette lighter. Standard models had whitewall 155/80R13 glass-belted radial tires; Scooters wore blackwalls. Coupes (except Scooter) had swing-out rear windows.

1979 Chevrolet, Monza Sport 2 + 2 two-door hatchback coupe

1979 Chevrolet, Monza two-door station wagon

1979 Chevrolet, Monza two-door coupe (CH)

MONZA -- SERIES 1H -- FOUR/V-6/V-8 -- Though unchanged in appearance, Monza added a few horsepower to the base 151 cu. in. (2.5-liter) four-cylinder engine, supplied by Pontiac. That engine had a redesigned cross-flow cylinder head and new Varajet two-stage, two-barrel carburetor. That meant a triple-venturi first stage and air valve secondary for power-on-demand. A new aluminum intake manifold cut weight. The engine was now all-metric design, with a new replaceable-element air cleaner. Optional engines: a 196 cu. in. (3.2-liter) V-6 on all models, a 231 cu. in. (3.8-liter) V-6, plus a 305 cu. in. (5.0-liter) V-8 available on all except the 'S' hatchback coupe and wagon. Four-cylinder and V-6 models could have standard four-speed manual, optional five-speed manual, or automatic transmission. The V-8, which had a new Dualjet carburetor, came with four-speed manual or optional three-speed automatic. Monza interiors sported new front seats and a sport steering wheel. The Value Series got a new interior look with new seat design and upgraded vinyl and cloth fabrics. Corrosion protection was improved on rear compartment pan and door panels (inner/outer). Bodyside moldings were standard. New radio choices were available. As in 1978, the Sport 2·+·2's grille was just one wide, squat opening stretching to fender tips, while the standard coupe carried a crossbar grille. All Monzas had energy-absorbing bumpers, standard A78 x 13 whitewall tires and full wheel covers, high-back bucket seats, heater/defroster, carpeting, AM radio, color-keyed instrument panel, tinted glass, center dome light, and cigarette lighter. All except the standard coupe held an interior console. Only 225 Monzas had a performance axle ratio installed this year, while 5,004 carried a five-speed transmission and 683 came with aluminum wheels. The Monza Spyder appearance package included front/rear spoilers; lower striping with Spyder name; black headlamp, parking light and belt moldings; black taillamp openings, sport mirrors and rear end panel; black lower body treatment from front to rear wheel openings; black windshield, back window, door and quarter-window moldings; and Rally II wheels. To add a bit of performance to looks, the separate Spyder equipment package included an F41 suspension, BR70 x 13/C radial tires and modified front stabilizer and rear shocks, as well as a day/night mirror. Spyder emblems went on the hood header panel and rear key-lock cover. A total of 9,679 Spyder equipment packages were produced, and 8,670 appearance packages.

1979 Chevrolet, Nova two-door coupe (AA)

NOVA -- SERIES 1X -- SIX/V-8 -- For its final year in the lineup, the compact Nova carried a new horizontally-ribbed grille, with single rectangular headlamps and inset clear vertical rectangular park/signal lamps with chrome bezels. The 'Chevrolet' insignia was on the heavy top bar of the grille. Separate 'Nova' letters stood on fender sides, somewhat forward of the door, in line with bodyside moldings. Two-door coupe and four-door bodies were again available in base or Custom series, along with the Nova hatchback coupe. Base engine continued to be the 250 cu. in. (4.1-liter) inline six, with optional 305 V-8. That V-8 actually lost 15 horsepower this year. Again, the three-speed manual transmission was standard with the six, four-speed with V-8 Novas. Turbo Hydra-matic was optional on both. Only in California or high altitude was the 350 four-barrel V-8 offered. A new steering column lock was supposed to thwart thieves. Rally wheels had a smaller center hub area with new Chevrolet bowtie emblem and chrome-accented vents. They were available separately, or as part of the Nova Rally option. A total of 2,299 Rally Novas were produced this year. Only 616 Novas came with a four-speed gearbox, 792 with the F41 sport suspension, and 303 with a performance axle ratio. Nova standard equipment included a built-in windshield radio antenna, heater/defroster, carpeting, locking glove compartment, manual steering and brakes, Freedom battery, and E78 x 14 blackwall tires. Nova Custom added a set of interior extras: cigarette lighter, glove box light, bright instrument cluster accents, right front door courtesy light switch, and day/night mirror. Nova's Rally Sport equipment package included lower bodyside and wheel opening stripes, a chrome diamond-pattern grille, black headlamp bezels, parking lamp accents, Rally wheels with trim rings and bright center hubs, and Rally nameplates.

1979 Chevrolet, Camaro Rally Sport two-door coupe (CP)

1979 Chevrolet, Camaro Berlinetta T-top two-door coupe (CH)

CAMARO -- SERIES 1F -- SIX/V-8 -- A new Berlinetta version, promoted as the "new way to take your pulse," took the place of the former Type LT Camaro. Berlinettas had body pin striping, a bright grille, and black rocker panels. Camaros got a new instrument panel and anti-theft steering column. The performance Z28 had new flared front wheel openings as well as a three-piece front air dam that wrapped around the sides, up into wheel openings. Z28 also had a blackout front end with center grille emblem. Its identifying decal moved from the front fender to the door. Both Z28 and Rally Camaros had a standard rear spoiler (but 81 examples were produced without one). The spoiler was a common option on other models. New radio options included a CB, cassette player or clock built into an AM/FM stereo. Both mast and windshield antennas were available. The base 250 cu. in. (4.1-liter) inline six had a lower axle ratio this year to raise gas mileage. Both 305 and 350 cu. in. V-8s were available. Only 2,438 Camaros were produced with a performance axle ratio, while 33,584 had the optional removable glass roof panels. Camaro standard equipment included power steering, Delco Freedom battery, front stabilizer bar, concealed two-speed windshield wipers, carpeting, heater/defroster, front bucket seats, center dome light, four-spoke sport steering wheel, day/night mirror, and FR78 x 14 steel-belted radial tires. The Berlinetta added whitewall tires on color-keyed custom styled wheels, body-color sport mirrors (left one remote-controlled), dual pin stripes, chrome headlamp bezels, soft fascia bumper systems (front and rear), bright windshield and back window moldings, and argent rear-panel appliqué. Camaro Z28 came with a standard 350 cu. in. four-barrel V-8; four-speed close-ratio manual gearbox; simulated hood air scoop (bolt-on, with black throat); black windshield and back window moldings; plus two-tone striping on front fenders and flares, air dam, door panels and rear deck panel. Also on Z28: front fender air louvers; body-color spoilers (front and rear); black grille, headlamp/taillamp bezels, rear end panel, and license mount; body-color sport mirrors, door handle inserts and back bumper; and white-letter P225/70R15 steel-belted tires on body-color 7 in. wheels.

1979 Chevrolet, Malibu Classic Landau two-door coupe (CP)

1979 Chevrolet, Malibu two-door coupe

1979 Chevrolet, Malibu Classic four-door sedan

MALIBU -- SERIES 1A -- V-6/V-8 -- Buyers may have been promised "a fresh new slice of apple pie," but mid-size Chevrolets didn't change much this year. Both Malibu and Malibu Classic had a new checkered-look horizontally-divided grille, along with new taillamps, for their second season in downsized form. The grille was actually in four horizontal sections, each one divided into two rows. Parking lamps and single rectangular

headlamps were structured as in 1978. Base engine was again the 200 cu. in. (3.3-liter) V-6, with an optional 305 cu. in. (5.0-liter) V-8. But one other option was added: a small-block 267 cu. in. (4.4-liter) V-8. Like other Chevrolet engines, Malibu's gained improvements in the EGR system and cold-trapped spark control system. Malibus came in Landau and sport coupe form, as well as sedans, Classic and Estate wagons. There was also a Special Equipment Order police car this year, succeeding the popular Nova police vehicle that had come into existence during the 1973-74 energy crisis. A total of 849 Malibus were built with the optional power sky roof, while 8,300 had the F41 sport suspension and 1,903 carried the MM4 four-speed transmission. Standard equipment included the 200 cu. in. V-6, three-speed manual shift, High Energy ignition, front stabilizer bar, heater/defroster, concealed wipers, inside day/night mirror, inside hood release, and locking glove compartment. Malibu Classic and Landau added dual horns and a special acoustical package. Malibu Classic models now carried an identifying script on the dashboard. Malibu Landau had a vinyl roof and silver sport wheel covers. Wagons had power brakes, wheel opening moldings, and full wheel covers.

1979 Chevrolet, Malibu Classic Estate Wagon

1979 Chevrolet, Monte Carlo two-door coupe

MONTE CARLO -- SERIES 1A -- V-6/V-8 -- Monte had a new grille with tight crosshatch pattern this year. Restyled wraparound angular side marker lamps and park/signal lamps were housed in a single bright bezel with horizontal divider bars. Taillamps were divided into three sections by vertical bars, with backup lenses in the section nearest the center. Body changes also included wide, bright lower body molding extensions. Landau models showed a new canopy-type roof with bright moldings behind the rear quarter windows. Seats had new cloth and vinyl fabrics. Like Malibu, Monte added a new engine possibility: the small-block 267 cu. in. (4.4-liter) V-8. Base engine was still the 200 cu. in. (3.3-liter) V-6. Also optional: a 231 V-6 and 305 V-8. All Montes came with standard front/rear stabilizer bars, heater/defroster, concealed wipers, electric clock, day/night mirror, locking glove compartment, dual horns, and P205/70R14 steel-belted radial tires. The 200 cu. in. V-6 and three-speed manual shift were standard, with manual brakes and steering. Monte Landaus had an automatic transmission, power brakes and steering, vinyl canopy roof, bodyside and rear striping, bright body sill moldings, visor vanity mirror (right side), and twin sport mirrors (left remote-controlled). A total of 7,830 Montes came with the optional power sky roof; 10,764 with removable glass roof panels.

1979 Chevrolet, Caprice Classic four-door sedan

1979 Chevrolet, Caprice Classic station wagon

1979 Chevrolet, Caprice Classic station wagon with wood grain Estate package.

IMPALA/CAPRICE CLASSIC -- SERIES 1B -- SIX/V-8 -- Full-size appearance changes for 1979 included front and rear refinements plus more subtle differences in side view. Impalas, as usual, had several styling differences to separate them from the costlier Caprice: a new "ladder" style grille with wide, squat holes; restyled park/signal lamps (inset in the bumper); narrow side marker lamps with horizontal dividers; and front fender end caps. Otherwise, the two full-size models remained similar, available in the same body styles: Sport coupe, Landau coupe, four-door sedan, and two- or three-seat wagon. Impala cost about $300 less than Caprice. Caprice's new grille, with wide-hole crosshatch pattern, was separated into ten side-by-side segments by dominant vertical bars. As before, the pattern repeated in slots below the bumper rub strip. Front fender extensions were reinforced fiberglass, molded continuously with the grille header for a full-width, flowing appearance. Front side marker lamps now had horizontal strip dividers. At the rear, Caprice had wider three-section taillamp clusters with a central Caprice crest. Backup lenses sat below each taillamp cluster. Both Impala and Caprice rear side marker lamps were restyled, with horizontal grid detailing. Both continued their quad rectangular headlamps. Base engine remained the 250 cu. in. (4.1-liter) inline six, which added five horsepower this year and ran a lower axle ratio than before. Wagons carried a standard 305 cu. in. (5.0-liter) V-8, which dropped from 145 to 130 horsepower. New, paler body colors were offered this year, including soft blues, greens and browns. Radios could have built-in tape players or CB transceivers. All full-size Chevrolets came with automatic transmission, power steering and brakes, Freedom battery, front stabilizer bar, heater/defroster, concealed two-speed wipers, carpeting, inside hood release, day/night mirror, locking glove compartment, and FR78 x 15 fiberglass-belted blackwall radial tires. Coupes had automatic front seatback locks. Caprice Classic added dual horns and wheel opening moldings. Caprice Classic Landau coupe added twin sport mirrors (left remote-controlled), a vinyl roof, and bodyside pin striping. Impala's Landau coupe added a vinyl roof, wheel opening moldings, and bodyside pin striping.

I.D. DATA: Chevrolet again used a 13-symbol Vehicle Identification Number (VIN), on a pad atop the dashboard, visible through the windshield. Coding was similar to 1978. Under Series, code 'S' now indicated

Camaro Berlinetta rather than LT. Code '77' under body/style was dropped. Model year code changed to '9' for 1979. Engine codes were as follows: 'E' = L4-97.6 2Bbl.; 'O' = L4-97.6 H.O.; 'V' = L4-151 2Bbl.; 'C' = V6-196 2Bbl.; 'M' = V6-200 2Bbl.; 'A' = V6-231 2Bbl.; 'D' = L6-250 1Bbl.; 'J' = V8-267 2Bbl.; 'G' = V8-305 2Bbl.; 'H' = V8-305 4Bbl.; 'L' = V8-350 4Bbl. Under assembly plants, code '2' for St. Therese, Quebec was dropped; code 'A' for Lakewood, GA added.

CHEVETTE (FOUR)

Model No.	Body/Style No.	Body Type & Seating	Factory Price	Shipping Weight	Prod. Total
1T	B08	2-dr. Hatch Cpe-4P	3794	1978	136,145
1T	B68	4-dr. Hatch Sed-4P	3914	2057	208,865

CHEVETTE SCOOTER (FOUR)

1T	J08	2-dr. Hatch Cpe-4P	3299	1929	24,099

MONZA (FOUR/V-6/V-8)

1H	M07	2-dr. Hatch 2+2-4P	3844	2630	56,871
1H	M27	2-dr. Cpe-4P	3617	2577	61,110
1H	M15	2-dr. Sta Wag-4P	3974	2631	15,190

MONZA SPORT (FOUR/V-6/V-8)

1H	R07	2-dr. Hatch 2+2-4P	4291	2676	30,662

Monza Engine Note: Prices shown are for four-cylinder engine. The 196 cu. in. V-6 cost $160 extra; the 305 V-8 cost $395. Only 8,180 Monzas had a V-8 engine.

NOVA (SIX/V-8)

1X	X27	2-dr. Cpe-6P	3955/4190	3135/3265	36,800
1X	X17	2-dr. Hatch-6P	4118/4353	3264/3394	4,819
1X	X69	4-dr. Sedan-6P	4055/4290	3179/3309	40,883

NOVA CUSTOM (SIX/V-8)

1X	Y27	2-dr. Cpe-6P	4164/4399	3194/3324	7,529
1X	Y69	4-dr. Sedan-6P	4264/4499	3228/3358	7,690

CAMARO (SIX/V-8)

1F	Q87	2-dr. Spt Cpe-4P	4677/4912	3305/3435	111,357
1F	Q87/Z85	2-dr. Rally Cpe-4P	5073/5308	N/A	19,101

CAMARO BERLINETTA (SIX/V-8)

1F	S87	2-dr. Spt Cpe-4P	5396/5631	3358/3488	67,236

CAMARO Z28 (V-8)

1F	Q87/Z28	2-dr. Spt Cpe-4P	---- /6115	---- / N/A	84,877

MALIBU (V-6/V-8)

1A	T27	2-dr. Spt Cpe-6P	4398/4588	2983/3111	41,848
1A	T19	4-dr. Sed-6P	4498/4688	2988/3116	59,674
1A	T35	4-dr. Sta Wag-6P	4745/4935	3155/3297	50,344

MALIBU CLASSIC (V-6/V-8)

1A	W27	2-dr. Spt Cpe-6P	4676/4866	3017/3145	60,751
1A	W27/Z03	2-dr. Lan Cpe-6P	4915/5105	N/A	25,213
1A	W19	4-dr. Sed-6P	4801/4991	3024/3152	104,222
1A	W35	4-dr. Sta Wag-6P	4955/5145	3183/3325	70,095

MONTE CARLO (V-6/V-8)

1A	Z37	2-dr. Spt Cpe-6P	4995/5185	3039/3169	225,073
1A	Z37/Z03	2-dr. Lan Cpe-6P	5907/6097	N/A	91,850

Malibu/Monte Carlo Engine Note: V-8 prices are for the small-block 267; the 305 V-8 cost $105 more. Only 3,812 Malibus had the 350 V-8 (code LM1).

1979 Chevrolet, Impala two-door coupe (CP)

IMPALA (SIX/V-8)

1B	L47	2-dr. Spt Cpe-6P	5497/5732	3495/3606	26,589
1B	L47/Z03	2-dr. Lan Cpe-6P	5961/6196	N/A	3,247
1B	L69	4-dr. Sedan-6P	5597/5832	3513/3624	172,717
1B	L35	4-dr. Sta Wag-6P	---- /6109	---- /4013	39,644
1B	L35/AQ4	4-dr. 3S Wag-8P	---- /6239	---- /4045	28,710

CAPRICE CLASSIC (SIX/V-8)

1B	N47	2-dr. Spt Cpe-6P	5837/6072	3535/3649	36,629
1B	N47/Z03	2-dr. Lan Cpe-6P	6234/6469	N/A	21,824
1B	N69	4-dr. Sedan-6P	5962/6197	3564/3675	203,017
1B	N35	4-dr. Sta Wag-6P	---- /6389	---- /4056	23,568
1B	N35/AQ4	4-dr. 3S Wag-8P	---- /6544	---- /4088	32,693

FACTORY PRICE AND WEIGHT NOTE: Where two prices and weights are shown, the figure to the left of the slash is for six-cylinder model, to right of slash for V-8.

BODY/STYLE NO. NOTE: Some models are actually option packages. Figure after the slash (e.g., Z03) is the number of the option package that comes with the model listed.

ENGINE DATA: BASE FOUR (Chevette): Inline. Overhead cam. Four-cylinder. Cast iron block and head. Displacement: 97.6 cu. in. (1.6 liters). Bore & stroke: 3.23 x 2.98 in. Compression ratio: 8.6:1. Brake horsepower: 70 at 5200 R.P.M. Torque: 82 lb.-ft. at 2400 R.P.M. Five main bearings. Hydraulic valve lifters. Carburetor: 2Bbl. Holley 5210C. VIN Code: E. **OPTIONAL HIGH-OUTPUT FOUR** (Chevette): Same as above except: Brake H.P.: 74 at 5200 R.P.M. Torque: 88 lb.-ft. at 2800 R.P.M. VIN Code: O. **BASE FOUR** (Monza): Inline. Overhead valve. Four-cylinder. Cast iron block. Displacement: 151 cu. in. (2.5 liters). Bore & stroke: 4.00 x 3.00 in. Compression ratio: 8.3:1. Brake horsepower: 90 at 4000 R.P.M. Torque: 128 lb.-ft. at 2400 R.P.M. Five main bearings. Hydraulic valve lifters. Carburetor: 2Bbl. Rochester 2SE. VIN Code: V. **OPTIONAL V-6** (Monza): 90-degree, overhead-valve V-6. Cast iron block and head. Displacement: 196 cu. in. (3.2 liters). Bore & stroke: 3.50 x 3.40 in. Compression ratio: 8.0:1. Brake horsepower: 105 at 4000 R.P.M. Torque: 160 lb.-ft. at 2000 R.P.M. Four main bearings. Hydraulic valve lifters. Carburetor: 2Bbl. Rochester M2ME. VIN Code: C. **BASE V-6** (Malibu, Monte Carlo): 90-degree, overhead-valve V-6. Cast iron block and head. Displacement: 200 cu. in. (3.3 liters). Bore & stroke: 3.50 x 3.48 in. Compression ratio: 8.2:1. Brake horsepower: 94 at 4000 R.P.M. Torque: 154 lb.-ft. at 2000 R.P.M. Four main bearings. Hydraulic valve lifters. Carburetor: 2Bbl. Rochester M2ME. VIN Code: M. OPTIONAL V-6 (Monza, Malibu, Monte Carlo): 90-degree, overhead-valve V-6. Cast iron block and head. Displacement: 231 cu. in. (3.8 liters). Bore & stroke: 3.80 x 3.40 in. Compression ratio: 8.0:1. Brake horsepower: 115 at 3800 R.P.M. Torque: 190 lb.-ft. at 2000 R.P.M. Four main bearings. Hydraulic valve lifters. Carburetor: 2Bbl. Rochester M2ME. VIN Code: A. BASE SIX (Nova, Camaro, Impala, Caprice): Inline. OHV. Six-cylinder. Cast iron block and head. Displacement: 250 cu. in. (4.1 liters). Bore & stroke: 3.88 x 3.53 in. Compression ratio: 8.0:1. Brake horsepower: 115 at 3800 R.P.M. Torque: 200 lb.-ft. at 1600 R.P.M. Seven main bearings. Hydraulic valve lifters. Carburetor: 1Bbl. Rochester 1ME. VIN Code: D. OPTIONAL V-8 (Malibu, Monte Carlo); 90-degree, overhead valve V-8. Cast iron block and head. Displacement: 267 cu. in. (4.4 liters). Bore & stroke: 3.50 x 3.48 in. Compression ratio: 8.2:1. Brake horsepower: 125 at 3800 R.P.M. Torque: 215 lb.-ft. at 2400 R.P.M. Five main bearings. Hydraulic valve lifters. Carburetor: 2Bbl. Rochester M2MC. VIN Code: J. BASE V-8 (Impala/Caprice wagon); OPTIONAL (Monza, Nova, Camaro, Impala, Caprice): 90-degree, overhead valve V-8. Cast iron block and head. Displacement: 305 cu. in. (5.0 liters). Bore & stroke: 3.74 x 3.48 in. Compression ratio: 8.4:1. Brake horsepower: 130 at 3200 R.P.M. Torque: 245 lb.-ft. at 2000 R.P.M. Five main bearings. Hydraulic valve lifters. Carburetor: 2Bbl. Rochester M2MC. VIN Code: G. OPTIONAL V-8 (Malibu, Monte Carlo): 90-degree, overhead valve V-8. Cast iron block and head. Displacement: 305 cu. in. (5.0 liters). Bore & stroke: 3.74 x 3.48 in. Compression ratio: 8.4:1. Brake horsepower: 160 at 4000 R.P.M. Torque: 235 lb.-ft. at 2400 R.P.M. Five main bearings. Hydraulic valve lifters. Carburetor: 4Bbl. Rochester M4MC. VIN Code: H. OPTIONAL V-8 (Nova, Malibu wagon, Impala, Caprice): 90-degree, overhead valve V-8. Cast iron block and head. Displacement: 350 cu. in. (5.7 liters). Bore & stroke: 4.00 x 3.48 in. Compression ratio: 8.2:1. Brake horsepower: 165-170 at 3800 R.P.M. Torque: 260-270 lb.-ft. at 2400 R.P.M. Five main bearings. Hydraulic valve lifters. Carburetor: 4Bbl. Rochester M4MC. VIN Code: L. BASE V-8 (Camaro Z28); OPTIONAL (Camaro): Same as 350 V-8 above except: Brake H.P.: 175 at 4000 R.P.M. Torque: 270 lb.-ft. at 2400 R.P.M.

CHASSIS DATA: Dimensions same as 1978, except Chevette Scooter overall length, 158.8 in. New Camaro Berlinetta had same dimensions as prior Type LT. Chevette tires were now 155/80R13 GBR.

TECHNICAL: Transmission: Three-speed manual transmission standard on Camaro, Nova, and Malibu/Monte six. Gear ratios: (1st) 3.50:1; (2nd) 1.89:1; (3rd) 1.00:1; (Rev) 3.62:1. Four-speed floor shift standard on Chevette: (1st) 3.75:1; (2nd) 2.16:1; (3rd) 1.38:1; (4th) 1.00:1; (Rev) 3.82:1. Four-speed floor shift standard on Monza four and V-6: (1st) 3.50:1; (2nd) 2.48:1; (3rd) 1.66:1; (4th) 1.00:1; (Rev) 3.50:1. Four-speed floor shift standard on Monza/Camaro/Nova (V8-305) and Camaro 350, optional on Malibu/Monza/Monte: (1st) 2.85:1; (2nd) 2.02:1; (3rd) 1.35:1; (4th) 1.00:1; (Rev) 2.85:1. Four-speed on Malibu V8-267: (1st) 3.11:1; (2nd) 2.20:1; (3rd) 1.47:1; (4th) 1.00:1; (Rev) 3.11:1. Camaro Z28 four-speed floor shift: (1st) 2.64:1; (2nd) 1.75:1; (3rd) 1.34:1; (4th) 1.00:1; (Rev) 2.55:1. Five-speed floor shift available on Monza: (1st) 3.40:1; (2nd) 2.08:1; (3rd) 1.39:1; (4th) 1.00:1; (5th) 0.80:1; (Rev) 3.36:1. Three-speed Turbo Hydra-matic standard on Monte Carlo Landau and Caprice/Impala, optional on others. Gear ratios: (1st) 2.52:1; (2nd) 1.52:1; (3rd) 1.00:1; (Rev) 1.93:1 except Caprice/Impala V8-305, Monza four and some Malibu six ratios: (1st) 2.74:1; (2nd) 1.57:1; (3rd) 1.00:1; (Rev) 2.07:1. Chevette four automatic trans.: (1st) 2.40:1; (2nd) 1.48:1; (3rd) 1.00:1; (Rev) 1.92:1. Standard final drive ratio: (Chevette) 3.70:1; (Monza four) 2.73:1 or 2.93:1 w/4-spd, 3.08:1 w/5-spd, 2.73:1 w/auto.; (Monza V-6) 2.73:1 exc. 2.93:1 w/5-spd; (Monza V-8) 3.08:1 w/4-spd, 2.29:1 w/auto.; (Nova) 2.56:1 w/six, 3.08:1 w/V-8 and 4-spd, 2.41:1 w/V-8 and auto.; (Camaro six) 2.56:1; (Camaro V-8) 3.08:1 w/4-spd, 2.41:1 or 3.08:1 w/auto.; (Z28) 3.73:1 w/4-spd, 3.42:1 w/auto.; (Malibu six) 2.73:1; (Malibu V-8) 2.29:1 exc. 2.73:1 w/auto.; (Malibu V-8 wag) 2.56:1 or 2.41:1; (Monte V-6) 2.73:1 or 2.41:1; (Monte V-8) 2.29:1; (Capr/Imp six) 2.56:1; (Capr/Imp V-8) 2.41:1 exc. Steering: (Chevette) rack and pinion; (others) recirculating ball. Suspension/Body: Same as 1976-78. Brakes: Front disc, rear drum. Fuel tank: (Chevette) 12.5 gal.; (Monza) 18.5 gal.; (Monza wag) 15 gal.; (Nova/Camaro) 21 gal.; (Malibu/Monte) 18.1 gal.; (Caprice/Imp) 20.7 gal.; (Caprice/Imp wag) 22 gal.

DRIVETRAIN OPTIONS: Engines: 1.6-liter H.O. four: Chevette ($60). 196 cu. in., 2Bbl. V-6: Monza ($160). 231 cu. in., 2Bbl. V-6: Monza ($200); Malibu ($40); Monte ($30). 267 cu. in., 2Bbl. V-8: Malibu/Monte ($190). 305 cu. in., 2Bbl. V-8: Monza ($395); Nova/Camaro ($235); Imp/Caprice cpe/sed ($235). 305 cu. in., 4Bbl. V-8: Malibu/Monte ($295). 350 cu. in., 4Bbl. V-8: Nova/Camaro ($360); Malibu wag ($360); Imp/Capr cpe/sed ($360); Imp/Capr wag ($125). Transmission/Differential: Four-speed manual shift: Nova (NC); Camaro/Malibu ($135). Close-ratio four-speed manual: Camaro (NC). Five-speed manual shift: Monza ($175). Turbo Hydra-matic: Chvt/Monza ($295); Nova/Camaro/Malibu/Monte ($335); Camaro Z28 ($59). Sport shifter: Chvt ($30). Positraction axle: Monza ($60); Nova/Camaro ($64); Malibu/Monte ($65); Imp/Capr ($68). Performance axle ratio: Monza ($17); Nova/Camaro/Malibu/Monte ($18); Imp/Capr ($19). Power Accessories: Power brakes: Chvt/Monza ($71); Nova/Camaro/Monte, Malibu cpe/sed ($76). Power steering: Monza ($146); Nova/Malibu/Monte ($163). Suspension: F40 H.D. susp.: Nova ($11-$36); Malibu cpe/sed, Monte ($22); Imp/Capr ($23). F41 sport susp.: Chvt ($33); Monza ($31); Nova ($45); Camaro, Malibu cpe/sed ($41); Imp/Capr cpe/sed ($42). Superlift rear shock absorbers: Imp/Capr ($56). Front stabilizer bar: Monza ($27). Other: Heavy-duty radiator ($31-$33) exc. Imp/Capr ($42). H.D. alternator (63-amp): Malibu/Monte ($5-$33); Imp/Capr ($34). H.D. battery ($19-$21). California emission system ($83) exc. Monza four ($150). High altitude emission ($35).

1979 Chevrolet, Monza Sport 2 + 2 Spyder two-door hatchback coupe

CHEVETTE/MONZA CONVENIENCE/APPEARANCE OPTIONS: Option Packages: Spyder equipment pkg.: Monza ($164). Spyder appearance pkg.: Monza ($231). Quiet sound group: Chvt ($35-$47); Monza ($29-$39). Auto. shoulder belt convenience group: Chvt ($144-$166). Deluxe appointment group (quiet sound, aux. lighting, clock): Chvt ($94-$137). Comfort/Convenience: Air conditioning ($496). Rear defogger, electric ($87). Tinted glass: Chvt ($60). Comfortilt steering wheel ($68). Special instrumentation (incl. tach): Chvt ($67); Monza ($50-$88). Electric clock ($21). Digital clock: Monza ($49). Cigarette lighter: Scooter ($7). Intermittent wipers ($35). Lighting and Mirrors: Aux. lighting: Chvt ($37-$44); Monza ($20-$37). Driver's remote sport mirror: Chvt ($25). Twin sport mirrors, left remote ($40). Day/night mirror ($10). Entertainment: AM radio: Scooter ($74). AM/FM radio: Chvt/Monza ($74); Scooter ($148). AM/FM stereo radio ($148). AM/FM stereo radio w/digital clock: Monza ($299). Stereo tape player w/AM radio: Monza ($159). Cassette or 8-track player with AM/FM stereo radio: Monza ($242). Rear speaker ($23). Exterior Trim: Removable sunroof: Monza ($180). Cabriolet vinyl roof: Monza ($156) incl. opera windows. Spoilers, front/rear: Monza ($97). Deluxe exterior (wheel opening, side window and rocker panel moldings): Chvt ($104). Tri-tone sport stripes: Chvt ($70). Sport striping: Monza wag ($84). Bodyside moldings: Scooter ($40). Wheel opening moldings: Monza ($21). Side window reveal moldings: Chvt ($67). Door edge guards ($12-$19). Roof carrier ($65). Rear air deflector: Monza ($28). Deluxe bumpers, front/rear: Scooter ($37). Bumper guards, front/rear: Chvt ($41-$78); Monza ($42); std. on wag. Interior Trim/Upholstery: Console: Monza cpe ($75). Bucket seats (sport cloth): Chvt ($11-$21). Knit cloth bucket seats: Monza ($21). Custom Chevette interior pkg. w/bucket seats: cloth ($181); vinyl ($160). Custom vinyl bucket seats: Monza ($159) exc. Sport (NC). Custom cloth bucket seats: Monza ($180) exc. Sport ($21). Folding rear seat: Monza ($97) but std. on 2·+·2. Rear seat delete: Chvt ($51 credit). Load floor carpet: Chvt ($21). Color-keyed floor mats ($21). Automatic shoulder belts: Chvt ($50). Deluxe seatbelts ($21). Wheels and Tires: Rally II wheels: Monza ($45-$88). Color-keyed deluxe wheel covers: Monza ($13-$43). Sport wheel covers: Chvt ($45). Wheel trim rings: Scooter ($37). 155/80-13 GBR WSW: Scooter ($37). 155/80-13 SBR BSW: Chvt ($11); Scooter ($42). 155/80-13 SBR WSW: Chvt ($42); Scooter ($79). 155/80-13 SBR WLT: Chvt ($55); Scooter ($92). B78 x 13 WSW: Monza ($19) exc. wag. (NC). BR70 x 13 SBR BSW: Monza ($137) exc. Spyder/wag (NC). BR70 x 13 SBR WSW: Monza ($138-$189). BR70 x 13 SBR WLT: Monza ($50-$205).

1979 Chevrolet, Camaro Z28 two-door coupe (CH)

NOVA/CAMARO/MALIBU/MONTE CARLO CONVENIENCE/APPEARANCE OPTIONS: Option Packages: Rally equipment: Nova ($211). Estate equipment: Malibu wag ($258). Interior decor/quiet sound group: Camaro ($64); std. on Berlinetta. Quiet sound group: Malibu ($51). Value appearance group (roof drip, side window and wheel opening moldings): Nova ($79). Security pkg.: Malibu wag ($37). Comfort/Convenience: Air conditioning: Nova/Camaro ($529-$562); Malibu/Monte ($562). Rear defogger (forced-air): Nova/Malibu ($55). Rear defogger (electric): Camaro/Malibu/Monte ($99). Cruise-master speed control ($103). Tinted glass: Camaro ($64); Malibu/Monte ($70). Comfortilt steering wheel ($75). Six-way power driver's seat: Malibu/Monte ($163). Power windows: Nova ($126-$178); Camaro/Monte ($132); Malibu ($132-$187). Power door locks: Nova/Malibu ($80-$120); Camaro/Monte ($86). Power trunk release: Malibu/Monte ($24). Power tailgate release: Malibu wag ($25). Electric clock: Nova, base Camaro ($23); Malibu ($23). Special instrumentation: Nova, base Camaro ($112); Malibu ($125); Monte ($102). Econominder gauge pkg.: Nova ($53). Gauge pkg.:

Malibu ($57); Monte ($34). Intermittent wipers ($38). Lighting, Horns and Mirrors: Aux. lighting ($31-$56). Dome reading light: Malibu/Monte ($20). Dual horns: Nova/Camaro, base Malibu ($9). Remote-control driver's mirror: Nova/Malibu/Monte ($18). Twin sport mirrors (left remote): Nova, base Camaro, Malibu/Monte ($43). Twin remote sport mirrors: Malibu/Monte ($68); Monte Lan ($25). Day/night mirror: Nova ($11). Visor vanity mirror: Malibu/Monte ($5). Lighted visor mirror: Malibu ($40); Monte ($35-$40). Entertainment: AM radio ($82-$85). AM/FM radio ($158). AM/FM stereo radio ($232). AM/FM stereo radio w/digital clock: Nova/Malibu ($395); Camaro ($372-$395). Stereo tape player w/AM radio ($244-$248). Stereo 8-track tape player with AM/FM stereo radio ($335). Cassette player with AM/FM stereo radio ($341). AM/FM/CB radio: Camaro/Malibu/Monte ($489). AM/FM stereo radio w/CB: Camaro/Malibu/Monte ($570). Rear speaker ($25). Dual front speakers: Malibu/Monte ($21). Windshield antenna ($27); incl. w/radios. Power antenna: Camaro/Malibu/Monte ($47). Exterior Trim: Removable glass roof panels: Camaro/Monte ($655). Power sky roof: Malibu cpe/sed, Monte ($529). Vinyl roof: Nova ($99); Camaro ($112); Malibu ($116); Monte ($131). Cabriolet roof: Nova ($190). Rear spoiler: Camaro Berlinetta ($58). Style trim pkg.: Camaro ($73). Two-tone paint: Nova ($55); Malibu ($67-$115); Monte ($120-$160). Swing-out rear side windows: Nova ($59). Bodyside moldings: Nova/Camaro ($43). Deluxe bodyside moldings: Nova/Malibu/Monte ($53). Door edge guards ($13-$21). Bright rocker moldings and extensions: Nova ($15-$37). Bright sill moldings: Monte ($44). Wheel opening moldings: Nova, Malibu cpe/sed ($23). Wide wheel opening moldings: Nova ($39). Side window sill moldings: Monte ($33). Side window reveal moldings: Nova/Malibu ($41). Roof drip moldings: Nova ($20); Camaro ($24). Bodyside pin striping: Nova ($30); Malibu ($48); Monte ($40). Rear window air deflector: Malibu wag ($30). Roof carrier: Malibu wag ($90). Bumper rub strips: Malibu ($41). Bumper rub strips and guards, front/rear: Nova ($79). Bumper guards, front/rear: Malibu ($46). Interior Trim/Upholstery: Interior decor pkg.: base Nova ($31). Console ($80). Vinyl bench seat: Malibu cpe/sed, Monte ($26). Sport cloth bench seat: Nova ($23); Malibu (NC). Knit cloth bench seat: Malibu wag ($28). Custom vinyl bench seat: Nova (NC). Custom vinyl bucket seats: Nova ($85); Camaro ($307). Vinyl bucket seats: Malibu cpe/sed, Monte ($85). Cloth bucket seats: Monte ($85). Sport cloth bucket seats: Camaro ($23). Custom knit cloth bucket seats: Camaro Berlinetta ($23); base Camaro ($330). Knit cloth 50/50 seating: Malibu cpe/sed ($172); Malibu wag ($198). Vinyl 50/50 seating: Malibu cpe/sed ($198); Malibu wag ($172). Custom cloth 55/45 seating: Monte ($368). Adj. driver's seatback: Camaro ($23). Litter container: Malibu/Monte ($8). Color-keyed mats ($23). Deluxe load-floor carpet: Malibu ($70). Deluxe seatbelts ($21-$23). Deluxe trunk trim: Malibu/Monte ($43). Wheels and Tires: Aluminum wheels: Camaro ($172-$315). Custom styled wheels: Camaro ($100-$143). Rally

wheels: Nova ($88); Camaro ($93) but std. on Rally; Malibu ($47-$90); Monte ($47). Wire wheel covers: Nova ($130); Malibu ($65-$160); Monte ($117); Monte Landau ($65). Full wheel covers: Nova/Camaro/Malibu ($43). Sport wheel covers (silver or gold): Malibu ($52-$95). E78 x 14 BSW: Camaro ($95-$119 credit). E78 x 14 WSW: Nova ($38-$47); Camaro ($58-$72 credit). FR78 x 14 SBR: Nova ($96-$119). FR78 x 14 SBR WSW: Nova ($135-$168); Camaro ($40-$49). FR78 x 14 SBR WLT: Nova ($148-$184); Camaro ($52-$65); Berlinetta ($13-$16). P185/75R14 GBR WSW: Malibu cpe/sed ($40). P195/75R14 GBR WSW: Malibu wag ($41). P195/75R14 SBR WSW: Malibu cpe/sed ($102); Malibu wag ($83). P205/70R14 SBR WSW: Monte ($44); Malibu cpe/sed ($149). Stowaway spare: Nova ($19); Camaro (NC).

IMPALA/CAPRICE CONVENIENCE/APPEARANCE OPTIONS: Option Packages: Estate equipment: wag ($262). Value appearance group: bodyside and wheel opening moldings, full wheel covers ($87). Comfort/Convenience: Four season air cond. ($605). Comfortron auto-temp air cond. ($688). Rear defogger, forced-air: cpe/sed ($57). Rear defogger, electric ($101). Cruise-Master speed control ($108). Tinted glass ($84). Comfortilt steering wheel ($77). Power door locks ($88-$122). Six-way power driver's seat ($166). Power windows ($122-$205). Power trunk release ($25). Power tailgate lock: wag ($40). Electric clock: Imp ($24). Digital clock: Imp ($55); Caprice ($31). Gauge pkg. ($54). Intermittent wipers ($39). Quiet sound group: Imp ($56). Lighting, Horns and Mirrors: Aux. lighting ($35-$50). Dual horns: Imp ($10). Driver's remote mirror ($19). Dual remote mirrors ($56). Dual sport mirrors, left remote ($44). Dual remote sport mirrors, body-color ($69) exc. Lan ($25). Visor vanity mirror ($6). Lighted visor mirror ($41). Entertainment: AM radio ($87). AM/FM radio ($161). AM/FM stereo radio ($236); w/digital clock, Imp ($401). Stereo tape player with AM radio ($265); with AM/FM stereo radio ($340). Cassette player with AM/FM stereo ($346). AM/FM/CB radio and power antenna ($503). AM/FM stereo with CB and power antenna ($578). Rear speaker ($26). Dual front speakers ($22). Power antenna ($48). Windshield antenna ($28); incl. w/radios. Exterior Trim: Power sky roof: cpe/sed ($625). Vinyl roof: cpe/sed ($145). Two-tone paint ($56). Custom two-tone ($87-$120). Pin striping ($33). Color-keyed bodyside moldings ($44). Door edge guards ($14-$21). Wheel opening moldings: Imp ($23). Bumper rub strips ($56). Bumper guards ($52). Interior Trim/Upholstery: Vinyl bench seat: cpe/sed ($27). Sport or knit cloth bench seat: wag ($27). Vinyl 50/50 seat ($240-$267). Knit cloth 50/50 seat: cpe/sed ($240); wag ($267). Special custom cloth 50/50 seat: cpe/sed ($397). Deluxe load-floor carpet: wag ($75). Deluxe cargo area carpet: wag ($107). Color-keyed mats ($24). Litter container ($8). Color-keyed seatbelts ($24-$27). Deluxe trunk trim ($46). Wheel Covers: Full wheel covers ($44). Sport wheel covers: Imp ($98); Caprice ($54). Wire wheel covers ($120).

Coupe/Sedan Tires: FR78 x 15 GBR WSW ($49). FR78 x 15 SBR BSW ($52). FR78 x 15 SBR WSW ($101). GR78 x 15 SBR WSW ($131). GR70 x 15 SBR WSW ($155). Wagon Tires: HR78 x 15 SBR WSW ($55).

HISTORY: Introduced: Sept. 28, 1978. Model year production (U.S.): 2,153,036 (incl. Corvettes but not incl. 44,927 Acadians and early 1980 Citations). Calendar year production: 2,238,226 (including 22,056 Sportvans, 48,568 Corvettes and 17,133 Acadians). Calendar year sales by U.S. dealers: 2,158,839 (incl. 30,630 Sportvans and 38,631 Corvettes) for a 25.9 percent market share. Model year sales by U.S. dealers: 2,257,751 (incl. 33,819 Sportvans and 39,816 Corvettes, plus 273,720 early 1980 Citations).

Historical Footnotes: Chevrolet fared rather well this year, despite a general slowdown in the auto industry. Chevettes sold particularly well. Sales of small cars were mandatory if the division expected to reach the CAFE limit of 19 mile-per-gallon fuel economy. Chevrolet built a non-production version of a 1979 turbo injected Chevette, to study optimal performance, economy and driveability.

1980

Chevettes had a new rear-end look for 1980. An aero restyling cut the weight of full-size models. Otherwise, apart from the new front-wheel drive Citation, this was a carryover year, devoted more to technical improvements than appearance changes. The old reliable in-line six-cylinder engine was gone, replaced by a V-6. Lockup torque converter clutches arrived on automatic transmissions. Over the past few years, the entire Chevrolet line had been downsized, signaling the beginning of a new era of smaller, lighter, fuel-efficient automobiles. This year also marked the first appearance of a diesel V-8, produced by Oldsmobile and installed (for an extra $915) in full-size station wagons.

1980 Chevrolet, Chevette four-door hatchback sedan

1980 Chevrolet, Chevette two-door hatchback coupe

CHEVETTE -- SERIES 1T -- FOUR -- Chevette gained a new aero-styled rear end this year. Restyled rear quarters held four-lens wraparound taillamps with larger, square backup lenses. Instead of the straight angled hatch of prior years, this year's version bent several inches above the taillamps to create a more vertical rear-end look. A Chevrolet badge was on the hatch, just above the right taillamp. The grille had a new Chevrolet emblem and rectangular headlamps. Also new: a round fuel filler door, revised license plate light, improved pressure-proportioning brake system, and new passive restraint system (a two-piece lap/shoulder belt setup). Once again, Chevette came with either a standard or high-output 1.6-liter engine, both with four-speed fully-synchronized manual transmission (or optional automatic). The standard overhead-cam four had a staged two-barrel carburetor, "tuned" aluminum intake manifold, and special valve porting. The high-output version had a high-speed camshaft and dual-takedown exhaust manifold. Chevettes came in 13 body colors this year: black, gray, red, red orange, white, bright yellow, and a selection of metallics: bright blue, dark blue, light blue, light camel, dark claret, dark green, or silver. Five two-tone combinations were available (except on the stripped-down Scooter). New to Chevette's option list: improved-wear steel-belted radial tires. Interiors held body-contoured, full foam front bucket seats that reclined (except Scooter's). Standard vinyl bucket seats came in black, camel, blue or carmine color (Scooter only in black or camel). Cloth bucket seats were available, as was a Custom interior in five two-tone combinations. All Chevettes had a built-in diagnostic connector, standard 155/80R13 glass-belted radial tires (whitewall except

Scooter), "smart switch" on the steering column, Freedom battery, rack-and-pinion steering, and full coil suspension. Front disc brakes had audible wear sensors. Improved automatic-transmission driveshaft balancing this year was meant to reduce noise. Chevette's flow-through ventilation system was redesigned for increased defroster airflow. Ball joints had a visible wear indicator. Bolt-on front fenders had plastic inner shields. Standard equipment (except on Scooters) also included an AM radio, center console, wheel trim rings, bodyside and sill moldings, brushed aluminum instrument panel moldings, lighter, glove box lock, sport steering wheel, color-keyed seat/shoulder belts, and right door jamb dome light switch. All models had vinyl-coated headliner, courtesy dome light, day/night mirror, cut-pile carpeting, front stabilizer bar, bumper guards and rub strips, high-pressure compact spare tire, and removable load floor carpet.

1980 Chevrolet, Monza Sport Spyder 2 + 2 two-door hatchback coupe (CH)

MONZA -- SERIES 1H -- FOUR/V-6 -- Apart from new black taillamp bezels and black grille center bars, Monza changed little this year. A restyled front air dam was integrated with wheel openings. Bumper guards were now standard. Emblems had a new finish. Bodyside moldings were sliced off at an angle to allow for new striping. The Spyder option included new hood decals and body stripes. Models included the 2 + 2 Sport hatchback, regular hatchback coupe, and notchback sedan. The station wagon was dropped, along with the V-8 option and green body color availability. Engine choices this year were the base 151 cu. in. (2.5-liter) four, or optional Buick 231 cu. in. (3.8-liter) V-6. Standard equipment included four-speed floor shift, manual front disc/rear drum brakes, A78 x 13 whitewall tires, front bucket seats, bumper guards (front/rear), vinyl bodyside moldings, AM radio, tinted glass, sport steering wheel, lighter, day/night mirror, carpeting, and Freedom battery. Monza's 2 + 2 hatchback added bumper rub strips, bright door frame and belt moldings, console, folding back seat, and bright/black rear quarter window moldings. The Monza Sport hatchback 2 + 2 with slope-back soft front end and bright-bezeled rectangular headlamps came with all the basic equipment, plus a black front air dam; bright/black windshield reveal molding; black wiper arms/blades; console; folding back seat; soft door trim panels with driver's side map pocket and armrest; bright door frame and belt moldings; body-color bumper rub strips and guards; bright/black rear quarter

window and back window moldings; full wheel covers; bright-trimmed wraparound taillamps; and body-color rear end panel. This year's Spyder equipment package, priced at $521, included Rally II wheels, front/rear spoilers, stripes with Spyder inserts, F41 suspension, BR70 x 13/C blackwall tires, modified front stabilizer bar and rear shock absorbers, and a Spyder emblem on the hood header panel. Black accents went on headlamps, parking lamps and belt moldings; taillamp openings; lower rocker panel, quarter panel and front fenders; plus windshield, rear window, quarter window and door moldings. The package also included sport mirrors. A total of 7,589 Spyder packages were installed.

1980 Chevrolet, Citation four-door hatchback sedan (CP)

1980 Chevrolet, Citation two-door Club Coupe (CP)

1980 Chevrolet, Citation X11 two-door hatchback coupe

1980 Chevrolet, Citation X11 two-door club coupe (CP)

CITATION -- SERIES 1X -- FOUR/V-6 -- Long before the model year began, in spring 1979, Chevrolet introduced the all-new front-drive Citation, described as "the most thoroughly tested new car in Chevy history." Chevrolet's General Manager Robert D. Lund called it "an affordable, functional family-size vehicle which is space efficient, economical to operate, comfortable and serviceable." Citation was claimed to offer "the exterior dimensions of a subcompact, the operating economy of a compact with a V-8, the interior room of a mid-size car and as much luggage capacity as many full-size sedans." Weighing about 2,500 pounds, it was 20 inches shorter and 800 pounds lighter than the compact Nova it replaced. Coupe, hatchback coupe and hatchback sedan models were offered, plus a sporty X-11 option on both two-door models. Citation's front-drive chassis held a MacPherson strut front suspension with transverse-mounted engine and transmission, computer-selected coil springs, front and rear stabilizer bars, and rack-and-pinion steering. The variable-rate rear suspension used rubber jounce bumpers as load-carrying springs. Citation's mini-frame construction mounted the powertrain on a separate, bolt-on "cradle" that also served as a mount for the front suspension. In addition to producing a quieter ride, this design allowed easy servicing by replacing the entire engine/powertrain module. Standard engine was a cast iron 151 cu. in. (2.5-liter) four, rated 90 horsepower, supplied by Pontiac. Chevrolet produced the optional powerplant: the industry's first transverse-mounted V-6, a compact 60-degree 173 cu. in. (2.8-liter) design made of cast iron. That engine could fit into the same underhood area as a four. Both engines used two-stage Varajet carburetors that metered fuel into the combustion chambers according to driving needs, increasing flow when passing. Citation had single rectangular headlamps, wraparound amber marker lamps, and vertical parking lamps behind the honeycomb grille with center Chevrolet emblem. On two-tone models, bodyside moldings separated the upper and lower colors, with pin striping on upper bodysides and fenders. A Citation nameplate was on the forward end of front fenders. Wide three-section taillamps included backup lamps in the center sections. Bodies came in 14 standard colors: beige, black, cinnabar, gray, red, silver, white, and yellow; plus six metallics (dark or light blue, light or medium camel, dark claret, or dark green). Thirteen two-tone combinations were also available. Six interior color trims were available in two trim levels. Standard vinyl bench seats came in black, camel, carmine or green. Custom vinyl and Sport and knit cloths were available, on bench or bucket seats. Citation was designed with easy servicing in mind. The cylinder head, oil pan, water pump, rear main bearing seal and engine front cover could all be removed without taking the engine out of the car. And even if it did have to come out, the mini-frame "cradle" made that job easier. Only eight bolts had to be removed, and suspension components loosened, to gain clearance for extracting the engine/transaxle unit. Both the engine and transaxle were removable separately too: the engine upward, transaxle downward. Since clutch repair on front-drives could be a problem, manual shift Citations had a constant-tension clutch cable to minimize the risk of early failure. Ball bearings at front and rear wheels were lifetime lubricated. Servicing of other components was also simplified, including the instrument panel cluster, taillamps, heater, and starter. Front fenders bolted onto the unitized body. Standard equipment included a four-speed manual transaxle with overdrive fourth gear, front disc/rear drum brakes (diagonal dual-braking), P185/80R13 glass-belted radial tires, front/rear stabilizer bars, compact spare tire, steel bumpers, concealed hatchback luggage compartment, dome light, and column-mounted turn signal/dimmer/wiper/washer control. Also standard: an inside hood release; locking glove box; inertia seatback latches; color-coded sliding door locks; and glass-belted radial tires. All except the base H11 coupe also had bright rocker panel, wheel opening and drip moldings; a cigarette lighter and ashtray; and push-button AM radio. Options included side window reveal moldings, tinted glass, remote swing-out side windows, bodyside pin striping, full wheel covers, intermittent wipers, roof rack, tilt steering, electric rear defogger, reclining passenger seat, removable pop-up sunroof, plus bumper guards and rub strips. The X11 sport package for hatchback and club coupe included a black-accented grille; black accents on headlamp bezels, taillamps, rocker panels, door lock pillars and rear license plate pocket; decal stripes; rear spoiler; pin striping; bright side window moldings; body-color sport mirrors; rally wheel trim; sport steering wheel; sport suspension; bumper rub strips; and white-letter P205/70R13 steel-belted radial tires. Large X11 identification was behind the door and on rear panel. X11 models could also have bucket seats, console, and special instrumentation (including tachometer, voltmeter, temp and oil pressure gauges). A total of 24,852 X11 equipment packages were installed this year.

1980 Chevrolet, Camaro Z28 two-door coupe (CP)

CAMARO -- SERIES 1F -- V-6/V-8 -- Camaro entered 1980 wearing a new grille with tighter crosshatch pattern and offering a revised engine selection. A lighter, more economical 229 cu. in. (3.8-liter) V-6 rated 115 horsepower replaced the old familiar 250 cu. in. inline six as standard powerplant. (California Camaros carried a 231 V-6.) There was also a new 267 cu. in. (4.4-liter) optional V-8 rated 120 horsepower, plus a 305 V-8 and the Z28 350 V-8 (not available in California). Automatic transmissions had a new torque converter clutch to eliminate slippage. Rally Sport Camaros came with an all-black "thin-line" grille, while Berlinetta carried a bright grille in the same style. The standard Sport Coupe grille had an emblem in the upper corner; Berlinetta had one in the center. Berlinettas had new standard wire wheel covers. Z28 grilles had a pattern of horizontal bars, with large 'Z28' emblem in the upper corner. Z28, billed as "the maximum Camaro," also had a new (functional) hood air-intake scoop facing to the rear, with an electrically-activated flap that opened when stepping hard on the gas. A side fender port let out hot engine air, and boosted pickup at the same time. Also new to Z28: rear fender flares. Body colors this year were white, black, silver, gold, red, bright blue, dark blue, bright yellow, lime green, red orange, bronze, charcoal, dark brown, and dark claret. Standard Camaro equipment included the 229 cu. in. V-6 engine, three-speed manual transmission, P205/705R14 SBR tires, body-color front/rear bumper covers, bucket seats, console, day/night mirror, and cigarette lighter. The Berlinetta coupe had whitewall tires; bright headlamp bezels, upper/lower grille, windshield and window reveal moldings; black rocker panels; dual horns; electric clock; special instruments; quiet sound group; sport mirrors; and wire wheel covers. Z28 came with P225/70R15 white-letter tires on body-color 15 x 7 in. wheels; black headlamp bezels, upper/lower grille, and reveal moldings; sport mirrors; body-color front spoiler and front flares; a hood scoop decal; front fender louvers; rear spoiler; plus sport suspension, power brakes and four-speed manual shift. Camaro's Rally Sport package included a rear spoiler, sport suspension, black rocker panels, black grille, black headlamp bezels, bright reveal moldings, sport mirrors, plus color-keyed Rally wheels.

side marker lamps all grew larger. At the rear were three-section wraparound taillamps with side marker lamps. New base engine was the 229 cu. in. (3.8-liter) V-6, with either a 267 (4.4-liter) or 305 (5.0-liter) V-8 optional. Wagons carried the 305 as standard; the big 350 was out of the lineup. Models included the two-door coupe, four-door sedan and four-door wagon; plus a Classic Landau. An Estate wagon package was optional. Malibus had a new, precisely controlled windshield washer (similar to Corvette's). Joining the option list: Rally wheels. The optional automatic transmission could now have a lock-up torque converter clutch. Only 202 Malibus came with a four-speed manual transmission. Malibu standard equipment included three-speed manual floor shift, front stabilizer bar, P185/75R14 tires, windshield and back window reveal moldings, roof drip moldings, day/night mirror, lighter, concealed wipers, and locking glove box. Wagons had P195/75R14 tires. Malibu Classic models added a stand-up hood ornament; wide wheel opening moldings; bright decklid and end cap moldings; dual horns; and full wheelcovers. The Landau coupe had sport wheel covers as well as bodyside and rear pin striping.

1980 Chevrolet, Malibu Classic Estate Wagon

1980 Chevrolet, Malibu two-door coupe (AA)

1980 Chevrolet, Monte Carlo T-top two-door coupe (with turbocharged V-6)

1980 Chevrolet, Malibu Classic four-door sedan

MALIBU -- SERIES 1A -- V-6/V-8 -- Though similar to the previous edition, Malibu sported a brighter, lightweight grille for 1980, made up of narrow vertical bars and divided by two subdued horizontal bars. Its nameplate was again in the lower corner (driver's side). Headlamps, parking lamps and

1980 Chevrolet, Monte Carlo Landau two-door coupe

MONTE CARLO -- SERIES 1A -- V-6/V-8 -- Monte wore a wider-spaced, heavier looking eggcrate grille this year, with 16 holes across in four rows. Also new were quad rectangular headlamps above wide rectangular parking lamps. Wraparound side marker lamps were replaced by separate horizontal lenses just ahead of the wheel, below 'Monte Carlo' script. New base engine was the Chevrolet-built 229 cu. in. (3.8-liter) V-6. But this year's option list included Buick's turbocharged 231 cu. in. V-6 that delivered 170 horsepower (compared to 115 from the base engine). Also available: 267 cu. in. (4.4-liter) and 305 (5.0-liter) V-8s, rated 120 and 155 horsepower, respectively. Three-speed manual shift was dropped, so all Montes now carried three-speed Turbo Hydra-matic as well as power brakes and steering. Turbo models had a special hood with raised center and identifying decal. A total of 13,839 turbo engines were installed for the model year. Standard Monte equipment included dual horns, day/night mirror, lighter, concealed wipers, front/rear stabilizer bars, and P205/70R14 steel-belted radial tires; plus moldings for window reveals, wheel openings, decklid, roof drip, and lower bodyside. New options: high-intensity halogen headlamps and a T-roof.

IMPALA/CAPRICE CLASSIC -- SERIES 1B -- V-6/V-8 -- In an attempt to boost gas mileage, both full-size models got a lighter weight standard engine: a 229 cu. in. (3.8-liter) V-6 with Dualjet carburetor and aluminum manifold. That powerplant replaced the old inline six. Wagons came with a standard 267 cu. in. (4.4-liter) V-8, also with Dualjet carburetor, introduced a year earlier on mid-sizes. For the first time, wagons could get an optional 350 cu. in. (5.7-liter) Oldsmobile-built diesel V-8 (except in California). All models could also get a 305 cu. in. (5.0-liter) gas V-8 with four-barrel. Sleek new aerodynamic styling on full-size models showed a lower hood, higher rear deck and restyled sides, along with a 100-pound weight loss. Impala's restyled grille had vertical bars over smaller segments. Caprice gained a new eggcrate grille design and three-lens taillamp assembly (with working center light). The new taillamp rear-end panel was removable. Unlike prior versions, the grille pattern was not repeated down in the bumper area. Landau models gained new roof moldings. Also new were a one-piece door beam, aluminum components in radiators and wagon bumpers, high-pressure easy-rolling tires, side-lift frame jack, and a 25-gallon fuel tank (formerly 21) to boost cruising range. Automatic transmissions added a new lockup torque converter clutch. New options included self-sealing tires, plus cornering lamps that worked with turn signals when headlamps were lit. EPA ratings of 18 MPG city, 26 highway, were the highest ever for a full-size Chevrolet. Reaching a step further, in mid-year an economy Impala emerged: the first full-size gas-engine car to achieve a 20 MPG city estimate. A total of 1,612 cars carried the special economy equipment package, while 13,843 had a diesel engine under the hood. Full-size models came in 14 body colors: beige, black, cinnabar, gray, silver, white, and yellow; plus metallic dark or light blue, light or medium camel, dark claret, or dark green. Ten two-tone combinations were offered, plus seven vinyl top colors. Standard front bench seats had cloth upholstery, but vinyl was available. Caprice could get an optional 50/50 split front seat. Standard equipment included Turbo Hydra-matic, power front disc/rear drum brakes, power steering, easy-roll steel-belted radial tires, acoustical headlining, one-piece carpeting, front stabilizer bar, and new compact spare tire. Full-size models had a built-in engine diagnostics connector, foot parking brake, cigarette lighter, heater/defroster, luggage compartment light, Freedom battery, and column lever for turn signal and dimmer.

1980 Chevrolet, Impala four-door sedan (PH)

1980 Chevrolet, Caprice Classic Landau two-door coupe

1980 Chevrolet, Caprice Classic four-door sedan (AA)

I.D. DATA: For the last time, Chevrolet used a 13-symbol Vehicle Identification Number (VIN), visible through the windshield on the driver's side. The first digit ('1') indicates Chevrolet division. Next is a letter identifying the series (car line): 'B' = Chevette; 'J' = Chevette Scooter; 'M' = Monza; 'R' = Monza Sport; 'H' = Citation coupe; 'X' = Citation; 'Q' = Camaro; 'S' = Camaro Berlinetta; 'T' = Malibu; 'W' = Malibu Classic; 'Z' = Monte Carlo; 'L' = Impala; 'N' = Caprice Classic. Symbols 3-4 indicate body type: '08' = 2-dr. hatchback coupe; '07' = 2-dr. (2 + 2) hatchback coupe; '11' = 2-dr. notchback; '27' = 2-dr. coupe; '87' = 2-dr. (4-pass.) sport coupe; '37' = 2-dr. (6-pass.) sport coupe; '47' = 2-dr. (6-pass.) coupe; '19' = 4-dr. (6-window) notchback sedan; '68' = 4-dr. (6-window) hatchback sedan; '69' = 4-dr. (4-window) notchback sedan; '35' = 4-dr. station wagon. Symbol five is the engine code: '9' = L4-97.6 2Bbl.; 'O' = L4-97.6 H.O.; 'V' = L4-151 2Bbl.; '5' = L4-151 2Bbl.; '7' = V6-173 2Bbl.; 'K' = V6-229 2Bbl.; 'A' = V6-231 2Bbl.; '3' = Turbo V6-231 4Bbl.; 'J' = V8-267 2Bbl.; 'H' = V8-305 4Bbl.; 'L' = V8-350 4Bbl; 'N' = V8-350 diesel. Next is a code for model year ('A' = 1980). Symbol seven denotes assembly plant: 'A' = Lakewood, GA; 'B' = Baltimore, MD; 'C' = South Gate, CA; 'D' = Doraville, GA; 'J' = Janesville, WI; 'K' = Leeds, MO; 'U' = Lordstown, OH; 'L' = Van Nuys, CA; 'N' = Norwood, OH; 'R' = Arlington, TX; 'S' = St. Louis, MO; 'T' = Tarrytown, NY; 'W' = Willow Run, MI; 'Y' = Wilmington, DE; 'Z' = Fremont, CA; '6' = Oklahoma City, OK; '1' = Oshawa, Ontario. The last six digits are the sequential serial number. A Body Number Plate on the upper horizontal surface of the shroud identifies model year, car division, series, style, body assembly plant, body number, trim combination, modular seat code, paint code, roof option, and build date code. Citations have a body style I.D. plate on the front tie bar, behind the right headlamp. A two- or three-symbol code (combined with a serial number) identifies each engine. Chevette engine numbers are on a pad at right of block, below No. 1 spark plug. Pontiac (151) fours have a number pad at the right side of the block, by distributor shaft hole. On sixes, the pad is at the right side of the block, to rear of distributor. On V-8s, that pad is just forward of the right cylinder head. Citation fours have an engine code on a pad at the left front of cylinder block, below the head; and an engine unit/code number label on timing cover. Citation V-6s have an engine unit/code label at rear (or front) of right rocker cover.

CHEVETTE (FOUR)

Model No.	Body/Style No.	Body Type & Seating	Factory Price	Shipping Weight	Prod. Total
1T	B08	2-dr. Hatch Cpe-4P	4289	1989	146,686
1T	B68	4-dr. Hatch Sed-4P	4418	2048	261,477

CHEVETTE SCOOTER (FOUR)

1T	J08	2-dr. Hatch Cpe-4P	3782	1985	40,998

MONZA (FOUR/V-6)

1H	M07	2-dr. Hatch 2+2-4P	4497/4722	2672	53,415
1H	M27	2-dr. Cpe-4P	4184/4409	2617	95,469

MONZA SPORT (FOUR/V-6)

1H	R07	2-dr. Hatch 2+2-4P	4921/5146	2729	20,534

1980 Chevrolet, Monza 2 + 2 two-door hatchback coupe (CP)

Monza Production Note: Figures do not include units built in fall 1980 as part of extended model year.

CITATION (FOUR/V-6)

1X	H11	2-dr. Cpe-5P	4491/4716	2391/2428	42,909
1X	X11	2-dr. Club Cpe-5P	4905/5130	2397/2434	100,340
1X	X08	2-dr. Hatch Cpe-5P	5032/5257	2417/2454	210,258
1X	X68	4-dr. Hatch Sed-5P	5153/5378	2437/2474	458,033

Citation Production Note: Figures include 187,229 Citations produced during the 1979 model year as early '80s.

CAMARO (V-6/V-8)

1F	P87	2-dr. Spt Cpe-4P	5499/5679	3218/3346	68,174
1F	P87/Z85	2-dr. Rally Cpe-4P	5916/6096	N/A	12,015

1980 Chevrolet, Camaro Berlinetta two-door coupe (AA)

CAMARO BERLINETTA (V-6/V-8)

1F	S87	2-dr. Spt Cpe-4P	6262/6442	3253/3381	26,679

CAMARO Z28 (V-8)

1F	P87/Z28	2-dr. Spt Cpe-4P	---- /7121	N/A	45,137

MALIBU (V-6/V-8)

1A	T27	2-dr. Spt Cpe-6P	5133/5313	2996/3117	28,425
1A	T19	4-dr. Sed-6P	5246/5426	3001/3122	67,696
1A	T35	4-dr. Sta Wag-6P	5402/5582	3141/3261	30,794

MALIBU CLASSIC (V-6/V-8)

1A	W27	2-dr. Spt Cpe-6P	5439/5619	3027/3148	28,425
1A	W27/Z03	2-dr. Lan Cpe-6P	5688/5868	N/A	9,342

1A	W19	4-dr. Sed-6P	5567/5747	3031/3152	77,938
1A	W35	4-dr. Sta Wag-6P	5654/5834	3167/3387	35,730

MONTE CARLO (V-6/V-8)

1A	Z37	2-dr. Spt Cpe-6P	6163/6343	3104/3219	116,580
1A	Z37/Z03	2-dr. Lan Cpe-6P	6411/6591	N/A	32,262

IMPALA (V-6/V-8)

1B	L47	2-dr. Spt Cpe-6P	6180/6360	3344/3452	10,756
1B	L69	4-dr. Sedan-6P	6289/6469	3360/3468	70,801
1B	L35	4-dr. Sta Wag-6P	----/6780	----/3892	11,203
1B	L35/AQ4	4-dr. 3S Wag-8P	----/6925	----/3924	6,767

CAPRICE CLASSIC (V-6/V-8)

1B	N47	2-dr. Spt Cpe-6P	6579/6759	3376/3484	13,919
1B	N47/Z03	2-dr. Lan Cpe-6P	7029/7209	N/A	8,857
1B	N69	4-dr. Sedan-6P	6710/6890	3410/3518	91,208
1B	N35	4-dr. Sta Wag-6P	----/7099	----/3930	9,873
1B	N35/AQ4	4-dr. 3S Wag-8P	----/7266	----/3962	13,431

FACTORY PRICE AND WEIGHT NOTE: Where two prices and weights are shown, the figure to the left of the slash is for six-cylinder model, to right of slash for the 267 cu. in. V-8 (305 V-8 cost $115 more). For Monza and Citation, prices and weights to left of slash are four-cylinder, to right for V-6 engine. All models had at least two price rises during the model year. The new Citation had an ample increase even before introduction.

BODY/STYLE NO. NOTE: Some models are actually option packages. Figure after the slash (e.g., Z03) is the number of the option package that comes with the model listed.

ENGINE DATA: BASE FOUR (Chevette): Inline. Overhead cam. Four-cylinder. Cast iron block and head. Displacement: 97.6 cu. in. (1.6 liters). Bore & stroke: 3.23 x 2.98 in. Compression ratio: 8.6:1. Brake horsepower: 70 at 5200 R.P.M. Torque: 82 lb.-ft. at 2400 R.P.M. Five main bearings. Hydraulic valve lifters. Carburetor: 2Bbl. Holley 5210C. VIN Code: 9. OPTIONAL HIGH-OUTPUT FOUR (Chevette): Same as above except: Brake H.P.: 74 at 5200 R.P.M. Torque: 88 lb.-ft. at 2800 R.P.M. VIN Code: O. BASE FOUR (Monza): Inline. Overhead valve. Four-cylinder. Cast iron block. Displacement: 151 cu. in. (2.5 liters). Bore & stroke: 4.00 x 3.00 in. Compression ratio: 8.2:1. Brake horsepower: 86 at 4000 R.P.M. Torque: 128 lb.-ft. at 2400 R.P.M. Five main bearings. Hydraulic valve lifters. Carburetor: 2Bbl. Rochester 2SE. VIN Code: V. BASE FOUR (Citation): Same as 151 cu. in. four above except: Brake H.P.: 90 at 4000 R.P.M. Torque: 134 lb.-ft. at 2400 R.P.M. VIN Code: 5. OPTIONAL V-6 (Citation): 60-degree, overhead-valve V-6. Cast iron block and head. Displacement: 173 cu. in. (2.8 liters). Bore & stroke: 3.50 x 3.00 in. Compression ratio: 8.5:1. Brake horsepower: 115 at 4800 R.P.M. Torque: 145 lb.-ft. at 2400 R.P.M. Four main bearings. Hydraulic valve lifters. Carburetor: 2Bbl. Rochester 2SE. VIN Code: 7. BASE V-6 (Camaro, Malibu, Monte Carlo, Impala, Caprice): 90-degree, overhead-valve V-6. Cast iron block and head. Displacement: 229 cu. in. (3.8 liters). Bore & stroke: 3.74 x 3.48 in. Compression ratio: 8.6:1. Brake horsepower: 115 at 4000 R.P.M. Torque: 175 lb.-ft. at 2000 R.P.M. Four main bearings. Hydraulic valve lifters. Carburetor: 2Bbl. Rochester M2ME. VIN Code: K. OPTIONAL V-6 (Monza); alternate for models above: 90-degree, overhead-valve V-6. Cast iron block and head. Displacement: 231 cu. in. (3.8 liters). Bore & stroke: 3.80 x 3.40 in. Compression ratio: 8.0:1. Brake horsepower: 110 at 3800 R.P.M. Torque: 190 lb.-ft. at 2000 R.P.M. Four main bearings. Hydraulic valve lifters. Carburetor: 2Bbl. Rochester M2ME. VIN Code: A. TURBOCHARGED V-6; OPTIONAL (Monte Carlo): Same as 231 cu. in. V-6 above, except: 4Bbl. Rochester M4ME carburetor. Brake H.P.: 170 at 4000 R.P.M. Torque: 265 lb.-ft. at 2400 R.P.M. VIN Code: 3. OPTIONAL V-8 (Camaro, Malibu, Monte Carlo, Impala, Caprice): 90-degree, overhead valve V-8. Cast iron block and head. Displacement: 267 cu. in. (4.4 liters). Bore & stroke: 3.50 x 3.48 in. Compression ratio: 8.3:1. Brake horsepower: 120 at 3600 R.P.M. Torque: 215 lb.-ft. at 2000 R.P.M. Five main bearings. Hydraulic valve lifters. Carburetor: 2Bbl. Rochester M2ME. VIN Code: J. OPTIONAL V-8 (Camaro, Malibu, Monte Carlo, Impala, Caprice): 90-degree, overhead valve V-8. Cast iron block and head. Displacement: 305 cu. in. (5.0 liters). Bore & stroke: 3.74 x 3.48 in. Compression ratio: 8.6:1. Brake horsepower: 155 at 4000 R.P.M. Torque: 240 lb.-ft. at 1600 R.P.M. Five main bearings. Hydraulic valve lifters. Carburetor: 4Bbl. Rochester M4ME. VIN Code: H. BASE V-8 (Camaro Z28): 90-degree, overhead valve V-8. Cast iron block and head. Displacement: 350 cu. in. (5.7 liters). Bore & stroke: 4.00 x 3.48 in. Compression ratio: 8.2:1. Brake horsepower: 190 at 4200 R.P.M. Torque: 280 lb.-ft. at 2400 R.P.M. Five main bearings. Hydraulic valve lifters. Carburetor: 4Bbl. Rochester M4ME. VIN Code: L. DIESEL V-8; OPTIONAL (Impala/Caprice wagon): 90-degree, overhead valve V-8. Cast iron block and head. Displacement: 350 cu. in. (5.7 liters). Bore & stroke: 4.06 x 3.39 in. Compression ratio: 22.5:1. Brake horsepower: 105 at 3200 R.P.M. Torque: 205 lb.-ft. at 1600 R.P.M. Five main bearings. Hydraulic valve lifters. Fuel injection. VIN Code: N.

CHASSIS DATA: Wheelbase: (Chevette 2-dr.) 94.3 in.; (Chvt 4-dr.) 97.3 in.; (Monza) 97.0 in.; (Citation) 104.9 in.; (Camaro) 108.0 in.; (Malibu/Monte) 108.1 in.; (Capr/Imp) 116.0 in. Overall length: (Chvt 2-dr.) 161.9 in.; (Chvt 4-dr.) 164.9 in.; (Monza) 179.9 in.; (Cit) 176.7 in.; (Camaro) 197.6 in.; (Malibu) 197.7 in.; (Malibu wag) 193.4 in.; (Monte) 200.4 in.; (Capr/Imp) 212.1 in.; (Capr/Imp wag) 215.1 in. Height: (Chvt) 52.3 in.; (Monza cpe) 50.1 in.; (Monza hatch) 50.2 in.; (Cit) 53.1 in.; (Camaro) 49.2 in.; (Malibu cpe) 53.3 in.; (Malibu sed) 54.2 in.; (Malibu wag) 54.5 in.; (Monte) 53.9 in.; (Capr/Imp cpe) 53.3 in.; (Capr/Imp sed) 55.9 in.; (Capr/Imp wag) 57.7 in. Width: (Chvt) 61.8 in.; (Monza) 65.4 in.; (Cit) 68.3 in.; (Camaro) 74.5 in.; (Malibu/Monte) 71.5 in.; (Malibu wag) 71.2 in.; (Capr/Imp) 75.3 in.; (Capr/Imp wag) 79.3 in. Front Tread: (Chvt) 51.2 in.; (Monza) 54.8 in.; (Cit) 58.7 in.; (Camaro) 61.3 in.; (Berlinetta) 61.6 in.; (Malibu/Monte) 58.5 in.; (Capr/Imp) 61.8 in.; (Capr/Imp wag) 62.2 in. Rear Tread: (Chvt) 51.2 in.; (Monza) 53.6 in.; (Cit) 57.0 in.; (Camaro) 60.0 in.; (Berlinetta) 60.3 in.; (Malibu/Monte) 57.8 in.; (Capr/Imp) 60.8 in.; (Capr/Imp wag) 64.1 in. Standard Tires: (Chvt) P155/80R13 GBR; (Monza) A78 x 13; (Cit) P185/80R13 GBR; (Camaro) P205/75R14 SBR; (Malibu) P185/75R14/B GBR; (Malibu wag) P195/75R14/B GBR; (Imp/Caprice) P205/75R15/B SBR; (Imp/Capr wag) P225/75R15/B SBR; (Monte) P205/70R14/B SBR.

TECHNICAL: Transmission: Three-speed manual transmission standard on Camaro and Malibu V-6. Gear ratios: (1st) 3.50:1; (2nd) 1.89:1; (3rd) 1.00:1; (Rev) 3.62:1. Four-speed floor shift standard on Chevette: (1st) 3.75:1; (2nd) 2.16:1; (3rd) 1.38:1; (4th) 1.00:1; (Rev) 3.82:1. Four-speed floor shift standard on Monza: (1st) 3.50:1; (2nd) 2.48:1; (3rd) 1.66:1; (4th) 1.00:1; (Rev) 3.50:1. Citation four-speed floor shift: (1st) 3.53:1; (2nd) 1.96:1; (3rd) 1.24:1; (4th) 0.81:1; (Rev) 3.42:1. Four-speed floor shift optional on Camaro/Malibu V8-305: (1st) 2.85:1; (2nd) 2.02:1; (3rd) 1.35:1; (4th) 1.00:1; (Rev) 2.85:1. Four-speed on Camaro V8-350: (1st) 3.42:1; (2nd) 2.28:1; (3rd) 1.45:1; (4th) 1.00:1; (Rev) 3.51:1. Three-speed Turbo Hydra-matic standard on Monte Carlo and Caprice/Impala, optional on others. Automatic gear ratios: (1st) 2.52:1; (2nd) 1.52:1; (3rd) 1.00:1; (Rev) 1.93:1 except Caprice/Impala V6/V8-267, Monza four, Malibu V-6 and Monte ratios: (1st) 2.74:1; (2nd) 1.57:1; (3rd) 1.00:1; (Rev) 2.07:1. Chevette automatic trans.: (1st) 2.40:1; (2nd) 1.48:1; (3rd) 1.00:1; (Rev) 1.92:1. Citation auto. trans.: (1st) 2.84:1; (2nd) 1.60:1; (3rd) 1.00:1; (Rev) 2.07:1. Standard final drive ratio: (Chevette) 3.70:1; (Monza four) 2.73:1; (Monza V-6) 2.93:1; (Citation) 3.34:1; (Camaro V-6) 2.73:1; (Camaro V-8) 2.56:1; (Malibu V-6) 2.73:1; (Malibu V-8) 2.29:1; (Malibu V-8 wag) 2.41:1; (Monte V-6) 2.41:1; (Monte V-8) 2.29:1; (Caprice/Imp V-6) 2.73 :1; (Caprice/Imp V-8) 2.41:1; (Caprice/Imp wag) 2.56:1. Steering: (Chevette/Citation) rack and pinion; (others) recirculating ball. Front Suspension: (Citation) MacPherson struts and coil springs; (others) control arms, coil springs and stabilizer bar. Rear Suspension: (Chevette) rigid axle, torque tube, longitudinal trailing radius arms, transverse linkage bar, coil springs and stabilizer bar; (Citation) rigid axle, trailing arm, control arms and stabilizer arm; (Camaro) rigid axle, semi-elliptic leaf springs and stabilizer bar; (others) rigid axle, lower trailing radius arms, upper oblique torque arms and coil springs, plus stabilizer bar on Monte and full-size. Brakes: Front disc, rear drum. Body construction: (Chevette/Citation) unibody; (Camaro) unibody with separate partial box frame; (others) separate body and perimeter box frame. Fuel tank: (Chvt) 12.5 gal.; (Monza) 18.5 gal.; (Citation) 14 gal.; (Camaro) 21 gal.; (Malibu/Monte) 18.1 gal.; (Malibu wag) 18.2 gal.; (Capr/Imp) 25 gal.; (Capr/Imp wag) 22 gal.

DRIVETRAIN OPTIONS: Engines: 1.6-liter H.O. four: Chevette ($60). 173 cu. in., 2Bbl. V-6: Citation ($225). 231 cu. in., 2Bbl. V-6: Monza ($225). Turbo 231 cu. in., 4Bbl. V-6: Monte ($500). 267 cu. in., 2Bbl. V-8: Camaro/Malibu/Monte/Imp/Caprice ($180). 305 cu. in., 4Bbl. V-8: Camaro/Malibu/Monte/Imp/Capr ($295); Imp/Capr wag ($115); Z28 ($50 credit). Diesel 350 cu. in. V-8: Imp/Capr wag ($915). Transmission/Differential: Four-speed manual shift: Camaro ($144); Malibu (N/A). Turbo Hydra-matic: Chvt/Monza ($320); Citation ($337); Camaro/Malibu ($358); Camaro Z28 ($63). Sport shifter: Chvt ($32). Limited-slip differential: Monza ($64); Camaro ($68); Malibu/Monte ($69); Imp/Capr ($73). Performance axle ratio: Monza ($18); Camaro/Malibu/Monte ($19); Imp/Capr ($20). Power Accessories: Power brakes: Chvt/Monza/Citation ($76); Camaro ($81). Power steering: Monza ($158); Citation/Malibu ($174). Suspension: F40 H.D. susp.: Citation ($21); Monte ($24). F40 H.D. shock absorbers: Imp/Capr ($25). F41 sport susp.: Chvt ($35); Monza ($33); Citation ($27); Camaro ($41); Imp/Capr cpe/sed ($45). Inflatable rear shock absorbers: Imp/Capr ($59). Front stabilizer bar: Monza ($29). Other: Heavy-duty radiator: Monza ($33). H.D. cooling: Chvt ($31-$58); Cit ($32-$59); Camaro/Malibu/Monte ($36-$63) Imp/Capr ($37-$64). Engine block heater: Imp/Capr wag ($16). H.D. alternator (63-amp): Malibu ($6-$35). H.D. alternator (70-amp): Cit ($11-$43); Monte ($32-$67); Imp/Capr ($33-$68). H.D. battery ($20-$22) exc. diesel ($44). California emission system ($250) exc. diesel ($83).

CHEVETTE/MONZA CONVENIENCE/APPEARANCE OPTIONS: Option Packages: Spyder equipment pkg.: Monza ($521). Quiet sound group: Chvt ($38-$50); Monza ($32-$42). Comfort/Convenience: Air conditioning ($531). Rear defogger, electric ($95). Tinted glass: Chvt ($64). Comfortilt steering wheel ($73). Tachometer: Chvt ($67). Gauge pkg. (incl. tach): Monza ($71-$94). Electric clock ($23). Cigarette lighter: Scooter ($8). Intermittent wipers ($37). Lighting and Mirrors: Aux. lighting: Chvt ($40-$41); Monza ($21-$27). Twin sport mirrors, left remote ($43). Driver's remote sport mirror: Chvt ($27). Entertainment: AM radio: Scooter ($79). AM/FM radio: Chvt/Monza ($64); Scooter ($143). AM/FM stereo radio ($101). AM/FM stereo radio w/digital clock: Monza ($252). Stereo 8-track tape player w/AM radio: Monza ($154). 8-track player with AM/FM: Monza ($176). Cassette player with AM/FM stereo radio: Monza ($188). Rear speaker ($18). Radio delete: Monza ($52 credit). Exterior Trim: Removable sunroof: Monza ($193). Cabriolet vinyl roof: Monza ($165) incl. opera windows. Spoilers, front/rear: Monza ($124). Deluxe exterior (wheel opening, side window and rocker panel moldings): Chvt ($112-$119). Exterior decor pkg. (wheel opening and side window moldings, wheel covers, luggage carrier): Monza ($139-$154). Two-tone paint: Chvt ($110). Sport stripes ($75). Bodyside moldings: Scooter ($43). Wheel opening moldings: Monza ($22). Side window reveal moldings: Chvt ($70-$77). Door edge guards ($13-$20). Roof carrier: Chvt ($70). Interior Trim/Upholstery: Console: Monza cpe ($80). Cloth bucket seats: Chvt ($12-$23); Monza ($23). Custom Chevette interior pkg. w/bucket seats: cloth ($183); vinyl ($160). Custom vinyl bucket seats:

Monza ($170) exc. Sport (NC). Custom cloth bucket seats: Monza ($193) exc. Sport ($23). Folding rear seat: Monza ($104) but std. on 2 + 2. Rear seat delete: Chvt ($54 credit). Color-keyed floor mats ($22). Automatic seat/shoulder belts: Chvt ($65). Wheels and Tires: Rally II wheels: Monza ($48-$94). Color-keyed deluxe wheel covers: Monza ($14-$46). Sport wheel covers: Chvt ($48). Wheel trim rings: Scooter ($40). P155/80-13/B GBR WSW: Scooter ($43). P175/70-13/B SBR BSW: Chvt ($53); Scooter ($95). P175/70-13/B SBR WSW: Chvt ($95); Scooter ($137). P175/70-13/B SBR WLT: Chvt ($109); Scooter ($152). B78 x 13/B WSW: Monza ($18). BR70 x 13/C SBR BSW: Monza ($154) exc. Sport ($116). BR70 x 13/C SBR WSW: Monza ($158-$196). BR70 x 13/C SBR WLT: Monza ($57-$211).

1980 Chevrolet, Citation two-door hatchback coupe (CP)

CITATION CONVENIENCE/APPEARANCE OPTIONS:
Option Packages: X-11 sport equipment pkg. ($501). Deluxe exterior pkg. ($102-$144). Quiet sound group ($52). Quiet sound/rear decor pkg. ($72). Comfort/Convenience: Air cond. ($564). Rear defogger, electric ($101). Cruise control ($105). Tinted glass ($70). Sport steering wheel (NC to $20). Comfortilt steering wheel ($75). Power windows ($133-$189). Power remote swing-out windows ($91). Power door locks ($87-$123). Gauge pkg. w/clock ($70). Special instruments incl. tachometer ($109). Electric clock ($25). Cigarette lighter: cpe ($8). Intermittent wipers ($39). Lighting, Horns and Mirrors: Aux. lighting ($41). Right door light switch: cpe ($8). Dual horns ($9). Driver's remote mirror ($18). Dual sport mirrors, left remote ($43). Entertainment: AM radio: cpe ($79). AM/FM radio: cpe ($143); others ($64). AM/FM stereo radio: cpe ($180); others ($101). 8-track player with AM/FM stereo: cpe ($255); others ($176). Cassette player with AM/FM stereo: cpe ($267); others ($188). CB with AM/FM stereo: cpe ($492); others ($413). Rear speaker ($18). Dual front/rear speakers ($40). Windshield antenna ($25); incl. w/radios. Radio delete ($52 credit). Exterior Trim: Removable sunroof ($240). Two-tone paint ($148) incl. pin striping and bodyside moldings. Bodyside pin striping ($32). Bodyside moldings ($43-$47). Bright rocker panel moldings: cpe ($20). Wheel opening moldings: cpe ($43). Door edge guards ($13-$20). Side window reveal moldings ($41-$65). Roof carrier ($86). Bumper guards ($45). Bumper rub strips ($40). Interior Trim/Upholstery: Console ($80). Reclining passenger seatback ($42-$70). Sport cloth bench seat ($23). Custom knit cloth bench seat ($189-$239). Custom vinyl bench seat ($166-$216). Custom bucket seats: knit cloth

($278-$328); vinyl ($255-$305). Locking glove compartment ($8). Color-keyed mats ($25). Wheels and Tires: Full wheel covers ($43). Wire wheel covers ($113-$156). Wheel trim rings ($48). Rally wheel trim ($35-$78). P185/80R13/B GBR WSW ($45). P185/80R13/B SBR BSW ($49). P185/80R13/B SBR WSW ($93). P205/70R13/B SBR WSW ($182). P205/70R13/B SBR WLT ($196).

1980 Chevrolet, Monte Carlo two-door coupe (CP)

1980 Chevrolet, Malibu Classic Landau two-door coupe (CP)

CAMARO/MALIBU/MONTE CARLO CONVENIENCE/ APPEARANCE OPTIONS: Option Packages: Estate equipment: Malibu wag ($276). Interior decor/quiet sound group: Camaro ($68); std. on Berlinetta. Quiet sound group: Malibu ($55). Value appearance group: Monte ($120-$129). Security pkg.: Malibu wag ($40). Comfort/Convenience: Air cond.: Camaro ($566); Malibu/Monte ($601). Rear defogger (forced-air): Malibu cpe/sed ($59). Rear defogger, electric ($107). Cruise control ($112). Tinted glass: Camaro ($68); Malibu/Monte ($75). Comfortilt steering wheel ($81). Six-way power driver's seat: Malibu/Monte ($175). Power windows: Camaro/Monte ($143); Malibu ($143-$202). Power door locks: Malibu ($93-$132); Camaro/Monte ($93). Power trunk release: Monte ($26). Electric clock: base Camaro, Malibu ($25). Gauge pkg.: Monte ($41). Gauge pkg. w/tach: base Camaro ($120); Malibu ($134); Monte ($109). Gauge pkg. w/clock: Malibu ($66). Intermittent wipers ($41). Lighting, Horns and Mirrors: High-intensity high-beam headlamps: Monte ($26). Aux. lighting: Camaro ($33-$40); Malibu ($33-$60); Monte ($33). Dual horns: Camaro, base Malibu ($10). Remote-control driver's mirror: Malibu/Monte ($19). Twin sport mirrors (left remote): base Camaro, Malibu/Monte ($46). Twin remote sport mirrors: Malibu ($73); Monte ($48-$73). Visor vanity mirror: Monte ($6). Lighted visor mirror: Monte ($37-$43). Entertainment: AM radio ($97). AM/FM radio ($153). AM/FM stereo radio ($192). AM/FM stereo radio w/digital clock: Malibu ($353); Camaro ($328-$353). Stereo 8-track tape player w/AM radio ($249). Stereo 8-track tape player with AM/FM stereo radio ($272). Cassette player with AM/FM stereo radio ($285). AM/FM/CB radio ($473). AM/FM stereo radio w/CB ($525). Rear speaker ($20). Dual front speakers: Monte ($14). Dual front and rear speakers: Malibu/Monte ($43). Windshield antenna ($27); incl. w/radios. Power antenna ($51). Exterior Trim: Removable glass roof panels: Camaro/Monte ($695). Power sky roof: Monte ($561). Vinyl roof: Malibu ($124); Monte ($140). Rear spoiler: Camaro Berlinetta ($62). Style trim pkg.: Camaro ($78). Two-tone paint: Malibu ($72-$123); Monte ($148-$171). Bodyside moldings: Camaro ($46). Deluxe bodyside moldings: Malibu/Monte ($57). Door edge guards ($14-$22). Bright sill moldings: Monte ($47). Wheel opening moldings: Malibu cpe/sed ($25). Side window sill moldings: Monte ($35). Side window reveal moldings: Malibu ($47). Roof drip moldings: Camaro ($26). Bodyside pin striping: Malibu ($51); Monte ($42). Rear window air deflector: Malibu wag ($32). Roof carrier: Malibu wag ($96). Bumper rub strips: Malibu ($44). Bumper guards, front/rear: Malibu ($49). Interior Trim/Upholstery: Console: Malibu cpe/sed, Monte ($86). Vinyl bench seat: Malibu cpe/sed, Monte ($28). Cloth bench seat: Malibu wag ($244). Custom vinyl bench seat: Malibu wag ($64). Cloth 50/50 seating: Malibu ($184-$244). Vinyl 50/50 seating: Malibu ($212-$244). Vinyl bucket seats: Malibu cpe/sed, Monte ($91). Cloth bucket seats: Camaro ($25); Malibu cpe/sed, Monte ($91). Custom vinyl bucket seats: base Camaro ($328). Custom cloth bucket seats: Berlinetta ($25); base Camaro ($353). Monte custom 55/45 seating: cloth ($366); vinyl ($394). Adj. driver's seatback: Camaro ($25). Litter container: Monte ($9). Color-keyed mats: Camaro/Malibu/Monte ($25). Deluxe load-floor carpet: Malibu wag ($75). Deluxe trunk trim: Monte ($46). Wheels and Tires: Aluminum wheels: Camaro ($184-$337). Custom styled wheels: Camaro ($107-$153). Rally wheels: Camaro ($100); Malibu ($50-$96); Monte ($50); Malibu Classic Landau (NC). Full wheel covers: Camaro/Malibu ($46). Sport wheel covers (silver or gold): Malibu ($56-$102). Wire wheel covers: Malibu ($69-$171); Monte ($69-$125). P185/75R14/B GBR WSW: Malibu cpe/sed ($45). P195/75R14/B GBR WSW: Malibu wag ($48). P195/75R14/B SBR WSW: Malibu cpe/sed ($118); Malibu wag ($96). P205/75R14 SBR WSW: Camaro ($51-$65). P205/75R14 SBR WLT: Camaro ($15-$81). P205/70R14/B SBR WSW: Monte ($51); Malibu cpe/sed ($171). P205/70R14/B SBR WLT: Malibu cpe/sed ($185). Stowaway spare: Camaro (NC).

IMPALA/CAPRICE CONVENIENCE/APPEARANCE OPTIONS:
Option Packages: Estate equipment: wag ($280). Value appearance group: Imp ($96). Comfort/Convenience: Four season air cond. ($647). Comfortron auto-temp air cond. ($738). Rear defogger, forced-air: cpe/sed ($61). Rear defogger, electric ($109). Cruise control ($118). Tinted glass ($90). Comfortilt steering wheel ($83). Power door locks ($95-$135). Six-way power driver's seat ($179). Power windows ($149-$221). Power trunk release ($27). Power tailgate lock: wag ($43). Electric clock: Imp ($26). Digital clock: Imp ($59); Caprice ($33). Gauge pkg. ($58). Intermittent wipers ($42). Quiet sound group: Imp ($60). Lighting, Horns and Mirrors: High-intensity high-beam headlamps ($27). Cornering lamps ($50). Aux. lighting ($37-$54). Dual horns: Imp ($11). Driver's remote mirror ($20). Dual remote mirrors ($60). Dual sport mirrors, left remote ($47). Dual remote body-color sport mirrors ($27-$74). Visor vanity mirror ($7). Lighted visor mirror ($44). Entertainment: AM radio ($99). AM/FM radio ($156). AM/FM stereo radio ($195); w/digital clock ($358-$384). Stereo 8-track tape player with AM radio ($253); with AM/FM stereo radio ($276). Cassette player with AM/FM stereo ($289). AM/FM/CB radio and power antenna ($480). AM/FM stereo with CB and power antenna ($533). Rear speaker ($21). Dual front/rear speakers ($44). Power antenna ($52). Windshield antenna ($28); incl. w/radios. Exterior Trim: Power sky roof ($670). Vinyl roof: cpe/sed ($155). Roof carrier: wag ($123). Two-tone paint ($60). Custom two-tone ($128). Pin striping ($35). Bodyside moldings ($48). Door edge guards ($15-$22). Wheel opening moldings: Imp ($25). Bumper rub strips, front/rear ($60). Bumper guards ($56). Interior Trim/Upholstery: Vinyl bench seat: cpe/sed ($29). Cloth 50/50 seat ($229-$276). Vinyl 50/50 seat ($247-$276). Custom cloth 50/50 seat: cpe ($412); sed ($437). Deluxe load-floor carpet: wag ($80). Deluxe cargo area carpet: wag ($114). Color-keyed mats: front ($15); rear ($11). Litter container ($9). Deluxe trunk trim ($49). Wheel Covers: Full wheel covers ($47). Sport covers: Imp ($105); Caprice ($58). Custom covers: Imp ($125); Caprice ($78). Wire covers: Caprice ($128). Coupe/Sedan Tires: P205/75R15 SBR WSW ($51). P215/75R15 SBR WSW ($82). P225/70R15 SBR WSW ($124). Wagon Tires: P225/75R15/B SBR WSW ($55). Puncture-sealant tires ($85).

HISTORY: Introduced: Oct. 11, 1979 except Citation, April 19, 1979, and Corvette, Oct. 25, 1979. Model year production (U.S.): 2,017,054 (incl. Corvettes and early 1980 Citations, but not incl. 19,631 Acadians). Calendar year production: 1,737,336 (including 44,190 Corvettes and 18,958 Acadians). Calendar year sales by U.S. dealers: 1,747,534 for a 26.6 percent market share. Model year sales by U.S. dealers: 1,831,953 (incl. 37,471 Corvettes, but not incl. 273,720 early 1980 Citations).

Historical Footnotes: While auto sales fell overall this year, Chevrolet remained GM's top seller (hardly a surprise). Model year sales dropped 20 percent, however. Chevette sales went up a bit, but other models declined. Camaro fell by nearly 44 percent, Monte and full-size models by about 40 percent. Full-size Chevrolet production fell by a whopping 66.3 percent. Only Chevette fared notably better than in 1979. The decline in full-size sales caused production to halt at South Gate, California and St. Louis plants. Only the Janesville, Wisconsin, facility continued to build full-size models. South Gate would be the site for production of the 1982 J-cars. Monzas, which still sold fairly well, continued to roll out of the plant at Lordstown, Ohio. Although Citation would soon be plagued by complaints and recalls, it was popular from the start. Chevrolet hoped the new front-drive would appeal to "a whole new generation of car buyers with values and attitudes far different from their parents and even their older brothers and sisters," declared General Manager Robert Lund. Those "new values" buyers for whom a car was "a functional part of their lives" would soon "revolutionize the marketplace." Citation had first been conceived in 1974, when fuel economy was uppermost in engineers' minds. Instead of being evolutionary, as was nearly always the case in earlier periods, it was designed from the ground up. The Chevrolet 60-degree V-6 engine built for Citation at Tonawanda, New York, was also distributed to the other GM division builders of X-bodied vehicles.

1981

Monza left the lineup this year, but the vacancy would soon be filled by the new (1982) front-drive Cavalier. Opening prices for 1981 were even higher compared to 1980 than 1980 was to '79--up by as much as $1,500. Monte Carlo got an aerodynamic restyle, while other models changed their front-end look. For the first time, a four-speed overdrive automatic transmission was installed on full-size Chevrolets with the 5.0-liter V-8. All GM automatic transmissions now had the lockup torque converter that had been introduced on some 1980 models. It offered a direct flywheel-to-driveshaft connection in one or two gears. All gas-engine models had GM's new Computer Command Control that adjusted the air/fuel mixture and spark timing to compensate for driving conditions, altitude, temperature and barometric pressure. It also included self-diagnostic features.

1981 Chevrolet, Chevette four-door hatchback sedan (AA)

CHEVETTE -- SERIES 1T -- FOUR -- Immodestly billed as "America's most popular subcompact," Chevette wore a new contemporary flush-mounted windshield with black outline molding. Also new: sporty argent-finish styled steel wheels and a bright-accented black grille. Standard powerplant was again the 98 cu. in. (1.6-liter) four, now with Computer Command Control to monitor the engine and reduce emissions. All models except the low-budget Scooter had a sport shifter in the floor console. Standard coupes had swing-out rear quarter windows, but Scooter's were fixed. A Rally trim option was available. For the first time power steering was available with automatic transmission and air conditioning--a lot of work for that little 1.6 engine to perform. Halogen headlamps and a rear wiper/washer were new options. Body colors were beige, black, red, white, bright yellow, and nine metallics: medium or light brown, champagne, silver, light or dark blue, maroon, dark green, or burnt orange. The custom interior included high contoured bucket seats up front, upholstered in cloth or vinyl. Standard equipment included the 1.6-liter engine, four-speed manual transmission, maintenance-free battery, energy-absorbing bumpers, front stabilizer bar, diagnostic connector, two-speed wipers, bumper guards and rub strips, day/night mirror, mini-console, vinyl interior, dome light, and P155/8013 fiberglass-belted whitewall tires. Scooter had blackwall tires and lacked various pieces of equipment standard on other models: an AM radio, bodyside moldings, color-keyed seat/shoulder belts, color-keyed instrument panel, sport steering wheel, lighter, and reclining front bucket seats.

1981 Chevrolet, Citation four-door hatchback sedan (AA)

CITATION -- SERIES 1X -- FOUR/V-6 -- Named *Motor Trend* "Car of the Year" for 1980, Citation was described (ironically, in view of imminent recalls and troubles) as the "most successful new car ever introduced." Following its huge introductory fanfare as an early 1980 model, Citation changed little for its second full year. The notchback coupe was dropped, so only hatchbacks remained: two-door or four-door. Citation had a 'Chevrolet' nameplate on the decklid, and 'Citation' nameplate at forward end of front fenders. Styling features included a body-color front valance panel, bright hood and windshield moldings, bright bumpers with body-color end caps, wide rocker panel moldings, and pin striping on decklid and quarter panels. The new brightchrome grille was arranged in a looser 8 x 4 hole pattern, with bowtie emblem in the center. Below was a new slotted air dam. Body colors this year were beige, black, red, white, and bright yellow; plus metallic light or dark blue, light or medium brown, champagne, dark green, maroon, burnt orange, or silver. Cloth or vinyl interiors came in beige, black, dark blue, camel or maroon (vinyl also in champagne). Engine choices again were the base 151 cu. in (2.5-liter) four or 60-degree 173 cu. in (2.8-liter) V-6, both with new Computer Command Control. The V-6 also added Electric Early Fuel Evaporation to improve emissions, by supplying electric current to a heater grid in the carburetor bore for better cold starts and warm-up. (1980 carburetor bases were heated by exhaust.) Engines also had a new Electronic Spark Timing system (ESC), plus a new Freedom II battery. Citation tires now took 30 psi air pressure. Engines offered improved service accessibility. A revised X11 package, which was mostly for looks in 1980, now included a high-output (135 horsepower) version of the V-6 engine. Chevrolet claimed that the X11 Citation package "gives you goose bumps." Carrying a Z09 RP0 code and $1,498 price tag, it included (for starters) a rear spoiler, body-color bumpers with black rub strips, tachometer, 'X11' decal on doors and rear spoiler, power brakes, and P215/60R14 steel-belted radials on 14 x 6.5 inch aluminum alloy wheels. A special lightweight fiberglass-reinforced, sheet-molded compound hood had a molded-in air inlet and 'High Output 660' emblem to show that the performance V-6 was underneath. Aero drag rated only 0.4. The X11 package also included low-drag, semi-metallic brake linings; a dual-snorkel air cleaner; quick-ratio rack-and-pinion steering; sport steering wheel; special instruments; twin sport mirrors; and large-diameter exhaust with dual tailpipes. The high-output V-6 had bigger valves, revised valve timing with higher lift and longer duration for better high-end volumetric efficiency, and an aluminum intake manifold. It produced 135 horsepower at 5400 R.P.M, and 145 lb.-ft. of torque at 2400. The F41 sport suspension included large-diameter stabilizer bars, higher-rate springs and firmer bushings, plus a numerically higher axle ratio. X11 also had black window moldings, headlamp bezels, and pillar louvers; black-accented grille and rocker panel moldings; and bucket seats. Also joining the option list were halogen headlamps and an automatic speed control with new "resume" feature, plus a reclining driver's seat backrest. Bucket seats could now be ordered with the standard interior. Citation's standard equipment included four-speed manual transmission, front stabilizer bar, P185/80R13 glass-belted radial tires on styled steel wheels, compact spare tire, two-speed wipers, bright roof drip moldings, push-button AM radio, day/night mirror, color-keyed steering wheel and seat/shoulder belts, and cut-pile carpeting.

1981 Chevrolet, Camaro Berlinetta two-door coupe (CP)

1981 Chevrolet, Camaro Z28 two-door coupe (PH)

CAMARO -- SERIES 1F -- V-6-/V-8 -- Rally Sport left the Camaro lineup this year, leaving only the base Sport Coupe, Berlinetta, and performance Z28. Not much changed, beyond the new Computer Command Control on all engines. Power brakes, formerly standard only on the Z28, were now universal. All Camaros got a space-saving compact spare tire (formerly an option) and lighter weight Freedom II battery, plus new low-drag front disc brakes. Optional automatic transmissions added a lockup torque converter clutch in third gear. The Z28's torque converter clutch was computer-controlled in both second and third gears. The basic Camaro coupe had an argent grille split (as before) into upper and lower sections, plus wraparound taillamps. Berlinetta's grille was bright-accented argent. Berlinetta came with a standard Quiet Sound Group including inner roof layer of sound-absorbing materials and inside roof covering of soft foam-backed headlining. Special paint and striping emphasized its "sculptured lines." Stripes came in silver, black, blue, beige, gold or red. Berlinetta identification was on the grille header panel, side pillars, and deck lid. Body sills were black (bright on the basic sport coupe). Base engine for both the standard sport coupe and posher Berlinetta remained the 229 cu. in. (3.8-liter) V-6 with three-speed manual transmission. Both 267 cu. in. (4.4-liter) and 305 cu. in. (5.0-liter) V-8s were optional, but required either four-speed or automatic. Z28 had a standard four-barrel 305 V-8 engine, with new wide-ratio four-speed manual transmission (optional on others). That gearbox's 3.42:1 low- gear ratio delivered both economy and low-end performance, hooked to 3.42:1 axle ratio. Z28 Camaros could also get a 350 cu. in. (5.7-liter) V-8 at no charge, but with automatic only. Even California Camaro fans could now get the 5.7-liter V-8 in their Z28s again. Camaro Z28 included a front air dam, front fender flares and air louvers, hood scoop with decal, rear spoiler, P225/70R15 raised white-letter tires on body-color 15 x 7 in. sport wheels, and contour bucket seats. Z28's distinctive grille was body-colored with horizontal bars. There was 'Z28' identification on the driver's side of the grille, and a decal on doors. Other Z28 features included black headlamp/taillamp bezels, rear end panel, license plate opening, parking light bezels, sill moldings, window and windshield moldings; plus tri-tone striping on the rear spoiler and lower bodyside, as well as on front air dam and fender flares. Front and rear bumper covers were body-color urethane. Z28's solenoid-activated hood air intake actually drew in air. So did its fender air scoops. Seven Z28 striping colors were available: silver, charcoal, blue, dark gold, gold, red and orange. Base Camaro sport coupes had the 229 V-6, three-speed manual transmission, power steering and brakes, P205/75R14 steel-belted radial tires, front stabilizer bar, multi-leaf rear springs, concealed two-speed wipers, front bucket seats with console, dome light, four-spoke sport steering wheel, day/night mirror, and body-colored bumpers. Berlinetta added whitewall tires and wire wheel covers, a gauge package (including tachometer), dual horns, sport mirrors (left-hand remote), and electric clock; plus moldings for door pillar, upper fender, hood panel, belt and roof drip. Z28 also included heavy-duty cooling, clock, gauge package, and sport mirrors. Standard colors were black, red, white, and bright yellow; plus metallic bright blue, light or dark blue, dark brown, charcoal, gold, maroon, orange or silver. Cloth or vinyl interiors came in beige, black, dark blue, camel, red or silver. Halogen headlamps were a new option. Camaro's basic body dated back to 1970, but downsizing would come for 1982.

hood ornament and front door pull strips. Body colors were beige, black, cream and white; plus metallic light or dark blue, light or medium brown, jade green, light jade green, maroon, light maroon, silver, or champagne. cloth and vinyl interiors came in camel, champagne, dark blue, jade or maroon; custom interiors could also have beige. Power steering was now standard. As before, Malibu came in coupe, sedan or station wagon form, plus a Landau coupe. Halogen headlamps were now optional. Standard engine again was the 229 cu. in. (3.8-liter) V-6, with three-speed manual or optional automatic transmission. Both optional V-8s (267 and 305 cu. in.) came only with automatic. The bigger one was available only in wagons (and in California Malibus). Basic Malibu equipment included power brakes, compact spare tire, front stabilizer bar, concealed two-speed wipers, day/night mirror, and locking glove compartment. Malibu Classic models had dual horns and side window reveal moldings (except coupe). The Malibu Classic Landau coupe added a vinyl roof and body pin striping, plus silver wheel covers. Wagons had wheel opening moldings. Cloth upholstery was standard except for wagons, which used vinyl.

1981 Chevrolet, Malibu Classic four-door sedan (AA)

1981 Chevrolet, Monte Carlo Landau two-door coupe (CP)

MALIBU -- SERIES 1A -- V-6/V-8 -- Although the mid-size Malibu didn't change drastically this year, it got several appearance alterations. The four-door sedan (now marketed as a "sport sedan") got a dramatically restyled, squarish formal roofline and back window section. (The profile looked similar to that of the 1980 Buick Century.) The new grille with prominent horizontal bars had bright upper and lower moldings that extended the full width of the front end. Malibu also had new headlamp bezels, triple-unit taillamps, and side marker lenses. Argent taillamp bezels had black accent. Full wheel covers were restyled, while the revised dash had a new glossy-black appliqué. Also new: high-pressure easy-roll tires, Delco maintenance-free Freedom II battery, and a jack that lifted the car from the side. Front ends held single rectangular headlamps. 'Chevrolet' nameplates were on the lower part of the grille (driver's side), as well as on the decklid (passenger side). 'Malibu' nameplates adorned the rear of quarter panels. Classic Landau coupes had a 'Landau' emblem on the "B" pillar. Malibus had an ornament with Chevrolet crest. Malibu Classic had a stand-up

1981 Chevrolet, Monte Carlo two-door coupe (PH)

MONTE CARLO -- SERIES 1A -- V-6/V-8 -- Monte's A-Special body got a major aerodynamic restyle this year, including a lowered hood and slightly higher rear deck. The new "subtle wedge shape" was claimed to cut wind drag by 10 percent. High-pressure radial tires helped boost gas mileage. The standard automatic transmission had a torque converter clutch controlled by the CCC system, for lockup in third gear. High-pressure (35 psi) tires cut rolling resistance. Also new: Freedom II battery and side-lift frame jack. Coil springs were computer selected to match a specific car's weight and equipment (but softer to compensate for the higher-pressure tires). New cast aluminum wheels were available. Wide rectangular parking lamps moved to the outer ends of the bumper, well below the quad rectangular headlamps and in line with the license plate. Body-color front/rear bumpers blended into fender sides. Wide lower bodyside moldings ran the full car length. Side marker lamps were recessed into lower moldings (front and rear). Cornering lamps were optional this year. A 'Monte Carlo' nameplate was on the front of the front fender. The crosshatch grille with bright chrome bars was arranged in a 6 x 3 pattern of large holes. 'Monte Carlo' script was on the 'B' pillar (or 'Landau' nameplate and crest for Landau coupes). Monte body colors were the same as Malibu. As before, base engine was the 229 cu. in. (3.8-liter) V-6, with optional turbocharged 231 cu. in. V-6 or a 267 cu. in. (4.4-liter) V-8. The 305 V-8 was now sold only in California. Standard equipment was similar to 1980, including automatic transmission, power steering and brakes, P195/75R14 steel-belted radial tires, compact spare tire, dual horns, concealed two-speed wipers, electric clock, locking glove compartment, body-color bumpers, and lighter. Also standard: wide lower bodyside, roof drip, rear quarter window and wheel opening moldings. Monte's Landau coupe added a vinyl roof, dual sport mirrors (driver's remote-controlled), a passenger visor mirror, side window sill moldings, 55/45 front seat, and body pin striping.

1981 Chevrolet, Caprice Classic Landau two-door coupe (CP)

IMPALA/CAPRICE CLASSIC -- SERIES 1B -- V-6/V-8 -- Impala's three-section argent-finished grille this year had strong horizontal bars and recessed vertical divider bars, forming large holes in an 8 x 3 pattern, with bowtie emblem in the center. Parking/turn signal lights were in the bumper. At the rear were three-unit bright-accented taillamps, plus 'Chevrolet' nameplate on deck lid. An 'Impala' nameplate stood on the pillar behind the rear door. Caprice had plain crosshatch grille this year, plus new side marker lamps, header moldings and headlamp bezels. Otherwise, the two looked much the same, though Caprice differed from Impala also in interior trim and option choices. Priced higher, however, Caprice (according to Chevrolet) "speaks of success. But not of excess." Both had tri-section taillamps, but Caprice's were bigger and added narrow vertical backup lamps alongside the license plate. Impala's small square backup lenses sat in each center taillamp section. Fourteen solid body colors were offered: beige, black, cream and white, plus 10 metallics (light and dark blue, light and medium brown, champagne, light jade green, jade green, light maroon, maroon, and silver). Nine two-tone combinations and seven vinyl top colors were available. Cloth interior colors were beige, dark blue, camel, champagne, jade and maroon. Vinyl came in all except beige. Caprice offered "richly elegant" velour upholstery. Full-size models with an optional 305 cu. in. (5.0-liter) V-8 got the new four-speed overdrive automatic transmission this year. The three-speed automatic continued with V-6 powerplants: standard 229 cu. in. (3.8-liter) in coupes and sedans. Wagons carried a standard 267 cu. in. (4.4-liter) V-8. Both transmissions had a computer-controlled torque converter clutch, which substituted a mechanical link for the customary fluid coupling in both third and fourth gears. A 350 cu. in. (5.7-liter) Oldsmobile diesel was offered again in wagons. Other changes included an easy-to-check plastic master cylinder reservoir, reduced-drag front disc brakes, Freedom II battery, new side-lift frame jack, and a "resume speed memory" for the optional cruise control. Corrosion protection at the underbody and fenders was improved, including durable Elpo dip plus frame assemblies immersed in hot-melt wax. A new compact

1981 Chevrolet, Impala two-door coupe (PH)

spare was mounted on a 16 in. wheel. Easy-roll tires were standard, puncture-sealant tires available. Both Impala and Caprice had standard 229 V-6 engine (267 V-8 in wagons) and automatic transmission, plus power brakes and steering, concealed two-speed wipers, color-keyed steering wheel and carpeting, day/night mirror, and locking glove compartment. Impala lacked standard dual horns, an electric clock, wheel opening moldings, stand-up hood ornament, and quiet sound group. The Caprice Classic Landau coupe had wire wheel covers, a vinyl roof, body pin striping, and dual sport mirrors (driver's remote-controlled). Wagons had vinyl upholstery; sedans and coupes cloth.

1981 Chevrolet, Caprice Classic four-door sedan

I.D. DATA: Chevrolet, like all GM passenger cars, got a new 17-symbol Vehicle Identification Number (VIN) this year. As before, it was on the upper left surface of the instrument panel, visible through the windshield. The first symbol indicates country ('1' USA.; '2' Canada). The second symbol denotes manufacturer ('G' General Motors). Symbol three indicates car make ('1' Chevrolet; '7' GM of Canada). Symbol four is restraint system ('A' non-passive; 'B' automatic belts; 'C' inflatable restraint). Symbol five is the car line/series: 'B' Chevette; 'J' Chevette Scooter; 'X' Citation; 'P' Camaro; 'S' Camaro Berlinetta; 'T' Malibu; 'W' Malibu Classic; 'Z' Monte Carlo; 'L' Impala; 'N' Caprice Classic. Symbols six and seven indicate body type: '08' 2-dr. hatchback coupe; '27' 2-dr. notchback coupe; '37' 2-dr. hardtop coupe; '47' 2-dr. hardtop coupe; '87' 2-dr. sport coupe; '68' 4-dr. hatchback sedan; '69' 4-dr. notchback sedan; '35' 4-dr. station wagon. Symbol eight is the engine code: '9' L4-98 2Bbl.; '5' L4-151 2Bbl.; 'X' V6-173 2Bbl.; 'Z' V6-173 H.O.; 'K' V6-229 2Bbl.; 'A' V6-231 2Bbl.; '3' Turbo V6-231 4Bbl.; 'J' V8-267 2Bbl.; 'H' V8-305 4Bbl.; 'L' V8-350 4Bbl.; 'N' Diesel V8-350. Next comes a check digit. Symbol ten indicates model year ('B' 1981). Symbol eleven is assembly plant: 'A' Lakewood; 'B' Baltimore; 'D' Doraville, GA; 'J' Janesville, WI; 'K' Leeds, MO; 'L' Van Nuys, CA; 'N' Norwood, OH; 'R' Arlington, TX; 'S' St. Louis; 'T' Tarrytown, NY; 'W' Willow Run, MI; 'Y' Wilmington, DE; 'Z' Fremont, CA; '1' Oshawa, Ontario; '6' Oklahoma City. The final size digits make up the sequential serial number for output from each assembly plant. Body Number Plates and engine identification code locations were similar to 1980.

CHEVETTE (FOUR)

Model No.	Body/Style No.	Body Type & Seating	Factory Price	Shipping Weight	Prod. Total
1T	B08	2-dr. Hatch Cpe-4P	5255	2000	114,621
1T	B68	4-dr. Hatch Sed-4P	5394	2063	250,616

CHEVETTE SCOOTER (FOUR)

Model No.	Body/Style No.	Body Type & Seating	Factory Price	Shipping Weight	Prod. Total
1T	J08	2-dr. Hatch Cpe-4P	4695	1945	55,211

CITATION (FOUR/V-6)

Model No.	Body/Style No.	Body Type & Seating	Factory Price	Shipping Weight	Prod. Total
1X	X08	2-dr. Hatch Cpe-5P	6270/6395	2404/2459	113,983
1X	X68	4-dr. Hatch Sed-5P	6404/6529	2432/2487	299,396

CAMARO (V-6/V-8)

Model No.	Body/Style No.	Body Type & Seating	Factory Price	Shipping Weight	Prod. Total
1F	P87	2-dr. Spt Cpe-4P	6780/6830	3222/3392	62,614

CAMARO BERLINETTA (V-6/V-8)

Model No.	Body/Style No.	Body Type & Seating	Factory Price	Shipping Weight	Prod. Total
1F	S87	2-dr. Spt Cpe-4P	7576/7626	3275/3445	20,253

CAMARO Z28 (V-8)

Model No.	Body/Style No.	Body Type & Seating	Factory Price	Shipping Weight	Prod. Total
1F	P87	2-dr. Spt Cpe-4P	----/8263	N/A	43,272

MALIBU (V-6/V-8)

Model No.	Body/Style No.	Body Type & Seating	Factory Price	Shipping Weight	Prod. Total
1A	T27	2-dr. Spt Cpe-6P	6498/6548	3037/3199	15,834
1A	T69	4-dr. Sed-6P	6614/6664	3028/3194	60,643
1A	T35	4-dr. Sta Wag-6P	6792/6842	3201/3369	29,387

MALIBU CLASSIC (V-6/V-8)

Model No.	Body/Style No.	Body Type & Seating	Factory Price	Shipping Weight	Prod. Total
1A	W27	2-dr. Spt Cpe-6P	6828/6878	3065/3227	14,255
1A	W27/Z03	2-dr. Lan Cpe-6P	7092/7142	N/A	4,622
1A	W69	4-dr. Sed-6P	6961/7011	3059/3225	80,908
1A	W35	4-dr. Sta Wag-6P	7069/7119	3222/3390	36,798

MONTE CARLO (V-6/V-8)

Model No.	Body/Style No.	Body Type & Seating	Factory Price	Shipping Weight	Prod. Total
1A	Z37	2-dr. Spt Cpe-6P	7299/7349	3102/3228	149,659
1A	Z37/Z03	2-dr. Lan Cpe-6P	8006/8056	N/A	38,191

IMPALA (V-6/V-8)

Model No.	Body/Style No.	Body Type & Seating	Factory Price	Shipping Weight	Prod. Total
1B	L47	2-dr. Spt Cpe-6P	7129/7179	3326/3458	6,067
1B	L69	4-dr. Sedan-6P	7241/7291	3354/3486	60,090
1B	L35	4-dr. Sta Wag-6P	----/7624	----/3897	11,345
1B	L35/AQ4	4-dr. 3S Wag-8P	----/7765	----/ N/A	8,462

CAPRICE CLASSIC (V-6/V-8)

Model No.	Body/Style No.	Body Type & Seating	Factory Price	Shipping Weight	Prod. Total
1B	N47	2-dr. Spt Cpe-6P	7534/7584	3363/3495	9,741
1B	N47/Z03	2-dr. Lan Cpe-6P	7990/8040	N/A	6,615
1B	N69	4-dr. Sedan-6P	7667/7717	3400/3532	89,573
1B	N35	4-dr. Sta Wag-6P	----/7948	----/3940	11,184
1B	N35/AQ4	4-dr. 3S Wag-8P	----/8112	----/ N/A	16,348

FACTORY PRICE AND WEIGHT NOTE: Where two prices and weights are shown, the figure to the left of the slash is for six-cylinder model, to right of slash for V-8 (267 and 305 V-8 were each $50 extra). For Citation, prices and weights to left of slash are four-cylinder, to right for V-6 engine. All models had at least one price rise during the model year, except Chevette, which enjoyed a $100 price cut.

BODY/STYLE NO. NOTE: Some models were actually option packages. Code after slash (e.g., Z03) is the number of the option package that comes with the model listed.

ENGINE DATA: BASE FOUR (Chevette): Inline. Overhead cam. Four-cylinder. Cast iron block and head. Displacement: 97.6 cu. in. (1.6 liters). Bore & stroke: 3.23 x 2.98 in. Compression ratio: 8.6:1. Brake horsepower: 70 at 5200 R.P.M. Torque: 82 lb.-ft. at 2400 R.P.M. Five main bearings. Hydraulic valve lifters. Carburetor: 2Bbl;. Holley 5210C. VIN Code: 9. BASE FOUR (Citation): Inline. Overhead valve. Four-cylinder. Cast iron block. Displacement: 151 cu. in. (2.5 liters). Bore & stroke: 4.00 x 3.00 in. Compression ratio: 8.2:1. Brake horsepower: 84 at 4000 R.P.M. torque: 125 lb.-ft. at 2400 R.P.M. Five main bearings. Hydraulic valve lifters. Carburetor: 2Bbl. Rochester 2SE. Pontiac-built. VIN Code: 5. OPTIONAL V-6 (Citation): 60-degree, overhead-valve V-6. Cast iron block and head. Displacement: 173 cu. in. (2.8 liters). Bore & stroke: 3.50 x 2.99 in. Compression ratio: 8.5:1. Brake horsepower: 110 at 4800 R.P.M. Torque: 145 lb.-ft. at 2400 R.P.M. Four main bearings. Hydraulic valve lifters. Carburetor: 2Bbl. Rochester 2SE. VIN Code: X. HIGH-OUTPUT V-6 (Citation): Same as 173 cu. in. V-6 above except C.R.: 8.9:1. Brake H.P.: 135 at 5400 R.P.M. Torque: 145 lb.-ft. at 2400 R.P.M. VIN Code: Z. BASE V-6 (Camaro, Malibu, Monte Carlo, Impala, Caprice): 90-degree, overhead-valve V-6. Cast iron block and head. Displacement: 229 cu. in. (3.8 liters). Bore & stroke: 3.74 x 3.48 in. Compression ratio: 8.6:1. Brake horsepower: 110 at 4200 R.P.M. Torque: 170 lb.-ft. at 2000 R.P.M. Four main bearings. Hydraulic valve lifters. Carburetor: 2Bbl. Rochester 2ME. VIN Code: K. CALIFORNIA V-6 (for models above): 90-degree, overhead-valve V-6. Cast iron block and head. Displacement: 231 cu. in. (3.8 liters). Bore & stroke: 3.80 x 3.40 in. Compression ratio: 8.0:1. Brake horsepower: 110 at 3800 R.P.M. Torque: 190 lb.-ft. at 1600 R.P.M. Four main bearings. Hydraulic valve lifters. Carburetor: 2Bbl. Rochester E2ME. Buick-built. VIN Code: A. TURBOCHARGED V-6; OPTIONAL (Monte Carlo): Same as 231 cu. in. V-6 above, except 4Bbl. Rochester E4ME carburetor. Brake H.P.: 170 at 4000 R.P.M. Torque: 275 lb.-ft. at 2400 R.P.M. VIN Code: 3. BASE V-8 (Caprice/Impala wagon); OPTIONAL (Camaro, Malibu, Monte Carlo, Impala, Caprice): 90-degree, overhead valve V-8. Cast iron block and head. Displacement: 267 cu. in. (4.4 liters). Bore & stroke: 3.50 x 3.48 in. Compression ratio: 8.3:1. Brake horsepower: 115 at 4000 R.P.M. Torque: 200 lb.-ft. at 2400 R.P.M. Five main bearings. Hydraulic valve lifters. Carburetor: 2Bbl. Rochester 2ME. VIN Code: J. OPTIONAL V-8 (Camaro, Malibu, Monte Carlo, Impala, Caprice): 90-degree, overhead valve V-8. Cast iron block and head. Displacement: 305 cu. in. (5.0 liters). Bore & stroke: 3.74 x 3.48 in. Compression ratio: 8.6:1. Brake horsepower: 150 at 3800 R.P.M. Torque: 240 lb.-ft. at 2400 R.P.M. Five main bearings. Hydraulic valve lifters. Carburetor: 4Bbl. Rochester 4ME. VIN Code: H. BASE V-8 (Camaro Z28): Same as 305 cu. in. V-8 above except: Brake H.P.: 165 at 4000 R.P.M. Torque: 245 lb.-ft. at 2400 R.P.M. M4ME carburetor. OPTIONAL V-8 (Camaro Z28): 90-degree, overhead valve V-8. Cast iron block and head. Displacement: 350 cu. in. (5.7 liters). Bore & stroke: 4.00 x 3.48 in. Compression ratio: 8.2:1. Brake horsepower: 175 at 4000 R.P.M. Torque: 275 lb.-ft. at 2400 R.P.M. Five main bearings. Hydraulic valve lifters. Carburetor: 4Bbl. Rochester 4ME. VIN Code: L. DIESEL V-8; OPTIONAL (Impala/Caprice): 90-degree, overhead valve V-8. Cast iron block and head. Displacement: 350 cu. in. (5.7 liters). Bore & stroke: 4.057 x 3.385 in. Compression ratio: 12.5:1. Brake horsepower: 105 at 3200 R.P.M. Torque: 200 lb.-ft. at 1600 R.P.M. Five main bearings. Hydraulic valve lifters. Fuel injection. Olds-built. VIN Code: N.

CHASSIS DATA: Wheelbase: (Chevette 2-dr) 94.3 in.; (Chvt 4-dr.) 97.3 in.; (Citation) 104.9 in.; (Camaro) 108.0 in.; (Malibu/Monte Carlo) 108.1 in.; (Caprice/Imp) 116.0 in. Overall length: (Chvt 2-dr.) 161.9 in; (Chvt 4-dr.) 164.9 in.; (Cit) 176.7 in.; (Camaro) 197.6 in.; (Malibu) 192.7 in.; (Malibu wag) 193.4 in.; (Monte) 200.4 in.; (Capr/Imp) 212.1 in.; (Capr/Imp wag) 215.1 in. Height: (Chvt) 52.9 in.; (Cit) 53.1 in.; (Camaro) 49.2 in.; (Malibu) 55.7 in.; (Malibu wag) 55.8 in.; (Monte) 53.9 in.; (Capr/Imp cpe) 54.6 in.; (Capr/Imp sed) 55.2 in.; (Capr/Imp wag) 57.1 in. Width: (Chvt) 61.8 in.; (Cit) 68.3 in.; (Camaro) 74.5 in.; (Malibu) 72.3 in.; (Malibu wag) 71.9 in.; (Monte) 71.8 in.; (Capr/Imp) 75.3 in.; (Capr/Imp wag) 79.3 in. Front Tread: (Chvt) 51.2 in.: (Cit) 58.7 in.; (Camaro) 61.3 in.; (Camaro Berlinetta) 61.6 in.; (Malibu/Monte) 58.5 in.; (Capr/Imp) 61.8 in.; (Capr/Imp wag) 62.2 in. Rear Tread: (Chvt) 51.2 in.; (Cit) 57.0 in.; (Camaro) 60.0 in.; (Camaro Berlinetta) 60.3 in.; (Malibu/Monte) 57.8 in.; (Capr/Imp) 60.8 in.; (Capr/Imp wag) 64.1 in. Standard Tires: (Chvt) P155/80R13 GBR; (Cit) P185/80R13 GBR; (Camaro) P205/75R14 SBR; (Camaro Z28) P225/70R15 WLT; (Malibu) P185/75R14 GBR; (Malibu wag) P195/75R14 GBR; (Monte) P195/75R14 SBR; (Imp/Capr) P205/75R15 SBR; (Imp/Capr wag) P225/75R15 SBR.

TECHNICAL: Transmission: Three-speed manual transmission standard on Camaro V-6. Gear ratios: (1st) 3.50:1; (2nd) 1.89:1; (3rd) 1.00:1; (Rev) 3.62:1 Four-speed floor shift standard on Chevette: (1st) 3.75:1; (2nd) 2.16:1; (3rd) 1.38:1; (4th) 1.00:1; (Rev) 3.82:1. Citation four-speed floor shift: (1st) 3.53:1; (2nd) 1.95:1; (3rd) 1.24:1; (4th) 0.81:1; (Rev) 3.42:1. Four-speed on Camaro V8305: (1st) 3.42:1; (2nd) 2.28:1; (3rd) 1.45:1; (4th) 1.00:1; (Rev) 3.51:1. Three-speed Turbo Hydra-matic standard on Monte Carlo and Caprice/Impala, optional on others. Gear ratios: (1st) 2.52:1; (2nd) 1.52:1; (3rd) 1.00:1; (Rev) 1.93:1 except Caprice/Impala V6231/V8305, Camaro V6-229 and Monte V6-231 ratios: (1st) 2.74:1; (2nd) 1.57:1; (3rd) 1.00:1; (Rev) 2.07:1 Base Chevette automatic trans.: (1st) 2.40:1; (2nd) 1.48:1; (3rd) 1.00:1; (Rev) 1.92:1. Citation auto. trans.: (1st) 2.84:1; (2nd) 1.60:1; (3rd) 1.00:1; (Rev) 2.07:1. Standard final drive ratio: (Chevette) 3.70:1; (Scooter) 3.36:1; (Citation) 3.32:1 w/manual, 2.84:1 w/auto.; (Camaro V-6) 2.73:1; (Camaro V-8) 2.56:1; (Camaro V8350) 3.08:1; (Z28) 3.42:1 w/4spd; (Malibu) 2.73:1 w/manual and V-6, 2.41:1 w/auto. and V-6, 2.29:1 w/V-8; (Monte V-6) 2.41:1; (Monte V8-267) 2.73:1; (Monte V8-305) 2.29:1; (Caprice/Imp V-6) 2.73:1; (Caprice/Imp V-8) 2.41:1. Steering: (Chevette/Citation) rack and pinion; (others) recirculating ball. Suspension/Body: same as 1980. Brakes: Front disc, rear drum. Fuel tank: (Chvt) 12.5 gal.: (Cit) 14 gal.: (Camaro) 21 gal.: (Malibu) 18.1 gal.: (Monte) 18.1 gal.: (Capr/Imp) 25 gal.: (Capr/Imp wag) 22 gal.

DRIVETRAIN OPTIONS: Engines: 173 cu. in., 2Bbl. V-6: Citation ($125). Turbo 231 cu. in., 4Bbl. V-6: Monte ($750). 267 cu. in., 2Bbl. V-8: Camaro/Malibu/Monte/Imp/Caprice ($50). 305 cu. in., 4Bbl. V-8: Camaro/Malibu/Monte/Imp/Capr ($50); Imp/Capr wag (NC). 350 cu. in., 4Bbl. V-8: Z28 (NC). Diesel 350 cu. in. V-8: Imp/Capr wag ($695). Transmission/Differential: Four-speed manual shift: Camaro ($141). Three-speed automatic: Chevette ($335); Citation/Camaro/Malibu ($349); Camaro Z28 ($61). Four-speed overdrive automatic trans.: Imp/Capr ($162). Limited-slip differential: Camaro/Malibu/Monte ($67); Imp/Capr ($71). Performance axle ratio: Camaro/Malibu/Monte ($19). Power Accessories: Power brakes: Chvt/Cit ($79). Power steering: Chvt ($164); Cit ($168). Suspension: F40 H.D. susp.: Cit/Malibu/Monte/Imp/Capr ($23) F41 sport susp.: Chvt ($37); Cit ($39); Camaro ($33); Malibu/Monte/Imp/Capr cpe/sed ($43). Inflatable rear shock absorbers: Imp/Capr ($57). Other: H.D. cooling ($34-$61). Engine block heater: Imp/Capr wag ($16). H.D. alternator (63-amp): Malibu ($6-$34). H.D. alternator (70-amp): Cit ($11-$45); Monte/Imp/Capr ($32-$66). H.D. battery ($20 exc. diesel ($40). California emission system ($46).

CHEVETTE CONVENIENCE/APPEARANCE OPTIONS: Comfort/Convenience: Air condition ($531). Rear defogger, electric ($102). Tinted glass ($70). Comfortilt steering wheel ($78). Tachometer ($70). Electric clock ($23). Cigarette lighter: Scooter ($8). Intermittent wipers ($41). Rear wiper/washer ($100). Quiet sound group ($40-$52). Lighting and Mirrors: Halogen headlamps ($36). Aux. lighting: Chvt ($42-$43). Twin sport mirrors, left remote ($43). Driver's remote sport mirror ($29). Entertainment: AM radio: Scooter ($78). AM/FM radio ($64); Scooter ($142). AM/FM stereo radio ($100). Rear speaker ($19). Exterior Trim: Deluxe exterior: wheel opening, side window and rocker panel moldings ($118-$125). Two-tone paint ($116). Sport stripes ($78). Bodyside moldings: Scooter ($42). Side window reveal moldings ($69-$76). Door edge guards ($13-$21). Roof carrier ($74). Interior Trim/Upholstery: Cloth bucket seats ($16-$28). Custom bucket seats: cloth ($249); vinyl ($221). Rear seat delete ($50 credit). Color-keyed floor mats ($23). Wheels and Tires: Rally wheel trim ($52). P175/7013 SBR BSW: Chvt ($60); Scooter ($108). P175/7013 SBR WSW: Chvt ($108); Scooter ($155). P175/7013 SBR WLTL: Chvt ($124); Scooter ($172).

CITATION CONVENIENCE/APPEARANCE OPTIONS: Option Packages: X-11 sport equipment pkg. ($1498). Deluxe exterior pkg. ($117-$151). Quiet sound/rear decor pkg. ($75). Comfort/Convenience: Air cond. ($585). Rear defogger, electric ($107). Cruise control w/resume ($123). Tinted glass ($75). Sport steering wheel (NC to $21). Comfortilt steering wheel ($81). Power windows ($140-$195). Remote swing-out windows ($95). Power door locks ($92-$132). Gauge pkg. w/clock ($73). Special instruments incl. tachometer ($114). Electric clock ($23). Intermit-

tent wipers ($41). Lighting, Horns and Mirrors: Halogen headlamps ($34). Aux. lighting ($43). Dual horns ($10). Driver's remote mirror ($19). Dual sport mirrors, left remote ($47). Entertainment: AM/FM radio ($64). AM/FM stereo radio ($100). Rear speaker ($19). Dual rear speakers ($28); incl. w/stereo radio. Dual rear speakers ($28); incl. w/stereo radio. Windshield antenna ($10). Power antenna ($47). Radio delete ($51 credit). Exterior Trim. Removable sunroof ($246). Two-tone paint ($155) incl. pin striping and bodyside moldings. Bodyside pin striping ($34). Roof carrier ($90). Bodyside moldings ($44). Door edge guards ($13-$21). Side window reveal moldings ($41-$50). Bumper guards ($48). Bumper rub strips ($43). Interior Trim/Upholstery: Console ($86). Reclining driver or passenger seatback ($41-$69). Sport cloth bench seat ($28). Custom cloth or vinyl bench seat ($391). Vinyl bucket seats ($91-$116). Sport cloth bucket seats ($119-$144). Custom cloth or vinyl bucket seats ($482-$507). Color-keyed mats ($25). Wheels and Tires: Full wheel covers ($46). Wire wheel covers ($117-$163). Wheel trim rings ($50). Rally wheel trim ($36-$82). P185/80R13 GBR WSW ($51). P185/80R13 SBR BSW ($54). P185/80R13 SBR WSW ($105). P205/70R13 SBR WSW ($206). P205/70R13 SBR WLT ($222).

CAMARO/MALIBU/MONTE CARLO CONVENIENCE/ APPEARANCE OPTIONS: Option Packages: estate equipment: Malibu wag ($271). Interior decor/quiet sound group: Camaro ($67). Quiet sound group: Malibu ($54). Security pkg.: Malibu wag ($39). Comfort/Convenience: Air cond.: Camaro ($560); Malibu/Monte ($585). Rear defogger, electric ($107). Cruise control w/resume ($132). Tinted glass ($75). Comfortilt steering wheel ($81). Six-way power driver's seat: Malibu/Monte ($173). Power windows: Camaro/Monte ($140); Malibu ($140-$195). Power door locks: Malibu ($93-$132); Camaro/Monte ($93). Power trunk release: Monte ($27). Electric clock: base Camaro, Malibu ($23). Gauge pkg. w/tach: base Camaro ($118). Gauge pkg. w/clock and trip odometer: Malibu ($80). Gauge pkg. w/trip odometer: Monte ($55). Intermittent wipers ($41). Lighting, Horns and Mirrors: Halogen headlamps: Camaro/Malibu ($36). Halogen high-beams: Monte ($27). Cornering lamps: Monte ($48). Aux. lighting: Camaro ($33-$39); Malibu ($33-$59); Monte ($33). Dual horns: Camaro, base Malibu ($10). Remote-control driver's mirror: Malibu/Monte ($19). Twin sport mirrors (left remote): base Camaro, Malibu/Monte ($47). Twin remote sport mirrors: Malibu ($73); Monte ($26-$73). Visor vanity mirror: Monte ($6). Lighted visor mirror: Monte ($36-$42). Entertainment: AM radio ($90). AM/FM radio ($142). AM/FM stereo radio ($178). Stereo 8-track tape player with AM/FM stereo radio ($252). Cassette player with AM/FM stereo radio ($264). AM/FM stereo radio w/CB ($487). Rear speaker ($19). Dual rear speakers: Malibu/Monte ($28). Windshield antenna ($25); include. w/ radios. Power antenna ($47). Exterior Trim: Removable glass roof panels: Camaro/Monte ($695). Power sky roof: Monte ($561). Vinyl roof: Malibu cpe ($115);

Malibu sed ($124); Monte ($130). Cabriolet vinyl roof: Malibu ($171). Padded opera roof: Monte ($232). Rear spoiler: Camaro ($60). Style trim pkg.: Camaro ($76). Two-tone paint: Malibu ($71-$121): Monte ($134-$188). Bodyside moldings: Camaro ($44). Deluxe bodyside moldings: Malibu/Monte ($53). Door edge guards: Camaro/Malibu ($13-$21). Wheel opening moldings: Malibu cpe/sed ($25). Side window sill moldings: Monte ($34). Side window reveal moldings: Malibu ($44). Roof drip moldings: Camaro ($25). Bodyside pin striping: Malibu ($50); Monte ($54). Rear window air deflector: Malibu wag ($32). Roof carrier: Malibu ($95). Bumper rub strips: Malibu ($43). Bumper guards, front/rear: Malibu ($48). Interior Trim/Upholstery: Custom interior (55/45 seating, center armrest, custom door panels and seats): Monte ($201-$387). Custom door/quarter trim panels: Monte ($27). Console: Malibu cpe/sed, Monte ($86). Vinyl bench seat: Malibu cpe/sed, Monte ($28). Cloth bench seat: Malibu wag ($28). Custom vinyl bench seat: Malibu wag ($63). Cloth 55/45 seating: Malibu ($181-$241); Monte ($208). Vinyl 55/45 seating: Malibu ($209-$241); Monte ($236); Monte Landau ($28). Vinyl bucket seats: Malibu cpe/sed ($91); Monte ($118). Cloth bucket seats: Camaro ($28); Malibu cpe/sed ($91); Monte ($118). Custom vinyl bucket seats: base Camaro ($322). Custom cloth bucket seats: Berlinetta ($28); base Camaro ($350). Adj. driver's seatback: Camaro ($23). Color-keyed mats ($25). Deluxe load-floor carpet; Malibu wag ($74). Deluxe trunk trim: Monte ($44). Wheels and Tires: Aluminum wheels: Camaro ($180-$331); Monte ($264-$319). Custom styled 14x7 wheels: Camaro ($151). Rally wheels: Camaro ($99); Malibu ($49-$95); Monte ($49); Malibu Classic Landau (NC). Full wheel covers: Camaro/Malibu ($46). Sport wheel covers (silver or gold): Malibu ($55-$101). Wire wheel covers: Malibu ($80-$181); Monte ($80-$135). Wheel cover locks: Berlinetta/Malibu/Monte ($34). P185/75R14 GBR WSW: Malibu cpe/sed ($48). P195/75R14 GBR WSW: Malibu wag ($51). P195/75R14 SBR WSW: Malibu cpe/sed ($125); Malibu wag ($102); Monte ($51). P205/75R14 SBR WSW: Camaro ($54). P205/75R14 SBR WLT: Camaro ($69); Berlinetta ($15). P205/70R14 SBR WSW: Monte ($107); Malibu cpe/sed ($183). P205/70R14 SBR WLT: Malibu cpe/sed ($198).

IMPALA/CAPRICE CONVENIENCE/APPEARANCE OPTIONS: Option Packages: Estate equipment: wag ($271). Value appearance group: bodyside and wheel opening moldings, full wheel covers ($93). Comfort/Convenience: Air cond. ($625). Comfortron autotemp air cond. ($708). Rear defogger, blower: cpe/sed ($59). Rear defogger, electric ($107). cruise control w/resume ($135). Tinted glass ($87). Comfortilt steering wheel ($81). Power door locks ($93-$132). Six-way power driver's seat ($173). Power windows ($143-$211). Power trunk release ($27). Power tailgate lock: wag ($43). Electric clock: Imp ($25). Digital clock: Imp ($59); Caprice ($36). Gauge pkg. w/trip odometer ($56). Intermittent wipers ($41). Quiet sound group:

Imp ($58). Lighting, Horns and Mirrors: Halogen high-beam headlamps ($27). Cornering lamps ($48). Aux. lighting ($36-$57). Dual horns: Imp ($10). Driver's remote mirror ($19). Dual remote mirrors ($58). Dual sport mirrors, left remote ($47). Dual remote body-color sport mirrors ($26-$73). Visor vanity mirror ($6). Lighted visor mirror ($42). Entertainment: AM radio ($90). AM/FM radio ($142). AM/FM stereo radio ($178). Stereo 8-track tape player with AM/FM stereo radio ($252). Cassette player with AM/FM stereo ($264). AM/FM stereo with CB and power antenna ($487). Rear speaker ($19). Dual rear speakers ($28). Power antenna ($47). Windshield antenna ($25); incl. w/radios. Exterior Trim: Power sky roof: cpe/sed ($650). Vinyl roof ($142). Roof carrier: wag ($119). Two-tone paint ($58). Custom two-tone ($124). Pin striping ($34). Color-keyed bodyside moldings ($44). Door edge guards ($13-$21). Wheel opening moldings: Imp ($25). Bumper rub strips, front/rear ($58). Bumper guards ($54). Interior Trim/Upholstery: Vinyl bench seat: cpe/sed ($28). Cloth bench seat: wag ($28). Cloth 50/50 seat ($222-$268). Vinyl 50/50 seat ($240-$268). Custom cloth 50/50 seat: cpe ($400); sed ($424). Deluxe load-floor carpet: wag ($77). Deluxe cargo area carpet: wag ($114). Color-keyed mats: front ($15); rear ($10). Deluxe trunk trim ($55). Wheel covers: Full wheel covers ($46). Sport wheel covers: Imp ($102); Caprice ($56). Custom wheel covers: Imp ($121); Capr ($75) Wire wheel covers: Capr ($135) Wire wheel cover locks ($34). Coupe/Sedan Tires: P205/75R15 SBR WSW ($54). P215/75R15 SBR WSW ($85). P225/70R15 SBR WSW ($132). Wagon Tires: P225/75R15 SBR WSW ($58). Puncture-sealant tires ($85-$105).

HISTORY: Introduced: Sept. 25, 1980. Model year production (U.S.): 1,582,575 (incl. Corvettes, but does not incl. 20,363 Acadians or early '82 Cavaliers). Of total production for U.S. market, 744,977 were four-cylinder, 590,984 sixes, and 392,632 V-8s. A total of 49,791 diesels and 3,027 turbos were installed. Calendar year production: 1,307,526 (incl. 27,990 Corvettes and 18,098 Acadians, but not incl. 139,837 early '82 Cavaliers). Calendar year sales by U.S. dealers: 1,442,281, for a 23.3 percent market share. Model year sales by U.S. dealers: 1,522,536 (incl. 33,414 Corvettes, but not incl. 43,855 early 1982 Cavaliers).

Historical Footnotes: Sales had been expected to take an upturn for 1981, but fell far short of expectations, dropping by about 265,000 for the model year (even including early '82 Cavaliers). And 1980 had hardly been a big year either. Only Chevette sold better in 1981 than 1980 (but only slightly). Citation had been the company's best seller for 1980, setting a first-year sales record for General Motors. But second-year sales slipped along with the other models. Full-size Chevrolets sold so poorly that there was speculation they would soon be dropped. Even with sagging sales, prices were raised at mid-year. Incentives (including rebates and reduced finance rates) were announced, but failed to bring in enough customers.

1982

Two all-new models (subcompact Cavalier and compact Celebrity) and a major restyle highlighted 1982. Biggest news was the downsized Camaro, even racier than before, which debuted with the family-size Celebrity in January 1982. Some hefty price increases arrived this year, too. Opening prices for the restyled Camaros were $976 to $1810 higher than 1981 equivalents. The remaining Malibu models rose by well over a thousand dollars. Unlike some years in this era, though, Chevrolets endured only a $15 price hike during the model year. On the mechanical front, Pontiac's four-cylinder engine (used in Citation, Camaro and Celebrity) added fuel injection. The fact that Malibu now wore a grille similar to full-size models helped fuel rumors that the big Chevrolets were doomed. But reports of their imminent demise proved premature.

1982 Chevrolet, Chevette four-door hatchback sedan (AA)

CHEVETTE -- SERIES 1T -- FOUR -- Both gas and diesel engines were offered on the subcompact Chevette this year. The 1.8-liter four-cylinder diesel, coupled to a new five-speed manual transmission, rated 40 MPG city and 55 MPG highway in EPA estimates. It was offered under both coupe and sedan hoods (but not Scooter), priced as a separate model rather than an option. The overhead-cam, 51-horsepower diesel had actually became available late in the 1981 model year, in limited numbers. Built by Isuzu, it had a cross-flow cylinder head and lightweight Bosch distributor-type fuel pump/injection system. The low-budget Scooter came in four-door hatchback form this year, as well as the carryover two-door (priced just under $5000). The four-door cost $241 more. Standard gasoline engine was the 1.6-liter four, with four-speed manual transmission. A new five-speed gearbox was also available, as well as automatic. The five-speed had been added as a late '81 option. Compression ratio of the gas engine rose from 8.6:1 in 1981 to 9.2:1 this year, as a redesigned cylinder head forced the air/fuel mixture into the combustion chamber with a more efficient swirling motion. Standard equipment (except on

Scooters) included an AM radio, color-keyed instrument panel, reclining front bucket seats, transmission floor control, and sport steering wheel. Chevettes did not change in appearance.

1982 Chevrolet, Cavalier two-door hatchback coupe (CP)

1982 Chevrolet, Cavalier Cadet four-door sedan (CH)

CAVALIER -- SERIES 1J -- FOUR -- Introduced on May 21, 1981, as an early '82 model, the new front-drive four-passenger Chevrolet was described as subcompact on the outside, with compact roominess inside. It was also called a "high-content vehicle" with an ample load of standard equipment, including radio, power brakes, reclining bucket seats, stabilizer bar, and remote trunk/hatch/tailgate release. Four models were offered: two-door and four-door sedans, two-door hatchback, and four-door wagon. Cavaliers came in three series: low-budget Cadet, base, and CL. Sole engine at first was a transverse-mounted 112 cu. in. (1.8-liter) four, rated 88 horsepower, with four-speed (overdrive) manual transmission. EPA ratings reached 30 MPG (city). A 2.0-liter four was announced, but arrived later. Cavaliers had a low, horizontal-style grille with bowtie emblem in the solid panel above. Single recessed rectangular headlamps flanked vertical park/signal lamps. Taillamps were split into two sections by a horizontal divider. Base Cavaliers had integrated bright bumper systems with black/argent rub strips; Plastisol R lower body stone chip protection; black wipers; amber rear turn signal lamps; bright hood molding and grille bars; a styled black outside mirror; body-color wraparound bumper end caps; and bodyside moldings. Rally wheels held trim rings. 'Cavalier' nameplates were on front fenders. Hatchbacks came with a flush-mount back window, soft-fascia front-end panel, wide-base Rally wheels, and flush-mount windshield; plus black grille, headlamp and parking lamp bezels. Body colors were white, black, light yellow, beige and red; plus metallic silver, light or dark blue, bright blue, light or dark jade, gold, maroon, or charcoal. After its first half-season, Cavalier got several powertrain changes (mainly in axle ratios and electronic control module) by the time the 1982 model year began. Carburetion and ignition calibration for models with air conditioning was revised to improve cold startups and low-speed response, using a new microchip. Models with air conditioning and automatic transmission got a 3.18:1 final drive ratio, while manual-shift Cavaliers switched from 2.96:1 to 3.32:1 after the start of the full model year. Automatic transmissions were modified too. As the model year began, Cavalier also got a full-width, three-passenger back seat (with optional split folding back), becoming a five-passenger vehicle rather than four. A bigger (2.0-liter), 90-horsepower four was announced, but arrived later. Cavalier's standard equipment included four-speed manual transaxle, P175/80R13 GBR tires on rally steel wheels, AM radio, electric side/rear window defoggers, lighter, digital clock, reclining front bucket seats, trip odometer, console, day/night mirror, color-keyed carpeting, locking glove compartment, front stabilizer bar, bodyside moldings, and bumper rub strips. Hatchbacks also had a gauge package and fold-down rear seat; wagons the fold-down seat and air deflector. Cavalier CL added power steering, AM/FM radio, whitewall tires, sport wheel covers, sport mirrors (left remote), tinted glass, rear stabilizer bar, gauges, intermittent wipers, leather-wrapped steering wheel, and halogen headlamps. CL hatchbacks had a tachometer and rear wiper/washer.

1982 Chevrolet, Citation two-door coupe (CH)

CITATION -- SERIES 1X -- FOUR/V-6 -- Electronic fuel injection became standard this year on the base 151 cu. in. (2.5-liter) four, supplied by Pontiac. This produced an estimated 4 MPG mileage increase. Also new were high-pressure (35 psi) easy-roll tires, geometry-tuned suspension, and a relocated rack-and-pinion steering mount. Citation again came in two-door and four-door hatchback form, along with an H11 five-passenger coupe. The high-performance two-door X11 package was offered again, including the HO 600 engine (a 135-horsepower version of the 2.8-liter V-6) and modified suspension components. Citation had a new horizontal grille for 1982, shaped similar to the 1981 crosshatch version. Eight body colors were new. New vinyl upholstery went on standard seats. Interiors came

in three new trim colors: charcoal, jadestone, and red-wood. New options included automatic speed control for use with manual transmission. The automatic transmission got a lockup torque converter clutch for high gear. The X11 sport equipment package included the high-output V-6 engine, power brakes, sport mirrors, rear spoiler, bucket seats, P215/60R14 tires on aluminum wheels, special instruments, sport steering wheel, F41 sport suspension, and bumper rub strips.

1982 Chevrolet, Camaro Berlinetta two-door coupe (CH)

1982 Chevrolet, Camaro Z28 two-door coupe

CAMARO -- SERIES 1F -- FOUR/V-6/V-8 -- An all-new Camaro arrived late in the model year, still rear-wheel drive but in a lighter-weight fastback form. In Chevrolet's words, the new version "captures the essence of the contemporary American performance expression." Offered again in three models, but with a contemporary aerodynamic shape and "aircraft-inspired interior," Camaro weighed some 470 pounds less than in 1981, though it was still no lightweight. The new body was nearly 10 inches shorter, riding a 101 inch wheelbase (down from 108). The fuel filler door was now on the quarter panel (driver's side), with a hatch release lock behind the license plate. Camaros had a new lift-up hatch back window. Standard Sport Coupe engine was now Pontiac's 151 cu. in. (2.5-liter), 90-horsepower "Iron Duke" four with electronic fuel injection. Options: a variant of Citation's 173 cu. in. (2.8-liter) V-6 rated 102 horsepower, or a four-barrel carbureted 305 cu. in. (5.0-liter) V-8 that produced 145 horsepower. The V-6 was standard in Berlinetta; V-8 standard in Z28. But the Z28 could also have an optional Cross-Fire fuel-injected 305 V-8, rated 165 horsepower, for an extra $450. That version was marked by a 'Cross Fire Injection' decal below the 'Z28' identifier (just behind the front wheel housing), plus operating air inlets. Camaro's optional three-speed automatic transmission had a torque converter lockup clutch. A four-speed manual gearbox was now standard on the base Camaro, so the old three-speed was gone for good. Four-wheel disc brakes were now available with V-8 engines. Inside, a new console held glove box, parking brake lever, and controls for heater, optional stereo radio and air conditioning. The instrument panel was black-finished to minimize reflections. Twin speedometer needles showed both MPH and kilometers per hour. Interior space was similar to before, even though outside dimensions had shrunk. The rear seat's backrest folded down, turning the rear section into a cargo area, accessible through the new hatch. For an extra $611, Z28s could have a new "Conteur" seat option from Lear-Siegler, with six adjustments (backrest bolster, thigh support, cushion bolster, lumbar and recliner). A six-way power seat was now optional on all models. Each model had its own styling features, including specific front air dam and rear fascia. All Camaros had deeply recessed quad rectangular headlamps and tri-color wraparound taillamps (not far removed from prior designs). Camaro's fastback profile included a compound S-shaped glass hatch. The flush-mounted windshield's 62-degree rake helped produce a 0.368 drag coefficient--one of the lowest ever tested by GM. Z28's front end had no upper grille opening, while its "ground effects" air dams reached lower to the ground. Z28s also rode special five-spoke aluminum wheels. Body colors for 1982 were white, silver, black, red, maroon, charcoal, light or dark blue, light or dark jade, gold, or dark gold. The new Camaro's body was unitized construction, but with bolt-on front sheet metal. Rear coils replaced the old leaf springs. The rear suspension now consisted of a longitudinal torque tube, short control arms ahead of the solid axle, and lateral track rod. Front suspension used modified MacPherson struts with coil springs and stabilizer bar. Z28s and the F41 sport suspension added a link-type rear stabilizer bar. Base Sport Coupe standard equipment included four-speed manual shift, power brakes and steering, front stabilizer bar, dual black sport mirrors, black windshield molding, concealed wipers, body-color wheels with hubcaps and P195/75R14 GBR tires, reclining front bucket seats, and a day/night mirror. Berlinetta added P205/70R14 SBR tires, body pin strip-

ing, body-color sport mirrors, black-accented lower body (with stripe), gold-accented aluminum spoke wheels, and higher-level acoustic package. Camaro Z28 equipment included five-spoke aluminum wheels (gold or charcoal accented) with P215/65R15 white-letter tires, a rear stabilizer bar, specially-tuned suspension, dual mufflers and tailpipes, body-color sport mirrors, front air dam, "ground effects" rocker molding area, and rear deck spoiler. Twin air scoops rode the special Z28 hood. A total of 6,360 Indy 500 Commemorative Editions of the Z28 were built this year, marking the use of a Camaro as Indy pace car. All the replicas had a silver/blue body, Indy 500 logos, red-accented silver aluminum wheels and Goodyear Eagle GT white-letter tires. Blue cloth/silver vinyl interiors held the Lear-Siegler Conteur driver's seat, along with special instruments, leather-wrapped steering wheel and AM/FM stereo radio. Chevrolet dealers were entitled to order one special edition apiece.

1982 Chevrolet, Celebrity two-door coupe (PH)

1982 Chevrolet, Celebrity four-door sedan (PH)

CELEBRITY -- SERIES 1A -- FOUR/V-6 -- The new front-wheel drive family sedan was designed to combine small-car economy with "big-car ride, comfort and style." When buying a Celebrity, declared Chevrolet general manager Robert D. Lund, customers wouldn't find that "they sacrificed comfort, space and prestige" for the sake of economy. Though roughly the same size inside as the Malibu it soon would replace, Celebrity weighed some 500 pounds less and stood a foot shorter in overall length. Wheelbase was identical to Citation's, but Celebrity measured almost a foot longer (188.3 inches overall). Celebrity came in two-door and four-door sedan form, with three five-passenger interior trim levels (base, CS and CL). The wedge-shape design (low nose and high deck) resulted from extensive wind-tunnel testing. Celebrity's 0.38 aero drag coefficient was the lowest rating ever for a mass-produced GM sedan. Celebrity wasn't introduced until after the first of the year, on January 14, 1982. Standard powertrain was a fuel-injected 151 cu. in. (2.5-liter) four-cylinder engine with three-speed automatic transaxle, which produced EPA estimates of 25 MPG city and 40 highway. Both gas and diesel V-6 engines were announced: a 173 cu. in. (2.8-liter) gasoline model and 4.3-liter diesel. But the diesel's appearance was delayed for a year. Gasoline models had an on-board computer system that included self-diagnostics. Celebrity's front end was similar to Cavalier, with a solid panel above the low grille; but the 8 x 4 hole crosshatch grille held a bowtie emblem in its center. Celebrity also carried quad rectangular headlamps over horizontal park/signal lamps. Wide tri-section taillamps stretched from license plate opening to quarter panel, divided by a horizontal bar. Celebrity came in a dozen solid colors plus six two-tones. Solids were white, light and dark blue, light and dark metallic jadestone or sandstone, light and dark metallic redwood, slate gray, silver metallic, and charcoal metallic. Two-tones were slate gray/silver metallic; dark blue/light blue metallic; dark blue/pastel sandstone; light/dark jadestone metallic; pastel sandstone/light redwood metallic; or dark/light redwood metallic. Cloth or vinyl interior trim came in slate gray, dark blue, jadestone, sandstone, doeskin and redwood. Standard equipment included the four-cylinder engine, power brakes, power rack-and-pinion steering, push-button AM radio, maintenance-free battery, front stabilizer bar, chrome bumpers with black rub strips and body-color end caps, and P185/80R13 GBR tires with full wheel covers. Also standard: black side window frames, bright drip and bodyside moldings, front bench seat with fixed armrest, side window defoggers, day/night mirror, and locking glove compartment.

1982 Chevrolet, Malibu Classic station wagon (CH)

1982 Chevrolet, Malibu Classic four-door sedan

MALIBU CLASSIC -- SERIES 1A -- V-6/V-8 -- This year's Malibu had a distinctive crosshatch grille similar to Caprice, flanked by quad rectangular headlamps that stood over horizontal quad park/signal lamps. A dozen body colors were available, with either cloth or vinyl interiors. A four-door sport sedan and four-door wagon were the only models. Base engine was the 229 cu. in. (3.8-liter) V-6. But Malibus could also have either the 267 cu. in. (4.4-liter) or 305 cu. in. (5.0-liter) gas V-6, or a choice of diesels: 4.3-liter V-6 or the big 5.7-liter V-8 from Oldsmobile. The small diesel, which arrived later in the model year, was Chevrolet's first V-6 version (actually produced by Oldsmobile). It had roller hydraulic valve lifters, a serpentine belt system, venturi-shaped prechamber, and a torque-pulse compensator for smoother power flow. The diesel had aluminum cylinder heads, intake manifold, water outlet and oil pump body. Base Malibus were gone, leaving only the Classic, in only sedan and station wagon form. Standard equipment included automatic transmission, power brakes and steering, notchback front bench seats with folding armrests, dual horns, front stabilizer bar, full wheel covers, and stand-up hood ornament. Bodies displayed a bright wide upper grille molding, bright back window and windshield reveal moldings, bright sill and roof drip moldings, and wide wheel opening moldings. Circular instrumentation was similar to Monte Carlo's. Inside were a lighter, dome light and day/night mirror. Sedans had bright decklid and end cap moldings, plus black-accented bright taillamp trim.

1982 Chevrolet, Monte Carlo two-door coupe (CH)

MONTE CARLO -- SERIES 1A -- V-6/V-8 -- A finely-textured crosshatch grille set off Monte's front end this year, divided into three sections by two horizontal bars. Quad rectangular headlamps sat alongside the grille, but wide parking lamps were recessed low in the bumper. The body carried on Monte's "subtle wedge shape," now available in a dozen solid body colors and six two-tones. The Landau coupe was dropped, leaving only one coupe model. Interiors could have either cloth or vinyl trim. A passenger-side mirror was now standard, and a fixed-mast radio antenna replaced the former windshield antenna. Monte rode high-pressure (35 psi) tires and stopped with low-drag brakes. Standard engine remained the 229 cu. in. (3.8-liter) V-6. Two gasoline V-8s were also available: 267 and 305 cu. in. So were a pair of diesels: either the new V-6 or the big Oldsmobile V-8. The turbo V-6 was out. Montes had standard automatic transmission, power brakes and steering, plus P195/75R14 SBR tires on 6 in. wheels. Also standard: body-color bumpers, bright roof drip and windshield reveal moldings, twin bright outside mirrors, bright lower bodyside and quarter window reveal moldings, a stand-up hood ornament, full wheel covers, wheel opening moldings, bright decklid and end cap moldings, full-width front seat with folding armrest, dome light, day/night mirror, dual horns, lighter, and trunk mat.

1982 Chevrolet, Impala four-door sedan (CP)

IMPALA/CAPRICE CLASSIC -- SERIES 1B -- V-6/V-8 -- Full-size Chevrolets looked about the same for 1982, but came in fewer models. The Caprice Landau coupe and Impala sport coupe were dropped. Only the three-seat Caprice wagon was offered, along with the sport coupe and four-door sedan. Impala's lineup included the sedan and twin wagons. Oldsmobile's 350 cu. in. (5.7-liter) diesel V-8 was now available on all models, not just the station wagon. Standard engine was the 229 cu. in. (3.8-liter) V-6, with three-speed automatic. Wagons had the 267 cu. in. (4.4-liter) V-8, which cost $70 extra on other models. Optional four-speed overdrive automatic boosted gas mileage on the optional 267 cu. in. (4.4-liter) or 305 (5.0-liter) gas engines. Impala had an argent grille, Caprice a chrome-plated grille. Impala lacked a stand-up hood ornament and had thinner rocker moldings. Its front side marker lenses stood slightly back from fender tips, while Caprice's wrapped around. Standard equipment included three-speed automatic transmission, power brakes and steering, two-speed wipers, front stabilizer bar, bright windshield reveal and roof drip moldings, bright window reveal and frame moldings, day/night mirror, lighter, and one-piece carpeting. Caprice also included full wheel covers, wheel opening moldings, carpeted lower door panels, headlamp-on reminder, dual horns, and bright wide sill moldings. Wagons had a power tailgate window and locking side compartment.

I.D. DATA: Chevrolet's 17-symbol Vehicle Identification Number (VIN) was again on the upper left surface of the instrument panel, visible through the windshield. Coding is similar to 1981, but the following codes were added: Under car line/series (symbol five), code 'D' =

Cavalier; 'E' = Cavalier hatch; 'W' = both Celebrity and Malibu. Under body type (symbols six and seven), code '19' = 4-dr. sedan; code '77' = 2-dr. hatchback coupe. Symbol eight is the engine code: 'C' = L4-98 2Bbl.; 'D' = L4-111 diesel; 'R' or '2' = L4-151 FI; 'X' or '1' = V6-173 2Bbl.; 'Z' = V6-173 H.O.; 'K' = V6-229 2Bbl.; 'V' = Diesel V6-262. 'J' = V8-267 2Bbl.; 'H' = V8-305 4Bbl.; '7' = V8-305 CFI; 'N' = Diesel V8-350. Model year (symbol ten) changed to 'C' for 1982. Codes combined with a serial number are also stamped on the engine. Chevette codes are on the right side of the block, below No. 1 plug. Cavalier's are on a pad on the right side of the block (facing the car), below the head. Pontiac 151 fours have coding on a pad at the left front of the block, below the head; or on a flange at left rear, above the starter. The V6-173 is coded on the block at the front of the right head, or on the left rocker cover. Other V-6s and V-8s have coding stamped on the left side of the bell housing flange.

CHEVETTE (FOUR)

Model No.	Body/Style No.	Body Type & Seating	Factory Price	Shipping Weight	Prod. Total
1T	B08	2-dr. Hatch Cpe-4P	5513	2002	51,431
1T	B68	4-dr. Hatch Sed-4P	5660	2063	111,661

CHEVETTE SCOOTER (FOUR)

| 1T | J08 | 2-dr. Hatch Cpe-4P | 4997 | 1957 | 31,281 |
| 1T | J68 | 4-dr. Hatch Sed-4P | 5238 | 2004 | 21,742 |

CHEVETTE DIESEL (FOUR)

| 1T | B08/Z90 | 2-dr. Hatch Cpe-4P | 6579 | N/A | 4,874 |
| 1T | B68/Z90 | 4-dr. Hatch Sed-4P | 6727 | N/A | 11,819 |

Chevette Production Note: Totals do not include Chevette diesels (4,252 coupes and 8,900 sedans) produced during the 1981 model year.

CAVALIER (FOUR)

1J	D27	2-dr. Coupe-5P	6966	2298	30,245
1J	E77	2-dr. Hatch Cpe-5P	7199	2364	22,114
1J	D69	4-dr. Sedan-5P	7137	2345	52,941
1J	D35	4-dr. Sta Wag-5P	7354	2405	30,853

1982 Chevrolet, Cavalier station wagon (CP)

CAVALIER CADET (FOUR)

1J	D27/Z11	2-dr. Coupe-5P	6278	N/A	2,281
1J	D69/Z11	4-dr. Sedan-5P	6433	N/A	9,511
1J	D35/Z11	4-dr. Sta Wag-5P	6704	N/A	4,754

CAVALIER CL (FOUR)

1J	D27/Z12	2-dr. Coupe-5P	7944	2315	6,063
1J	E77/Z12	2-dr. Hatch Cpe-5P	8281	2381	12,792
1J	D69/Z12	4-dr. Sedan-5P	8137	2362	15,916
1J	D35/Z12	4-dr. Sta Wag-5P	8452	2422	7,587

CITATION (FOUR/V-6)

1X	H11	2-dr. Coupe-5P	6297/6515	2404/2468	9,102
1X	X08	2-dr. Hatch Cpe-5P	6754/6972	2413/2477	29,613
1X	X68	4-dr. Hatch Sed-5P	6899/7024	2447/2511	126,932

CAMARO (V-6/V-8)

1F	P87	2-dr. Spt Cpe-4P	7755/7925	2846/3025	78,761

CAMARO BERLINETTA (V-6/V-8)

1F	S87	2-dr. Spt Cpe-4P	9266/9436	2880/3094	39,744

CAMARO Z28 (V-8)

1F	P87	2-dr. Spt Cpe-4P	---- /9700	---- /3005	63,563

Camaro Engine Note: Prices and weights before slash are for V-6 engine, after slash for V-8. Base Camaro Sport Coupes were also available with a four-cylinder engine, priced at $7,631 and weighing 2,770 pounds. The Z28 could have an optional CFI V-8 for an additional $450.

Z28 Production Note: A total of 6,360 Indy 500 Commemorative Editions were built, in addition to standard Z28s. Chevrolet figures also show over 1,300 Z28E hatchback models for export.

CELEBRITY (FOUR/V-6)

1A	W27	2-dr. Coupe-5P	8313/8438	2609/2669	19,629
1A	W19	4-dr. Sedan-5P	8463/8588	2651/2711	72,701

MALIBU CLASSIC (V-6/V-8)

1A	W69	4-dr. Spt Sed-6P	8137/8207	3097/3228	70,793
1A	W35	4-dr. Sta Wag-6P	8265/8335	3247/3387	45,332

MONTE CARLO (V-6/V-8)

1A	Z37	2-dr. Spt Cpe-6P	8177/8247	3116/3245	92,392

IMPALA (V-6/V-8)

1B	L69	4-dr. Sedan-6P	7918/7988	3368/3492	47,780
1B	L35	4-dr. Sta Wag-6P	---- /8516	---- /3938	10,654
1B	L35/AQ4	4-dr. 3S Wag-8P	---- /8670	---- / N/A	6,245

CAPRICE CLASSIC (V-6/V-8)

1B	N47	2-dr. Spt Cpe-6P	8221/8291	3380/3500	11,999
1B	N69	4-dr. Sedan-6P	8367/8437	3417/3541	86,126
1B	N35/AQ4	4-dr. 3S Wag-9P	---- /9051	---- /4019	25,385

FACTORY PRICE AND WEIGHT NOTE: For Citation and Celebrity, prices and weights to left of slash are for four-cylinder, to right for V-6 engine. For Camaro, Malibu, Monte Carlo and full-size models, figures to left of slash are for six-cylinder model, to right of slash for V-8 (267 and 305 V-8 were each $70 extra). Diesel engines cost considerably more (see option prices).

BODY/STYLE NO. NOTE: Some models were actually option packages. Code after the slash (e.g., AQ4) is the number of the option package that comes with the model listed.

ENGINE DATA: BASE FOUR (Chevette): Inline. Overhead cam. Four-cylinder. Cast iron block and head. Displacement: 98 cu. in. (1.6 liters). Bore & stroke: 3.23 x 2.98 in. Compression ratio: 9.2:1. Brake horsepower: 65 at 5200 R.P.M. Torque: 80 lb.-ft. at 3200 R.P.M. Five main bearings. Hydraulic valve lifters. Carburetor: 2Bbl. Holley 6510C. VIN Code: C. DIESEL FOUR (Chevette): Inline. Overhead cam. Four-cylinder. Cast iron block and head. Displacement: 111 cu. in. (1.8 liters). Bore & stroke: 3.31 x 3.23 in. Compression ratio: 22.0:1. Brake horsepower: 51 at 5200 R.P.M. Torque: 72 lb.-ft. at 2000 R.P.M. Five main bearings. Solid valve lifters. Fuel injection. VIN Code: D. BASE FOUR (Cavalier): Inline. Overhead valve. Four-cylinder. Cast iron block and head. Displacement: 112 cu. in. (1.8 liters). Bore & stroke: 3.50 x 2.91 in. Compression ratio: 9.0:1. Brake horsepower: 88 at 5100 R.P.M. Torque: 100 lb.-ft. at 2800 R.P.M. Five main bearings. Hydraulic valve lifters. Carburetor: 2Bbl. Rochester E2SE. VIN Code: G. BASE FOUR (Citation, Celebrity, Camaro): Inline. Overhead valve. Four-cylinder. Cast iron block and head. Displacement: 151 cu. in. (2.5 liters). Bore & stroke: 4.00 x 3.00 in. Compression ratio: 8.2:1. Brake horsepower: 90 at 4000 R.P.M. Torque: 132 lb.-ft. at 2800 R.P.M. Five main bearings. Hydraulic valve lifters. Throttle-body fuel injection. Pontiac-built. VIN Code: R or 2. BASE V-6 (Camaro Berlinetta); OPTIONAL (Citation, Celebrity, Camaro): 60-degree, overhead-valve V-6. Cast iron block and head. Displacement: 173 cu. in. (2.8 liters). Bore & stroke: 3.50 x 2.99 in. Compression ratio: 8.5:1. Brake horsepower: 102-112 at 4800 R.P.M. (Camaro, 102). Torque: 142-145 lb.-ft. at 2400 R.P.M. (Camaro, 142). Four main bearings. Hydraulic valve lifters. Carburetor: 2Bbl. Rochester E2SE. VIN Code: X or 1. HIGH-OUTPUT V-6 (Citation): Same as 173 cu. in. V-6 above except: C.R.: 8.9:1. Brake H.P.: 135 at 5400 R.P.M. Torque: 145 lb.-ft. at 2400 R.P.M. VIN Code: Z. BASE V-6 (Malibu, Monte Carlo, Impala, Caprice): 90-degree, overhead-valve V-6. Cast iron block and head. Displacement: 229 cu. in. (3.8 liters). Bore & stroke: 3.74 x 3.48 in. Compression ratio: 8.6:1. Brake horsepower: 110 at 4200 R.P.M. Torque: 170 lb.-ft. at 2000 R.P.M. Four main bearings. Hydraulic valve lifters. Carburetor: 2Bbl. Rochester E2ME. VIN Code: K. DIESEL V-6 (Malibu, Monte Carlo): 90-degree, overhead-valve V-6. Cast iron block and aluminum head. Displacement: 262 cu. in. (4.3 liters). Bore & stroke: 4.057 x 3.385 in. Compression ratio: 22.5:1. Brake horsepower: 85 at 3600 R.P.M. Torque: 165 lb.-ft. at 1600 R.P.M. Four main bearings. Hydraulic valve lifters. Fuel injection. VIN Code: V. BASE V-8 (Caprice/Impala wagon); OPTIONAL (Malibu, Monte Carlo, Impala, Caprice): 90-degree, overhead valve V-8. Cast iron block and head. Displacement: 267 cu. in. (4.4 liters). Bore & stroke: 3.50 x 3.48 in. Compression ratio: 8.3:1. Brake horsepower: 115 at 4000 R.P.M. Torque: 205 lb.-ft. at 2400 R.P.M. Five main bearings. Hydraulic valve lifters. Carburetor: 2Bbl. Rochester E2ME. VIN Code: J. BASE V-8 (Camaro Z28); OPTIONAL (Camaro, Malibu, Monte Carlo, Impala, Caprice): 90-degree, overhead valve V-8. Cast iron block and head. Displacement: 305 cu. in. (5.0 liters). Bore & stroke: 3.74 x 3.48 in. Compression ratio: 8.6:1. Brake horsepower: 145 at 4000 R.P.M. Torque: 240 lb.-ft. at 2000 R.P.M. Five main bearings. Hydraulic valve lifters. Carburetor: 4Bbl. Rochester E4ME. VIN Code: H. OPTIONAL V-8 (Camaro Z28): Same as 305 cu. in. V-8 above with dual CFI: Brake H.P.: 165 at 4200 R.P.M. Torque: 240 lb.-ft. at 2400 R.P.M. VIN Code: 7. DIESEL V-8; OPTIONAL (Impala/Caprice): 90-degree, overhead valve V-8. Cast iron block and head. Displacement: 350 cu. in. (5.7 liters). Bore & stroke: 4.057 x 3.385 in. Compression ratio: 22.5:1. Brake horsepower: 105 at 3200 R.P.M. Torque: 200 lb.-ft. at 1600 R.P.M. Five main bearings. Hydraulic valve lifters. Fuel injection. Olds-built. VIN Code: N.

CHASSIS DATA: Wheelbase: (Chevette 2-dr.) 94.3 in.; (Chvt 4-dr.) 97.3 in.; (Cavalier) 101.2 in.; (Citation/Celebrity) 104.9 in.; (Camaro) 101.0 in.; (Malibu/Monte Carlo) 108.1 in.; (Caprice/Imp) 116.0 in. Overall length: (Chvt 2-dr.) 161.9 in.; (Chvt 4-dr.) 164.9 in.; (Cav cpe) 170.4 in.; (Cav hatch) 173.5 in.; (Cav sed) 172.4 in.; (Cav wag) 173.0 in.; (Cit) 176.7 in.; (Camaro) 187.8 in.; (Celeb) 188.3 in.; (Malibu) 192.7 in.; (Malibu wag) 193.3 in.; (Monte) 200.4 in.; (Imp/Capr) 212.2 in.; (Imp/Capr wag) 215.1 in. Height: (Chvt) 52.9 in.; (Cav cpe) 52.0 in.; (Cav sed) 53.9 in.; (Cav wag) 54.4 in.; (Cit) 53.9 in.; (Camaro) 50.0 in.; (Celeb) 53.7 in.; (Malibu) 55.7 in.; (Malibu wag) 55.8 in.; (Monte) 54.3 in.; (Imp/Capr cpe) 56.4 in.; (Imp/Capr wag) 58.1 in. Width: (Chvt) 61.8 in.; (Cav cpe) 66.0 in.; (Cav sed/wag) 66.3 in.; (Cit) 68.3 in.; (Camaro) 72.8 in.; (Celeb cpe) 69.3 in.; (Celeb sed) 68.8 in.; (Malibu) 72.3 in.; (Malibu wag) 71.9 in.; (Monte) 71.8 in.; (Imp/Capr) 75.3 in.; (Imp/Capr wag) 79.3 in. Front Tread: (Chvt) 51.2 in.; (Cav) 55.4 in.; (Cit/Celeb) 58.7 in.; (Camaro) 60.7 in.; (Malibu/Monte) 58.5 in.; (Imp/Capr) 61.8 in.; (Imp/Capr wag) 62.2 in. Rear Tread: (Chvt) 51.2 in.; (Cav) 55.2 in.; (Cit/Celeb) 57.0 in.; (Camaro) 61.6 in.; (Malibu/Monte) 57.8 in.; (Imp/Capr 60.8 in.; (Imp/Capr wag) 64.1 in. Standard Tires: (Chvt) P155/80R13 GBR; (Cav) P175/80R13 GBR; (Cit/Celeb) P185/80R13 GBR; (Camaro) P195/75R14 GBR; (Camaro Berlinetta) P205/70R14 SBR; (Camaro Z28) P215/65R15 SBR; (Malibu) P185/75R14 GBR; (Malibu wag) P195/75R14 GBR; (Monte) P195/75R14 SBR; (Imp/Capr) P205/75R15 SBR; (Imp/Capr wag) P225/75R15 SBR. Wheel size: (Camaro) 14 x 6 in.; (Berlinetta) 14 x 7 in.; (Z28) 15 x 7 in.

TECHNICAL: Transmission: Four-speed floor shift standard on Chevette: Gear ratios (1st) 3.75:1; (2nd) 2.16:1; (3rd) 1.38:1; (4th) 1.00:1; (Rev) 3.82:1. Four-speed floor shift on four-cylinder Cavalier/Citation: (1st) 3.53:1; (2nd) 1.95:1; (3rd) 1.24:1; (4th) 0.81:1 or 0.73:1; (Rev) 3.42:1. Citation H.O. V-6 four-speed manual trans.: (1st) 3.31:1; (2nd) 1.95:1; (3rd) 1.24:1; (4th) 0.81:1; (Rev) 3.42:1. Camaro four/V-6 four-speed manual trans.: (1st) 3.50:1; (2nd) 2.48:1; (3rd) 1.66:1; (4th) 1.00:1; (Rev) 3.50:1. Four-speed on Camaro V8-305: (1st) 3.42:1; (2nd) 2.28:1; (3rd) 1.45:1; (4th) 1.00:1; (Rev) 3.51:1. Camaro V8-305 TBI four-speed manual trans.: (1st) 2.88:1; (2nd) 1.91:1; (3rd) 1.33:1; (4th) 1.00:1; (Rev) 2.78:1. Chevette five-speed manual shift: (1st) 3.76:1; (2nd) 2.18:1; (3rd) 1.36:1; (4th) 1.00:1; (5th) 0.86:1; (Rev) 3.76:1. Three-speed Turbo Hydramatic standard on Monte Carlo and Caprice/Impala, optional on others. Automatic gear ratios: (1st) 2.52:1; (2nd) 1.52:1; (3rd) 1.00:1; (Rev) 1.93:1 except Caprice/Impala V6-231/V8-305, Camaro and Malibu/Monte diesel V-6: (1st) 2.74:1; (2nd) 1.57:1; (3rd) 1.00:1; (Rev) 2.07:1. Chevette automatic trans.: (1st) 2.40:1; (2nd) 1.48:1; (3rd) 1.00:1; (Rev) 1.92:1. Cav/Cit/Celeb-

rity auto. trans.: (1st) 2.84:1; (2nd) 1.60:1; (3rd) 1.00:1; (Rev) 2.07:1. Four-speed overdrive automatic transmission on Caprice/Impala: (1st) 2.74:1; (2nd) 1.57:1; (3rd) 1.00:1; (4th) 0.67:1; (Rev) 2.07:1. Four-speed overdrive automatic on Capr/Imp w/V-6: (1st) 3.06:1; (2nd) 1.63:1; (3rd) 1.00:1; (4th) 0.70:1; (Rev) 2.29:1. Standard final drive ratio: (Chevette) 3.36:1; (Cavalier) 3.32:1 w/manual, 2.84:1 w/auto.; (Cav wag) 3.65:1; (Citation) 3.32:1 w/4-speed, 2.84:1 w/auto. exc. H.O. V-6, 3.65:1 w/4-spd, 3.33:1 w/auto.; (Camaro four) 3.42:1 w/4-spd, 3.08:1 w/auto.; (Camaro V-6) 3.23:1 w/4-spd, 3.08:1 w/auto.; (Camaro V-8) 2.73:1; (Camaro "Cross-Fire" V-8) 3.23:1 w/4-spd, 2.23:1 w/auto. exc. (Z28) 2.93:1. (Celebrity) 2.84:1; (Malibu V-6) 2.41:1; (Malibu V-8) 2.29:1; (Malibu wag) 2.73:1 w/V-6, 2.56:1 w/V8-267, 2.41:1 or 2.73:1 w/V8-305; (Monte V-6) 2.41:1; (Monte V-8) 2.29:1; (Capr/Imp V-6) 2.73:1; (Capr/Imp V-8) 2.41:1 or 2.73:1 exc. 3.08:1 w/4-spd and V8-305. Steering: (Cavalier/Chevette/Citation/Celebrity) rack and pinion; (others) recirculating ball. Front suspension: (Chevette/Cavalier/Citation/Celeb) MacPherson struts, lower control arms, coil springs, stabilizer bar; (Camaro) modified MacPherson struts, control arms, coil springs, stabilizer bar; (Malibu/Monte/Capr/Imp) upper and lower control arms, coil springs, stabilizer bar. Rear suspension: (Chevette) rigid axle, coil springs, trailing links; (Cavalier) beam axle, trailing arms, variable-rate coil springs; (Citation) beam "twist" axle, trailing arms, control arms, stabilizer bar; (Celeb) beam "twist" axle, trailing arms, coil springs, Panhard rod, stabilizer bar; (Camaro) torque arm, solid axle, lower control arms, track bar and coil springs, plus link-type rear stabilizer bar for F41 sport suspension and Z28; (Malibu/Monte/Capr/Imp) coil springs, four-link live axle, lower trailing radius arms and upper oblique torque arms, plus stabilizer bar on some models. Brakes: Front disc, rear drum. Four-wheel discs available with Camaro V-8. Body construction: (Chvt/Cav/Cit/Celeb) unit; (Camaro) unitized with partial front frame and bolt-on front sheet metal; (Malibu/Monte/Capr/Imp) separate body and frame. Fuel tank: (Chvt) 12.5 gal.; (Cav) 14 gal.; (Cit) 15.9 gal.; (Camaro) 16 gal.; (Celeb) 15.7 gal.; (Celeb V-6) 16.4 gal.; (Malibu) 18.1 gal.; (Malibu wag) 18.2 gal.; (Monte) 18.1 gal.; (Capr/Imp) 25 gal.; (Capr/Imp wag) 22 gal.

DRIVETRAIN OPTIONS: Engines: 173 cu. in., 2Bbl. V-6: Citation, base Camaro, Celeb ($125). 267 cu. in., 2Bbl. V-8: Malibu/Monte/Imp/Caprice ($70). 305 cu. in., 4Bbl. V-8: Camaro ($295); Berlinetta ($170); Malibu wag, Monte/Imp/Capr ($70); Imp/Capr wag (NC). 305 cu. in., dual CFI V-8: Camaro ($450). Diesel 260 cu. in. V-6: Celeb ($775). Diesel 350 cu. in. V-8: Malibu/Monte/Imp/Capr ($825); Imp/Capr wag ($653). Transmission/Differential: Three-speed automatic trans.: Chevette ($380); Cavalier ($370); Citation/Camaro ($396); Camaro Z28 ($72). Four-speed overdrive automatic trans.: Imp/Capr ($172). Limited-slip differential: Camaro/Malibu/Monte ($76); Imp/Capr ($80). Special final drive ratio (2.84:1 or 3.18:1): Cavalier ($20). Performance axle ratio: Camaro, Malibu/Imp/Capr wag ($21). Power Accessories: Power brakes: Chvt/Cit ($93). Power four-wheel disc brakes: Camaro ($179).

Power steering: Chvt ($190); Cav ($180); Cit ($195). Suspension: F40 H.D. suspension: Cit/Celeb/Monte/Imp/Capr ($26). F41 sport suspension: Cav ($10-$46); Cit/Celeb ($33); Camaro/Monte/Imp/Capr cpe/sed ($49). Rear stabilizer bar: Cavalier ($36). Inflatable rear shock absorbers: Imp/Capr wag ($64). Other: H.D. radiator: Cavalier ($37-$65). H.D. cooling: Chvt/Cit/Camaro/Celeb/Malibu/Monte/Imp/Capr ($40-$70). Cold climate pkg.: Malibu/Monte/Imp/Capr diesel ($99). Diesel engine and fuel line heater: Celeb ($49). H.D. battery: Cav ($22); others ($25) exc. diesel ($50). California emission system: Chvt/Cit/Malibu/Monte/Imp/Capr (N/A); Cav ($46); Camaro/Celeb ($65); Celeb diesel ($205).

CHEVETTE CONVENIENCE/APPEARANCE OPTIONS: Comfort/Convenience: Air conditioning ($595). Rear defogger, electric ($120). Tinted glass ($82). Comfortilt steering wheel ($95). Quartz electric clock ($32). Cigarette lighter: Scooter ($10). Rear wiper/washer ($117). Quiet sound group ($48-$60). Lighting and Mirrors: Halogen headlamps ($10). Aux. lighting ($41-$42). Twin sport mirrors, left remote ($50). Driver's remote sport mirror ($33). Entertainment: AM radio: Scooter ($78). AM/FM radio ($75); Scooter ($153). AM/FM stereo radio ($106). Rear speaker ($20). Radio delete ($51 credit). Exterior Trim: Deluxe exterior ($131-$138). Two-tone paint ($133). Sport stripes ($89). Bodyside moldings: Scooter ($45). Door edge guards ($15-$25). Roof carrier ($87). Interior Trim/Upholstery: Cloth bucket seats ($16-$28). Custom cloth bucket seats ($160). Rear seat delete ($50 credit). Color-keyed floor mats ($25). Wheels and Tires: Rally wheel trim ($59). P155/80R13 SBR WSW ($51). P175/70R13 SBR WSW ($122) exc. Scooter ($173).

CAVALIER CONVENIENCE/APPEARANCE OPTIONS: Comfort/Convenience: Air cond. ($625). Cruise control w/resume ($145-$155). Tinted glass: base ($82). Six-way power driver's seat ($183). Comfortilt steering wheel ($88). Power windows ($152-$216). Power door locks ($99-$142). Remote swing-out side windows ($55). Gauge pkg. ($46). Special instruments ($78-$124). Intermittent wipers ($44). Rear wiper/washer ($109). Lighting, Horns and Mirrors: Halogen headlamps: base ($38). Aux. lighting ($72-$81). Dual sport mirrors, left remote ($51). Dual electric remote sport mirrors ($79-$130). Right visor mirror ($7). Lighted visor mirror ($38-$45). Entertainment: AM/FM radio: base ($64). AM/FM stereo radio ($100) exc. CL ($36). AM/FM stereo radio w/8-track player ($179) exc. CL ($115). AM/FM stereo radio w/cassette ($217) exc. CL ($153). Rear speaker ($20-$32); dual ($30-$42). Radio delete ($71-$138 credit). Exterior Trim: Removable sunroof ($261). Two-tone paint ($164). Pin striping ($53). Sport striping ($95). Wheel opening moldings ($26). Door edge guards ($14-$22). Roof carrier ($98). Bumper guards ($51). Interior Trim/Upholstery: Cloth bucket seats ($28). Color-keyed mats: front ($15); rear ($10). Cargo area cover ($60). Wheels and Tires: Aluminum wheels ($272-$317). P175/80R13 GBR WSW

($55). P195/70R13 SBR BSW ($133) exc. CL ($78). P195/70R13 SBR WSW ($188) exc. CL ($133). P195/70R13 SBR WLT ($205) exc. CL ($150). Puncture-sealant tires ($94).

CITATION/CELEBRITY CONVENIENCE/APPEARANCE OPTIONS: Option Packages: X-11 sport equipment pkg.: Citation ($1744). Deluxe exterior pkg.: Citation ($118-$169). Exterior molding pkg. (rocker panel and wheel opening moldings): Celeb ($53). Max. efficiency pkg. (rear spoiler and decals): Cit ($42). Quiet sound/rear decor pkg.: Cit ($87). Comfort/Convenience: Air cond. ($675). Rear defogger, electric ($125). Cruise control ($155-$165). Tinted glass ($88). Comfortilt steering wheel ($95). Six-way power driver's seat: Celeb ($197). Power windows ($165-$235). Remote swing-out side windows: Cit ($108). Power door locks ($106-$152). Gauge pkg. w/clock: Cit ($104). Gauge pkg. w/trip odometer: Celeb ($64). Electric clock: Cit ($32). Digital clock: Celeb ($60). Intermittent wipers ($47). Lighting, Horns and Mirrors: Halogen high-beam headlamps: Celeb ($10). Aux. lighting: Cit ($50). Dual horns: Cit ($12). Driver's remote mirror ($22). Dual sport mirrors, left remote ($55). Dual remote mirrors: Celeb ($86). Entertainment: AM/FM radio ($75-$82). AM/FM stereo radio ($106-$118). AM/FM stereo w/8-track: Celeb ($282). AM/FM stereo w/cassette: Celeb ($277). Dual rear speakers ($30); incl. w/stereo radio. Windshield antenna: Cit ($12). Power antenna: Cit ($55). Radio delete ($56 credit). Exterior Trim: Removable sunroof: Cit ($275). Vinyl roof: Celeb ($140). Two-tone paint: Cit ($176) incl. pin striping and bodyside moldings; Celeb ($148). Bodyside pin striping: Cit ($39); Celeb ($57). Bodyside moldings: Cit ($47). Door edge guards ($15-$25). Bumper guards ($56-$60). Bumper rub strips: Cit ($50). Interior Trim/Upholstery: Console ($100). Reclining driver and passenger seatbacks ($96). Sport cloth bench seat: Cit ($28). Custom cloth or vinyl bench seat: Cit ($418). Sport cloth bucket seats: Citation ($131-$160) exc. w/X-11 (NC). Custom cloth bucket seats: Cit ($397-$534). Vinyl bench seat: Celeb ($28). Celebrity custom bench seat: cloth ($109-$179); vinyl ($137-$207). Celebrity 45/45 seating: cloth ($133); vinyl ($161). Special custom cloth 45/45 seat: Celeb ($399-$459). Color-keyed mats: front ($16); rear ($11). Wheels and Tires: Full wheel covers: Cit ($52). Sport wheel covers: Celeb ($62). Wire wheel covers: Celeb ($153). Wheel cover locks: Celeb ($39). Rally wheels: Cit ($41-$93); Celeb ($153). P185/80R13 GBR WSW ($58). P185/80R13 SBR BSW ($64). P185/80R13 SBR WSW ($122). P205/70R13 SBR BSW: Celeb ($179). P205/70R13 SBR WSW: Celeb ($245). P205/70R13 SBR WLT: Cit ($267). P185/75R14 SBR WSW: Celeb ($157). P215/60R14 SBR WLT: Citation X-11 ($92). Puncture-sealant tires ($106).

CAMARO/MALIBU/MONTE CARLO CONVENIENCE/APPEARANCE OPTIONS: Option Packages: Estate equipment: Malibu wag ($307). Quiet sound group: Camaro ($72-$82). Security pkg.: Malibu wag ($44). Comfort/Convenience: Air cond. ($675). Rear defogger, electric ($125). Cruise control ($155-$165). Tinted glass ($88). Comfortilt steering wheel ($95). Six-way power driver's seat: Camaro/Monte ($197). Power windows: Camaro/Monte ($165); Malibu ($235). Power door locks: Malibu ($152); Camaro/Monte ($106). Power trunk release: Monte ($32). Power hatch release: Camaro ($32). Power tailgate window release: Malibu wag ($33). Electric clock: base Camaro, Malibu/Monte ($32). Digital clock: Berlinetta/Z28 ($28). Gauge pkg. w/trip odometer: Malibu/Monte ($95). Special instruments: base Camaro ($149). Intermittent wipers ($47). Rear wiper/washer: Camaro ($117). Lighting, Horns and Mirrors: Halogen high-beam headlamps ($10). Cornering lamps: Monte ($55). Aux. lighting: Camaro ($52); Malibu/Monte ($38). Dual horns: Camaro ($12). Remote-control driver's mirror: Malibu ($22). Twin sport mirrors (left remote): base Camaro, Monte ($48); Malibu ($55). Twin remote sport mirrors: Monte ($79). Twin electric remote sport mirrors: Camaro ($89-$137). Lighted visor mirror: Monte ($48). Entertainment: AM radio: Camaro/Monte ($111). AM/FM radio: ($165-$172). AM/FM stereo radio: Camaro ($258-$282); Malibu/Monte ($196). Stereo 8-track tape player with AM/FM stereo radio: Camaro ($390-$446); Malibu/Monte ($282). Cassette player with AM/FM stereo radio: Camaro ($385-$441); Malibu/Monte ($283). Dual rear speakers: Camaro ($30-$54); Malibu/Monte ($30). Fixed mast antenna ($41); incl. w/radios. Power antenna ($55). Exterior Trim: Removable glass roof panels: Camaro/Monte ($790). Landau vinyl roof: Monte ($232). Rear spoiler: Camaro ($69). Two-tone paint: Malibu ($138); Monte ($214). Bodyside moldings: Camaro ($47). Deluxe bodyside moldings: Malibu/Monte ($57). Door edge guards ($15-$25). Side window sill and rear hood moldings: Monte ($45). Roof drip moldings: Camaro ($29). Bodyside pin striping: Malibu ($57); Monte ($61). Rear window air deflector: Malibu wag ($36). Roof carrier: Malibu wag ($115). Bumper rub strips: Malibu ($50). Bumper guards, front/rear: Malibu ($56). Interior Trim/Upholstery: Vinyl bench seat: Malibu cpe/sed, Monte ($28). Cloth bench seat: Malibu wag ($28). Custom cloth bench seat: Malibu sed, Monte ($358). Cloth or vinyl 55/45 seating: Malibu/Monte ($133-$161). Cloth bucket seats: Camaro ($28). Custom cloth or vinyl bucket seats: base Camaro/Z28 ($299). Cloth LS contour bucket seats: Camaro ($312). Custom cloth LS contour bucket seats: Camaro ($611). Color-keyed mats: Malibu/Monte ($27); Camaro front ($16); Camaro rear ($11). Deluxe load-floor carpet: Malibu wag ($84). Deluxe trunk trim: Camaro ($164); Monte ($47). Wheels and Tires: Aluminum wheels: Monte ($362). Rally wheels: Camaro ($112); Malibu/Monte ($56). Full wheel covers: Camaro ($52). Sport wheel covers (silver or gold): Malibu ($62). Wire wheel covers: Malibu/Monte ($153). Wheel cover locks: Malibu/Monte ($39). P185/75R14 GBR WSW: Malibu cpe/sed ($58). P195/75R14 GBR WSW: Camaro, Malibu wag ($62). P195/75R14 SBR BSW: Camaro ($65). P195/75R14 SBR WSW: Camaro ($127); Malibu cpe/sed ($151); Malibu wag ($123); Monte ($62). P205/70R14 SBR BSW: base Camaro ($123). P205/70R14 SBR WSW:

Camaro ($189); Berlinetta ($66); Monte ($124). P205/70R14 SBR WLT: Camaro ($211). Puncture-sealant tires: Malibu/Monte ($105).

1982 Chevrolet, Caprice Classic Estate Wagon (CP)

IMPALA/CAPRICE CONVENIENCE/APPEARANCE OPTIONS: Option Packages: Estate equipment: wag ($307). Value appearance group: bodyside and wheel opening moldings, full wheel covers ($113). Comfort/Convenience: Air cond. ($695). Rear defogger, electric ($125). Cruise control ($155). Tinted glass ($102). Comfortilt steering wheel ($95). Power door locks ($106-$152). Six-way power driver's seat ($197). Power windows ($165-$240). Power trunk release ($32). Power tailgate lock: wag ($49). Electric clock: Imp ($32). Digital clock: Imp ($66); Caprice ($34). Gauge pkg. w/trip odometer ($64). Intermittent wipers ($47). Quiet sound group: Imp ($66-$72). Lighting and Mirrors: Halogen high-beam headlamps ($10). Cornering lamps ($55). Aux. lighting ($42-$64). Driver's remote mirror ($22). Dual remote mirrors ($65). Dual sport mirrors, left remote ($55). Dual remote body-color sport mirrors ($86). Lighted visor mirror ($48). Entertainment: AM radio ($99). AM/FM radio ($153). AM/FM stereo radio ($184). Stereo 8-track tape player with AM/FM stereo radio ($270). Cassette player with AM/FM stereo ($271). Dual rear speakers ($30). Power antenna ($55). Windshield antenna ($29); incl. w/radios. Exterior Trim: Vinyl roof: cpe/sed ($165). Roof carrier: wag ($140). Two-tone paint ($65). Custom two-tone ($141). Pin striping ($39). Color-keyed bodyside moldings ($51). Door edge guards ($15-$25). Bumper rub strips, front/rear ($66). Bumper guards ($62). Interior Trim/Upholstery: Vinyl bench seat: cpe/sed ($28). Cloth bench seat: wag ($28). Cloth 50/50 seat ($238-$285). Custom cloth 50/50 seat: cpe ($428); sed ($452). Deluxe load-floor carpet: wag ($89). Deluxe cargo area carpet: wag ($129). Color-keyed mats: front ($16); rear ($11). Deluxe trunk trim ($59). Wheels and Tires: Full wheel covers ($52). Sport wheel covers: Imp ($115); Caprice ($63). Wire wheel covers ($153). Wire wheel cover locks ($39). P205/75R15 SBR WSW: cpe/sed ($66). P225/70R15 SBR WSW: cpe/sed ($159). P225/75R15 SBR WSW: wag ($71). Puncture-sealant tires ($106-$131).

HISTORY: General introduction was Sept. 24, 1981 but Cavalier debuted May 21, 1981; Chevette/Citation/Corvette on Dec. 12, 1981; and Camaro/Celebrity not until Jan. 14, 1982. Model year production (U.S.): 1,131,748 (incl. Corvettes and early '82 Cavaliers but not incl. 10,655 Acadians). Total production for the U.S. market was made up of 524,694 four-cylinder, 356,314 sixes, and 351,518 V-8s. A total of 48,654 diesels were installed. Calendar year production (U.S.): 1,004,244 (including 22,838 Corvettes plus Acadians, but not incl. 139,837 early '82 Cavaliers). Calendar year sales by U.S. dealers: 1,260,620, for a 21.8 percent market share. Model year sales by U.S. dealers: 1,234,988 (incl. 22,086 Corvettes but not incl. 43,855 early 1982 Cavaliers), for a 22.3 percent share.

Historical Footnotes: Cavalier debuted in a national media preview in Washington, D.C., amid sales predictions of 345,000 for 1982. Production began slowly and sales proved disappointing, even after early delivery shortages were remedied. Additional assembly plants (at Leeds and Janesville) were prepared to begin Cavalier production in spring 1982. Chevrolet called 1982 the "year of the diesel." Diesel power was now available on Chevettes, Caprice/Impalas, Malibus and Monte Carlos, and soon would arrive on the new Celebrity. Of the 14 engine sizes available this year in cars and light trucks, five were diesels. General manager Robert D. Lund estimated that over 300,000 Chevrolet vehicles built in 1982 might have diesel engines. That prediction turned out to be overly optimistic. Within a couple of years the highly-touted diesel powerplant would begin to fade away, victim of driveability problems, stable gasoline prices, and general lack of customer interest. In one illuminating survey that held portents of the future, Chevrolet discovered that nearly 37 percent of Camaros purchased in 1980 were bought by women. That was higher than any other Chevrolet passenger car, and well above the industry average of 24.5 percent. Twin slogans for the restyled Camaro also suggested what was to come as the decade unrolled. "Excess is out. Efficiency is in" predicted the rising emphasis on fuel-efficiency and modest size. "Brute power is out. Precision is in" seemed to toll the death knell for the big V-8, but it would be around for some time yet.

1983

After the three major new product introductions for 1982, this year focused on powertrain refinements for performance and economy. Changes included new five-speed manual gearboxes available for Camaro, Chevette and Cavalier, plus a bigger Cavalier engine. All Citations could get the high-output (135 horsepower) V-6 this year. Mid-year arrivals included a Cavalier convertible, notchback Citation X11, and available four-speed manual transaxle in Celebrity. But the most notable news of all was probably the reworked 1984 Corvette, which debuted in spring and missed the '83 model year completely.

1983 Chevrolet, Chevette S two-door hatchback coupe (AA)

CHEVETTE -- SERIES 1T -- FOUR -- Chevette enjoyed a rather dramatic restyling this year, gaining a deep front air dam that flowed into flared wheel housings, body-color bumpers (but black on Scooters), and a number of blackout body trim pieces. Even so, apart from a higher position of front side marker lamps and front fender script, basic appearance was quite similar to before. Scooters, priced as low as $4997, gained reclining front bucket seats as standard. Chevette's crosshatch grille sported a familiar bowtie emblem in its center. A new 'Chevette S' sport decor package included black and red accents, special wheel trim rings, black grille, black headlamp bezels, and black wheels. Red accents went on bodyside moldings and nameplates. The sport package came in five body colors, others in ten. Four interior colors were offered. Two four-cylinder engine choices were available (1.6-liter gas and 1.8-liter diesel), plus three transmissions: four- and five-speed manual, and three-speed automatic. Five-speed was standard with the diesel, and offered for the first time with the gas engine (though it had been announced earlier). Scooter equipment included a color-keyed front air dam, black steel bumpers with end caps and guards, black grille, dome lamp, day/night mirror, black moldings (windshield, hatch window reveal, roof drip), vinyl reclining front bucket seats, front stabilizer, and styled steel wheels. Standard models added color-keyed bumpers, lighter, mini console, locking glove box, black grille with argent accent, color-keyed dash, black bodyside and rocker moldings, and an AM radio. Diesel Chevettes had standard power brakes.

1983 Chevrolet, Cavalier two-door coupe (JG)

1983 Chevrolet, Cavalier four-door sedan

1983 Chevrolet, Cavalier CL two-door hatchback coupe

CAVALIER -- SERIES 1J -- FOUR -- Appearance was similar to 1982, but a modified standard equipment list allowed significant price cuts to the subcompact Cavalier. The new base prices ($5888 to $6633) were $389 to $1868 lower than equivalent 1982 values. But quite a few items that had been standard now joined the option list. Seven models and three trim levels were available. Top-of-the-line was now the CS, while CL became an option package (priced at $577 to $696), containing many of the former CL series items. The budget-priced Cadet series was dropped, along with the base hatchback coupe. All Cavaliers had beige/charcoal instrument panels and consoles, replacing the former brushed aluminum/woodgrain. Two-door CS models got a new easy-entry passenger seat that slid forward automatically when folded down for access to the back. Standard equipment remaining in the list included radial tires, power brakes, front stabilizer bar, vinyl reclining front bucket seats, and side window defoggers. Cavaliers came in ten body colors and five interior colors. On the mechanical side, Cavalier became Chevrolet's first front-drive with a five-speed manual transaxle available. It offered two overdrive ratios (0.92:1 in fourth and 0.75:1 in fifth gear), plus a 3.91:1 first gear ratio. Four-speed overdrive manual remained standard, with three-speed automatic optional. Also new was a bigger (2.0-liter) fuel-injected engine with higher compression and torque. A "cyclonic" cylinder head gave faster fuel burning. New, "more aggressive" axle ratios boosted performance. A new convertible arrived later in the model year (January), built by American Sunroof in Lansing, Mich-

igan. Produced in limited numbers, it was the first Chevrolet ragtop since 1975. Cavalier's new standard equipment list included bright bumpers with black/argent rub strips, black grille, black left-hand outside mirror, day/night inside mirror, console with rear ashtray and coin tray, four-spoke charcoal steering wheel, styled steel wheels with P175/80R13 GBR tires, compact spare tire, two-speed wiper/washers, and black moldings (glass and drip). CS models added a lighter, locking glove compartment, halogen headlamps, color-keyed dash, AM radio, three-spoke color-keyed steering wheel, black/argent bodyside moldings, and bright side window moldings. CS hatchbacks also had color-keyed bumpers, fold-down rear seat and special instruments; all but hatchbacks had a bright grille rather than the standard black. The new Cavalier convertible carried tinted glass, power steering, power windows, and twin sport mirrors (left remote). Added to the option list were an electric rear defogger, power hatch or trunk release, electronic-tuning radios, split folding rear seatback, and black/argent bodyside moldings.

1983 Chevrolet, Citation two-door hatchback coupe (JG)

CITATION -- SERIES 1X -- FOUR/V-6 -- Little changed on Citation except for upgraded front seats and a restyled instrument panel. Interiors held new low-back front seats with adjustable headrests. Of the five interior colors, maroon and dark brown were new. Maroon was also a new addition to the body color selection. Base engine was still the fuel-injected 151 cu. in. (2.5-liter) four. The high-output V-6 was now optional on all models, not just as part of the X-11 option package. Citation was still offered as a two-door hatchback, two-door notchback, or four-door hatchback. Joining the option list this year was a Sport Decor package that included exterior graphics, rear spoiler, rally wheels, color-keyed bumpers, and sport mirrors. The X-11 package was again offered for the two-door hatchback and, later in the model year, for the notchback as well. It included special graphics, a bubble hood with nameplates, and high-output V-6 engine. Because of equipment changes, the package cost about $700 less than in 1982. The revised X-11 also included bucket seats, sport mirrors, rear spoiler, P215/60R14 SBR tires on 14 in. aluminum alloy wheels, black grille, nameplates, sport steering wheel, power brakes, F41 sport suspension, modified exhaust, color-keyed bumpers with rub strips, sport decal, and black moldings (windshield, window and drip). Price tag was now $998, and 1,934 were installed.

1983 Chevrolet, Camaro Z28 T-top two-door coupe (JG)

CAMARO -- SERIES 1F -- V-6/V-8 -- Camaro's looks changed little this year after the 1982 aero restyle, but more powertrain combinations were available. Engine choices were as before: base 151 cu. in. (2.5-liter) fuel-injected four on the Sport Coupe, Berlinetta's standard 173 cu. in. (2.8-liter) V-6, and two 305 cu. in. (5.0-liter) V-8s. Standard V-8 was carbureted, but Z28 could have the Cross-Fire fuel-injected version. Camaros with the CFI engine had functional dual air intake hood scoops. Five-speed overdrive manual was now optional on the base Sport Coupe, standard on others. New four-speed overdrive automatic (with lockup torque converter) was also available. A new high-output 305 V-8 engine with revised cam and four-barrel carburetor arrived late in the model year, developing 190 horsepower. A total of 3,223 H.O. V-8s were installed in Camaros this year. Optional "Conteur" multi-adjustment driver's seats got matching passenger seats. Stereo radios offered electronic tuning. Z28 had new three-tone upholstery featuring multiple Camaro logos. Body colors this year were white, black and red, plus seven metallics: silver, light or dark blue, light or dark brown, charcoal, and dark gold. Maroon was dropped from the body color list, and brown replaced maroon as an interior choice; but colors otherwise remained the same as before. Camaros again had a rear glass hatch, reclining front bucket seats, and standard power steering. Joining the option list: a rear compartment cover to hide cargo. Optional mats now were carpeted instead of plain rubber.

1983 Chevrolet, Celebrity CL four-door sedan (AA)

CELEBRITY -- SERIES 1A -- FOUR/V-6 -- Arriving late this year, the luxury aerodynamic five-passenger family car got the diesel V-6 option (announced earlier) for the first time. A new four-speed overdrive automatic transmission also joined the mid-year option list. Chevrolet's biggest front-drive kept its standard 151 cu. in. (2.5-liter) fuel-injected four, with optional 2.8-liter gas V-6 as well as the diesel. Standard equipment included automatic transmission, power brakes and steering. Interiors came in five colors and two CL trim levels, one with 45/45 seating. A center console was optional. Ten body colors were offered. All radio options now had electronic tuning and the 8-track tape players were dropped, but little else changed.

MALIBU -- SERIES 1A -- V-6/V-8 -- This would be the final season for the rear-drive six-passenger Malibu, whose family-carrying duties were being taken over by the front-drive Celebrity. Base engine was the 229 cu. in. (3.8-liter) V-6, with V-6 and V-8 diesels available as well as the 305 gas V-8. Only two bodies were offered: four-door sedan and four-door wagon. The Malibu Classic nameplate was dropped (replaced by the luxury CL option), so only one series remained this year, stressing economy. Notchback bench or 55/45 split front seats with fold-down armrests came in cloth or vinyl. Several trim items were added to the option list, including rocker panel and wheel opening moldings. Malibu's standard equipment included power brakes and steering, automatic transmission, locking glove compartment, lighter, dome light, compact spare tire, front stabilizer bar, and two-speed wiper/washers. Bodies held bright sill, rear window and windshield reveal, roof drip and belt moldings.

1983 Chevrolet, Monte Carlo CL two-door coupe (AA)

MONTE CARLO -- SERIES 1A -- V-6/V-8 -- Monte's front end gained a bolder, more aggressive look with its new large-segmented (bigger holes) crosshatch grille. Both gas and diesel V-6 and V-8 engines were available, but the small-block 267 cu. in. gas V-8 was dropped, replaced by the 305 cu. in. (5.0-liter) V-8. For the first time in three years, the 305 V-8 was available under both Malibu and Monte Carlo hoods. Standard engine was the 229 cu. in. (3.8-liter) V-6. Monte came in ten body colors and five interior colors, in two trim levels (including a luxury CL option). A revived interest in rear-drive mid-sizes kept Monte in the lineup, offering six-passenger coupe roominess. Standard equipment included power brakes and steering, full wheel covers, front stabilizer bar, body-color bumpers, bright windshield and quarter-window reveal moldings, twin bright mirrors, chromed headlamp bezels, bright lower bodyside moldings, wheel opening and roof drip moldings, dual horns, and a stand-up hood ornament. Montes rode P195/75R14 SBR tires and carried a compact spare. Inside was a full-width front seat with folding armrest, door pull straps, leather-like dash appliqué, day/night mirror, color-keyed steering wheel, locking glove compartment, lighter, and courtesy lights. In addition to the base model, a new Monte Carlo SS coupe joined the lineup late in the season, powered by a high-output version of the carbureted 305 cu. in. V-8.

1983 Chevrolet, Caprice Classic station wagon

1983 Chevrolet, Caprice Classic four-door sedan (JG)

IMPALA/CAPRICE CLASSIC -- SERIES 1B -- V-6/V-8 -- Continuing demand kept the twin full-size Chevrolets around, but they lost a number of models this year. All that remained of the Impala name was a four-door sedan, while Caprice fielded a sedan and nine-passenger (three-seat) station wagon. No two-door models were left. Base sedan engine remained the 229 cu. in. (3.8-liter) V-6. The Caprice wagon continued with the 305 cu. in. (5.0-liter) V-8. Options included the 305 gas V-8, 350 diesel V-8, new four-speed overdrive automatic transmission with 0.79:1 top gear, and a higher-number (3.08:1) axle ratio. The 267 cu. in. V-8 was gone. Black was again offered as one of the ten possible body colors, after being unavailable in 1982. Interior trims came in five colors: dark blue, light green, silver, maroon, and dark brown. Caprice sedans could have a CL luxury interior package. Impala standard equipment included three-speed automatic transmission, power brakes and steering, cloth bench seat, day/night mirror, two-speed wiper/washers, front stabilizer bar, trunk mat, lighter, and lights for dome, trunk and glove compartment. Impala also wore bright roof drip, windshield and back window reveal, window frame, door frame and lower bodyside moldings. Caprice added overdrive automatic transmission, a quartz electric clock, dual

horns, full wheel covers, wheel opening moldings, bright wide lower bodyside moldings, dash and ashtray lights, and a headlamps-on warning buzzer. Wagons had a power tailgate window. Caprice sedans had cloth seats, wagons vinyl.

I.D. DATA: Chevrolets again had a 17-symbol Vehicle Identification Number (VIN) on the upper left surface of the instrument panel, visible through the windshield. Symbol one indicates country: '1' = U.S.A.; '2' = Canada. Next is a manufacturer code: 'G' = General Motors. Symbol three is car make: '1' = Chevrolet; '2' = GM of Canada. Symbol four denotes restraint system: 'A' = non-passive (standard); 'B' = passive (automatic belts); 'C' = passive (inflatable). Symbol five is car line/series: 'B' = Chevette; 'J' = Chevette Scooter; 'D' = Cavalier; 'E' = Cavalier hatchback; 'H' = Citation coupe; 'X' = Citation; 'P' = Camaro; 'S' = Camaro Berlinetta; 'W' = Celebrity or Malibu; 'Z' = Monte Carlo; 'L' = Impala; 'N' = Caprice. Symbols six-seven reveal body type: '08' = 2-dr. hatch coupe; '11' = 2-dr. notchback coupe; '27' = 2-dr. notchback coupe (or convertible); '37' = special 2-dr. notch coupe; '77' = 2-dr. hatch coupe; '87' = 2-dr. sport coupe; '19' = 4-dr. 6-window notchback sedan; '68' = 4-dr. hatch sedan; '69' = 4-dr. 4-window notchback sedan; '35' = 4-dr. station wagon. Next is the engine code: 'C' = L4-98 2Bbl.; 'D' = L4-111 diesel; 'P' = L4-121 FI; 'R' or '2' = L4-151 FI; 'X' or '1' = V6-173 2Bbl.; 'Z' = H.O. V6-173; 'K' or '9' = V6-229 2Bbl.; 'T' or 'V' = V6-262 diesel; 'H' = V8-305 4Bbl.; 'S' = V8-305 FI; 'N' = V8-350 diesel. Next is a check digit, followed by 'D' for model year 1983. Symbol eleven indicates assembly plant: 'B' = Baltimore; 'J' = Janesville, WI; 'L' = Van Nuys, CA; 'N' = Norwood, OH; 'R' = Arlington, TX; 'T' = Tarrytown, NY; 'X' = Fairfax, KS; 'Y' = Wilmington, DE; '1' = Oshawa, Ontario; '6' = Oklahoma City, OK; '7' = Lordstown, OH. The final six digits are the sequential serial number. Engine number coding is similar to 1982.

CHEVETTE (FOUR)

Model No.	Body/Style No.	Body Type & Seating	Factory Price	Shipping Weight	Prod. Total
1T	B08	2-dr. Hatch Cpe-4P	5469	2029	37,537
1T	B68	4-dr. Hatch Sed-4P	5616	2090	81,297

CHEVETTE SCOOTER (FOUR)

1T	J08	2-dr. Hatch Cpe-4P	4997	1971	33,488
1T	J68	4-dr. Hatch Sed-4P	5333	2040	15,303

CHEVETTE DIESEL (FOUR)

1T	B08/Z90	2-dr. Hatch Cpe-4P	6535	N/A	439
1T	B68/Z90	4-dr. Hatch Sed-4P	6683	N/A	1,501

CAVALIER (FOUR)

1J	C27	2-dr. Coupe-5P	5888	2315	23,028
1J	C69	4-dr. Sedan-5P	5999	2335	33,333
1J	C35	4-dr. Sta Wag-5P	6141	2395	27,922

CAVALIER CS (FOUR)

1J	D27	2-dr. Coupe-5P	6363	2305	22,172
1J	E77	2-dr. Hatch Cpe-5P	6549	2370	25,869
1J	D69	4-dr. Sedan-5P	6484	2357	52,802
1J	D35	4-dr. Sta Wag-5P	6633	2417	32,834
1J	D27/Z08	2-dr. Conv. Cpe-5P	10990	N/A	627

CITATION (FOUR/V-6)

1X	H11	2-dr. Coupe-5P	6333/6483	2394/2457	6,456
1X	X08	2-dr. Hatch Cpe-5P	6788/6938	2403/2466	14,323
1X	X68	4-dr. Hatch Sed-5P	6934/7084	2442/2505	71,405

CAMARO (V-6/V-8)

1F	P87	2-dr. Spt Cpe-4P	8186/8386	2878/3035	63,806

CAMARO BERLINETTA (V-6/V-8)

1F	S87	2-dr. Spt Cpe-4P	9881/10106	2864/3056	27,925

CAMARO Z28 (V-8)

1F	P87	2-dr. Spt Cpe-4P	---- /10336	---- /3061	62,100

Camaro Engine Note: Prices and weights before slash are for V-6 engine, after slash for V-8. Base Camaro Sport Coupes were also available with a four-cylinder engine, priced at $8036 and weighing 2803 pounds. The Z28 could have an optional CFI V-8 for an additional $450.

Z28 Production Note: Chevrolet production figures also show 550 Z28E hatchback sport coupes built for export.

CELEBRITY (FOUR/V-6)

1A	W27	2-dr. Coupe-5P	8059/8209	2629/2689	19,221
1A	W19	4-dr. Sedan-5P	8209/8359	2649/2709	120,608

MALIBU CLASSIC (V-6/V-8)

1A	W69	4-dr. Spt Sed-6P	8084/8309	3106/3214	61,534
1A	W35	4-dr. Sta Wag-6P	8217/8442	3249/3376	55,892

MONTE CARLO (V-6/V-8)

1A	Z37	2-dr. Spt Cpe-6P	8552/8777	3128/3236	91,605

MONTE CARLO 'SS' (V-8)

1A	Z37/Z65	2-dr. Spt Cpe-6P	---- /10249	---- /3242	4,714

IMPALA (V-6/V-8)

1B	L69	4-dr. Sedan-6P	8331/8556	3356/3460	45,154

CAPRICE CLASSIC (V-6/V-8)

1B	N69	4-dr. Sedan-6P	8802/9027	3402/3506	122,613
1B	N35	4-dr. 3S Wag-9P	---- /9518	---- /3975	53,028

FACTORY PRICE AND WEIGHT NOTE: For Citation and Celebrity, prices and weights to left of slash are for four-cylinder, to right for V-6 engine. For Camaro, Malibu, Monte Carlo and full-size models, figures to left of slash are for six-cylinder model, to right of slash for 305 cu. in. V-8. Diesel V-6 and V-8 engines cost considerably more (see option prices).

BODY/STYLE NO. NOTE: Some models were actually option packages. Code after the slash (e.g., Z65) is the number of the option package that comes with the model listed.

ENGINE DATA: BASE FOUR (Chevette): Inline. Overhead cam. Four-cylinder. Cast iron block and head. Displacement: 98 cu. in. (1.6 liters). Bore & stroke: 3.23 x 2.98 in. Compression ratio: 9.0:1. Brake horsepower: 65 at 5200 R.P.M. Torque: 80 lb.-ft. at 3200 R.P.M. Five main bearings. Hydraulic valve lifters. Carburetor: 2Bbl. VIN Code: C. DIESEL FOUR (Chevette): Inline. Overhead cam. Four-cylinder. Cast iron block and head. Displacement: 111 cu. in. (1.8 liters). Bore & stroke: 3.31 x 3.23 in. Compression ratio: 22.0:1. Brake horsepower: 51 at 5200 R.P.M. Torque: 72 lb.-ft. at 2000 R.P.M. Five main bearings. Solid valve lifters. Fuel injection. VIN Code: D. BASE FOUR (Cavalier): Inline. Overhead valve. Four-cylinder. Cast iron block and head. Displacement: 121 cu. in. (2.0 liters). Bore & stroke: 3.50 x 3.15 in. Compression ratio: 9.3:1. Brake horsepower: 88 at 4800 R.P.M. Torque: 110 lb.-ft. at 2400 R.P.M. Five main bearings. Hydraulic valve lifters. Throttle-body fuel injection. VIN Code: P. BASE FOUR (Citation, Celebrity, Camaro): Inline. Overhead valve. Four-cylinder. Cast iron block and head. Displacement: 151 cu. in. (2.5 liters). Bore & stroke: 4.00 x 3.00 in. Compression ratio: 8.2:1. Brake horsepower: 92 at 4000 R.P.M. Torque: 134 lb.-ft. at 2800 R.P.M. Five main bearings. Hydraulic valve lifters. Throttle-body fuel injection. Pontiac-built. VIN Code: R exc. (Camaro) 2. BASE V-6 (Camaro Berlinetta); OPTIONAL (Citation, Celebrity, Camaro): 60-degree, overhead-valve V-6. Cast iron block and head. Displacement: 173 cu. in. (2.8 liters). Bore & stroke: 3.50 x 2.99 in. Compression ratio: 8.5:1. Brake horsepower: 112 at 4800 R.P.M. (Camaro, 107 at 4800). Torque: 145 lb.-ft. at 2100 R.P.M. Four main bearings. Hydraulic valve lifters. Carburetor: 2Bbl. Rochester E2SE. VIN Code: X exc. (Camaro) 1. HIGH-OUTPUT V-6 (Citation): Same as 173 cu. in. V-6 above except: C.R.: 8.9:1. Brake H.P.: 135 at 5400 R.P.M. Torque: 145 lb.-ft. at 2400 R.P.M. VIN Code: Z. BASE V-6 (Malibu, Monte Carlo, Impala, Caprice): 90-degree, overhead-valve V-6. Cast iron block and head. Displacement: 229 cu. in. (3.8 liters). Bore & stroke: 3.74 x 3.48 in. Compression ratio: 8.6:1. Brake horsepower: 110 at 4000 R.P.M. Torque: 190 lb.-ft. at 1600 R.P.M. Four main bearings. Hydraulic valve lifters. Carburetor: 2Bbl. Rochester E2ME. VIN Code: K or 9. (NOTE: California models used a Buick 231 V-6.) DIESEL V-6 (Malibu, Celebrity, Monte Carlo): 90-degree, overhead-valve V-6. Cast iron block and head. Displacement: 262 cu. in. (4.3 liters). Bore & stroke: 4.057 x 3.385 in. Compression ratio: 22.8:1. Brake horsepower: 85 at 3600 R.P.M. Torque: 165 lb.-ft. at 1600 R.P.M. Four main bearings. Hydraulic valve lifters. Fuel injection. VIN Code: T or V. BASE V-8 (Camaro Z28, Impala/Caprice wagon); OPTIONAL (Camaro, Malibu, Monte Carlo, Impala, Caprice): 90-degree, overhead valve V-8. Cast iron block and head. Displacement: 305 cu. in. (5.0 liters). Bore & stroke: 3.74 x 3.48 in. Compression ratio: 8.6:1. Brake horsepower: 150 at 4000 R.P.M. Torque: 240 lb.-ft. at 2400 R.P.M. Five main bearings. Hydraulic valve lifters. Carburetor: 4Bbl. Rochester E4ME. VIN Code: H. HIGH-OUTPUT V-8 (Monte Carlo SS); OPTIONAL (Camaro): Same as 305 cu. in. V-8 above, except: Brake H.P.: 175 at 4800 R.P.M. Torque: 235 lb.-ft. at 3200 R.P.M. OPTIONAL FUEL-INJECTED V-8 (Camaro Z28): Same as 305 cu. in. V-8 above, with dual CFI: Brake H.P.: 175 at 4200 R.P.M. Torque: 250 lb.-ft. at 2800 R.P.M. VIN Code: S. DIESEL V-8; OPTIONAL (Malibu, Monte Carlo, Impala/Caprice): 90-degree, overhead valve V-8. Cast iron block and head. Displacement: 350 cu. in. (5.7 liters). Bore & stroke: 4.057 x 3.385 in. Compression ratio: 22.5:1. Brake horsepower: 105 at 3200 R.P.M. Torque: 200 lb.-ft. at 1600 R.P.M. Five main bearings. Hydraulic valve lifters. Fuel injection. Olds-built. VIN Code: N.

CHASSIS DATA: Dimensions and tires were virtually identical to 1982, except for slight growth in overall length of Cavalier coupe to 170.9 in.

TECHNICAL: Transmission: Four-speed floor shift standard on Chevette: Gear ratios (1st) 3.75:1; (2nd) 2.16:1; (3rd) 1.38:1; (4th) 1.00:1; (Rev) 3.82:1. Four-speed floor shift on Cavalier/Citation: (1st) 3.53:1; (2nd) 1.95:1; (3rd) 1.24:1; (4th) 0.81:1 or 0.73:1; (Rev) 3.42:1. Citation H.O. V-6 four-speed manual trans.: (1st) 3.31:1; (2nd) 1.95:1; (3rd) 1.24:1; (4th) 0.81:1; (Rev) 3.42:1. Camaro four/V-6 four-speed manual trans.: (1st) 3.50:1; (2nd) 2.48:1; (3rd) 1.66:1; (4th) 1.00:1; (Rev) 3.50:1. Cavalier five-speed manual: (1st) 3.91:1; (2nd) 2.04:1; (3rd) 1.33:1; (4th) 0.92:1; (5th) 0.75:1; (Rev) 3.50:1. Camaro four/V-6 five-speed manual: (1st) 3.50:1; (2nd) 2.14:1; (3rd) 1.36:1; (4th) 1.00:1; (5th) 0.78:1; (Rev) 3.39:1. Camaro V8-305 five-speed manual: (1st) 2.95:1; (2nd) 1.94:1; (3rd) 1.34:1; (4th) 1.00:1; (5th) 0.73:1; (Rev) 2.76:1. Chevette five-speed manual shift: (1st) 3.76:1; (2nd) 2.18:1; (3rd) 1.36:1; (4th) 1.00:1; (5th) 0.86:1; (Rev) 3.76:1. Three-speed Turbo Hydra-matic standard on Celebrity, Malibu, Monte Carlo and Caprice/Impala. Malibu/Monte/Caprice/Imp gear ratios: (1st) 2.52:1; (2nd) 1.52:1; (3rd) 1.00:1; (Rev) 1.93:1. Camaro four/V-6 and Malibu/Monte diesel V-6: (1st) 2.74:1; (2nd) 1.57:1; (3rd) 1.00:1; (Rev) 2.07:1. Chevette automatic trans.: (1st) 2.40:1; (2nd) 1.48:1; (3rd) 1.00:1; (Rev) 1.92:1. Cavalier/Citation/Celebrity auto. trans.: (1st) 2.84:1; (2nd) 1.84:1; (3rd) 1.00:1; (Rev) 2.07:1. Four-speed overdrive automatic transmission on Caprice/Impala: (1st) 2.74:1; (2nd) 1.57:1; (3rd) 1.00:1; (4th) 0.67:1; (Rev) 2.07:1. Four-speed overdrive automatic on Camaro V8-305, Caprice/Imp diesel: (1st) 3.06:1; (2nd) 1.63:1; (3rd) 1.00:1; (4th) 0.70:1; (Rev) 2.29:1. Standard final drive ratio: (Chevette) 3.36:1; (Cavalier) 3.32:1 exc. 2.83:1 w/5-spd and 3.18:1 w/auto.; (Citation four) 2.42:1 or 2.39:1; (Cit V-6) 2.69:1 or 2.53:1; (Cit H.O. V-6) 2.96:1 or 3.06:1; (Camaro V-6) 3.42:1 w/five-spd, 3.08:1 or 3.23:1 w/auto.; (Camaro V-8) 3.73:1 w/five-spd, 3.08:1 or 2.93:1 w/auto.; (Z28) 3.23:1; (Celeb four) 2.39:1; (Celeb V-6) 2.84:1; (Malibu/Monte V-6) 2.41:1; (Malibu/Monte V-8) 2.29:1; (Caprice/Imp V-6) 2.56:1 or 2.73:1; (Caprice/Imp V-8) 2.41:1, 2.73:1 or 2.93:1. Steering: (Cavalier/Chevette/Citation/Celebrity) rack and pinion; (others) recirculating ball. Suspension/Brakes/Body: Same as 1982. Fuel tank: (Chvt) 12.5 gal.; (Cav) 14 gal.; (Cit) 15.9 gal.; (Camaro) 16.2 gal. exc. 15.8 with four-cyl. or CFI V-8; (Celeb) 15.7 gal. approx.; (Malibu/Monte) 18.1 gal.; (Capr/Imp) 25 gal.; (Capr/Imp wag) 22 gal.

DRIVETRAIN OPTIONS: Engines: 173 cu. in., 2Bbl. V-6: Citation, base Camaro, Celeb ($150). H.O. 173 cu. in., 2Bbl. V-6: Citation ($300). 305 cu. in., 4Bbl. V-8: Camaro ($350); Berlinetta ($225); Malibu/Monte, Imp/Caprice sed ($225). H.O. 305 cu. in., 4Bbl. V-8: Camaro ($505). 305 cu. in. CFI V-8: Camaro Z28 ($450). Diesel 260 cu. in. V-6: Celeb/Monte, Malibu sed ($500). Diesel 350 cu. in. V-8: Malibu/Monte/Imp/Caprice ($700); Caprice wag ($525). Transmission/Differential: Three-speed automatic trans.: Chevette/Cavalier ($395); Chvt diesel ($380); Citation/Camaro ($425); Berlinetta ($195). Five-speed manual trans.: Chevette/Cavalier ($75); base Camaro ($125). Four-speed overdrive automatic trans.: base Camaro ($525); Berlinetta/Z28 ($295); Imp/Caprice ($175). Limited-slip differential: Camaro/Malibu/Monte/Imp/Capr ($95). Performance axle ratio Chvt/Cav/Camaro/Malibu/Monte, Imp/Capr wag ($21). Power Accessories: Power brakes: Chevette ($95); Citation ($100). Power four-wheel disc brakes: Camaro V-8 ($179). Power steering: Chvt/Cav ($199); Cit ($210). Suspension: F40 H.D. susp.: Cav/Cit/Celeb/Malibu/Monte/Imp/Capr ($26). F41 sport suspension: Cit/Celeb ($33); Cav/Camaro/Monte, Imp/Capr sed ($49). Rear stabilizer bar: Cavalier ($36). Inflatable rear shock absorbers: Caprice wag ($64). Other: H.D. cooling ($40-$70). Cold climate pkg.: Malibu/Monte/Imp/Capr diesel ($99). Diesel engine and fuel line heater: Celeb ($49). H.D. battery ($25) exc. diesel ($50). California emission system ($75) exc. diesel ($215).

CHEVETTE CONVENIENCE/APPEARANCE OPTIONS: Option Packages: Sport decor pkg.: black grille, headlamp bezels and wheels; bodyside moldings, trim rings and decals ($95). Deluxe exterior: side window reveal moldings, argent wheels and trim rings ($150-$165). Comfort/Convenience: Air conditioning ($625). Rear defogger, electric ($125). Tinted glass ($90). Comfortilt steering wheel ($99). Cigarette lighter: Scooter ($10). Rear wiper/washer ($117). Lighting and Mirrors: Aux. lighting ($41-$42). Twin sport mirrors, left remote ($51). Driver's remote sport mirror ($33). Entertainment: AM radio: Scooter ($83). AM/FM radio ($82); Scooter ($165). AM/FM stereo radio ($109). Radio delete ($51 credit). Exterior Trim: Two-tone paint ($133). Sport stripes ($89). Bodyside moldings: Scooter ($45). Door edge guards ($15-$25). Interior Trim/Upholstery: Cloth bucket seats ($28). Custom cloth bucket seats ($130). Color-keyed floor mats ($25). Wheels and Tires: Wheel trim rings ($52). P155/80R13 GBR WSW ($51). P175/70R13 SBR BSW ($119). P175/70R13 SBR WSW ($173).

CAVALIER CONVENIENCE/APPEARANCE OPTIONS: Option Packages: CL equipment pkg.: custom interior, quiet sound group, visor mirror, leather-wrapped steering wheel, sport mirrors and wheel covers, warning chimes ($577-$696). Comfort/Convenience: Air cond. ($625). Cruise control w/resume ($170). Rear defogger, electric ($125). Tinted glass ($90). Six-way power driver's seat ($210). Comfortilt steering wheel ($99). Power windows ($180-$255). Power door locks ($120-$170). Remote swing-out side windows ($55). Power hatch or trunk release ($40). Power liftgate release ($35). Gauge pkg. w/trip odometer ($69). Special instruments incl. tach ($70-$139). Lighter: base ($14). Intermittent wipers ($49). Rear wiper/washer ($117). Lighting, Horns and Mirrors: Halogen headlamps ($10). Aux. lighting ($72-$95). Dual sport mirrors, left remote ($51). Dual electric remote sport mirrors ($89-$137). Right visor mirror ($7). Entertainment: AM/FM radio: base ($112). AM/FM stereo radio ($171) exc. CS ($82). Electronic-tuning AM/FM stereo radio w/clock ($277) exc. CS ($177). Electronic-tuning AM/FM stereo radio w/cassette ($377) exc. CS ($277). Electronic-tuning AM/FM stereo seek/scan radio w/cassette and clock ($555) exc. CS ($455). Dual rear speakers ($30-$42); premium ($25). Fixed-mast antenna: base ($41) but incl. w/radios. Radio delete ($56 credit). Exterior Trim: Removable sunroof ($295). Two-tone paint ($176). Pin striping ($53). Sport striping ($95). Bodyside moldings, black/argent ($45). Wheel opening moldings ($30). Door edge guards ($15-$25). Roof carrier ($98). Bumper guards ($56). Interior Trim/Upholstery: Cloth bucket seats ($28). Split-folding rear seatback ($50). Color-keyed mats: front ($15); rear ($10). Cargo area cover ($64). Wheels and Tires: Aluminum wheels ($272-$369). Wheel trim rings ($52). P175/80R13 GBR WSW ($54). P195/70R13 SBR BSW ($169). P195/70R13 SBR WSW ($231). P195/70R13 SBR WLT ($253).

CITATION/CELEBRITY CONVENIENCE/APPEARANCE OPTIONS:

Option Packages: X-11 sport equipment pkg.: Citation ($998). Sport decor pkg. (rear spoiler, rally wheels, sport mirrors, color-keyed bumpers w/rub strips, decal): Citation ($299). Deluxe exterior pkg.: Cit ($118-$218). Exterior molding pkg. (rocker panel and wheel opening moldings): Celeb ($53). Value appearance group: Cit ($55-$63). Quiet sound group: Cit cpe ($43). Quiet sound/rear decor pkg.: Cit ($92). Comfort/Convenience: Air conditioning ($725). Rear defogger, electric ($135). Cruise control w/resume ($170). Tinted glass ($105). Sport steering wheel: Cit ($22). Comfortilt steering wheel ($105). Six-way power driver's seat: Celeb ($210). Power windows ($180-$255). Remote swing-out side windows: Cit ($108). Power door locks ($120-$170). Gauge pkg. w/clock and trip odometer: Cit ($104). Gauge pkg. w/tachometer: Cit ($149). Gauge pkg. w/trip odometer: Celeb ($64). Electric clock: Cit ($35). Digital clock: Celeb ($39). Lighter: Cit cpe ($10). Intermittent wipers ($49). Lighting, Horns and Mirrors: Halogen high-beam headlamps: Celeb ($10). Aux. lighting ($50). Dual horns: Cit ($12). Driver's remote mirror ($22). Dual sport mirrors, left remote ($59). Dual remote mirrors: Celeb ($89). Entertainment: AM radio: Cit cpe ($83). AM/FM radio: Cit hatch, Celeb ($82); Cit cpe ($165). AM/FM stereo radio: Cit ($109) exc. cpe ($192). AM/FM stereo w/cassette: Cit ($209) exc. cpe ($292). Celebrity electronic-tuning AM/FM stereo radio w/clock ($177); w/cassette ($277); with seek/scan and cassette ($455). Dual rear speakers ($30); incl. w/stereo radio. Premium dual rear speakers: Celeb ($25) but incl. with seek/scan radio. Radio delete ($56 credit). Exterior Trim: Vinyl roof: Celeb ($155). Two-tone paint: Cit ($176-$184) incl. pin striping and bodyside moldings; Celeb ($148). Bodyside pin striping: Cit ($39-$47); Celeb ($57). Bodyside moldings: Cit ($55). Door edge guards ($15-$25). Bumper guards ($56). Bumper rub strips: Cit ($50). Interior Trim/Upholstery: Console ($100). Reclining driver and passenger seatbacks: Celeb ($90). Sport

cloth bench seat: Cit ($28). Custom trim w/cloth bench seat: Cit ($467). Vinyl bench seat: Celeb ($28). Celebrity custom bench seat: cloth ($179-$250); vinyl ($109-$207). Celebrity 45/45 seating: cloth ($100); custom cloth ($250-$330). Sport cloth bucket seats: Cit ($221-$250). Custom trim w/cloth bucket seats: Cit ($467-$492). Color-keyed mats: front ($17); rear ($12). Deluxe seatbelts: Cit cpe ($26). Wheels and Tires: Full wheel covers: Cit ($52). Sport wheel covers: Celeb ($63). Wire wheel covers: Celeb ($153). Wheel cover locks: Celeb ($39). Rally wheels: Cit ($60-$112); Celeb ($56). P185/80R13 GBR WSW ($58). P185/80R13 SBR BSW ($65). P185/80R13 SBR WSW ($123). P195/74R14 GBR WSW: Celeb ($129). P195/75R14 SBR WSW: Celeb ($194). P205/70R13 SBR WSW: Celeb ($245). P205/70R13 SBR WLT: Cit ($267). P215/60R14 SBR WLT: Citation X-11 ($92). Puncture-sealant tires: Celeb ($106).

1983 Chevrolet, Monte Carlo SS two-door coupe (JG)

CAMARO/MALIBU/MONTE CARLO CONVENIENCE/ APPEARANCE OPTIONS:

Option Packages: Estate equipment: Malibu wag ($307). Quiet sound group: Camaro ($72-$82); Malibu ($66). Security pkg.: Malibu wag ($44). Comfort/Convenience: Air cond. ($725). Rear defogger, electric ($135). Cruise control w/resume ($170). Tinted glass ($105). Comfortilt steering wheel ($105). Six-way power driver's seat: Camaro/Monte ($210). Power windows: Camaro/Monte ($180); Malibu ($255). Power door locks: Malibu ($170); Camaro/Monte ($120). Power trunk opener: Monte ($40). Power hatch release: Camaro ($40). Power tailgate window release: Malibu wag ($40). Electric clock: base Camaro, Malibu/Monte ($35). Digital clock: base Camaro ($39). Gauge pkg. w/trip odometer: Malibu/Monte ($95). Special instruments incl. tach: base Camaro ($149). Intermittent wipers ($49). Rear wiper/washer: Camaro ($120). Lighting, Horns and Mirrors: Halogen high-beam headlamps ($10). Cornering lamps: Monte ($55). Aux. lighting: Camaro ($52); Malibu ($49-$56); Monte ($28). Dual horns: Camaro/Malibu ($12). Remote-control driver's mirror: Malibu ($22). Twin sport mirrors (left remote): base Camaro, Monte ($51); Malibu ($59). Twin remote sport mirrors: Monte ($81). Twin electric remote sport mirrors: Camaro ($89-$137). Entertainment: AM radio ($112). AM/FM radio ($171). AM/FM stereo radio ($198). Cassette player with AM/FM stereo radio: Malibu/Monte ($298). Camaro electronic-tuning AM/FM stereo radio w/clock ($267-$302); w/cassette and clock ($367-$402); w/cassette and seek/scan ($520-$555). Dual rear speakers ($30). Fixed mast antenna ($41); incl. w/radios. Power antenna: Camaro/Monte ($60). Exterior Trim: Removable glass roof panels: Camaro/Monte ($825). Landau vinyl roof: Monte ($240). Rear spoiler: Camaro ($69). Two-tone paint: Malibu ($138); Monte ($214). Bodyside moldings, black: Camaro ($55). Deluxe bodyside moldings: Malibu/Monte ($57). Rocker panel moldings: Malibu ($25). Wheel opening moldings: Malibu ($30). Side window reveal moldings: Malibu ($44). Door edge guards ($15-$25). Side window sill moldings: Monte ($45). Roof drip moldings: Camaro ($29). Bodyside pin striping: Malibu ($57); Monte ($61). Rear window air deflector: Malibu wag ($36). Roof carrier: Malibu wag ($125). Bumper rub strips: Malibu ($50). Bumper guards: Malibu ($56). Interior Trim/Upholstery: Vinyl bench seat: Monte ($28). Cloth bench seat: Malibu ($28). Custom cloth bench seat: Malibu ($161); Monte ($358). Custom vinyl bench seat: Malibu ($133). Cloth or vinyl 55/45 seating: Malibu ($233-$261); Monte ($133-$161). Cloth bucket seats: Camaro ($28). Custom cloth or vinyl bucket seats: base Camaro ($299); Z28 ($227). Cloth LS conteur bucket seats: Camaro ($375). Custom cloth LS conteur bucket seats: Camaro ($650). Color-keyed mats: Malibu/Monte ($27); Camaro front ($20); Camaro rear ($15). Cargo area cover: Camaro ($64). Deluxe load-floor carpet: Malibu wag ($84). Deluxe trunk trim: Camaro ($164); Monte ($47). Wheels and Tires: Aluminum wheels: Monte ($362). Rally wheels: Camaro ($112); Malibu ($108); Monte ($56). Full wheel covers: Camaro/Malibu ($52). Sport wheel covers: Malibu ($115). Wire wheel covers: Malibu ($190); Monte ($153). Wheel cover locks: Monte ($39). P185/75R14 GBR WSW: Malibu sed ($58). P195/75R14 GBR WSW: Camaro, Malibu wag ($62). P195/75R14 SBR BSW: Camaro ($64). P195/75R14 SBR WSW: Camaro ($126); Malibu sed ($151); Malibu wag ($122); Monte ($62). P205/70R14 SBR BSW: base Camaro ($123). P205/70R14 SBR WSW: Camaro ($189); Berlinetta ($66); Monte ($124). P205/70R14 SBR WLT: Camaro ($211). P205/75R14 SBR BSW: Malibu ($95). P205/75R14 SBR WSW: Malibu ($151).

IMPALA/CAPRICE CONVENIENCE/APPEARANCE OPTIONS:

Option Packages: Estate equipment: wag ($307). Value appearance group: bodyside and wheel opening moldings, full wheel covers ($118). Comfort/Convenience: Air cond. ($725). Rear defogger, electric ($135). Cruise control w/resume ($170). Tinted glass ($105). Comfortilt steering wheel ($105). Power door locks ($170). Six-way power driver's seat ($210). Power windows ($255). Power trunk opener ($40). Power tailgate lock: wag ($49). Electric clock: Imp ($35). Digital clock: Imp ($66); Caprice ($34). Gauge pkg. w/trip odometer ($64). Intermittent wipers ($49). Quiet sound group: Imp ($66). Lighting and Mirrors: Halogen high-beam headlamps ($10). Cornering lamps ($55). Aux. lighting ($32-$42). Driver's remote mirror ($22). Dual remote mirrors ($65). Dual sport mirrors, left remote ($59). Dual remote body-color sport mirrors ($89). Lighted visor mirror ($48). Enter-

tainment: AM radio ($112). AM/FM radio ($171). AM/FM stereo radio ($198). Cassette player with AM/FM stereo ($298). Dual rear speakers ($30). Power antenna ($60). Windshield antenna ($29); incl. w/radios. Exterior Trim: Vinyl roof: sed ($180). Roof carrier: wag ($150). Custom two-tone paint ($141). Pin striping ($39). Bodyside moldings ($55). Door edge guards ($25). Bumper rub strips ($66). Bumper guards ($62). Interior Trim/Upholstery: Vinyl bench seat: sed ($28). Cloth bench seat: wag ($28). Cloth 50/50 seat ($257-$285). Custom cloth 50/50 seat: sed ($452). Deluxe load-floor carpet: wag ($89). Deluxe cargo area carpet: wag ($129). Color-keyed mats: front ($17); rear ($12). Deluxe trunk trim ($59). Wheels and Tires: Full wheel covers ($52). Sport wheel covers: Imp ($115); Caprice ($63). Wire wheel covers ($153). Wire wheel cover locks ($39). P205/75R15 SBR WSW: sed ($66). P225/70R15 SBR WSW: sed ($159). P225/75R15 SBR WSW: wag ($71). Puncture-sealant tires ($106-$132).

HISTORY: Introduced: Sept. 23, 1982 excl. Camaro Nov. 8, 1982. Model year production (U.S.): 1,012,649 (incl. Corvettes but not incl. 11,640 Acadians). Total production for U.S. market was made up of 500,305 four-cylinder, 350,722 sixes and 374,668 V-8s. A total of 12,480 diesels were installed. Calendar year production (U.S.): 1,294,184 (including 28,174 Corvettes). Calendar year sales by U.S. dealers: 1,347,447 (incl. 28,144 Corvettes), for a 19.8 percent market share. Model year sales by U.S. dealers: 1,306,951 (incl. 25,891 Corvettes) for a 20.2 percent share.

Historical Footnotes: The nation's economic condition may have improved during 1983, but Chevrolet's status remained shaky. Model year sales rose by close to six percent, but domestic cars in general fared far better--up by nearly 17 percent. Both at Chevrolet and in the industry generally, most of that increase came from mid- and full-size models. Robert C. Stempel, Chevrolet's general manager, promoted a new "pricing strategy which finds more than half of Chevrolet's 1983 passenger car models carrying lower sticker prices than they did in '82." Some of the reduction, though, was due to elimination of formerly standard equipment--a practice that would become common in the years ahead. Citation sales fell sharply, down from a healthy 321,023 in 1981 and so-so 209,545 in 1982 to a piddling 116,460 this year. No doubt, the well-publicized recall of 1980 models contributed to much of the decline. NHTSA had ordered that recall for alleged brake problems as this model year began. That action would soon change popular opinion of the X-car in general and Citation in particular. A week-long sales seminar at the Citation plant at Tarrytown, New York this year couldn't do much for sales if the buying public truly turned against the X-car. The newer Cavalier and Celebrity performed better, showing ample sales gains, partly as a result of marketing Cavalier as a sporty economy car. Far fewer Chevette diesels were sold than in 1982: only 1,940 total. Camaro was named *Motor Trend* "Car of the Year" for 1982. In a GM reshuffling, Chevrolet became part of the new Chevrolet-Pontiac-GM of Canada Group, which was to emphasize small cars. That group was headed by Lloyd E. Reuss, formerly Buick's general manager. Robert C. Stempel of Chevrolet moved over to the new Buick-Oldsmobile-Cadillac group, which focused on large cars. Robert D. Burger then became Chevrolet's general manager.

1984

This year saw the arrival of only one new body style, the Celebrity station wagon, along with a "re-launching" of the troubled X-car (as Citation II). Malibu was dropped, its role as a mid-size family car having been usurped by the front-drive Celebrity. Scooter was gone too, but Monte Carlo added a high-performance SS model to lure enthusiasts and Celebrity fielded a Eurosport option. Otherwise, 1984 was mainly a year for engineering changes.

1984 Chevrolet, Chevette CS four-door hatchback sedan (CP)

CHEVETTE -- SERIES 1T -- FOUR -- Except for a new passenger door map pocket, the rear-drive subcompact showed virtually no change for 1984. Once again, Chevette came with either a 1.6-liter gasoline four or a 1.8-liter diesel, which could (according to Chevrolet) deliver fuel mileage in the 60 MPG neighborhood. Diesels added a fuel-line heater. Both two-door and four-door hatchbacks were again available, in two trim levels. Joining the option list: new chrome bumpers and sport wheel covers. The stripped-down Scooter was abandoned, but Chevettes still came in two series: base and CS. Base Chevettes came with black bumpers (with guards and end caps), vinyl reclining front bucket seats, fold-down rear seat, front stabilizer bar, four-speed manual transmission, two-speed wip-

ers, styled steel wheels, and a passenger map pocket. Chevette CS added color-keyed bumpers, a cigarette lighter, mini-console, AM radio, and black bodyside moldings. Diesels included a five-speed transmission and power brakes. Chevette's CS Sport Decor package (price $95) included a black grille, black headlamps with red accents, bodyside moldings, black bumper with end caps, and black styled wheels with bright trim rings and decals. A Custom Exterior package included black window frames with narrow bright side window moldings, plus argent styled steel wheels with trim rings. CS displayed a 'Chevette' nameplate ahead of front doors; base models did not.

1984 Chevrolet, Cavalier CS station wagon (CP)

1984 Chevrolet, Cavalier Type 10 two-door coupe

CAVALIER -- SERIES 1J -- FOUR -- Cavalier's new wind-tunnel-tuned front end got a new grille, quad headlamps and bumper this year. The crosshatch-pattern grille, tapered inward at the base, had a Chevrolet bowtie in the center and occupied the entire opening, with no solid upper panel as before. Wide rectangular park/signal lamps moved down below the rub strips in the body-colored bumpers. Quad rectangular headlamps were recessed. Cavaliers now came in eight body colors and four interior colors. Sedans and wagons came in base or CS trim, but the base/CS two-door coupe and hatchback were dropped. The sporty Type 10, initially offered only in hatchback form, added the convertible and two-door notchback coupe to its body list. Type 10 models carried their special nameplates on bodysides, just ahead of the rear wheels. CS Cavaliers wore an identifier just ahead of the front door. More examples of the convertible, offered in limited number during 1983, were expected to find buyers this year. A total of 5,161 Cavaliers are reported to have come with an Olympic Special Appearance package. Cavalier's standard suspension got larger-diameter stabilizer bars and softer front bushings. The rear stabilizer bar on the optional F41 sport suspension was also larger in diameter. Standard equipment included power brakes, four-speed manual transaxle (with over drive), argent grille, charcoal instrument panel, bright window moldings, color-keyed bumpers, vinyl front reclining bucket seats, front stabilizer bar, and four-spoke charcoal steering wheel. P175/80R13 GBR tires rode styled steel wheels. Type 10 added a black grille, color-keyed dash with black trim plate, cigarette lighter and ashtray light, AM radio, three-spoke color-keyed steering wheel, glove compartment lock, black window moldings, and bodyside moldings. Cavalier CS models had a bright grille. Convertible equipment was similar to Type 10 but with tinted glass, warning chimes, bright rocker panel moldings, power steering and windows, and dual black sport mirrors (left remote-controlled). An optional CL Custom Interior package included modified door and quarter trim, custom reclining seats with adjustable head restraints, and fender nameplates. On the Type 10 hatchback, it also included a leather steering wheel and split folding seat. This year's options added a leather-wrapped steering wheel and rear window louvers, plus a rear spoiler and sport wheel covers.

engines. Engine mounts were revised to reduce vibration at idle. The high-performance X11 equipment package, offered on both notchback and hatchback coupes. attempted to capitalize on a good record in SCCA showroom stock racing. Citation again came with a 151 cu. in. (2.5-liter) four-cylinder engine or optional V-6. Standard equipment included bright bumpers and grille, day/night mirror, four-speed manual transmission, styled steel wheels, two-speed wiper/washers, low-back vinyl bench front seat, locking glove box, and bright windshield and fender moldings. Hatchbacks also had a lighter, AM radio, black back window molding, rocker panel and wheel opening moldings. The X11 package included P215/60R14 SBR tires on cast aluminum wheels, hood scoop, sport suspension, color-keyed bumpers with black rub strips, power brakes, AM radio; and on hatchbacks, a cigarette lighter and removable cargo cover. Package price was $981 for an X11 hatchback, or $911 when installed on the coupe.

1984 Chevrolet, Camaro Berlinetta two-door coupe (CP)

1984 Chevrolet, Citation II X11 two-door hatchback coupe (AA)

1984 Chevrolet, Citation II four-door hatchback sedan

CITATION II -- SERIES 1X -- FOUR/V-6 -- Chevrolet's X-car got a slightly different name this year, supposedly in response to the many improvements it had received during the preceding three years. But renamed or not, it was still essentially a carryover. All-season steel-belted radial tires were standard on all models. New body badges identified

1984 Chevrolet, Camaro Z28 T-top two-door coupe (with High Output 5.0-liter V-8)

CAMARO -- SERIES 1F -- V-6/V-8 -- Berlinetta gained the most attention this year. That model's new "space-age instrumentation" included digital readouts, a pivoting pedestal-mounted radio, and dual adjustable fingertip control pods that could be moved close to the steering wheel. The Corvette-inspired cockpit also sported a roof console, plus adjustable low-back seats. A digital display ahead of the driver showed road speed (miles or kilometers per hour) plus odometer or engine speed. An adjoining vertical-bar tachometer flashed more urgently as engine speed increased, while a monitor farther to the right signaled low fluid levels or other trouble spots. At the left were conventional needle-type gauges. The twin pods contained switches for lights and instrument displays, plus wiper and climate control. Other push-button controls were in the floor console, while the overhead console contained a swivel map light and small storage pouch. A remote-controlled, electronically-tuned AM/FM stereo radio with digital clock was standard; tape player and graphic equalizer optional. The radio could swivel for easy operation by either the driver or passenger. Buttons for optional cruise control were on Berlinetta's steering wheel, not the column. Berlinettas could be spotted by their gold-colored body trim. On the mechanical side, Cross-Fire Injection was dropped, but the Z28 could have an optional high-output 5.0-liter engine (RPO code L69) rated 190 horsepower, hooked to either five-speed manual or four-speed automatic transmission. That H.O. V-8 (introduced in spring 1983) was the most powerful carbureted engine offered in a Chevrolet. It had a higher-lift, longer-duration camshaft, retuned valve system, and 9.5:1 compression. The H.O. engine also had a specially-calibrated Rochester Quadrajet carb, dual-snorkel cold-air intake, large-diameter exhaust and tailpipes, and wide-mouth (Corvette-type) catalytic converter. Steel-belted radial tires were now made standard on the Sport Coupe with four-cylinder engine, thus standard on all Camaros. All except Z28 now carried fourth-generation All-Season tires. Once again, 173 cu. in. (2.8-liter) V-6 and 305 cu. in. (5.0-liter) V-8 engines were available. The three-speed automatic transmission was dropped, replaced by a four-speed overdrive unit. A hydraulic clutch was now used with all manual gearboxes. The base Camaro Sport Coupe still came with a choice of four, six or eight cylinder power. Camaro's basic "grille" hardly qualified for that name, consisting of no more than three side-by-side slots in the front panel flanked by rectangular headlamps. The Z28 didn't even have those slots in its upper panel, but displayed subtle '5.0-Liter H.O.' badges on its back bumper and rocker panels (and air cleaner), plus dual tailpipes at the back. Base Sport Coupe equipment was similar to 1983, now with SBR tires and color-keyed front/rear bumpers with black accents. Body colors were the same as 1983, but added Dark Gold. In addition to the electronic instrumentation and roof console, Berlinetta equipment included an AM/FM stereo electronic-tuning radio, digital clock, hood and sail panel decals, lockable fuel filler door, sport aluminum hood, dual horns, five-speed manual gearbox, smooth-ride suspension, intermittent wipers, and custom vinyl reclining front bucket seats with adjustable head restraints. Berlinettas carried color-keyed sport mirrors and lower accent body paint with striping. Their 14 x 7 in. wheels were gold/aluminum finned. Z28 equipment was similar to 1983. Other models could have Berlinetta's roof console for an extra $50, while a locking rear storage cover cost $80.

1984 Chevrolet, Celebrity station wagon (AA)

1984 Chevrolet, Celebrity Eurosport four-door sedan (AA)

CELEBRITY -- SERIES 1A -- FOUR/V-6 -- Like Cavalier, the mid-size Celebrity boasted a new front-end design this year. The taller grille wore a center bowtie emblem and filled the entire space, lacking the solid upper panel of the prior version. Its top was roughly aligned with the top of the headlamps, and the cross-hatch pattern was made up of thin vertical slots with two horizontal divider bars. New police and taxi packages were based on the standard four-door sedan platform. A new four-door station wagon came with either two seats or a rear-facing third seat, and a rear opening wider than the Malibu that it replaced. Eurosport versions of each body style included specially-tuned suspension, unique blackout trim, and special decals. The Eurosport name was on front doors, in block letters. A high-output 173 cu. in. (2.8-liter) V-6 engine, similar to Citation's but with slightly less horsepower, became optional on coupes and sedans. Only 2,945 of them were installed this year. A four-speed manual gearbox was offered for the first time, standard equipment with the base four (or V-6 diesel). Also new: four-speed overdrive automatic with V-6 engines. Celebrity's standard equipment included chrome bumpers with end caps and black rub strips (with white inserts), side window defoggers, black left mirror, AM radio, front and rear stabilizer bars, power steering, and full wheel covers. Also standard: two-passenger vinyl front bench seat with folding center armrest, black windshield/window moldings, bright headlamp bezels, wide bodyside moldings, and a concealed spare tire. Wagons had a three-passenger vinyl bench front seat, power brakes, tailgate-ajar light, and hidden floor stowage area. The

Eurosport package included an F41 sport suspension, sport steering wheel, P195/7514 SBR tires on 6 in. rally wheels, red accent striping, blackout decor, black bodyside moldings, and red-finish nameplates. The price was $226 for coupe or sedan, $191 on wagons. A total of 26,844 Eurosport packages were installed for the year.

1984 Chevrolet, Caprice Classic two-door coupe (CP)

1984 Chevrolet, Monte Carlo two-door coupe (CP)

MONTE CARLO -- SERIES 1G -- V-6/V-8 -- Two options returned to Monte Carlo's lineup this year: bucket seats and a console. Also joining the list was the four-speed overdrive automatic transmission. With the loss of Malibu, Monte remained the only rear-drive mid-size Chevrolet. The diesel V-6 engine was dropped, but the V-8 diesel remained available with a $700 price tag. The high-output 305 cu. in. (5.0-liter) V-8 in the high-performance Monte Carlo SS (added to the lineup in spring 1983) got a boost to 180 horsepower to become what Chevrolet called a "street version of current NASCAR point leader." The SS powertrain also consisted of a high-stall-speed automatic transmission, dual exhausts, 3.42:1 axle ratio, and low-profile Goodyear Eagle GT white-letter P215/65R15 tires on 7 in. rally wheels. Cleanly styled SS Montes carried no body brightwork and wore a wind-tunnel-tuned nose plus a rear spoiler, producing a drag coefficient of just .375. The simple, slightly-angled blackout grille was flanked by quad rectangular headlamps. Wide recessed parking/signal lamps sat below the bumper rub strips. Monte SS bodies were painted only in dark metallic blue or white. Large door decals identified the SS, which also displayed an easy-to-spot "ground effects" front panel. Base Monte standard equipment included power brakes and steering, three-speed automatic transmission, cloth-upholstered bench seats with folding armrest, P195/75R14 SBR tires, compact spare tire, full wheel covers, wheel opening and roof drip moldings, dual chrome mirrors, dual horns, two-speed wiper/washers, and courtesy lights. Monte Carlo SS eliminated the wheel opening moldings but added gauges, black roof drip moldings, a rear spoiler, tachometer, sport suspension, and sport mirrors (left remote). A total of 7,281 Montes had the optional removable glass roof panels.

IMPALA/CAPRICE CLASSIC -- SERIES 1B -- V-6/V-8 -- After a year's absence, the Caprice Classic two-door coupe returned for 1984. The coupe and wagon came only in Caprice Classic trim, while sedans were sold under both Caprice and Impala names. Standard engine was again the 229 cu. in. (3.8-liter) V-6, with 305 cu. in. (5.0-liter) gas V-8 or 5.7-liter diesel optional. External appearance was unchanged. The wiper/washer controls moved from the dashboard to the turn signal lever. Optional cruise control gained incremental acceleration/deceleration, which allowed speed changes down to just 1 MPH at a time. Gas-engine wagons had standard heavy-duty suspension, while diesel wagons had standard four-speed overdrive automatic transmission. Impala's standard equipment included the V-6 engine, power brakes and steering, three-speed automatic transmission, front stabilizer bar, full wheel covers, cloth bench seat, padded door trim panels, trunk mat, day/night mirror, and bright moldings (windshield, door frame and roof drip). Also dome, trunk and glove box lights. Caprice equipment was similar, but added a folding center armrest, quartz clock, wheel opening moldings, color-keyed steering wheel with woodgrain insert, headlamps-on warning buzzer, and lower-carpeted door trim panels with pull straps. Caprice sport coupes and sedans had bumper rub strips. Wagons had vinyl bench seating plus the overdrive automatic transmission. A Landau equipment package with vinyl roof cost an extra $306.

I.D. DATA: Coding of the 17-symbol Vehicle Identification Number (VIN) was similar to 1983. Symbol five (car line/series) was now: 'J' = base Chevette; 'B' = Chevette CS; 'C'= Cavalier; 'D' = Cavalier CS; 'E' = Cavalier Type 10; 'H' = Citation coupe; 'X' = Citation; 'P' = Camaro; 'S' = Camaro Berlinetta; 'W' = Celebrity ; 'G' = Monte Carlo; 'L' = Impala; 'N' = Caprice. Body type (symbols six-seven) added code '47' for full-size 2-dr. sport coupe. Code 'S' for V8-305 FI engine was dropped. Code 'G' for H.O. V8-305 4Bbl. was added. The model year code changed to 'E' for 1984.

CHEVETTE (FOUR)

Model No.	Body/Style No.	Body Type & Seating	Factory Price	Shipping Weight	Prod. Total
1T	J08	2-dr. Hatch Cpe-4P	4997	1988	66,446
1T	J68	4-dr. Hatch Sed-4P	5333	2051	28,466

CHEVETTE CS (FOUR)

Model No.	Body/Style No.	Body Type & Seating	Factory Price	Shipping Weight	Prod. Total
1T	B08	2-dr. Hatch Cpe-4P	5489	2032	47,032
1T	B68	4-dr. Hatch Sed-4P	5636	2091	94,897

CHEVETTE DIESEL (FOUR)

1T	J08/Z90	2-dr. Hatch Cpe-4P	5500	N/A		1,495
1T	J68/Z90	4-dr. Hatch Sed-4P	5851	N/A		1,180

CHEVETTE CS DIESEL (FOUR)

1T	B08/Z90	2-dr. Hatch Cpe-4P	5999	N/A		1,000
1T	B68/Z90	4-dr. Hatch Sed-4P	6161	N/A		3,384

CAVALIER (FOUR)

1J	C69	4-dr. Sedan-5P	6222	2320	90,023
1J	C35	4-dr. Sta Wag-5P	6375	2392	50,718

CAVALIER CS (FOUR)

1J	D69	4-dr. Sedan-5P	6666	2334	110,295
1J	D35	4-dr. Sta Wag-5P	6821	2405	58,739

1984 Chevrolet, Cavalier Type 10 two-door convertible (AA)

CAVALIER TYPE 10 (FOUR)

1J	E27	2-dr. Coupe-5P	6477	2300	103,204
1J	E77	2-dr. Hatch Cpe-5P	6654	2350	44,146
1J	E27/Z08	2-dr. Conv. Cpe-4P	11299	2515	5,486

CITATION II (FOUR/V-6)

1X	H11	2-dr. Coupe-5P	6445/6695	2382/2454	4,936
1X	X08	2-dr. Hatch Cpe-5P	6900/7150	2399/2471	8,783
1X	X68	4-dr. Hatch Sed-5P	7046/7296	2435/2507	83,486

CAMARO (V-6/V-8)

1F	P87	2-dr. Spt Cpe-4P	8245/8545	2907/3091	127,292

CAMARO BERLINETTA (V-6/V-8)

1F	S87	2-dr. Spt Cpe-4P	10895/11270	2919/3157	33,400

CAMARO Z28 (V-8)

1F	P87	2-dr. Spt Cpe-4P	---- /10620	---- /3107	100,416

Camaro Engine Note: Prices and weights before slash are for V-6 engine, after slash for V-8. Base Camaro Sport Coupes were also available with a four-cylinder engine, priced at $7,995 and weighing 2,813 pounds. The Z28 could have an optional high-output V-8 for an additional $530.

Z28 Production Note: Chevrolet production figures also show 478 Z28E hatchback sport coupes.

CELEBRITY (FOUR/V-6)

1A	W27	2-dr. Coupe-5P	7711/7961	2587/2719	29,191
1A	W19	4-dr. Sedan-5P	7890/8140	2623/2755	200,259
1A	W35	4-dr. Sta Wag-5P	8214/8464	2771/2894	48,295
1A	W35/AQ4	4-dr. 3S Wag-8P	8429/8679	N/A	31,543

MONTE CARLO (V-6/V-8)

1G	Z37	2-dr. Spt Cpe-6P	8936/9311	3085/3200	112,730

MONTE CARLO 'SS' (V-8)

1G	Z37/Z65	2-dr. Spt Cpe-6P	---- /10700 ---- /3336		24,050

IMPALA (V-6/V-8)

1B	L69	4-dr. Sedan-6P	8895/9270	3352/3450	55,296

1984 Chevrolet, Caprice Classic four-door sedan (CP)

CAPRICE CLASSIC (V-6/V-8)

1B	N47	2-dr. Spt Cpe-6P	9253/9628	3363/3461	19,541
1B	N69	4-dr. Sedan-6P	9399/9774	3396/3494	135,970
1B	N35	4-dr. 3S Wag-8P	---- /10210	---- /3952	65,688

FACTORY PRICE AND WEIGHT NOTE: For Citation and Celebrity, prices and weights to left of slash are for four-cylinder, to right for V-6 engine. For Camaro, Monte Carlo and full-size models, figures to left of slash are for six-cylinder model, to right of slash for 305 cu. in. V-8. Celebrity diesel V-6 cost $250 more than gas V-6. Diesel V-8 was $325 more than gas V-8.

BODY/STYLE NO. NOTE: Some models were actually option packages. Code after the slash (e.g., Z65) is the number of the option package that comes with the model listed.

ENGINE DATA: BASE FOUR (Chevette): Inline. Overhead cam. Four-cylinder. Cast iron block and head. Displacement: 98 cu. in. (1.6 liters). Bore & stroke: 3.23 x 2.98 in. Compression ratio: 9.0:1. Brake horsepower: 65 at 5200 R.P.M. Torque: 80 lb.-ft. at 3200 R.P.M. Five main bearings. Hydraulic valve lifters. Carburetor: 2Bbl. VIN Code: C. **DIESEL FOUR** (Chevette): Inline. Overhead cam. Four-cylinder. Cast iron block and head. Displacement: 111 cu. in. (1.8 liters). Bore & stroke: 3.31 x 3.23 in. Compression ratio: 22.0:1. Brake horsepower: 51 at 5000 R.P.M. Torque: 72 lb.-ft. at 2000 R.P.M. Five main bearings. Solid valve lifters. Fuel injection. VIN Code: D. **BASE FOUR** (Cavalier): Inline. Overhead valve. Four-cylinder. Cast iron block and head. Displacement: 121 cu. in. (2.0 liters). Bore & stroke: 3.50 x 3.15 in. Compression ratio: 9.3:1. Brake horsepower: 88 at 4800 R.P.M. Torque: 110 lb.-ft. at 2400 R.P.M. Five main bearings. Hydraulic valve lifters. Throttle-body fuel injection. VIN Code: P. **BASE FOUR** (Citation, Celebrity, Camaro): Inline. Overhead valve. Four-cylinder. Cast iron block and head. Displacement: 151 cu. in. (2.5 liters). Bore & stroke: 4.00 x 3.00 in. Compression ratio: 9.0:1. Brake horsepower: 92 at 4000 R.P.M. Torque: 132 lb.-ft. at 2800 R.P.M. Five main bearings. Hydraulic valve lifters. Throttle-body fuel injection. Pontiac-built. VIN Code: R exc. (Camaro) 2. BASE V-6 (Camaro Berlinetta); OPTIONAL (Citation, Celebrity, Camaro): 60-degree, overhead-valve V-6. Cast iron block and head. Displacement: 173 cu. in. (2.8 liters). Bore & stroke: 3.50 x 2.99 in. Compression ratio: 8.5:1. Brake horsepower: 112 at 4800 R.P.M. (Camaro, 107 at 4800). Torque: 145 lb.-ft. at 2100 R.P.M. Four main bearings. Hydraulic valve lifters. Carburetor: 2Bbl. VIN Code: X exc. (Camaro) 1. HIGH-OUTPUT V-6; OPTIONAL (Citation, Celebrity): Same as 173 cu. in. V-6 above except: C.R.: 8.9:1. Brake H.P.: 135 at 5400 R.P.M. (Celebrity, 130 H.P.). Torque: 145 lb.-ft. at 2400 R.P.M. VIN Code: Z. BASE V-6 (Monte Carlo, Impala, Caprice): 90-degree, over-head-valve V-6. Cast iron block and head. Displacement: 229 cu. in. (3.8 liters). Bore & stroke: 3.74 x 3.48 in. Compression ratio: 8.6:1. Brake horsepower: 110 at 4000 R.P.M. Torque: 190 lb.-ft. at 1600 R.P.M. Four main bearings. Hydraulic valve lifters. Carburetor: 2Bbl. VIN Code: 9. (NOTE: California models used a Buick 231 V-6.) DIESEL V-6 (Celebrity): 90-degree, overhead-valve V-6. Cast iron block and head. Displacement: 262 cu. in. (4.3 liters). Bore & stroke: 4.057 x 3.385 in. Compression ratio: 22.8:1. Brake horsepower: 85 at 3600 R.P.M. Torque: 165 lb.-ft. at 1600 R.P.M. Four main bearings. Hydraulic valve lifters. Fuel injection. VIN Code: T. BASE V-8 (Camaro Z28, Caprice wagon): OPTIONAL (Camaro, Monte Carlo, Impala, Caprice): 90-degree, overhead valve V-8. Cast iron block and head. Displacement: 305 cu. in. (5.0 liters). Bore & stroke: 3.74 x 3.48 in. Compression ratio: 8.6:1. Brake horsepower: 150 at 4000 R.P.M. Torque: 240 lb.-ft. at 2400 R.P.M. Five main bearings. Hydraulic valve lifters. Carburetor: 4Bbl. VIN Code: H. HIGH-OUTPUT V-8 (Monte Carlo SS): Same as 305 cu. in. V-8 above, except: Brake H.P.: 180 at 4800 R.P.M. Torque: 235 lb.-ft. at 3200 R.P.M. VIN Code: G. HIGH-OUTPUT V-8; OPTIONAL (Camaro Z28): Same as 305 cu. in. V-8 above, except: C.R.: 9.5:1. Brake H.P.: 190 at 4800 R.P.M. Torque: 240 lb.-ft. at 3200 R.P.M. VIN Code: G. DIESEL V-8; OPTIONAL (Monte Carlo, Impala/Caprice): 90-degree, overhead valve V-8. Cast iron block and head. Displacement: 350 cu. in. (5.7 liters). Bore & stroke: 4.057 x 3.385 in. Compression ratio: 22.1:1. Brake horsepower: 105 at 3200 R.P.M. Torque: 200 lb.-ft. at 1600 R.P.M. Five main bearings. Hydraulic valve lifters. Fuel injection. Olds-built. VIN Code: N.

CHASSIS DATA: Wheelbase: (Chevette 2-dr.) 94.3 in.; (Chvt 4-dr.) 97.3 in.; (Cavalier) 101.2 in.; (Citation/Celebrity) 104.9 in.; (Camaro) 101.0 in.; (Monte Carlo) 108.0 in.; (Imp/Caprice) 116.0 in. Overall length: (Chvt 2-dr.) 161.9 in.; (Chvt 4-dr.) 164.9 in.; (Cav cpe/conv) 172.4 in.; (Cav sed) 174.3 in.; (Cav wag) 174.5 in.; (Cit) 176.7 in.; (Camaro) 187.8 in.; (Celeb) 188.3 in.; (Celeb wag) 190.8 in.; (Monte) 200.4 in.; (Monte SS) 202.4 in.; (Impala) 212.2 in.; (Caprice sed) 212.8 in.; (Capr wag) 215.1 in. Height: (Chvt) 52.8 in.; (Cav cpe) 51.9 in.; (Cav hatch) 51.7 in.; (Cav conv) 52.7 in.; (Cav sed) 53.8 in.; (Cav wag) 54.3 in.; (Cit) 53.9 in.; (Camaro) 50.0 in.; (Camaro Z28) 50.3 in.; (Celeb) 53.9 in.; (Celeb wag) 54.3 in.; (Monte) 54.4 in.; (Monte SS) 55.0 in.; (Imp/Capr sed) 56.4 in.; (Capr wag) 58.1 in. Width: (Chvt) 61.8 in.; (Cav cpe/conv) 66.0 in.; (Cav sed/wag) 66.3 in.; (Cit) 68.3 in.; (Camaro) 72.8 in.; (Celeb) 69.3 in.; (Monte) 71.8 in.; (Imp/Capr) 75.4 in.; (Capr wag) 79.3 in. Front Tread: (Chvt) 51.2 in.; (Cav) 55.4 in.; (Cit/Celeb) 58.7 in.; (Camaro) 60.7 in.; (Monte) 58.5 in.; (Imp/Capr) 61.7 in.; (Caprice wag) 62.2 in. Rear Tread: (Chvt) 51.2 in.; (Cav) 55.2 in.; (Cit/Celeb) 57.0 in.; (Camaro) 61.6 in.; (Monte) 57.8 in.; (Imp/Capr) 60.7 in.; (Caprice wag) 64.1 in. Standard Tires: (Chvt) P155/80R13 GBR; (Cav) P175/80R13 GBR; (Cit/Celeb) P185/80R13 SBR; (Celeb wag) P185/75R14 SBR; (Camaro) P195/75R14 SBR; (Camaro Berlinetta) P205/70R14 SBR; (Camaro Z28) P215/65R15 WLT SBR; (Monte) P195/75R14 SBR; (Monte SS) P215/65R15; (Imp/Capr) P205/75R15 SBR; (Caprice wag) P225/75R15 SBR.

TECHNICAL: Transmission: Four-speed floor shift standard on Chevette. Gear ratios (1st) 3.75:1; (2nd) 2.16:1; (3rd) 1.38:1; (4th) 1.00:1; (Rev) 3.82:1. Four-speed floor shift on Cavalier/Citation/Celebrity: (1st) 3.53:1; (2nd) 1.95:1; (3rd) 1.24:1; (4th) 0.81:1 or 0.73:1; (Rev) 3.42:1. Citation H.O. V-6 four-speed manual trans.: (1st) 3.31:1; (2nd) 1.95:1; (3rd) 1.24:1; (4th) 0.81:1; (Rev) 3.42:1. Camaro four four-speed manual trans.: (1st) 3.50:1; (2nd) 2.48:1; (3rd) 1.66:1; (4th) 1.00:1; (Rev) 3.50:1. Cavalier five-speed manual: (1st) 3.91:1; (2nd) 2.15:1; (3rd) 1.33:1; (4th) 0.92:1; (5th) 0.74:1; (Rev) 3.50:1. Camaro four five-speed manual: (1st) 3.76:1; (2nd) 2.18:1; (3rd) 1.42:1; (4th) 1.00:1; (5th) 0.86:1; (Rev) 3.76:1. Camaro V-6 five-speed manual: (1st) 3.50:1; (2nd) 2.14:1; (3rd) 1.36:1; (4th) 1.00:1; (5th) 0.78:1; (Rev) 3.39:1. Camaro V8-305 five-speed manual.: (1st) 2.95:1; (2nd) 1.94:1; (3rd) 1.34:1; (4th) 1.00:1; (5th) 0.73:1; (Rev) 2.76:1. Chevette five-speed manual shift: (1st) 3.76:1; (2nd) 2.18:1; (3rd) 1.36:1; (4th) 1.00:1; (5th) 0.86:1; (Rev) 3.76:1. Three-speed Turbo Hydra-matic standard on Monte Carlo and Imp/Caprice: (1st) 2.74:1; (2nd) 1.57:1; (3rd) 1.00:1; (Rev) 2.07:1. Monte/Imp/Caprice w/V6-229: (1st) 2.52:1; (2nd) 1.52:1; (3rd) 1.00:1; (Rev) 1.93:1. Chevette auto. trans.: (1st) 2.40:1; (2nd) 1.48:1; (3rd) 1.00:1; (Rev) 1.92:1. Cav/Cit/Celeb auto. trans.: (1st) 2.84:1; (2nd) 1.60:1; (3rd) 1.00:1; (Rev) 2.07:1. Four-speed overdrive automatic on Imp/Caprice: (1st) 2.74:1; (2nd) 1.57:1; (3rd) 1.00:1; (4th) 0.67:1; (Rev) 2.07:1. Four-speed overdrive automatic on Celebrity: (1st) 2.92:1; (2nd) 1.57:1; (3rd) 1.00:1; (4th) 0.70:1; (Rev) 2.38:1. Four-speed overdrive automatic on Camaro: (1st) 3.06:1; (2nd) 1.63:1; (3rd) 1.00:1; (4th) 0.70:1; (Rev) 2.29:1. Standard final drive ratio: (Chevette) 3.36:1 or 3.62:1; (Cavalier) 3.32:1 or 4.10:1 w/4-spd, 3.83:1 w/5-spd or 3.73:1 w/auto.; (Citation four) 3.32:1 or 3.65:1 exc. 2.39:1 or 2.84:1 w/auto.; (Cit V-6) 3.32:1 exc. 2.53:1 w/auto.; (Cit H.O. V-6) 3.65:1 exc. 3.33:1 w/auto.; (Camaro four) 3.42:1 exc. 3.73:1 w/auto. or 5-spd; (Camaro V-6) 3.42:1 w/5-spd, 3.20:1 w/auto.; (Camaro V-8) 3.20:1 or 3.78:1 w/5-spd, 3.08:1 or 3.73:1 w/auto.; (Z28) 3.20:1 w/auto.; (Celebrity four) 3.65:1 exc. 2.39:1 w/auto.; (Celeb V-6) 2.84:1 or 3.06:1; (Celeb H.O. V-6)

3.33:1; (Monte V-6) 2.41:1 or 2.73:1; (Monte V-8) 3.42:1 or 3.73:1; (Monte H.O. V-8) 3.42:1 or 3.73:1; (Monte SS) 3.42:1; (Imp/Caprice V-6) 2.73:1 or 3.23:1; (Imp/Capr V-8) 2.73:1 or 3.08:1. Steering, Suspension, Brakes and Body: Same as 1982-83. Fuel tank: (Chvt) 12.2 gal.; (Cav) 13.6 gal.; (Cit four) 14.6 gal.; (Cit V-6) 15.1 gal.; (Camaro four) 15.5 gal.; (Camaro V-6) 16.2 gal.; (Celeb four) 15.7 gal.; (Celeb V-6) 16.4 gal.; (Monte) 18.1 gal.; (Imp/Capr) 25 gal.; (Caprice wag) 22 gal.

DRIVETRAIN OPTIONS: Engines: 173 cu. in., 2Bbl. V-6: Citation, base Camaro, Celeb ($250). H.O. 173 cu. in., 2Bbl. V-6: Citation ($400). 305 cu. in., 4Bbl. V-8: Camaro ($550); Berlinetta ($375); Monte, Imp/Caprice cpe/sed ($375). H.O. 305 cu. in., 4Bbl. V-8: Camaro Z28 ($530). Diesel 260 cu. in. V-6: Celeb ($500). Diesel 350 cu. in. V-8: Monte/Imp/Caprice ($700). Transmission/Differential: Five-speed manual trans.: Chevette/Cavalier ($75); base Camaro ($125). Three-speed automatic trans.: Chevette/Cavalier ($395); Chvt diesel ($380); Citation/Celeb ($425). Four-speed overdrive automatic trans.: base Camaro ($525); Berlinetta/Z28 ($295); Celeb (N/A); Monte, Imp/Capr cpe/sed ($175). Limited-slip differential: Camaro/Monte/Imp/Capr ($95). Performance axle ratio ($21). Power Accessories: Power brakes: Chevette ($95); Citation, Celeb cpe/sed ($100). Power four-wheel disc brakes: Camaro V-8 ($179). Power steering: Chvt/Cav ($204); Cit ($215). Suspension: F40 H.D. susp.: Cav/Cit/Celeb/Monte/Imp/Capr ($26). F41 sport suspension: Cit/Celeb ($33); Cav ($44-$49); Camaro/Monte, Imp/Capr cpe/sed ($49). Inflatable rear shock absorbers: Celeb/Caprice wag ($64). Other: H.D. cooling ($40-$70). Engine block heater ($20). Cold climate pkg.: Monte/Imp/Caprice diesel ($99). Diesel engine and fuel line heater: Celeb ($49). H.D. battery ($26) exc. diesel ($52). California emission system ($99).

CHEVETTE CONVENIENCE/APPEARANCE OPTIONS: Option Packages: Sport decor pkg.: black grille, headlamp bezels and wheels; bodyside moldings, trim rings and decals ($95). Deluxe exterior: side window reveal moldings, argent wheels and trim rings ($152-$167). Comfort/Convenience: Air conditioning ($630). Rear defogger, electric ($130). Tinted glass ($95). Comfortilt steering wheel ($104). Cigarette lighter: Scooter ($10). Lighting and Mirrors: Twin sport mirrors, left remote ($53). Driver's remote sport mirror ($34). Entertainment: AM radio: Scooter ($83). AM/FM radio ($82); Scooter ($165). AM/FM stereo radio ($109). Radio delete ($51 credit). Exterior Trim: Two-tone paint ($133). Rear spoiler ($69). Bodyside moldings: Scooter ($45). Door edge guards ($15-$25). Chrome bumpers ($25). Interior Trim/Upholstery: Cloth bucket seats ($28). Custom cloth bucket seats ($130). Color-keyed floor mats ($25). Wheels and Tires: Sport wheel covers ($97). Wheel trim rings ($52). P155/80R13 GBR WSW ($51). P175/70R13 SBR BSW ($119). P175/70R13 SBR WSW ($173).

CAVALIER CONVENIENCE/APPEARANCE OPTIONS: Option Packages: CL equipment pkg.: custom interior w/reclining seats, quiet sound group, three-spoke leather-wrapped steering wheel, custom door/quarter trim ($275-$375); incl. split folding rear seat on hatch/wagon. Comfort/Convenience: Air cond. ($630). Cruise control ($175). Rear defogger, electric ($130). Tinted glass ($95). Six-way power driver's seat ($215). Leather-wrapped steering wheel ($74-$95). Comfortilt steering wheel ($99). Power windows ($185-$260). Power door locks ($125-$175). Power hatch or trunk release ($40). Power liftgate release ($35). Gauge pkg. w/trip odometer ($69). Special instruments incl. tach ($139). Lighter: base ($14). Intermittent wipers ($50). Rear wiper/washer ($120). Lighting and Mirrors: Halogen headlamps ($10). Aux. lighting ($72-$95). Dual sport mirrors, left remote ($53). Right visor mirror ($7). Entertainment: AM radio: base ($112). AM/FM radio ($171) exc. CS/10 ($82). Electronic-tuning AM/FM stereo radio: CS/10 ($177). Elect.-tuning AM/FM stereo radio w/clock ($277) exc. CS/10 ($177). Elect.-tuning AM/FM stereo radio w/cassette ($377) exc. CS/10 ($277). Elect.-tuning AM/FM stereo seek/scan radio w/cassette, equalizer and clock ($605) exc. CS/10 ($505). Dual rear speakers ($30-$42); premium ($25). Fixed-mast antenna: base ($41) but incl. w/radios. Radio delete ($56 credit). Exterior Trim: Removable sunroof ($300). Rear spoiler ($69). Rear window louvers ($199). Pin striping ($53). Sport striping ($95). Bodyside moldings, black/argent ($45). Wheel opening moldings ($30). Wheel opening and rocker panel moldings ($55). Door edge guards ($15-$25). Roof carrier ($105). Bumper guards ($56). Interior Trim/Upholstery: Cloth or CS bucket seats ($28). Split-folding rear seatback ($50). Color-keyed mats: front ($15); rear ($10). Cargo area cover ($69). Wheels and Tires: Aluminum wheels ($369). Sport wheel covers w/black wheels ($97). Wheel trim rings ($52). P175/80R13 GBR WSW ($54). P195/70R13 SBR BSW ($169). P195/70R13 SBR WSW ($231). P195/70R13 SBR WLT ($253).

CITATION/CELEBRITY CONVENIENCE/APPEARANCE OPTIONS: Option Packages: X-11 sport equipment pkg.: Citation ($919-$981). Eurosport pkg.: Celeb cpe/sed ($226); wag ($191). Sport decor pkg. (rear spoiler, rally wheels, sport mirrors, color-keyed bumpers w/rub strips, decal): Citation ($249). Deluxe exterior pkg.: Cit ($68-$168). Exterior molding pkg. (black rocker panel and wheel opening moldings): Celeb ($55). Value appearance group: Cit ($55-$63). Quiet sound group: Cit cpe ($43). Quiet sound/rear decor pkg.: Cit ($92). Security pkg.: Celeb wag ($44). Comfort/Convenience: Air cond. ($725-$730). Rear defogger, electric ($140). Cruise control ($175). Tinted glass ($110). Sport steering wheel: Cit ($22). Comfortilt steering wheel ($110). Six-way power driver's seat: Celeb ($215). Power windows ($185-$260). Remote swing-out side windows: Cit ($108). Power door locks ($125-$175). Citation gauge pkg. w/clock and trip odometer ($104); w/tachometer ($149). Gauge pkg. w/trip odometer: Celeb ($64). Electric clock: Cit ($35). Digital clock: Celeb ($39). Lighter: Cit cpe ($10). Intermittent wipers ($50). Rear wiper/washer: Celeb ($120). Lighting, Horns and Mirrors: Halogen high-beam headlamps: Celeb ($10). Aux. lighting: Cit ($50); Celeb ($43-$57). Dome reading lamp: Celeb ($24). Dual horns: Cit

($12). Driver's remote mirror ($23). Dual sport mirrors, left remote ($61). Dual remote mirrors: Celeb ($91). Entertainment: AM radio: Cit cpe ($83). AM/FM radio: Cit hatch, Celeb ($82); Cit cpe ($165). AM/FM stereo radio: Cit ($109) exc. cpe ($192). AM/FM stereo w/cassette: Cit ($209) exc. cpe ($292). Celebrity electronic-tuning AM/FM stereo radio w/clock ($177); w/cassette ($277); with seek/scan, equalizer and cassette ($505). Dual rear speakers ($30); incl. w/stereo radio. Premium dual rear speakers: Celeb ($25) but incl. with elect. tuning radio. Radio delete ($56 credit). Exterior Trim: Vinyl roof: Celeb ($160). Two-tone paint: Cit ($176-$184) incl. pin striping and bodyside moldings; Celeb ($148). Bodyside pin striping: Cit ($39-$47); Celeb ($57). Bodyside moldings: Cit ($55). Door edge guards ($15-$25). Rear window air deflector: Celeb wag ($40). Swing-out quarter vent windows: Celeb ($75). Swing-out tailgate: Celeb ($105). Roof carrier: Celeb wag ($105). Bumper guards ($56). Bumper rub strips: Cit ($50). Citation Interior Trim/Upholstery: Console ($105). Sport cloth bench seat ($28). Custom trim w/cloth bench seat ($195); w/custom cloth bucket seats ($367-$392). Sport cloth bucket seats ($221-$250). Color-keyed mats: front ($17); rear ($12). Deluxe seatbelts: cpe ($26). Celebrity Interior Trim/Upholstery: Console ($105). Reclining driver and passenger seatbacks ($90). Two-pass. vinyl front bench seat: cpe/sed ($28). Three-pass. vinyl front bench seat: sed ($78). Three-pass. cloth front bench seat ($28-$50). CL custom cloth 45/45 seat ($250-$330). CL three-pass. custom bench seating: vinyl ($229); cloth ($257). CL two-pass. custom cloth bench seating ($109-$179). 45/45 cloth seating ($100). Cloth bucket seats ($147). Color-keyed mats: front ($17); rear ($12). Deluxe luggage area trim: wag ($40). Citation Wheels/Tires: Rally wheels ($56). P185/80R13 SBR WSW ($58). P205/70R13 SBR WLT ($202). P215/60R14 SBR WLT: X-11 ($92). Celebrity Wheels/Tires: Aluminum wheels ($306-$362). Sport wheel covers ($65). Wire wheel covers ($159). Wheel cover locks ($39). Rally wheels ($56). P185/80R13 SBR WSW ($58). P185/75R14 SBR BSW ($36). P185/75R14 SBR WSW ($58-$94). P195/70R14 SBR BSW ($28). P195/75R14 SBR BSW ($31-$67). P195/75R14 SBR WSW ($93-$129). P205/70R13 SBR WSW ($180).

1984 Chevrolet, Monte Carlo SS two-door coupe (CP)

CAMARO/MONTE CARLO CONVENIENCE/APPEARANCE OPTIONS: Comfort/Convenience: Air conditioning ($730). Rear defogger, electric ($140).

Cruise control ($175-$185). Tinted glass ($110). Comfortilt steering wheel ($110). Six-way power driver's seat ($215). Power windows ($185). Power door locks ($125). Power trunk opener: Monte ($40). Power hatch release: Camaro ($40). Electric clock ($35). Gauge pkg. w/trip odometer: Monte ($95). Gauge pkg. incl. tach: Camaro ($149). Intermittent wipers ($50). Rear wiper/washer: Camaro ($120). Quiet sound group: Camaro ($72-$82). Lighting, Horns and Mirrors: Halogen high-beam headlamps ($10). Cornering lamps: Monte ($55). Aux. lighting: Camaro ($37-$72); Monte ($28). Dual horns: Camaro ($12). Twin sport mirrors (left remote): base Camaro, Monte ($53). Twin remote sport mirrors: Monte ($83); SS ($30). Twin electric remote sport mirrors: Camaro ($91-$139). Entertainment: AM radio ($112). AM/FM radio ($171). AM/FM stereo radio: Monte ($198). Cassette player with AM/FM stereo radio: Monte ($298). Camaro electronic-tuning AM/FM stereo radio ($263); w/clock ($267-$302); w/cassette and clock ($367-$402); w/cassette, clock and seek/scan ($570-$605). Dual rear speakers ($30). Fixed mast antenna ($41); incl. w/radios. Power antenna ($60). Exterior Trim: Removable glass roof panels ($825). Landau vinyl roof: Monte ($245). Rear spoiler: Camaro ($69). Two-tone paint: Monte ($214). Bodyside moldings, black: Camaro ($55). Deluxe bodyside moldings: Monte ($57). Door edge guards ($15). Side window sill moldings: Monte ($45). Roof drip moldings: Camaro ($29). Bodyside pin striping: Monte ($61). Interior Trim/Upholstery: Console: Camaro ($50); Monte ($105). Vinyl bench seat: base Monte ($28). Cloth 55/45 seating: base Monte ($133). Cloth bucket seats: Camaro ($28); Monte ($147). Custom cloth or vinyl bucket seats: base Camaro ($359); Z28 ($287). Custom cloth CL 55/45 seating: base Monte ($385). Cloth LS contour bucket seats: Camaro ($375). Custom cloth LS contour bucket seats: Camaro ($650). Mats w/carpeted inserts: Camaro front ($20); Camaro rear ($15). Color-keyed mats: Monte ($27). Cargo area cover: Camaro ($69). Deluxe trunk trim: Camaro ($164); Z28 ($84). Locking rear storage cover: Camaro ($80). Wheels and Tires: Aluminum wheels: Monte ($362). Rally wheels: Camaro ($112); Monte ($56). Full wheel covers: Camaro ($52). Wire wheel covers: Monte ($159). Wheel cover locks: Monte ($39). P195/75R14 GBR WSW: Camaro ($62). P195/75R14 SBR WSW: Monte ($62). P205/70R14 SBR BSW: base Camaro ($58). P205/70R14 SBR WSW: Camaro ($124); Berlinetta ($66); Monte ($124). P205/70R14 SBR WLT: Camaro ($146). P215/65R15 SBR BSW: Z28 ($92 credit).

IMPALA/CAPRICE CONVENIENCE/APPEARANCE OPTIONS: Option Packages: Estate equipment: wag ($307). Landau equipment pkg.: vinyl roof, sport mirrors and reveal moldings ($306). Comfort/Convenience: Air cond. ($730). Rear defogger, electric ($140). Cruise control ($175). Tinted glass ($110). Comfortilt steering wheel ($110). Power door locks ($125-$175). Six-way power driver's seat ($215). Power windows ($185-$260). Power trunk opener ($40). Power tailgate lock: wag ($50). Electric clock: Imp ($35). Digital clock: Imp ($66); Caprice ($34). Gauge pkg. w/trip odometer ($64).

Intermittent wipers ($50). Quiet sound group: Imp ($66). Lighting and Mirrors: Halogen high-beam headlamps ($10). Cornering lamps ($55). Aux. lighting ($32-$42). Driver's remote mirror ($23). Dual remote mirrors ($67). Dual sport mirrors, left remote ($61). Dual remote body-color sport mirrors ($91) exc. Landau ($30). Lighted visor mirror ($48). Entertainment: Same as 1983. AM radio ($112). AM/FM radio ($171). AM/FM stereo radio ($198). Cassette player with AM/FM stereo ($298). Dual rear speakers ($30). Power antenna ($60). Windshield antenna ($29); incl. w/radios. Exterior Trim: Vinyl roof: sed ($185). Roof carrier: wag ($110). Custom two-tone paint ($141). Pin striping ($39). Bodyside moldings ($55). Door edge guards ($15-$25). Rear window air deflector: wag ($40). Bumper rub strips ($66). Bumper guards ($62). Interior Trim/Upholstery: Reclining passenger seatback ($45). Vinyl bench seat: Imp sed ($28). Cloth bench seat: wag ($28). Cloth 50/50 seating: Caprice ($195-$225). Deluxe load-floor carpet: wag ($89). Deluxe cargo area carpet: wag ($129). Color-keyed mats: front ($17); rear ($12). Deluxe trunk trim ($59). Wheels and Tires: Sport wheel covers ($65). Wire wheel covers ($159). Wire wheel cover locks ($39). P205/75R15 SBR WSW: cpe/sed ($66). P225/70R15 SBR WSW: cpe/sed ($159). P225/75R15 SBR WSW: wag ($71). Puncture-sealant tires ($106-$132).

HISTORY: Introduced: Sept. 22, 1983. Model year production (U.S.): 1,658,868 (incl. Corvettes but not incl. 18,314 Acadians). Total production for the U.S. market included 871,578 four-cylinder, 466,797 sixes and 507,774 V-8s. A total of 11,452 diesels were installed. Calendar year production (U.S.): 1,471,462 (including 35,661 Corvettes). Calendar year sales by U.S. dealers: 1,565,143 (incl. 30,424 Corvettes) for a 19.7 percent market share. Model year sales by U.S. dealers: 1,585,902 (incl. 27,986 Corvettes) for a 20.1 percent share.

Historical Footnotes: Model year sales finished nearly 23 percent higher than the 1983 result, with all lines (except Citation) performing well. Sales of that forlorn X-car fell by more than half. As demand for Citations slowed, production was halted at the Oklahoma plant and cut to one shift at Tarrytown, New York. Cavalier continued as America's best selling car, with Celebrity not far behind. Two new imports, Sprint (built by Suzuki) and Spectrum (by Isuzu) would soon give Chevrolet another toehold on the rising small-car market. Sprint went on sale late in the 1984 model year, Spectrum later, both as '85 models. To help plan for the enthusiast's market, surveys revealed that nearly two-thirds of Camaro buyers were under age 35. *Road & Track* magazine called the '84 Camaro one of the dozen top enthusiast cars, and it tied with Trans Am for best Sports GT in its price league. The International Race of Champions returned to the racing circuit during 1984, after a three-year absence. Co-sponsored by Chevrolet, Anheuser-Busch, Goodyear and True Value Hardware, the races would put a dozen of the world's top drivers behind the wheel of identically-prepared Camaro Z28s. That IROC racing series had begun in 1974 using Porsches, then switched to Camaros. With heavy TV coverage, this year's races would draw considerable attention to Camaro and perhaps help pave the way for the soon-to-come IROC-Z production models. On another level, Chevrolet hosted a traveling Chevy Sports Hall of Fame show in urban shopping malls this year, as part of greatly increased advertising and promotional expenditures.

1985

Chevrolet claimed this year to offer "America's highest-mileage car, America's fastest car...America's most popular full-size car and America's most popular car, regardless of size." Still, 1985 was a year of refinement and evolution rather than revolution. But several intriguing models and engines were announced, including the new IROC-Z Camaro, performance Z24 Cavalier, and 4.3-liter V-6 engine with fuel injection. That 130-horsepower powerplant was the standard eight in Caprice and Monte Carlo, intended to tempt V-8 fans who might appreciate a bit better gas mileage. Also new was a multi-port fuel-injected version of the 2.8-liter V-6, identified by 'MFI' logo when installed in a Cavalier, Celebrity, Citation II or Camaro. Unfortunately, the Z24 Cavalier didn't actually arrive until the 1986 model year, nearly a year later than scheduled. The old reliable 305 cu. in. (5.0-liter) V-8 got a boost in compression ratio and new Electronic Spark Control.

1985 Chevrolet, Chevette CS four-door hatchback sedan (CP)

CHEVETTE -- SERIES 1T -- FOUR -- In the face of a flurry of front-drive subcompacts, Chevette hung on with rear-wheel drive. Little changed this year, except that the base Chevette was dropped, leaving only the CS version, again in two- or four-door hatchback form. Base powertrain remained the 1.6-liter gas four with four-speed manual transmission. The diesel four was still available, but only a handful were sold. A five-speed manual gearbox was now available on all models (formerly only on two-doors without air conditioning).

Diesels could no longer get automatic. Of the 10 body colors, eight were new this year. Also new: Custom two-tone combinations. Four-doors now had standard Custom Cloth front bucket seats. New bodyside moldings had argent inserts. Returning to the option list was a Z13 Sport Decor graphic package, including black grille, bumpers and wheels, plus black bodyside moldings with red inserts.

equipment, though similar to Type 10, included black/argent bodyside moldings and a bright grille. Convertibles came with a power top, power windows (drop-down rear quarter), black/argent bumper rub strips, tinted glass, black sport mirrors, and bright rocker panel moldings. Convertible interiors held cloth or vinyl custom reclining bucket seats.

1985 Chevrolet, Cavalier four-door sedan (AA)

1985 Chevrolet, Citation II X11 two-door hatchback coupe (AA)

CAVALIER -- SERIES 1J -- FOUR/V-6 -- Two-door Cavaliers got new taillamps, wheels and hubcaps, plus a new steering wheel. An upshift light was added to manual-gearbox models. Base models had upgraded seats. The lineup again included two-door notchbacks and hatchbacks, four-door sedans and wagons, plus the convertible. The convertible officially became a separate line this year, rather than an option package. Both Type 10 and convertible models got a "cockpit" styled instrument panel, with switches in control pods at the sides of the cluster. Cavaliers also got new interior trim colors and "Star Wars" instrumentation. Of the dozen body colors, ten were new this year. Cavaliers again had a crosshatch-pattern grille, angled inward at the base with bowtie emblem in the middle, and flanked by recessed quad rectangular headlamps. Parking lights were below the bumper rub strips. The base 121 cu. in. (2.0-liter) four, rated 85 horsepower, got refinements to improve durability and economy. But the biggest news for Cavalier was the availability of a 2.8-liter V-6 with multi-port fuel injection. Arriving later in the season, the V-6 was rated 125 horsepower, standard with the announced Z24 sports package but available in all models. That Z24 package, scheduled for spring 1985 arrival, was to include flared rocker panels, specific fascia, rally wheels, and digital instruments. But it didn't actually appear until the 1986 model year. Cavalier standard equipment included four-speed manual (overdrive) transmission, power brakes, front/rear ashtrays, color-keyed bumpers with black/argent rub strips, side window defogger, argent grille, day/night mirror, front stabilizer bar, styled steel wheels, fixed quarter windows, black windshield and back window moldings, and vinyl reclining bucket seats. Type 10 Cavaliers included black/red bumper rub strips, lighter, black grille, AM radio, color-keyed sport steering wheel, black/red bodyside moldings, plus black window and belt moldings. CS

1985 Chevrolet, Citation II four-door hatchback sedan

CITATION II -- SERIES 1X -- FOUR/V-6 -- All the final Citations were hatchbacks, as the notchback coupe was dropped this year. X-cars had been plagued by problems, including court battles, largely for alleged brake flaws on the 1980 models. A new dashboard included a horizontal-style radio. Electronic-tuning models were now available, with or without a cassette tape player. A dozen body colors were offered (nine new this year). Citation's X11 package now included a 130-horsepower 173 cu. in. (2.8-liter) V-6 with multi-port fuel injection. That powerplant was also available separately, in all models. The base 151 cu. in. (2.5-liter) four added hydraulic roller valve lifters this year, while the carbureted 2.8 V-6 continued in its prior form. The X11 package also included power brakes, sport steering wheel, sport cloth bucket seats, domed hood with air inlet, body-color bumpers, X11 decals, rear deck spoiler, F41 sport suspension, and P215/60R14 SBR tires on newly-styled Rally wheels. Black headlamp bezels, grille, B-pillar/window frames and taillamp frames completed the package. Aluminum wheels were optional.

1985 Chevrolet, Camaro Z28 two-door coupe

CAMARO -- SERIES 1F -- FOUR/V-6/V-8 -- Most appealing to connoisseurs was the new IROC-Z, styled along the lines of the racing models that performed in the International Race of Champions and with a nod to Corvette. IROC-Z was packaged as a Z28 option. In appearance, it could be spotted by twin foglamps inset in the grille opening (alongside the license plate mount), a low front air dam, ornamental hood louvers, and striping at rocker panel level. IROC-Z had a solid angled front panel between deeply recessed quad headlamps, with parking lamps just below the crease line. Deep body-color "ground effects" skirting encircled the entire car. Special 16 x 8 in. aluminum wheels held Corvette-inspired P245/50VR16 Goodyear Eagle GT unidirectional tires. Near the base of each door were large 'IROC-Z' decals. The IROC-Z chassis featured Delco/Bilstein rear shock absorbers, special struts and springs, special rear stabilizer, and reinforced front frame rails. The IROC-Z could have any of three 305 cu. in. (5.0-liter) V-8s: standard four-barrel with five-speed manual gearbox (four-speed overdrive automatic available), a high-output L69 carbureted V-8 with five-speed, or the new LB9 tuned-port fuel injection (TPI) version. The TPI came only with four-speed automatic. Individually-tuned runners channeled incoming air to each cylinder in the TPI V-8, while computer-controlled port injectors delivered precisely-metered fuel. In limited-production IROC-Z dress, the factory claimed a 0-60 MPH time in the seven-second area, and 15-second quarter-mile acceleration times. "Ordinary" Z28s could have only the standard or TPI versions, not the carbureted H.O. Z28s in general had a selection of changes in appearance details, including grille and parking lamps, deeper ground-effects rocker panels, hood louvers, deeper chin spoiler, three-element taillamps, larger rear bumper fascia, and new body nameplates. Inside were new speedometer graphics and tachometer. Berlinetta got a new standard 173 cu. in. (2.8-liter) V-6 with multi-port fuel injection and only one option: the carbureted 5.0-liter V-8. Also new were body graphics and subtly-patterned interior fabrics. The base Sport Coupe again came with either a four, V-6 or V-8 engine under the hood. Like the Z28, it had new body styling, a wider selection of optional sound systems with electronic-tuning radios, and revised optional instrument cluster graphics. All Camaros had new "wet arm" windshield wipers, with washer outlets mounted on the blades. The double-needle speedometer was abandoned. Split rear seatbacks were a new option, and cast aluminum wheels (standard on Z28) were available on the base Camaro. Body colors this year were white, silver, copper, red maroon, black, medium gray, dark or bright blue, yellow or light yellow, and light brown.

1985 Chevrolet, Celebrity Eurosport four-door sedan (AA)

1985 Chevrolet, Celebrity Eurosport two-door coupe

CELEBRITY -- SERIES 1F -- FOUR/V-6 -- Like other models, Celebrity got a new optional 173 cu. in. (2.8-liter) V-6 with multi-port fuel injection, available on all models. Also optional: a carbureted 2.8 and a 4.3-liter V-6 diesel, plus the standard 151 cu. in. (2.5-liter) four. All models now had 14 in. wheels and standard power brakes. Gas engines had new hydraulic mounts, plus the availability of four-speed overdrive automatic transmission. The Eurosport option package added gas-charged shock absorbers. Of the dozen body colors, nine were new this year. Station wagons could get a new woodgrain Estate Package. Coupes and sedans could be ordered with a new Celebrity Classic padded vinyl roof. Interior trim styles and colors were also new. The lineup continued as a two-door coupe, four-door sedan, and two- or three-seat wagons. The Eurosport package included black-finish body hardware with red accents, specific nameplates (inside and out), Rally wheels, red-accented bodyside molding rub strips, sport steering wheel, special F41 sport suspension, and gas-charged front struts and rear shocks. 'Eurosport' block lettering was at the forward edge of front doors; a '2.8FI' engine identifier on the decklid.

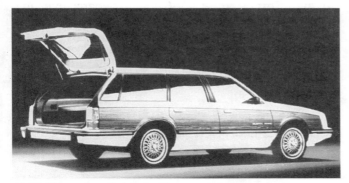

1985 Chevrolet, Celebrity Estate station wagon

1985 Chevrolet, Monte Carlo two-door coupe (CP)

1985 Chevrolet, Monte Carlo SS two-door coupe

MONTE CARLO -- SERIES 1G -- V-6/V-8 -- Under the hood of standard Montes was a new base 262 cu. in. (4.3-liter) V-6. Chevrolet claimed that the new 4.3 V-6 would be as economical as the prior carbureted 3.8, and nearly as "frisky" as a V-8. Standard Sport Coupes got new cloth interior trim and five new interior colors, plus new standard wheel covers. Still, the Monte Carlo SS, "cousin to the Grand National stock cars" on the NASCAR circuit, received the strongest promotion. Formerly offered only in white or blue body colors, this year's SS came in silver, maroon, white or black. Interiors could be gray or maroon, either bench or bucket style. This street version of the NASCAR racing car had special instruments, sport suspension, rear spoiler, sport mirrors and steering wheel, plus P215/65R15 white-letter radial tires on special rally wheels, Apart from 'Monte Carlo SS' lettering on the doors and decklid, the body was nearly devoid of ornamentation. The blackout grille was a simple crosshatch pattern, flanked by recessed quad rectangular headlamps with deeply inset park/signal lamps below the forward crease line. Taillamp lenses sat nearly flush with the decklid panel. Monte SS again carried a high-output (RPO code L69) version of the familiar 305 cu. in. (5.0-liter) V-8, now with four-speed overdrive automatic transmission. SS mufflers grew in capacity; axles got larger ring gears. Removable black roof panels were to become available on SS later in the model year.

1985 Chevrolet, Caprice Classic Landau two-door coupe (AA)

IMPALA/CAPRICE CLASSIC -- SERIES 1B -- V-6/V-8 -- Full-size Chevrolets had some changes to produce a more controlled ride, plus an economical new 262 cu. in. (4.3-liter) V-6 engine rated 130 horsepower. That new base engine was described as "a standard V-6 that acts like a V-8." All full-size models now wore fourth-generation All-Season tires. Four-speed overdrive automatic was available across the board. For the last time, the 5.7-liter diesel V-8 was optional (except in California). The lineup again included Caprice Classic two-door, four-door and station wagon, plus the four-door Impala sedan. Interiors received their most extensive reworking since 1977, all presumably to give a more contemporary, less stodgy look and feel. Wagons again came with a standard 305 cu. in. (5.0-liter) V-8, which was optional in other models. This year, it got a boost in compression (and horsepower), plus a new exhaust system. Caprice had a bold crosshatch grille, parking lamps inset into the bumper, wraparound cornering lamps, and quad rectangular headlamps. A 'Caprice Classic' script was at the forward end of front fenders. Impalas had standard AM radio, folding front center armrest, power brakes and steering, three-speed automatic transmission, lighter, padded door panels, argent grille, day/night mirror, cloth bench seats, full wheel covers, two-speed wiper/washers, and bright moldings. Caprice added a quartz clock, dual horns, wheel opening and lower bodyside moldings, headlamps-on buzzer, and bumper rub strips (except wagons). Wagons included vinyl bench seating, a locking side compartment, heavy-duty front/rear suspension, power liftgate window, and overdrive automatic transmission, along with the V-8 engine.

I.D. DATA: Chevrolets again had a 17-symbol Vehicle Identification Number (VIN) on the upper left surface of the instrument panel, visible through the windshield. Symbol one indicates country: '1' = U.S.A.; '2' = Canada. Next is a manufacturer code: 'G' = General Motors. Symbol three is car make: '1' = Chevrolet; '7' = GM of Canada. Symbol four denotes restraint system: 'A' = non-passive (standard); 'B' = passive (automatic belts); 'C' = passive (inflatable). Symbol five is car line/series: 'B' = Chevette; 'C'= Cavalier; 'D' = Cavalier CS; 'E' = Cavalier Type 10; 'X' = Citation; 'P' = Camaro; 'S' = Camaro Berlinetta; 'W' = Celebrity; 'Z' = Monte Carlo; 'L' = Impala; 'N' = Caprice. Symbols six-seven reveal body type: '08' = 2-dr. hatch coupe; '27' = 2-dr. notchback coupe (or convertible); '37' = special 2-dr. notch coupe; '47' = full-size 2-dr. sport coupe; '77' = 2-dr. hatch coupe; '87' = 2-dr. sport coupe; '19' = 4-dr. 6-window notchback sedan; '68' = 4-dr. 6-window hatch sedan; '69' = 4-dr. 4-window notchback sedan; '35' = 4-dr. station wagon. Next is the engine code: 'C' = L4-98 2Bbl.; 'D' = L4-111 diesel; 'P' = L4-121 FI; 'R' or 'Z' = L4-151 FI; 'X' = V6-173 2Bbl.; 'S' or 'W' = V6-173 MFI; 'Z' = V6-262 FI; 'T' = V6-262 diesel; 'H' = V8-305 4Bbl.; 'G' = H.O. V8-305 4Bbl.; 'F' = V8-305 TPI; 'N' V8-350 diesel. Next is a check digit, followed by 'F' for model year 1985. Symbol eleven indicates assembly plant: 'B' = Baltimore; 'J' = Janesville, WI; 'L' = Van Nuys, CA; 'N' = Norwood, OH; 'R' = Arlington, TX; 'T' = Tarrytown, NY; 'X' = Fairfax, KS; 'Y' = Wilmington, DE; '1' = Oshawa, Ontario; '6' = Oklahoma City, OK; '7' = Lordstown, OH. The final six digits are the sequential serial number. Engine number coding is similar to 1981-84.

CHEVETTE CS (FOUR)

Model No.	Body/Style No.	Body Type & Seating	Factory Price	Shipping Weight	Prod. Total
1T	B08	2-dr. Hatch Cpe-4P	5340	2032	57,706
1T	B68	4-dr. Hatch Sed-4P	5690	2091	65,128

CHEVETTE CS DIESEL (FOUR)

1T	B08/Z90	2-dr. Hatch Cpe-4P	5850	N/A	203
1T	B68/Z90	4-dr. Hatch Sed-4P	6215	N/A	462

CAVALIER (FOUR)

1J	C69	4-dr. Sedan-5P	6477	2320	86,597
1J	C35	4-dr. Sta Wag-5P	6633	2392	34,581

CAVALIER CS (FOUR)

1J	D69	4-dr. Sedan-5P	6900	2334	93,386
1J	D35	4-dr. Sta Wag-5P	7066	2405	33,551

CAVALIER TYPE 10 (FOUR)

1J	E27	2-dr. Coupe-5P	6737	2300	106,021
1J	E77	2-dr. Hatch Cpe-5P	6919	2350	25,508
1J	E27/Z08	2-dr. Conv. Cpe-4P	11693	2515	4,108

Cavalier Engine Note: A V-6 engine became available during the model year, priced at $560.

CITATION II (FOUR/V-6)

1X	X08	2-dr. Hatch Cpe-5P	6940/7200	2399/2471	7,443
1X	X68	4-dr. Hatch Sed-5P	7090/7350	2435/2507	55,279

CAMARO (V-6/V-8)

1F	P87	2-dr. Spt Cpe-4P	8698/8998	2907/3091	97,966

CAMARO BERLINETTA (V-6/V-8)

1F	S87	2-dr. Spt Cpe-4P	11060/11360	2919/3157	13,649

CAMARO Z28 (V-8)

1F	P87	2-dr. Spt Cpe-4P	---- /11060	---- /3107	68,199

Camaro Engine Note: Prices and weights before slash are for V-6 engine, after slash for V-8. Base Camaro Sport Coupes were also available with a four-cylinder engine, priced at $8,363 and weighing 2,813 pounds. The Z28 could have an optional fuel-injected or carbureted (IROC-Z) high-output V-8 for an additional $695.

Z28 IROC-Z Production Note: A total of 21,177 Z28s had the IROC-Z performance package (RPO Code B4Z). Chevrolet production figures also show 204 Z28E hatchback sport coupes.

CELEBRITY (FOUR/V-6)

1A	W27	2-dr. Coupe-5P	8102/8362	2587/2719	29,010
1A	W19	4-dr. Sedan-5P	8288/8548	2623/2755	239,763
1A	W35	4-dr. Sta Wag-5P	8479/8739	2771/2894	45,602
1A	W35/AQ4	4-dr. 3S Wag-8P	8699/8959	N/A	40,547

MONTE CARLO (V-6/V-8)

1G	Z37	2-dr. Spt Cpe-6P	9540/9780	3085/3093	83,573

MONTE CARLO 'SS' (V-8)

1G	Z37/Z65	2-dr. Spt Cpe-6P	---- /11380	---- /3336	35,484

IMPALA (V-6/V-8)

1B	L69	4-dr. Sedan-6P	9519/9759	3352/3366	53,438

CAPRICE CLASSIC (V-6/V-8)

1B	N47	2-dr. Spt Cpe-6P	9888/10128	3363/3377	16,229
1B	N69	4-dr. Sedan-6P	10038/10278	3396/3410	139,240
1B	N35	4-dr. 3S Wag-8P	---- /10714	---- /3952	55,886

FACTORY PRICE AND WEIGHT NOTE: For Citation and Celebrity, prices and weights to left of slash are for four-cylinder, to right for V-6 engine. For Camaro, Monte Carlo and full-size models, figures to left of slash are for six-cylinder model, to right of slash for 305 cu. in. V-8. Celebrity diesel V-6 cost the same as gas V-6. Diesel V-8 for Caprice/Impala was also priced the same as gas V-8. Optional engine prices rose during the model year.

BODY/STYLE NO. NOTE: Some models were actually option packages. Code after the slash (e.g., Z65) is the number of the option package that comes with the model listed.

ENGINE DATA: BASE FOUR (Chevette): Inline. Overhead cam. Four-cylinder. Cast iron block and head. Displacement: 98 cu. in. (1.6 liters). Bore & stroke: 3.23 x 2.98 in. Compression ratio: 9.0:1. Brake horsepower: 65 at 5200 R.P.M. Torque: 80 lb.-ft. at 3200 R.P.M. Five main bearings. Hydraulic valve lifters. Carburetor: 2Bbl. VIN Code: A. DIESEL FOUR (Chevette): Inline. Overhead cam. Four-cylinder. Cast iron block and head. Displacement: 111 cu. in. (1.8 liters). Bore & stroke: 3.31 x 3.23 in. Compression ratio: 22.0:1. Brake horsepower: 51 at 5000 R.P.M. Torque: 72 lb.-ft. at 2000 R.P.M. Five main bearings. Fuel injection. VIN Code: B. BASE FOUR (Cavalier): Inline. Overhead valve. Four-cylinder. Cast iron block and head. Displacement: 121 cu. in. (2.0 liters). Bore & stroke: 3.50 x 3.15 in. Compression ratio: 9.0:1. Brake horsepower: 85 at 4800 R.P.M. Torque: 110 lb.-ft. at 2400 R.P.M. Five main bearings. Hydraulic valve lifters. Throttle-body fuel injection. VIN Code: P. BASE FOUR (Citation, Celebrity, Camaro): Inline. Overhead valve. Four-cylinder. Cast iron block and head. Displacement: 151 cu. in. (2.5 liters). Bore & stroke: 4.00 x 3.00 in. Compression ratio: 9.0:1. Brake horsepower: 92 at 4400 R.P.M. (Camaro, 88 at 4400). Torque: 134 lb.-ft. at 2800 R.P.M. (Camaro, 132 at 2800). Five main bearings. Hydraulic valve lifters. Throttle-body fuel injection. Pontiac-built. VIN Code: R exc. (Camaro) 2. OPTIONAL V-6 (Citation, Celebrity): 60-degree, overhead-valve V-6. Cast iron block and head. Displacement: 173 cu. in. (2.8 liters). Bore & stroke: 3.50 x 2.99 in. Compression ratio: 8.5:1. Brake horsepower: 112 at 4800 R.P.M. Torque: 145 lb.-ft. at 2100 R.P.M. Four main bearings. Hydraulic valve lifters. Carburetor: 2Bbl. VIN Code: X. HIGH-OUTPUT V-6 (Camaro Berlinetta); OPTIONAL (Cavalier, Citation, Camaro, Celebrity): Same as 173 cu. in. V-6 above except with multi-port fuel injection--C.R.: 8.9:1. Brake H.P.: 135 at 5100 R.P.M. (Cavalier, 125 at 4800; Citation/Celebrity, 130 at 4800). Torque: 165 lb.-ft. at 3600 R.P.M. (Cavalier/Citation/Celeb, 155 at 3600). VIN Code: W exc. (Camaro) S. BASE V-6 (Monte Carlo, Impala, Caprice): 90-degree, overhead-valve V-6. Cast iron block and head. Displacement: 262 cu. in. (4.3 liters). Bore & stroke: 4.00 x 3.48 in. Compression ratio: 9.3:1. Brake horsepower: 130 at 3600 R.P.M. Torque: 210 lb.-ft. at 2000 R.P.M. Four main bearings. Hydraulic valve lifters. Fuel injection. VIN Code: Z. DIESEL V-6 (Celebrity): 90-degree, overhead-valve V-6. Cast iron block and head. Displacement: 262 cu. in. (4.3 liters). Bore & stroke: 4.057 x 3.385 in. Compression ratio: 22.8:1. Brake horsepower: 85 at 3600 R.P.M. Torque: 165 lb.-ft. at 1600 R.P.M. Four main bearings. Hydraulic valve lifters. Fuel injection. VIN Code: T. BASE V-8 (Camaro Z28, Caprice wagon): OPTIONAL (Camaro, Monte Carlo, Impala, Caprice): 90-degree, overhead valve V-8. Cast iron block and head. Displacement: 305 cu. in. (5.0 liters). Bore & stroke: 3.74 x 3.48 in. Compression ratio: 9.5:1. Brake horsepower: 155 at 4200 R.P.M. (Monte, 150 at 4000; Caprice/Imp, 165 at 4200). Torque: 245 lb.-ft. at 2000 R.P.M. (Monte, 240 at 2000; Caprice/Imp, 245 at 2400). Five main bearings. Hydraulic valve lifters. Carburetor: 4Bbl. VIN Code: H. HIGH-OUTPUT V-8 (Monte Carlo SS): Same as 305 cu. in. V-8 above, except--Brake H.P.: 180 at 4800 R.P.M. Torque: 235 lb.-ft. at 3200 R.P.M. VIN Code: G. OPTIONAL HIGH-OUTPUT V-8 (Camaro Z28/IROC-Z): Same as 305 cu. in. V-8 above, except: Brake H.P.: 190 at 4800 R.P.M. Torque: 240 lb.-ft. at 3200 R.P.M. RPO Code: L69. VIN Code: G. OPTIONAL HIGH-OUTPUT V-8 (Camaro Z28/IROC-Z): Same as 305 cu. in. V-8 above, but with tuned port fuel injection: Brake H.P.: 215 at 4400 R.P.M. Torque: 275 lb.-ft. at 3200 R.P.M. RPO Code: LB9. VIN Code: F. DIESEL V-8; OPTIONAL (Impala/Caprice): 90-degree, overhead valve V-8. Cast iron block and head. Displacement: 350 cu. in. (5.7 liters). Bore & stroke: 4.057 x 3.385 in. Compression ratio: 22.1:1. Brake horsepower: 105 at 3200 R.P.M. Torque: 200 lb.-ft. at 1600 R.P.M. Five main bearings. Hydraulic valve lifters. Fuel injection. Olds-built. VIN Code: N.

CHASSIS DATA: Wheelbase: (Chevette 2-dr.) 94.3 in.; (Chvt 4-dr.) 97.3 in.; (Cavalier) 101.2 in.; (Citation/Celeb) 104.9 in.; (Camaro) 101.0 in.; (Monte Carlo) 108.0 in.; (Imp/Caprice) 116.0 in. Overall length: (Chvt 2-dr.) 161.9 in.; (Chvt 4-dr.) 164.9 in.; (Cav cpe/conv) 172.4 in.; (Cav sed) 174.3 in.; (Cav wag) 174.5 in.; (Cit) 176.7 in.; (Camaro) 188.0 in.; (Camaro Z28) 192.0 in.; (Celeb) 188.3 in.; (Celeb wag) 190.8 in.; (Monte) 200.4 in.; (Monte SS) 202.4 in.; (Imp/Capr sed) 212.8 in.; (Caprice wag) 215.1 in. Height: (Chvt) 52.8 in.; (Cav cpe) 50.2 in.; (Cav conv) 52.7 in.; (Cav sed) 52.1 in.; (Cav wag) 52.8 in.; (Cit) 53.9 in.; (Camaro) 50.0 in.; (Camaro Z28) 50.3 in.; (Celeb) 54.1 in.; (Celeb wag) 54.3 in.; (Monte) 54.4 in.; (Monte SS) 54.9 in.; (Imp/Capr sed) 56.4 in.; (Caprice wag) 58.2 in. Width: (Chvt) 61.8 in.; (Cav cpe/conv) 66.0 in.; (Cav sed/wag) 66.3 in.; (Cit) 68.3 in.; (Camaro) 72.8 in.; (Celeb) 69.3 in.; (Monte) 71.8 in.; (Imp/Capr) 75.4 in.; (Caprice wag) 79.3 in. Front Tread: (Chvt) 51.2 in.; (Cav) 55.4 in.; (Cit/Celeb) 58.7 in.; (Camaro) 60.7 in.; (Camaro Berlinetta/Z28) 60.0 in.; (Monte) 58.5 in.; (Imp/Capr) 61.7 in.; (Caprice wag) 62.2 in. Rear Tread: (Chvt) 51.2 in.; (Cav) 55.2 in.; (Cit/Celeb) 57.0 in.; (Camaro) 61.6 in.; (Camaro Berlinetta/Z28): 60.9 in.; (Monte) 57.8 in.; (Imp/Capr) 60.7 in.; (Caprice wag) 64.1 in. Standard Tires: (Chvt) P155/80R13 GBR; (Cav) P175/80R13 GBR; (Cav Type 10) P215/60R14 SBR; (Cit) P185/80R13 SBR; (Celeb) P185/75R14 SBR; (Camaro) P195/75R14 SBR; (Camaro Berlinetta) P205/70R14 SBR; (Camaro Z28) P215/65R15 WLT SBR; (Monte) P195/75R14 SBR; (Monte SS) P215/65R15 SBR; (Imp/Capr) P205/75R15 SBR; (Caprice wag) P225/75R15 SBR.

TECHNICAL: Transmission: Four-speed floor shift standard on Chevette: Gear ratios (1st) 3.75:1; (2nd) 2.16:1; (3rd) 1.38:1; (4th) 1.00:1; (Rev) 3.82:1. Four-speed floor shift on Cavalier/Citation/Celebrity: (1st) 3.53:1; (2nd) 1.95:1; (3rd) 1.24:1; (4th) 0.81:1 or 0.73:1; (Rev) 3.42:1. Citation V-6 FI and Cavalier V-6 four-speed manual trans.: (1st) 3.31:1; (2nd) 1.95:1; (3rd) 1.24:1; (4th) 0.90:1; (Rev) 3.42:1. Camaro four four-speed manual trans.: (1st) 3.50:1; (2nd) 2.48:1; (3rd) 1.66:1; (4th) 1.00:1; (Rev) 3.50:1. Cavalier five-speed manual: (1st) 3.73:1; (2nd) 2.15:1; (3rd) 1.33:1; (4th) 0.92:1; (5th) 0.74:1; (Rev) 3.50:1. Camaro four five-speed manual: (1st) 3.76:1; (2nd) 2.18:1; (3rd) 1.42:1; (4th) 1.00:1; (5th) 0.86:1; (Rev) 3.76:1. Camaro V-6 five-speed manual: (1st) 3.50:1; (2nd) 2.14:1; (3rd) 1.36:1; (4th) 1.00:1; (5th) 0.78:1; (Rev) 3.39:1. Camaro V-8 five-speed manual.: (1st) 2.95:1; (2nd) 1.94:1; (3rd) 1.34:1; (4th) 1.00:1; (5th) 0.73:1; (Rev) 2.76:1. Chevette five-speed manual shift: (1st) 3.76:1; (2nd) 2.18:1; (3rd) 1.36:1; (4th) 1.00:1; (5th) 0.86:1; (Rev) 3.76:1. Three-speed Turbo Hydra-matic standard on Monte Carlo and Imp/Caprice: (1st) 2.74:1; (2nd) 1.57:1; (3rd) 1.00:1; (Rev) 2.07:1. Chevette automatic trans.: (1st) 2.40:1; (2nd) 1.48:1; (3rd) 1.00:1; (Rev) 1.92:1. Cavalier/Citation/Celebrity auto. trans.: (1st) 2.84:1; (2nd) 1.60:1; (3rd) 1.00:1; (Rev) 2.07:1. Four-speed overdrive automatic transmission on Monte Carlo: (1st) 2.74:1; (2nd) 1.57:1; (3rd) 1.00:1; (4th) 0.67:1; (Rev) 2.07:1. Four-speed overdrive automatic on Celebrity: (1st) 2.92:1; (2nd) 1.57:1; (3rd) 1.00:1; (4th) 0.70:1; (Rev) 2.38:1. Four-speed overdrive automatic on Camaro/Capr/Imp: (1st) 3.06:1; (2nd) 1.63:1; (3rd) 1.00:1; (4th) 0.70:1; (Rev) 2.29:1. Standard final drive ratio: (Chevette) 3.36:1 or 3.62:1; (Cavalier) 3.32:1 on notchback, 3.65:1 on others exc. 3.83:1 w/5-spd, 3.18:1 or 3.43:1 w/auto., 3.65:1 w/V-6 and 4-spd; (Citation) 3.32:1 w/4-spd, 2.39:1 or 2.53:1 w/auto.; (Cit H.O. V-6) 3.65:1 w/4-spd, 2.84:1 or 3.18:1 w/auto.; (Camaro four) 3.73:1; (Camaro V-6) 3.42:1; (Camaro V-8) 3.23:1 exc. 3.08:1 w/auto.; (Camaro TPI V-8) 3.23:1; (Camaro H.O. V-8) 3.73:1; (Celebrity four) 3.65:1 w/4-spd, 2.39:1 w/auto.; (Celeb V-6) 2.84:1 or 3.06:1; (Monte) 2.29:1 or 2.41:1; (Monte H.O. V-8) 3.73:1; (Imp/Caprice V-6) 2.56:1 or 3.08:1; (Imp/Capr V-8) 2.73:1 or 3.08:1. Steering/Suspension/Brakes/Body: same as 1982-84. Fuel tank: (Chvt) 12.2 gal.; (Cav) 13.6 gal.; (Cit) 14.6 or 15.1 gal.; (Camaro) 15.5 or 16.2 gal.; (Celeb) 15.7 or 16.4 gal.; (Monte) 17.6 or 18.1 gal.; (Imp/Capr) 25 gal.; (Caprice wag) 22 gal.

DRIVETRAIN OPTIONS: (Note: Prices of many options rose soon after the model year began.) Engines: 173 cu. in., 2Bbl. V-6: Cavalier ($560); Citation ($260); base Camaro ($335) Celeb ($260). H.O. 173 cu. in., 2Bbl. V-6: Citation/Celeb ($435). 305 cu. in., 4Bbl. V-8: Camaro ($635); Berlinetta ($300); Monte, Imp/Caprice cpe/sed ($240). H.O. 305 cu. in., 4Bbl. V-8: Camaro IROC-Z ($680). 350 cu. in., TPI V-8: Camaro Z28 ($680). Diesel 260 cu. in. V-6: Celeb ($260). Diesel 350 cu. in. V-8: Imp/Caprice ($240) exc. wag (NC). Transmission/Differential: Five-speed manual trans.: Chevette/Cavalier ($75); Camaro (NC). Three-speed automatic trans.: Chevette/Cavalier ($425); Citation/Celeb ($425). Four-speed overdrive automatic trans.: Camaro ($395); Celeb ($600); base Monte, Imp/Caprice cpe/sed ($175). Limited-slip differential: Camaro/Monte/Imp/Capr ($95). Performance axle ratio ($21). Power Accessories: Power brakes: Chevette ($100); Citation ($100). Power four-wheel disc brakes: Camaro V-8 ($179). Power steering: Chevette/Cavalier ($215); Citation ($215). Suspension: F40 H.D. susp.: Cav/Cit/Celeb/Imp/Capr ($26). F41 sport susp.: Cit ($33); Cav ($44-$49); Cama-

ro/Monte, Imp/Capr cpe/sed ($49). Inflatable rear shock absorbers: Celeb/Caprice wag ($64). Other: H.D. cooling ($40-$70). Engine block heater ($20). Cold climate pkg.: Imp/Capr diesel ($99). Diesel engine and fuel line heater: Celeb ($49). H.D. battery ($26) exc. diesel ($52). California emission system ($99).

CHEVETTE CONVENIENCE/APPEARANCE OPTIONS: Option Packages: Sport decor pkg.: black grille, wheels, bodyside moldings, bumpers; black trim w/red accents ($95). Custom exterior: black window moldings, styled argent wheels and bright trim rings ($152-$167). Comfort/Convenience: Air conditioning ($645). Rear defogger, electric ($135). Tinted glass ($99). Comfortilt steering wheel ($115). Lighting and Mirrors: Twin sport mirrors, left remote ($53). Driver's remote sport mirror ($34). Entertainment: AM/FM radio ($82). AM/FM stereo radio ($109). Radio delete ($51 credit). Exterior Trim: Two-tone paint ($133). Rear spoiler (N/A). Door edge guards ($15-$25). Chrome bumpers ($25). Interior Trim/Upholstery: Cloth bucket seats: cpe ($28). Custom cloth bucket seats: cpe ($130). Color-keyed floor mats ($25). Wheels and Tires: Sport wheel covers ($45-$97). Wheel trim rings ($52). P155/80R13 GBR WSW ($51). P175/70R13 SBR BSW ($118). P175/70R13 SBR WSW ($172).

1985 Chevrolet, Cavalier Type 10 two-door convertible (CP)

CAVALIER CONVENIENCE/APPEARANCE OPTIONS: Option Packages: CL custom interior pkg.: reclining seats w/adj. head restraints, quiet sound group, sport steering wheel, console (for manual shift), custom door/quarter trim ($251-$325); incl. split folding rear seat on hatch/wagon. Comfort/Convenience: Air cond. ($645). Cruise control w/resume ($175). Rear defogger, electric ($135). Tinted glass ($99). Six-way power driver's seat ($225). Black sport steering wheel ($22-$40). Comfortilt steering wheel ($115). Power windows ($195-$270). Power door locks ($130-$180). Power hatch or trunk release ($40). Power liftgate release ($40). Electronic instrument cluster ($295). Gauge pkg. w/trip odometer ($69); incl. tach ($139). Digital clock: 10/conv. ($39). Lighter: base ($14). Intermittent wipers ($50). Rear wiper/washer ($125). Lighting and Mirrors: Halogen headlamps ($25). Aux. lighting ($43-$95). Dual black sport mirrors, left remote ($53). Right visor mirror ($7). Entertainment: AM radio: base ($112). AM/FM radio ($82) exc. base ($171). Electronic-tuning

AM/FM stereo radio ($138) exc. base ($238); w/clock ($177) exc. base ($277); with seek/scan (N/A). Electronic-tuning AM/FM stereo seek/scan radio w/cassette ($319) exc. base ($419). Electronic-tuning AM stereo/FM seek/scan radio w/cassette, equalizer and clock ($494-$504) exc. base ($594). Dual rear speakers ($30-$42); premium ($25). Extended-range sound system: 10/Z24/conv. ($35). Fixed-mast antenna: base ($41) but incl. w/radios. Radio delete ($56 credit). Exterior Trim: Removable sunroof ($310). Rear spoiler: Type 10 ($69). Rear window louvers: Type 10 hatch ($199). Custom two-tone paint: CS ($176); Type 10 ($123). Pin striping ($53). Bodyside moldings, black ($45). Wheel opening moldings: conv. ($30). Wheel opening and rocker panel moldings ($55). Door edge guards ($15-$25). Wagon roof carrier ($105). Bumper guards ($56). Interior Trim/Upholstery: Cloth or sport cloth reclining bucket seats ($28). Custom CL reclining bucket seats: CS/10/conv. (NC). Split-folding rear seatback: wag/hatch ($50). Color-keyed mats: front ($18); rear ($15). Cargo area cover: wag/hatch ($69). Wheels and Tires: Aluminum wheels, 13 x 5.5 in. ($285); 14 x 6 in. (N/A). Styled 14 in. wheels: 10/conv. ($52). Sport wheel covers ($97). Wheel trim rings ($52). P175/80R13 SBR WSW ($54). P195/70R13 SBR BSW ($104). P195/70R13 SBR WSW ($166). P195/70R13 SBR RWL ($188). P215/60R14 SBR BSW: 10/conv. ($246). P215/60R14 SBR RWL: 10/conv. ($338); Z24 ($92).

CITATION/CELEBRITY CONVENIENCE/APPEARANCE OPTIONS: Option Packages: X-11 sport equipment pkg.: Citation ($941). Eurosport pkg.: Celeb ($199). Sport decor pkg. (rear spoiler, rally wheels, sport mirrors, color-keyed bumpers w/rub strips, black grille and moldings, black-accent trim, decal): Citation cpe ($249). Exterior molding pkg. (rocker panel and wheel opening moldings): Celeb ($55). CL custom interior (deluxe door trim w/cloth insert, custom cloth seats, rear ashtray, custom steering wheel): Citation cpe, reclining bucket seats ($392); Citation sed, bench seat ($195). Quiet sound/rear decor pkg.: Cit ($92). Security pkg.: Celeb wag ($44). Comfort/Convenience: Air conditioning ($730). Rear defogger, electric ($140). Cruise control ($175). Tinted glass ($110). Sport steering wheel: Cit ($22). Comfortilt steering wheel ($110). Six-way power driver's seat: Celeb ($215). Power windows ($185-$260). Power door locks ($125-$175). Power trunk or liftgate release: Celeb ($40). Gauge pkg. w/trip odometer: Cit ($69); Celeb ($64). Gauge pkg. w/tachometer: Cit ($149). Digital clock: Celeb ($39). Intermittent wipers ($50). Rear wiper/washer: Celeb ($120). Lighting, Horns and Mirrors: Halogen headlamps: Celeb ($22). Aux. lighting: Cit ($50); Celeb ($43-$57). Dome reading lamp: Celeb ($24). Dual horns ($12). Driver's remote mirror ($23). Dual sport mirrors, left remote ($61). Dual remote sport mirrors: Celeb ($91). Entertainment: AM/FM radio ($82). Electronic-tuning AM/FM stereo radio ($138); w/clock ($177); w/cassette, clock and seek/scan ($319). Electronic-tuning AM stereo/FM radio w/clock, seek/scan, equalizer and cassette: Celeb ($504). Dual rear speakers ($30). Extended-range rear speakers: Celeb ($35). Radio de-

lete ($56 credit). Exterior Trim: Removable sunroof: Celeb ($300). Padded vinyl roof: Celeb ($270). Two-tone paint: Cit ($176) incl. pin striping and bodyside moldings; Celeb ($148). Bodyside pin striping: Cit ($39); Celeb ($57). Bodyside moldings, black: Cit ($55). Side window reveal moldings: Cit ($45-$55). Door edge guards ($15-$25). Rear window air deflector: Celeb wag ($40). Rear quarter vent windows: Celeb ($75). Swing-out tailgate: Celeb wag ($105). Decklid or roof (wagon) luggage carrier: Celeb ($100-$105). Bumper guards ($56). Bumper rub strips: Cit ($50). Interior Trim/Upholstery: Console ($105). Reclining driver and passenger seatbacks: Celeb ($90). Cloth bench seat: Cit ($28). Reclining cloth bucket seats: Cit ($243). Celebrity cpe/sed vinyl front bench seat: two-pass. ($28). Celebrity sed vinyl front bench seat: three-pass. ($78). Celebrity three-pass. cloth front bench seat ($28-$50). Celebrity CL three-pass. custom bench seating: vinyl ($229); cloth ($229-$257). Celebrity CL two-pass. custom cloth bench seating ($109-$179). Celebrity 45/45 cloth seating ($100). Celebrity CL custom cloth 45/45 seat ($250-$330). Cloth bucket seats: Celeb ($147). Color-keyed mats: front ($17); rear ($12). Deluxe trunk or wagon luggage area trim: Celeb ($40-$47). Wheels and Tires: Aluminum wheels: Cit ($306); Celeb ($306-$362). Sport wheel covers: Celeb ($65). Locking wire wheel covers: Celeb ($190). Rally wheels ($56). P185/80R13 SBR WSW: Cit ($58). P185/75R14 SBR WSW: Celeb ($58). P195/70R14 Eagle GT SBR BSW: Celeb ($60). P195/75R14 SBR BSW: Celeb ($30). P195/75R14 SBR WSW: Celeb ($92). P205/70R13 SBR WLT: Cit ($202). P215/60R14 SBR WLT: Cit ($92).

1985 Chevrolet, Camaro IROC-Z28 two-door coupe

CAMARO/MONTE CARLO CONVENIENCE/APPEARANCE OPTIONS: Option Packages: IROC-Z sport equipment pkg.: Camaro Z28 ($659). Comfort/Convenience: Air conditioning ($730). Rear defogger ($140). Cruise control w/resume ($175-$185). Tinted glass ($110). Comfortilt steering wheel ($110). Six-way power driver's seat ($215). Power windows ($185). Power door locks ($125). Power trunk opener: Monte ($40). Power hatch release: Camaro ($40). Electric clock ($35). Gauge pkg. w/trip odometer: Monte ($95). Gauge pkg. incl. tach: base Camaro ($149). Intermittent wipers ($50). Rear wiper/washer: Camaro ($120). Quiet sound group: Camaro ($72-$82). Lighting, Horns and Mirrors: Halogen headlamps ($22). Cornering lamps: Monte ($55). Aux. lighting: Camaro ($37-$72); Monte ($28). Dual horns: Camaro ($12). Twin sport mirrors (left remote): base Camaro, Monte ($53). Twin remote sport mirrors: Monte ($83); SS ($30). Twin electric remote sport mirrors: Camaro ($91-$139). Entertainment: AM/FM radio ($82). AM/FM stereo radio: Monte ($109). Cassette player with AM/FM stereo radio: Monte ($198). Electronic-tuning AM/FM stereo radio: base Camaro/Z28 ($173); w/clock ($177-$212); w/cassette, clock and seek/scan ($319-$354). Camaro seek/scan AM stereo/FM w/cassette, equalizer and clock ($469-$504). Seek/scan AM/FM stereo w/remote control: Berlinetta ($242). Dual rear speakers ($30). Power antenna ($60). Radio delete: Camaro ($56 credit); Berlinetta ($256 credit). Exterior Trim: Removable glass roof panels ($825). Landau vinyl roof: Monte ($245). Rear spoiler: Camaro ($69). Two-tone paint: Monte ($214). Bodyside moldings, black: Camaro ($55). Deluxe vinyl bodyside moldings: Monte ($57). Door edge guards ($15). Side window sill moldings: Monte ($45). Bodyside pin striping: Monte ($61). Interior Trim/Upholstery: Console: Monte ($105). Roof console: Camaro/Z28 ($50). Vinyl bench seat: base Monte ($28). Cloth 55/45 seating: base Monte ($133). Cloth bucket seats: Camaro ($28); Monte ($147). Custom cloth bucket seats: base Camaro/Z28 ($359). Custom cloth CL 55/45 seating: base Monte ($385). Custom cloth LS contour bucket seats: Camaro Z28 ($650). Split folding back seat: Camaro ($50). Mats w/carpeted inserts: Camaro front ($20); rear ($15). Color-keyed mats: Monte front ($17); rear ($12). Cargo area cover: Camaro ($69). Deluxe trunk trim: Camaro ($164); Z28 ($84). Locking rear storage cover: base Camaro ($80). Wheels and Tires: Aluminum wheels: Monte ($362); Camaro ($225); std. Z28. Rally wheels: base Camaro ($112); Monte ($56). Full wheel covers: base Camaro ($52). Locking wire wheel covers: Monte ($159). P195/75R14 SBR WSW: base Camaro ($62). P195/75R14 SBR WSW: Monte ($62). P205/70R14 SBR BSW: base Camaro ($58). P205/70R14 SBR WSW: Camaro ($124); Berlinetta ($66); Monte ($124). P205/70R14 SBR WLT: base Camaro ($146). P235/60VR15 SBR BSW: Z28 ($85).

IMPALA/CAPRICE CONVENIENCE/APPEARANCE OPTIONS: Option Packages: Estate equipment: wag ($307). Landau equipment pkg.: vinyl roof, sport mirrors and reveal moldings ($306). Comfort/Convenience: Air cond. ($730). Rear defogger, electric ($140). Cruise control ($175). Tinted glass ($110). Comfortilt steering wheel ($110). Power door locks ($125-$175). Six-way power driver's seat ($215). Power windows ($185-

$260). Power trunk opener ($40). Power tailgate lock: wag ($50). Electric clock: Imp ($35). Gauge pkg. w/trip odometer ($64). Intermittent wipers ($50). Quiet sound group: Imp ($66). Lighting and Mirrors: Halogen headlamps ($22). Cornering lamps ($55). Aux. lighting ($32-$42). Driver's remote mirror ($23). Dual remote mirrors ($67). Dual sport mirrors, left remote ($61). Dual remote color-keyed sport mirrors ($91) exc. Landau ($30). Lighted right visor mirror ($48). Entertainment: AM/FM radio ($82). Electronic-tuning AM/FM stereo radio ($138); w/clock ($142-$177); w/cassette and seek/scan ($264-$319); w/cassette, seek/scan, equalizer and clock ($394-$464). Dual rear speakers ($30); extended-range ($35). Power antenna ($60). Radio delete ($56 credit). Exterior Trim: Vinyl roof: sed ($185). Roof carrier: wag ($110). Custom two-tone paint ($141). Pin striping ($39). Bodyside moldings ($55). Wheel opening moldings: Imp ($30). Door edge guards ($15-$25). Rear window air deflector: wag ($40). Bumper rub strips ($66). Bumper guards ($62). Interior Trim/Upholstery: Reclining passenger seatback ($45). Vinyl bench seat: Imp sed ($28). Cloth bench seat: wag ($28). Cloth 50/50 seating: Caprice ($195-$225). Deluxe load-floor carpet: wag ($89). Deluxe cargo area carpet: wag ($129). Color-keyed mats: front ($17); rear ($12). Mats w/carpet insert: front ($25); rear ($20). Deluxe trunk trim ($59). Wheels and Tires: Sport wheel covers ($65). Wire wheel covers: Caprice ($159). Wire wheel cover locks ($39). P205/75R15 SBR WSW: cpe/sed ($66). P225/70R15 SBR WSW: cpe/sed ($157). P225/75R15 SBR WSW: wag ($71). Puncture-sealant tires ($105-$130).

HISTORY: General introduction was Oct. 2, 1984, but Camaro/Cavalier debuted on Nov. 8 and Chevette on Nov. 21. The new imported subcompact Sprint was introduced on May 30, 1984, and the Sprint on Nov. 15. Model year production (U.S.): 1,415,097 (incl. Corvettes but not incl. early '86 Novas and 8,992 Acadians). Of total production for sale in U.S., 695,893 were four-cylinder, 449,156 six, and 420,410 V-8. A total of 2,167 diesels were installed. Calendar year production (U.S.): 1,708,970 (incl. 46,304 Corvettes). Calendar year sales by U.S. dealers: 1,600,200 (incl. 37,956 Corvettes), for a 19.5 percent market share. Model year sales by U.S. dealers: 1,595,504 (incl. 37,878 Corvettes), for a 19.0 percent share.

Historical Footnotes: Model year sales rose only slightly over 1984, due mainly to the popularity of Cavalier and Celebrity, which ranked 1st and 3rd in the national ranking. Even so, Chevrolet's market share dropped a full percentage point, down to 19 percent. Only 5,485 Cavalier convertibles had been built in the 1984 model year, but production was even lower in 1985. Prices rose a fairly modest 2.3 percent for 1985. (Chevette was cut in price, by $121 to $183.) Chevettes and Cavaliers arrived a bit late as the 1984 model year was extended to take advantage of their stronger CAFE fuel economy ratings. Chevrolet was the only GM division not receiving either a new C-body or N-body car this year. This year's ad theme was "Today's Chevrolet" and focused on the new IROC-Z and awaited Cavalier Z24, as well as the multi-port fuel-injection V-6 engine. The new subcompact Japanese imports, Spectrum and Sprint, arrived to give Chevrolet a stronger grasp on the small-car market. The three-cylinder Sprint (from Suzuki) debuted on the West Coast in May 1984. Spectrum (built by Isuzu) arrived in November 1984, first sold only on the east coast. The new California-built Nova, a joint venture by Chevrolet and Toyota, would arrive as an early '86 model. Its initial sales looked good, requiring the addition of a second shift to the plant in Fremont, California, by winter 1985. Also contributing to Chevrolet's versatility in the marketplace was the new Astro passenger van, intended to compete with the twin Chrysler minivans. A prototype "Customer Communications Systems" began test operation at selected Chevrolet dealerships. Prospects could view the benefits of Chevrolet ownership via touch-screen computer videodisc with bold graphics. A "Commitment to Excellence" program provided enhanced pre-delivery inspection of each new car sold by a dealer, an orientation drive by the salesperson, and customer benefit package mailed to the owner after purchase.

1986

Chevrolet's ill-fated Citation X-car finally bit the dust, but its place in the lineup was taken up by the new subcompact Nova, produced in a joint venture between Chevrolet and Toyota. The rear-drive Chevette was still hanging on, but its days were numbered. Front-drive had become the rule for small cars--and quite a few large ones as well. On the sporty front, Cavalier's Z24 package finally arrived, creating an obvious small-scale rival to the Camaro Z28. And for peak performance, the IROC-Z package returned for the Z28. Monte Carlo added a new luxury model, but the Impala name dropped out of the Chevrolet list after nearly three decades of service. Diesel engines left the lineup, except for a handful installed in Chevettes.

1986 Chevrolet, Chevette four-door hatchback sedan

CHEVETTE -- SERIES 1T -- FOUR -- A new bowtie emblem went on Chevette's grille this year and one new body color (yellow beige) was offered. New Cus-

tom seat cloth became standard on the four-door, optional on the two-door. All-season P155/80R13 SBR blackwall tires were made standard. As before, the 1.6-liter four and four-speed manual gearbox were standard, with diesel four and three-speed automatic available. Diesels were no longer available in California. A $95 Sport Decor package included a black grille and bumpers, black bodyside moldings with red inserts, and black wheels; plus red 'Chevette S' and 'Chevrolet' decals on front fender and hatch. Though antiquated in mechanical design, the rear-drive Chevette was promoted not only as an entry-level car, but as a vehicle for fleets and light delivery.

1986 Chevrolet, Nova four-door hatchback sedan (CH)

1986 Chevrolet, Nova four-door sedan

NOVA -- SERIES 1S -- FOUR -- Produced in a joint venture between Chevrolet and Toyota, the five-passenger front-drive subcompact Nova went on sale in June 1985 in half the states. For the full 1986 model year, it was made available nationwide, and a four-door hatchback joined the original four-door notchback sedan. Riding a 95.7 inch wheelbase, Nova weighed about 200 pounds less than an equivalent Cavalier. Hatchbacks had split-folding rear seats, for carrying both passengers and cargo. Nova wore a black crosshatch grille with three horizontal divider bars and seven vertical divider bars, with center bowtie emblem. Wrap around cornering lamps flanked quad rectangular headlamps, with parking lamps inset low in the bumper. The original 97 cu. in. (1.6-liter) four-cylinder engine rated 70 horsepower, while the full-year version added four more. New engine mounts were meant to reduce idle shake, and the optional air conditioner got a larger compressor. A five-speed manual (overdrive) transaxle was standard, with three-speed automatic available. Standard equipment included power brakes, rack-and-pinion steering, AM radio, black bumpers with silver stripe, side window defoggers, cloth door panels with map pockets, full console, and a locking fuel filler door. Also standard: tinted glass, temperature gauge, locking glove box, day/night mirror, black left mirror (remote-controlled), temporary spare tire, trip odometer, cloth/vinyl low-back reclining front bucket seats, and an audible warning system. Argent styled wheels held P155/80R13 SBR blackwall tires. Wiper/washers had a mist cycle. Bodies carried narrow black bodyside, roof drip and windshield moldings. Hatchbacks had a black rear spoiler. Nova's option list was unusually small: just a series of packages rather than individual items. Step-up CL option packages each included a set of extras, in addition to the items indicated in the option lists. Those extra features included a custom cloth interior, wide bodyside moldings, bright belt and roof drip moldings, black door frames and rocker panels, console with storage box, trunk carpet and light, tilt steering column, remote trunk and fuel filler door openers, right visor vanity mirror, soft steering wheel, driver's seat with vertical adjustment and lumbar support, and passenger assist grips.

1986 Chevrolet, Cavalier Z24 two-door coupe (CP)

1986 Chevrolet, Cavalier Z24 two-door hatchback coupe (PH)

CAVALIER -- SERIES 1J -- FOUR/V-6 -- After nearly a year's delay, Cavalier's new Z24 performance package (obviously inspired by Camaro's Z28) finally arrived to become a highlight of 1986. Offered in either two-door coupe or two-door hatchback form, it carried a 173 cu. in. (2.8-liter) V-6 with multi-port fuel injection, four-speed manual transaxle, 14 in. Eagle GT radial tires on Rally wheels, and sports package with all-around ground-effects skirting similar to Z28. A cockpit-style instrument panel displayed "Star Wars" electronic instrumentation. Control pods sat on each side of the

steering wheel. The simple Z24 grille had four horizontal bars, with bowtie emblem at the center. Park/signal lamps sat at bumper level, below the quad rectangular headlamps. Also new this year was the sporty RS series (replacing the former Type 10). This one had standard F41 sport suspension, power steering, All-Season radial tires, and a distinctive exterior look. 'Cavalier RS' and engine identifier badges were red. Five different RS bodies were offered: four-door sedan and wagon, two-door coupe and hatchback, and the convertible. Base and CS Cavaliers came in four-door sedan or wagon form, as well as two-door bodies. A new Electronic Control Module reduced current drain when the car was idle, and included improved self-diagnostic features. New options this year were a decklid rack (for notchback coupes and sedans), plus new seat cloth and door panel trim for the CL custom interior. Base Cavaliers had standard power brakes, color-keyed bumpers with rub strips, full console with storage, side window defoggers, an argent grille, black left-hand mirror, day/night mirror, compact spare tire, two-speed wiper/washer, vinyl reclining bucket seats, and front stabilizer bar. Styled steel argent wheels held P175/80R13 SBR tires. Cavaliers had bright belt, drip, door and window moldings; plus black windshield and back window moldings. Cavalier CS added an AM radio and fixed-mast antenna, lighter, locking glove box, bright grille, and black bodyside moldings. RS models had black bumper rub strips with red accents, a cockpit-style console, power steering, black sport steering wheel, sport suspension, wheel trim rings, red-accented black bodyside moldings, and a set of black moldings (drip, rocker panel, belt, door, window). Convertibles lacked some of those moldings but included a boot cover, tinted glass, and front/rear courtesy lights. Z24 added an air dam, electronic instrument cluster, tachometer and trip odometer, dual black sport mirrors, and black bodyside and drip moldings.

1986 Chevrolet, Camaro two-door coupe (CP)

1986 Chevrolet, Camaro IROC-Z28 two-door coupe (CH)

CAMARO -- SERIES 1F -- V-6/V-8 -- Base Camaro Sport Coupes could take on the tone of the famed Z28 this year. When ordered with either optional engine (2.8-liter V-6 or 5.0-liter V-8), the base coupe also came equipped with a sport suspension, P215/65R15 blackwall tires on 15 x 7 in. styled steel wheels, and sport-tone exhaust. Even four-cylinder Camaros got the sport suspension and 14 in. styled wheels. With V-6 power, a five-speed manual gearbox was included (four-speed automatic optional). With a V-8 option, the four-speed automatic was installed. Appearance changes this year included black accents on headlamps and front fascia vents, lower body stripes (with black or charcoal finish below), black sport mirrors, and Rally wheels. Sport Coupe taillamps had a new black accent band. New 'Chevrolet' lettering replaced the Camaro name on rear fascia. New Sport Coupe standard equipment included styled wheels with trim rings, raised-letter SBR tires, retuned exhaust system with dual tailpipes, black sport mirrors, blackout rockers and fascia, and special stripes. An upshift indicator was added to manual-gearbox models. All Camaros got an air conditioning cutout switch, for use when full power was needed. The full-opening rear hatch had a new automatic closure. All Camaros had wet-arm windshield wipers. New standard items included an automatic rear hatch pulldown latch, plus softer-feel leather for steering wheel, shift lever and parking brake lever. Five engines were available: the "Iron Duke" four (from Pontiac), MFI 173 cu. in. (2.8-liter) V-6, standard 305 cu. in. (5.0-liter) V-8, high-output carbureted 5.0 V-8, and Tuned-port injection 5.0 V-8. Bodyside moldings now came in eight colors or black (black only on Sport Coupe). All 12 body colors (eight of them new) were applied using a new basecoat/clearcoat process. New to the option list were halogen foglamps (as on the IROC-Z), available on all models; an automatic day/night mirror; color-keyed bodyside moldings; and an AM radio with digital clock. The top-performance IROC-Z, introduced a year earlier, was virtually unchanged except for new colors. Same with Z28 in general, except for new colors on lower panels and accent stripes. IROC-Z had no grille opening at all in the front, but two foglamps alongside the license plate opening and parking lamps farther outboard. Quad rectangular headlamps were deeply recessed, flanking a solid angled body panel with tiny emblem in the center. Base Sport Coupe standard equipment included an AM radio, power steering and brakes, five-speed manual transmission, front/rear stabilizer bars, cockpit-style instrument panel, center console with stowage, side window defoggers, remote-controlled left mirror, day/night inside mirror, vinyl reclining front bucket seats, and tape stripes. P205/70R14 SBR all-season tires (P215/65R15 with V-6 or V-8) rode Rally steel wheels with trim rings. Bodies had black lower body accent, plus black windshield and drip moldings and color-keyed bumpers. Berlinetta added an electronic-tuning AM/FM stereo radio with digital clock, dual horns, electronic instruments, locking rear storage cover, dome and map lights, color-keyed sport mirrors (left remote), intermittent wipers, roof console, full

wheel covers, and a tachometer. Bodies showed color-keyed lower accent paint with striping; interiors held custom cloth reclining front bucket seats. Standard Berlinetta tires were P205/70R14 SBR. Berlinetta lacked rocker panel moldings and a rear stabilizer bar. Z28 added an air dam, gauge package, color-keyed sport mirrors, visor vanity mirror (passenger), AM radio with digital clock, rear spoiler, leather-wrapped steering wheel, tachometer, and P215/65R15 tires on color-keyed aluminum wheels. The IROC-Z Sport Equipment package (RPO code B4Z, for Z28) included P245/50VR16 Goodyear Eagle GT tires on 16 in. aluminum wheels, halogen foglamps, and special suspension components: special front struts and springs, rear springs, larger-diameter stabilizer bar, and Delco/Bilstein gas-filled shock absorbers. IROC-Z also had front frame reinforcement and specific steering gear valving. All that plus body-color lower ground-effect panels, door panel decals, and lower-body accent stripes.

1986 Chevrolet, Celebrity four-door sedan (with Classic option package including wire wheel covers and vinyl roof) (CH)

1986 Chevrolet, Celebrity Eurosport two-door coupe

CELEBRITY -- SERIES 1A -- FOUR/V-6 -- Celebrity wore a new finely-louvered grille with center bowtie emblem for a new front-end look--the most notable styling revision since the family mid-size was introduced in 1982. New wraparound side marker lamps flowed past the quad rectangular headlamps, with prominent bright bezels surrounding the entire assembly. New full wheel covers were standard. 'Celebrity' lettering was on the front door, engine identification at the forward end of front fenders, small parking lamps below the bumper rub strip. The new rear-end look consisted of three rectangular lamps, with side marker lamps included in the outboard unit. A new three-passenger front seat gave Celebrity six-passenger capacity rather than the previous five. At mid-year, a landau roof coupe option became available. Diesel engines were gone, and Celebrity's base prices were up by over $600. Standard engine was the 151 cu. in. (2.5-liter) four, with either carbureted or multi-port fuel injected 173 cu. in. (2.8-liter) V-6 optional. A new valve cover and gaskets improved oil sealing in all engines. Modified exhaust systems improved noise isolation. A fully galvanized floor pan was added at mid-year. A new variable-displacement air conditioning compressor for four-cylinder models was designed for quieter, more economical operation. New options included 55/45 front seating, a tachometer, AM radio with digital clock, and passenger visor mirror (standard or illuminated). Wagons could have an Estate package for $325. Both coupes and sedans could have a padded vinyl roof for $270. Celebrity Eurosports came in three new solid colors: silver metallic, light brown metallic, and black. Grilles, wheels and moldings matched the body color. The $225 Eurosport package included a sport suspension, sport steering wheel, P195/75R14 SBR tires on Rally wheels with trim rings, bodyside moldings with red accent stripes, color-accented bumper rub strips, and gas shock absorbers. Red 'Eurosport' nameplates on the doors made the model easy to identify.

1986 Chevrolet, Monte Carlo SS two-door coupe (CP)

1986 Chevrolet, Monte Carlo SS two-door Aerocoupe (PH)

MONTE CARLO -- SERIES 1G -- V-6/V-8 -- Monte was moderately restyled for 1986, and a new luxury LS model joined the base and SS coupes after the start of the model year. Standard Montes kept their 1985-style grilles and quad rectangular headlamps, but the LS was different. An aerodynamic LS front end held wide flush-mount composite headlamps and a wide-look finely-

crosshatched grille with 11 vertical dividers and distinctive center crest emblem. Parking lamps (also wide) sat below the bumper rub strips. Engine identification was on the forward end of the front fender. The LS had wide and bright bodyside moldings, semi-wraparound taillamps, and restyled standard wheels. All Montes got new aerodynamic sport mirrors (black on base model, body-color optional). Sport Coupe and LS Montes got new wheel covers. Retuned suspensions used harder bushings and stiffer shock valving. Inside was a new color-keyed two-spoke steering wheel. P205/70R14 tires with improved rolling resistance were optional on the Sport Coupe. Delco 2000 Series electronically-tuned radios were on the option list. Also optional: a tachometer and passenger visor vanity mirror (plain or illuminated). Monte Carlo SS had new aluminum wheels, plus gas-pressure shock absorbers (front and rear). Engine choices were the same as 1985: 262 cu. in. (4.3-liter) V-6 or 305 cu. in. (5.0-liter) V-8, with a high-output, 180-horsepower 305 under SS hoods. All Monte Carlos had standard power brakes and steering, three-speed overdrive automatic (four-speed on SS), AM radio with digital clock, cloth bench seats, dual black mirrors, dual-note horn, full wheel covers, color-keyed bumpers, and front stabilizer bar. Bodies held bright wheel opening, belt, window/windshield reveal, lower bodyside and roof drip moldings. Monte Carlo SS had a rear spoiler, black sport steering wheel, tachometer, black grille and moldings, sport mirrors (left remote-controlled), gauge package, and P215/65R15 white-letter tires. Rarest of the SS Montes is the striking Aero-coupe fastback. Only 200 were built--a tiny fraction of Monte Carlo output.

1986 Chevrolet, Caprice Classic Brougham four-door sedan (CP)

CAPRICE CLASSIC -- SERIES 1B -- V-6/V-8 -- With a history dating back to 1958, the Impala name departed this year, but a new Caprice Classic Brougham Sedan joined the full-size lineup (at the top). Three other Classic models were offered (two-door sport coupe, four-door sedan and four-door wagon), plus a basic lower-priced four-door Caprice sedan. All models had the same, somewhat rounded front-end look this year. That included a new grille and bumper filler panel, flush-mounted crest, and new bezels for headlamps and marker lamps. Coupes and sedans also had restyled tri-section taillamps in a full-width end panel, plus a new filler panel and bumper rub strip. Each taillamp section was split horizontally. Base prices were $700-$800 higher than in 1985. Four-speed overdrive automatic was now optional with the base 262 cu. in. (4.3-liter) V-6 engine. The diesel V-8 was dropped, but the 305 cu. in. (5.0-liter) gasoline V-8 remained optional (standard on wagons). Engines used a new poly-V alternator drive belt. Power window and seat controls moved to the top of new front door armrest extensions. The new Brougham Sedan package included a full vinyl roof, cloth 55/45 pillow-style front seats with center armrest, front-door dome/map and warning lights, bright brushed metal center pillar appliqué, and 'Brougham' identification. Standard equipment on the basic Caprice sedan included an AM radio, power brakes and steering, three-speed automatic transmission, full wheel covers, folding front center armrest, cloth bench seats, day/night mirror, front stabilizer bar, two-speed wiper/washers, bright moldings (roof drip, windshield, belt and sill), and lower carpet door trim panels. Caprice Classic added a quartz clock, cloth-insert door trim panels, dual-note horn, wheel opening and bright wide lower bodyside moldings, and headlamps-on buzzer. Coupes and sedans had bumper rub strips. Wagons had a power tailgate window, heavy-duty suspension, and overdrive automatic transmission. Caprice and Pontiac's Parisienne were the last traditional rear-drive full-size family sedans left in the GM lineup, regularly threatened with extinction but continuing to find quite a few buyers.

I.D. DATA: Chevrolets again had a 17-symbol Vehicle Identification Number (VIN) on the upper left surface of the instrument panel, visible through the windshield. Symbol one indicates country: '1' = U.S.A.; '2' = Canada. Next is a manufacturer code: 'G' = General Motors. Symbol three is car make: '1' = Chevrolet; '7' = GM of Canada. Symbol four denotes restraint system: 'A' = non-passive (standard); 'B' = passive (automatic belts); 'C' = passive (inflatable). Symbol five is car line/series: 'B' = Chevette; 'K' = Nova; 'C'= Cavalier; 'D' = Cavalier CS; 'E' = Cavalier RS; 'F' = Cavalier Z24; 'P' = Camaro; 'S' = Camaro Berlinetta; 'W' = Celebrity; 'Z' = Monte Carlo; 'L' = Impala; 'N' = Caprice. Symbols six-seven reveal body type: '08' = 2-dr. hatch coupe; '27' = 2-dr. notchback coupe; '37' = special 2-dr. notchback coupe; '47' = full-size 2-dr. sport coupe; '67' = 2-dr. convertible coupe; '77' = 2-dr. hatch coupe; '87' = 2-dr. sport coupe; '19' = 4-dr. 6-window notchback sedan; '68' = 4-dr. 6-window hatch sedan; '69' = 4-dr. 4-window notchback sedan; '35' = 4-dr. station wagon. Next is the engine code: 'C' = L4-98 2Bbl.; '4' = L4-97 2Bbl.; 'D' = L4-111 diesel; 'P' = L4-121 FI; 'R' or '2' = L4-151 FI; 'X' = V6-173 2Bbl.; 'S' or 'W' = V6-173 MFI; 'Z' = V6-262 FI; 'H' or 'Y' = V8-305 4Bbl.; 'G' = H.O. V8-305 4Bbl.; 'F' = V8-305 TPI. Next is a check digit, followed by 'G' for model year 1986. Symbol eleven indicates assembly plant: 'B' = Baltimore; 'J' = Janesville, WI; 'L' = Van Nuys, CA; 'N' = Norwood, OH; 'R' = Arlington, TX; 'T' = Tarrytown, NY; 'X' = Fairfax, KS; 'Y' = Wilmington, DE; '1' = Oshawa, Ontario; '6' = Oklahoma City, OK; '7' = Lordstown, OH.

The final six digits are the sequential serial number. Engine number coding is similar to 1981-85.

CHEVETTE CS (FOUR)

Model No.	Body/Style No.	Body Type & Seating	Factory Price	Shipping Weight	Prod. Total
1T	B08	2-dr. Hatch Cpe-4P	5645	2022	48,756
1T	B68	4-dr. Hatch Sed-4P	5959	2083	54,164

CHEVETTE CS DIESEL (FOUR)

| 1T | B08/Z90 | 2-dr. Hatch Cpe-4P | 6152 | 2194 | 124 |
| 1T | B68/Z90 | 4-dr. Hatch Sed-4P | 6487 | 2255 | 200 |

NOVA (FOUR)

| 1S | K19 | 4-dr. Sedan-4P | 7435 | 2016 | 124,961 |
| 1S | K68 | 4-dr. Hatch Sed-4P | 7669 | 2057 | 42,788 |

Nova Production Note: An additional 27,943 Nova sedans were built late in the 1985 model year, placed on sale in June 1986.

CAVALIER (FOUR/V-6)

1J	C27	2-dr. Coupe-5P	6706/7316	2231/2351	57,370
1J	C69	4-dr. Sedan-5P	6888/7498	2274/2394	86,492
1J	C35	4-dr. Sta Wag-5P	7047/7657	2344/2464	30,490

CAVALIER CS (FOUR/V-6)

1J	D77	2-dr. Hatch Cpe-5P	7373/7983	2287/2407	8,046
1J	D69	4-dr. Sedan-5P	7350/7960	2306/2426	89,168
1J	D35	4-dr. Sta Wag-5P	7525/8135	2355/2475	23,101

CAVALIER RS (FOUR/V-6)

1J	E27	2-dr. Coupe-5P	7640/8250	2257/2377	53,941
1J	E77	2-dr. Hatch Cpe-5P	7830/8440	2319/2439	7,504
1J	E69	4-dr. Sedan-5P	7811/8451	2299/2419	17,361
1J	E35	4-dr. Sta Wag-5P	7979/8589	2371/2491	6,252
1J	E67	2-dr. Conv. Cpe-4P	12530/13140	----/2376	5,785

CAVALIER Z24 (V-6)

| 1J | F27 | 2-dr. Spt Cpe-5P | ----/8878 | ----/2451 | 36,365 |
| 1J | F77 | 2-dr. Hatch Cpe-5P | ----/9068 | ----/2513 | 10,226 |

CAMARO (V-6/V-8)

| 1F | P87 | 2-dr. Spt Cpe-4P | 9285/9685 | 2912/3071 | 99,517 |

CAMARO BERLINETTA (V-6/V-8)

| 1F | S87 | 2-dr. Spt Cpe-4P | 11902/12302 | 2983/3162 | 4,479 |

CAMARO Z28 (V-8)

| 1F | P87/Z28 | 2-dr. Spt Cpe-4P | ----/11902 | ----/3121 | 38,547 |

CAMARO IROC-Z (V-8)

| 1F | P87/B4Z | 2-dr. Spt Cpe-4P | ----/12561 | N/A | 49,585 |

Camaro Engine Note: Prices and weights before slash are for V-6 engine, after slash for V-8. Base Camaro Sport Coupes were also available with a four-cylinder engine, priced at $8,935 and weighing 2,781 pounds.

Z28 Production Note: Chevrolet production figures also show 91 Z28E hatchback sport coupes built for export. IROC-Z was actually a $659 option package for the Z28, not a separate model.

CELEBRITY (FOUR/V-6)

1A	W27	2-dr. Coupe-6P	8735/9170	2609/2720	29,223
1A	W19	4-dr. Sedan-6P	8931/9366	2638/2749	291,760
1A	W35	4-dr. Sta Wag-6P	9081/9516	2790/2881	36,655
1A	W35/AQ4	4-dr. 3S Wag-8P	9313/9748	N/A	47,245

MONTE CARLO (V-6/V-8)

| 1G | Z37 | 2-dr. Spt Cpe-6P | 10241/10631 | 3046/3120 | 50,418 |
| 1G | Z37/Z09 | 2-dr. LS Cpe-6P | 10451/10841 | 3046/3170 | 27,428 |

MONTE CARLO 'SS' (V-8)

1G	Z37/Z65	2-dr. Spt Cpe-6P	---- /12466 ---- /3293	41,164
1G	Z37/Z65	2-dr. Aerocpe-6P	---- /14191 ---- /3440	200

CAPRICE (V-6/V-8)

1B	L69	4-dr. Sedan-6P	10243/10633 3399/3499	50,751

CAPRICE CLASSIC (V-6/V-8)

1B	N47	2-dr. Spt Cpe-6P	10635/11025 3411/3511	9,869
1B	N69	4-dr. Sedan-6P	10795/11185 3428/3528	67,772
1B	N69/B45	4-dr. Brghm-6P	11429/11819 N/A	69,320
1B	N69/B45	4-dr. LS Brghm-6P	N/A N/A	2,117
1B	N35	4-dr. 3S Wag-8P	---- /11511 ---- /3977	45,183

FACTORY PRICE AND WEIGHT NOTE: For Cavalier and Celebrity, prices and weights to left of slash are for four-cylinder, to right for V-6 engine. For Camaro, Monte Carlo and Caprice, figures to left of slash are for six-cylinder model, to right of slash for 305 cu. in. V-8.

BODY/STYLE NO. NOTE: Some models were actually option packages. Code after the slash (e.g., B45) is the number of the option package that comes with the model listed.

ENGINE DATA: BASE FOUR (Chevette): Inline. Overhead cam. Four-cylinder. Cast iron block and head. Displacement: 98 cu. in. (1.6 liters). Bore & stroke: 3.23 x 2.98 in. Compression ratio: 9.0:1. Brake horsepower: 65 at 5200 R.P.M. Torque: 80 lb.-ft. at 3200 R.P.M. Five main bearings. Hydraulic valve lifters. Carburetor: 2Bbl. VIN Code: C. **DIESEL FOUR** (Chevette): Inline. Overhead cam. Four-cylinder. Cast iron block and head. Displacement: 111 cu. in. (1.8 liters). Bore & stroke: 3.31 x 3.23 in. Compression ratio: 22.0:1. Brake horsepower: 51 at 5000 R.P.M. Torque: 72 lb.-ft. at 2000 R.P.M. Five main bearings. Solid valve lifters. Fuel injection. VIN Code: D. **BASE FOUR** (Nova): Inline. Overhead cam. Four-cylinder. Cast iron block and head. Displacement: 97 cu. in. (1.6 liters). Bore & stroke: 3.19 x 3.03 in. Compression ratio: 9.0:1. Brake horsepower: 74 at 5200 R.P.M. Torque: 86 lb.-ft. at 2800 R.P.M. Solid valve lifters. Carburetor: Asian 2Bbl. VIN Code: 4. **BASE FOUR** (Cavalier): Inline. Overhead valve. Four-cylinder. Cast iron block and head. Displacement: 121 cu. in. (2.0 liters). Bore & stroke: 3.50 x 3.15 in. Compression ratio: 9.0:1. Brake horsepower: 85 at 4800 R.P.M. Torque: 110 lb.-ft. at 2400 R.P.M. Five main bearings. Throttle-body fuel injection. VIN Code: P. **BASE FOUR** (Celebrity, Camaro): Inline. Overhead valve. Four-cylinder. Cast iron block and head. Displacement: 151 cu. in. (2.5 liters). Bore & stroke: 4.00 x 3.00 in. Compression ratio: 9.0:1. Brake horsepower: 92 at 4400 R.P.M. (Camaro, 88 at 4400). Torque: 134 lb.-ft. at 2800 R.P.M. (Camaro, 130 at 2800). Five main bearings. Hydraulic valve lifters. Throttle-body fuel injection. Pontiac-built. VIN Code: R or 2. **OPTIONAL V-6** (Celebrity): 60-degree, overhead-valve V-6. Cast iron block and head. Displacement: 173 cu. in. (2.8 liters). Bore & stroke: 3.50 x 2.99 in. Compression ratio: 8.0:1. Brake horsepower: 112 at 4800 R.P.M. Torque: 145 lb.-ft. at 2100 R.P.M. Four main bearings. Hydraulic valve lifters. Carburetor: 2Bbl. VIN Code: X. **HIGH-OUTPUT V-6** (Camaro Berlinetta, Cav-

alier Z24); OPTIONAL (Cavalier, Camaro, Celebrity): Same as 173 cu. in. V-6 above except multi-port fuel injection: C.R.: 8.5:1 (Camaro 8.9:1). Brake H.P.: 135 at 5100 R.P.M. (Cavalier, 120 at 4800; Celebrity, 125 at 4800). Torque: 160 lb.-ft. at 3900 R.P.M. (Cavalier, 155 at 3600; Celeb, 160 at 3600). VIN Code: W or S. **BASE V-6** (Monte Carlo, Caprice): 90-degree, overhead-valve V-6. Cast iron block and head. Displacement: 262 cu. in. (4.3 liters). Bore & stroke: 4.00 x 3.48 in. Compression ratio: 9.3:1. Brake horsepower: 140 at 4000 R.P.M. Torque: 225 lb.-ft. at 2000 R.P.M. Four main bearings. Hydraulic valve lifters. Fuel injection. VIN Code: Z. **BASE V-8** (Camaro Z28, Caprice wagon): OPTIONAL (Camaro, Monte Carlo, Caprice): 90-degree, overhead valve V-8. Cast iron block and head. Displacement: 305 cu. in. (5.0 liters). Bore & stroke: 3.74 x 3.48 in. Compression ratio: 9.5:1. Brake horsepower: 155 at 4200 R.P.M. (Monte, 150 at 4000; Caprice, 165 at 4200; Z28, 165 at 4400). Torque: 245 lb.-ft. at 2000 R.P.M. (Monte, 240 at 2000; Caprice, 245 at 2400; Z28, 250 at 2000). Five main bearings. Hydraulic valve lifters. Carburetor: 4Bbl. VIN Code: H exc. (Caprice) Y. **HIGH-OUTPUT V-8** (Monte Carlo SS): Same as 305 cu. in. V-8 above, except: Brake H.P.: 180 at 4800 R.P.M. Torque: 225 lb.-ft. at 3200 R.P.M. VIN Code: G. **OPTIONAL HIGH-OUTPUT V-8** (Camaro Z28/IROC-Z): Same as 305 cu. in. V-8 above, except: Brake H.P.: 190 at 4800 R.P.M. Torque: 240 lb.-ft. at 3200 R.P.M. VIN Code: G. **OPTIONAL HIGH-OUTPUT V-8** (Camaro Z28/IROC-Z): Same as 305 cu. in. V-8 above, but with tuned port fuel injection: Brake H.P.: 190 at 4000 R.P.M. Torque: 285 lb.-ft. at 2800 R.P.M. VIN Code: F.

CHASSIS DATA: Wheelbase: (Chevette cpe) 94.3 in.; (Chvt sed) 97.3 in.; (Nova) 95.7 in.; (Cavalier) 101.2 in.; (Celebrity) 104.9 in.; (Camaro) 101.0 in.; (Monte Carlo) 108.0 in.; (Caprice) 116.0 in. Overall length: (Chvt cpe) 161.9 in.; (Chvt sed) 164.9 in.; (Nova) 166.3 in.; (Cav cpe/conv) 172.4 in.; (Cav sed) 174.3 in.; (Cav wag) 174.5 in.; (Camaro) 188.0 in.; (Camaro Z28) 192.0 in.; (Celeb) 188.3 in.; (Celeb wag) 190.8 in.; (Monte) 200.4 in.; (Monte SS) 202.4 in.; (Monte LS) 203.3 in.; (Caprice cpe) 212.8 in.; (Capr sed) 212.2 in.; (Capr wag) 215.1 in. Height: (Chvt) 52.8 in.; (Nova) 52.7 in.; (Cav cpe) 50.2 in.; (Cav conv) 52.7 in.; (Cav sed) 52.1 in.; (Cav wag) 52.8 in.; (Camaro) 50.0 in.; (Camaro Z28) 50.3 in.; (Celeb) 54.1 in.; (Celeb wag) 54.3 in.; (Monte) 54.4 in.; (Monte SS) 54.9 in.; (Caprice) 56.4 in.; (Caprice wag) 58.2 in. Width: (Chvt) 61.8 in.; (Nova) 64.4 in.; (Cav cpe/conv) 66.0 in.; (Cav sed/wag) 66.3 in.; (Camaro) 72.8 in.; (Celeb) 69.3 in.; (Monte) 71.8 in.; (Caprice) 75.4 in.; (Capr wag) 79.3 in. Front Tread: (Chvt) 51.2 in.; (Nova) 56.1 in.; (Cav) 55.4 in.; (Celeb) 58.7 in.; (Camaro) 60.7 in.; (Camaro Z28) 60.0 in.; (Monte) 58.5 in.; (Caprice) 61.7 in.; (Capr wag) 62.2 in. Rear Tread: (Chvt) 51.2 in.; (Nova) 55.3 in.; (Cav) 55.2 in.; (Celeb) 57.0 in.; (Camaro) 61.6 in.; (Camaro Z28): 60.9 in.; (Monte) 57.8 in.; (Caprice) 60.7 in.; (Capr wag) 64.1 in. Standard Tires: (Chvt/Nova) P155/80R13 SBR; (Cav) P175/80R13 SBR; (Cav RS) P195/70R13 SBR; (Cav Z24) P215/60R14 SBR; (Celeb)

P185/75R14 SBR; (Celeb Eurosport) P195/75R14 SBR; (Camaro) P205/70R14 SBR; (Camaro Z28) P215/65R15 SBR; (Camaro IROC-Z) P245/50VR16 SBR; (Monte) P195/75R14 SBR; (Monte SS) P215/65R15 SBR; (Caprice) P205/75R15 SBR; (Caprice wag) P225/75R15 SBR.

TECHNICAL: Transmission: Four-speed manual shift standard on Chevette and Celebrity. Four-speed overdrive manual shift standard on Cavalier. Five-speed manual shift standard on Chevette diesel, Nova, Camaro. Three-speed Turbo Hydra-matic standard on Monte Carlo and Caprice: (1st) 2.74:1; (2nd) 1.57:1; (3rd) 1.00:1; (Rev) 2.07:1. Chevette automatic trans.: (1st) 2.40:1; (2nd) 1.48:1; (3rd) 1.00:1; (Rev) 1.92:1. Nova auto. trans.: (1st) 2.30:1; (2nd) 1.55:1; (3rd) 1.00:1; (Rev) 2.81:1. Cavalier/Celebrity auto. trans.: (1st) 2.84:1; (2nd) 1.60:1; (3rd) 1.00:1; (Rev) 2.07:1. Four-speed overdrive automatic transmission on Monte Carlo: (1st) 2.74:1; (2nd) 1.57:1; (3rd) 1.00:1; (4th) 0.67:1; (Rev) 2.07:1. Four-speed overdrive automatic on Celebrity: (1st) 2.92:1; (2nd) 1.56:1; (3rd) 1.00:1; (4th) 0.70:1; (Rev) 2.38:1. Four-speed overdrive automatic on Camaro/Caprice: (1st) 3.06:1; (2nd) 1.63:1; (3rd) 1.00:1; (4th) 0.70:1; (Rev) 2.29:1. Standard final drive ratio: (Chevette) 3.36:1; (Nova) 3.72:1 w/5-spd, 3.42:1 w/auto.; (Cavalier four) 3.32:1 w/4-spd, 3.83:1 w/5-spd, 3.18:1 w/auto.; (Cavalier V-6) 3.65:1 w/4-spd, 3.18:1 w/auto.; (Camaro four) 3.73:1; (Camaro V-6) 3.42:1; (Camaro V-8) 2.73:1 or 3.23:1; (Celebrity four) 3.65:1 w/4-spd, 2.39:1 w/auto.; (Celeb V-6) 2.84:1 or 3.06:1; (Celeb wag) 2.84:1; (Monte V-6) 2.29:1 or 2.41:1; (Monte V-8) 2.41:1 or 3.73:1; (Caprice V-6) 2.56:1; (Capr V-8) 2.73:1. Steering: (Cavalier/Chevette/Nova/Celebrity) rack and pinion; (others) recirculating ball. Front Suspension: (Chevette/Monte/Caprice) unequal-length control arms, coil springs, stabilizer bar; (Nova) MacPherson struts w/coil springs and lower control arms; (Cavalier/Camaro/Celeb) MacPherson struts with coil springs, lower control arms and stabilizer. Rear Suspension: (Chevette) rigid axle and torque tube w/four links and track bar, coil springs, stabilizer; (Nova) fully independent MacPherson struts, dual links, coil springs and stabilizer bar; (Cavalier) semi-independent with beam axle, trailing arms, coil springs, stabilizer available; (Camaro) rigid axle and torque tube with longitudinal control arms, Panhard rod, coil springs and stabilizer; (Celeb) beam twist axle with integral stabilizer, trailing arms, Panhard rod and coil springs; (Monte/Caprice) rigid axle with four links, control arms, coil springs, stabilizer available. Brakes: Front disc, rear drum; four-wheel discs available on Camaro V-8. Body construction: Unibody except (Camaro) unibody with partial frame; (Monte/Caprice) separate body and frame. Fuel tank: (Chvt) 13.2 gal.; (Cav) 13.6 gal.; (Camaro) 15.5 gal.; (Camaro V-8) 16.2 gal.; (Celeb) 15.7 or 16.4 gal.; (Monte) 17.6 or 18.1 gal.; (Capr) 24.5 gal.; (Capr wag) 22 gal.

DRIVETRAIN OPTIONS: Engines: 173 cu. in., 2Bbl. V-6: Cavalier ($670); base Camaro ($350); Celeb ($435). 173 cu. in., MFI V-6: Celeb ($560). 305 cu. in., 4Bbl. V-8: base Camaro ($750); Berlinetta ($400); base Monte, Caprice cpe/sed ($390). H.O. 305 cu. in., 4Bbl. V-8: Camaro Z28 ($695). 350 cu. in., TPI V-8: Camaro Z28 ($695). Transmission/Differential: Five-speed manual trans.: Chevette/Cavalier ($75). Three-speed automatic trans.: Chevette ($425); Cavalier ($465); Celeb ($490). Four-speed overdrive auto. trans.: Camaro ($465); Celeb ($665); base Monte, Caprice cpe/sed ($175). Limited-slip differential: Camaro/Monte/Caprice ($100). Performance axle ratio ($21). Power Accessories: Power brakes: Chevette ($100). Power four-wheel disc brakes: Camaro V-8 ($179). Power steering: Chvt/Cav ($215). Suspension: F40 H.D. susp.: Cav/Celeb/Caprice ($26). F41 sport susp.: Cav ($44-$49); Monte, Caprice cpe/sed ($49). Inflatable rear shock absorbers: Celeb/Caprice wag ($64). Other: H.D. cooling ($40-$70). Engine block heater ($20). H.D. battery ($26). California emission system ($99).

CHEVETTE CONVENIENCE/APPEARANCE OPTIONS: Option Packages: Sport Decor pkg.: black grille, headlamp bezels, bodyside moldings w/red accents; black bumpers; black wheels w/bright trim rings and red decals ($95). Custom exterior: black window moldings, styled argent wheels and bright trim rings ($152-$167). Comfort/Convenience: Air conditioning ($645). Rear defogger, electric ($135). Tinted glass ($99). Comfortilt steering wheel ($115). Lighting and Mirrors: Twin sport mirrors, left remote ($53). Driver's remote sport mirror ($34). Entertainment: AM/FM radio ($82). AM/FM stereo radio ($109). Radio delete ($51 credit). Exterior Trim: Two-tone paint ($133). Door edge guards ($15-$25). Chrome bumpers ($25). Interior Trim/Upholstery: Cloth bucket seats: cpe ($28). Custom cloth bucket seats: cpe ($130). Color-keyed floor mats ($25). Wheels and Tires: Sport wheel covers ($45-$97). Wheel trim rings ($52). P155/80R13 SBR WSW ($51).

NOVA CONVENIENCE/APPEARANCE OPTIONS: Nova had only one individual option: two-tone paint ($176). All other options came in packages, as follows. Pkg. 1: Five-speed trans., AM radio, P155/80R13 BSW tires (NC). Pkg. 2: Pkg. 1 plus power steering and automatic trans. ($610). Pkg. 3: Pkg. 1 plus air conditioning, electronic-tuning AM/FM stereo seek/scan radio w/digital clock, dual mirrors (left remote), power steering, electric rear defogger and halogen headlamps ($1180). Pkg. 4: Same as pkg. 3 plus automatic trans. ($1575). Pkg. 5: Automatic trans., P155/80R13 tires, AM/FM with clock, power steering and air cond. ($1525). CL Pkg. 1: Five-speed trans., air cond., P155/80R13 BSW tires, seek/scan AM/FM stereo radio with digital clock, dual mirrors (left remote), power steering, rear defogger, halogen headlamps and Custom CL features ($1730). CL Pkg. 2: Same as CL 1 plus automatic trans. ($2125). CL Pkg. 3: Same as CL 1 plus AM/FM stereo radio w/cassette player and clock, aluminum wheels, P175/70R13 SBR BSW tires, intermittent wipers, cruise control and (on hatchback) rear wiper/washer ($2515-$2640). CL Pkg. 4: Same as CL 3, but with automatic trans. and P155/80R13 tires, plus power door locks ($2620-$2745).

1986 Chevrolet, Cavalier RS two-door convertible (CH)

1986 Chevrolet, Cavalier CL four-door sedan

1986 Chevrolet, Cavalier RS four-door sedan

CAVALIER CONVENIENCE/APPEARANCE OPTIONS: Option Packages: CL custom interior pkg.: reclining bucket seats, quiet sound group, sport steering wheel, console, custom door/quarter trim w/carpet inserts, fender nameplates ($251-$325); incl. split folding rear seat on hatch/wagon. Comfort/Convenience: Air cond. ($645). Cruise control w/resume ($175). Rear defogger, electric ($135). Tinted glass ($99). Six-way power driver's seat ($225). Black sport steering wheel ($22-$40). Comfortilt steering wheel ($115). Power windows ($195-$270). Power door locks ($130-$180). Power hatch or trunk release ($40). Power liftgate release ($40). Electronic instrument cluster ($295). Gauge pkg. w/trip odometer ($69); incl. tach ($139). Digital clock: RS/Z24 ($39). Lighter: base ($14). Intermittent wipers ($50). Rear wiper/washer ($125). Lighting and Mirrors: Halogen headlamps ($25). Aux. lighting ($43-$95). Dual black sport mirrors, left remote ($53). Entertainment: AM radio: base ($112). Electronic-tuning seek/scan AM/FM stereo radio ($158) exc. base ($258); w/clock ($197) exc. base ($297); w/cassette ($319) exc. base ($419).

Electronic-tuning AM stereo/FM seek/scan radio w/cassette, equalizer and clock ($494-$504) exc. base ($594). Premium dual rear speakers ($25). Extended-range sound system: RS/Z24/conv. ($35). Fixed-mast antenna: base ($41) but incl. w/radios. Radio delete ($56 credit). Exterior Trim: Removable sunroof ($310). Rear spoiler: RS/Z24 ($69). Rear window louvers ($199). Custom two-tone paint: CS ($176); RS ($123). Pin striping ($53). Bodyside moldings, black: base ($45). Wheel opening moldings, black: conv. ($30). Wheel opening and rocker panel moldings ($55). Door edge guards ($15-$25). Wagon roof carrier ($105). Decklid luggage rack ($100). Bumper guards ($56). Interior Trim/Upholstery: Cloth reclining bucket seats: base/CS ($28). Sport cloth reclining bucket seats: Z24 (NC). Custom CL cloth bucket seats: CS/RS/Z24 (NC). Custom CL vinyl bucket seats: RS/Z24 (NC). Split-folding rear seatback: wag/hatch ($50). Color-keyed mats: front ($18); rear ($15). Cargo area cover: wag/hatch ($69). Deluxe seat/shoulder belts: base ($26). Wheels and Tires: Aluminum wheels, 13 in. ($233-$285); 14 in., Z24 ($173). Rally 14 in. wheels: conv. ($56). Sport wheel covers ($45-$97). Wheel trim rings: base/CS ($52). P175/80R13 SBR WSW: base/CS ($54). P195/70R13 SBR BSW: base/CS ($104). P195/70R13 SBR WSW: base/CS ($166). P195/70R13 SBR RWL: base/CS ($188); RS ($84). P215/60R14 SBR BSW: RS ($142). P215/60R14 SBR RWL: RS ($234); Z24 ($92).

1986 Chevrolet, Cavalier RS station wagon

CELEBRITY/CAPRICE CONVENIENCE/APPEARANCE OPTIONS: Option Packages: Eurosport pkg.: Celeb ($225). Estate equipment: Capr wag ($307). Landau equipment (vinyl roof, sport mirrors and reveal moldings): Capr ($306). Exterior molding pkg. (rocker panel and wheel opening moldings): Celeb ($55). Security pkg.: Celeb wag ($44). Quiet sound group: base Capr ($66). Comfort/Convenience: Air cond. ($750). Rear defogger, electric ($145-$150). Cruise control ($175). Tinted glass ($115). Comfortilt steering wheel ($115). Six-way power driver's seat ($215-$225). Power windows ($195-$270). Power door locks ($130-$180). Power trunk or liftgate release ($40). Power tailgate lock: Capr wag ($50). Gauge pkg. w/trip odometer ($64). Tachometer: Celeb ($90). Quartz clock: base Capr ($39). Intermittent wipers ($50). Rear wiper/washer: Celeb ($125). Lighting, Horns and Mirrors: Halogen headlamps ($25). Cornering lamps: Capr

($55). Aux. lighting: Celeb ($51-$67); Capr ($32-$42). Dome reading lamp: Celeb ($24). Dual horns: Celeb ($12). Driver's remote mirror ($23). Dual sport mirrors, left remote ($61). Dual remote sport mirrors ($91) exc. Capr Lan ($30). Right visor mirror: Celeb ($7). Lighted visor mirror ($50). Entertainment: AM radio w/digital clock: Celeb ($39). Electronic-tuning seek/scan AM/FM stereo radio ($158); w/clock ($162-$197); w/cassette, clock and seek/scan ($284-$319). Seek/scan AM/FM stereo radio w/cassette, equalizer and clock: Capr ($394-$464). Seek/scan AM stereo/FM radio w/clock, equalizer and cassette: Celeb ($504). Extended-range rear speakers ($35). Power antenna: Capr ($65). Radio delete ($56 credit). Exterior Trim: Removable sunroof: Celeb ($310). Padded vinyl roof: Celeb ($270). Vinyl roof: Capr sed ($185). Two-tone paint ($141-$148). Bodyside pin striping ($39-$57). Bodyside moldings: Capr ($55). Wheel opening moldings: base Capr ($30). Door edge guards ($15-$25). Rear window air deflector: wag ($40). Rear quarter vent windows: Celeb ($75). Swing-out tailgate: Celeb wag ($105). Decklid luggage carrier: Celeb ($100). Roof carrier: wag ($105-$110). Bumper rub strips: Capr ($66). Bumper guards ($56-$62). Celebrity Interior: Console ($110). Reclining passenger seatback ($45); both ($90). Cloth bench seat: wag ($28). Vinyl bench seat: cpe/sed ($28). Cloth 55/45 seat ($133). CL custom cloth 45/45 seat ($200-$330). CL custom cloth 55/45 seating ($305-$435). Cloth reclining bucket seats ($147). Color-keyed rubber mats: front ($17); rear ($12). Carpeted mats: front ($25); rear ($20). Deluxe trunk or wagon luggage area trim ($40-$47). Caprice Interior: Reclining passenger seatback: Classic ($45). Vinyl bench seat: base sed ($28). Cloth bench seat: wag ($28). Cloth 50/50 seating: Classic ($195-$225). Vinyl 50/50 seating ($195). Deluxe load-floor carpet: wag ($89). Deluxe cargo area trim: wag ($129). Mats w/carpet insert: front ($25); rear ($20). Deluxe trunk trim ($59). Celebrity Wheels/Tires: Aluminum wheels ($306-$362). Sport wheel covers ($65). Locking wire wheel covers ($199). Rally wheels ($56). P185/75R14 SBR WSW ($58). P195/70R14 Eagle GT SBR BSW: Eurosport ($80). P195/75R14 SBR BSW ($30). P195/75R14 SBR WSW ($92). Caprice Wheels/Tires: Sport wheel covers ($65). Wire wheel covers w/locks ($199). P205/75R15 SBR WSW: cpe/sed ($66). P225/70R15 SBR WSW: cpe/sed ($157). P225/75R15 SBR WSW: wag ($71). Puncture-sealant tires ($115-$140).

1986 Chevrolet, Camaro Berlinetta two-door coupe

1986 Chevrolet, Camaro Z28 two-door coupe

CAMARO/MONTE CARLO CONVENIENCE/APPEARANCE OPTIONS: Option Packages: IROC-Z sport equipment pkg.: Camaro Z28 ($659). Comfort/Convenience: Air cond. ($750). Rear defogger (electric) ($145). Cruise control w/resume ($175-$185). Tinted glass ($115). Comfortilt steering wheel ($115). Six-way power driver's seat ($225). Power windows ($195). Power door locks ($130). Power trunk opener: Monte ($40). Power hatch release: Camaro ($40). Tachometer: Monte ($90). Gauge pkg. w/trip odometer: Monte ($69). Gauge pkg. incl. tach: base Camaro ($149). Intermittent wipers ($50). Rear wiper/washer: Camaro ($125). Quiet sound group: Camaro ($82). Lighting, Horns and Mirrors: Halogen headlamps ($25). Halogen foglamps: Camaro ($60). Aux. lighting: Camaro ($37-$72); Monte ($28). Dual horns: Camaro ($12). Twin sport mirrors (left remote): Monte ($53). Twin remote sport mirrors: Monte ($83); SS ($30). Twin electric remote sport mirrors: Camaro ($91). Automatic day/night mirror: Camaro ($80). Right visor mirror: Monte ($7); lighted ($50). Entertainment: AM radio w/digital clock: base ($39). Electronic-tuning seek/scan AM/FM stereo radio: base Camaro ($193); Electronic-tuning seek/scan AM/FM stereo radio w/clock: Camaro ($197-$232); w/cassette and clock ($319-$354); w/AM stereo and cassette ($469-$504). Seek/scan AM/FM stereo w/remote control and cassette: Berlinetta ($242). Monte seek/scan electronic-tuning AM/FM stereo radio ($158); w/clock ($197); w/cassette ($319); with AM stereo and cassette ($494). Premium rear speakers: Monte ($25). Power antenna: Camaro ($60). Radio delete ($56 credit) exc. Berlinetta ($256 credit); Z28 ($95 credit). Exterior Trim: Removable glass roof panels: Camaro ($846); Monte ($875). Landau vinyl roof: Monte ($245). Rear spoiler: Camaro ($69). Rear window louvers: Camaro ($210). Two-tone paint: Monte ($214). Bodyside moldings, black: Camaro ($55). Deluxe vinyl bodyside moldings: Monte ($57). Door edge guards ($15). Side window sill moldings: Monte ($45). Bodyside pin striping: Monte ($61). Interior Trim/Upholstery: Console: Monte ($110). Roof console: Camaro/Z28 ($50). Vinyl bench seat: Monte ($28). Cloth 55/45 seating: base Monte ($133). Cloth bucket seats: Camaro ($28); Monte ($147). Custom cloth bucket seats: base Camaro/Z28 ($359). Custom cloth CL 55/45 seating: base Monte ($385). Split folding back seat: Camaro ($50). Mats w/carpeted inserts: front ($20); rear ($15). Cargo area cover: Camaro ($69). Deluxe trunk trim: Camaro ($164); Z28 ($84). Locking rear storage cover: Z28 ($80). Wheels and Tires: Aluminum wheels: Monte ($362); Berlinetta ($225). Wheel locks: Berlinetta/Z28

($16). Rally wheels: Monte ($56). Locking wire wheel covers: Monte ($199). P195/70R14 SBR BSW Eagle GT: Berlinetta ($80). P195/75R14 SBR WSW: Monte ($62). P205/70R14 SBR WSW: Berlinetta ($66); Monte ($124). P215/65R15 SBR BSW: Z28 ($92 credit). P215/65R15 SBR RWL: Camaro four ($92). P235/60VR15 SBR BSW: Z28 ($85).

HISTORY: Introduced: Oct. 3, 1985. Model year production (U.S.): 1,564,303 (incl. Corvettes but not incl. 21,643 Acadians). Total production for sale in U.S. consisted of 867,823 four-cylinder, 433,461 sixes, and 448,221 V-8s. Only 588 leftover diesels were installed. Calendar year production (U.S.): 1,518,794 (including 28,410 Corvettes). Calendar year sales by U.S. dealers: 1,558,476, for a 19.5 percent market share. Model year sales by U.S. dealers: 1,587,024 (incl. 35,969 Corvettes) for a 19.7 percent share.

Historical Footnotes: The new joint-venture Nova, produced by Chevrolet and Toyota, helped Chevrolet sales come close to the 1985 figure. Total sales still dropped a bit for the model year. Even so, Chevrolet's domestic market share managed to grow somewhat. A total of 170,661 Novas were sold during the full model year, but Cavalier and Celebrity were still the top sellers. Actually, Celebrity pulled ahead and made No. 1 this year. As Nova production increased, the outmoded rear-drive Chevette's days were numbered, especially when Chevrolet announced in late 1985 that the Lakewood, Georgia, plant that assembled Chevettes would be converted to rear-drive production. Chevette sales shrunk to 75,761, prompting a price cut for 1987 and abandonment early in that model year. With the new Nova (based on Toyota's Corolla) and the twin Japanese imports sold under the Chevrolet banner (Spectrum and Sprint), Chevrolet offered a total of five small cars. Chevrolet's General Manager Robert D. Burger predicted that subcompacts and smaller cars would "account for nearly 40 percent of total car sales in this country in 1986." The company was especially interested in attracting first-time, younger buyers, who might later want to move up to a "better" Chevrolet model. In addition to the small-car lineup, Chevrolet claimed to have America's fastest car (Corvette), most popular car (Cavalier), most popular mid- and full-size cars (Celebrity and Caprice), and favorite sporty 2 + 2 (Camaro). Low-interest loans (7.7 percent) were offered by GM late in the 1985 model year, and 8.8 percent rates arrived for 1986. One Illinois dealer opened experimental operations in a shopping mall, in an attempt to lure buyers who might otherwise be missed. A Women's Marketing Committee was formed to develop approaches to attract female buyers, whose role in auto purchasing was gaining steadily by the mid-1980s. Among other innovations was a pre-approved credit plan for women customers, through General Motors Acceptance Corporation. Dealers also held "Car Care Clinics" for women. Nova's manufacturing facility was called New United Motor Manufacturing, Inc. (NUMMI), located at Fremont, California.

Late in the model year, two new Chevrolet models arrived: the front-drive Corsica and Beretta. Rather than heading straight for new-car dealers, they first had a tryout as rental vehicles. In addition to all the domestic models, Chevrolet marketed the sub-compact Sprint (built by Suzuki) and slightly larger Spectrum (from Isuzu).

CHEVETTE — SERIES 1T — FOUR — Chevette's diesel engine option was dropped this year, but few other changes were evident for the subcompact's final season. Sole powerplant was the 1.6-liter gasoline four, with standard four-speed manual gearbox, optional five-speed, or optional three-speed automatic.

1987 Chevrolet, Nova four-door sedan (PH)

NOVA — SERIES 1S — FOUR — Taillamps were a little wider this year, and bumpers turned to body color. Otherwise, little changed in the front-drive Nova, built in California as a joint venture between GM and Toyota. New standard equipment included a rear-window defogger. Notchback and hatchback four-door sedans were offered, powered by a 1.6-liter four that produced 74 horsepower and standard five-speed gearbox. An automatic transmission was available only as part of an option package.

1987 Chevrolet, Cavalier RS four-door sedan

1987 Chevrolet, Cavalier Z24 two-door hatchback coupe (PH)

CAVALIER — SERIES 1J — FOUR/V-6 — Customers for Chevrolet's popular J-body subcompact had quite a variety to choose from this year: five body styles and four trim levels. Both the 2.0-liter four-cylinder and 2.8-liter V-6 engines went into Generation II versions, and added the option of a five-speed Getrag-designed manual gearbox. With a new Computer Controlled Coil Ignition sending power to its spark plugs, the four-cylinder engine no longer had need for a distributor. Standard in the performance-oriented Z24 and optional in the RS convertible, the V-6 added a new aluminum cylinder head, new fuel injectors, and electronic spark control for a rating of 125 or 130 horsepower. One belt now drove all the accessories under V-6 hoods. Modifications to the Z24 included a fresh-air induction hood, low-restriction exhaust system, and the installation of new 14-inch aluminum wheels.

1987 Chevrolet, Camaro IROC-Z28 two-door convertible

1987 Chevrolet, Camaro IROC-Z28 two-door coupe (PH)

CAMARO — SERIES 1F — V-6/V-8 — Biggest news for performance fans was the arrival of the 350 cu. in. (5.7-liter) V-8 with roller lifters as an option for the IROC-Z. Both the four-cylinder engine and the high-output carbureted 5.0-liter V-8 were dropped this year, giving the 173 cu. in. (2.8-liter) Generation II V-6 new duty as Camaro's base powerplant. A new LT model (actually a set of option packages) replaced the former Berlinetta. A 165-horsepower carbureted 5.0-liter V-8 was optional in the base and LT Camaros, and standard under Z28 hoods. But the Z28 could also be ordered with a tuned-port injection version of that V-8, delivering 215 horsepower. All Camaros could have either a five-speed manual gearbox or four-speed overdrive automatic, except the IROC-Z with 5.7-liter V-8, which came only with automatic. Otherwise, Camaros changed little in appearance apart from new wet-arm wipers and the mounting of the required center high-mount stoplight on the rear spoiler (if installed).

CORSICA/BERETTA — SERIES 1L — FOUR/V-6 — Intended to replace the ill-starred Citation, which was dropped after 1985, the new compact Corsica sedan and Beretta coupe rode a 103.4-inch wheelbase and carried either a 121-cu. in. (2.0-liter) four or optional 2.8-liter V-6. A five-speed gearbox was standard. Though both appeared late in the 1987 model year they were actually early '88 models. See 1988 listing for further details.

1987 Chevrolet, Celebrity Classic four-door sedan (PH)

CELEBRITY — SERIES 1A — FOUR/V-6 — During 1986, Chevrolet's front-drive A-body mid-size took over Cavalier's role as most popular American automobile. This year's front end held composite aerodynamic headlamps with integral side marker lamps, while engine compartments contained Generation II engines: either a 2.5-liter four or 2.8-liter V-6. The four-cylinder engine added six horsepower as a result of reworked fuel metering, a restyled intake manifold and lighter pistons. New aluminum cylinder heads helped knock a few pounds off the V-6 weight, while horsepower rose to 135. For the first time, a Getrag-designed five-speed gearbox was offered with the V-6, which formerly came only with automatic. Standard transmission was a three-speed automatic, with four-speed automatic available (V-6 only).

MONTE CARLO — SERIES 1G — V-6/V-8 — Both LS and SS rear-drive Montes were offered this year in the mid-size coupe body. Also available again was the stylish fastback Aerocoupe, only 200 of which had appeared in 1986. Base powerplant for the LS was the 262 cu. in. (4.3-liter) V-6 with throttle-body fuel injection and new roller valve lifters. Optional again was the carbureted 305 cu. in. (5.0-liter) V-8, producing 150 horsepower. The SS had a high-output version of the V-8, rated 180 horsepower. Six-cylinder Montes came with a standard three-speed automatic, while V-8s sent their power through a four-speed. Aerodynamic composite headlamps, introduced for 1986 on the LS, also went on the SS this time around. Otherwise, apart from a few design revisions in the back end, little change was evident.

1987 Chevrolet, Caprice Classic Brougham LS four-door sedan (PH)

CAPRICE — SERIES 1B — V-6/V-8 — On the outside, full-size Chevrolet coupes, sedans and wagons got new stand-up hood ornaments this year, plus composite headlamps that combined high and low beams into a single unit. Joining the upscale Classic Brougham was a new Brougham LS sedan, aiming even further upscale with its formal Landau vinyl roof. A new base station wagon joined the former Classic wagon, both carrying a standard 307 cu. in. (5.0-liter) V-8 engine. Coupes and sedans came with a standard 262 cu. in. (4.3 liter) V-6, with a 305 cu. in. V-8 optional. All three engines added roller lifters this year, and both V-8s used four-barrel carburetors.

I.D. DATA: Chevrolets again had a 17-symbol Vehicle Identification Number (VIN) on the upper left surface of the instrument panel, visible through the windshield. Symbol one indicates country: '1' - USA.; '2' - Canada. Next is a manufacturer code: 'G' - General Motors. Symbol three is car make: '1' - Chevrolet; '7' - GM of Canada. Symbol four denotes restraint system: 'A' - non-passive (standard); 'B' - passive (automatic belts); 'C' - passive (inflatable). Symbol five is car line/series. Symbols six-seven reveal body type. Next is the engine code, followed by a check digit, ten 'H' for model year 1987. Symbol eleven indicates assembly plant. The final six digits are the sequential serial number. Engine number coding is similar to 1981-86.

CHEVETTE CS (FOUR)

Model No.	Body/Style No.	Body Type & Seating	Factory Price	Shipping Weight	Prod. Total
1T	B08	2-dr. Hatch Cpe-4P	4995	2078	26,135
1T	B68	4-dr. Hatch Sed-4P	5495	2137	20,073

NOVA (FOUR)

1S	K19	4-dr. Sedan-4P	8258	2206	123,782
1S	K68	4-dr. Hatch Sed-4P	8510	2253	26,224

CAVALIER (FOUR/V-6)

1J	C27	2-dr. Coupe-5P	7255/7915	2300/----	53,678
1J	C69	4-dr. Sedan-5P	7449/8109	2345/----	84,445
1J	C35	4-dr. Sta Wag-5P	7614/8275	2401/----	25,542

CAVALIER CS (FOUR/V-6)

1J	D77	2-dr. Hatch Cpe-5P	7978/8638	2359/----	3,480
1J	D69	4-dr. Sedan-5P	7953/8613	2355/----	50,625
1J	D35	4-dr. Sta Wag-5P	8140/8800	2411/----	15,023

CAVALIER RS (FOUR/V-6)

1J	E27	2-dr. Coupe-5P	8318/8978	2360/----	36,353
1J	E77	2-dr. Hatch Cpe-5P	8520/9180	2408/----	2,818
1J	E69	4-dr. Sedan-5P	8499/9159	2397/----	15,482
1J	E35	4-dr. Sta Wag-5P	8677/9337	2460/----	5,575
1J	E67	2-dr. Conv. Cpe-4P	13446/14106	2519/----	5,826

CAVALIER Z24 (V-6)

1J	F27	2-dr. Spt Cpe-5P	----/9913	----/2511	42,890
1J	F77	2-dr. Hatch Cpe-5P	----/10115	----/2560	4,517

CAMARO (V-6/V-8)

1F	P87	2-dr. Spt Cpe-4P	9995/10395	3062/3181	83,890
1F	P67	2-dr. Conv Cpe-4P	----/14794	N/A	263

CAMARO Z28 (V-8)

1F	P87/Z28	2-dr. Spt Cpe-4P	12819	3228	52,863
1F	P67/Z28	2-dr. Conv Cpe-4P	17218	N/A	744

CAMARO IROC-Z (V-8)

1F	P87/Z28	2-dr. Spt Cpe-4P	13488	N/A	Note 1
1F	P67/Z28	2-dr. Conv Cpe-4P	17917	N/A	Note 1

CORSICA (FOUR/V-6)

1L	T69	4-dr. Sedan-5P	8995/9655	2491/2609	8,973

BERETTA (FOUR/V-6)

1L	V37	2-dr. Coupe-5P	9555/10215	2550/2648	8,072

CELEBRITY (FOUR/V-6)

1A	W27	2-dr. Coupe-5P	9995/10605	2685/2769	18,198
1A	W19	4-dr. Sedan-5P	10265/10875	2715/2799	273,864
1A	W35	4-dr. Sta Wag-6P	10425/11035	2847/2931	33,894
1A	W35/AQ4	4-dr. 3S Wag-8P	10672/11382	N/A	36,568

MONTE CARLO (V-6/V-8)

1G	Z37	2-dr. LS Cpe-6P	11306/11746	3283/3389	72,993

MONTE CARLO 'SS' (V-8)

1G	Z37/Z65	2-dr. Spt Cpe-6P	13463	3473	Note 2
1G	Z37/Z16	2-dr. Aerocpe-6P	14838	3526	6,052

CAPRICE (V-6/V-8)

1B	L69	4-dr. Sedan-6P	10995/11435	3510/3603	56,266
1B	L35	4-dr. 3S Wag-8P	----/11995	----/4114	11,953

CAPRICE CLASSIC (V-6/V-8)

1B	N47	2-dr. Coupe-6P	11392/11802	3512/3605	3,110
1B	N69	4-dr. Sedan-6P	11560/12000	3527/3620	53,802
1B	U69	4-dr. Brghm-6P	12549/12989	3476/3669	51,341
1B	U69/B6N	4-dr. LS Brghm-6P	13805/14245	N/A	23,641
1B	N35	4-dr. 3S Wag-8P	----/12586	----/4125	23,387

Note 1: IROC-Z production included in Z28 total.

Note 2: Monte Carlo SS sport coupe production included in LS total.

FACTORY PRICE AND WEIGHT NOTE: For Cavalier, Corsica, Beretta and Celebrity, prices and weights to left of slash are for four-cylinder, to right for V-6 engine. For Camaro, Monte Carlo and Caprice, figures to left of slash are for six-cylinder model, to right of slash for least expensive V-8.

BODY/STYLE NO. NOTE: Some models were actually option packages. Code after the slash (e.g., Z28) is the number of the option package that comes with the model listed.

ENGINE DATA: BASE FOUR (Chevette): Inline. Overhead cam. Four-cylinder. Cast iron block and head. Displacement: 98 cu. in. (1.6 liters). Bore & stroke: 3.23 x 2.98 in. Compression ratio: 9.0:1 Brake horsepower: 65 at 5600 RPM. Torque: 80 lb.-ft. at 3200 RPM. Five main bearings. Hydraulic valve lifters. Carburetor: 2Bbl. BASE FOUR (Nova): Inline. Overhead cam. Four-cylinder. Cast iron block and head. Displacement: 97 cu. in. (1.6 liters). Bore & stroke: 3.19 x 3.03 in. Compression ratio: 9.0:1. Brake horsepower: 74 at 5200 RPM. Torque: 86 lb.-ft. at 2800 RPM. Solid valve lifters. Carburetor: Aisan 2Bbl. BASE FOUR (Cavalier, Corsica/Beretta): Inline. Overhead valve. Four-cylinder. Cast iron block and aluminum head. Displacement: 121 cu. in. (2.0 liters). Bore & stroke: 3.50 x 3.15 in. Compression ratio: 9.0:1. Brake horsepower: 90 at 5600 RPM. Torque: 108 lb.-ft. at 3200 RPM. Five main bearings. Hydraulic valve lifters. Throttle-body fuel injection. BASE FOUR (Celebrity): Inline. Overhead valve. Four-cylinder. Cast iron block and head. Displacement: 151 cu. in (2.5 liters). Bore & stroke: 4.00 x 3.00 in. Compression ratio: 9.0:1. Brake horsepower: 98 at 4400 RPM. Torque: 135 lb.-ft. at 3200 RPM. Five main bearings. Hydraulic valve lifters. Throttle-body fuel injection. BASE V-6 (Camaro, Cavalier Z24); OPTIONAL (Cavalier RS conv., Celebrity): 60-degree, overhead valve V-6. Cast iron block and head. Displacement: 173 cu. in. (2.8 liters). Bore & stroke: 3.50 x 2.99 in. Compression ratio: 8.9:1 Brake horsepower: (Cavalier) 125/130 at 4500; (Corsica/Beretta) 125 at 4500; (Camaro) 135 at 4900; (Celebrity) 125 at 4500. Torque: (Cavalier) 160/165 at 3600; (Corsica/Beretta) N/A; (Camaro) 160 at 3900; (Celeb) 160 at 3600. Multi-port fuel injection. BASE V-6 (Monte Carlo, Caprice); 90-degree, overhead valve V-6. Cast iron block and head. Displacement: 262 cu. in. (4.3 liters). Bore & stroke: 4.00 x 3.48 in. Compression ratio: 9.3:1. Brake horsepower: (Caprice) 140 at 3200 RPM; (Monte) 145 at 4200. Torque: 225 lb.-ft. at 2000 RPM. Four main bearings. Hydraulic valve lifters. Throttle-body fuel injection. BASE V-8 (Camaro Z28, Caprice wagon); OPTIONAL (Camaro, Monte Carlo, Caprice); 90-degree, overhead valve V-8. Cast iron block and head. Displacement: 305 cu. in. (5.0 liters). Bore & stroke: 3.74 x 3.48 in. Compression ratio: (Camaro) 9.3:1 (Monte/Caprice) 9.5:1. Brake horsepower: (Camaro) 165 at 4400 RPM; (Monte) 150 at 4000; (Caprice) 170 at 4400. Torque: (Camaro) 245/250 lb.-ft. at 2800 RPM (Monte) 240 at 2000; (Caprice) 250 at 2800. Five main bearings. Hydraulic valve lifters. Carburetor: 4Bbl. HIGH-OUTPUT V-8 (Monte Carlo SS): Same as 305 cu. in. V-8 above, except: BHP: 180 at 4800 RPM. Torque: 225 lb.-ft. at 3200 RPM. OPTIONAL HIGH-OUTPUT V-8 (Camaro Z28): Same as 305 cu. in. V-8 above, but with turned port fuel injection: BHP: 215 at 4400 RPM (190 at 4000 with automatic). Torque: 250 lb.-ft. at 3200 RPM (295 at 2800 with automatic). OPTIONAL V-8 (Caprice wagon): 90-degree, overhead valve V-8. Cast iron block and head. Displacement: 307 cu. in. (5.0 liters). Bore & stroke: 3.80 x 3.38 in. Compression ratio: 8.0:1 Brake horsepower: 140 at 3200 RPM. Torque: 225 lb.-ft. at 2000 RPM. Five main bearings. Hydraulic

roller valve lifters. Carburetor: 4Bbl. OPTIONAL V-8 (Camaro IROC-Z): 90-degree, overhead valve V-8. Cast iron block and head. Displacement: 350 cu. in. (5.7 liters). Bore & stroke: 4.00 x 3.48 in. Compression ratio: 9.0:1 Brake horsepower: 225 at 4400 RPM. Torque: 330 lb.-ft. at 2800 RPM.

1987 Chevrolet, Monte Carlo SS two-door Aerocoupe

CHASSIS DATA: Wheelbase: (Chevette cpe) 94.3 in.; (Chvt sed) 97.3 in.; (Nova) 95.7 in.; (Cavalier) 101.2 in.; (Camaro) 101.0 in.; (Corsica/Beretta) 103.4 in.; (Celebrity) 104.9 in.; (Monte Carlo) 108.0 in.; (Caprice) 116.0 in. Overall length: (Chvt cpe) 161.9 in.; (Chvt sed) 164.9 in.; (Nova) 166.3 in.; (Cav cpe/conv) 172.4 in.; (Cav sed) 174.3 in.; (Cav wag) 174.5 in.; (Camaro) 188.0 in.; (Camaro Z28/IROC-Z) 192.0 in.; (Corsica) 183.4 in.; (Beretta) 187.2 in.; (Celeb) 188.3 in.; (Celeb wag) 190.8 in.; (Monte) 200.4 in.; (Caprice cpe) 212.8 in.; (Capr sed) 212.2 in.; (Capr wag) 215.1 in. Height: (Chvt) 52.8 in.; (Nova sed) 53.0 in.; (Nova hatch) 52.8 in.; (Cav cpe) 50.2 in.; (Cav conv) 52.7 in.; (Cav sed) 52.1 in.; (Cav wag) 52.8 in.; (Camaro) 50.0 in.; (Corsica) 52.7 in.; (Beretta) 52.6 in.; (Celeb) 54.1 in.; (Celeb Wag) 54.3 in.; (Monte) 54.4 in.; (Caprice) 56.4 in.; (Caprice wag) 58.2 in. Width: (Chvt) 61.8 in.; (Nova) 64.4 in.; (Cap cpe/conv) 66.0 in.; (Cav sed/wag) 66.3 in.; (Camaro) 72.8 in.; (Corsica) 68.2 in.; (Beretta) 68.0 in.; (Celeb) 69.3 in.; (Monte) 71.8 in.; (Caprice) 75.4 in.; (Capr wag) 79.3 in. Front Tread: (Chvt) 51.2 in.; (Nova) 56.1 in.; (Cav) 55.4 in.; (Camaro) 60.7 in.; (Corsica/Beretta) 55.6 in.; (Celeb) 58.7 in.; (Monte) 58.5 in.; (Caprice) 61.7 in.; (Capr wag) 62.2 in. Rear Tread: (Chvt)

51.2 in.; (Nova) 55.3 in.; (Cav) 55.2 in.; (Camaro) 61.6 in.; (Corsica) 55.1 in.; (Beretta) 56.5 in.; (Celeb) 57.0 in.; (Monte) 57.8 in.; (Caprice (60.7 in.; (Capr wag) 64.1 in. Standard Tires: (Chvt/Nova) P155/80R13; (Cav) P185/80R13; (Cav RS) P195/70R13; (Cav Z24) P215/60R14; (Camaro) P205/70R14; (Camaro Z28) P215/65R15; (Corsica/Beretta) P185/80R13; (Celeb) P185/75R14; (Celeb Eurosport) P195/75R14; (Monte) P195/75R14; (Monte SS) P215/65R15; (Caprice) P205/75R15; (Caprice wag) P225/75R15.

TECHNICAL: Transmission: Four-speed manual shift standard on Chevette. Four-speed overdrive manual shift standard on Cavalier. Five-speed manual shift standard on Nova, Cavalier Z24, Corsica/Beretta and Camaro. Three-speed automatic standard on Celebrity, Monte Carlo and Caprice. Steering: (Cavalier/Chevette/Nova/Corsica/Beretta/Celebrity) rack and pinion; (others) recirculating ball. Front Suspension: (Chevette/Monte/Caprice) unequal-length control arms, coil springs, stabilizer bar; (Nova) MacPherson struts w/coil springs and lower control arms; (Corsica/Beretta) MacPherson struts with coil springs; (Cavalier/Camaro/Celeb) MacPherson struts with coil springs, lower control arms and stabilizer bar. Rear Suspension: (Chevette) rigid axle and torque tube w/four links and track bar, coil springs; (Nova) fully independent MacPherson struts, dual links, coil springs and stabilizer bar; (Cavalier) semi-independent with beam axle, trailing arms, coil springs, stabilizer bar available; (Camaro) rigid axle and torque tube with longitudinal control arms, Panhard rod, coil springs and stabilizer bar; (Corsica/Beretta) trailing twist axle with coil springs; (Celeb) beam twist axle with integral stabilizer, trailing arms, Panhard rod and coil springs; (Monte/Caprice) rigid axle with four links, coil springs, stabilizer available. Brakes: front disc, rear drum; four-wheel discs available on Camaro. Body construction: unibody except (Monte/Caprice) separate body and frame. Fuel tank (Chvt) 12.2 gal.; (Nova) 13.2 gal.; (Cav) 13.6 gal.; (Camaro) 15.5 gal; (Corsica/Beretta) 13.6 gal.; (Celeb) 15.7 gal.; (Monte V-6) 17.6 gal.; (Monte V-8) 18.1 gal.; (Capr) 24.5 gal.; (Capr wag) 22 gal.

DRIVETRAIN OPTIONS: Engines: 173 cu. in. V-6; Cavalier RS conv ($660); Celeb ($610); 305 cu. in., 4Bbl. V-8: Camaro ($400); Monte Carlo LS, Caprice cpe/sed ($440). 305 cu. in., TPI V-8; Camaro Z28 ($745). 350 cu. in., TPI V-8: Camaro IROC-Z ($1045). Transmission/Differential: Five-speed manual trans.: Chevette/Cavalier ($75); Celeb ($440 credit). Three-speed automatic trans.: Chevette ($450); Cavalier ($490); Cavalier Z24 ($415). Four-speed overdrive auto. trans.: Camaro ($490); Celeb V-6 ($175); Monte LS, Caprice cpe/sed ($175). Limited-slip differential: Camaro/Monte/Caprice ($100). Performance axle ratio: Chevette/Camaro/Celeb/Monte/Caprice ($21). Power Accessories: Power brakes: Chevette ($105). Power four-wheel disc brakes: Camaro ($179). Power steering: Chvt/Cav ($225). Suspension: F40 H.D. susp.: Cav/Celeb. Caprice ($26). F41 sport susp.: Cav ($44-$49); Monte LS, Caprice ($49). Inflatable rear shock absorbers: Celeb/Caprice ($64).

CHEVETTE CONVENIENCE/APPEARANCE OPTIONS: Air conditioning ($675). Heavy-duty battery ($26). Chromed bumpers ($25). Heavy-duty cooling system, w/o air conditioning ($70), w/air conditioning ($40). Custom exterior pkg. 3-door ($139). 5-door ($154). Rear defogger ($145). California emissions pkg. ($99). Tinted glass ($105). Engine block heater ($20). Left remote & right manual mirrors ($53). Left remote mirror ($34). Bodyside moldings ($50). AM/FM radio ($92). AM/FM stereo ($119). AM delete ($51 credit). Exterior sport decor ($132). Tilt steering column ($125). Cloth bucket seats ($28). Custom cloth bucket seats ($130). Custom two-tone paint ($183).

NOVA CONVENIENCE/APPEARANCE OPTIONS: Custom two-tone paint ($176). Option Package 2 ($630). Automatic transmission, power steering. Option Package 3 ($1120), Pkg. 2 plus 5-speed, air conditioning, AM/FM stereo (electronic-tune). Option Package 4 ($1530), Pkg. 3 plus automatic transmission, Option Package 5 ($1480), Pkg. 4 but without rear defogger. CL Option Package 1, 4-door ($2405). 5-door ($2710). Automatic transmission, AM/FM stereo, left remote and right manual mirrors, power steering, air conditioning, Halogen headlamps, P175/70R13 tires. CL Option Package 2, 4-door ($2625). 5-door ($2450). CL pkg. 1 plus 5-speed, cassette stereo, intermittent wipers, cruise control, rear wiper/washer (5-door). CL Option Package 3, 4-door ($3200). 5-door ($3630). CL pkg. 2 plus automatic transmission, power windows and door locks, full wheel covers (4-door), aluminum wheels (5-door).

NOTE: All CL Option Packages include windshield tint and wide black bodyside molding, bodyside stripes, remote decklid and fuel filler releases, luggage compartment trim and lamp, driver's seat height and lumbar support adjustments, velour seat trim, console storage box and armrest, right visor mirror, passenger assist grips and tilt steering column.

CAVALIER CONVENIENCE/APPEARANCE OPTIONS: Air conditioning ($675). Heavy-duty battery ($26). Deluxe seatbelts, base ($26). Roof rack, wagons ($115). Decklid rack, 2- and 4-doors ($115). CL Custom Interior, 3-doors ($271). Wagons ($295). RS & Z24 2-doors ($221). CS & RS 4-doors ($245). Cargo area cover ($69). Rear defogger ($145). Power door locks, 2- and 3-doors ($145); 4- and 5-doors ($195). California emissions system ($99). Gauge package ($69). Tinted glass (std. on conv) ($105). Halogen headlamps ($25). Engine block heater ($20). Electronic instrument cluster (std. on Z24) ($295). Auxiliary lighting. All exc. wagons & convertible ($52). Wagon ($58). RS conv. ($35). Left remote & right manual mirrors ($53). Bodyside moldings, base ($50). AM radio, base ($122). AM/FM stereo (electronic-tuning), base ($307). Others ($207). Above w/cassette, base ($429). Others ($329). Above w/equalizer, RS & Z24 ($479). AM delete all exc. base ($56 credit). Fixed-mast antenna w/o factory radio ($41). Power liftgate release ($50). Split folding rear seat (N/A 2- and 4-doors) ($50). Cruise control ($175).

Rear spoiler ($200). Tilt steering column ($125). Removable glass sunroof ($350). Remote trunk/liftgate release ($50). Cast aluminum wheels ($212). Power windows, 2- and 3-doors ($210); 4-doors, wagons ($285). Intermittent wipers ($55). Rear wiper/washer, 3-doors and wagons ($125). Cloth bucket seats, base & CS ($28). Two tone paint: CS ($176); RS ($123).

CAMARO CONVENIENCE/APPEARANCE OPTIONS: Air conditioning ($775). Heavy-duty battery ($26). Engine oil cooler ($110). Locking rear storage cover ($80). Rear defogger ($145). Power door locks ($145). California emissions pkg. ($99). Gauge pkg., Sport Coupe ($149). Tinted glass ($120). Rear window louvers ($210). Deluxe luggage compartment trim, Sport Coupe ($164). Z28 ($84). Bodyside moldings ($60). Power antenna ($70). T-top roof ($866). Split folding rear seatback ($50). Rear spoiler, Sport Coupe ($69). Cast aluminum wheels w/locks ($215). Sound systems, Sport Coupe, AM/FM stereo cassette ($364). AM/FM stereo ET, EQ ($242). AM/FM stereo ET w/cassette & EQ ($514). Delco-GM/Bose music system ($1127). AM mono radio ($39). Sport Coupe Option Pkg. 2 ($1212). Tinted glass, air conditioning, tilt steering column, AM/FM stereo. Sound systems w/Sport Coupe Pkg. 2 AM/FM stereo cassette ($122). AM/FM stereo w/cassette & EQ ($272). Delco-GM/Bose music system ($885). AM/FM stereo delete ($298 credit). Sport Coupe Option Pkg. 3 ($1628). Pkg. 2 plus four floor mats, bodyside moldings, intermittent wipers, rear spoiler, cruise control, AM/FM stereo w/cassette and extended range speakers. Sport Coupe Option Pkg. 4 ($2126). Pkg. 3 plus power windows and door locks, power hatch release, cargo cover. Halogen headlamps, auxiliary lighting. Sound systems w/Sport Coupe Option Pkgs. 3 or 4, AM/FM stereo w/cassettes & EQ ($150). Delco-GM/Bose music system ($763). AM/FM stereo delete ($420 credit). LT Option Pkg. 1. ($1522). Tinted glass, air conditioning, tilt steering column, AM-FM stereo, full wheel covers, bodyside stripes, custom interior, quiet sound group. Sound systems w/LT Option Pkg. 1. AM/FM cassette ($122). AM/FM w/cassette & EQ ($272). Delco-GM/Bose music system ($885). AM/FM delete ($298 credit). LT Option Pkg. 2 ($1938). Pkg. 1 plus floormats, bodyside moldings, intermittent wipers, rear spoiler, cruise control, AM/FM ST ET cassette w/extended range speakers. LP Option Pkg. 3 ($2387). Pkg. 2 plus power windows and door locks, power hatch release, cargo cover Halogen headlamps. LT Option Pkg. 4 ($2858). Pkg. 3 plus power seat, interior roof console, automatic day/night mirror, power remote mirrors, Halogen fog lamps. Sound Systems w/LT Option Pkg. 2, 3 or 4. AM/FM stereo ET w/cassette & EQ ($150). Delco-GM/Bose music system ($763). AM/FM stereo ET cassette delete ($420 credit). Sound Systems. Z28. AM/FM ET cassette ($325). AM/FM stereo ET ($203). AM/FM w/cassette & EQ ($475). Delco-GM/Bose music system ($1088). Z28 Option Pkg. 2 ($1999). Sport equipment, tinted glass, air conditioning, tilt steering wheel, floormats, bodyside moldings, intermittent wipers, cruise control. AM/FM stereo ET cas-

sette with extended range speakers. Z28 Option Pkg. 3, w/o cargo cover ($2470), w/cargo cover ($2539). Pkg. 2 plus power windows and door locks, power hatch release, auxiliary lighting. Halogen headlamps, cargo cover, power mirrors, power seat, automatic day/night mirror, interior roof console. Halogen fog lamps. Sound system w/Z28 Option Pkg. 2 or 3. AM/FM stereo ET w/cassette & EQ ($150). Delco-GM/Bose music system ($763). AM/FM ET w/cassette, deleted ($381 credit). IROC Option Pkg. 1 ($669). Halogen fog lamps, uprated suspension, P245/50VR16 tires on aluminum wheels. Sound systems w/IROC Pkg. 1. AM/FM stereo ET w/cassette ($325). AM/FM stereo ET ($203). AM-FM stereo ET w/cassette & EQ ($475). Delco-GM/Bose music system ($1088). IROC Option Pkg. 2 ($2409). Pkg. 1 plus sport equipment, tinted glass, air conditioning, tilt steering column, floor mats, intermittent wipers, AM/FM stereo ET cassette with extended range speakers, power windows and door locks, power hatch release. Sound Systems w/IROC Pkg. 2 AM/FM stereo ET w/cassette & EQ ($150). Delco-GM/Bose music system ($763). AM/FM stereo ET w/cassette & EQ ($150). Delco-GM/Bose music system ($763). AM/FM stereo ET w/cassette, deleted ($381 credit). IROC Option Pkg. 3 ($3273). W/o cargo cover ($3204). Pkg. 2 plus power mirrors, cruise control, bodyside moldings, cargo cover, auxiliary lighting, automatic day/night mirror, power seat, interior roof console, AM/FM stereo ET with cassette and equalizer, extended range speakers. Sound systems w/IROC Pkg. 3. Delco-GM/Bose music system ($613). AM/FM stereo ET w/cassette & EQ delete ($531 credit).

CORSICA/BERETTA CONVENIENCE/APPEARANCE OPTIONS: See 1988 listing.

CELEBRITY CONVENIENCE/APPEARANCE OPTIONS: Air conditioning ($775). Rear window air deflector, wagon ($40). Heavy-duty battery ($26). Bumper guards ($56). Roof carrier (wagon) or decklid rack (others) ($115). Center console w/shift lever ($110). Heavy-duty cooling system. W/air conditioning ($40). W/o air conditioning ($70). Rear defogger ($145). Power door locks. Coupe ($145). Sedans, wagons ($195). California emissions pkg. ($99). Estate equipment wagon ($325). Eurosport Package ($240). (Sport suspension, sport steering wheel, P195/75R14 all season tires, rally wheels, side moldings and rub strips w/specific color treatment and black-out decor.) Gauge package (incl. trip odometer) ($64). Tinted glass ($120). Engine block heater ($20). Auxiliary lighting. Coupe ($52). Sedan ($64). 2-seat wagon ($70). 3-seat wagon ($56). Coupe w/sunroof ($28). Sedan w/sunroof ($40). 2-seat wagon w/sunroof ($46). 3-seat wagon w/sunroof ($32). Deluxe luggage compartment trim ($47). Left remote mirror ($23). Left remote & right manual mirrors ($61). Dual remote mirrors ($91). Right visor mirror ($7). Illuminated right visor mirror ($50). Exterior molding pkg. ($55). Sound systems. AM radio ($39). AM/FM stereo ET ($168). Above w/cassette ($329). Above w/graphic equalizer ($514). Extended range speakers ($35). Deluxe rear compartment decor ($40).

Power driver's seat ($240). Reclining front seatbacks (each) ($45). Cargo area security pkg., wagon ($44). Cruise control ($175). Tilt steering column ($125). Removable glass sunroof ($350). Tachometer ($90). Power trunk or liftgate release ($50). Locking wire wheel covers ($199). Cast aluminum wheels: w/o Eurosport ($199); w/Eurosport ($143). Rally wheels ($56). Swing-out rear vent windows, wagon ($75). Swing-out tailgate window, wagon ($105). Power windows, coupe ($210). Sedan & Wagon ($285). Intermittent wipers ($55). Rear wiper/washer, wagon ($125).

MONTE CARLO CONVENIENCE/APPEARANCE OPTIONS: Air conditioning ($775). Heavy-duty battery ($26). Console ($110). Heavy-duty cooling: w/o A/C ($70); w/A/C ($40). Rear defogger ($145). Power door locks ($145). California emissions system ($99). Gauge package, LS ($69). Tinted glass ($120). Halogen headlamps, SS ($25). Engine block heater ($20). Auxiliary lighting: w/o T-top roof ($33); w/T-top roof ($15). Left remote & right manual mirrors, LS ($53). Dual remote mirrors, LS ($83). SS ($30). Sound systems. AM/FM stereo ET ($168). W/cassette & equalizer ($329). AM radio delete ($56 credit). Power antenna ($70). Premium rear speakers ($25). T-top roof ($895). 6-way power driver's seat (55/45 seat req.) ($240). Cruise control ($175). Tilt steering column ($125). Tachometer LS ($90). Power trunk lid release ($50). Locking wire wheel covers ($199). Styled rally wheels ($56). Cast aluminum wheels ($230). Power windows ($210). Intermittent wipers ($55). Custom two-tone paint ($214). Padded vinyl Landau roof ($260). Cloth 55/45 seat ($133). Cloth bucket seats ($147). Vinyl bench seat ($28). Custom cloth CL 55/45 seat ($385).

CAPRICE CONVENIENCE/APPEARANCE OPTIONS: Air conditioning ($775). Rear air deflector, wagons ($65). Heavy-duty battery ($26). Bumper rub strips, base ($66). Bumper guards ($62). Roof luggage rack ($115). Heavy-duty cooling: w/o A/C ($70); w/A/C ($40). Rear defogger ($145). Power door locks, 2-doors ($145). 4-doors, wagons ($195). California emissions system ($99). Estate equipment ($307). Deluxe load floor carpeting, wagons ($89). Gauge package ($64). Tinted glass ($120). Engine block heater ($20). Cornering lamps ($55). Auxiliary lighting base ($50). Classic ($32). Deluxe luggage compartment trim ($59). Left remote mirror ($23). Dual remote mirrors: w/o Landau roof ($91); w/Landau roof ($30). Left remote & right manual mirrors, base ($61). Illuminated passenger visor mirror ($50). Bodyside moldings ($60). Quiet Sound Group, base ($66). Sound Systems. AM/FM stereo ET, Classic & Brougham ($129). Base ($168). AM/FM stereo ET cassette, Classic & Brougham ($290). Base ($329). W/equalizer, Classic & Brougham ($435). Classic wagon ($400). Base sedan ($474). Base wagon ($439). AM radio delete base ($56 credit). Classic & Brougham ($95 credit). Power antenna ($70). Extended range speakers ($35). Deluxe rear compartment decor, wagons ($129). Power seats ($240 each). Passenger seat recliner

($45). Cruise control ($175). Tilt steering wheel ($125). Power tailgate lock ($60). Puncture sealant tires, exc. wagon ($125). Wagon ($150). Remote trunk release ($50). Locking wire wheel covers ($199). Power windows, 2-doors ($210). 4-doors, wagons ($285). Intermittent wipers ($55). Custom two-tone paint ($141). Landau roof & sport mirrors (std. on LS) ($321). Full vinyl roof (std. on Brougham) ($200). Cloth bench seat, base wagon ($28). Vinyl bench seat, base sedan ($28). Vinyl 50/50 seat, base sedan ($225). Base wagon ($195). Cloth 50/50 seat, base sedan ($195). Base wagon ($225). Classic ($195).

1987 Chevrolet, Chevette S two-door hatchback coupe

HISTORY: Introduced: October 9, 1986. Model year production: 1,553,252 (incl. 30,632 Corvettes, 63,570 imported Sprints and 91,708 imported Spectrums). Calendar year production (U.S.): 1,516,449 (including 28,514 Corvettes). Model year sales by U.S. dealers: 1,391,281 (incl. 25,266 Corvettes but not including imports).

1988

After introduction as early '88 models, the Corsica sedan and Beretta coupe entered their first full model year. The subcompact Chevette was gone, while the Monte Carlo coupe, favored by stock car racers, had just one more season before it, too, would disappear. Cavalier enjoyed a restyle that gave it a rounded, aerodynamic look, not unlike the Corsica/Beretta duo. Also departed: Camaro's Z28, but the IROC-Z took over its spot in the performance lineup.

1988 Chevrolet, Nova Twin-Cam four-door sedan

NOVA — SERIES 1S — FOUR — Customers for the joint-venture Toyota/Chevrolet subcompact had a second power-plant choice this year: a 16-valve, dual-overhead-cam version of the 97 cu. in. (1.6-liter) four, producing 110 horsepower. This was Chevrolet's first multi-valve engine. The Twin-Cam Nova sedan came in just one color choice: basic black metallic, with gray interior. Standard Twin-Cam equipment included disc brakes all around and P175/70HR13 Goodyear Eagle GT tires on aluminum wheels. Base Nova engine remained the 74-horsepower four, with five-speed gearbox. Twin-Cam buyers could get a four-speed automatic instead of the five-speed manual, but the base four-door sedan and hatchback offered only a three-speed automatic option. All three models now had an AM/FM stereo radio and rear defogger.

1988 Chevrolet, Cavalier Z24 two-door coupe

1988 Chevrolet, Cavalier Z24 two-door convertible

CAVALIER — SERIES 1J — FOUR/V-6 — Cavalier's formerly lengthy model list shrunk this year to base, RS and Z24 levels. Fresh sheet metal gave the subcompact a more aerodynamic appearance, with a new grille and composite headlamps in a rounded front end. Back-end changes included a new decklid, taillamps and bumper. Coupes even got a new roof profile. A 2.8-liter V-6 engine was standard

in the sporty Z24, which came in coupe and convertible form, but optional only in the station wagon this year. Other models came only with the 2.0-liter four. The former RS convertible was dropped, as was the hatchback coupe. Analog instruments (including a tachometer) were standard on the Z24, with electronic instruments optional. All models came with a standard five-speed manual gearbox or optional three-speed automatic.

1988 Chevrolet, Camaro two-door coupe

CAMARO — SERIES 1F — V-6/V-8 — Most noticeable of the Camaro changes this year may have been the absence of a Z28. Only the base sport coupe and IROC-Z were offered, with the latter gaining status as a specific model rather than an option package. With the demise of the Z28, the base coupe added standard equipment including a rear spoiler, aluminum wheels, lower bodyside panels, and body-color mirrors. Base powerplant remained the 2.8-liter V-6, rated 125 horsepower. The optional 5.0-liter V-8 (standard on the IROC-Z) switched from a four-barrel carburetor to throttle-body fuel injection, gaining five horsepower in the process. Two multi-point fuel-injected V-8 options were offered on the IROC-Z: a high-output 5.0-liter rated at 220 horsepower with five-speed manual shift (but 195 horsepower with automatic), or the 350-cu. in. (5.7-liter) edition that came only with four-speed automatic. Barely a thousand Camaro convertibles had been produced during the 1987 model year, but for this full season their numbers rose to 5,620.

1988 Chevrolet, Corsica four-door sedan

CORSICA/BERETTA — SERIES 1L — FOUR/V-6 — For their first complete year of production, the compact

Corsica sedan and Beretta coupe found a sizable share of customers, though little changed from their debut in early 1987. Base remained the 2.0-liter four hooked to five-speed manual gearbox. With a 2.8-liter V-6 and three-speed automatic optional. Models with the V-6 and manual gearbox added on upshift indicator light. A digital clock was included with the standard AM/FM stereo radio. Corsica sedan with the V-6 gained some suspension revisions, including bigger stabilizer bars.

1988 Chevrolet, Celebrity Eurosport VR two-door coupe

CELEBRITY — SERIES 1A — FOUR/V-6 — Appearance changed little this year, but Chevrolet's mid-size coupe, sedan and wagon gained a tougher 2.5-liter. Tech IV base engine with balance shafts. Low-friction pistons went into the 2.8-liter V-6, optional in each model. Standard transmission was a three-speed automatic, but V-6 Celebritys could get either a four-speed automatic, or, with the Eurosport option package, a Getrag five-speed manual gearbox. That Eurosport edition included special body trim as well as an F41 sport suspension and bigger (P195/75R14) tires, with the option of even larger P195/70R14 Goodyear Eagle GT+4 rubber. Standard equipment included outside mirrors on both sides.

MONTE CARLO — SERIES 1G — V-6/V-8 — For its final season in the lineup, the rear-drive mid-size coupe came in LS and SS form, the latter with a standard 305 cu. in. (5.0-liter) V-8 under its hood, rated 180 horsepower. Base powerplant for the LS remained a 262 cu. in. (4.3-liter) V-6, with a less powerful V-8 option available. Both came with a standard four-speed overdrive automatic transmission, replacing the former three-speed. New standard equipment also included tinted glass, twin mirrors, and AM/FM stereo with built-in clock. The fast-back SS Aerocoupe faded away this year.

CAPRICE — SERIES 1B — V-6/V-8 — No more full-size coupes were offered, but the four-door sedan and station wagon carried on (the latter only in Classic form). Caprice Classic sedans could have base, Brougham or Brougham LS trim. Standard equipment now included tinted glass, a remote-control driver's mirror (manual on the passenger side), automatic headlamp on/off, and an AM/FM stereo radio with built-in clock. Base engine for sedans remained the 262 cu. in. (4.3-liter) V-6, with 305 cu. in. (5.0-liter) V-8 optional. Under the Classic wagon hood was a 307 cu. in. (5.0-liter) V-8. Four-speed overdrive automatic was standard on all models.

I.D. DATA: Chevrolets again had a 17-symbol Vehicle Identification Number (VIN) on the upper left surface of the instrument panel, visible through the windshield. Symbol one indicates country: '1' - U.S.A.; '2' - Canada. Next is a manufacturer code: 'G' - General Motors. Symbol three is car make: '1' - Chevrolet; '7' - GM of Canada. Symbol four denotes restraint system: 'A' - non-passive (standard); 'B' - passive (automatic belts); 'C' - passive (inflatable). Symbol five is car line/series. Symbols six-seven reveal body type. Next is the engine code, followed by a check digit, the 'J' for model year 1988. Symbol eleven indicates assembly plant. The final six digits are the sequential serial number. Engine number coding is similar to 1981-87.

NOVA (FOUR)

Model No.	Body/Style No.	Body Type & Seating	Factory Price	Shipping Weight	Prod. Total
1S	K19	4-dr. Sedan-4P	8795	2211	87,263
1S	K68	4-dr. Hatch Sed-4P	9050	2257	18,570
1S	L19	4-dr. Twin-Cam Sed-4P	11395	N/A	3,300

CAVALIER (FOUR)

1J	C37	2-dr. Coupe-5P	8120	2359	34,470
1J	C37/WV9	2-dr. VL Cpe-5P	6995	N/A	43,611
1J	C69	4-dr. Sedan-5P	8195	2363	107,438
1J	C35	4-dr. Sta Wag-5P	8490	2413	29,806

Cavalier Engine Note: A V-6 engine cost $660 additional.

CAVALIER RS (FOUR)

| 1J | E37 | 2-dr. Coupe-5P | 9175 | 2371 | 24,359 |
| 1J | E69 | 4-dr. Sedan-5P | 9385 | 2414 | 18,852 |

CAVALIER Z24 (V-6)

| 1J | F37 | 2-dr. Coupe-5P | 10725 | 2558 | 55,658 |
| 1J | F67 | 2-dr. Conv Cpe-4P | 15990 | 2665 | 8,745 |

CAMARO (V-6/V-8)

| 1F | P87 | 2-dr. Spt Cpe-4P | 10995/11395 | 3054/3228 | 66,605 |
| 1F | P87/Z08 | 2-dr. Conv Cpe-4P | ----/16255 | ----/3350 | 1,859 |

CAMARO IROC-Z (V-8)

| 1F | P87/Z28 | 2-dr. Spt Cpe-4P | 13490 | 3229 | 24,050 |
| 1F | P87/Z08 | 2-dr. Conv Cpe-4P | 18015 | 3352 | 3,761 |

CORSICA (FOUR/V-6)

| 1L | T69 | 4-dr. Sedan-5P | 9555/10215 | 2589/2688 | 291,163 |

BERETTA (FOUR/V-6)

| 1L | V37 | 2-dr. Coupe-5P | 10135/10795 | 2608/2707 | 275,098 |

CELEBRITY (FOUR/V-6)

1A	W27	2-dr. Coupe-5P	10585/11195	2727/2793	11,909
1A	W19	4-dr. Sedan-5P	11025/11635	2765/2833	195,205
1A	W35/B5E	4-dr. Sta Wag-6P	11350/11960	2903/2970	23,759
1A	W35/AQ4	4-dr. 3S Wag-8P	11590/12200	N/A	27,583

MONTE CARLO (V-6/V-8)

| 1G | Z37 | 2-dr. LS Cpe-6P | 12330/12770 | 3212/3267 | 13,970 |

MONTE CARLO 'SS' (V-8)

| 1G | Z37/Z65 | 2-dr. Spt Cpe-6P | 14320 | 3239 | 16,204 |

CAPRICE (V-6/V-8)

| 1B | L69 | 4-dr. Sedan-6P | 12030/12470 | 3540/3633 | 60,900 |

CAPRICE CLASSIC (V-6/V-8)

1B	N69	4-dr. Sedan-6P	12575/13015	3556/3649	42,292
1B	U69	4-dr. Brghm-6P	13645/14085	3607/3700	33,685
1B	U69/B6N	4-dr. LS Brghm-6P	14820/15260	N/A	21,586
1B	N35	4-dr. 3S Wag-8P	----/14340	----/4158	30,645

FACTORY PRICE AND WEIGHT NOTE: For Corsica, Beretta and Celebrity, prices and weights to left of slash are for four-cylinder, to right for V-6 engine. For Camaro, Monte Carlo and Caprice, figures to left of slash are for six-cylinder model, to right of slash for least expensive V-8.

BODY/STYLE NO. NOTE: Some models were actually packages. Code after the slash (e.g., Z28) is the number of the option package that comes with the model listed.

ENGINE DATA: BASE FOUR (Nova): Inline. Overhead cam. Four-cylinder. Cast iron block and head. Displacement: 97 cu. in. (1.6 liters). Bore & stroke: 3.19 x 3.03 in. Compression ratio: 9.0:1 Brake horsepower: 74 at 5200 RPM. Torque: 86 lb.-ft. at 2800 RPM. Solid valve lifters. Carburetor: Aisan 2Bbl. BASE FOUR (Twin-Cam Nova): Same as 97 cu. in. four above, but with dual overhead camshafts (16 valves). Compression ratio: 9.4:1. Brake horsepower: 110 at 6600 RPM. Torque: 98 lb.-ft. at 4800 RPM. BASE FOUR (Cavalier, Corsica/Beretta): Inline. Overhead valve. Four-cylinder. Cast iron block and aluminum head. Displacement: 121 cu. in. (2.0 liters). Bore & stroke: 3.50 x 3.15 in. Compression ratio: 9.0:1. Brake horsepower: 90 at 5600 RPM. Torque: 108 lb.-ft. at 3200 RPM. five main bearings. Hydraulic valve lifters. Throttle-body fuel injection. BASE FOUR (Celebrity): Inline. Overhead valve. Four-cylinder. Cast iron block and head. Displacement: 151 cu. in. (2.5 liters). Bore & stroke: 4.00 x 3.00 in. Compression ratio: 8.3:1. Brake horsepower: 98 at 4800 RPM. Torque: 135 lb.-ft. at 3200 RPM. Five main bearings. Hydraulic valve lifters. Throttle-body fuel injection. BASE V-6 (Camaro, Cavalier Z24); OPTIONAL (Cavalier wagon, Corsica/Beretta, Celebrity): 60-degree, overhead-valve V-6. Cast iron block and head. Displacement: 173 cu. in. (2.8 liters). Bore & stroke: 3.50 x 2.99 in. Compression ratio: 8.9:1. Brake horsepower: (Cavalier/Celeb) 125 at 4500; (Corsica/Beretta) 130 at 4700; (Camaro) 135 at 4900. Torque: (Cavalier/Celeb/Corsica/Beretta) 160 at 3600; (Camaro) 160 at 3900. Multi-port fuel injection. BASE V-6 (Monte Carlo, Caprice): 90-degree, overhead-valve V-6. Cast iron block and head. Displacement: 262 cu. in. (4.3 liters). Bore & stroke: 4.00 x 3.48 in. Compression ratio: 9.3:1. Brake horsepower: (Caprice) 140 at 4200 RPM; (Monte) 145 at 4200. Torque: 225 lb.-ft. at 2000 RPM. Four main bearings. Hydraulic valve lifters. Throttle-body fuel injection. OPTIONAL V-8 (Monte Carlo, Caprice sedan): 90-degree, overhead valve V-8. Cast iron block and head. Displacement: 305 cu. in. (5.0 liters). Bore & stroke: 3.74 x 3.48 in. Compression ratio: 9.3:1. Brake horsepower: (Monte) 150 at 4000 RPM; (Caprice) 170 at 4400. Torque: (Monte) 240 lb.-ft. at 2000 RPM; (Caprice) 250 at 2800. Five main bearings. Hydraulic valve lifters. Carburetor: 4Bbl. BASE V-8 (Camaro IROC-Z): OPTIONAL (Camaro): Same as 305 cu. in. V-8 above but with throttle-body fuel injection. Compression ratio: 9.3:1. Brake horsepower: 170 at 4000 RPM. Torque: 255 lb.-ft. 2400 RPM. OPTIONAL V-8 (Camaro IROC-Z): Same as 305 cu. in. V-8 above, with port fuel injection. Compression ratio: 9.3:1. Brake horsepower: 220 at 4400 RPM (195

hp with automatic). Torque: 290 lb.-ft. at 3200 RPM. HIGH-OUTPUT V-8 (Monte Carlo SS): Same as 305 cu. in. V-8 above, except - BHP: 180 at 4800 RPM. Torque: 225 lb.-ft. at 3200 RPM. BASE V-8 (Caprice wagon): 90-degree over-head valve V-8. Cast iron block and head. Displacement: 307 cu. in. (5.0 liters). Bore & stroke: 3.80 x 3.38 in. Compression ratio: 8.0:1. Brake horsepower: 140 at 3200 RPM. Torque: 225 lb.-ft. at 2000 RPM. Five main bearings. Hydraulic roller valve lifters. Carburetor: 4Bbl. OPTIONAL V-8 (Camaro IROC-Z): 90-degree, overhead valve V-8. Cast iron block and head. Displacement: 350 cu. in. (5.7 liters). Bore & stroke: 4.00 x 3.48 in. Compression ratio: 9.3:1. Brake horsepower: 230 at 4400 RPM. Torque: 330 lb.-ft. at 3200 RPM.

CHASSIS DATA: Wheelbase: (Nova) 95.7 in.; (Cavalier) 101.2 in.; (Camaro) 101.0 in.; (Corsica/Beretta) 103.4 in.; (Celebrity) 104.9 in.; (Monte Carlo) 108.0 in.; (Caprice) 116.0 in. Overall length: (Nova) 166.3 in.; (Cav cpe/sed) 174.5 in.; (Cav conv) 178.7 in.; (Cav wag) 177.9 in.; (Camaro) 192.0 in.; (Corsica) 183.4 in.; (Beretta) 187.2 in.; (Celeb) 188.3 in.; (Celeb wag) 190.8 in.; (Monte) 200.4 in.; (Caprice sed) 212.2 in.; (Capr wag) 215.1 in. Height: (Nova sed) 53.0 in.; (Nova hatch) 52.8 in.; (Cav cpe) 50.2 in.; (Cav conv) 52.7 in.; (Cav sed) 52.1 in.; (Cav wag) 52.8 in.; (Camaro) 50.0 in. (Corsica) 52.7 in.; (Beretta) 55.3 in.; (Celeb) 54.1 in.; (Celeb wag) 54.3 in.; (Monte) 54.4 in.; (Caprice) 56.4 in.; (Caprice wag) 58.2 in. Width: (Nova) 64.4 in.; (Cav cpe/conv) 66.0 in.; (Cav sed/wag) 66.3 in.; (Camaro) 72.8 in.; (Corsica/Beretta) 68.2 in.; (Celeb) 69.3 in.; (Monte) 71.8 in.; (Caprice) 75.4 in.; (Capr wag) 79.3 in. Front Tread: (Nova) 56.1 in.; (Cav) 55.4 in.; (Camaro) 60.7 in.; (Corsica/Beretta) 55.6 in.; (Celeb) 58.7 in.; (Monte) 58.5 in.; (Caprice) 61.7 in.; (Capr wag) 62.2 in. Rear Tread: (Nova) 55.3 in.; (Cav) 55.2 in.; (Camaro) 61.6 in.; (Corsica) 55.1 in.; (Beretta) 56.6 in.; (Celeb) 57.0 in.; (Monte) 57.8 in.; (Caprice) 60.7 in.; (Capr wag) 64.1 in. Standard Tires: (Nova) P155/80R13; (Nova Twin-Cam) P175/70HR13; (Cav) P185/80R13; (Cav Z24) P215/60R14; (Camaro) P215/65R15; (Corsica/Beretta) P185/80R13; (Celeb) P185/75R14; (Celeb Eurosport) P195/75R14; (Monte) P195/75R14; (Monte SS) P215/65R15; (Caprice) P205/75R15; (Caprice wag) P225/75R15.

TECHNICAL: Transmission: Five-speed manual shift standard on Nova, Cavalier, Corsica/Beretta and Camaro. Three-speed automatic standard on Celebrity. Four-speed overdrive automatic standard on Monte Carlo and Caprice. Steering: (Cavalier/Nova/Corsica/Beretta/Celebrity) rack and pinion; (others) recirculating ball. Front Suspension: (Monte/Caprice) unequal-length control arms, coil springs, stabilizer bar; (Nova) MacPherson struts w/coil springs and lower control arms; (Corsica/Beretta) MacPherson struts with coil springs; (Cavalier/Camaro/Celeb) MacPherson struts with coil springs, lower control arms and stabilizer bar. Rear Suspension: (Nova) fully independent MacPherson struts, dual links, coil springs and stabilizer bar; (Cavalier) semi-independent with beam axle, trailing arms, coil springs, stabilizer bar available; (Camaro) rigid axle and torque tube with longitudinal control arms. Panhard rod, coil springs and stabilizer bar; (Corsica/Beretta) trailing twist axle with coil springs; (Celeb) beam twist axle with integral stabilizer, trailing arms, Panhard rod and coil springs; (Monte/Caprice) rigid axle with four links, coil springs, stabilizer available. Brakes: front disc, rear drum; four-wheel discs standard on Twin-Cam Nova and available on Camaro. Body construction: unibody except (Monte/Caprice) separate body and frame. Fuel tank: (Nova) 13.2 gal.; (Cav) 13.6 gal.; (Camaro) 15.5 gal.; (Corsica/Beretta) 13.6 gal.; (Celeb) 15.7 gal.; (Monte V-6) 17.6 gal.; (Monte V-8) 18.1 gal.; (Caprice) 24.5 gal.; (Caprice wag) 22 gal.

1988 Chevrolet, Beretta GT two-door coupe

DRIVETRAIN OPTIONS: Engines: 173 cu. in. V-6: Cavalier wagon ($660); Corsica/Beretta ($660); Celeb ($610). 305 cu. in. V-8: Camaro ($400); Monte Carlo LS, Caprice sed ($440). 305 cu. in., TPI V-8: Camaro IROC-Z ($745). 350 cu. in. V-8: Camaro IROC-Z ($1045). Transmission/Differential: Five-speed manual trans.: Celeb ($440 credit). Three-speed automatic trans.: Cavalier ($415); Corsica/Beretta ($490). Four-speed overdrive auto. trans.: Camaro ($490); Celeb V-6 ($175). Limited-slip differential: Camaro/Monte/Caprice ($100). Performance axle ratio: Camaro/Monte/Caprice ($21). Power Accessories: Power four-wheel disc brakes: Camaro ($179). Power steering: base Cav ($225). Suspension: FE2 sport suspension: Cav base/RS ($27). F40 H.D. susp.: Corsica/Beretta/Celeb/Caprice ($26). F41 sport susp.: Corsica/Beretta, Monte LS, Caprice ($49). Inflatable rear shock absorbers: Celeb/Caprice ($64).

NOVA CONVENIENCE/APPEARANCE OPTIONS: Option Pkg. 2, Incl Auto Trans: P155/80R-13 All Sea-sons Blackwall tires; Elect Tuned AM/FM Stereo w/Seek & Scan & Digital Clock; Pwr Strg ($645). Opt. Pkg. 3 Incl 5-Spd Trans; P155/80R-13 All Seasons Blackwall Tires; Elect Tuned AM/FM Stereo w/Seek & Scan & Digital Clock; Pwr Steering; Air Cond ($900). Opt. Pkg. 4 Incl Auto Trans; P155/80R-13 All Seasons Blackwall Tires; Elect Tuned AM/FM Stereo w/Seek & Scan & Digital Cock; Pwr Steering; Air Cond; Pwr Door Locks ($1515). Nova CL Opt. Pkg. 5 (1SK19 only) Incl. 5-Spd Trans; P175/70R-13 All Seasons Blackwall Tires: Elect Tuned AM/FM Stereo w/Seek & Scan & Digital Clock; Pwr Strg; Air Cond; Custom CL Feature Pkg: Speed Control, w/resume feature; Intermittent Wipers; Pwr. Dr. Locks ($2119). Nova CL Opt. Pkg. 6 (1SK19 only), Incl Auto Trans; P175/70R-13 All Seasons Blackwall Tires; Elect Tuned AM/FM Stereo w/seek & Scan & Digital Clock; Pwr Strg; Air Cond; Custom CL Feature Pkg: Spd Control w/resume feature; Intermittent Wipers; Pwr Dr Locks ($2539). Twin Cam Opt. Pkg. 2, (ISL19 only) Incl Twin Cam Eng; Auto Trans; P175/70HR-13 High Perf Blackwall Tires; Elect Tuned AM/FM Stereo w/Seek & Scan & Digital Clock; Pwr Strg; Tachometer; Alum Wheels ($790). Twin Cam Opt. Pkg. 3, (1SL19 only) Incl Twin Cam Eng; 5-Spd Trans; P175/70HR-13 High Perf Blackwall Tires; Elect Tuned AM/FM Stereo w/Seek & Scan & Digital Clock; Pwr Strg; Tachometer; Alum Wheels; Air Cond ($675). Twin Cam Opt. Pkg. 4, (1SL19 only) Incl Twin Cam Eng; Auto Trans; P175/70HR-13 High Perf. Blackwall Tires; Elect Tuned AM/FM Stereo w/Seek & Scan & Digital Clock; Pwr Strg; Tachometer; Alum Wheels; Air Cond ($1465). Twin Cam Opt. Pkg. 5, (1SL19 only) Incl Twin Cam Eng; 5-Spd Trans; P175/70HR-13 High Perf. Blackwall tires; Elect. Tuned AM/FM Stereo w/Seek & Scan & Digital Clock; Pwr. Strg; Alum Wheels; Air Cond; Spd Control w/resume feature; Intermittent Wipers; Pwr. Dr. Locks; Pwr Windows & Tachometer ($1370). Twin Cam Opt Pkg. 6 (1SL19 only) Incl Twin Cam Eng; Auto Trans; P175/70HR-13 High perf. Blackwall Tires; Elect Tuned AM/FM Stereo w/Seek & Scan & Digital Clock; Pwr Strg; Tachometer, Alum Wheels; Air Cond; Spd Control w/resume; Intermittent Wipers; Pwr. Dr. Locks; Pwr. Windows ($2160). Color-Keyed Mats Carpeted. Front only ($25); Rear only ($15).

CAVALIER CONVENIENCE/APPEARANCE OPTIONS: VL Opt. Pkg. (1JC37/WV9 only): Incl Air Cond; Tinted Glass, Spt LH Remote & RH Man Mirrors, Black Body Side moldings, Pwr Strg ($1078). VL Opt. Pkg. 3 (1JC37/WV9 only): Air Cond; Tinted Glass, Spt LH Remote & RH Manual Mirrors, Blk Body Side Moldings; Pwr Strg; Carpeted Mats; Aux Lighting; Spd Control, w/resume speed; Comfortilt Strg Wheel; Intermittent Windshield Wiper System ($1488). Cavalier Opt. Pkg. 2: Air Cond; Tinted Glass; Spt. LH Remote & RH Manual Mirrors ($1078). Sta Wgn Opt. Pkg. 3: Air Cond; Tinted Glass; Spt LH Remote & RH Manual Mirrors; Black Body Side Moldings; Pwr Strg.; Carpeted Mats, F&R; Roof Carrier; Pwr. Liftgate Release; Comfortilt Wheel; Intermittent Windshield Wiper System ($1436). Sta Wag Opt. Pkg. 4: Air Cond; Tinted Glass; Spt LH Remote &

RH Manual Mirrors; Black Body Side Moldings; Pwr Strg; Carpeted Mats, F & R; Roof Carrier; Pwr Liftgate Release; Comfortilt Strg Wheel; Intermittent Windshield Wiper System; Pwr Door Lock System; Lighting; Spd Control w/resume ($1834). Opt. Pkg. 3 (1JC37-1JC69): Air Cond; Tinted Glass; Spt LH Remote & RH Manual Mirrors; Black Body Side Moldings; Pwr Strg; Carpeted Mats, F&R; Aux Lighting; Spd Control w/resume; Comfortilt Strg Wheel; Intermittent Windshield Wiper System ($1488). RS Opt. Pkg. 2 (1JE37-1JE69): Air Cond; Carpeted Mats, F&R; Tinted Glass; Speed Control w/resume; Comfortilt Wheel; Intermittent Windshield Wiper System ($1138). RS Opt. Pkg. 2 (1JE37-1JE69): Air Cond; Carpeted Mats, F&R; Tinted Glass; Elect Speed Control w/resume; Comfortilt Strg Wheel; Intermittent Windshield Wiper System; Pwr Door Lock System; Aux Lighting; AM/FM Stereo w/Seek & Scan, Stereo Cass. Tape & Digital Clock; Incl extd range sound system; Pwr Trunk Opener; Pwr Windows; RS Coupe ($1677). RS Sedan ($1802). Z24 Opt. Pkg. 2: Air Cond; Carpeted Mats, F&R; Tinted Glass; Speed Control w/resume; Comfortilt Strg Wheel; Intermittent Windshield Wiper System ($1138). Z24 Opt. Pkg. 3: Air Cond; Carpeted Mats, F&R; Tinted Glass; Speed Control w/resume speed; Comfortilt Strg Wheel; Intermittent Windshield Wiper System; Pwr Door Lock System; Aux Lighting; Elect Tuned AM/FM Stereo w/Seek & Scan, Stereo Cass. Tape & Digital Clock, Incl extd range sound system; Pwr Trunk Release; Pwr Windows ($1687). Convertible Opt. Pkg. 2: Air Cond; Carpeted Mats, F&R; Aux Lighting; AM/FM Stereo w/Seek & Scan, Stereo Cass. Tape & Digital Clock; Incl extd range sound system; Pwr Trunk Release; Spd Control w/resume; Comfortilt Strg. Wheel; Intermittent Windshield Wiper System ($1270). Cloth Bucket Seats ($28). Vinyl Bucket Seats (NC). Sport Cloth Bucket Seats Wgn only (incl Split Folding Rear Seat) ($325). Air Conditioning (Incl increased cooling) ($675). Arm Rest, Center Console ($58). H.D. Battery ($26). Frt License Plate Bracket (NC). Roof Carrier Bright ($115). Deck Lid Carrier: Bright ($115). Black ($115). Rear Window Defogger ($145). Pwr Door Lock System: Coupes ($145). Sedans & Wagons ($195). Calif. Emission System ($99). Carpeted Color-Keyed Mats, F&R ($33). Gauge Pkg. w/o Tachometer, (trip odometer, temp, voltmeter & oil pressure gauges) ($69). Gauge Pkg. w/Tachometer, (trip odometer, temp, voltmeter & oil pressure gauges) ($139). Tinted Glass, All windows ($105). Eng. Block Heater ($20). Electronic Instrument Cluster (Incl conventional tachometer): RS only ($295), Z24 only ($156). Body Side Moldings ($50). Door Edge Guards, Blk RS Coupe ($15). RS Sedan ($25). VL ($32). Elect Tuned AM/FM Stereo w/Seek & Scan & Digital Clock (Incl extd range sound system), Elect Tuned AM/FM Stereo w/Seek & Scan, Stereo Cass. Tape & Digital Clock (Incl extd. range sound system) VL ($454); others ($122). Elect Tuned AM Stereo & FM Stereo w/Seek & Scan, Stereo Cass. Tape w/Search & Repeat, Graphic Equalizer & Digital Clock (Incl Z24/RS) ($272) or ($150) extd. range sound system; Pwr. Base Steering ($225). Removable Sunroof ($350). Tires: P185/80R-13 All Seasons Steel Belted Radial White Stripe ($68). P205/70R-13 All Seasons Steel Belted Radial Blackwall ($124). P205/70R-13 All Seasons Steel Belted Radial White Lettered ($212). P215/60R-14 Steel Belted Radial White Outline Lettered ($102). Wheel Trim rings ($39). Alum Wheels 13x5.5-in. ($212). Pwr Windows: Coupes ($210). Sedans & Wagons ($285).

CAMARO CONVENIENCE/APPEARANCE OPTIONS: Spt Coupe Opt. Pkg. 2: Air Cond; Tinted Glass; Bodyside Color-Keyed Moldings ($920). Spt Coupe Opt. Pkg. 3: Air Cond; Tinted Glass; Bodyside Color-Keyed Moldings; Carpeted Mats, F&R; Pwr Hatch Release; Electronic Speed Control w/resume speed; Comfortilt Strg Wheel; Pwr Windows; Intermittent Windshield Wiper System ($1555). Spt Coupe Opt. Pkg. 4: Air Cond; Tinted Glass; Body Side Color-Keyed Moldings; Color-Keyed Carpeted Mats, F&R; Pwr Hatch Release; Spd Control w/resume speed; Comfortilt Strg Wheel; Pwr Windows; Intermittent Windshield Wiper System; Rear Compartment Cargo Cover; Dome & Reading Lamp; Pwr Dr Lock System; Halogen Headlamps, High & Low Beam; Aux Lighting; Elect Tuned AM/FM Stereo w/Seek & Scan, Stereo Radio w/Seek & Scan, Stereo Cass. Tape & Digital Clock (Incl extended range sound system) ($1939). IROC-Z Opt. Pkg. 2: IROC-Z Equip; Air Cond; Pwr Dr Lock System; Carpeted Mats, F&R; Tinted Glass; Pwr Hatch Release; Aux Lightning; Bodyside Color-Keyed Moldings; Elect Tuned AM/FM Stereo w/Seek & Scan, Stereo Cass. Tape & Digital Clock (Incl extd range sound system); Elect Spd Control w/resume speed; Comfortilt Steering Wheel; Pwr Windows; Intermittent Windshield Wiper System ($1846). IROC-Z Opt. Pkg. 3: IROC-Z Equip; Air Cond; Pwr Dr Lock System; Color-Keyed Carpeted Mats, F&R; Tinted Glass; Pwr Hatch Release; Aux Lighting; Bodyside Color-Keyed Moldings; Elect Spd Control w/resume speed; Comfortilt Strg Wheel; Pwr Windows; Intermittent Windshield Wiper System; Rear Comp. Cargo Cover; Dome & Reading Lamp; Halogen Headlamps, High & Low Beam; Spt. Elect Twin Remote Mirrors; Pwr Driver Seat; Elect Tuned AM/FM Stereo w/Seek & Scan, Stereo Cass. Tape, Graphic Equalizer & Digital Clock (Incl extd range sound system) ($2410); w/UU8 Radio, Add ($613). Convertible Opt. Pkg. 2: Air Cond; Tinted Glass; Bodyside Color-Keyed Moldings ($920). Convertible Opt. Pkg. 3: Air Cond; Tinted Glass; Bodyside Color-Keyed Moldings; Color-Keyed Carpeted Mats, F&R; Elect Spd Control, w/resume speed; Comfortilt Strg Wheel; Pwr Windows; Intermittent Windshield Wiper System ($1505). Convertible Opt Pkg. 4: Air Cond; Tinted Glass; Bodyside Color-Keyed Moldings; Carpeted Color-Keyed Mats, F&R; Elect Spd Control, w/resume speed; Comfortilt Strg Wheel; Pwr Windows; Intermittent Windshield Wiper System; Pwr Dr Locks; Halogen Headlamps (High & Low Beam); Elect. Tuned AM/FM Stereo w/Seek & Scan, Stereo Cass. Tape & Digital Clock (Incl extd range sound system) ($1747). IROC-Z Convertible Opt. Pkg. 2: IROC-Z Equip; Air Cond; Pwr Door Lock System; Carpeted Color-Keyed Mats, F&R; Tinted Glass; Bodyside Color-Keyed Molding; Elect Tuned AM/FM Stereo w/Seek &

Scan; Stereo Cass. Tape & Digital Clock (Incl extd range sound system); Elect Spd Control, w/resume speed; Comfortilt Strg Wheel; Pwr Windows; Intermittent Windshield Wiper System ($1747). IROC-Z Convertible Opt. Pkg. 3: IROC-Z Equip; Air Cond; Pwr Dr Lock System; Carpeted Color-Keyed Mats, F&R; Tinted Glass; Bodyside, Color-Keyed Moldings; Elect Spd Control, w/resume speed; Comfortilt Strg Wheel; Pwr Windows; Intermittent Windshield Wiper System; Halogen headlamps (High & Low Beam); Twin Remote Spt Mirrors; Pwr Driver's Seat; Elect Tuned AM Stereo/FM Stereo w/Seek & Scan, Stereo Cass. Tape, Graphic Equalizer & Digital Clock (Incl Extd Range Sound System) ($2218). Custom Cloth Bucket Seats ($277). Custom Leather Bucket Seats ($750). Air Cond (Incl increased cooling) ($775). Ltd. Slip Differential ($100). Performance Axle Ratio ($212). H.D. Battery ($26). Frt. License Plate Bracket (NC). Pwr F&R Disc Brakes ($179). Eng Oil Cooler ($110). Locking Rear Storage Cover ($80). Decal & Stripe delete ($60 credit). Rear Window Electric Defogger ($145). Pwr Door Lock System ($145). Calif. Emission System ($99). Tinted Glass, All Windows ($120). Eng. Block Heater ($20). Rear Window Louvers ($210). Deluxe Luggage Comp Trim, Spt Cpe (Incl Lckg Rear Comp Storage Cover) ($164). IROC-Z Sport Cpe ($84). Bodyside Color-Keyed Molding on IROC-Z Spt Cpe & Blk on Spt Cpe ($60). Blk Dr Edge Guards ($15). Elect Tuned AM Stereo/FM Stereo w/Seek & Scan, Stereo Cass. Tape w/Search & Repeat, Graphic Equalizer & Digital Clock ($150/$272). Elect Tuned AM/FM Stereo w/Seek & Scan, Stereo Cass. Tape & Digital Clock ($122). Elect Tuned Delco/Bose Music System, Incl AM/FM Stereo w/Seek & Scan, Stereo Cass. Tape & Digital Clock, special tone & balance control and four spkrs; Pwr Antenna ($70). Removable Roof Panels, Incl locks ($866). Split, Folding Rear Seatbacks ($50). Alum Wheels, 16-in, Incl Wheel Locks & P245/50 VR16 Blackwall Tires ($468). Pwr. Windows ($210).

CORSICA CONVENIENCE/APPEARANCE OPTIONS: UM6 Radio ($122). UX1 Radio ($272). Option Pkg. 2: Incl. A/C; Tinted Glass ($870). W/UM6 Radio ($122). W/UX1 Radio ($272). Opt. Pkg. 3: Incl A/C, Tinted Glass; Carpeted Mats, F&R; Dual Horns; Elect Spd Control, w/resume speed; Comfortilt Strg Wheel; Intermittent Wipers ($1270). W/UM6 Radio ($122). W/UX1 Radio ($272). Opt. Pkg. 4: Incl A/C; Tinted Glass; Carpeted Mats, F&R; Dual Horns; Elect Spd Control w/resume speed; Comfortilt Strg Wheel; Intermittent Wipers; Pwr Dr Lock System; Aux Lighting; Elect Tuned AM/FM Stereo w/Seek & Scan, Stereo Cass. Tape & Digital Clock (incl extd range sound system); Pwr Trunk Opener; Pwr Windows ($1986). W/UX1 Radio ($150). LT Opt. Pkg. 1 ($234). W/UM6 Radio ($122). W/UX1 Radio ($272). LT Opt. Pkg. 2: A/C; Tinted Glass ($1104). W/UM6 Radio ($122). W/UX1 Radio ($272). Lt Opt. Pkg 3: Incl AC; Tinted Glass; Carpeted Mats, F&R; Dual Horns; Spd Control w/resume speed; Comfortilt Strg Wheel; Intermittent Wipers ($1504). W/UM6 Radio ($122). W/UX1 Radio ($272). Lt Opt. Pkg. 4: Incl A/C; Tinted Glass; Carpeted Mats, F&R; Dual Horns;

Spd Control, w/resume speed; Comfortilt Strg Wheel; Intermittent Wipers; Pwr Dr Lock System; Aux Lighting; Elect Tuned AM/FM Stereo w/Seek & Scan, Stereo Cass. Tape & Digital Clock (Incl extd range sound system); Pwr Trunk Opener; Pwr Windows ($2220). Vinyl Bucket Seats ($28). Custom Cloth CL Bucket Seats ($275). Custom Two-Tone Paint ($123). Air Cond ($750). H.D. Battery ($26). Frt Lic Plate Brackets (NC). Console ($60). Rear Window Elect Defogger ($145). Pwr Dr Lock System ($195). Calif. Emission System ($99). Gauge Pkg. w/Tach, Incl Voltmeter, Oil Pressure, Temp. Gauges & Trip Odometer ($139). Tinted Glass, All Windows ($120). Eng Block Heater ($20). Body Side Striping ($57). TIRES: P195/70 R-14 All Seasons SBR Blackwall ($104), P195/70 R-14 All Seasons SBR White Stripe ($166). P185/80 R-13 All Seasons SBR White Stripe ($68). Spt Wheel Covers ($45). Styled Wheels ($56). Alum Wheels, Incl Locks ($215). W/Z1 LT Equipment Pkg ($159). Pwr Windows ($285). Intermittent Windshield Wiper System ($55).

1988 Chevrolet, Beretta GTU two-door coupe

BERETTA CONVENIENCE/APPEARANCE OPTIONS: UM6 Radio ($122). UX1 Radio ($272). Opt. Pkg. 2: Incl A/C; Carpeted Mats, F&R ($783). W/UM6 Radio ($122). W/UX1 Radio ($272). Opt. Pkg. 3: Incl A/C; Carpeted Mats, F&R; Aux Lighting; Elect Spd Control, w/resume speed; Comfortilt Strg. Wheel; Intermittent Wipers ($1170). W/UM6 Radio ($122). W/UX1 Radio ($272). Opt. Pkg. 4: Incl A/C; Carpeted Mats, F&R; Aux Lighting; Elect Spd Control, w/resume speed; Comfortilt Strg Wheel; Intermittent Wipers; Pwr Dr. Lock System; Elect Tuned AM/FM Stereo w/Seek & Scan, Stereo Cass. Tape & Digital Clock (incl extd range sound system); Pwr Trunk Opener; Pwr Windows ($1697). W/UX1 Radio ($150). GT Opt. Pkg. 1: Incl A/C ($1716). W/UM6 Radio ($122). W/UX1 Radio ($272). GT Opt. Pkg. 2: Incl A/C; Carpeted Mats, F&R; Electronic Spd Control, w/resume speed; Comfortilt Strg. Wheel; Intermittent Wipers ($2104). W/UM6 Radio ($122). W/UX1 Radio ($272). GT Opt. Pkg 3: Incl A/C; Carpeted Mats, F&R; Elect Spd Control, w/resume speed; Comfortilt Strg Wheel; Intermittent Wipers; Pwr Dr Lock System; Aux Lighting; Elect Tuned AM/FM Stereo w/Seek & Scan, Stereo Cass. Tape & Digital Clock; Pwr Trunk Opener ($2663). W/UX1 Radio ($150). Custom Two-Tone ($123). Air Cond ($750). H.D. Battery ($26). Frt Lic Plate Bracket (NC). Elect Rear Window Defogger ($145). Pwr Dr Lock System ($145). Calif. Emission System ($99). Eng Block Heater ($20). Elect Instrumentation; Bar Graph Speedometer & Digital Readout, Incl Tach ($156). Z51 Performance Hdlg. Pkg. Incl Spt Susp; 15-in. Styled Wheels; P205/60R-15 Tires & Ext Body Emblems ($153). Removable Sunroof ($350). TIRES: P195/70 R-14 All Seasons SBR Ply White Stripe ($72). Styled Wheels ($56). Alum Wheels, Incl Locks ($215). W/Z21 GT Equip Pkg ($159). Pwr Windows ($210). Intermittent Windshield Wiper System ($55).

CELEBRITY CONVENIENCE/APPEARANCE OPTIONS: Opt. Pkg. 2: Incl Air Cond; Color-Keyed Floor Mats, F&R; Ext Mldg. Pkg; Spd Control w/resume speed; Comfortilt Steering Wheel; Intermittent Windshield Wiper System ($1164). Opt. Pkg 3: Incl Air Cond; Color-Keyed Flr Mats, F&R; Ext Mldg Pkg; Spd Control, w/resume speed; Comfortilt Steering Wheel; Intermittent Windshield Wiper System; Bumper Guards; Pwr Dr Lock System; Gauge Pkg w/Trip Odometer; Aux Lighting; Remote Spt Mirrors; Dr Edge Guards; Power Trunk Opener; Pwr Windows; Coupe ($1725). Sedan ($1861). Eurosport Opt Pkg. 1 ($230). Eurosport Opt Pkg. 2: Air Cond; Color-Keyed Flr Mats, F&R; Gauge Pkg w/Trip Odometer; Molding Pkg; Elect Spd Control, w/resume speed; Comfortilt Strg Wheel; Intermittent Windshield Wiper System ($1458). Eurosport Opt. Pkg. 3: Air Cond; Color-Keyed Flr Mats, F&R; Gauge Pkg. w/Trip Odometer; Mldg. Pkg; Elect Spd Control, w/resume speed; Comfortilt Strg Wheel; Intermittent Windshield Wiper System; Pwr Dr Lock System; Aux Lighting; Spt Twin Remote Mirrors; Black Dr Edge Guard Moldings; AM/FM Radio w/Seek & Scan, Stereo Cass. Tape & Digital Clock (Incl Ext Range Sound System); Pwr Trunk Opener; Pwr Windows; Eurosport Coupe ($2020). Eurosport Sedan ($2157). Wagon Opt. Pkg. 2: Incl Air Cond; Color-Keyed Flr Mats, F&R; Pwr Liftgate Release; Ext Pkg Molding; Roof Carrier; Spd Control, w/resume speed; Comfortilt Strg Wheel; Intermittent Windshield Wiper System ($1304). Wagon Opt. Pkg. 3: Incl Air Cond; Color-Keyed Flr Mats, F&R; Pwr Liftgate Release, Ext Mldg. Pkg; Roof Carrier; Elect Spd Control, w/resume speed; Comfortilt Strg Wheel; Intermittent Windshield Wiper System; Bumper Guards; Pwr Door Lock System, Gauge Pkg w/trip odometer; Aux Lighting; Spt Twin Remote Mirrors; Black Moldings; Dr Edge Guard; AM/FM Radio Stereo w/Seek & Scan, Stereo Cass. Tape & Digital Clock (Incl ext. range sound system); Dlx Pwr Rear Compartment Decor; Cargo Area Security Pkg. Pwr Windows ($2159). Eurosport Wgn Opt. Pkg. 1 ($230). Eurosport Wgn Opt. Pkg. 2: Incl Air Cond; Roof Carrier; Flr Mats, F&R; Gauge Pkg w/Trip Odometer; Pwr Liftgate Release; Ext Mldg Pkg; Spd Control w/resume speed; Comfortilt Strg Wheel; Intermittent Windshield Wiper System ($1598). Eurosport Wgn Opt Pkg 3: Incl Air Cond; Roof Carrier; Flr Mats, F&R; Gauge Pkg w/Trip Odometer; Pwr Liftgate Release; Ext Mldg Pkg; Spd Control w/resume speed; Comfortilt Strg Wheel; Intermittent Windshield Wiper

System; Pwr Door Locks; Aux Lighting; Spt Twin Remote Mirrors; Black Dr Edge Guard; AM/FM Stereo Radio w/Seek & Scan, Stereo Cass. Tape & Digital Clock (Incl Ext Range Sound System); Dlx Pwr Rear Compartment Decor; Cargo Area Sec Pkg; Pwr Windows ($2333). Cloth Bench Seat Wagon ($28). Cloth Bucket Seats w/console ($257). Cloth 45/55 Seat ($133). Vinyl Bench Seat, Coupe & Sedan ($28). Custom Cloth CL 45/55 (Incl split, individual folding second seatback on wgn), Sedan ($385). Coupe ($305). Wagon ($435). Custom Cloth CL 45/55 w/console (Incl split, individual folding second seatback on wgn), Sedan ($335). Coupe ($255). Wagon ($385). Custom Two-Tone Paint; Incl lower body accent & ext. mldg. pkg; w/1SB or 1SC Pkg ($93). W/1SA Pkg ($148). Air Cond ($775). Rear Window Air Deflector ($40). H.D. Battery ($26). Frt. License Plate Bracket (NC). H.D. Cooling: w/o Air Cond ($70); w/Air Cond ($40). Electric Rear Window Defogger ($145). Pwr Door Lock System, Coupe ($145). Sedan & Wagon ($195). Calif. Emission System ($99). Eng. Block Heater ($20). Elect Tuned AM/FM Stereo Radio w/Seek & Scan, Stereo Cass. Tape & Digital Clock (incl extd range sound system) ($122). Pwr 6-way Frt Seat ($240). Body Striping ($57). Tachometer ($90). TIRES: P185/75R14 All Season Steel Belted Radial White Stripe ($68). P195/75 R14 All Seasons Steel Belted Radial Blackwall ($40). P195/75 R14 All Seasons Steel Belted Radial White Stripe ($102). P195/70 R14 All Seasons Steel Belted Radial Black Lettered ($90). Sport Wheel Covers ($65). Wire Wheel Covers, w/Locks ($199). Alum Wheels w/o ZV8 Eurosport Equip Pkg ($199). W/ZV8 Eurosport Equip Pkg ($143). Rally Wheels, Incl styled wheels, special hubcaps & trim rings ($56). Pwr Windows, coupe ($210). Sedan & Wagon ($285). Rear Window Wiper/Washer ($125).

MONTE CARLO CONVENIENCE/APPEARANCE OPTIONS: LS Opt. Pkg. 2: Air Cond; Color-Keyed Carpeted Mats, F&R; Aux Lighting; Deluxe Body Side Moldings; Spd Control, w/resume speed; Comfortilt Strg Wheel; Intermittent Windshield Wiper System ($1243). LS Opt. Pkg. 3: Air Cond; Color-Keyed Carpeted Mats, F&R; Aux Lighting; Deluxe Body Side Molding; Spd Control w/resume speed; Comfortilt Strg Wheel; Intermittent Windshield Wiper System; Power Dr Locks; Gauge Pkg w/Trip Odometer; Spt Twin Remote Mirrors; Dr Edge Guards; Side Window Sill; AM/FM Radio, w/Seek & Scan, Stereo Cass. Tape & Digital Clock (incl extd range sound system); Power Trunk Opener; Pwr Window ($1854). SS Opt. Pkg. 2: Air Cond; Color-Keyed Carpeted Mats, F&R; Pwr Dr Lock System; Halogen Headlamps (High & Low Beam); Aux Lighting; Spt Twin Remote Mirrors; AM/FM Radio Stereo, w/Seek & Scan, Stereo Cass. Tape & Digital Clock (Incl extd range sound system); Spd Control, w/resume speed; Comfortilt Strg Wheel; Pwr Trunk Opener; Pwr Windows; Intermittent Windshield Wiper System ($1790). Vinyl Bench Seat ($28). Cloth 45/55 Seat ($133). Cloth Bucket Seats ($257). Custom Cloth CL 45/55 Seat ($385). Custom Two-Tone Paint, incl upper body accent & color-keyed striping ($214). Padded Vinyl Landau Roof ($260). Air Conditioning ($775). Ltd Slip Differential ($100). Performance Axle Ratio ($21). H.D. Battery ($26). Frt License Plate Bracket (NC). H.D. Cooling: w/o Air Cond ($70); w/Air Cond ($40). Rear Window Electric Defogger ($145). Pwr Door Lock System ($145). Calif. Emission System ($99). Eng Block Heater ($20). Lighted right visor mirror ($50). Elect Tuned AM/FM Stereo Radio w/Seek & Scan, Stereo Cass. Tape & Digital Clock (Incl extd range sound system) ($122). Elect Tuned AM Stereo & FM Stereo w/Seek & Scan, Stereo Cass. Tape w/Search & Repeat, Graphic Equalizer & Digital Clock (Incl extd range sound system) ($150/$272). Pwr Antenna ($70). Removable Roof Panels, Incl locks, w/o 1SB or 1SC Opt Pkg ($895). W/1SB or 1SC Opt Pkg ($877). Pwr 6-Way Driver's Seat w/45/55 Seat ($240). Body Striping ($61). Tachometer, Spt Cpe ($90). TIRES: P195/75 R-14 All Season Steel Belted Radial White Stripe ($72). P205/70 R-14 All Seasons Steel Belted Radial White Stripe ($134). Wire Wheel Covers w/Locks ($199). Rally Wheels, Incl special hubcaps & trim rings ($56). Alum Wheels ($230).

CAPRICE CONVENIENCE/APPEARANCE OPTIONS: Caprice Sdn Opt. Pkg. 2: Incl Air Cond; Carpeted Colored-keyed Mats, F&R; Body Side Wheel Opening Moldings; Spd Control w/resume speed; Comfortilt Strg Wheel ($1185). Caprice Sdn Opt Pkg. 3: Incl Air Cond; Carpeted Color-Keyed Mats, F&R; Body Side Moldings; Wheel Opening Moldings; Spd Control w/resume speed; Comfortilt Strg Wheel; Dr. Lock System; Aux Lighting; Intermittent Windshield Wiper System ($1452). Caprice Classic Sdn Opt. Pkg 2: Incl Air Cond; Carpeted Color-Keyed Mats, F&R; Body Side Moldings, Spd Control w/resume speed; Comfortilt Strg Wheel; Intermittent Windshield Wiper System ($1210). Caprice Classic Sdn Opt. Pkg. 3: Incl Air Cond; Carpeted Color-Keyed Mats, F&R; Body Side Moldings; Spd Control, w/resume speed; Comfortilt Strg Wheel; Intermittent Windshield Wiper System; Bumpers Guards, F&R; Power Dr Lock System; Aux Lighting; Twin Remote Sport Mirrors; Pwr Trunk Opener; Pwr Windows ($1814). Caprice Classic Sdn Opt. Pkg. 4: Incl Air Cond; Carpeted Color-Keyed Mats, F&R; Body Side Moldings; Spd Control w/resume speed; Comfortilt Strg Wheel; Intermittent Windshield Wiper System; Bumper Guards, F&R; Pwr Dr Lock System; Aux Lighting; Twin Remote Sport Mirrors; Pwr Trunk Opener; Pwr Windows; Gauge Pkg w/trip odometer; Twilight Sentinel Headlamps; Cornering Lamps; Deluxe Luggage Compartment Trim; Lighted RH Visor Mirror; Dr. Edge Guard Moldings; Pwr Antenna; AM/FM Radio w/Seek & Scan w/Cass. Tape & Digital Clock, Incl dual rear spkrs ($2259). Caprice Classic Wgn Opt. Pkg. 2: Incl Roof Carrier; Color-Keyed Body Side Moldings; exc w/BX3 Estate which is woodgrain moldings; Spd Control; Comfortilt Strg Wheel; Pwr Tailgate Lock; Intermittent Windshield Wiper System ($590). Caprice Classic Wgn Opt Pkg. 3: Incl Roof Carrier; Color-Keyed Body Side Moldings; exc w/BX3 Estate which is woodgrain moldings; Spd Control, w/resume speed; Comfortilt Strg Wheel; Pwr Tailgate Lock; Dlx Load Flr Carpeting; Carpeted Color-Keyed Mats, F&R; Aux Lighting; Spt Twin Remote Mirrors; Pwr Windows ($1241). (1SD) Caprice Classic Wgn Opt. Pkg. 4: Incl Roof Carrier; Color-Keyed Body Side Moldings; exc w/BX3 Estate which is woodgrain moldings; Spd Control, w/resume speed; Comfortilt Strg Wheel; Pwr Tailgate Lock; Intermittent Windshield Wiper System; Pwr Dr Lock System; Dlx Load Floor Carpeting; Carpeted Mats, F&R; Aux Lighting; Spt Twin Remote Mirrors; Pwr Windows; F&R Bumper Guards; Gauge Pkg w/Trip Odometer; Twilight Sentinel Headlamps; Cornering Lamps; Dlx Rear Comp Decor; Pwr Antenna; AM/FM Stereo Radio w/Seek & Scan, Stereo Cass. Tape & Digital Clock, Incl dual rear spkrs ($1714). Caprice Classic Brhgm Opt Pkg. 2: Incl Air Cond; Bumper Guards, F&R; Pwr Door Lock System; Carpeted Mats, F&R; Spt Twin Remote Mirrors; Body Side Moldings; Pwr Six-Way Driver's Seat; Electronic Spd Control, w/resume speed; Comfortilt Strg Wheel; Pwr Trunk Opener; Pwr Windows; Intermittent Windshield Wiper System; AM/FM Stereo Radio w/Seek & Scan, Stereo Cass. Tape & Digital Clock, Incl rear spkrs ($2219). Caprice Classic Brghm Opt. Pkg 3: Incl Air Cond; Bumper Guards, F&R; Pwr Dr Lock System; Color-Keyed Carpeted Mats, F&R; Spt Twin Remote Mirrors; Body Side Moldings; Pwr Six-Way Driver's Seat; Elect Spd Control, w/resume speed; Comfortilt Strg Wheel; Elect Trunk Opener; Pwr Windows; Intermittent Windshield Wiper System; Gauge Pkg w/Trip Odometer; Twilight Sentinel Headlamps; Cornering Lamps; Deluxe Luggage Comp Trim; RH Visor Illum Mirror; Dr Edge Guard; Pwr Antennas; Elect Tuned AM/FM Stereo Radio w/Seek & Scan, Stereo Cass. Tape, Graphic Equalizer & Digital Clock, (Incl extd range sound system) ($2697). Vinyl Bench Seat, Caprice Sedan ($28). Caprice Classic Wagon, delete ($172 credit). Vinyl 50/50 Seat, Caprice Sedan ($260). Caprice Classic Wagon ($58). Cloth 50/50 Seat, Caprice Sedan ($230). Caprice Classic Wagon ($230). Leather 45/55 Seat ($550). Custom Two-Tone Paint, Incl body accent, color-keyed striping & o/s door handle inserts ($141). Roof, Full Vinyl ($200). Air Cond ($775). Rear Window Air Deflector ($65). Ltd Slip Differential ($100). Performance Axle Ratio ($21). H.D. Battery ($26). Frt. License Plate Bracket (NC). H.D. Cooling: w/o Air Cond ($70); w/Air Cond ($40). Rear Window Electric Defogger ($145). Pwr Dr Lock System ($195). Calif. Emission System ($99). Estate Equipment ($307). Eng. Block Heater ($20). Elect Tuned AM/FM Stereo Radio w/Seek & Scan, Stereo Cass. Tape & Digital Clock, Incl dual rear spkrs ($122). Elect Tuned AM/FM Stereo w/Seek & Scan, Stereo Cass. Tape, Graphic Equalizer & Digital Clock, Caprice Sdn, Classic Sdn & Brghm only (Incl extd range sound system) ($145/$267). Caprice Classic Wgns only, Incl dual rear spkrs; Ext Range Sound System ($35). Power 6-Way Seat; Driver's side w/5050 or 45/55 Seat ($240). Pass. side w/50/50 or 45/55 Seat ($240). Body Striping ($61). TIRES: P205/75R-15 All Seasons Steel Belted Radial White Stripe ($76). P225/70R-15 Steel Belted Radial White Stripe ($188). P225/75R-15 All Seasons Steel Belted Radial White Stripe (NC). Custom Wheel Covers, Std/Brghm ($65). Wire Wheel Covers, w/Locks ($134). All exc. Brghm ($199).

HISTORY: Introduced: Oct. 1, 1987. Model year production: 1,709,742 (incl. 22,789 Corvettes, 53,250 imported Sprints and 61,357 imported Spectrums). Model year sales by U.S. dealers: 1,340,840 (incl. 25,425 Corvettes but not including imports)

1989

Two familiar names left the Chevrolet lineup: Nova (the short-lived Toyota/Chevy joint venture) and Monte Carlo. Sales were strong for the Corsica and Beretta pair, at least when considered together rather than as separate models. In fact, the pair ranked first in sales for part of the calendar year. Chevrolet imports took on the Geo name this year: The former Chevrolet Sprint became Geo Metro, while the Spectrum simply added the Geo designation.

1989 Chevrolet, Cavalier Z24 two-door coupe

1989 Chevrolet, Cavalier Z24 two-door convertible

CAVALIER — SERIES 1J — FOUR/V-6 — Little was new in Chevrolet's subcompact, apart from a new self-aligning steering wheel with energy-absorbing hub. The RS coupe and sedan models were dropped, but re-placed by RS option packages (including sport suspension and 14-inch tires) for the three base Cavaliers. Other models included the Value Leader (VL) coupe and the Z24.coupe and convertible, which added gas-pressurized shock absorbers. A 130-horse-power V-6 continued as standard under Z24 hoods, but others carried the 2.0 liter four. The station wagon was available with either engine. All models had rear shoulder belts this year.

1989 Chevrolet, Camaro RS two-door coupe

CAMARO — SERIES 1F — V-6/V-8 — Two versions of the rear-drive Camaro were available again this year, but the cheaper of the pair was now called RS. Both the RS and IROC-Z came in hatchback coupe or convertible form, and both added a "pass-key" theft-deterrent system as standard equipment. That piece of equipment should have been welcome news to customers, since Camaros ranked as the most popular vehicle among car thieves. The RS coupe actually debuted first in California, with a standard 2.8-liter V-6 engine, as a model intended to keep insurance costs down. Both the IROC-Z duo and the RS convertible had a standard 170-horsepower V-8, and the IROC-Z also had a choice of 220-horsepower 5.0-liter V-8 or the big 5.7-liter V-8 with 10 more horses.

1989 Chevrolet, Corsica four-door hatchback sedan

CORSICA/BERETTA — SERIES 1L — FOUR/V-6 — A sporty new LTZ edition gave the compact Corsica sedan the appearance of a performance boost, if not the reality. As for the Beretta coupe, its former GT option package became a full-fledged model this year, wearing 15-inch tires on aluminum wheels. Corsica also added a four-door hatchback sedan to its regular notchback version, with a standard rollup cargo cover. Both the GT and LTZ carried the 173 cu. in. (2.8-liter) V-6 engine and sport suspension, while base models had either the standard 2.0-liter four or the V-6 as an option. The LTZ also included a decklid luggage rack. Tires in the base models grew to P185/70R14 size for the Corsica, P195/70R14 for Beretta. Later in the model year, a GTU Beretta arrived as the sportiest of the lot.

CELEBRITY — SERIES 1A — FOUR/V-6 — Only the four-door sedan and station wagon remained in the mid-size front-drive lineup, as the coupe departed. Both the base 151-cu. in. (2.5-liter) four and the optional 2.8-liter V-6 came with standard three-speed automatic, white V-6 Celebritys could have a four-speed overdrive automatic instead. Due to weak sales, the five-speed manual gearbox (formerly a credit option) was abandoned this year.

1989 Chevrolet, Caprice Classic four-door sedan

CAPRICE — SERIES 1B — V-8 — All Caprice models now came with a V-8 engine and standard air conditioning, as the base sedan V-6 disappeared. Instead of the former four-barrel carburetor, the 305-cu. in. (5.0-liter) V-8 now had throttle-body fuel injection. Horsepower remained the same as before, while torque got a slight boost. Caprice wagons still had their own carbureted V-8, displacing 307 cubic inches and delivering 140 horsepower (30 less than the sedan's). This version of the full-size Chevrolet had been around since 1977, and a restyle was anticipated soon.

I.D. DATA: Chevrolets again had a 17-symbol Vehicle Identification Number (VIN) on the upper left surface of the instrument panel, visible through the windshield. Symbol one indicates country: '1' - U.S.A.; '2' - Canada. Next is a manufacturer code: 'G' - General Motors. Symbol three is car make: '1' - Chevrolet; '7' - GM of Canada. Symbol four denotes restraint system: 'A' - non-passive (standard); 'B' - passive (automatic belts); 'C' - passive (inflatable). Symbol five is car line/series. Symbols six-seven reveal body type. Next is the engine code, followed by a check digit, then 'K' for model year 1989. Symbol eleven indicates assembly plant. The final six digits are the sequential serial number. Engine number coding is similar to 1981-88.

CAVALIER (FOUR)

Model No.	Body/Style No.	Body Type & Seating	Factory Price	Shipping Weight	Prod. Total
1J	C37	2-dr. Coupe-5P	8395	2418	Note 1
1J	C37/WV9	2-dr. VL Cpe-5P	7375	N/A	Note 1
1J	C69	4-dr. Sedan-5P	8595	2423	107,569
1J	C35	4-dr. Sta Wag-5P	8975	2478	28,549

Cavalier Engine Note: Station wagon could have a V-6 engine for $660 additional.

CAVALIER Z24 (V-6)

| 1J | F37 | 2-dr. Coupe-5P | 11325 | N/A | Note 1 |
| 1J | F67 | 2-dr. Conv Cpe-4P | 16615 | 2729 | 13,075 |

Note 1: Total Cavalier coupe production was 227,433 with no further breakout available.

CAMARO (V-6/V-8)

| 1F | P87 | 2-dr. RS Cpe-4P | 11495/11895 | 3082/3285 | Note 1 |
| 1F | P67 | 2-dr. RS Conv-4P | ----/16995 | ----/3116 | Note 2 |

CAMARO IROC-Z (V-8)

| 1F | P87/Z28 | 2-dr. Spt Cpe-4P | 14145 | 3264 | Note 1 |
| 1F | P67/Z28 | 2-dr. Conv Cpe-4P | 18945 | N/A | Note 2 |

Note 1: Total Camaro coupe production was 103,554 with no further breakout available.

Note 2: Total Camaro convertible production was 7,185 with no further breakout available.

CORSICA (FOUR/V-6)

1L	T69	4-dr. Sedan-5P	9985/10645	2595/2690	Note 1
1L	Z69	4-dr. LTZ Sed-5P	----/12825	N/A	Note 1
1L	T68	4-dr. Hatch-5P	10375/1103	52648/----	26,578

Note 1: Total Corsica sedan production was 204,589 with no further breakout available.

BERETTA (FOUR/V-6)

1L	V37	2-dr. Coupe-5P	10575/11235	2631/2727	Note 1
1L	W37	2-dr. GT Cpe-5P	----/12685	N/A	Note 1
1L	W37	2-dr. GTU Cpe-5P	N/A	N/A	Note 1

Note 1: Total Beretta coupe production was 180,242 with no further breakout available.

CELEBRITY (FOUR/V-6)

1A	W19	4-dr. Sedan-6P	11495/12280	2751/2819	162,482
1A	W35/B5E	4-dr. Sta Wag-6P	11925/12710	2888/2928	Note 1
1A	W35/AQ4	4-dr. 3S Wag-8P	12175/12960	N/A	Note 1

Note 1: Total Celebrity station wagon production was 39,179 with no further breakout available.

CAPRICE (V-8)

1B	L69	4-dr. Sedan-6P	13865	3693	Note 1
1B	N69	4-dr. Sedan-6P	14445	N/A	Note 1
1B	U69	4-dr. Brghm-6P	15615	N/A	Note 1
1B	U69/B6N	4-dr. LS Brghm-6P	16835	N/A	Note 1
1B	N35	4-dr. 3S Wag-8P	15025	4192	23,789

Note 1: Total Caprice sedan production was 173,255 with no further breakout available.

FACTORY PRICE AND WEIGHT NOTE: For Corsica, Beretta and Celebrity, prices and weights to left of slash are for four-cylinder, to right for V-6 engine. For Camaro RS, figures to left of slash are for six-cylinder model, to right of slash for V-8.

BODY/STYLE NO. NOTE: Some models were actually option packages. Code after the slash (e.g., B6N) is the number of the option package that comes with the model listed.

ENGINE DATA: BASE FOUR (Cavalier, Corsica/Beretta): Inline. Overhead valve. Four-cylinder. Cast iron block and aluminum head. Displacement: 121 cu. in. (2.0 liters). Bore & stroke: 3.50 x 3.15 in. Compression ratio: 9.0:1 Brake horsepower: 90 at 5600 RPM. Torque: 108 lb.-ft. at 3200 RPM. Five main bearings. Hydraulic valve lifters. Throttle-body fuel injection. **BASE FOUR** (Celebrity): Inline. Overhead valve. Four-cylinder. Cast iron block and head. Displacement: 151 cu. in. (2.5 liters). Bore & stroke: 4.00 x 3.00 in. Compression ratio: 8.3:1. Brake horsepower: 98 at 4800 RPM (later, 110 horsepower). Torque: 135 lb.-ft. at 3200 RPM. Five main bearings. Hydraulic valve lifters. Throttle-body fuel injection. **BASE V-6** (Camaro RS coupe, Cavalier Z24, Corsica LTZ, Beretta GT); **OPTIONAL** (Cavalier wagon, Corsica/Beretta, Celebrity): 60-degree, overhead-valve V-6. Cast iron block and head. Displacement: 173 cu. in. (2.8 liters). Bore & stroke: 3.50 x 2.99 in. Compression ratio: 8.9:1. Brake horsepower: (Celeb) 125 at 4500; (Cavalier) 130 at 4500; (Corsica/Beretta) 130 at 4700; (Camaro) 135 at 4900. Torque: (Cavalier/Celeb/Corsica/Beretta) 160 at 3600; (Camaro) 160 at 3900. Multi-port fuel injection. **BASE V-8** (Caprice sedan); 90-degree, overhead valve V-8. Cast iron block and head. Displacement: 305 cu. in. (5.0 liters). Bore & stroke: 3.74 x 3.48 in. Compression ratio: 9.3:1. Brake horsepower: 170 at 4000 RPM. Torque: 250 lb.-ft. at 2400 RPM. Five main bearings. Hydraulic valve lifters. Throttle-body fuel injection. **BASE V-8** (Camaro RS convertible, IROC-Z); **OPTIONAL** (Camaro RS coupe): Same as 305 cu. in. V-8 above but with throttle-body fuel injection. Compression ratio: 9.3:1. Brake horsepower: 170 at 4000 RPM. Torque: 255 lb.-ft. at 2400 RPM. **OPTIONAL** (Camaro IROC-Z): Same as 305 cu. in. V-8 above, with port fuel injection. Compression ratio: 9.3:1. Brake horsepower: 220 at 4400 RPM (195 with automatic). Torque: 290 lb.-ft. 3200 RPM (295 at 2800 with automatic). **BASE V-8** (Caprice wagon): 90-degree, overhead valve V-8. Cast iron block and head. Displacement: 307 cu. in. (5.0 liters). Bore & stroke: 3.80 x 3.38 in. Compression ratio: 8.0:1 Brake horsepower: 140 at 3200 RPM. Torque: 255 lb.-ft. at 2000 RPM. Five main bearings. Hydraulic roller valve lifters. Carburetor: 4Bbl. **OPTIONAL V-8** (Camaro IROC-Z): 90-degree, overhead valve V-8. Cast iron block and head. Displacement: 350 cu. in. (5.7 liters). Bore & stroke: 4.00 x 3.48 in. Compression ratio: 9.3:1. Brake horsepower: 230 at 4400 RPM. Torque: 330 lb.-ft. at 3200 RPM.

CHASSIS DATA: Wheelbase: (Cavalier) 101.2 in.; (Camaro) 101.1 in.; (Corsica/Beretta) 103.4 in.; (Celebrity) 104.9 in.; (Caprice) 116.0 in. Overall length: (Cav cpe/sed) 178.4 in.; (Cav conv) 178.7 in.; (Cav wag) 174.5 in.; (Camaro) 192.0 in.; (Corsica) 813.4 in.; (Beretta) 187.2 in.; (Celeb) 188.3 in.; (Celeb wag) 190.8 in.; (Caprice sed) 212.2 in.; (Capr wag) 215.7 in. Height: (Cavalier) 52.0-52.8 in.; (Camaro cpe) 50.0 in.; (Camaro conv) 50.3 in.; (Corsica) 56.2 in.; (Beretta) 55.3 in.; (Celeb) 54.1 in.; (Celeb wag) 54.3 in.; (Caprice) 56.4 in.; (Caprice wag) 58.2 in. Width: (Cav cpe/conv) 66.0 in.; (Cav sed/wag) 66.3 in.; (Camaro) 72.8 in.; (Corsica/Beretta) 68.2 in.; (Celeb) 69.3 in.; (Caprice) 75.4 in.; (Capr wag) 79.3 in. Front Tread: (Cav) 55.4 in.; (Camaro) 60.7 in.; (Corsica/Beretta) 55.6 in.; (Celeb) 58.7 in.; (Caprice) 61.7 in.; (Capr wag) 62.2 in. Rear Tread: (Cav) 55.2 in.; (Camaro) 61.6 in.; (Corsica) 55.1 in.; (Beretta) 56.6 in.; (Celeb) 57.0 in.; (Caprice) 60.7 in.; (Capr wag) 64.1 in. Standard Tires: (Cav) P185/80R13; (Cav Z24) P215/60R14; (Camaro) P215/65R15; (Corsica) P185/75R14; (Beretta) P195/75R14; (Corsica LTZ/Beretta GT) P205/60R15; (Celeb) P185/75R14; (Celeb Eurosport) P195/75R14; (Caprice) P205/75R15; (Caprice wag) P225/75R15.

TECHNICAL: Transmission: Five-speed manual shift standard on Cavalier, Corsica/Beretta and Camaro. Three-speed automatic standard on Celebrity. Four-speed overdrive automatic standard on Caprice. Steering: (Cavalier/Corsica/Beretta/Celebrity) rack and pinion; (others) recirculating ball. Front Suspension: (Cavalier/Camaro/Celebrity) MacPherson struts with coil springs, lower control arms and stabilizer bar; (Corsica/Beretta) MacPherson struts with coil springs; (Caprice) unequal-length control arms, coil springs, stabilizer bar. Rear Suspension: (Cavalier) semi-independent with beam axle, trailing arms, coil springs, stabilizer bar available; (Camaro) rigid axle and torque tube with longitudinal control arms, Panhard rod, coil springs and stabilizer bar; (Corsica/Beretta) trailing twist axle with control arms and coil springs; (Celeb) beam twist axle with integral stabilizer, trailing arms, Panhard rod and coil springs; (Caprice) rigid axle with four links, coil springs, stabilizer available. Brakes: front disc, rear drum; four-wheel discs available on Camaro. Body construction: unibody except (Caprice) separate body and frame. Fuel tank: (Cav) 13.6 gal.; (Camaro) 15.5 gal.; (Corsica/Beretta) 13.6 gal.; (Celeb) 15.7 gal.; (Caprice) 24.5 gal.; (Caprice wag) 22 gal.

DRIVETRAIN OPTIONS: Engines: 173 cu. in. V-6; Cavalier wagon ($660); Corsica/Beretta ($660); Celeb ($610). 305 cu. in. V-8: Camaro RS cpe ($400); Caprice sed ($440). 305 cu. in., TPI V-8: Camaro IROC-Z ($745). 350 cu. in. V-8; Camaro IROC-Z ($1045). Transmission/Differential: Five-speed manual trans.: Celeb ($440 credit). Three-speed automatic trans.: Cavalier ($415); Corsica/Beretta ($490). Four-speed overdrive auto. trans.: Camaro ($490); Celeb V-6 ($175). Limited-slip differential: Camaro/Caprice ($100). Performance axle ratio: Caprice ($21). Power Accessories: Power four-wheel disc brakes: Camaro ($179). Suspension: FE2 sport suspension: Cavalier ($27). F40 H.D. Susp.: Celeb/Caprice ($26). F41 sport susp.: Corsica/Beretta, Caprice ($49). Inflatable rear shock absorbers: Celeb/Caprice ($64)

CAVALIER CONVENIENCE/APPEARANCE OPTIONS: VL Preferred Equip. Grp. 1: Aux Lighting, Pwr

Strg; w/5 Spd Trans; H.D. Battery ($303); w/Auto Trans. ($277). VL Preferred Equip. Grp. 2: Incl Color-Keyed Carpeted Mats, F&R; Tinted Glass; Aux Lighting; Spt LH Remote & RH Manual Mirrors; Body Side Moldings; Pwr Strg; w/5 Spd Trans; H.D. Battery ($544). W/Auto Trans ($518). VL Preferred Equip. Grp. 3: Incl Air Cond; Color-Keyed Carpeted Mats, F&R; Tinted Glass; Aux Lighting; Spt LH Remote & RH Manual Mirrors; Body Side Moldings; Electronic Spd Control; w/resume speed; Pwr Strg; Comfortilt Wheel; Intermittent Windshield Wiper System; W/5 Spd Trans; H.D. Battery ($1604). W/Auto Trans ($1578). Cavalier Preferred Equip. Grp. 1 (1JC35, 1JC37, 1JC69): Incl Aux Lighting, Pwr Strg; w/2.0 Liter Eng & 5 Spd Trans or 2.8 Liter Eng., Coupe & Sedan ($303). Wagon ($309). W/Auto Trans. & 2.0 Liter Eng., Coupe & Sedan ($277). Wagon ($283). Cavalier Preferred Equip. Grp. 2 (1JC35, 1JC37, 1JC69): Color-Keyed Carpeted Mats, F&R; Tinted Glass; Aux Lighting; Spt. LH Remote & RH Manual Mirrors; Body Side Moldings; Pwr Strg; H.D. Battery; 2.0 Liter Eng & 5 Spd Trans or 2.8 Liter Eng.; Sedan ($544). Wagon ($550). W/Auto Trans & 2.0 Liter Eng., Coupe & Sedan ($518). Wagon ($524). Cavalier Preferred Equipment Grp. 3 (1JC37, 1JC69): Air Cond; Color-Keyed Carpeted Mats, F&R; Tinted Glass; Aux Lighting; Spt LH Remote & RH Manual Mirrors; Body Side Moldings; Spd Control, Electronic Spd w/resume speed; Pwr Strg; Comfortilt Wheel; Intermittent Windshield Wiper System; w/5 Spd Trans; H.D. Battery ($1604). W/Auto Trans & LL8 2.0 Liter Eng. ($1578). Station Wgn Preferred Equip. Grp. 3: Air Cond; Roof Carrier; Color-Keyed Carpeted Mats, F&R; Tinted Glass; Aux Lighting; Spt LH Remote & RH Manual Mirrors; Body Side Moldings; Spd Control, w/resume speed; Comfortilt Strg Wheel; Intermittent Windshield Wiper System, w/LL8 2.0 Liter Eng & 5 Spd Trans. or LB6 2.8 Liter Eng.; H.D. Battery ($1725). W/Auto Trans & LL8 2.0 Liter Eng. ($1699). Cavalier Preferred Equip. Grp 4 (1JC37, 1JC69): Air Cond; Pwr Dr Lock System; Color-Keyed Carpeted Mats, F&R; Tinted Glass; Aux Lighting; Spt LH Remote & RH Manual Mirrors; Body Side Moldings; Elect. Tuned AM/FM Stereo Radio w/Seek & Scan, Stereo Cass. Tape & Digital Clock; Extd range sound system; Spd Control, w/resume; Pwr Strg; Comfortilt Strg Wheel; Pwr Windows; H.D. Battery; Intermittent Windshield Wiper System; Coupe ($2101). Sedan ($2226). W/Auto Trans & 2.0 Liter Eng., Coupe ($2075). Sedan ($2200). RS Equipment Pkg, Coupe ($696). Sedan ($705). RS Preferred Equip. Grp. 1 (1JC35, 1JC37, 1JC69): Color-Keyed Carpeted Mats, F&R; Tinted Glass; Aux Lighting; H.D. Battery; 2.0 Liter Eng. & 5 Spd Trans. or 2.8 Liter Eng., Coupe ($911). Sedan ($921). Wagon ($927). W/Auto Trans & 2.0 Liter Eng., Coupe ($885). Sedan ($895). Wagon ($901). RS Preferred Equip. Grp. 2 (1JC35, 1JC37, 1JC69): Air Cond; Color-Keyed Carpeted Mats, F&R; Tinted Glass; Aux Lighting; Spd Control, w/resume speed; Comfortilt Strg Wheel; Intermittent Windshield Wiper System; H.D. Battery; w/2.0 Liter Eng & 5 Spd Trans or 2.8 Liter Eng ($1971). Coupe ($1981). Sedan ($1981). Wagon ($1989). W/Auto Trans & 2.0 Liter Eng., Coupe ($1945).

Sedan ($1955). Wagon ($1961). RS Preferred Equip. Grp. 3 (1JC37, 1JC69): Air Cond; Decklid Carrier (Cpe only); Pwr Dr Lock System; Color-Keyed Carpeted Mats, F&R; Tinted Glass; Aux Lighting; H.D. Battery; AM/FM Stereo w/Seek & Scan; Stereo Cass. Tape & Digital CL Clock; Extd range sound system; Elect Spd Control, w/resume speed; Comfortilt Strg Wheel; Pwr Windows; Intermittent Windshield Wiper System; w/5 Spd Trans. RS Coupe ($2633). RS Sedan ($2653). W/Auto Trans & 2.0 Liter Eng RS Coupe ($2607). RS Sedan ($2627). RS Wagon Preferred Equip. Grp. 3: Air Cond; Roof Carrier; Pwr Dr Lock System; Color-Keyed Carpeted Mats, F&R; Tinted Glass; Aux Lighting; AM/FM Stereo Radio, w/Seek & Scan, Stereo Cass. Tape & Digital Clock; Extd range sound system; Electronic Spd Control, w/resume speed; Comfortilt Strg Wheel; Intermittent Windshield Wiper System; 2.0 Liter Eng & 5 Spd Trans. or 2.8 Liter Eng ($2724). W/Auto Trans & 2.0 Liter Eng ($2698). Z24 Cpe Preferred Equip. Grp. 1: Air Cond; H.D. Battery; Tinted Glass; Aux Lighting. Z24 Cpe. Preferred Equip. Grp. 2: Air Cond; H.D. Battery; Color-Keyed Carpeted Mats, F&R; Tinted Glass; Aux Lightning; Elect Tuned AM/FM Stereo Radio, w/Seek & Scan, Stereo Cass. Tape & Digital Clock, Extd range sound system; Spd Control, w/resume speed; Comfortilt Strg Wheel; Intermittent Windshield Wiper System ($1390). Z24 Cpe Preferred Equip. Grp. 2: Air Cond; H.D. Battery; Pwr Dr Lock System; Color-Keyed Carpeted Mats, F&R; Tinted Glass; Aux Lighting; Elect Tuned AM Stereo/FM Stereo Radio, w/Seek & Scan, Stereo Cass. Tape w/Search and Repeat; Graphic Equalizer & Digital Clock; Extd range sound; Elect Spd Control, w/resume speed; Comfortilt Strg Wheel; Pwr Trunk Opener; Pwr Windows; Intermittent Windshield Wiper System ($1965). Z24 Convertible Preferred Equip. Grp. 1: Air Cond; H.D. Battery; Aux Lighting; AM/FM Stereo Radio, w/Seek & Scan Stereo Cass. Tape & Digital Clock; Extd range sound system ($858). Z24 Convertible preferred Equip. Grp. 2: Air Cond; H.D. Battery; Aux Lighting; Color-Keyed Carpeted Mats, F&R; Elect Tuned AM Stereo, FM Stereo Radio, w/Seek & Scan, Stereo Cass. Tape w/Search & Repeat; Graphic Equalizer & Digital Clock; Extd range sound system; Pwr Trunk Opener; Spd Control, w/resume speed; Comfortilt Strg Wheel; Intermittent Windshield Wiper System ($1456). Cloth Bucket Seats ($28). Sport Cloth bucket Seats, Incl arm rest & Split Fldg Rear Seat, Coupe ($459). Sedan ($483). Wagon ($383). Air Cond ($695). Frt License Plate Bracket (NC). Roof Carrier Bright or Black ($115). Deck Lid Carrier Black ($115). Electric Rear Window Defogger ($150). Pwr Door Lock System ($155). Sedans & Wagon ($205). Calif. Emission System ($100). Color-Keyed Carpeted Mats, F&R ($33). Tinted Glass, All Windows ($105). Eng Block Heater ($20). Electronic Instrument Cluster, Incl conventional tachometer ($156). Body Side Molding ($50). Radio: VL ($332); Elect tuned AM/FM Stereo Radio, w/Seek & Scan, Stereo Cass. Tape & Digital Clock, Extd range sound system; VL ($454); base/Z24 ($122); Elect Tuned AM Stereo & FM Stereo, w/Seek & Scan, Stereo Cass. Tape w/Search & Repeat, Graphic Equalizer & Digital Clock, Extd range sound system, Z24/RS ($150/$272). Removable Sunroof ($350). TIRES: P185/80R13 All Seasons SBR White Stripe ($68). P195/70R14 All Seasons SBR Blk Lettered, Incl in RS Equip ($129). P215/60R14 SBR White Outline Lettered ($102). Pwr Trunk Opener ($50). Wheel Trim Rings ($39). Styled Steel 14-in. Wheels (NC). Alum Wheels 13x5.5-in. ($265). Pwr Windows ($295).

CAMARO CONVENIENCE/APPEARANCE OPTIONS: RS Cpe Preferred Equip. Grp. 1: H.D. Battery; Tinted Glass; Aux Lighting; Body Side Moldings ($255). RS Cpe Preferred Equip. Grp. 2: Air Cond; Pwr Dr Locks; H.D. Battery; Color-Keyed Carpeted Mats, F&R; Tinted Glass; Aux Lighting; Body Side Moldings; Elect. Tuned AM/FM Stereo Radio, w/Seek & Scan, Stereo Cass. Tape & Digital Clock; Extd range sound system; Spd Control, w/resume speed; Comfortilt Strg Wheel; Intermittent Windshield Wiper System ($1727). RS Cpe Preferred Equip. Grp. 3: Air Cond; H.D. Battery; Cargo Cover; Pwr Dr Lock System; Carpeted Mats, F&R; Tinted Glass; Halogen Headlamps, High & Low Beam; Aux Lighting; Mirror w/Dual Reading Lamps; Body Side Moldings; Elect Tuned AM/FM Stereo Radio, w/Seek & Scan, Stereo Cass. Tape & Digital Clock; Extd range sound system; Electronic Spd Control, w/resume speed; Comfortilt Strg Wheel; Intermittent Windshield Wiper System; IROC-Z Preferred Equip. Grp. 1: Tinted Glass; H.D. Battery; Aux Lighting; Body Side Mldgs: w/o 5.7 Liter Eng. ($255); w/5.7 Liter Eng ($229). IROC-Z Preferred Equip. Gr. 2: Air Cond; Pwr Dr Lock System; Carpeted Mats, F&R; Tinted Glass; Pwr Hatch Release; Aux Lighting; Body Side Molding; Elect Tuned AM/FM Stereo Radio, w/Seek & Scan, Stereo Cass. Tape & Digital Clock, extd range sound system; Spd Control, w/resume speed; H.D. Battery; Comfortilt Strg Wheel; Intermittent Windshield Wiper System, w/o 5.7 Liter Eng ($1777). IROC-Z Preferred Equip. Grp 3: Air Cond; Pwr Dr Lock System; Cargo Cover; Color-Keyed Carpeted Mats, F&R; Tinted Glass; Halogen Headlamps, High & Low Beam; Pwr Hatch Release; Aux Lighting; Mirror, w/Dual Reading Lamps; Twin Remote Sport Mirrors; Body Side Moldings; Elect. Tuned AM Stereo/FM Stereo Radio, w/Seek & Scan Stereo Cass. Tape w/Search & Repeat; Graphic Equalizer & Digital Clock, extd range sound system; Pwr Driver's Seat; Electronic Spd Control, w/resume speed; H.D. Battery; Comfortilt Strg Wheel; Pwr Windows; Intermittent Windshield Wiper System: w/o 5.7 Liter Eng ($2605); w/B2L 5.7 Liter Eng ($2579). RS Convertible Preferred Equip. Grp. 1: H.D. Battery; Tinted Glass; Body Side Moldings ($206). RS Convertible Preferred Equip. Grp. 2: Air Cond; H.D. Battery; Pwr Dr Lock System; Color-Keyed Carpeted Mats, F&R; Tinted Glass; Body Side Moldings; Elect Tuned AM/FM Stereo Radio, w/Seek & Scan, Stereo Cass. Tape & Digital Clock; Extd range sound system; Electronic Spd Control, w/resume speed; Comfortilt Strg Wheel; Intermittent Windshield Wiper System ($1678). RS Convertible Preferred Equip. Grp 3: Air Cond; H.D. Battery; Pwr Dr Lock System; Color-Keyed Carpeted Mats, F&R; Tinted Glass; Halogen Headlamps, High & Low Beam; Body Side Moldings; Elect Tuned AM/FM

Stereo Radio, w/Seek & Scan, Stereo Cass. Tape & Digital Clock; Extd range sound system; Electronic Spd Control, w/resume speed; Comfortilt Strg Wheel; Pwr Windows; Intermittent Windshield Wiper System ($1923). IROC-Z Convertible Preferred Equip. Grp. 1: H.D. Battery; Tinted Glass; Body Side Moldings ($206). IROC-Z Convertible Preferred Equip. Grp. 2: Air Cond; H.D. Battery; Pwr Dr Lock System; Carpeted Mats, F&R; Tinted Glass; Body Side Moldings; Elect Tuned AM/FM Stereo Radio, w/Seek & Scan; Stereo Cass. Tape & Digital Clock; Extd range sound system; Spd Control, w/resume speed; Comfortilt Strg Wheel; Intermittent Windshield Wiper System ($1678). IROC-Z Convertible Preferred Equip. Grp. 3: Air Cond; H.D. Battery; Pwr Dr Lock System; Carpeted Mats, F&R; Tinted Glass; Halogen Headlamps, High & Low Beam; Twin Remote Sport Mirrors; Body Side Moldings; Elect Radio Tuned AM Stereo/FM Stereo Radio, w/Seek & Scan, Stereo Cass. Tape w/Search & Repeat, Graphic Equalizer & Digital Clock; Extd range sound system; Pwr Driver's Seat; Spd Control, w/resume speed; Comfortilt Strg Wheel; Pwr Windows; Intermittent Windshield Wiper System ($2414). Custom Cloth Bucket Seats ($277). Custom Leather Bucket Seats ($750). Air Cond ($795). Ltd Slip Differential ($100). Performance Axle Ratio; Incl Dual Exhaust ($177). Frt Lic Plate Bracket (NC). Pwr F&R Disc Brakes ($179). Eng Oil Cooler ($110). Lckng Rear Storage Cover ($80). Decal & Stripe Delete ($60 credit). Electric Rear Window Defogger ($150). Pwr Door Lock system ($155). Calif. Emission System ($100). Pwr Hatch Release ($50). Eng Block Heater ($20). Rear Window Louvers ($210). Deluxe Luggage Comp. Trim, RS Cpe only, Incl Lckng Rear Comp Storage Cover ($164). IROC-Z Cpe ($84). Spt Twin Remote Mirrors ($91). Dr. Edge Guards Blk ($15). Elect Tuned AM Stereo/FM Stereo Radio, w/Seek & Scan, Stereo Cass. Tape w/Search & Repeat, Graphic Equalizer & Digital Clock ($150/$272). Elect Tuned AM/FM Stereo, w/Seek & Scan, Stereo Cass. Tape & Digital Clock ($122). Elect Tuned Delco/Bose Music System, Incl AM/FM Stereo, w/Seek & Scan, Stereo Cass. Tape & Digital Clock, special tone & balance control & 4 Spkrs ($613/$885). Electronically tuned AM/FM Stereo Radio, w/Seek & Scan, Compact Disc Player & Digital Clock ($124/$396). Pwr Antenna ($70). Removable Roof Panels, Incl Locks ($866). Split Fldg Rear Seatback ($50). Cast Alum 16-in. Wheels, Incl Wheel Locks & P245/50 VF16 SBR Blackwall Tires ($520).

CORSICA CONVENIENCE/APPEARANCE OPTIONS: Preferred Equip. Grp. 1: H.D. Battery; Carpeted Mats, F&R; Tinted Glass; Aux Lighting, Sedan ($243). Hatchback ($235). Preferred Equip. Grp. 2: Air Cond; H.D. Battery; Tinted Glass; Carpeted Mats, F&R; Aux Lighting; Spd Control, w/resume speed; Comfortilt Strg Wheel; Intermittent Windshield Wiper System ($1378). Hatchback ($1370). Preferred Equip. Grp. 3: Air Cond; H.D. Battery; Power Dr Lock System; Carpeted Mats, F&R; Tinted Glass; Aux Lighting; Elect Tuned AM/FM Stereo Radio, w/Seek & Scan, Stereo Cass. Tape & Digital Clock, Extd range sound system; Spd Control, w/resume speed; Comfortilt Strg Wheel; Trunk/Hatch Opener; Pwr Windows; Intermittent Windshield Wiper System;

Sedan ($2050). Hatchback ($2042). LT Preferred Equip. Grp. 1: H.D. Battery; Carpeted Mats, F&R; Tinted Glass; Aux Lighting; Sedan ($487), Hatchback ($479). LT Preferred Equip. Grp. 2: Air Cond; H.D. Battery; Carpeted Mats, F&R; Gauge Pkg w/Tachometer; Tinted Glass; Aux Lighting; Spd Control, w/resume speed; Comfortilt Strg Wheel; Intermittent Windshield Wiper System; Sedan ($1761). Hatchback ($1753). LT Preferred Equip. Grp. 3: Air Cond; H.D. Battery; Pwr Dr Lock System; Carpeted Mats, F&R; Gauge Pkg w/Tachometer; Tinted Glass; Aux Lighting; Elect Tuned AM/FM Stereo Radio, w/Seek & Scan, Stereo Cass. Tape & Digital Clock; Extd range sound system; Electronic Spd Control, w/resume speed; Comfortilt Strg Wheel; Pwr Trunk/hatch Opener; Pwr Windows; Intermittent Windshield Wiper System; Sedan ($2433). Hatchback ($2425). LTZ Preferred Equip. Grp. 1: H.D. Battery; Carpeted Mats, F&R; Tinted Glass; Electronic Spd Control, w/resume speed; Comfortilt Strg Wheel; Intermittent Windshield Wiper System ($544). LTZ Preferred Equip. Grp. 2: H.D. Battery; Pwr Dr Lock System; Carpeted Mats, F&R; Tinted Glass; Elect Tune AM/FM Stereo Radio, w/Seek & Scan, Stereo Cass. Tape & Digital Clock, Extd range sound system; Electronic Spd Control, w/resume speed; Comfortilt Strg Wheel; Pwr Trunk Opener; Pwr Windows; Intermittent Windshield Wiper System ($1216). Custom Cloth CL Bucket Seats, Sedan ($425). Hatchback ($275). LTZ (NC). Custom Two-Tone Paint ($123). Air Cond, Incl w/LTZ ($770). H.D. Battery ($26). Frt License Plate Bracket (NC). Deck Lid Carrier Blk, Incl w/LTZ ($115). Flr Mounted Console ($60). Rear Window Electric Defogger ($150). Pwr Door Lock System ($205). Calif. Emission System ($100). Gauge Pkg w/Tachometer, voltmeter, oil pressure, temp. gauges & trip odometer, Incl w/LTZ ($139). Eng. Block Heater ($20). Aux Lighting: courtesy, instrument panel eng & dual reading lamp, Incl w/LTZ Sedan ($64). Hatchback only ($56). Elect Tuned AM/FM Stereo Radio w/Seek & Scan, Stereo Cass. Tape & Digital Clock, Incl extd sound system ($122). Elect Tuned AM Stereo/FM Stereo w/Seek & Scan, Stereo Cass. Tape w/Search & Repeat, Graphic Equalizer & Digital Clock, Incl extd range sound system ($150/$272). Body Side Striping ($57). TIRES: P195/70 R14 All Seasons SBR Blk Lettered, incl w/LT ($93). P185/75 R14 All Season SBR White Stripe ($68). Styled Wheels, Incl w/LT Equip Pkg ($265). w/o LT Equip Pkg ($210). Intermittent Windshield Wiper System ($55).

BERETTA CONVENIENCE/APPEARANCE OPTIONS: Preferred Equip. Grp. 1: H.D. Battery; Carpeted Mats, F&R; Aux Lighting ($91). Preferred Equip. Grp. 2: Air Cond; H.D. Battery; Carpeted Mats, F&R; Aux Lighting; Spd Control, w/resume speed; Elect Comfortilt Strg. Wheel, Intermittent Wipers ($1226). Preferred Equip. Grp. 3: Air Cond; H.D. Battery; Pwr Dr Lock System; Carpeted Mats, F&R; Aux Lighting; Elect Tuned AM/FM Stereo w/Seek & Scan, Stereo Cass. Tape & Digital Clock; Incl extd range sound system; Spd Control, w/resume speed; Comfortilt Strg Wheel; Pwr Trunk Opener; Pwr Windows; Intermittent Windshield Wiper System ($1773). GT Preferred Equip. Grp. 1: H.D. Battery; Color-Keyed Carpeted Mats, F&R; Aux Lighting; Electronic Spd Control, w/resume speed; Comfortilt Strg Wheel; Intermittent Wipers ($458). GT Preferred Equip. Grp. 2: H.D. Battery; Pwr Dr Lock System; Carpeted Mats, F&R; Aux Lighting; Elect Tuned AM/FM Stereo Radio w/Seek & Scan, Stereo Cass. Tape & Digital Clock; Extd range sound system; Electronic Spd Control, w/resume speed; Comfortilt Strg Wheel; Pwr Trunk Opener; Intermittent Wipers ($1003). Custom Two-Tone Paint ($123). Air Cond Incl w/GT ($770). H.D. Battery ($26). Frt Lic Plate Bracket (NC). Deck Lid Carrier Blk ($115). Electric Rear Window Defogger ($150). Pwr Dr Lock System ($155). Calif. Emission System ($100). Eng Block Heater ($20). Electronic Instrumentation Speedometer Bar Graph & Digital Readout, Tachometer ($156). Aux Lighting, Incl Eng & dual reading lamps ($32). Elect Tuned AM/FM Stereo Radio w/Seek & Scan, Stereo Cass. Tape & Digital Clock, Extd range sound system ($122). Elect Tuned AM Stereo/FM Stereo w/Seek & Scan, Stereo Cass. Tape w/Search & Repeat, Graphic Equalizer & Digital Clock, Incl extd range sound system ($150/$272). Removable Sunroof ($350). Alum Wheels, w/Locks ($210). Intermittent Windshield Wiper System ($55).

1989 Chevrolet, Beretta GT two-door coupe

1989 Chevrolet, Celebrity CL Eurosport four-door sedan

CELEBRITY CONVENIENCE/APPEARANCE OPTIONS: Preferred Equip. Grp. 1: Air Cond; Color-Keyed Flr Mats, F&R; Aux Lighting; Ext Molding Pkg; 2.5 Liter Eng ($931), w/LB6 2.8 Liter Eng ($957). Preferred Equip. Grp. 2: Air Cond; Pwr Dr Lock System; Color-Keyed Mats, F&R; Gauge Pkg w/Trip odometer; Aux Lighting; Ext Mldg Pkg; Spd Control, w/resume speed; Comfortilt Strg Wheel; Intermittent Windshield Wiper System; ($1565): 2.5 Liter Eng ($1565); 2.8 Liter Eng ($1591). Preferred Equip. Grp. 3: Air Cond; Pwr Dr. Lock System; Color-Keyed Mats, F&R; Gauge Pkg w/Trip Odometer; Aux Lighting; Spt Twin Remote Mirrors; Ext Pkg Moldings; Elect Tuned AM/FM Stereo Radio w/Seek & Scan, Stereo Cass. Tape & Digital Clock; Incl extd range sound system; Spd Control, w/resume speed; Comfortilt Strg Wheel; Pwr Trunk Opener; Pwr Windows; Intermittent Windshield Wiper System: 2.5 Liter Eng ($2062); 2.8 Liter Eng ($2088). Eurosport Equip Pkg ($230). Eurosport Preferred Equip. Grp. 1: Eurosport Equip; Air Cond; Color-Keyed Mats, F&R; Aux Lighting; Ext Molding Pkg; 2.5 Liter Eng ($1161). 2.8 Liter Eng ($1187); Eurosport Preferred Equip. Grp. 2: Eurosport Equip; Air Cond; Pwr Dr Lock System; Color-Keyed Mats, F&R; Gauge pkg w/Trip Odometer; Aux Lighting; Exterior Molding Pkg; Spd Control, w/resume speed; Comfortilt Strg Wheel; Intermittent Windshield Wiper System; 2.5 Liter Eng ($1795). 2.8 Liter Eng ($1821). Eurosport preferred Equip. Grp. 3: Eurosport Equip; Air Cond; Pwr Dr Lock System; Color-Keyed Mats, F&R; Gauge Pkg w/Trip Odometer; Aux Lighting; Spt Twin Remote Mirrors; Ext Molding Pkg; AM/FM Stereo Radio w/Seek & Scan, Stereo Cass. Tape & Digital Clock, Extd range sound system; Electronic Spd Control, w/resume speed; Comfortilt Strg Wheel; Pwr Trunk Opener; Pwr Windows; Intermittent Windshield Wiper System: 2.5 Liter Eng ($2292). 2.8 Liter Eng ($2318). Wgn Preferred Equip Grp. 1: Air Cond; Color-Keyed Mats, F&R; Aux Lighting; Ext Molding Pkg: w/2.5 Liter Eng ($923). w/LB6 2.5 Liter Eng ($949). Wgn Preferred Equip Grp. 2: Air Cond; Chrome Roof Carrier; Pwr Dr Lock System; Color-Keyed Mats, F&R; Gauge Pkg w/Trip Odometer; Pwr Liftgate Release; Aux Lighting; Ext Molding Pkg; Electronic Spd Control, w/resume speed; Comfortilt Strg Wheel; Intermittent Windshield Wiper System: 2.5 Liter Eng ($1722). 2.8 Liter Eng ($1748). Wgn Preferred Equip. Grp. 3: Air Cond; Chrome Roof Carrier; Pwr Dr Lock System; Color-Keyed Mats, F&R; Gauge Pkg w/Trip Odometer; Pwr Liftgate Release; Aux Lighting; Spt Twin Remote Mirrors; Molding Pkg; AM/FM Stereo Radio w/Seek & Scan, Stereo Cass. Tape & Digital Clock, Extd range sound system; Deluxe Rear Compartment Decor; Cargo Area Security pkg; Electronic Spd Control, w/resume speed; Comfortilt Strg Wheel; Pwr Windows; Intermittent Windshield Wiper System: 2.5 Liter Eng ($2253). 2.8 Liter Eng ($2279). Eurosport Wgn Preferred Equip. Grp. 1: Eurosport Equip. Pkg; Air Cond; Color-Keyed Mats, F&R; Aux Lighting; Exterior Mldg. Pkg: 2.5 Liter Eng ($1153). 2.8 Liter Eng, Incl H.D. Battery ($1179). Eurosport Wgn Preferred Equip. Grp. 2: Eurosport Equip. Pkg; Air Cond; Roof Carrier; Pwr Dr Lock System; Color-Keyed Mats, F&R; Gauge pkg w/Trip Odometer; Pwr Liftgate Release; Aux Lighting; Exterior Mldg. Pkg; Electronic Spd Control, w/resume speed; Comfortilt Strg Wheel; Intermittent Windshield Wiper System: 2.5 Liter Eng ($1952). 2.8 Liter Eng ($1978). Eurosport Wgn Preferred Equip. Grp. 3: Eurosport Equip. Pkg; Air Cond; Roof Carrier; Pwr Dr Lock System; Flr Mats, F&R; Gauge pkg w/Trip Odometer; Pwr Liftgate Release; Aux Lighting; Spt Twin Remote Mirrors; Ext Mldg Pkg; AM/FM Stereo Radio w/Seek & Scan, Stereo Cass. Tape & Digital Clock, Extd range sound system; Deluxe Rear Compartment Decor; Cargo Security Pkg; Spd Control, w/resume speed; Comfortilt Strg Wheel; Pwr Windows; Intermittent Windshield Wiper System: 2.5 Liter Eng ($2483). 2.8 Liter Eng ($2509). Cloth Bucket Seats w/console ($257). Cloth 55/45 Seat ($133). Custom Cloth CL 55/45 Sedan ($385). Wagon Incl split individual fldg second seatback, Wagon ($435). Custom Cloth CL 45/45 w/console, Sedan ($335). Incl split individual fldg second seatback, Wagon ($385). Custom Two-Tone paint, Incl Lwr body accent & Ext Mldg. Pkg. w/1SB, 1SC or 1SD Pkg ($93); w/1SA Pkg ($148). Air Cond; Incl increased cooling ($795). Rear Window Air Deflector ($40). Frt Lic Plate Bracket (NC). H.D. Cooling: w/o Air Cond ($70); w/Air Cond ($40). Rear Window Electric Defogger ($150). Pwr Dr Lock System ($205). Calif. Emission System ($100). Color-Keyed Mats, Front ($17). Rear ($12). Gauge Pkg. Incl Voltmeter, Trip Odometer & Temp Gauges ($64). Eng Block Heater ($20). Exterior Molding Pkg, Incl rocker panel & wheel opening mldgs, Incl w/Custom Two-Tone Paint ($55). Elect Tuned AM/FM Stereo Radio w/Seek & Scan, Stereo Cass. Tape & Digital Clock, Extd range sound system ($122). Deluxe Rear Compartment Decor ($40). 6-way Pwr Driver's Seat ($250). Reclining Seatback, Driver & Pass ($90). Cargo Area Security Pkg ($44). TIRES: P185/75R14 All Seasons SBR White Stripe ($68). P195/70R14 All Seasons SBR White Stripe ($68). P195/70R14 All Seasons SBR Blackwall ($90). Sport Wheel Covers ($656). Wire Wheel Covers, w/Locks ($215). Alum Wheels ($195). Rally Wheels, Incl w/Eurosport Equip., Incl styled wheels, special hubcaps & trim rings ($56). Rear Window Wiper/Washer ($125).

CAPRICE CONVENIENCE/APPEARANCE OPTIONS: Sdn Preferred Equip. Grp. 1: H.D. Battery; Color-Keyed Carpeted Mats, F&R; Body Side Moldings; Wheel Opening Mldgs; Extd Range Spkrs ($196). Sdn Preferred Equip. Grp. 2: H.D. Battery; Pwr Dr Lock System; Carpeted Mats, F&R; Aux Lighting; Body Side Mldgs; Wheel Opening Mldgs; Extd Range Spkrs; Spd Control, w/resume speed; Comfortilt Strg Wheel; Intermittent Windshield Wiper System ($816). Classic Sdn Preferred Equip. Grp. 1: H.D. Battery; Carpeted Mats, F&R; Aux Lighting; Spt Twin Remote Mirrors; Body Side Mldgs; Extd Range Spkrs; Spd Control, w/resume speed; Comfortilt Strg Wheel; P205/75R15 All Seasons SBR Ply White Stripe; Pwr Trunk Opener; Intermittent Windshield Wiper System ($719). Classic Sdn Preferred Equip Grp 2: H.D. Battery; Pwr Dr Lock System; Color-Keyed Carpeted Mats, F&R; Aux Lighting; Deluxe Luggage Comp Trim; Spt Twin Remote Mirrors; RH Lighted Visor Mirror; Body Side Moldings, Elect Tuned AM/FM Stereo Radio, w/Seek & Scan, Stereo Cass. Tape, Digital Clock & Pwr Antenna; extd range sound system; Elect Spd Control, w/resume speed; Comfortilt Strg Wheel; P205/75R15 All Seasons SBR White Stripe Tires; Pwr

Trunk Opener; Pwr Windows; Intermittent Windshield Wiper System; w/50/50 Seats, Incl driver & pass pwr seats ($2020); w/Bench Seat ($1520). Classic Wgn Preferred Equip. Grp. 1: H.D. Battery; Dlx Load Flr Carpeting; Aux Lighting; Spt Twin Remote Mirrors; Body Side Mldgs; Color-Keyed, exc. Estate which is woodgrain ($237). Caprice Classic Wgn Preferred Equip Grp. 2: H.D. Battery; Roof Carrier; Pwr Dr Lock System; Incl Tailgate Lock; Dlx Load Floor Carpeting, F&R; Aux Lighting; Spt Twin Remote Mirrors; Body Side Mldgs; Color-Keyed, exc Estate which is woodgrain; Elect Tuned AM/FM Stereo Radio w/Seek & Scan, Stereo Cass. Tape; Pwr Antenna & Digital Clock, Dual Rear spkrs; Electronic Spd Control, w/resume speed; Comfortilt Strg Wheel; Pwr Windows; Intermittent Windshield Wiper System ($1514). Caprice Classic Wgn Preferred Equip. Grp. 3: H.D. Battery; Roof Carrier; Pwr Dr Lock System; Incl Tailgate Lock; Color-Keyed Carpeted Mats, F&R; Gauge Pkg w/Trip Odometer; Twilight Sentinel Headlamps; Cornering Lamps; Aux Lighting; RH Lighted Visor Mirror; Spt Twin Remote Mirrors; Body Side Mldgs; Color-Keyed, exc Estate which is woodgrain; Elect Tuned AM/FM Stereo Radio, w/Seek & Scan, Stereo Cass. Tape, Graphic Equalizer, Pwr Antenna & Digital Clock; Dual Rear spkrs. Dlx Rear Comp Decor; Electronic Spd Control, w/resume speed; Comfortilt Strg Wheel; Pwr Windows; Intermittent Windshield Wiper System; w/50/50 Seats, Incl Driver & Pass Pwr Seats w/Bench Seat ($2393). w/Bench Seat ($1893). Caprice Classic Brghm Preferred Equip. Grp. 1: H.D. Battery; Carpeted Mats, F&R; Gauge Pkg w/Trip Odometer; Twilight Sentinel; RH Visor Illum Mirror; Spt Twin Remote Mirrors; Body Side Mldgs; Extd Range Spkrs; P205/75R15 All Seasons SBR White Stripe Tires; Pwr Trunk Opener ($496). Caprice Brghm Preferred Equip Grp 2: H.D. Battery; Pwr Dr Lock System, Carpeted Mats, F&R; Gauge Pkg w/Trip Odometer; Twilight Sentinel Cornering Lamps; Dlx Luggage Comp Trim; Lighted RH Visor Mirror; Spt Twin Remote Mirrors; Body Side Mldgs; Elect Tuned AM/FM Stereo Radio, w/Seek & Scan Stereo Cass. Tape; Pwr Antenna & Digital Clock; Extd range sound system; Pwr Six-Way Driver & Pass Seats; Spd Control, w/resume speed; Comfortilt Strg Wheel; P205/75R15 All Seasons SBR White Stripe Tires; Pwr Trunk Opener; Wire Wheel Covers, w/Locks; Pwr Windows; Intermittent Windshield Wiper System ($2317). Caprice Classic Brghm LS Preferred Equip. Grp. 1: H.D. Battery; Pwr Dr Lock System; Color-Keyed Carpeted Mats, F&R; Gauge Pkg w/Trip Odometer; Twilight Sentinel Headlamps; Lighted RH Visor Mirror; Spt Twin Remote Mirrors; Body Side Mldgs; Elect Tuned AM/FM Stereo Radio, w/Seek & Scan, Stereo Cass. Tape; Power Antenna & Digital Clock; Extd range sound system; Six-Way Pwr Driver & Pass Seats; Spd Control, w/resume speed; Comfortilt Strg Wheel; P205/75R15 All Seasons SBR White Stripe Tires; Pwr Trunk Opener; Wire Wheel Covers, w/locks; Pwr Windows; Intermittent Windshield Wiper System ($2203). Caprice Classic Brghm LS Preferred Equip Grp. 2: H.D. Battery; Pwr Dr Lock System; Color-Keyed Carpeted Mats, F&R; Gauge pkg w/Trip Odometer; Twilight Sentinel Headlamps; Cornering Lamps; Dlx Luggage Comp Trim; RH Visor Illum Mirror; Spt Twin Remote Mirrors; Body Side Mldgs; Elect Tuned AM/FM Stereo Radio, w/Seek & Scan, Stereo Cass. Tape, Graphic Equalizer & Pwr Antenna & Digital Clock, Extd range sound system; Pwr 6-Way Driver & Pass Seats; Electronic Spd Control, w/resume speed; Comfortilt Strg Wheel; P205/75R15 All Seasons SBR White Stripe Tires; Pwr Trunk Opener; Wire Wheel Covers, w/Locks; Pwr Windows; Intermittent Windshield Wiper System ($2427). Vinyl Bench Seat, Caprice Sdn ($28). Caprice Classic Wgn ($172). Vinyl 50/50 Seat, Caprice Sdn ($305). Caprice Classic Wgn ($103). Cloth 50/50 Seat ($275). Cloth 45/55 Seat (NC). Leather 45/55 Seat ($550). Custom Two-Tone paint, Incl Lwr body accent color-keyed striping & outside door handle inserts ($141). Full Vinyl Roof Cover ($200). Rear Window Air Deflector ($65). Frt Lic Plate Bracket (NC). Trunk Cargo net ($30). H.D. Cooling ($40). Rear Window Electric Defogger ($150). Pwr Dr. Lock System, Sedans ($205). Wgn, Incl Tailgate Lock ($265). Calif. Emission System ($100). Estate Equip ($307). Eng Block Heater ($20). Elect Tuned AM/FM Stereo, w/Seek & Scan, Stereo Cass. Tape & Digital Clock ($122/$227). Elect Tuned AM/FM Stereo, w/Seek & Scan, Stereo Cass. Tape, Graphic Equalizer & Digital Clock ($110/$337). Pin Striping, Color-Keyed ($61). TIRES: P205/75R15 All Seasons SBR White Stripe ($76). P225/70R15 SBR White Stripe ($188). P225/75R15 All Seasons SBR White (NC). Custom Wheel Covers, Std/Brghm ($65). Wire Wheel Covers, w/Locks, Brghm ($150). All others ($215).

HISTORY: Chevrolet's market share for U.S.-made passenger cars in model year 1989 was 17.5 percent, representing 1,295,455 units. The Caprice was the top-selling U.S. car in the full-size market segment.

1990

Lumina was the new name for 1990, a front-drive mid-size coupe and sedan to replace the Monte Carlo coupe (dropped after 1988) and the Celebrity sedan, which faded away this year. Its natural rival was the popular Ford Taurus. In addition to the coupe and sedan, a Lumina APV (All Purpose Vehicle) emerged this year, one of three futuristically-styled GM minivans in which composite body panels were bonded to a steel frame. Oldsmobile's Silhouette and Pontiac's Trans Sport were the others in the dramatic front-drive trio, each of which took on a distinct personality.

1990 Chevrolet, Cavalier four-door sedan

CAVALIER — SERIES 1J — FOUR/V-6 — All Cavaliers had a solid top this year, as the convertible faded away. The standard four-cylinder engine grew from 2.0 to 2.2 liters (133 cu. in.) adding five horsepower in the process. At the same time, the V-6, optional under station wagon hoods and standard in the Z24, grew to 190 cu. in. (3.1 liters), for an increase of 10 horsepower. Both the VL (Value Leader) model and the step-up RS option package now were offered in all three body styles: coupe, sedan and station wagon. All except the VL now had standard tinted glass and power steering. Each engine came with a standard five-speed gearbox, but the four-cylinder version was built by Isuzu, the V-6's by Muncie-Getrag. Three-speed automatic remained optional. Exhaust systems were made of stainless steel.

1990 Chevrolet, Camaro RS two-door coupe

CAMARO — SERIES 1F — V-6/V-8 — Only for a short model run did this year's Camaros become available, as the face-lifted '91 models were scheduled to arrive in spring 1990. The Camaro RS got a larger base V-6 engine: 190 cu. in. (3.1 liters) versus the former 2.8-liter. Both the RS and IROC-Z added a driver's air bag, for the coupe and convertible. A five-speed manual gearbox remained standard, but Camaros with the optional four-speed overdrive automatic got a modified torque converter with higher lockup points for improved gas mileage. New standard equipment included Halogen headlamps, tinted glass, intermittent wipers and a tilt steering wheel. New 16-inch alloy wheels became standard on the IROC-Z convertible (optional on the coupe). IROC-Z also had a standard limited-slip differential. Leather upholstery joined the interior option list, while the instrument panel switched to new yellow graphics.

1990 Chevrolet, Beretta GTZ two-door coupe (PH)

CORSICA/BERETTA — SERIES 1L — FOUR/V-6 — A high-performance GTZ Beretta coupe replaced the former GTU this year, powered by GM's high-output Quad Four dual-overhead-cam engine and rated 180 horsepower. With the demise of Cavalier's convertible came the promise of an open Beretta, arriving late in the season. Instead of being fully open-air, that ragtop featured a structural roof bar, which was not intended to serve as a rollbar but to add integrity to the body and minimize wind drafts to passengers. Corsica added standard equipment this year, with base models carrying the same gear as the prior season's LT series, including black body trim. Corsica LTZ added adjustable lumbar supports, and carried 15-inch tires on alloy wheels as well as stabilizer bars at front and rear. Corsica/Beretta's base four-cylinder engine grew from 2.0 to 2.2 liters, while the V-6 went from 2.8 to 3.1 liters, GTZ had a unique grille and extended rocker panels, plus 16-inch alloy wheels instead of the usual 15-nchers. All Berettas came with a standard five-speed manual gearbox, and all but the GTZ could get the optional three-speed automatic. Corsicas had either an Isuzu-built five-speed or, with V-6 power, a Muncie-Getrag unit, as well as the automatic option. Fuel capacities grew to 15.6 gallons with the adoption of a new molded tank.

1990 Chevrolet, Celebrity Eurosport station wagon

CELEBRITY — SERIES 1A — FOUR/V-6 — After losing its coupe a year earlier, the mid-size front-drive Celebrity also lost the four-door sedan this time. So only the station wagon remained, as the others were replaced by the new Lumina. Both two-seat (six-passenger) and three-seat (eight-passenger) versions were available, in base trim or with the Eurosport package. A dozen more horsepower found their way into the base four-cylinder engine, as a result of modifications in the cylinder walls and heads. Eurosport Celebritys carried a new 190 cu. in. (3.1-liter) V-6, rated 135 horsepower, with four-speed overdrive automatic transmission. That V-6 was optional on the base model, which used a standard three-speed automatic. New standard equipment included intermittent wipers. Scotchgard fabric protection, map pockets in front doors, and heavy-duty suspension.

1990 Chevrolet, Lumina two-door coupe (PH)

1990 Chevrolet, Lumina Euro two-door coupe (PH)

LUMINA — SERIES 1W — FOUR/V-6 — A sedan led off the front-drive Lumina lineup, arriving in late spring 1989, followed by a coupe in the fall. The mid-size sedan evolved from the coupe design introduced for 1988 as the Buick Regal, Oldsmobile Cutlass Supreme and Pontiac Grand Prix. Base and Eurosport models were offered, with a 151 cu. in. (2.5-liter) four-cylinder engine standard in the base model and a 191 cu. in. (3.1-liter) V-6 in the Euro. Both engines drove a standard three-speed automatic, with four-speed overdrive automatic optional in V-6 models. Standard equipment included disc brakes and independent suspension on all four wheels, plus power steering, tinted glass, intermittent wipers, and an AM/FM radio. The Euro edition was air conditioned, displayed blackout body trim and a decklid spoiler, and contained a sport suspension with larger (15-inch) tires than the base model.

1990 Chevrolet, Lumina Euro four-door sedan (PH)

1990 Chevrolet, Caprice Classic Brougham LS four-door sedan

CAPRICE — SERIES 1B — V-8 — Not much changed in the full-size rear-drive Chevrolet, as a completely different, more rounded Caprice was expected as an early '91 model, to replace the traditional boxy sedan and wagon. This carryover Caprice still was powered by one of two 5.0-liter V-8s: 305 cubic inches and 170 horsepower for the sedan, but 307 cid and 140 horses for the wagon. Both engines had throttle-body fuel injection and hooked to a four-speed overdrive automatic transmission. Under the hood, new quick-connect fuel lines were supposed to speed up servicing. Interiors had new Scotchgard fabric protection. Two new metallic red body colors were offered.

I.D. DATA: Chevrolets again had a 17-symbol Vehicle Identification Number (VIN) on the upper left surface of the instrument panel, visible through the windshield. Symbol one indicates country: '1' - U.S.A.; '2' - Canada. Next is a manufacturer code: 'G' - General Motors. Symbol three is car make: '1' - Chevrolet; '7' - GM of Canada. Symbol four denotes restraint system: 'A' - non-passive (standard); 'B' - passive (automatic belts); 'C' - passive (inflatable). Symbol five is car line/series. Symbols six-seven reveal body type. Next is the engine code, followed by a check digit, then 'L' for model year 1990. Symbol eleven indicates assembly plant. The final six digits are the sequential serial number. Engine number coding is similar to 1981-89.

CAVALIER (FOUR/V-6)

Model No.	Body/Style No.	Body Type & Seating	Factory Price	Shipping Weight	Prod. Total
1J	C37	2-dr. Coupe-5P	8620	2291	Note 1
1J	C69	4-dr. Sedan-5P	8820	2295	Note 2
1J	C35	4-dr. Sta Wag-5P	9195	2295	Note 3

CAVALIER VL (FOUR/V-6)

1J	C37/WV9	2-dr. Coupe-5P	7577	2291	Note 1
1J	C69/WV9	4-dr. Sedan-5P	8165	2291	Note 2
1J	C35/WV9	4-dr. Sta Wag-5P	8165	2295	Note 3

Cavalier Engine Note: A V-6 engine cost $685 additional.

CAVALIER Z24 (V-6)

1J	F37	2-dr. Coupe-5P	11505	2489	Note 1

Note 1: Total Cavalier coupe production was 185,071 with no further breakout available.

Note 2: Total Cavalier sedan production was 103,384 with no further breakout available.

Note 3: Total Cavalier station wagon production was 22,046 with no further breakout available.

CAMARO (V-6/V-8)

1F	P87	2-dr. RS Cpe-4P	10995/11345	2975/3143	Note 1
1F	P67	2-dr. RS Conv-4P	----/16880	----/3270	Note 2

CAMARO IROC-Z (V-8)

1F	P87/Z28	2-dr. Spt Cpe-4P	14555	3149	Note 1
1F	P67/Z28	2-dr. Conv Cpe-4P	20195	3272	Note 2

Note 1: Total Camaro coupe production was 77,810 with no further breakout available.

Note 2: Total Camaro convertible production was 5,279 with no further breakout available.

CORSICA (FOUR/V-6)

1L	T69	4-dr. Sedan-5P	9495/10180	2520/2525	Note 1
1L	Z69	4-dr. LTZ Sed-5P	----/12795	----/2545	Note 1
1L	T68	4-dr. Hatch-5P	9895/10580	2540/2545	13,001

Note 1: Total Corsica sedan production was 181,520 with no further breakout available.

BERETTA (FOUR/V-6)

1L	V37	2-dr. Coupe-5P	10320/11005	2540/----	Note 1
1L	W37	2-dr. GT Cpe-5P	----/12500	----/2676	Note 1
1L	W37	2-dr. GTZ Cpe-5P	----/13750	N/A	Note 1

Note 1: Total Beretta coupe production was 99,721 with no further breakout available.

CELEBRITY (V-6)

1A	W35	4-dr. Sta Wag-6P	12395	2809	Note 1
1A	W35	4-dr. Sta Wag-8P	12645	N/A	Note 1

Note 1: Total Celebrity station wagon production was 29,205 with no further breakout available.

LUMINA (FOUR/V-6)

1W	L27	2-dr. Coupe-6P	12140/12800	2953/----	Note 1
1W	L69	4-dr. Sedan-6P	12340/13000	3033/----	Note 2

LUMINA EUROSPORT (V-6)

1W	N27	2-dr. Coupe-6P	14040	N/A	Note 1
1W	N69	4-dr. Sedan-6P	14340	N/A	Note 2

Note 1: Total Lumina coupe production was 43,912 with no further breakout available.

Note 2: Total Lumina sedan production was 156,135 with no further breakout available.

CAPRICE (V-8)

1B	L69	4-dr. Sedan-6P	14525	3406	Note 1

CAPRICE CLASSIC (V-8)

1B	N69	4-dr. Sedan-6P	15125	3355	Note 1
1B	U69	4-dr. Brghm-6P	16325	3470	Note 1
1B	U69-B6N	4-dr. LS Brghm-6P	17525	3475	Note 1
1B	N35	4-dr. 3S Wag-8P	15725	4041	12,305

Note 1: Total Caprice sedan production was 211,552 with no further breakout available.

FACTORY PRICE AND WEIGHT NOTE: For Corsica and Beretta, prices and weights to left of slash are for four-cylinder, to right for V-6 engine. For Camaro RS, figures to left of slash are for six-cylinder model, to right of slash for V-8.

BODY/STYLE NO. NOTE: Some models were actually option packages. Code after the slash (e.g., B6N) is the number of the option package that comes with the model listed.

ENGINE DATE: BASE FOUR (Cavalier, Corsica/Beretta): Inline. Overhead valve. Four-cylinder. Cast iron block and aluminum head. Displacement: 133 cu. in. (2.2 liters). Bore & stroke: 3.50 x 3.46 in. Compression ratio: 9.0:1 Brake horsepower: 95 at 5200 RPM. Torque: 120 lb.-ft. at 3200 RPM. Five main bearings. Hydraulic valve lifters. Throttle-body fuel injection. BASE QUAD FOUR (Beretta GTZ): Inline. Dual overhead cam (16-valve). Four-cylinder. Cast iron block and aluminum head. Displacement: 138 cu. in. (2.3 liters). Bore & stroke: 3.63 x 3.35 in. Compression ratio: 10.0:1. Brake horsepower: 180 at 6200 RPM. Torque: 160 lb.-ft. at 5200 RPM. Port fuel injection. BASE FOUR (Celebrity, Lumina): Inline. Overhead valve. Four-cylinder. Cast iron block and head. Displacement: 151 cu. in. (2.5 liters). Bore & stroke: 4.00 x 3.00 in. Compression ratio: 8.3:1. Brake horsepower: 110 at 5200 RPM. Torque: 135 lb.-ft. at 3200 RPM. Five main bearings. Hydraulic valve lifters. Throttle-body fuel injection. BASE V-6 (Camaro RS coupe, Cavalier Z24, Corsica LTZ, Beretta GT/con, Lumina Eurosport); OPTIONAL (Cavalier wagon, Corsica/Beretta, Celebrity, Lumina): Overhead-valve V-6. Cast iron block and head. Displacement: 191 cu. in. (3.1 liters). Bore & stroke: 3.50 x 3.31 in. Compression ratio: 8.8:1. Brake horsepower: (Celeb/Lumina) 135 at 4400 RPM; (Cavalier) 135 at 4500; (Corsica/Beretta) 135 at 4200; (Camaro) 144 at 4400. Torque: (Cavalier/Celeb/Corsica/Beretta/Camaro) 180 at 3600; Multi-port fuel injection. BASE V-8 (Caprice sedan): 90-degree, overhead-valve V-8. Cast iron block and head. Displacement: 305 cu. in. (5.0 liters). Bore & stroke: 3.74 x 3.48 in. Compression ratio: 9.3:1. Brake horsepower: 170 at 4000 RPM. Torque: 255 lb.-ft. at 2400 RPM. Five main bearings. Hydraulic roller valve lifters. Throttle-body fuel injection. BASE V-8 (Camaro RS convertible, IROC-Z): OPTIONAL (Camaro RS coupe): Same as 305 cu. in. V-8 above but with throttle-body fuel injection. Compression ratio: 9.3:1. Brake horsepower: 170 at 4000 RPM. Torque: 255 lb.-ft. at 2400 RPM. OPTIONAL V-8 (Camaro IROC-Z): Same as 305 cu. in. V-8 above, with port fuel injection. Compression ratio: 9.3:1. Brake horsepower: 220 at 4400 RPM. Torque: 290 lb.-ft. at 3200 RPM. BASE V-8 (Caprice wagon): 90-degree, overhead valve V-8. Cast iron block and head. Displacement: 307 cu. in. (5.0 liters). Bore & stroke: 3.80 x 3.38 in. Compression ratio: 8.0:1. Brake horsepower: 140 at 3200 RPM. Torque: 255 lb.-ft. at 2000 RPM. Five main bearings. Hydraulic roller valve lifters. Carburetor: 4Bbl. OPTIONAL V-8 (Camaro IROC-Z): 90-degree, overhead valve V-8. Cast iron block and head. Displacement: 350 cu. in. (5.7 liters). Bore & stroke: 4.00 x 3.48 in. Compression ratio: 9.3:1. Brake horsepower: 230 at 4400 RPM. Torque: 330 lb.-ft. at 3200 RPM.

CHASSIS DATA: Wheelbase: (Cavalier) 101.2 in.; (Camaro) 101.0 in.; (Corsica/Beretta) 103.4 in.; (Celebrity) 104.9 in.; (Lumina) 107.5 in.; (Caprice) 116.0 in. Overall length: (Cav cpe/sed) 178.4 in.; (Cav wag) 174.5 in.; (Camaro) 192.0 in.; (Corsica) 183.4 in.; (Beretta) 187.2 in.; (Celeb) 190.8 in.; (Lumina cpe) 198.4 in.; (Lumina sed) 197.6 in.; (Caprice sed) 212.2 in.; (Capr wag) 215.7 in. Height: (Cavalier) 52.0-52.8 in.; (Camaro cpe) 50.0 in.; (Camaro conv) 50.3 in.; (Corsica) 56.2 in.; (Beretta) 52.6 in.; (Celeb) 54.3 in.; (Lumina cpe) 53.3 in.; (Lumina sed) 53.6 in.; (Caprice) 56.4 in.; (Caprice wag) 58.2 in. Width: (Cav cpe) 66.0 in.; (Cav sed/wag) 66.3 in.; (Camaro) 72.8 in.; (Corsica) 68.2 in.; (Beretta) 68.0 in.; (Celeb) 69.3 in.; (Lumina) 71.0-71.1 in.; (Caprice) 75.4 in.; (Capr wag) 79.3 in. Front Tread: (Cav) 55.8 in.; (Camaro) 60.0 in.; (Corsica/Beretta) 55.6 in.; (Celeb) 58.7 in.; (Lumina) 59.5 in.; (Caprice) 61.7 in.; (Capr wag) 62.2 in. Rear Tread: (Cav) 55.2 in.; (Camaro) 60.9 in.; (Corsica/Beretta) 55.1 in.; (Beretta) 56.6 in.; (Celeb) 57.0 in.; (Lumina) 58.0 in.; (Caprice) 60.7 in.; (Capr wag) 64.1 in. Standard Tires: (Cav) P185/80R13; (Cav Z24) P215/60R14; (Camaro) P215/65R15; (Camaro IROC-Z conv) P245/50ZR16; (Corsica) P185/75R14; (Beretta) P185/70R14; (Corsica LTZ/Beretta GT) P205/60R15; (Beretta conv/GTZ) 205/55R16; (Celeb) P185/75R14; (Lumina) P195/75R14; (Lumina Euro) P195/70R15; (Caprice) P205/75R15; (Caprice wag) P225/75R15.

TECHNICAL: Transmission: Five-speed manual shift standard on Cavalier, Corsica/Beretta and Camaro. Three-speed automatic standard on Celebrity and Lumina. Four-speed overdrive automatic standard on Caprice. Steering: (Camaro/Caprice) recirculating ball; (others) rack and pinion. Front Suspension: (Cavalier) MacPherson struts with coil springs, lower control arms and stabilizer bar; (Corsica/Beretta) MacPherson struts with coil springs; (Camaro) modified MacPherson struts with coil springs; (Celeb) MacPherson struts with coil springs, lower control arms; (Lumina) MacPherson struts with coil springs and stabilizer bar; (Caprice) unequal-length control arms, coil springs, stabilizer bar. Rear Suspension: (Cavalier) trailing crank arm with twist beam axle and coil springs; (Camaro) Salisbury axle and torque arm with ICA, coil springs and track bar; (Corsica/Beretta) trailing twist axle with coil springs; (Celeb) trailing arms with stamped control arms and open section; (Lumina) MacPherson struts with transverse leaf spring and stabilizer bar; (Caprice) rigid axle with four links, coil springs, stabilizer available. Brakes: front disc, rear drum; four-wheel discs standard on Lumina. Body construction: unibody except (Caprice) separate body and frame. Fuel tank: (Cav) 13.6 gal.; (Camaro) 15.5 gal.; (Corsica/Beretta) 15.6 gal.; (Celeb) 15.7 gal.; (Lumina) 17.1 gal.; (Caprice) 24.5 gal.; (Caprice wag) 22 gal.

DRIVETRAIN OPTIONS: Engines: 3.1-liter V-6: Cavalier wagon ($685); Corsica/Beretta ($685); Celeb/Lumina ($660). 305 cu. in. V-8; Camaro RS cpe ($350); Caprice sed ($440). 350 cu. in., V-8: Camaro IROC-Z ($300). Transmission/Differential: Three-speed automatic trans.: Cavalier ($465); Corsica/Beretta ($540). Four-speed overdrive auto. trans.: Camaro ($515); Celeb/Lumina V-6 ($200). Limited-slip differential: Caprice ($100). Performance axle ratio: ($21). Performance axle ratio w/dual exhausts: Camaro ($466). Suspension: F40 H.D. susp.: Caprice ($26). F41 sport susp.: Caprice ($49). Inflatable rear shock absorbers: Celeb/Caprice ($64).

1990 Chevrolet, Cavalier Z24 two-door coupe

CAVALIER CONVENIENCE/APPEARANCE OPTIONS: VL Preferred Equip. Grp 1: Pwr Strg; Body Side Moldings ($275). VL Preferred Equip. Grp 2: Pwr Strg; Tinted Glass; Spt LH Remote & RH Manual Mirrors; Body Side Moldings; Carpeted Mats ($443). Cavalier Preferred Equip. Grp 1: Folding split back rear seat; Intermittent Windshield Wiper System; Spt LH Remote & RH Manual Mirrors; Body Side Molding; Carpeted mats ($318). Cavalier Preferred Equip Grp 2 (1JC37, 1JC69 only): Air Cond; Electronic Spd Control, w/resume speed; Comfortilt Strg Wheel; Split Back, Folding Rear Seat; Intermittent Windshield Wiper System; Spt. LH Remote & RH Manual Mirrors; Body Side Moldings; Color-Keyed Carpeted Mats ($1368). Cavalier Wgn Preferred Equip. Grp 2: Air Cond; Spd Control, w/resume speed; Comfortilt Strg Wheel; Roof Carrier; Fldg. Rear Seat Split Back; Intermittent Windshield Wiper System; Spt LH Remote & RH Manual Mirrors; Body Side Moldings; Color-Keyed Carpeted mats, F&R ($1483). Cavalier Preferred Equip. Grp. 3 (1JC37, 1JC69 only): Air Cond; Elect Tuned AM/FM Stereo Radio, w/Seek & Scan, Stereo Cass. Tape & Digital Clock w/extended range sound system; Pwr Windows; Pwr Dr Lock System; Spd Control; w/resume speed; Comfortilt Strg Wheel; Folding Rear Seat Split Back; Intermittent Windshield Wiper System; Spt LH Remote & RH Manual Mirrors; Body Side Moldings; Carpeted Mats, Coupe ($1913). Sedan ($2018). Preferred Equip. Grp 3 (1JC35): Air Cond; Elect Tuned AM/FM Stereo Radio, w/Seek & Scan, Stereo Cass. Tape & Digital Clock, extended range sound system; Pwr Windows; Pwr Dr Lock System, Spd Control, w/resume speed; Comfortilt Strg Wheel; Roof Carrier; Split Back, Fldg Rear Seat; Intermittent Windshield Wiper System; Spt LH Remote & RH Manual Mirrors; Body Side Moldings, Carpeted Mats; F&R ($2133). Z24 Cpe Preferred Equip Grp 1: Air Cond; Dome Reading Lamp ($744). Z24 Cpe Preferred Equip. Grp. 2: Air Cond; Elect Tuned AM/FM Stereo Radio, w/Seek & Scan, Stereo Cass. Tape & Digital Clock, extended range sound system; Spd Control w/resume speed; Comfortilt Strg Wheel; Intermittent Windshield Wiper System; Color-Keyed Carpeted Mats, F&R; Dome Reading Lamp ($1302). Z24 Cpe Preferred Equip. Grp 3: Air Cond; Elect Tuned AM Stereo/FM Stereo Radio, w/Seek & Scan, Stereo Tape w/Search & Repeat, Graphic Equalizer & Digital Clock, extended range sound system; Pwr Windows; Pwr Door Lock System; Electronic Spd Control, w/resume speed; Comfortilt Strg Wheel; Intermittent Windshield Wiper System; Pwr Trunk Opener; Carpeted Mats, F&R; Dome Reading Lamp ($1907). Air Cond ($720). Frt License Plate Bracket (NC). Deck Lid Carrier, Black ($115). Roof Carrier ($115). Rear Window Defogger Electric ($160). Pwr Door Lock System, Coupes ($175). Sedans & Wgns ($175). Calif. Emission System ($100). Tinted Glass, All Windows ($105). Body Side Moldings, Std/Z24 ($50). Elect Tuned AM/FM Stereo, w/Seek & Scan & Digital Clock, extended range sound system, VL ($332). Elect Tuned AM/FM Stereo, w/Seek & Scan, Stereo Cass. Tape & Digital Clock, extended range sound system, VL ($472); others ($140); Elect Tuned

AM Stereo & FM Stereo, w/Seek & Scan, Stereo Cass. Tape w/Search & Repeat, Graphic Equalizer & Digital Clock, extended range sound system ($150/$290). R/S Sport Pkg ($405). Removable Sunroof ($350). TIRES: P185/80R13 All Seasons Steel Belted Radial White Stripe ($68). P195/70R14 All Seasons Steel Belted Radial Blackwall ($156). P215/60R14 All Seasons Steel Belted Radial White Outline Lettered ($102). Aluminum Painted Wheels ($265). Styled Steel Wheels (NC).

CAMARO CONVENIENCE/APPEARANCE OPTIONS: RS Coupe Preferred Equip. Grp 1: Air Cond; Elect Tuned AM/FM Stereo Radio, w/Seek & Scan, Stereo Cass. Tape & Digital Clock, extended range sound system; Pwr Dr Lock System; Spd Control, w/resume speed; Body Side Moldings ($1410). RS Coupe Preferred Equip. Grp. 2: Air Cond; Elect Tuned AM/FM Stereo Radio, w/Seek & Scan, Stereo Cass. Tape & Digital Clock, extd range sound system; Pwr Windows; Pwr Dr Lock; Electronic Spd Control, w/resume speed; Pwr Hatch Release; Cargo Cover; Body Side Moldings; Carpeted Mats, F&R; Mirror w/Dual Reading Lamps ($1782). IROC-Z Preferred Equip. Grp. 1: Air Cond; Body Side Moldings ($865). IROC-Z Preferred Equip. Grp. 2: Air Cond; Elect Tuned AM/FM Stereo Radio, w/Seek & Scan; Stereo Cass. Tape & Digital Clock, extd. range sound system; Pwr Windows; Pwr Dr Lock System; Electronic Spd Control, w/resume speed; Pwr Hatch Release; Cargo Cover; Body Side Moldings; Carpeted Mats, F&R ($1759). IROC-Z Preferred Equip. Grp. 3: Air Cond; Elect Tuned AM/FM Stereo Radio, w/Seek & Scan, Stereo Cass. Tape & Digital Clock, extd range sound system; Pwr Windows; Pwr Seat, drivers side only; Pwr Dr Lock System; Electronic Spd Control, w/resume speed; Pwr Hatch Release; Spt Electric Twin Remote Mirrors; Cargo Cover; Body Side Moldings; Carpeted Mats, F&R; Mirror, w/Dual Reading Lamps ($2143). RS Convertible Preferred Equip. Grp. 1: Air Cond; Elect Tuned AM/FM Stereo Radio, w/Seek & Scan, Stereo Cass. Tape & Digital Clock, extended range sound system; Body Side Moldings; Carpeted Mats, F&R ($1040). RS Convertible Preferred Equip. Grp 2: Air Cond; Elect Tuned AM/FM Stereo Radio, w/Seek & Scan, Stereo Cass. Tape & Digital Clock, extended range sound system; Pwr Windows; Pwr Dr Lock System; Spd Control, w/resume speed; Body Side Moldings; Carpeted Mats, F&R ($1640). IROC-Z Convertible Preferred Equip. Grp 1: Air Cond; Body Side Moldings ($865). IROC-Z Convertible Preferred Equip. Grp. 2: Air Cond; Elect Tuned AM/FM Stereo Radio, w/Seek & Scan, Stereo Cass. Tape & Digital Clock, extended range sound system; Spd Control, w/resume speed; Body Side Moldings; Carpeted Mats, F&R ($1640). IROC-Z Convertible Preferred Equip. Grp 3: Air Cond; Elect Tuned AM/FM Stereo Radio, w/Seek & Scan, Stereo Cass. Tape & Digital Clock, extended range sound system; Pwr Windows; Pwr Seat, Driver Side only; Pwr Dr Lock System; Electronic Spd Control, w/resume speed; Spt Electric Twin Remote Mirrors; Body Side Moldings; Carpeted Mats, F&R ($2001). Custom Cloth Bucket Seats ($327). Custom Leather Bucket Seats ($800). Air Cond, Incl increased cooling

($805). Frt License Plate Bracket (NC). Decal & Stripe Delete ($60 credit). Rear Window Defogger ($160). Pwr Door Lock System ($175). Calif. Emission System ($100). Pwr Hatch Release ($50). Engine Block Heater ($20). Rear Window Louvers ($210). Spt. Twin Remote Electric Mirrors ($91). Elect Tuned AM/FM Stereo, w/Seek & Scan, Stereo Cass. Tape & Digital Clock ($140). Elect Tuned Delco/Bose Music System, Incl AM/FM Stereo w/Seek & Scan, Stereo Cass. Tape & Digital Clock, special tone & balance control & 4 spkrs ($875/$1015). Removable Glass Roof Panels, Incl locks ($866). Cast Alum Wheels 16-in., incl wheel locks & P245/50 ZR16 SBR Blackwall Tires ($520).

1990 Chevrolet, Corsica four-door hatchback sedan

CORSICA CONVENIENCE/APPEARANCE OPTIONS: LT Preferred Equip. Grp. 1: Tinted Glass; Intermittent Windshield Wiper System; Carpeted Mats, F&R; Map Lamps w/Consolette ($232). LT Preferred Equip. Grp 2: Air Cond; Spd Control, w/resume speed; Comfortilt Strg Wheel; Tinted Glass; Intermittent Windshield Wiper System; Carpeted Mats, F&R; Map Lamps w/Consolette ($1342). LT Preferred Equip. Grp 3: Air Cond; Elect Tuned AM/FM Stereo Radio, w/Seek & Scan, Stereo Cass. Tape & Digital Clock, extended range sound system; Pwr Windows; Pwr Dr Lock System; Electronic Spd Control, w/resume speed; Comfortilt Strg Wheel; Tinted Glass; Intermittent Windshield Wiper System; Trunk/hatch Opener; Carpeted Mats, F&R; Map Lamps w/Consolette ($2042). LTZ Preferred Equip. Grp. 1: Electronic Spd Control, w/resume speed; Comfortilt Strg Wheel; Carpeted mats, F&R ($363). LTZ Preferred Equip. Grp 2: Elect Tuned AM/FM Stereo Radio, w/Seek & Scan, Stereo Cass. Tape & Digital Clock, extended range sound system; Pwr Windows; Pwr Dr Lock System; Electronic Spd Control, w/resume speed; Comfortilt Strg Wheel; Pwr Trunk Opener; Carpeted Mats, F&R ($106). Custom Cloth CL Bucket Seats, Sedan ($425). Hatchback ($275). Sport Cloth Bucket, Incl w/LTZ (NC). Custom Two-Tone Paint ($123). Air Cond, Incl increased cooling, Std on LTZ ($780). Frt License Plate Bracket (NC). Deck Lid Carrier, Black ($115). Floor Mounted Console ($60). Electric Rear Window Defogger ($160). Pwr Door Lock System ($215). Calif. Emission System ($100). Gauge Pkg w/Tachometer, Incl Voltmeter, Oil Pressure, Temperature Gauges & Trip Odometer, Std on LTZ ($139). Elect Tuned AM/FM Stereo Radio, w/Seek & Scan, Stereo Cass. Tape & Digital Clock, Incl extended range sound system ($140). Elect Tuned AM Stereo/FM Stereo Radio, w/Seek & Scan, Stereo Cass. Tape w/Search & Repeat, Graphic Equalizer & Digital Clock, Incl extended range sound system ($150/$290). TIRES: P185/75 R14 All Seasons SBR White Stripe ($68). Styled Wheels ($56).

1990 Chevrolet, Corsica LTZ four-door sedan

1990 Chevrolet, Beretta two-door coupe

BERETTA CONVENIENCE/APPEARANCE OPTIONS: Preferred Equip. Grp. 1: Intermittent Windshield Wiper System; Carpeted Mats, F&R; Map Lamps w/Consolette ($112). Preferred Equip. Grp. 2: Air Cond; Spd Control, w/resume speed; Comfortilt Strg Wheel; Intermittent Windshield Wiper System; Carpeted Mats, F&R; Map Lamps w/Consolette ($1222). Preferred Equip. Grp. 3: Air Cond; Elect Tuned AM/FM Stereo Radio, w/Seek & Scan; Stereo Cass. Tape & Digital Clock, Extd range sound system; Pwr Windows; Pwr Dr Lock System; Electronic Spd Control, w/resume speed; Comfortilt Strg Wheel; Intermittent Windshield Wiper System; Pwr Trunk Opener; Carpeted Mats, F&R; Map Lamps w/Consolette ($1817). GT Preferred Equip. Grp. 1: Electronic Spd Control, w/resume speed; Comfortilt Strg Wheel; Intermittent Windshield Wiper System; Carpeted Mats, F&R; Map Lamps w/Consolette ($442). GT Preferred Equip. Grp. 2: Elect Tuned AM/FM Stereo Radio, w/Seek & Scan, Stereo Cass. Tape & Digital Clock, Extd range sound system; Pwr Windows; Pwr Dr Lock System; Electronic Spd Control, w/resume speed; Comfortilt Strg Wheel; Intermittent Windshield Wiper System; Pwr Trunk Opener; Carpeted Mats, F&R; Map Lamps w/Consolette ($1037). GTZ

Preferred Equip. Grp. 1: Electronic Spd Control, w/resume speed; Comfortilt Strg Wheel; Carpeted Mats, F&R ($363). GTZ Preferred Equip. Grp. 2: Elect Tuned AM/FM Stereo Radio, w/Seek & Scan; Stereo Cass. Tape & Digital Clock, Extd range sound system; Pwr Windows; Pwr Dr Lock System; Electronic Spd Control, w/resume speed; Comfortilt Strg Wheel; Pwr Trunk Opener; Carpeted Mats, F&R ($958). Custom Two-Tone Paint ($123). Air Cond, Incl w/GT & GTZ ($780). Frt License Plate Bracket (NC). Deck Lid Carrier, Black ($115). Rear Window Defogger, Electric ($160). Pwr Door Lock System ($175). Electronic Instrumentation; Speedometer Bar Graph & Digital readout, Incl Tachometer ($156). Elect Tuned AM/FM Stereo Radio, w/Seek & Scan, Stereo Cass. Tape & Digital Clock, Incl extd range sound system ($140). Elect Tuned AM Stereo/FM Stereo, Radio w/Seek & Scan, Stereo Cass. Tape w/Search & Repeat, Graphic Equalizer & Digital Clock, Incl extd range sound system ($150/$290). Manual Sunroof, Removable ($350). Alum Wheels, w/Locks ($210).

CELEBRITY CONVENIENCE/APPEARANCE OPTIONS: Wgn Preferred Equip. Grp. 1: Air Cond; Molding Pkg; Aux Lighting; Color-Keyed Mats, F&R ($921). Wgn Preferred Equip. Grp. 2: Air Cond; Pwr Dr Lock System; Electronic Spd Control, w/resume speed; Comfortilt Strg Wheel; Roof Carrier (blk); Gauge Pkg w/Trip Odometer; Ext Molding Pkg; Pwr Liftgate Release; Aux Lighting; Color-Keyed Mats, F&R ($1710). Wgn Preferred Equip. Grp. 3: Air Cond; Elect Tuned AM/FM Stereo Radio, w/Seek & Scan, Stereo Cass. Tape & Digital Clock, extd range sound system; Pwr Windows; Pwr Dr Lock System; Spd Control, w/ resume speed; Comfortilt Strg Wheel; Roof Carrier (blk); Gauge Pkg w/Trip Odometer; Exterior Molding Pkg; Pwr Liftgate Release; Cargo Area Security Pkg; Aux Lighting; Deluxe Rear Compartment Decor; Spt Twin Remote Mirrors; Color-Keyed Mats, F&R ($2269). Eurosport Wgn Base Equip. Grp: Air Cond; 3.1L Eng; 4 Spd Auto Trans ($1895). Eurosport Wgn Preferred Equipment Grp 1: Air Cond; 3.1L Eng; 4 Spd Auto Trans; Molding Pkg; Aux Lighting; Color-Keyed Mats, F&R ($2011). Eurosport Wgn Preferred Equip. Grp. 2: Air Cond; 3.1L Eng; 4 Spd Auto Trans; Pwr Dr Lock System; Electronic Spd Control, w/resume speed; Comfortilt Strg Wheel; Roof Carrier (blk); Gauge Pkg, w/Trip Odometer; Exterior Molding Pkg; Pwr Liftgate Release; Aux Lighting; Color-Keyed Mats, F&R ($2800). Eurosport Wgn Preferred Equip. Grp. 3: Air Cond; 3.1L Eng; 4 Spd Auto Trans; Elect Tuned AM/FM Stereo Radio, w/Seek & Scan, Stereo Cass. Tape & Digital Clock, extd range sound system; Pwr Windows; Pwr Dr Lock System; Electronic Spd Control, w/resume speed; Comfortilt Steering Wheel; Roof Carrier (blk); Gauge Pkg w/Trip Odometer; Molding Pkg; Pwr Liftgate Release; Cargo Area Security Pkg; Aux Lighting; Deluxe Rear Compartment Decor; Spt Twin Remote Mirrors; Color-Keyed Mats, F&R ($3349). Cloth 55/45 Seat ($133). Air Cond ($805). Frt License Plate Bracket (NC). Electric Rear Window Defogger ($160). Calif. Emission System ($100). Pwr Dr Lock System ($215). 6-Way Pwr Seat, Driver's Side

($270). Elect Tuned AM/FM Stereo Radio, w/Seek & Scan, Stereo Cass. Tape & Digital Clock, Incl extd range sound system ($140). Pwr Reclining Seatbacks, Driver & Pass ($110). TIRES: P185/75R14 All Seasons Steel Belted Radial White Stripe ($68). Sport Wheel Covers ($65). Cast Alum Wheels ($195). Rear Window Wiper/Washer ($125).

LUMINA CONVENIENCE/APPEARANCE OPTIONS:

Preferred Equip. Grp 1: Air Cond; Electronic Spd Control, w/resume speed; Comfortilt Strg Wheel; Carpeted Mats, F&R ($1180). Lumina Preferred Equip. Grp. 2: Air Cond; Pwr Windows; Pwr Dr Lock System; Spd Control, w/resume speed; Comfortilt Strg Wheel; Pwr Trunk Opener; Pwr Mirrors; Spt. Twin Remote Mirrors; Carpeted Mats, F&R; Coupe ($1665). Sedan ($1770). Euro Preferred Equip. Grp. 1: Electronic Spd Control, w/resume speed; Comfortilt Strg Wheel; Gauge Pkg w/Tachometer; Carpeted Mats, F&R ($475). Euro Preferred Equip. Grp. 2: Elect Tuned AM/FM Stereo Radio, w/Seek & Scan, Stereo Cass. Tape & Digital Clock, extd range sound system; Pwr Windows; Pwr Dr Lock System; Electronic Pwr Spd Control, w/resume speed; Comfortilt Strg Wheel; Pwr Trunk Opener; Gauge Pkg. w/Tachometer; Spt Twin Remote Mirrors; Carpeted Mats, F&R; Coupe ($1100). Sedan ($1205). Custom Cloth Bucket Seats w/console ($299). Custom Cloth 60/40 Seat ($199). Cloth 60/40 Seat ($159). Air Cond, Std/Euro ($805). Frt License Plate Bracket (NC). Electric Rear Window Defogger ($160). Pwr Door Lock System; Coupe ($175). Sedan ($215). Calif. Emission System ($100). Elect Tuned AM/FM Stereo Radio, w/Seek & Scan; Stereo Cass. Tape & Digital Clock, Incl extd range sound system ($140). Pwr 6-way Driver's Seat ($270). Rear Spoiler, Delete ($128 credit). TIRES: P195/75 R14 All Seasons Steel Belted Radial White Stripe ($72). P215/60 R16 All Seasons Steel Belted Radial Black Wall ($76). Alum Wheels ($250).

CAPRICE CONVENIENCE/APPEARANCE OPTIONS:

Caprice Sdn Preferred Equip. Grp. 1: Body Side Moldings; Carpeted Mats, F&R; Extended Range Spkrs; Wheel Opening Moldings ($170). Caprice Sdn Preferred Equip. Grp. 2: Pwr Dr Lock System; Spd Control, w/resume speed; Comfortilt Strg Wheel; Body Side Moldings; Intermittent Windshield Wiper System; Aux Lighting; Color-Keyed Carpeted Mats, F&R; Extd Range Spkrs; Wheel Opening Moldings ($820). Caprice Classic Sdn Preferred Equip. Grp. 1: Spd Control, w/resume speed; Comfortilt Strg Wheel; P205/75R15 All Seasons SBR White Stripe Tires; Body Side Moldings; Intermittent Windshield Wiper System; Pwr Trunk Opener; Aux Lighting; Color-Keyed Carpeted Mats, F&R; Extd Range Spkrs; Spt Twin Remote Mirrors ($713). Caprice Classic Sdn Preferred Equip Grp 2: Elect Tuned AM/FM Stereo Radio, w/Seek & Scan, Stereo Cass. Tape, Digital Clock & Pwr Antenna; Extd range sound system; Pwr Windows; Pwr 6-Way Driver & Pass Seats; Pwr Dr Lock System; Spd Control, w/resume speed; Comfortilt Strg Wheel; P205/75R15 All Seasons SBR White Stripe Tires; Body Side Moldings; Luggage Compartment Trim; Intermittent Windshield Wiper System; Pwr Trunk Opener; Aux Lighting; RH Visor Illum Mirror; Carpeted Mats; Spt Twin Remote Mirrors; w/50/50 Seats, Incl Driver & Pass Pwr Seats ($1547). Caprice Classic Wgn Preferred Equip. Grp. 1: Body Side Moldings; Aux Lighting; Dlx Load Flr Carpeting; Spt Twin Remote Mirrors ($211). Caprice Classic Wgn Preferred Equip. Grp. 2: Elect Tuned AM/FM Stereo Radio, w/Seek & Scan, Stereo Cass. Tape; Pwr Antenna & Digital Clock; Dual Rear Spkrs; Pwr Windows; Pwr Dr Lock System, Incl Tailgate Lock; Spd Control, w/resume speed; Comfortilt Strg Wheel; Roof Carrier; Body Side Moldings; Aux Lighting; Intermittent Windshield Wiper System; Dlx Load Floor Carpeting; Carpeted Mats, Spt Twin Remote Mirrors ($1556). Caprice Classic Wgn Preferred Equip. Grp. 3: Elect Tuned AM/FM Stereo Radio, w/Seek & Scan; Stereo Cass. Tape, Graphic Equalizer, Pwr Antenna & Digital Clock; Dual Rear Spkrs; Pwr Windows; Pwr Dr Lock System, Incl Tailgate Lock; Pwr 6-way Drive & Pass Seats; Spd Control, w/resume speed; Deluxe Rear Compartment Decor; Comfortilt Strg Wheel; Roof Carrier; Gauge Pkg w/Trip Odometer; Body Side Moldings; Twilight Sentinel Headlamps; Intermittent Windshield Wiper System; Aux Lighting; Cornering Lamps; RH Visor Illum Mirror; Carpeted Mats; Spt Twin Remote Mirrors; w/50/50 Seats, Incl Driver & Pass Pwr Seats ($2475). W/Bench Seat ($1935). Caprice Classic Brghm Preferred Equip. Grp. 1: P205/75R15 SBR White Stripe Tires; Gauge Pkg W/Trip Odometer; Body Side Moldings; Twilight Sentinel; Pwr Trunk Opener; RH Visor Illum Mirror; Carpeted Mats; Extd Range Spkrs; Spt Twin Remote Mirrors ($470), Caprice Brghm Preferred Equip. Grp. 2: Elect Tuned AM/FM Stereo Radio, w/Seek & Scan, Stereo Cass. Tape, Pwr Antenna & Digital Clock, Extd Range Sound System; Pwr Windows; Pwr 6-way Driver & Pass Seats; Pwr Dr Lock System; Electronic Spd Control, w/resume speed; Wire Wheel Covers, w/locks; Comfortilt Strg Wheel; P205/75R15 All Seasons SBR White Stripe Tires; Gauge Pkg w/Trip Odometer; Body Side Moldings; Twilight Sentinel Headlamps; Dlx Luggage Comp Trim; Intermittent Windshield Wiper System; Cornering Lamps; Pwr Trunk Opener; RH Visor Illum Mirror; Carpeted Mats; Spt Twin Remote Mirrors ($2384). Caprice Classic Brghm LS Preferred Equip Grp 1: Elect Tuned AM/FM Stereo Radio, w/Seek & Scan, Stereo Cass. Tape, Pwr Antenna & Digital Clock, Extd Range Sound System, Pwr Windows, Pwr 6-way Driver & Pass Seats; Pwr Dr Lock System; Electronic Spd Control w/resume speed; Wire Wheel Covers, w/Locks; Comfortilt Strg Wheel; P205/75R15 All Seasons SBR White Stripe Tires; Gauge Pkg w/Trip Odometer; Body Side Moldings; Twilight Sentinel; Intermittent Windshield Wiper System; Pwr Trunk Opener; RH Visor Illum Mirror; Carpeted Mats; Spt Twin Remote Mirrors ($2270). Caprice Classic Brghm LS Preferred Equip. Grp. 2: Elect Tuned AM/FM Stereo Radio w/Seek & Scan, Stereo Cass. Tape, Graphic Equalizer, Pwr Antenna & Digital Clock; Extd Range Sound System; Pwr Windows; Pwr 6-way Driver & Pass Seats; Pwr Dr Lock System; Electronic Spd Control, w/resume speed; Wire Wheel Covers, w/Locks; Comfortilt Strg Wheel; P205/75R15 All Seasons SBR White Stripe Tires; Gauge Pkg w/Trip Odometer; Body Side Moldings; Twilight Sentinel Headlights; Dlx Luggage Compartment Trim; Intermittent Windshield Wiper System; Cornering Lamps; Pwr Trunk Opener; RH Visor Illum

Mirror; Carpeted Mats; Spt Twin Remote Mirrors ($2494). Vinyl Bench Seat, Caprice Sedan ($28). Caprice Classic Wgn ($172). Vinyl 50/50 Seat, Caprice Sedan ($305). Caprice Classic Wgn ($103). Cloth 50/50 Seat ($275). Cloth 45/55 Seat (NC). Leather 45/55 Seat ($550). Custom Two-Tone Paint; Incl lower body accent, color-keyed striping & o/s door handle inserts ($141). Full Vinyl Roof Cover ($200). Air Deflector, Rear Window ($65). Frt License Plate Bracket (NC). Trunk Cargo Net ($30). H.D. Cooling ($40). Electric Rear Window Defogger $160). Pwr Dr Lock System, Sedans ($215). Wgn, Incl Tailgate Lock ($290). Calif. Emission System ($100). Estate Equipment ($307). Engine block heater ($20). Elect Tuned AM/FM Stereo, w/Seek & Scan, Stereo Cass. Tape & Digital Clock ($140/$250). Elect Tuned AM/FM Stereo, w/Seek & Scan, Stereo Cass. Tape, Graphic Equalizer & Digital Clock ($110/$360). Pin Striping, Color-Keyed ($61). TIRES: P205/75R15 All Seasons SBR White Stripe ($76). P225/79R15 SBR White Stripe ($188). Custom Wheel Covers, Std/Brghm ($65). Wire Wheel Covers, w/Locks ($150). Brghm ($150). All except Brghm ($215).

HISTORY: Chevrolet's market share for U.S.-made passenger cars in model year 1990 was 12.9 percent, representing 785,918 units. A Chevrolet Beretta paced the 1990 Indianapolis 500 with Chevrolet Motor Division General Manager Jim Perkins at the wheel.

1991

The Camaro Z28 returned this year (introduced early in 1990 as a 1991 model) and replaced the IROC-Z, which was dropped. The Celebrity, down to only a station wagon the year previous, was also dropped. Also new for 1991 (and also introduced in early 1990) was the new-design Caprice and Caprice Classic sedans, which featured a more rounded appearance. A convertible joined the Cavalier RS lineup after the previous year's discontinuation of the Cavalier Z24 ragtop. A Z34 Performance Coupe was added to the Lumina lineup, and featured a 3.4-liter DOHC V-6 rated at 200 horsepower.

1991 Chevrolet, Cavalier RS two-door convertible

CAVALIER — SERIES 1J — FOUR/V-6 — In January 1991, an RS convertible joined the lineup, which again consisted of VL (Value Leader) and step-up RS series and a Z24 coupe. The VL and RS series each consisted of coupe, sedan and station wagon. Standard equipment included stainless steel exhaust and an electric tailgate release on wagons. New-for-1991 were a Z51 Performance Package, a Z24 appearance package, all new interiors, and revamped front end panels, headlamps, fascias, grilles and taillamps. The J-car Cavalier (a platform shared with the Pontiac Sunbird) featured a 2.2-liter four-cylinder engine in all VL and RS sedans and station wagons. A 3.1-liter V-6 was the standard powerplant of the Z24 coupe and RS convertible, and was optional on station wagons. A five-speed manual transmission with overdrive was the base unit while a three-speed automatic was optional across-the-board.

1991 Chevrolet, Camaro Z28 two-door coupe

CAMARO — SERIES 1F — V-6/V-8 — The 1991 Camaro lineup debuted in early 1990. Gone was the IROC-Z name, replaced with the return of the Z28. Both the Z28 and RS series each offered coupe and convertible models. Standard equipment included the PASS-Key theft deterrent system and driver's side airbag. New equipment included 16-inch wheels for the Z28 (optional on the RS), aero-styled rocker panels, high profile rear spoiler for the Z28, two new exterior colors, heavy-duty battery and the high-mounted stop lamp was relocated. Standard engine in the RS coupe was the 3.1-liter V-6. The 5.0-liter V-8 was the base powerplant in the RS convertible and the Z28 line. The Z28 could be ordered with the 5.7-liter TPI V-8. Base transmission was the five-speed manual while a four-speed automatic was optional across-the-board. Removable T-tops were also offered as optional equipment.

CORSICA/BERETTA — SERIES 1L — FOUR/V-6 — Aside from dropping the LTZ from its 1991 lineup, the Corsica and Beretta offerings remained much the same as the year previous. Corsica was available as a LT sedan and hatchback while the Beretta was offered in three levels as a coupe: base, GT and GTZ. Standard features included Scotchgard fabric protector for interiors, driver's side airbag and stainless steel exhaust. New-for-1991 included an improved four-speaker sound system, improved ride and handling and redesigned instrumentation. A Z52 Sport Package was optional on the Corsica. Corsica LT and base Beretta were powered by a 2.2-liter four-cylinder engine. Beretta GTZ featured a 2.3-liter High Output Quad 4 engine rated at

180 horsepower. A 3.1-liter V-6 was the standard powerplant on the Beretta GT, and was optional on all other Corsica and Beretta models. The five-speed automatic transaxle was standard and a three-speed automatic was optional.

1991 Chevrolet, Lumina Z34 two-door coupe

LUMINA — SERIES 1W — FOUR/V-6 — A Z34 coupe joined the Lumina lineup for 1991, which also included a base coupe and sedan and Euro coupe and sedan. Standard equipment included four-wheel independent suspension and four-wheel disc brakes. New features included a new grille treatment, a luggage rack on the base models, panel lamp with delay illumination, trunk cargo net and Delco Bose sound system. Aluminum wheels were optional equipment. Base Luminas had the 2.5-liter four-cylinder engine with three-speed automatic transmission as standard. A 3.1-liter V-6 was optional on base Luminas and standard on Euro models. A four-speed automatic overdrive transmission was optional across-the-board.

1991 Chevrolet, Caprice station wagon

1991 Chevrolet, Caprice Classic LTZ four-door sedan

CAPRICE — SERIES 1B — V-8 — All-new, 1991 Caprice and Caprice Classic sedans were unveiled in early 1990, joined by a Caprice station wagon and Ca-

price Classic LTZ sedan during the traditional 1991 model year. Totally redesigned inside and out, the exterior appearance was more aerodynamic with rounded edges. Standard equipment included air conditioning, simulated wood interior trim accents and driver's side airbag. New features included an anti-lock braking system, rear door child security locks, luggage area cargo net and two-way tailgate with wiper on the station wagon. Optional equipment included a ride and handling package, twilight sentinel headlamps, keyless remote door lock and trunk opener and tilt steering wheel. Standard powerplant across-the-board was the 5.0-liter V-8 mated to a four-speed automatic transmission. The new LTZ featured a 5.7-liter V-8 capable of 0-60 mph in under 10 seconds.

I.D. DATA: Chevrolets again had a 17-symbol Vehicle Identification Number (VIN) on the upper left surface of the instrument panel, visible through the windshield. Symbol one indicates country: '1' - U.S.A.; '2' - Canada. Next is a manufacturer code: 'G' - General Motors. Symbol three is car make: '1' - Chevrolet; '7' - GM of Canada. Symbols four and five denote car line/series: B/L - Caprice; B/N - Caprice Classic; F/P - Camaro; J/C - Cavalier; J/F - Cavalier Z24; L/T - Corsica; L/V - Beretta; L/W - Beretta GT; L/Z - Beretta GTZ; W/L - Lumina; W/N - Lumina Euro and W/P - Lumina Z34. Symbol six is the body style: '1' - 2-dr coupe/sedan, '2' - 2-dr hatchback, '3' - 2-dr convertible, '4' - 2-dr station wagon, '5' - 4-dr sedan, '6' - 4-dr hatchback, '8' - 4-dr station wagon. Symbol seven is the restraint system: '1' - active (manual) belts, '3' - active (manual) belts w/ driver's side airbag, '4' - passive (automatic belts). Symbol eight is the engine code: 'A' - 2.3-liter four-cyl.; 'E' and 'F' - 5.0-liter V-8; 'G' - 2.2-liter four-cyl.; 'J' - 5.7-liter V-8; 'R' - 2.5-liter four-cyl.; 'T' - 3.1-liter V-6; 'X' - 3.4-liter V-6; '7' and '8' - 5.7-liter V-8. This is followed by symbol nine, which is a check digit. Symbol ten is 'M' for model year 1991. Symbol eleven indicates assembly plant. The final six digits are the sequential serial number.

CAVALIER VL (FOUR/V-6)

Model No.	Body/Style No.	Body Type & Seating	Factory Price	Shipping Weight	Prod. Total
1J	C37/WV9	2-dr. Coupe-5P	7995	2480	Note 1
1J	C69/WV9	4-dr. Sedan-5P	8270	2491	Note 2
1J	C35/WV9	4-dr. Sta Wag-5P	9225	2587	Note 3

CAVALIER RS (FOUR/Convertible only V-6)

Model No.	Body/Style No.	Body Type & Seating	Factory Price	Shipping Weight	Prod. Total
1J	C37	2-dr. Coupe-5P	9065	2436	Note 1
1J	C69	4-dr. Sedan-5P	9265	2444	Note 2
1J	C67	2-dr. Conv-5P	15214	2753	5,882
1J	C35	4-dr. Sta Wag-5P	10270	2587	Note 3

Cavalier Engine Note: A V-6 engine cost $685 additional.

CAVALIER Z24 (V-6)

Model No.	Body/Style No.	Body Type & Seating	Factory Price	Shipping Weight	Prod. Total
1J	F37	2-dr. Coupe-5P	12050	2688	Note 1

Note 1: Total Cavalier coupe production was 171,759 with no further breakout available.

Note 2: Total Cavalier sedan production was 125,713 with no further breakout available.

Note 3: Total Cavalier station wagon production was 23,493 with no further breakout available.

CAMARO RS (V-6/V-8)

1F	P87	2-dr. Cpe-4P	12180/12530	3103/3263	Note 1
1F	P67	2-dr. Conv-4P	17960/18310	3203/3363	Note 2

CAMARO Z-28 (V-8)

1F	P87/Z28	2-dr. Cpe-4P	15455	3319	Note 1
1F	P67/Z28	2-dr. Conv-4P	20815	3400	Note 2

Note 1: Total Camaro coupe production was 92,306 with no further breakout available.

Note 2: Total Camaro convertible production was 8,532 with no further breakout available.

CORSICA LT (FOUR/V-6)

1L	T69	4-dr. Sedan-5P	10070/10755	2638/2742	187,981
1L	T68	4-dr. Hatch-5P	10745/11430	2706/2810	2,525

BERETTA (FOUR/V-6)

1L	V37	2-dr. Coupe-5P	10365/11050	2649/2749	Note 1
1L	W37	2-dr. GT Cpe-5P	----/13150	----/2797	Note 1
1L	Z37	2-dr. GTZ Cpe-5P	14550/----	2795/----	Note 1

Note 1: Total Beretta coupe production was 69,868 with no further breakout available.

LUMINA (FOUR/V-6)

1W	L27	2-dr. Coupe-6P	12670/13330	3111/3239	Note 1
1W	L69	4-dr. Sedan-6P	12870/13530	3192/3320	Note 2

LUMINA EURO (V-6)

1W	N27	2-dr. Coupe-6P	14795	3239	Note 1
1W	N69	4-dr. Sedan-6P	14995	3321	Note 2

LUMINA Z34 (V-6)

1W	P27	2-dr. Coupe-6P	17275	3374	Note 1

Note 1: Total Lumina coupe production was 36,345 with no further breakout available.

Note 2: Total Lumina sedan production was 159,482 with no further breakout available.

CAPRICE (V-8)

1B	L19	4-dr. Sedan-6P	16515	3907	Note 1
1B	L35	4-dr. 3S Wag-8P	17875	4354	15,000

CAPRICE CLASSIC (V-8)

1B	N19	4-dr. Sedan-6P	18470	3951	Note 1
1B	N19/B4U	4-dr. Sedan-6P	N/A	N/A	Note 1

Note 1: Total Caprice sedan production was 89,297 with no further breakout available.

FACTORY PRICE AND WEIGHT NOTE: For Corsica/Beretta and Lumina, prices and weights to left of slash are for four-cylinder, to right for V-6 engine. For Camaro RS, figures to left of slash are for six-cylinder model, to right of slash for V-8.

BODY/STYLE NO. NOTE: Some models were actually option packages. Code after the slash (e.g., B4U) is the number of the option package that comes with the model listed.

ENGINE DATE: BASE FOUR (Cavalier, Corsica/Beretta): Inline. Overhead valve. Four-cylinder. Cast iron block and aluminum head. Displacement: 133 cu. in. (2.2 liters). Bore & stroke: 3.50 x 3.46 in. Compression ratio: 9.0:1 Brake horsepower: 95 at 5200 RPM. Torque: 120 lb.-ft. at 3200 RPM. Hydraulic valve lifters. Throttle-body fuel injection. BASE QUAD FOUR (Beretta GTZ): Inline. Dual overhead cam (16-valve). Four-cylinder. Cast iron block and aluminum head. Displacement: 138 cu. in. (2.3 liters). Bore & stroke: 3.63 x 3.35 in. Compression ratio: 10.0:1. Brake horsepower: 180 at 6200 RPM. Torque: 160 lb.-ft. at 5200 RPM. Hydraulic valve lifters. Port fuel injection. BASE FOUR (Lumina): Inline. Overhead valve. Four-cylinder. Cast iron block and head. Displacement: 151 cu. in. (2.5 liters). Bore & stroke: 4.00 x 3.00 in. Compression ratio: 8.3:1. Brake horsepower: 105 at 4800 RPM. Torque: 135 lb.-ft. at 3200 RPM. Hydraulic valve lifters. Throttle-body fuel injection. BASE V-6 (Camaro RS coupe, Cavalier Z24, Beretta GT, Lumina Euro); OPTIONAL (Cavalier wagon, Corsica/Beretta/Beretta GTZ, Lumina): Overhead-valve V-6. Cast iron block and head. Displacement: 191 cu. in. (3.1 liters). Bore & stroke: 3.50 x 3.31 in. Compression ratio: 8.8:1. Brake horsepower: 140 at 4400 RPM. Torque: 180 lb.-ft. at 3800 RPM. Hydraulic valve lifters. Port fuel injection. BASE V-6 (Lumina Z34): Dual overhead cam (16-valve). V-6. Cast iron block and aluminum head. Displacement: 207 cu. in. (3.4 liters). Bore & stroke: 3.62 x 3.31 in. Compression ratio: 9.25:1. Brake horsepower: 210 at 5200 RPM. Torque: 215 lb.-ft. at 4000 RPM. Hydraulic valve lifters. Port fuel injection. BASE V-8 (Camaro RS conv., Camaro Z28, Caprice/Caprice Classic/Caprice Classic LTZ): 90-degree, overhead-valve V-8. Cast iron block and head. Displacement: 305 cu. in. (5.0 liters). Bore & stroke: 3.74 x 3.48 in. Compression ratio: 9.3:1. Brake horsepower: 230 at 4400 RPM. Torque: 255 lb.-ft. at 2400 RPM. Hydraulic valve lifters. Port fuel injection (except Caprice/Caprice Classic/Caprice Classic LTZ - Throttle-body fuel injection). OPTIONAL (Camaro RS coupe): Same as 305 cu. in. V-8 above except - Brake horsepower: 170 at 4000 RPM. OPTIONAL V-8 (Camaro Z28 coupe, Caprice Classic LTZ): 90-degree, overhead-valve V-8. Cast iron block and head. Displacement: 350 cu. in. (5.7 liters). Bore & stroke: 4.00 x 3.48 in. Compression ratio: 9.3:1. Brake horsepower: 245 at 4400 RPM. Torque: 345 lb.-ft. at 3200 RPM. Hydraulic valve lifters. Port fuel injection.

CHASSIS DATA: Wheelbase: (Cavalier) 101.3 in.; (Camaro) 101.0 in.; (Corsica/Beretta) 103.4 in.; (Lumina) 107.5 in.; (Caprice) 115.9 in. Overall length: (Cav cpe/sed) 182.3 in.; (Cav wag) 181.1 in.; (Camaro) 192.6 in.; (Corsica/Beretta) 183.4 in.; (Lumina cpe) 198.4 in.; (Lumina sed) 198.3 in.; (Lumina Z34) 199.3 in.; (Caprice sed) 214.1 in.; (Capr wag) 217.3 in. Height: (Cavalier sed) 52.9 in.; (Cavalier cpe/Z24) 51.3; (Cavalier wag) 52.8; (Camaro) 50.4 in.; (Corsica/Beretta) 56.2 in.; (Lumina cpe) 53.3 in.; (Lumina sed) 53.6 in.; (Caprice) 56.7 in.; (Caprice wag) 60.9 in. Width: (Cavalier) 66.3 in.; (Camaro) 72.4 in.; (Corsica/Beretta) 68.2 in.; (Lumina cpe) 71.7 in.; (Lumina sed) 71.0 in.; (Caprice sed) 77.0 in.; (Capr wag) 79.6 in. Front Tread: (Cavalier) 55.9 in.; (Cavalier conv/Z24) 55.8 in.; (Camaro) 60.0 in.; (Corsica/Beretta) 55.6 in.; (Lumina) 59.5 in.; (Caprice sed) 61.8 in.; (Caprice wag) 62.1 in. Rear Tread: (Cavalier) 55.4 in.; (Cavalier conv/Z24) 55.2 in.; (Camaro) 60.9 in.; (Corsica/Beretta) 55.1 in.; (Lumina) 58.0 in.; (Caprice sed) 60.7 in.; (Caprice wag) 64.1 in. Standard Tires: (Cavalier) P185/75R14; (Cavalier Z24) P205/60R15; (Camaro RS) P215/65R15; (Camaro Z28) P235/55R16; (Corsica/Beretta) P185/75R14; (Beretta GT) P195/70R14; (Lumina) P195/75R14; (Lumina Euro) P205/70R15; (Lumina Z34) P225/60R16; (Caprice sed) P215/75R15; (Caprice wag) P225/75R15; (Caprice Classic LTZ) P235/70VR15.

TECHNICAL: Transmission: Five-speed manual shift standard on Cavalier, Corsica/Beretta, Camaro and Lumina Z34. Three-speed automatic standard on Lumina. Four-speed overdrive automatic standard on Caprice. Steering: (Camaro/Caprice) recirculating ball; (others) rack and pinion. Front Suspension: (Cavalier) MacPherson struts with coil springs, lower control arms and stabilizer bar; (Corsica/Beretta) MacPherson struts with coil springs; (Camaro) modified MacPherson struts with coil springs; (Lumina) MacPherson struts with coil springs and stabilizer bar; (Caprice) unequal-length control arms, coil springs, stabilizer bar. Rear Suspension: (Cavalier) trailing crank arm with twist beam axle and coil springs; (Camaro) Salisbury axle and torque arm with ICA, coil springs and track bar; (Corsica/Beretta) trailing twist axle with coil springs; (Lumina) Tubular struts with transverse leaf spring and stabilizer bar; (Caprice) Salisbury four link coil springs, stabilizer available. Brakes: front disc, rear drum; four-wheel discs standard on Lumina; anti-lock on Caprice. Body construction: unibody except (Caprice) separate body and frame. Fuel tank: (Cavalier) 13.6 gal.; (Camaro) 15.5 gal.; (Corsica/Beretta) 15.6 gal.; (Lumina) 17.1 gal.; (Caprice sed) 23.0 gal.; (Caprice wag) 22.0 gal.

DRIVETRAIN OPTIONS: Engines: 3.1-liter V-6: Cavalier wagon ($685); Corsica/Beretta ($685); Lumina ($660). 5.0-liter V-8: Camaro RS cpe ($350). 5.7-liter V-8: Camaro Z28 ($300). Transmission/Differential: Three-speed automatic trans.: Cavalier ($495); Corsica/Beretta ($555). Four-speed overdrive auto. trans.: Camaro ($530); Lumina V-6 ($200). Limited-slip differential: Caprice ($100). Performance axle ratio w/dual exhausts: Camaro ($675). Suspension: F41 sport susp.: Caprice ($49). Auto leveling susp.: Caprice wag ($175).

CAVALIER CONVENIENCE/APPEARANCE OPTIONS: VL Preferred Equip. Grp 1: Elect Tuned AM/FM Stereo Radio, w/Seek & Scan & Digital Clock, w/extended range sound system; Tinted glass, all windows; Spt. LH Remote & RH Manual Mirrors; Color-Keyed Carpeted Mats, F&R ($500). VL Station Wagon Preferred Equip. Grp: Elect Tuned AM/FM Stereo Radio, w/Seek & Scan & Digital Clock, w/extended range sound system; Spt LH Remote & RH Manual Mirrors; Color-Keyed Carpeted Mats, F&R ($395). RS Preferred Equip. Grp 1 (1JC37, 1JC69 only): Folding Split Back Rear Seat; Intermittent Windshield Wiper System; Spt LH Remote & RH Manual Mirrors; Instrument Panel Mounted Reading Lamp; Dual Covered Visor Vanity Mirrors; Color-Keyed Carpeted Mats, F&R; Cargo Retaining Net ($327). RS Station Wagon Preferred Equip Grp: Folding Split Back Rear Seat; Intermittent Windshield Wiper System; Spt. LH Remote & RH Manual Mirrors; Instrument Panel Mounted Reading Lamp; Dual Covered Visor Vanity Mirrors; Color-Keyed Carpeted Mats ($197). RS Preferred Equip. Grp 2 (1JC37, 1JC69 only): Air Cond; Elect Spd Control, w/resume speed; Comfortilt Strg Wheel; Folding Split Back Rear Seat; Intermittent Windshield Wiper System; Spt LH Remote & RH Manual Mirrors; Instrument Panel Mounted Reading Lamp; Dual Covered Visor Vanity Mirrors; Color-Keyed Carpeted Mats, F&R; Cargo Retaining Net ($1442). RS Preferred Equip. Grp. 3 (1JC37, 1JC69 only): Air Cond; Elect Tuned AM/FM Stereo Radio, w/Seek & Scan, Stereo Cass. Tape & Digital Clock w/extended range sound system; Pwr Windows; Pwr Door Lock System; Pwr Trunk Opener; Spd Control; w/resume speed; Comfortilt Strg Wheel; Folding Split Back Rear Seat; Intermittent Windshield Wiper System; Spt LH Remote & RH Manual Mirrors; Instrument Panel Mounted Reading Lamp; Dual Covered Visor Vanity Mirrors; Color-Keyed Carpeted Mats, F&R: Coupe ($2117). Sedan ($2222). Preferred Equip. Grp 1 RS Convertible: Air Cond; Intermittent Windshield Wiper System; Instrument Panel Mounted Reading Lamp; Color-Keyed Carpeted Mats ($848). Preferred Equip. Grp 2 RS Convertible: Air Cond.; Elect Tuned AM/FM Stereo Radio, w/Seek & Scan, Stereo Cass. Tape & Digital Clock, w/extended range sound system; Elect Spd Control, w/resume speed; Comfortilt Strg Wheel; Intermittent Windshield Wiper System; Instrument Panel Mounted Reading Lamp; Color-Keyed Carpeted Mats, F&R; Cargo Retaining Net ($1388). Z24 Preferred Equip. Grp 1: Air Cond; Elect Tuned AM/FM Stereo Radio, w/Seek & Scan, Stereo Cass. Tape & Digital Clock, w/extended range sound system; Elect Spd Control, w/resume speed; Comfortilt Strg Wheel; Intermittent Windshield Wiper System; Color-Keyed Carpeted Mats, F&R; Dome Reading Lamp ($1377). Z24 Preferred Equip. Grp. 2: Air Cond; Elect Tuned AM/FM Stereo Radio, w/Seek & Scan, Stereo Cass. Tape & Digital Clock, w/extended range sound system; Spd Control w/resume speed; Pwr Windows; Pwr Door Lock System; Pwr Trunk Opener; Comfortilt Strg Wheel; Intermittent Windshield Wiper System; Color-Keyed Carpeted Mats, F&R; Dome Reading Lamp ($1912). Air Cond ($745). Frt License Plate Bracket (NC). Cargo Retaining Net ($30). Deck Lid Carrier, Black ($115). Roof Carrier ($115). Electric Rear Window Defogger ($170). Dome Reading Lamp ($24). Pwr Door Lock System, Cpe ($210). Sed & Wag ($250). Flr Mats, F&R ($33). Tinted Glass ($105). Reading Lamp, Instr. Panel Mounted ($5). Folding Split Back Rear Seat: Sed ($150); Wag ($50). Spd Control, w/resume speed ($225). Spoiler, Z24 ($110). Comfortilt Strg Wheel ($145). Removable Sunroof ($350). Pwr Trunk Opener ($60). Pwr Windows: Cpe (265); Sed & Wag ($330). Intermittent Wipers ($65). Eng. Block Htr ($20). Calif. Emission System ($100). Z51 Perf Handling Pkg: P195/70R14 tires; Level II Spt Susp.; Gauge Pkg w/tach ($205). TIRES: P185/75R14 All Seasons Steel Belted Radial Blackwall (NC). P195/70R14 All Seasons Steel Belted Radial Blackwall (NC). P205/60R15 Steel Belted Radial Blackwall (NC). P205/60R15 Steel Belted Radial White Outline Lettered ($98).

CAMARO CONVENIENCE/APPEARANCE OPTIONS: RS Coupe Preferred Equip. Grp 1: Air Cond; Elect Tuned AM/FM Stereo Radio, w/Seek & Scan, Stereo Cass. Tape, w/Search & Repeat & Digital Clock, w/extended range sound system; Body Side Moldings; Color-Keyed Carpeted Mats ($1085). RS Coupe Preferred Equip. Grp. 2: Air Cond; Elect Tuned AM/FM Stereo Radio, w/Seek & Scan, Stereo Cass. Tape, w/Search & Repeat & Digital Clock, w/extended range sound system; Pwr Windows; Pwr Door Locks; Elect Spd Control, w/resume speed; Pwr Hatch Release; Cargo Cover; Body Side Moldings; Color-Keyed Carpeted Mats, F&R; Mirror, w/Dual Reading Lamps ($1937). RS Convertible Preferred Equip. Grp. 1: Air Cond; Elect Tuned AM/FM Stereo Radio, w/Seek & Scan, Stereo Cass. Tape, w/Search & Repeat & Digital Clock, w/extended range sound system; Body Side Moldings; Color-Keyed Carpeted Mats ($1085). RS Convertible Preferred Equip. Grp. 2: Air Cond; Elect Tuned AM/FM Stereo Radio, w/Seek & Scan, Stereo Cass. Tape, w/Search & Repeat & Digital Clock, w/extended range sound system; Pwr Windows; Pwr Door Locks; Elect Spd Control, w/resume speed; Body Side Moldings; Color-Keyed Carpeted Mats ($1785). Z28 Preferred Equip. Grp. 1: Air Cond; Body Side Moldings; Color-Keyed Carpeted Mats, F&R ($925). Z28 Preferred Equip. Grp. 2: Air Cond; Elect Tuned AM/FM Stereo Radio, w/Seek & Scan; Stereo Cass. Tape, w/Search & Repeat & Digital Clock, w/extended range sound system; Pwr Windows; Pwr Door Lock System; Elect Spd Control, w/resume speed; Pwr Hatch Release; Cargo Cover; Body Side Moldings; Color-Keyed Carpeted Mats, F&R; Mirror, w/Dual Reading Lamps ($1937). Z28 Preferred Equip. Grp. 3: Air Cond; Elect Tuned AM/FM Stereo Radio, w/Seek & Scan; Stereo Cass. Tape, w/Search & Repeat & Digital Clock, w/extended range sound system; Pwr Windows; Pwr Door Lock System; Elect Spd Control, w/resume speed; Pwr Hatch Release; Cargo Cover; Body Side Moldings; Color-Keyed Carpeted Mats, F&R; Mirror, w/Dual Reading Lamps; Pwr Driver's Seat; Spt Elect Twin Remote Mirrors ($2333). Z28 Convertible Preferred Equip. Grp 1: Air Cond; Body Side Moldings; Color-Keyed Carpeted Mats, F&R ($925). Z28 Convertible Preferred Equip. Grp. 2: Air Cond; Elect Tuned AM/FM Stereo Radio, w/Seek & Scan, Stereo Cass. Tape, w/Search & Repeat & Digital Clock, w/extended range sound system; Pwr Windows; Pwr Door Locks; Elect Spd Control, w/resume speed; Body Side Moldings; Color-Keyed Carpeted Mats, F&R ($1785). Z28 Convertible Preferred Equip. Grp 3: Air Cond; Elect Tuned AM/FM Stereo Radio, w/Seek & Scan, Stereo Cass. Tape, w/Search & Repeat & Digital Clock, w/extended range sound system; Pwr Windows; Pwr Door Locks; Elect Spd Control, w/resume speed; Body Side Moldings; Color-Keyed Carpeted Mats, F&R; Pwr Driver's Seat; Spt Elect Twin Remote Mirrors ($2181). 5.0-liter V-8 ($350). 5.7-liter V-8 ($300). Custom Cloth Bucket Seats ($327). Custom Leather Bucket Seats ($850). Air Cond, Incl increased cooling ($830). Frt License Plate Bracket (NC). Elect Rear Window Defogger ($170). Pwr Door Lock System ($210). Calif. Emission System ($100).

Pwr Hatch Release ($60). Eng. Block Htr ($20). Rear Window Louvers ($210). Spt. Elect Twin Remote Mirrors ($91). Delco/Bose Elect Tuned AM/FM Stereo, w/Seek & Scan, Stereo Cass. Tape & Digital Clock ($1015). Removable Glass Roof Panels, Incl locks ($895). TIRES: P235/55R16 Steel Belted Radial Blackwall ($170). P245/50ZR16 Steel Belted Radial Blackwall ($400). Cast Alum Wheels 16-in. (NC).

CORSICA CONVENIENCE/APPEARANCE OPTIONS: LT Preferred Equip. Grp. 1: Intermittent Windshield Wiper System; Color-Keyed Carpeted Mats, F&R; Rearview Mirror, w/Reading Lamps ($121). LT Preferred Equip. Grp 2: Air Cond; Elect Spd Control, w/resume speed; Comfortilt Strg Wheel; Intermittent Windshield Wiper System; Color-Keyed Carpeted Mats, F&R; Rearview Mirror, w/Reading Lamps ($1296). LT Preferred Equip. Grp 3: Air Cond; Elect Tuned AM/FM Stereo Radio, w/Seek & Scan, Stereo Cass. Tape & Digital Clock, w/extended range sound system; Pwr Windows; Pwr Door Lock System; Elect Spd Control, w/resume speed; Comfortilt Strg Wheel; Intermittent Windshield Wiper System; Trunk/hatch Opener; Color-Keyed Carpeted Mats, F&R; Rearview Mirror, w/Reading Lamps ($2146). Custom Two-Tone Paint ($123). Air Cond, Incl increased cooling ($805). Frt License Plate Bracket (NC). Deck Lid Carrier, Black ($115). B19 Comfort Convenience Pkg: Luggage Area Cargo Net; 4-Way Adj. Pass Seat; Sliding Sun Shade Ext. & Visor Mirrors: Hatchback ($85); Notchback ($235). Electric Rear Window Defogger ($170). Pwr Door Lock System ($250). Calif. Emission System ($100). Gauge Pkg w/Tach, Incl Voltmeter, Oil Pressure, Temperature Gauges & Trip Odometer ($139). Eng. Block Htr ($20). Rearview Mirror, w/Reading Lamp ($23). Elect Spd Control, w/resume speed ($225). Comfortilt Strg Wheel ($145). Pwr Trunk Release ($60). Intermittent Wipers ($65). Pwr Driver's Side Window ($350). Z52 Spt Handling Pkg: 15-in. alum wheels; Level III Spt Susp.; Body Side Mldgs, w/red inserts; Spt Strg Wheel ($395). TIRES: P185/75R14 All Seasons Steel Belted Radial White Stripe ($68). Styled Wheels ($56).

BERETTA CONVENIENCE/APPEARANCE OPTIONS: Preferred Equip. Grp. 1: Intermittent Windshield Wiper System; Color-Keyed Carpeted Mats, F&R; Rearview Mirror, w/Reading Lamps; Visor Mirrors, w/Sun Shade Ext. ($141). Preferred Equip. Grp. 2: Air Cond; Elect Spd Control, w/resume speed; Comfortilt Strg Wheel; Intermittent Windshield Wiper System; Color-Keyed Carpeted Mats, F&R; Rearview Mirror, w/Reading Lamps; Visor Mirrors, w/Sun Shade Ext. ($1316). Preferred Equip. Grp. 3: Air Cond; Elect Tuned AM/FM Stereo Radio, w/Seek & Scan; Stereo Cass. Tape & Digital Clock, w/extended range sound system; Pwr Windows; Pwr Door Lock System; Pwr Trunk Opener; Elect Spd Control, w/resume speed; Comfortilt Strg Wheel; Intermittent Windshield Wiper System; Color-Keyed Carpeted Mats, F&R; Rearview Mirror, w/Reading Lamps; Visor Mirrors, w/Sun Shade Ext. ($2061). GT Preferred Equip. Grp. 1: Elect Spd Control, w/resume speed;

Comfortilt Strg Wheel; Intermittent Windshield Wiper System; Color-Keyed Carpeted Mats, F&R; Rearview Mirror, w/Reading Lamps ($491). GT Preferred Equip. Grp. 2: Elect Tuned AM/FM Stereo Radio, w/Seek & Scan, Stereo Cass. Tape & Digital Clock, w/extended range sound system; Pwr Windows; Pwr Door Lock System; Pwr Trunk Opener; Elect Spd Control, w/resume speed; Comfortilt Strg Wheel; Intermittent Windshield Wiper System; Color-Keyed Carpeted Mats, F&R; Rearview Mirror, w/Reading Lamps ($1176). GTZ Preferred Equip. Grp. 1: Elect Spd Control, w/resume speed; Comfortilt Strg Wheel; Intermittent Windshield Wiper System; Color-Keyed Carpeted Mats, F&R ($403). GTZ Preferred Equip. Grp. 2: Elect Tuned AM/FM Stereo Radio, w/Seek & Scan; Stereo Cass. Tape & Digital Clock, w/extended range sound system; Pwr Windows; Pwr Door Lock System; Pwr Trunk Opener; Elect Spd Control, w/resume speed; Comfortilt Strg Wheel; Intermittent Windshield Wiper System; Color-Keyed Carpeted Mats, F&R ($1088). 3.1-liter V-6 ($685). Air Cond, Incl increased cooling ($805). Frt License Plate Bracket (NC). Deck Lid Carrier, Black ($115). Flr Mounted Console ($60). Elect Rear Window Defogger ($170). Pwr Door Lock System ($210). Color-Keyed Carpeted Flr Mats ($18). Calif. Emission System ($100). Gauge Pkg, w/Tach, Voltmeter, Oil Pressure, Temp Gauges, Trip Odometer ($139). Eng. Block Htr ($20). Elect Spd Control, w/resume speed ($225). Rear Spoiler ($110). Comfortilt Strg Wheel ($145). Manual Sunroof, Removable ($350). F41 Spt Susp. ($49). Pwr Trunk Opener ($60). Intermittent Wipers ($65). Pwr Windows ($275). TIRES: P195/70R14 All Seasons Steel Belted Radial Blackwall ($93).

LUMINA CONVENIENCE/APPEARANCE OPTIONS: Preferred Equip. Grp 1: Air Cond; Comfortilt Strg Wheel; Color-Keyed Carpeted Mats, F&R ($1020). Lumina Preferred Equip. Grp. 2: Air Cond; Elect Spd Control, w/resume speed; Comfortilt Strg Wheel; Deck Lid Carrier, Blk; Luggage Area Cargo Retaining Net; Color-Keyed Carpeted Mats, F&R ($1390). Lumina Preferred Equip. Grp. 3: Air Cond; Elect Spd Control, w/resume speed; Pwr Windows; Pwr Door Lock System; Pwr Trunk Opener; Comfortilt Strg Wheel; Deck Lid Carrier, Blk; Luggage Area Cargo Retaining Net; Spt Twin Remote Mirrors; Color-Keyed Carpeted Mats, F&R: Cpe ($1955); Sed ($2060). Euro Preferred Equip. Grp. 1: Elect Spd Control, w/resume speed; Comfortilt Strg Wheel; Gauge Pkg w/Tach; Cargo Area Retaining Net; Color-Keyed Carpeted Mats, F&R ($545). Euro Preferred Equip. Grp. 2: Elect Tuned AM/FM Stereo Radio, w/Seek & Scan, Stereo Cass. Tape & Digital Clock, w/extended range sound system; Pwr Windows; Pwr Door Lock System; Pwr Trunk Opener; Elect Spd Control, w/resume speed; Comfortilt Strg Wheel; Gauge Pkg. w/Tach; Cargo Area Retaining Net; Spt Twin Remote Mirrors; Color-Keyed Carpeted Mats, F&R: Cpe ($1250); Sed ($1355). Z34 Preferred Equip. Grp. 1: Delco/Bose Elect Tuned AM/FM Stereo Radio, w/Seek & Scan, Stereo Cass. Tape & Digital Clock, w/extended range sound system; Pwr Windows; Pwr Door Lock System; Pwr Trunk Opener ($870). Custom Cloth Bucket Seats w/console ($299). Custom Cloth 60/40 Seat ($199). Cloth 60/40 Seat ($159). 3.1-liter V-6 ($660). Air Cond, Std/Euro ($830). Frt License Plate Bracket (NC). Electric Rear Window Defogger ($170). Pwr Door Lock System: Cpe ($210); Sed ($250). Pwr Windows: Cpe ($265); Sed ($330). Pwr Trunk Opener ($60). Cargo Area Retaining Net ($30). Color-Keyed Carpeted Mats ($20). Calif. Emission System ($100). Deck Lid Carrier ($115). Trans Oil Cooler ($75). Gauge Pkg, w/Tach ($100). Spt Twin Remote Mirrors ($30). Pwr 6-way Driver's Seat ($305). Elect Spd Control, w/resume speed ($225). Comfortilt Strg Wheel ($145). Rear Spoiler, Delete ($128 credit). TIRES: P195/75R14 All Seasons Steel Belted Radial White Stripe ($72). P215/60R16 All Seasons Steel Belted Radial Blackwall ($112).

CAPRICE CONVENIENCE/APPEARANCE OPTIONS: Caprice Sed Preferred Equip. Grp. 1: Pwr Windows; Pwr Door Lock System; Pwr Trunk Opener; Elect Spd Control, w/resume speed; Comfortilt Strg Wheel; Color-Keyed Carpeted Mats, F&R ($1065). Caprice Sed Preferred Equip. Grp. 2: Elect Tuned AM/FM Stereo Radio, w/Seek & Scan, Stereo Cass. Tape & Digital Clock, w/extended range sound system; Pwr Windows; Pwr Door Lock System; Pwr Trunk Opener; Elect Spd Control, w/resume speed; Comfortilt Strg Wheel; Pwr 6-Way Driver's Seat; Elect Twin Remote Mirrors; Rearview Mirror Dual Reading Lamps; Illum RH Visor, w/mirror; Color-Keyed Carpeted Mats, F&R ($1766). Caprice Classic Sed Preferred Equip. Grp. 1: Elect Tuned AM/FM Stereo Radio, w/Seek & Scan, Stereo Cass. Tape & Digital Clock, w/extended range sound system; Pwr 6-Way Driver's Seat; Elect Spd Control, w/resume speed; Comfortilt Strg Wheel; Pwr Trunk Opener; Illum RH Visor, w/mirror; Color-Keyed Carpeted Mats, F&R ($983). Caprice Classic Sed Preferred Equip Grp 2: Delco/Bose Elect Tuned AM/FM Stereo Radio, w/Seek & Scan, Stereo Cass. Tape & Digital Clock; Pwr 6-Way Driver & Pass Seats; Pwr Door Lock System; Pwr Trunk Opener; Elect Spd Control, w/resume speed; Comfortilt Strg Wheel; Elect Twin Remote Mirrors; Pwr Twilight Sentinel Headlamp System; Dual Reading Lamps, w/Elect Compass in Rearview Mirror; Illum RH Visor ($1748). Caprice Station Wagon Preferred Equip. Grp. 1: Elect Tuned AM/FM Stereo Radio, w/Seek & Scan, Stereo Cass. Tape & Digital Clock, w/extended range sound system; Pwr Windows; Pwr Door Lock System; Pwr Tailgate Lock; Elect Spd Control, w/resume speed; Comfortilt Strg Wheel; Color-Keyed Carpeted Mats, F&R ($1245) Caprice Station Wagon Preferred Equip. Grp. 2: Elect Tuned AM/FM Stereo Radio, w/Seek & Scan, Stereo Cass. Tape & Digital Clock, w/extended range sound system; Pwr 6-Way Driver's Seat; Pwr Windows; Pwr Door Lock System; Pwr Tailgate Lock; Dlx Rear Comp Decor; Elect Twin Remote Mirrors; Elect Spd Control, w/resume speed; Comfortilt Strg Wheel; Dual Reading Lamps in Rearview Mirror; Illum RH Visor; Color-Keyed Carpeted Mats, F&R ($1890). Cloth 55/45 Seat ($223). Leather 45/55 Seat ($645). Custom Two-Tone Paint, Incl lower body accent, color-keyed striping & o/s door handle inserts ($141). Limited Slip Rear Axle

($100). Frt License Plate Bracket (NC). Electric Rear Window Defogger ($170). Pwr Door Lock System: Sed ($250); Wag, Incl Tailgate Lock ($325). Calif. Emission System ($100). LTZ Option Pkg: 3.23 Limited Slip Axle; Spt Susp., w/H.D. frame, brakes, cooling; Dual Pwr Mirrors; Leather-wrapped Strg Wheel; Digital Instrumentation, Incl Tach; P235/70VR15 tires; Keyless Entry System ($825). Engine block heater ($20). Pin Striping, Color-Keyed ($61). Auto Leveling Susp. ($175). F41 Ride/Handling Pkg ($49). V92 Trailering Pkg: Sed ($220); Wag ($171). TIRES: P215/75R15 All Seasons Steel Belted Radial White Stripe ($80). P225/70R15 Steel Belted Radial White Stripe ($176). Custom Wheel Covers ($215).

HISTORY: Chevrolet's market share for U.S.-made passenger cars in model year 1991 was 10.9 percent, representing 895,569 units. The Chevy Caprice was voted *Motor Trend* magazine's "Car of the Year" in 1991.

1992

After a two-year absence, the Z24 convertible returned to the Cavalier lineup. The other all-new-for-1992 model was the Lumina 3.4 sedan. A special 25th Anniversary exterior appearance package, named the Heritage Edition, was available on all Camaro models. Anti-lock brakes became standard equipment on all Cavalier, Corsica, Beretta and Lumina Euro and Z34 models. The Corsica hatchback was dropped. The 2.2-liter four-cylinder engine powering the Cavalier and Beretta was upgraded from its 95 horsepower rating the year previous to 110 horsepower.

1992 Chevrolet, Cavalier RS two-door convertible

1992 Chevrolet, Cavalier RS four-door sedan

1992 Chevrolet, Cavalier Z34 two-door coupe

CAVALIER — SERIES 1J — FOUR/V-6 — The Cavalier lineup now offered two ragtops: one in the RS series and the new convertible in the Z24 series. Anti-lock brakes and power door locks were now standard equipment in all Cavaliers. The base 2.2-liter four-cylinder engine received multi-port fuel injection this year and its horsepower rating increased from 95 to 110. Cavalier again offered three series. The VL (Value Leader) series consisted of coupe, sedan and station wagon, while the RS series had those same three body styles plus a convertible. The Z24 series offered a coupe and the aforementioned ragtop. Standard equipment included the 2.2-liter engine and five-speed manual transmission (except on station wagons, which had the three-speed automatic as standard). The Z24 was powered by the 3.1-liter V-6, which was the option engine for the RS convertible and station wagon.

1992 Chevrolet, Camaro RS "Heritage Edition" two-door convertible

1992 Chevrolet, Camaro RS two-door coupe

CAMARO — SERIES 1F — V-6/V-8 — Twenty-five years after the debut of the Camaro, Chevrolet marked the anniversary with a "Heritage Edition" package, available on 1992 RS and Z28 models. Both series featured coupe and convertible models. Standard power plant for the RS line was the 3.1-liter V-6. The 5.0-liter V-8 was the base engine in the Z28 line, and optional for the RS coupe and ragtop. The Z28 coupe could be ordered with the 5.7-liter V-8. Base transmission was the five-speed manual while a four-speed automatic was optional across-the-board.

1992 Chevrolet, Corsica LT four-door sedan

1992 Chevrolet, Beretta two-door coupe

1992 Chevrolet, Beretta GT two-door coupe

1992 Chevrolet, Beretta GTZ two-door coupe

CORSICA/BERETTA — SERIES 1L — FOUR/V-6 —
The Corsica LT lineup now consisted of just the sedan as the hatchback sedan was dropped. The Beretta

lineup remained unchanged from the year previous, with three coupes offered: base, GT and GTZ. Anti-lock brakes became standard equipment this year. The base 2.2-liter four-cylinder engine was fitted with multi-port fuel injection, which gave it a 15-horsepower boost (from 95 to 110). The Corsica, base Beretta and Beretta GT were powered by a 2.2-liter engine. Beretta GTZ featured a 2.3-liter High Output Quad 4 engine rated at 180 horsepower. A 3.1-liter V-6 was the option engine for all four models. The five-speed manual transmission was standard and a three-speed automatic was optional on all except the Beretta GTZ with Quad 4 power.

1992 Chevrolet, Lumina four-door sedan

1992 Chevrolet, Lumina Euro two-door coupe

1992 Chevrolet, Lumina Euro four-door sedan

1992 Chevrolet, Lumina Euro 3.4 four-door sedan

1992 Chevrolet, Lumina Z34 two-door coupe

LUMINA — SERIES 1W — FOUR/V-6 — The Lumina lineup was expanded this year to include an option package called the Euro 3.4 sedan, powered by the 3.4-liter V-6 mated to a four-speed automatic transmission. The remainder of the lineup returned from 1991, and featured a base coupe and sedan, Euro coupe and sedan and Z34 coupe. The Lumina featured four-wheel disc brakes and anti-lock brakes were now standard equipment on the Euro and Z34 models. Base Luminas had the 2.5-liter four-cylinder engine with three-speed automatic transmission as standard. Euro models featured the 3.1-liter V-6 and three-speed automatic as standard, and optional on base Luminas. The Z34 also used the aforementioned 3.4-liter V-6 coupled to a five-speed manual transmission.

1992 Chevrolet, Caprice four-door sedan

1992 Chevrolet, Caprice station wagon

1992 Chevrolet, Caprice Classic four-door sedan

CAPRICE — SERIES 1B — V-8 — Totally new the year previous, the 1992 Caprice and Caprice Classic lineup was unchanged from 1991. Caprice offered a base sedan and station wagon while Caprice Classic featured a base sedan and LTZ sedan. Standard powerplant across-the-board was the 5.0-liter V-8 mated to a four-speed automatic transmission. The 5.7-liter V-8 was now offered as an option engine in the Caprice station wagon.

I.D. DATA: Chevrolets again had a 17-symbol Vehicle Identification Number (VIN) on the upper left surface of the instrument panel, visible through the windshield. Symbol one indicates country: '1' - U.S.A.; '2' - Canada. Next is a manufacturer code: 'G' - General Motors. Symbol three is car make: '1' - Chevrolet; '7' - GM of Canada. Symbols four and five denote car line/series: B/L - Caprice; B/N - Caprice Classic; F/P - Camaro; J/C - Cavalier; J/F - Cavalier Z24; L/T - Corsica; L/V - Beretta; L/W - Beretta GT; L/Z - Beretta GTZ; W/L - Lumina; W/N - Lumina Euro and W/P - Lumina Z34. Symbol six is the body style: '1' - 2-dr coupe/sedan, '2' - 2-dr hatchback, '3' - 2-dr convertible, '4' - 2-dr station wagon, '5' - 4-dr sedan, '6' - 4-dr hatchback, '8' - 4-dr station wagon. Symbol seven is the restraint system: '1' - active (manual) belts, '2' - active (manual) belts w/driver's and passenger's airbag, '3' - active (manual) belts w/driver's side airbag, '4' - passive (automatic) belts, '5' - passive (automatic) belts w/driver's side airbag. Symbol eight is the engine code: 'A' - 2.3-liter four-cyl.; 'E' and 'F' - 5.0-liter V-8; 'J' and 'P' - 5.7-liter V-8; 'R' - 2.5-liter four-cyl.; 'T' - 3.1-liter V-6; 'X' - 3.4-liter V-6; '4' - 2.2-liter four-cyl.; '7' - 5.7-liter V-8. This is followed by symbol nine, which is a check digit. Symbol ten is 'N' for model year 1992. Symbol eleven indicates assembly plant. The final six digits are the sequential serial number.

CAVALIER VL (FOUR/V-6)

Model No.	Body/Style No.	Body Type & Seating	Factory Price	Shipping Weight	Prod. Total
1J	C37/WV9	2-dr. Coupe-5P	9999	2509	Note 1
1J	C69/WV9	4-dr. Sedan-5P	8999	2520	Note 2
1J	C35/WV9	4-dr. Sta Wag-5P	10099	2617	Note 3

CAVALIER RS (FOUR/V-6)

1J	C37	2-dr. Coupe-5P	9999	2509	Note 1
1J	C69	4-dr. Sedan-5P	10199	2520	Note 2
1J	C67	2-dr. Conv-5P	15395	2672	Note 4
1J	C35	4-dr. Sta Wag-5P	11199	2617	Note 3

Cavalier Engine Note: A V-6 engine cost $610 additional.

CAVALIER Z24 (V-6)

1J	F37	2-dr. Coupe-5P	12995	2689	Note 1
1J	F67	2-dr. Conv-5P	18305	2826	Note 4

Note 1: Total Cavalier coupe production was 126,117 with no further breakout available.

Note 2: Total Cavalier sedan production was 70,786 with no further breakout available.

Note 3: Total Cavalier station wagon production was 19,685 with no further breakout available.

Note 4: Total Cavalier convertible production was 9,045 with no further breakout available.

CAMARO RS (V-6/V-8)

1F	P87	2-dr. Cpe-4P	12075/12444	3103/3384	Note 1
1F	P67	2-dr. Conv-4P	18055/18424	3203/3484	Note 2

CAMARO Z-28 (V-8)

1F	P87/Z28	2-dr. Cpe-4P	16055	3319	Note 1
1F	P67/Z28	2-dr. Conv-4P	21500	3400	Note 2

Note 1: Total Camaro coupe production was 66,191 with no further breakout available.

Note 2: Total Camaro convertible production was 3,816 with no further breakout available.

CORSICA LT (FOUR/V-6)

1L	T69	4-dr. Sedan-5P	10999/11609	2638/2742	144,833

BERETTA (FOUR/V-6)

1L	V37	2-dr. Coupe-5P	10999/11609	2649/2749	Note 1
1L	W37	2-dr. GT Cpe-5P	12575/13185	2697/2797	Note 1
1L	Z37	2-dr. GTZ Cpe-5P	15590/15440	2795/2895	Note 1

Note 1: Total Beretta coupe production was 52,451 with no further breakout available.

LUMINA (FOUR/V-6)

1W	L27	2-dr. Coupe-6P	13200/13860	3115/3224	Note 1
1W	L69	4-dr. Sedan-6P	13400/14060	3220/3328	Note 2

LUMINA EURO (V-6)

1W	N27	2-dr. Coupe-6P	15600	3256	Note 1
1W	N69	4-dr. Sedan-6P	15800	3361	Note 2

LUMINA Z34 (V-6)

1W	P27	2-dr. Coupe-6P	18400	3447	Note 1

Note 1: Total Lumina coupe production was 38,037 with no further breakout available.

Note 2: Total Lumina sedan production was 198,269 with no further breakout available.

CAPRICE (V-8)

1B	L19	4-dr. Sedan-6P	17300	3907	Note 1
1B	L35	4-dr. 3S Wag-8P	18700	4354	13,400

CAPRICE CLASSIC (V-8)

1B	N19	4-dr. Sedan-6P	19300	3951	Note 1
1B	N19/B4U	4-dr. Sedan-6P	N/A	N/A	Note 1

Note 1: Total Caprice sedan production was 103,381 with no further breakout available.

FACTORY PRICE AND WEIGHT NOTE: For Corsica/Beretta and Lumina, prices and weights to left of slash are for four-cylinder, to right for V-6 engine. For Camaro RS, figures to left of slash are for six-cylinder model, to right of slash for V-8.

BODY/STYLE NO. NOTE: Some models were actually option packages. Code after the slash (e.g., B4U) is the number of the option package that comes with the model listed.

ENGINE DATA: BASE FOUR (Cavalier, Corsica/Beretta, Beretta GT): Inline. Overhead valve. Four-cylinder. Cast iron block and aluminum head. Displacement: 133 cu. in. (2.2 liters). Bore & stroke: 3.50 x 3.46 in. Compression ratio: 9.0:1 Brake horsepower: 110 at 5200 RPM. Torque: 130 lb.-ft. at 3200 RPM. Hydraulic valve lifters. Port fuel injection. BASE QUAD FOUR (Beretta GTZ): Inline. Dual overhead cam (16-valve). Four-cylinder. Cast iron block and aluminum head. Displacement: 138 cu. in. (2.3 liters). Bore & stroke: 3.62 x 3.35 in. Compression ratio: 10.0:1. Brake horsepower: 180 at 6200 RPM. Torque: 160 lb.-ft. at 5200 RPM. Hydraulic valve lifters. Port fuel injection. BASE FOUR (Lumina): Inline. Overhead valve. Four-cylinder. Cast iron block and head. Displacement: 151 cu. in. (2.5 liters). Bore & stroke: 4.00 x 3.00 in. Compression ratio: 8.3:1. Brake horsepower: 105 at 4800 RPM. Torque: 135 lb.-ft. at 3200 RPM. Hydraulic valve lifters. Throttle-body fuel injection. BASE V-6 (Camaro RS, Cavalier Z24, Lumina Euro); OPTIONAL (Cavalier RS convertible/wagon, Corsica/Beretta/Beretta GT/Beretta GTZ, Lumina): Overhead-valve V-6. Cast iron block and head. Displacement: 191 cu. in. (3.1 liters). Bore & stroke: 3.50 x 3.31 in. Compression ratio: 8.8:1. Brake horsepower: 140 at 4200 RPM. Torque: 180 lb.-ft. at 3600 RPM. Hydraulic valve lifters. Port fuel injection. BASE V-6 (Lumina Euro 3.4/Lumina Z34): Dual overhead cam (24-valve). V-6. Cast iron block and aluminum head. Displacement: 207 cu. in. (3.4 liters). Bore & stroke: 3.62 x 3.31 in. Compression ratio: 9.3:1. Brake horsepower: 210 at 5000 RPM. Torque: 215 lb.-ft. at 4000 RPM. Hydraulic valve lifters. Port fuel injection. BASE V-8 (Camaro Z28, Caprice/Caprice Classic/Caprice Classic LTZ): 90-degree, overhead-valve V-8. Cast iron block and head. Displacement: 305 cu. in. (5.0 liters). Bore & stroke: 3.74 x 3.48 in. Compression ratio: 9.3:1. Brake horsepower: 170 at 4200 RPM for Caprice/230 at 4400 RPM for Camaro. Torque: 255 lb.-ft. at 2400 RPM for Caprice/285-300 lb.-ft. for Camaro. Hydraulic valve lifters. Throttle-body fuel injection for Caprice/Port fuel injection for Camaro. OPTIONAL (Camaro RS): Same as 305 cu. in. V-8 above except - Brake horsepower: 170 at 4000 RPM. OPTIONAL V-8 (Camaro Z28 coupe, Caprice wagon): 90-degree, overhead-valve V-8. Cast iron block and head. Displacement: 350 cu. in. (5.7 liters). Bore & stroke: 4.00 x 3.48 in. Compression ratio: 9.3:1 for Caprice/9.8:1 for Camaro. Brake horsepower: 180 at 4000 RPM for Caprice/245 at 4400 RPM for Camaro. Torque: 300 lb.-ft. at 2400 RPM for Caprice/345 lb.-ft. at 3200 RPM for Camaro. Hydraulic valve lifters. Throttle-body fuel injection for Caprice/Port fuel injection for Camaro.

CHASSIS DATA: Wheelbase: (Cavalier) 101.3 in.; (Camaro) 101.0 in.; (Corsica/Beretta) 103.4 in.; (Lumina) 107.5 in.; (Caprice) 115.9 in. Overall length: (Cav cpe/sed) 182.3 in.; (Cav wag) 181.1 in.; (Camaro) 192.6 in.; (Corsica/Beretta) 183.4 in.; (Lumina) 198.3 in.; (Lumina Euro 3.4) 199.3 in.; (Caprice sed) 214.1 in.; (Capr wag) 217.3 in. Height: (Cavalier cpe/wag) 52.0 in.; (Cavalier sed) 53.6; (Camaro) 50.4 in.; (Corsica/Beretta) 56.2 in.; (Lumina cpe) 53.3 in.; (Lumina sed) 53.6 in.; (Caprice) 56.7 in.; (Caprice wag) 60.9 in. Width: (Cavalier) 66.3 in.; (Camaro) 72.4 in.; (Corsica/Beretta) 68.2 in.; (Lumina cpe) 71.7; (Lumina sed) 71.0 in.; (Caprice sed) 77.0 in.; (Capr wag) 79.6 in. Front Tread: (Cavalier) 55.9 in.; (Cavalier conv) 55.8 in.; (Camaro) 60.0 in.;

(Corsica/Beretta) 55.6 in.; (Lumina) 59.5 in.; (Caprice sed) 61.8 in.; (Caprice wag) 62.1 in. Rear Tread: (Cavalier) 55.4 in.; (Cavalier conv/Z24) 55.2 in.; (Camaro) 60.9 in.; (Corsica/Beretta) 55.1 in.; (Lumina) 58.0 in.; (Caprice sed) 60.3 in.; (Caprice wag) 64.1 in. Standard Tires: (Cavalier) P185/75R14; (Cavalier Z24) P205/60R15; (Camaro RS) P215/65R15; (Camaro Z28) P235/55R16; (Corsica/Beretta) P185/75R14; (Beretta GT) P195/70R14; (Lumina) P195/75R14; (Lumina Euro) P205/70R15; (Lumina Z34) P225/60R16; (Caprice sed) P215/75R15; (Caprice wag) P225/75R15; (Caprice Classic LTZ) P235/70VR15.

TECHNICAL: Transmission: Five-speed manual shift standard on Cavalier, Corsica/Beretta, Camaro and Lumina Z34. Three-speed automatic standard on Cavalier wagon and Lumina. Four-speed overdrive automatic standard on Caprice. Steering: (Camaro/Caprice) recirculating ball; (others) rack and pinion. Front Suspension: (Cavalier) MacPherson struts with coil springs, lower control arms and stabilizer bar; (Corsica/Beretta) MacPherson struts with coil springs; (Camaro) modified MacPherson struts with coil springs; (Lumina) MacPherson struts with coil springs and stabilizer bar; (Caprice) unequal-length control arms, coil springs, stabilizer bar. Rear Suspension: (Cavalier) trailing crank arm with twist beam axle and coil springs; (Camaro) Salisbury axle and torque arm with ICA, coil springs and track bar; (Corsica/Beretta) trailing twist axle with coil springs; (Lumina) Tubular struts with transverse leaf spring and stabilizer bar; (Caprice) Salisbury four link coil springs, stabilizer available. Brakes: front disc, rear drum; four-wheel discs standard on Lumina; antilock brakes standard on Cavalier, Beretta/Corsica, Lumina Euro/Lumina Z34 and Caprice. Body construction: unibody except (Caprice) separate body and frame. Fuel tank: (Cavalier) 13.6 gal.; (Camaro) 15.5 gal.; (Corsica/Beretta) 15.6 gal.; (Lumina) 17.1 gal.; (Caprice sed) 23.0 gal.; (Caprice wag) 22.0 gal.

DRIVETRAIN OPTIONS: Engines: 3.1-liter V-6: Cavalier RS conv/wag ($610); Corsica/Beretta/Beretta GT ($610); Lumina ($660). 5.0-liter V-8: Camaro RS ($369). 5.7-liter V-8: Camaro Z28 cpe ($300); Caprice wag ($250). Transmission/Differential: Three-speed automatic trans.: Cavalier ($495); Corsica/Beretta ($555). Four-speed overdrive auto. trans.: Camaro ($530); Lumina V-6 ($200). Limited-slip differential: Caprice ($100). Performance axle ratio w/dual exhausts: Camaro ($675). Suspension: F41 sport susp.: Caprice ($49). Auto leveling susp.: Caprice wag ($175).

CAVALIER CONVENIENCE/APPEARANCE OPTIONS: VL Preferred Equip. Grp 1: Elect Tuned AM/FM Stereo Radio, w/Seek & Scan & Digital Clock, w/extended range sound system; Tinted glass, all windows; Spt. LH Remote & RH Manual Mirrors; Bodyside Moldings; Color-Keyed Carpeted Mats, F&R ($550). VL Station Wagon Preferred Equip. Grp: Elect Tuned AM/FM Stereo Radio, w/Seek & Scan & Digital Clock, w/extended range sound system; Spt LH Remote & RH Manual Mirrors; Bodyside Moldings; Color-Keyed Car-

peted Mats, F&R ($332). RS Preferred Equip. Grp 1 (1JC37, 1JC69 only): Air Cond; Folding Split Back Rear Seat; Intermittent Windshield Wiper System; Spt LH Remote & RH Manual Mirrors; Pwr Trunk Opener; Dome Mounted Reading Lamp; Dual Covered Visor Vanity Mirrors; Color-Keyed Carpeted Mats, F&R; Dlx Luggage Comp Trim ($672). RS Preferred Equip. Grp 2 (1JC37, 1JC69 only): Air Cond; Folding Split Back Rear Seat; Elect Spd Control, w/resume speed; Pwr Windows; Comfortilt Strg Wheel; Intermittent Windshield Wiper System; Spt LH Remote & RH Manual Mirrors; Pwr Trunk Opener; Dome Mounted Reading Lamp; Dual Covered Visor Vanity Mirrors; Color-Keyed Carpeted Mats, F&R; Dlx Luggage Comp Trim; Cargo Retaining Net ($1277). RS Station Wagon Preferred Equip Grp 1 (1JC35): Air Cond; Folding Split Back Rear Seat; Intermittent Windshield Wiper System; Spt. LH Remote & RH Manual Mirrors; Dome Mounted Reading Lamp; Dual Covered Visor Vanity Mirrors; Color-Keyed Carpeted Mats ($561). RS Station Wagon Preferred Equip. Grp 2 (1JC35): Air Cond; Elect Tuned AM/FM Stereo Radio, w/Seek & Scan & Digital Clock, w/extended range sound system; Elect Spd Control, w/resume speed; Pwr Windows; Roof Carrier; Comfortilt Strg Wheel; Folding Split Back Rear Seat; Intermittent Windshield Wiper System; Spt LH Remote & RH Manual Mirrors; Dome Mounted Reading Lamp; Dual Covered Visor Vanity Mirrors; Color-Keyed Carpeted Mats, F&R; Cargo Retaining Net ($1316). Preferred Equip. Grp 1 RS Convertible: Air Cond; Intermittent Windshield Wiper System; Instrument Panel Mounted Reading Lamp; Color-Keyed Carpeted Mats ($848). Preferred Equip. Grp 2 RS Convertible: Air Cond.; Elect Tuned AM/FM Stereo Radio, w/Seek & Scan, Stereo Cass. Tape & Digital Clock, w/extended range sound system; Elect Spd Control, w/resume speed; Comfortilt Strg Wheel; Intermittent Windshield Wiper System; Instrument Panel Mounted Reading Lamp; Color-Keyed Carpeted Mats, F&R; Cargo Retaining Net ($744). Z24 Coupe Preferred Equip. Grp 1: Air Cond; Comfortilt Strg Wheel; Intermittent Windshield Wiper System; Mech Trunk Opener; Color-Keyed Carpeted Mats, F&R; Dome Reading Lamp ($623). Z24 Coupe Preferred Equip. Grp. 2: Air Cond; Elect Tuned AM/FM Stereo Radio, w/Seek & Scan, Stereo Cass. Tape & Digital Clock, w/extended range sound system; Spd Control w/resume speed; Pwr Windows; Mech Trunk Opener; Comfortilt Strg Wheel; Intermittent Windshield Wiper System; Color-Keyed Carpeted Mats, F&R; Dome Reading Lamp; Cargo Area Retaining Net ($1083). Z24 Convertible Preferred Equip. Grp 1: Air Cond; Intermittent Windshield Wiper System; Color-Keyed Carpeted Mats, F&R; Dome Reading Lamp ($354). Z24 Coupe Preferred Equip. Grp. 2: Air Cond; Elect Tuned AM/FM Stereo Radio, w/Seek & Scan, Stereo Cass. Tape & Digital Clock, w/extended range sound system; Spd Control w/resume speed; Mech Trunk Opener; Comfortilt Strg Wheel; Intermittent Windshield Wiper System; Color-Keyed Carpeted Mats, F&R; Dome Reading Lamp; Cargo Area Retaining Net ($744). Air Cond ($745). Frt License Plate Bracket (NC). Cargo Retaining Net ($30). Deck Lid Carrier, Black ($115). Roof Carrier ($115). Electric Rear Window Defogger ($170). Dome Reading Lamp ($24). Tinted Glass ($105). Flr Mats, F&R ($33). Folding Split Back Rear Seat: Sed ($150); Wag ($50). Vinyl Bucket Seat, conv only ($75). Elect Spd Control, w/resume speed ($225). Spoiler, Z24 ($110). Comfortilt Strg Wheel ($145). Removable Sunroof ($350). Mech Trunk Opener ($11). Pwr Windows: Cpe (265); Sed & Wag ($330). Intermittent Wipers ($65). Eng. Block Htr ($20). Calif. Emission System (NA). Z51 Perf Handling Pkg: P195/70R14 tires; Level II Spt Susp.; Gauge Pkg w/tach, RS only ($224). TIRES: P185/75R14 All Seasons Steel Belted Radial Blackwall (NC). P195/70R14 All Seasons Steel Belted Radial Blackwall (NC). P205/60R15 Steel Belted Radial Blackwall (NC). P205/60R15 Steel Belted Radial White Outline Lettered ($98).

CAMARO CONVENIENCE/APPEARANCE OPTIONS: RS Coupe Preferred Equip. Grp 1: Air Cond; Elect Tuned AM/FM Stereo Radio, w/Seek & Scan, Stereo Cass. Tape, w/Search & Repeat & Digital Clock, w/extended range sound system; Body Side Moldings; Color-Keyed Carpeted Mats ($535). RS Coupe Preferred Equip. Grp. 2: Air Cond; Elect Tuned AM/FM Stereo Radio, w/Seek & Scan, Stereo Cass. Tape, w/Search & Repeat & Digital Clock, w/extended range sound system; Pwr Windows; Pwr Door Locks; Elect Spd Control, w/resume speed; Pwr Hatch Release; Cargo Cover; Body Side Moldings; Color-Keyed Carpeted Mats, F&R; Mirror, w/Dual Reading Lamps ($1037). RS Convertible Preferred Equip. Grp. 1: Air Cond; Elect Tuned AM/FM Stereo Radio, w/Seek & Scan, Stereo Cass. Tape, w/Search & Repeat & Digital Clock, w/extended range sound system; Body Side Moldings; Color-Keyed Carpeted Mats ($1085). RS Convertible Preferred Equip. Grp. 2: Air Cond; Elect Tuned AM/FM Stereo Radio, w/Seek & Scan, Stereo Cass. Tape, w/Search & Repeat & Digital Clock, w/extended range sound system; Pwr Windows; Pwr Door Locks; Elect Spd Control, w/resume speed; Body Side Moldings; Color-Keyed Carpeted Mats ($885). Z28 Coupe Preferred Equip. Grp. 1: Air Cond; Body Side Moldings; Color-Keyed Carpeted Mats, F&R ($375). Z28 Preferred Equip. Grp. 2: Air Cond; Elect Tuned AM/FM Stereo Radio, w/Seek & Scan; Stereo Cass. Tape, w/Search & Repeat & Digital Clock, w/extended range sound system; Pwr Windows; Pwr Door Lock System; Elect Spd Control, w/resume speed; Pwr Hatch Release; Cargo Cover; Body Side Moldings; Color-Keyed Carpeted Mats, F&R; Mirror, w/Dual Reading Lamps ($1037). Z28 Preferred Equip. Grp. 3: Air Cond; Elect Tuned AM/FM Stereo Radio, w/Seek & Scan; Stereo Cass. Tape, w/Search & Repeat & Digital Clock, w/extended range sound system; Pwr Windows; Pwr Door Lock System; Elect Spd Control, w/resume speed; Pwr Hatch Release; Cargo Cover; Body Side Moldings; Color-Keyed Carpeted Mats, F&R; Mirror, w/Dual Reading Lamps; Pwr Driver's Seat; Spt Elect Twin Remote Mirrors ($1333). Z28 Convertible Preferred Equip. Grp 1: Air Cond; Body Side Moldings; Color-Keyed Carpeted Mats, F&R ($375). Z28 Convertible Preferred

Equip. Grp. 2: Air Cond; Elect Tuned AM/FM Stereo Radio, w/Seek & Scan, Stereo Cass. Tape, w/Search & Repeat & Digital Clock, w/extended range sound system; Pwr Windows; Pwr Door Locks; Elect Spd Control, w/resume speed; Body Side Moldings; Color-Keyed Carpeted Mats, F&R ($885). Z28 Convertible Preferred Equip. Grp 3: Air Cond; Elect Tuned AM/FM Stereo Radio, w/Seek & Scan, Stereo Cass. Tape, w/Search & Repeat & Digital Clock, w/extended range sound system; Pwr Windows; Pwr Door Locks; Elect Spd Control, w/resume speed; Body Side Moldings; Color-Keyed Carpeted Mats, F&R; Pwr Driver's Seat; Spt Elect Twin Remote Mirrors ($1181). 5.0-liter V-8 ($369). 5.7-liter V-8 ($300). Custom Cloth Bucket Seats ($327). Custom Leather Bucket Seats ($850). Air Cond, Incl increased cooling ($830). Frt License Plate Bracket (NC). Rear Comp Cover ($69). Elect Rear Window Defogger ($170). Pwr Door Lock System ($210). Calif. Emission System (NA). Carpeted Mats ($20). Pwr Hatch Release ($60). Pwr Windows ($265). Elect Spd Control, w/resume speed ($225). Pwr Driver's Seat ($305). Eng. Block Htr ($20). Rear Window Louvers ($210). Spt. Elect Twin Remote Mirrors ($91). Heritage Edition Pkg ($175). Removable Glass Roof Panels, Incl locks ($895). TIRES: P235/55R16 Steel Belted Radial Blackwall ($219). P245/50ZR16 Steel Belted Radial Blackwall ($400). Cast Alum Wheels 16-in. (NC).

CORSICA CONVENIENCE/APPEARANCE OPTIONS: LT Preferred Equip. Grp. 1: Air Cond; Intermittent Windshield Wiper System; Color-Keyed Carpeted Mats, F&R ($603). LT Preferred Equip. Grp 2: Air Cond; Comfortilt Strg Wheel; Pwr Door Lock System; Intermittent Windshield Wiper System; Color-Keyed Carpeted Mats, F&R; Rearview Mirror, w/Reading Lamps ($1623). LT Preferred Equip. Grp 3: Air Cond; Elect Tuned AM/FM Stereo Radio, w/Seek & Scan, Stereo Cass. Tape & Digital Clock, w/extended range sound system; Pwr Windows; Pwr Door Lock System; Elect Spd Control, w/resume speed; Comfortilt Strg Wheel; Console, w/armrest; Intermittent Windshield Wiper System; Pwr Trunk Opener; Color-Keyed Carpeted Mats, F&R; Rearview Mirror, w/Reading Lamps ($1623). Custom Two-Tone Paint ($123). Air Cond, Incl increased cooling ($805). Frt License Plate Bracket (NC). Deck Lid Carrier, Black ($115). B19 Comfort Convenience Pkg: Luggage Area Cargo Net; Split Folding Rear Seat; Sliding Sun Shade Ext. & Visor Mirrors; Full Trunk Trim ($223). Electric Rear Window Defogger ($170). Pwr Door Lock System ($250). Calif. Emission System (NA). Gauge Pkg w/Tach, Incl Voltmeter, Oil Pressure, Temperature Gauges & Trip Odometer ($139). Eng. Block Htr ($20). Elect Spd Control, w/resume speed ($225). Comfortilt Strg Wheel ($145). Console, w/center armrest ($60). Intermittent Wipers ($65). Pwr Driver's Side Window ($340). Z52 Spt Handling Pkg: 15-in. alum wheels; Level II Spt Susp.; Body Side Mldgs, w/red inserts; Spt Strg Wheel ($395). TIRES: P185/75R14 All Seasons Steel Belted Radial White Stripe ($68). Styled Wheels ($56).

BERETTA CONVENIENCE/APPEARANCE OPTIONS: Preferred Equip. Grp. 1: Air Cond; Intermittent

Windshield Wiper System; Color-Keyed Carpeted Mats, F&R ($603). Preferred Equip. Grp. 2: Air Cond; Comfortilt Strg Wheel; Intermittent Windshield Wiper System; Color-Keyed Carpeted Mats, F&R; Pwr Door Locks ($758). Preferred Equip. Grp. 3: Air Cond; Elect Tuned AM/FM Stereo Radio, w/Seek & Scan; Stereo Cass. Tape & Digital Clock, w/extended range sound system; Pwr Windows; Pwr Trunk Opener; Elect Spd Control, w/resume speed; Comfortilt Strg Wheel; Intermittent Windshield Wiper System; Console, w/armrest; Color-Keyed Carpeted Mats, F&R; ($1518). GT Preferred Equip. Grp. 1: Air Cond; Intermittent Windshield Wiper System; Color-Keyed Carpeted Mats, F&R; Rearview Mirror, w/Reading Lamps ($626). GT Preferred Equip. Grp. 2: Air Cond; Pwr Door Lock System; Comfortilt Strg Wheel; Intermittent Windshield Wiper System; Color-Keyed Carpeted Mats, F&R; Rearview Mirror, w/Reading Lamps ($781). GT Preferred Equip. Grp. 3: Air Cond; Elect Tuned AM/FM Stereo Radio, w/Seek & Scan; Stereo Cass. Tape & Digital Clock, w/extended range sound system; Pwr Door Lock System; Pwr Trunk Opener; Pwr Windows; Elect Spd Control, w/resume speed; Comfortilt Strg Wheel; Intermittent Windshield Wiper System; Color-Keyed Carpeted Mats, F&R; Rearview Mirror, w/Reading Lamps ($1481). GTZ Preferred Equip. Grp. 1: Comfortilt Strg Wheel; Pwr Door Lock System; Color-Keyed Carpeted Mats, F&R ($188). GTZ Preferred Equip. Grp. 2: Pwr Windows; Pwr Door Lock System; Pwr Trunk Opener; Elect Spd Control, w/resume speed; Comfortilt Strg Wheel; Color-Keyed Carpeted Mats, F&R ($688). 3.1-liter V-6 ($610). Air Cond, Incl increased cooling ($805). Frt License Plate Bracket (NC). Deck Lid Carrier, Black ($115). Console, w/armrest ($60). Elect Rear Window Defogger ($170). Pwr Door Lock System ($210). Color-Keyed Carpeted Flr Mats ($18). Calif. Emission System (NA). Gauge Pkg, w/Tach, Voltmeter, Oil Pressure, Temp Gauges, Trip Odometer ($139). Eng. Block Htr ($20). Elect Spd Control, w/resume speed ($225). Rear Spoiler ($110). Comfortilt Strg Wheel ($145). Manual Sunroof, Removable ($350). F41 Spt Susp. ($49). Pwr Trunk Opener ($60). Intermittent Wipers ($65). Pwr Windows ($275). Rearview Mirror. w/Reading Lamps ($23). Convenience Pkg: Luggage Area Cargo Net; Sliding Sun Shade Ext., Map Lights and Visor Mirrors; Full Trunk Trim ($223). TIRES: P195/70R14 All Seasons Steel Belted Radial Blackwall ($93).

LUMINA CONVENIENCE/APPEARANCE OPTIONS: Preferred Equip. Grp 1: Air Cond; Comfortilt Strg Wheel; Color-Keyed Carpeted Mats, F&R ($820). Lumina Preferred Equip. Grp. 2: Air Cond; Elect Spd Control, w/resume speed; Comfortilt Strg Wheel; Deck Lid Carrier, Blk; Luggage Area Cargo Retaining Net; Color-Keyed Carpeted Mats, F&R ($990). Lumina Preferred Equip. Grp. 3: Air Cond; Elect Spd Control, w/resume speed; Pwr Windows; Pwr Door Lock System; Pwr Trunk Opener; Comfortilt Strg Wheel; Deck Lid Carrier, Blk; Luggage Area Cargo Retaining Net; Spt Twin Remote Mirrors; Color-Keyed Carpeted Mats, F&R: Cpe ($1355); Sed ($1260). Euro Preferred Equip. Grp. 1: Elect Spd Control, w/resume speed; Comfortilt Strg

Wheel; Gauge Pkg w/Tach; Cargo Area Retaining Net; Color-Keyed Carpeted Mats, F&R ($345). Euro Preferred Equip. Grp. 2: Elect Tuned AM/FM Stereo Radio, w/Seek & Scan, Stereo Cass. Tape & Digital Clock, w/extended range sound system; Pwr Windows; Pwr Door Lock System; Pwr Trunk Opener; Elect Spd Control, w/resume speed; Comfortilt Strg Wheel; Gauge Pkg. w/Tach; Cargo Area Retaining Net; Spt Twin Remote Mirrors; Color-Keyed Carpeted Mats, F&R: Cpe ($650); Sed ($555). Euro 3.4 Preferred Equip Grp. 1 (WBA1 only): Custom Cloth Bucket Seats; Elect Spd Control, w/resume speed; Comfortilt Strg Wheel; Gauge Pkg. w/Tach; Cargo Area Retaining Net; Color-Keyed Carpeted Mats, F&R ($2230). Euro 3.4 Preferred Equip. Grp. 2 (WBA1 only): Elect Tuned AM/FM Stereo Radio, w/Seek & Scan; Stereo Cass. Tape & Digital Clock, w/extended range sound system; Custom Cloth Bucket Seats; Elect Spd Control, w/resume speed; Comfortilt Strg Wheel; Pwr Windows; Pwr Door Lock System; Pwr Trunk Opener; Dual Remote Spt Mirrors; Gauge Pkg. w/Tach; Cargo Area Retaining Net; Color-Keyed Carpeted Mats, F&R ($2440). Z34 Preferred Equip. Grp. 1: Pwr Windows; Pwr Door Lock System; Pwr Trunk Opener ($335). Custom Cloth Bucket Seats w/console ($334). Custom Cloth 60/40 Seat ($284). Cloth 60/40 Seat ($194). 3.1-liter V-6 ($660). BYP Euro 3.4 Pkg: 3.4-liter V-6; 4-Spd Auto Trans; Custom Cloth Bucket Seats; 16-in. Cast Alum Wheels; FE3 Spt Susp.; Stainless Steel Dual Exhaust ($1885). Air Cond, Std/Euro ($830). Frt License Plate Bracket (NC). 4-Wheel Anti-Lock Brakes ($450). Armrest ($50). Electric Rear Window Defogger ($170). Pwr Door Lock System: Cpe ($210); Sed ($250). Pwr Windows: Cpe ($265); Sed ($330). Pwr Trunk Opener ($60). Cargo Area Retaining Net ($30). Calif. Emission System (NA). Deck Lid Carrier ($115). Trans Oil Cooler ($75). Gauge Pkg, w/Tach ($100). Spt Twin Remote Mirrors ($30). Pwr 6-way Driver's Seat ($270). Elect Spd Control, w/resume speed ($225). Comfortilt Strg Wheel ($145). Rear Spoiler, Delete ($128 credit). TIRES: P195/75R14 All Seasons Steel Belted Radial White Stripe ($72). P215/60R16 All Seasons Steel Belted Radial Blackwall ($112).

CAPRICE CONVENIENCE/APPEARANCE OPTIONS: Caprice Sed Preferred Equip. Grp. 1: Elect Spd Control, w/resume speed; Color-Keyed Carpeted Mats, F&R ($270). Caprice Sed Preferred Equip. Grp. 2: Pwr Windows; Pwr Door Lock System; Pwr Trunk Opener; Elect Spd Control, w/resume speed; Elect Twin Remote Mirrors; Color-Keyed Carpeted Mats, F&R ($998). Caprice Sed Preferred Equip. Grp. 3: Elect Tuned AM/FM Stereo Radio, w/Seek & Scan, Stereo Cass. Tape & Digital Clock; Pwr Windows; Pwr Door Lock System; Pwr Trunk Opener; Elect Spd Control, w/resume speed; Elect Twin Remote Mirrors; Pwr 6-Way Driver's Seat; Pwr Antenna; Rearview Mirror, w/dual reading lamps; Illum Visor Mirror; Color-Keyed Carpeted Mats, F&R ($1621). Caprice Classic Sed Preferred Equip. Grp. 1: Elect Tuned AM/FM Stereo Radio, w/Seek & Scan, Stereo Cass. Tape & Digital Clock, w/extended range sound system; Pwr 6-Way Driver's Seat; Elect Spd Control, w/resume speed; Comfortilt Strg Wheel; Pwr Trunk Opener; Illum RH Visor, w/mirror; Color-Keyed Carpeted Mats, F&R ($916). Caprice Classic Sed Preferred Equip Grp 2: Elect Tuned AM/FM Stereo Radio, w/Seek & Scan, Stereo Cass. Tape & Digital Clock; Pwr 6-Way Driver & Pass Seats; Pwr Door Lock System; Pwr Trunk Opener; Elect Spd Control, w/resume speed; Comfortilt Strg Wheel; Elect Twin Remote Mirrors; Pwr Twilight Sentinel Headlamp System; Dual Reading Lamps, w/Elect Compass in Rearview Mirror; Illum RH Visor; Color-Keyed Carpeted Mats ($1826). Caprice Classic LTZ Preferred Equip. Grp. 1: B4U Pkg including Leather-Wrapped Steering Wheel; Digital Strg Wheel, w/Analog Tach, Voltmeter, Temp & Oil Pressure Gauges; Keyless Remote Entry, w/Trunk Release; Elect Tuned AM/FM Stereo Radio, w/Seek & Scan, Stereo Cass. Tape & Digital Clock, w/extended range sound system; Pwr 6-Way Driver's Seat; Elect Twin Remote Mirrors; Elect Spd Control, w/resume speed; Comfortilt Strg Wheel; Illum RH Visor; Color-Keyed Carpeted Mats, F&R ($1538). Caprice Classic LTZ Preferred Equip. Grp. 2: B4U Pkg including Leather-Wrapped Steering Wheel; Digital Strg Wheel, w/Analog Tach, Voltmeter, Temp & Oil Pressure Gauges; Keyless Remote Entry, w/Trunk Release; Elect Tuned AM/FM Stereo Radio, w/Seek & Scan, Stereo Cass. Tape & Digital Clock, w/extended range sound system; Pwr 6-Way Driver's Seat; Elect Twin Remote Mirrors; Elect Spd Control, w/resume speed; Comfortilt Strg Wheel; Rearview Mirror, w/dual reading lamps and compass; Illum RH Visor; Twilight Sentinel Headlamp System; Color-Keyed Carpeted Mats, F&R ($2363). Caprice Station Wagon Preferred Equip. Grp. 1: Cruise Control; Color-Keyed Carpeted Mats, F&R ($270). Caprice Station Wagon Preferred Equip. Grp. 2: Elect Tuned AM/FM Stereo Radio, w/Seek & Scan, Stereo Cass. Tape & Digital Clock, w/extended range sound system; Pwr 6-Way Driver's Seat; Pwr Windows; Pwr Door Lock System; Pwr Tailgate Lock; Cruise Control; Elect Twin Remote Mirrors; Color-Keyed Carpeted Mats, F&R ($1483). Caprice Station Wagon Preferred Equip. Grp. 3: Elect Tuned AM/FM Stereo Radio, w/Seek & Scan, Stereo Cass. Tape & Digital Clock, w/extended range sound system; Pwr 6-Way Driver's & Pass Seat; Pwr Windows; Pwr Door Lock System; Pwr Tailgate Lock; Pwr Antenna; Rear Comp Cover; Dlx Rear Comp Decor; Illum RH Visor Mirror; Rearview Mirror, w/dual reading lamps and compass; Cruise Control; Elect Twin Remote Mirrors; Color-Keyed Carpeted Mats, F&R ($2050). Cloth 55/45 Seat ($223). Leather 45/55 Seat ($645). Custom Two-Tone Paint, Incl lower body accent, color-keyed striping & o/s door handle inserts ($141). 5.7-liter V-8, wag only ($250). Limited Slip Rear Axle ($100). Frt License Plate Bracket (NC). Electric Rear Window Defogger ($170). Pwr Door Lock System: Sed ($250); Wag, Incl Tailgate Lock ($325). Calif. Emission System (NA). LTZ Option Pkg: 3.23 Limited Slip Axle; Spt Susp., w/H.D. frame, brakes, cooling; Dual Pwr Mirrors; Leather-wrapped Strg Wheel; Surface Mounted Hood Orn; Digital Instrumentation, Incl Tach; P235/70VR15 tires; Keyless Entry System ($825). Engine block heater ($20). Pin Striping, Color-Keyed ($61). Auto Leveling Susp. ($175). F41

Ride/Handling Pkg ($49). V92 Trailering Pkg: Sed ($220); Wag ($171). TIRES: P215/75R15 All Seasons Steel Belted Radial White Stripe ($80). P225/70R15 Steel Belted Radial White Stripe ($176). Custom Wheel Covers ($215).

HISTORY: Chevrolet's market share for U.S.-made passenger cars in model year 1992 was 10.1 percent, representing 630,183 units.

1993

The biggest bowtie news for 1993 was the total redesign of the Camaro—billed as the fourth generation of the "closest thing to a 'Vette"—now offered only in coupe form with the dropping of the ragtop. Other changes for the year included the redesign of the rear appearance of the Caprice, now featuring more open wheel wells. All Caprice models offered were now in the Caprice Classic series. On the base Lumina sedan, the 2.2-liter four-cylinder engine replaced the 2.5-liter four as the standard powerplant.

1993 Chevrolet, Cavalier VL two-door coupe

CAVALIER — SERIES 1J — FOUR/V-6 — Several refinements and a lower price were the only changes to the Cavalier lineup from the previous year. Improvements included reduced engine noise for both the four-cylinder and V-6 engine offerings, as well as an improved clutch "feel" for the five-speed manual transmission. Other refinements were a glass backlight as standard equipment for convertible models and an optional rear window defogger; Z24 sport cloth trim and seatback storage pockets for RS models; a split-folding rear seat as standard equipment on the RS station wagon and an optional compact disc player on VL (Value Leader) models. Cavalier again offered three series. The VL (Value Leader) series consisted of coupe, sedan and station wagon, while the RS series had those same three body styles plus a convertible. The Z24 series offered a coupe and convertible. Standard equipment again included the 2.2-liter engine and five-speed manual transmission (except on station wagons, which had the three-speed automatic as standard). The Z24 was powered by the 3.1-liter V-6, which was the option engine for the RS series.

1993 Chevrolet, Camaro two-door coupe

1993 Chevrolet, Camaro Z28 two-door coupe

CAMARO — SERIES 1F — V-6/V-8 — The fourth generation Camaro made its debut as a 1993 model, and was a totally new product from nose to tail. It was longer, taller and wider than its third-generation predecessor. Gone were the convertible models and the RS series, leaving only a base coupe and Z28 coupe. Standard features included driver and passenger side airbags, anti-lock brakes, wraparound instrument panel, a state-of-the-art sound system and GM's PASS-KEY II theft-deterrent system. The base coupe was powered by the 3.4-liter V-6 mated to a five-speed manual transmission. The Z28 coupe received Corvette's 5.7-liter LT1 V-8 fitted with a Borg-Warner T56 six-speed manual transmission. A four-speed automatic is optional in both coupes. The Camaro's air-conditioning system was charged with R-134a refrigerant—the first GM passenger car to use this non-ozone depleting CFC substitute.

Also new was the short and long control-arm (SLA) front suspension. While the base coupe had front disc and rear drum brakes, the Z28 offered four-wheel disc brakes as standard equipment.

CORSICA/BERETTA — SERIES 1L — FOUR/V-6 — No changes occurred in the Corsica/Beretta lineup for 1993, but several refinements were implemented. Larger mufflers across-the-board offered a quieter ride. A brake-transmission shift interlock was a new safety feature that required the driver to apply the brake before shifting out of "Park." Scotchgard fabric protection was applied to all models' carpeting and mats. The Corsica LT sedan and three Beretta coupes—base, GT and GTZ—was again the lineup. The 2.2-liter four-cylinder was standard powerplant on all but the GTZ, which used the 2.3 DOHC Quad 4 engine. The five-speed manual transmission was standard across-the-board. A three-speed automatic was optional in the Beretta series. The 3.1-liter V-6 was optional for all four models.

1993 Chevrolet, Lumina Euro 3.4 four-door sedan

LUMINA — SERIES 1W — FOUR/V-6 — The Lumina was again available as a coupe or sedan with either base or Euro trim, a sporty Euro 3.4 sedan and the Z34 coupe. Automatic power door locks were now standard equipment. The 2.2-liter four-cylinder engine was the standard powerplant for the base series coupe and sedan, replacing the previous year's 2.5-liter four. The Hydra-matic 4T60-E electronically-controlled four-speed automatic transmission was the new standard offering for the Lumina Euro 3.4 sedan and was optional equipment on Luminas ordered with the 3.1-liter V-6 and the Z34 coupe. The 3.1-liter V-6 was the standard powerplant for the Euro coupe and sedan, and the option engine for the base Luminas. The Euro 3.4 sedan and Z34 coupe were powered by the 3.4-liter DOHC V-6. In all but the Euro 3.4 sedan, the three-speed automatic transmission was standard with the aforementioned Hydra-matic four-speed automatic optional.

1993 Chevrolet, Caprice Classic LS four-door sedan

CAPRICE — SERIES 1B — V-8 — The base Caprice sedan and station wagon from the previous year were elevated into the Caprice Classic series, joining the newly-named Caprice Classic LS sedan and option-package LTZ sedan. All Caprice Classic models received a new rear treatment including more open wheel wells, a widening of the bodyside moldings and rear axle, and adding a chrome trunk lid molding and new taillights with chrome detailing. The Caprice Classic series featured added acoustical insulation to reduce wind, engine and road noise as well as new interior fabrics and trim. The 5.0-liter V-8 was again the standard powerplant on all models except the LTZ sedan, which was powered by the 5.7-liter V-8 producing 180 horsepower. The four-speed automatic transmission was used across-the-board.

I.D. DATA: Chevrolets again had a 17-symbol Vehicle Identification Number (VIN) on the upper left surface of the instrument panel, visible through the windshield. Symbol one indicates country: '1' - U.S.A.; '2' - Canada. Next is a manufacturer code: 'G' - General Motors. Symbol three is car make: '1' - Chevrolet; '7' - GM of Canada. Symbols four and five denote car line/series: B/N - Caprice Classic; F/P - Camaro; J/C - Cavalier; J/F - Cavalier Z24; L/T - Corsica; L/V - Beretta; L/W - Beretta GT; L/Z - Beretta GTZ; W/L - Lumina; W/N - Lumina Euro and W/P - Lumina Z34. Symbol six is the body style: '1' - 2-dr coupe/sedan, '2' - 2-dr hatchback, '3' - 2-dr convertible, '4' - 2-dr station wagon, '5' - 4-dr sedan, '6' - 4-dr hatchback and '8' - 4-dr station wagon. Symbol seven is the restraint system: '1' - active (manual) belts, '2' - active (manual) belts w/driver's and passenger's side airbags, '3' - active (manual) belts w/driver's side airbag, '4' - passive (automatic) belts, '5' - passive (automatic) belts w/driver's side airbag. Symbol eight is the engine code: 'A' - 2.3-liter four-cyl.; 'E' - 5.0-liter V-8; 'J' and 'P' - 5.7-liter V-8; 'S' and 'X' - 3.4-liter V-6; 'T' and 'W' - 3.1-liter V-6; '4' - 2.2-liter four-cyl.; '7' - 5.7-liter V-8. This is followed by symbol nine, which is a check digit. Symbol ten is 'P' for model year 1993. Symbol eleven indicates assembly plant. The final six digits are the sequential serial number.

CAVALIER VL (FOUR/V-6)

Model No.	Body/Style No.	Body Type & Seating	Factory Price	Shipping Weight	Prod. Total
1J	C37/WV9	2-dr. Coupe-5P	8520	2509	Note 1
1J	C69/WV9	4-dr. Sedan-5P	8620	2520	Note 2
1J	C35/WV9	4-dr. Sta Wag-5P	9735	2623	Note 3

CAVALIER RS (FOUR/V-6)

1J	C37	2-dr. Coupe-5P	9520	2515	Note 1
1J	C69	4-dr. Sedan-5P	9620	2526	Note 2
1J	C67	2-dr. Conv-5P	15395	2678	Note 4
1J	C35	4-dr. Sta Wag-5P	10785	2623	Note 3

Cavalier Engine Note: A V-6 engine cost $610 additional.

CAVALIER Z24 (V-6)

1J	F37	2-dr. Coupe-5P	12500	2695	Note 1
1J	F67	2-dr. Conv-5P	18305	2832	Note 4

Note 1: Total Cavalier coupe production was 127,229 with no further breakout available.

Note 2: Total Cavalier sedan production was 96,545 with no further breakout available.

Note 3: Total Cavalier station wagon production was 19,207 with no further breakout available.

Note 4: Total Cavalier convertible production was 8,609 with no further breakout available.

CAMARO (V-6)

1F	P87	2-dr. Cpe-4P	13339	3241	Note 1

CAMARO Z-28 (V-8)

1F	P87/Z28	2-dr. Cpe-4P	16799	3373	Note 1

Note 1: Total Camaro coupe production was 39,103 with no further breakout available.

CORSICA LT (FOUR/V-6)

1L	T69	4-dr. Sedan-5P	11395/11995	2665/2763	148,232

BERETTA (FOUR/V-6)

1L	V37	2-dr. Coupe-5P	11395/11995	2649/2749	Note 1
1L	W37	2-dr. GT Cpe-5P	12995/13595	2749/2797	Note 1
1L	Z37	2-dr. GTZ Cpe-5P	15995/15845	2795/2895	Note 1

Note 1: Total Beretta coupe production was 42,263 with no further breakout available.

LUMINA (FOUR/V-6)

1W	L27	2-dr. Coupe-6P	13905/14690	3052/3169	Note 1
1W	L69	4-dr. Sedan-6P	13400/14010	3180/3288	Note 2

LUMINA EURO (V-6)

1W	N27	2-dr. Coupe-6P	15600	3193	Note 1
1W	N69	4-dr. Sedan-6P	15800	3312	Note 2
1W	N69/BYP	4-dr. 3.4 Sedan	NA	NA	Note 2

LUMINA Z34 (V-6)

1W	P27	2-dr. Coupe-6P	18400	3374	Note 1

Note 1: Total Lumina coupe production was 30,166 with no further breakout available.

Note 2: Total Lumina sedan production was 191,189 with no further breakout available.

CAPRICE CLASSIC (V-8)

1B	L19	4-dr. Sed-6P	17995	3995	Note 1
1B	L35	4-dr. 3S Wag-8P	19575	4471	10,607
1B	N19	4-dr. LS Sed-6P	19995	3988	Note 1
1B	N19/B4U	4-dr. LTZ Sed-6P	N/A	N/A	Note 1

Note 1: Total Caprice sedan production was 90,041 with no further breakout available.

FACTORY PRICE AND WEIGHT NOTE: For Corsica/Beretta and Lumina, prices and weights to left of slash are for four-cylinder, to right for V-6 engine.

BODY/STYLE NO. NOTE: Some models were actually option packages. Code after the slash (e.g., B4U, BYP) is the number of the option package that comes with the model listed.

ENGINE DATA: BASE FOUR (Cavalier, Corsica/Beretta, Beretta GT, Lumina): Inline. Overhead valve. Four-cylinder. Cast iron block and aluminum head. Displacement: 133 cu. in. (2.2 liters). Bore & stroke: 3.50 x 3.46

in. Compression ratio: 9.0:1 Brake horsepower: 110 at 5200 RPM. Torque: 130 lb.-ft. at 3200 RPM. Hydraulic valve lifters. Port fuel injection. BASE QUAD FOUR (Beretta GTZ): Inline. Dual overhead cam (16-valve). Four-cylinder. Cast iron block and aluminum head. Displacement: 138 cu. in. (2.3 liters). Bore & stroke: 3.62 x 3.35 in. Compression ratio: 10.0:1. Brake horsepower: 175 at 6200 RPM. Torque: 155 lb.-ft. at 5200 RPM. Hydraulic valve lifters. Port fuel injection. BASE V-6 (Cavalier Z24, Lumina Euro); OPTIONAL (Cavalier RS, Corsica/Beretta/Beretta GT/Beretta GTZ, Lumina): Overhead-valve V-6. Cast iron block and head. Displacement: 191 cu. in. (3.1 liters). Bore & stroke: 3.50 x 3.31 in. Compression ratio: 8.9:1. Brake horsepower: 140 at 4200 RPM. Torque: 185 lb.-ft. at 3200 RPM. Hydraulic valve lifters. Port fuel injection. BASE V-6 (Camaro): 60-degree, overhead-valve V-6. Cast iron block and head. Displacement: 207 cu. in. (3.4 liters). Bore & stroke: 3.62 x 3.31 in. Compression ratio: Camaro: 9.0:1. Brake horsepower: 160 at 4600 RPM. Torque: 200 lb.-ft. at 3600 RPM. Hydraulic valve lifters. Sequential fuel injection. BASE V-6 (Lumina Euro 3.4/Lumina Z34): Dual overhead cam (24-valve). V-6. Cast iron block and aluminum head. Displacement: 207 cu. in. (3.4 liters). Bore & stroke: 3.62 x 3.31 in. Compression ratio: 9.2:1. Brake horsepower: 200 at 5000 RPM. Torque: 215 lb.-ft. at 4000 RPM. Hydraulic valve lifters. Port fuel injection. BASE V-8 (Caprice Classic): 90-degree, overhead-valve V-8. Cast iron block and head. Displacement: 305 cu. in. (5.0 liters). Bore & stroke: 3.74 x 3.48 in. Compression ratio: 9.3:1. Brake horsepower: 170 at 4200 RPM. Torque: 255 lb.-ft. at 2400 RPM. Hydraulic valve lifters. Throttle-body fuel injection for Caprice. BASE V-8 (Camaro Z28, Caprice Classic LTZ): 90-degree, overhead-valve V-8. Cast iron block and head. Displacement: 350 cu. in. (5.7 liters). Bore & stroke: 4.00 x 3.48 in. Compression ratio: Z28: 10.5:1; LTZ: 9.3:1. Brake horsepower: Z28: 275 at 5000 RPM; LTZ: 180 at 4000 RPM. Torque: Z28: 325 lb.-ft. at 2400 RPM; LTZ: 300 lb.-ft. at 2400 RPM. Hydraulic valve lifters. Z28: Port fuel injection; LTZ: Throttle-body fuel injection.

CHASSIS DATA: Wheelbase: (Cavalier) 101.3 in.; (Camaro) 101.1 in.; (Corsica/Beretta) 103.4 in.; (Lumina) 107.5 in.; (Caprice) 115.9 in. Overall length: (Cav cpe/sed) 182.3 in.; (Cav wag) 181.1 in.; (Camaro) 193.2 in.; (Corsica/Beretta) 183.4 in.; (Lumina) 198.3 in.; (Caprice sed) 214.1 in.; (Capr wag) 217.3 in. Height: (Cavalier cpe) 52.0 in.; (Cavalier sed/wag) 53.6; (Camaro) 51.3 in.; (Corsica/Beretta) 56.2 in.; (Lumina cpe) 53.3 in.; (Lumina Euro) 53.6 in.; (Caprice) 55.7 in.; (Caprice wag) 60.9 in. Width: (Cavalier) 66.3 in.; (Camaro) 74.1 in.; (Corsica/Beretta) 68.2 in.; (Lumina cpe) 71.7; (Lumina sed) 71.0 in.; (Caprice sed) 77.0 in.; (Capr wag) 79.6 in. Front Tread: (Cavalier) 55.8 in.; (Camaro) 60.7 in.; (Corsica/Beretta) 55.8 in.; (Lumina) 59.5 in.; (Caprice sed) 61.8 in.; (Caprice wag) 62.1 in. Rear Tread: (Cavalier) 56.6 in.; (Camaro) 60.6 in.; (Corsica/Beretta) 56.6 in.; (Lumina) 58.0 in.; (Caprice sed) 62.3 in.; (Caprice wag) 64.1 in. Standard Tires: (Cavalier) P185/75R14; (Cavalier Z24) P205/60R15; (Camaro) P215/60R16; (Camaro Z28) P235/55R16; (Corsica/Beretta) P185/75R14; (Beretta GT) P205/60R15; (Beretta GTZ) P205/ZR5516; (Lumina) P195/75R14; (Lumina Euro) P205/70R15; (Lumina Z34) P225/60R16; (Caprice sed) P215/75R15; (Caprice wag) P225/75R15; (Caprice Classic LTZ) P235/70R15.

TECHNICAL: Transmission: Five-speed manual shift standard on Cavalier, Corsica/Beretta, Camaro and Lumina Z34. Six-speed manual shift standard on Camaro Z28. Three-speed automatic standard on Cavalier wagon and Lumina. Four-speed overdrive automatic standard on Caprice Classic. Steering: (Caprice Classic) recirculating ball; (others) rack and pinion. Front Suspension: (Cavalier) MacPherson struts with coil springs, lower control arms and stabilizer bar; (Corsica/Beretta) MacPherson struts with coil springs; (Camaro) SLA/Coil over monotube gas shocks, tubular stabilizer bar w/links; (Lumina) MacPherson struts with coil springs and stabilizer bar; (Caprice) unequal-length control arms, coil springs, stabilizer bar. Rear Suspension: (Cavalier) trailing crank arm with twist beam axle and coil springs; (Camaro) Solid axle/torque arm, trailing arm, coil springs, track bar, monotube gas shocks and solid stabilizer bar w/links; (Corsica/Beretta) trailing twist axle with coil springs; (Lumina) Tubular struts with transverse leaf spring and stabilizer bar; (Caprice) Salisbury four link coil springs, stabilizer available. Brakes: front disc, rear drum; four-wheel discs standard on Lumina, Camaro Z28; anti-lock brakes standard on all except base Lumina. Body construction: unibody except (Caprice Classic) separate body and frame. Fuel tank: (Cavalier) 15.2 gal.; (Camaro) 15.5 gal.; (Corsica/Beretta) 15.6 gal.; (Lumina cpe) 16.5 gal.; (Lumina sed) 17.1 gal.; (Caprice sed) 23.0 gal.; (Caprice wag) 22.0 gal.

DRIVETRAIN OPTIONS: Engines: 3.1-liter V-6: Cavalier RS ($610); Corsica/Beretta/Beretta GT ($600); Lumina ($610). 5.7-liter V-8: Caprice Classic wag ($250). Transmission/Differential: Three-speed automatic trans.: Cavalier ($495); Corsica/Beretta ($555). Four-speed overdrive auto. trans.: Camaro ($530); Lumina V-6 ($200). Limited-slip differential: Caprice ($100). Suspension: F41 sport susp.: Caprice ($49). Auto leveling susp.: Caprice wag ($175).

CAVALIER CONVENIENCE/APPEARANCE OPTIONS: VL Preferred Equip. Grp 1 (1JC37, 1JC69 only): Elect Tuned AM/FM Stereo Radio, w/Seek & Scan & Digital Clock, w/extended range sound system; Tinted glass, all windows; Spt. LH Remote & RH Manual Mirrors; Bodyside Moldings ($564). VL Preferred Equip. Grp 2 (1JC37, 1JC69 only): Elect Tuned AM/FM Stereo Radio, w/Seek & Scan & Digital Clock, w/extended range sound system; Elect Spd Control, w/resume speed; Tinted glass, all windows; Intermittent Wiper System; Mech Trunk Opener; Spt. LH Remote & RH Manual Mirrors; Bodyside Moldings ($865). VL Station Wagon Preferred Equip. Grp 1: Elect Tuned AM/FM Stereo Radio, w/Seek & Scan & Digital Clock, w/extended range sound system; Spt LH Remote & RH Manual Mirrors; Bodyside Moldings ($459). VL Station Wagon Preferred Equip. Grp 2: Elect Tuned AM/FM

Stereo Radio, w/Seek & Scan & Digital Clock, w/extended range sound system; Elect Spd Control, w/resume speed; Spt LH Remote & RH Manual Mirrors; Intermittent Wiper System; Bodyside Moldings ($749). RS Preferred Equip. Grp 1 (1JC37, 1JC69 only): Air Cond; Elect Tuned AM/FM Stereo Radio, w/Seek & Scan & Digital Clock, w/extended range sound system; Elect Spd Control, w/resume speed; Comfortilt Strg Wheel; Cargo Retaining Net ($1285). RS Station Wagon Preferred Equip. Grp. 1 (1JC35): Air Cond; Elect Tuned AM/FM Stereo Radio, w/Seek & Scan & Digital Clock, w/extended range sound system; Elect Spd Control, w/resume speed; Comfortilt Strg Wheel ($1255). RS Convertible Preferred Equip. Grp 1 (1JC67 only): Air Cond; Elect Tuned AM/FM Stereo Radio, w/Seek & Scan & Digital Clock, w/extended range sound system; Elect Spd Control, w/resume speed; Comfortilt Strg Wheel; Cargo Retaining Net ($1285). Z24 Coupe Preferred Equip. Grp 1: Air Cond; Elect Tuned AM/FM Stereo Radio, w/Seek & Scan & Digital Clock, w/extended range sound system; Elect Spd Control, w/resume speed; Comfortilt Strg Wheel; Cargo Retaining Net ($1285). Z24 Convertible Preferred Equip. Grp 1: Air Cond; Elect Tuned AM/FM Stereo Radio, w/Seek & Scan & Digital Clock, w/extended range sound system; Elect Spd Control, w/resume speed; Comfortilt Strg Wheel; Cargo Retaining Net ($1285). Air Cond ($745). Frt License Plate Bracket (NC). Deck Lid Carrier, Black ($115). Roof Carrier ($115). Dual Spt Mirrors ($30). Bodyside Mldgs ($50). Electric Rear Window Defogger ($170). Pwr Windows: Cpe ($265); Sed ($330). Tinted Glass ($105). Split Folding Rear Seat ($150). Vinyl Bucket Seat, conv only ($75). Elect Spd Control, w/resume speed ($225). Spoiler, Z24 ($110). Comfortilt Strg Wheel ($145). Removable Sunroof ($350). Eng. Block Htr ($20). Calif. Emission System ($100). Z51 Perf Handling Pkg: P195/70R14 tires; Level II Spt Susp.; Gauge Pkg w/tach ($224). TIRES: P205/60R15 Steel Belted Radial White Outline Lettered ($98).

CAMARO CONVENIENCE/APPEARANCE OPTIONS: Coupe Preferred Equip. Grp. 1: Air Cond; Elect Spd Control, w/resume speed; Fog Lamps; Remote Hatch Release ($1240). Coupe Preferred Equip. Grp. 2: Air Cond; Pwr Windows; Pwr Door Locks; Elect Spd Control, w/resume speed; Remote Hatch Release; Fog Lamps; Spt Twin Remote Mirrors; Leather-wrapped Strg Wheel/Trans Shifter/Prk Brake Handle; Illum Remote Keyless Entry ($2036). Z28 Coupe Preferred Equip. Grp. 1: Air Cond; Elect Spd Control, w/resume speed; Remote Hatch Release; Eng. Oil Cooler; Fog Lamps ($1350). Z28 Coupe Preferred Equip. Grp. 2: Air Cond; Pwr Windows; Pwr Door Lock System; Elect Spd Control, w/resume speed; Eng. Oil Cooler; Fog Lamps; Remote Hatch Release; Spt Twin Remote Mirrors; Leather-wrapped Strg Wheel/Trans Shifter/Prk Brake Handle; Illum Remote Keyless Entry ($2146). Air Cond ($895). Frt License Plate Bracket (NC). Elect Rear Window Defogger ($170). Pwr Door Lock System ($220). Calif. Emission System ($100). Bodyside Mldgs ($60). GU5 Axle, w/Eng. Oil Cooler ($110). 1LE Perf Pkg: Eng. Oil Cooler and Special Handling Susp. Sys-

tem ($310). 4-Spd Automatic Trans. ($595). Pwr Driver's Seat ($270). Removable Glass Roof Panels, Incl locks ($895). TIRES: P235/55R16 Steel Belted Radial Blackwall, stnd/Z28 ($132). P245/50ZR16 Steel Belted Radial Blackwall ($144). Cast Alum Wheels, 16-in., stnd/Z28 ($275).

CORSICA CONVENIENCE/APPEARANCE OPTIONS: LT Preferred Equip. Grp. 1: Air Cond; Intermittent Windshield Wiper System; Color-Keyed Carpeted Mats, F&R ($603). LT Preferred Equip. Grp 2: Air Cond; Comfortilt Strg Wheel; Pwr Door Lock System; Intermittent Windshield Wiper System; Color-Keyed Carpeted Mats, F&R ($798). LT Preferred Equip. Grp 3: Air Cond; Elect Tuned AM/FM Stereo Radio, w/Seek & Scan, Stereo Cass. Tape & Digital Clock, w/extended range sound system; Pwr Windows; Pwr Door Lock System; Elect Spd Control, w/resume speed; Comfortilt Strg Wheel; Console, w/armrest; Intermittent Windshield Wiper System; Pwr Trunk Opener; Color-Keyed Carpeted Mats, F&R ($1623). Custom Two-Tone Paint ($123). 3.1-liter V-6 ($600). Air Cond, Incl increased cooling ($805). Frt License Plate Bracket (NC). Deck Lid Carrier, Black ($115). B19 Comfort Convenience Pkg: Luggage Area Cargo Net; Split Folding Rear Seat; Sliding Sun Shade Ext. & Visor Mirrors; Full Trunk Trim ($223). Electric Rear Window Defogger ($170). Pwr Door Lock System ($250). Calif. Emission System ($100). Gauge Pkg w/Tach, Incl Voltmeter, Oil Pressure, Temperature Gauges & Trip Odometer ($111). Eng. Block Htr ($20). Color-Keyed Carpeted Mats ($33). Elect Spd Control, w/resume speed ($225). Comfortilt Strg Wheel ($145). Console, w/center armrest ($60). Intermittent Wipers ($65). Pwr Windows ($340). Z52 Spt Handling Pkg: 15-in. alum wheels; Level II Spt Susp.; Body Side Mldgs, w/red inserts; Spt Strg Wheel ($395). 3-Spd Auto Trans ($555). TIRES: P185/75R14 All Seasons Steel Belted Radial White Stripe ($68). Styled Wheels, 14-in. ($56).

BERETTA CONVENIENCE/APPEARANCE OPTIONS: Preferred Equip. Grp. 1: Air Cond; Intermittent Windshield Wiper System; Color-Keyed Carpeted Mats, F&R ($603). Preferred Equip. Grp. 2: Air Cond; Comfortilt Strg Wheel; Pwr Door Locks; Intermittent Windshield Wiper System; Color-Keyed Carpeted Mats, F&R ($758). Preferred Equip. Grp. 3: Air Cond; Elect Tuned AM/FM Stereo Radio, w/Seek & Scan; Stereo Cass. Tape & Digital Clock, w/extended range sound system; Pwr Windows; Pwr Trunk Opener; Elect Spd Control, w/resume speed; Comfortilt Strg Wheel; Intermittent Windshield Wiper System; Console, w/armrest; Color-Keyed Carpeted Mats, F&R ($1518). GT Preferred Equip. Grp. 1: Air Cond; Intermittent Windshield Wiper System; Color-Keyed Carpeted Mats, F&R; Rearview Mirror, w/Reading Lamps ($626). GT Preferred Equip. Grp. 2: Air Cond; Pwr Door Lock System; Comfortilt Strg Wheel; Intermittent Windshield Wiper System; Color-Keyed Carpeted Mats, F&R; Rearview Mirror, w/Reading Lamps ($781). GT Preferred Equip. Grp. 3: Air Cond; Elect Tuned AM/FM Stereo Radio, w/Seek & Scan; Stereo Cass. Tape &

Digital Clock, w/extended range sound system; Pwr Door Lock System; Pwr Trunk Opener; Pwr Windows; Elect Spd Control, w/resume speed; Comfortilt Strg Wheel; Intermittent Windshield Wiper System; Color-Keyed Carpeted Mats, F&R; Rearview Mirror, w/Reading Lamps ($1481). GTZ Preferred Equip. Grp. 1: Comfortilt Strg Wheel; Pwr Door Lock System; Color-Keyed Carpeted Mats, F&R ($188). GTZ Preferred Equip. Grp. 2: Elect Tuned AM/FM Stereo Radio, w/Seek & Scan; Stereo Cass. Tape & Digital Clock, w/extended range sound system; Pwr Windows; Pwr Door Lock System; Pwr Trunk Opener; Elect Spd Control, w/resume speed; Comfortilt Strg Wheel; Color-Keyed Carpeted Mats, F&R ($688). 3.1-liter V-6 ($600). Air Cond, Incl increased cooling ($805). Frt License Plate Bracket (NC). Deck Lid Carrier, Black ($115). Console, w/armrest ($60). Elect Rear Window Defogger ($170). Pwr Door Lock System ($210). Calif. Emission System ($100). Color-Keyed Carpeted Mats ($33). Gauge Pkg, w/Tach, Voltmeter, Oil Pressure, Temp Gauges, Trip Odometer ($111). Eng. Block Htr ($20). Elect Spd Control, w/resume speed ($225). Rear Spoiler ($110). Comfortilt Strg Wheel ($145). Manual Sunroof, Removable ($350). Pwr Trunk Opener ($60). Intermittent Wipers ($65). Pwr Windows ($275). Rearview Mirror. w/Reading Lamps ($23). B19 Comfort Convenience Pkg: Split Fldg Rear Seat; Luggage Area Cargo Net; Sliding Sun Shade Ext., Map Lights and Visor Mirrors; Full Trunk Trim ($223). 3-Spd Auto Trans ($555). TIRES: P195/70R14 All Seasons Steel Belted Radial Blackwall ($93).

LUMINA CONVENIENCE/APPEARANCE OPTIONS:
Preferred Equip. Grp 1: Air Cond; Comfortilt Strg Wheel; Color-Keyed Carpeted Mats, F&R ($520). Lumina Preferred Equip. Grp. 2: Air Cond; Comfortilt Strg Wheel; Deck Lid Carrier, Blk; Luggage Area Cargo Retaining Net; Color-Keyed Carpeted Mats, F&R ($690). Lumina Preferred Equip. Grp. 3: Air Cond; Elect Tuned AM/FM Stereo Radio, w/Seek & Scan; Stereo Cass. Tape & Digital Clock, w/extended range sound system; Elect Spd Control, w/resume speed; Pwr Windows; Pwr Trunk Opener; Comfortilt Strg Wheel; Deck Lid Carrier, Blk; Luggage Area Cargo Retaining Net; Spt Twin Remote Mirrors; Color-Keyed Carpeted Mats, F&R: ($1150). Euro Preferred Equip. Grp. 1: Elect Spd Control, w/resume speed; Comfortilt Strg Wheel; Gauge Pkg w/Tach; Cargo Area Retaining Net; Color-Keyed Carpeted Mats, F&R ($345). Euro Preferred Equip. Grp. 2: Elect Tuned AM/FM Stereo Radio, w/Seek & Scan, Stereo Cass. Tape & Digital Clock, w/extended range sound system; Pwr Windows; Pwr Trunk Opener; Elect Spd Control, w/resume speed; Comfortilt Strg Wheel; Gauge Pkg. w/Tach; Cargo Area Retaining Net; Spt Twin Remote Mirrors; Color-Keyed Carpeted Mats, F&R ($440). Euro 3.4 Preferred Equip Grp. 1: Elect Tuned AM/FM Stereo Radio, w/Seek & Scan, Stereo Cass. Tape & Digital Clock, w/extended range sound system; Pwr Windows; Pwr Trunk Opener; Elect Spd Control, w/resume speed; Comfortilt Strg Wheel; Gauge Pkg. w/Tach; Cargo Area Retaining Net; Spt Twin Remote Mirrors; Color-Keyed Carpeted Mats,

F&R ($405). Z34 Preferred Equip. Grp. 1: Pwr Windows; Pwr Trunk Opener ($125). Custom Cloth Bucket Seats w/console ($334). Custom Cloth 60/40 Seat ($284). Cloth 60/40 Seat ($194). 3.1-liter V-6 ($610). BYP Euro 3.4 Pkg: 3.4-liter V-6; 4-Spd Auto Trans; Custom Cloth Bucket Seats; 16-in. Cast Alum Wheels; FE3 Spt Susp.; Stainless Steel Dual Exhaust ($1885). Air Cond, Std/Euro ($830). Frt License Plate Bracket (NC). 4-Wheel Anti-Lock Brakes ($450). Armrest ($50). Electric Rear Window Defogger ($170). Pwr Windows: Cpe ($265); Sed ($330). Pwr Trunk Opener ($60). Cargo Area Retaining Net ($30). Calif. Emission System ($100). Deck Lid Carrier ($115). Trans Oil Cooler ($75). Gauge Pkg, w/Tach ($100). Spt Twin Remote Mirrors ($30). Pwr 6-way Driver's Seat ($270). Elect Spd Control, w/resume speed ($225). Comfortilt Strg Wheel ($145). Rear Spoiler, Delete ($128 credit). 4-Spd Auto Trans ($200). TIRES: P195/75R14 All Seasons Steel Belted Radial White Stripe ($72). P215/60R16 All Seasons Steel Belted Radial Blackwall ($112).

CAPRICE CONVENIENCE/APPEARANCE OPTIONS:
Caprice Classic Sed Preferred Equip. Grp. 1: Elect Spd Control, w/resume speed; Color-Keyed Carpeted Mats, F&R ($270). Caprice Classic Sed Preferred Equip. Grp. 2: Pwr Windows; Pwr Door Lock System; Pwr Trunk Opener; Elect Spd Control, w/resume speed; Elect Twin Remote Mirrors; Color-Keyed Carpeted Mats, F&R ($498). Caprice Classic Sed Preferred Equip. Grp. 3: Elect Tuned AM/FM Stereo Radio, w/Seek & Scan, Stereo Cass. Tape & Digital Clock; Pwr Windows; Pwr Door Lock System; Pwr Trunk Opener; Elect Spd Control, w/resume speed; Elect Twin Remote Mirrors; Pwr 6-Way Driver's Seat; Pwr Antenna; Rearview Mirror, w/dual reading lamps; Illum Visor Mirror; Door Edge Guards; Color-Keyed Carpeted Mats, F&R ($1177). Caprice Classic LS Sed Preferred Equip. Grp. 1: Elect Tuned AM/FM Stereo Radio, w/Seek & Scan, Stereo Cass. Tape & Digital Clock, w/extended range sound system; Pwr 6-Way Driver's Seat; Elect Spd Control, w/resume speed; Elect Twin Remote Mirrors; Illum RH Visor, w/mirror; Color-Keyed Carpeted Mats, F&R: ($926); on LTZ ($848). Caprice Classic LS Sed Preferred Equip Grp 2: Delco/Bose Elect Tuned AM/FM Stereo Radio, w/Seek & Scan, Stereo Cass. Tape & Digital Clock; Pwr 6-Way Driver & Pass Seats; Remote Keyless Entry, w/Trunk Release; Elect Spd Control, w/resume speed; Pwr Antenna; Elect Twin Remote Mirrors; Pwr Twilight Sentinel Headlamp System; Auto Day/Night Rearview Mirror; Color-Keyed Carpeted Mats: ($1581); on LTZ ($1618). Caprice Classic Station Wagon Preferred Equip. Grp. 1: Elect Spd Control, w/resume speed; Color-Keyed Carpeted Mats, F&R ($270). Caprice Classic Station Wagon Preferred Equip. Grp. 2: Elect Tuned AM/FM Stereo Radio, w/Seek & Scan, Stereo Cass. Tape & Digital Clock, w/extended range sound system; Pwr 6-Way Driver's Seat; Pwr Windows; Pwr Door Lock System; Pwr Tailgate Lock; Elect Spd Control, w/resume speed; Elect Twin Remote Mirrors; Color-Keyed Carpeted Mats, F&R ($1493). Caprice Station Wagon Preferred Equip. Grp. 3: Elect Tuned AM/FM Stereo Radio, w/Seek & Scan, Stereo Cass. Tape & Digital Clock, w/extended range sound system; Pwr 6-

Way Driver's & Pass Seat; Pwr Windows; Pwr Door Lock System; Pwr Tailgate Lock; Pwr Antenna; Rear Comp Cover; Dlx Rear Comp Decor; Illum RH Visor Mirror; Rearview Mirror, w/dual reading lamps; Elect Spd Control, w/resume speed; Elect Twin Remote Mirrors; Color-Keyed Carpeted Mats, F&R ($2186). Custom Cloth 55/45 Seat ($342). Cloth 55/45 Seat ($223). Leather 45/55 Seat ($645). Custom Two-Tone Paint, Incl lower body accent, color-keyed striping & o/s door handle inserts ($141). 5.7-liter V-8, wag only ($250). Limited Slip Rear Axle ($100). Frt License Plate Bracket (NC). Electric Rear Window Defogger ($170). Cargo Net ($30). Pwr Door Lock System: Sed ($250); Wag, Incl Tailgate Lock ($325). Calif. Emission System ($100). LTZ Option Pkg: 3.08 Limited Slip Axle; Spt Susp., w/H.D. frame, brakes, cooling; Dual Pwr Mirrors; Leather-wrapped Strg Wheel; Digital Instrumentation, Incl Tach; P235/70R15 tires; Keyless Entry System; Bodyside Mldgs ($1075). Door Edge Guards ($20). Engine block heater ($20). Elect Spd Control, w/resume speed ($225). Color-Keyed Carpeted Mats ($45). Illum. RH Visor Mirror ($38). Pwr Trunk Opener ($60). Reading Lamps, F&R ($51). Pwr 6-Way Driver's Seat ($305). Elect Twin Remote Mirrors ($78). Pin Striping, Color-Keyed ($61). Woodgrain Ext. ($595). Auto Leveling Susp. ($175). F41 Ride/Handling Pkg ($49). V92 Trailering Pkg: Sed ($220); Wag ($171). TIRES: P215/75R15 All Seasons Steel Belted Radial White Stripe ($80). P225/70R15 Steel Belted Radial White Stripe ($176). P235/70R15 All Seasons Steel Belted Radial White Stripe ($90). Wire Wheel Covers ($215). Dlx Wheel Covers ($70).

HISTORY: Chevrolet's market share for U.S.-made passenger cars in model year 1993 was 9.4 percent, representing 562,910 units (figures do not include 39,103 Camaros produced in model year 1993 due to that model's late introduction in January). A Camaro Z28, driven by Chevrolet General Manager Jim Perkins, paced the 1993 Indianapolis 500. The Impala SS, based on the Caprice Classic LTZ sedan, made its debut as a concept car at the 1993 Chicago Auto Show in February.

1994

Revamped lineups and refinements were the norm at Chevrolet in 1994. New models joining the bowtie brigade were convertible models in the Camaro series, the previous year's concept Impala SS was now a production model and Beretta offered a Z26 coupe to replace the discontinued GT and GTZ models. Also, the Lumina coupe was available only in the Euro and Z34 series. The standard 2.2-liter four-cylinder engine offered in Cavalier and Corsica/Beretta was redesigned for 1994. The 3.1-liter V-6 was also new and the new standard powerplant in the Lumina replacing the previous year's 2.2-liter four. The Caprice Classic also received a new standard engine in the 4.3-liter V-8, which replaced the former year's 5.0-liter V-8.

1994 Chevrolet, Cavalier VL two-door coupe

1994 Chevrolet, Cavalier RS four-door sedan

1994 Chevrolet, Cavalier Z24 two-door convertible

CAVALIER — SERIES 1J — FOUR/V-6 — With an all-new Cavalier due the following year, 1994's lineup was much like before with the exception of the discontinuance of the VL (Value Leader) series station wagon. The VL series consisted of coupe and sedan, while the RS series—with an updated appearance package—offered coupe, sedan, convertible and station wagon models. The Z24 series again offered a coupe and convertible. New standard equipment included tinted windows, automatic door unlock with ignition turned off, right-hand outside mirror and more durable rear brake drums. The upgraded 2.2-liter four-cylinder engine was again the standard engine, but offered 10 more horsepower over the previous year's version. The five-speed manual transmission was the base offering except on the station wagon, which again had the three-speed automatic as standard. The Z24 was powered by the 3.1-liter V-6, which was the option engine for the RS series.

1994 Chevrolet, Camaro two-door coupe

1994 Chevrolet, Camaro two-door convertible

1994 Chevrolet, Camaro Z28 two-door coupe

1994 Chevrolet, Camaro Z28 two-door convertible

CAMARO — SERIES 1F — V-6/V-8 — The convertible returned to the Camaro lineup after a one-year absence. Offered in both base and Z28 series, the ragtops joined the coupes offered in those two series. New standard features included a new keyless entry system, "flood light" interior illumination and a compact disc system with new coaxial speakers available for the first time in convertible models. Base models were powered by the 3.4-liter V-6. Coupes utilized the five-speed manual transmission as standard while the convertibles had the 4L60-E electronic four-speed automatic transmission as base offering. The Z28s again used Corvette's 5.7-liter LT1 V-8 fitted to a Borg-Warner T56 six-speed manual transmission. The four-speed automatic was the option transmission in Z28s. The Z28's 5.7-liter V-8 received sequential fuel injection for 1994 to provide a smoother idle and lower emissions. The T56 six-speed transmission utilized Computer-Aided Gear Selection to improve fuel economy.

1994 Chevrolet, Corsica four-door sedan

1994 Chevrolet, Beretta two-door coupe

1994 Chevrolet, Beretta Z26 two-door coupe

CORSICA/BERETTA — SERIES 1L — FOUR/V-6 — Gone on the 1994 Corsica sedan was the LT designation used in previous years. For Beretta, the previous GT and GTZ coupes were no longer offered, replaced by a single coupe named the Z26. This performance coupe was joined by the base Beretta coupe, while the Corsica sedan was the only model offered in that series. Changes to the Corsica/Beretta included power automatic door locks and air conditioning joining the list of standard features. Also, a new Mid-Function Integrated Control and Alarm Module (MICAM) provided battery rundown protection, turn signal warning and delayed lighting. The air conditioning system used the non-ozone depleting R134a refrigerant. Front suspension on both series was redesigned to obtain a smoother ride, and rear brake drums were sturdier. Base Beretta and Corsica used the upgraded-for-1994 2.2-liter four-cylinder engine mated to a five-speed manual transmission as standard equipment. The Z26 used the 2.3-liter High Output Quad 4 engine fitted with the five-speed manual transmission as base offering. The 3.1-liter V-6 was optional across-the-board. The three-speed automatic transmission was optional on all except the Z26, which used the 4T60-E four-speed automatic as the option transmission.

1994 Chevrolet, Lumina Euro four-door sedan

1994 Chevrolet, Lumina Z34 two-door coupe

LUMINA — SERIES 1W — V-6 — With the loss of the base coupe, Lumina's lineup consisted of the base sedan, Euro coupe and sedan, Euro 3.4 sedan and the Z34 coupe. The 2.2-liter four-cylinder engine formerly offered as standard powerplant in base Lumina was replaced with the 3.1-liter V-6 with multi-port fuel injection, also used in the Lumina Euro series. All Luminas used only the 4T60-E four-speed automatic transmission. Base powerplant for the Euro 3.4 sedan and Z34 coupe was the 3.4-liter DOHC V-6, which was revised with improved fuel, ignition, air control and electrical systems. It was a short year for the 1994 Luminas as the all-new '95 Lumina sedans—as well as their Monte Carlo coupe counterparts—were debuted in May of 1994.

1994 Chevrolet, Caprice Classic station wagon

1994 Chevrolet, Caprice Classic LS four-door sedan

CAPRICE CLASSIC/IMPALA — SERIES 1B — V-8 — The Caprice Classic LTZ was discontinued, and in its place the former concept car named the Impala SS joined the Caprice Classic series. The Impala name had not been used since 1969, and the 1994 Impala SS represented the first time the Impala name was used on a sedan. The Caprice Classic series also consisted of the base sedan and station wagon and LS. New standard features included the new 4.3-liter V-8 with sequential

fuel injection, which replaced the former 5.0-liter V-8 base engine, PASS-KEY II security system and dual airbags. The Impala SS was powered by the 260-horsepower LT1 Corvette V-8, which was the option engine for the base and LS Caprice Classic sedans. Across-the-board, the 4T60-E four-speed automatic transmission was used. The Impala SS featured five-spoke 17 x 8.5-inch aluminum wheels, monochromatic black paint with body-colored moldings, a unique grille, rear deck spoiler and Impala SS emblems. The rear quarter windows were subtly reshaped with inserts. Four-wheel disc brakes with anti-lock braking system (ABS) and a special Ride and Handling Suspension with De Carbon shock absorbers were standard equipment. The interior of the Impala SS featured a console, leather-wrapped steering wheel, black satin-finished trim and gray cloth upholstery. Gray leather upholstery was optional.

1994 Chevrolet, Impala SS four-door sedan

I.D. DATA: Chevrolets again had a 17-symbol Vehicle Identification Number (VIN) on the upper left surface of the instrument panel, visible through the windshield. Symbol one indicates country: '1' or '4' - U.S.A.; '2' - Canada. Next is a manufacturer code: 'G' - General Motors. Symbol three is car make: '1' - Chevrolet; '7' - GM of Canada. Symbols four and five denote car line/series: B/L - Caprice Classic; B/N - Caprice Classic LS; F/P - Camaro; J/C - Cavalier; J/F - Cavalier Z24; L/D - Corsica; L/V - Beretta; L/W - Beretta Z26; W/L - Lumina; W/N - Lumina Euro and W/P - Lumina Z34. Symbol six is the body style: '1' - 2-dr coupe/sedan, '2' - 2-dr hatchback, '3' - 2-dr convertible, '4' - 2-dr station wagon, '5' - 4-dr sedan, '6' - 4-dr hatchback and '8' - 4-dr station wagon. Symbol seven is the restraint system: '1' - active (manual) belts, '2' - active (manual) belts w/driver's and passenger's side airbags, '3' - active (manual) belts w/driver's side airbag, '4' - passive (automatic) belts, '5' - passive (automatic) belts w/driver's side airbag, '6' - passive (automatic) belts w/driver's and passenger's side airbags. Symbol eight is the engine code: 'A' - 2.3-liter four-cyl.; 'J' and 'P' - 5.7-liter V-8; 'M' and 'T' - 3.1-liter V-6; 'S' and 'X' - 3.4-liter V-6; 'W' - 4.3-liter V-6; '4' - 2.2-liter four-cyl. This is followed by symbol nine, which is a check digit. Symbol ten is 'R' for model year 1994. Symbol eleven indicates assembly plant. The final six digits are the sequential serial number.

CAVALIER VL (FOUR/V-6)

Model No.	Body/Style No.	Body Type & Seating	Factory Price	Shipping Weight	Prod. Total
1J	C37/WV9	2-dr. Coupe-5P	8845	2509	Note 1
1J	C69/WV9	4-dr. Sedan-5P	8995	2520	Note 2

CAVALIER RS (FOUR/V-6)

1J	C37	2-dr. Coupe-5P	10715	2515	Note 1
1J	C69	4-dr. Sedan-5P	11315	2526	Note 2
1J	C67	2-dr. Conv-5P	16995	2678	Note 3
1J	C35	4-dr. Sta Wag-5P	11465	2623	18,149

Cavalier Engine Note: A V-6 engine cost $834 additional.

CAVALIER Z24 (V-6)

1J	F37	2-dr. Coupe-5P	13995	2695	Note 1
1J	F67	2-dr. Conv-5P	19995	2858	Note 3

Note 1: Total Cavalier coupe production was 147,528 with no further breakout available.

Note 2: Total Cavalier sedan production was 98,966 with no further breakout available.

Note 3: Total Cavalier convertible production was 7,932 with no further breakout available.

CAMARO (V-6)

1F	P87	2-dr. Cpe-4P	13399	3247	Note 1
1F	P67	2-dr. Conv-4P	18745	3342	Note 2

CAMARO Z-28 (V-8)

1F	P87/Z28	2-dr. Cpe-4P	16799	3424	Note 1
1F	P67/Z28	2-dr. Conv-4P	22075	3524	Note 2

Note 1: Total Camaro coupe production was 112,539 with no further breakout available.

Note 2: Total Camaro convertible production was 7,260 with no further breakout available.

CORSICA (FOUR/V-6)

1L	D69	4-dr. Sedan-5P	13145/13865	2665/2763	143,296

BERETTA (FOUR/V-6)

1L	V37	2-dr. Coupe-5P	12415/13690	2649/2749	Note 1
1L	W37	2-dr. Z26 Cpe-5P	15310/15835	2749/2797	Note 1

Note 1: Total Beretta coupe production was 64,277 with no further breakout available.

LUMINA (V-6)

1W	L69	4-dr. Sedan-6P	15305	3333	Note 2

LUMINA EURO (V-6)

1W	N27	2-dr. Coupe-6P	16875	3369	Note 1
1W	N69	4-dr. Sedan-6P	16515	3269	Note 2
1W	N69/BYP	4-dr. 3.4 Sedan	NA	NA	Note 2

LUMINA Z34 (V-6)

1W	P27	2-dr. Coupe-6P	19310	3440	Note 1

Note 1: Total Lumina coupe production was NA.

Note 2: Total Lumina sedan production was 82,766 with no further breakout available.

CAPRICE CLASSIC/IMPALA (V-8)

1B	L19	4-dr. Sed-6P	18995	4036	Note 1
1B	L35	4-dr. 3S Wag-8P	21180	4449	7,719
1B	N19	4-dr. LS Sed-6P	21435	4054	Note 1

IMPALA SS (V-8)

1B	N19/BN5	4-dr. Sed-6P	21920	4218	Note 1

Note 1: Total Caprice Classic/Impala SS sedan production was 96,329 with no further breakout available.

FACTORY PRICE AND WEIGHT NOTE: For Corsica/Beretta, prices and weights to left of slash are for four-cylinder, to right for V-6 engine.

BODY/STYLE NO. NOTE: Some models were actually option packages. Code after the slash (e.g., BYP) is the number of the option package that comes with the model listed.

ENGINE DATA: BASE FOUR (Cavalier, Corsica/Beretta): Inline. Overhead valve. Four-cylinder. Cast iron block and aluminum head. Displacement: 133 cu. in. (2.2 liters). Bore & stroke: 3.50 x 3.46 in. Compression ratio: 9.0:1 Brake horsepower: 120 at 5200 RPM. Torque: 130 lb.-ft. at 4000 RPM. Hydraulic valve lifters. Port fuel injection. **BASE QUAD FOUR (Beretta Z26):** Inline. Dual overhead cam (16-valve). Four-cylinder. Cast iron block and aluminum head. Displacement: 138 cu. in. (2.3 liters). Bore & stroke: 3.62 x 3.35 in. Compression ratio: 10.0:1. Brake horsepower: 175 at 6200 RPM. Torque: 150 lb.-ft. at 5200 RPM. Hydraulic valve lifters. Port fuel injection. **BASE V-6 (Cavalier Z24, Lumina/Lumina Euro); OPTIONAL (Cavalier RS, Corsica/Beretta/Beretta Z26):** Overhead-valve V-6. Cast iron block and head. Displacement: 191 cu. in. (3.1 liters). Bore & stroke: 3.50 x 3.31 in. Compression ratio: 8.9:1. Brake horsepower: 140 at 4200 RPM. Torque: 185 lb.-ft. at 3200 RPM. Hydraulic valve lifters. Port fuel injection. **BASE V-6 (Camaro):** 60-degree, overhead-valve V-6. Cast iron block and head. Displacement: 207 cu. in. (3.4 liters). Bore & stroke: 3.62 x 3.31 in. Compression ratio: 9.0:1. Brake horsepower: 160 at 4600 RPM. Torque: 200 lb.-ft. at 3600 RPM. Hydraulic valve lifters. Sequential fuel injection. **BASE V-6 (Lumina Euro 3.4/Lumina Z34); OPTIONAL (Lumina Euro):** Dual overhead cam (24-valve). V-6. Cast iron block and aluminum head. Displacement: 207 cu. in. (3.4 liters). Bore & stroke: 3.62 x 3.31 in. Compression ratio: 9.3:1. Brake horsepower: 200 at 5000 RPM. Torque: 215 lb.-ft. at 4000 RPM. Hydraulic valve lifters. Sequential fuel injection. **BASE V-8 (Caprice Classic/Caprice Classic LS):** Overhead-valve V-8. Cast iron block and head. Displacement: 265 cu. in. (4.3 liters). Bore & stroke: 3.75 x 3.48 in. Compression ratio: 9.9:1. Brake horsepower: 200 at 5200 RPM. Torque: 245 lb.-ft. at 2400 RPM. Hydraulic valve lifters. Sequential fuel injection. **BASE V-8 (Camaro Z28, Impala SS); OPTIONAL (Caprice Classic/Caprice Classic LS):** 90-degree, overhead-valve V-8. Cast iron block and head. Displacement: 350 cu. in. (5.7 liters). Bore & stroke: 4.00 x 3.48 in. Compression ratio: 10.5:1. Brake horsepower: Z28: 275 at 5000 RPM; Impala SS: 260 at 5000

RPM. Torque: Z28: 325 lb.-ft. at 2000 RPM; Impala SS: 330 lb.-ft. at 3200 RPM. Hydraulic valve lifters. Sequential fuel injection.

CHASSIS DATA: Wheelbase: (Cavalier) 101.3 in.; (Camaro) 101.1 in.; (Corsica/Beretta) 103.4 in.; (Lumina) 107.5 in.; (Caprice) 115.9 in. Overall length: (Cav cpe/sed) 182.3 in.; (Cav wag) 181.1 in.; (Camaro) 193.2 in.; (Corsica/Beretta) 183.4 in.; (Lumina) 198.3 in.; (Caprice/Impala sed) 214.1 in.; (Capr wag) 217.3 in. Height: (Cavalier cpe) 52.0 in.; (Cavalier sed/wag) 53.6; (Camaro cpe) 51.3 in.; (Camaro conv) 52.0 in.; (Corsica/Beretta) 56.2 in.; (Lumina cpe) 53.3 in.; (Lumina Euro) 53.6 in.; (Caprice/Impala) 55.7 in.; (Caprice wag) 60.9 in. Width: (Cavalier) 66.3 in.; (Camaro) 74.1 in.; (Corsica/Beretta) 68.2 in.; (Lumina cpe) 71.7; (Lumina sed) 71.0 in.; (Caprice/Impala sed) 77.0 in.; (Capr wag) 79.6 in. Front Tread: (Cavalier) 55.8 in.; (Camaro) 60.7 in.; (Corsica/Beretta) 55.9 in.; (Lumina) 59.5 in.; (Caprice sed) 61.8 in.; (Caprice wag) 62.1 in. Rear Tread: (Cavalier) 56.6 in.; (Camaro) 60.6 in.; (Corsica/Beretta) 56.6 in.; (Lumina) 58.0 in.; (Caprice sed) 62.3 in.; (Caprice wag) 64.1 in. Standard Tires: (Cavalier) P185/75R14; (Cavalier Z24) P205/60R15; (Camaro) P215/60R16; (Camaro Z28) P235/55R16; (Corsica/Beretta) P185/75R14; (Beretta Z26) P205/60R15; (Lumina) P195/75R14; (Lumina Euro) P205/70R15; (Lumina Z34) P225/60R16; (Caprice sed) P215/75R15; (Caprice wag) P225/75R15; (Impala SS) P255/50ZR17.

TECHNICAL: Transmission: Five-speed manual shift standard on Cavalier, Corsica/Beretta and Camaro. Six-speed manual shift standard on Camaro Z28. Three-speed automatic standard on Cavalier wagon. Four-speed overdrive automatic standard on Lumina and Caprice Classic/Impala SS. Steering: (Caprice Classic) recirculating ball; (others) rack and pinion. Front Suspension: (Cavalier) MacPherson struts with coil springs, lower control arms and stabilizer bar; (Corsica/Beretta) MacPherson struts with coil springs; (Camaro) SLA/Coil over monotube gas shocks, tubular stabilizer bar w/links; (Lumina) MacPherson struts with coil springs and stabilizer bar; (Caprice) unequal-length control arms, coil springs, stabilizer bar. Rear Suspension: (Cavalier) trailing crank arm with twist beam axle and coil springs; (Camaro) Solid axle/torque arm, trailing arm, coil springs, track bar, monotube gas shocks and solid stabilizer bar w/links; (Corsica/Beretta) trailing twist axle with coil springs; (Lumina) Tubular struts with transverse leaf spring and stabilizer bar; (Caprice) Salisbury four link coil springs, stabilizer available. Brakes: front disc, rear drum; four-wheel discs standard on Lumina, Camaro Z28; anti-lock brakes standard on all except base Lumina. Body construction: unibody except (Caprice Classic) separate body and frame. Fuel tank: (Cavalier) 15.2 gal.; (Camaro) 15.5 gal.; (Corsica/Beretta) 15.2 gal.; (Lumina) 16.5 gal.; (Caprice Classic/Impala SS sed) 23.0 gal.; (Caprice wag) 22.0 gal.

DRIVETRAIN OPTIONS: Engines: 3.1-liter V-6: Cavalier RS ($834); Corsica ($720); Beretta ($1275); Beretta Z26 ($555). 5.7-liter V-8: Caprice Classic ($325). Trans-mission/Differential: Three-speed automatic trans.: Cavalier ($495); Corsica/Beretta ($555). Four-speed overdrive auto. trans.: Camaro ($750). Limited-slip differential: Caprice Classic: Sed ($250); Wag ($100). Suspension: F41 sport susp.: Caprice Classic ($49). Auto leveling susp.: Caprice Classic wag ($175).

CAVALIER CONVENIENCE/APPEARANCE OPTIONS: VL Preferred Equip. Grp 1 (1JC37, 1JC69 only): Intermittent Wiper System; Mech Trunk Opener; Dual Covered Visor Mirrors, w/map straps; Bodyside Moldings; Color-Keyed Carpeted Mats, F&R ($173). VL Preferred Equip. Grp 2 (1JC37, 1JC69 only): Tilt Strg Wheel; Elect Spd Control, w/resume speed; Intermittent Wiper System; Mech Trunk Opener; Dual Covered Visor Mirrors, w/map straps; Bodyside Moldings; Color-Keyed Carpeted Mats, F&R ($543). RS Preferred Equip. Grp 1 (1JC37, 1JC69 only): Tilt Strg Wheel; Elect Spd Control, w/resume speed ($370). RS Station Wagon Preferred Equip. Grp. 1 (1JC35): Tilt Strg Wheel; Elect Spd Control, w/resume speed; Intermittent Wiper System ($435). RS Convertible Preferred Equip. Grp 1 (1JC67 only): Tilt Strg Wheel; Elect Spd Control, w/resume speed ($370). Z24 Coupe Preferred Equip. Grp 1: Elect Spd Control, w/resume speed; Pwr Windows; Split Fldg Rear Seat; Cargo Retaining Net ($670). 3.1-liter V-6 ($834). Air Cond ($785). Frt License Plate Bracket (NC). Roof Carrier ($115). Electric Rear Window Defogger ($170). Pwr Windows: Cpe ($265); Sed ($330). Split Folding Rear Seat ($180). Vinyl Bucket Seat, conv only ($75). Spoiler ($110). Removable Sunroof ($350). Eng. Block Htr ($20). Calif. Emission System ($100). 3-Spd Auto Trans ($495). TIRES: P205/60R15 Steel Belted Radial White Outline Lettered ($98).

CAMARO CONVENIENCE/APPEARANCE OPTIONS: Coupe Preferred Equip. Grp. 1: Air Cond; Elect Spd Control, w/resume speed; Fog Lamps; Remote Trunk Release ($1240). Coupe Preferred Equip. Grp. 2: Air Cond; Pwr Windows; Pwr Door Locks; Elect Spd Control, w/resume speed; Remote Trunk Release; Fog Lamps; Spt Twin Remote Mirrors; Leather-wrapped Strg Wheel/Trans Shifter/Prk Brake Handle; Illum Remote Keyless Entry ($2036). Convertible Preferred Equip. Grp. 1: Air Cond; Elect Spd Control, w/resume speed; Fog Lamps; Remote Trunk Release ($1240). Convertible Preferred Equip. Grp. 2: Air Cond; Pwr Windows; Pwr Door Locks; Elect Spd Control, w/resume speed; Remote Trunk Release; Fog Lamps; Spt Twin Remote Mirrors; Leather-wrapped Strg Wheel/Trans Shifter/Prk Brake Handle; Illum Remote Keyless Entry ($2036). Z28 Coupe Preferred Equip. Grp. 1: Air Cond; Elect Spd Control, w/resume speed; Remote Trunk Release; Eng. Oil Cooler; Fog Lamps ($1350). Z28 Coupe Preferred Equip. Grp. 2: Air Cond; Pwr Windows; Pwr Door Lock System; Elect Spd Control, w/resume speed; Eng. Oil Cooler; Fog Lamps; Remote Trunk Release; Spt Twin Remote Mirrors; Leather-wrapped Strg Wheel/Trans Shifter/Prk Brake Handle; Illum Remote Keyless Entry ($2146). Z28 Convertible Preferred Equip. Grp. 1: Air Cond; Elect Spd Control, w/resume speed; Remote Trunk Release; Eng. Oil Cooler; Fog Lamps ($1350). Z28 Convertible Preferred Equip. Grp. 2: Air Cond; Pwr Windows; Pwr Door Lock System; Elect Spd Control, w/resume speed; Eng. Oil Cooler; Fog Lamps; Remote Trunk Release; Spt Twin Remote Mirrors; Leather-wrapped Strg Wheel/Trans Shifter/Prk Brake Handle; Illum Remote Keyless Entry ($2146). Air Cond ($895). Frt License Plate Bracket (NC). Elect Rear Window Defogger ($170). Calif. Emission System ($100). Bodyside Mldgs ($60). GU5 Axle, w/Eng. Oil Cooler ($175). 1LE Perf Pkg: Eng. Oil Cooler and Special Handling Susp. System ($310). 4-Spd Automatic Trans. ($750). Pwr Driver's Seat ($270). Removable Glass Roof Panels, Incl locks ($895). Rear Mats ($15). TIRES: P235/55R16 Steel Belted Radial Blackwall, stnd/Z28 ($132). P245/50ZR16 Steel Belted Radial Blackwall ($225). Cast Alum Wheels, 16-in., stnd/Z28 ($275).

CORSICA CONVENIENCE/APPEARANCE OPTIONS: Preferred Equip. Grp. 1: Day/Night Rear View Mirror, w/reading lamps; LH & RH Visor Mirrors; Luggage Area Cargo Net; Intermittent Wiper System; Color-Keyed Carpeted Mats, F&R ($165). Preferred Equip. Grp 2: Tilt Strg Wheel; Elect Spd Control, w/resume speed; Split Fldg Rear Seat; Day/Night Rear View Mirror, w/reading lamps; LH & RH Visor Mirrors; Pwr Trunk Opener; Luggage Area Cargo Net; Intermittent Wiper System; Color-Keyed Carpeted Mats, F&R ($745). 3.1-liter V-6 ($720). Frt License Plate Bracket (NC). Elect Rear Window Defogger ($170). Eng. Block Htr ($20). Pwr Windows ($340). TIRES: P185/75R14 All Seasons Steel Belted Radial White Stripe ($68). Styled Wheels, 14-in. ($56).

BERETTA CONVENIENCE/APPEARANCE OPTIONS: Preferred Equip. Grp. 1: Day/Night Rear View Mirror, w/reading lamps; LH & RH Visor Mirrors; Luggage Area Cargo Net; Intermittent Wiper System; Color-Keyed Carpeted Mats, F&R ($165). Preferred Equip. Grp. 2: Tilt Strg Wheel; Elect Spd Control, w/resume speed; Split Fldg Rear Seat; Day/Night Rear View Mirror, w/reading lamps; LH & RH Visor Mirrors; Pwr Trunk Opener; Luggage Area Cargo Net; Intermittent Wiper System; Color-Keyed Carpeted Mats, F&R ($745). Z26 Preferred Equip. Grp. 1: Tilt Strg Wheel; Pwr Trunk Opener; Elect Spd Control, w/resume speed; Color-Keyed Carpeted Mats, F&R ($463). 3.1-liter V-6: base cpe ($1275); Z26 ($555). Frt License Plate Bracket (NC). Elect Rear Window Defogger ($170). Calif. Emission System ($100). Gauge Pkg, w/Tach, Voltmeter, Oil Pressure, Temp Gauges, Trip Odometer ($111). Eng. Block Htr ($20). Rear Spoiler, stnd/Z26 ($110). Manual Sunroof, Removable ($350). Pwr Windows ($275). 3-Spd Auto Trans ($555). TIRES: P195/70R14 Steel Belted Radial Blackwall ($93). P205/60R15 Steel Belted Radial Blackwall, stnd/Z26 ($175). P205/55R16 Steel Belted Radial Blackwall ($372).

LUMINA CONVENIENCE/APPEARANCE OPTIONS: Preferred Equip. Grp. 1: Pwr Windows; Pwr Trunk Opener; Comfortilt Strg Wheel; Deck Lid Carrier, Blk;

Luggage Area Cargo Retaining Net; Spt Twin Remote Mirrors ($790). Euro Preferred Equip. Grp. 1: Pwr Windows (stnd/Cpe); Pwr Trunk Opener; Elect Spd Control, w/resume speed; Gauge Pkg. w/Tach; Cargo Area Retaining Net; Spt Twin Remote Mirrors: Cpe ($445); Sed ($775). Euro 3.4 Preferred Equip Grp. 1: Pwr Windows; Pwr Trunk Opener; Elect Spd Control, w/resume speed; Gauge Pkg. w/Tach; Cargo Area Retaining Net; Spt Twin Remote Mirrors ($775). Z34 Preferred Equip. Grp. 1: NA. Custom Cloth Bucket Seats w/console ($50). Custom Cloth 60/40 Seat ($90). BYP Euro 3.4 Pkg ($1376). Frt License Plate Bracket (NC). 4-Wheel Anti-Lock Brakes ($450). Electric Rear Window Defogger ($170). Calif. Emission System ($100). Deck Lid Carrier ($115). Cellular Phone Provision ($45). Pwr 6-way Driver's Seat ($270). Elect Spd Control, w/resume speed ($225). Comfortilt Strg Wheel ($145). Rear Spoiler, Delete ($128 credit). TIRES: P195/75R14 All Seasons Steel Belted Radial White Stripe ($72). P215/60R16 All Seasons Steel Belted Radial Blackwall ($112).

CAPRICE CLASSIC/IMPALA CONVENIENCE/APPEARANCE OPTIONS: Caprice Classic Sed Preferred Equip. Grp. 1: Elect Spd Control, w/resume speed; Pwr Windows; Pwr Door Lock System; Pwr Trunk Opener; Elect Twin Remote Mirrors ($953). Caprice Classic Sed Preferred Equip. Grp. 2: Elect Tuned AM/FM Stereo Radio, w/Seek & Scan, Stereo Cass. Tape & Digital Clock, w/extended range sound system; Pwr 6-Way Driver's Seat; Pwr Antenna; Pwr Windows; Pwr Door Lock System; Pwr Trunk Opener; Elect Spd Control, w/resume speed; Rearview Mirror, w/dual reading lamps; Illum RH Visor Mirror; Elect Twin Remote Mirrors ($1607). Caprice Classic LS Sed Preferred Equip. Grp. 1: Pwr 6-Way Pass. Seat; Pwr Antenna; Auto Day/Night Rearview Mirror; Rear Window Defogger, w/heated outside rearview mirrors; Remote Keyless Entry, w/Trunk Release; Twilight Sentinel Headlamp System ($860). Caprice Classic Station Wagon Preferred Equip. Grp. 1: Elect Spd Control, w/resume speed; Pwr Windows; Pwr Door Lock System, w/tailgate lock; Pwr 6-Way Driver's Seat; Elect Twin Remote Mirrors ($1273). Caprice Classic Station Wagon Preferred Equip. Grp. 2: Elect Spd Control, w/resume speed; Pwr Windows; Pwr Door Lock System, w/tailgate lock; Pwr 6-Way Driver's Seat; Elect Twin Remote Mirrors Pwr Antenna; Auto Day/Night Rearview Mirror; Rear Window Defogger, w/heated outside rearview mirrors; Dlx Rear Comp. Decor; Rear Comp. Security Cover; Illum RH Visor Mirror; Rear Comp. Reading Lamps ($2146). Impala SS Preferred Equip. Grp. 1: Pwr Antenna; Auto Day/Night Rearview Mirror; Rear Window Defogger, w/heated outside rearview mirrors; Pwr 6-Way Pass. Seat; Remote Keyless Entry, w/trunk release; Twilight Sentinel Headlamp System ($860). Custom Cloth 55/45 Seat ($342). Cloth 55/45 Seat ($223). Leather 45/55 Seat ($645). Custom Two-Tone Paint, Incl lower body accent, outside door handle inserts ($141). 5.7-liter V-8, stnd/Impala SS ($325). Limited Slip Rear Axle: Sed ($250); Wag ($100). Frt License Plate Bracket (NC). Electric Rear Window Defogger ($170). Cargo Net ($30). Pwr Door Lock System: Sed ($250); Wag, Incl Tailgate Lock ($325). Calif. Emission System ($100). Elect Spd Control, w/resume speed ($225). Pin Striping, Color-Keyed ($61). Woodgrain

Ext. ($595). Auto Leveling Susp. ($175). B4U Sport Susp. ($508). F41 Ride/Handling Pkg ($49). V92 Trailering Pkg ($21). TIRES: P215/75R15 All Seasons Steel Belted Radial White Stripe ($80). P225/70R15 All Seasons Steel Belted Radial White Stripe ($176). P235/70R15 All Seasons Steel Belted Radial White Stripe ($90). Wire Wheel Covers ($215). Dlx Wheel Covers ($70).

HISTORY: Chevrolet's market share for U.S.-made passenger cars in model year 1994 was 10.12 percent, representing 610,060 units.

1995

Nineteen ninety-five marked the return of the Monte Carlo name to Chevrolet's lineup after a six-year absence. Once again, the favorite on the NASCAR circuit, this new Monte Carlo was the coupe counterpart to an all-new design Lumina sedan lineup that lost the Euro series and Z34 coupe offered previously. The Cavalier was also all-new-for-1995. Gone was the Value Leader (VL) series and the station wagon. The Cavalier lineup now consisted of a base coupe and sedan, LS sedan and convertible and Z24 coupe. The Caprice Classic LS sedan was also discontinued for 1995. Daytime Running Lamps became standard equipment for Corsica/Beretta offerings, while all Cavalier models had dual airbags. Traction control was available for Camaro Z28 models after December of 1994. All or part of the 1995 Lumina, Monte Carlo and Cavalier lines were in dealerships by midyear 1994.

1995 Chevrolet, Cavalier LS two-door convertible

1995 Chevrolet, Cavalier LS four-door sedan

1995 Chevrolet, Cavalier Z24 two-door coupe

CAVALIER — SERIES 1J — FOUR — A new design from the ground up, the 1995 Cavalier featured a two-inch wider track and three-inch longer wheelbase, yet it was two inches shorter than the previous year's offering to provide better maneuverability. One benefit gained from Cavalier's redesign was a more spacious interior. Standard equipment included dual airbags and four-wheel anti-lock brakes. Handling was improved with a new "progressive ride" suspension system. A torque axis mounting system reduced engine vibration. The Z24 coupe featured PASS-LOCK theft-deterrent system, fog lamps, P205/55R16 radials on 16-inch aluminum wheels, Level II sport suspension, aero rocker moldings, rear spoiler and dual, stainless steel exhaust. The 2.2-liter four-cylinder engine was again the standard offering with the base coupe and sedan fitted with the five-speed manual transmission. The LS sedan and convertible used the three-speed automatic. The Z24 coupe featured the 2.3-liter Quad 4 engine mated to the five-speed manual transmission as standard. This Quad 4 was the option engine on the LS series, while the three-speed automatic was the option transmission on the base series and the 4T40-E four-speed automatic was optional on the Z24. The LS series convertible was assembled off-site by Genasys, a joint venture corporation established by ASC and Lansing Automotive Division.

CAMARO — SERIES 1F — V-6/V-8 — Camaro returned in 1995 with the same lineup as the year previous, that being a coupe and convertible offered in each of the base and Z28 series. New features included body-colored outside dual sport mirrors on base models, an optional monochromatic roof treatment on Z28 coupes and base coupes with T-tops, as well as optional chrome-plated wheel covers and aluminum wheels. Also available on the Z28 were speed-rated performance tires (including a 150 mph speedometer) and optional Acceleration Slip Regulation (ASR). The base coupe was powered by the 3.4-liter V-6 fitted to a five-speed manual transmission as standard while the convertible used the LT1 (Corvette) 5.7-liter V-8 mated to an electronic four-speed automatic transmission as base offering. The Z28s again featured the LT1 5.7-liter V-8 fitted to a Borg-Warner T56 six-speed manual transmission as standard equipment. The four-speed automatic was the option transmission in Z28s.

CORSICA/BERETTA — SERIES 1L — FOUR/V-6 — The big changes for 1995 were the Beretta Z26 received the 3.1-liter V-6 with sequential fuel injection as its standard engine, and Corsica and Beretta models gained Daytime Running Lamps to make them easier to see. The rear suspension of both series' models was revised, using a "spring on center" design to enhance ride comfort and quietness. Again, the base Beretta and Corsica used the 2.2-liter four-cylinder engine as standard equipment. The Z26 featured the aforementioned 3.1-liter V-6, which was optional for Corsica and base Beretta. Corsica used the three-speed automatic while Beretta and Z26 were fitted with the five-speed manual transmission as base offerings. The three-speed automatic was optional on the Beretta coupe while the four-speed automatic was the option transmission on the Corsica and Z26.

1995 Chevrolet, Lumina LS four-door sedan

LUMINA — SERIES 1W — V-6 — Chevrolet touted the Lumina as having 67 percent of its components new-for-1995. Also, the number of parts comprising a Lumina decreased from 3,200 in 1994 to 2,300 in 1995. The revised lineup consisted of a base sedan and LS sedan with the Euro series—including the Euro 3.4 sedan—and the Z34 coupe of the year previous all discontinued. Aside from all-new exterior and interior styling, new standard features on the Lumina included dual airbags, theft-deterrent system, air conditioning and power door locks. Anti-lock brakes are standard on the LS sedan and optional on the base sedan. The 3.1-liter V-6 was the standard engine in both Lumina models. The 3.4-liter DOHC was the option powerplant in the LS sedan. The base sedan used a three-speed automatic as standard while the four-speed automatic was optional. The four-speed automatic was the lone offering for the LS sedan.

1995 Chevrolet, Monte Carlo LS two-door coupe

1995 Chevrolet, Monte Carlo Z34 two-door coupe

MONTE CARLO — SERIES 1W — V-6 — Last used in 1988, the Monte Carlo name returned to Chevrolet in the form of an LS coupe and performance-oriented Z34 coupe. Safety features of the Monte Carlo included dual airbags, four-wheel anti-lock brake system, PASS-KEY II theft-deterrent system, safety-cage construction and side-guard door beams. The LS coupe used the 3.1-liter V-6 with sequential fuel injection as standard equipment. The Z34 coupe featured the 3.4-liter DOHC V-6 with sequential fuel injection as base offering. Both coupes had the four-speed automatic transmission as standard equipment.

CAPRICE CLASSIC/IMPALA — SERIES 1B — V-8 — With the discontinuation of the LS sedan, the Caprice Classic lineup in 1995 was represented by the base sedan and station wagon. Joining the series under another name was the Impala SS, which returned after its debut the year previous (not counting its time as a concept car on the auto show tour in 1993). New features on the Caprice Classic models included new paint colors, revised rear quarter panel/window styling, and re-designed, relocated, fold-away outside rearview mirrors. Also available as an option was a custom interior package that enhanced comfort and convenience. The Caprice Classic sedan was powered by the 4.3-liter V-8 with sequential fuel injection. The Caprice Classic station wagon and Impala SS were powered by the LT1 (Corvette) 5.7-liter V-8, which was also the option engine for the Caprice Classic sedan. The four-speed automatic transmission was standard in all three models.

I.D. DATA: Chevrolets again had a 17-symbol Vehicle Identification Number (VIN) on the upper left surface of the instrument panel, visible through the windshield. Symbol one indicates country: '1' or '4' - U.S.A.; '2' - Canada. Next is a manufacturer code: 'G' - General Motors. Symbol three is car make: '1' - Chevrolet; '7' - GM of Canada. Symbols four and five denote car line/series: B/L - Caprice Classic/Impala SS; F/P - Camaro; J/C - Cavalier; J/F - Cavalier Z24 and LS; L/D - Corsica; L/V - Beretta; L/W - Beretta Z26; W/L - Lumina; W/N - Lumina LS; W/W - Monte Carlo LS and W/X - Monte Carlo Z34. Symbol six is the body style: '1' - 2-dr coupe, '2' - 2-dr, '3' - 2-dr convertible, '4' - 2-dr station wagon, '5' - 4-dr sedan, '6' - 4-dr and '8' - 4-dr station wagon. Symbol seven is the restraint system: '1' - active (manual) belts, '2' - active (manual) belts w/driver's and passenger's side airbags, '3' - active (manual) belts w/driver's side airbag, '4' - passive (automatic) belts,

'5' - passive (automatic) belts w/driver's side airbag, '6' - passive (automatic) belts w/driver's and passenger's side airbags. Symbol eight is the engine code: 'D' - 2.3-liter four-cyl.; 'J' and 'P' - 5.7-liter V-8; 'M' - 3.1-liter V-6; 'S' and 'X' - 3.4-liter V-6; 'W' - 4.3-liter V-8; '4' - 2.2-liter four-cyl. This is followed by symbol nine, which is a check digit. Symbol ten is 'S' for model year 1995. Symbol eleven indicates assembly plant. The final six digits are the sequential serial number.

CAVALIER (FOUR)

Model No.	Body/Style No.	Body Type & Seating	Factory Price	Shipping Weight	Prod. Total
1J	C37	2-dr. Coupe-5P	10060	2617	Note 1
1J	C69	4-dr. Sedan-5P	10265	2676	Note 2

CAVALIER LS (FOUR)

1J	F69	4-dr. Sedan-5P	12465	2736	Note 2
1J	F67	2-dr. Conv-5P	17210	2838	6,060

CAVALIER Z24 (FOUR)

1J	F37	2-dr. Coupe-5P	13810	2788	Note 1

Note 1: Total Cavalier coupe production was 88,909 with no further breakout available.

Note 2: Total Cavalier sedan production was 56,700 with no further breakout available.

CAMARO (V-6)

1F	P87	2-dr. Cpe-4P	14250	3251	Note 1
1F	P67	2-dr. Conv-4P	19495	3342	Note 2

CAMARO Z-28 (V-8)

1F	P87/Z28	2-dr. Cpe-4P	17915	3390	Note 1
1F	P67/Z28	2-dr. Conv-4P	23095	3480	Note 2

Note 1: Total Camaro coupe production was 115,365 with no further breakout available.

Note 2: Total Camaro convertible production was 7,360 with no further breakout available.

CORSICA (FOUR/V-6)

1L	D69	4-dr. Sedan-5P	13890/14610	2745/2885	142,073

BERETTA (FOUR/V-6)

1L	V37	2-dr. Coupe-5P	12995/14270	2756/2896	Note 1
1L	W37	2-dr. Z26 Cpe-5P	----- /16295	---- /2990	Note 1

Note 1: Total Beretta coupe production was 71,762 with no further breakout available.

LUMINA (V-6)

1W	L69/Z7H	4-dr. Sedan-6P	15460	3330	Note 1

LUMINA LS (V-6)

1W	N69/Z7E	4-dr. Sedan-6P	16960	3372	Note 1

Note 1: Total Lumina sedan production was 242,112 with no further breakout available.

MONTE CARLO LS (V-6)

1W	W27/Z7F	2-dr. Coupe-6P	16760	3276	Note 1

MONTE CARLO Z34 (V-6)

1W	X27/Z7G	2-dr. Coupe-6P	18960	3451	Note 1

Note 1: Total Monte Carlo coupe production was 93,150 with no further breakout available.

CAPRICE CLASSIC (V-8)

1B	L19	4-dr. Sed-6P	20310	4061	Note 1
1B	L35	4-dr. 3S Wag-8P	22840	4473	5,030

IMPALA SS (V-8)

1B	L19/BL5	4-dr. Sed-6P	22910	4036	Note 1

Note 1: Total Caprice Classic/Impala SS sedan production was 75,707 with no further breakout available.

FACTORY PRICE AND WEIGHT NOTE: For Corsica/Beretta, prices and weights to left of slash are for four-cylinder, to right for V-6 engine.

ENGINE DATA: BASE FOUR (Cavalier, Corsica/Beretta): Inline. Overhead valve. Four-cylinder. Displacement: 133 cu. in. (2.2 liters). Bore & stroke: 3.50 x 3.46 in. Compression ratio: 9.0:1. Brake horsepower: 120 at 5200 RPM. Port fuel injection. BASE QUAD FOUR (Cavalier Z24): Inline. Dual overhead cam (16-valve). Four-cylinder. Displacement: 138 cu. in. (2.3 liters). Bore & stroke: 3.63 x 3.35 in. Compression ratio: 9.5:1. Brake horsepower: 150 at 6000 RPM. Port fuel injection. BASE V-6 (Beretta Z26, Lumina/Lumina LS, Monte Carlo LS); OPTIONAL (Corsica/Beretta): Overhead-valve V-6. Displacement: 191 cu. in. (3.1 liters). Bore & stroke: 3.51 x 3.31 in. Compression ratio: 9.6:1. Brake horsepower: 155 at 5200 RPM. Sequential fuel injection. BASE V-6 (Camaro cpe): 60-degree, overhead-valve V-6. Displacement: 207 cu. in. (3.4 liters). Bore & stroke: 3.62 x 3.31 in. Compression ratio: 9.0:1. Brake horsepower: 160 at 4600 RPM. Sequential fuel injection. BASE V-6 (Monte Carlo Z34): Dual overhead cam (24-valve) V-6. Displacement: 207 cu. in. (3.4 liters). Bore & stroke: 3.62 x 3.31 in. Compression ratio: 9.3:1. Brake horsepower: 210 at 5200 RPM. Sequential fuel injection. BASE V-8 (Caprice Classic sed): Overhead-valve V-8. Displacement: 265 cu. in. (4.3 liters). Bore & stroke: 3.75 x 3.48 in. Compression ratio: 9.9:1. Brake horsepower: 200 at 5200 RPM. Sequential fuel injection. BASE V-8 (Camaro conv/Camaro Z28, Caprice Classic wag/Impala SS); OPTIONAL (Caprice Classic sed): 90-degree, overhead-valve V-8. Displacement: 350 cu. in. (5.7 liters). Bore & stroke: 4.00 x 3.48 in. Compression ratio: All except Caprice Classic wag: 10.5:1; Caprice Classic wag: 10.0:1. Brake horsepower: Camaro conv/Z28: 275 at 5000 RPM; Caprice Classic wag/Impala SS: 260 at 4800 RPM. Sequential fuel injection.

CHASSIS DATA: Wheelbase: (Cavalier) 104.1 in.; (Camaro) 101.1 in.; (Corsica/Beretta) 103.4 in.; (Lumina/Monte Carlo) 107.5 in.; (Caprice Classic/Impala SS) 115.9 in. Overall length: (Cavalier) 180.3 in.; (Camaro) 193.2 in.; (Corsica) 183.4 in.; (Beretta) 187.3 in.; (Lumina) 200.9 in.; (Monte Carlo) 200.7 in.; (Caprice Classic/Impala SS sed) 214.1 in.; (Caprice Classic wag) 217.3 in. Height: (Cavalier cpe) 53.2 in.; (Cavalier sed) 54.8; (Cavalier Z24) 53.9 in.; (Camaro cpe) 51.3 in.; (Camaro conv) 52.0 in.; (Corsica) 54.2 in.; (Beretta) 53.0 in.; (Lumina) 55.2 in.; (Monte Carlo) 53.8 in.; (Caprice Classic/Impala SS sed) 55.7 in.; (Caprice Classic wag) 60.9 in. Width: (Cavalier) 67.4 in.; (Camaro) 74.1

in.; (Corsica) 68.5 in.; (Beretta) 67.9; (Lumina) 72.5; (Monte Carlo) 71.9 in.; (Caprice Classic/Impala SS sed) 77.5 in.; (Caprice Classic wag) 79.6 in. Standard Tires: (Cavalier) P195/70R14; (Cavalier LS) P195/65R15; (Cavalier Z24) P205/55R16; (Camaro) P215/60R16; (Camaro Z28) P235/55R16; (Corsica/Beretta) P195/70R14; (Beretta Z26) P205/60R15; (Lumina/Lumina LS/Monte Carlo LS) P205/70R15; (Monte Carlo Z34) P225/60R16; (Caprice Classic sed) P215/75R15; (Caprice Classic wag) P225/75R15; (Impala SS) P255/50ZR17.

TECHNICAL: Transmission: Five-speed manual shift standard on Cavalier, Beretta and Camaro cpe. Six-speed manual shift standard on Camaro Z28. Three-speed automatic standard on Cavalier LS, Corsica and Lumina. Four-speed overdrive automatic standard on Camaro conv, Lumina LS, Monte Carlo and Caprice Classic/Impala SS. Steering: (Caprice Classic) recirculating ball; (others) rack and pinion. Brakes: front disc, rear drum; four-wheel discs standard on Camaro Z28 and Impala SS; anti-lock brakes standard on all except base Lumina. Body construction: unibody except (Caprice Classic) separate body and frame. Fuel tank: (Cavalier) 15.2 gal.; (Camaro) 15.5 gal.; (Corsica/Beretta) 15.2 gal.; (Lumina) 16.5 gal.; (Monte Carlo) 17.1 gal.; (Caprice Classic/Impala SS sed) 23.0 gal.; (Caprice wag) 22.0 gal.

DRIVETRAIN OPTIONS: Engines: 2.3-liter four-cylinder: Cavalier LS ($395). 3.1-liter V-6: Beretta ($1275); Corsica ($720). 3.4-liter V-6: Lumina LS ($995). 5.7-liter V-8: Caprice Classic sed ($550). Transmission/Differential: Three-speed automatic trans.: Cavalier ($495); Beretta ($555). Four-speed overdrive auto. trans.: Beretta Z26 (NC); Corsica (NC); Camaro cpe/Z28 ($775); Lumina (NC). Limited-slip differential: Caprice Classic: Sed ($250); Wag ($100). Suspension: B4U sport susp.: Caprice Classic sed ($508). F41 sport susp.: Caprice Classic ($49). Auto leveling susp.: Caprice Classic wag ($175).

CAVALIER CONVENIENCE/APPEARANCE OPTIONS: Coupe Preferred Equip. Grp 1: Intermittent Wiper System; Mech Trunk Opener; Dual Covered Visor Mirrors, w/map straps; Bodyside Moldings; Mud Guards; Color-Keyed Carpeted Mats, F&R ($210). Coupe Preferred Equip. Grp 2: Tilt Strg Wheel; Elect Spd Control, w/resume speed; Intermittent Wiper System; Mech Trunk Opener; Dual Covered Visor Mirrors, w/map straps; Bodyside Moldings; Mud Guards; Color-Keyed Carpeted Mats, F&R ($580). Sedan Preferred Equip. Grp 1: Intermittent Wiper System; Mech Trunk Opener; Dual Covered Visor Mirrors, w/map straps; Bodyside Moldings; Mud Guards; Color-Keyed Carpeted Mats, F&R ($193). Sedan Preferred Equip. Grp. 2: Tilt Strg Wheel; Elect Spd Control, w/resume speed; Intermittent Wiper System; Mech Trunk Opener; Dual Covered Visor Mirrors, w/map straps; Bodyside Moldings; Mud Guards; Color-Keyed Carpeted Mats, F&R ($563). LS Sedan Preferred Equip. Grp 1: Tilt Strg Wheel; Elect Spd Control, w/resume speed; Intermittent

Wiper System ($435). LS Sedan Preferred Equip. Grp 2: Tilt Strg Wheel; Elect Spd Control, w/resume speed; Intermittent Wiper System; Elect Twin Remote Mirrors; Pwr Windows; Pwr Door Locks ($1101). LS Convertible Preferred Equip. Grp 1: Tilt Strg Wheel; Elect Spd Control, w/resume speed; Intermittent Wiper System ($435). LS Convertible Preferred Equip. Grp 2: Tilt Strg Wheel; Elect Spd Control, w/resume speed; Intermittent Wiper System; Elect Twin Remote Mirrors; Pwr Windows; Pwr Door Locks ($996). Z24 Coupe Preferred Equip. Grp 1: Elect Spd Control, w/resume speed; Intermittent Wiper System ($290). Z24 Coupe Preferred Equip. Grp 2: Elect Spd Control, w/resume speed; Intermittent Wiper System; Elect Twin Remote Mirrors; Pwr Windows; Pwr Door Locks ($851). Air Cond ($785). W27 Appearance Pkg (base coupe only): Body color fascias & side moldings, 15-in. bolt-on wheel covers, P195/65R15 tires ($200). Frt License Plate Bracket (NC). Electric Rear Window Defogger ($170). Pwr Door Locks: Cpe/Conv ($210); Sed ($250). Vinyl Bucket Seats, conv only ($50). Elect Sun Roof, cpe only ($595). Eng. Block Htr ($20). Calif. Emission System ($100). 4-Spd auto trans.: Z24 ($695); LS conv ($200). 15-in. alum wheels, LS models ($259).

CAMARO CONVENIENCE/APPEARANCE OPTIONS: Coupe Preferred Equip. Grp. 1: Air Cond; Elect Spd Control, w/resume speed; Fog Lamps; Remote Trunk Release ($1240). Coupe Preferred Equip. Grp. 2: Air Cond; Pwr Windows; Pwr Door Locks; Elect Spd Control, w/resume speed; Remote Trunk Release; Fog Lamps; Spt Twin Remote Mirrors; Leather-wrapped Strg Wheel/Trans Shifter/Prk Brake Handle; Illum Remote Keyless Entry ($2036). Convertible Preferred Equip. Grp. 1: Air Cond; Elect Spd Control, w/resume speed; Fog Lamps; Remote Trunk Release ($1240). Convertible Preferred Equip. Grp. 2: Air Cond; Pwr Windows; Pwr Door Locks; Elect Spd Control, w/resume speed; Remote Trunk Release; Fog Lamps; Spt Twin Remote Mirrors; Leather-wrapped Strg Wheel/Trans Shifter/Prk Brake Handle; Illum Remote Keyless Entry ($2036). Z28 Coupe Preferred Equip. Grp. 1: Air Cond; Elect Spd Control, w/resume speed; Remote Trunk Release; Eng. Oil Cooler; Fog Lamps; 4-Way Adj Driver's Seat ($1385). Z28 Coupe Preferred Equip. Grp. 2: Air Cond; Pwr Windows; Pwr Door Lock System; Elect Spd Control, w/resume speed; Eng. Oil Cooler; Fog Lamps; Remote Trunk Release; 4-Way Adj Driver's Seat; Spt Twin Remote Mirrors; Leather-wrapped Strg Wheel/Trans Shifter/Prk Brake Handle; Illum Remote Keyless Entry ($2181). Z28 Convertible Preferred Equip. Grp. 1: Air Cond; Elect Spd Control, w/resume speed; Remote Trunk Release; Eng. Oil Cooler; Fog Lamps ($1350). Z28 Convertible Preferred Equip. Grp. 2: Air Cond; Pwr Windows; Pwr Door Lock System; Elect Spd Control, w/resume speed; Eng. Oil Cooler; Fog Lamps; Remote Trunk Release; Spt Twin Remote Mirrors; Leather-wrapped Strg Wheel/Trans Shifter/Prk Brake Handle; Illum Remote Keyless Entry ($2146). Acceleration Slip Regulation, Z28 only ($450). Frt License Plate Bracket (NC). Elect Rear Window Defogger ($170). Calif. Emission System ($100). Bodyside Mldgs

($60). Pwr Door Lock System ($220). GU5 Axle, Z28 only ($250). 1LE Perf Pkg, Z28 cpe only: Eng. Oil Cooler and Special Handling Susp. System ($310). 4-Spd auto trans. ($750). Pwr Driver's Seat ($270). Leather Bucket Seats ($499). Sunshades ($25). Removable Glass Roof Panels, Incl locks ($970). Rear Mats ($15). TIRES: P235/55R16 Steel Belted Radial Blackwall, stnd/Z28 ($132). P245/50ZR16 Steel Belted Radial Blackwall, w/150 mph speedometer, Z28 only ($225). Dlx chrome wheel covers ($35). Cast Alum Wheels, 16-in., stnd/Z28 ($275).

CORSICA CONVENIENCE/APPEARANCE OPTIONS: Preferred Equip. Grp. 1: Day/Night Rear View Mirror, w/reading lamps; LH & RH Visor Mirrors; Luggage Area Cargo Net; Intermittent Wiper System; Color-Keyed Carpeted Mats, F&R ($165). Preferred Equip. Grp 2: Tilt Strg Wheel; Elect Spd Control, w/resume speed; Split Fldg Rear Seat; Day/Night Rear View Mirror, w/reading lamps; LH & RH Visor Mirrors; Pwr Trunk Opener; Luggage Area Cargo Net; Intermittent Wiper System; Color-Keyed Carpeted Mats, F&R ($745). 3.1-liter V-6 ($720). Frt License Plate Bracket (NC). Elect Rear Window Defogger ($170). Eng. Block Htr ($20). Pwr Windows ($340). TIRES: P195/70R14 All Seasons Steel Belted Radial White Stripe ($68). Styled Wheels, 14-in. ($56).

BERETTA CONVENIENCE/APPEARANCE OPTIONS: Preferred Equip. Grp. 1: Day/Night Rear View Mirror, w/reading lamps; LH & RH Visor Mirrors; Luggage Area Cargo Net; Intermittent Wiper System; Color-Keyed Carpeted Mats, F&R ($165). Preferred Equip. Grp. 2: Tilt Strg Wheel; Elect Spd Control, w/resume speed; Split Fldg Rear Seat; Day/Night Rear View Mirror, w/reading lamps; LH & RH Visor Mirrors; Pwr Trunk Opener; Luggage Area Cargo Net; Intermittent Wiper System; Color-Keyed Carpeted Mats, F&R ($745). Z26 Preferred Equip. Grp. 1: Tilt Strg Wheel; Pwr Trunk Opener; Elect Spd Control, w/resume speed; Color-Keyed Carpeted Mats, F&R ($463). 3.1-liter V-6: base cpe ($1275). Frt License Plate Bracket (NC). Elect Rear Window Defogger ($170). Calif. Emission System ($100). Gauge Pkg, w/Tach & Trip Odometer, stnd Z26 ($111). Eng. Block Htr ($20). Rear Spoiler, stnd/Z26 ($110). Manual Sunroof, Removable ($350). Pwr Windows ($275). 3-Spd Auto Trans ($555). TIRES: P205/60R15 Steel Belted Radial Blackwall, stnd/Z26 ($175). P205/55R16 Steel Belted Radial Blackwall ($372).

LUMINA CONVENIENCE/APPEARANCE OPTIONS: Preferred Equip Grp. 1: Pwr Windows; Pwr Trunk Opener; Elect Spd Control, w/resume speed; Cargo Area Retaining Net; Spt Twin Remote Mirrors ($707). LS Preferred Equip. Grp. 1: Pwr Trunk Opener; Elect Spd Control, w/resume speed; Cargo Area Retaining Net; Spt Twin Remote Mirrors; Remote Keyless Entry ($590). Dual Control HVAC System, LS only ($100). Custom Cloth Bucket Seats w/console ($48). Frt License Plate Bracket (NC). 4-Wheel Anti-Lock Brakes, stnd LS ($575). Electric Rear Window Defogger ($170).

Calif. Emission System ($100). Remote Keyless Entry ($220). Cellular Phone Provision ($43). Pwr 6-way Driver's Seat ($300). Elect Spd Control, w/resume speed ($217). TIRES: P225/60R16 All Seasons Steel Belted Radial Blackwall ($175). P225/60R16 All Seasons Steel Belted Radial Blackwall, LS only ($190). 15-in. bolt-on chrome wheel cover, stnd/LS ($100).

MONTE CARLO CONVENIENCE/APPEARANCE OPTIONS: LS Preferred Equip Grp. 1: Pwr Trunk Opener; Elect Spd Control, w/resume speed; Cargo Area Retaining Net; Spt Twin Remote Mirrors; Remote Keyless Entry ($590). Custom Cloth Bucket Seats, w/console, LS only ($48). Custom Leather Bucket Seats, w/console: LS ($675); Z34 ($627). Frt License Plate Bracket (NC). Electric Rear Window Defogger ($170). Calif. Emission System ($100). Dual Control HVAC System ($100). 6-Way Pwr Driver's Seat ($300). Eng Block Htr ($19). Elect Spd Control, w/resume speed ($217). Strg Wheel Radio Controls ($121). Cellular Phone Provision ($43). TIRES: P225/60R16 All Seasons Steel Belted Radial Blackwall ($175). 16-in. alum wheels, stnd Z34 ($300).

CAPRICE CLASSIC CONVENIENCE/APPEARANCE OPTIONS: Caprice Classic Sed Preferred Equip. Grp. 1: Elect Spd Control, w/resume speed; Pwr Windows; Pwr Trunk Opener; Elect Twin Remote Mirrors ($703). Caprice Classic Sed Preferred Equip. Grp. 2: Elect Tuned AM/FM Stereo Radio, w/Seek & Scan, Stereo Cass. Tape & Digital Clock, w/extended range sound system; Pwr 6-Way Driver's Seat; Pwr Antenna; Pwr Windows; Pwr Trunk Opener; Elect Spd Control, w/resume speed; Rearview Mirror, w/dual reading lamps; Illum RH Visor Mirror; Elect Twin Remote Mirrors ($1382). Caprice Classic Sed Preferred Equip. Grp. 3: Elect Tuned AM/FM Stereo Radio, w/Seek & Scan, Stereo Cass. Tape & Digital Clock, w/extended range sound system; Rear Courtesy Lamps; Auto Day/Night Rearview Mirror, w/reading lamps; Pwr 6-Way Driver's Seat; Pwr Pass. Seat; Twilight Sentinel Headlamp System; Pwr Antenna; Pwr Windows; Pwr Trunk Opener; Elect Spd Control, w/resume speed; Remote Keyless Entry; Illum RH Visor Mirror; Elect Twin Remote Mirrors ($2016). Caprice Classic Station Wagon Preferred Equip. Grp. 1: Elect Spd Control, w/resume speed; Pwr Windows; Pwr 6-Way Driver's Seat; Elect Twin Remote Mirrors ($948). Caprice Classic Station Wagon Preferred Equip. Grp. 2: Elect Spd Control, w/resume speed; Pwr Windows; Pwr 6-Way Driver's Seat; Elect Twin Remote Mirrors; Pwr Antenna; Auto Day/Night Rearview Mirror; Rear Window Defogger, w/heated outside rearview mirrors; Dlx Rear Comp. Decor; Rear Comp. Security Cover; illum RH Visor Mirror; Rear Comp. Reading Lamps ($1821). Custom Leather Seats ($775). Custom Two-Tone Paint ($141). Frt License Plate Bracket (NC). Electric Rear Window Defogger ($170). Heat Reflective Windshield ($52). B18 Interior Pkg: Cargo Net, Front Courtesy Lamps, LH Covered Visor Mirror, Custom Trim Door Panels ($130). Cellular Phone Provision ($45). Cargo Net ($30). Pwr 6-Way Driver's Seat ($305). Calif. Emission System ($100). Elect Spd Control, w/resume speed ($225). Pin Striping ($61). Woodgrain Ext. ($595).

V92 Trailering Pkg ($21). TIRES: P215/75R15 All Seasons Steel Belted Radial White Stripe ($80). P225/70R15 All Seasons Steel Belted Radial White Stripe ($176). P235/70R15 All Seasons Steel Belted Radial White Stripe ($90). Alum wheels, w/locks ($250). Wire Wheel Covers ($215). Dlx Wheel Covers ($70).

IMPALA SS CONVENIENCE/APPEARANCE OPTIONS: Impala SS Preferred Equip. Grp. 1: Pwr Antenna; Auto Day/Night Rearview Mirror; Rear Window Defogger, w/heated outside rearview mirrors; Pwr 6-Way Pass. Seat; Remote Keyless Entry, w/trunk release; Twilight Sentinel Headlamp System ($890). Frt License Plate Bracket (NC). Electric Rear Window Defogger ($205). Calif. Emission System ($100). Eng Block Htr ($20). Heat Reflective Windshield ($52).

HISTORY: Chevrolet's market share for U.S.-made passenger cars in model year 1995 was 8.44 percent, representing 568,329 units (these figures do not include Camaro models for which numbers are not available). A Chevrolet Corvette paced the Indianapolis 500 in 1995.

1996

Three Chevrolet series made their final appearance in 1996: Beretta, Corsica and Caprice Classic (including the Impala SS). With so many models in their final year of production, 1996 was not a year of big change for Chevrolet. The Camaro line added an intermediate RS coupe and convertible, positioned between the base and Z28 coupes and ragtops. Also, the 3.4-liter V-6 that was formerly standard in Camaro was replaced by a 3.8-liter V-6 rated at 200 horsepower. In the Cavalier line, the new DOHC 2.4-liter four-cylinder engine that was standard in the Z24 was made optional in the LS sedan and convertible. Daytime Running Lamps were made standard equipment in the Cavalier, as was the new PassLock antitheft system. Enhanced Traction Control was also standard on the Cavalier LS with the four-speed automatic transmission. A new four-wheel disc brake system was standard on the Lumina LS sedan and Monte Carlo Z34 coupe.

1996 Chevrolet, Cavalier LS four-door sedan

CAVALIER — SERIES 1J — FOUR — After an all-new design Cavalier was debuted the year previous, the 1996 model was only slightly revised. The Z24 coupe received a new standard powerplant in the form of a DOHC 2.4-liter four-cylinder engine with sequential fuel injection, which was also the option engine in the LS sedan and convertible. The new PassLock antitheft system and Daytime Running Lamps became standard equipment on Cavalier models. Remote entry was an option on all Cavaliers except the base sedan. The LS line came standard with the electronic four-speed automatic transmission, which featured Enhanced Traction Control. The 2.2-liter four-cylinder engine was again the standard powerplant for the base and LS Cavalier models. The five-speed manual transmission was standard on the base coupe and sedan and Z24. The three-speed automatic was the option transmission for the base models.

1996 Chevrolet, Camaro RS two-door coupe

CAMARO — SERIES 1F — V-6/V-8 — With the addition of an intermediate RS coupe and convertible, buyers now had their choice of three Camaro coupes and three convertibles offered in base, RS or Z28 trim. The standard powerplant of the base and RS models was the 3.8-liter V-6, which replaced the 3.4-liter V-6 formerly offered as base engine. A new V-6 Performance Handling Package was offered as was a new second gear select switch on V-6-powered Camaros fitted with automatic transmissions. This switch allowed for second gear starts for improved launch on slippery surfaces. T-tops were again available as optional equipment on coupes, and an antitheft system was also available for all Camaro models as an option. The Z28 again used the 5.7-liter V-8 as its standard engine. The base and RS lines featured the five-speed manual transmission as base offering while the Z28 had the six-speed manual transmission as standard. The four-speed automatic was the option transmission for all Camaro models.

CORSICA/BERETTA — SERIES 1L — FOUR/V-6 — The 1996 lineup for Corsica and Beretta in their final year of production remained unchanged from the previous year. The 3.1-liter V-6 used in the Z26 was revised for better performance. Again, the base Beretta and Corsica used the 2.2-liter four-cylinder engine as standard equipment. Corsica again used the three-speed automatic while Beretta and Z26 were fitted with the five-speed manual transmission as base offerings. The three-speed automatic was optional on the Beretta coupe while the four-speed automatic was the option transmission on the Corsica and Z26.

1996 Chevrolet, Lumina LS four-door sedan (with optional aluminum wheels)

LUMINA — SERIES 1W — V-6 — Optional equipment on the 1996 Lumina two-sedan line included dual-zone temperature controls and steering wheel-mounted radio controls. The LS sedan had a leather seat option. This model also offered a new four-wheel disc brake system. The 3.1-liter V-6 was again the standard engine in both the base and LS models. The upgraded 3.4-liter DOHC was the option powerplant in the LS sedan. The four-speed automatic was the only transmission offered in Luminas.

MONTE CARLO — SERIES 1W — V-6 — The LS and Z34 coupes returned as Monte Carlo's 1996 lineup. New features included radio controls on the steering wheel, which was standard equipment on the Z34 and optional on the LS coupe. Both the 3.1-liter V-6 standard in the LS coupe and the DOHC 3.4-liter V-6 standard in the Z34 were refined to offer better performance. The Z34 was also fitted with a new four-wheel disc brake system. Both coupes again had the four-speed automatic transmission as standard equipment.

1996 Chevrolet, Caprice Classic four-door sedan

1996 Chevrolet, Caprice Classic station wagon

CAPRICE CLASSIC/IMPALA — SERIES 1B — V-8 — With 1996 being the final year for production of the Caprice Classic and Impala SS, it was the end of the full-size front-engine, rear-drive automobile offerings from Chevrolet. It was also the demise of the large station wagon, with the minivan and sport utility vehicle now the vehicles of choice for family transportation. The final lineup for Caprice Classic was again comprised of a sedan and station wagon, as well as the Impala SS sedan. The Caprice Classic sedan was again powered by the 4.3-liter V-8 with sequential fuel injection. The Caprice Classic station wagon and Impala SS were again powered by the LT1 (Corvette) 5.7-liter V-8, which was the option engine for the Caprice Classic sedan. The four-speed automatic transmission was again standard in all three models.

I.D. DATA: Chevrolets again had a 17-symbol Vehicle Identification Number (VIN) on the upper left surface of the instrument panel, visible through the windshield. Symbol one indicates country: '1' or '4' - U.S.A.; '2' - Canada. Next is a manufacturer code: 'G' - General Motors. Symbol three is car make: '1' - Chevrolet; '7' - GM of Canada. Symbols four and five denote car line/series: B/L - Caprice Classic/Impala SS; F/P - Camaro; J/C - Cavalier; J/F - Cavalier Z24 and LS; L/D - Corsica; L/V - Beretta; L/W - Beretta Z26; W/L - Lumina; W/N - Lumina LS; W/W - Monte Carlo LS and W/X - Monte Carlo Z34. Symbol six is the body style: '1' - 2-dr coupe, '3' - 2-dr, '3' - 2-dr convertible, '4' - 2-dr station wagon, '5' - 4-dr sedan, '6' - 4-dr and '8' - 4-dr station wagon. Symbol seven is the restraint system: '1' - active (manual) belts, '2' - active (manual) belts w/driver's and passenger's side airbags, '3' - active (manual) belts w/driver's side airbag, '4' - passive (automatic) belts, '5' - passive (automatic) belts w/driver's side airbag, '6' - passive (automatic) belts w/driver's and passenger's side airbags, '7' - active (manual) belt driver and passive (automatic) belt passenger w/driver's and passenger's side airbag. Symbol eight is the engine code: 'K' - 3.8-liter V-6; 'M' - 3.1-liter V-6; 'P' - 5.7-liter V-8 (LT1); 'T' - 2.4-liter four-cyl.; 'W' - 4.3-liter V-8; 'X' - 3.4-liter V-6; '4' - 2.2-liter four-cyl.; '5' - 5.7-liter V-8 (LT4). This is followed by symbol nine, which is a check digit. Symbol ten is 'T' for model year 1996. Symbol eleven indicates assembly plant. The final six digits are the sequential serial number.

CAVALIER (FOUR)

Model No.	Body/Style No.	Body Type & Seating	Factory Price	Shipping Weight	Prod. Total
1J	C37	2-dr. Coupe-5P	10500	2617	Note 1
1J	C69	4-dr. Sedan-5P	10700	2676	Note 2

CAVALIER LS (FOUR)

1J	F69	4-dr. Sedan-5P	12900	2736	Note 2
1J	F67	2-dr. Conv-5P	17500	2838	10

CAVALIER Z24 (FOUR)

1J	F37	2-dr. Coupe-5P	14200	2788	Note 1

Note 1: Total Cavalier coupe production was 145,229 with no further breakout available.

Note 2: Total Cavalier sedan production was 116,447 with no further breakout available.

CAMARO (V-6)

1F	P87	2-dr. Cpe-4P	14990	3306	Note 1
1F	P67	2-dr. Conv-4P	21270	3440	Note 2

CAMARO RS (V-6)

1F	P87	2-dr. Cpe-4P	17490	3306	Note 1
1F	P67	2-dr. Conv-4P	22720	3440	Note 2

CAMARO Z-28 (V-8)

1F	P87/Z28	2-dr. Cpe-4P	19390	3466	Note 1
1F	P67/Z28	2-dr. Conv-4P	24490	3593	Note 2

Note 1: Total Camaro coupe production was 54,525 with no further breakout available.

Note 2: Total Camaro convertible production was 6,837 with no further breakout available.

CORSICA (FOUR/V-6)

1L	D69	4-dr. Sedan-5P	14385/15105	2745/2885 148,652

BERETTA (FOUR/V-6)

1L	V37	2-dr. Coupe-5P	13490/14765	2756/2896	Note 1
1L	W37	2-dr. Z26 Cpe-5P	---- /16690	---- /2990	Note 1

Note 1: Total Beretta coupe production was 42,476 with no further breakout available.

LUMINA (V-6)

1W	L69	4-dr. Sedan-6P	16355	3330	Note 1

LUMINA LS (V-6)

1W	N69	4-dr. Sedan-6P	18055	3372	Note 1

Note 1: Total Lumina sedan production was 224,573 with no further breakout available.

MONTE CARLO LS (V-6)

1W	W27/Z7F	2-dr. Coupe-6P	17255	3306	Note 1

MONTE CARLO Z34 (V-6)

1W	X27/Z7G	2-dr. Coupe-6P	19455	3436	Note 1

Note 1: Total Monte Carlo coupe production was 80,717 with no further breakout available.

CAPRICE CLASSIC (V-8)

1B	L19	4-dr. Sed-6P	19905	4061	Note 1
1B	L35	4-dr. 3S Wag-8P	22405	4473	485

IMPALA SS (V-8)

1B	L19/1SS	4-dr. Sed-6P	24405	4036	Note 1

Note 1: Total Caprice Classic/Impala SS sedan production was 69,096 with no further breakout available.

FACTORY PRICE AND WEIGHT NOTE: For Corsica/Beretta, prices and weights to left of slash are for four-cylinder, to right for V-6 engine.

ENGINE DATA: BASE FOUR (Cavalier, Corsica/Beretta): Inline. Overhead valve. Four-cylinder. Displacement: 133 cu. in. (2.2 liters). Bore & stroke: 3.50 x 3.46 in. Compression ratio: 9.0:1. Brake horsepower: 120 at 5200 RPM. Sequential fuel injection. BASE V-6 (Cavalier Z24); OPTIONAL (Cavalier LS): Overhead valve V-6. Displacement: 146 cu. in. (2.4 liters). Bore & stroke: 3.54 x 3.70 in. Compression ratio: 9.5:1. Brake horsepower: 150 at 6000 RPM. Sequential fuel injection. BASE V-6 (Beretta Z26, Lumina/Lumina LS, Monte Carlo LS): Overhead-valve V-6. Displacement: 191 cu. in. (3.1 liters). Bore & stroke: 3.51 x 3.31 in. Compression ratio:

9.6:1. Brake horsepower: 155 at 5200 RPM. Sequential fuel injection. BASE V-6 (Camaro/Camaro RS): Overhead valve V-6. Displacement: 231 cu. in. (3.8 liters). Bore & stroke: 3.80 x 3.40 in. Compression ratio: 9.4:1. Brake horsepower: 200 at 5200 RPM. Sequential fuel injection. BASE V-6 (Monte Carlo Z34); OPTIONAL (Lumina LS): Dual overhead cam (24-valve) V-6. Displacement: 207 cu. in. (3.4 liters). Bore & stroke: 3.62 x 3.31 in. Compression ratio: 9.7:1. Brake horsepower: 215 at 5200 RPM. Sequential fuel injection. BASE V-8 (Caprice Classic sed): Overhead valve V-8. Displacement: 265 cu. in. (4.3 liters). Bore & stroke: 3.74 x 3.00 in. Compression ratio: 9.4:1. Brake horsepower: 200 at 5200 RPM. Sequential fuel injection. BASE V-8 (Camaro Z28, Caprice Classic wag/Impala SS); OPTIONAL (Caprice Classic sed): 90-degree, overhead valve V-8. Displacement: 350 cu. in. (5.7 liters). Bore & stroke: 4.00 x 3.48 in. Compression ratio: Z28: 10.4:1; Caprice Classic wag/Impala SS: 10.0:1. Brake horsepower: Z28: 285 at 5200 RPM; Caprice Classic wag/Impala SS: 260 at 5000 RPM. Sequential fuel injection.

CHASSIS DATA: Wheelbase: (Cavalier) 104.1 in.; (Camaro) 101.1 in.; (Corsica/Beretta) 103.4 in.; (Lumina/Monte Carlo) 107.5 in.; (Caprice Classic/Impala SS) 115.9 in. Overall length: (Cavalier) 180.3 in.; (Camaro) 193.2 in.; (Corsica) 183.4 in.; (Beretta) 187.3 in.; (Lumina) 200.9 in.; (Monte Carlo) 200.7 in.; (Caprice Classic/Impala SS sed) 214.1 in.; (Caprice Classic wag) 217.3 in. Height: (Cavalier cpe) 53.2 in.; (Cavalier sed) 54.8; (Cavalier Z24) 53.9 in.; (Camaro cpe) 51.3 in.; (Camaro conv) 52.0 in.; (Corsica) 54.2 in.; (Beretta) 53.0 in.; (Lumina) 55.2 in.; (Monte Carlo) 53.8 in.; (Caprice Classic/Impala SS sed) 55.7 in.; (Caprice Classic wag) 60.9 in. Width: (Cavalier) 67.4 in.; (Camaro) 74.1 in.; (Corsica) 68.0 in.; (Beretta) 67.9; (Lumina) 72.5; (Monte Carlo) 72.5 in.; (Caprice Classic/Impala SS sed) 77.5 in.; (Caprice Classic wag) 79.6 in. Standard Tires: (Cavalier) P195/70R14; (Cavalier LS) P195/65R15; (Cavalier Z24) P205/55R16; (Camaro) P215/60R16; (Camaro RS/Camaro Z28) P235/55R16; (Corsica/Beretta) P195/70R14; (Beretta Z26) P205/60R15; (Lumina/Lumina LS/Monte Carlo LS) P205/70R15; (Monte Carlo Z34) P225/60R16; (Caprice Classic sed) P215/75R15; (Caprice Classic wag) P225/75R15; (Impala SS) P255/50ZR17.

TECHNICAL: Transmission: Five-speed manual shift standard on Cavalier/Cavalier Z24, Beretta/Beretta Z26 and Camaro/Camaro RS. Six-speed manual shift standard on Camaro Z28. Three-speed automatic standard on Corsica. Four-speed overdrive automatic standard on Cavalier LS, Lumina/Lumina LS, Monte Carlo LS and Caprice Classic/Impala SS. Steering: (Caprice Classic) recirculating ball; (others) rack and pinion. Brakes: front disc, rear drum; four-wheel discs standard on Camaro Z28, Lumina LS, Monte Carlo Z34 and Impala SS; anti-lock brakes standard on all except base Lumina. Body construction: unibody except (Caprice Classic) separate body and frame. Fuel tank: (Cavalier) 15.2 gal.; (Camaro) 15.5 gal.; (Corsica/Beretta) 15.2 gal.; (Lumina) 16.5 gal.; (Monte Carlo) 17.1 gal.; (Caprice Classic/Impala SS sed) 23.0 gal.; (Caprice wag) 22.0 gal.

DRIVETRAIN OPTIONS: Engines: 2.4-liter four-cylinder: Cavalier LS ($395). 3.1-liter V-6: Beretta ($1275); Corsica ($720). 3.4-liter V-6: Lumina LS ($1095). 5.7-liter V-8: Caprice Classic sed ($550). Transmission/Differential: Three-speed automatic trans.: Cavalier ($550); Beretta ($555). Four-speed overdrive auto. trans.: Beretta Z26 (NC); Corsica (NC); Camaro/RS/Z28 ($790).

CAVALIER CONVENIENCE/APPEARANCE OPTIONS: Coupe Preferred Equip. Grp 1: Intermittent Wiper System; Mech Trunk Opener; Dual Covered Visor Mirrors, w/map straps; Bodyside Moldings; Mud Guards; Color-Keyed Carpeted Mats, F&R ($240). Coupe Preferred Equip. Grp 2: Tilt Strg Wheel; Elect Spd Control, w/resume speed; Pwr Mirrors; Intermittent Wiper System; Mech Trunk Opener; Dual Covered Visor Mirrors, w/map straps; Bodyside Moldings; Mud Guards; Color-Keyed Carpeted Mats, F&R ($696). Coupe Preferred Equip. Grp 3: Tilt Strg Wheel; Elect Spd Control, w/resume speed; Pwr Mirrors; Pwr Windows; Remote Keyless Entry, Incl Pwr Locks; Intermittent Wiper System; Mech Trunk Opener; Dual Covered Visor Mirrors, w/map straps; Bodyside Moldings; Mud Guards; Color-Keyed Carpeted Mats, F&R ($1295). Sedan Preferred Equip. Grp 1: Intermittent Wiper System; Mech Trunk Opener; Dual Covered Visor Mirrors, w/map straps; Bodyside Moldings; Mud Guards; Color-Keyed Carpeted Mats, F&R ($223). Sedan Preferred Equip. Grp. 2: Tilt Strg Wheel; Elect Spd Control, w/resume speed; Intermittent Wiper System; Mech Trunk Opener; Dual Covered Visor Mirrors, w/map straps; Bodyside Moldings; Mud Guards; Color-Keyed Carpeted Mats, F&R ($593). LS Sedan Preferred Equip. Grp 1: Tilt Strg Wheel; Elect Spd Control, w/resume speed; Intermittent Wiper System ($435). LS Sedan Preferred Equip. Grp 2: Tilt Strg Wheel; Elect Spd Control, w/resume speed; Intermittent Wiper System; Elect Twin Remote Mirrors; Pwr Windows; Remote Keyless Entry, Incl Pwr Locks ($1225). LS Convertible Preferred Equip. Grp 1: Tilt Strg Wheel; Elect Spd Control, w/resume speed; Intermittent Wiper System ($435). LS Convertible Preferred Equip. Grp 2: Tilt Strg Wheel; Elect Spd Control, w/resume speed; Intermittent Wiper System; Elect Twin Remote Mirrors; Pwr Windows; Remote Keyless Entry, Incl Pwr Locks ($1120). Z24 Coupe Preferred Equip. Grp 1: Elect Spd Control, w/resume speed; Intermittent Wiper System ($290). Z24 Coupe Preferred Equip. Grp 2: Elect Spd Control, w/resume speed; Intermittent Wiper System; Elect Twin Remote Mirrors; Pwr Windows; Remote Keyless Entry, Incl Pwr Locks ($975). Air Cond ($795). W27 Appearance Pkg (base coupe only): Body color fascias & side moldings, 15-in. bolt-on wheel covers, P195/65R15 tires ($255). Frt License Plate Bracket (NC). Electric Rear Window Defogger ($170). Pwr Door Locks: Cpe ($210); Sed ($250). Vinyl Bucket Seats, conv only ($50). Elect Sun Roof, cpe only ($670). Eng. Block Htr ($20). Calif. Emission System ($100). 4-Spd auto trans.: ($795). 15-in. alum wheels, LS models ($295).

CAMARO CONVENIENCE/APPEARANCE OPTIONS: Coupe Preferred Equip. Grp. 1: Air Cond; Elect Spd Control, w/resume speed; Fog Lamps; Remote Trunk Release ($1240). Coupe Preferred Equip. Grp. 2: Air Cond; Pwr Windows; Pwr Door Locks; Elect Spd Control, w/resume speed; Remote Trunk Release; Fog Lamps; Spt Twin Remote Mirrors; Leather-wrapped Strg Wheel/Trans Shifter/Prk Brake Handle; Illum Remote Keyless Entry; Antitheft Alarm System ($2126). Convertible Preferred Equip. Grp. 1: Pwr Door Locks; Elect Spd Control, w/resume speed; Fog Lamps; Remote Trunk Release ($565). Convertible Preferred Equip. Grp. 2: Pwr Windows; Pwr Door Locks; Elect Spd Control, w/resume speed; Remote Trunk Release; Fog Lamps; Spt Twin Remote Mirrors; Leather-wrapped Strg Wheel/Trans Shifter/Prk Brake Handle; Illum Remote Keyless Entry; Antitheft Alarm System ($1231). RS Coupe Preferred Equip. Grp. 1: Pwr Door Locks; Elect Spd Control, w/resume speed; Fog Lamps; Remote Trunk Release ($565). RS Coupe Preferred Equip. Grp. 2: Pwr Windows; Pwr Door Locks; Elect Spd Control, w/resume speed; Fog Lamps; Remote Trunk Release; Spt Twin Remote Mirrors; Leather-wrapped Strg Wheel/Trans Shifter/Prk Brake Handle; Illum Remote Keyless Entry; Antitheft Alarm System ($1231). RS Convertible Preferred Equip. Grp. 1: Pwr Door Locks; Elect Spd Control, w/resume speed; Fog Lamps; Remote Trunk Release ($565). RS Convertible Preferred Equip. Grp. 2: Pwr Windows; Pwr Door Locks; Elect Spd Control, w/resume speed; Fog Lamps; Remote Trunk Release; Spt Twin Remote Mirrors; Leather-wrapped Strg Wheel/Trans Shifter/Prk Brake Handle; Illum Remote Keyless Entry; Antitheft Alarm System ($1231). Z28 Coupe Preferred Equip. Grp. 1: Pwr Door Locks; Elect Spd Control, w/resume speed; Remote Trunk Release; Fog Lamps; 4-Way Adj Driver's Seat ($600). Z28 Coupe Preferred Equip. Grp. 2: Pwr Windows; Pwr Door Locks; Elect Spd Control, w/resume speed; Fog Lamps; Remote Trunk Release; 4-Way Adj Driver's Seat; Spt Twin Remote Mirrors; Leather-wrapped Strg Wheel/Trans Shifter/Prk Brake Handle; Illum Remote Keyless Entry; Antitheft Alarm System ($1266). Z28 Convertible Preferred Equip. Grp. 1: Pwr Door Locks; Elect Spd Control, w/resume speed; Remote Trunk Release; Fog Lamps ($565). Z28 Convertible Preferred Equip. Grp. 2: Pwr Windows; Pwr Door Lock System; Elect Spd Control, w/resume speed; Fog Lamps; Remote Trunk Release; Spt Twin Remote Mirrors; Leather-wrapped Strg Wheel/Trans Shifter/Prk Brake Handle; Illum Remote Keyless Entry; Antitheft Alarm System ($1231). Acceleration Slip Regulation, Z28 only ($450). Frt License Plate Bracket (NC). Elect Rear Window Defogger ($170). Calif. Emission System ($100). Bodyside Mldgs ($60). Pwr Door Lock System ($220). GU5 Axle, Z28 only ($250). 1LE Perf Pkg, Z28 cpe only: Incl Special Handling Susp. System ($310). Y87 Performance Handling Pkg, base & RS only: Incl Ltd Slip Axle, 4-Wheel Disc Brakes, Dual Exhaust & Spt Strg Ratio ($400). 4-Spd auto trans. ($790). 6-Way Pwr Driver's Seat ($270). Leather Bucket Seats ($499). Sunshades ($25). Removable Glass Roof Panels, Incl locks ($970). TIRES: P235/55R16 Steel Belted Radial Blackwall, stnd/RS & Z28 ($132). P245/50ZR16 Steel Belted Radial Blackwall, Z28 only ($225). Cast Alum Wheels, 16-in., stnd/Z28 ($275).

CORSICA CONVENIENCE/APPEARANCE OPTIONS:

Preferred Equip. Grp. 1: Dual Reading Lamps; LH & RH Visor Mirrors; Luggage Area Cargo Net; Intermittent Wiper System; Color-Keyed Carpeted Mats, F&R ($165). Preferred Equip. Grp 2: Tilt Strg Wheel; Elect Spd Control, w/resume speed; Split Fldg Rear Seat; Dual Reading Lamps; LH & RH Visor Mirrors; Pwr Trunk Opener; Luggage Area Cargo Net; Intermittent Wiper System; Color-Keyed Carpeted Mats, F&R ($745). 3.1-liter V-6 ($720). Frt License Plate Bracket (NC). Elect Rear Window Defogger ($170). Elect Spd Control, w/resume speed ($225). Eng. Block Htr ($20). Pwr Windows ($340). TIRES: P195/70R14 All Seasons Steel Belted Radial White Stripe ($68). Styled Wheels, 14-in. ($56).

BERETTA CONVENIENCE/APPEARANCE OPTIONS:

Preferred Equip. Grp. 1: Day/Night Rear View Mirror, w/reading lamps; LH & RH Visor Mirrors; Luggage Area Cargo Net; Intermittent Wiper System; Color-Keyed Carpeted Mats, F&R ($165). Preferred Equip. Grp. 2: Tilt Strg Wheel; Elect Spd Control, w/resume speed; Split Fldg Rear Seat; Day/Night Rear View Mirror, w/reading lamps; LH & RH Visor Mirrors; Pwr Trunk Opener; Luggage Area Cargo Net; Intermittent Wiper System; Color-Keyed Carpeted Mats, F&R ($745). Z26 Preferred Equip. Grp. 1: Tilt Strg Wheel; Pwr Trunk Opener; Elect Spd Control, w/resume speed; Color-Keyed Carpeted Mats, F&R ($463). 3.1-liter V-6: base cpe ($1275). Frt License Plate Bracket (NC). Elect Rear Window Defogger ($170). Calif. Emission System ($100). Gauge Pkg, w/Tach & Trip Odometer, stnd Z26 ($111). Eng. Block Htr ($20). Rear Spoiler, stnd/Z26 ($110). Manual Sunroof, Removable ($350). Pwr Windows ($275). TIRES: P205/60R15 Steel Belted Radial Blackwall, stnd/Z26 ($175). P205/55R16 Steel Belted Radial Blackwall, Z26 only ($372).

LUMINA CONVENIENCE/APPEARANCE OPTIONS:

Preferred Equip Grp. 1: Pwr Windows; Pwr Trunk Opener; Elect Spd Control, w/resume speed; Cargo Area Retaining Net; Spt Twin Remote Mirrors; Flr Mats, F&R ($736). LS Preferred Equip. Grp. 1: Pwr Trunk Opener; Elect Spd Control, w/resume speed; Driver & Pass. Temp Control; Remote Keyless Entry; Flr Mats, F&R ($625). Dual Control HVAC System ($100). Custom Cloth Bucket Seats, LS only ($48). 60/40 Bench Seat, Leather Trim, LS only ($627). Bucket Seats, Leather Trim, LS only ($675). 60/40 Bench Seat, Cloth Trim, stnd LS ($150). Frt License Plate Bracket (NC). 4-Wheel Anti-Lock Brakes, stnd LS ($575). Electric Rear Window Defogger ($170). Calif. Emission System ($100). Remote Keyless Entry ($220). Pwr Driver's Seat ($300). Rear Integrated Child's Seat ($195). Elect Spd Control, w/resume speed ($217). Color-Keyed Carpeted Mats, F&R ($15). TIRES: P225/60R16 All Seasons Steel Belted Radial Blackwall ($175). P225/60R16 All Seasons Steel Belted Radial Blackwall, LS only ($190). 15-in. bolt-on chrome wheel cover, stnd/LS ($100). 16-in. alum wheels ($300).

MONTE CARLO CONVENIENCE/APPEARANCE OPTIONS:

LS Preferred Equip Grp. 1: Pwr Trunk Opener; Elect Spd Control, w/resume speed; Cargo Area Retaining Net; Driver & Pass. Temp Control ($403). Custom Cloth Bucket Seats, w/console, LS only ($48). Custom Leather Bucket Seats, w/console: LS ($675); Z34 ($627). Frt License Plate Bracket (NC). Electric Rear Window Defogger ($170). Calif. Emission System (NC). Dual Control HVAC System ($100). Pwr Driver's Seat ($300). Eng Block Htr ($19). Elect Spd Control, w/resume speed ($217). Strg Wheel Radio Controls ($171). TIRES: P225/60R16 All Seasons Steel Belted Radial Blackwall ($175). 16-in. alum wheels, stnd Z34 ($300).

CAPRICE CLASSIC CONVENIENCE/APPEARANCE OPTIONS:

Caprice Classic Sed Special Value Pkg 1: Elect Spd Control, w/resume speed; Pwr Windows; Pwr Trunk Opener; Pwr Antenna; Auto Day/Night Rearview Mirrors, w/dual reading lamps; Rear Window Defogger; Rear Comp. Reading Lamps; Elect Twin Remote Heated Mirrors; Dlx Wheel Covers; Full-size Spare Tire; P215/75R15 Tires (NC). Caprice Classic Sed Special Value Pkg 2: Elect Spd Control, w/resume speed; Pwr Windows; Pwr Trunk Opener; Pwr Antenna; Auto Day/Night Rearview Mirrors, w/dual reading lamps; Rear Window Defogger; Rear Comp. Reading Lamps; Cornering Lamps; Illum RH Covered Visor Mirror; Pwr Seats, driver & pass.; Elect Twin Remote Heated Mirrors; Alum Wheels; Full-size Spare Tire; P215/75R15 Tires (NC). Caprice Classic Sed Special Value Pkg 3: Elect Tuned AM/FM Stereo Radio, w/Seek & Scan, CD Player, w/extended range sound system; Custom Interior Pkg; Elect Spd Control, w/resume speed; Pwr Windows; Pwr Trunk Opener; Remote Keyless Entry; Twilight Sentinel Headlamp System; Heat Reflective Windshield; Pwr Antenna; Auto Day/Night Rearview Mirrors, w/dual reading lamps; Rear Window Defogger; Rear Comp. Reading Lamps; Cornering Lamps; Illum RH Covered Visor Mirror; Pwr Seats, driver & pass.; Elect Twin Remote Heated Mirrors; Alum Wheels; Full-size Spare Tire; P215/75R15 Tires (NC). Caprice Classic Station Wagon Special Value Pkg 1: Custom Interior Pkg; Elect Spd Control, w/resume speed; Pwr Windows; Heat Reflective Windshield; Pwr Antenna; Auto Day/Night Rearview Mirrors, w/dual reading lamps; Rear Window Defogger; Dlx Rear Comp. Pkg: Incl Reading Lamps & Security Cover; Illum RH Covered Visor Mirror; Pwr Seats, driver & pass.; Elect Twin Remote Heated Mirrors; Auto Leveling Susp.; Wire Wheel Covers; Full-size Spare Tire (NC). Frt License Plate Bracket (NC). G80 Axle, w/eng oil cooler ($250). Calif. Emission System (NC). Leather Seats ($775). Pin Striping ($61). Woodgrain Ext. ($595). Eng Block Htr ($20). V92 Trailering Pkg ($21). TIRES: P215/75R15 All Seasons Steel Belted Radial White Stripe ($80). P225/70R15 All Seasons Steel Belted Radial White Stripe ($176). P235/70R15 All Seasons Steel Belted Radial White Stripe ($90). Alum wheels, w/locks ($180). Wire Wheel Covers ($145).

IMPALA SS CONVENIENCE/APPEARANCE OPTIONS:

Impala SS Preferred Equip. Grp. 1: Auto Day/Night Rearview Mirror; Pwr Pass. Seat; Twilight Sentinel Headlamp System ($490). Frt License Plate Bracket (NC). Calif. Emission System (NC). Eng Block Htr ($20). Heat Reflective Windshield ($52).

HISTORY: Chevrolet's market share for U.S.-made passenger cars in model year 1996 was 9.56 percent, representing 491,665 units (these figures do not include Camaro/Lumina/Monte Carlo models for which numbers are not available).

1997

Chevrolet's ranks were a bit thinner in 1997 with the discontinuation of Corsica/Beretta and Caprice Classic/Impala SS from the previous year. One new series was introduced to help bolster the lineup, and that was the return of the Malibu name to a pair of sedans offered in base and LS trim. A 30th Anniversary Package was available on Camaro Z28s, with a orange stripe on white paint scheme reminiscent of the 1969 Camaro that paced that year's Indianapolis 500. An intermediate RS coupe joined the Cavalier series, positioned between the base and LS models. All Cavalier models were stiffened to meet tougher side-impact standards. An upscale, sporty LTZ sedan joined the Lumina line as a third offering.

CAVALIER — SERIES 1J — FOUR — All the models offered in the Cavalier series were stiffened in 1997 to meet tougher side-impact standards. This included the all-new RS (Rally Sport) coupe, which was an intermediate offering positioned between the base Cavalier and LS lines. The 2.2-liter four-cylinder engine was again standard equipment in all Cavaliers except the Z24. The performance coupe used the DOHC 2.4-liter four as its base offering, which was the option engine for the LS line. The five-speed manual transmission was again standard on the base coupe and sedan and Z24 as well as the new RS coupe and the option for the LS convertible. The four-speed automatic was standard equipment on the LS sedan and convertible and the option transmission for the Z24. The three-speed automatic was the option transmission for the base models and RS coupe.

1997 Chevrolet, Malibu four-door sedan

MALIBU — SERIES 1N — FOUR/V-6 — The replacement for the discontinued Corsica sedan, the Malibu returned to the Chevrolet lineup after a 13-year absence in the form of base and LS sedans. The Malibu featured four-wheel independent suspension and a hydroformed front frame for structural integrity. It could go up to 100,000 miles between tune-ups, its extended-life coolant lasted five years or 150,000 miles, and its transmission fluid was good for the life of the car. Standard equipment included anti-lock brakes, dual airbags, Automatic Daytime Running Lamps and five-mph bumpers. The Malibu also featured battery run-down protection. The Malibu's standard 2.4-liter DOHC four-cylinder generated 150 horsepower and 155 pound-feet of torque. The LS sedan used the 3.1-liter V-6 with sequential fuel injection, producing 155 horsepower and 185 pound-feet of torque. This was also the option engine in the base sedan. The four-speed automatic transmission was the lone offering in the Malibu line.

1997 Chevrolet, Camaro Z28 30th Anniversary Edition two-door convertible

CAMARO — SERIES 1F — V-6/V-8 — The Camaro observed its 30th Anniversary in 1997 and Chevrolet marked the occasion by offering a 30th Anniversary Package for its Z28 line. The package consisted of a Arctic White with Hugger Orange stripes paint scheme, reminiscent of the 1969 Camaro that paced that year's Indianapolis 500. Also part of the package were door handles finished in white as were the five-spoke aluminum wheels and front fascia intake. Seats in this Anniversary Z28 were also Arctic White with cloth black-and-white houndstooth inserts. In addition, the floor mats and headrests had 30th Anniversary five-color embroidery. Standard features on all Camaros included Automatic Daytime Running Lamps, four-wheel anti-lock disc brakes, dual airbags, electronically controlled AM/FM stereo with cassette player and extended range speakers and a reinforced steel safety cage that included steel side-door beams and front and rear crush zones. The Camaro lineup again was comprised of three coupes and three convertibles offered in base, RS or Z28 trim. The standard powerplant of the base and RS models was the 3.8-liter V-6 that produced 200 horsepower. The Z28 again used the 5.7-liter V-8 as its standard engine. The base and RS lines again featured the five-speed manual transmission as base offering while the Z28 had the six-speed manual transmission as standard. The four-speed automatic was the option transmission for all Camaro models.

1997 Chevrolet, Lumina four-door sedan

1997 Chevrolet, Lumina LS four-door sedan

1997 Chevrolet, Lumina LTZ four-door sedan

LUMINA — SERIES 1W — V-6 — The 1997 Lumina line was increased by one with the addition of an upscale LTZ sports sedan joining the base and LS sedan offerings. Several new paint colors were offered and other new features included an engine oil wear indicator in the instrument panel. Also, a power sunroof was available as an option. The 3.1-liter V-6 was again the standard engine in both the base and LS models. The 3.4-liter DOHC V-6 was used in the LTZ sedan. The four-speed automatic was the only transmission offered in Luminas.

MONTE CARLO — SERIES 1W — V-6 — Aside from new paint colors, the 1997 Monte Carlo LS and Z34 coupes were basically carry-over models from the year previous.

The 3.1-liter V-6 returned as the standard engine in the LS coupe and the DOHC 3.4-liter V-6 remained as the standard offering in the Z34. Both coupes again had the four-speed automatic transmission as standard equipment.

I.D. DATA: Chevrolets again had a 17-symbol Vehicle Identification Number (VIN) on the upper left surface of the instrument panel, visible through the windshield. Symbol one indicates country: '1' or '4' - U.S.A.; '2' - Canada. Next is a manufacturer code: 'G' - General Motors. Symbol three is car make: '1' - Chevrolet; '7' - GM of Canada. Symbols four and five denote car line/series: F/P - Camaro; J/C - Cavalier; J/F - Cavalier Z24 and LS; N/D - Malibu; N/E - Malibu LS; W/L - Lumina LS; W/N - Lumina LTZ; W/W - Monte Carlo LS and W/X - Monte Carlo Z34. Symbol six is the body style: '1' - 2-dr coupe, '2' - 2-dr, '3' - 2-dr convertible, '5' - 4-dr sedan, '6' - 4-dr and '8' - 4-dr station wagon. Symbol seven is the restraint system: '2' - active (manual) belts w/driver's and passenger's side airbags, '4' - active (manual) belts w/driver's and passenger's side airbags, frontal and side. Symbol eight is the engine code: 'G' - 5.7-liter V-8 (LS1); 'K' - 3.8-liter V-6; 'M' - 3.1-liter V-6; 'P' - 5.7-liter V-8 (LT1); 'T' - 2.4-liter four-cyl.; 'X' - 3.4-liter V-6; '4' - 2.2-liter four-cyl. This is followed by symbol nine, which is a check digit. Symbol ten is 'V' for model year 1997. Symbol eleven indicates assembly plant. The final six digits are the sequential serial number.

CAVALIER (FOUR)

Model No.	Body/Style No.	Body Type & Seating	Factory Price	Shipping Weight	Prod. Total
1J	C37	2-dr. Coupe-5P	10980	2584	Note 1
1J	C69	4-dr. Sedan-5P	11180	2630	Note 2

CAVALIER RS (FOUR)

1J	C37/WP2	2-dr. Coupe-5P	12225	2617	Note 1

CAVALIER LS (FOUR)

1J	F69	4-dr. Sedan-5P	13380	2729	Note 2
1J	F67	2-dr. Conv-5P	17765	2899	1,108

CAVALIER Z24 (FOUR)

1J	F37	2-dr. Coupe-5P	14465	2749	Note 1

Note 1: Total Cavalier coupe production was 171,225 with no further breakout available.

Note 2: Total Cavalier sedan production was 142,803 with no further breakout available.

MALIBU (FOUR/V-6)

1N	D69	4-dr. Sedan-5P	15470/15865	3051/3077	Note 1

MALIBU LS (V-6)

1N	E69	4-dr. Sedan-5P	18190	3077	Note 1

Note 1: Total Malibu sedan production was 100,266 with no further breakout available.

CAMARO (V-6)

1F	P87	2-dr. Cpe-4P	16215	3294	Note 1
1F	P67	2-dr. Conv-4P	21770	3446	Note 2

CAMARO RS (V-6)

1F	P87	2-dr. Cpe-4P	17970	3307	Note 1
1F	P67	2-dr. Conv-4P	23170	3455	Note 2

CAMARO Z-28 (V-8)

1F	P87/Z28	2-dr. Cpe-4P	20115	3433	Note 1
1F	P67/Z28	2-dr. Conv-4P	25520	3589	Note 2

Note 1: Total Camaro coupe production was 48,292 with no further breakout available.

Note 2: Total Camaro convertible production was 6,680 with no further breakout available.

LUMINA (V-6)

1W	L69	4-dr. Sedan-6P	16945	3360	Note 1

LUMINA LS (V-6)

1W	N69/Z7H	4-dr. Sedan-6P	19145	3388	Note 1

LUMINA LTZ (V-6)

1W	NA	4-dr. Sedan-6P	19455	NA	Note 1

Note 1: Total Lumina sedan production was 234,626 with no further breakout available.

MONTE CARLO LS (V-6)

1W	W27/Z7F	2-dr. Coupe-6P	17445	3320	Note 1

MONTE CARLO Z34 (V-6)

1W	X27/Z7G	2-dr. Coupe-6P	19945	3455	Note 1

Note 1: Total Monte Carlo coupe production was 72,555 with no further breakout available.

FACTORY PRICE AND WEIGHT NOTE: For Malibu, prices and weights to left of slash are for four-cylinder, to right for V-6 engine.

ENGINE DATA: BASE FOUR (Cavalier/Cavalier RS/Cavalier LS): Inline. Overhead valve. Four-cylinder. Displacement: 133 cu. in. (2.2 liters). Bore & stroke: 3.50 x 3.46 in. Compression ratio: 9.0:1. Brake horsepower: 120 at 5200 RPM. Torque: 130 lb.-ft. at 4000 RPM. Sequential fuel injection. BASE V-6 (Cavalier Z24); OPTIONAL (Cavalier LS): Dual overhead cam V-6. Displacement: 146 cu. in. (2.4 liters). Bore & stroke: 3.54 x 3.70 in. Compression ratio: 9.5:1. Brake horsepower: 150 at 5600 RPM. Torque: 155 lb.-ft. at 4400 RPM. Sequential fuel injection. BASE V-6 (Malibu LS, Lumina/Lumina LS, Monte Carlo LS); OPTIONAL (Malibu): Overhead-valve V-6. Displacement: 191 cu. in. (3.1 liters). Bore & stroke: 3.51 x 3.31 in. Compression ratio: 9.6:1. Brake horsepower: 160 at 5200 RPM. Torque: 185 lb.-ft. at 4000 RPM. Sequential fuel injection. BASE V-6 (Camaro/Camaro RS): Overhead valve V-6. Displacement: 231 cu. in. (3.8 liters). Bore & stroke: 3.80 x 3.40 in. Compression ratio: 9.4:1. Brake horsepower: 200 at 5200 RPM. Torque: 225 lb.-ft. at 4000 RPM. Sequential fuel injection. BASE V-6 (Lumina LTZ, Monte Carlo Z34): Dual overhead cam (24-valve) V-6. Displacement: 207 cu. in. (3.4 liters). Bore & stroke: 3.62 x 3.31 in. Compression ratio: 9.7:1. Brake horsepower: 215 at 5200 RPM. Torque: 220 lb.-ft. at 4000 RPM. Sequential fuel injection. BASE V-8 (Camaro Z28): 90-degree, overhead valve V-8. Displacement: 350 cu. in. (5.7 liters). Bore & stroke: 4.00 x 3.48 in. Compression ratio: 10.4:1. Brake horsepower: 285 at 5200 RPM. Torque: 325 lb.-ft. at 2400 RPM. Sequential fuel injection.

CHASSIS DATA: Wheelbase: (Cavalier) 104.1 in.; (Malibu) 107.0 in.; (Camaro) 101.1 in.; (Lumina/Monte Carlo) 107.5 in. Overall length: (Cavalier) 180.3 in.; (Malibu) 190.4 in.; (Camaro) 193.2 in.; (Lumina) 200.9 in.; (Monte Carlo) 200.7 in. Height: (Cavalier cpe) 53.2 in.; (Cavalier sed) 54.8; (Cavalier conv) 53.9 in.; (Malibu) 56.4 in.; (Camaro cpe) 51.3 in.; (Camaro conv) 52.0 in.; (Lumina) 55.2 in.; (Monte Carlo) 53.8 in. Width: (Cavalier) 67.4 in.; (Malibu) 69.4 in.; (Camaro) 74.1 in.; (Lumina) 72.5; (Monte Carlo) 72.5 in. Standard Tires: (Cavalier) P195/70R14; (Cavalier RS) P195/65R15; (Cavalier LS) P195/65R15; (Cavalier Z24) P205/55R16; (Malibu) P215/60R15; (Camaro) P215/60R16; (Camaro RS/Camaro Z28) P235/55R16; (Lumina/Monte Carlo LS) P205/70R15; (Lumina LS) P225/60R16; (Monte Carlo Z34) P225/60R16.

TECHNICAL: Transmission: Five-speed manual shift standard on Cavalier/Cavalier RS/Cavalier Z24 and Camaro/Camaro RS. Six-speed manual shift standard on Camaro Z28. Four-speed overdrive automatic standard on Cavalier LS, Malibu/Malibu LS, Lumina/Lumina LS/Lumina LTZ, Monte Carlo LS/Monte Carlo Z34. Steering: (All) rack and pinion. Brakes: front disc, rear drum; four-wheel discs standard on Camaro Z28, Lumina LS, Monte Carlo Z34; anti-lock brakes standard on all except base Lumina. Body construction: unibody. Fuel tank: (Cavalier) 15.2 gal.; (Malibu) 15.0 gal.; (Camaro) 15.5 gal.; (Lumina) 16.5 gal.; (Monte Carlo) 17.1 gal.

DRIVETRAIN OPTIONS: Engines: 2.4-liter four-cylinder: Cavalier LS ($395). 3.1-liter V-6: Malibu ($395). Three-speed automatic trans.: Cavalier/Cavalier RS ($550). Four-speed overdrive auto. trans.: Cavalier Z24 ($795); Camaro/RS/Z28 ($815). Five-speed manual trans.: Cavalier LS conv. (NC).

CAVALIER CONVENIENCE/APPEARANCE OPTIONS: Coupe Preferred Equip. Grp 1: Intermittent Wiper System; Mech Trunk Opener; Dual Covered Visor Mirrors, w/map straps; Bodyside Moldings; Mud Guards; Cargo Net; Color-Keyed Carpeted Mats, F&R ($240). Coupe Preferred Equip. Grp 2: Tilt Strg Wheel; Elect Spd Control, w/resume speed; Pwr Mirrors; Intermittent Wiper System; Mech Trunk Opener; Dual Covered Visor Mirrors, w/map straps; Bodyside Moldings; Mud Guards; Cargo Net; Color-Keyed Carpeted Mats, F&R ($696). Coupe Preferred Equip. Grp 3: Tilt Strg Wheel; Elect Spd Control, w/resume speed; Pwr Mirrors; Pwr Windows; Remote Keyless Entry, Incl Pwr Locks; Intermittent Wiper System; Dual Covered Visor Mirrors, w/map straps; Bodyside Moldings; Mud Guards; Cargo Net; Color-Keyed Carpeted Mats, F&R ($1295). Sedan Preferred Equip. Grp 1: Intermittent Wiper System; Mech Trunk Opener; Dual Covered Visor Mirrors, w/map straps; Bodyside Moldings; Mud Guards; Cargo Net; Color-Keyed Carpeted Mats, F&R ($223). Sedan Preferred Equip. Grp. 2: Tilt Strg Wheel; Elect Spd Control, w/resume speed; Intermittent Wiper System; Mech Trunk Opener; Dual Covered Visor Mirrors, w/map straps; Bodyside Moldings; Mud Guards; Cargo Net; Color-Keyed Carpeted Mats, F&R ($593). RS Coupe Preferred Equip. Grp. 1: Tilt Strg Wheel; Elect Spd Control, w/resume speed; Pwr Windows ($456). RS Coupe Preferred Equip. Grp. 2: Tilt Strg

Wheel; Elect Spd Control, w/resume speed; Pwr Windows; Remote Keyless Entry, Incl Pwr Locks ($1055). LS Sedan Preferred Equip. Grp 1: Tilt Strg Wheel; Elect Spd Control, w/resume speed; Intermittent Wiper System ($435). LS Sedan Preferred Equip. Grp 2: Tilt Strg Wheel; Elect Spd Control, w/resume speed; Intermittent Wiper System; Elect Twin Remote Mirrors; Pwr Windows; Remote Keyless Entry, Incl Pwr Locks ($1225). LS Convertible Preferred Equip. Grp 1: Tilt Strg Wheel; Elect Spd Control, w/resume speed; Intermittent Wiper System ($435). LS Convertible Preferred Equip. Grp 2: Tilt Strg Wheel; Elect Spd Control, w/resume speed; Intermittent Wiper System; Elect Twin Remote Mirrors; Pwr Windows; Remote Keyless Entry, Incl Pwr Locks ($1120). Z24 Coupe Preferred Equip. Grp 1: Elect Spd Control, w/resume speed; Intermittent Wiper System ($290). Z24 Coupe Preferred Equip. Grp 2: Elect Spd Control, w/resume speed; Intermittent Wiper System; Elect Twin Remote Mirrors; Pwr Windows; Remote Keyless Entry, Incl Pwr Locks ($975). Air Cond ($795). W27 Appearance Pkg (base coupe only): Body color fascias & side moldings, 15-in. bolt-on wheel covers, P195/65R15 tires ($255). Frt License Plate Bracket (NC). Electric Rear Window Defogger ($170). Pwr Door Locks: Cpe ($210); Sed ($250). Vinyl Bucket Seats ($50). Elect Sun Roof, cpe only ($670). Eng. Block Htr ($20). Calif. Emission System ($170). 15-in. alum wheels, RS/LS models ($295).

MALIBU CONVENIENCE/APPEARANCE OPTIONS:
Preferred Equip. Grp. 1: Pwr Windows; Pwr Door Locks, Pwr Ext. Mirrors ($676). Preferred Equip. Grp. 2: Elect Spd Control, w/resume speed; Pwr Windows; Pwr Door Locks, Pwr Ext. Mirrors; Remote Keyless Entry; Dual Mirror-Mounted Reading Lamps ($1059). Remote Keyless Entry ($135). 6-Way Pwr Driver's Seat, stnd/LS ($305). Custom Cloth Recl. Frnt. Bucket Seat w/Splt Fldg Rear Seat & Cargo Net, stnd/LS ($210). Mud Guards ($50). Frt License Plate Bracket (NC). Electric Rear Window Defogger ($170). Eng Block Htr ($20). Calif. Emission System ($170). Color-Keyed Carpeted Mats, F&R, stnd/LS ($30). 15-in. alum wheels, stnd/LS ($295).

CAMARO CONVENIENCE/APPEARANCE OPTIONS:
Coupe Preferred Equip. Grp. 1: Elect Spd Control, w/resume speed; Fog Lamps; Remote Trunk Release ($345). Coupe Preferred Equip. Grp. 2: Pwr Windows; Pwr Door Locks; Elect Spd Control, w/resume speed; Remote Trunk Release; Fog Lamps; Elect Spt Twin Remote Mirrors; Leather-wrapped Strg Wheel/Trans Shifter/Prk Brake Handle; Illum Remote Keyless Entry; Antitheft Alarm System ($1231). Convertible Preferred Equip. Grp. 1: Pwr Door Locks; Elect Spd Control, w/resume speed; Fog Lamps; Remote Trunk Release ($565). Convertible Preferred Equip. Grp. 2: Pwr Windows; Pwr Door Locks; Elect Spd Control, w/resume speed; Remote Trunk Release; Fog Lamps; Elect Spt Twin Remote Mirrors; Leather-wrapped Strg Wheel/Trans Shifter/Prk Brake Handle; Illum Remote Keyless Entry; Antitheft Alarm System ($1231). RS Coupe Preferred Equip. Grp. 1: Pwr Door Locks; Elect Spd Control, w/resume speed; Fog Lamps; Remote Trunk Release ($565). RS Coupe Preferred Equip. Grp. 2: Pwr

Windows; Pwr Door Locks; Elect Spd Control, w/resume speed; Fog Lamps; Remote Trunk Release; Elect Spt Twin Remote Mirrors; Leather-wrapped Strg Wheel/Trans Shifter/Prk Brake Handle; Illum Remote Keyless Entry; Antitheft Alarm System ($1231). RS Convertible Preferred Equip. Grp. 1: Pwr Door Locks; Elect Spd Control, w/resume speed; Fog Lamps; Remote Trunk Release ($565). RS Convertible Preferred Equip. Grp. 2: Pwr Windows; Pwr Door Locks; Elect Spd Control, w/resume speed; Fog Lamps; Remote Trunk Release; Elect Spt Twin Remote Mirrors; Leather-wrapped Strg Wheel/Trans Shifter/Prk Brake Handle; Illum Remote Keyless Entry; Antitheft Alarm System ($1231). Z28 Coupe Preferred Equip. Grp. 1: Pwr Door Locks; Elect Spd Control, w/resume speed; Remote Trunk Release; Fog Lamps; 4-Way Adj Driver's Seat ($600). Z28 Coupe Preferred Equip. Grp. 2: Pwr Windows; Pwr Door Locks; Elect Spd Control, w/resume speed; Fog Lamps; Remote Trunk Release; 4-Way Adj Driver's Seat; Elect Spt Twin Remote Mirrors; Leather-wrapped Strg Wheel/Trans Shifter/Prk Brake Handle; Illum Remote Keyless Entry; Antitheft Alarm System ($1266). Z28 Convertible Preferred Equip. Grp. 1: Pwr Door Locks; Elect Spd Control, w/resume speed; Remote Trunk Release; Fog Lamps ($565). Z28 Convertible Preferred Equip. Grp. 2: Pwr Windows; Pwr Door Lock System; Elect Spd Control, w/resume speed; Fog Lamps; Remote Trunk Release; Elect Spt Twin Remote Mirrors; Leather-wrapped Strg Wheel/Trans Shifter/Prk Brake Handle; Illum Remote Keyless Entry; Antitheft Alarm System ($1231). Z4C 30th Anniversary Edition Pkg: Incl White Monochromatic Ext. w/ Orange Stripes, White 5-spoke Alum Wheels, 30th Anniversary Embroidered Emblems on Flr Mats and Headrests ($575). Acceleration Slip Regulation, Z28 only ($450). Frt License Plate Bracket (NC). Elect Rear Window Defogger ($170). Calif. Emission System ($170). Bodyside Mldgs ($60). Pwr Door Lock System ($220). GU5 Axle, Z28 only ($300). 1LE Perf Pkg, Z28 cpe only: Incl Special Handling Susp. System ($1175). Y87 Performance Handling Pkg, base & RS only: Incl Ltd Slip Axle, 4-Wheel Disc Brakes, Dual Exhaust & Spt Strg Ratio ($400). Remote CD Changer ($595). 6-Way Pwr Driver's Seat ($270). Leather Bucket Seats ($499). Removable Glass Roof Panels, Incl locks ($995). TIRES: P235/55R16 Steel Belted Radial Blackwall, stnd/Z28 ($132). P245/50ZR16 Steel Belted Radial Blackwall, Z28 only ($225). Cast Alum Wheels, 16-in., stnd/Z28 ($275).

LUMINA CONVENIENCE/APPEARANCE OPTIONS:
Preferred Equip Grp. 1: Pwr Windows; Pwr Trunk Opener; Elect Spd Control, w/resume speed; Cargo Net; Elect Spt Twin Remote Mirrors; Flr Mats, F&R ($758). LS Preferred Equip. Grp. 1: Pwr Trunk Opener; Driver & Pass. Temp Control; Remote Keyless Entry; Rear Window Defogger; Flr Mats, F&R ($590). Dual Control HVAC System ($100). 60/40 Bench Seat, Leather Trim ($645). 60/40 Bench Seat, Custom Cloth Trim ($150). Frt License Plate Bracket (NC). 4-Wheel Anti-Lock Brakes, stnd LS ($575). Electric Rear Window Defogger ($170). Calif. Emission System ($170). Remote Keyless Entry ($220). Pwr Driver's Seat ($305). Rear Integrated Child's Seat ($195). Elect Spd Control, w/resume speed ($225). Elect Sunroof ($700). Eng Block Htr ($20). Strg Wheel Radio Controls

($171). TIRES: P225/60R16 All Seasons Steel Belted Radial Blackwall ($175). 15-in. bolt-on chrome wheel cover ($100). 16-in. alum wheels ($300).

MONTE CARLO CONVENIENCE/APPEARANCE OPTIONS: LS Preferred Equip Grp. 1: Pwr Trunk Opener; Elect Spd Control, w/resume speed; Cargo Net; Driver & Pass. Temp Control ($415). Custom Cloth Bucket Seats, w/console, LS only ($150). Custom Leather Bucket Seats, w/console: LS ($695); Z34 ($645). Frt License Plate Bracket (NC). Electric Rear Window Defogger ($170). Calif. Emission System ($170). Dual Control HVAC System ($100). Pwr Driver's Seat ($305). Elect Sunroof ($700). Eng Block Htr ($19). Elect Spd Control, w/resume speed ($225). Strg Wheel Radio Controls ($171). TIRES: P225/60R16 All Seasons Steel Belted Radial Blackwall ($175). 16-in. alum wheels, stnd Z34 ($300).

HISTORY: *Motor Trend* magazine voted the Chevrolet Malibu its 1997 "Car of the Year." In conjunction with SLP Engineering, Chevrolet offered a limited edition (1,000 produced) Z28 SS Camaro in 30th Anniversary Edition colors of orange stripes on white. The SS Z28 was powered by the LT1 V-8 rated at 305 horsepower. It featured a hood scoop with functional forced-air induction, performance exhaust system, Hurst six-speed shifter and Bilstein sport suspension package.

1998

The Geo Division of General Motors—activated in 1989 and aligned with Chevrolet via having its Geo line of joint-venture (with Japanese makers) automobiles sold through Chevy dealerships—was discontinued in 1998, and the surviving Metro and Prizm series of small cars were now badged as Chevrolets. The Generation III all-aluminum block V-8, introduced the previous year in the Corvette, was now used in the Camaro Z28 and SS (a Camaro Performance/Appearance Package in 1998). The Cavalier LS convertible previously offered was discontinued and replaced with a Z24 ragtop. The OnStar communications system was optional equipment for Lumina and Monte Carlo, while the 3.8-liter V-6 became the option engine for Lumina LTZ and Monte Carlo Z34.

1998 Chevrolet, Metro two-door hatchback coupe

1998 Chevrolet, Metro LSi two-door hatchback coupe

1998 Chevrolet, Metro LSi four-door sedan

METRO — SERIES 1M — THREE/FOUR — Rebadged as a Chevrolet for 1998, this entry-level series offered a base hatchback coupe and LSi hatchback coupe and sedan. In the switchover from Geo, 1998 Chevrolet Metro models received redesigned front and rear fascias, new seat fabrics, composite headlamps, revised wheel covers and one new exterior color—California Gold Metallic. Standard features included four-wheel independent suspension, stainless steel muffler and tailpipe, full-folding rear seats. A split-folding rear seat with pass-through feature was optional equipment on the LSi sedan. The base Metro used the inline 1.0-liter three-cylinder engine mated to a five-speed manual transmission as standard equipment. The LSi series featured the revised 1.3-liter four-cylinder powerplant with multi-port fuel injection. The five-speed manual transmission was the base offering on LSi models, while the three-speed automatic was optional.

1998 Chevrolet, Prizm four-door sedan

1998 Chevrolet, Prizm LSi four-door sedan

PRIZM — SERIES 1S — FOUR — A pair of former Geo sedans rebadged as Chevrolet models in 1998, the base Prizm sedan and Prizm LSi sedan were the first economy-class sedans to offer side-impact airbags (optional equipment). Standard features included Daytime Running Lamps, Automatic Exterior Lamp Control system (activated at dusk to return exterior lamps from daytime power to full, normal power), dual trip odometers and an on-board refueling vapor recovery system. The Prizm's hoodline was also lowered in 1998 to improve aerodynamics and enhance front visibility. Standard powerplant in the Prizm was the new-for-1998 DOHC 1.8-liter four-cylinder engine with sequential fuel injection. The five-speed manual transmission was the base transmission for both sedans, while the three-speed automatic and electronic four-speed automatic with fourth gear overdrive were both optional.

1998 Chevrolet, Cavalier RS two-door coupe

1998 Chevrolet, Cavalier two-door coupe

1998 Chevrolet, Cavalier LS four-door sedan

CAVALIER — SERIES 1J — FOUR — The Cavalier LS convertible was discontinued in 1998, replaced by a ragtop in the Z24 series. The Z24 convertible featured the 150-horsepower DOHC 2.4-liter four-cylinder engine, power top, air conditioning, Remote Keyless Entry, power door locks, new front-passenger safety belt adjuster and 15-inch cross-lace design aluminum wheels. In the Cavalier line, changes included a redesigned manual transmission shifter, new seat sew pattern on LS sedan and Z24 model interiors and electric odometer/trip odometer on base Cavaliers. Standard features included Daytime Running Lamps, theater lighting, PassLock theft-deterrent system and four-wheel anti-lock brakes. A rear spoiler, standard equipment on the RS coupe and Z24 models, was optional on the LS sedan. The 2.2-liter four-cylinder engine, standard in all Cavaliers except the Z24 models, was refined for 1998, with revisions made to the pistons and composite intake manifold to reduce engine noise levels. Base powerplant for Z24s—and optional for the LS sedan—was the DOHC 2.4-liter four-cylinder engine. The five-speed manual transmission was standard on all Cavaliers except the LS sedan, which used the 4T40-E electronic four-speed automatic—the option transmission across-the-board on Cavaliers. The 3T40 three-speed automatic was also optional on base series Cavaliers.

1998 Chevrolet, Malibu four-door sedan

1998 Chevrolet, Malibu LS four-door sedan

MALIBU — SERIES 1N — FOUR/V-6 — The Malibu for 1998 underwent minor refinement after its launch the year previous. Leather seating—in light gray or neutral—was optional in the LS sedan. The base Malibu sedan was now offered with an oak interior color. Both sedans could be ordered with 15-inch, machine-faced, aluminum wheels with revised center caps—standard on the LS sedan and optional on the base sedan. Also, the six-way power driver's seat standard in the LS sedan was now optional in the base sedan. Standard engine in the base Malibu was the 2.4-liter DOHC four-cylinder powerplant. The LS sedan used the 3.1-liter V-6 as its standard offering, which was also the option engine in the base sedan. The 4T40-E electronic four-speed automatic transmission was again the only offering in the Malibu line.

1998 Chevrolet, Camaro Z28 two-door coupe

CAMARO — SERIES 1F — V-6/V-8 — Chevrolet did not allow the Camaro to rest on its 30th Anniversary laurels from the year previous. The 1998 Camaro received significant changes of which the discontinuation of the RS coupe and convertible offered previously led the list. In place of the RS series, Chevrolet offered an optional Sport Appearance Package available on both the base or Z28 coupes and convertibles (except on Z28 SS models). A factory-direct SS Performance/Appearance Package was optional on the Z28 models in 1998, as opposed to the previous year's off-site assembling of this limited edition performance model by SLP Engineering. The Camaro's exterior appearance was revised for 1998, including a redesigned hood, front fenders and front fascia, composite headlamps with reflector optics and optional foglamps. A new four-wheel disc brake system was standard on all Camaros, as was a one-piece, all-welded exhaust system used to reduce noise and vibration. The Z28 received the new-generation 5.7-liter LS1 aluminum-block V-8 also used in the Corvette. The LS1 offered more horsepower (305 vs. 285) than the previous year's LT1 V-8. The standard powerplant of the base models was again the 3.8-liter

V-6 fitted to the five-speed manual transmission. The 4L60-E four-speed automatic was the standard offering for Z28 models and the option transmission for base Camaros. Z28s used the six-speed manual as the option transmission.

1998 Chevrolet, Lumina four-door sedan

1998 Chevrolet, Lumina LS four-door sedan

1998 Chevrolet, Lumina LTZ four-door sedan

LUMINA — SERIES 1W — V-6 — The trio of Lumina sedans, base, LS and LTZ, offered the year previous returned for 1998 with several refinements. The Lumina line offered the optional OnStar system that combined a cellular phone with Global Positioning System (GPS) satellite technology and a 24-hour OnStar Center. The Lumina's Soft Ride Suspension received a 2mm larger (32mm) front stabilizer bar to help reduce lean in cornering maneuvers. The LTZ sedan received the Series II 3.8-liter V-6 as its option engine, replacing the 3.4-liter V-6 offered previously. The Series II 3.8-liter V-6 produced 200 horsepower and generated 225 pound-feet of torque. This option engine was teamed with the 4T65-E electronic four-speed automatic overdrive transmission and Ride & Handling Suspension, which received revised four-stage valving in front struts for a finer degree of ride control. The Lumina's Daytime Running Lamp system also was revised for 1998, its high-beam lamps illuminated at reduced intensity instead of the low-beam lamps. The 3.1-liter V-6 was again the standard engine in all Lumina sedans. The 4T60-E electronic four-speed automatic was the base transmission offered in all Luminas.

1998 Chevrolet, Monte Carlo LS two-door coupe

1998 Chevrolet, Monte Carlo Z34 two-door coupe

MONTE CARLO — SERIES 1W — V-6 — Monte Carlo in 1998 received the revised Daytime Running Lamp system, accommodations for the optional OnStar communications system and four new exterior colors. The 3.4-liter V-6 formerly used to power the Z34 was replaced by the Series II 3.8-liter V-6 fitted to a 4T65-E electronic four-speed automatic overdrive transmission. The 3.1-liter V-6 was again the standard engine in the LS coupe, coupled with the 4T60-E four-speed automatic overdrive transmission.

I.D. DATA: Chevrolets again had a 17-symbol Vehicle Identification Number (VIN) on the upper left surface of the instrument panel, visible through the windshield. Symbol one indicates country: '1' or '4' - U.S.A.; '2' - Canada. Next is a manufacturer code: 'G' - General Motors. Symbol three is car make: '1' - Chevrolet; '7' - GM of Canada. Symbols four and five denote car line/series: F/P - Camaro; J/C - Cavalier; J/F - Cavalier Z24 and LS; M/R - Metro/Metro LSi; N/D - Malibu; N/E - Malibu LS; S/K - Prizm/Prizm LSi; W/L - Lumina LS; W/N - Lumina LTZ; W/W - Monte Carlo LS and W/X - Monte Carlo Z34. Symbol six is the body style: '1' - 2-dr coupe, '2' - 2-dr, '3' - 2-dr convertible, '5' - 4-dr sedan, '6' - 4-dr and '8' - 4-dr station wagon. Symbol seven is the restraint system: '2' - active (manual) belts w/driver's and passenger's side airbags, '4' - active (manual) belts w/driver's and passenger's side airbags, frontal and side. Symbol eight is the engine code: 'G' - 5.7-liter V-8 (LS1); 'K' - 3.8-liter V-6; 'M' - 3.1-liter V-6; 'T' - 2.4-liter four-cyl.; '2' - 1.3-liter four-cyl.; '4' - 2.2-liter four-

cyl.; '6' - 1.0-liter three-cyl.; '8' - 1.4-liter four-cyl. This is followed by symbol nine, which is a check digit. Symbol ten is 'W' for model year 1998. Symbol eleven indicates assembly plant. The final six digits are the sequential serial number.

NOTE: * As this book went to press, the production figures for 1998 Chevrolet automobiles were not yet available.

METRO (THREE)

Model No.	Body/Style No.	Body Type & Seating	Factory Price	Shipping Weight	Prod. Total
1M	R08	2-dr. Htchbk Cpe-4P	8655	1895	*

METRO LSi (FOUR)

Model No.	Body/Style No.	Body Type & Seating	Factory Price	Shipping Weight	Prod. Total
1M	R08/B4M	2-dr. Htchbk Cpe-4P	9455	1895	*
1M	R69/B4M	4-dr. Sedan-4P	10055	1984	*

PRIZM (FOUR)

1S	K19	4-dr. Sedan-5P	12045	NA	*

PRIZM LSi (FOUR)

1S	K19/B4M	4-dr. Sedan-5P	14615	NA	*

CAVALIER (FOUR)

1J	C37	2-dr. Coupe-5P	11610	2584	*
1J	C69	4-dr. Sedan-5P	11810	2630	*

CAVALIER RS (FOUR)

1J	C37/WP2	2-dr. Coupe-5P	12870	2584	*

CAVALIER LS (FOUR)

1J	F69	4-dr. Sedan-5P	14250	2630	*

CAVALIER Z24 (FOUR)

1J	F37	2-dr. Coupe-5P	15710	2749	*
1J	F67	2-dr. Conv-5P	19410	2899	*

MALIBU (FOUR/V-6)

1N	D69	4-dr. Sedan-5P	15670/16165	3100/NA	*

MALIBU LS (V-6)

1N	E69	4-dr. Sedan-5P	18470	NA	*

CAMARO (V-6)

1F	P87	2-dr. Cpe-4P	16625	3331	*
1F	P67	2-dr. Conv-4P	22125	3468	*

CAMARO Z-28 (V-8)

1F	P87/Z28	2-dr. Cpe-4P	20470	3439	*
1F	P67/Z28	2-dr. Conv-4P	27450	3574	*

LUMINA (V-6)

1W	L69	4-dr. Sedan-6P	17245	3330	*

LUMINA LS (V-6)

1W	L69/BV2	4-dr. Sedan-6P	19245	3372	*

LUMINA LTZ (V-6)

1W	N69	4-dr. Sedan-6P	19745	3420	*

MONTE CARLO LS (V-6)

1W	W27	2-dr. Coupe-6P	17795	3239	*

MONTE CARLO Z34 (V-6)

1W	X27	2-dr. Coupe-6P	20295	3452	*

FACTORY PRICE AND WEIGHT NOTE: For Malibu, prices and weights to left of slash are for four-cylinder, to right for V-6 engine.

ENGINE DATA: BASE THREE (Metro): Inline. Single overhead cam. Three-cylinder. Displacement: 61 cu. in. (1.0 liters). Bore & stroke: 2.91 x 3.03 in. Compression ratio: 9.5:1. Brake horsepower: 55 at 5700 RPM. Torque: 58 lb.-ft. at 3300 RPM. Throttle-body fuel injection. BASE FOUR (Metro LSi): Inline. Single overhead cam. Four-cylinder. Displacement: 79 cu. in. (1.3 liters). Bore & stroke: 2.91 x 2.97 in. Compression ratio: 9.5:1. Brake horsepower: 79 at 6000 RPM. Torque: 75 lb.-ft. at 3000 RPM. Multi-port fuel injection. BASE FOUR (Prizm/Prizm LSi): Inline. Dual overhead cam. Four-cylinder. Displacement: 109.5 cu. in. (1.8 liters). Bore & stroke: 3.11 x 3.60 in. Compression ratio: 10.1:1. Brake horsepower: 120 at 5600 RPM. Torque: 127 lb.-ft. at 4400 RPM. Sequential fuel injection. BASE FOUR (Cavalier/Cavalier RS/Cavalier LS): Inline. Overhead valve. Four-cylinder. Displacement: 134 cu. in. (2.2 liters). Bore & stroke: 3.50 x 3.46 in. Compression ratio: 9.0:1. Brake horsepower: 115 at 5000 RPM. Torque: 135 lb.-ft. at 3600 RPM. Sequential fuel injection. BASE V-6 (Cavalier Z24, Malibu); OPTIONAL (Cavalier LS): Dual overhead cam V-6. Displacement: 146 cu. in. (2.4 liters). Bore & stroke: 3.54 x 3.70 in. Compression ratio: 9.5:1. Brake horsepower: 150 at 5600 RPM. Torque: 155 lb.-ft. at 4400 RPM. Sequential fuel injection. BASE V-6 (Malibu LS, Lumina/Lumina LS/Lumina LTZ, Monte Carlo LS); OPTIONAL (Malibu): Overhead-valve V-6. Displacement: 191 cu. in. (3.1 liters). Bore & stroke: 3.51 x 3.31 in. Compression ratio: 9.6:1. Brake horsepower: 150 at 4800 RPM. Torque: 180 lb.-ft. at 3200 RPM. Sequential fuel injection. BASE V-6 (Camaro, Monte Carlo Z34); OPTIONAL (Lumina LTZ): Overhead valve V-6. Displacement: 231 cu. in. (3.8 liters). Bore & stroke: 3.80 x 3.40 in. Compression ratio: 9.4:1. Brake horsepower: 200 at 5200 RPM. Torque: 225 lb.-ft. at 4000 RPM. Sequential fuel injection. BASE V-8 (Camaro Z28): 90-degree, overhead valve V-8. Displacement: 350 cu. in. (5.7 liters). Bore & stroke: 3.90 x 3.48 in. Compression ratio: 10.1:1. Brake horsepower: 305 at 5200 RPM. Torque: 335 lb.-ft. at 4000 RPM. Sequential fuel injection.

CHASSIS DATA: Wheelbase: (Metro) 93.1 in.; (Prizm) 97.1 in.; (Cavalier) 104.1 in.; (Malibu) 107.0 in.; (Camaro) 101.1 in.; (Lumina/Monte Carlo) 107.5 in. Overall length: (Metro cpe) 149.4 in.; (Metro sed) 164.0 in.; (Prizm) 175.0 in.; (Cavalier cpe) 180.1 in.; (Cavalier sed/conv) 180.7 in.; (Malibu) 190.4 in.; (Camaro) 193.5 in.; (Lumina) 200.9 in.; (Monte Carlo) 200.7 in. Height: (Metro cpe) 54.7 in.; (Metro sed) 55.4 in.; (Prizm) 53.5 in.; (Cavalier cpe) 53.0 in.; (Cavalier sed) 54.7; (Cavalier conv) 53.7 in.; (Malibu) 56.4 in.; (Camaro cpe) 51.3 in.; (Camaro conv) 52.0 in.; (Lumina) 55.2 in.; (Monte Carlo) 53.8 in. Width: (Metro) 62.6 in.; (Prizm) 66.7 in.; (Cavalier) 67.9 in.; (Malibu) 69.4 in.; (Camaro) 74.1 in.; (Lumina/Monte Carlo) 72.5 in. Front Tread: (Metro) 54.5 in.; (Prizm) 57.9 in.; (Cavalier) 57.6 in.; (Malibu) 59.1 in.; (Camaro) 60.7 in.; (Lumina/Monte Carlo) 59.5 in. Rear Tread: (Metro) 53.5 in.; (Prizm) 57.5 in.; (Cavalier) 56.4 in.; (Malibu) 59.3 in.; (Camaro) 60.6 in.; (Lumina/Monte Carlo) 59.0 in. Standard Tires: (Metro) P155/80R13; (Prizm) P185/65R14; (Cavalier) P195/70R14; (Cavalier RS/LS) P195/65R15; (Cavalier Z24) P205/55R16; (Malibu) P215/60R15; (Camaro) P215/60R16; (Camaro Z28) P235/55R16; (Lumina/Monte Carlo LS) P205/70R15; (Lumina LS/LTZ, Monte Carlo Z34) P225/60R16.

TECHNICAL: Transmission: Five-speed manual shift standard on Metro/Metro LSi, Prizm/Prizm LSi, Cavalier/Cavalier RS/Cavalier Z24 and Camaro. Four-speed overdrive automatic standard on Cavalier LS, Malibu/Malibu LS, Camaro Z28, Lumina/Lumina LS/Lumina LTZ, Monte Carlo LS/Monte Carlo Z34. Steering: (All) rack and pinion. Brakes: front disc, rear drum; four-wheel discs standard on Camaro/Camaro Z28, Lumina LTZ (equipped with 3.8-liter V-6 option engine), Monte Carlo Z34; anti-lock brakes standard on all except Metro/Metro LSi, base Lumina. Body construction: unibody. Fuel tank: (Metro) 10.6 gal.; (Prizm) 13.2 gal.; (Cavalier) 15.2 gal.; (Malibu) 15.0 gal.; (Camaro) 15.5 gal.; (Lumina) 16.6 gal.; (Monte Carlo) 16.6 gal.

DRIVETRAIN OPTIONS: Engines: 2.4-liter four-cylinder: Cavalier LS ($450). 3.1-liter V-6: Malibu ($495). 3.8-liter V-6 ($450). Three-speed automatic trans.: Metro LSi ($645). Prizm ($645). Cavalier ($600). Four-speed overdrive auto. trans.: Prizm ($850). Cavalier/RS/Z24 ($780); Camaro ($815). Six-speed manual trans.: Camaro Z28 (NA)

METRO CONVENIENCE/APPEARANCE OPTIONS: Coupe Preferred Equip. Grp. 1: Incl w/model (NC). Coupe Preferred Equip. Grp. 2: Bodyside Mldgs.; 3-spoke Wheels; Color-Keyed Carpeted Mats, F&R ($179). Coupe Preferred Equip. Grp. 3: Air Cond, w/CFC-free Refrigerant; Elect Tuned AM/FM Stereo Radio, w/Seek, Four Speakers and Digital Clock; Bodyside Mldgs.; 3-spoke Wheels; Color-Keyed Carpeted Mats, F&R ($1294). LSi Coupe Preferred Equip. Grp. 1: Incl w/model (NC). LSi Coupe Preferred Equip. Grp. 2: Air Cond, w/CFC-free Refrigerant; Elect Tuned AM/FM Stereo Radio and Cass. Player, w/Seek & Scan, Tone Select, Four Speakers and Digital Clock; Color-Keyed Carpeted Mats, F&R ($1375). LSi Sedan Preferred Equip. Grp. 1: Incl w/model (NC). LSi Sedan Preferred Equip. Grp. 2: Air Cond, w/CFC-free Refrigerant; Pwr Steering; Elect Tuned AM/FM Stereo Radio and Cass. Player, w/Seek, Tone Select, Four Speakers and Digital Clock; Color-Keyed Carpeted Mats, F&R ($1665). Air Cond, w/CFC-free Refrigerant ($785). Z05 Convenience Pkg: Dual Manual Remote Mirrors, Remote Trunk Release, Split Fldg Rear Seat & Trunk Light ($125). 4-Wheel Anti-Lock Brakes ($565). Pwr Door Locks ($220). Rear Window Defogger ($160). Calif. Emission System ($170). Color-Keyed Carpeted Mats, F&R ($40). Bodyside Mldgs. ($50). Pwr Steering ($290). Tachometer ($70). Rear Window Wiper/Washer System, cpe only ($125).

PRIZM CONVENIENCE/APPEARANCE OPTIONS: Sedan Preferred Equip. Grp. 1: Incl w/model (NC). Sedan Preferred Equip. Grp. 2: Air Cond, w/CFC-free Refrigerant; Elect Tuned AM/FM Stereo Radio, w/Seek, Four Speakers and Digital Clock; Wheel Covers; Color-

Keyed Carpeted Mats, F&R ($1222). Sedan Preferred Equip. Grp. 3: Air Cond, w/CFC-free Refrigerant; Pwr Door Locks, Elect Tuned AM/FM Stereo Radio and Cass. Player, w/Seek & Scan, Four Speakers and Digital Clock; Elect Spd Control, w/resume speed; Wheel Covers; Color-Keyed Carpeted Mats, F&R ($1847). LSi Sedan Preferred Equip. Grp. 1: Incl w/model (NC). LSi Sedan Preferred Equip. Grp. 2: FE2 Handling Pkg; Tilt Strg Wheel; Elect Tuned AM/FM Stereo Radio and Cass. Player, w/Seek & Scan, Tone Select, Four Speakers, Theft Deterrent and Digital Clock; Pwr Windows ($550). Air Cond, w/CFC-free Refrigerant ($795). 4-Wheel Anti-Lock Brakes ($645). FE2 Handling Pkg ($70). Child's Safety Seat, rear pass. position ($125). Elect Spd Control, w/resume speed ($185). Rear Window Defogger ($180). Pwr Door Locks ($220). Pwr Windows, LSi only ($300). Calif. Emission System ($170). Color-Keyed Carpeted Mats, F&R ($40). Elect Sun Roof ($675). Tilt Strg Wheel ($80). Tachometer ($70). Intermittent Wiper System ($55). Wheel Covers ($55). 14-in. Alloy Wheels ($335).

CAVALIER CONVENIENCE/APPEARANCE OPTIONS: Coupe Preferred Equip. Grp 1: Intermittent Wiper System; Mech Trunk Opener; Dual Covered Visor Mirrors, w/map straps; Mud Guards; Cargo Net; Color-Keyed Carpeted Mats, F&R ($515). Coupe Preferred Equip. Grp 2: Tilt Strg Wheel; Elect Spd Control, w/resume speed; Pwr Mirrors; Intermittent Wiper System; Mech Trunk Opener; Dual Covered Visor Mirrors, w/map straps; Mud Guards; Cargo Net; Color-Keyed Carpeted Mats, F&R ($990). Sedan Preferred Equip. Grp 1: Intermittent Wiper System; Mech Trunk Opener; Dual Covered Visor Mirrors, w/map straps; Ext. Appearance Pkg: Bodyside Moldings, Body-Color Fascias and 15-inch Bolt-on Wheel Covers; Mud Guards; Cargo Net; Color-Keyed Carpeted Mats, F&R ($498). RS Coupe Preferred Equip. Grp. 1: Pwr Windows; Pwr Mirrors; Remote Keyless Entry, Incl Pwr Locks & Trunk Release ($714). LS Sedan Preferred Equip. Grp 1: Pwr Windows; Pwr Mirrors; Remote Keyless Entry, Incl Pwr Locks & Trunk Release ($819). Air Cond ($795). Frt License Plate Bracket (NC). Electric Rear Window Defogger ($180). Pwr Door Locks: Cpe ($220); Sed ($260). Rear Spoiler ($125). Vinyl Bucket Seats ($50). Elect Sun Roof ($595). Eng. Block Htr ($30). Calif. Emission System ($170). 15-in. alum wheels ($295).

MALIBU CONVENIENCE/APPEARANCE OPTIONS: Preferred Equip. Grp. 1: Pwr Windows; Pwr Door Locks, Pwr Ext. Mirrors ($700). Preferred Equip. Grp. 2: Elect Spd Control, w/resume speed; Pwr Windows; Pwr Door Locks, Pwr Ext. Mirrors; Remote Keyless Entry; Dual Mirror-Mounted Reading Lamps ($1100). Remote Keyless Entry ($150). 6-Way Pwr Driver's Seat ($310). Custom Cloth Recl. Frnt. Bucket Seat w/Splt Fldg Rear Seat ($225). Leather Bucket Seat ($475). Mud Guards ($60). Elect Sun Roof ($595). Electric Rear Window Defogger ($180). Elect Spd Control, w/resume speed ($225). Eng Block Htr ($30). Calif. Emission System ($170). Color-Keyed Carpeted Mats, F&R ($40). 15-in. alum wheels ($310).

CAMARO CONVENIENCE/APPEARANCE OPTIONS: Coupe Preferred Equip. Grp. 1: Elect Spd Control, w/resume speed; Fog Lamps; Pwr Door Locks; Remote Trunk Release ($565). Coupe Preferred Equip. Grp. 2: Pwr Windows; Pwr Door Locks; Elect Spd Control, w/resume speed; Remote Trunk Release; Fog Lamps; Elect Spt Twin Remote Mirrors; Leather-wrapped Strg Wheel/Trans Shifter/Prk Brake Handle; Illum Remote Keyless Entry; Antitheft Alarm System ($1231). Convertible Preferred Equip. Grp. 1: Pwr Windows; Pwr Door Locks; Elect Spd Control, w/resume speed; Fog Lamps; Remote Trunk Release; Elect Spt Twin Remote Mirrors; Leather-wrapped Strg Wheel/Trans Shifter/Prk Brake Handle; Illum Remote Keyless Entry; Antitheft Alarm System; Bodyside Mldgs.; Color-Keyed Carpeted Mats, F&R ($1306). Z28 Coupe Preferred Equip. Grp. 1: Pwr Windows; Pwr Door Locks; Elect Spd Control, w/resume speed; Fog Lamps; Remote Trunk Release; Elect Spt Twin Remote Mirrors; Leather-wrapped Strg Wheel/Trans Shifter/Prk Brake Handle; Illum Remote Keyless Entry; Antitheft Alarm System; Bodyside Mldgs.; Color-Keyed Carpeted Mats, =&R ($1576). Z28 Convertible Preferred Equip. Grp. 1: Pwr Windows; Pwr Door Locks; Elect Spd Control, w/resume speed; Fog Lamps; Remote Trunk Release; Elect Spt Twin Remote Mirrors; Leather-wrapped Strg Wheel/Trans Shifter/Prk Brake Handle; Illum Remote Keyless Entry; Antitheft Alarm System; Bodyside Mldgs.; Color-Keyed Carpeted Mats, F&R (NC). Acceleration Slip Regulation, Z28 only ($450). Frt License Plate Bracket (NC). Elect Rear Window Defogger ($170). Calif. Emission System ($170). Bodyside Mldgs ($60). Y3F Sport Appearance Pkg: Front & Rear Fascia Ext., Rocker Mldgs and Spoiler Ext. ($1755). WU8 SS Performance/Appearance Pkg: 320 HP Eng. Upgrade, Forced Air Induction Hood, Spoiler, 17-in. alum wheels, High Perf. Ride & Handling Pkg and SS Badging, Z28 only ($3500). GU5 Axle, Z28 only ($300). 1LE Perf Pkg, Z28 cpe only: Incl Special Handling Susp. System ($1175). Y87 Performance Handling Pkg, Incl Ltd Slip Axle, Dual Exhaust & Spt Strg Ratio ($225). Remote Keyless Entry ($225). 6-Way Pwr Driver's Seat ($270). Leather Bucket Seats ($499). Eng Block Htr ($20). Removable Glass Roof Panels, Incl locks ($995). TIRES: P235/55R16 Steel Belted Radial Blackwall ($132). P245/50ZR16 Steel Belted Radial Blackwall, Z28 only ($225). Chrome Alum Wheels, 16-in.: Camaro ($775); Z28 ($500).

LUMINA CONVENIENCE/APPEARANCE OPTIONS: Preferred Equip Grp. 1: Pwr Windows; Pwr Trunk Opener; Elect Spd Control, w/resume speed; Cargo Net; Elect Spt Twin Remote Mirrors; Color-Keyed Carpeted Mats, F&R ($758). LS Preferred Equip. Grp. 1: Pwr Trunk Opener; Driver & Pass. Temp Control; Remote Keyless Entry; Color-Keyed Carpeted Mats, F&R ($645). LTZ Preferred Equip. Grp. 1: Strg Wheel Radio Controls; Pwr Trunk Opener; Driver & Pass. Temp Control; Remote Keyless Entry; Color-Keyed Carpeted Mats, F&R ($816). 60/40 Bench Seat, Leather Trim ($645). 60/40 Bench Seat, Custom Cloth Trim ($150). Frt License Plate Bracket (NC). 4-Wheel Anti-Lock

Brakes ($575). Electric Rear Window Defogger ($170). Calif. Emission System ($170). Remote Keyless Entry ($220). Pwr Windows ($328). Elect Spd Control, w/resume speed ($225). 6-Way Pwr Driver's Seat ($305). Elect Sunroof ($700). Eng Block Htr ($20). RS9 Sport Perf Pkg: 3.8-liter V-6 and 16-in. alum wheels, LTZ only ($500). TIRES: P225/60R16 All Seasons Steel Belted Radial Blackwall ($175). 15-in. bolt-on chrome wheel cover ($100). 16-in. alum wheels ($300).

MONTE CARLO CONVENIENCE/APPEARANCE OPTIONS: LS Preferred Equip Grp. 1: Pwr Trunk Opener; Elect Spd Control, w/resume speed; Cargo Net; Driver & Pass. Temp Control; Remote Keyless Entry ($635). Custom Cloth Bucket Seats, w/console ($200). Custom Leather Bucket Seats, w/console: LS ($695); Z34 ($645). Frt License Plate Bracket (NC). Electric Rear Window Defogger ($170). Calif. Emission System ($170). Pwr Driver's Seat ($305). Elect Sunroof ($700). Eng Block Htr ($19). Rear Deck Spoiler ($175). Elect Spd Control, w/resume speed ($225). TIRES: P225/60R16 All Seasons Steel Belted Radial Blackwall ($175). 16-in. alum wheels ($300).

HISTORY: A 1998 Corvette convertible was selected to pace the Indianapolis 500 with professional golfer Greg "The Shark" Norman the driver.

(Continued from page 199)

The Monte Carlo returned to the Chevrolet fold in 1995 after a six-year absence. It was brought back as the coupe counterpart to the now all-sedan, new-design Lumina series (as well as being an instant powerhouse on the NASCAR circuit). With Lumina's revamp, gone were the former Euro and Z34 coupes. Cavalier was also new-for-1995. The VL models were dropped, as was the station wagon. One of the new Cavalier models was the LS convertible, which was assembled off-site by Genasys, a joint venture corporation established by ASC and Lansing Automotive Division. Beretta's Z26 coupe now used the 3.1-liter V-6 with sequential fuel injection as its standard engine. The Impala SS sedan and Caprice Classic station wagon both featured Corvette's LT1 5.7-liter V-8 as their source of power.

The 1996 Chevrolet lineup was not altered much from the previous year's with the exception of the addition of an RS coupe and convertible to the Camaro series, positioned between base and Z28 lines. Making their final appearances were the Beretta, Corsica and Caprice Classic/Impala SS models, all to be dropped by model year's end. With the discontinuance of Caprice Classic and Impala SS, this also meant the end of Chevrolet's full-size front-engine, rear-drive offerings—the backbone of Chevy production since its initial 1912 Classic Six touring car originated this configuration. In addition to the RS series coming on line, Camaro's former standard engine, the 3.4-liter V-6, was replaced by the 3.8-liter V-6. Cavalier's Z24 line also received a new standard powerplant in the form of the DOHC 2.4-liter four-cylinder engine.

To offset the loss of Beretta, Corsica, Caprice Classic/Impala SS from '96, the 1997 Chevrolet ranks received the Malibu, selected as *Motor Trend* magazine's "Car of the Year." The Malibu name was missing from Chevrolet for 13 years, and returned in the form of base and LS sedans. Camaro, now observing three decades of production, offered a 30th Anniversary Package for its Z28 models. This package included an orange-stripe-on-white-finish paint scheme reminiscent of the Camaro that paced the 1969 Indianapolis 500. An RS coupe was added to the Cavalier lineup, positioned between the base and LS models. Lumina added a third sedan to its ranks in the form of an upscale, sporty LTZ sedan powered by the DOHC 3.4-liter V-6.

After years of being sold at Chevrolet dealerships across the country, the Geo Division of General Motors was disbanded in 1998 and its two-model line of cars were now badged as Chevrolets. Metro and Prizm were the new additions to the 1998 Chevrolet lineup, as well as a Cavalier Z24 convertible that replaced the former LS ragtop that was dropped. Corvette's Generation III all-aluminum block LS1 V-8, introduced the year previous, was now used in the Camaro Z28 and SS model, which was now offered as a Camaro Performance/Appearance Package. The Series II 3.8-liter V-6 was now the standard engine in the Lumina LTZ and Monte Carlo Z34.

Approaching the 21st century, Chevrolet was offering "high-tech" equipment such as OnStar Stolen Vehicle Tracking/Emergency Communication System, Pass-Key II Theft Deterrent System, Traction Control, Reduced Force Airbags and Side-Impact Airbags and a host of other safety features that the automaker hopes will keep it competitive in the auto industry of the new millennium. These advances and, more importantly, the past 86 years of Chevy automobiles are indicators that the competition should keep an eye on Chevrolet.

STANDARD CATALOG OF
CORVETTE
1976-1998

With the introduction of the 45th Anniversary 1997 Corvette (foreground), there were five generations of America's sports car in existence.

By 1976, Corvette's shapely aerodynamic body was eight years old. Yet it would remain in this form for half a dozen more years, attracting performance-minded drivers even though the engine choices were far milder than they had been. After all, what else was there? As Chevrolet proclaimed, Corvette was "America's only true production sports car." Only the Stingray coupe body remained for 1976, as convertible Corvettes became extinct. Removable roof panels would be the closet one could come to open-topped motoring. Corvettes remained fiberglass-bodied, of course; but this year a partial steel underbody was added. Customers had a choice of wide- or close-ratio four-speed gearboxes, and the standard or special (L82) 350 cu. in. V-8 engine. The latter engine, installed in 5,720 cars, had finned aluminum rocker covers and special cylinder heads. Sales hit a record level.

Next year, the Stingray name faded away, but not much else changed. Less than 16 percent of Corvettes came with either the close-ratio or wide-ratio four-speed transmission—a figure typical of this period. Most customers, it seemed, wanted Corvette's performance—but didn't wish to shift for themselves.

An aero restyling of the basic body arrived for Corvette's 25th anniversary year, adding a fastback roofline and large wraparound back window. The high-performance (L82) V-8 added horsepower with a new dual-snorkel air-intake system and lower-restriction exhaust components. Nearly one-third of this year's Corvettes sported optional Silver Anniversary two-tone silver paint. Even more striking were the Indy Pace Car replicas, with black-over-silver paint and a host of extras. They sold for well above retail at the time, and remain among the more desirable Corvettes today.

Some of those Pace Car features found their way onto standard models for 1979, including bolt-on spoilers and lightweight bucket seats. Both the base and special V-8s now had the dual-snorkel intake. Production slid upward for the model year, but sales slipped a bit. Another modest restyling came in 1980, lowering the hood profile and recessing the grille (and taking off some weight). Lift-off roof panels were made of microscopic glass beads. Front and rear spoilers were now molded into place. Corvette 350 cu. in. V-8s produced as much as 230 horsepower, but speedometers now peaked at 85 MPH.

382

In another weight-cutting move, a fiberglass-reinforced Monoleaf rear spring was installed on automatic-transmission models in 1981. A new-190 horsepower, 350 cu. in. (5.7-liter) engine had cast magnesium rocker covers and stainless steel exhaust manifolds. In an attempt to keep-up with a rising problem, the theft alarm added a starter interrupt.

A new Corvette was in the works, but the 1982 version had some strong points of its own: essentially, a strong new drivetrain in the last of the old bodies. The "Cross Fire" fuel-injected V-8 used throttle-body injectors, but produced only 10 more horsepower (200) than the former version. For the first time since 1955, all Corvettes had automatic shift. A built-to-order Collector Edition featured silver-beige metallic paint and a frameless glass hatch. That was the first 'Vette to carry a price tag above $20,000. Sales sagged dramatically, perhaps because customers were waiting for the next (fourth) generation.

No Corvettes at all were built for the 1983 model year, but the aerodynamic '84 edition (debuting in spring 1983) was worth the wait. The buff books fawned over it with superlatives. Technical changes included an aluminum driveshaft and fiberglass springs. A new transmission was offered—four-speed manual with automatic overdrive in top three gears—but only one in eight Corvettes carried it. The overdrive was locked out during hard acceleration. This year's dual-injector V-8 produced 205 horsepower. One other little change: Corvette's price tag soared past the $23,000 mark.

Horsepower jumped by 25 for 1985, with a new tuned-port fuel-injected 350 V-8. Next year, a convertible arrived—first open Corvette since 1975. Anti-lock braking also became standard, as did a new VATS anti-theft system. Four-speed overdrive automatic was standard, but a four-speed manual (overdrive in top three gears) cost no more. A switch to aluminum heads for the TPI engine produced a few problems, so early models kept the old cast iron heads. All convertibles (roadsters) were sold as Indy Pace Cars. It can easily be said that all Corvettes are collectible, yet some more so than others. The 1978 Pace Car Replica is one; the '82 Collector Edition another. Neither qualifies as rare, though, as quite a few were produced. No doubt, strong demand will keep the '86 convertible on the desirable list.

Though little changed from the previous model, the 1987 Corvette Y-body coupe and convertible highlighted state-of-the-art technology throughout. From an electronic instrument panel with eight possible gauge readouts in four locations to aluminum cylinder heads and a high-performance stereo speaker system, the Chevrolet luxury sports car was aimed at buyers who wanted the latest in automotive features, regardless of cost.

Some early 1987 Corvettes experienced problems with cracking of their new aluminum cylinder heads. The problem was ultimately solved, but did have a negative affect on production operations. The 5.7-liter Corvette V-8 was also fitted with new roller lifters which reduced friction and bumped horsepower to 240.

After new for the year was an optional Z52 suspension setup, a low-tire-pressure indicating system and Bosch four-wheel anti-lock braking. In the works was a change to recently developed Goodyear 17-inch tires with a rac-

ing-style 45 percent aspect ratio, plus a much-desired gearbox change. At a plant in Brewer, Me., the North American branch of Germany's Zahnrad Fabrik Friedrichshafen AG (better known to car buffs as ZF) was busy developing a new six-speed manual transmission for the Corvette. Unfortunately, the new transmission was not ready in 1987, when 86 percent of Corvettes came with Turbo Hydramatic and 14 percent with four-speeds.

Corvette production continued to be housed in Chevrolet's Bowling Green, Ky., factory. Model year production totaled 30,632 (including 10,625 convertibles) although model year sales of 25,266 units fell short of the 35,969 sold in 1986.

For 1988, the Corvette remained available as a hatchback coupe or a roadster, with prices starting just below $30,000. Increased excitement was generated by a new 5.7-liter V-8 that jumped horsepower from 235 to 245. The 17-inch tires were now made available for cars with the Z52 option. However, the ZF six-speed remained on the Vette owners' "wish list" and 81.2 percent of the cars has a four-speed manual with lock-up overdrive.

Production of 1988 Corvettes began on Aug. 24, 1987, and stopped on July 28, 1988. During that period, 'Vettes were built on a single shift at the Bowling Green factory, with workers cranking out an average of 11 cars per hour. Output totaled 22,789 units, of which 7,407 were ragtops. Model year sales of 25,425 units again accounted for an .03 percent share of the domestic car market.

A reaction injected molded (RIM) structural composite front bumper beam was new for all 1989 Corvettes and all could also be had with the long-awaited ZF gearbox. Corvette was one of the few American cars to start offering air bags this season. Both coupes and roadsters were powered by a 5.7-liter tuned port injected V-8, which was rated 245 nhp @ 4300 rpm for coupes and 240 nhp @ 4000 rpm for convertibles. A much-heralded ZR-1 "King-of-the-Hill" Corvette whas scheduled for mid-1989 release, but its due date was ultimately delayed.

Model year output went in the right direction, rising to 26,412 units, of which 9,749 were open cars. Transmission attachments ran a bit higher for automatics (84.4 percent) despite the availability of the six-speed. Nearly all 1989 Corvettes came 100 percent loaded with options with some exceptions being a Bose sound system used in 91.4 percent, a rear window defogger in 63.1 percent and power seats in 96.9 percent.

An exciting addition to the 1990 Corvette lineup was the ZR-1 coupe, which was engineered in conjunction with Lotus of England and the Mercury Marine Div. of Brunswick Corp., in Stillwater, Okla. It bowed in September 1989, as a 1990 model, and production of 3,000 copies was scheduled for Bowling Green.

The ZR-1's prime attraction was a special high-performance 5.7-liter aluminum double overhead cam V-8 (RPO LT5), which featured four valves per cylinder and 375 horses, and mated to the ZF transmission. The car's body also had a wider rear roof bow and quarter panel section made of traditional SMC plastic materials produced by GenCorp at its Reinforced Plastics Div. plant in Marion, Ind. A price tag of $59,495 made the ZR-1 America's most expensive production car.

To go along with ZR-1 performance image, power on standard L98-powered coupes and convertibles was made 245 nhp (or 250 nhp with sport mufflers). The basic price for a Corvette jumped $434 to $32,479. New for 1990 convertibles was an optional removable hardtop.

During the 1987-1990 period, Chevrolet Motor Div. operated as a branch of General Motors Corp., with its headquarters in Warren, Mich. Robert D. Burger was general manager through mid-1989, when Jim C. Perkins—an enthusiast and Classic Chevy collector—took over the command post.

The most talked about change for 1991 Corvettes was the restyling of the coupe's and convertible's rear to more closely resemble the ZR-1, the price of which increased $4,643 to $64,138 for what was essentially a carry-over model from 1990.

This same scenario occurred in 1992 as the ZR-1 did not change drastically, but its price climbed to $65,318. The standard Corvette models received a more potent (by 300 horsepower) 5.7-liter V-8. Acceleration Slip Regulation was also a new feature on 'Vettes this year.

It was the 40th Anniversary of the Corvette in 1993. The occasion was marked by Chevrolet offering an optional special appearance package, available on all models, that included "ruby red" exterior and interior, anniversary badging on the hood, deck and side-gills, and seat headrests embroidered with the anniversary logo. The ZR-1's LT5 V-8 got a power boost, now rated at 405 horsepower, which was an increase of 20 over the previous powerplant used. The '93 'Vette also introduced GM's Passive Keyless Entry System, and was the first North American automobile to use recycled sheet-molded-compound body panels.

Chevrolet constructed this 1979 Turbo-Corvette with fuel injection as an "idea" vehicle. The production Corvette, with a 5.7-liter V-8 engine, got a boost from its regular 195 bhp to an estimated 260 bhp by adding the special equipment. Chevrolet engineers were testing the potential for performance with smaller engines that is possible by turbocharging. Air came in through the air cleaner, traveled through the turbocharger, up through the chrome pipe to the manifold and intake ports for each cylinder, where the air was mixed with metered injected fuel.

Some "tweaking" was done to 1994 Corvettes, with several safety and ride-enhancing items installed. The price of a ZR-1 was now $67,443. Corvettes now offered brake-transmission shift interlock, dual airbags, sequential fuel injection and a refined interior including new carpeting and door panel trim. The ZR-1 received new wheels. The 4L60-E electronic four-speed overdrive automatic transmission standard in Corvettes was also refined to provide smoother shift points.

The ZR-1, now priced at just over $68,000, made its final appearance in 1995. The biggest change on Corvettes this year was a new gill panel located behind the front wheel openings that instantly identified these 'Vettes as '95 models. Changes included the addition of heavy-duty brakes with larger front rotors and the use of de Carbon gas-charged shock absorbers for improved ride quality. A Corvette paced the 1995 Indianapolis 500, the third time (1978 and 1986, previously) for America's sports car to lead the pack at Indy.

It was a year of transition at Bowling Green, Ky., with the fourth-generation Corvette in its final year in 1996. With the ZR-1 now history, Chevrolet introduced two special versions of the Corvette in the form of a Grand Sport Edition and Collector Edition. The Grand Sport, in its Admiral Blue, White Stripe and red "hash mark" on the left front fender finish, evoked memories of the brutish racing Corvettes from 1962-'63 and raced by legends including A.J. Foyt and Roger Penske. The modern version was powered by the 330 horsepower LT4 V-8 coupled to a T56 six-speed manual transmission. The Collector Edition Corvette was finished in Sebring Silver and featured badging and embroidered seat headrests with the Collector Edition logo. Also available was a Z51 Performance & Handling Package offered only on the Corvette coupe for enthusiasts who wanted to run their cars in autocross or gymkhana events.

The fifth-generation Corvette of 1997 received rave reviews in the press, and after a mid-model year (January 1997) launch sold over 9,000 copies in coupe form only. Everything was new about this Corvette including the frame construction and blunt tail styling. The LS1 5.7-liter V-8 was more compact and more potent, producing 350 horsepower and 345 pound-feet of torque. The cockpit was reminiscent of the original Corvette of 1953 in that it utilized a twin-pod design. It was the first all-new Corvette in 13 years and only the sixth major change in the car's 44-year history.

Now observing its 45th year in 1998, the Corvette lineup added a convertible to go with the coupe launched the year previous. The refinements included magnesium wheels with a bronze tint and Daytime Running Lamps. Price of a coupe reached $37,995 with the ragtop costing $44,425. For the fourth time, a Corvette was selected to be the pace car for the Indianapolis 500. The 1998 pacer 'Vette was finished in purple and yellow and was driven by professional golfer Greg "the Shark" Norman.

Rumors of the demise of the Corvette have been steady in recent years, but after 45 years of production and with it being a proven image-enhancing product for Chevrolet, the Corvette's future cannot be dismissed so easily.

1976

1976 Chevrolet, Corvette Stingray two-door coupe (PH)

STINGRAY -- SERIES Y -- V-8 -- Unlike some advertisers, Chevrolet was correct in billing the fiberglass-bodied Corvette as "America's only true production sports car." The big-block V-8 had disappeared after 1974, leaving a 350 cu. in. (5.7-liter) small-block as the powerplant for all Corvettes in the next decade. Two V-8s were offered this year, both with four-barrel carburetor. The base L48 version now developed 180 horsepower (15 more than in 1975). An optional L82 V-8 produced 210. That one had special heads with larger valves, impact-extruded pistons, and finned aluminum rocker covers. The standard V-8 drove a new, slightly lighter weight automatic transmission: the Turbo Hydra-matic 350, which was supposed to improve shifting at wide-open throttle. Optional engines kept the prior Turbo Hydra-matic 400, but with a revised torque converter. A wide-range four-speed manual gearbox (with 2.64:1 first gear ratio) was standard; close-ratio version available at no extra cost. A new Carburetor Outside Air Induction system moved intake from the cowl to above the radiator. The convertible was dropped this year, so only the Stingray coupe remained, with twin removable roof panels. A partial steel underbody replaced the customary fiberglass, to add strength and improve shielding from exhaust system heat. A new one-piece bar Corvette nameplate was on the rear, between twin-unit taillamps (which were inset in the bumper cover). Of the ten body colors, eight were Corvette exclusives. This year's colors were red, silver, Classic white, bright yellow, bright blue, dark green, buckskin, dark brown, mahogany, and orange flame. Corvettes had side marker lights with reflectors, parking lamps that went on with headlamps, lane-change turn signals, and two-speed wiper/washers. Inside was a new, smaller-diameter four-spoke sports steering wheel with crossed-flags medallion, which came from Vega. Not everyone appreciated its lowly origin, so it lasted only this year. A grained vinyl trimmed instrument panel (with stitched seams) held a 160 MPH speedometer with trip odometer, and 7000 R.P.M. electronic tachometer. A key lock in left front fender set the anti-theft alarm. Corvettes had fully independent suspension and four-wheel disc brakes. Wide GR70 SBR tires rode 15 x 8 in. wheels. A total of 5,368 Corvettes had the FE7 Gymkhana suspension installed; 5,720 came with the L82 V-8; and 2,088 had the M21 four-speed close-ratio manual gearbox. Cast aluminum wheels were a new option, installed on 6,253 cars. Standard equipment included bumper guards, flush retracting headlamps, Soft-Ray tinted glass, Hide-A-Way wipers, wide-view day/night mirror, and center console with lighter and ashtray. Behind the seatbacks were three carpeted storage compartments. Bucket seats had textured-vinyl upholstery and deep-pleated saddle-stitched seat panels (black, dark firethorn, light buckskin or white). Interior leather trim was now available in seven colors.

I.D. DATA: Like other GM vehicles, Corvette had a 13-symbol Vehicle Identification Number (VIN) atop the dashboard, visible through the windshield on the driver's side. The VIN appears in the form: 1Z37()6S4()()()()(). The '1' indicates Chevrolet division; 'Z' is Corvette series; '37' = body type (2-dr. sport coupe). Fifth symbol is an engine code: 'L' = base L48 V-8 and 'X' = optional L82 V-8. Next is model year: '6' = 1976. The letter 'S' indicates assembly plant (St. Louis). Finally comes a six-digit sequential serial number, starting with 400001. That sequential serial number is repeated on the engine block itself, stamped on a pad just ahead of the cylinder head on the right (passenger) side, combined with a three-letter identification suffix. Cast into the top rear (right side) of the block is a date built code. The first letter of that four-symbol code shows the month the block was cast. The next number (or numbers) reveals the day of the month, while the final digit indicates year.

CORVETTE

Model No.	Body/Style No.	Body Type & Seating	Factory Price	Shipping Weight	Prod. Total
1Y	Z37	2-dr. Cpe-2P	7605	3445	46,558

ENGINE DATA: BASE V-8: 90-degree, overhead valve V-8. Cast iron block and head. Displacement: 350 cu. in. (5.7 liters). Bore & stroke: 4.00 x 3.48 in. Compression ratio: 8.5:1. Brake horsepower: 180 at 4000 R.P.M. Torque: 270 lb.-ft. at 2400 R.P.M. Five main bearings. Hydraulic valve lifters. Carburetor: 4Bbl. Rochester M4MC. RPO Code: L48. VIN Code: L. OPTIONAL V-8: Same as above, except Compression ratio: 9.0:1. Brake horsepower: 210 at 5200 R.P.M. Torque: 255 lb.-ft. at 3600 R.P.M. RPO Code: L82. VIN Code: X.

CHASSIS DATA: Wheelbase: 98.0 in. Overall length: 185.2 in. Height: 48.0 in. Width: 69.0 in. Front Tread: 58.7 in. Rear Tread: 59.5 in. Wheel Size: 15 x 8 in. Standard Tires: GR70 x 15.

TECHNICAL: Transmission: Four-speed fully synchronized manual transmission (floor shift) standard. Gear ratios: (1st) 2.64:1; (2nd) 1.75:1; (3rd) 1.34:1; (4th) 1.00:1; (Rev) 2.55:1. Close-ratio four-speed fully synchronized manual trans. optional: (1st) 2.43:1; (2nd) 1.61:1; (3rd) 1.23:1; (4th) 1.00:1; (Rev) 2.35:1. Three-speed automatic optional: (1st) 2.52:1; (2nd) 1.52:1; (3rd) 1.00:1; (Rev) 1.94:1. Three-speed automatic ratios with L82 engine: (1st) 2.48:1; (2nd) 1.48:1; (3rd) 1.00:1; (Rev) 2.08:1. Standard final drive ratio: 3.36:1 w/4-spd, 3.08:1 w/auto. exc. with optional L82 engine 3.55:1 w/4-spd, 3.55:1 or 3.70:1 with close-ratio four-speed, or 3.36:1 w/auto. Positraction standard. Steering: Recirculating ball. Front Suspension: unequal-length control arms with ball joints, coil springs and stabilizer bar. Rear Suspension: Independent with trailing-link, transverse semi-elliptic leaf spring. Brakes: Four-wheel disc (11.75 in. disc dia.). Ignition: HEI electronic. Body construction: Separate fiberglass body and box-type ladder frame with cross-members. Fuel tank: 18 gal.

CORVETTE OPTIONS: Special L82 350 cu. in., 4Bbl. V-8 engine ($481). Close-ratio four-speed manual transmission (NC). Turbo Hydra-matic (NC); but ($134) w/L82 V-8. High-altitude or highway axle ratio ($13). Gymkhana suspension ($35). Power brakes ($59). Power steering ($151). Heavy-duty battery ($16). California emissions system ($50). Four Season air cond. ($523). Rear defogger ($78). Tilt/tele-scopic steering wheel ($95). Power windows ($107). Map light ($10). Push-button AM/FM radio ($187). AM/FM stereo radio ($281). Vinyl interior (NC). Custom interior ($164). Aluminum wheels ($299). GR70 x 15/B SBR WSW tires ($37). GR70 x 15/B SBR WLT ($51).

HISTORY: Introduced: Oct. 2, 1975. Model year production: 46,558. Calendar year production: 47,425. Calendar year sales by U.S. dealers: 41,673. Model year sales by U.S. dealers: 41,027.

Historical Footnotes: Though largely a carryover from 1975, Corvette set a new sales record. Basic design dated back to 1968.

1977

1977 Chevrolet, Corvette two-door coupe (PH)

SERIES Y -- V-8 -- Since the Stingray front fender nameplate departed this year, Chevrolet's sports car no longer had a secondary title. Changes were fairly modest this year, mainly hidden (such as steel hood reinforcement) or inside. New crossed-flags emblems stood between the headlamps, and on the fuel filler door. A thinner blacked-out pillar gave windshield and side glass a more integrated look. Corvette's console was restyled in an aircraft-type cluster design, with individual-look gauges. A voltmeter replaced the former ammeter. "Door ajar" and "headlamp up" warning lights were abandoned. New heater/air conditioning controls, ashtray and lighter were on the horizontal surface. A recessed pocket was now behind the shift lever. Power window switches moved to the new console. The manual shift lever was almost an inch higher, with shorter travel. Automatic transmission levers added a pointer, and both added a new black leather boot. A shorter steering column held a multi-function control lever. This year's steering wheel had a leather-wrapped rim. Of the ten body colors, seven were new and eight exclusive to Corvette. Colors were: Classic white, black, medium red and silver, plus Corvette dark or light blue, orange, dark red, tan or yellow. The Custom interior, formerly an extra-cost option, was now standard. "Dynasty" horizontal-ribbed cloth upholstery was framed with leather (the first cloth trim offered on Corvette), or buyers could have the customary all-leather seat panels. Leather came in ten colors, cloth in six. Two new trim colors were available: red and blue. Door panel inserts were satin finish black instead of the prior woodgrain. Both instrument panel and door trim lost their embossed stitch lines. New padded sunshades could swivel to side windows. Passenger-side roof pillars held a soft vinyl coat hook. Powertrains were the same as in 1976, but power brakes and steering were now standard. A total of 6,148 Chevrolets came with the special L82 V-8 engine under the hood, while 7,269 had optional Gymkhana suspension. Only 5,743 Corvettes had the M20 four-speed manual gearbox, and 2,060 the M26 close-ratio four-speed. And just 289 came with trailering equipment. New options included AM/FM stereo radio with tape player, cruise control (for automatic only), and a luggage carrier that could hold the roof panels. Glass roof panels were announced, but delayed for another year.

I.D. DATA: Coding of the 13-symbol Vehicle Identification Number (VIN) was the same as 1976, but it moved to the windshield side pillar (still visible through the windshield). Model year code changed to '7' for 1977.

CORVETTE

Model No.	Body/Style No.	Body Type & Seating	Factory Price	Shipping Weight	Prod. Total
1Y	Z37	2-dr. Cpe-2P	8648	3448	49,213

ENGINE DATA: BASE V-8: 90-degree, overhead valve V-8. Cast iron block and head. Displacement: 350 cu. in. (5.7 liters). Bore & stroke: 4.00 x 3.48 in. Compression ratio: 8.5:1. Brake horsepower: 180 at 4000 R.P.M. Torque: 270 lb.-ft. at 2400 R.P.M. Five main bearings. Hydraulic valve lifters. Carburetor: 4Bbl. Rochester

M4MC. RPO Code: L48. VIN Code: L. OPTIONAL V-8: Same as above, except C.R.: 9.0:1. B.H.P.: 210 at 5200 R.P.M. Torque: 255 lb.-ft. at 3600 R.P.M. bearings. RPO Code: L82. VIN Code: X.

CHASSIS DATA: Wheelbase: 98.0 in. Overall length: 185.2 in. Height: 48.0 in. Width: 69.0 in. Front Tread: 58.7 in. Rear Tread: 59.5 in. Standard Tires: GR70 x 15.

TECHNICAL: Transmission: Four-speed manual transmission (floor shift) standard. Gear ratios: (1st) 2.64:1; (2nd) 1.75:1; (3rd) 1.34:1; (4th) 1.00:1; (Rev) 2.55:1. Close-ratio four-speed manual trans. optional: (1st) 2.43:1; (2nd) 1.61:1; (3rd) 1.23:1; (4th) 1.00:1; (Rev) 2.35:1. Three-speed automatic optional: (1st) 2.48:1; (2nd) 1.48:1; (3rd) 1.00:1; (Rev) 2.08:1. Standard final drive ratio: 3.36:1. Steering/Suspension/Body: same as 1976. Brakes: Four-wheel disc. Ignition: Electronic. Fuel tank: 17 gal.

CORVETTE OPTIONS: L82 350 cu. in., 4Bbl. V-8 engine ($495). Close-ratio four-speed manual transmission (NC). Turbo Hydra-matic (NC); but ($146) w/L82 V-8. Highway axle ratio ($14). Gymkhana suspension ($38). Heavy-duty battery ($17). Trailer towing equipment ($83). California emissions system ($70). High-altitude emissions ($22). Air conditioning ($553). Rear defogger ($84). Cruise-master speed control ($88). Tilt/telescopic leather steering wheel ($165). Power windows ($116). Convenience group ($22). Sport mirrors, left remote ($36). AM/FM radio ($187). AM/FM stereo radio ($281); with stereo tape player ($414). Luggage carrier/roof panel ($73). Color-keyed floor mats ($22). Aluminum wheels ($321). GR70 x 15/B SBR WL tires ($57).

HISTORY: Introduced: Sept. 30, 1976. Model year production: 49,213 (Chevrolet initially reported 49,034 units). Calendar year production: 46,345. Calendar year sales by U.S. dealers: 42,571. Model year sales by U.S. dealers: 40,764.

1978

1978 Chevrolet, Corvette Silver Anniversary two-door coupe (CH)

SERIES Y -- V-8 -- To mark Corvette's 25th anniversary, the 1978 model got a major aerodynamic restyling with large wraparound back window and a fastback roofline. This was the first restyle since 1968. Two special editions were produced, one well known and the other little more than an optional paint job. New tinted glass lift-out roof panels were wired into the standard anti-theft system. A 24-gallon "fuel cell" replaced the former 17-gallon tank, filling space made available by a new temporary spare tire. Six of the ten body colors were new this year. Seven interiors were available (four new). Inside was a restyled, padded instrument panel with face-mounted round instruments and a new locking glove box (to replace the former map pocket). The restyled interior had more accessible rear storage area, with a roll shade to hide luggage. The wiper/washer control moved from the steering column back to the instrument panel, but turn signal and dimmer controls remained on the column. Door trim was now cut-and-sew design with soft expanded vinyl (or cloth). As in 1977, seats had leather side bolsters, with either leather or cloth seating area in a fine rib pattern. Corvette's optional L82 high-performance 350 V-8 reached 220 horsepower, as a result of a new dual-snorkel cold-air intake system, larger-diameter exhaust and tailpipes, and lower-restriction mufflers. The automatic transmission used with the optional V-8 lost weight and had a low-inertia, high-stall torque converter. Base engines used a Muncie four-speed manual gearbox with higher first/second gear ratios than before; the performance V-8 used a close-ratio Borg-Warner. Axle ratios in California and at high altitude switched from 3.08:1 to 3.55:1. A total of 12,739 optional L82 engines were installed, while 3,385 Corvettes had the M21 four-speed close-ratio gearbox and 38,614 had automatic. Glass roof panels, promised earlier, actually became available this year. What Chevrolet described as "aggressive" 60-series white-letter tires also joined the option list for the first time. An optional AM/FM/CB stereo radio used a tri-band power antenna on the rear deck. Each of this year's Corvettes could have Silver Anniversary emblems on the nose and rear deck. A total of 15,283 displayed the $399 special two-tone silver paint option: silver metallic on top, with charcoal silver on the lower body. Pinstripes accentuated fender upper profiles, wheel openings, front fender vents, hood, and rear license cavity. Interiors were also silver. Various other options were required, including aluminum wheels. For a considerably higher price, buyers could have the Limited Edition replica of the Indy Pace Car with distinctive black-over-silver paint and red accent striping. Equipment in this "Indy Package" (RPO code Z78) included a special silver interior with new lightweight highback seats, special front/rear spoilers, P255/60R15 white-letter tires on alloy wheels, and lift-off glass canopy roof panels. It contained nearly all Corvette options, plus special decals (unless the customer specified that they be omitted). Upholstery was silver leather, or leather with smoke (gray) cloth inserts.

I.D. DATA: Corvette's 13-symbol Vehicle Identification Number (VIN), visible through the windshield, altered its coding a bit this year. The VIN appears in the form:

1Z87()8S()()()()()(). The '1' indicates Chevrolet division; 'Z' is Corvette series; '87' = body type (2-dr. sport coupe). Fifth symbol is an engine code: 'L' = base L48 V-8 and 'H' = optional L82 V-8. Next is model year: '8' = 1978. The letter 'S' indicates assembly plant (St. Louis). Finally comes a six-digit sequential serial number, starting with 400001 for standard model but 900001 for Pace Car replicas. This step was taken to make it more difficult to produce counterfeit pace cars. As before, the serial number is repeated on the engine block itself, stamped on a pad just ahead of the cylinder head on the right side. A date built code is also cast into the top rear (right side) of the block. The first letter of that four-symbol code shows the month the block was cast. The next number(s) reveal the day of the month, while the final digit indicates year.

CORVETTE

Model No.	Body/Style No.	Body Type & Seating	Factory Price	Shipping Weight	Prod. Total
1Y	Z87	2-dr. Cpe-2P	9446	3401	40,275

CORVETTE LIMITED EDITION (PACE CAR REPLICA)

1Y	Z87/Z78	2-dr. Cpe-2P	13653	N/A	6,501

1978 Chevrolet, Corvette Limited Edition Indianapolis 500 Pace Car (PH)

ENGINE DATA: BASE V-8: 90-degree, overhead valve V-8. Cast iron block and head. Displacement: 350 cu. in. (5.7 liters). Bore & stroke: 4.00 x 3.48 in. Compression ratio: 8.2:1. Brake horsepower: 185 at 4000 R.P.M. Torque: 280 lb.-ft. at 2400 R.P.M. Five main bearings. Hydraulic valve lifters. Carburetor: 4Bbl. RPO Code: L48. VIN Code: L. **OPTIONAL V-8:** Same as above, except C.R.: 8.9:1. B.H.P.: 220 at 5200 R.P.M. Torque: 260 lb.-ft. at 3600 R.P.M. RPO Code: L82. VIN Code: H.

CHASSIS DATA: Wheelbase: 98.0 in. Overall length: 185.2 in. Height: 48.0 in. Width: 69.0 in. Front Tread: 58.7 in. Rear Tread: 59.5 in. Wheel size: 15 x 8 in. Standard Tires: P225/70R15 SBR. Optional Tires: P225/60R15.

TECHNICAL: Transmission: Four-speed manual transmission (floor shift) standard. Gear ratios: (1st) 2.85:1;

(2nd) 2.02:1; (3rd) 1.35:1; (4th) 1.00:1; (Rev) 2.85:1. Close-ratio four-speed manual available at no extra charge: (1st) 2.43:1; (2nd) 1.61:1; (3rd) 1.23:1; (4th) 1.00:1; (Rev) 2.35:1. Three-speed automatic optional: (1st) 2.52:1; (2nd) 1.52:1; (3rd) 1.00:1; (Rev) 1.94:1. Standard final drive ratio: 3.36:1 w/4-spd, 3.08:1 w/auto. exc. L82 V-8, 3.70:1 w/4-spd and 3.55:1 w/auto. Steering/Suspension/Body: Same as 1976-77. Brakes: Four-wheel disc (11.75 in. disc dia.). Ignition: Electronic. Fuel tank: 24 gal.

CORVETTE OPTIONS: L82 350 cu. in., 4Bbl. V-8 engine ($525). Close-ratio four-speed manual transmission (NC). Turbo Hydra-matic (NC). Highway axle ratio ($15). Gymkhana suspension ($41). Heavy-duty battery ($18). Trailer towing equipment inc. H.D. radiator and Gymkhana pkg. ($89). California emissions system ($75). High-altitude emissions ($33). Air conditioning ($605). Rear defogger, electric ($95). Cruise-master speed control ($99). Tilt/telescopic leather steering wheel ($175). Power windows ($130). Convenience group ($84). Sport mirrors, left remote ($40). AM/FM radio ($199). AM/FM stereo radio ($286); with stereo tape player ($419). AM/FM stereo radio w/CB and power antenna ($638). Power antenna ($49). 25th anniversary paint ($399). Aluminum wheels ($340). P225/70R15/B SBR WL tires ($51). P225/60R15/B SBR WL tires ($216).

HISTORY: Introduced: Oct. 6, 1977. Model year production: 46,772 (but some industry sources have reported a total of 47,667). Calendar year production: 48,522. Calendar year sales by U.S. dealers: 42,247. Model year sales by U.S. dealers: 43,106.

Historical Footnotes: The limited-edition Pace Car replica was created to commemorate the selection of Corvette as Pace Car for the 62nd Indy 500 race on May 28, 1978. A production run of 2,500 was planned. But so many potential buyers who saw it at the New York Auto Show in February wanted one that the goal quickly expanded to 6,500--roughly one for every Chevrolet dealer. Buyers also had to endure a selection of "Forced RPOs," meaning items installed at the factory whether wanted or not. Those mandatory extras included power windows, air conditioning, sport mirrors, tilt/telescope steering, rear defogger, AM/FM stereo with either an 8-track tape player or CB radio, plus power door locks and a heavy-duty battery. Before long, the original $13,653 list price meant little, as speculators eagerly paid double that amount and more. A year later, as is usually the case, the price retreated to around original list. Even though so many were built, it's still a desirable model. Dave McLellan was now head of engineering for Corvettes, working on the next generation.

1979

SERIES Y -- V-8 -- "The Corvette evolution continues," declared this year's catalog. Not much of that evolution was visible, however, after the prior year's massive restyle.

Under the hood, the base engine got the dual-snorkel air intake introduced in 1978 for the optional L82 V-8. That added 10 horsepower. The L82 V-8 had a higher-lift cam, special heads with larger valves and higher compression, impact-extruded pistons, forgedsteel crankshaft, and finned aluminum rocker covers. The "Y" pipe exhaust system had new open-flow mufflers, while the automatic transmission got a higher numerical (3.55:1) rear axle ratio. All Corvettes now had the highback bucket seats introduced on the 1978 limited-edition Indy Pace Car. A high pivot point let the seat backrest fold flat on the passenger side, level with the luggage area floor. An AM/FM radio was now standard. Of ten body colors, only one (dark green metallic) was new this year. The others were Classic white, black and silver, plus Corvette dark or light blue, yellow, light beige, red, and dark brown. Interiors came in black, red, light beige, dark blue, dark brown, oyster, or dark green. Corvettes had black roof panel and window moldings. Bolt-on front and rear spoilers (also from the Pace Car) became available. Buyers who didn't want the full Gymkhana suspension could now order heavy-duty shocks alone. Standard equipment included the L48 V-8 with four-barrel carb, either automatic transmission or four-speed manual gearbox (close-ratio version available), power four-wheel disc brakes, and limited-slip differential. Other standards: tinted glass; front stabilizer bar; concealed wipers/washers; day/night inside mirror; wide outside mirror; anti-theft alarm system; four-spoke sport steering wheel; electric clock; trip odometer; heater/defroster; bumper guards; and luggage security shade. Tires were P225/70R15 steel-belted radial blackwalls on 15 x 8 in. wheels. Corvettes had four-wheel independent suspension. Bucket seats came with cloth/leather or all-leather trim. The aircraft-type console held a 7000 R.P.M. tachometer, voltmeter, oil pressure, temp and fuel gauges. Seat inserts could have either leather or cloth trim.

1979 Chevrolet, Corvette two-door coupe (PH)

I.D. DATA: Coding of the 13-symbol Vehicle Identification Number (VIN) was similar to 1978. Engine codes changed to '8' = base L48 and '4' = optional L82.

Model year code changed to '9' for 1979. Serial numbers began with 400001.

CORVETTE

Model No.	Body/Style No.	Body Type & Seating	Factory Price	Shipping Weight	Prod. Total
1Y	Z87	2-dr. Spt Cpe-2P	10220	3372	53,807

ENGINE DATA: BASE V-8: 90-degree, overhead valve V-8. Cast iron block and head. Displacement: 350 cu. in. (5.7 liters). Bore & stroke: 4.00 x 3.48 in. Compression ratio: 8.2:1. Brake horsepower: 195 at 4000 R.P.M. Torque: 285 lb.-ft. at 3200 R.P.M. Five main bearings. Hydraulic valve lifters. Carburetor: 4Bbl. RPO Code: L48. VIN Code: 8. OPTIONAL V-8: Same as above, except C.R.: 8.9:1. B.H.P.: 225 at 5200 R.P.M. Torque: 270 lb.-ft. at 3600 R.P.M. RPO Code: L82. VIN Code: 4.

CHASSIS DATA: Wheelbase: 98.0 in. Overall length: 185.2 in. Height: 48.0 in. Width: 69.0 in. Front Tread: 58.7 in. Rear Tread: 59.5 in. Wheel Size: 15 x 8 in. Standard Tires: P225/70R15 SBR. Optional Tires: P225/60R15.

TECHNICAL: Transmission: Four-speed manual transmission (floor shift) standard. Gear ratios: (1st) 2.85:1; (2nd) 2.02:1; (3rd) 1.35:1; (4th) 1.00:1; (Rev) 2.85:1. Close-ratio four-speed manual trans. optional: (1st) 2.43:1; (2nd) 1.61:1; (3rd) 1.23:1; (4th) 1.00:1; (Rev) 2.35:1. Three-speed automatic optional: (1st) 2.52:1; (2nd) 1.52:1; (3rd) 1.00:1; (Rev) 1.93:1. Standard final drive ratio: 3.36:1 w/4-spd, 3.55:1 w/auto. Steering: Recirculating ball. Front Suspension: Control arms, coil springs and stabilizer bar. Rear Suspension: Independent, with single transverse leaf spring and lateral struts. Brakes: Four-wheel disc (11.75 in. disc dia). Ignition: Electronic. Body construction: Fiberglass, on separate frame. Fuel tank: 24 gal.

CORVETTE OPTIONS: L82 350 cu. in., 4Bbl. V-8 engine ($565). Close-ratio four-speed manual transmission (NC). Turbo Hydra-matic (NC). Highway axle ratio ($19). Gymkhana suspension ($49). H.D. shock absorbers ($33). Heavy-duty battery ($21). Trailer towing equipment inc. H.D. radiator and Gymkhana suspension ($98). California emissions system (N/A). High-altitude emissions (N/A). Four season air cond. ($635). Rear defogger, electric ($102). Cruise-master speed control ($113). Tilt/telescopic leather-wrapped steering wheel ($190). Power windows ($141). Power windows and door locks ($272). Convenience group ($94). Sport mirrors, left remote ($45). AM/FM stereo radio ($90); with 8-track or cassette player ($228-$234). AM/FM stereo radio w/CB and power antenna ($439). Dual rear speakers ($52). Power antenna ($52). Removable glass roof panels ($365). Aluminum wheels ($380). P225/70R15 SBR WL tires ($54). P225/60R15 Aramid-belted radial WL tires ($226).

HISTORY: Introduced: Sept. 25, 1978. Model year production: 53,807 (Chevrolet initially reported a total of 49,901 units.) Calendar year production: 48,568. Calendar year sales by U.S. dealers: 38,631. Model year sales by U.S. dealers: 39,816.

Historical Footnotes: For what it's worth, 7,949 Corvettes this year were painted in Classic White, while 6,960 carried silver paint. Only 4,385 Corvettes had the MM4 four-speed manual gearbox, while 4,062 ran with the close-ratio M21 version.

1980

1980 Chevrolet, Corvette two-door coupe

SERIES Y -- V-8 -- Corvette lost close to 250 pounds in a more streamlined restyle. Hood and doors were lighter, glass thinner. Bodies held new fiberglass bumper structures. Lift-off roof panels were made of lightweight, low-density microscopic glass beads. Body panels were urethane-coated. Weight cuts also hit the powertrain. The differential housing and supports were made of aluminum. The 350 cu. in. (5.7-liter) V-8 had a new aluminum intake manifold, while California 305 (5.0-liter) V-8s had a stainless exhaust manifold. Hoods showed a new low profile. The front bumper had an integrated lower air dam, and the bumper cover now extended to wheel openings. Two-piece front cornering lamps worked whenever the lights were switched on. A deeply recessed split grille held integral parking lamps. Front fender air vents contained functional black louvers. New front/rear spoilers were molded in, integrated with bumper caps, no longer the bolt-on type. New emblems included an engine identifier for the optional L82 V-8. Turbo Hydra-matic transmissions added a lockup torque converter that engaged at about 30 MPH, while the four-speed manual got new gear ratios. California 'Vettes could only have a 305 V-8 and automatic this year. The base V-8 lost five horsepower, while the optional version gained five. New standard equipment this year included the formerly optional power windows, tilt/telescopic steering wheel, and Four Season

air conditioner. Rally wheels held P225/70R15/B blackwall SBR tires with trim rings and center caps. Body colors were: black, silver, red, yellow, white, dark green, dark blue, dark claret, dark brown, or frost beige. Interiors came in black, red, oyster, claret, dark blue, or doeskin. Dashes held a new 85 MPH speedometer. Only two storage bins stood behind the seat, where three used to be.

I.D. DATA: Coding of the 13-symbol Vehicle Identification Number (VIN) was similar to 1978-79. Engine codes were '8' = base L48 V-8, '6' = optional L82 V-8, and 'H' = California V-8. Model year code changed to 'A' for 1980. Serial numbers began with 400001.

CORVETTE

Model No.	Body/Style No.	Body Type & Seating	Factory Price	Shipping Weight	Prod. Total
1Y	Z87	2-dr. Cpe-2P	13140	3206	40,614

ENGINE DATA: BASE V-8: 90-degree, overhead valve V-8. Cast iron block and head. Displacement: 350 cu. in. (5.7 liters). Bore & stroke: 4.00 x 3.48 in. Compression ratio: 8.2:1. Brake horsepower: 190 at 4200 R.P.M. Torque: 280 lb.-ft. at 2400 R.P.M. Five main bearings. Hydraulic valve lifters. Carburetor: 4Bbl. RPO Code: L48. VIN Code: 8. OPTIONAL V-8: Same as above, except C.R.: 9.0:1. B.H.P.: 230 at 5200 R.P.M. Torque: 275 lb.-ft. at 3600 R.P.M. RPO Code: L82. VIN Code: 6. CALIFORNIA V-8: 90-degree, overhead valve V-8. Cast iron block and head. Displacement: 305 cu. in. (5.0 liters). Bore & stroke: 3.74 x 3.48 in. Compression ratio: 8.5:1. Brake horsepower: 180 at 4200 R.P.M. Torque: 255 lb.-ft. at 2000 R.P.M. Five main bearings. Hydraulic valve lifters. Carburetor: 4Bbl. Roch. M4ME. RPO Code: LG4. VIN Code: H.

CHASSIS DATA: Wheelbase: 98.0 in. Overall length: 185.3 in. Height: 48.1 in. Width: 69.0 in. Front Tread: 58.7 in. Rear Tread: 59.5 in. Wheel size: 15 x 8 in. Standard Tires: P225/70R15/B SBR. Optional Tires: P255/60R15/B.

TECHNICAL: Transmission: Four-speed manual transmission (floor shift) standard. Gear ratios: (1st) 2.88:1; (2nd) 1.91:1; (3rd) 1.33:1; (4th) 1.00:1; (Rev) 2.78:1. Three-speed Turbo Hydra-matic optional: (1st) 2.52:1; (2nd) 1.52:1; (3rd) 1.00:1; (Rev) 1.93:1. Standard final drive ratio: 3.07:1 w/4-spd, 3.55:1 w/auto. Steering/Suspension/Body/Brakes: Same as 1979. Fuel tank: 24 gal.

CORVETTE OPTIONS: L82 350 cu. in., 4Bbl. V-8 engine ($595). 305 cu. in., 4Bbl. V-8 ($50 credit). Turbo Hydra-matic (NC). Gymkhana suspension ($55). H.D. shock absorbers ($35). Heavy-duty battery ($22). Trailer towing equipment incl. H.D. radiator and Gymkhana suspension ($105). California emissions system ($250). Rear defogger, electric ($109). Cruise-master speed control ($123). Power door locks ($140). AM/FM stereo radio ($46); with 8-track ($155); w/cassette player ($168). AM/FM stereo radio w/CB and power antenna ($391). Dual rear speakers ($31). Power antenna ($56). Radio delete ($126 credit). Removable glass roof panels ($391). Roof panel carrier ($125). Aluminum wheels ($407). P225/70R15/B SBR WL tires ($62). P255/60R15/B SBR WL tires ($426).

HISTORY: Introduced: Oct. 25, 1979. Model year production: 40,614 (but Chevrolet reported a total of 40,564 units). Calendar year production: 44,190. Model year sales by U.S. dealers: 37,471.

Historical Footnotes: Production continued at the St. Louis plant, but a new GMAD operation at Bowling Green, Kentucky was planned to begin production of the next-generation Corvettes. Chevrolet engineers released a TurboVette that used a Garrette AiResearch turbocharger and fuel injection, but press people who drove it discovered performance more sluggish than a regular L82 V-8 could dish out. Only 5,726 Corvettes had the MM4 four-speed manual gearbox. And only 5,069 carried the special L82 engine. A total of 9,907 had the Gymkhana suspension.

1981

1981 Chevrolet, Corvette two-door coupe (PH)

SERIES Y -- V-8 -- Probably the most significant change this year was hidden from view. Corvettes with Turbo Hydra-matic had a new fiberglass-reinforced Monoleaf rear spring that weighed just eight pounds (33 pounds less than the multi-leaf steel spring it replaced). Obviously, it also eliminated interleaf friction. Manual-shift models kept the old spring, as did those with optional Gymkhana suspension. Side glass was thinner, in a further attempt to cut weight. A new L81 version of the 350 cu. in. V-8 arrived this year, rated 190 horsepower, with lightweight magnesium rocker covers. New stainless steel free-flow exhaust manifolds weighed 14 pounds less than the previous cast iron. A new thermostatically-controlled auxiliary electric fan boosted cooling, and allowed use of a smaller main fan. Air cleaners had a new chromed cover. Computer Command Control controlled fuel metering as well as the torque converter lockup clutch, which operated in second and third gears. Manual transmission was available in all 50 states, the first time in several years that Californians could have a stick shift. A quartz crystal clock was now standard. Corvette's standard anti-theft alarm added a starter interrupt device. Joining the option list: a six-way power seat. Electronic-tuning radios could have built-in cassette or 8-track tape players, or a CB transceiver. Body colors this year were black, white, red, yellow, beige,

and five metallics: silver, dark or bright blue, maroon, or charcoal. Four two-tone combinations were available. Interiors came in black, red, silver, rust, camel or blue. Corvette's ample standard equipment list included either four-speed manual or automatic transmission (same price), four-wheel power disc brakes, limited-slip differential, power steering, tinted glass, twin remote-control sport mirrors, and concealed two-speed wipers. Also standard: halogen high-beam retractable headlamps, air conditioning, power windows, tilt/telescope leather-wrapped steering wheel, tachometer, AM/FM radio, trip odometer, courtesy lights, and a luggage compartment security shade. Buyers had a choice of cloth/vinyl or leather/vinyl upholstery. Corvettes rode P225/70R15 steel-belted radial blackwall tires on 15 x 8 in. wheels. The optional Gymkhana suspension (price $54) was also included with the trailer towing package.

I.D. DATA: Corvettes had a new 17-symbol Vehicle Identification Number (VIN), again visible through the windshield on the driver's side. The VIN took the form: 1G1AY8764B()()()()()()(). The '1G1A' portion indicates U.S.A., General Motors, Chevrolet Division, and non-passive restraint system. 'Y' denotes Corvette series. '87' indicates 2-door sport coupe body style. '6' is the engine code. '4' is a check digit. Model year 1981 is revealed by the 'B'. Next is a code for assembly plant: either 'S' for St. Louis or '5' for Bowling Green. The last six digits are the sequential serial number, starting with 400001 for St. Louis models and 100001 for Corvettes built at Bowling Green, Kentucky. As before, the serial number is repeated on the engine block, stamped on a pad just ahead of the cylinder head on the right side. A date built code is also cast into the top rear (right side) of the block. The first letter of that four-symbol code shows the month the block was cast. The next number(s) reveal the day of the month, while the final digit indicates year.

CORVETTE

Model No.	Body/Style No.	Body Type & Seating	Factory Price	Shipping Weight	Prod. Total
1Y	Y87	2-dr. Cpe-2P	15248	3179	40,606

ENGINE DATA: BASE V-8: 90-degree, overhead valve V-8. Cast iron block and head. Displacement: 350 cu. in. (5.7 liters). Bore & stroke: 4.00 x 3.48 in. Compression ratio: 8.2:1. Brake horsepower: 190 at 4200 R.P.M. Torque: 280 lb.-ft. at 1600 R.P.M. Five main bearings. Hydraulic valve lifters. Carburetor: 4Bbl. RPO Code: L81. VIN Code: 6.

CHASSIS DATA: Wheelbase: 98.0 in. Overall length: 185.3 in. Height: 48.1 in. Width: 69.0 in. Front Tread: 58.7 in. Rear Tread: 59.5 in. Wheel Size: 15 x 8 in. Standard Tires: P225/70R15 SBR. Optional Tires: P225/60R15.

TECHNICAL: Transmission: Four-speed manual trans. (floor shift) standard. Gear ratios: (1st) 2.88:1; (2nd) 1.91:1; (3rd) 1.33:1; (4th) 1.00:1; (Rev) 2.78:1. Three-speed Turbo Hydra-matic optional: (1st) 2.52:1; (2nd) 1.52:1; (3rd) 1.00:1; (Rev) 1.93:1. Standard final drive ratio: 2.72:1 w/4-spd, 2.87:1 w/auto. Steering/Suspension/Body/Brakes: Same as 1979-80. Fuel tank: 24 gal

CORVETTE OPTIONS: Turbo Hydra-matic (NC). Performance axle ratio ($19). Gymkhana suspension ($54). H.D. shock absorbers ($35). Trailer towing equipment incl. H.D. radiator and Gymkhana suspension ($104). California emissions system ($48). Rear defogger, electric ($109). Cruise-master speed control w/resume ($141). Six-way power driver's seat ($173). Power door locks ($135). AM/FM stereo radio ($95). Electronic-tuning AM/FM stereo radio with 8-track ($385); w/cassette player ($423); w/8-track and CB ($709); w/cassette and CB ($747). Power antenna ($52). Radio delete ($118 credit). Removable glass roof panels ($391). Roof panel carrier ($124). Aluminum wheels ($404). P225/70R15 SBR WL tires ($67). P255/60R15 SBR WL tires ($460).

HISTORY: Introduced: Sept. 25, 1980. Model year production: 40,606 (but Chevrolet first reported a total of 40,593 units). Calendar year production: 27,990. Model year sales by U.S. dealers: 33,414.

Historical Footnotes: Of the total output this model year, 8,995 Corvettes came out of the new plant at Bowling Green, Kentucky, which began production in June 1981. Despite some weak years in the industry, Corvette sales remained strong through this period.

1982

1982 Chevrolet, Corvette two-door coupe (CH)

SERIES Y -- V-8 -- For the first time since 1955, no stick shift Corvettes were produced. Every one had four-speed automatic, now with lockup in every gear except first. Under the hood, though, was a new kind of 350 cu. in. V-8 with Cross-Fire fuel injection. Twin throttle-body injectors with computerized metering helped boost horsepower to 200 (10 more than 1982), and cut emissions at the same time. This was the first fuel-injected Corvette in nearly two decades, and a much different breed now that mini-computerization had arrived. In the gas tank was a new electric fuel pump. Externally, this final version of the big Corvettes

changed little. But this year's Collector Edition displayed quite a few special features, highlighted by a frameless glass lift-up hatch instead of the customary fixed backlight. Unique silver-beige metallic paint was accented by pinstripes and fading shadow treatment on hood, fenders and doors, plus distinctive cloisonné emblems. Special finned wheels were similar to the cast aluminum wheels dating back to 1967 (finale for the last prior Corvette era). Removable glass roof panels had special bronze color and solar screening. Crossed-flags emblems read "Corvette Collector Edition" around the rim. Inside was a matching silver-beige metallic interior with multi-tone leather seats and door trim. Even the hand-sewn leather-wrapped steering wheel kept the theme color, and its leather-covered horn button had a cloisonné emblem. Tires were P255/60R15 Goodyear SBR WLT Eagle GT. Back to non-collector models, standard body colors were white, red and black, plus metallic charcoal, silver, silver blue, silver green, dark blue, bright blue, gold, or dark claret. Four two-tones were available. Interiors came in dark red, charcoal, dark blue, camel, silver gray, silver beige, or silver green. Standard equipment included power brakes and steering, P225/70R15/B SBR tires on steel wheels with center hub and trim rings, cornering lamps, front fender louvers, halogen high-beam retractable headlamps, dual remote sport mirrors, and tinted glass. The body-color front bumper had a built-in air dam. Also standard: luggage security shade, air conditioning, push-button AM/FM radio, concealed wipers, power windows, time-delay dome/courtesy lamps, headlamp-on reminder, lighted visor vanity mirror, tilt/telescoping leather-wrapped steering wheel, 7000 R.P.M. tachometer, analog clock with sweep second hand, day/night mirror, lighter, and trip odometer. Bucket seats could be all cloth or leather-trimmed.

I.D. DATA: Coding of the 17-symbol Vehicle Identification Number (VIN) was similar to 1981, but several of the codes changed. The VIN took the form: 1G1AY()()8()C51()()()()(). For symbols 6-7 (body type), '87' = standard model and '07' = Collector Edition. The next symbol ('8') is the engine code. Next is a check digit: '6' for standard model, '1' for Collector. Model year code 'C' = 1982, and '5' indicates the new Bowling Green assembly plant. Six-digit sequential serial numbers began with 100001.

CORVETTE

Model No.	Body/Style No.	Body Type & Seating	Factory Price	Shipping Weight	Prod. Total
1Y	Y87	2-dr. Spt Cpe-2P	18290	3213	18,648

CORVETTE COLLECTOR EDITION

1Y	Y07	2-dr. Hatch Cpe-2P	22537	3222	6,759

ENGINE DATA: BASE V-8: 90-degree, overhead valve V-8. Cast iron block and head. Displacement: 350 cu. in. (5.7 liters). Bore & stroke: 4.00 x 3.48 in. Compression ratio: 9.0:1. Brake horsepower: 200 at 4200 R.P.M. Torque: 285 lb.-ft. at 2800 R.P.M. Five main bearings. Hydraulic valve lifters. Cross-fire fuel injection (twin TBI). RPO Code: L83. VIN Code: 8.

CHASSIS DATA: Wheelbase: 98.0 in. Overall length: 185.3 in. Height: 48.4 in. Width: 69.0 in. Front Tread: 58.7 in. Rear Tread: 59.5 in. Wheel Size: 15 x 8 in. Standard Tires: P225/70R15 SBR (Collector Edition, P255/60R15).

1982 Chevrolet, Corvette Collector Edition two-door coupe

TECHNICAL: Transmission: THM 700-R4 four-speed overdrive automatic (floor shift). Gear ratios: (1st) 3.06:1; (2nd) 1.63:1; (3rd) 1.00:1; (4th) 0.70:1; (Rev) 2.29:1. Standard final drive ratio: 2.72:1 exc. 2.87:1 w/aluminum wheels. Steering: Recirculating ball (power assisted). Front Suspension: Upper/lower A-arms, coil springs, stabilizer bar. Rear Suspension: Fully independent with half-shafts, lateral struts, control arms, and transverse leaf spring. Brakes: Power four-wheel discs (11.75 in. dia.). Ignition: Electronic. Body construction: Separate fiberglass body and ladder-type steel frame. Fuel tank: 24 gal.

CORVETTE OPTIONS: Four-speed manual trans. (NC). Gymkhana suspension ($61). H.D. cooling ($57). California emissions system (N/A). Rear defogger, electric ($129). Cruise control w/resume ($165). Six-way power driver's seat ($197). Power door locks ($155). Twin electric remote-control sport mirrors ($125). AM/FM stereo radio ($101). Electronic-tuning AM/FM stereo radio with 8-track ($386); w/cassette player ($423); w/cassette and CB ($755) exc. ($458) on Collector Edition. Power antenna ($60). Radio delete ($124 credit). Removable glass roof panels ($443). Roof panel carrier ($144). Custom two-tone paint ($428) w/lower body accents and multi-color striping. Aluminum wheels ($458). P225/70R15 SBR WL tires ($80).

HISTORY: Introduced: Dec. 12, 1981. Model year production: 25,407. Calendar year production: 22,838. Model year sales by U.S. dealers: 22,086.

Historical Footnotes: All Corvettes now came from the factory at Bowling Green, Kentucky. Production fell dramatically this year, reaching the lowest total since 1967. No doubt, some buyers preferred to wait for the next generation to arrive. Still, this was the end of the big 'Vette era: "An enthusiast's kind of Corvette. A most civilized one," according to the factory catalog. *Road & Track* called it "truly the last of its series," though one with an all-new drivetrain. The Collector Edition earned the dubious distinction of being the first Corvette to cost more than $20,000. They were built to order, rather than according to a predetermined schedule. Special VIN plates were used, to prevent swindlers from turning an ordinary 'Vette into a special edition (which had happened all too often with the Pace Car replicas of 1978).

1983

The 1983 Corvettes were not EPA certified; those produced were used for tests and then destroyed.

1984

1984 Chevrolet, Corvette two-door coupe (CP)

SERIES Y -- V-8 -- The eagerly-awaited sixth-generation Corvette for the eighties missed the 1983 model year completely, but arrived in spring 1983 in an all-new form. An aerodynamic exterior featuring an "acute" windshield rake (64 degrees) covered a series of engineering improvements. A one-piece, full width fiberglass roof (no T-bar) was removable; transparent acrylic lift-off panel with solar screen optional. At the rear was a frameless glass back window/hatch, above four round taillamps. Hidden headlamps were joined by clear, integrated halogen foglamps and front cornering lamps. Dual sport mirrors were electrically remote-controlled. The unit body (with partial front frame) used a front-hinged "clamshell" hood with integral twin-duct air intake. Sole engine was again the L83 350 cu. in. (5.7-liter) V-8 with Cross-Fire fuel injection. Stainless steel headers led into its exhaust system. Air cleaner and valve train had cast magnesium covers. After being unavailable in the 1982 model, a four-speed manual gearbox returned as the standard transmission (though not until January 1984). A four-plus-three-speed automatic, with computer-activated overdrive in every gear except 1st, was offered at no extra cost. It used a hydraulic clutch. Overdrive was locked out during rigorous acceleration above specified speeds, and when a console switch was activated. Under the chassis were an aluminum driveshaft, forged aluminum suspension arms, and fiberglass transverse leaf springs. Power rack-and-pinion steering and power four-wheel disc brakes were standard. Optional Goodyear 50-series "uni-directional" tires were designed for mounting on a specific wheel. Inside, an electronic instrument panel featured both analog and digital LCD readouts, in either English or metric measure. A Driver Information System between speedometer and tach gave a selection of switch-chosen readings. At the driver's left was the parking brake. Body colors were red, black, white, and seven metallics: gold, light or medium blue, light bronze, dark bronze, silver or gray. Two-tone options were light/medium blue, silver/gray, and light/dark bronze. Standard interiors came in graphite, blue, bronze, saddle or gray cloth; optional leather in graphite, saddle, bronze, dark red or gray. Corvette's ample standard equipment list included an advanced (and very necessary) theft-prevention system with starter-interrupt. Other standard equipment: air conditioning, power windows, electronic-tuning seek/scan AM/FM stereo radio with digital clock, reclining bucket seats, leather-wrapped tilt/telescope steering wheel, luggage security shade, and side window defoggers.

I.D. DATA: Coding of the 17-symbol Vehicle Identification Number (VIN), visible through the windshield, was similar to prior models. The VIN took the form: 1G1AY078()E5100001. The '1G1A' portion indicates U.S.A., General Motors, Chevrolet Division, and non-passive restraint system (standard seatbelts). 'Y' denotes Corvette series. '07' indicates 2-door hatchback coupe body style. '8' is the engine code. Next is a check digit, followed by 'E' for the 1984 model year and '5' for the Bowling Green, KY assembly plant. Finally comes the six-digit sequential serial number, starting with 100001. Engine identification numbers again were stamped on a pad on the block, at the front of the right cylinder head. That number reveals assembly plant, date built, and a three-letter engine code.

CORVETTE

Model No.	Body/Style No.	Body Type & Seating	Factory Price	Shipping Weight	Prod. Total
1Y	Y07	2-dr. Hatch Cpe-2P	23360	3088	51,547

NOTE: Of the total production, 240 Corvettes were modified for use with leaded gasoline (for export).

ENGINE DATA: BASE V-8: 90-degree, overhead valve V-8. Cast iron block and head. Displacement: 350 cu. in. (5.7 liters). Bore & stroke: 4.00 x 3.48 in. Compression ratio: 9.0:1. Brake horsepower: 205 at 4200 R.P.M. Torque: 290 lb.-ft. at 2800 R.P.M. Five main bearings. Hydraulic valve lifters. Dual TBI (CFI). RPO Code: L83. VIN Code: 8.

CHASSIS DATA: Wheelbase: 96.2 in. Overall length: 176.5 in. Height: 46.7 in. Width: 71.0 in. Front Tread: 59.6 in. Rear Tread: 60.4 in. Wheel Size: 15 x 7 in. Standard Tires: P215/65R15. Optional Tires: Eagle P255/50VR16 on 16 x 8 in. wheels.

TECHNICAL: Transmission: THM 700-R4 four-speed overdrive automatic (floor shift) standard. Gear ratios: (1st) 3.06:1; (2nd) 1.63:1; (3rd) 1.00:1; (4th) 0.70:1; (Rev) 2.29:1. Four-speed manual transmission optional: (1st) 2.88:1; (2nd) 1.91:1; (3rd) 1.33:1; (4th) 1.00:1; (overdrive) 0.67:1; (Rev) 2.78:1. Standard final drive ratio: 2.73:1 w/auto., 3.07:1 w/4-spd (3.31:1 optional). Steering: Rack and pinion (power-assisted). Front Suspension: Single fiberglass composite monoleaf transverse spring with unequal-length aluminum control arms and stabilizer bar. Rear Suspension: Fully independent five-link system with transverse fiberglass single-leaf spring, aluminum upper/lower trailing links, and strut/tie rod assembly. Brakes: Four-wheel power disc. Body construction: Unibody with partial front frame. Fuel tank: 20 gal.

CORVETTE OPTIONS: Four-speed overdrive manual trans. (NC). California emission system ($75). Performance axle ratio ($22). Performance handling pkg.: H.D. springs/shocks, front/rear stabilizers, special bushings and P255/50VR16 tires on 16 x 9-1/2 in. wheels ($600). Delco/Bilstein shock absorbers ($189). Engine oil cooler ($158). H.D. cooling ($57). Rear defogger system incl. mirrors ($160). Electronic cruise control w/resume ($185). Six-way power driver's seat ($210). Power door locks ($165). Electronic-tuning AM/FM stereo radio with seek/scan, clock and cassette player ($153). Delco-GM/Bose music system: AM/FM seek/scan stereo radio w/clock, cassette and four speakers ($895). CB radio ($215). Radio delete ($276 credit). Lift-off transparent roof panels ($595). Custom two-tone paint ($428) w/lower body accents. Custom adj. sport cloth bucket seats ($625). Leather bucket seats ($400). P255/50VR16 SBR BSW tires on 16 in. aluminum wheels ($561).

HISTORY: Introduced: March 25, 1983. Model year production: 51,547 (in extended model year). Calendar year production: 35,661. Calendar year sales by U.S. dealers: 30,424. Model year sales by U.S. dealers: 53,877 (including 25,891 sold during the 1983 model year).

Historical Footnotes: *Car and Driver* called the new Corvette "the most advanced production car on the planet." *Motor Trend* described it as "the best-handling production car in the world, regardless of price." Heady praise indeed. During its year-and-a-half model run, orders poured in well ahead of schedule, even though the new edition cost over $5,000 more than the 1982 version. The body offered the lowest drag coefficient of any Corvette: just 0.341. Testing at GM's Proving Grounds revealed 0.95G lateral acceleration--the highest ever for a production car. Only 6,443 Corvettes had a four-speed manual transmission, and only 410 came with a performance axle ratio, but 3,729 had Delco/Bilstein shocks installed.

1985

1985 Chevrolet, Corvette two-door coupe (CP)

SERIES Y -- V-8 -- Two details marked the 1985 Corvette as different from its newly-restyled 1984 predecessor: a 'Tuned Port Injection' nameplate on fender molding, and straight tailpipes at the rear. That nameplate identified a new 350 cu. in. (5.7-liter) V-8 under the hood, with port fuel injection and a 230-horsepower rating. Peak torque reached 330 lb.-ft, compared to 290 from the prior Cross-Fire V-8. City fuel economy ratings went up too. Otherwise, the only evident change was a slight strengthening in the intensity of the red and silver body colors. Corvette's smoothly sloped nose, adorned by nothing other than the circular emblem, held retracting halogen headlamps. Wide parking/signal lamps nearly filled the space between license plate and outer edge. Wide horizontal side marker lenses were just ahead of the front wheels. The large air cleaner of '82 was replaced by an elongated plenum chamber with eight curved aluminum runners. Mounted ahead of the radiator, it ducted incoming air into the plenum through a Bosch hot-wire mass airflow sensor. Those tuned runners were meant to boost power at low to medium R.P.M., following a principle similar to that used for the tall intake stacks in racing engines. Electronic Spark Control sensed knocking and adjusted timing to fit fuel octane. Under the chassis, the '85 carried a reworked suspension (both standard and optional Z51) to soften the ride without losing control. The Z51 handling package now included 9.5-inch wheels all around, along with Delco-Bilstein gas-charged shock absorbers and heavy-duty cooling. Stabilizer bars on the Z51 were thicker. Spring rates on both suspensions were reduced. Cast aluminum wheels held P255/50VR16 Eagle GT tires. Master cylinders used a new large-capacity plastic booster. Manual gearboxes drove rear axles with 8.5-inch ring gears. Instrument cluster graphics had a bolder look. Roof panels added more solar screening. An optional leather-trimmed sport seat arrived at mid-year. Corvette standard equipment included an electronic information center, air conditioning, limited-slip differential, power four-wheel disc brakes, power steering, cornering lamps, and seek/scan AM/FM stereo radio with four speakers and automatic power antenna. Also standard: a lighter, digital clock, tachometer, intermittent wipers, halogen foglamps, and side window defoggers. Corvettes had contour high-back cloth bucket seats, power windows, a trip odometer, theft-deterrent system with starter interrupt, compact spare tire, dual electric remote-control sport mirrors, and tinted glass. Bodies held black belt, windshield and bodyside moldings, plus color-keyed rocker panel moldings. Four-speed overdrive automatic transmission was standard, with four-speed manual (overdrive in three gears) available at no extra cost.

I.D. DATA: Coding of the 17-symbol Vehicle Identification Number (VIN) was similar to 1984. Model year code changed to 'F' for 1985.

CORVETTE

Model No.	Body/Style No.	Body Type & Seating	Factory Price	Shipping Weight	Prod. Total
1Y	Y07	2-dr. Hatch Cpe-2P	24873	3088	39,729

ENGINE DATA: BASE V-8: 90-degree, overhead valve V-8. Cast iron block and head. Displacement: 350 cu. in. (5.7 liters). Bore & stroke: 4.00 x 3.48 in. Compression ratio: 9.0:1. Brake horsepower: 230 at 4000 R.P.M. Torque: 330 lb.-ft. at 3200 R.P.M. Five main bearings. Hydraulic valve lifters. Tuned-port fuel injection. RPO Code: L98. VIN Code: 8.

CHASSIS DATA: Wheelbase: 96.2 in. Overall length: 176.5 in. Height: 46.4 in. Width: 71.0 in. Front Tread: 59.6 in. Rear Tread: 60.4 in. Wheel Size: 16 x 8.5 in. Standard Tires: P255/50VR16 SBR.

TECHNICAL: Transmission: THM 700-R4 four-speed overdrive automatic standard. Gear ratios: (1st) 3.06:1; (2nd) 1.63:1; (3rd) 1.00:1; (4th) 0.70:1; (Rev) 2.29:1. Four-speed overdrive manual transmission available at no extra charge: (1st) 2.88:1; (2nd) 1.91:1; (3rd) 1.33:1; (4th) 1.00:1; (Rev) 2.78:1; planetary overdrive ratios: (2nd) 1.28:1; (3rd) 0.89:1; (4th) 0.67:1. Standard final drive ratio: 3.07:1 or 2.73:1. Steering/Suspension/Brakes/Body: Same as 1984. Fuel tank: 20.0 gal.

CORVETTE OPTIONS: Four-speed overdrive manual trans. (NC). California emission system ($99). Performance axle ratio ($22). Delco/Bilstein shock absorbers ($189). H.D. cooling ($225). Performance handling pkg.

(Z51): H.D. springs and front/rear stabilizers, Delco/Bilstein shocks and H.D. cooling ($470). Rear defogger system incl. mirrors ($160). Electronic cruise control w/resume ($185). Six-way power driver's seat ($215). Power door locks ($170). Electronic-tuning AM/FM stereo radio with seek/scan, clock and cassette player ($122). Delco-GM/Bose music system: AM/FM seek/scan stereo radio w/clock, cassette and four speakers ($895). Radio delete ($256 credit). Lift-off transparent roof panels ($595). Custom two-tone paint ($428) w/lower body accents. Custom adj. sport cloth bucket seats ($625). Leather bucket seats ($400).

HISTORY: Introduced: October 2, 1984. Model year production: 39,729. Calendar year production: 46,304. Calendar year sales by U.S. dealers: 37,956. Model year sales by U.S. dealers: 37,878.

Historical Footnotes: Chevrolet claimed a 17 percent reduction in 0-60 MPH times with the TPI powerplant. To save weight, Corvettes used not only the fiberglass leaf springs front and rear, but over 400 pounds of aluminum parts (including steering/suspension components and frame members). A total of 14,802 Corvettes had the Z51 performance handling package installed, 9,333 had Delco/Bilstein shocks ordered separately, and only 9,576 had a four-speed manual transmission. Only 16 Corvettes are listed as having a CB radio, and only 82 with an economy rear axle ratio.

1986

SERIES Y -- V-8 -- One new body style and an engineering development were the highlights of 1986. Corvette added a convertible during the model year, the first since 1975. And computerized anti-lock braking system (ABS) was made standard. During hard braking, the system (based on a Bosch ABS II design) detected any wheel that was about to lock, then altered braking pressure in a pulsating action to prevent lockup from happening. Drivers could feel the pulses in the pedal. This safety innovation helped the driver to maintain traction and keep the car under directional control, without skidding, even on slick and slippery surfaces. Corvette's engine was the same 350 cu. in. (5.7-liter) 230-horsepower, tuned-port fuel-injected V-8 as 1985, but with centrally-positioned copper-core spark plugs this year. New aluminum cylinder heads had sintered metal valve seats and increased intake port flow, plus higher (9.5:1) compression. The engine had an aluminum intake manifold with tuned runners, magnesium rocker covers, and outside-air induction system. Both four-plus-three manual and four-speed overdrive automatic transmissions were available, now with an upshift indicator light on the instrument cluster. Three monolith catalytic converters in a new dual exhaust system kept emissions down during warm-up. Cast alloy wheels gained a new raised hub emblem and a brushed-aluminum look. The instrument cluster was tilted to cut glare. The sport seat from 1985 was made standard this year, with leather optional. Electronic air conditioning, announced earlier, arrived as a late option. Otherwise, standard equipment was similar to 1985. A new electronic Vehicle Anti-Theft System (VATS) was also made standard. A small electrically-coded pellet was embedded in the ignition key, while a decoder was hidden in the car. When the key was placed in the ignition, its resistance code was "read." Unless that code was compatible, the starter relay wouldn't close and the Electronic Control Module wouldn't activate the fuel injectors. Corvettes came in one new solid color this year (yellow), plus a white/silver metallic two-tone. Carryover body colors were white, black, bright red, silver metallic, medium gray metallic, and gold metallic. New this year were five metallics: medium blue, silver beige, copper, medium brown, and dark red. Corvette's back end held four round recessed lenses, with 'Corvette' block letters in the center. The license plate sat in a recessed housing. Cloth seats had lateral support and back-angle adjustments. Roadsters (convertibles) had a manual top with velour inner liner. The yellow console button that ordinarily controlled Corvette's hatch release opened a fiberglass panel behind the seats to reveal the top storage area. Cast alloy 16 x 8-1/2 in. aluminum alloy wheels held unidirectional P255/50VR16 Goodyear Eagle GT SBR tires.

I.D. DATA: Coding of the 17-symbol Vehicle Identification Number (VIN) was similar to 1984-85, but body type codes were now either '07' for hatchback coupe or '67' for the new convertible. Model year code changed to 'G' for 1986.

1986 Chevrolet, Corvette two-door convertible (CMD)

CORVETTE

Model No.	Body/Style No.	Body Type & Seating	Factory Price	Shipping Weight	Prod. Total
1Y	Y07	2-dr. Hatch Cpe-2P	27027	3086	27,794
1Y	Y67	2-dr. Conv. Cpe-2P	32032	N/A	7,315

ENGINE DATA: BASE V-8: 90-degree, overhead valve V-8. Cast iron block and head. Displacement: 350 cu.

in. (5.7 liters). Bore & stroke: 4.00 x 3.48 in. Compression ratio: 9.5:1. Brake horsepower: 230 at 4000 R.P.M. Torque: 330 lb.-ft. at 3200 R.P.M. Five main bearings. Hydraulic valve lifters. Tuned-port fuel injection. RPO Code: L98. VIN Code: 8.

CHASSIS DATA: Wheelbase: 96.2 in. Overall length: 176.5 in. Height: 46.4 in. Width: 71.0 in. Front Tread: 59.6 in. Rear Tread: 60.4 in. Wheel Size: 16 x 8.5 in. (9.5 in. wide with optional Z51 suspension). Standard Tires: P245/50VR16 or P255/50VR16 SBR.

TECHNICAL: Transmission: THM 700-R4 four-speed overdrive automatic transmission standard. Gear ratios: (1st) 3.06:1; (2nd) 1.63:1; (3rd) 1.00:1; (4th) 0.70:1; (Rev) 2.29:1. Four-speed manual overdrive transmission available at no extra charge. Standard final drive ratio: 3.07:1 w/manual, 2.59:1 or 3.07:1 w/auto. Steering/Suspension: Same as 1984-85. Brakes: Anti-lock; power four-wheel disc. Ignition: Electronic. Body construction: Fiberglass; separate ladder frame with cross-members. Fuel tank: 20.0 gal.

CORVETTE OPTIONS: Four-speed overdrive manual trans. with upshift indicator (NC). California emission system ($99). Performance axle ratio ($22). Performance handling pkg. (Z51): H.D. springs and front/rear stabilizers, Delco/Bilstein shocks, H.D. radiator and boost fan, engine cooler and P255/50VR16 Eagle BSW tires ($470). Delco/Bilstein shock absorbers ($189). H.D. radiator ($40). Radiator boost cooling fan ($75). Engine oil cooler ($110). Custom feature pkg.: rear defogger, dual heated electric remote mirrors, map lights, console lighting ($195). Electronic air cond. ($150). Rear defogger system incl. mirrors ($165). Electronic cruise control w/resume ($185). Six-way power driver's seat ($225). Power door locks ($175). Electronic-tuning AM/FM stereo radio with seek/scan, clock and cassette player ($122). Delco-GM/Bose music system: AM/FM seek/scan stereo radio w/clock, cassette and four speakers ($895). Radio delete ($256 credit). Removable roof panel ($595); dual panels ($895) incl. blue or bronze transparent panel. Custom two-tone paint ($428) w/lower body accents. Leather bucket seats ($400). Leather adj. sport bucket seats ($1025).

HISTORY: Introduced: October 3, 1985. Model year production: 35,109. Calendar year production (U.S.): 28,410. Model year sales by U.S. dealers: 35,969.

Historical Footnotes: Styled like the Corvette roadster that would serve as '86 Indy Pace Car, the new convertible went on sale late in the model year. The actual pace car was bright yellow, differing from showroom models only in its special track lights. Chevrolet considered "pace car" to be synonymous with "open top," so all convertibles were considered pace car models. Special decals were packed in the car, but not mounted. Corvette was the only street-legal vehicle to pace the Indy race since 1978 (also a Corvette). Instead of a conversion by an outside company, as had become the practice for most 1980s ragtops, Cor-

vette's roadster was built by Chevrolet, right alongside the coupe. Problems with cracking of the new aluminum cylinder heads meant the first '86 models had old cast iron heads. Those difficulties soon were remedied. It was estimated that the new anti-theft system would require half an hour's work to overcome, which would dissuade thieves who are typically in a hurry. A total of 6,242 Corvettes had removable roof panels installed, and 12,821 came with the Z51 performance handling package. Only 6,835 Corvettes carried the MM4 four-speed manual transmission.

1987

1987 Chevrolet, Corvette two-door coupe

CORVETTE — SERIES Y — V-8 — Except for the addition of roller hydraulic lifters to the Corvette's 350 cu. in. (5.7-liter) V-8, little changed this year. Horsepower got a boost to 240 (from the former 230), and gas mileage rated a trifle higher. Joining the option list was an electronic tire-pressure monitor, which signaled a dashboard light to warn of low pressure in any tire. Two four-speed transmissions were available: manual or automatic. Standard equipment included power steering, power four-wheel disc brakes (with anti-locking), air conditioning, a theft-deterrent system, tinted glass, twin remote-control mirrors, power windows, intermittent wipers, tilt/telescope steering column, and AM/FM seek/scan radio.

1987 Chevrolet, Corvette two-door convertible

I.D. DATA: Coding of the 17-symbol Vehicle Identification Number (VIN) was similar to 1984-86. Model year code changed to 'H' for 1987.

CORVETTE

Model No.	Body/Style No.	Body Type & Seating	Factory Price	Shipping Weight	Prod. Total
1Y	Y07	2-dr. Hatch Cpe-2P	27999	3216	20,007
1Y	Y67	2-dr. Conv. Cpe-2P	33172	3279	10,625

ENGINE DATA: BASE V-8: 90-degree, overhead valve V-8. Cast iron block and head. Displacement: 350 cu. in. (5.7 liters). Bore & stroke: 4.00 x 3.48 in. Compression ratio: 9.0:1. Brake horsepower: 240 at 4000 RPM. Torque: 345 lb.-ft. at 3200 RPM. Five main bearings. Hydraulic valve lifters. Tuned-port fuel injection.

CHASSIS DATA: Wheelbase: 96.2 in. Overall length: 176.5 in. Height: (hatch) 46.7 in.; (conv) 46.4 in. Width: 71.0 in. Front Tread: 59.6 in. Rear Tread: 60.4 in. Standard Tires: P245/60VR15 Goodyear Eagle GT.

TECHNICAL: Transmission: four-speed overdrive manual or automatic. Standard final drive ratio: 3.07:1 w/manual, 2.59:1 or 3.07:1 w/auto. Steering: rack and pinion (power assisted). Suspension (front): unequal-length control arms, single-leaf transverse spring and stabilizer bar. Suspension (rear): upper/lower control arms with five links, single-leaf transverse spring, stabilizer bar. Brakes: Anti-lock; power four-wheel disc. Body construction: fiberglass; separate ladder frame with cross-members. Fuel tank: 20.0 gal.

CORVETTE OPTIONS: Automatic air conditioning ($150). Performance axle ratio ($22). Engine oil cooler ($110). Rear defogger & heated outside mirrors ($165). Power door locks ($190). Calif. emissions system ($99). Radiator cooling boost fan ($75). Dual heated power mirrors ($35). Illuminated left visor mirror ($58). Performance Handling Pkg. ($795). Heavy-duty radiator ($40). AM/FM cassette ($132). Delco-GM/Bose music stereo electronic-tuning cassette system ($905). AM/FM delete ($256 credit). Removable roof panel ($615). Removable roof panel ($615). Dual removable roof panels ($915). 6-way power driver's seat ($240). Delco-Bilstein shock absorbers ($189). Tire low pressure indicator ($325). Leather seats ($400). Leather sport seats ($1025). Custom two-tone paint ($428).

HISTORY: Introduced: October 9, 1986. Model Year Production: 30,632. Calendar year production (U.S.): 28,514. Model year sales by U.S. dealers: 25,266.

1988

CORVETTE — SERIES Y — V-8 — By 1988, approximately 900,000 Corvettes had been produced in the 35 years America's sports car had been produced, beginning in 1953. Little changed in Corvette's appearance this year, except for restyled six-slot wheels. Optional 17-inch wheels looked similar to the standard 16-inchers, but held massive P275/40ZR17 Goodyear Eagle GT tires. Suspension modifications were intended to improve control during hard braking, while brake components were toughened, including the use of thicker rotors. Under the hood, the standard 350 cu. in. (5.7-liter) V-8 could breathe more easily with a pair of modified aluminum cylinder heads. Performance also got a boost via a new camshaft, though horsepower only rose by five. Both a convertible and a hatchback coupe were offered.

1988 Chevrolet, Corvette two-door coupe

I.D. DATA: Coding of the 17-symbol Vehicle Identification Number (VIN) was similar to 1984-87. Model year code changed to 'J' for 1988.

1988 Chevrolet, Corvette two-door convertible

CORVETTE

Model No.	Body/Style No.	Body Type & Seating	Factory Price	Shipping Weight	Prod. Total
1Y	Y07	2-dr. Hatch Cpe-2P	29480	3229	15,382
1Y	Y67	2-dr. Conv. Cpe-2P	34820	3299	7,407

ENGINE DATA: BASE V-8: 90-degree, overhead valve V-8. Cast iron block and head. Displacement: 350 cu. in. (5.7 liters). Bore & stroke: 4.00 x 3.48 in. Compression ratio: 9.5:1. Brake horsepower: 245 at 4000 RPM. Torque: 345 lb.-ft. at 3200 RPM. Five main bearings. Hydraulic valve lifters. Tuned-port fuel injection.

CHASSIS DATA: Wheelbase: 96.2 in. Overall length: 176.5 in. Height: (hatch) 46.7 in.; (conv) 46.4 in. Width: 71.0 in. Front Tread: 59.6 in. Rear Tread: 60 in. Standard Tires: P255/50ZRI6 Goodyear Eagle GT (Z-rated).

TECHNICAL: Transmission: four-speed overdrive manual or automatic. Steering: rack and pinion (power assisted). Suspension (front): unequal-length control arms, single-leaf transverse spring and stabilizer bar. Suspension (rear): upper/lower control arms with five links, single-leaf transverse spring, stabilizer bar. Brakes: Anti-lock; power four-wheel disc. Body construction: fiberglass; separate ladder frame with cross-members. Fuel tank: 20.0 gal.

1988 Chevrolet, Corvette 35th Anniversary two-door coupe (PH)

CORVETTE OPTIONS: Leather Bucket Seats ($400). AB Leather Adjust. Spt Bucket Seats ($1025). Solid Exterior Color Paint (NC). Electronic Control Air cond ($150). Performance ratio axle ($22). Engine oil cooler ($110). Rear Window Defogger System & Outside Rearview Mirrors ($165). Calif. Emission System ($99). Radiator cooling boost fan ($75). Performance Handling Pkg: H.D. Radiator, Radiator Cooling Boost Fan, Eng. Oil Cooler, Pwr Strg oil cooler, FG3 Delco Bilstein Shock Absorbers, H.D. F&R Springs, H.D. Frame, 17 x 9.5-in. Alum Wheels, P275/0ZR 17 blackwall tires, H.D. front & rear Stabilizers ($1295). (Z52) Sports Handling Pkg Includes H.D. Radiator; Radiator Cooling Boost Fan; Eng. Oil Cooler; FG3 Delco Bilstein Shock Absorbers; H.D. F&R Springs. 17 x 9.5-in. Alum Wheels P275/40ZR-17 blackwall tires; H.D. front & rear Stabi-

lizers ($970). Eng. Block Heater ($20). Twin Remote Heated Mirrors ($35). Lighted Visor Mirrors ($58). H.D. Radiator ($40). Elect Tuned Delco/Bose Music System, incl AM/FM Stereo w/Seek & Scan, Stereo Cass Tape & Digital Clock, special tone & balance control, 4 speakers and Pwr Antenna ($773). Removable Roof Panels. Transparent, blue tint or bronze tint ($615). Dual body color-keyed roof panel & blue or bronze transparent roof panel ($915). Pwr 6-way Seats. Driver's Side only ($240). Pass. Side only ($240). Delco/Bilstein Shock Absorbers ($189).

HISTORY: Introduced: October 1, 1987. Model year production: 22,789. Calendar year production: 22,878. Model year sales by U.S. dealers: 25,425. Chevrolet produced 2,050 35th Anniversary Edition Corvette coupes, each with a build sequence number and special badging. This option listed for $4,795. The 35th Anniversary Edition Corvettes featured a custom two-tone paint scheme consisting of a white body color, painted white wheels and black roof bow with transparent black roof panels. The white scheme was carried out through the interior trim, which included 35th Anniversary badges embroidered on the seat backs.

1989

1989 Chevrolet, Corvette two-door convertible

CORVETTE — SERIES Y — V-8 — Most of the Corvette publicity this year centered on the eagerly-awaited ZR-1, claimed to be the world's fastest production automobile. After several announcements proved premature, the ZR-1 was delayed until the 1990 model year. Meanwhile, the "ordinary" Corvette added a new ZF six-speed manual gearbox with two overdrive ratios. To meet fuel-economy standards, the ingenious transmission was designed so a computer sent a signal that prevented shifts from first to second gear unless the gas pedal hit the floor. Instead, a blocking pin forced the shifter directly into fourth gear, for improved economy during light-throttle operation. Joining the option list was a new FX3 Delco-Bilstein Selective Ride Control system, with a switch to select the desired degree of shock-absorber damping for Touring, Sport or Competition driving. Only coupes with manual shift and the Z51 Performance Handling Package could get the ride control option. For the first time since 1975, a removable fiberglass hardtop became available for the convertible, but later in the model year.

I.D. DATA: Coding of the 17-symbol Vehicle Identification Number (VIN) was similar to 1984-88. Model year code changed to 'K' for 1989.

CORVETTE

Model No.	Body/Style No.	Body Type & Seating	Factory Price	Shipping Weight	Prod. Total
1Y	Y07	2-dr. Hatch Cpe-2P	31545	3229	16,663
1Y	Y67	2-dr. Conv. Cpe-2P	36785	3269	9,749

ENGINE DATA: BASE V-8: 90-degree, overhead valve V-S. Cast iron block and head. Displacement: 350 cu. in. (5.7 liters). Bore & stroke: 4.00 x 3.48 in. Compression ratio: 9.5:1 Brake horsepower: 245 at 4300 RPM. Torque: 340 lb.-ft. at 3200 RPM. Five main bearings. Hydraulic valve lifters. Tuned-port fuel injection.

1989 Chevrolet, Corvette two-door coupe (PH)

CHASSIS DATA: Wheelbase: 96.2 in. Overall length: 176.5 in. Height: (hatch) 46.7 in.; (conv) 46.4 in. Width: 71.0 in. Front Tread: 59.6 in. Rear Tread: 60:4 in. Standard Tires: P275/40VR17 Goodyear Eagle GT (Z-rated).

TECHNICAL: Transmission: four-speed overdrive manual or automatic. Steering: rack and pinion (power assisted). Suspension (front): unequal-length control arms, single-leaf transverse spring and stabilizer bar. Suspension (rear): upper/lower control arms with five links, single-leaf transverse spring stabilizer bar. Brakes: Anti-lock; power four-wheel disc. Body construction: fiberglass; separate ladder frame with crossmembers. Fuel tank: 20.0 gal.

CORVETTE OPTIONS: Preferred Equipment Group Includes Electronic Air Cond; Elect Tuned Delco/Bose Music System (AM/FM Stereo Radio w/Seek & Scan, Stereo Cass. Tape & Digital Clock, special tone & balance control & 4 spkrs); Pwr Six-Way Driver's Seat ($1193). Corvette Convertible Base Equip Grp Incl w/Mid (NC). Elect Tuned Delco/Bose Music System (AM/FM Stereo w/Seek & Scan, Stereo Cass Tape & Digital Clock, special tone & balance control & 4 spkrs) ($773). Leather bucket seats ($425). Leather Adjustable Sport Bucket seats ($1050). Solid Exterior Paint (NC). Electronic Control Air Cond ($170). Performance Ratio Axle ($22). Luggage Carrier ($140). Eng Oil Cooler ($110). Calif. Emission System ($100). Radiator Cooling Boost Fan ($75). Z51 Performance Pkg: Eng Oil Cooler Radiator Fan & H.D Radiator ($575). (FX3) Electronic Selective Ride ($1695). Eng Block Heater ($20). Low Tire Pressure Warning Indicator ($325).

Lighted Visor Mirror, Driver ($58). H.D. Radiator ($40). Roof Panels Removable, Blue or Bronze Tint ($615). Dual body color-keyed Roof Panel & Blue or Bronze Transparent Roof Panel ($915). Removable Hardtop ($1995). Six-way power seats, Driver's Side only ($250). Pass. Side only ($250).

HISTORY: Model year production: 26,412. Calendar year production: 25,279. Model year sales by U.S. dealers: 23,928

1990

1990 Chevrolet, Corvette two-door ZR-1 coupe

CORVETTE — SERIES Y — V-8 — Finally, after months of hoopla and a few false starts, the superperformance ZR-1 Corvette arrived. Intended for production in limited quantity, with a price tag higher than any General Motors product, the ZR-1 became a collectible long before anyone ever saw one "in the flesh," with customers eager to pay far above the suggested retail price for the few examples that became available. Under the ZR-1 hood was a Lotus-designed 32-valve, dual-overhead-cam, 350 cu. in. (5.7-liter) V-8, built by Mercury Marine in Oklahoma. Although the displacement was identical to the standard Corvette V-8, this was an all-new powerplant with different bore and stroke dimensions. Wider at the rear than a standard model, partly to contain the huge 315/35ZR17 back tires, the ZR-1 was easy to spot because of its convex back end and rectangular taillamps. Ordinary Corvettes continued to display a concave rear end with round taillamps. Standard ZR-1 equipment included an FX3 Selective Ride adjustable suspension, which was also available on standard Corvettes with the six-speed manual gearbox. Four-speed overdrive automatic was available (at no cost) only on the regular Corvette. New standard equipment included an engine oil cooler, 17-inch alloy wheels, and improved ABS II-S anti-lock braking. The convertible added a new back light made of flexible "Ultrashield" for improved scratch resistance and visibility. An air bag was installed in the new steering wheel on all Corvettes, and a revised dashboard mixed digital and analog instruments.

I.D. DATA: Coding of the 17-symbol Vehicle Identification Number (VIN) was similar to 1984-89. Model year code changed to 'L' for 1989.

1990 Chevrolet, Corvette two-door convertible (PH)

CORVETTE

Model No.	Body/Style No.	Body Type & Seating	Factory Price	Shipping Weight	Prod. Total
1Y	Y07	2-dr. Hatch Cpe-2P	31979	3223	16,016
1Y	Y67	2-dr. Conv. Cpe-2P	37264	3263	7,630
1Y	N/A	2-dr. ZR1 Cpe-2P	58995	3465	N/A

ENGINE DATA: BASE V-8: 90-degree, overhead valve V-8. Cast iron block and head. Displacement: 350 cu. in. (5.7 liters). Bore & stroke: 4.00 x 3.48 in. Compression ratio: 9.5:1. Brake horsepower: 245 at 4000 RPM. Torque: 340 lb.-ft. at 3200 RPM. Five main bearings. Hydraulic valve lifters. Tuned-port fuel injection. ZR-1 V-8: 90-degree dual, overhead cam V-8. Cast aluminum block and head. Displacement: 350 cu. in. (5.7 liters). Bore & stroke: 3.90 x 3.66 in. Compression ratio: 11.0:1. Brake horsepower: 370 at 5800 RPM. Torque: 370 lb.-ft. at 5600 RPM. Five main bearings. Hydraulic valve lifters. Tuned-port fuel injection.

CHASSIS DATA: Wheelbase: 96.2 in. Overall length: 176.5 in.; (ZR-1) 177.4 in. Height: (hatch) 46.7 in.; (conv) 46.4 in. Width: 71.0 in.; (ZR-1) 74.0 in. Front Tread: 59.6 in.; (ZR-1) 59.6 in. Rear Tread: 60.4 in.; (ZR-1) 61.9 in. Standard Tires: P275/40ZR17 Goodyear Eagle GT (ZR-1, 315/35ZR17 in rear).

TECHNICAL: Transmission: four-speed overdrive manual or automatic. Steering: rack and pinion (power assisted). Suspension (front): unequal-length control arms, single leaf transverse spring and stabilizer bar. Suspension (rear): upper/lower control arms with five links, single-leaf transverse spring, stabilizer bar. Brakes: Anti-lock power four-wheel disc. Body construction: fiberglass; separate ladder frame with cross-members. Fuel tank: 20.0 gal.

CORVETTE OPTIONS: Preferred Equip. Grp. Incl Electronic Air cond; Elect Tuned Delco/Bose Music System (AM/FM Stereo w/Seek & Scan, Stereo Cass. Tape & Digital Clock, special tone & balance control & 4 spkrs); Pwr 6-way Driver's Seat ($1273). Pkg w/U1F Radio, Add ($396). Leather Bucket Seats ($425). Leather Adjustable Spt Bucket Seat ($1050). Solid Exterior Color Paint (NC). Electronic Air Cond ($180). Performance Ratio Axle ($22). Luggage Carrier ($140). Eng Oil Cooler ($110). Calif. Emission System ($100). Z51 Performance Handling Pkg: Incl Eng Oil Cooler & H.D. Brakes ($460). (FX3) Electronic Selective Ride ($1695). Eng. Block Heater ($20). Low Tire Pressure Warning Indicator ($325). (UU8) Elect Tuned Delco/Bose Music System (AM/FM Stereo w/Seek & Scan, Stereo Cass. Tape & Digital Clock, special tone & balance control & 4 spkrs) ($823). (U1F) Elect Tuned Delco-Bose Music System, (AM/FM Stereo w/Seek & Scan, Stereo Cass Tape, Compact Disc Player, Digital Clock special tone & balance control & 4 spkrs) ($1219). Roof Panels, Blue Tint or Bronze Tint ($615). Dual body color-keyed roof panel & Blue or Bronze Transparent Roof Panel ($915). Removable Hard Top ($1995). Pwr 6-way Seats, Driver's Side only ($270). Passenger side only ($270).

HISTORY: Model year production: 23,646. Calendar year production: 22,154. Model year sales by U.S. dealers: 22,690.

1991

1991 Chevrolet, Corvette two-door coupe

CORVETTE — SERIES Y — V-8 — Not a year of great change after the launch of the ZR-1 the previous year. Standard Corvettes were restyled at the rear to more closely resemble the ZR-1. All models were again equipped with ABS II-S anti-lock braking and driver's side airbag as well as an anti-theft system. The ZR-1 was again powered by the 32-valve DOHC 5.7-liter V-8 matched with a six-speed transaxle. Corvette models used the 5.7-liter TPI V-8 fitted with the four-speed overdrive automatic or optional six-speed manual transmission.

I.D. DATA.: Coding of the 17-symbol Vehicle Identification Number (VIN) was similar to 1984-90. Fourth and fifth symbols designate car line/series as follows: Y/Y - Corvette; Y/Z - ZR-1. Model year code changed to 'M' for 1991.

CORVETTE

Model No.	Body/Style No.	Body Type & Seating	Factory Price	Shipping Weight	Prod. Total
1Y	Y07	2-dr. Hatch Cpe-2P	32455	3223	Note 1
1Y	Y67	2-dr. Conv. Cpe-2P	38770	3263	5,672
1Y	N/A	2-dr. ZR1 Cpe-2P	64138	3465	Note 1

Note 1: Total Corvette coupe production was 14,967 with no further breakout available.

1991 Chevrolet, Corvette two-door convertible

ENGINE DATA: BASE V-8: 90-degree, overhead valve V-8. Cast iron block and head. Displacement: 350 cu. in. (5.7 liters). Bore & stroke: 4.00 x 3.48 in. Compression ratio: 10.0:1 Brake horsepower: 245 at 4000 RPM. Torque: 340 lb.-ft. at 3200 RPM. Five main bearings. Hydraulic valve lifters. Tuned-port fuel injection. ZR-1 V-8: 90-degree dual overhead cam V-8. Cast aluminum block and head. Displacement: 350 cu. in. (5.7 liters). Bore & stroke: 3.90 x 3.66 in. Compression ratio: 11.0:1 Brake horsepower: 375 at 5800 RPM. Torque: 370 lb.-ft. at 4800 RPM. Five main bearings. Hydraulic valve lifters. Tuned-port fuel injection.

CHASSIS DATA: Wheelbase: 96.2 in. Overall length: 178.6 in.; (ZR-1) 178.5 in. Height: (hatch) 46.7 in.; (conv) 46.4 in. Width: 71.0 in.; (ZR-1) 73.2 in. Front Tread: 59.6 in.; (ZR-1) 59.6 in. Rear Tread: 60.4 in.; (ZR-1) 61.9 in. Standard Tires: P275/40ZR17 Goodyear Eagle GT; (ZR-1) P315/35ZR17 in rear).

TECHNICAL: Transmission: four-speed overdrive automatic. Steering: rack and pinion (power assisted). Suspension (front): unequal-length control arms, single leaf transverse spring and stabilizer bar. Suspension (rear): upper/lower control arms with five links, single-leaf transverse spring, stabilizer bar. Brakes: Anti-lock: power four-wheel disc. Body construction: fiberglass; separate ladder frame with cross-members. Fuel tank: 20.0 gal.

CORVETTE OPTIONS: Coupe Preferred Equip. Grp. 1: Air Cond; Elect Tuned Delco/Bose Music System (AM/FM Stereo w/Seek & Scan, Stereo Cass Tape & Digital Clock, special tone & balance control & 4 spkrs); Pwr 6-way Driver's Seat ($1333). Pkg w/U1F Radio, Add ($396). Leather Bucket Seats ($475). Leather Adjustable Spt Bucket Seat ($1100). Solid Exterior Color,

Paint (NC). Electronic Air Cond ($205). Performance Ratio Axle ($50). Luggage Carrier ($140). Eng Oil Cooler ($110). Calif. Emission System ($100). ZO7 Adjustable Handling Pkg: Engine Oil Cooler, Heavy-Duty Brakes and Bilstein Adjustable Ride Control System ($2155). FX3 Elect Selective Ride ($1695). Eng. Block Heater ($20). Low Tire Pressure Warning Indicator ($325). Roof Panels, Blue Tint or Bronze Tint ($650). Dual body color-keyed roof panel & Blue or Bronze Transparent Roof Panel ($915). Removable Hard Top ($1995). Pwr 6-way Seats, Driver's Side only ($305). Passenger side only ($305).

HISTORY: Calendar year sales totaled 17,472 Corvettes. Model year production totaled 20,639.

1992

1992 Chevrolet, Corvette two-door coupe

CORVETTE — SERIES Y — V-8 — Another year of little change in the makeup of the Corvette line. The ZR-1 was basically a carry-over from the year previous. Standard Corvette models received an upgraded 300 horsepower 5.7-liter V-8 as well as Acceleration Slip Regulation. The ZR-1 was again powered by the 32-valve DOHC 5.7-liter V-8 matched with a six-speed transaxle. Corvette models used the aforementioned more powerful 5.7-liter V-8 fitted with the four-speed overdrive automatic or optional six-speed manual transmission.

1992 Chevrolet, Corvette two-door convertible (1,000,000th Corvette produced on July 2, 1992, posed with a 1953 Corvette).

I.D. DATA.: Coding of the 17-symbol Vehicle Identification Number (VIN) was similar to 1984-91. Fourth and fifth symbols designate car line/series as follows: Y/Y - Corvette; Y/Z - ZR-1. Model year code changed to 'N' for 1992.

CORVETTE

Model No.	Body/Style No.	Body Type & Seating	Factory Price	Shipping Weight	Prod. Total
1Y	Y07	2-dr. Hatch Cpe-2P	33635	3223	Note 1
1Y	Y67	2-dr. Conv. Cpe-2P	40145	3269	5,875
1Y	N/A	2-dr. ZR1 Cpe-2P	65318	3465	Note 1

Note 1: Total Corvette coupe production was 14,604 with no further breakout available.

ENGINE DATA: BASE V-8: 90-degree, overhead valve V-8. Cast iron block and head. Displacement: 350 cu. in. (5.7 liters). Bore & stroke: 4.00 x 3.48 in. Compression ratio: 10.3:1 Brake horsepower: 300 at 5000 RPM. Torque: 330 lb.-ft. at 4000 RPM. Five main bearings. Hydraulic valve lifters. Tuned-port fuel injection. ZR-1 V-8: 90-degree dual overhead cam V-8. Cast aluminum block and head. Displacement: 350 cu. in. (5.7 liters). Bore & stroke: 3.90 x 3.66 in. Compression ratio: 11.0:1 Brake horsepower: 375 at 5800 RPM. Torque: 370 lb.-ft. at 4800 RPM. Five main bearings. Hydraulic valve lifters. Tuned-port fuel injection.

CHASSIS DATA: Wheelbase: 96.2 in. Overall length: 178.6 in.; (ZR-1) 178.5 in. Height: (hatch) 46.3 in.; (conv) 47.3 in. Width: 71.1 in.; (ZR-1) 73.1 in. Front Tread: 57.7 in.; (ZR-1) 57.7 in. Rear Tread: 59.0 in.; (ZR-1) 60.6 in. Standard Tires: P275/40ZR17 Goodyear Eagle GT; (ZR-1) P315/35ZR17 in rear).

TECHNICAL: Transmission: four-speed overdrive automatic. Steering: rack and pinion (power assisted). Suspension (front): unequal-length control arms, single leaf transverse spring and stabilizer bar. Suspension (rear): upper/lower control arms with five links, single-leaf transverse spring, stabilizer bar. Brakes: Anti-lock: power four-wheel disc. Body construction: fiberglass; separate ladder frame with cross-members. Fuel tank: 20.0 gal.

CORVETTE OPTIONS: Coupe Preferred Equip. Grp. 1: Air Cond; Elect Tuned Delco/Bose Music System (AM/FM Stereo w/Seek & Scan, Stereo Cass Tape & Digital Clock, special tone & balance control & 4 spkrs); Pwr 6-way Driver's Seat ($1333). Pkg w/U1F Radio, Add ($396). Arctic White Leather Bucket Seats ($555). Arctic White Adjustable Leather Bucket Seats ($1180). Leather Bucket Seats ($475). Solid Exterior Color, Paint (NC). Electronic Air Cond ($205). G92 Performance Ratio Axle ($50). Luggage Carrier ($140). Calif. Emission System ($100). ZO7 Adjustable Handling Pkg: Heavy-Duty Brakes and Bilstein Adjustable Ride Control System ($2045). FX3 Elect Selective Ride ($1695). Low Tire Pressure Warning Indicator ($325). Roof Panels, Blue Tint or Bronze Tint ($650). Dual body color-keyed roof panel & Blue or Bronze Transparent Roof Panel ($950). Removable Hard Top ($1995). Pwr 6-way Seats, Driver's Side only ($305). Passenger side only ($305).

HISTORY: Calendar year sales totaled 19,819 Corvettes. Model year production totaled 20,479.

1993 Chevrolet, Corvette 40th Anniversary two-door convertible

CORVETTE — SERIES Y — V-8 — Corvette for 1993 marked its 40th Anniversary with a special appearance package that included an exclusive "ruby red" exterior and interior with color-keyed wheel centers, headrest embroidery and bright emblems on the hood, deck and side-gills. This anniversary package was optional equipment on all models. The ZR-1's LT5 5.7-liter V-8 was upgraded this year and featured significant horsepower and torque increases. Improved air flow from cylinder head and valvetrain refinements boosted the ZR-1's horsepower rating from its former 375 to 405. The 1993 Corvette also introduced GM's first Passive Keyless Entry System, whereby simply leaving or approaching the Corvette automatically unlocked or locked the appropriate doors. The '93 'Vette was also the first North American automobile to use recycled sheet-molded-compound body panels. The ZR-1 again used a six-speed transaxle. Standard Corvette models were again powered by the 5.7-liter V-8 fitted with the four-speed overdrive automatic or optional six-speed manual transmission.

I.D. DATA.: Coding of the 17-symbol Vehicle Identification Number (VIN) was similar to 1984-92. Fourth and fifth symbols designate car line/series as follows: Y/Y - Corvette; Y/Z - ZR-1. Model year code changed to 'P' for 1993.

CORVETTE

Model No.	Body/Style No.	Body Type & Seating	Factory Price	Shipping Weight	Prod. Total
1Y	Y07	2-dr. Hatch Cpe-2P	34595	3333	Note 1
1Y	Y67	2-dr. Conv. Cpe-2P	41195	3383	5,712
1Y	N/A	2-dr. ZR1 Cpe-2P	66278	3503	Note 1

Note 1: Total Corvette coupe production was 15,968 with no further breakout available.

ENGINE DATA: BASE V-8: 90-degree, overhead valve V-8. Cast iron block and head. Displacement: 350 cu. in. (5.7 liters). Bore & stroke: 4.00 x 3.48 in. Compression ratio: 10.5:1 Brake horsepower: 300 at 5000 RPM. Torque: 340 lb.-ft. at 3600 RPM. Five main bearings. Hydraulic valve lifters. Tuned-port fuel injection. ZR-1 V-8: 90-degree dual overhead cam V-8. Cast aluminum block and head. Displacement: 350 cu. in. (5.7 liters). Bore & stroke: 3.90 x 3.66 in. Compression ratio: 11.0:1 Brake horsepower: 405 at 5800 RPM. Torque: 385 lb.-ft. at 5200 RPM. Five main bearings. Hydraulic valve lifters. Tuned-port fuel injection.

CHASSIS DATA: Wheelbase: 96.2 in. Overall length: 178.5 in.; (ZR-1) 178.5 in. Height: (hatch) 46.3 in.; (conv) 47.3 in. Width: 70.7 in.; (ZR-1) 73.1 in. Front Tread: 57.7 in.; (ZR-1) 57.7 in. Rear Tread: 59.1 in.; (ZR-1) 60.6 in. Standard Tires: (front) P255/45ZR15 Goodyear Eagle GT/(rear) P285/40ZR17 Goodyear Eagle GT; (ZR-1) P315/35ZR17 in rear.

TECHNICAL: Transmission: four-speed overdrive automatic. Steering: rack and pinion (power assisted). Suspension (front): unequal-length control arms, single leaf transverse spring and stabilizer bar. Suspension (rear): upper/lower control arms with five links, single-leaf transverse spring, stabilizer bar. Brakes: Anti-lock: power four-wheel disc. Body construction: fiberglass; separate ladder frame with cross-members. Fuel tank: 20.0 gal.

CORVETTE OPTIONS: Coupe Preferred Equip. Grp. 1: Air Cond; Elect Tuned Delco/Bose Music System (AM/FM Stereo w/Seek & Scan, Stereo Cass Tape & Digital Clock, special tone & balance control & 4 spkrs); Pwr 6-way Driver's Seat ($1333). Pkg w/U1F Radio, Add ($396). Arctic White Leather Bucket Seats ($555). Arctic White Adjustable Leather Bucket Seats ($1180). Leather Bucket Seats ($475). Adjustable Leather Bucket Seats ($1100). Solid Exterior Color, Paint (NC). Electronic Air Cond ($205). G92 Performance Ratio Axle ($50). Luggage Carrier ($140). Calif. Emission System ($100). ZO7 Adjustable Handling Pkg: Heavy-Duty Brakes and Bilstein Adjustable Ride Control System ($2045). Z25 40th Anniversary Appearance Pkg: Ruby Red Interior Trim, Pwr Adjustable Pass. Seat, 40th Anniv. Emblems ($1455). FX3 Elect Selective Ride ($1695). Low Tire Pressure Warning Indicator ($325). Roof Panels, Blue Tint or Bronze Tint ($650). Dual body color-keyed roof panel & Blue or Bronze Transparent Roof Panel ($950). Removable Hard Top ($1995). Pwr 6-way Seats, Driver's Side only ($305). Passenger side only ($305).

HISTORY: Calendar year sales totaled 20,487 Corvettes. Model year production totaled 21,590.

1994

CORVETTE — SERIES Y — V-8 — Several refinements focused on safety and smoother operation were the order for 1994 Corvette models. A passenger side airbag was added so all Corvettes now offered dual airbags. In addition, other interior changes included new carpeting, door trim panels, seats, steering wheel, instrument panel and console. Other new equipment included an optional rear axle ratio, revised spring rates, heated glass convertible backlight and new exterior colors. The

ZR-1 also received new wheels for 1994. The 5.7-liter V-8 powering the standard Corvettes now used sequential fuel injection, which provided smoother idle, better driveability and lower emissions. That engine was also mated to the refined 4L60-E electronic four-speed automatic overdrive transmission that provided a more consistent shift feel. A brake-transmission shift interlock safety feature was also new-for-'94. The ZR-1 again used the LT5 5.7-liter V-8 fitted with a six-speed manual transmission, which was again optional for standard Corvette models.

1994 Chevrolet, Corvette ZR-1 two-door coupe

I.D. DATA.: Coding of the 17-symbol Vehicle Identification Number (VIN) was similar to 1984-93. Fourth and fifth symbols designate car line/series as follows: Y/Y - Corvette; Y/Z - ZR-1. Model year code changed to 'R' for 1994.

CORVETTE

Model No.	Body/Style No.	Body Type & Seating	Factory Price	Shipping Weight	Prod. Total
1Y	Y07	2-dr. Hatch Cpe-2P	36185	3317	Note 1
1Y	Y67	2-dr. Conv. Cpe-2P	42960	3358	5,320
1Y	N/A	2-dr. ZR1 Cpe-2P	67443	3503	Note 1

Note 1: Total Corvette coupe production was 17,868 with no further breakout available.

1994 Chevrolet, Corvette two-door convertible

ENGINE DATA: BASE V-8: 90-degree, overhead valve V-8. Cast iron block and head. Displacement: 350 cu. in. (5.7 liters). Bore & stroke: 4.00 x 3.48 in. Compression ratio: 10.5:1 Brake horsepower: 300 at 5000 RPM. Torque: 340 lb.-ft. at 3600 RPM. Five main bearings. Hydraulic valve lifters. Sequential fuel injection. ZR-1 V-8: 90-degree dual overhead cam V-8. Cast aluminum block and head. Displacement: 350 cu. in. (5.7 liters). Bore & stroke: 3.90 x 3.66 in. Compression ratio: 11.0:1 Brake horsepower: 405 at 5800 RPM. Torque: 385 lb.-ft. at 5200 RPM. Five main bearings. Hydraulic valve lifters. Tuned-port fuel injection.

CHASSIS DATA: Wheelbase: 96.2 in. Overall length: 178.5 in.; (ZR-1) 178.5 in. Height: (hatch) 46.3 in.; (conv) 47.3 in. Width: 70.7 in.; (ZR-1) 73.1 in. Front Tread: 57.7 in.; (ZR-1) 57.7 in. Rear Tread: 59.1 in.; (ZR-1) 60.6 in. Standard Tires: (front) P255/45ZR17 Goodyear Eagle GT/(rear) P285/40ZR17 Goodyear Eagle GT; (ZR-1) P315/35ZR17 in rear.

TECHNICAL: Transmission: four-speed overdrive automatic. Steering: rack and pinion (power assisted). Suspension (front): unequal-length control arms, single leaf transverse spring and stabilizer bar. Suspension (rear): upper/lower control arms with five links, single-leaf transverse spring, stabilizer bar. Brakes: Anti-lock: power four-wheel disc. Body construction: fiberglass; separate ladder frame with cross-members. Fuel tank: 20.0 gal.

CORVETTE OPTIONS: Coupe Preferred Equip. Grp. 1: Air Cond; Elect Tuned Delco/Bose Music System (AM/FM Stereo w/Seek & Scan, Stereo Cass Tape & Digital Clock, special tone & balance control & 4 spkrs); Pwr 6-way Driver's Seat ($1333). Pkg w/U1F Radio, Add ($396). Convertible Preferred Equip. Grp. 1: Air Cond; Elect Tuned Delco/Bose Music System (AM/FM Stereo w/Seek & Scan, Stereo Cass Tape & Digital Clock, special tone & balance control & 4 spkrs); Pwr 6-way Driver's Seat ($1333). Pkg w/U1F Radio, Add ($396). Leather Bucket Seats (NC). Adjustable Leather Bucket Seats ($625). Solid Exterior Color, Paint (NC). G92 Performance Ratio Axle ($50). Calif. Emission System ($100). ZO7 Adjustable Handling Pkg: Heavy-Duty Brakes and Bilstein Adjustable Ride Control System ($2045). FX3 Elect Selective Ride ($1695). Low Tire Pressure Warning Indicator ($325). Roof Panels, Blue Tint or Bronze Tint ($650). Dual body color-keyed roof panel & Blue or Bronze Transparent Roof Panel ($950). Removable Hard Top ($1995). Pwr 6-way Seats, Driver's Side only ($305). Passenger side only ($305). TIRES: Ext Mobility P255/45ZR17 (front) and P285/40ZR17 (rear), requires low tire pressure warning indicator ($70).

HISTORY: Calendar year sales totaled 21,839 Corvettes. Model year production totaled 23,330.

1995

CORVETTE — SERIES Y — V-8 — The big news of 1995 was the final appearance of the ZR-1 performance coupe after several years of availability (announced in 1989, but not offered until 1990). Changes on the Corvette included the addition of heavy-duty brakes with larger front rotors as standard equipment as were new low-rate springs (except ZR-1) and de Carbon gas-charged shock absorbers for improved ride quality. Aside from one new exterior color offered, Corvettes featured a new gill panel behind the front wheel openings to quickly distinguish the '95 models from predecessors. Other improvements included reinforced interior stitching and a quieter-running cooling fan. Engine/transmission offerings remained unchanged from the year previous.

1995 Chevrolet, Corvette two-door convertible

I.D. DATA.: Coding of the 17-symbol Vehicle Identification Number (VIN) was similar to 1984-94. Fourth and fifth symbols designate car line/series as follows: Y/Y - Corvette; Y/Z - ZR-1. Model year code changed to 'S' for 1995.

CORVETTE

Model No.	Body/Style No.	Body Type & Seating	Factory Price	Shipping Weight	Prod. Total
1Y	Y07	2-dr. Hatch Cpe-2P	36785	3203	Note 1
1Y	Y67	2-dr. Conv. Cpe-2P	43665	3360	3,980
1Y	N/A	2-dr. ZR1 Cpe-2P	68043	3512	Note 1

Note 1: Total Corvette coupe production was 15,960 with no further breakout available.

ENGINE DATA: BASE V-8: 90-degree, overhead valve V-8. Cast iron block and head. Displacement: 350 cu. in. (5.7 liters). Bore & stroke: 4.00 x 3.48 in. Compression ratio: 10.5:1 Brake horsepower: 300 at 5000 RPM. Torque: 340 lb.-ft. at 3600 RPM. Five main bearings. Hydraulic valve lifters. Sequential fuel injection. ZR-1 V-8: 90-degree dual overhead cam V-8. Cast aluminum block and head. Displacement: 350 cu. in. (5.7 liters). Bore & stroke: 3.90 x 3.66 in. Compression ratio: 11.0:1 Brake horsepower: 405 at 5800 RPM. Torque: 385 lb.-ft. at 5200 RPM. Five main bearings. Hydraulic valve lifters. Tuned-port fuel injection.

CHASSIS DATA: Wheelbase: 96.2 in. Overall length: 178.5 in.; (ZR-1) 178.5 in. Height: (hatch) 46.3 in.; (conv) 47.3 in. Width: 70.7 in.; (ZR-1) 73.1 in. Front Tread: 57.7 in.; (ZR-1) 57.7 in. Rear Tread: 59.1 in.; (ZR-1) 60.6 in. Standard Tires: (front) P255/45ZR17 Goodyear Eagle GT/(rear) P285/40ZR17 Goodyear Eagle GT; (ZR-1) P275/40ZR17 in front.

TECHNICAL: Transmission: four-speed overdrive automatic. Steering: rack and pinion (power assisted). Suspension (front): unequal-length control arms, single leaf transverse spring and stabilizer bar. Suspension (rear): upper/lower control arms with five links, single-leaf transverse spring, stabilizer bar. Brakes: Anti-lock: power four-wheel disc. Body construction: fiberglass; separate ladder frame with cross-members. Fuel tank: 20.0 gal.

CORVETTE OPTIONS: Coupe Preferred Equip. Grp. 1: Air Cond; Elect Tuned Delco/Bose Music System (AM/FM Stereo w/Seek & Scan, Stereo Cass Tape & Digital Clock, special tone & balance control & 4 spkrs); Pwr 6-way Driver's Seat ($1333). Pkg w/U1F Radio, Add ($396). Convertible Preferred Equip. Grp. 1: Air Cond; Elect Tuned Delco/Bose Music System (AM/FM Stereo w/Seek & Scan, Stereo Cass Tape & Digital Clock, special tone & balance control & 4 spkrs); Pwr 6-way Driver's Seat ($1333). Pkg w/U1F Radio, Add ($396). Leather Bucket Seats (NC). Adjustable Leather Bucket Seats ($625). G92 Performance Ratio Axle ($50). Calif. Emission System ($100). ZO7 Adjustable Handling Pkg: FX3 Elect Selective Ride and Bilstein Adjustable Ride Control System ($2045). FX3 Elect Selective Ride ($1695). Low Tire Pressure Warning Indicator ($325). Roof Panels, Blue Tint or Bronze Tint ($650). Dual body color-keyed roof panel & Blue or Bronze Transparent Roof Panel ($950). Removable Hard Top ($1995). Pwr 6-way Seats, Driver's Side only ($305). Passenger side only ($305). TIRES: Ext Mobility P255/45ZR17 (front) and P285/40ZR17 (rear), requires low tire pressure warning indicator ($70).

HISTORY: Calendar year sales totaled 18,966 Corvettes. Model year production totaled 19,478. For the third time in its existence (also 1978 and 1986), Corvette was selected as the pace car for the Indianapolis 500. The 1995 dark purple metallic over arctic white Corvette was driven by 1960 Indy 500 winner Jim Rathmann.

1996

CORVETTE — SERIES Y — V-8 — Nineteen ninety-six was a landmark year for Corvette enthusiasts. With the demise of the ZR-1, Chevrolet offset the void by introducing two new special edition Corvettes: Grand Sport and Collector Edition models. The Grand Sport evoked memories of its 1962-'63 racing predecessors, sporting Admiral Blue Metallic Paint, white stripe and red "hash marks" on the left front fender and black five-spoke aluminum wheels. Powering the Grand Sport (and optional in all other Corvettes) was the 330 horsepower LT4 5.7-liter V-8 featuring a specially prepared crankshaft, steel camshaft and water pump gears driven by a roller chain. The LT4 was available only with the six-speed manual transmission. The Collector Edition Corvette was produced as a tribute to the final year of production of the fourth-generation Corvette (the fifth-generation model to debut the following year). It featured exclusive Sebring Silver paint, "Collector Edition" emblems, silver five-spoke aluminum wheels and LT1 5.7-liter V-8 fitted with a four-speed automatic transmission (LT4 V-8 and six-speed manual transmission were both optional). On all Corvettes, 1996 marked the introduction of the optional Selective Real Time Damping system that employed sensors at each wheel to measure movement. Data retrieved from each wheel and the Pow-

ertrain Control Module was processed by an electronic controller that calculated the damping mode to provide optimum control. Also optional was a Z51 Performance Handling Package available on the Corvette coupe, and tuned for autocross and gymkhana competition. Standard Corvette models again used the 5.7-liter V-8 with sequential fuel injection and four-speed automatic transmission.

1996 Chevrolet, Corvette two-door coupe

I.D. DATA.: Coding of the 17-symbol Vehicle Identification Number (VIN) was similar to 1984-95. Fourth and fifth symbols designate car line/series as follows: Y/Y - Corvette. Model year code changed to 'T' for 1996.

1996 Chevrolet, Corvette two-door convertible

CORVETTE

Model No.	Body/Style No.	Body Type & Seating	Factory Price	Shipping Weight	Prod. Total
1Y	Y07	2-dr. Hatch Cpe-2P	37225	3298	Note 1
1Y	Y67	2-dr. Conv. Cpe-2P	45060	3360	Note 2

Note 1: Total Corvette coupe production was 16,833 with no further breakout available for base/Grand Sport/Collector Edition.

Note 2: Total Corvette convertible production was 4,185 with no further breakout available for base/Grand Sport/Collector Edition.

ENGINE DATA: BASE V-8 (Corvette/Corvette Collector Edition): 90-degree, overhead valve V-8. Cast iron block and head. Displacement: 350 cu. in. (5.7 liters). Bore & stroke: 4.00 x 3.48 in. Compression ratio: 10.4:1 Brake horsepower: 300 at 5000 RPM. Torque: 335 lb.-ft. at 4000 RPM. Five main bearings. Hydraulic valve lifters. Sequential fuel injection. BASE V-8 (Corvette Grand Sport); OPTIONAL (Corvette/Corvette Collector Edition): 90-degree, overhead valve High Output V-8. Cast iron block and aluminum head. Displacement: 350 cu. in. (5.7 liters). Bore & stroke: 4.00 x 3.48 in. Compression ratio: 10.8:1. Brake horsepower: 330 at 5800 RPM. Torque: 340 lb.-ft. at 4500 RPM. Five main bearings. Hydraulic valve lifters. Sequential fuel injection.

CHASSIS DATA: Wheelbase: 96.2 in. Overall length: 178.5 in. Height: (hatch) 46.3 in.; (conv) 47.3 in. Width: (hatch) 70.7 in.; (conv) 73.1 in. Front Tread: 57.7 in. Rear Tread: 59.1 in. Standard Tires: (front) P255/45ZR17/(rear) P285/40ZR17; (Grand Sport coupe) (front) P275/40-ZR17/(rear) P315/35ZR17; (Grand Sport convertible) (front) P255/45ZR17/(rear) P285/40ZR17.

1996 Chevrolet, Corvette Collectors Edition two-door convertible

TECHNICAL: Transmission: four-speed overdrive automatic. Steering: rack and pinion (power assisted). Suspension (front): independent SLA forged-aluminum upper and lower control arms and steering knuckle, transverse monoleaf spring, steel stabilizer bar, spindle offset. Suspension (rear): independent five-link design with tow and camber adjustment, forged-aluminum control links and steering knuckle, transverse monoleaf spring, steel tie rods and stabilizer bar, tubular U-joint aluminum driveshaft. Brakes: Anti-lock: power four-wheel disc. Body construction: fiberglass; separate ladder frame with cross-members. Fuel tank: 20.0 gal.

1996 Chevrolet, Corvette Grand Sport two-door convertible

CORVETTE OPTIONS: Coupe Preferred Equip. Grp. 1: Air Cond; Elect Tuned Delco/Bose Music System (AM/FM Stereo w/Seek & Scan, Stereo Cass Tape & Digital Clock, special tone & balance control & 4 spkrs); Pwr 6-way Driver's Seat ($1333). Pkg w/U1F Radio, Add ($396). Convertible Preferred Equip. Grp. 1: Air Cond; Elect Tuned Delco/Bose Music System (AM/FM Stereo w/Seek & Scan, Stereo Cass Tape & Digital Clock, special tone & balance control & 4 spkrs); Pwr 6-way Driver's Seat ($1333). Pkg w/U1F Radio, Add ($396). LT4 5.7-liter V-8 ($1450). Leather Bucket Seats (NC). Adjustable Leather Bucket Seats ($625). G92 Performance Ratio Axle ($50). Calif. Emission System (NC). Z51 Performance Handling

Pkg: Bilstein Adjustable Ride Control System ($350). F45 Selective Real Time Damping System ($1695). Z16 Grand Sport Edition: Incl Admiral Blue w/White Stripe & Red Hash Marks, Rear Wheel Flares, 17-in. Black Five-Spoke Alum Wheels, Perforated Sport Seats w/Grand Sport Embroidery ($3250). Z15 Collector Edition: Incl Sebring Silver Paint, 17-in. Silver Five-Spoke Alum Wheels, Perforated Sport Seats w/Collector Edition Embroidery ($1250). Low Tire Pressure Warning Indicator ($325). Roof Panels, Blue Tint or Bronze Tint ($650). Dual body color-keyed roof panel & Blue or Bronze Transparent Roof Panel ($950). Removable Hard Top ($1995). Pwr 6-way Seats, Driver's Side only ($305). Passenger side only ($305). TIRES: Ext Mobility P255/45ZR17 (front) and P285/40ZR17 (rear), requires low tire pressure warning indicator ($70).

HISTORY: Calendar year sales totaled 17,805 Corvettes. Model year production totaled 22,000.

1997

CORVETTE — SERIES Y — V-8 — Another landmark year for Corvette in that the 1997 model was the first all-new model in 13 years and only the sixth major change in the car's 44-year history. The fifth-generation Corvette was offered only as a coupe in its debut year. Among the equipment featured on the new 'Vette was a new, more compact LS1 5.7-liter V-8 that produced 350 horsepower and 345 pound-feet of torque. A rear-mounted transaxle opened up more interior space and helped maintain a near 50:50 front-to-rear weight distribution. Electronic Throttle Control allowed engineers a limitless range of throttle progression. The 1997 Corvette's underbody structure was the stiffest in the car's history and consisted of two full-length, hydro-formed perimeter frame rails coupled to a backbone tunnel. The rails consisted of a single piece of tubular steel, replacing the 14 parts used previously. The cockpit of the all-new Corvette featured a twin-pod design reminiscent of the original, 1953 Corvette. The instrument panel contained traditional backlit, analog gauges and a digital Driver Information Center that comprised a display of 12 individual readouts in four languages. The new-design blunt tail section allowed for smoother airflow and resulting 0.29 coefficient of drag. Corvette was offered with the 4L60-E electronic four-speed overdrive automatic as the base offering and six-speed manual transmission as optional.

I.D. DATA.: Coding of the 17-symbol Vehicle Identification Number (VIN) was similar to 1984-96. Fourth and fifth symbols designate car line/series as follows: Y/Y - Corvette. Model year code changed to 'V' for 1997.

CORVETTE

Model No.	Body/Style No.	Body Type & Seating	Factory Price	Shipping Weight	Prod. Total
1Y	Y07	2-dr. Cpe-2P	37495	3229	9,092

ENGINE DATA: BASE V-8: Overhead valve V-8. Cast aluminum block and head. Displacement: 346 cu. in.

(5.7 liters). Bore & stroke: 3.90 x 3.62 in. Compression ratio: 10.1:1. Brake horsepower: 345 at 5600 RPM. Torque: 350 lb.-ft. at 4400 RPM. Hydraulic valve lifters. Sequential fuel injection.

1997 Chevrolet, Corvette two-door coupe

DATA: Wheelbase: 104.5 in. Overall length: 179.7 in. Height: 47.7 in. Width: 73.6 in. Front Tread: 62.0 in. Rear Tread: 62.1 in. Standard Tires: (front) P245/45ZR17/(rear) P275/40ZR18.

TECHNICAL: Transmission: four-speed overdrive automatic. Steering: rack and pinion (power assisted). Suspension (front): independent SLA forged-aluminum upper and lower control arms and steering knuckle, transverse monoleaf spring, steel stabilizer bar, spindle offset. Suspension (rear): independent five-link design with tow and camber adjustment, cast-aluminum upper and lower control arms and knuckle, transverse monoleaf spring, steel tie rods and stabilizer bar, tubular U-jointed metal matrix composite driveshaft. Brakes: Anti-lock: power four-wheel disc. Body construction: fiberglass; integral perimeter frame with center backbone/all-welded steel body frame construction. Fuel tank: 19.1 gal.

CORVETTE OPTIONS: Dual Zone Air Cond ($365). Adjustable Leather Bucket Seats, requires 6-Way Pwr Pass. Seat ($625). G92 Performance Ratio Axle, N/A with 6-speed manual trans. ($100). Calif. Emission System ($170). JL4 Active Handling System ($500). Z51 Performance Handling Pkg: Bilstein Adjustable Ride Control System ($350). F45 Continuously Variable Real Time Damping, N/A with Z51 Pkg ($1695). AAB Memory Pkg, recalls settings for OSRV Mirrors/Radio/HVAC/Pwr Seats ($150). Remote CD Changer ($600). UN0 Delco/Bose Music System ($100). License Plate Frame ($15). Fog Lamps ($65). Luggage Shade & Cargo Net ($50). Floor Mats, front ($25). Bodyside Mldgs ($75). Dual body color-keyed roof panel & Blue Transparent Roof Panel ($950). Roof Panel, Blue Tint ($650). Pwr 6-way Seats, Pass. side only ($305).

1998

1998 Chevrolet, Corvette two-door coupe

CORVETTE — SERIES Y — V-8 — In its 45th year, the Corvette returned to offering convertible and coupe models with the debut of a "topless" version of the 'Vette. The convertible's glass rear window was heated, and the top had an Express-Down feature that released the tonneau cover and automatically lowered windows part way at the touch of a button. New-for-'98 was the magnesium wheel option featuring lightweight wheels with a unique bronze tone. Two new exterior colors were offered and a new light oak leather interior color was available. Standard features included stainless steel exhaust system, Extended Mobility Tires capable of running for 200 miles with no air pressure, dual heated electric remote breakaway outside rearview mirrors, Daytime Running Lamps and five-mph front and rear bumpers. The LS1 V-8 and four-speed automatic transmission were again the standard offering, with the T56 six-speed manual transmission optional.

I.D. DATA.: Coding of the 17-symbol Vehicle Identification Number (VIN) was similar to 1984-97. Fourth and fifth symbols designate car line/series as follows: Y/Y - Corvette. Model year code changed to 'W' for 1998.

CORVETTE

Model No.	Body/Style No.	Body Type & Seating	Factory Price	Shipping Weight	Prod. Total
1Y	Y07	2-dr. Cpe-2P	37995	3245	Note 1
1Y	Y67	2-dr. Conv-2P	44425	3246	Note 1

Note 1: Production figures for 1998 Corvettes were not available at the time this book went to press.

ENGINE DATA: BASE V-8: Overhead valve V-8. Cast aluminum block and head. Displacement: 346 cu. in. (5.7 liters). Bore & stroke: 3.90 x 3.62 in. Compression ratio: 10.1:1. Brake horsepower: 345 at 5600 RPM. Torque: 350 lb.-ft. at 4400 RPM. Hydraulic valve lifters. Sequential fuel injection.

CHASSIS DATA: Wheelbase: 104.5 in. Overall length: 179.7 in. Height: 47.7 in. Width: 73.6 in. Front Tread: 62.0 in. Rear Tread: 62.1 in. Standard Tires: (front) P245/45ZR17/(rear) P275/40ZR18.

1998 Chevrolet, Corvette two-door convertible

TECHNICAL: Transmission: four-speed overdrive automatic. Steering: rack and pinion (power assisted). Suspension (front): independent SLA forged-aluminum upper and lower control arms and steering knuckle, transverse monoleaf spring, steel stabilizer bar, spindle offset. Suspension (rear): independent five-link design with tow and camber adjustment, cast-aluminum upper and lower control arms and knuckle, transverse monoleaf spring, steel tie rods and stabilizer bar, tubular U-jointed metal matrix composite driveshaft. Brakes: Anti-lock: power four-wheel disc. Body construction: fiberglass; integral perimeter frame with center backbone/all-welded steel body frame construction. Fuel tank: 19.1 gal.

CORVETTE OPTIONS: Custom Magnesium Wheels ($3000). Dual Zone Air Cond ($365). Adjustable Leather Bucket Seats, requires 6-Way Pwr Pass. Seat ($625). G92 Performance Ratio Axle, N/A with 6-speed manual trans. ($100). Calif. Emission System ($170). JL4 Active Handling System ($500). Z51 Performance Handling Pkg: Bilstein Adjustable Ride Control System ($350). F45 Continuously Variable Real Time Damping, N/A with Z51 Pkg ($1695). AAB Memory Pkg, recalls settings for OSRV Mirrors/Radio/HVAC/Pwr Seats ($150). Remote CD Changer ($600). UN0 Delco/Bose Music System ($100). License Plate Frame ($15). Fog Lamps ($65). Luggage Shade & Cargo Net ($50). Floor Mats, front ($25). Bodyside Mldgs ($75). Dual body color-keyed roof panel & Blue Transparent Roof Panel ($950). Roof Panel, Blue Tint ($650). Pwr 6-way Seats, Pass. side only ($305).

HISTORY: For the fourth time (1978, 1986, 1995, 1998), a Corvette was selected to pace the Indianapolis 500 with professional golfer Greg "the Shark" Norman driving the purple and yellow pace car. Corvette made its long-awaited return to Trans-Am racing successful by placing first in the 1998 season-opening event on the street circuit at Long Beach, Calif., in the #8 AutoLink Corvette driven by veteran road racer Paul Gentilozzi.

Chevrolet's Indianapolis 500 Pace Cars

The pace car has been a part of the Indianapolis 500 race tradition for 87 years, beginning with the inaugural 1911 race that was paced by a Stoddard Dayton with Carl G. Fisher performing the driving duties. During those years, Chevrolet has been given the pace car honor 11 times. The Indy 500s paced by a Chevrolet were: 1948, 1955, 1967, 1969, 1978, 1982, 1986, 1990, 1993, 1995 and 1998. Camaro and Corvette account for eight pace cars (four each) with Beretta, Bel Air and Fleetmaster rounding out the list.

For 1948, Chevy's Fleetmaster convertible powered by the trustworthy (and only choice) 216.5 cid Stovebolt six served as the official pace car for the Indy 500.

What a change it was only seven years later when Chevy's all-new inside, outside and under the hood 1955 Bel Air convertible powered by the famous first-time Chevy 265 cid V-8 small-block engine paced the 1955 race.

By 1967, the first year for Chevy's performance car, the Camaro SS convertible became the "leader of the pack" at Indy. Power for this handsome convertible came from a 396 cid V-8 big-block powerplant.

For 1969, Camaro was again up front, with another RS/SS convertible. Power was again supplied by a 396 cid/375 hp big-block V-8.

In 1978, the Indy 500 was finally paced by America's only sports car—the Corvette—that was by now full-grown and 25 years old, as well as being long overdue as a pace car. A 350 cid/220 hp V-8 engine powered this handsome entry.

By 1982, the T-top Z28 Camaro made that model's third Indianapolis 500 appearance. An aluminum block

The 1948 Chevrolet Fleetmaster was the first Chevy chosen as an official pace car. It was essentially a carry-over 1947 model—the best-selling car in America during that year. It was driven by three-time Indianapolis 500 winner Wilbur Shaw. Power was provided by an inline six-cylinder engine that produced 90 horsepower at 3300 rpm. The gray two-door convertible had a wheelbase of 116 inches and was available only with the three-speed manual transmission.

and head example of Chevy's 350 cid small-block (rated at 250 hp) propelled this Camaro.

A Corvette roadster was selected to pace the 1986 Memorial Day Classic, honoring a joint anniversary of 75 years for both Chevrolet Division and the Indianapolis 500.

For 1990, the Beretta convertible paced the Indy 500. Powered by a 3.4-liter experimental V-6 engine bored out from a 3.1-liter unit, this Beretta hoped to reinforce the "Hot One" image that began at Chevrolet in the mid-1950s. The electric yellow Beretta convertible was powered by the aforementioned 3.4-liter V-6 rated at 225 hp.

Camaro made its fourth appearance at the "Brickyard" as the pace car for the 1993 Indy 500. The Z28 T-top coupe was powered by the 275 hp LT1 small-block V-8.

In 1995, Corvette returned for its third time as pace car for the Indianapolis 500. The Corvette convertible used the 300 hp 5.7-liter V-8 for power.

Just three years later, in 1998, Corvette again was chosen to pace the Indy 500, its fourth stint as pace car. The Corvette convertible was powered by the 345 hp LS1 5.7-liter V-8.

The 1955 Chevrolet Bel Air was on the cutting edge of the automotive technology at the time it was selected for duty as the Indianapolis 500 pace car. It featured the "Power Pack" small-block V-8 engine known as the "Turbo Fire," which produced 180 horsepower. Thomas H. Keating, Chevrolet sales manager, was the driver of this attractive red and white convertible. A movie camera was placed in the car to film the racers on the pace lap through a cut out in the trunk. Speedway owner Tony Hulman is pictured holding the checkered flag and Mauri Rose is pictured leaning on the driver's door.

The initial year of production for the 1967 Chevrolet Camaro SS was also when it made its debut as the pace car of the Indy 500. The Camaro SS convertible's 396 cid V-8 engine produced 375 horsepower at 4800 rpm in stock form. The actual pace car was modified by the Chevrolet Experimental Department, and no exact horsepower figures were reported. Three-time Indy 500 winner Mauri Rose drove the striking Ermine white machine trimmed with bright blue lettering. Chevrolet sold 100 pace car replicas to the public that year.

Making a return engagement to pace the 1969 Indianapolis 500 was the Chevy Camaro convertible, this time a 1969 RS/SS model. Driven by 1960 Indy 500 winner Jim Rathmann, this Camaro featured an Ermine white exterior, this time accented by bright orange lettering and twin rally stripes. Other features included the familiar V-8 engine, 15-inch Rallye wheels, front and rear spoilers, sports-styled steering wheel, push-button radio, floor console, power convertible top, special instrumentation, houndstooth and white vinyl interior, front shoulder safety belts and tinted glass. Chevrolet produced 3,675 replicas for sale to the public. The actual pace car was powered by a high-performance version of the 396 cid big-block engine while replicas could be ordered with either that engine or a 350 cid small-block V-8.

Twenty-five years after its introduction to the public, the Chevrolet Corvette was selected to pace the 1978 Indy 500. Jim Rathmann was the driver. The 1978 Corvette featured the L82 small-block V-8 capable of producing 220 horsepower at 5200 rpm. The exterior of this pace car featured a black and silver two-tone paint job. Other exterior features included a front air dam, rear deck lid spoiler, polished aluminum spoke wheels, glass roof panels and sport mirrors. A total of 6,502 1978 Corvette pace car replicas were produced.

For the third time, a Camaro was selected to pace the Indianapolis 500 in 1982. Jim Rathmann saw duty, also for the third time, as the pace car driver. The 1982 Chevy Camaro Z28 was equipped with a hybrid small-block V-8 that produced 250 horsepower at 4600 rpm. The actual Camaro used as the pace car was the first Z28 built at GM's facility in Van Nuys, Calif. The Z28 pace car featured 15-inch aluminum wheels with P245/60R blackwall tires. The suspension system incorporated front and rear stabilizer bars, high-rate coil springs, modified front MacPherson struts and a torque arm with Panhard rod in the rear. Stopping power was provided by disc brakes all-around. The exterior of the Z28 was silver and blue, with the interior featuring dark blue seats with sewn-in Z28 logos. Chevrolet produced 6,360 Z28 pace car replicas.

Chevrolet's first Corvette convertible in 10 years was selected as the official pace car of the 1986 Indy 500. Turned out by Corvette's Bowling Green, Kentucky, plant, the 1986 Corvette was powered by a 350 cid (5.7-liter) V-8 engine producing 230 horsepower at 4000 rpm. A four-speed manual transmission with computer-controlled overdrive provided smooth shifting, and heavy-duty four-wheel anti-lock brakes provided the stopping power. All soft top 1986 Corvettes were considered pace car replicas, and were designated Z51. The bright yellow Corvette was piloted by U.S. Air Force Brigadier General (retired) Chuck Yeager, the first pilot to shatter the sound barrier as a test pilot.

The bright yellow 1990 Chevrolet Beretta driven by Jim Perkins, general manager of Chevrolet and vice-president of General Motors, was the first six-cylinder Chevy to be chosen as Indianapolis 500 pace car since the Fleetmaster paced the 1948 race. With a 103.4-inch wheelbase, the Beretta featured a 60-degree 3. 4-liter V-6 engine rated at 225 horsepower, an electronically controlled automatic transmission and aluminum alloy wheels. Chevy produced 4,500 special-edition Beretta coupes to commemorate the event. Of these, 1,500 were made available in the brilliant yellow of the actual pace car and 3,000 more were offered in a distinctive turquoise color.

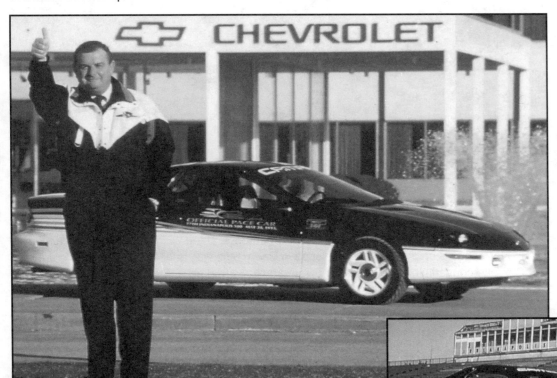

In 1993, Chevrolet debuted the third-generation of its Camaro Z28 and it was selected to pace that year's Indy 500. It marked the fourth time a Camaro paced the May classic. Driven by Jim Perkins, the Camaro Z28 was powered by a 275 horsepower version of the LT1 small-block V-8. Other performance features included a four-speed electronically controlled automatic transmission and four-wheel anti-lock brakes. The Z28's appearance was the most radical to date, as it sported removable T-top glass panels, two-tone black over white paint job and multi-colored "ribbon" striping along the body panels. These stripes continued into the interior where they highlighted the bucket seats. Chevy produced only 645 pace car replicas.

The third Chevrolet Corvette to pace the Indy 500 was a 1995 convertible with unique two-tone paint (dark purple metallic over Arctic white) with "ribbon" striping and a white convertible top. Jim Perkins was again assigned the driving duty. The sleek convertible featured a standard 300 horsepower 5.7-liter V-8 engine with automatic transmission, as well as ZR-1 five-spoke wheels. The interior featured leather seats. Replicas were near duplicates of the pace car, and only 527 were produced.

A year after the introduction of the fifth-generation Corvette, and the year of the debut of the convertible model, the Corvette was selected to pace the 1998 Indianapolis 500—the sports car's fourth appearance at the "Brickyard" as pace car. Professional golfer Greg "the Shark" Norman was chosen to drive. Finished in Radar blue with bright yellow wheels, graphics and interior accents, the 1998 Corvette convertible pace car was powered by the standard 345 horsepower LS1 5.7-liter V-8. Chevrolet produced 1,158 replicas.

The Many

Stories of

Chevrolet

Chevrolet—First With Low Cost
Luxury

Chevrolet for 1932 was a luxury revolution on wheels. It was, indeed, a mini-Cadillac.

Chevrolet got off to a wobbly start in 1913, couldn't seem to find its reach, and by 1921 sales had dropped to a trickle. Losses that year almost reached $10 million, a vast sum in those days. Model T was out-selling Chevrolet 16 to one and gaining.

The Chevrolet got up from this front seat on Death Row and built the broad base on which the modern General Motors was founded. Since GM came to be the mainstream of the US auto industry, Chevrolet led the United States, indeed the World in auto production.

This magnificent feat of imagination and courage perhaps unprecedented in American business, rests squarely on two Chevrolets—1925 Model K and 1932 Model named strangely Confederate Series BA. They were the beginning and the end of an automobile revolution.

In the beginning the small car production trouble was two-fold. When cars were built like birds' nests, one at a time, the way Rolls-Royce still is, only rich people could afford them. This method didn't produce many cars, but there weren't many rich people, either, so until World War I there was a nice balance in the business between supply and demand with little incentive to upset it. The only lower priced cars the established industry could conceive were

still costly. Packard Single Six of 1921 sold for $2795, half the price of its big brother Twin Six but still five times too much for average Americans.

The looks of a low priced car before World War I weighed heavily against it. The deep rutted roads of the day demanded high wheels, and the body, set on a straight rail frame built up a high edifice. A long wheelbase car could carry this off, but foreshortened such a car looked awkward. That small cars should be ugly was taken for granted then. Henry Leland, past master of mechanical excellence, founder of Cadillac drove for his personal transportation a 1907 one cylinder Cadillac Model M Coupe that looked for all the world like a traveling telephone booth.

Henry Ford solved half of this small car dilemma. Nineteen twenty five was the year he dropped his price to $290 for a new touring car. If you wanted a low priced car, here it was. Like a mule it had no pride of ancestry, no hope of posterity. But nobody ever called it beautiful. It left the buyer with a crying psychological need. After World War I, the new motoring public wanted to take pride in its cars.

The Chevrolet stroke of genius was to understand this

1925 Chevrolet Coach

1928 Chevrolet Coach

The 1924 Chevrolet was a most influential automobile. It showed that grace, style and color could be an integral part of the low-priced automobile. Prices started at $510 for the Touring Car.

when Henry Ford didn't. Chevrolet set out to make the owner proud of his car. The sales record shows the result.

Henry Ford produced 1,749,827 units in 1924, compared to 262,100 for Chevrolet. Only three years later, these figures were almost exactly reversed. Chevrolet sales soared to 1,749,998 cars while Ford fell to an abysmal 356,188 and then he shut down the Model T production line forever. In 1925 buyers were no longer looking for bare bones transportation. They were looking for low cost luxury and Chevrolet undertook to give it to them.

Model K Chevrolet of 1926 may have revolutionized the industry, but there was nothing revolutionary about the car. It just looked better. A lot better.

The radiator shell used bright metal. Caddies waiting on the curb for a ride to a golf club I remember used to stand up when they saw a car coming with a shiny radiator, the mark of affluence. Now Chevrolet had one, too.

Duco made a great difference. You could have a Chevrolet in any color but black, and Chevrolets stood out in the drab traffic of the day in their bright coats of long lasting Duco paint.

The basics of Model K weren't so different. It was simply last year's car made more attractive. The body was

longer, allowing more leg room. "All closed bodies featured a one-piece windshield with an automatic wiper, dome light and a Klaxon horn. The clutch was improved and a new rear end replaced the one that had given so much trouble," according to A. P. Sloan, GM President. Balloon tires, bumpers and moto-meters were available. The sedans normally featured disc wheels like Packard; nickel trim, a neat visor and cowl parking lights produced a stylish image entirely new to the low priced field.

Seven years later Chevrolet's low cost luxury revolution was complete. New models in 1932 joined the General Motors family with no more implications of inferiority than younger brothers. George Dammann's Chevrolet book pictures a 1932 Chevrolet Roadster without a background to betray its scale which could easily be taken for a Cadillac Sixteen. It could even be argued that the Chevrolet was the better automobile—simpler, easier to drive and take care of and a strong competitor on the highway. Chevrolet had proved a low cost car could be handsome, complete and capable.

Chevrolet had won for General Motors the ascendancy in the automobile world it has enjoyed ever since.

The Day Chevy Nearly Sank

By A. Stanley Kramer

For one tense moment, despite substantial sales, Chevrolet nearly went out of business. The year was 1920. As president of General Motors, W. C. Durant had expanded the company's operations tremendously from 1915 until then.

In 1915 Durant had moved Chevrolet's headquarters from Flint, Mich. to New York City. In the next few years he bought Maxwell's Terrytown, N.Y. assembly plant and made arrangements with investors in Canada and St. Louis, which made possible the assembly of the popular 490 Chevrolet in Flint, St. Louis, Tarrytown, Oshawa (Canada), Oakland, Calif., and Fort Worth, Texas. (The 490 got its name from the $490 Henry Ford charged for his Model T touring car, targeted as the competition. However, six weeks after the introduction of the 490, Ford lowered his price to $440.)

In 1916 factory sales soared to 70,701, then to 125,882 in 1917. They dropped slightly in 1918 and 1919 but bounced back to 150,226 in 1920—accounting for a large share of GM's total North American sales of 393,075 cars.

But Chevrolet's future was nowhere near as solid as these figures might indicate. As GM president, Durant had expanded GM's operations dazzlingly. But his entire personal fortune was committed to the support of its shares on Wall Street. When business fell off sharply in September 1920, Durant and his empire were in deep trouble. They were saved from disaster only through the intervention of the vast resources of the duPont family whose quick action alone kept GM alive. But at a price. Durant had to resign on Nov. 30, 1920 to be succeeded by Pierre

S. duPont, who also made himself general manager of Chevrolet.

Alfred P. Sloan Jr. then became, as he wrote in *My Years with General Motors*, "sort of executive vice president in charge of all operations, reporting to Mr. duPont."

Sloan described the near debacle graphically. "Someone had the idea of having a survey made of the General Motors properties, with recommendations as to what might be done in the way of a reconstruction program. The job was entrusted to a firm of consulting engineers of high standing. The most illuminating recommendation was that the whole Chevrolet operation should be liquidated. There was no chance, they said, to make it a profitable business. We could not hope to compete. I was much upset because I feared the prestige of the authors might overcome our arguments to the contrary." Pierre duPont listened patiently and at length to Sloan's pleas to carry on the business. Sloan recalled, "I went to Mr. duPont and told him what we thought we might accomplish if we built a good product and sold it aggressively."

It was a tense moment. Millions of dollars and the working lives of thousands of people hung in the balance. President Pierre thought long and hard. Then he smiled, something he was not famous for.

"Forget the report," he said, "We will go ahead and see what we can do."

The rest is important American history. Like the bumblebee who flew very well despite aeronautic engineers' overwhelming proof that its wings were too small and its fuselage too thick for flight, Chevrolet flew too, and has been flying high ever since.

Saga Of Copper Cooled Chevy

By Rich Taylor

Charles F. Kettering

Charles F. Kettering, the brilliant "boss Ket," figures prominently in the early history of General Motors, and indeed, the automobile. He invented the self-starter, the high-tension ignition system, the high-compression engine, freon refrigerant, the two-cycle Diesel and leaded gasoline. Indeed, Kettering had only one significant failure, and that was one that seems like it would have been the simplest of all...the air-cooled engine.

Boss Ket started work on his air-cooled engine in 1918. At that time he was the director of Daytona Engineering Laboratories, which was the research division of General Motors. Now in 1918, the air-cooled engine was nothing new ...Franklin was only the best known of dozens of air-cooled engine manufacturers.

Every air-cooled engine in production was made by laborously welding cooling fins onto the block, or carefully casting integral fins when the block was made. Either way was very expensive and time-consuming. Kettering wanted to invent a way to air-cool an engine that would be cheap enough for mass-production and more efficient than anything anybody else was doing.

His solution was to use cast iron cylinders that were smooth on the outside. Then he took sheet copper and pleated it into a series of continuous, vertical fins. These would be welded to the outside of the cast iron cylinders, and since copper transfers heat more efficiently than cast iron, Kettering figured his engine would be super-efficient and easy to build. The only problem was, he couldn't devise a way to weld the copper fins to the cast iron cylinders.

In 1919, Kettering reported to the new board of directors that he had solved the problem. A high-temperature bonding oven would literally fuse the fins to the cylinder at 1400 degrees. A year later, when Billy C. Durant was forced to leave GM and Pierre S. duPont took over, Kettering wrote to duPont. "The small air-cooled engine is now ready to push toward a production basis," he said.

duPont agreed. The Chevrolet Model 490 had been in production without change since 1913, and was desperately in need of sprucing up. duPont ordered Kettering to build a prototype four-cylinder "copper-cooled" engine that would fit into the existing Model 490 and share at least some parts with the existing 171 cubic inch Four. Kettering started work on a 135 cubic inch Four, with overhead valves borrowed from the water-cooled 490 and four individually-cast cylinders wrapped in copper fins. The bottom end was just a modified version of the existing engine.

In January of 1921, Pierre duPont decided that the new air-cooled engine deserved a whole new car, and he ordered Chevrolet general manager K. W. Zimmerschied to come up with a brand-new body and chassis for 1923. A month later, duPont decided that Oakland also needed to be revamped, and directed Kettering to simultaneously design a six-cylinder air-cooled engine for an all-new Oakland which would sell for around $1000..twice as much as the new Chevrolet.

In May, 1921, Kettering had test cars fitted with the new four and six-cylinder engines ready to run. Unfortunately, neither ran very well. The air flow around the vertical copper fins simply wasn't enough to cool the cylinders. Kettering designed a shroud to surround the cylinders and lead into a front-mounted fan. Air was sucked up beneath the car, flowed past the cylinders and exhausted out the sides of the hood. You'd think that Kettering would have designed it so the air would flow in the grille and be blown down and back by the fan, to be sucked out the bottom by the partial vacuum which exists beneath any moving car.

Chevrolet's Zimmerschied didn't have much faith in the four-cylinder air-cooled engine, so Kettering had switched his allegiance to George Hannum, the general manager of

Oakland, who was much more receptive to the whole idea. In October, 1921, Kettering shipped two six-cylinder test cars up to Hannum in Pontiac, Michigan.

After the cars had been driven for two weeks, Hannum sent a letter to Kettering, with a copy to Pierre duPont. "To get this car to the point where we are ready to put our OK on same, it will take at least six months. To bridge this time, we are planning on bringing in a complete new water-cooled line." Kettering was so furious that on the same day duPont indefinitely postponed the air-cooled Oakland project, he wrote a letter signed by all the members of the GM Executive Committee that reaffirmed their faith in Kettering, in the air-cooled concept and in the four-cylinder Chevrolet version.

duPont also ordered Kettering to try and get the air-cooled engine into production by September, 1922. And to help him, he gave an unprecedented order. The chief engineers of Chevrolet, Oakland and Buick were transferred to Dayton where they would work for Kettering. Pierre duPont was pinning everything on Kettering's untried engine.

Alfred Sloan was a member of the Executive Committee, as was Charles Mott. In January, 1922, they met with Chevrolet's Zimmerschied in the Hotel Statler in Detroit. The three men secretly decided that the copper-cooled motor was too much of a gamble for General Motors. They would let Kettering and duPont go along planning on the copper-cooled, but Sloan and Zimmerschied would secretly modernize the water-cooled Model 490, just in case.

General Motors was in a real mess. All sorts of corporate infighting was going on, and nobody knew exactly who was running the company. On February 1, 1922, duPont hired William S. Knudsen away from Ford and made him assistant to Charles Mott, with sweeping powers. Knudsen went down to Dayton, talked with Kettering and ordered that Chevrolet stop production of the water-cooled 490 and immediately start building the copper-cooled engine.

Zimmerschied told Knudsen where to get off. But Knudsen had Pierre duPont's backing, and Zimmerschied didn't. Knudsen was made vice-president of Chevrolet operations, and duPont named himself general manager of Chevrolet. Zimmerschied was given a vague executive post with no power.

Chevrolet began tooling up for production of the new engine in April of 1922, expecting to make ten per day by September and fifty per day by December. But Kettering wouldn't approve the tooling. He rightly claimed that the copper-cooled engine wasn't quite ready for production, and he needed just a little more time to work the bugs out.

By June, it was obvious even to duPont and Knudsen that the engine would never be ready. Sloan and Mott were allowed to take the lineup of bodies that had been designed for the new car and fit them to a spruced-up version of the Model 490 chassis. This would give them a new Superior 490 line for 1923. If and when the air-cooled engine was ready, it could be fitted to the Superior 490 without chassis modifications.

The Superior 490 used a longer 103 inch wheelbase version of the old 490 frame, with quarter-elliptic leaf springs front and rear, rigid axles, demountable rims on wooden spoke wheels and external contracting brakes on the rear wheels only. The engine was the tried and true water-cooled 490, now entering its tenth year, the transmission was the same old 3-speed, the differential a spiral bevel gear.

The Superior 490 line was priced from right around $500, just upscale of the Model T, to just under $900, or just downscale of the Oakland. The new line contained a two-passenger sedanette, a closed five passenger sedan and a closed two passenger coupe.

Throughout the summer of 1922, Pierre duPont kept putting off the introduction date of the copper-cooled motor, as Kettering kept asking for more development time. Finally, in November, 1922, duPont sent a letter to Kettering and the Executive Committee. "Chevrolet will proceed with the development of its Copper-Cooled model cautiously, in such a way that the hazard to the Corporation is at all times kept at a minimum."

Chevrolet was seemingly off the hook. But in the same letter, duPont now ordered Kettering to get back to work on the six-cylinder version and have it ready for Oldsmobile to start building by August of 1923. Indeed, he even ordered Oldsmobile—which had so far not been involved in the air-cooled debacle at all—not to do any development work on water-cooled engines starting from receipt of the letter on November 16, 1922. If you read between the lines, it's obvious that there was a terrific struggle going on for control of General Motor, with duPont and Knudsen on one side and Mott and Sloan on the other. The divisions were being swapped around, only pawns in their game.

Knudsen ordered Chevrolet to actually produce Copper-Cooled cars beginning in December, 1922. The price

William S. Knudsen

was set at $200 more that the equivalent water-cooled model. The cars were identical except that the starter location was moved, the generator was belt-driven, the clutch used multiple discs instead of a single disc, the distributor had one of Kettering's automatic spark advancers and the emergency brake acted on the driveshaft.

Between December and May, Knudsen built only 759 Copper-Cooled cars. And on May 10, 1923, the executive battle over who would control GM was finally won by Alfred Sloan. Pierre duPont resigned. Sloan's first move was to ask for a status report on the six-cylinder Copper-Cooled engine that was supposedly being readied for Oldsmobile. duPont was so sure of Kettering's engine that he had ordered Oldsmobile to sell off its entire stock of water-cooled cars at a $50 loss on each one, in order to clear the pipeline for fabulous new air-cooled cars which would come along in less than 3 months.

The engineer's report on the Copper-Cooled Six was exactly two paragraphs long.

"The Copper-Cooled Six preignites badly after driving at moderate speeds in air temperatures from sixty to seventy degrees. It shows a serious loss of compression and power when hot, though the power is satisfactory when the engine is warming up from a cold condition.

"These major difficulties plus several minor ones which

can be reported in detail, if you so desire, lead us to the conclusion that the job is not in shape for immediate production. We recommend that we set it aside for further development and it be left out of consideration as far as immediate production is concerned.''

As a result of this devastating report, Sloan ordered Oldsmobile to get going on a water-cooled car. He also ordered Knudsen not only to stop building the four-cylinder air-cooled cars, but to buy back and destroy any 759 which had been sold. Knudsen scrapped 239 which were still on the production lines, plus about 150 cars that were being driven by Chevrolet managers and 300 that were bought back from dealer's showrooms.

Only 100 had actually been sold to retail customers, and Chevrolet field service men were able to buy back all but two coupes. One had been purchased in Detroit by Henry Ford, curiously enough, just to see what all the fuss was about. It's in the Henry Ford Museum at Greenfield Village today. The other coupe was bought by a Mr. Samuel Elliot of Boston, who being a typical crusty New Englander, simply refused to give it up. It's now in Harrah's collection.

Charles F. Kettering was understandably upset when he learned that Sloan had canned his car, and threatened to resign. Sloan handled him beautifully. He suggested that Kettering himself introduce a new line of cars, called Copper-Cooled, to be built in Dayton and distributed through General Motors dealers. Kettering diddled around all summer, and in September, 1923 he gave a number of test engines to the engineering department at the University of Michigan.

The student engineers discovered something that Kettering had overlooked. While the inlet manifold temperatures of the water-cooled 490 engine were 125 degrees at all four cylinders, the inlets of the Copper-Cooled were 134, 122, 127 and 160 degrees, front to back. And while the cylinder head temperature of the front cylinder was only 380 degrees, the back cylinder was 450 degrees.

The evidence is obvious. The reason the Copper-Cooled engine didn't work is because Kettering never figured out an adequate way to get equal amounts of cooling air to each cylinder. The uneven temperatures led to detonation, higher temperatures and eventually, piston seizure.

Faced with this thermodynamic evidence, and with no interest in the engine from GM, Kettering abandoned the Copper-Cooled. It's nothing more than a reminder of the way in which a few ambition-blinded executives in the wrong positions can make a total muddle of a large corporation within a matter of months. If not for Alfred Sloan, Pierre duPont and Charles Kettering might have totally bankrupt General Motors by selling a car that simply didn't run.

Curiously enough, it was while trying to find a way to stop the detonation which destroyed his copper-cooled engine that Kettering began investigating the properties of gasoline itself. He discovered that the addition of tetraethyl lead to the gasoline raised the octane rating and made the engine run cooler, with less detonation. In a well-cooled engine, it permitted higher compression ratios for much more power. So in two respects, really, the Copper-Cooled Chevrolet was a success. It helped put Alfred Sloan into the presidency of General Motors, and it led to the discovery of leaded gasoline. That's more than you can say for many more successful cars.

The brilliant Charles F. Kettering had only one significant failure . . . his air-cooled engine for the Chevrolet car.

1928

A Milestone Year for Chevrolet and General Motors Corp.

By Robert C. Ackerson

Riding in any automobile that is older than you is almost by definition a humbling experience. And when the automobile is well over half a century in age it also becomes a memorable one. In the case of Laddie MacKenzie's 1928 National Series AB Chevrolet sedan (with barely 22,000 miles on the odometer) it assumes even additional importance since Chevrolets of this vintage are, in automotive history, significant vehicles.

The first Chevrolet of 1911 was powered by a six cylinder engine but three years later the "Chevrolet Four" debuted and that car says General Motors, "first made the Chevrolet name famous." The 1914 model was the first Chevrolet to wear the soon to be world famous bow-

tie logo and began Chevrolet's long use of overhead valves. In a 1914 advertisement Chevrolet noted the advantages of this arrangement, explaining to readers, "Gasoline is introduced directly into the cylinder head and exploded there. The full force of the explosion comes in direct contact with the piston head. For this reason Chevrolet power is maximum with minimum fuel."

Chevrolet was as is common knowledge directly involved in the machinations of William Durant and his second coming as the master of General Motors. This colorful if ultimately tragic (for Durant) episode in automotive history has been, and appropriately so, well researched and recorded. But, in terms of its actual impact upon the development of the American automotive industry, Chevrolet, by the end of World War I was yet to be heard from. From that point events moved with great rapidity. While the Model T Ford was reaching its peak sales year in 1923 with 2,091,000 cars sold, Alfred Sloan was beginning his long tenure as General Motors president. Under Sloan and his immediate predecessor, Pierre S. duPont GM had become a corporation with clearly defined and clarified responsibilities for every key individual at each crucial level of operation. It was a firm with an awesome ability to gather and interpret statistics and at the same time operate in a decentralized fashion that spurred innovation and creativity. On the other hand, Henry Ford had proudly announced in 1922 that "The Ford factories and enterprises have no organization, no specific duties attaching to any position, no line of succession or of authority, very few titles, and no conferences." He should have added that Ford was also losing its grip upon industry leadership. In 1924, '25 an '26, Model T sales fell and whereas in 1921 Ford controlled 55.7 percent of the market, a decade later its share was 24.9 percent. General Motors, over the same time, moved its new car sales from 12.7 percent to 43.9 percent. In 1925 General Motors introduced the six cylinder Pontiac and in its annual report informed stockholders that "The Corporation has established the fundamental policy of building a car for every purse and purpose." This meant that at the lower end of the market would be found a Chevrolet that was extremely competitive to what Ford had to offer; was capable of instilling in owners a high degree of loyalty and, for those individuals experiencing upward mobility, create satisfied car buyers who would cheerfully seek out a Pontiac or Oldsmobile dealer when their dreams of affluence became reality. It all paid off extremely handsomely. In 1928 General Motors reported a profit of $296,256,223, truly a milestone of American industrial development. In January of that year the four millionth Chevrolet was completed and before the year ended the fifth millionth, an AB Coach was manufactured.

Sandwiched as it was between the arrival of the 1928 Ford Model A and the new six cylinder Chevrolet the following year, it's been easy for automotive history to ignore that last (that is until 1962) of the Chevrolet Fours. This has been unfortunate. Not only did it help (with sales of 769,9927) GM make that just mentioned mountain of money, but it was also a very fine automobile. Chevrolet which already had the new engine on tap and ready to go was still able to report in 1928 that "this great new car is everywhere hailed as an amazing revelation in automotive value." With its larger 107 inch wheelbase (which represented a four inch increase from 1927) and tasteful restyling it was, said Chevrolet, an automobile of "arresting new beauty." Perhaps a bit overstated, Chevrolet. The 1928 model still looked a little top heavy but a new grille shape and a winged wheel embellishment for the bow tie overseeing the front end were nice touches and, like other American automobiles, the Chevrolet's lines were beginning to soften into the more pleasing shapes that were waiting for the 1930's to arrive.

Chevrolet also spoke of the "thrilling new acceleration" of its 171 cid engine which with a higher, 4.5:1 compression ratio was capable of producing 35 horsepower. With a weight of 2,435 pounds the Chevrolet was in reality a modest performer but with new, four-wheel mechanical brakes it was for 1928 a well balanced family car, that Chevrolet appropriately proclaimed, "The first choice the nation for 1928."

With its additional four inches of wheelbase positioned in the hood section, the 1928 National Series Chevrolet was obviously paving the way for 1928 and that little four-cylinder engine seemed out of place under its spacious

hood. But let's give credit where it's due. The 1928 model was indeed "the bigger and better Chevrolet"; an automobile that maintained Chevrolet's reputation as an outstanding value. Neither extreme nor flashy, it none-the-less was an automobile like millions of Chevrolets that followed. Reliable beyond reproach and constructed with integrity it was very much "the world's most luxurious low-priced automobile."

1928 "National" 2dr "BA" Coach

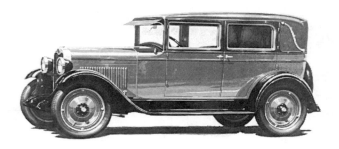

1928 Imperial Landau

1928 Coupe

Chevy's Postwar

Woodie Wagons

By John Gunnell

Postwar Chevrolets with wood framed or wood grain trimmed bodies are not exactly rare vehicles, since whatever Chevy built was made in relatively high numbers. On the other hand, using an individual model basis, there were fewer years of Chevrolet "woodies" (or semi-woodies) than there was for the major competition — Ford.

Chevy's most interesting postwar woodies came, undoubtedly, in the years immediately following the end of the fighting overseas. From 1946 to 1948 there were station wagons, suburban Carryalls, school buses and even Aerosedans, put together with real wood body framing or appliques. Some were products of the Chevrolet factories, while others were constructed by body building firms such as Campbell or Cantrell. All of these vehicles hold special interest to collectors today and will be the main focus of this article. We will, however, talk about some later woodie collectibles, too.

For the 1946 season, the Chevrolet station wagon was a late year addition to the line, since it took time to get assemblies rolling after the war's duration. The wagon, quite obviously, did not have top priority in production schedules. When it finally appeared, it was part of the 116 inch wheelbase Fleetmaster line in the Model DK series.

The station wagon was rated an 8-passenger model (3 seats) and was priced $1,712, which worked out to just under fifty-cents per pound. Power was supplied by the tried-and-true 3-1/2 x 3-3/4 inch bore and stroke Chevrolet six, with 216.5 cubic inches of displacement and 90 horsepower to 3,300 R.P.M. Only 804 examples were built.

Similar to station wagons in general styling were a number of privately built wood wagons or Carryalls constructed on the Model DP, 115 inch wheelbase half-ton commerical chassis or the Model DR, 124-1/2 inch wheelbase three-quarter ton chassis. Both of these chassis were available in two forms called "chassis-cowl" or "chassis-cowl-windshield". The names aptly describe what you got for your money, which was $744 and $764 respectively for the lighter model and $833 and $853 respectively for the heaviest.

We have no documentation that any of these type vehicles were built in 1946, though there have been several letters from readers indicating this was so. Hopefully some deeper research will surface eventually. It is definitely recorded (in the Crestline book *Sixty Years of Chevrolet*) that truck-based wood wagons were built in Bombay, India during 1946. Some came with masonite panels, teakwood framing and with righthand steering. Another book, *Great American Wagons & Woodies*, indicates the half ton edition had white ash framing with mahogany panels and that these wooden components were supplied by Cantrell, a Long Island, N.Y. body firm. Therefore, it would not be surprising if some of these truck/station wagons were also made for the domestic market.

1947

Except for price, there was no great change in the Chevrolet wood-bodied station wagon for 1947. It was continued with the same specifications as the previous year, but now cost $1,893. Both series and model designations were slightly revised, making the wagon part of the Chevy Model EK, or Series 2100 line. The model number was 2109. The wooden sections of the bodies came from the Ionia body Co. of Michigan, or from Cantrell, in New York. For 1947 Chevrolet had a bolder grille with horizontal bars extending into the front fenders. Production amounted to 4,912 station wagons.

There is little doubt that wood-bodied commercial vehicles were built on the 1947 Chevrolet truck chassis, too. Again, there is very little documentation for these models, though Cantrell appears to have been the big supplier in this field. One interesting rig, seen recently at New England car shows, is a restored woodbodied Chevrolet school bus constructed on the large 1½ ton chassis. The body on this particular bus — with a 1947 serial number — was made by a New England firm named Campbell. The bus has had an excellent owner restoration and is quite a sight to see.

Of even greater interest to collectors was the appearance of several 1947 fastback Aerosedans with so-called "Country Club" wood trim. These cars had white ash framing and mahogany paneling placed over the sheet-metal on the front doors and rear body quarters. This made the Chevrolet the same look as the Chrysler Town & Country or the Ford/Mercury Sportsman models. By 1948, some convertibles got this treatment, too.

There is some bit of controversy over the source of the wood trim. It was first thought to be a factory feature made by either Chevrolet or Fisher body. However, the Country Club edition does not appear in any Chevrolet literature or parts manuals. It seems that the wood trim was produced as an aftermarket kit by Engineered Enterprises

of Detroit and may have been installed on some cars by authorized Chevrolet dealers.

1948

Featuring the 1948 Chevrolet station wagon was another price increase, a slight reduction in weight and a better looking grille. General specifications stayed about the same, with the wagon now part of the Series 2100 FK Fleetmaster line. It had an overall length of 207½ inches and tipped the scales at 3,430 pounds with a $2,103 basic price tag. As in the two previous years, 6.00 x 16 size tires were used. Production climbed to 10,171 units as the postwar wagon boom began to get into gear.

Seen again this year were Cantrell built Chevy Carryalls with wood bodies and a variety of other custom made woodies, as well as Country Club kits for dealer installation on Aerosedans and convertibles. All these are now highly desirable collector cars (and trucks), although there is still considerable historical research needed in this area.

1949

The 1949 model year was marked by new postwar styling, replacing the basically prewar look carried over in 1946-48. The new model lineup included two sleekly streamlined wagons, though only one was a true woodie.

It was the model 2109 version and proved to be a milestone of Chevrolet history . . . the last wood-bodied wagon ever made.

This car no longer had a fabric covered slat roof like earlier station wagons, but instead featured an all-steel top, complete with headliner. One distinction was wood framed body construction at the rear quarter area. The 3,485 pound car could seat 8-passengers on its three vinyl covered seats and sold for $2,267. A 216.5 cubic inch engine was carried over as the powerplant with no big changes. New specifications included a 115 inch wheelbase; 198 inch overall length and 15 x 6.70 tires.

The wood wagon was considered a part of the Styleline DeLuxe model range or the 2100 GK series and production began in January, 1949. The more modern look dictated inside storage of the spare tire (a new feature) and a number of other touches that made it more passenger car like. No longer did the Chevy wagon look like a relative of the company's trucks and Carryalls.

In terms of sales figures, the wood wagon was not a popular model this year. There was a marked buyer preference for the all-steel Model 2119 station wagon, which seemed a lot more durable machine. This car had all the good features of the woodie edition — including simulated wood graining — and was only $10 costlier. As a consequence, sales of the all-steel, 3,485 pound wagon hit 6,006 units.

Also seen in 1949 was the Cantrell-bodied Suburban Carryall, still being made in the body builder's Huntington, Long Island factory. This remained a custom built station wagon type vehicle constructed — in most cases — on the Chevrolet 1/2-ton truck chassis. The body was 218 inches long.; 63 inches wide and 60 inches high with a load space that measured 86 inches. This truck/wagon carried the GP Series designation and had a 116-inch wheelbase and a 216.5 cubic inch truck engine. It was

1947 Fleetline 2dr with wood kit.

undoubtedly built on the commercial range chassis-cowl-windshield offering, which Cantrell purchased for about $900 and then the wood body was added to it. The cost of the finished product is not known, but was likely in the $1,800 range. The use of the Chevy cowl and windshield meant that the front windows rolled up and down. The remainder of the body sections had sliding glass. The Cantrell Carryall Suburban was produced through the 1955 model year.

1950

For the 1950 model year Chevrolet's station wagon production jumped to 37,100 units or 24.5 percent of U.S. wagon production. It was a big increase and was reflective of the all-steel model's popularity. There was only one wagon available, as body style number 50-1062. This made the car part of the Styleline DeLuxe 2100 HK series, with a 115 inch wheelbase and 198¼ inch overall length.

As usual, the wagon came with a standard three-speed manual transmission and a 216.5 cubic inch displacement six as standard equipment. However, the engine was now rated 92 horsepower at 5,400 R.P.M., which represented a slight increase. A bigger change in the powerplant department was the optional combination of Powerglide automatic transmission with a new 235.5 cubic inch displacement six. This motor had a 6.70:1 compression ratio and developed 105 horsepower. In a surprise move, the price of the station wagon dropped by $25 (to $1,994), while the weight jumped to 3,460 pounds.

In reality, the all-steel body and lower price were just two factors that boosted wagon sales. There were some additional considerations, such as Powerglide automatic transmission becoming available and the fact that Ford's only offering for the year was a two-door station wagon with somewhat less utilitarian appeal than the four-door Chevy.

1951

There are several different sources for production totals of 1951 Chevrolet wagons. *The Production Figure Book for U.S. Cars* says that 23,586 were made, while the 1952 edition of *Ward's Automotive Yearbook* estimates Chevy's wagon output at 38,000 units and 19.7 percent of industry. In any case, there was just one all-steel edition sold. It carried body style number 51-1062, in the Styleline DeLuxe 2100 HK series and was priced $2,191 with a 3,450 pound weight. Overall length was down to 197-7/8 inches and detail changes to the grille, parking lamps, side spear trim and hood ornament were seen. Otherwise, the car was very much like the 1950 product with simulated wood trim, standard fender skirts and a two-piece tailgate.

1952

Chevrolet's station wagon line included just one model again in 1952. This was essentially the same car as the year before with a toothier grille and some small trim revi-

The Custom Country Club Coupe . . . Beautiful wood panelling adds the smart effect of long lines to the cozy intimacy of this popular close-coupled Custom Country Club Coupe.

1948 Coupe with optional wood trim.

sions. Power choices remained unchanged as well. According to *Ward's* Chevy made 25,000 wagons this season, although other sources give a figure of just 12,756 units. A footnote in the *Ward's 1954 Automotive Yearbook* seems to indicate their figures include station wagons mounted on truck chassis. This is interesting, since the suggestion would then be that some 12,000 Carryall station wagons make up the difference in totals. That's about the closest we've ever come to Carryall production figures. This might be of interest to truck buffs. (All of the Carryalls did not have wood bodies).

1953

In 1953, Chevrolet began the practice of building station wagons in more than one series. The lineup now included two 2100 B Deluxe "210" station wagons and the lower priced 1500 A Special "150". The first used body style number 53-1062 and was called the Two-Ten Townsman; the second was style number 53-1062F or Two-Ten Handyman; the third was the 53-1262F One-Fifty Handyman. The main difference between the wagons was in trim level. Only the Two-Ten Townsman featured wood grain trim.

This DeLuxe wagon was a handsome rendition of Chevy's new for 1953 sheetmetal. It used the old 115 inch wheelbase and had a 198-7/8 inch overall length, but came with a 235.5 cubic inch displacement engine, regardless of transmission. When linked to the conventional three-speed, the motor used solid lifters and had a 7.1:1 compression ratio with horsepower rating of 108 at 3,600 R.P.M. The Powerglide version was 7.5:1 compres-

sioned, with hydraulic lifters and 115 horsepower at 3,600 R.P.M.

The wood grain trimmed Townsman was priced $2,123 and tipped the scales at 3,495. It had a fold-down third seat to provide accommodations for 8-9 passengers. For those who needed cargo space, the center seat could be removed. Thus, with the rear seat folded into the down postion, a large amount of carrying space was produced. In the floor behind the rear set was a hidden compartment for storage of the spare tire and tools.

An interesting note about all 1949-54 station wagons was the fact that the wood graining was added with a decal or transfer. Repair kits included a bonding agent a top coat; one-quarter pint cans of solid or highlight Di-Noc and two Squee Gees.

In addition to wood grain trim, the Townsman was distinquished by the use of sliding rear quarter windows. Production of the fanciest Chevrolet wagon went no higher than 7,988 units this year. This was considerably lower than Two-Ten Handyman (18,258 units) and One-Fifty Handyman (22,408 units) production totals.

1954

In an attempt to pump-up sales of the more luxurious station wagon, the Townsman edition was made a part of the topline Bel-Air series for 1954. Using body style number 54-1062D, the car had a steeper $2,283 factory base price and weighed in, with 3,540 pounds, as the heaviest model of the year. Only a small band of simulated wood grain trim was seen. The nine passenger car turned out to be a slow seller, with production of only 8,156 units.

1947 Station Wagon

1947 Station Wagon

The 1954 wagon was about the same as the 1953 model, except for the addition of Bel Air contrast trim, full wheel covers, fender skirts and revised treatments for the bumpers, grille, lights and hood ornament. The engine was of the same capacity, but got a number of internal improvements to compression ratio and lubrication. The standard motor was a 7.5:1 compression, 115 horsepower version of the 235 cubic inch mill. Optional, with Powerglide, was a 8.0:1 compression edition with 125 horsepower . . . the most powerful engine any Chevrolet had known.

It was not in engineering, however, that the 1954 Townsman wagon stood historically significant. Of greater interest was the fact that it became the last wood grain trimmed Chevrolet to appear until 1966! In an unusual move, the company went a full 12 years before returning to the use of wood-type appliques for station wagons.

Bel Air

An American Success Story

By Terry Boyce

Postwar car buyers were ready for a car like the Bel Air, Chevrolet's new-for-1950 hardtop Sport Coupe.

Offering the style and approaching the openness of a convertible, but without the leak and noise problems inherent in that body type, the hardtop was also the most modern design of the moment. Less than a year before, General Motors had released a trio of upper-bracket special hardtop models - the Buick Roadmaster Riviera, Cadillac Coupe deVille and Olds 98 Holiday. Expensive and in short supply, these beautiful luxury cars attracted a lot of attention. Now, for 1950, Chevrolet brought this sensational styling to the low-priced bracket.

The first Bel Air was, not surprisingly, a success. Sales were strong and would get stronger. The basic body was face-lifted for 1951, then continued into 1952 with only minimal additional changes. Often, these six cylinder Sports Coupes left the show rooms of Main Street America laden with many of the accessory goodies offered by Chevrolet. Sun shades, front and rear bumper end guards, wheel discs, a radio and a heater were among the popular items.

A stop at the local auto supply store could result in the addition of blue dot taillights, a spot light or two and, no doubt, a lucite "necker knob" for the steering wheel.

By 1953, Chevrolet felt the Bel Air name would carry the Chevrolet top series well, so it was expanded to a more complete series of body styles, including a convertible, and two- and four-door sedans in addition to the Sport Coupe. Every Bel Air had a contrasting paint band on the rear fender, with the series script mounted there; adding a roof of the same color made a handsome "two-tone" at minimal cost. Bel Air trim levels were top notch, too, with quality fabrics and brightly colored vinyl or leather for the Sport Coupe and convertible.

Working with the same basic body as 1953, Chevrolet stylists came up with a really pleasing 1954 Bel Air lineup. A new grille and front bumper ensemble gave the car a more substantial, richer appearance. There was a new model, too, the Beauville four-door station wagon: the first Chevrolet wagon offered with Bel Air interior and exterior decor. This interesting model featured vestigal wood body side panels, the last sliver of the warmly toned age of the woodie wagons.

The 1954 Bel Airs were quiet, nicely appointed and retained Chevrolet's traditional durability. They were a fitting summation of the GM Division's six-cylinder era.

But, car buyers were looking for more than traditional values in cars by 1954. They were demanding and getting performance and excitement. Chevrolet responded in 1955 with a single master stroke that almost overnight revolutionized the meaning of the name Chevrolet - yet without losing the following that had so long made the marque America's number one best selling car-line.

About the only thing that wasn't new for 1955 were the series designations. The Bel Air script was still affixed to top line Chevrolet models, with their new low and crisp styling, high-revving optional V-8s and wrap-around windshields. America loved this new Chevrolet right from the first, so it was not surprising that the 1956 models were more of the same, but with a new, more up-level front appearance, slightly sleeker lines and even more horsepower.

For 1957, a third version appeared, a handsome restyle that had more than a little Cadillac influence. By now the V-8's reputation was made; its legend had begun. Topping the engine charts this year were Rochester fuel-injected engines offering as much as one horsepower per cubic inch.

There were new body styles during this classic era. During mid-1955 yet another station wagon appeared.

This was a two-door job with hardtop style door windows and one of the prettiest roof lines ever to grace a

1951 Bel Air

1952 Bel Air 2dr Hardtop

1954 Bel Air 4dr Sedan

car of this body type. It said Nomad on the tailgate, but the Bel Air script appeared on the rear fenders. New for 1956 was the Sport Sedan, an effort to expand the popular "hardtop" concept to a.four-door body style. Though never as popular as the Bel Air two-door hardtop, the Sport Sedan found favor with families who liked a sporting-style car.

The 1955-57 Chevrolets with their tightly packaged yet eye-pleasing styling, perky power teams and exceptional

Dream car of a generation - a '57 Bel Air hardtop "factory fuelie."

Capping a sensational line of 1955 Bel Air models was the beautiful Nomad wagon.

Eclipsed by the new Bel Air Impala Sport Coupe pictured here, the 1958 Bel Air two-door hardtop, though brightly trimmed and plushly upholstered, was still down-line.

durability were held dear by many owners who found the Chevrolets that followed not nearly as appealing. As late as 1963, Chevrolet marketing managers were still trying to figure a way to pry the '55-'57 models away from their original owners. It was no coincidence that the 1964 Chevelle was very comparable to these cars in size and equipment.

But, by this time, there was a whole new market for 1955-57 Bel Airs. The baby boom was going to high school and the cars of choice in mid-sixties school parking lots were - you know it - '55-'57 Chevys An impromptu poll at any 20th or 25th anniversary reunion is sure to turn up a surprising percentage of former Bel Air hardtop owners. And, there will likely be a few lucky persons who still have one.

But two decades ago, as the 1958 models were being styled, it appeared that lower, wider and heavier were the ways to go. And, to go along with this theme of more of everything, it seemed that new models were in order to top the Chevrolet line. Thus, greeting 1958 car shoppers were a pair of Impalas, a Sport Coupe and convertible. For this one year - although no one but historians remember - these were technically "Bel Air Impalas," special models topping the Bel Air line, which was still trimmed inside and out in top-level finery throughout its series lineup.

For 1959, however, the Impala expanded to become Chevrolet's top series and the Bel Air was relegated to the mid-line slot. There wasn't even a Bel Air Sport Coupe this year (although, strangely, there was a Bel Air Sport Sedan). The 1960 Bel Air lineup did include the Sport Coupe once again, but with its truly mundane interior it attracted only a fraction of the sales scored by the colorful Impala.

Standard Catalog of Chevrolet

The High Performance Cars From Chevrolet

by Robert C. Ackerson

1955 was a pivotal year in Chevrolet history. Prior to that time Chevrolet had more or less accepted a second best position when it came to performance to its great rival, Ford. This really wasn't as self defeating as it sounds because since 1936 Chevrolet had let its arch rival in sales and that after all was said and done, was really what the automobile business was all about.

Without downgrading the profound impact of Henry Ford and the Model T and Model A Fords upon the automobile industry and indeed virtually every facet of our lives, it's equally important to recognize Chevrolet's role in the same frame of reference.

In the years following William C. Durants' second and final exodus from the leadership of General Motors, his successor, Alfred P. Sloan served as the chief architect of the design of a new corporate philosophy which was to

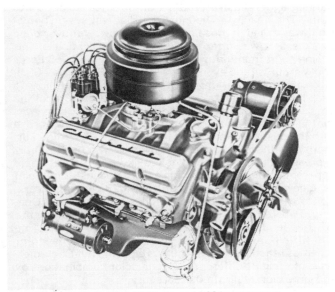

Chev's new, little V-8 for 1955 carried 162 horsepower.

prove fabulously successful. In part his policy was to design automobiles in each price bracket of the market that offered just a bit more to the customer than their competitors. This "bit more" was a composite of factors such as riding comfort, styling innovations and interior appointments that in total conveyed an impression to the customer that he was getting more value for his dollar when he purchased a General Motors product. Thus reasoned Sloan, he would have little objection to paying a slightly higher price.

As General Motors' entry in the low price field, Chevrolet was perhaps the prime example of just how successful Sloan's strategy was.

It took time for Sloan to fully implement this plan but by the late 20s Chevrolet was openly referring to its cars as "Bigger and Better . . ." offering "an order of elegance never before thought possible in a low priced car." When the decade had begun, Ford was of course clearly in a position of superiority but as the years passed the Model T's sales margin over the Chevrolet steadily dwindled. In terms of meeting the desires of the buying public as compared to meeting the transportation needs of the nation, the Model T was clearly in a state of decline. In 1924 Model T sales reached a figure of 1,870,000 but dropped the following year to 1,675,000. In the same time span Chevrolet moved from 280,000 sales to an impressive 470,000. The following year (1926) price reductions failed to stem the tide and Ford sales dropped nearly 400,000 while Chevrolet, under General Manager William S. Knudsen, saw its sales continue upward to reach 732,000.

After its peak year in 1923 when 2,091,000 were produced, the Model T had by 1927 clearly reached the end of the road.

Chevrolet moved ahead of Ford (which had to shut down for six months to prepare for the manufacture of the Model A) in 1927 and maintained this lead into 1928 when 786,670 Chevrolets were produced compared to Ford's total of 713,528. The following year Ford made a great comeback producing 1,715,100 cars which was virtually double the comparable Chevrolet figure.

Yet in spite of this trouncing, Chevrolet sales in 1929 stood at an all time high and the fact that its 1929 models were powered by a new 194cid overhead valve engine must be seen as a major step forward in the design of the modern low priced car in America. Furthermore under Knudsen, Chevrolet had managed to make the change over to the six cylinder engine in record time. Certainly this application of the "Bigger and Better" philosophy was a prime mover in pushing Henry Ford toward production of a V8 in 1932 and Walter Chrysler's concurrent act of offering hydraulic brakes on his Plymouth, and in 1933 a six cylinder engine as well.

During the middle thirties, the number one position in automobile producers swung back and forth between Ford and Chevrolet but in 1936 Chevrolet established a lead of nearly 180,000 cars over Ford and for the next 22 years was the nation's top automobile producer.

Yet Ford remained the nation's sweetheart when it came to performance. In reality however, by the early fifties Ford's right to this amorous relationship with the public was based more on fancy than fact. Granted that Chevrolet's trusty old six was getting a bit long in the tooth (it had been introduced in 1929 and had received a major redesign in 1936), Ford's flathead V-8 was also in need of replacement.

A comparison of the performance of the 1952 Ford and Chevrolet reveals just how similar their relative performance had become:

	Ford V-8 (110bhp)	**Ford Six** (101bhp)	**Chevy Six** (92bhp)
0-60mph	20.47 sec	19.45 sec	20.46 sec
10-60 in high gear	26.93 sec	24.40 sec	23.83 sec
30-60 in high gear	17 sec	15.34 sec	15.68 sec
Top speed	86.70 mph	86.28 mph	80.93 mph

Furthermore in the last Mexican Road Race of 1954 C.D. Evans drove a 1954 Chevrolet to a class victory. As set up for this race Evan's Chevrolet had a top speed of approximately 104mph.

The impact of this racing success upon Chevrolet sales was probably minimal but both behind the scenes and in public Chevrolet was gradually shedding its conservative image. The visual segment of this transformation was of course the Corvette, the hidden element centered around the arrival of Ed Cole at Chevrolet as its new Chief Engineer in May, 1952. Cole, who had earlier worked on the design of the Cadillac ohv V-8 of 1948, was, if any one individual is to be singled out, the man who "made" the 1955 Chevrolet.

1955 was a great year for the Big Three (and a corresponding disaster fo what remained of the independents). With the exception of Lincoln and the senior GM cars (Buick, Oldsmobile and Cadillac); Ford, General Motors and Chrysler offered cars with all-new styling, and major engineering advances.

Even as the new cars were making their debut amidst the holiday mood which prevailed at new car announcement time back in those days it was clear that the new Chevrolet was the fairest of them all.

From every angle the 1955 models represented a major watershed in Chevrolet's long history. For once the adage "All New" was justified as a description of the Chevrolet. For example, the 1955 Chevrolet contained some 4,500 different parts of which 3,825 were changed from their 1954 model counterparts. And that styling. Seldom has there been an American car that bore such a styling change from its predecessors and yet managed somewhat to resemble them. It doesn't seem at all improper to refer to the 1955 Chevrolet's front end as a classic design. Nothing was overdone, there were no extremes. Even today that simple yet elegant egg crate grille still remains as one of the best ever to appear on an American production car. A close look at the Chevy's head and parking lights illustrates GM's unmatched attention to detail. The headlights had just the slightest suggestion of what was called in those days an eyebrow. Not over done to excess, it was a far more graceful application of this styling point than that which appeared on the 1955 Fords and Mercurys (and even worse, on 1955 Packards). Similarly, the front parking lights were a simple teardrop shape, hard to criticize from any point of view. One of the amazing things about the styling of the '55 Chevy was that in spite of it being an all new body style that broke with the past it still managed to look like a Chevrolet. Furthermore, there were some individuals who unabashedly expressed the view that it looked like a "little Cadillac." Apparently this similarity didn't hurt because Chevrolet set a new production record of 1,830,028 passenger cars.

A total of 14 different body styles in three lines (One-Fifty, Two-Ten and Bel Air) were offered, each sharing the notched fender line which Harley Earl was so fond of. The mid-fifties saw the use of two and three tone color schemes reach a pretty ridiculous extreme but Chevrolet, while offering 21 different two-tone color combinations by and large didn't fall into this category.

Beneath the Chevrolet's finely proportioned body was a new chassis that was 5 stiffer and 18% lighter than the one it replaced. Both front and rear suspension were major steps forward from their 1954 counterparts. In the front a ball joint suspension with tilted coil springs and new control arm geometry combined with outrigger positioned rear springs (9" longer than in 1954) to give the new Chevrolet vastly improved handling.

Walt Woron (*Motor Trend,* December, 1954) summed up his impression of the quality of the new Chevy's handling by going out on a limb and writing: "I wouldn't be afraid to stack it up against many of the so-called sports cars." *Road & Track* was a bit less enthusiastic about the Chevrolet's prowess in this area, noting in its February, 1955 issue that there was "plenty of room for improvement in this department."

The new Chevrolets were first shown to the press at GM's Proving Ground on October 12, 1954. The Chevy's new styling, exciting as it was, took a back seat to its new 265cid V-8. Much has been written about this engine and deservedly so. In terms of durability, versatility, production costs (Roger Huntington once estimated that Chevrolet could build this V-8 for just a little more than what it cost Ford and Plymouth to build their V-8s), and sheer ability to produce gobs of power it stands as one of the finest American engines ever produced.

In both its wedge-type combustion chamber shape and its over-square design (3¾" bore and 3" stroke) the Chevrolet V-8 was similar to the earlier Oldsmobile and Cadillac V-8s. Although its displacement was at 265 cubic inches relatively modest, the Chevrolet V-8s fairly gener-

ous 3¾" bore allowed large, 1¾" intake and exhaust valves to be used. Likewise the exhaust ports were for an engine of this size, huge.

Anyone having their first look at Chevy's "Turbo-Fire" V-8 was impressed by its incredibly compact dimensions. Its block measured only 22" in length and total engine width a mere 26½."

Most Chevy V-8s destined for use in family sedans and wagons carried a single 2-barrel carburetor and were rated at 162bhp gross (137bhp, net). If a standard transmission was ordered the V-8 was equipped with solid valve lifters whereas Powerglide V-8 used hydraulic tappets. In both cases the horsepower rating remained unchanged.

Eager to avoid a problem similar to that which Ford experienced in 1954 with the camshafts of their new ohv V-8, Chevrolet went to great lengths to make certain that their new engine was as trouble free as possible. A step in this direction was the electronical balancing of each engine after its assembly. Furthermore, the new V-8 passed the usual tests for durability with flying colors. In one such trial a V-8 ran for 35 hours at 5,500 rpm without

The 50 millionth General Motors car — a 1955 Chevrolet Bel Air Sport Coupe. Built and introduced on November 23, 1954, it marked the first time any auto manufacturer had reached this milestone. The '55 Chev can easily be counted as one of the most attractive post-war cars.

This '57 Two-Ten Sport Sedan is a natural progression from the "all new" '55s and pretty '56s.

failure.

Right from their initial press preview the evidence was overwhelming that the Chevrolet had become, virtually overnight, one of the world's best performing sedans. Mixed in among the various production models at GMs Proving Ground for th October 12, 1954 Press Day was "Ed Cole's Baby," a four door Bel Air equipped with what was to become part of the jargon used by automobile minded America, the "power-pack." The official title for this performance option was the "Plus Power Package" but this term never caught on. Whatever you wanted to call it, A Chevy duly equipped was a car to be reckoned with. For $55 the buyer received a 4-barrel carburetor, an intake maniforld with larger ports, and dual exhausts. Horsepower went up to 180 (160 net). In this form the V-8 weighed just 469 pounds dry.

What a great car a '55 Chevy with power pack was. For well under $2,500 you could get a nicely appointed Two-Ten coupe with the 180bhp engine and three-speed overdrive transmission that could hustle you from zero to 60mph in 9.7 seconds. Mounted on a 115" wheelbase and weighing just under 3,400 pounds the Chevy was a lithe little machine with only 18.9 pounds for each horsepower to tote around.

Furthermore it was a fairly economical car. *Road & Track* (February, 1955) reported obtaining an average 24.4mpg for some 300 miles of driving around which included "cruising at 80 . . . occasionally hitting 90 . . . getting 100mph (in second gear overdrive) and making lots of use of the kickdown.

As would be expected, Chevrolets were in abundance at the 1955 Daytona Speed Week. While not the fastest cars on the sand the power-pack Chevys were near the top. In the flying mile competition the fastest Chevy was clocked at 112.877mph. The only faster were the Chrysler 300 (127.580mph), Cadillac (120.478mph), Buick Century (116.345mph) and a Chrysler New Yorker (114.631mph). In acceleration over a one mile distance from a standing start the Chevrolet's power and light weight (almost 200 pounds less than a comparable Ford) put it very near the top of the pile. Only Cadillac with a speed of 80.428mph proved superior to the Chevrolet's best run of

This is the 1957 Bel Air convertible. It is quickly becoming one of the most desirable collector cars in America; with or without speed equipment.

placement of 283 cubic inches was to be a familiar figure in a couple of years. Numerous Chevrolets with this larger bore plus a longer ¼" stroke allowing a 306cid prowled not only the nation's dragstrips but its highways as that grand old American tradition known as street racing took on a new and far more interesting form.

Chevrolet's slogan for 1956, "The Hot One's Even Hotter" indicated that it had no intention of relinquishing its position as one of America's great high performance automobiles. Things got off to a fast start on September 9,1955 when Zora Arkus-Duntov drove a pseudo-disguised '56 Chevrolet to set a new stock car record up the 12.42 mile run (which also included 170 sharp turns) to the summit of Pikes Peak, 14,110 feet above sea level.

Duntov's time of 17 minutes, 24.05 seconds shattered Cannonball Baker's old mark of 19 minutes, 25.7 seconds which had stood for 21 years. Both Baker and NASCAR President Bill France were interested on-lookers to Duntov's achievement. After the run was completed, officials from NASCAR, which sanctioned the run, tore the car

Bel Air Beauville Station Wagon

The 1955-1957 wagons haven't escaped the loving eye of collectors. The car came in both two and four-door models.

78.158mph. For the record, some comparative speeds were: Chrysler 300 (77.436mph), Ford (73.428mph) and Plymouth (72.072mph).

It's also worth noting that given the greater rolling resistance the sand at Daytona offered to tires of a car passing over it, it's fair to say that a 180bhp Chevy was a good deal quicker and faster than its Daytona speeds would indicate.

In June, shortly after the 1955 Indianapolis "500" at which a red and white Chevrolet Bel Air convertible served as the Pace Car the 195bhp hotter cammed V-8 which had been an option in the Corvette became available for all Chevrolets.

At this point Chevrolet became *The Car* at National Hot Rod Association drag strips from coast to coast. A similar situation existed in NASCAR stock car competition where Chevrolet won 13 of 25 short track events in 1955. In addition, Chevrolets finished second 11 times, and third 12 times. Its closest competitor, Dodge won only five races.

During the 1955 racing season some hot rodders jumped the gun on Chevrolet and took it upon themselves to increase its internal dimensions. Frank McGurk of Inglewood, California produced pistons for Chevrolet engines that were bored out an additional ⅛". The resulting dis-

down and certified it as a stock car. Eventually Chevrolet also made it available for press use, the only change made being the replacement of its heavy duty clutch with a standard unit.

The 1956 Chevrolets underwent a fairly substantial sheet metal change that was, as face lifts go, quite successful. 19 models were available including nine passenger sedan and the then current hot styling idea from Detroit, the four door hardtop.

1956 Chevrolets also offered seat belts and shoulder harnesses as options. Like Ford and virtually all American producers, Chevrolet found customer interest in these features rather limited.

The 1955 Chevrolet's suspension was carried over into 1956 with only minor changes, the most notable being a slight tilting of the front control arm which reduced nose dive in extreme braking situations by 45%. At the rear 1" wider rear spring hangers which helped fight spring compression resulting from the axle's side-thrusts under acceleration were small but worthwhile changes.

The initial high performance offering for 1956, the Super Turbo-Fire V-8 was rated at 205bhp with a 9.25:1 compression ratio. This engine used the same cam as the 170bhp V-8 which was available only with Powerglide.

Anyone who loved the sounds emitting from the twin

pipes of a '55 Power-pack Chevy was bound to be a little disappointed after his first audio experience with its 1956 counterpart for the 205bhp engine used longer mufflers and shorter exhaust pipes which made them somewhat quieter than the '55s.

The 205bhp V-8s, when hitched to a three speed transmission used a high capacity clutch of coil spring design in place of the diaphragm spring unit used on less powerful Chevrolets.

Like all Chevy V-8s the 205bhp version had a remarkably flat torque curve which was a major explanation of its phenomenal performance. At 3000rpm, torque was a respectable 268 ft.-lbs. and even at 4,600rpm where its peak horsepower of 205 was reached, stood at an impressive 234 ft.-lbs.

This gave a 205bhp Chevrolet a pretty snappy performance, especially when it was teamed up with a three speed/overdrive transmission. 60mph came up from a standing start in just 8.5 or nine seconds flat and top speed with a 3.70 rear axle was a nifty 111mph. Naturally Chevrolets that were tuned to within an inch of their lives could substantially improve on these figures.

Just before the 1956 Daytona Speed Weeks, Chevrolet made the Corvette 225bhp V-8 with dual-four barrel carburetors, 8.25:1 compression ratio and solid valve lifters optional in any model.

The 1956 version of Daytona's annual orgy of speed was marked by a high level of factory participation that followed at times a no-holds-barred format. This kept NASCAR officials charged with insuring that the cars running were bonafide production models hopping.

Quite a few Chevys at Daytona developed a strange tendency towards losing their fan belts during speed runs which had the effect of increasing their top end potential by several miles per hour. Nearly as quickly as they finished their runs however a NASCAR official was on hand to disqualify them. One such Chevrolet made one run through the flying mile at 136.62mph before receiving its pink slip from NASCAR.

Eventually the fastest "legal" Chevrolet recorded a new class record of 121.335mph for the flying mile with a second Chevy reaching 81.335mph for the standing start mile run. In this event Chevrolet could not quite equal the winning speed of a Dodge D-500 of 81.78mph. It's also worth noting that prior to the Daytona Speed Week a 240bhp Plymouth Fury had been clocked at 82.52mph for the standing start mile. Overall at the 1956 Daytona Speed Week, Ford with 584 points to Chevrolet's 566 was awarded the Pure Oil Manufacturers Trophy.

The last year for the Chevrolet body introduced in 1955 was the 1957 model run. To many Chevrolet fans 1957 is the year as far as they are concerned. Whether or not the styling of the '57 is superior to that of the '55 and '56 models is obviously a matter of personal choice, but judging from the current *Old Cars Price Guide* the '57s seem to have the edge.

Both Ford and Plymouth broke with the normal three year cycle of new body designs and emerged with new bodies and in Plymouth's case a fairly sophisticated torsion bar suspension for 1957. It's definitely a tribute to the quality of the 1955 Chevrolet's styling that it could be sufficiently updated to enable Chevrolet to finish in a virtual deadheat with Ford in the 1957 production race. According to Ray Miller's *Chevrolet-U.S.A.-1*, Ford produced 1,522,408 1957 model cars to Chevrolet's 1,522,549.

It's hard to determine which was the greater catalyst to sales, Chevrolet's styling or its ability to perform. In both cases Chevrolet was loaded for bear. Although my personal preferences leans to the '55s as the best looking Chevrolet of the 1955-57 era, the current and apparently timeless greater appeal of the '57 as a collector's car seems to put me in the minority.

"Sweet, Smooth and Sassy" was how Chevrolet described its 1957 models with that last adjective obviously intended as a succinct description of its performance capability. Even if the '57s had been visually unchanged the availability of the "Ramjet" fuel injection system on any Chevrolet would have assured Chevy of a good deal of favorable publicity.

With the introduction of this system Chevrolet became the first American car to offer fuel injection on its passenger cars. More over its top form, the "Super Turbo-Fire 283," with 283bhp at 6,200 rpm became a member of the elite "one horsepower per cubic inch club" which had always had a distinctly European character to it.

It's no wonder that with this engine to back its ad claims up, that Chevrolet could print advertisements with copy that read: "Chevy Comes to the Line *Loaded* for '57! That's the big scoop this season — for Chevrolet has more goodies under that bold hood that you'll find this side of Stuttgart!"

Built by GM's Rochester Products Division, which provided them to Chevrolet completely adjusted and ready for installation. Chevrolet's fuel injection system was a continuous flow unit in which a fuel pump supplied fuel to a fuel bowl where a high pressure gear pump, driven by a cable stemming from the distributor housing sent it on to the fuel control valve. This pump was capable of providing up to 200 pounds pressure. At the fuel control valve a spill plunger, controlled by the pressure inside the valve chamber determined, along with diaphragms by both airflow through an air meter and past a throttle valve, the volume of gas going to the injector nozzles. At the nozzles air was mixed with the gas with the combination then sprayed into each intake port.

In a fuel injected Chevrolet there was no acceleration lag as was the case occasionally with Chevys equipped with dual four barrel carbs, although some early F.I. Chevrolets did experience problems that caused a fuel cut-off during acceleration. A second problem, rough idling which occurred when the fuel nozzles got warm was solved by slightly increasing their length which extended them into the airstream. Furthermore the fuel injection system was unaffected by altitude and the position of the car. Thus there was no fuel starvation in hard cornering.

Chevrolet V-8s for 1957 were offered both in 265 and 283 cubic inch versions. The 265cid, 162bhp V-8 was available only when linked either to a three speed or overdrive equipped Chevrolet.

The larger V-8 derived its extra cubic inches from a growth in bore to 3.875" from 3.75" and came in 185, 220, 245, 250, 270 and 283 horsepower rating. All V-8s of 220 and more horsepower using manual transmissions had semi-centrifugal clutches which Chevrolet claimed produced greater force on the pressure plate.

The 270hp V-8 with two four-barrel carburetors used the famous Duntov cam and solid valve lifters of the 283hp fuel injected engine.

This seemed destined to end the flow of high performance cars from Chevrolet or any other manufacturer for that matter. But the American competitive spirit and the half-century old love affair Americans had enjoyed with their automobiles were twin forces too powerful for any scrap of paper to stifle and for Chevrolet and its compatriot competitors. The best was yet to come.

William L. Mitchell — Proponent Of "Good Automotive Design"

Probably no individual in the past half century has had so great an impact on international design trends as has William L. Mitchell.

Although his name may not be familiar to everyone, his work certainly is.

Mitchell served as Vice President of Design for General Motors Corporation from 1958 until his retirement in July, 1977. In that capacity, Mitchell was responsible for the appearance of the wide variety of products produced by GM's domestic divisions and foreign subsidiaries. Chief among those products, which ranged from small appliances to massive earthmoving equipment, were the cars and trucks of GM's automotive division.

In the nineteen years Mitchell held that position, he was responsible for the design of more than 100,000,000 individual Chevrolet, Pontiac, Oldsmobile, Buick, Cadillac, and G.M.C. car and truck models. His innovative approach to design resulted in exciting, trend setting vehicles that firmly established GM as the automotive style leader while setting design standards for the entire industry.

Many of the designs conceived by Mitchell were immediately acclaimed as "classics" and proved to be among the best selling automobiles in history. The 1938 Cadillac 60 Special, The Chevrolet Corvette Sting Ray, the Buick Riviera, the Chevrolet Camaro, the Oldsmobile Toronado, the Cadillac Eldorado, and the last two Cadillac Seville models, including the 1980, are among them. These vehicles had a profound effect on the taste levels and lifestyles of every American as well as millions more people around the world.

Mitchell joined GM as a member of the Cadillac design staff at twenty-three years of age. A year later, in 1936, he became Chief Designer for Cadillac. His first production car, the 1938 Cadillac 60 Special, has been described as the vehicle that ushered in the "modern era" of automotive design. It was certainly a departure from any car produced up to that time. It had a much lower profile, no running boards, a tremendously increased amount of window area, and the slenderest possible roof supports which gave it an appearance similar to the hardtop designs Mitchell would later introduce.

Under Mitchell's design stewardship, Cadillac became the most prestigious, most wanted car in America, and the name itself became a synonym for excellence.

1963 Corvette

William L. Mitchell (Right)

1958 Chevrolet Impala On Its Way to Fame

By Pat Chappell

1958 Impala convertible.

IMPALA. Webster defines it as "a gracefull fast-running antelope from the African plains." But for GM's Chevrolet Division in 1958 it was the beginning of a new image. The first Impala is now becoming one of Chevy's more collectible entries.

In 1958 Chevrolet introduced the Impala, which in time expanded to an incredibly successful model line. Additionally, 1958 was a unique one-year-only body design. The original Impala was limited to the highly collectible two-door hardtop coupe and convertible body styles, exclusive not only in trim but in sheet metal which differed from the cowl back. The name Impala had originated for a 1956 GM show car, and 1958 production styling bore a definite relationship to both the 1955 Biscayne and the 1956 Corvette Impala Motorama entries.

The first Impala was introduced by Chevrolet Division on Oct. 31, 1957, weighing in at 3,650 pounds on a 117.5 inch wheelbase, 209 inches long, 77 inches wide and 56 inches high.

For 1958 Chevrolet regained the title of "U.S.A. Number 1," capturing the sales lead it had lost to Ford the year before. Coming back with a brand new design, more powerful engines (the 348 cid V8 Turbo Thrust made its debut), a new Cadillac-inspired X-member frame, all coil-spring suspension, and an "upper" Bel Air series of fleet-footed Impalas, the Division handily outsold Ford by a

1958 Impala Trim

quarter million units. It also gleaned 30 percent of the passenger car market for the first time in history while Ford dropped to 22.3 percent and Plymouth to 9.6 percent.

Chevrolet for 1958 was completely different from the Division's entries of 1955-57 and those to follow in 1959. A one-year offering was quite unusual for any division.

Clare MacKichan, head of the Chevrolet Design Studio during that era, said '58 styling was axed after one year because "in 1959 we went to a shared body shell with Pontiac, Oldsmobile and Buick. This was an effort to save money in the corporation. The idea was to make the outer surfaces different so that nobody would know they were shared, but the things underneath that cost the major amount of money would be shared."

The 1958 Chevy Impala — limited to 125,480 two-door hardtops and 55,989 convertibles — represented 15 percent of total production of 1,217,047 for the model year. It was an attractive model in many ways, but particularly pleasing to the eye were the sheet metal variations.

The Impala sport coupe had its own distinctive roof which wore a chrome-edged, rear facing dummy air scoop in the curved contour crease molded into the back of its roof. Other sheet metal special to the Impala involved the lower body from the "A" piller back: different dimensions in doors, rear compartment lid, and rear fender panel extensions. Understandably, these sheet metal changes dictated special glass. Though the Impala was the same size and weight as the Bel Air sport coupe, the rear deck was longer, resulting in a shorter interior compartment.

The two-tone paint treatment was handled differently for the Impala with the secondary color application limited to the roof of the sport coupe and the fabric top of the convertible. Distinctive wheel covers, stainless steel rocker panel trim, and a large, dummy chrome plated air

1958 Impala with Continental Kit

develop. Hidden in the shadow of these highly popular cars for the last decade, the Impala is just recently emerging into popularity among automotive enthusiasts.

The Impala attracts young, middle-aged and older automotive hobbyists and collectors alike. It lends itself comfortably to both stock and modified restorations. Strictly stock ones often wear numerous factory accessories like continental kit, dual rear-mounted antennae, simulated exhaust ports on the rear quarter, and wonder-bar radios mounted in the dashboard.

With the growing interest in 1958 Chevys in general, it was inevitable they would be accepted in the hobby club structure. Welcomed by VCCA, and more recently by AACA, as well as VMCCA and CHVA, it was actually the National Impala Association and The Late Great Chevrolet Association (1958-1964 Chevrolets) that started helping members with technical information and parts availability.

Editorial Director Bob Snowden, of the Late Great Chevys, said that presently more parts are available for 1958 Chevys than the other years within the club, and even more are on the way.

Impala owners are faced with the same problem that 1955-1957 Chevy Nomad owners used to have: finding trim parts and sheet metal particular to the model. But Impala owners, unlike Nomad owners, have *numbers* on their side. Consider the following. From 1955-1957 only 23,000 Nomads were produced. For 1958, 181,000 Impalas were built — eight times as many. Even if only one-eighth of the Impalas survive (and it's estimated about one-fourth do), the number of 1958 Impalas which remain would be equal to the *original* production of Chevy

1958 Impala 2dr Hardtop

scoop directly in front of the rear wheel well were all variations on the basic 1958 theme. From the rear, the Impala was particularly identifiable: The triple taillamp arrangement graced the right and left of the automobile.

The Impala's interior, designed by Ed Donaldson, had many hallmarks identifying it. The competition style two-spoke deep hub steering wheel was trimmed with an Impala medallion. The door trim panels had brushed anodized aluminum inserts which were color coordinated to match the horizontally striped seat upholstery which blended with the exterior paint.

Collector interest in the 1958 Chevy Impala, unlike its older brothers, 1955-57 Chevys, has been slow to

Nomads, i.e. 23,000 — a considerable and ripe market for reproduction manufacturers.

Even though 1958 Chevy Impalas, like 1955-1957 Nomads, had numerous rust problems involving the headlight area, lower front fenders, rocker panels, rear wheel well, lower rear quarters and floors, we've seen a good many Nomads develop — via N.O.S. and repro parts — from virtual rust buckets to sound restorations during the last decade.

And, like the Nomad, from the "A" pillar forward, the first Impala was basically the same as any other Chevy that year, and 1,217,000 1958 Chevys were manufactured, so many parts and sheet metal are still available.

Chevy II's 'Super-Thrift' 4

By Robert C. Ackerson

1962 Chevy II 300 4dr Sedan (Center)

Everyone knows how terrible the Detroit auto industry treats the poor, gullible, misguided consumer. Remember all those nasty high performance cars of the sixties that were stuffed down our unwilling throats? Recall all those scenes of thousands of young people being brainwashed by crafty ad copy writers into purchasing those undesirable Road Runners, Chargers, 427 Super Sport Chevys, Mach I Mustangs and of course that absolutely outrageous GTO?

That's the way many self ordained critics of the automobile industry would like automotive history to be written. The only problem is that it wasn't that way at all and it still isn't. We bought what we bought back then because we wanted to; it's as simple as that. If you were hooked on foreign-econo cars you drove a VW Bug. If power was your game a Road Runner with a 440-Six pack was tucked away in your garage. Freedom was the name of the game. You shopped around, took a lot of test drives, tried your hand at haggling and then found it hard to wait till the day you took delivery.

Mort Sahl once said that "If the government made a car in America I guess it would be a two-door gray Valiant." Now don't get me wrong, I've nothing against two-door gray Valiants but the idea that someone else is going to decide what's best for me doesn't square very well with Jefferson's belief that we *all* possess the right to pursue happiness without some super-sized government getting into the act.

A far better way of deciding what kind of automobiles are to be built is to let the buyer decide which are best suited to his needs and economic positions. In other words let him pick the car that will make him happy. It's a pretty simple idea and furthermore it works!

After all that's been said and written about the Edsel the reason for its demise was simple, that not many people wanted it; in other words ownership of an Edsel didn't make many people happy.

Almost at the same time the Edsel bit the dust, Chevrolet was choking on some airborne dirt kicked up by the sales success of the Ford Falcon. Ed Cole had high hopes for the Corvair but in sales it was no match for the Falcon. The old marketplace sent a loud and clear message back to Chevrolet. American economy car buyers (apparently) liked their economy cars straight forward and practical. No fancy rear-engine and swing-axle jive for them. Within months Chevrolet responded with its "Car H" project. Its goal was to develop an automobile of "maximum functionalism with thrift . . . to provide good basic transportation for the average American family and at the most reasonable cost. This includes not only the original purchase price but also more economical operating and maintenance expenses."

The end result of the Car H project was of course the Chevy II which debuted in 1962 and which as the Nova was in production until 1979 when the Citation was introduced. Although it was extremely orthodox in design, the Chevy II did possess several interesting technical features, the most interesting being its single leaf rear spring which was subjected to laboratory testing that duplicated 1,500,000 miles of highway driving.

But, to anyone who has looked under the hood of a Chevrolet Citation, the Chevy II's most interesting feature was its four cylinder engine for the X-cars gutsy little four-banger is really nothing more than that Chevy II engine brought up to date.

When Chevrolet put the Chevy II into production most journalists were more interested, after taking a few measurements, in reporting that a 327 cid V8 would fit under its hood rather than detailing the features of the Chevy II's four-cylinder engine. Such bias was understandable since this was the early spring of the great age of American performance cars and in that environment a U.S.-built four-banger was nothing more than a white crow.

As a result, sales of Chevy II's with the 153 cid-four never amounted to anything. For example they were installed in only 2% of all 1963 Chevy II's. Yet at the same time some 12% of the Chevy II's assembled were equipped with the Super Sport trim package that carried a $161.40 price tag . . . *Car Life* magazine (December 1963) thus concluded "This luxury-oriented market of today just isn't interested in 4 cyl. engines . . . The slightly improved gas mileage and lower first cost, as compared to a six, doesn't mean a thing. This is one area where GM market forecasters guessed wrong." Yet Chevy continued the four through 1970 after which it remained dormant until resurfacing as Pontiac's Iron Duke in 1977.

One reason why Chevrolet persisted so long with the four was the low cost of keeping it in production. A new automated assembly line was used for both the four and six cylinder engine and since both shared many parts with the 283 V8 (such as pistons, rods and some valve-train components) they were not expensive to produce. At the same time the little four was one tough engine. Along with the 194 cid six, it had chalked up nearly one million miles of pre-production testing and its simple but rugged design along with five bearing crankshaft and high-chrome cast iron cylinder head, gave it an excellent record of reliability at the hands of its owner.

Compared to the 194 six and 283 V8 the four was a lightweight engine, tipping the scales at just 360 pounds; comparative weights for the other engines were 455 and 596 pounds respectively. When compared to the four-cylinder engine Pontiac used for its early Tempest, the Chevy II four was 21% smaller in displacement but weighed 35% less! With fairly good breathing characteristics the little four developed 90 hp at 4400 rpm and 152 lb. ft. of torque at 2400 rpm. This latter output equalled just about one lb. ft. per cubic inch. In late 1961 Chevrolet published a power curve for the 153 cid four that placed its net horsepower and torque output at 75 and 144 respectively.

Obviously a Chevy II with this engine was not a performance car. With Powerglide its zero to 60 mph time was 20 seconds. A three speed stick model didn't do too bad though, reaching 60 mph in 17 seconds. This wasn't "Chevy Two Much" performance but remember that with just 360 pounds of engine weight on its front wheels a four cylinder model was the best handling Chevy II and both metallic brake linings and genuine, knock-off wirewheels were available. A 2-door Chevy II in the lowest priced "100" series had a base price of $1827 and with the aforementioned options would have made for a neat, sporty and economical car in the early sixties. Today it would make for a neat, sporty, economical and *different* car to share a collector's garage with a Nova 396SS.

Late Sixties 4-cylinder Chevy II's were available with Torque-Drive, a semi-automatic transmission priced at approximately $65. That price is significant because for just $59 Chevy II customers could opt for the larger six cylinder engine.

Thus there were no tears shed when the four-cylinder Chevy engine was phased out. Lots of cars and engines have been described as being before their time but somehow, such pompous declarations don't seem to be appropriate for what was really just a simple no-nonsense economy engine. But what the heck, with gas prices creeping up to the $1.50 per gallon mark somebody might just speak out and say, "hey, remember that little 4-cylinder Chevy II that came out back in '62? Now that *was* a better idea!"

A Legacy of Muscle Kept Growing Through Chevelle's Short Life

By R. Perry Zavitz

The beginning of the 1978 models unfortunately brought an end to the Chevelle. With the drastic change in dimensions and design of the intermediate Chevrolet, it perhaps seemed an opportune time to break with the past and drop the Chevelle name. Over its 14 year life-span, some 5,000,000 units of that popular model were built and sold.

While demand for compact cars remained too strong to ignore, and the standard size models grew with abandon during the early-mid 60s, a chasm developed between the two. For 1962 Ford fielded a redesigned Fairlane to fit into the obvious gap. By 1965 Plymouth evolved a Belvedere for middleweight class.

The only new car when the 1964 models first appeared was the Chevelle, Chevrolet's entry in the in-between size. Overall length was 193.9 inches for all models but the station wagon. That made the Chevelle 16 inches shorter than the full-size Chevrolets, but 11 inches longer than the Chevy II. It was comparable in length and wheelbase to the contemporary Fairlane. Incidently, the first Chevelle had the same wheelbase and was 1.1 inch shorter overall than the Chevrolet of one decade before.

That Chevrolet had a choice of just one engine — two if you consider the higher output standard with Powerglide. By contrast, the Chevelle was introduced with seven engine choices. They ranged from the small 194 cid, 120 hp. six, and the larger 230 cid. 155 hp. six, through the 283 cid. V-8 with 195 or 220 hp.

Four different transmissions were available — the standard three-speed manual, Powerglide automatic, overdrive, and four-speed manual. Only with the 283 V-8's could any of these four transmissions be ordered. Transmission options were limited on the other engines, nevertheless, a total of 20 engine/transmission combinations were obtainable.

Chevelle came in 11 models in three series. The 300 series (no relation to the Chrysler 300) offered two and four-door sedans, and two and four-door station wagons. The Malibu, the name still used in 1978, offered a four-door sedan, two-door hardtop, convertible, six-pass. wagon, and nine-pass. wagon. The top series Malibu Super Sport had a two-door hardtop and a convertible. Prices spread from $2,231 for the 300 two-door to $3,240 for the Malibu four-door station wagon.

Oh yes, there was one more related model. The El Camino returned after a three year hiatus, utilizing the 115 inch Chevelle wheelbase, and front end styling.

Styling for the Chevelle could be described as contemporary conservative, but pleasant. Nothing about the styling would excite anyone, but by the same token nothing would upset anyone — a wise way to introduce a new car.

Production took place in Baltimore, Md. Kansas City, Mo. and a new plant at Fremont, Calif. A total of 338,286 Chevelles were built in its first model year. A very substantial sum indeed for a new model, and it accounted for 4.3% of the industry's production for the model year. Of all '64 Chevrolets, 14.5% were Chevelles. Sales of the Chevelle during calendar 1964 were a success, and lead Fairlane by a five to four margin.

The 1965 Chevelle got a redesigned grille, but otherwise its styling remained much the same as before. Yet the car managed to grow about three inches longer. The 300 series had a two-door wagon instead of a four-door wagon. A new 300 DeLuxe series had a four-door wagon, as well as two and four-door sedans. The Malibu line remained as before, but with nine pass. wagon discontinued. The Malibu Super Sport offered a two-door hardtop and convertible again.

Engine availabilities were changed to include the 327 cid V-8 in Chevelle's second year. The rating of the larger six and the most potent V-8 were raised to 140 and 350 h.p. respectively. There was no 220 h.p. V-8 for '65.

Probably the rarest of all Chevelle models was the SS 396, of which only 201 were built.

The special batch of super Chevelles was assembled at the Kansas City assembly plant early in 1965. The special RPO Z-16 package built around the new 375 hp. engine was designed to effectively showcase it. The cost for the option package was $1501.05, shoving the price of a Chevelle SS hardtop so equipped to more than $4500.

Besides the very heavy duty engine, the buyer got a four-speed, special exterior and interior trim, vinyl top, fake Chevy mag wheels, Goodyear gold line tires, bumper guards and even Delco's new AM-FM Multiplex stereo system. On the dash a 160 mph speedometer and a tach red lining at 5800 rpm reminded the driver that he was not chauffeuring just a jazzed up car with no real guts.

Chevrolet had to do considerable beefing underneath the Chevelle to provide for the punishment of the 375 h.p. 396. Convertible frames, with bracing, were used, although all 201 units were apparently hardtops. The

1970 Chevelle SS-454

driveline was strengthened in many areas. Sometimes the modifications, as in the case of the brakes, involved the mere substitution of units from the big Chevs of the same year. The engine itself was the same as the 425 h.p. Corvette 396 introduced concurrently, except that it used hydraulic lifters instead of the 'Vette's solids.

Motor Trend tested one of the very few '65 SS 396s to reach California late in 1965. They called it, "...the hottest and finest car of its type ever made."

The Chevy 396, which emerged from the famous 1963 Chevrolet racing engine, would appear in many subsequent Chevelles. But none could ever match the power or scarcity of the first 201 '65 SS 396s, just as *Motor Trend* inadvertently predicted.

1969 Malibu Convertible

1969 Malibu Convertible Interior

Prices were reduced on 1964's comparable models. They started at $2,109 for the 300 two-door — the lowest basic list price of any Chevelle. The most expensive was the Malibu Super Sport convertible at $2,690. Production of the '65 model increased modestly to 343,894.

Entirely new styling appeared on the 1966 Chevelles. Still a bit conservative, perhaps the most unusual styling feature was found on the two-door hardtops. The flat rear window was on a steeper slope than the rear quarter roof panels. The result was a flying buttress shape. This was fashionable in the mid 60's, but was originated by John Fitch on his Sprint conversions of the first generation Corvairs.

Wheelbase was stretched an inch to 116 inches, but overall length remained approximately the same. Although 12 models were offered as before, there was an omission and an addition. The 300 two-door wagon was gone, but in the Malibu lineup Chevelle's first four-door hardtop appeared. The Super Sport also became known as the SS 396.

The standard engine for the SS 396 was rated at 325 h.p. but 360 h.p. was optional. The extra muscle came from a four-bbl carburetor, special camshaft, and dual exhausts. Neither of these 396 engines could be ordered for any other series. They were for the Super Sports only.

There were changes in the optional V-8s for Chevelle, although the standard 283 cid, 195 h.p., V-8 remained. The 220 h.p. 283 V-8 was back after skipping the '65 models. Only one of the 327 cid. V-8s could be had. It was the 275 h.p. version.

A new model year production record was set again, when 412,155 Chevelles were built. That sum pushed the total number of Chevelles over the 1,000,000 mark.

With only minor styling alterations, the 1967 Chevelle did not sell as well as the '66. Model year production amounted to 369,133. Yet that was the car's second best year. Overall production of the '67 models was down. Chevelle still carved out for itself a 4.8% slice of the production pie, like it had done the year before. The Fairlane was not faring quite as well.

The same models were made available in the '67 lineup, with one addition. A luxurious four-door six-pass. station wagon was introduced. Called Concours, it was separate from all other series. It was easily identifiable because of the woodgrain trim along the sides and across the lower part of the tailgate.

Some changes occurred in the engine compartment for '67. The 194 cid. six was dropped. The 230 cid. six became standard. The 250 cid. 155 h.p. six of the full-size Chevrolets was available optionally for the first time in the Chevelle. What was referred to as the standard V-8, the 195 h.p. motor, was the only 283 cid. V-8 available. The optional 327 V-8 could be had in either 275 h.p. or 325 h.p. potencies. The 396 V-8 was still only available in the Super Sport models. The advertised horsepower of the high-output version was reduced to 350 h.p.

No fewer than six transmission choices were offered. In addition to the previous four, a new special three-speed floor mounted stick shift was available with any engine. It was standard in the SS 396. An option in those models, but not in the other lines was GM's Turbo Hydra-Matic.

A new body appeared on the 1968 Chevelle. The sedans and wagons kept their 116 inch wheelbase, while growing to 201 inches overall. The coupes and convertibles were four inches shorter in both wheelbase and overall length. In this case the term coupe was used in the literal sense. It comes from the French word for "cut". These models were in effect cut shorter than the sedans.

The 14 models offered again represented a few changes. The four-door sedan was no longer offered in the 300, but a four-door wagon was. New to the 300 DeLuxe line was a two-door hardtop. There were four Chevelle wagons and all were four-door six-pass., models. The 300 version was called Nomad, and the 300 DeLuxe was the Nomad Custom. What a disappointment to the lovers of Chevrolet's most prestigious station wagon of '55 to '57 to find that name relegated to the marque's most austere wagons. It was probably the deliberate strategy of the sales and advertising people to cash in on the renowned image of the original Nomad. The Malibu wagon had no special name, and the Concours was no longer called a station wagon, but Estate wagon — a title borrowed from Buick.

There seems to be no evidence that the name manipulation caused difficulties. Production of the '68 Chevelle set a new record of 422,893. A production record was set in June when 49,792 Chevelles were made. To our knowledge that monthly total has not been exceeded even though model year totals have since surpassed that of '68.

Again a few changes in engine availabilities were made. The faithful old 283 V-8 was retired in '67. For 1968, the standard V-8 for Chevelle was a 307 cid motor, which developed an even 200 h.p. and was offered in addition to the 275 and 325 h.p. editions.

Chevelle had been on a two year cycle of complete restyling. The 1969 model was the off year, which often means a slight easing of a car's acceptance. Such was not the case for Chevelle, however. An increase raised the model year's production to 439,611, which was a record. That figure also represents another peak. It was 5.2% of all '69 model cars produced. That was Chevelle's greatest proportion. Also, during the '69 model run, the 2,000,000th Chevelle was built.

Series changes were made for '69. The 300 line was abandoned. The bottom line then became the 300 DeLuxe, which consisted of coupe, sedan, and hardtop. Malibu offered the same body types as before, except the station wagon. All the wagons were in a separate series of their own. The Nomad was again at the cheap end of the range (although at $2,668 its base price was $196 more than the first Nomad). Next up the wagon ladder were the Greenbriers. One was a two-seat wagon and the other a three-seat model.

(Does the name Greenbrier sound vaguely familiar? The larger Corvair station wagon of '61 to '64 — the van styled model — was called Greenbrier. But going even further into the past, there was a Nash Rambler station wagon called Greenbrier in 1953.)

The Concours also came in two and three-seat models. That is a total of five wagons, but with V-8 power two more were offered. The Concours Estate — those with woodgrain side trim — were available in two and three-seat editions. Dual-action tailgate was standard on the three-seat Greenbrier and all Concours and Concours Estate wagons. This tailgate, which also doubled as a door if you wished, was optional on the other two Chevelle wagons.

There was a Concours Sport Sedan, but it was a special exterior and interior trim option on the Malibu Sport Sedan, the four-door hardtop. Alas, the SS 396 also became an option. Offered on any coupe or the convertible for an extra $348, it meant the same as before — a 396 cid V-8 of 325 h.p. or 350 h.p. Chevelle. SS 396 insignia announced this option on virtually all sides of the car.

Another engine was retired. A 350 cid. V-8 of 255 h.p. or 300 h.p. replaced the three versions of the former 327 cid. V-8. Transmission availabilities remained the same, except for the deletion of overdrive. It is surprising to some that overdrive was offered on Chevrolets for so many years. Many people associate overdrive with Studebaker, Nash and Ford, but seldom with Chevrolet. Yet Chevrolet offered it sometimes when it was

1970 Chevelle Malibu (Non-SS) Convertible

1970 Chevelle SS-396 Sport Coupe

450

unavailable on some of those other cars.

Right on schedule, the 1970 Chevelle received a new body. The two wheelbases continued, but overall length grew an inch, although station wagons were an inch shorter than previously.

The 300 DeLuxe name was eliminated but not replaced. A coupe and sedan were in the unnamed series. Malibu offered the same body types as before. Among the wagons, six-cylinder engines were restricted to the two-seat models of Nomad, Greenbrier, and Concours. But V-8 power could be had in all these as well as the three-seat versions of the Greenbrier, Concours, and both Concours Estate models.

SS was an option on the Malibu two-door hardtop and convertible. The cost of this package was raised to $446, and included a special hood, black accented grille, and wide oval white lettered tires. Standard SS power became the 396 cid, 350 h.p. V-8, which had been the optional version. A new option was the whopping 454 cid. V-8 rated

1971 Malibu SS-454

at 360 h.p.

Other engine availability changes included a re-rating of the less potent 350 cid, V-8 to 250 h.p., down five. Another new optional engine was a 400 cid. V-8, which developed 350 h.p. (Actually this engine had a displacement of 402.3 cubic inches. It had the same stroke but 1/32 inch greater bore than the 396 cid motor).

One more transmission option disappeared. Just one three-speed manual shift was available. It could be had only with the six and the two least powerful V-8's.

Production for the '70 models was down about 10%. But so was total production for the model year, so Chevelle held onto its record share of 5.2% of total U.S.

production.

Styling changes for 1971 were minor, as might be expected. The main difference was the change to single headlights. All previous Chevelles used the dual headlight system. But at the rear, dual round taillights were inserted in the bumper.

The model range for '71 was unchanged from the year before. However, the six-cylinder engine was no longer obtainable in a growing number of body types. The Malibu four-door hardtop and convertible, as well as all wagons except the Nomad had V-8 power only.

Washington was moving into Motown, and one of the evidences of this was beginning to show up in the engine horsepower ratings. Indirectly because of exhaust emission regulations, output was reduced in many cases. The six was reduced to 145 h.p. The standard 307 V-8 remained at 200 h.p. but the optional 350's developed 245 and 270 h.p. — down five and 30 h.p. respectively. The 400 (402) V-8 was down 10% to 300 h.p. Contrary to

1972 Chevelle Malibu Sport Coupe

the trend was the 454 V-8. Its output was raised five to 365 h.p. Interestingly, an optional version producing 425 h.p. was available.

The SS package was made available on the Malibu two-door hardtop and convertible with any optional V-8 engine. The 454 V-8 was only available with the SS package, though. A hardtop with the 425 h.p. engine had a ratio of just under eight pounds per horsepower. That compared with about seven and a half pounds per h.p. for a '71 Corvette with the same engine. Pricewise the 425 h.p. SS Chevelle was about 40% less than the similar powered Corvette.

Production of the 1971 model Chevelle was down to 327,157 for its lowest total thus far. Some consolation

Standard Catalog of Chevrolet

was gained when the 3,000,000th Chevelle was built.

Several serious external influences were beginning to be felt in Detroit. The car market was behaving in an erratic manner. Certain models would be hot selling items for a few months, then interest would suddenly shift to an entirely different type of car. Perhaps such uncertainties were a factor for the 1972 Chevelle retaining for a third year its old body style. The pattern had been to change every second year without fail. Minor grillework alterations were the greatest external changes for the '72 models.

Even the model choices were static for '72. A new option package called Heavy Chevy was offered on the basic Sport Coupe hardtop. In this package, the standard engine was the 307 cid. V-8, but any other V-8, except the 454, could be ordered. Adding to the performance image, the Heavy Chevy had a special domed hood with lock pins, black grille, special side striping just below the belt line, and Heavy Chevy decals. Rally style wheels with center caps and bright big nuts also appealed to performance oriented youth. To state it simply, the Heavy Chevy was an economical SS. The SS continued as a Malibu hardtop coupe and convertible option. Any optional V-8 was available, but the 454 V-8 was exclusive with the SS.

Engine output had to be rated as net horsepower, proclaimed Washington. Actually it was a realistic move, because so much power robbing pollution paraphernalia had to be a permanent part of the engines that gross horsepower figures were meaningless exaggerations. The net ratings for '72 Chevelle engines were 110 h.p. for the six; 130 h.p. for the 307 V-8; 165 h.p. and 175 h.p. for the 350 V-8; 240 h.p. for the 400 V-8; and 270 h.p. for the 454 cid. V-8. The high-output 454 V-8 was not available.

With stifled engines, and market vagaries, the Chevelle did not sell as well in '72 as '71. However, production of 357,820 exceeded the previous year's model year total. This contradiction was probably a result of the spasmodic market.

The 1973 Chevelle donned brand new styling. On its established wheelbases, the new models were five inches, and wagons seven inches longer than before. Part of the reason for extra length was the new front bumper, which absorbed minor impacts without damage.

A record number of 17 basic models were fielded by Chevelle. The bottom line finally received a name, DeLuxe. It included a two-door coupe and four-door sedan. So did the Malibu. A new top line called Laguna also offered a coupe and sedan.

The convertible was missing in the '73 range. Equally significant, though less noticed perhaps, was the fact that the hardtop had also become extinct as far as Chevelle was concerned. The coupes and sedans were called Colonade hardtops by Chevrolet, but these models did not have a cut-off B-pillar and could not be opened above it. So, at least in our definition of the term, the Chevelle hardtop was defunct.

No fewer than 11 Chevelle station wagons were offered. Imagine nearly twice as many wagons as all other Chevelle body types combined! The Nomad name was replaced by DeLuxe. The lowest priced DeLuxe wagon had a six-cylinder motor — the only such powered Chevelle wagon.

The V-8 wagon list included a two-seat and a three-seat model in each of five series or sub-series. There were DeLuxe, Malibu, Malibu Estate, Laguna, and Laguna Estate lines. The Malibu Estate and Laguna Estate wagons each had woodgrain exterior trim. The Concours name was laid aside, then picked up later by Nova.

Incidently, all Laguna models had front end styling totally unlike the DeLuxe and Malibu. A distinctive one-piece urethane panel covered the whole front end, except for the headlights and grille of course. It served as the the bumper. Painted body color, it was dent resistant, and mounted to the new energy absorbing bumper system.

Further engine tinkering reduced net horsepower ratings still more. The six was only 100 h.p. (It was 21 years since the standard Chevrolet engine output was that low, but a comparison of gross and net horsepower is perhaps unfair.) The 307 V-8 yielded a modest 115 h.p. The lesser 350 V-8 was 145 h.p. but the other version still developed 175 h.p. net. The 400 V-8 was not available. The giant 454 was choked off at just 245 h.p. Transmission choices were dwindling too. Powerglide was no longer offered.

Standard engine for the Laguna series was the 145 h.p. 350 V-8. The Heavy Chevy was lifted from the option list, but the SS continued. It was offered on the Malibu coupe, and surprisingly on the Malibu station wagons. Power for the SS was either of the 360 V-8 versions, or the 454 V-8.

1973 model Chevelle production dropped to 328,533.

Minor appearance changes for the 1974 Chevelles were not unexpected. An extra wide Mercedes style grille embellished the front of the Malibu and Malibu Classic models. These were the new names for the lower and middle priced series. Coupe and sedan body types were offered in each line. In addition, the Malibu Classic offered a Landau coupe. It came with a vinyl covered roof, and a few other trim goodies like pin-striping, and dual mirrors.

With an unpredictable market and a serious energy crisis to face, it is understandable that the assortment of station wagons was reduced. All had V-8 power, which in retrospect turned out to be the wrong move at that time. There were two and three-seat wagons in the Malibu, Malibu Classic and Malibu Classic Estate series.

There were no Laguna wagons for '74. In fact, the Laguna line was limited to just a coupe. It was officially renamed the Laguna Type S-3.

No SS package was available for '74. Therefore the 454 engine was available on any V-8 model. Engine choices and net horsepower ratings were otherwise unchanged.

For the first time, model year production fell below 300,000 but a highlight of the year was the 4,000,000th Chevelle.

We have traced the Chevelle beyond the point where it can hardly be considered an old car, so we had better draw this review to a quick conclusion before we get kicked out of this newspaper. It should be pointed out, however, that for its remaining three model years Chevelle used the same body styling begun with the '73 models.

In 14 model years the Chevelle had grown in overall length from 193.9 inches to 209.7 (215.4 for the wagons). It was literally just one silly centimeter shorter than the '64 Impala, when the Chevelle was first introduced.

More regulations from Capital Hill have set strict minimum fuel consumption standards. To meet them the car makers, among other approaches, have been reducing size to reduce weight. No more heavy Chevys. That is why the 1978 Malibu shrunk. Coincidently the Chevelle name was left off. The Chevelle has ended, but the Malibu lingers on.

Dream Cars

The term, "Dream Car" is believed to have been penned in connection with the General Motors Motorama car shows of the early and mid-Fifties. Harley Earl, then head of General Motors Styling, used the Motorama shows to bring to the public the stylists' ideas of future automobiles.

All too often the inspired design of a stylist was hacked at and watered down by all the different committees his design passed through on its way to production. Earl used the Motorama to wake up corporate management as to what could be done given a clean slate and few restraints. The result brought forth dozens of inspired (and not-so-inspired) car designs that influenced future production more than anyone ever imagined.

Practically every auto company jumped onto the "Dream Car" bandwagon. Chrysler's Virgil Exner began an association with Ghia that lasted for over a decade.

Ford's early show cars began their second 50 years with new excitement and flair. But it was GM that really pushed the idea to the fullest. Earl's brilliant Le Sabre and Charles Chayne's Buick XP-300 had the automotive world buzzing with excitement. The public was still "starved" for anything new. World War II was still a recent memory and Europe, particularly Germany and Italy, were still in a huge rebuilding program. "Dream Cars" caught the public's fancy and millions of people thronged to auto shows all across the nation.

Among the many examples of Harley Earl's Advanced Styling Studio products, Chevrolets were abundant. The following photographs show some of the extreme styling ideas where a "no-holds-barred" approach was encouraged. Not only did some of yesterday's dreams become tomorrow's realities, but today, in the Nineties, collectors are unearthing some of these Motorama cars, and restoring them.

1953 Corvette. The Corvette was shown at the New York Auto Show in January of 1953. It was supposedly strictly a show car but public reaction was so great that Chevrolet rushed the car into production. And, on July 1, 1953, the first Corvette rolled off the line at Flint, Mich.

1958 Corvette XP 700. What began as a personal car for William Mitchell, head of GM styling, became a test bed for future Corvettes. The car started out as a stock '58 Corvette. The rear end treatment found its way to the '61 Corvette. By 1959 the XP 700 was elevated to "show car" status.
(Applegate & Applegate photo)

1960 Cerv I. The Chevrolet Engineering Research Vehicle (CERV) was used mainly for testing of suspension and steering componets.

1963 Corvette Mako Shark I XP-755. Here Mitchell has taken the 1958 XP-700 closer to the production Corvette of 1968. The engine is a supercharged version of the new 409 cubic inch powerplant. Note the functional external competition exhausts. The plastic roof is both tinted and treated inside with vaporized aluminum to deflect sunlight. The Shark door handles were flush type, with opening handles that flipped out when an integral button was pressed. (GM photo)

1962 Corvair Monza GT Coupe. William Mitchell went all out with this version of the Corvair. He named it, like the '61 Sebring Spyder, after a famous sportscar racing track — Monza, Italy. Retaining the Corvair rear engine, the fiberglass body had several unusual styling features. Entry to the car was gained when the entire forward part of the passenger compartment hinged forward in one piece. The extreme slant of the windshield was possible when the two seats were moved close together, thus allowing the rakish slant.

1964 Corvette Coupe Rondine. Built by Pininfarina in Italy, this one-of-a-kind features a reverse-slant roofline and much smoother, less aggressive front end treatment. (Applegate & Applegate photo)

1963 Corvair Super Spyder. Bill Mitchell carried the Sebring Spyder of 1962 a little farther into the "Dream Car" zone with the Super Spyder. Note the external exhaust at the rear. The front end received more aggressive styling also. This car, along with the Corvair Monza GT and Monza roadster, made its public debut at various sports car racing facilities across the country.

1965 Corvette Mako Shark II. With modification, the style set forth by the Mako II Corvette "Dream Car," became the production 'Vette for 1967.' There were no less than 17 electric motors to run such things as headlights, wipers that retracted under the hood, adjustable headrests suspended from the roof, movable venetian blind rear window shades, adjustable clutch, brake and steering wheel (all electrically adjustable), adjustable rear spoiler, remote controlled gas filler, and a retractable rear license plate (none of the above made the production version except the headlights)! (Applegate & Applegate photo)

1963 Corvair Testudo. Built by the Italian coachmaker, Bertone, this Corvair-based show car was designed by Giorgia Giugiaro, who gave the world dozens of wild and not-so-wild automobiles. To enter, the entire cockpit cap swung forward (similar to the Corvair Monza FT).

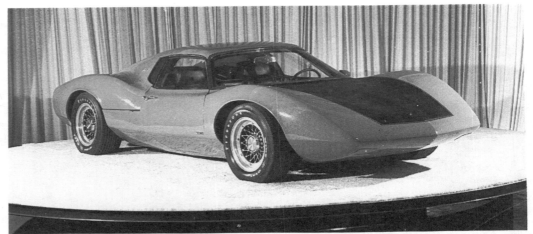

67 Astro II XP-880. Frank Winchell and Larry Nies of Chevrolet set about to design the new mid-engined Corvette for the '70s. The Astro II is the result. It had a spot-welded steel backbone frame. The radiator was mounted in the rear so that hot radiator hoses wouldn't have to pass through the passenger compartment. Engine used was the Mk IV 390 h.p. unit with power passing through a two-speed torque converter of a 1963 Pontiac Tempest transaxle. (GM photo)

1973 XP-987 GT Corvette 2-Rotor, GM was heavily into the development of the radical Wankel rotary engine in the early '70s. Two famous show cars developed during this time and this is the first one. Originally not called a Corvette, this snappy two-passenger sportscar was also considered a replacement for the German GM division's little "mini-Corvette," the Opel GT. Horsepower from the 2-rotor was about 180. The front end treatment saw production on the Chevy Monza 2-plus-2 in 1975. (Applegate & Applegate photo)

1967 Corvair Astro I. A bored-out Corvair flat six cylinder engine, displacing 176 cubic inches, powered this far out GT coupe. Unlike the earlier 1963 Monza GT, the entire pod over the passenger compartment swung up and backwards for entry (the GT's pod swung forward). The Astro was built on an 88-inch chassis and the engine put out 240 h.p. (GM photo)

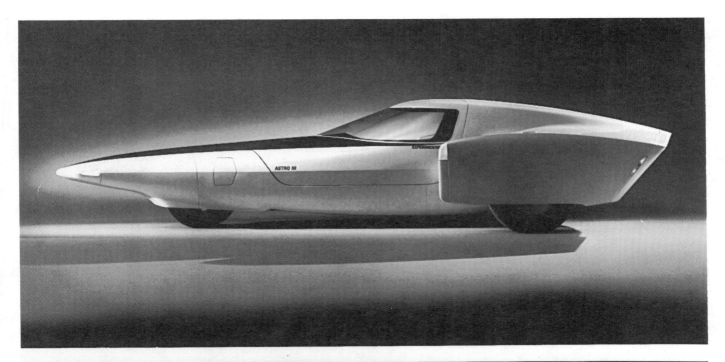

1969 Astro III. The Astro III is a two-passenger show car that features a tricycle-type wheel arrangement. It was designed with turbine-power in mind. Closed-circuit television provides rear vision. (Chevrolet photo)

GM's Fabulous Motorama Cars

by Pat Chappell

As General Motors Corporation celebrates its 75th Anniversary we can't help thinking about all the fabulous show cars and experimental models which came from the advanced styling studios of GM. The highlight in the opinion of many was the era of GM's extravagant road shows, the Motoramas. Held eight times from 1949 to 1961, these showcases of styling and engineering were a natural outgrowth of Alfred P. Sloan's yearly industrialists' luncheons which had been held in New York City in January since 1931. Over the years, Motorama played to an audience of 10.5 million people in a total of eight major cities. They were something from the golden age of postwar styling of which dreams are made. They were the grandfather of all automobile shows, before and after — the creme de la creme. What is most important, they were the first public viewing of what was to come.

Some of these show cars would go into limited production with varying degrees of change from the original. These included the Chevrolet Corvette and Nomad, Buick Skylark, Oldsmobile Fiesta, and Cadillac Eldorado Brougham. Many innovations appearing in Motoramas came on the market within a year or two of their preview. Eventually many production vehicles carried names which originated at the shows: Biscayne, Bonneville, Corvair, Cutlass, Firebird, Impala, Le Mans, Le Sabre, and Wildcat.

Newsweek called the show "a moving mountain of logistical problems." Reporters referred to the crowds at the 1955 Boston showing as "something like the equivalent of nine consecutive holiday double-headers at Fenway Park." *Collier's* saw the Motorama as "show business on wheels...GM's top salesman, its best prognosticator and barometer of business." Harley Earl, head of GM's Styling Section during those years, saw his experimental cars as "small opinion laboratories." William Mitchell, director of styling under Earl, spoke of these show cars as "the dessert in our regular meals." William F. Hufstader to whose budget Motorama was charged as vice-president of distribution for GM stated: "automobiles can't be sold out of catalogues. You have to see them to appreciate them. Motorama gives us the opportunity to display our wares in the best possible setting."

These successful shows were the responsibility of Spencer D. Hopkins, who headed GM's sales section. He was assisted by T.H. Roberts, show manager and a 34-year GM veteran. Leroy E. Kiefer was director of product and exhibit designs, and Harold B. Stubbs was the display man. The first event in 1949 was called "Transportation Unlimited" (not Motorama), and over half a million people attended the New York and Boston showings. Attendance dropped off the following year to 320,000 with a single show at the Waldorf. In 1951 and 1952 no show was held due to involvement in the Korean War and necessary military commitments.

But it was full steam ahead for 1953. That year the term "Motorama" was applied to the GM traveling exhibits which were to become memorable. Perhaps you were there at the Waldorf in 1953 and may remember ... seeing a Chevrolet Corvette for the first time (it would be in production by five months); rubbing elbows with other enthusiasts like yourself, which totalled almost one and a half million by the time the Motorama toured Miami, Los Angeles, San Francisco, Dallas, and Kansas City. Or was it the fiberglass Buick Wildcat you remember, gleaming black with vivid green upholstery about which a fan-of-the-times was heard to remark: "that's the special, the super duper, the non-stop car..." Oldsmobile's entry was a fiberglass Starfire; Cadillac's Le Mans, Eldorado and Orleans graced the ballroom floor; and Pontiac fielded its Landau.

No one seemed to know how much this extravaganza cost. One reliable magazine reported the show cost GM one and a half million dollars, while a second source estimated over four million. Spencer D. Hopkins, director, was quoted by a third publication as saying: "the Motorama costs about three times as much as most people think it does."

It was a big bucks production. It was an important time for the movers and shakers of the auto industry to combine the trip east with the inauguration of President Eisenhower in Washington that January. They flocked in from Michigan, with the "Detroiter," a crack train that ran between Detroit and NYC, carrying two extra sections the

"Corvair" was first used as a GM name for this 1954 Motorama fastback entry.

week before the show. Five hundred GM people, plus officials from other auto manufacturers, fled en masse as Motown moved to Manhattan. Meanwhile, over the road, the gigantic parade of GM trucks and vans had been enroute carrying cars, scenery, props, and a troupe of entertainers. The show was attended by 700 reporters, publishers, company officials, and celebrities and was kicked off with a high-level press party headed by Paul Garrett, GM's public relations vice-president. The next day at noon 500 auto manufacturers and banking executives met with the Company's top brass for luncheon on the Waldorf's Starlight Roof, followed by a private viewing of the show cars in the Grand Ballroom. Some have referred to the 1953 Motorama as the birthplace of the American sports car — not only was it the first glimpse of the Corvette, but four of the five divisions showed sports type experimental cars created with fiberglass bodies. These plastic beauties literally stole the show!

After the Motorama of 1953, one imagines those in charge may have commented: "That's a tough act to follow." But follow they did with a return to Waldorf-Astoria, revisiting Miami, Los Angeles and San Francisco. Dallas and Kansas City were replaced by Chicago, which at the time promised a better drawing. Attendance was excellent for 1954, with almost two million people visiting the multimillion dollar show. By then, the contemporary press had given up on exact figures. Overall, GM had retooled for 25 new production models and 11 experimental cars, and was coming off a 3.5 million car year with 45.6 percent of the market. Expansion was the name of the game with a one billion dollar program under way for 1954 and 1955.

We were to see new design features from previous show cars on actual production Buicks, Oldsmobiles, and Cadillacs for 1954: wrap-around windshields, cut-down doors via beltline dips, an overall lower and longer look. The show cars were breathtaking: one can hardly forget Buick's Wildcat II. This fiberglass convertible, only 48 inches high on a 100-inch wheelbase powered by a 220 hp V-8 engine, featured clam-shell fenders which resembled Stutz-Bearcat. The experimental "Corvette Nomad"

made its debut that January. It made a great impact on the attending public. So much so that Harley Earl phoned Clare MacKichan, head of Chevrolet Design Studio, back in Detroit. The message: "When I get back in two days I want to see that whole car (the Nomad) and how you would do it on a 1955 Chevrolet." We *were* to see the end product a year later at the 1955 Motorama.

With the unwritten law that each show must be a little more spectacular than the last, Harley Earl and his advanced styling studio, and Spencer Hopkins and his staff started planning for 1955's Motorama shortly after the '54 show was put to bed. It debuted at the Waldorf in January 1955, then toured Miami, Los Angeles, and San Francisco. Chicago, which had a good dealer show of its own, was replaced by Boston because of pressure from New England dealers. Turned out to be a good move, with Boston topping the other four cities with almost 600,000 attendees in nine days. Over two million attended the '55 Motorama during its five city tour. *Business Week* reported the extravaganza cost GM two million dollars. GM reported that the show sold $1.2 million worth of cars in the NYC stand alone, with 50 people a minute swarming the show at the Waldorf. Over a hundred exhibits displayed GM's huge line of products ranging from household appliances to earth movers. But the dream cars were the stars.

In many ways, the dream cars were different in 1955 from the previous years when they were almost all flashy sports models. Many noted that they looked as if they might be next year's production models. Indeed, the Chevrolet Nomad, which had been ordered by Harley Earl from the "Corvette Nomad" in 1954's Motorama would be available to buyers shortly, as would its kissing cousin, Pontiac's Safari wagon. Cadillac's Eldorado Brougham, a four passenger, four-door hardtop would be available in limited quantities by 1957. Oldsmobile's Delta "88", Chevy's Biscayne, and Buick's Wildcat III never made it to the dealer's showroom, but their names did and so did many of their features. GMC's delivery truck entry, called Expedier or L'Universelle, certainly predicted the tremendous popularity of vans in years to come.

1956 Chevrolet Impala

The Impala, Chevrolet's 1956 Motorama entry, suggested lines for 1958 production cars.

The traveling Motorama road show was something of a legend in its own time, and looking back some 30 years later, we can't help but be amazed at the logistics of the undertaking. Spencer Hopkins once remarked: "Moving the Motorama around is like moving to a new house. The carpet is the last thing you take from the old house and the first thing you put in the new one." Carpets? For 1955's show GM had five trucks for carpets...plus seven trucks for the dismantled 72-ton steel stage with five giant hydraulic arms. The entire caravan consisted of 99 red, white and blue trailers and trucks with over 1000 crates. Three hundred fifty people worked full time to run the Motorama, including 115 truck drivers, 125 in the show troupe, 115 men participating from GM's 33 divisions who oversaw the setting up and staging of their own exhibits. Additionally, part-time help was hired in each city in the form of guards, porters, local musicians, and college girls to hand out souvenirs. *Newsweek* described the phenomenon which was the Motorama show: "the cars burst onstage through a cloud of smoke, whirling on turntables on the ends of the stage's arms over a 900-square foot pool of water while the orchestra thumped from a bandshell suspended overhead..." Wow!

Suddenly it was 1956, and the gigantic show was on the road again, with repeat visits to New York in January, Miami in February, Los Angeles and San Francisco in March, and Boston in April. The Motorama continued to be a lavish display of all of GM's products which whet the appetite of the buying public and predicted what might be available in the future. The GM caravan grew even larger with 125 trucks and trailers insured for a cool five million. The props weren't cheap either, with 26 cutaway models costing between $90,000 and $100,000 each. The dream cars had cost from $200,000 to $250,000 each to produce. Remember, this was in 1956 dollars! Over two million attended the '56 viewing, and along with production models a show car was exhibited from each division. Setting the theme for the show was the titanium bodied Firebird II which combined the thinking of all five divisions. Its predecessor, Firebird I, shown at the 1954 Motorama,

was a single-seat, jet-shaped gas turbined rear-engined car which reportedly was unfit for highways due to its torrid exhaust. Firebird II, a continuation of GM's gas turbine development, was a much safer model because its power plant was placed forward. Its clear plastic top, hinged in the center, opened in gullwing fashion. We were, in time, to see a Firebird go into production from GM's Pontiac Division. However, it was to be a much milder version than its namesake.

Chevrolet's Impala predicted some of the things to come for that division in 1958, especially the name which has by now become ubiquitous. The Impala show car was eight inches lower than the regular production 1956 Chevys, and its fiberglass body was trimmed with stainless steel. Driver safety had been considered with a padded bar across the instrument panel and a steering wheel with padded center strut contoured to the chest of the driver. Pontiac's entry, Club de Mer, "strictly for use in straightaway time trials" as one auto magazine noted, was powered by a 300-horsepower V8. Oldsmobile's Golden Rocket was an extrmely aerodynamic looking two-passenger sports car. Buick's Centurion was another fiberglass beauty, four inches shorter than regular production Specials. Cadillac's town car, though it resembled the Eldorado Brougham, was designed to be chauffeur driven, aimed at the "youthful wealthy." All in all, it was a beautiful field of cars, as it was a fabulously exciting era of dream machines.

No Motorama was held in 1957, due to the rebirth of the National Automobile Show held at New York's Coliseum December 8-16, 1956, and sponsored by the Automobile Manufacturers Association. This was the first postwar National Automobile Show, a tradition which had begun at Madison Square Garden in 1900 and continued through 1940, when the threat of World War II intervened, causing the cancellation of the 1941 show. Postwar readjustments, the Korean War, and a lack of suitable show facilities were some of the reasons for the long hiatus.

The newly constructed $35 million Coliseum exhibition hall had three floors devoted to the show. Five automobile

The Corvette Nomad, show car from 1954 Motorama, was the birth of the 1955-1957 production Nomad.

manufacturers displayed 124 1957 passenger cars, and 11 truck manufacturers brought 66 trucks and busses. GM's Chevrolet Division showed its 36th millionth Chevrolet, Cadillac's $12,500 Eldorado Brougham was present, as was Pontiac's Bonneville Special convertible. The theme was "America on the Move," and it was a united effort to promote automobile sales. It gave the viewing public an opportunity to compare style against style, price against price, and quality against quality with all makes and models under the same roof.

The GM Motorama was absent from the scene in 1958, but returned for 1959, playing to a total of 600,000 in New York City and Boston. The next and final Motorama was held in 1961 in New York, San Francisco, and Los Angeles with a healthy turnout of over one million attending.

All good things come to an end, as did the fabulous GM Motoramas. Reasons for its demise were varied. Certainly the revival of the National Auto Show was one; the fact that television was drawing larger and larger audiences in the home setting was another. The tremendous annual expense was a factor, and the fear that competition was ripping off GM's brilliant styling ideas was pretty evident. Some even felt the 1964 World's Fair offered a good bit of competition.

Show cars and experimental models were still built by the advanced styling studios, and from time to time they were shown and on display in major auto shows. But the annual gala event which had brought so much excitement and pleasure to the 10.5 million lucky attendees was gone...forever.

Rumors abound about the whereabouts of all those Motorama vehicles. Were they all destroyed? Are they secretly squirreled away in the inner sanctum of GM's property? Are they in the hands of GM designers of private collectors? Have marque club enthusiasts reconstructed any according to specifications?

As General Motors prepared for its 75th Anniversary Auto Expo to be held September 24 at the Technical Center in Warren, Michigan, we had been wondering how many of these famous Motorama cars would suddenly make another appearance. Wouldn't it be exciting to see them, after all these years, alongside the production models they influenced?

A WORD ABOUT OLD CHEVROLETS...

The market for cars more than 20 years old is strong. Some buyers of pre-1980 cars are collectors who invest in vehicles likely to increase in value the older they get. Other buyers prefer the looks, size, performance and reliability of yesterday's better-built automobiles.

With a typical 1998 model selling for $20,000 or more, some Americans find themselves priced out of the new-car market. Late-model used cars are pricey, too, although short on distinctive looks and roominess. The old cars may use a little more gas, but they cost a lot less.

New cars and late-model used cars depreciate rapidly in value. They can't tow large trailers or mobile homes. Their high-tech engineering is expensive to maintain or repair. In contrast, well-kept old cars are mechanically simpler, but very powerful. They appreciate in value as they grow more scarce and collectible.

Selecting a car and paying the right price for it are two considerations old car buyers face. What models did Chevrolet offer in 1958? Which 1963 Chevy is worth the most today? What should one pay for a 1970 Impala convertible?

The *Standard Catalog of Chevrolet 1912-1998* answers such questions. The following Price Guide section shows most models made between 1912 and 1991. It helps to gauge what they sell for in six different, graded conditions. Models built since 1991 are generally considered "used cars" of which few, as yet, have achieved collectible status.

The price estimates contained in this book are current as of the publishing date of mid-1998. After that date, more current prices may be obtained by referring to *Old Cars Price Guide*, which is available from Krause Publications, 700 E. State St., Iola, WI 54990, telephone (715)445-2214.

HOW TO USE THE PRICE GUIDE

On the following pages is a **CHEVROLET PRICE GUIDE.** The worth of an old car is a "ballpark" estimate at best. The estimates contained in this book are based upon national and regional data compiled by the editors of *Old Cars News & Marketplace* and *Old Cars Price Guide*. These data include actual bids and prices at collector car auctions and sales, classified and display advertising of such vehicles, verified reports of private sales and input from experts.

Price estimates are listed for cars in six different states of condition. These conditions (1-to-6) are illustrated and explained in the **VEHICLE CONDITION SCALE** on the following pages. Values are for complete vehicles — not parts cars — except as noted. Modified car values are not included, but can be estimated by figuring the cost of restoring the subject vehicle to original condition and adjusting the figures shown here accordingly.

Appearing below is a section of chart taken from the **CHEVROLET PRICE GUIDE** to illustrate the following elements:

A. MAKE The make of car, or marque name, appears in large, boldface type at the beginning of each value section.

B. DESCRIPTION The extreme left-hand column indicates vehicle year, model name, body type, engine configuration and, in some cases, wheelbase.

C. CONDITION CODE The six columns to the right are headed by the numbers one through six (1-6) which correspond to the conditions described in the **VEHICLE CONDITION SCALE** on the following page.

D. PRICE The price estimates, in dollars, appear below their respective condition code headings and across from the vehicle descriptions.

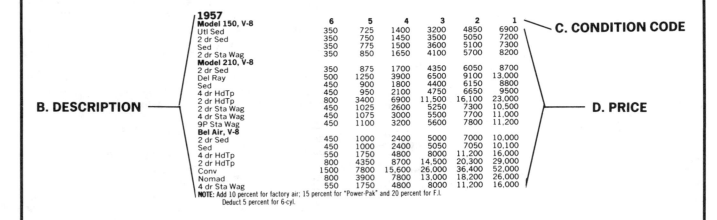

A. MAKE —— **CHEVROLET**

1957

Model 150, V-8	6	5	4	3	2	1
Utl Sed	350	725	1400	3200	4850	6900
2 dr Sed	350	750	1450	3500	5050	7200
Sed	350	775	1500	3600	5100	7300
2 dr Sta Wag	350	850	1650	4100	5700	8200
Model 210, V-8						
2 dr Sed	350	875	1700	4350	6050	8700
Del Ray	500	1250	3900	6500	9100	13,000
Sed	450	900	1800	4400	6150	8800
4 dr HdTp	450	950	2100	4750	6650	9500
2 dr HdTp	800	3400	6900	11,500	16,100	23,000
2 dr Sta Wag	450	1025	2600	5250	7300	10,500
4 dr Sta Wag	450	1075	3000	5500	7700	11,000
9P Sta Wag	450	1100	3200	5600	7800	11,200
Bel Air, V-8						
2 dr Sed	450	1000	2400	5000	7000	10,000
Sed	450	1000	2400	5050	7050	10,100
4 dr HdTp	550	1750	4800	8000	11,200	16,000
2 dr HdTp	800	4350	8700	14,500	20,300	29,000
Conv	1500	7800	15,600	26,000	36,400	52,000
Nomad	800	3900	7800	13,000	18,200	26,000
4 dr Sta Wag	550	1750	4800	8000	11,200	16,000

NOTE: Add 10 percent for factory air; 15 percent for "Power-Pak" and 20 percent for F.I. Deduct 5 percent for 6-cyl.

C. CONDITION CODE

D. PRICE

VEHICLE CONDITION SCALE

Excellent

1) EXCELLENT: Restored to current maxiumum professional standards of quality in every area, or perfect original with components operating and appearing as new. A 95-plus point show vehicle that is not driven.

Fine

2) FINE: Well-restored, or a combination of superior restoration and excellent original. Also, an *extremely* well-maintained original showing very minimal wear.

Very Good

3) **VERY GOOD:** Completely operable original or ''older restoration'' showing wear. Also, a good amateur restoration, all presentable and serviceable inside and out. Plus, combinations of well-done restoration and good operable components or a partially restored vehicle with all parts necessary to complete and/or valuable NOS parts.

Good

4) **GOOD:** A driveable vehicle needing no or only minor work to be functional. Also, a deteriorated restoration or a very poor amateur restoration. All components may need restoration to be ''excellent,'' but the vehicle is mostly useable ''as is.''

Restorable

5) RESTORABLE: Needs *complete* restoration of body, chassis and interior. May or may not be running, but isn't weathered, wrecked or stripped to the point of being useful only for parts.

Parts Car

6) PARTS VEHICLE: May or may not be running, but is weathered, wrecked and/or stripped to the point of being useful primarily for parts.

CHEVROLET PRICE GUIDE

CHEVROLET

	6	5	4	3	2	1
1912						
Classic Series, 6-cyl.						
Tr	1150	3700	6200	12,400	21,700	31,000
1913						
Classic Series, 6-cyl.						
Tr	1050	3400	5700	11,400	20,000	28,500
1914						
Series H2 & H4, 4-cyl.						
Rds	850	2750	4600	9200	16,100	23,000
Tr	900	2800	4700	9400	16,500	23,500
Series C, 6-cyl.						
Tr	1000	3250	5400	10,800	18,900	27,000
Series L, 6-cyl.						
Tr	1200	3850	6400	12,800	22,400	32,000
1915						
Series H2 & H4, 4-cyl.						
Rds	800	2500	4200	8400	14,700	21,000
Tr	850	2750	4600	9200	16,100	23,000
Series H3, 4-cyl.						
2P Rds	900	2900	4800	9600	16,800	24,000
Series L, 6-cyl.						
Tr	1150	3700	6200	12,400	21,700	31,000
1916						
Series 490, 4-cyl.						
Tr	700	2300	3800	7600	13,300	19,000
Series H2, 4-cyl.						
Rds	650	2100	3500	7000	12,300	17,500
Torp Rds	700	2300	3800	7600	13,300	19,000
Series H4, 4-cyl.						
Tr	800	2500	4200	8400	14,700	21,000
1917						
Series F2 & F5, 4-cyl.						
Rds	650	2050	3400	6800	11,900	17,000
Tr	700	2150	3600	7200	12,600	18,000
Series 490, 4-cyl.						
Rds	600	1900	3200	6400	11,200	16,000
Tr	600	1900	3200	6400	11,200	16,000
HT Tr	650	2050	3400	6800	11,900	17,000
Series D2 & D5, V-8						
Rds	950	3000	5000	10,000	17,500	25,000
Tr	1000	3100	5200	10,400	18,200	26,000
1918						
Series 490, 4-cyl.						
Tr	650	2050	3400	6800	11,900	17,000
Rds	600	1900	3200	6400	11,200	16,000
Cpe	350	975	1600	3200	5600	8000
Sed	350	840	1400	2800	4900	7000
Series FA, 4-cyl.						
Rds	650	2050	3400	6800	11,900	17,000
Tr	700	2150	3600	7200	12,600	18,000
Sed	350	975	1600	3200	5600	8000
Series D, V-8						
4P Rds	950	3000	5000	10,000	17,500	25,000
Tr	1000	3100	5200	10,400	18,200	26,000
1919						
Series 490, 4-cyl.						
Rds	500	1550	2600	5200	9100	13,000
Tr	550	1700	2800	5600	9800	14,000
Sed	350	840	1400	2800	4900	7000
Cpe	350	900	1500	3000	5250	7500
Series FB, 4-cyl.						
Rds	550	1800	3000	6000	10,500	15,000
Tr	600	1900	3200	6400	11,200	16,000
Cpe	450	1080	1800	3600	6300	9000
2d Sed	350	1020	1700	3400	5950	8500
4d Sed	350	975	1600	3200	5600	8000
1920						
Series 490, 4-cyl.						
Rds	500	1550	2600	5200	9100	13,000
Tr	550	1700	2800	5600	9800	14,000
Sed	350	1020	1700	3400	5950	8500
Cpe	450	1080	1800	3600	6300	9000
Series FB, 4-cyl.						
Rds	550	1800	3000	6000	10,500	15,000
Tr	600	1900	3200	6400	11,200	16,000
Sed	450	1140	1900	3800	6650	9500
Cpe	400	1200	2000	4000	7000	10,000
Cpe	100	300	500	1000	1750	2500
1921						
Series 490, 4-cyl.						
Rds	650	2050	3400	6800	11,900	17,0C0
Tr	650	2050	3400	6800	11,900	17,000
Cpe	450	1080	1800	3600	6300	9000
C-D Sed	450	1140	1900	3800	6650	9500
Series FB, 4-cyl.						
Rds	650	2100	3500	7000	12,300	17,500
Tr	700	2150	3600	7200	12,600	18,000
Cpe	400	1200	2000	4000	7000	10,000
4d Sed	450	1140	1900	3800	6650	9500
1922						
Series 490, 4-cyl.						
Rds	650	2050	3400	6800	11,900	17,000
Tr	700	2150	3600	7200	12,600	18,000
Cpe	400	1200	2000	4000	7000	10,000
Utl Cpe	450	1140	1900	3800	6650	9500
Sed	450	1080	1800	3600	6300	9000

	6	5	4	3	2	1
Series FB, 4-cyl.						
Rds	650	2050	3400	6800	11,900	17,000
Tr	700	2150	3600	7200	12,600	18,000
Sed	450	1080	1800	3600	6300	9000
Cpe	400	1200	2000	4000	7000	10,000
1923						
Superior B, 4-cyl.						
Rds	650	2050	3400	6800	11,900	17,000
Tr	700	2150	3600	7200	12,600	18,000
Sed	450	1080	1800	3600	6300	9000
2d Sed	450	1080	1800	3600	6300	9000
Utl Cpe	450	1140	1900	3800	6650	9500
DeL Tr	400	1300	2200	4400	7700	11,000
1924						
Superior, 4-cyl.						
Rds	650	2050	3400	6800	11,900	17,000
Tr	700	2150	3600	7200	12,600	18,000
DeL Tr	700	2200	3700	7400	13,000	18,500
Sed	350	1020	1700	3400	5950	8500
DeL Sed	450	1050	1750	3550	6150	8800
2P Cpe	450	1140	1900	3800	6650	9500
4P Cpe	450	1080	1800	3600	6300	9000
DeL Cpe	950	1100	1850	3700	6450	9200
2d Sed	350	1020	1700	3400	5950	8500
1925						
Superior K, 4-cyl.						
Rds	800	2500	4200	8400	14,700	21,000
Tr	850	2650	4400	8800	15,400	22,000
Cpe	400	1200	2000	4000	7000	10,000
Sed	450	1080	1800	3600	6300	9000
2d Sed	450	1080	1800	3600	6300	9000
1926						
Superior V, 4-cyl.						
Rds	800	2500	4200	8400	14,700	21,000
Tr	850	2650	4400	8800	15,400	22,000
Cpe	400	1300	2200	4400	7700	11,000
Sed	400	1200	2000	4000	7000	10,000
2d Sed	400	1200	2000	4000	7000	10,000
Lan Sed	400	1250	2100	4200	7400	10,500
1927						
Model AA, 4-cyl.						
Rds	800	2500	4200	8400	14,700	21,000
Tr	850	2650	4400	8800	15,400	22,000
Utl Cpe	400	1300	2150	4300	7500	10,700
2d Sed	400	1200	2000	4000	7000	10,000
Sed	400	1200	2000	4000	7000	10,000
Lan Sed	400	1250	2100	4200	7400	10,500
Cabr	650	2050	3400	6800	11,900	17,000
Imp Lan	550	1800	3000	6000	10,500	15,000
1928						
Model AB, 4-cyl.						
Rds	800	2500	4200	8400	14,700	21,000
Tr	850	2650	4400	8800	15,400	22,000
Utl Cpe	400	1300	2200	4400	7700	11,000
Sed	400	1250	2100	4200	7400	10,500
2d Sed	400	1250	2100	4200	7400	10,500
Cabr	700	2150	3600	7200	12,600	18,000
Imp Lan	550	1800	3000	6000	10,500	15,000
Conv Cabr	700	2300	3800	7600	13,300	19,000
1929						
Model AC, 6-cyl.						
Rds	850	2650	4400	8800	15,400	22,000
Tr	850	2750	4600	9200	16,100	23,000
Cpe	500	1550	2600	5200	9100	13,000
Spt Cpe	550	1700	2800	5600	9800	14,000
Sed	400	1300	2200	4400	7700	11,000
Imp Sed	450	1450	2400	4800	8400	12,000
Conv Lan	700	2300	3800	7600	13,300	19,000
2d Sed	400	1300	2200	4400	7700	11,000
Conv Cabr	750	2400	4000	8000	14,000	20,000
1930						
Model AD, 6-cyl.						
Rds	850	2750	4600	9200	16,100	23,000
Spt Rds	900	2900	4800	9600	16,800	24,000
Phae	900	2900	4800	9600	16,800	24,000
2d Sed	400	1300	2200	4400	7700	11,000
Cpe	500	1550	2600	5200	9100	13,000
Spt Cpe	550	1700	2800	5600	9800	14,000
Clb Sed	450	1500	2500	5000	8800	12,500
Spec Sed	450	1450	2400	4800	8400	12,000
Sed	450	1400	2300	4600	8100	11,500
Con Lan	700	2300	3800	7600	13.300	19.000
1931						
Model AE, 6-cyl.						
Rds	900	2900	4800	9600	16,800	24,000
Spt Rds	1000	3100	5200	10,400	18,200	26,000
Cabr	850	2750	4600	9200	16,100	23,000
Phae	900	2900	4800	9600	16,800	24,000
2d Sed	450	1450	2400	4800	8400	12,000
5P Cpe	550	1700	2800	5600	9800	14,000
5W Cpe	550	1800	3000	6000	10,500	15,000
Spt Cpe	650	2050	3400	6800	11,900	17,000
Cpe	600	1900	3200	6400	11,200	16,000
2d DeL Sed	550	1700	2800	5600	9800	14,000
Sed	450	1500	2500	5000	8800	12,500
Spl Sed	500	1600	2700	5400	9500	13,500
Lan Phae	950	3000	5000	10,000	17,500	25,000

1932

	6	5	4	3	2	1
Model BA Standard, 6-cyl.						
Rds	1050	3350	5600	11,200	19,600	28,000
Phae	1050	3350	5600	11,200	19,600	28,000
Lan Phae	1000	3250	5400	10,800	18,900	27,000
3W Cpe	650	2050	3400	6800	11,900	17,000
5W Cpe	700	2150	3600	7200	12,600	18,000
Spt Cpe	700	2300	3800	7600	13,300	19,000
2d Sed	500	1550	2600	5200	9100	13,000
Sed	550	1700	2800	5600	9800	14,000
5P Cpe	700	2150	3600	7200	12,600	18,000
Model BA DeLuxe, 6-cyl.						
Spt Rds	1100	3500	5800	11,600	20,300	29,000
Lan Phae	1050	3350	5600	11,200	19,600	28,000
Cabr	1000	3250	5400	10,800	18,900	27,000
3W Bus Cpe	700	2150	3600	7200	12,600	18,000
5W Cpe	700	2300	3800	7600	13,300	19,000
Spt Cpe	750	2400	4000	8000	14,000	20,000
2d Sed	550	1700	2800	5600	9800	14,000
Sed	550	1800	3000	6000	10,500	15,000
Spl Sed	600	1900	3200	6400	11,200	16,000
5P Cpe	700	2300	3800	7600	13,300	19,000

1933

	6	5	4	3	2	1
Mercury, 6-cyl.						
2P Cpe	450	1450	2400	4800	8400	12,000
RS Cpe	500	1550	2600	5200	9100	13,000
2d Sed	450	1140	1900	3800	6650	9500
Master Eagle, 6-cyl.						
Spt Rds	900	2900	4800	9600	16,800	24,000
Phae	950	3000	5000	10,000	17,500	25,000
2P Cpe	450	1450	2400	4800	8400	12,000
Spt Cpe	500	1550	2600	5200	9100	13,000
2d Sed	450	1170	1975	3900	6850	9800
2d Trk Sed	400	1200	2000	4000	7000	10,000
Sed	400	1200	2000	4000	7000	10,000
Conv	700	2200	3700	7400	13,000	18,500

1934

	6	5	4	3	2	1
Standard, 6-cyl.						
Sed	450	1140	1900	3800	6650	9500
Spt Rds	800	2500	4200	8400	14,700	21,000
Phae	850	2650	4400	8800	15,400	22,000
Cpe	400	1200	2000	4000	7000	10,000
2d Sed	450	1130	1900	3800	6600	9400
Master, 6-cyl.						
Spt Rds	850	2650	4400	8800	15,400	22,000
Bus Cpe	450	1450	2400	4800	8400	12,000
Spt Cpe	450	1500	2500	5000	8800	12,500
2d Sed	400	1200	2000	4000	7100	10,100
Twn Sed	400	1300	2200	4400	7600	10,900
Sed	400	1250	2100	4200	7300	10,400
Conv	750	2400	4000	8000	14,000	20,000

1935

	6	5	4	3	2	1
Standard, 6-cyl.						
Rds	650	2050	3400	6800	11,900	17,000
Phae	700	2300	3800	7600	13,300	19,000
Cpe	450	1400	2300	4600	8100	11,500
2d Sed	400	1250	2100	4200	7400	10,500
Sed	400	1300	2150	4300	7600	10,800
Master, 6-cyl.						
5W Cpe	450	1450	2400	4800	8400	12,000
Spt Cpe	450	1500	2500	5000	8800	12,500
2d Sed	400	1300	2150	4300	7500	10,700
Sed	400	1300	2200	4400	7700	11,000
Spt Sed	400	1350	2250	4500	7800	11,200
Twn Sed	400	1300	2150	4300	7600	10,800

1936

	6	5	4	3	2	1
Standard, 6-cyl.						
Cpe	450	1400	2300	4600	8100	11,500
Sed	400	1250	2100	4200	7400	10,500
Spt Sed	400	1300	2150	4300	7600	10,800
2d Sed	400	1250	2100	4200	7300	10,400
Cpe PU	450	1400	2350	4700	8300	11,800
Conv	550	1700	2800	5600	9800	14,000
Master, 6-cyl.						
5W Cpe	450	1450	2400	4800	8400	12,000
Spt Cpe	450	1500	2500	5000	8800	12,500
2d Sed	400	1300	2150	4300	7500	10,700
Twn Sed	400	1300	2150	4300	7600	10,800
Sed	400	1300	2200	4400	7600	10,900
Spt Sed	400	1300	2200	4400	7700	11,000

1937

	6	5	4	3	2	1
Master, 6-cyl.						
Conv	900	2900	4800	9600	16,800	24,000
Cpe	450	1400	2350	4700	8200	11,700
Cpe PU	450	1500	2450	4900	8600	12,300
2d Sed	400	1300	2200	4400	7600	10,900
2d Twn Sed	400	1300	2200	4400	7700	11,000
4d Trk Sed	400	1350	2200	4400	7800	11,100
4d Spt Sed	400	1350	2250	4500	7800	11,200
Master DeLuxe, 6-cyl.						
Cpe	450	1500	2450	4900	8600	12,300
Spt Cpe	450	1500	2500	5000	8800	12,500
2d Sed	400	1200	2000	4000	7000	10,000
2d Twn Sed	400	1200	2000	4000	7100	10,100
4d Trk Sed	400	1200	2000	4000	7000	10,000
4d Spt Sed	400	1200	2000	4000	7100	10,100

1938

	6	5	4	3	2	1
Master, 6-cyl.						
Conv	950	3000	5000	10,000	17,500	25,000
Cpe	450	1400	2350	4700	8200	11,700
Cpe PU	450	1500	2450	4900	8600	12,300
2d Sed	400	1300	2200	4400	7700	11,000
2d Twn Sed	400	1350	2200	4400	7800	11,100
4d Sed	400	1300	2200	4400	7700	11,000
4d Spt Sed	400	1350	2200	4400	7800	11,100
Master DeLuxe, 6-cyl.						
Cpe	450	1500	2500	5000	8800	12,500
Spt Cpe	500	1500	2550	5100	8900	12,700
2d Sed	400	1350	2200	4400	7800	11,100
2d Twn Sed	400	1350	2250	4500	7800	11,200
4d Sed	400	1350	2200	4400	7800	11,100
4d Spt Sed	400	1350	2250	4500	7800	11,200

1939

	6	5	4	3	2	1
Master 85, 6-cyl.						
Cpe	450	1400	2350	4700	8300	11,800
2d Sed	400	1250	2050	4100	7200	10,300
2d Twn Sed	400	1250	2100	4200	7300	10,400
4d Sed	400	1250	2050	4100	7200	10,300
4d Spt Sed	400	1250	2100	4200	7300	10,400
Sta Wag	850	2650	4400	8800	15,400	22,000
Master DeLuxe, 6-cyl.						
Cpe	400	1350	2250	4500	7900	11,300
Spt Cpe	450	1400	2300	4600	8100	11,600
2d Sed	400	1350	2250	4500	7900	11,300
2d Twn Sed	450	1350	2300	4600	8000	11,400
4d Sed	400	1350	2250	4500	7900	11,300
4d Spt Sed	400	1250	2100	4200	7300	10,400
Sta Wag	750	2400	4000	8000	14,000	20,000

1940

	6	5	4	3	2	1
Master 85, 6-cyl.						
2d Cpe	450	1450	2400	4800	8400	12,000
2d Twn Sed	400	1250	2100	4200	7400	10,600
4d Spt Sed	400	1250	2100	4200	7400	10,500
4d Sta Wag	950	3000	5000	10,000	17,500	25,000
Master DeLuxe, 6-cyl.						
2d Cpe	450	1500	2500	5000	8800	12,500
Spt Cpe	500	1550	2600	5200	9100	13,000
2d Twn Sed	400	1300	2200	4400	7700	11,000
4d Spt Sed	400	1300	2200	4400	7700	11,000
Special DeLuxe, 6-cyl.						
2d Cpe	500	1550	2600	5200	9100	13,000
2d Spt Cpe	500	1600	2700	5400	9500	13,500
2d Twn Sed	450	1400	2300	4600	8100	11,500
4d Spt Sed	450	1350	2300	4600	8000	11,400
2d Conv	900	2900	4800	9600	16,800	24,000
4d Sta Wag	1000	3100	5200	10,400	18,200	26,000

1941

	6	5	4	3	2	1
Master DeLuxe, 6-cyl.						
2P Cpe	450	1450	2400	4800	8400	12,000
4P Cpe	450	1500	2500	5000	8800	12,500
2d Twn Sed	400	1250	2100	4200	7300	10,400
4d Spt Sed	400	1250	2050	4100	7200	10,300
Special DeLuxe, 6-cyl.						
2P Cpe	500	1550	2600	5200	9100	13,000
4P Cpe	550	1700	2800	5600	9800	14,000
2d Sed	450	1400	2300	4600	8100	11,600
4d Spt Sed	450	1400	2300	4600	8100	11,500
4d Flt Sed	450	1450	2400	4800	8400	12,000
2d Conv	950	3000	5000	10,000	17,500	25,000
4d Sta Wag	1150	3600	6000	12,000	21,000	30,000
2d Cpe PU	550	1700	2800	5600	9800	14,000

1942

	6	5	4	3	2	1
Master DeLuxe, 6-cyl.						
2P Cpe	450	1450	2400	4800	8400	12,000
4P Cpe	450	1450	2450	4900	8500	12,200
2d Cpe PU	450	1500	2500	5000	8800	12,500
2d Twn Sed	400	1300	2150	4300	7600	10,800
2d Twn Sed	400	1300	2200	4400	7600	10,900
Special DeLuxe, 6-cyl.						
2P Cpe	450	1500	2500	5000	8800	12,500
2d 5P Cpe	500	1500	2550	5100	8900	12,700
2d Twn Sed	400	1300	2200	4400	7700	11,000
4d Spt Sed	400	1350	2200	4400	7800	11,100
2d Conv	1050	3350	5600	11,200	19,600	28,000
4d Sta Wag	950	3000	5000	10,000	17,500	25,000
Fleetline, 6-cyl.						
2d Aero	450	1400	2300	4600	8100	11,500
4d Spt Mstr	400	1350	2250	4500	7800	11,200

1946-1948

	6	5	4	3	2	1
Stylemaster, 6-cyl.						
2d Bus Cpe	450	1500	2500	5000	8800	12,500
2d Spt Cpe	500	1500	2550	5100	8900	12,700
2d Twn Sed	400	1300	2200	4400	7700	11,000
4d Spt Sed	400	1350	2200	4400	7800	11,100
Fleetmaster, 6-cyl.						
2d Spt Cpe	500	1550	2600	5200	9100	13,000
2d Twn Sed	450	1350	2300	4600	8000	11,400
4d Spt Sed	450	1400	2300	4600	8100	11,500
2d Conv	1100	3500	5800	11,600	20,300	29,000
4d Sta Wag	950	3000	5000	10,000	17,500	25,000
Fleetline, 6-cyl.						
2d Aero	450	1450	2400	4800	8400	12,000
4d Spt Mstr	450	1400	2350	4700	8300	11,800

1949-1950

	6	5	4	3	2	1
Styleline Special, 6-cyl.						
2d Bus Cpe	400	1300	2200	4400	7700	11,000
2d Spt Cpe	450	1350	2300	4600	8000	11,400
2d Sed	400	1200	2000	4000	7100	10,100
4d Sed	400	1200	2050	4100	7100	10,200
Fleetline Special, 6-cyl.						
2d Sed	400	1200	2050	4100	7100	10,200
4d Sed	400	1250	2050	4100	7200	10,300
Styleline DeLuxe, 6-cyl.						
Spt Cpe	450	1450	2400	4800	8400	12,000
2d Sed	400	1250	2050	4100	7200	10,300
4d Sed	400	1250	2100	4200	7300	10,400
2d HT Bel Air (1950 only)	600	1900	3200	6400	11,200	16,000
2d Conv	1000	3100	5200	10,400	18,200	26,000
4d Woodie Wag (1949 only)	650	2050	3400	6800	11,900	17,000
4d Mtl Sta Wag	450	1450	2400	4800	8400	12,000
Fleetline DeLuxe, 6-cyl.						
2d Sed	450	1350	2300	4600	8000	11,400
4d Sed	450	1400	2300	4600	8100	11,500

1951-1952

	6	5	4	3	2	1
Styleline Special, 6-cyl.						
2d Bus Cpe	400	1350	2200	4400	7800	11,100
2d Spt Cpe	450	1400	2300	4600	8100	11,500
2d Sed	400	1250	2050	4100	7200	10,300
4d Sed	400	1200	2050	4100	7100	10,200
Styleline DeLuxe, 6-cyl.						
2d Spt Cpe	450	1450	2400	4800	8400	12,000
2d Sed	400	1300	2150	4300	7600	10,800
4d Sed	400	1300	2150	4300	7500	10,700
2d HT Bel Air	600	1900	3200	6400	11,200	16,000
2d Conv	1000	3100	5200	10,400	18,200	26,000

	6	5	4	3	2	1
Fleetline Special, 6-cyl						
2d Sed (1951 only)	450	1130	1900	3800	6600	9400
4d Sed (1951 only)	450	1120	1875	3750	6500	9300
4d Sta Wag	450	1450	2400	4800	8400	12,000
Fleetline DeLuxe, 6-cyl.						
2d Sed	400	1350	2200	4400	7800	11,100
4d Sed (1951 only)	400	1300	2200	4400	7700	11,000
1953						
Special 150, 6-cyl.						
2d Bus Cpe	450	1140	1900	3800	6650	9500
2d Clb Cpe	450	1150	1900	3850	6700	9600
2d Sed	950	1100	1850	3700	6450	9200
4d Sed	450	1090	1800	3650	6400	9100
4d Sta Wag	450	1450	2400	4800	8400	12,000
DeLuxe 210, 6-cyl.						
2d Clb Cpe	450	1400	2300	4600	8100	11,500
2d Sed	400	1250	2100	4200	7400	10,500
4d Sed	400	1250	2100	4200	7300	10,400
2d HT	650	2050	3400	6800	11,900	17,000
2d Conv	1050	3350	5600	11,200	19,600	28,000
4d Sta Wag	450	1500	2500	5000	8800	12,500
4d 210 Townsman Sta Wag	500	1500	2550	5100	8900	12,700
Bel Air						
2d Sed	450	1400	2300	4600	8100	11,600
4d Sed	450	1400	2300	4600	8100	11,500
2d HT	700	2150	3600	7200	12,600	18,000
2d Conv	1150	3700	6200	12,400	21,700	31,000
1954						
Special 150, 6-cyl.						
2d Utl Sed	450	1080	1800	3600	6300	9000
2d Sed	950	1100	1850	3700	6450	9200
4d Sed	450	1090	1800	3650	6400	9100
4d Sta Wag	450	1450	2400	4800	8400	12,000
Special 210, 6-cyl.						
2d Sed	400	1250	2100	4200	7400	10,500
2d Sed Delray	450	1450	2400	4800	8400	12,000
4d Sed	400	1250	2100	4200	7300	10,400
4d Sta Wag	450	1500	2500	5000	8800	12,500
Bel Air, 6-cyl.						
2d Sed	450	1400	2350	4700	8200	11,700
4d Sed	450	1400	2300	4600	8100	11,600
2d HT	700	2300	3800	7600	13,300	19,000
2d Conv	1200	3850	6400	12,800	22,400	32,000
4d Sta Wag	550	1800	3000	6000	10,500	15,000
1955						
Model 150, V-8						
2d Utl Sed	450	1140	1900	3800	6650	9500
2d Sed	400	1200	2000	4000	7100	10,100
4d Sed	400	1200	2000	4000	7000	10,000
4d Sta Wag	400	1300	2200	4400	7700	11,000
Model 210, V-8						
2d Sed	400	1300	2200	4400	7700	11,000
2d Sed Delray	450	1450	2400	4800	8400	12,000
4d Sed	400	1200	2000	4000	7000	10,000
2d HT	800	2500	4200	8400	14,700	21,000
2d Sta Wag	450	1400	2300	4600	8100	11,500
4d Sta Wag	400	1350	2250	4500	7800	11,200
Bel Air, V-8						
2d Sed	450	1450	2450	4900	8500	12,200
4d Sed	450	1450	2400	4800	8400	12,000
2d HT	950	3000	5000	10,000	17,500	25,000
2d Conv	1600	5050	8400	16,800	29,400	42,000
2d Nomad	800	2500	4200	8400	14,700	21,000
4d Sta Wag	550	1700	2800	5600	9800	14,000

NOTE: Add 10 percent for A/C; 15 percent for "Power-Pak".
    Deduct 10 percent for 6-cyl.

1956						
Model 150, V-8						
2d Utl Sed	450	1080	1800	3600	6300	9000
2d Sed	450	1140	1900	3800	6650	9500
4d Sed	450	1120	1875	3750	6500	9300
4d Sta Wag	400	1200	2000	4000	7000	10,000
Model 210, V-8						
2d Sed	450	1140	1900	3800	6650	9500
2d Sed Delray	450	1400	2300	4600	8100	11,500
4d Sed	400	1200	2000	4000	7000	10,000
4d HT	400	1300	2200	4400	7700	11,000
2d HT	750	2400	4000	8000	14,000	20,000
2 dr Sta Wag	400	1250	2050	4100	7200	10,300
4d Sta Wag	400	1200	2000	4000	7000	10,000
4d 9P Sta Wag	400	1200	2000	4000	7100	10,100
Bel Air, V-8						
2d Sed	400	1300	2200	4400	7700	11,000
4d Sed	400	1300	2200	4400	7700	11,000
4d HT	500	1550	2600	5200	9100	13,000
2d HT	900	2900	4800	9600	16,800	24,000
2d Conv	1550	4900	8200	16,400	28,700	41,000
2d Nomad	700	2300	3800	7600	13,300	19,000
4d 9P Sta Wag	550	1700	2800	5600	9800	14,000

NOTE: Add 10 percent for A/C; 15 percent for "Power-Pak".
    Deduct 10 percent for 6-cyl.

1957						
Model 150, V-8						
2d Utl Sed	450	1080	1800	3600	6300	9000
2d Sed	450	1120	1875	3750	6500	9300
4d Sed	450	1120	1875	3750	6500	9300
2d Sta Wag	400	1250	2100	4200	7400	10,500
Model 210, V-8						
2d Sed	400	1200	2000	4000	7000	10,000
2d Sed Delray	450	1400	2300	4600	8100	11,500
4d Sed	400	1250	2100	4200	7400	10,500
4d HT	400	1300	2200	4400	7700	11,000
2d HT	700	2150	3600	7200	12,600	18,000
2d Sta Wag	450	1400	2300	4600	8100	11,500
4d Sta Wag	400	1300	2200	4400	7700	11,000
4d 9P Sta Wag	400	1350	2200	4400	7800	11,100
Bel Air, V-8						
2d Sed	450	1450	2400	4800	8400	12,000
4d Sed	450	1400	2350	4700	8300	11,800
4d HT	500	1550	2600	5200	9100	13,000
2d HT	1000	3100	5200	10,400	18,200	26,000
2d Conv	1700	5400	9000	18,000	31,500	45,000
2d Nomad	750	2400	4000	8000	14,000	20,000
4d Sta Wag	550	1700	2800	5600	9800	14,000

NOTE: Add 10 percent for A/C; 15 percent for "Power-Pak" and 20 percent for F.I.
    Deduct 10 percent for 6-cyl.

1958						
Delray, V-8						
2d Utl Sed	350	1000	1650	3350	5800	8300
2d Sed	350	1020	1700	3400	5950	8500
4d Sed	350	1020	1700	3400	5950	8500
Biscayne, V-8						
2d Sed	350	1040	1750	3500	6100	8700
4d Sed	350	1040	1700	3450	6000	8600
Bel Air, V-8						
2d Sed	400	1250	2100	4200	7400	10,500
4d Sed	400	1250	2100	4200	7400	10,600
4d HT	450	1450	2400	4800	8400	12,000
2d HT	550	1700	2800	5600	9800	14,000
2d Impala	1150	3600	6000	12,000	21,000	30,000
2d Imp Conv	1600	5150	8600	17,200	30,100	43,000
Station Wagons, V-8						
2d Yeo	400	1200	2000	4000	7100	10,100
4d Yeo	400	1200	2000	4000	7000	10,000
4d 6P Brookwood	400	1250	2050	4100	7200	10,300
9P Brookwood	400	1250	2100	4200	7300	10,400
4d Nomad	450	1450	2400	4800	8400	12,000

NOTE: Add 10 percent for Power-Pak & dual exhaust on 283 V-8.
    Add 20 percent for 348.
    Add 30 percent for 348 Tri-Power set up.
    Add 15 percent for A/C.
    Deduct 10 percent for 6-cyl.

1959						
Biscayne, V-8						
2d Utl Sed	350	975	1600	3200	5600	8000
2d Sed	350	1000	1650	3300	5750	8200
4d Sed	350	1000	1650	3350	5800	8300
Bel Air, V-8						
2d Sed	350	1040	1750	3500	6100	8700
4d Sed	450	1050	1750	3550	6150	8800
4d HT	400	1200	2000	4000	7000	10,000
Impala, V-8						
4d Sed	450	1080	1800	3600	6300	9000
4d HT	400	1300	2200	4400	7700	11,000
2d HT	650	2050	3400	6800	11,900	17,000
2d Conv	1100	3500	5800	11,600	20,300	29,000
Station Wagons, V-8						
4d Brookwood	450	1080	1800	3600	6300	9000
4d Parkwood	450	1130	1900	3800	6600	9400
4d Kingswood	400	1200	2000	4000	7000	10,000
4d Nomad	400	1250	2100	4200	7400	10,500

NOTE: Add 10 percent for A/C.
    Add 5 percent for 4-speed transmission.
    Deduct 10 percent for 6-cyl.
    Add 30 percent for 348 Tri-Power set up.

1960						
Biscayne, V-8						
2d Utl Sed	350	870	1450	2900	5100	7300
2d Sed	350	950	1500	3050	5300	7600
4d Sed	350	950	1550	3100	5400	7700
Biscayne Fleetmaster, V-8						
2d Sed	350	950	1550	3150	5450	7800
4d Sed	350	975	1600	3200	5500	7900
Bel Air, V-8						
2d Sed	350	1000	1650	3350	5800	8300
4d Sed	350	1020	1700	3400	5900	8400
4d HT	450	1140	1900	3800	6650	9500
2d HT	400	1300	2200	4400	7700	11,000
Impala, V-8						
4d Sed	450	1050	1750	3550	6150	8800
4d HT	400	1300	2200	4400	7700	11,000
2d HT	700	2150	3600	7200	12,600	18,000
2d Conv	1050	3350	5600	11,200	19,600	28,000
Station Wagons, V-8						
4d Brookwood	450	1080	1800	3600	6300	9000
4d Kingswood	450	1120	1875	3750	6500	9300
4d Parkwood	450	1140	1900	3800	6650	9500
4d Nomad	400	1200	2000	4000	7000	10,000

NOTE: Add 10 percent for A/C.
    Deduct 10 percent for 6-cyl.
    Add 30 percent for 348 Tri-Power set up.

1961						
Biscayne, V-8						
2d Utl Sed	350	830	1400	2950	4830	6900
2d Sed	350	900	1500	3000	5250	7500
4d Sed	350	850	1450	2850	4970	7100
Bel Air, V-8						
2d Sed	350	950	1550	3100	5400	7700
4d Sed	350	950	1500	3050	5300	7600
4d HT	450	1080	1800	3600	6300	9000
2d HT	700	2150	3600	7200	12,600	18,000
Impala, V-8						
2d Sed	350	975	1600	3200	5600	8000
4d Sed	350	975	1600	3250	5700	8100
4d HT	450	1140	1900	3800	6650	9500
2d HT*	600	1900	3200	6400	11,200	16,000
2d Conv*	900	2900	4800	9600	16,800	24,000
Station Wagons, V-8						
4d Brookwood	350	1020	1700	3400	5950	8500
4d Parkwood	450	1080	1800	3600	6300	9000
4d Nomad	400	1200	2000	4000	7000	10,000

NOTE: Add 10 percent for Power-Pak & dual exhaust on 283 V-8.
    Add 15 percent for A/C.
    Add 35 percent for 348 CID.
    *Add 40 percent for Super Sport option.
    Add 50 percent 409 V-8.
    Deduct 10 percent for 6-cyl.

1962						
Chevy II, 4 & 6-cyl.						
2d Sed	350	850	1450	2850	4970	7100
4d Sed	350	840	1400	2800	4900	7000
2d HT	500	1550	2600	5200	9100	13,000
2d Conv	550	1800	3000	6000	10,500	15,000
4d Sta Wag	350	1020	1700	3400	5950	8500
Biscayne, V-8						
2d Sed	350	880	1500	2950	5180	7400
4d Sed	350	900	1500	3000	5250	7500
4d Sta Wag	350	1000	1650	3350	5800	8300

Bel Air, V-8	6	5	4	3	2	1
2d Sed	350	950	1500	3050	5300	7600
4d Sed	350	950	1550	3100	5400	7700
2d HT	700	2300	3800	7600	13,300	19,000
4d Sta Wag	400	1200	2000	4000	7000	10,000
Bel Air 409 muscle car						
2d Sed (380 HP)	550	1700	2800	5600	9800	14,000
2d HT (380 HP)	900	2900	4800	9600	16,800	24,000
2d Sed (409 HP)	600	1900	3200	6400	11,200	16,000
2d HT (409 HP)	1000	3100	5200	10,400	18,200	26,000
Impala, V-8						
4d Sed	350	975	1600	3200	5600	8000
4d HT*	400	1200	2000	4000	7000	10,000
2d HT*	650	2050	3400	6800	11,900	17,000
2d Conv*	1000	3100	5200	10,400	18,200	26,000
4d Sta Wag	400	1300	2200	4400	7700	11,000

*NOTE: Add 15 percent for Super Sport option.
   Add 15 percent for Power-Pak & dual exhaust.
   Add 15 percent for A/C.
   Add 35 percent for 409 CID.
   Deduct 10 percent for 6-cyl except Chevy II.

1963

Chevy II and Nova, 4 & 6-cyl.	6	5	4	3	2	1
4d Sed	350	800	1350	2700	4700	6700
2d HT*	450	1450	2400	4800	8400	12,000
2d Conv*	550	1800	3000	6000	10,500	15,000
4d Sta Wag	350	975	1600	3200	5600	8000

*NOTE: Add 15 percent for Super Sport option.

Biscayne, V-8	6	5	4	3	2	1
2d Sed	350	780	1300	2600	4550	6500
4d Sed	350	790	1350	2650	4620	6600
4d Sta Wag	350	900	1500	3000	5250	7500
Bel Air, V-8						
2d Sed	350	790	1350	2650	4620	6600
4d Sed	350	800	1350	2700	4700	6700
4d Sta Wag	350	975	1600	3200	5600	8000
Impala, V-8						
4d Sed	350	975	1600	3200	5600	8000
4d HT	400	1200	2000	4000	7000	10,000
2d HT*	700	2300	3800	7600	13,300	19,000
2d Conv*	950	3000	5000	10,000	17,500	25,000
4d Sta Wag	400	1200	2000	4000	7000	10,000

NOTE: Add 15 percent for Power-Pak & dual exhaust.
   Add 15 percent for A/C.
   Add 35 percent for 409 CID.
   Add 15 percent for Super Sport option.
   Deduct 10 percent for 6-cyl except Chevy II.

1964

Chevy II and Nova, 4 & 6-cyl.	6	5	4	3	2	1
2d Sed	350	820	1400	2700	4760	6800
4d Sed	350	830	1400	2950	4830	6900
2d HT	450	1450	2400	4800	8400	12,000
4d Sta Wag	350	1000	1650	3300	5750	8200

NOTE: Add 10 percent for 6-cyl.

Nova Super Sport Series, 6-cyl.	6	5	4	3	2	1
2d HT	550	1800	3000	6000	10,500	15,000

NOTE: Add 25 percent for V8.
   Add 10 percent for 4 speed trans.

Chevelle	6	5	4	3	2	1
2d Sed	350	780	1300	2600	4550	6500
4d Sed	350	790	1350	2650	4620	6600
2d Sta Wag	350	1020	1700	3400	5900	8400
4d Sta Wag	350	1000	1650	3300	5750	8200
Malibu Series, V-8						
4d Sed	350	790	1350	2650	4620	6600
2d HT*	550	1700	2800	5600	9800	14,000
2d Conv*	850	2650	4400	8800	15,400	22,000
4d Sta Wag	350	975	1600	3200	5600	8000

NOTE: Add 15 percent for Super Sport option.
   Deduct 10 percent for 6-cyl.

Biscayne, V-8	6	5	4	3	2	1
2d Sed	350	780	1300	2600	4550	6500
4d Sed	350	790	1350	2650	4620	6600
4d Sta Wag	350	900	1500	3000	5250	7500
Bel Air, V-8						
2d Sed	350	790	1350	2650	4620	6600
4d Sed	350	800	1350	2700	4700	6700
4d Sta Wag	450	1080	1800	3600	6300	9000
Impala, V-8						
4d Sed	350	900	1500	3000	5250	7500
4d HT	450	1140	1900	3800	6650	9500
2d HT*	700	2150	3600	7200	12,600	18,000
2d Conv*	1000	3100	5200	10,400	18,200	26,000
4d Sta Wag	400	1300	2200	4400	7700	11,000

*NOTE: Add 15 percent for Super Sport option.
   Add 15 percent for Power-Pak & dual exhaust.
   Add 15 percent for A/C.
   Add 35 percent for 409 CID.
   Deduct 10 percent for 6-cyl.

1965

Chevy II, V-8	6	5	4	3	2	1
4d Sed	350	790	1350	2650	4620	6600
2d Sed	350	790	1350	2650	4620	6600
4d Sta Wag	350	820	1400	2700	4760	6800
Nova Series, V-8						
4d Sed	350	800	1350	2700	4700	6700
2d HT	450	1450	2400	4800	8400	12,000
4d Sta Wag	350	975	1600	3200	5600	8000
Nova Super Sport, V-8						
2d Spt Cpe	550	1800	3000	6000	10,500	15,000
Chevelle						
2d Sed	350	770	1300	2550	4480	6400
4d Sed	350	780	1300	2600	4550	6500
2d Sta Wag	350	1020	1700	3400	5950	8500
4d Sta Wag	350	1020	1700	3400	5950	8500
Malibu, V-8						
4d Sed	350	820	1400	2700	4760	6800
2d HT	600	1900	3200	6400	11,200	16,000
2d Conv	850	2650	4400	8800	15,400	22,000
4d Sta Wag	350	975	1600	3250	5700	8100
Malibu Super Sport, V-8						
2d HT	750	2400	4000	8000	14,000	20,000
2d Conv	1000	3250	5400	10,800	18,900	27,000

NOTE: Add 100 percent for RPO Z16 SS-396 option on hardtop only.
   Add 35 percent for 396 CID, 325 hp.

Biscayne, V-8	6	5	4	3	2	1
2d Sed	350	770	1300	2550	4480	6400
4d Sed	350	780	1300	2600	4550	6500
4d Sta Wag	350	800	1350	2700	4700	6700
Bel Air, V-8						
2d Sed	350	820	1400	2700	4760	6800
4d Sed	350	830	1400	2950	4830	6900
4d Sta Wag	350	900	1500	3000	5250	7500
Impala, V-8						
4d Sed	350	975	1600	3200	5600	8000
4d HT*	450	1140	1900	3800	6650	9500
2d HT	550	1800	3000	6000	10,500	15,000
2d Conv	900	2900	4800	9600	16,800	24,000
4d Sta Wag	350	1020	1700	3400	5950	8500
Impala Super Sport, V-8						
2d HT	600	1900	3200	6400	11,200	16,000
2d Conv	1000	3100	5200	10,400	18,200	26,000

NOTE: Add 20 percent for Power-Pak & dual exhaust.
   Add 15 percent for A/C.
   Add 35 percent for 409 CID.
   Add 35 percent for 396 CID, 325 hp.
   Add 50 percent for 396 CID, 425 hp.
   Add 40 percent for 409 CID, 340 hp.
   Add 50 percent for 409 CID, 400 hp.
   Deduct 10 percent for 6-cyl.
   Add 10 percent for Caprice models.

1966

Chevy II Series 100	6	5	4	3	2	1
2d Sed	350	790	1350	2650	4620	6600
4d Sed	350	800	1350	2700	4700	6700
4d Sta Wag	350	830	1400	2950	4830	6900
Nova Series, V-8						
2d HT	450	1080	1800	3600	6300	9000
4d Sed	350	820	1400	2700	4760	6800
4d Sta Wag	350	840	1400	2800	4900	7000
Nova Super Sport						
2d HT	550	1800	3000	6000	10,500	15,000

NOTE: Add 60 percent for High Performance pkg.

Chevelle	6	5	4	3	2	1
2d Sed	350	770	1300	2550	4480	6400
4d Sed	350	780	1300	2600	4550	6500
4d Sta Wag	350	800	1350	2700	4700	6700
Malibu, V-8						
4d Sed	350	820	1400	2700	4760	6800
4d HT	350	840	1400	2800	4900	7000
2d HT	600	1900	3200	6400	11,200	16,000
2d Conv	850	2650	4400	8800	15,400	22,000
4d Sta Wag	350	840	1400	2800	4900	7000
Super Sport, '396' V-8						
2d HT	900	2900	4800	9600	16,800	24,000
2d Conv	1150	3600	6000	12,000	21,000	30,000

NOTE: Deduct 10 percent for 6-cyl. Chevelle.
   Add 10 percent for 396 CID, 360 hp.
   Add 30 percent for 396 CID, 375 hp.

Biscayne, V-8	6	5	4	3	2	1
2d Sed	350	780	1300	2600	4550	6500
4d Sed	350	790	1350	2650	4620	6600
4d Sta Wag	350	820	1400	2700	4760	6800
Bel Air, V-8						
2d Sed	350	840	1400	2800	4900	7000
4d Sed	350	850	1450	2850	4970	7100
4d 3S Wag	350	975	1600	3200	5600	8000
Impala, V-8						
4d Sed	350	900	1500	3000	5250	7500
4d HT	450	1140	1900	3800	6650	9500
2d HT	650	2050	3400	6800	11,900	17,000
2d Conv	850	2650	4400	8800	15,400	22,000
4d Sta Wag	400	1200	2000	4000	7000	10,000
Impala Super Sport, V-8						
2d HT	750	2400	4000	8000	14,000	20,000
2d Conv	950	3000	5000	10,000	17,500	25,000
Caprice, V-8						
4d HT	450	1450	2400	4800	8400	12,000
2d HT	700	2150	3600	7200	12,600	18,000
4d Sta Wag	400	1300	2200	4400	7700	11,000

NOTE: Add 35 percent for 396 CID.
   Add 40 percent for 427 CID, 390 hp.
   Add 50 percent for 427 CID, 425 hp.
   Add approx. 40 percent for 427 CID engine when available.
   Add 15 percent for A/C.

1967

Chevy II, 100, V-8, 110" wb	6	5	4	3	2	1
2d Sed	200	750	1275	2500	4400	6300
4d Sed	350	770	1300	2550	4480	6400
4d Sta Wag	350	790	1350	2650	4620	6600
Chevy II Nova, V-8, 110" wb						
4d Sed	350	780	1300	2600	4550	6500
2d HT	450	1400	2300	4600	8100	11,500
4d Sta Wag	350	900	1500	3000	5250	7500
Chevy II Nova SS, V-8, 110" wb						
2d HT	450	1500	2500	5000	8800	12,500

NOTE: Add 60 percent for High Performance pkg.

Chevelle 300, V-8, 115" wb	6	5	4	3	2	1
2d Sed	350	770	1300	2550	4480	6400
4d Sed	350	780	1300	2600	4550	6500
Chevelle 300 DeLuxe, V-8, 115" wb						
2d Sed	350	800	1350	2700	4700	6700
4d Sed	350	820	1400	2700	4760	6800
4d Sta Wag	350	975	1600	3200	5600	8000
Chevelle Malibu, V-8, 115" wb						
4d Sed	350	840	1400	2800	4900	7000
4d HT	350	975	1600	3200	5600	8000
2d HT	550	1700	2800	5600	9800	14,000
2d Conv	800	2500	4200	8400	14,700	21,000
4d Sta Wag	350	900	1500	3000	5250	7500
Chevelle Concours, V-8, 115" wb						
4d Sta Wag	350	1020	1700	3400	5950	8500
Chevelle Super Sport 396, 115" wb						
2d HT	950	3000	5000	10,000	17,500	25,000
2d Conv	1100	3500	5800	11,600	20,300	29,000

NOTE: Add 10 percent for 396 CID, 350 hp.
   Add 30 percent for 396 CID, 375 hp.

Biscayne, V-8, 119" wb	6	5	4	3	2	1
2d Sed	350	780	1300	2600	4550	6500
4d Sed	350	790	1350	2650	4620	6600
4d Sta Wag	350	900	1500	3000	5250	7500

	6	5	4	3	2	1
Bel Air, V-8, 119" wb						
2d Sed	350	860	1450	2900	5050	7200
4d Sed	350	870	1450	2900	5100	7300
4d 3S Sta Wag	350	975	1600	3200	5600	8000
Impala, V-8, 119" wb						
4d Sed	350	900	1500	3000	5250	7500
4d HT	350	975	1600	3200	5600	8000
2d HT	500	1550	2600	5200	9100	13,000
2d Conv	800	2500	4200	8400	14,700	21,000
4d 3S Sta Wag	450	1080	1800	3600	6300	9000
Impala SS, V-8, 119" wb						
2d HT	550	1700	2800	5600	9800	14,000
2d Conv	800	2500	4200	8400	14,700	21,000
Caprice, V-8, 119" wb						
2d HT	550	1800	3000	6000	10,500	15,000
4d HT	400	1300	2200	4400	7700	11,000
4d 3S Sta Wag	400	1200	2000	4000	7000	10,000

NOTES: Add approximately 40 percent for SS-427 engine options when available in all series.
Add 40 percent for SS-396 option.
Add 15 percent for A/C.

	6	5	4	3	2	1
Camaro, V-8						
2d IPC	1000	3100	5200	10,400	18,200	26,000
2d Cpe	550	1800	3000	6000	10,500	15,000
2d Conv	800	2500	4200	8400	14,700	21,000
2d Z28 Cpe	1300	4200	7000	14,000	24,500	35,000
2d Yenko Cpe	2800	8900	14,800	29,600	51,800	74,000

NOTES: Deduct 5 percent for Six, (when available).
Add 10 percent for Rally Sport Package (when available; except incl. w/Indy Pace Car).
Add 10 percent for SS-350 (when available; except incl. w/Indy Pace Car).
Add 15 percent for SS-396 (L-35/325 hp; when available).
Add 35 percent for SS-396 (L-78/3/5 hp; when available).
Add 10 percent for A/C.

1968

	6	5	4	3	2	1
Nova 307 V8						
2d Cpe	350	820	1400	2700	4760	6800
4d Sed	200	720	1200	2400	4200	6000

NOTE: Deduct 5 percent for 4 or 6-cyl.
Add 25 percent for 327 CID.
Add 30 percent for 350 CID.
Add 35 percent for 396 CID engine.

	6	5	4	3	2	1
Chevelle 300						
2d Sed	200	650	1100	2150	3780	5400
4d Sta Wag	200	660	1100	2200	3850	5500
Chevelle 300 DeLuxe						
4d Sed	200	650	1100	2150	3780	5400
4d HT	200	700	1200	2350	4130	5900
2d Cpe	200	650	1100	2150	3780	5400
4d Sta Wag	200	720	1200	2400	4200	6000
Chevelle Malibu						
4d Sed	200	660	1100	2200	3850	5500
4d HT	350	780	1300	2600	4550	6500
2d HT	450	1450	2400	4800	8400	12,000
2d Conv	750	2400	4000	8000	14,000	20,000
4d Sta Wag	350	780	1300	2600	4550	6500

NOTE: Add 10 percent for 396 CID, 350 hp.
Add 30 percent for 396 CID, 375 hp.

	6	5	4	3	2	1
Chevelle Concours Estate						
4d Sta Wag	350	840	1400	2800	4900	7000
Chevelle SS-396						
2d 2d HT	800	2500	4200	8400	14,700	21,000
2d Conv	1000	3250	5400	10,800	18,900	27,000
Biscayne						
2d Sed	200	650	1100	2150	3780	5400
4d Sed	200	660	1100	2200	3850	5500
4d Sta Wag	200	720	1200	2400	4200	6000
Bel Air						
2d Sed	200	660	1100	2200	3850	5500
4d Sed	200	670	1150	2250	3920	5600
4d 2S Sta Wag	350	780	1300	2600	4550	6500
4d 3S Sta Wag	350	840	1400	2800	4900	7000
Impala						
4d Sed	200	720	1200	2400	4200	6000
4d HT	350	860	1450	2900	5050	7200
2d HT	450	1080	1800	3600	6300	9000
2d Cus Cpe	450	1140	1900	3800	6650	9500
2d Conv	700	2300	3800	7600	13,300	19,000
4d 2S Sta Wag	350	975	1600	3200	5600	8000
4d 3S Sta Wag	350	975	1600	3250	5700	8100
Caprice						
4d HT	350	975	1600	3200	5600	8000
2d HT	400	1300	2200	4400	7700	11,000
4d 2S Sta Wag	350	1020	1700	3400	5950	8500
4d 3S Sta Wag	450	1080	1800	3600	6300	9000
Chevelle 300						

NOTE: Only 1,270 Nova 4's were built in 1968.

	6	5	4	3	2	1
Camaro, V-8						
2d Cpe	550	1700	2800	5600	9800	14,000
2d Conv	700	2150	3600	7200	12,600	18,000
2d Z28	800	2500	4200	8400	14,700	21,000
2d Yenko Cpe	2100	6700	11,200	22,400	39,200	56,000

NOTES: Deduct 5 percent for Six, (when available).
Add 10 percent for A/C.
Add 15 percent for Rally Sport Package (when available).
Add 25 percent for SS package.
Add 15 percent for SS-350 (when available; except Z-28).
Add 25 percent for SS-396 (L35/325 hp; when available).
Add 35 percent for SS-396 (L78/375 hp; when available).
Add 40 percent for SS-396 (L89; when available).
Add approx. 40 percent for 427 engine options when availble.

1969

	6	5	4	3	2	1
Nova Four						
2d Cpe	200	700	1075	2150	3700	5300
4d Sed	200	700	1050	2100	3650	5200
Nova Six						
2d Cpe	200	650	1100	2150	3780	5400
4d Sed	200	700	1075	2150	3700	5300
Chevy II, Nova V-8						
2d Cpe	200	660	1100	2200	3850	5500
4d Sed	200	650	1100	2150	3780	5400
2d Yenko Cpe	2100	6700	11,200	22,400	39,200	56,000

NOTES: Add 25 percent for Nova SS.
Add 30 percent for 350 CID.
Add 35 percent for 396 CID.
Add 10 percent for Impala "SS".
Add 25 percent for other "SS" equipment pkgs.

	6	5	4	3	2	1
Chevelle 300 DeLuxe						
4d Sed	200	675	1000	2000	3500	5000
2d HT	350	900	1500	3000	5250	7500
2d Cpe	200	660	1100	2200	3850	5500
4d Nomad	200	685	1150	2300	3990	5700
4d Dual Nomad	200	720	1200	2400	4200	6000
4d GB Wag	200	660	1100	2200	3850	5500
4d 6P GB Dual Wag	200	660	1100	2200	3850	5500
4d 9P GB Dual Wag	200	670	1150	2250	3920	5600
Chevelle Malibu, Concours, V-8						
4d Sed	200	660	1100	2200	3850	5500
4d HT	200	720	1200	2400	4200	6000
2d HT	450	1450	2400	4800	8400	12,000
Conv	700	2300	3800	7600	13,300	19,000
4d HT	350	900	1500	3000	5250	7500
4d 9P Estate	200	670	1150	2250	3920	5600
4d 6P Estate	200	660	1100	2200	3850	5500

NOTE: Add 10 percent for 396 CID, 350 hp.
Add 30 percent for 396 CID, 375 hp.

	6	5	4	3	2	1
Chevelle Malibu SS-396						
2d HT	700	2300	3800	7600	13,300	19,000
2d Conv	950	3000	5000	10,000	17,500	25,000

NOTE: Add 60 percent for Yenko Hardtop.

	6	5	4	3	2	1
Biscayne						
2d Sed	200	675	1000	2000	3500	5000
4d Sed	200	675	1000	1950	3400	4900
4d Sta Wag	200	700	1050	2100	3650	5200
Bel Air						
2d Sed	200	660	1100	2200	3850	5500
4d Sed	200	675	1000	2000	3500	5000
4d 6P Sta Wag	200	670	1150	2250	3920	5600
4d 9P Sta Wag	200	670	1200	2300	4060	5800
Impala, V-8						
4d Sed	200	660	1100	2200	3850	5500
4d HT	350	840	1400	2800	4900	7000
2d HT	350	1020	1700	3400	5950	8500
2d Cus Cpe	350	1040	1750	3500	6100	8700
2d Conv	550	1800	3000	6000	10,500	15,000
4d 6P Sta Wag	200	670	1200	2300	4060	5800
4d 9P Sta Wag	200	720	1200	2400	4200	6000

NOTE: Add 35 percent for Impala SS 427 option.

	6	5	4	3	2	1
Caprice, V-8						
4d HT	350	975	1600	3200	5600	8000
2d Cus Cpe	450	1140	1900	3800	6650	9500
4d 6P Sta Wag	200	720	1200	2400	4200	6000
4d 9P Sta Wag	350	840	1400	2800	4900	7000
Camaro, V-8						
2d Spt Cpe	600	1900	3200	6400	11,200	16,000
2d Conv	800	2500	4200	8400	14,700	21,000
2d Z28	800	2500	4200	8400	14,700	21,000
2d IPC	950	3000	5000	10,000	17,500	25,000
2d ZL-1*	2850	9100	15,200	30,400	53,200	76,000
2d Yenko	1700	5400	9000	18,000	31,500	45,000

NOTES: Deduct 5 percent for Six, (when available).
Add 5 percent for Rally Sport (except incl. w/Indy Pace Car).
Add 10 percent for SS-350 (when avail.; except incl. w/Indy Pace Car).
Add 25 percent for SS-396 (L78/375 hp; when available).
Add 35 percent for SS-396 (L89/375 hp, alum. heads; when available).
Add approx. 40 percent for 427 engine options when available.
*The specially trimmed coupe with the aluminum 427 block.

1970

	6	5	4	3	2	1
Nova Four						
2d Cpe	200	675	1000	2000	3500	5000
4d Sed	200	675	1000	1950	3400	4900
Nova Six						
2d Cpe	200	700	1050	2050	3600	5100
4d Sed	200	675	1000	2000	3500	5000
Nova, V-8						
2d Cpe	200	700	1050	2100	3650	5200
4d Sed	200	700	1050	2050	3600	5100
2d Yenko Cpe	1950	6250	10,400	20,800	36,400	52,000
Chevelle						
2d Cpe	350	820	1400	2700	4760	6800
4d Sed	200	660	1100	2200	3850	5500
4d Nomad	200	720	1200	2400	4200	6000
Greenbrier						
4d 6P Sta Wag	200	660	1100	2200	3850	5500
4d 8P Sta Wag	200	660	1100	2200	3850	5500
Malibu, V-8						
4d Sed	200	670	1150	2250	3920	5600
4d HT	200	720	1200	2400	4200	6000
2d HT	400	1300	2200	4400	7700	11,000
2d Conv	700	2150	3600	7200	12,600	18,000
4d Concours Est Wag	350	790	1350	2650	4620	6600
Chevelle Malibu SS 396						
2d HT	800	2500	4200	8400	14,700	21,000
2d Conv	1000	3100	5200	10,400	18,200	26,000
Chevelle Malibu SS 454						
2d HT	950	3000	5000	10,000	17,500	25,000
2d Conv	1150	3600	6000	12,000	21,000	30,000

NOTE: Add 30 percent for 396 CID, 375 hp.
Add 50 percent for LS6 engine option.

	6	5	4	3	2	1
Monte Carlo						
2d HT	450	1450	2400	4800	8400	12,000

NOTE: Add 35 percent for SS 454.

	6	5	4	3	2	1
Biscayne						
4d Sed	150	650	950	1900	3300	4700
4d Sta Wag	150	650	975	1950	3350	4800
Bel Air						
4d Sed	200	700	1050	2050	3600	5100
4d 6P Sta Wag	200	700	1075	2150	3700	5300
4d 9P Sta Wag	200	660	1100	2200	3850	5500
Impala, V-8						
4d Sed	200	670	1200	2300	4060	5800
4d HT	350	900	1500	3000	5250	7500

	6	5	4	3	2	1
2d Spt Cpe	350	975	1600	3200	5600	8000
2d Cus Cpe	350	975	1600	3200	5600	8000
2d Conv	450	1450	2400	4800	8400	12,000
4d 6P Sta Wag	350	780	1300	2600	4550	6500
4d 9P Sta Wag	350	840	1400	2800	4900	7000
Caprice, V-8						
4d HT	350	975	1600	3200	5600	8000
2d Cus Cpe	450	1140	1900	3800	6650	9500
4d 6P Sta Wag	350	860	1450	2900	5050	7200
4d 9P Sta Wag	350	900	1500	3000	5250	7500

NOTE: Add 35 percent for SS 454 option.
Add 25 percent for Rally Sport and/or Super Sport options.

	6	5	4	3	2	1
Camaro, V-8						
2d Cpe	400	1300	2200	4400	7700	11,000
2d Z28	550	1800	3000	6000	10,500	15,000

NOTE: Deduct 5 percent for Six, (except Z-28).
Add 35 percent for the 375 horsepower 396, (L78 option).
Add 35 percent for Rally Sport and/or Super Sport options.

1971

	6	5	4	3	2	1
Vega						
2d Sed	200	675	1000	2000	3500	5000
2d HBk	200	700	1050	2050	3600	5100
2d Kammback	200	700	1050	2100	3650	5200

NOTE: Add 5 percent for GT.

	6	5	4	3	2	1
Nova, V-8						
4d Sed	200	675	1000	2000	3500	5000
2d Sed	200	700	1050	2100	3650	5200
2d SS	350	820	1400	2700	4760	6800
Chevelle						
2d HT	400	1300	2200	4400	7700	11,000
2d Malibu HT	600	1900	3200	6400	11,200	16,000
2d Malibu Conv	800	2500	4200	8400	14,700	21,000
4d HT	350	975	1600	3200	5600	8000
4d Sed	200	660	1100	2200	3850	5500
4d Concours Est Wag	350	840	1400	2800	4900	7000
Chevelle Malibu SS						
2d HT	650	2050	3400	6800	11,900	17,000
2d Conv	850	2750	4600	9200	16,100	23,000
Chevelle Malibu SS-454						
2d HT	750	2400	4000	8000	14,000	20,000
2d Conv	1000	3100	5200	10,400	18,200	26,000
Monte Carlo						
2d HT	500	1550	2600	5200	9100	13,000

NOTE: Add 35 percent for SS 454. Add 25 percent for SS 402 engine option.

	6	5	4	3	2	1
Biscayne, V-8, 121" wb						
4d Sed	150	650	975	1950	3350	4800
Bel Air, V-8, 121" wb						
4d Sed	200	700	1050	2100	3650	5200
Impala, V-8, 121" wb						
4d Sed	200	660	1100	2200	3850	5500
4d HT	200	745	1250	2500	4340	6200
2d HT	350	975	1600	3200	5600	8000
2d HT Cus	350	1000	1650	3300	5750	8200
2d Conv	550	1800	3000	6000	10,500	15,000
Caprice, V-8, 121" wb						
4d HT	350	840	1400	2800	4900	7000
2d HT	350	1020	1700	3400	5950	8500
Station Wags, V-8, 125" wb						
4d Brookwood 2-S	200	650	1100	2150	3780	5400
4d Townsman 3-S	200	685	1150	2300	3990	5700
4d Kingswood 3-S	200	700	1200	2350	4130	5900
4d Est 3-S	200	720	1200	2400	4200	6000

NOTE: Add 35 percent for SS 454 option.

	6	5	4	3	2	1
Camaro, V-8						
2d Cpe	400	1300	2200	4400	7700	11,000
2d Z28	550	1700	2800	5600	9800	14,000

NOTE: Add 35 percent for Rally Sport and/or Super Sport options.

1972

	6	5	4	3	2	1
Vega						
2d Sed	200	675	1000	2000	3500	5000
2d HBk	200	700	1050	2050	3600	5100
2d Kammback	200	700	1050	2100	3650	5200

NOTE: Add 15 percent for GT.

	6	5	4	3	2	1
Nova						
4d Sed	200	700	1050	2100	3650	5200
2d Sed	200	700	1075	2150	3700	5300

NOTE: Add 25 percent for SS.

	6	5	4	3	2	1
Chevelle						
2d Malibu Spt Cpe	550	1700	2800	5600	9800	14,000
2d Malibu Conv	800	2500	4200	8400	14,700	21,000
4d HT	350	975	1600	3200	5600	8000
4d Sed	200	660	1100	2200	3850	5500
4d Concours Est Wag	350	840	1400	2800	4900	7000
Chevelle Malibu SS						
2d HT	650	2050	3400	6800	11,900	17,000
2d Conv	850	2750	4600	9200	16,100	23,000
Chevelle Malibu SS-454						
2d HT	700	2300	3800	7600	13,300	19,000
2d Conv	950	3000	5000	10,000	17,500	25,000
Monte Carlo						
2d HT	500	1550	2600	5200	9100	13,000

NOTE: Add 35 percent for 454 CID engine. Add 25 percent for 402 engine option.

	6	5	4	3	2	1
Biscayne, V-8, 121" wb						
4d Sed	150	650	975	1950	3350	4800
Bel Air, V-8, 121" wb						
4d Sed	200	675	1000	1950	3400	4900
Impala, V-8, 121" wb						
4d Sed	200	700	1050	2100	3650	5200
4d HT	200	745	1250	2500	4340	6200
2d HT Cus	350	975	1600	3200	5600	8000
2d HT	350	900	1500	3000	5250	7500
2d Conv	500	1550	2600	5200	9100	13,000
Caprice, V-8, 121" wb						
4d Sed	200	660	1100	2200	3850	5500
4d HT	350	900	1500	3000	5250	7500
2d HT	350	1020	1700	3400	5950	8500
Station Wagons, V-8, 125" wb						
4d Brookwood 2-S	200	685	1150	2300	3990	5700
4d Townsman 3-S	200	700	1200	2350	4130	5900
4d Kingswood 3-S	200	720	1200	2400	4200	6000
4d Est 3-S	350	780	1300	2600	4550	6500

NOTE: Add 35 percent for 454 option.
Add 30 percent for 402 option.

	6	5	4	3	2	1
Camaro, V-8						
2d Cpe	450	1450	2400	4800	8400	12,000
2d Z28	550	1800	3000	6000	10,500	15,000

NOTE: Add 35 percent for Rally Sport and/or Super Sport options.

1973

	6	5	4	3	2	1
Vega						
2d Sed	200	670	1150	2250	3920	5600
2d HBk	200	700	1050	2050	3600	5100
2d Sta Wag	200	700	1050	2100	3650	5200
2d Nova Custom V8						
2d Cpe	200	650	1100	2150	3780	5400
4d Sed	200	700	1075	2150	3700	5300
2d HBk	200	660	1100	2200	3850	5500
Chevelle Malibu V8						
2d Cpe	200	670	1150	2250	3920	5600
4d Sed	200	660	1100	2200	3850	5500

NOTE: Add 15 percent for SS option.

	6	5	4	3	2	1
Laguna V8						
4d Sed	200	670	1150	2250	3920	5600
2d Cpe	350	900	1500	3000	5250	7500
4d 3S DeL Sta Wag	200	675	1000	2000	3500	5000
4d 3S Malibu Sta Wag	200	700	1050	2050	3600	5100
4d 3S Malibu Est Wag	200	700	1050	2100	3650	5200
4d 3S Laguna Sta Wag	200	660	1100	2200	3850	5500
4d 3S Laguna Est Wag	200	685	1150	2300	3990	5700
Monte Carlo V8						
2d Cpe	350	780	1300	2600	4550	6500
2d Cpe Lan	350	840	1400	2800	4900	7000
Bel Air						
4d	200	670	1150	2250	3920	5600
4d 2S Bel Air Sta Wag	200	650	1100	2150	3780	5400
4d 3S Bel Air Sta Wag	200	660	1100	2200	3850	5500
Impala V8						
2d Cpe Spt	350	780	1300	2600	4550	6500
2d Cpe Cus	350	800	1350	2700	4700	6700
4d Sed	200	685	1150	2300	3990	5700
4d HT	200	720	1200	2400	4200	6000
4d 3S Impala Wag	200	720	1200	2400	4200	6000
Caprice Classic V8						
2d Cpe	350	840	1400	2800	4900	7000
4d Sed	200	685	1150	2300	3990	5700
4d HT	350	780	1300	2600	4550	6500
2d Conv	600	1900	3200	6400	11,200	16,000
4d 3S Caprice Est Wag	350	780	1300	2600	4550	6500
Camaro, V-8						
2d Cpe	450	1450	2400	4800	8400	12,000
2d Z28	550	1700	2800	5600	9800	14,000

NOTE: Add 35 percent for Rally Sport and/or Super Sport options.

1974

	6	5	4	3	2	1
Vega						
2d Cpe	200	675	1000	2000	3500	5000
2d HBk	200	700	1050	2050	3600	5100
2d Sta Wag	200	700	1050	2100	3650	5200
Nova						
2d Cpe	200	650	1100	2150	3780	5400
2d HBk	200	670	1150	2250	3920	5600
4d Sed	200	650	1100	2150	3780	5400
Nova Custom						
2d Cpe	200	660	1100	2200	3850	5500
2d HBk	200	670	1150	2250	3920	5600
4d Sed	200	660	1100	2200	3850	5500

NOTE: Add 10 percent for Spirit of America option where applied.

	6	5	4	3	2	1
Malibu						
2d Col Cpe	200	720	1200	2400	4200	6000
4d Col Sed	200	670	1150	2250	3920	5600
4d Sta Wag	200	700	1050	2100	3650	5200
Malibu Classic						
2d Col Cpe	200	685	1150	2300	3990	5700
2d Lan Cpe	200	650	1100	2150	3780	5400
4d Col Sed	200	700	1050	2050	3600	5100
4d Sta Wag	200	675	1000	2000	3500	5000
Malibu Classic Estate						
4d Sta Wag	200	700	1050	2050	3600	5100
Laguna Type S-3, V-8						
2d Cpe	350	1020	1700	3400	5950	8500
Monte Carlo						
2d 'S' Cpe	200	720	1200	2400	4200	6000
2d Lan	350	780	1300	2600	4550	6500
Bel Air						
4d Sed	200	675	1000	2000	3500	5000
4d Sta Wag	200	675	1000	2000	3500	5000
Impala						
4d Sed	200	700	1075	2150	3700	5300
4d HT Sed	200	670	1200	2300	4060	5800
2d Spt Cpe	350	780	1300	2600	4550	6500
2d Cus Cpe	350	820	1400	2700	4760	6800
4d Sta Wag	200	700	1050	2050	3600	5100
Caprice Classic						
4d Sed	200	650	1100	2150	3780	5400
4d HT Sed	200	720	1200	2400	4200	6000
2d Cus Cpe	350	860	1450	2900	5050	7200
2d Conv	550	1800	3000	6000	10,500	15,000
4d Sta Wag	200	660	1100	2200	3850	5500

NOTES: Add 20 percent for Nova SS package.
Add 12 percent for Malibu with canopy roof.
Add 20 percent for 454 V-8.
Add 15 percent for Nova with 185 horsepower V-8.
Add 25 percent for Impala 'Spirit of America' Sport Coupe.

	6	5	4	3	2	1
Camaro, V-8						
2d Cpe	450	1400	2300	4600	8100	11,500
2d LT Cpe	450	1450	2400	4800	8400	12,000

NOTE: Add 10 percent for Z28 option.

1975

	6	5	4	3	2	1
Vega						
2d Cpe	200	675	1000	2000	3500	5000
2d HBk	200	700	1050	2050	3600	5100
2d Lux Cpe	200	700	1050	2050	3600	5100
4d Sta Wag	200	700	1050	2100	3650	5200
4d Est Wag	200	700	1075	2150	3700	5300
2d Cosworth	350	975	1600	3200	5600	8000
Nova						
2d 'S' Cpe	200	700	1050	2050	3600	5100
2d Cpe	200	700	1050	2050	3600	5100
2d HBk	200	700	1050	2100	3650	5200
4d Sed	200	700	1050	2100	3650	5200
Nova Custom						
2d Cpe	200	700	1050	2100	3650	5200
2d HBk	200	700	1075	2150	3700	5300
4d Sed	200	700	1050	2100	3650	5200

	6	5	4	3	2	1
Nova LN, V-8						
4d Sed	200	700	1075	2150	3700	5300
2d Cpe	200	650	1100	2150	3780	5400
Monza						
2d 2 plus 2	200	660	1100	2200	3850	5500
2d Twn Cpe	200	700	1050	2100	3650	5200
Malibu						
2d Col Cpe	200	660	1100	2200	3850	5500
2d Col Sed	200	675	1000	2000	3500	5000
4d Sta Wag	200	700	1050	2050	3600	5100
Malibu Classic						
2d Col Cpe	200	720	1200	2400	4200	6000
2d Lan	200	745	1250	2500	4340	6200
4d Col Sed	200	700	1050	2100	3650	5200
4d Sta Wag	200	700	1050	2050	3600	5100
4d Est Wag	200	700	1050	2100	3650	5200
Laguna Type S-3, V-8						
2d Cpe	450	1080	1800	3600	6300	9000
Monte Carlo						
2d 'S' Cpe	350	780	1300	2600	4550	6500
2d Lan	350	840	1400	2800	4900	7000
Bel Air						
4d Sed	200	700	1050	2050	3600	5100
4d Sta Wag	200	675	1000	2000	3500	5000
Impala						
4d Sed	200	700	1075	2150	3700	5300
4d HT	200	650	1100	2150	3780	5400
2d Spt Cpe	200	720	1200	2400	4200	6000
2d Cus Cpe	200	730	1250	2450	4270	6100
2d Lan	350	780	1300	2600	4550	6500
4d Sta Wag	200	650	1100	2150	3780	5400
Caprice Classic						
4d Sed	200	650	1100	2150	3780	5400
4d HT	200	660	1100	2200	3850	5500
2d Cus Cpe	350	780	1300	2600	4550	6500
2d Lan	350	780	1300	2600	4550	6500
2d Conv	550	1800	3000	6000	10,500	15,000
4d Sta Wag	200	720	1200	2400	4200	6000

NOTES: Add 10 percent for Nova SS.
Add 15 percent for SS option on Chevelle wagon.
Add 20 percent for Monte Carlo or Laguna 454.
Add 15 percent for 454 Caprice.
Add 15 percent for canopy top options.
Add 10 percent for Monza V-8.

	6	5	4	3	2	1
Camaro, V-8						
Cpe	400	1200	2000	4000	7000	10,000
Type LT	400	1300	2200	4400	7700	11,000

NOTE: Add 30 percent for Camaro R/S.

1976

	6	5	4	3	2	1
Chevette, 4-cyl.						
2d Scooter	150	650	950	1900	3300	4700
2d HBk	200	675	1000	1950	3400	4900
Vega, 4-cyl.						
2d Sed	200	675	1000	2000	3500	5000
2d HBk	200	700	1050	2050	3600	5100
2d Cosworth HBk	350	975	1600	3200	5600	8000
2d Sta Wag	200	700	1050	2100	3650	5200
2d Est Sta Wag	200	700	1075	2150	3700	5300
Nova, V-8						
2d Cpe	200	700	1050	2050	3600	5100
2d HBk	200	700	1050	2100	3650	5200
4d Sed	200	675	1000	2000	3500	5000
Nova Concours, V-8						
2d Cpe	200	700	1050	2100	3650	5200
2d HBk	200	700	1075	2150	3700	5300
4d Sed	200	700	1050	2050	3600	5100
Monza, 4-cyl.						
2d Twn Cpe	200	675	1000	1950	3400	4900
2d HBk	200	675	1000	1950	3400	4900
Malibu, V-8						
2d Sed	200	700	1050	2050	3600	5100
4d Sed	200	675	1000	2000	3500	5000
4d 2S Sta Wag ES	200	675	1000	2000	3500	5000
4d 3S Sta Wag ES	200	675	1000	2000	3500	5000
Malibu Classic, V-8						
2d Sed	200	660	1100	2200	3850	5500
2d Lan Cpe	200	685	1150	2300	3990	5700
4d Sed	200	675	1000	2000	3500	5000
Laguna Type S-3, V-8						
2d Cpe	350	1020	1700	3400	5950	8500
Monte Carlo, V-8						
2d Cpe	350	780	1300	2600	4550	6500
2d Lan Cpe	350	840	1400	2800	4900	7000
Impala, V-8						
4d Sed	150	650	975	1950	3350	4800
4d Spt Sed	200	675	1000	1950	3400	4900
2d Cus Cpe	200	660	1100	2200	3850	5500
4d 2S Sta Wag	200	675	1000	1950	3400	4900
4d 3S Sta Wag	200	675	1000	2000	3500	5000
Caprice Classic, V-8						
4d Sed	200	675	1000	2000	3500	5000
4d Spt Sed	200	700	1050	2050	3600	5100
2d Cpe	350	780	1300	2600	4550	6500
2d Lan Cpe	350	800	1350	2700	4700	6700
4d 2S Sta Wag	200	675	1000	2000	3500	5000
4d 3S Sta Wag	200	700	1050	2050	3600	5100
Camaro, V-8						
2d Cpe	450	1080	1800	3600	6300	9000
2d Cpe LT	400	1200	2000	4000	7000	10,000

1977

	6	5	4	3	2	1
Chevette, 4-cyl.						
2d HBk	150	550	850	1650	2900	4100
Vega, 4-cyl.						
2d Spt Cpe	150	575	875	1700	3000	4300
2d HBk	150	575	900	1750	3100	4400
2d Sta Wag	150	600	900	1800	3150	4500
2d Est Wag	150	600	950	1850	3200	4600
Nova, V-8						
2d Cpe	150	600	900	1800	3150	4500
2d HBk	150	600	950	1850	3200	4600
4d Sed	150	575	900	1750	3100	4400
Nova Concours, V-8						
2d Cpe	150	600	950	1850	3200	4600
2d HBk	150	650	950	1900	3300	4700
4d Sed	150	600	900	1800	3150	4500

	6	5	4	3	2	1
Monza, 4-cyl.						
2d Twn Cpe	150	600	900	1800	3150	4500
2d HBk	150	600	900	1800	3150	4500
Malibu, V-8						
2d Cpe	150	575	900	1750	3100	4400
4d Sed	150	600	900	1800	3150	4500
4d 2S Sta Wag	150	550	850	1650	2900	4100
3S Sta Wag	150	550	850	1675	2950	4200
Malibu Classic, V-8						
2d Cpe	150	600	900	1800	3150	4500
2d Lan Cpe	200	675	1000	2000	3500	5000
4d Sed	150	600	950	1850	3200	4600
4d 2S Sta Wag	150	575	875	1700	3000	4300
4d 3S Sta Wag	150	575	900	1750	3100	4400
Monte Carlo, V-8						
2d Cpe	200	660	1100	2200	3850	5500
2d Lan Cpe	200	720	1200	2400	4200	6000
Impala, V-8						
2d Cpe	200	675	1000	2000	3500	5000
4d Sed	150	600	900	1800	3150	4500
4d 2S Sta Wag	150	600	900	1800	3150	4500
4d 3S Sta Wag	150	600	950	1850	3200	4600
Caprice Classic, V-8						
2d Cpe	200	700	1050	2100	3650	5200
4d Sed	150	650	950	1900	3300	4700
4d 2S Sta Wag	150	600	950	1850	3200	4600
4d 3S Sta Wag	150	650	950	1900	3300	4700
Camaro, V-8						
2d Spt Cpe	350	975	1600	3200	5600	8000
2d Spt Cpe LT	350	1020	1700	3400	5950	8500
2d Spt Cpe Z28	450	1080	1800	3600	6300	9000

1978

	6	5	4	3	2	1
Chevette						
2d Scooter	150	475	775	1500	2650	3800
2d HBk	150	475	775	1500	2650	3800
4d HBk	150	500	800	1550	2700	3900
Nova						
2d Cpe	150	575	900	1750	3100	4400
2d HBk	150	575	900	1750	3100	4400
4d Sed	150	575	875	1700	3000	4300
Nova Custom						
2d Cpe	150	600	900	1800	3150	4500
4d Sed	150	575	900	1750	3100	4400
Monza						
2d Cpe 2 plus 2	150	600	950	1850	3200	4600
2d 'S' Cpe	150	600	900	1800	3150	4500
2d Cpe	150	575	900	1750	3100	4400
4d Sta Wag	150	550	850	1650	2900	4100
4d Est Wag	150	550	850	1675	2950	4200
2d Spt Cpe 2 plus 2	200	675	1000	2000	3500	5000
2d Spt Cpe	150	650	975	1950	3350	4800
Malibu						
2d Spt Cpe	150	600	950	1850	3200	4600
4d Sed	150	600	900	1800	3150	4500
4d Sta Wag	150	600	900	1800	3150	4500
Malibu Classic						
2d Spt Cpe	150	650	950	1900	3300	4700
4d Sed	150	600	950	1850	3200	4600
4d Sta Wag	150	600	950	1850	3200	4600
Monte Carlo						
2d Cpe	200	675	1000	2000	3500	5000
Impala						
2d Cpe	200	675	1000	2000	3500	5000
4d Sed	150	650	950	1900	3300	4700
4d Sta Wag	150	650	950	1900	3300	4700
Caprice Classic						
2d Cpe	200	700	1075	2150	3700	5300
4d Sed	200	675	1000	2000	3500	5000
4d Sta Wag	200	700	1050	2050	3600	5100
Camaro, V-8						
2d Cpe	200	720	1200	2400	4200	6000
2d LT Cpe	350	780	1300	2600	4550	6500
2d Z28 Cpe	350	840	1400	2800	4900	7000

1979

	6	5	4	3	2	1
Chevette, 4-cyl.						
4d HBk	150	500	800	1550	2700	3900
2d HBk	150	500	800	1550	2700	3900
2d Scooter	150	475	775	1500	2650	3800
Nova, V-8						
4d Sed	150	575	900	1750	3100	4400
2d Sed	150	575	875	1700	3000	4300
2d HBk	150	600	900	1800	3150	4500
Nova Custom, V-8						
4d Sed	150	600	900	1800	3150	4500
2d Sed	150	575	900	1750	3100	4400

NOTE: Deduct 5 percent for 6-cyl.

	6	5	4	3	2	1
Monza, 4-cyl.						
2d 2 plus 2 HBk	150	650	950	1900	3300	4700
2d	150	600	950	1850	3200	4600
4d Sta Wag	150	550	850	1675	2950	4200
2d Spt 2 plus 2 HBk	150	650	975	1950	3350	4800
Malibu, V-8						
4d Sed	150	600	950	1850	3200	4600
2d Spt Cpe	150	650	975	1950	3350	4800
4d Sta Wag	150	650	950	1900	3300	4700
Malibu Classic, V-8						
4d Sed	150	650	950	1900	3300	4700
2d Spt Cpe	200	675	1000	1950	3400	4900
2d Lan Cpe	200	675	1000	2000	3500	5000
4d Sta Wag	150	650	975	1950	3350	4800

NOTE: Deduct 5 percent for 6-cyl.

	6	5	4	3	2	1
Monte Carlo, V-8						
2d Spt Cpe	200	675	1000	2000	3500	5000
2d Lan Cpe	200	660	1100	2200	3850	5500

NOTE: Deduct 10 percent for 6-cyl.

	6	5	4	3	2	1
Impala, V-8						
4d Sed	150	650	975	1950	3350	4800
2d Sed	150	650	950	1900	3300	4700
2d Lan Cpe	200	675	1000	1950	3400	4900
4d 2S Sta Wag	150	650	950	1900	3300	4700
4d 3S Sta Wag	150	650	975	1950	3350	4800
Caprice Classic, V-8						
4d Sed	200	675	1000	2000	3500	5000
2d Sed	200	700	1050	2050	3600	5100
2d Lan Cpe	200	700	1050	2100	3650	5200

(continuation)

	6	5	4	3	2	1
4d Sed	150	600	950	1850	3200	4600
2d VL Cpe	150	550	850	1675	2950	4200
2d Cpe	150	600	900	1800	3150	4500
4d Sta Wag	150	650	975	1950	3350	4800
2d Z24 Cpe, V-6	350	830	1400	2950	4830	6900
2d Z24 Conv, V-6	950	1100	1850	3700	6450	9200
Beretta						
2d Cpe, 4-cyl.	200	700	1050	2100	3650	5200
2d Cpe, V-6	200	730	1250	2450	4270	6100
2d GT Cpe, V-6	200	745	1250	2500	4340	6200
Corsica						
4-cyl.						
4d NBk	150	650	950	1900	3300	4700
4d HBk	150	650	975	1950	3350	4800
V-6						
4d NBk	200	700	1050	2100	3650	5200
4d NBk LTZ	200	670	1200	2300	4060	5800
4d HBk	200	700	1075	2150	3700	5300
Celebrity						
4-cyl.						
4d Sed	150	600	900	1800	3150	4500
4d Sta Wag	150	650	950	1900	3300	4700
V-6						
4d Sed	150	600	950	1850	3200	4600
4d Sta Wag	200	675	1000	1950	3400	4900
Caprice, V-8						
4d Sed	200	745	1250	2500	4340	6200
4d Sed Classic	350	790	1350	2650	4620	6600
4d Classic Brgm Sed	350	860	1450	2900	5050	7200
4d Classic Sta Wag	350	1020	1700	3400	5950	8500
4d LS Sed	350	1000	1650	3300	5750	8200
Camaro						
V-6						
2d RS Cpe	200	720	1200	2400	4200	6000
V-8						
2d RS Cpe	350	780	1300	2600	4550	6500
2d RS Conv	450	1450	2400	4800	8400	12,000
2d IROC-Z Cpe	350	1020	1700	3400	5950	8500
2d IROC-Z Conv	550	1700	2800	5600	9800	14,000

1990

	6	5	4	3	2	1
Cavalier, 4-cyl.						
2d Cpe	150	550	850	1675	2950	4200
4d Sed	150	575	875	1700	3000	4300
4d Sta Wag	150	575	900	1750	3100	4400
2d Z24, V-6	350	780	1300	2600	4550	6500
Beretta, 4-cyl.						
2d Cpe	200	700	1050	2100	3650	5200
2d GTZ Cpe	200	745	1250	2500	4340	6200

NOTE: Add 10 percent for V-6.

	6	5	4	3	2	1
Corsica, 4-cyl.						
4d LT	150	650	975	1950	3350	4800
4d LT HBk	200	675	1000	1950	3400	4900
4d LTZ	200	720	1200	2400	4200	6000

NOTE: Add 10 percent for V-6.

	6	5	4	3	2	1
Celebrity, 4-cyl.						
4d Sta Wag	200	675	1000	2000	3500	5000

NOTE: Add 10 percent for V-6.

	6	5	4	3	2	1
Lumina, 4-cyl.						
2d Cpe	200	660	1100	2200	3850	5500
4d Sed	200	660	1100	2200	3850	5500
2d Euro Cpe	350	780	1300	2600	4550	6500
4d Euro Sed	350	780	1300	2600	4550	6500
Caprice, V-8						
4d Sed	350	780	1300	2600	4550	6500
4d Classic Sed	350	975	1600	3200	5600	8000
4d Classic Sta Wag	350	1020	1700	3400	5950	8500
4d Brgm Sed	350	1020	1700	3400	5950	8500
4d LS Sed	450	1080	1800	3600	6300	9000
Camaro						
V-6						
2d RS Cpe	200	720	1200	2400	4200	6000
V-8						
2d RS Cpe	350	790	1350	2650	4620	6600
2d RS Conv	400	1300	2200	4400	7700	11,000
2d IROC-Z Cpe	450	1080	1800	3600	6300	9000
2d IROC-Z Conv	500	1550	2600	5200	9100	13,000

1991

	6	5	4	3	2	1
Cavalier, 4-cyl.						
4d VL Sed	125	450	700	1400	2450	3500
2d VL Cpe	125	400	700	1375	2400	3400
4d VL Sta Wag	125	450	750	1450	2500	3600
4d RS Sta Wag	150	475	775	1500	2650	3800
2d RS Cpe	150	475	750	1475	2600	3700
2d RS Conv, V-6	350	840	1400	2800	4900	7000
4d RS Sta Wag	150	500	800	1550	2700	3900
2d Z24, V-6	200	720	1200	2400	4200	6000

NOTE: Add 10 percent for V-6.

	6	5	4	3	2	1
Beretta, 4-cyl.						
2d Cpe	150	600	900	1800	3150	4500
2d GT Cpe, V-6	350	820	1400	2700	4760	6800
2d GTZ Cpe	350	780	1300	2600	4550	6500
4d NBk Corsica	150	500	800	1600	2800	4000
4d HBk Corsica	150	550	850	1675	2950	4200

NOTE: Add 10 percent for V-6.

	6	5	4	3	2	1
Lumina, 4-cyl.						
4d Sed	150	650	950	1900	3300	4700
2d Cpe	150	650	975	1950	3350	4800

NOTE: Add 10 percent for V-6.

	6	5	4	3	2	1
4d Euro Sed, V-6	200	685	1150	2300	3990	5700
2d Euro Sed, V-6	350	830	1400	2950	4830	6900
2d Z34 Cpe, V-6	350	900	1500	3000	5250	7500
Camaro, V-6						
2d Cpe	200	720	1200	2400	4200	6000
2d Conv	400	1200	2000	4000	7000	10,000
Camaro, V-8						
2d RS Cpe	350	780	1300	2600	4550	6500
2d RS Conv	400	1250	2100	4200	7400	10,500
2d Z28 Cpe	350	1020	1700	3400	5950	8500
2d Z28 Conv	450	1500	2500	5000	8800	12,500
Caprice, V-8						
4d Sed	200	700	1200	2350	4130	5900
4d Sta Wag	350	900	1500	3000	5250	7500
4d Sed Classic	350	870	1450	2900	5100	7300

CORVAIR

	6	5	4	3	2	1
1960						
Standard, 6-cyl.						
4d Sed	350	900	1500	3000	5250	7500
2d Cpe	350	975	1600	3200	5600	8000
DeLuxe, 6-cyl.						
4d Sed	350	950	1500	3050	5300	7600
2d Cpe	350	1000	1650	3300	5750	8200
Monza, 6-cyl.						
2d Cpe	400	1300	2150	4300	7500	10,700
1961						
Series 500, 6-cyl.						
4d Sed	350	900	1500	3000	5250	7500
2d Cpe	350	975	1600	3200	5600	8000
4d Sta Wag	350	950	1550	3150	5450	7800
Series 700, 6-cyl.						
4d Sed	350	975	1600	3200	5500	7900
2d Cpe	350	1020	1700	3400	5950	8500
4d Sta Wag	350	1000	1650	3300	5750	8200
Monza, 6-cyl.						
4d Sed	350	975	1600	3250	5700	8100
2d Cpe	450	1160	1950	3900	6800	9700
Greenbrier, 6-cyl.						
4d Spt Wag	350	1020	1700	3400	5950	8500

NOTE: Add $1,200. for A/C.

	6	5	4	3	2	1
1962-1963						
Series 500, 6-cyl.						
2d Cpe	350	975	1600	3250	5700	8100
Series 700, 6-cyl.						
4d Sed	350	975	1600	3250	5700	8100
2d Cpe	350	1040	1700	3450	6000	8600
4d Sta Wag (1962 only)	350	1000	1650	3350	5800	8300
Series 900 Monza, 6-cyl.						
4d Sed	350	1040	1700	3450	6000	8600
2d Cpe	400	1200	2000	4000	7100	10,100
2d Conv	450	1400	2300	4600	8100	11,500
4d Sta Wag (1962 only)	350	1040	1750	3500	6100	8700
Monza Spyder, 6-cyl.						
2d Cpe	400	1250	2100	4200	7400	10,600
2d Conv	450	1450	2400	4800	8400	12,000
Greenbrier, 6-cyl.						
4d Spt Wag	350	1000	1650	3350	5800	8300

NOTE: Add $1,600. for K.O. wire wheels.
  Add $800. for A/C.

	6	5	4	3	2	1
1964						
Series 500, 6-cyl.						
2d Cpe	350	1000	1650	3350	5800	8300
Series 700, 6-cyl.						
4d Sed	350	975	1600	3250	5700	8100
Series 900 Monza, 6-cyl.						
4d Sed	350	1020	1700	3400	5950	8500
2d Cpe	400	1200	2000	4000	7100	10,100
2d Conv	400	1300	2200	4400	7700	11,000
Monza Spyder, 6-cyl.						
2d Cpe	400	1250	2100	4200	7400	10,600
2d Conv	450	1450	2400	4800	8400	12,000
Greenbrier, 6-cyl.						
4d Spt Wag	350	1040	1700	3450	6000	8600

NOTE: Add $1,600. for K.O. wire wheels.
  Add $800. for A/C except Spyder.

	6	5	4	3	2	1
1965						
Series 500, 6-cyl.						
4d HT	350	820	1400	2700	4760	6800
2d HT	350	900	1500	3000	5250	7500
Monza Series, 6-cyl.						
4d HT	350	900	1500	3000	5250	7500
2d HT	450	1140	1900	3800	6650	9500
2d Conv	450	1400	2300	4600	8100	11,500

NOTES: Add 20 percent for 140 hp engine.
  Add 30 percent for 180 hp engine.

	6	5	4	3	2	1
Corsa Series, 6-cyl.						
2d HT	450	1140	1900	3800	6650	9500
2d Conv	450	1450	2400	4800	8400	12,000
Greenbrier, 6-cyl.						
4d Spt Wag	350	975	1600	3200	5600	8000

NOTE: Add $1,000. for A/C.

	6	5	4	3	2	1
1966						
Series 500, 6-cyl.						
4d HT	350	840	1400	2800	4900	7000
2d HT	350	950	1500	3050	5300	7600
Monza Series, 6-cyl.						
4d HT	350	950	1550	3100	5400	7700
2d HT	450	1140	1900	3800	6650	9500
2d Conv	450	1450	2400	4800	8400	12,000

NOTES: Add 20 percent for 140 hp engine.
  Add 30 percent for 180 hp engine.

	6	5	4	3	2	1
Corsa Series, 6-cyl.						
2d HT	400	1200	2000	4000	7100	10,100
2d Conv	450	1500	2500	5000	8800	12,500

NOTE: Add $1,000. for A/C.

	6	5	4	3	2	1
1967						
Series 500, 6-cyl.						
2d HT	350	900	1500	3000	5250	7500
4d HT	350	840	1400	2800	4900	7000
Monza, 6-cyl.						
4d HT	350	950	1550	3100	5400	7700
2d HT	450	1140	1900	3800	6650	9500
2d Conv	450	1400	2300	4600	8100	11,500

NOTES: Add $1,000. for A/C.
  Add 20 percent for 140 hp engine.

	6	5	4	3	2	1
1968						
Series 500, 6-cyl.						
2d HT	350	900	1500	3000	5250	7500
Monza, 6-cyl.						
2d HT	450	1140	1900	3800	6650	9500
2d Conv	450	1400	2300	4600	8100	11,500

NOTE: Add 20 percent for 140 hp engine.

	6	5	4	3	2	1
1969						
Series 500, 6-cyl.						
2d HT	350	1020	1700	3400	5950	8500
Monza						
2d HT	400	1300	2200	4400	7700	11,000
2d Conv	450	1450	2400	4800	8400	12,000

NOTE: Add 20 percent for 140 hp engine.

CORVETTE

	6	5	4	3	2	1
1953						
6-cyl. Conv	3600	11,500	19,200	38,400	67,200	96,000

NOTE: Add $1,800. & up for access. hardtop.

	6	5	4	3	2	1
1954						
6-cyl Conv	2050	6600	11,000	22,000	38,500	55,000

NOTE: Add $1,800. & up for access. hardtop.

	6	5	4	3	2	1
1955						
6-cyl Conv	2500	7900	13,200	26,400	46,200	66,000
8-cyl Conv	2500	7900	13,200	26,400	46,200	66,000

NOTE: Add $1,800. & up for access. hardtop.

	6	5	4	3	2	1
1956						
Conv	2250	7200	12,000	24,000	42,000	60,000

NOTE: All post-1955 Corvettes are V-8 powered.
Add $1,800. & up for removable hardtop.
Add 20 percent for two 4 barrel carbs.

	6	5	4	3	2	1
1957						
Conv	2350	7450	12,400	24,800	43,400	62,000

NOTES: Add $1,800. for hardtop.
Add 50 percent for F.I., 250 hp.
Add 75 percent for F.I., 283 hp.
Add 25 percent for two 4 barrel carbs, 245 hp.
Add 35 percent for two 4 barrel carbs, 270 hp.
Add 15 percent for 4-speed trans.
Add 150 percent for 579E option.

	6	5	4	3	2	1
1958						
Conv	1800	5750	9600	19,200	33,600	48,000

NOTES: Add $1,800. for hardtop; 30 percent for F.I.
Add 25 percent for two 4 barrel carbs, 245 hp.
Add 35 percent for two 4 barrel carbs, 270 hp.
Add 40 percent for F.I., 250 hp.
Add 60 percent for F.I., 290 hp.

	6	5	4	3	2	1
1959						
Conv	1700	5400	9000	18,000	31,500	45,000

NOTES: Add $1,800. for hardtop.
Add 40 percent for F.I., 250 hp.
Add 60 percent for F.I., 290 hp.
Add 25 percent for two 4 barrel carbs, 245 hp.
Add 35 percent for two 4 barrel carbs, 270 hp.

	6	5	4	3	2	1
1960						
Conv	1700	5400	9000	18,000	31,500	45,000

NOTES: Add $1,800. for hardtop.
Add 40 percent for F.I., 275 hp.
Add 60 percent for F.I., 315 hp.
Add 25 percent for two 4 barrel carbs, 245 hp.
Add 35 percent for two 4 barrel carbs, 270 hp.

	6	5	4	3	2	1
1961						
Conv	1750	5500	9200	18,400	32,200	46,000

NOTES: Add $1,800. for hardtop.
Add 40 percent for F.I., 275 hp.
Add 60 percent for F.I., 315 hp.
Add 25 percent for two 4 barrel carbs, 245 hp.
Add 35 percent for two 4 barrel carbs, 270 hp.

	6	5	4	3	2	1
1962						
Conv	1750	5650	9400	18,800	32,900	47,000

NOTE: Add $1,800. for hardtop; 30 percent for F.I.

	6	5	4	3	2	1
1963						
Spt Cpe	1600	5050	8400	16,800	29,400	42,000
Conv	1550	4900	8200	16,400	28,700	41,000
GS					value not estimable	

NOTES: Add 30 percent for F.I.; $4,500. for A/C.
Add $1,800. for hardtop; $3,000. for knock off wheels.
Z06 option, value not estimable.

	6	5	4	3	2	1
1964						
Spt Cpe	1350	4300	7200	14,400	25,200	36,000
Conv	1550	4900	8200	16,400	28,700	41,000

NOTES: Add 30 percent for F.I.; $4,500. for A/C.
Add 30 percent for 327 CID, 365 hp.
Add $1,800. for hardtop; $3,000. for knock off wheels.

	6	5	4	3	2	1
1965						
Spt Cpe	1350	4300	7200	14,400	25,200	36,000
Conv	1550	4900	8200	16,400	28,700	41,000

NOTES: Add 40 percent for F.I.; $4,500. for A/C.
Add 60 percent for 396 CID.
Add $3,000. for knock off wheels; 50 percent for 396 engine.
Add $1,800. for hardtop.

	6	5	4	3	2	1
1966						
Spt Cpe	1350	4300	7200	14,400	25,200	36,000
Conv	1550	4900	8200	16,400	28,700	41,000

NOTES: Add $4,500. for A/C; 20 percent for 427 engine - 390 hp.
Add 50 percent for 427 engine - 425 hp.
Add $3,000. for knock off wheels; $1800. for hardtop.

	6	5	4	3	2	1
1967						
Spt Cpe	1400	4450	7400	14,800	25,900	37,000
Conv	1600	5050	8400	16,800	29,400	42,000

NOTES: Add $4,500. for A/C. L88 & L89 option not estimable. 30 percent for 427 engine - 390 hp. Add 50 percent for 427 engine - 400 hp, 70 percent for 427 engine - 435 hp; $4,000. for aluminum wheels; $1800. for hardtop.

	6	5	4	3	2	1
1968						
Spt Cpe	1000	3100	5200	10,400	18,200	26,000
Conv	1150	3600	6000	12,000	21,000	30,000

NOTES: Add 40 percent for L89 427 - 435 hp aluminum head option. L88 engine option not estimable. Add 40 percent for 427, 400 hp.

	6	5	4	3	2	1
1969						
Spt Cpe	1000	3100	5200	10,400	18,200	26,000
Conv	1150	3600	6000	12,000	21,000	30,000

NOTES: Add 40 percent for 427 - 435 hp aluminum head option. L88 engine option not estimable. Add 40 percent for 427, 400 hp.

	6	5	4	3	2	1
1970						
Spt Cpe	950	3000	5000	10,000	17,500	25,000
Conv	1100	3500	5800	11,600	20,300	29,000

OTES: Add 70 percent for LT-1 option. ZR1 option not estimable.

	6	5	4	3	2	1
1971						
Spt Cpe	900	2900	4800	9600	16,800	24,000
Conv	1050	3350	5600	11,200	19,600	28,000

NOTES: Add 50 percent for LT-1 option; 30 percent for LS 5 option; 75 percent for LS 6 option.

	6	5	4	3	2	1
1972						
Spt Cpe	900	2900	4800	9600	16,800	24,000
Conv	1050	3350	5600	11,200	19,600	28,000

NOTES: Add 50 percent for LT-1 option.
Add 30 percent for LS 5 option.
Add 25 percent for air on LT 1.

	6	5	4	3	2	1
1973						
Spt Cpe	850	2650	4400	8800	15,400	22,000
Conv	1000	3100	5200	10,400	18,200	26,000

NOTE: Add 10 percent for L82.

	6	5	4	3	2	1
1974						
Spt Cpe	700	2300	3800	7600	13,300	19,000
Conv	900	2900	4800	9600	16,800	24,000

NOTE: Add 10 percent for L82.

	6	5	4	3	2	1
1975						
Spt Cpe	750	2400	4000	8000	14,000	20,000
Conv	1000	3100	5200	10,400	18,200	26,000

NOTE: Add 10 percent for L82.

	6	5	4	3	2	1
1976						
Cpe	700	2300	3800	7600	13,300	19,000

NOTE: Add 10 percent for L82.

	6	5	4	3	2	1
1977						
Cpe	700	2300	3800	7600	13,300	19,000

NOTE: Add 10 percent for L82.

	6	5	4	3	2	1
1978						
Cpe	850	2750	4600	9200	16,100	23,000

Note: Add 10 percent for anniversary model.
Add 25 percent for pace car.
Add 10 percent for L82 engine option.

	6	5	4	3	2	1
1979						
Cpe	750	2400	4000	8000	14,000	20,000

NOTE: Add 10 percent for L82 engine option.

	6	5	4	3	2	1
1980						
Corvette, V-8						
Cpe	750	2400	4000	8000	14,000	20,000

NOTE: Add 20 percent for L82 engine option.

	6	5	4	3	2	1
1981						
Corvette, V-8						
Cpe	750	2400	4000	8000	14,000	20,000

	6	5	4	3	2	1
1982						
Corvette, V-8						
2d HBK	800	2500	4200	8400	14,700	21,000

NOTE: Add 20 percent for Collector Edition.

1983

NOTE: None manufactured.

	6	5	4	3	2	1
1984						
Corvette, V-8						
2d HBk	700	2150	3600	7200	12,600	18,000

	6	5	4	3	2	1
1985						
Corvette, V-8						
2d HBk	700	2150	3600	7200	12,600	18,000

	6	5	4	3	2	1
1986						
Corvette, V-8						
2d HBk	700	2300	3800	7600	13,300	19,000
Conv	850	2750	4600	9200	16,100	23,000

NOTE: Add 10 percent for pace car.

	6	5	4	3	2	1
1987						
Corvette, V-8						
2d HBk	700	2300	3800	7600	13,300	19,000
Conv	850	2750	4600	9200	16,100	23,000

	6	5	4	3	2	1
1988						
Corvette, V-8						
2d Cpe	600	1850	3100	6200	10,900	15,500
Conv	800	2500	4200	8400	14,700	21,000

	6	5	4	3	2	1
1989						
Corvette, V-8						
2d Cpe	700	2300	3800	7600	13,300	19,000
Conv	850	2650	4400	8800	15,400	22,000

	6	5	4	3	2	1
1990						
Corvette, V-8						
2d HBk	850	2750	4600	9200	16,100	23,000
Conv	1000	3250	5400	10,800	18,900	27,000
2d HBk ZR1	1700	5400	9000	18,000	31,500	45,000

	6	5	4	3	2	1
1991						
Corvette, V-8						
2d HBk	1100	3500	5800	11,600	20,300	29,000
Conv	1200	3850	6400	12,800	22,400	32,000
2d HBk ZR1	1800	5750	9600	19,200	33,600	48,000

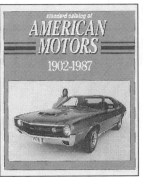
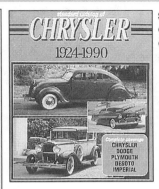
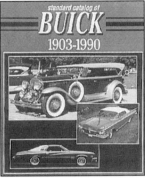
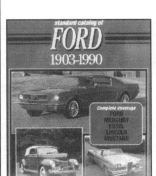

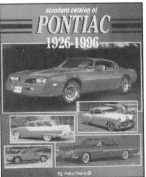
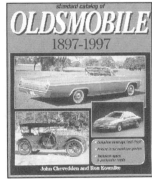

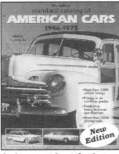

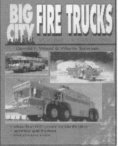

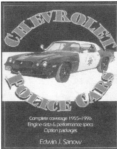

	6	5	4	3	2	1
Impala, V-8						
4d Sed	150	650	950	1900	3300	4700

NOTE: Deduct 10 percent for V6 cyl.

	6	5	4	3	2	1
Caprice Classic, V-8						
4d Sed	200	675	1000	1950	3400	4900
2d Sed	200	675	1000	2000	3500	5000
4d Sta Wag	200	675	1000	1950	3400	4900

NOTE: Deduct 10 percent for V-6 cyl.

1985

	6	5	4	3	2	1
Sprint, 3-cyl.						
2d HBk	125	450	700	1400	2450	3500
Chevette, 4-cyl.						
4d HBk	125	450	750	1450	2500	3600
2d HBk	125	450	700	1400	2450	3500

NOTE: Deduct 20 percent for diesel.

	6	5	4	3	2	1
Spectrum, 4-cyl.						
4d HBk	125	450	750	1450	2500	3600
2d HBk	125	450	750	1450	2500	3600
Nova, 4-cyl.						
4d HBk	125	450	750	1450	2500	3600
Cavalier						
2d T Type Cpe	150	550	850	1675	2950	4200
2d T Type HBk	150	575	875	1700	3000	4300
T Type Conv	200	660	1100	2200	3850	5500

NOTE: Deduct 10 percent for 4-cyl.
NOTE: Deduct 5 percent for lesser models.

	6	5	4	3	2	1
Citation, V-6						
4d HBk	150	550	850	1675	2950	4200
2d HBk	150	550	850	1675	2950	4200

NOTE: Deduct 10 percent for 4-cyl.

	6	5	4	3	2	1
Celebrity, V-6						
4d Sed	150	575	875	1700	3000	4300
2d Cpe	150	575	875	1700	3000	4300
4d Sta Wag	150	575	900	1750	3100	4400

NOTE: Deduct 10 percent for 4-cyl.
Deduct 30 percent for diesel.

	6	5	4	3	2	1
Camaro, V-8						
2d Cpe Spt	350	800	1350	2700	4700	6700
2d Cpe Berlinetta	350	830	1400	2950	4830	6900
2d Cpe Z28	350	860	1450	2900	5050	7200
2d Cpe IROC-Z	350	950	1500	3050	5300	7600

NOTE: Deduct 30 percent for 4-cyl.
Deduct 20 percent for V-6.

	6	5	4	3	2	1
Monte Carlo, V-8						
2d Cpe Spt	200	730	1250	2450	4270	6100
2d Cpe SS	350	820	1400	2700	4760	6800

NOTE: Deduct 20 percent for V-6 where available.

	6	5	4	3	2	1
Impala, V-8						
4d Sed	150	650	975	1950	3350	4800

NOTE: Deduct 20 percent for V-6.

	6	5	4	3	2	1
Caprice Classic, V-8						
4d Sed	200	675	1000	2000	3500	5000
2d Cpe	200	675	1000	2000	3500	5000
4d Sta Wag	200	700	1050	2100	3650	5200

NOTE: Deduct 20 percent for V-6.
Deduct 30 percent for diesel.

1986

	6	5	4	3	2	1
Chevette						
2d Cpe	125	450	750	1450	2500	3600
4d Sed	150	475	750	1475	2600	3700
Nova						
4d Sed	150	475	750	1475	2600	3700
4d HBk	150	475	775	1500	2650	3800
Cavalier						
2d Cpe	150	500	800	1600	2800	4000
4d Sed	150	550	850	1650	2900	4100
4d Sta Wag	150	550	850	1675	2950	4200
2d Conv	200	720	1200	2400	4200	6000
Cavalier Z24						
2d Cpe	200	670	1200	2300	4060	5800
2d HBk	200	685	1150	2300	3990	5700
Camaro						
2d Cpe	350	820	1400	2700	4760	6800
2d Cpe Berlinetta	350	840	1400	2800	4900	7000
2d Cpe Z28	350	900	1500	3000	5250	7500
2d Cpe IROC-Z	350	975	1600	3200	5600	8000
Celebrity						
2d Cpe	150	575	900	1750	3100	4400
4d Sed	150	600	900	1800	3150	4500
4d Sta Wag	150	600	950	1850	3200	4600
Monte Carlo						
2d Cpe	350	780	1300	2600	4550	6500
2d Cpe LS	350	840	1400	2800	4900	7000
Monte Carlo SS						
2d Cpe	350	975	1600	3200	5600	8000
2d Cpe Aero	400	1200	2000	4000	7000	10,000
Caprice						
4d Sed	200	660	1100	2200	3850	5500
Caprice Classic						
2d Cpe	200	685	1150	2300	3990	5700
4d Sed	200	670	1150	2250	3920	5600
4d Sta Wag	200	720	1200	2400	4200	6000
Caprice Classic Brougham						
4d Sed	200	700	1200	2350	4130	5900
4d Sed LS	200	720	1200	2400	4200	6000

1987

	6	5	4	3	2	1
Sprint, 3-cyl.						
2d HBk	125	450	750	1450	2500	3600
4d HBk	150	475	750	1475	2600	3700
2d HBk ER	150	475	750	1475	2600	3700
2d HBk Turbo	150	475	775	1500	2650	3800
Chevette, 4-cyl.						
2d HBk	125	450	750	1450	2500	3600
4d HBk	150	475	750	1475	2600	3700
Spectrum, 4-cyl.						
2d HBk	150	500	800	1550	2700	3900
4d HBk	150	500	800	1550	2700	3900
2d HBk EX	150	475	775	1500	2650	3800
4d HBk Turbo	150	500	800	1600	2800	4000
Nova, 4-cyl.						
4d HBk	150	475	775	1500	2650	3800
4d Sed	150	500	800	1550	2700	3900
Cavalier, 4-cyl.						
4d Sed	150	500	800	1600	2800	4000
2d Cpe	150	500	800	1550	2700	3900
4d Sta Wag	150	550	850	1650	2900	4100

	6	5	4	3	2	1
4d Sed GS	150	550	850	1650	2900	4100
2d HBk GS	150	500	800	1600	2800	4000
4d Sta Wag GS	150	550	850	1675	2950	4200
4d Sed RS	150	550	850	1675	2950	4200
2d Cpe RS	150	550	850	1650	2900	4100
2d HBk RS	150	550	850	1650	2900	4100
2d Conv RS	200	745	1250	2500	4340	6200
4d Sta Wag	150	550	850	1675	2950	4200

NOTE: Add 10 percent for V-6.

	6	5	4	3	2	1
Cavalier Z24 V-6						
2d Spt Cpe	200	700	1200	2350	4130	5900
2d Spt HBk	200	670	1200	2300	4060	5800
Beretta						
2d Cpe 4-cyl.	150	650	950	1900	3300	4700
2d Cpe V-6	200	675	1000	2000	3500	5000
Corsica						
4d Sed 4-cyl.	150	650	975	1950	3350	4800
4d Sed V-6	200	700	1050	2050	3600	5100
Celebrity						
4d Sed 4-cyl.	150	600	950	1850	3200	4600
2d Cpe 4-cyl.	150	600	900	1800	3150	4500
4d Sta Wag 4-cyl.	150	650	950	1900	3300	4700
4d Sed V-6	150	650	975	1950	3350	4800
2d Cpe V-6	150	650	950	1900	3300	4700
4d Sta Wag V-6	200	675	1000	1950	3400	4900
Camaro						
2d Cpe V-6	350	830	1400	2950	4830	6900
2d Cpe LT V-6	350	840	1400	2800	4900	7000
2d Cpe V-8	350	860	1450	2900	5050	7200
2d Cpe LT V-8	350	870	1450	2900	5100	7300
2d Cpe Z28 V-8	350	950	1550	3100	5400	7700
2d Cpe IROC-Z V-8	350	1000	1650	3300	5750	8200
2d Conv IROC-Z V-8	600	1900	3200	6400	11,200	16,000

NOTE: Add 20 percent for 350 V-8 where available.

	6	5	4	3	2	1
Monte Carlo						
2d Cpe LS V-6	350	790	1350	2650	4620	6600
2d Cpe LS V-8	350	820	1400	2700	4760	6800
2d Cpe SS V-8	350	975	1600	3200	5600	8000
2d Cpe Aero V-8	450	1080	1800	3600	6300	9000
Caprice, V-6						
4d Sed	200	670	1150	2250	3920	5600
Caprice Classic V-6						
4d Sed	200	670	1200	2300	4060	5800
2d Cpe	200	685	1150	2300	3990	5700
4d Sed Brgm	200	700	1200	2350	4130	5900
2d Cpe Brgm	200	670	1200	2300	4060	5800
Caprice, V-8						
4d Sed	200	670	1200	2300	4060	5800
4d Sta Wag	200	730	1250	2450	4270	6100
Caprice Classic V-8						
4d Sed	200	720	1200	2400	4200	6000
2d Cpe	200	700	1200	2350	4130	5900
4d Sta Wag	200	750	1275	2500	4400	6300
4d Sed Brgm	200	730	1250	2450	4270	6100
2d Cpe Brgm	200	720	1200	2400	4200	6000

1988

	6	5	4	3	2	1
Sprint, 3-cyl.						
2d HBk	100	360	600	1200	2100	3000
4d HBk	125	380	650	1300	2250	3200
2d Metro	100	330	575	1150	1950	2800
2d Turbo	100	350	600	1150	2000	2900
Spectrum, 4-cyl.						
2d HBk Express	100	325	550	1100	1900	2700
4d Sed	100	350	600	1150	2000	2900
2d HBk	100	330	575	1150	1950	2800
4d Turbo Sed	125	370	650	1250	2200	3100
Nova, 4-cyl.						
5d HBk	125	450	700	1400	2450	3500
4d Sed	125	400	700	1375	2400	3400
4d Sed Twin Cam	150	550	850	1650	2900	4100
Cavalier						
4d Sed	125	400	700	1375	2400	3400
2d Cpe	125	450	750	1450	2500	3600
4d Sta Wag	125	400	700	1375	2400	3400
4d RS Sed	150	500	800	1550	2700	3900
2d RS Cpe	150	500	800	1600	2800	4000
2d Z24 Cpe V-6	200	675	1000	2000	3500	5000
2d Z24 Conv V-6	200	720	1200	2400	4200	6000
Beretta, 4-cyl.						
2d Cpe	150	550	850	1675	2950	4200
2d Cpe V-6	150	600	900	1800	3150	4500
Corsica, V-4						
4d Sed	150	500	800	1600	2800	4000
4d Sed V-6	150	575	875	1700	3000	4300
Celebrity, 4-cyl.						
4d Sed	125	450	750	1450	2500	3600
2d Cpe	125	450	700	1400	2450	3500
4d Sta Wag	150	500	800	1550	2700	3900
4d Sed V-6	150	500	800	1550	2700	3900
2d Cpe V-6	150	475	775	1500	2650	3800
4d Sta Wag V-6	150	550	850	1650	2900	4100
Monte Carlo						
2d Cpe V-6	200	660	1100	2200	3850	5500
2d Cpe V-8	200	720	1200	2400	4200	6000
2d SS Cpe V-8	450	1080	1800	3600	6300	9000
Caprice, V-6						
4d Sed	200	675	1000	2000	3500	5000
4d Classic Sed	200	660	1100	2200	3850	5500
4d Brgm Sed	200	720	1200	2400	4200	6000
4d LS Brgm Sed	350	780	1300	2600	4550	6500
Caprice, V-8						
4d Sed	200	720	1200	2400	4200	6000
4d Classic Sed	350	780	1300	2600	4550	6500
4d Sta Wag	350	840	1400	2800	4900	7000
4d Brgm Sed	350	840	1400	2800	4900	7000
4d LS Brgm Sed	350	900	1500	3000	5250	7500
Camaro						
V-6						
2d Cpe	200	660	1100	2200	3850	5500
V-8						
2d Cpe	200	720	1200	2400	4200	6000
2d Conv	400	1200	2000	4000	7000	10,000
2d IROC-Z Cpe	350	1020	1700	3400	5950	8500
2d IROC-Z Conv	500	1550	2600	5200	9100	13,000

1989

Cavalier, 4-cyl.

	6	5	4	3	2	1
4d 2S Sta Wag	200	700	1050	2050	3600	5100
4d 3S Sta Wag	200	700	1050	2100	3650	5200

NOTE: Deduct 15 percent for 6-cyl.

Camaro, V-8

	6	5	4	3	2	1
2d Spt Cpe	200	670	1200	2300	4060	5800
2d Rally Cpe	350	770	1300	2550	4480	6400
2d Berlinetta Cpe	350	790	1350	2650	4620	6600
2d Z28 Cpe	350	830	1400	2950	4830	6900

NOTE: Deduct 20 percent for 6-cyl.

1980

Chevette, 4-cyl.

	6	5	4	3	2	1
2d HBk Scooter	100	360	600	1200	2100	3000
2d HBk	125	370	650	1250	2200	3100
4d HBk	125	380	650	1300	2250	3200

Citation, 6-cyl.

	6	5	4	3	2	1
4d HBk	125	450	700	1400	2450	3500
2d HBk	125	400	700	1375	2400	3400
2d Cpe	125	450	750	1450	2500	3600
2d Cpe Clb	150	475	750	1475	2600	3700

NOTE: Deduct 10 percent for 4-cyl.

Monza, 4-cyl.

	6	5	4	3	2	1
2d HBk 2 plus 2	125	400	700	1375	2400	3400
2d HBk Spt 2 plus 2	125	450	750	1450	2500	3600
2d Cpe	125	450	700	1400	2450	3500

NOTE: Add 10 percent for V-6.

Malibu, V-8

	6	5	4	3	2	1
4d Sed	125	450	750	1450	2500	3600
2d Cpe Spt	150	475	775	1500	2650	3800
4d Sta Wag	150	475	750	1475	2600	3700

NOTE: Deduct 10 percent for V-6.

Malibu Classic, V-8

	6	5	4	3	2	1
4d Sed	150	475	750	1475	2600	3700
2d Cpe Spt	150	500	800	1550	2700	3900
2d Cpe Lan	150	500	800	1600	2800	4000
4d Sta Wag	150	475	775	1500	2650	3800

NOTE: Deduct 10 percent for 6-cyl.

Camaro, 6-cyl.

	6	5	4	3	2	1
2d Cpe Spt	200	730	1250	2450	4270	6100
2d Cpe RS	200	750	1275	2500	4400	6300
2d Cpe Berlinetta	350	770	1300	2550	4480	6400

Camaro, V-8

	6	5	4	3	2	1
2d Cpe Spt	350	780	1300	2600	4550	6500
2d Cpe RS	350	800	1350	2700	4700	6700
2d Cpe Berlinetta	350	820	1400	2700	4760	6800
2d Cpe Z28	350	840	1400	2800	4900	7000

Monte Carlo, 6-cyl.

	6	5	4	3	2	1
2d Cpe Spt	200	650	1100	2150	3780	5400
2d Cpe Lan	200	660	1100	2200	3850	5500

Monte Carlo, V-8

	6	5	4	3	2	1
2d Cpe Spt	200	670	1200	2300	4060	5800
2d Cpe Lan	200	700	1200	2350	4130	5900

Impala, V-8

	6	5	4	3	2	1
4d Sed	150	500	800	1550	2700	3900
2d Cpe	150	500	800	1600	2800	4000
4d 2S Sta Wag	150	500	800	1600	2800	4000
4d 3S Sta Wag	150	550	850	1650	2900	4100

NOTE: Deduct 12 percent for 6-cyl. sedan and coupe only.

Caprice Classic, V-8

	6	5	4	3	2	1
4d Sed	150	500	800	1600	2800	4000
2d Cpe	150	550	850	1675	2950	4200
2d Cpe Lan	150	575	900	1750	3100	4400
4d 2S Sta Wag	150	550	850	1650	2900	4100
4d 3S Sta Wag	150	550	850	1675	2950	4200

1981

Chevette, 4-cyl.

	6	5	4	3	2	1
2d HBk Scooter	125	370	650	1250	2200	3100
2d HBk	125	380	650	1300	2250	3200
4d HBk	125	400	675	1350	2300	3300

Citation, 6-cyl.

	6	5	4	3	2	1
4d HBk	125	450	750	1450	2500	3600
2d HBk	125	450	700	1400	2450	3500

NOTE: Deduct 10 percent for 4-cyl.

Malibu, V-8

	6	5	4	3	2	1
4d Sed Spt	150	475	750	1475	2600	3700
2d Cpe Spt	150	475	775	1500	2650	3800
4d Sta Wag	150	475	775	1500	2650	3800

NOTE: Deduct 10 percent for 6-cyl.

Malibu Classic, V-8

	6	5	4	3	2	1
4d Sed Spt	150	475	775	1500	2650	3800
2d Cpe Spt	150	500	800	1550	2700	3900
2d Cpe Lan	150	500	800	1600	2800	4000
4d Sta Wag	150	500	800	1550	2700	3900

Camaro, 6-cyl.

	6	5	4	3	2	1
2d Cpe Spt	200	745	1250	2500	4340	6200
2d Cpe Berlinetta	350	770	1300	2550	4480	6400

Camaro, V-8

	6	5	4	3	2	1
2d Cpe Spt	350	790	1350	2650	4620	6600
2d Cpe Berlinetta	350	820	1400	2700	4760	6800
2d Cpe Z28	350	860	1450	2900	5050	7200

Monte Carlo, 6-cyl.

	6	5	4	3	2	1
2d Cpe Spt	200	660	1100	2200	3850	5500
2d Cpe Lan	200	670	1150	2250	3920	5600

Monte Carlo, V-8

	6	5	4	3	2	1
2d Cpe Spt	200	700	1200	2350	4130	5900
2d Cpe Lan	200	720	1200	2400	4200	6000

Impala, V-8

	6	5	4	3	2	1
4d Sed	150	500	800	1600	2800	4000
2d Cpe	150	550	850	1650	2900	4100
4d 2S Sta Wag	150	550	850	1650	2900	4100
4d 3S Sta Wag	150	550	850	1675	2950	4200

NOTE: Deduct 12 percent for 6-cyl. on sedan and coupe only.

Caprice Classic, V-8

	6	5	4	3	2	1
4d Sed	150	550	850	1675	2950	4200
2d Cpe	150	575	875	1700	3000	4300
2d Cpe Lan	150	600	900	1800	3150	4500
4d 2S Sta Wag	150	575	875	1700	3000	4300
4d 3S Sta Wag	150	575	900	1750	3100	4400

NOTE: Deduct 15 percent for 6-cyl. coupe and sedan only.

1982

Chevette, 4-cyl.

	6	5	4	3	2	1
2d HBk	125	400	700	1375	2400	3400
4d HBk	125	450	700	1400	2450	3500

NOTE: Deduct 5 percent for lesser models.

Cavalier, 4-cyl.

	6	5	4	3	2	1
4d Sed CL	150	500	800	1600	2800	4000
2d Cpe CL	150	550	850	1650	2900	4100
2d Hatch CL	150	550	850	1675	2950	4200
4d Sta Wag CL	150	550	850	1675	2950	4200

NOTE: Deduct 5 percent for lesser models.

Citation, 6-cyl.

	6	5	4	3	2	1
4d HBk	150	475	775	1500	2650	3800
2d HBk	150	475	750	1475	2600	3700
2d Cpe	150	475	775	1500	2650	3800

NOTE: Deduct 10 percent for 4-cyl.

Malibu, V-8

	6	5	4	3	2	1
4d Sed	150	550	850	1650	2900	4100
4d Sta Wag	150	550	850	1675	2950	4200

NOTE: Deduct 10 percent for 6-cyl.

Celebrity, 6-cyl.

	6	5	4	3	2	1
4d Sed	150	550	850	1675	2950	4200
2d Cpe	150	575	875	1700	3000	4300

NOTE: Deduct 10 percent for 6-cyl.

Camaro, 6-cyl.

	6	5	4	3	2	1
2d Cpe Spt	200	750	1275	2500	4400	6300
2d Cpe Berlinetta	350	780	1300	2600	4550	6500

Camaro, V-8

	6	5	4	3	2	1
2d Cpe Spt	350	800	1350	2700	4700	6700
2d Cpe Berlinetta	350	830	1400	2950	4830	6900
2d Cpe Z28	350	880	1500	2950	5180	7400

NOTE: Add 20 percent for Indy pace car.

Monte Carlo, 6-cyl.

	6	5	4	3	2	1
2d Cpe Spt	200	685	1150	2300	3990	5700

Monte Carlo, V-8

	6	5	4	3	2	1
2d Cpe Spt	200	730	1250	2450	4270	6100

Impala, V-8

	6	5	4	3	2	1
4d Sed	150	575	900	1750	3100	4400
4d 2S Sta Wag	150	575	900	1750	3100	4400
4d 3S Sta Wag	150	600	900	1800	3150	4500

NOTE: Deduct 12 percent for 6-cyl. on sedan only.

Caprice Classic, V-8

	6	5	4	3	2	1
4d Sed	150	600	950	1850	3200	4600
2d Spt Cpe	150	650	950	1900	3300	4700
4d 3S Sta Wag	150	650	950	1900	3300	4700

NOTE: Deduct 15 percent for 6-cyl. coupe and sedan only.

1983

Chevette, 4-cyl.

	6	5	4	3	2	1
2d HBk	125	450	700	1400	2450	3500
4d HBk	125	450	750	1450	2500	3600

NOTE: Deduct 5 percent for lesser models.

Cavalier, 4-cyl.

	6	5	4	3	2	1
4d Sed CS	150	500	800	1550	2700	3900
2d Cpe CS	150	500	800	1600	2800	4000
2d HBk CS	150	550	850	1650	2900	4100
4d Sta Wag CS	150	550	850	1650	2900	4100

NOTE: Deduct 5 percent for lesser models.

Citation, 6-cyl.

	6	5	4	3	2	1
4d HBk	150	475	775	1500	2650	3800
2d HBk	150	475	750	1475	2600	3700
2d Cpe	150	475	775	1500	2650	3800

NOTE: Deduct 10 percent for 4-cyl.

Malibu, V-8

	6	5	4	3	2	1
4d Sed	150	550	850	1675	2950	4200
4d Sta Wag	150	575	875	1700	3000	4300

NOTE: Deduct 10 percent for 6-cyl.

Celebrity, V-6

	6	5	4	3	2	1
4d Sed	150	575	875	1700	3000	4300
2d Cpe	150	575	900	1750	3100	4400

NOTE: Deduct 10 percent for 4-cyl.

Camaro, 6-cyl.

	6	5	4	3	2	1
2d Cpe Spt	350	770	1300	2550	4480	6400
2d Cpe Berlinetta	350	790	1350	2650	4620	6600

Camaro, V-8

	6	5	4	3	2	1
2d Cpe Spt	350	620	1400	2700	4760	6800
2d Cpe Berlinetta	350	840	1400	2800	4900	7000
2d Cpe Z28	350	900	1500	3000	5250	7500

Monte Carlo, 6-cyl.

	6	5	4	3	2	1
2d Cpe Spt	200	670	1200	2300	4060	5800

Monte Carlo, V-8

	6	5	4	3	2	1
2d Cpe Spt SS	350	820	1400	2700	4760	6800
2d Cpe Spt	200	745	1250	2500	4340	6200

Impala, V-8

	6	5	4	3	2	1
4d Sed	150	600	900	1800	3150	4500

NOTE: Deduct 12 percent for 6-cyl.

Caprice Classic, V-8

	6	5	4	3	2	1
4d Sed	150	650	950	1900	3300	4700
4d Sta Wag	150	650	950	1900	3300	4700

NOTE: Deduct 15 percent for 6-cyl.

1984

Chevette CS, 4-cyl.

NOTE: Deduct 10 percent for V-6 cyl.

	6	5	4	3	2	1
2d HBk	125	450	750	1450	2500	3600

NOTE: Deduct 5 percent for lesser models.

Cavalier, 4-cyl.

	6	5	4	3	2	1
4d Sed	150	475	750	1475	2600	3700
4d Sta Wag	150	500	800	1600	2800	4000

Cavalier Type 10, 4-cyl.

	6	5	4	3	2	1
2d Sed	150	475	775	1500	2650	3800
2d HBk	150	500	800	1550	2700	3900
2d Conv	200	660	1100	2200	3850	5500

Cavalier CS, 4-cyl.

	6	5	4	3	2	1
4d Sed	150	500	800	1550	2700	3900
4d Sta Wag	150	500	800	1600	2800	4000

Citation, V-6

	6	5	4	3	2	1
4d HBk	150	550	850	1650	2900	4100
2d HBk	150	550	850	1650	2900	4100
2d Cpe	150	550	850	1675	2950	4200

NOTE: Deduct 5 percent for 4-cyl.

Celebrity, V-6

	6	5	4	3	2	1
4d Sed	150	500	800	1600	2800	4000
2d Sed	150	500	800	1600	2800	4000
4d Sta Wag	150	550	850	1650	2900	4100

NOTE: Deduct 5 percent for 4-cyl.

Camaro, V-8

	6	5	4	3	2	1
2d Cpe	350	790	1350	2650	4620	6600
2d Cpe Berlinetta	350	820	1400	2700	4760	6800
2d Cpe Z28	350	850	1450	2850	4970	7100

NOTE: Deduct 10 percent for V-6 cyl.

Monte Carlo, V-8

	6	5	4	3	2	1
2d Cpe	200	720	1200	2400	4200	6000
2d Cpe SS	350	800	1350	2700	4700	6700

NOTE: Deduct 15 percent for V-6 cyl.